REGULATION OF LAWYERS

ASPEN CASEBOOK SERIES

Regulation of Lawyers
Problems of Law and Ethics

Twelfth Edition

Stephen Gillers

Elihu Root Professor of Law
New York University School of Law

Copyright © 2021 Stephen Gillers.

Published by Wolters Kluwer in New York.

Wolters Kluwer Legal & Regulatory U.S. serves customers worldwide with CCH, Aspen Publishers, and Kluwer Law International products. (www.WKLegaledu.com)

No part of this publication may be reproduced or transmitted in any form or by any means, electronic or mechanical, including photocopy, recording, or utilized by any information storage or retrieval system, without written permission from the publisher. For information about permissions or to request permissions online, visit us at www.WKLegaledu.com, or a written request may be faxed to our permissions department at 212-771-0803.

To contact Customer Service, e-mail customer.service@wolterskluwer.com, call 1-800-234-1660, fax 1-800-901-9075, or mail correspondence to:

Wolters Kluwer
Attn: Order Department
PO Box 990
Frederick, MD 21705

Printed in the United States of America.

1 2 3 4 5 6 7 8 9 0

ISBN 978-1-5438-2586-2

Library of Congress Cataloging-in-Publication Data

Names: Gillers, Stephen, 1943- author.
Title: Regulation of lawyers : problems of law and ethics / Stephen
   Gillers, Elihu Root Professor of Law, New York University School of Law.
Description: Twelfth edition. | New York : Wolters Kluwer, [2020] | Series:
   Aspen casebook series | Includes bibliographical references and index. |
   Summary: "Professional Responsibility casebook with problems/notes and
   engaging mix of materials"—Provided by publisher.
Identifiers: LCCN 2020043074 (print) | LCCN 2020043075 (ebook) | ISBN
   9781543825862 (hardcover) | ISBN 9781543825879 (ebook)
Subjects: LCSH: Legal ethics—United States. | Lawyers—United
   States–Discipline. | Practice of law—United States. | LCGFT: Casebooks
   (Law)
Classification: LCC KF306 .G55 2020 (print) | LCC KF306 (ebook) | DDC
   174/.30973—dc23
LC record available at https://lccn.loc.gov/2020043074
LC ebook record available at https://lccn.loc.gov/2020043075

SUSTAINABLE FORESTRY INITIATIVE   Certified Sourcing
www.sfiprogram.org
SFI-000028

About Wolters Kluwer Legal & Regulatory U.S.

Wolters Kluwer Legal & Regulatory U.S. delivers expert content and solutions in the areas of law, corporate compliance, health compliance, reimbursement, and legal education. Its practical solutions help customers successfully navigate the demands of a changing environment to drive their daily activities, enhance decision quality and inspire confident outcomes.

Serving customers worldwide, its legal and regulatory portfolio includes products under the Aspen Publishers, CCH Incorporated, Kluwer Law International, ftwilliam.com, and MediRegs names. They are regarded as exceptional and trusted resources for general legal and practice-specific knowledge, compliance and risk management, dynamic workflow solutions, and expert commentary.

As with the eleven prior editions, this one is dedicated
with love and pride to my strolling-in-the-city companions,
Gillian Gillers and Heather Gillers,
les enfants du paradis.

Summary of Contents

Contents   xi
Preface: Performance in Law, Performance of Law   xxv
Acknowledgments   xxxi
A Word About Case Editing   xxxiii

Chapter I   **The What, Who, How, When, and Why**
                   of "Legal Ethics"   1

Part One

THE ATTORNEY-CLIENT RELATIONSHIP   17

Chapter II   **Defining the Attorney-Client Relationship**   19
Chapter III   **Protecting the Attorney-Client Relationship**
                   Against Outside Interference   85
Chapter IV   **Lawyers, Money, and the Ethics of Legal Fees**   109

Part Two

CONFLICTS OF INTEREST   153

Chapter V   **Concurrent Conflicts of Interest**   155
Chapter VI   **Successive Conflicts of Interest**   237

Part Three

SPECIAL LAWYER ROLES   269

Chapter VII   **Ethics in Advocacy**   271
Chapter VIII   **Special Issues in Criminal Prosecutions**   367
Chapter IX   **Negotiation and Transactional Matters**   401
Chapter X   **Lawyers for Companies and Other Organizations**   427
Chapter XI   **Judges**   461

Part Four

AVOIDING AND REDRESSING PROFESSIONAL FAILURE   499

Chapter XII	**Control of Quality: Reducing the Likelihood of Professional Failure**	501
Chapter XIII	**Control of Quality: Remedies for Professional Failure**	543
Chapter XIV	**Control of Quality: Nonlawyers in the Law Business (and Related Issues)**	605

Part Five

FIRST AMENDMENT RIGHTS OF LAWYERS AND JUDICIAL CANDIDATES   635

Chapter XV	**Free Speech Rights of Lawyers and Judicial Candidates**	637
Chapter XVI	**Marketing Legal Services**	663

Answers to Self-Assessment Questions	687
Table of Cases	707
Table of Codes, Rules, and Restatement Provisions	715
Index	719

Contents

Preface: Performance in Law, Performance of Law   xxv
Acknowledgments   xxxi
A Word About Case Editing   xxxiii

Chapter I   **The What, Who, How, When, and Why of "Legal Ethics"**   1

A.   Does Legal Ethics Have a Theory?   2
B.   Does Legal Ethics Have a Politics?   5
C.   Normative and Behavioral Arguments   6
D.   Judges vs. Lawmakers   7
E.   Congress   8
F.   Rules of Professional Conduct   8
     A *Very* Brief History of Lawyer Ethics Rules: 1908 to Today   9
G.   Ethics Rules vs. the Borderless Market for Legal Services: A Paradox   12
H.   Ethics Rules as Authority   12
I.   Other Sources   13
J.   Behavioral Legal Ethics   14
K.   Real Ethics   14
L.   What Is Professionalism?   14

Part One

THE ATTORNEY-CLIENT RELATIONSHIP   17

Chapter II   **Defining the Attorney-Client Relationship**   19

A.   Is There a Client Here?   20
B.   What Do Lawyers Owe Clients?   22
    1.   Competence   22
       Competence Includes Judgment   24
    2.   Confidentiality   24
       The Case of the Innocent Lifer   24
       "Lori Is on Opioids"   25

How Does *Your Garden*™ Grow?   26
   Perez v. Kirk & Carrigan   26
Privileged Communication and Confidential
   Information: What Is the Difference?   31
Organizational Clients   36
   Slip and Fall (Part I)   36
   Upjohn Co. v. United States   37
Should There Even Be an Attorney-Client Privilege for
   Corporations?   41
Exceptions to Privilege and Confidentiality   42
Self-Defense and Legal Claims   42
Waiver (or Consent)   44
The Crime-Fraud Exception to the Privilege   45
The Crime-Fraud Privilege Exception Applied   47
The Confidentiality Exceptions for Crimes and Frauds
   and to Prevent Death and Bodily Harm   47
The Difference Between the Crime-Fraud and Physical
   Harm Exceptions to Privilege and Confidentiality
   Pithily Stated   48
The Effect of the Confidentiality Exceptions on Privilege   48
The "Fiduciary" Exception   50
Noisy Withdrawal   51
Lawyers and Social Media: Risks, Benefits, and
   Best Practices   51
3. Lawyers Are Agents   54
   Taylor v. Illinois   54
   Choice Hotels International v. Grover   57
When a Lawyer Abandons a Client the Agency Ends   59
Vicarious Admissions   60
4. Lawyers Are Fiduciaries   60
5. Loyalty and Diligence   61
6. The Duty to Inform and Advise   62
   Nichols v. Keller   62
The Client's Right to Know   64
In a Box   65
C. Autonomy of Attorneys and Clients   66
1. Criminal Cases   66
   Lesser Included Offenses   66
   "Long Black Veil"   67
   "I Want to Die"   68
   Jones v. Barnes   70
   Case Note: McCoy v. Louisiana   73
2. Civil Cases   75
   "It's the Right and Decent Thing to Do"   75

"Accept the Offer" 76
Olfe v. Gordon 78
The Scope of the Client's Autonomy 79
Clients with Diminished Capacity 79
D. Terminating the Relationship 80
1. Termination by the Client 80
2. Termination by the Lawyer 81
3. Termination by Drift 82
4. Episodic Clients 82
Self-Assessment Questions 83

Chapter III Protecting the Attorney-Client Relationship Against
Outside Interference 85

A. Communicating with Another Lawyer's Clients 85
1. Civil Matters 88
Slip and Fall (Part II) 88
"We Want to Know What Reach Tekkno Is Saying" 89
Niesig v. Team I 90
How Large Is the Circle of Secrecy? 93
When Government Is the "Represented Person" 94
Testers 95
"The Adverse Client . . ." 97
2. Criminal Matters 97
The Case of the Cooperating Target 97
United States v. Carona 100
B. Improper or Accidental Acquisition of Confidential
Information 104
"It's the Discovery Wellmost Suppressed" 104
Inadvertent Disclosure and Metadata 106
Self-Assessment Questions 107

Chapter IV Lawyers, Money, and the Ethics of Legal Fees 109

A. The Role of the Marketplace 111
Brobeck, Phleger & Harrison v. Telex Corp. 111
Time or Value? Or Does Value = Time? 115
B. Unethical Fees and Billing Practices 117
"Sparrow Owes Robin a Refund" 117
"What Are You Worth?" 117
Case Note: In re Fordham 119
Are *Fordham* and *Brobeck* Compatible? 121
Inflating Bills and Other Abuses 121
Courts and Billing Guidelines Make Lawyers Defend
Every Dollar 122

	Billing Judgment	124
	Post-Retainer Fee Agreements	124
	Should a Lawyer Be Required to Put Fee Agreements in Writing?	125
C.	Contingent Fees	126
	A Lawyer's Advantage When Negotiating a Contingent Fee	127
	Contingent Fees and Conflicts of Interest	127
	Prohibitions on Contingent Fees in Criminal and Matrimonial Cases	129
	A Radical Proposal or Client Protection?	129
D.	Minimum Fee Schedules	131
	Goldfarb v. Virginia State Bar	132
	Case Note: North Carolina State Board of Dental Examiners v. Federal Trade Commission	134
E.	Court-Awarded Fees	136
	1. What's the Right Amount?	136
	Fee-Shifting Cases	136
	Common Fund and Derivative Cases	137
	2. Settlement Conditioned on Fee Waiver	138
	Case Note: Evans v. Jeff D.	138
	The Effect of Evans v. Jeff D. on Civil Rights Class Actions	142
	Questions and Comments About *Jeff D.*	142
F.	Mandatory Pro Bono Plans	144
	"Should We Adopt Mandatory Pro Bono?"	144
	Deborah L. Rhode, Cultures of Commitment: Pro Bono for Lawyers and Law Students	146
	Jonathan R. Macey, Mandatory Pro Bono: Comfort for the Poor or Welfare for the Rich?	148
	Self-Assessment Questions	152

Part Two

CONFLICTS OF INTEREST

		153
Chapter V	**Concurrent Conflicts of Interest**	155
	Conflicts of Interest: Definition and Context	155
A.	Client-Lawyer Conflicts	160
	1. A Lawyer's Business and Financial Interests	160
	Lawyer. Realtor. Any Problem?	160
	In re Neville	161
	A Lawyer's Financial Interests	164
	Deals with Clients	164
	Interests Adverse to Clients	165

2. Media Rights 167
3. Financial Assistance 168
    Becca Dionne Is Puzzled 168
4. Fee-Payer Interests 171
5. Related Lawyers, Significant Others, and Friends 172
6. Can a Lawyer's Gender, Religion, or Race Create a
    Conflict? 173
    Implicit Bias in the Jury Room 173
    How Roger Baldwin Picked a Lawyer 176
    The Schempp Case 177

B. Client-Client Conflicts 178
1. Criminal Cases (Defense Lawyers) 178
    Murder One, Murder Two 178
    Did Officer Schwarz Get the Effective Assistance
        of Counsel? 179
    Cuyler v. Sullivan 181
    Turning Conflicts into Sixth Amendment Claims After
        Cuyler v. Sullivan 185
    Holloway Error 186
    Disqualification of Defense Counsel 188
    Murder at the Ballgame 189
    Wheat v. United States 190
    Wheat's Harvest 196
    Criminal Case Disqualification and the "Automatic
        Reversal" Debate 197
    Can a Conflicted Lawyer Advise a Current Client on
        Whether to Waive Her Conflict? 198
2. Criminal Cases (Prosecutors) 200
    Forfeiture Plus Prosecution 200
    Young v. United States ex rel. Vuitton et Fils S.A. 200
    Prosecutors Avec Deux Chapeaux 203
    People v. Adams 204
3. Civil Cases 207
    "Will You Represent Us Both?" 207
    "My Birthday Poodle" 207
    "If You're Adverse to Gyro, You're Adverse to Us" 208
    "Significant and Direct Financial Harm" 209
    Fiandaca v. Cunningham 209
    "Directly Adverse" Conflicts 213
    Imputed Conflicts 214
    Standing to Object 215
    Should the Rules Let a Lawyer Act Adversely to a
        Current Firm Client on a Matter That Is *Unrelated* to
        the Representation of That Client? 216

Confidentiality and Privilege in Multiple Client
   Representations   218
Appealability of Civil Disqualification Orders   221
Malpractice and Fee Forfeiture Based on Conflicts   222
   Simpson v. James   222
What Did Oliver and James Do Wrong?   226
Consent and Waiver   227
   4. The Insurance Triangle   228
      Ed's Daughter Was Driving   228
      Client Identity and the Obligation to Defend   229
C. The Advocate-Witness Rule   231
   Policies Behind the Advocate-Witness Rule   231
   Giuffre v. Dershowitz   232
Self-Assessment Questions   234

Chapter VI   Successive Conflicts of Interest   237

A. Private Practice   237
   Divorce and Default   237
   "What Do I Owe Haywood Tallman?"   238
   "Stop the High Rise"   239
   Analytica, Inc. v. NPD Research   240
   The "Substantial Relationship" Test   244
   Can *Playbook* Create a Substantial Relationship?   246
   The Loyalty Duty to Former Clients (*or* It's Not Only
      About Confidences)   248
   Who Counts as a *Client* Under the Former Client
      Conflict Rule?   249
   "Like a Hot Potato": Is the Client Former or Current?   250
   "Thrust Upon" Conflicts   251
   Standing and Waiver   251
   The Appearance of Impropriety   252
   Conflicts in Class Actions   252
B. Imputed Disqualification and Migratory Lawyers   253
   "You Don't Know Anything"   253
   "Can We Hire Taylor Monk?"   254
   A Conflict Bouquet   255
   Cromley v. Board of Education   255
   Why Didn't *Cromley* Ask . . .?   258
   Presumptions in Imputed Disqualification   259
   Removing Conflicts from a Former Firm   262
C. Government Service   262
   Investigating Landlords   262
   Armstrong v. McAlpin   263
   The Revolving Door in the Model Rules: The Two Issues   265
Self-Assessment Questions   267

Part Three

SPECIAL LAWYER ROLES												269

Chapter VII Ethics in Advocacy										271

  A. Four Views of Adversary Justice									276
        Simon Rifkind and Marvin Frankel: Two Views on the
           Role of Truth in the Adversary System						276
           Simon H. Rifkind, The Lawyer's Role and
               Responsibility in Modern Society						276
           Marvin E. Frankel, Partisan Justice						279
        Faking It: Lawyers and Actors, Lawyers As Actors				282
           Shakespeare, Hamlet								282
           Robert C. Post, On the Popular Image of the
               Lawyer: Reflections in a Dark Glass					282
        The Advocate in Literature							284
           Anthony Trollope, Orley Farm						284
           "Adversary Justice Is Good for Lawyers But Bad for
               Justice"								285
  B. Are Lawyers Morally Accountable for Their Choice of
      Clients or What They Do for Them?							287
           Ronald S. Sullivan, Jr., Defends Harvey Weinstein			288
           Lawyers for Opponents of Marriage Equality				289
  C. (Courtroom) Truth and Confidences							291
           "Out Carousing with Mikey"						291
           Nix v. Whiteside								294
           "Streets for Bikes Not Trucks"						302
        After *Nix*, Open Questions?							303
           "Maybe I Was Insane"							308
        Robert Bennett's Letter to Judge Susan Webber Wright			311
        Summary: Variables in Analyzing Issues Concerning
           Witness Perjury and False Testimony					312
  D. Fostering Falsity or Advancing Truth?							313
    1. Literal Truth									315
      a. The Parable of Billy and the Cookies					316
      b. The Romance of Annie and Bill					316
      c. In the Matter of William Jefferson Clinton				317
      d. The Law of Perjury (and Rules Governing "False"
          Statements)								319
      e. The Law of Contempt						324
          "Did You Talk to Cassie?"						324
    2. Cross-Examining the Truthful Witness					326
          Daniel J. Kornstein, A Tragic Fire—A Great
            Cross-Examination							327
          Ann Ruben & Emily Ruben, Letter to the Editor			329

3. Appeals to Bias   331
    People v. Marshall   331
4. The Boundaries of Proper Argument   336
    "I Hang a Key on a Nail"   337
    The Eyewitness (Part I)   337
    They Eyewitness (Part II)   338
    Zapata v. Vasquez   338
    The Subin-Mitchell Debate   342
        Harry Subin, The Criminal Lawyer's "Different
            Mission": Reflections on the "Right" to Present a
            False Case   342
        John Mitchell, Reasonable Doubts Are Where You
            Find Them: A Response to Professor Subin's
            Position on the Criminal Lawyer's "Different
            Mission"   343
        Harry Subin, Is This Lie Necessary? Further
            Reflections on the Right to Present a False Defense   345
    Questions   346
        "Maxwell's Silver-Handled .38"   348
        Phantom Profits   349
5. Spoliation   349
E. Hardball and Incivility   351
    Mullaney v. Aude   353
    She Had to Explain "Slut Shaming"   356
F. Misstating Facts, Precedent, or the Record   359
G. The Obligation to Reveal Adverse Legal Authority   362
    Thul v. OneWest Bank, FSB   362
Self-Assessment Questions   363

Chapter VIII   Special Issues in Criminal Prosecutions   367

A. Real Evidence   367
    The Client's Loaded .45 (Part I)   367
    Lawyers and Real Evidence: An Introduction   367
1. Real Evidence and Legal Ethics   369
    In re Ryder   369
2. Real Evidence and Criminal Law   373
    The Client's Loaded .45 (Part II)   373
3. Real Evidence and the Attorney-Client Privilege   376
    The Client's Loaded .45 (Part III)   376
    People v. Meredith   377
    The Turnover Duty   380
    Does the Source Matter?   381
        "The White Women on the Walls Have to Go"   382
    The Rules Today (So Far as Can Be Known)   384

B. Some Issues Concerning Prosecutors   384
    1. Constitutional and Ethical Disclosure Obligations   385
        "We Can Make No Promises But . . ."   386
        Is the Rule 3.8(d) Turnover Duty Broader Than *Brady*?   389
    2. Ethical Issues in Making the Charging Decision   392
        The People of the State of Montana v. Anita Winslow
            and Abel Mertz   392
    3. Victim's Interest in How a Prosecutor Decides   395
        Contributions to Justice   396
        Whose Reasonable Doubt?   397
Self-Assessment Questions   399

Chapter IX   Negotiation and Transactional Matters   401

A. Lawyers as Negotiators: An Introduction   402
B. Negotiation: The Risks to Lawyers   403
    1. The "Bad Client" Problem   403
        The Bad Builder's Good Lawyer   403
        "Come to the Cabaret"   406
        The Noisy Withdrawal   408
    2. The Lawyer's Own Statements   410
        True or False in Negotiation Land   410
        What Does "Material" Mean?   411
        Can Others Rely on an Opposing Lawyer's
            Representations of Fact?   411
        Graycas, Inc v. Proud   411
        Lessons for Lawyers: Watch What You Say?   415
        Can Others Rely on an Opposing Lawyer's Legal
            Opinions   417
        Hoyt Properties v. Production Resource Group   417
    3. Exploiting an Opponent's Mistake   419
        The Case of the Dead Witness   419
        Negotiation Mistakes (Part I)   420
        Negotiation Mistakes (Part II)   420
        Negotiation Mistakes (Part III)   420
        Mok v. 21 Mott St. Restaurant Corp.   421
    What Does *Mok* Stand For?   422
    Some Special Situations   423
Self-Assessment Questions   425

Chapter X   Lawyers for Companies and Other Organizations   427

    Introduction: "Who's Your Client?"   427
A. Companies Behaving Badly: "Where Were the Lawyers?"   428

Should We Forbid Secret Settlements That Conceal
Danger?   433
B. Conflicts and Confidentiality in Entity Representation   434
1. Internal Investigations   434
"Please, Just Find Out What Happened"   434
In re Grand Jury Subpoena Under Seal   435
"Who's Your Client?" (Reprise)   439
What About Government Lawyers?   440
2. Change of Corporate Control   442
"We're Still on the Same Side"   442
Tekni-Plex, Inc. v. Meyner & Landis   443
3. Conflict and Privilege Issues in Representing a Member
of a Corporate Family   448
"We Have Never Done Work for the Parent"   448
Corporate Family Conflicts   448
4. Closely Held Entities   451
*Murphy & Demory, Ltd., et al. v. Admiral Daniel
J. Murphy, U.S.N. (Ret.)*   451
C. Sarbanes-Oxley, Dodd-Frank, and the Rule 1.13
Amendments   454
Cash for Confidences   457
Self-Assessment Questions   459

Chapter XI   Judges   461

Introduction to Judicial Ethics   462
Ex Parte Communications   464
A. Conflicts and Disqualification   465
Abortion on Appeal   465
"My Daughter Abby Is a Lawyer"   466
"The City Gets the Money, Not the Judge"   466
What Judicial Conflicts Violate the Due Process Clause?   467
Caperton v. A.T. Massey Coal Co.   467
John Roberts's 40 Socratic Questions and Andrew
Frey's Strategic Decision   473
Williams v. Pennsylvania   475
Campaign Contributions and (the Appearance of)
Partiality   475
Ethical and Statutory Disqualification   477
Case Note: Liljeberg v. Health Services Acquisition Corp.   478
Who Decides?   484
A Judge's Personal Relationships or Interests   484
Source of Knowledge: The Extrajudicial Source
Doctrine (or Factor)   487
Law Clerks   488

A Judge's Duty to Reveal   489

B. Expressions of Gender, Racial, and Other Bias   490
    The Judge and the Boy Scouts   490
    "Where You Live, Not Who You Are"   492
    Courtroom Bias   493
    Discriminatory Organizations   494
Self-Assessment Questions   496

Part Four

AVOIDING AND REDRESSING PROFESSIONAL FAILURE   499

Chapter XII   Control of Quality: Reducing the Likelihood of Professional Failure   501

A. Admission to the Bar   502
  1. Geographical Exclusion   504
  2. Geographical Restriction   504
  3. Education and Examination   505
  4. Character Inquiries   506
    Borrowing from the Moot Court Account   506
    The Racist Bar Applicant   506
    In re Glass   508
    Frequently Cited Grounds for Delaying or Denying
      Admission to the Bar   513
  5. Admission in a Federal System   515
B. Transient Lawyers and Multijurisdictional Firms: Local
    Interests Confront a National Bar   516
  1. Admissions Pro Hac Vice   517
    Leis v. Flynt   517
    Justice and the Traveling Lawyer   520
    What About the Defendant's Interests?   522
  2. Services Other Than Litigation   522
    Food Pantry Law   522
    Employment Law Professor   523
    *Birbrower, Montalbano, Condon & Frank, P.C. v.
      Superior Court*   524
    Why Is *Birbrower* a Problem and What Is the Solution?   528
    The View from Canada and the European Union 530
C. Unauthorized Practice of Law   531
    "The Landlords' Lawyers Are a Mean Bunch"   531
    Linder v. Insurance Claims Consultants, Inc.   533
    Three Limitations on State UPL Rules: The Supremacy
      Clause, the First Amendment, and Antitrust Laws   537
Self-Assessment Questions   540

**Chapter XIII Control of Quality: Remedies for
Professional Failure**   543

A. Malpractice and Breach of Fiduciary Duty   543
    1. Liability to Clients   544
            When Sally Left Ari . . .   544
            Togstad v. Vesely, Otto, Miller & Keefe   546
        Was Miller Just a Nice Guy?   551
        What Is the Required Standard of Care?   551
        Breach of Fiduciary Duty or Malpractice?   552
            Tante v. Herring   553
    2. Liability to Third Parties for Professional Negligence   555
    3. Vicarious Liability   556
B. Proving Lawyer Liability   556
    1. Use of Ethics Rules and Expert Testimony   556
            Smith v. Haynsworth, Marion, McKay & Geurard   557
        Fee Forfeiture Due to Rule Violations   559
            Rodriguez v. Disner   559
        Fee Forfeiture (and Disgorgement)   561
    2. Causation and Defenses   562
            Viner v. Sweet   563
        The "But For" Test in Malpractice and Fiduciary Duty
            Claims: Additional Issues   566
        Causation in Criminal Cases   569
            Arenns v. Dobbins   569
C. Lawyer Liability to Third Persons   571
        Negligent Misrepresentation   572
        Consumer Protection Laws   572
        Criminal Law   573
        Violation of Escrow Agreements   573
D. Discipline   574
    1. Why Do Lawyers Violate the Rules?   574
    2. Purposes of Discipline   575
    3. Sanctions   576
    4. Disciplinary Systems   577
    5. Acts Justifying Discipline   577
        a. Dishonesty   577
            The Defense Sting   577
            A Research Shortcut   578
            In re Warhaftig   579
            In re Disciplinary Proceedings Against Siderits   581
        Deceit, Dishonesty, Etcetera   582
        b. Neglect and Lack of Candor   583
        c. Sex with a Client   584
        d. The Lawyer's "Private" Life and Conduct
            Unrelated to Practice   586

e.	Discrimination in Choice of Clients	587
f.	Racist and Sexist Conduct in Law Practice	588
	In re Jordan Schiff	589
	The Rule 8.4(g) Debate	592
	"Affirmative Action Hurts Those It Promises to Help"	593
	LGBTQ Policy	595
	"Inappropriate Touching"	596
g.	Failure to Report Another Lawyer's Misconduct	596
6.	Defenses	597
E.	Constitutional Protection in Criminal Cases	597
	"She Didn't Call My Alibi"	597
	The Ineffectiveness Test in a System of Procedural Defaults	601
	Self-Assessment Questions	602

Chapter XIV   Control of Quality: Nonlawyers in the Law Business (and Related Issues) — 605

A.	Nonprofit Entities and Intermediaries	607
1.	Public Interest Organizations	607
	NAACP v. Button	607
	Maintenance, Barratry, Champerty, and Change: What Did *Button* Decide?	612
	In re Primus	616
2.	Labor Unions	620
	United Transportation Union v. State Bar of Michigan	622
	The United Freelancers Association	625
B.	For-Profit Enterprises	625
	"Can Viktor Be Our Partner?"	625
	"Can We Make This Deal?"	626
	AmazonLaw.com	627
	Nonlawyers at the Borders	630
	Self-Assessment Questions	633

Part Five

FIRST AMENDMENT RIGHTS OF LAWYERS AND JUDICIAL CANDIDATES — 635

Chapter XV   Free Speech Rights of Lawyers and Judicial Candidates — 637

A.	Public Comment About Pending Cases	637
	Case Note: Gentile v. State Bar of Nevada	639
	Questions and Comments About *Gentile*	643
	People v. Harvey Weinstein	645

Immunity for Allegedly Defamatory Statements
    During Litigation   646
B. Public Comment About Judges   646
    #SourOnHoney   646
    In re Holtzman   647
  Questions and Comments About *Holtzman*   650
C. Judicial Campaign Speech   651
    "I Got These Questionnaires"   651
    Republican Party of Minnesota v. White   653
  Gray Areas Post-*White*   659
  How About Supreme Court Nominees?   661
Self-Assessment Questions   661

Chapter XVI Marketing Legal Services   663

  "The Top Ten"   663
  Marketing Legal Services: An Introduction   664
A. Defining the Borders: *Bates* and *Ohralik*   665
    Ohralik v. Ohio State Bar Ass'n   668
  A Prophylactic Rule   671
B. Defining the Center: *Zauderer* and *Shapero*   672
  1. Targeted Advertisements   672
    Zauderer v. Office of Disciplinary Counsel   672
  2. Targeted Mail   676
    Shapero v. Kentucky Bar Ass'n   676
  The Response to *Shapero* and the Response to
    the Response   680
C. Defining the Methodology   681
  1. How Does the Court Know Things?   682
  2. Professionalism and Money   683
Self-Assessment Question   684

Answers to Self-Assessment Questions   687
Table of Cases   707
Table of Codes, Rules, and Restatement Provisions   715
Index   719

Preface:
Performance in Law, Performance of Law

Imagine that you are going to spend substantial time in a distant island nation. You're excited because you've heard a lot of good things about the place, but you're also a little anxious. Much will resemble home, but many customs will be new. You don't want to embarrass yourself or, worse, get kicked off the island. You buy a guidebook to tell you how to act in different business and social situations. What should you expect?

This book is a guidebook of sorts. Its silent subtitle could be *How to Perform in the Law.* It tells you how to act in a new place—Lawyerland—a place where most readers of this book will spend decades of their working life. You need to know the customs or, more accurately, the rules in order to thrive.

How to act. In *The Performance of Self in Everyday Life,* the sociologist Erving Goffman compared everyday face-to-face encounters to acting, to a series of performances. In chapter 7A, Robert Post draws on Goffman's study of performance and acting to help understand the popular perception of American lawyers. "All the world's a stage," Jacques declared in *As You Like It,* anticipating Goffman by centuries. Law practice is also a stage, on which, updating Jacques, a lawyer in her lifetime will play many parts.

* * *

Here are three things about this book and the class it serves.

First, this is your second most important class. A bold statement, but true. Say you become an antitrust lawyer. The criminal procedure class you loved will fade in your memory. Or if you become a criminal defense lawyer, you won't need to know much about copyright. But whatever work you do as a lawyer, you will practice what you learn here every day you go to work. Other courses teach lessons that bear on a client's problems. This book is about your work as a lawyer. You're the client.

Knowledge of these rules enables you to stay safe and to protect your clients from the misconduct of other lawyers. Also, representing lawyers and law firms in trouble (or needing advice to avoid trouble) is now an established practice area, one that might appeal to you.

Second, the book contains many problems. Some are one paragraph, others a page or more. Many are based on or composites of real events that I've heard or read about. Many of the problems are dense and messy, like life. They arose yesterday or will tomorrow. A problem may not have all the information required to answer it. Just like practice. You may have to identify what more you need to know.

Lawyers know that finding solutions to problems that arise in practice benefits from conversation. So, too, here. Listening to others in class and articulating your own tentative responses will produce a better result than thinking alone.

Third, this book has a personality, a voice: mine. In that way, it is unlike some other casebooks. Its voice is conversational. Sometimes, it takes a position. I invite you to disagree. "I" appears with some frequency as the subject of a sentence.

As you approach the starting line of your legal career, most important are the rules that constrain your behavior. You will want to know—in such areas as competence, fees, advocacy, confidentiality, conflicts of interest, negotiation, and the client-lawyer relationship—what you may or must do or not do, with confidence that your conduct will not land you before a disciplinary committee, create civil or criminal liability, invite court sanction, forfeit your fee, or damage your reputation.

Ethics, a useful shorthand, does not accurately describe all lessons learned here. The law business is heavily regulated. The regulations are growing more complex. This has led to new terms—*the law governing lawyers* and *the law of lawyering*—lest anyone be fooled by the word "ethics" into believing that the subject is simply about how to be a good person and a lawyer at the same time (although it's about that, too). It sometimes seems that the public thinks both are not possible.

Avoid two errors.

Do not believe that the right way to act—toward clients, courts, adversaries, or colleagues—will be intuitively obvious. Sure, sometimes it will be. But no one needs to teach you not to lie or steal. The rules here may be obscure, some may be counterintuitive, and others are subtle in application. Application in turn calls for judgment, and judgment is mostly learned through experience. But it can start now.

Do not assume your employer will provide all the protection you need. Most law offices do have systems to detect and avoid mistakes and people to whom lawyers can turn for advice. But the best systems and resources are still not perfect, and anyway, the professional responsibility of a lawyer cannot be delegated wholesale to others. Furthermore, you need to know enough to know when you need to seek advice or do research.

* * *

A broader perspective from which to view the laws and rules that regulate lawyers looks at their effect on civil society and the administration of justice. These laws and rules help define the nature and work of the entire profession and therefore the behavior of our legal institutions and the quality of our social justice. For example, a rule that prohibits, requires, or allows a lawyer to reveal a client's confidential information to protect others from harm will guide a lawyer's own behavior, but it can also affect what information clients are willing to share with their lawyers. Many rules reflect an effort to reconcile competing interests between clients and others.

As you enter law practice, you are likely more interested in such questions as "How must I behave?" and "How can I stay out of trouble?" than in asking, "What are the consequences to civil society and justice if one or another version of a particular rule is applied to the 1.3 million American lawyers?" Still, the last question is important and, if not as immediate, may arise in the course of your professional life. You may someday be in a position to resolve the broader questions — as a member of a bar committee, a legislator, a government lawyer, or a judge.

Asking about the consequences to justice and civil society if a rule is resolved one way rather than another — and saying which resolution is best — engenders different answers among both lawyers and the public. Why is that? In part, because the answers depend on political and moral values more fundamental than the "ethics" that inform various codes. And political and moral values of different people differ.

In addressing the questions here, we must be honest about the interests we mean to protect. Those of society generally? Those of a particular client population? The legal profession's? Your own? Law school and law practice, it is sometimes said, encourage more rather than less self-interest. In transition as you are, your answers may vary from what they would have been when you applied to law school, and they will likely be different five years after you graduate.

* * *

You will enter a profession in greater transition than at any other time in American history. Three forces are reshaping the U.S. law industry: technology, globalization, and competition from new sources. As it happens, while I was writing this preface the Wall St. Journal ran an article entitled "Would You Trust a Lawyer Bot With Your Legal Needs?" by Asa Fitch (August 10, 2020.) And the Utah Supreme Court adopted reforms that allow nonlawyers to own law firms, an idea that, until recently, would have been unthinkable. Lyle Moran, "Utah Embraces Nonlawyer Ownership of Law Firms as Part of Broad Reforms," (ABA Journal August 14, 2020). Arizona did, too. See chapter 14B.

Will artificial intelligence replace some lawyer tasks? Will it replace some lawyers? Will it reduce the cost of some legal services? Yes, yes, and yes. It has already happened.

These three forces are upsetting a lawyer regulatory system that has served the United States well for more than a century, a system based on geography. In that system, lawyers get licensed by a place and serve clients from an office in that place. But technology has challenged the use of geography as the basis for regulation and licensure. The Internet does not recognize borders. Neither may a client's problems. An algorithm does not need a law license. Technology and globalization have encouraged competition from lawyers outside the U.S. and the ability of non-law businesses to offer legal services at lower cost. Chapters 12C and 14B address these trends.

* * *

This is the twelfth edition of the book. I started working on it in 1982 shortly before the birth of the first of two amazing daughters to whom all editions have been dedicated. I sent the manuscript to the publisher just after the birth of the second daughter in 1984. The daughters are now out in the world, but the book has never left home.

You think a lot about what a casebook is and can be when you live with one so long. The book's primary purpose is to provide information, but that's just the beginning. The minimum editorial task would allow me to pick good cases and other materials, edit them, order them logically, add interstitial notes and questions, and put the product between covers. Voila! A casebook. Of course, one must begin this way, but if nothing more were possible (even if not required), I wonder if I would have kept at it so long. Luckily, more is possible while still serving the book's goal—to teach the subject.

For starters, we can strive for humor, variety, clarity, and good writing. The enterprise will not likely support the wit and moral imagination of an Orwell essay or the originality of a Vonnegut novel—assuming counterfactually that I had the talent to write either (in which case I'd probably be in a different line of work)—but a casebook is a book, after all, and it should have an authorial presence in so far as possible. That's what makes the book mine.

And then there are the stories lawyers tell each other. The legal profession is a culture of storytellers and stories. Harrison Tweed (1885-1969), a president of the New York City Bar Association, once said: "I have a high opinion of lawyers. With all their faults, they stack up well against those in every other occupation or profession. They are better to work with or play with or fight with or drink with than most other varieties of mankind." These words are inscribed on a wall at the Association's headquarters. As a young lawyer, I thought Tweed was overly effusive, even sanctimonious. At the time, I was inclined to agree with the character in George Bernard Shaw's play *The Doctor's Dilemma* who said that "all professions are conspiracies against the laity." I still find Tweed a bit over the top and Shaw's observation spot-on. But now I think that Tweed was onto something. The profession and its members *are* fascinating to study. Its stories *are* fascinating to hear.

As with the study of any culture, understanding the bar requires density of information. We must know a thousand small details about the actual life within the society of lawyers, not merely a few doctrines and theories, if we are going to understand Lawyerland truly. I have tried to include some of those details here. I have tried to include stories lawyers tell each other and stories about lawyers from the popular and legal press.

I invite your views on the book. What was dull? What worked well? How can the book be improved? Have you encountered a quote or story somewhere (true or fictional) that you think nicely highlights an issue? This edition is indebted to past users who alerted me to interesting sources. All comments will be gratefully acknowledged.

Stephen Gillers
Stephen.Gillers@NYU.edu
September 2020

Acknowledgments

Beginning with the first edition of this book in 1985 and ever since, I have been fortunate to have help from generations of students at New York University School of Law. Among the students who assisted with the last edition was Lindsey E. Smith, class of 2018. When it came time for me to consider a twelfth edition, I reached out to Lindsey, now in practice, to see if I could persuade her to assist again. She said yes. Her hundreds of contributions, though invisible to readers, are quite visible to me and greatly improve the book. Her consummate skill as a close reader of text and thorough researcher are equaled only by the conscientiousness she brings to the tasks.

My former colleague Norman Dorsen, who died in 2017, was my co-author on the first two editions of this casebook and my mentor and friend for fifty years. Other demands on his time caused Professor Dorsen to trust succeeding editions to my sole care. Nevertheless, in countless ways this edition, like its predecessors, benefits from Professor Dorsen's early work and his good advice over the decades. Also, as he several times reminded me, he had the connection to Little, Brown, the original publisher. "I got the client," he'd joke.

I thank the D'Agostino/Greenberg Fund for financial assistance that aided this twelfth edition.

My understanding of the subject of legal ethics has been immeasurably enhanced by my conversations across forty years with one person whom I mention last but am grateful to most: Professor Barbara S. Gillers, whose decades of professional work on lawyer regulation—in a government law office, in private practice, and with bar associations local and national—has put her on the front lines of most of the developing issues recounted here. She has left private practice, but not the subject. For three years, until August 2020, she chaired (and was previously a member of) the American Bar Association's Standing Committee on Ethics and Professional Responsibility. She served as vice chair of the New York State Bar Association's Committee on Standards of Attorney Conduct. She was the chair and a member of the ethics committee of the New York City Bar Association. Now as an adjunct professor at New York University School of Law, she teaches a class in legal ethics and a seminar on legal ethics for public interest lawyers. Our ethics partnership has been invaluable to our work in the field.

I am grateful for permission to reprint excerpts from the following:

Marvin E. Frankel, from Partisan Justice by Marvin E. Frankel. Copyright © 1980 by Marvin E. Frankel. Reprinted by permission of Farrar, Straus & Giroux. All rights reserved.

Daniel J. Kornstein, A Tragic Fire—A Great Cross-Examination, N.Y.L.J., Mar. 28, 1986, at 2. Copyright © 1986 by Daniel J. Kornstein. Reprinted by permission. All rights reserved.

Jonathan R. Macey, Mandatory Pro Bono: Comfort for the Poor or Welfare for the Rich?, 77 Cornell L. Rev. 1115 (1992). Copyright © 1992 by Cornell Law Review. Reprinted by permission. All rights reserved.

John B. Mitchell, Reasonable Doubts Are Where You Find Them: A Response to Professor Subin's Position on the Criminal Lawyer's Different Mission, 1 Geo. J. Legal Ethics 339 (1987). Copyright © 1987 by Georgetown Journal of Legal Ethics. Reprinted by permission. All rights reserved.

Robert C. Post, On the Popular Image of the Lawyer: Reflections in a Dark Glass, 75 Cal. L. Rev. 379, 379-380, 387-389 (1987). Copyright © 1987 by Robert C. Post. Reprinted by permission. All rights reserved.

Deborah Rhode, Cultures of Commitment: Pro Bono for Lawyers and Law Students, 67 Fordham L. Rev. 2415 (1999). Copyright © 1999 by Fordham Law Review. Reprinted by permission.

Simon H. Rifkind, The Lawyer's Role and Responsibility in Modern Society, 30 The Record of the Assoc. Of the Bar of the City of N.Y. 534 (1975). Copyright © 1975 by Simon H. Rifkind. Reprinted by permission.

Ann Ruben and Emily Ruben, Letters to the Editor, N.Y.L.J., Apr. 14, 1986, at 2. Copyright © 1986 by Ann and Emily Ruben. Reprinted by permission. All rights reserved.

A Word About Case Editing

No case is reprinted unedited. Omissions are identified with ellipses or brackets where helpful, but there is no identification where only case citations or other authorities are deleted. Case citations do not include subsequent history denying review except that United States Supreme Court denials of certiorari are indicated for principal cases. In a few instances, decisions have been vacated on jurisdictional grounds and these are indicated. Where a holding other than the one for which the case is cited has been overruled or limited by statute or a later case, that fact is not shown. Internal quotes and brackets are sometimes omitted from quotations within cases for ease of reading.

REGULATION OF LAWYERS

I

The What, Who, How, When, and Why of "Legal Ethics"

The Preface explained why, especially today, law students really need to know the rules and laws that will govern their careers as lawyers. These rules and laws have a long history, at least 1,500 years, according to Professor Carol Andrews. "By the end of the Roman Empire," she writes,

> the advocate's oath was remarkably similar to modern oaths. An oath reportedly used in the era of Justinian (sixth century A.D.) required advocates to swear that:
>
> > [T]hey will undertake with all their power and strength, to carry out for their clients what they consider to be true and just, doing everything with it is possible for them to do. However, they, with their knowledge and skill, shall not prosecute a lawsuit with a bad conscience when they know [beforehand] that the case entrusted to them is dishonest or utterly hopeless or composed of false allegations. But even if, while the suit is proceeding, it were to become known [to them] that it is of that sort [i.e., dishonest], let them withdraw from the case, utterly separating themselves from any such common cause.
>
> . . .
>
> Parliament also regulated the early English lawyers known as attorneys (the predecessor of modern solicitors). In 1402, Parliament formally required that attorneys take an oath. The 1402 Act did not specify any form of the attorney's oath, but the oath probably was some form of the following pledge to "do no falsehood:"
>
> > You shall doe noe Falsehood nor consent to anie to be done in the Office of Pleas of this Courte wherein you are admitted an Attorney. And if you shall knowe of anie to be done you shall give Knowledge thereof to the Lord Chiefe Baron or other his Brethren that it may be reformed; you shall Delay noe Man for Lucre Gaine or Malice; you shall increase noe Fee but you shall be contented with the old Fee accustomed. And

1

> further you shall use yourselfe in the Office of Attorney in the said office
> of Pleas in this Courte according to your best Learninge and Discrecion.
> So helpe you God.[*]

As the Preface also explained, "legal ethics" inadequately describes the subject of this book and the courses that may use it. The term is fine as a shorthand, but our subject is broader. Rules that govern how lawyers and judges may, must, or must not behave have many sources. I will list them here, but first we need to ask two big questions.

A. DOES LEGAL ETHICS HAVE A THEORY?

A colleague once told me that "the problem with legal ethics" was that it lacked a theory. He meant to be helpful. He taught legal history, so I wondered, but did not ask, "Does legal history have a theory?" Why is the lack of a theory a "problem"?

Then I got to thinking. Do the various rules and laws subsumed under the title Regulation of Lawyers derive from an overarching Theory of Everything, or at least a Theory of Pretty Much Everything — one (nearly) grand design that explains (most of) it? Academics (me, your teacher) favor theories. They are part of the academic toolkit, if not all of it. We cannot choose the right rule until we know our goals. We cannot identify our goals until we know the norms and values we wish to advance. And why? So we need a theory.

In truth, we may never find that theory, or we may disagree about what it is, or we may see our theory temporarily ascendant, then repudiated by the next generation of scholars. More distant generations may resurrect our theory when we're no longer around to enjoy the recognition. And so it goes. None of this does, or should, stop us from the search for a theory. In asking the questions, we learn a lot.[†]

Outside the academy, people must subordinate theory to pragmatism. To what works. Michael Ignatieff was a Harvard political science professor before returning to his native Canada, getting elected to Parliament, and briefly serving as a Liberal Party leader. So he was in a good position to understand how ideas (a synonym for theory) worked differently in different environments. On August 5, 2007, he published a New York Times

---

[*] Carol Rice Andrews, The Lawyer's Oath: Both Ancient and Modern, 22 Geo. J. Legal Ethics 3 (Winter 2009).

[†] To borrow from Rainer Maria Rilke's *Letters to a Young Poet* (1903): "And the point is to live everything. Live the questions now. Perhaps then, someday far in the future, you will gradually, without even noticing it, live your way into the answer."

Magazine article, "Getting Iraq Wrong," in which he tried to understand his own mistake in initially supporting the war in Iraq:

> The philosopher Isaiah Berlin once said that the trouble with academics and commentators is that they care more about whether ideas are interesting than whether they are true. Politicians live by ideas just as much as professional thinkers do, but they can't afford the luxury of entertaining ideas that are merely interesting. They have to work with the small number of ideas that happen to be true and the even smaller number that happen to be applicable to real life. In academic life, false ideas are merely false and useless ones can be fun to play with. In political life, false ideas can ruin the lives of millions and useless ones can waste precious resources. An intellectual's responsibility for his ideas is to follow their consequences wherever they may lead. A politician's responsibility is to master those consequences and prevent them from doing harm.*

What does this mean for legal ethics? All legal rules must be pragmatic ("applicable to real life") because they tell people how to behave. And legal ethics rules must be pragmatic because they tell lawyers how to behave when advising other people how to behave. As Ignatieff wrote, we "can't afford the luxury of entertaining ideas that are merely interesting." Or more precisely, we can, but it's not enough. Our ideas must also lead to rules that make sense to those who must obey them. Lawyers and judges know this instinctively.

Legal theories need stories and vice versa. Lawyers are storytellers, and not only trial lawyers. Stories help lawyers make sense of their work, which combines the abstract and the particular. Every client matter is a story. A client wants an estate plan or to start a business or tax advice because of events in the client's life, which tell a story. Lawsuits tell conflicting stories. So although we can and will talk theoretically about the scope of a lawyer's duty of loyalty or confidentiality, we test and come to understand these concepts through stories. This book seeks to do that with many problems, some based on real events, in addition to cases and case notes.

---

* The same thought appears elsewhere in Berlin's work:

> In one of his most famous essays, Isaiah Berlin quotes a fragment from the Greek poet Archilochus: "The fox knows many things, but the hedgehog knows one big thing" ("The Hedgehog and the Fox"). The contrast is a metaphor for the crucial distinction at the heart of Berlin's thought between monist and pluralist accounts of moral value. According to monism, a single value or narrow set of values overrides all others, while on the pluralist view human goods are multiple, conflicting and incommensurable. Monism, Berlin believes, harbors political dangers that pluralism avoids. While the great authoritarian visions of politics have all rested on monist foundations, pluralism is naturally aligned with toleration, moderation and liberalism. George Crowder, Hedgehog and Fox, 38 Australian J. Pol. Sci. 333 (July 2003).

Another philosopher, former New York Yankees shortstop Yogi Berra, is reputed to have expressed the same idea more concisely: "In theory there is no difference between theory and practice, in practice there is."

Lawyers and judges are foxes in the work they do, and this book is mostly a fox book.

With all this in mind, let us identify perspectives (even if not fully formed theories) that might help explain the law and rules governing lawyers. Each finds some support (or criticism) in primary or secondary authority.

1. **"The Client Is the Center of the Universe, if Not the Whole Universe."** The dominant, rarely questioned ideology of the American bar is that the laws and rules governing lawyers must permit and often require lawyers to protect the rights and autonomy of clients in a complex legal world. Lawyers must be free to act for a client in any lawful manner that achieves the client's goal. Protecting a client's autonomy requires an environment in which the client is encouraged to be candid. The rules must therefore assure clients that lawyers cannot and will not betray a client's trust, reveal her secrets, or cause her harm. In addition, lawyers must diligently pursue a client's goals. So long as the means and ends are lawful, a lawyer should be free to push forward even if the whole world would consider her ends or means unjust to others. If a lawyer cannot do that for a particular matter, she must decline the representation.

2. **"Lawyers and the Legal Profession Also Deserve Autonomy."** Lawyers are not technicians robotically obligated to ignore the wrongfulness of a client's instructions or to do whatever works, however distasteful. They are moral agents entitled to decline to be the instruments of injury and injustice to others even when lawful. The lawyer's autonomy is not limited to declining to accept a matter she finds repugnant. It includes the right, even after accepting a matter, to refuse to use means or to pursue ends the lawyer finds offensive. The rules must allow for a lawyer's autonomy. But how much?

3. **"The Bad Client Problem."** Some clients are willing to use lawyers to commit frauds or crimes that harm others or the administration of justice. Of course, lawyers cannot knowingly assist them. Rule 1.2(d). But a lawyer may later learn that her labors assisted a client's criminal or fraudulent scheme. These bad clients deserve no concern. The rules governing lawyers must permit, perhaps even require, lawyers to protect the victims of a client's past, ongoing, or prospective illegal conduct, at least where the lawyer has been the unwitting facilitator of the client's scheme, and even if doing so harms the client.

4. **"The Tempted Lawyer Problem."** Faced with conflicting interests, lawyers may be tempted to abuse a client's trust for their own benefit or the benefit of other clients or third parties. Alas, some lawyers will succumb to the temptation. Although most will not, the mere existence of a conflict can be a problem because clients who view their lawyers as facing conflicting interests may hesitate fully to trust them. Because client trust is crucial to enabling lawyers to advise and protect a client, the rules governing lawyers should forbid lawyers (absent client consent) ever to occupy positions in which the risk of betrayal is too high. But what is too high?

5. **"The Poor Lawyer Problem."** Not all lawyers are above average all of the time. Even those who are usually above average may perform below average on occasion, and below average lawyers may work especially hard and perform above average. When a lawyer seriously messes up, the law should afford a remedy to clients who suffer. Just as important, the rules should adopt prophylactic measures that promote competence in the first place, so that the amount of messing up is small.

6. **"The Justice and Fairness Model."** Lawyers are the intermediaries between the law on paper and its application to the real problems of actual clients. We cannot have the rule of law without lawyers, at least not in a modern society. No matter how beautiful a legal theory may be, it is only a theory until lawyers implement it. Legal theories have many goals. *Justice* and *fairness* are two. We may disagree on what justice or fairness requires, abstractly or in a particular situation, but we seem to accept that the law should aspire toward both. Consequently, so should rules for lawyers, who are the bridge between theory and practice.

7. **"The Professional Conspiracy Theory."** Why do we need legal ethics rules at all? Lawyers are just one kind of agent. Why aren't the legal rules that govern other agents sufficient? This theory posits that the ethics rules exist mainly to protect the interests of lawyers and to impede what, in their absence, would be legislative (rather than judicial) control of the bar. Judges, lawyers in robes, are more likely than lawmakers to favor the bar. True, the bar can no longer be so obvious about protecting its economic self-interest as in the days of minimum fee schedules. But that only means it has better learned how to showcase its devotion to the public interest and the clients' interest. Look closer and it turns out that the interests the rules mostly protect are those of the bar.

8. **"The 'In Service of Other Theories' Theory."** Legal ethics does not need a theory. We have quite enough theories and theory makers already, thank you very much. Instead, the proper content of any ethical rule should respond to theories developed in other areas of legal and jurisprudential studies. The ethics rules can then adapt themselves as appropriate to serve contract theory, feminist legal theory, adversary justice theory, criminal law theory, constitutional theory, law and economics theory, and so on. Let scholars in those fields do the heavy theory lifting. The ethics rules will tag along, implementing the insights and values they propound.

B. DOES LEGAL ETHICS HAVE A POLITICS?

Do the rules, or does a particular rule, favor one political, economic, or social ideology over others? Is there a clear political left, right, and center in the world of legal ethics? I don't think so. Alignments get scrambled when we move from the political realm to the world of lawyer regulation. In debates about a rule, a political adversary may support you and a political ally may oppose you. Lawyers favor rules that are best for their clients, their practices, or both. Lawyers who, for example, represent class action plaintiffs and those who represent class action defendants may support different rules, making class actions easier or harder to bring, but it will be because the rule helps or hurts their clients, and not (or not only) because the lawyers are politically conservative or progressive. The same is true for criminal defense lawyers and prosecutors. I may be naïve about this, so you should ask this question again as you work through the book.

One exception here are rules and laws that prevent or impede a person's access to the courts because of ideological opposition to the rights she is trying to protect. Two examples are the Virginia laws that prevented the NAACP from using the courts to implement Brown v. Board of Education and South Carolina's effort to discipline a public interest lawyer after she wrote to a potential client whose government benefits were conditioned on her agreement to be sterilized, offering to represent her. See chapter 14A.

Of particular concern are rules or laws that at one time impeded or still impede access to legal advice and representation. These rules and laws appear throughout the book. Examples include the minimum fee schedules once set by bar associations (now forbidden, see chapter 4D), laws prohibiting unauthorized law practice (chapter 12C), and a rule that prevents a lawyer from assisting a needy client with living expenses while her case moves slowly through the courts (chapter 5A3).

C. NORMATIVE AND BEHAVIORAL ARGUMENTS

Here, as elsewhere, a rule can be defended or criticized from two perspectives. One is normative. We can say, for example, that confidentiality rules are morally right because they respect a client's dignity and humanity by giving her a protected space in which to confide in a legal advisor who is on her side. That maximizes the client's autonomy within the law, which is complex and which she cannot navigate alone.

A behavioral prediction also operates here. It is that clients will in fact be more candid the greater the assurance of confidentiality. We may or may not intuitively accept its accuracy. It is only a prediction, not proof. Some predictions are so intuitively likely that the lack of proof may not matter. Others may be questionable (and questioned), and yet the inquiry goes no further, perhaps because proof would be expensive and difficult to get. This is true about the never-ending debate over whether exceptions to the duty of confidentiality will discourage client candor. See chapter 2B2. Even if confidentiality rules are not needed to encourage client candor, the normative justification for them remains.

D. JUDGES VS. LAWMAKERS

Judges promulgate most professional conduct rules for lawyers. What gives them the right?

Courts claim that their inherent authority to regulate the bar inheres in their judicial power under state and federal constitutions. They may also cite specific or general constitutional language. Persels & Assocs. v. Banking Comm'r, 122 A.3d 592 (Conn. 2015) ("[T]he judiciary wields the sole authority to license and regulate the general practice of law in Connecticut.") (citing state constitution). A court may invalidate legislation that purports to regulate lawyers even when it does not contradict the court's own rules. This has been called *negative* inherent power. Not only do we get to make the rules for lawyers, the courts insist, lawmakers cannot make any regardless of what we do or don't do. One effect of the inherent power doctrine is to prevent popular regulation (via legislation) to control the conduct of lawyers. Although that may sound undemocratic, the doctrine insulates the bar (and the administration of justice) from political interference.

Here are some examples.

State ex rel. Fiedler v. Wisconsin Senate, 454 N.W.2d 770 (Wis. 1990), invalidated a law that imposed a continuing legal education requirement on attorneys who wished to be appointed as guardians ad litem. The court held that "once an attorney has been determined to have met the legislative and judicial threshold requirements and is admitted to practice law, he or she is subject to the judiciary's inherent and exclusive authority to regulate the practice of law."

Irwin v. Surdyk's Liquor, 599 N.W.2d 132 (Minn. 1999), held that statutorily imposed limitations on attorney's fee awards violated separation of powers. Even where the legislature's only goal is to protect clients as consumers, courts may say no. See also Preston v. Stoops, 285 S.W.3d 606 (Ark. 2008) (refusing to apply deceptive trade practices law to out-of-state lawyers because "any action by the General Assembly to control the practice of law would be a violation of the separation-of-powers doctrine").

Some courts are more tolerant of legislative activity. The Kansas Supreme Court allowed the legislature to include lawyers in the Kansas Consumer Protection Act (KCPA):

> A statutory regulation governing the practice of law is effective only when it accords with the inherent power of the judiciary, because licensed attorneys are officers of the court. This court has nevertheless recognized the legitimate authority of the legislature to enact statutes that have direct or indirect effects on the practice of law when those statutes reinforce the objective of the judiciary. . . .
>
> The purpose of the consumer protection laws in Kansas is protection of the public. This intent is consistent with the Kansas Rules of Professional Conduct. The KCPA harmonizes with the goals of this court when it regulates the practice of law, and the statute provides a private cause of action that supplements the regulatory power of this court.

Hays v. Ruther, 313 P.3d 782 (Kan. 2013). In Colorado, Crowe v. Tull, 126 P.3d 196 (Colo. 2006), held that the state's consumer protection law could be used to sue lawyers for false advertising. While emphasizing its "inherent and plenary powers . . . to regulate . . . the practice of law," the court wrote that "some overlap between judicial rulemaking and legislative policy is constitutionally permissible as long as the overlap does not create a substantial conflict."

Unauthorized practice of law is a controversial area in which judges and lawmakers may clash. Lawmakers may authorize "nonlawyers" to provide a particular service that lawyers also offer. That can reduce its cost by increasing the number of (less expensive) people who offer the service. If the provision is challenged, a court may invalidate it on the ground that the specified service constitutes "the practice of law" (a broad and fluid term), for which the court alone may license practitioners. See chapters 12C and 14B.

E. CONGRESS

The federal government has broad power to regulate lawyers notwithstanding the tradition of state regulation. See the discussion of the Sarbanes-Oxley and Dodd-Frank legislation in chapter 10C. See also Milavetz, Gallop & Milavetz, P.A. v. United States, 559 U.S. 229 (2010) (regulation of bankruptcy lawyers). Congress can make rules for lawyers who work for the federal government. 28 U.S.C. §530B, called the McDade Amendment after its sponsor, Rep. Joseph McDade, does just that. See chapter 3A2.

F. RULES OF PROFESSIONAL CONDUCT

The dominant influence here is the American Bar Association's Model Rules of Professional Conduct (RPC or Rules). Some may question the wisdom of allowing the regulated to write even the first draft of the regulations. This skepticism has occasionally proved justified, but less so in recent years.

Proponents argue that self-regulation is the hallmark of a profession. (For the profession's affirmation of this view, see the Rules' Preamble.) This loops us into a debate about professions: What makes an occupation a profession? Whatever the answer, why should professionals get to regulate themselves? Asked less charitably, the question might be whether the claim to self-regulation is simply a way to maintain power over rules governing the sale of a product—legal help—and its cost.

But how much power do lawyers really have? The ABA is a private organization with no right to impose its rules on anyone. That is why its Rules of Professional Conduct are preceded by the word "Model." Before any rule can actually govern any lawyer's behavior, a court must adopt it. Courts once accepted the ABA's (or a state bar's) recommendations with little change.

Some still do, but fewer lately. The Model Rules, adopted in 1983, generated substantial professional and even popular debate, as have their periodic amendments. Some courts have shown less deference to the bar's wishes, including courts in California, Florida, New York, Massachusetts, and New Jersey. Still, even if lawyers do not have the final say, we must not discount their influence.

A *Very* Brief History of Lawyer Ethics Rules: 1908 to Today

1. **The Canons and the Code.** The ABA's first effort to codify ethical rules was the 1908 Canons of Professional Ethics, which (with amendments) remained in effect—if of diminishing relevance—for 62 years.* Effective in 1970, the ABA (and soon thereafter all states, in some form) adopted the Code of Professional Responsibility (the Code or Model Code). The Code is divided into nine Canons, numerous Ethical Considerations (ECs), which are said to be "aspirational," and many Disciplinary Rules (DRs). The courts in some states, like New York, did not adopt the ECs but would cite them.

2. **The Kutak Commission and Watergate.** The Code's inadequacy became quickly apparent. In 1977, the ABA formed a new commission, chaired by Robert J. Kutak, an energetic and visionary Nebraska lawyer. Meanwhile, perhaps because so many lawyers were implicated in the burglary of the Democratic National Committee's office during the 1972 presidential campaign (referred to today simply as "Watergate," the venue of the burglary) and in the attempted cover-up, and because of the rapid growth of the bar, professional and popular interest in legal ethics increased.

   Watergate also explains why in the 1970s the ABA first required law schools to teach legal ethics as a condition of ABA approval, which is needed nearly everywhere in the United States for admission to the bar. Blame John Dean, Richard Nixon's White House Counsel. In a 2000 interview, Dean said that the Senate Watergate committee had asked him for a list of "everybody that I thought had been involved in Watergate. Then I put an asterisk beside the names of all the lawyers. They asked me, 'What are all those asterisks?' and they really did jump out. I said to myself, 'How did all those lawyers get involved?'" (There were 21 lawyers on the list.) Dean answered his own question: Some, like Nixon and G. Gordon Liddy, who was part of Nixon's reelection

---

* Was there a U.S. legal ethics code in the nineteenth century? See Norman Spaulding, The Myth of Civic Republicanism: Interrogating the Ideology of Antebellum Legal Ethics, 171 Fordham L. Rev. 1397 (2003) (arguing that "the morally activist concept of lawyering so often said to prevail among nineteenth-century civic republican legal elites is more mythical than real"); Russell Pearce, Rediscovering the Republican Origins of the Legal Ethics Codes, 6 Geo. J. Legal Ethics 241 (1992).

campaign, did not believe the law applied to them. Some did not understand the law. And others "simply remained loyal to Richard Nixon."*

Dean's testimony was a watershed moment for the bar. Were law schools turning out ethically challenged graduates? Was there something about law school or law practice that turned good law students into bad people? Whatever the right answers, there emerged the requirement of mandatory legal ethics instruction as a condition of ABA approval, which may explain why you are taking the course that assigned this book.

The work of the Kutak Commission prompted extensive debate within and outside the bar. After six years and several drafts, the ABA House of Delegates adopted the Model Rules of Professional Conduct on August 2, 1983. The Rules use a "Restatement" format, with black letter rules followed by comments. Each comment, according to the Scope section as it reads today, "explains and illustrates the meaning and purpose of the Rule." They are "intended as guides to interpretation, but the text of each Rule is authoritative." Elsewhere, the Scope tells us that comments "do not add obligations to the Rules but provide guidance for practicing in compliance with the Rules."

Whereas state adoption of the 1970 Model Code was swift, adoption of the Rules was glacial. New Jersey was first in 1984. But not until 2009 did two of the three remaining holdouts, New York and Maine, go along. That left California. In 2019, after many years of study and false starts, the state Supreme Court approved a new set of rules that more closely tracks the ABA text than did its predecessor. No state has adopted the Rules unchanged and the changes are not nationally uniform.

3. **The Ethics 2000 Commission.** In 1997, the ABA appointed a new commission to study the Model Rules and recommend amendments. Although its official name was the Commission on Evaluation of the Rules of Professional Conduct, it soon became known as the Ethics 2000 (or E2K) Commission because it was charged to report in the year 2000. It did issue a report in November 2000, but then made significant changes. The ABA House of Delegates began debating the report at its August 2001 meeting and continued through 2002. The House adopted nearly all of the recommendations.

4. **The Task Force on Corporate Responsibility.** In July 2002, as part of the Sarbanes-Oxley Act, which responded to a wave of corporate scandals (e.g., Enron, Tyco, WorldCom) that alarmed many, Congress

---

* Interview with John Dean by Michael Taylor, SFGate.com, Feb. 4, 2000. By 1980 or thereabouts, Dean was no longer famous. Then came investigations of the Trump administration, which turned Dean into a frequent commentator on CNN as an expert on White House shenanigans. Who says there are no second acts in American life?

passed and President Bush signed legislation that, among other things, required the Securities and Exchange Commission (SEC) to adopt specific rules governing lawyers appearing and practicing before the SEC and authorized the agency to adopt additional rules as it might choose. This was a controversial event in the history of the regulation of the bar because it gave explicit authority to (and in part required) a federal agency to make rules governing an important and lucrative area of legal work. Whatever the SEC did would affect many lawyers and clients. More threatening, other federal agencies might seek statutory authority to regulate lawyers who practice before them.

Before the ink was dry on the legislation, the ABA charged a Task Force to propose rules and policies responsive to the corporate scandals. That was meant to show that the profession could react appropriately and thereby to discourage the SEC from adopting rules broader than the legislation required. The effort did not entirely succeed, although it did lead to significant agency deference. The federal threat also led the ABA to accept two confidentiality exceptions that the Ethics 2000 Commission had proposed but that the ABA had rejected just a year earlier. See Rule 1.6(b)(2) and (b)(3), discussed in chapter 2B2. The ABA was also moved to amend Rule 1.13, which describes the duties of lawyers for organizations, to permit those lawyers to disclose confidential information to outsiders when the unlawful conduct of officials poses a likely threat of serious harm to the company. See chapter 10C.

5. **The MJP and 20/20 Commissions.** In 2002, the Multijurisdictional Practice (MJP) Commission proposed, and the ABA adopted, dramatic amendments to Rule 5.5 (which forbids lawyers to engage in the unauthorized practice of law or to aid others in doing so). The amendments recognize that lawyers increasingly need to cross state and national borders, physically or virtually, to represent clients in jurisdictions in which they are not admitted. They created "safe harbors" whereby a lawyer in one state could render legal services in another state without risking an unauthorized practice charge. In 2009, the ABA created the 20/20 Commission (so named to encourage foresight) and charged it to study advances in technology and the rise of cross-border practice, globally and nationally, and to recommend how lawyer conduct rules should respond. All of its recommendations were accepted, among them a requirement that lawyers "keep abreast of changes in the law and its practice, including the benefits and risks associated with relevant technology." Rule 1.1 cmt. [8]. Rule 5.5 was amended to create safe harbors for foreign lawyers practicing in the United States.

6. **One Size Fits (Almost) All.** A jurisdiction's ethics rules apply to all lawyers admitted in it, mostly without regard to their practice settings or the identity of their clients. A lawyer in a solo practice in suburban San Diego whose practice focuses on real estate, wills, and similar work for individual clients is governed by nearly all of the same rules

as the San Francisco lawyer whose field is international banking, is a partner in a 1,500-lawyer Montgomery Street firm, and whose clients are among the Fortune 500. The Rules do make some distinctions, however. There are rules for trial lawyers, a rule for prosecutors, and a rule aimed at lawyers for corporations and other organizations. Mostly, though, the Rules do not recognize differences in practice settings, client identity, or the size of a law office. That may have made sense a century ago, but does it make sense today? On the other hand, is there any way to avoid it? Is it feasible to write entirely different sets of rules depending on the nature of a lawyer's practice or the identity of her clients?

G. ETHICS RULES VS. THE BORDERLESS MARKET FOR LEGAL SERVICES: A PARADOX

The Model Rules are only that. A model. States deviate, sometimes in significant ways, including from each other. So we must interrupt this story to recognize a remarkable fact. There is greater dissimilarity in state ethics rules today than during the era of the Model Code (the 1970s), before the growth of our current national and international legal economy. As far as I can tell, no two states have identical rules. State courts want it *their* way. Yet even as these discrepancies have emerged, the American legal profession has become more mobile. Lawyers freely practice across state and national borders, both physically and virtually—via email, fax, satellite, and audio and video conferencing. The laws of each state are immediately available to lawyers anywhere. Those laws are often much alike. Federal and international law is identical everywhere. A Florida construction lawyer will be better able to represent a builder in New York than a New York lawyer whose practice is limited to criminal defense. How can we reconcile disparities among state ethics rules with the fact that lawyers (and not just large-firm lawyers) increasingly view the entire nation, and for some the world, as the relevant market for their area of practice?

We can't. The incongruity of having an expanding national and international legal economy, on one hand, and discrepant local rules, on the other, has created "cracks" in the regulatory machinery. One consequence has been a (perhaps) unavoidably vague choice-of-rule rule for when a lawyer's work crosses borders. See Rule 8.5. But this rule also differs among U.S. jurisdictions.

H. ETHICS RULES AS AUTHORITY

Jurisdictions give the professional conduct rules varying degrees of respect. The New York Court of Appeals said the (former) Code "is essentially the legal profession's document of self-governance, embodying principles of ethical conduct for attorneys as well as rules for professional discipline. While unquestionably important, and respected by the courts, the code does not have the force of law." Niesig v. Team I, 558 N.E.2d 1030 (N.Y. 1990). Rather, the court will look to the rules "as guidelines to be applied with due regard for the broad range of interests at stake." People v. Herr, 658 N.E.2d 1032 (N.Y. 1995). This view is hard to reconcile with the fact that it is the courts (not "the legal profession") that adopt the rules, enforce them through discipline, cite them to resolve legal issues, and admit evidence of a rule's requirements to prove the violation of a legal duty. See chapter 13B1. Other jurisdictions reject this view. See, e.g., Post v. Bregman, 707 A.2d 806 (Md. 1998) (the rules "constitute[] a statement of public policy by the only entity in this State having the Constitutional authority to make such a statement, and [they have] the force of law").

I. OTHER SOURCES

Beyond the Rules are interpretations of them by bar committees in all states and at the ABA. A lawyer may write (or sometimes telephone) for advice about prospective conduct. Compliance with the advice demonstrates a lawyer's good faith, although the opinions are ordinarily not binding on a disciplinary committee or court. Opinions are published as guidelines for other lawyers and for whatever persuasive force (ranging from none to considerable) they may have with judges. Published opinions omit identifying information.

Many bar groups, including the ABA, do not await a lawyer's query before choosing to write on important new issues. As such, their work takes on the character of advisory opinions on broad questions meant to guide lawyers and courts. The ABA's opinions are particularly influential because its ethics committee is interpreting the organization's own widely copied document. Opinions are available on the ABA's website (americanbar.org/cpr), state and local bar websites, and Lexis, Westlaw, and Bloomberg Law.

Other secondary sources include:

- The Georgetown Journal of Legal Ethics, inspired by Father Robert Drinan, which has become essential reading for anyone working in this field.
- The multivolume Lawyers' Manual on Professional Conduct, published electronically. Not only does the Manual monitor court decisions and other developments; it also provides summaries of important ethics opinions (and for ABA opinions, the full text).
- The two-volume Restatement of the Law Governing Lawyers, a 14-year project that aimed to restate the rules governing the U.S. legal profession.

J. BEHAVIORAL LEGAL ETHICS

This book is about rules lawyers must obey. Their oath of office requires that they do so. When a lawyer violates a rule, he may be aware of his misconduct but hope to gain a perceived advantage without detection; in other words, a "bad apple." But it may also be that he missed the ethical issue entirely—just didn't recognize it—or that he saw it but "reasoned" his way out of it so he could do what he wanted.

Research in behavioral and cognitive psychology explains how such things happen—why good people stray. Recent scholarship applies this research to lawyers. It is called *behavioral legal ethics*. (For one dramatic example of a court's use of behavioral legal ethics, see United States v. Kentucky Bar in chapter 5B1.) Understanding the lessons of behavioral legal ethics can provide self-awareness that helps avoid misconduct. A good source is Jennifer Robbennolt & Jean Sternlight, Behavioral Legal Ethics, 45 Ariz. St. L.J. 1107 (2013).

K. REAL ETHICS

Are we forgetting something? Colloquially, the subject is called legal *ethics*. Does it have anything to do with real ethics—the kind moral philosophers study in the tradition of Plato, Kant, and Mill? Yes and no. The title of the model ABA document has moved further and further away from ethics, as such, and toward descriptions that are rather law-like. Indeed, the documents that courts adopt *are* law, if by law we mean rules that carry state penalties if violated. Whereas the 1908 Canons had "Professional Ethics" in its title, the 1970 Code substituted "Professional Responsibility," and the 1983 Rules opted for "Professional Conduct."

But "ethics" lives on. Appeals to ethics let the bar proclaim its allegiance to ancient ideals, although the profession has made little or no effort to seek the views of moral philosophers. Real ethicists and academics who study the professions have nonetheless measured the "ethics" of lawyers against the standards of their disciplines. Richard Wasserstrom's prominent article, Lawyers as Professionals: Some Moral Issues, 5 Hum. Rts. 1 (1975), was one of the first to do so. (Some day I will attend a legal ethics conference wearing a button reading WWAD: What Would Aristotle Do?)

L. WHAT IS PROFESSIONALISM?

In the mid-1980s, the word "professionalism" appeared with some frequency in bar publications and was heard increasingly at bar meetings. The ABA and some local bar groups formed committees on professionalism (or committees on the profession) to study the topic and write reports. Many meetings were held. Many reports were written, most saying the same things. Their definitions of a "profession" share a theme: A professional subordinates self-interest and private gain to the interests of clients or to the public good generally. But the professionalism committees also recognized the financial needs of lawyers. Some forthrightly acknowledged that law practice shares many of the attributes of a business. It most certainly does. The search seems to be for the proper balance between professionalism and business. Some trends are said to take the profession too far in the wrong direction. We are warned against "over-commercialization." Mostly, the reports' conclusions are vague and aspirational.

No one can say for sure how it came about that so many lawyers in so many bar associations decided, seemingly simultaneously, to spend so many hours at bar dinners debating what it means to be a profession and drafting codes of professionalism for others to put on their shelves. I offer two possibilities:

- The advent of lawyer advertising following the *Bates* decision in 1977 (see chapter 16A) led to some offensive marketing schemes, which, coupled with pervasive, if tamer, efforts at self-promotion, conveyed the impression that lawyers were fixated on making money. An emphasis on professionalism might then be seen as an antidote or at least the public appearance of one.
- As the number of lawyers in the nation dramatically increased relative to its nonlawyer population (from 1 in every 625 persons in 1960 to 1 in every 245 persons by 2020 according to the Census Bureau and the ABA), a need arose to remind lawyers that they were members of an elite club, or if (alas) the club was no longer quite so elite, it behooved lawyers to behave otherwise (at least in public).

Professionalism now has a permanent, if less prominent, home in the legal world. You may hear talk of it wherever lawyers congregate. Even lawyers too young to remember whether the particular Camelot ever existed will invoke the kinder, gentler time when courtesy was king, no one fought dirty, and lawyers treated each other like, well, professionals. Bar chatter is spiced with anecdotes of other lawyers' (usually an adversary's) monstrous behavior, often accompanied by a shake of the head, lips pressed together. Tsk tsk. What's this world coming to? Meanwhile, some lawyers seek to turn the perceived decline to their advantage by proudly (and loudly) proclaiming their readiness to "go right up to the line" for their clients. This presumes, of course, that there is a line, like the one down the center of a highway, and that its location is obvious. Much of this book is meant to tell you that if that was ever so, it is no longer. Proceed with caution.

PART ONE

THE ATTORNEY-CLIENT RELATIONSHIP

II

Defining the Attorney-Client Relationship

In the beginning is the client. But also before the beginning and after the end. Which is another way of saying that some rules apply even before a person formally becomes a client (if she ever does) and continue long after the work is done.

Lawyers love to quote Henry Brougham, the great British barrister and Lord Chancellor of the nineteenth century, who said that "an advocate, in the discharge of his duty, knows but one person in all the world, and that person is his client."* How professionally liberating. *One person. In all the world.* But like many grand pronouncements, it is not entirely true. Lawyers also have obligations to courts, adversaries, partners, and associates. Still, duties to clients are the main concern of ethical and legal rules governing lawyers and will be ours. Whether these duties, in addition to being more numerous, should always be viewed as more important than preventing harm to others, the demands of "justice," or the "public interest"—and if so, when—are questions for debate. Indeed, debate is inevitable.

Debate is more likely in law schools and bar committees than in law offices. In the tumult of daily practice, lawyers have brief time to ponder *The Big Questions.* Many lawyers would agree with a prominent Connecticut lawyer's response to me when, recently admitted to the bar, I asked if he did public interest cases. It probably sounded like a challenge. It probably was. "I serve the public interest by fighting for the private interests of each of my clients, one at a time," he instructed, slowly emphasizing each word. Is he right? Lord Brougham would say yes. Rejecting any qualifiers, Brougham went on to say that the "hazards and costs to other persons" are of no concern to the lawyer, who "must not regard the alarm, the torments, the destruction which he may bring upon others. . . . [H]e must go on reckless of the consequences, though it should be his unhappy fate to involve his

---

* Trial of Queen Caroline 8 (J. Nightingale ed., 1821).

19

country in confusion."* No ambiguity there. Is that what legal ethics rules (should) require, tolerate, or encourage?

Not exactly. Lawyers have a tendency to describe their commitment to clients with a fervor generally associated with speakers at revival meetings, Fourth of July orators, and deans at alumni events. If nothing else, it plays well; but, to be fair, the passion is often truly felt. Passion, however, is not a reliable guide for conduct. We do have rules, after all, and some subordinate a client's interests to other interests and values. Sometimes, in fact, the clash is between the interests of two (or more) current or former clients.

A further word about Lord Brougham (who has an encore in chapter 7). The Lord made his comments while representing the Queen of England against a criminal charge of adultery. We might view his description of the advocate's role as a threat to expose the King. If so, it worked.†

A. IS THERE A CLIENT HERE?

A threshold question that recurs throughout this book is: What makes someone a client? That question is answered by case law, not the Rules. But much can turn on the answer, such as whether a lawyer has a conflict that restricts his or her practice and the practice of colleagues, whether a lawyer may be liable in malpractice or subject to discipline, and whether a person's communications with a lawyer are confidential or privileged. For lovers of ambiguity, the question (is or was X a client?) will often lack an easy answer. Lawyers do love ambiguity. You can see why. Ambiguity creates contests that require the assistance of counsel. Much of what lawyers do in litigation is find ambiguity when clarity disserves their clients. In transactional matters, lawyers avoid ambiguities that may harm their clients, but not those that a client may later exploit to advantage.

Lawyers hate ambiguity that creates dilemmas for lawyers, however, especially if guessing wrong can be costly. But as lawyers often tell clients whose personal or commercial lives are governed by complex rules, the answer to the question "Can I do that?" may be "Not clear. Arguments exist pro and con. What's your risk tolerance?" The same goes for lawyers.

The vast majority of lawyer-client relationships are still formed by contracts, leaving no doubt. The relationship can also be implied.

> An attorney-client relationship is formed when: (1) a person manifests to a lawyer the person's intent that the lawyer provide legal services for the person; and . . . (b) the lawyer fails to manifest lack of consent to do so, and the lawyer knows or reasonably should know that the person reasonably relies on the lawyer to provide the services.

---

* *Id.* 333

† For a riveting account of the trial and of Lord Brougham's prowess as a lawyer, see Jane Robins, *The Trial of Queen Caroline* (Free Press 2006).

Atty. Grievance Comm'n. v. Kreamer, 946 A.2d 500 (Md. 2008) (quoting the Restatement). Court assignment of lawyers to represent indigent criminal defendants is the other common route to a professional relationship.

But that's not the end of it. "The client is no longer simply the person who walks into a law office," Judge Arthur Sprecher presciently wrote in 1978 in Westinghouse Electric Corp. v. Kerr-McGee Corp., 580 F.2d 1311 (7th Cir. 1978), capturing in a short, understated sentence an emerging trend whose reality has since become commonplace. So, for example, in *Togstad* (chapter 13A), a lawyer had a professional relationship with (and malpractice liability to) Mrs. Togstad although he *declined* to accept her case. Mr. Togstad was his client, too, although the two apparently never met. As we shall see in the material on conflicts of interest, companies that are members of trade groups may be deemed clients of lawyers who represent the groups, at least for certain purposes. Rule 1.18 protects persons who consult lawyers but do not ultimately retain them.

Courts are alert to what persons claiming to be clients might reasonably have believed, especially so if they have given the lawyer confidential information. In Analytica, Inc. v. NPD Research (chapter 6A), a company wanted to give an employee stock as a reward for good service. The company disclosed financial information to a law firm the employee had hired to advise on how to minimize taxes from the transfer. On a motion to disqualify the law firm from later suing the company in a matter in which the financial information could be used against it, the court said the company was a former client even though it had not itself retained the firm.

Duties in the professional relationship are, as we shall see, based in part on the law of agency. Even when a client-lawyer relationship is established, it will have a finite scope, as do principal-agent relationships generally. The Rules and cases use the word "matter" to describe the scope of a lawyer's retainer and therefore the extent of her authority and duties. So, for example, when the Brobeck firm was retained to file a certiorari petition for Telex (see chapter 4A), it had no duty to advise Telex on its personnel policies. The matter was the petition, nothing else.

The Telex retainer agreement was detailed, but often the scope of the relationship will be unclear. If a lawyer is retained to bring a negligence claim following a car crash, she has no responsibility for the client's copyright claim. But must the lawyer also protect the client's no-fault insurance benefits arising from the crash, even though that service was never mentioned? The client may look at the retainer holistically, while the lawyer may define it by reference to a particular service. So the client thinks, "This lawyer will help me get the money I'm owed because of this accident," while the lawyer thinks, "I'm retained only to sue the other driver for negligence, not to get no-fault payments from the client's own insurer." Courts expect lawyers to be sensitive to, and to clarify, any ambiguity. The nature of the clarification will depend on the client's sophistication.

The conventional image of the client-lawyer relationship posits two people who have agreed that one will provide a defined service to the other for a fee. However, no formality or fee is necessary, nor must the participants be limited to two. (Sometimes, however, the agreement must be in writing. See chapter 4B.) There may be several or many lawyers and several or many clients. Nor must the client be a person. Corporations, trade associations, labor unions, estates, and governments may all be clients.

Another type of client is the class. "The responsibility of class counsel to absent class members whose control over their attorneys is limited does not permit even the appearance of divided loyalties of counsel. In addition, class counsel's fiduciary duty is to the class as a whole and it includes reporting potential conflict issues." Rodriguez v. West Publ'g Corp., 563 F.3d 948 (9th Cir. 2009). Some courts recognize a fiduciary duty to members of a "putative" (not yet certified) class. "Beyond their ethical obligations to their clients, class attorneys, purporting to represent a class, also owe the entire class a fiduciary duty once the class complaint is filed." In re Gen. Motors Corp. Pick-Up Truck Fuel Tank Prods. Liab. Litig., 55 F.3d 768 (3d Cir. 1995); Fla. Bar v. Adorno, 60 So. 3d 1016 (Fla. 2011) (even if Adorno had no attorney-client relationship with putative class members, he violated his fiduciary duty to them when he settled the action for named plaintiffs only).

B. WHAT DO LAWYERS OWE CLIENTS?

1. Competence

> About half of the practice of a decent lawyer is telling would-be clients that they are damned fools and should stop.[*]
> —Elihu Root, U.S. Secretary of State (1905-1909)

> A Washington, D.C. judge declared a mistrial in a murder case Friday, saying he was "astonished" at the performance of the defense lawyer who confessed to jurors he'd never tried a case before.
> —ABA Journal, April 4, 2011

The very first rule in the Model Rules requires lawyers to provide clients with "competent" representation, defined to require "the legal knowledge, skill, thoroughness and preparation reasonably necessary for the representation." Rule 1.1. Incompetence has many parents: ignorance, inexperience, neglect, lack of time, and high volume.

---

* Quoted, inter alia, in In re Haggerty, 542 B.R. 849 (Bankr. N.D. Ind. 2015); Triplett v. Colvin, 2013 WL 6169562 (N.D. Ill. 2013); and Andrus v. Dep't. of Transp., 117 P.3d 1152 (Wash. Ct. App. 2005). The message here is that sometimes it is wise to tell a client to forget about it, for their own good and yours. Many clients don't want to hear "forget about it," and many lawyers don't want to say "forget about it" because it turns away business. That's no excuse.

The Florida Supreme Court has ruled that public defenders may withdraw from matters if their case volume threatens effective representation. "[W]hen understaffing creates a situation where indigent [defendants] are not afforded effective assistance of counsel, the public defender may be allowed to withdraw." Pub. Defender v. State, 115 So. 3d 261 (Fla. 2013) (rejecting legislation that prohibited granting permission to withdraw on this basis). A lawyer has a duty to decline more work than he can competently handle, but that might not be easy for junior lawyers. If the person assigning the work is a lawyer, she has a duty not to assign more work than a subordinate can perform competently. ABA Opinion 06-441 makes the point:

> If workload prevents a lawyer from providing competent and diligent representation to existing clients, she must not accept new clients. If the clients are being assigned through a court appointment system, the lawyer should request that the court not make any new appointments. . . . [L]awyer supervisors must, working closely with the lawyers they supervise, monitor the workload of the supervised lawyers to ensure that the workloads do not exceed a level that may be competently handled by the individual lawyers.

Incompetent work can lead to malpractice liability (chapter 13A). It rarely leads to discipline. (Contrast neglect, where a lawyer does *no work at all* and which can and does lead to discipline.) But it does happen. Although Joe Pegram had no criminal law experience, he accepted a felony case and charged $20,000 for representation through trial. He affiliated with experienced co-counsel, but continued alone after that lawyer dropped out and even though he knew he would be unable to try the case. He was hoping to negotiate a plea, but could not. So he withdrew on the first day of trial. He was reprimanded for taking work he was not competent to handle. In re Pegram, 167 So.3d 230 (Miss. 2014). Stephen Barns accepted a job as a company's chief legal officer, but later admitted that "he had never organized a corporate structure for anyone other than himself" and that he had "entered an area of law that he knew nothing about." Columbus Bar Ass'n v. Barns, 123 N.E.3d 922 (Ohio 2018) (public reprimand).

If suspicions about a lawyer's competence persist, you might expect these to deter new clients. After all, poorly reviewed movies discourage ticket buyers. But this assumes knowledgeable law consumers and available information. Sophisticated buyers of legal services, like big companies that retain lawyers with the advice of in-house lawyers, can shop for quality and monitor performance. Not so those who rarely hire lawyers. Consumers may do more research when buying a car than when hiring a lawyer because more information is easily available about cars. The market is imperfect.

The Sixth Amendment has an additional competence requirement. It guarantees the effective assistance of counsel in criminal cases. See chapter 13E. Each state can choose its own definition of competence for malpractice and discipline, but the Sixth Amendment guarantee is the same nationwide.

Malpractice, discipline, and the Sixth Amendment are enforced in retrospect by inspecting what the lawyer did or failed to do. We also attempt to reduce the risk of incompetence prospectively by imposing education and examination requirements for admission to the bar. See chapter 12A.

Competence Includes Judgment

Among the most important qualities a lawyer can have is good judgment, which is part of competence. Malpractice includes the failure to exercise reasonable judgment. See, e.g., Williamson v. Bratt, 2010 WL 4102999 (Mich. Ct. App. 2010) ("An attorney owes a duty to exercise reasonable skill, care, discretion, and judgment in representing a client."). Judgment distinguishes what should be done from what can be done. I sometimes think of it as learned intuition, which requires years of experience. Problem-solving in law school classes, especially clinics, can begin to develop judgment. Students, preferably in small groups, can talk through options and risks, including those that might not have occurred to each of them alone, and collectively identify the best response. But developing judgment takes more than the limited opportunities law schools can offer. It requires time in practice. Watching seasoned lawyers helps. They teach by example whether they know it or not.

2. *Confidentiality*

The Case of the Innocent Lifer*

In March 2008, CBS News correspondent Bob Simon reported this story on *60 Minutes*:

> Alton Logan was convicted of killing a security guard at a McDonald's in Chicago in 1982. Police arrested him after a tip and got three eyewitnesses to identify him. Logan, his mother and brother all testified he was at home asleep when the murder occurred. But a jury found him guilty of first degree murder. . . . Logan, who maintains he didn't commit the murder, thought they were "crazy" when he was arrested for the crime.
>
> Attorneys Dale Coventry and Jamie Kunz knew Logan had good reason to think that, because they knew he was innocent. And they knew that because their client, Andrew Wilson, who they were defending for killing two policemen, confessed to them that he had also killed the security guard at McDonald's — the crime Logan was charged with.
>
> "We got information that Wilson was the guy and not Alton Logan. So we went over to the jail immediately almost and said, 'Is that true? Was

---

* This is the first of this book's many problems. Mostly, problems precede the materials that will then help you solve the problems. The advantage is that you can have the problems in mind as you read the text.

that you?' And he said, 'Yep it was me,'" Kunz recalled. "He just about hugged himself and smiled. I mean he was kind of gleeful about it. It was a very strange response," Kunz said, recalling how Wilson had reacted.

"How did you interpret that response?" Simon asked.

"That it was true and that he was tickled pink," Kunz said.

---

1. Wilson gave his lawyers written authority to reveal his guilt after he died. He lived 26 years. All the while Logan was imprisoned. After his release, Logan sued Chicago and settled for $10.25 million.
2. Under the Model Rules (which were not then the Illinois rules), what options and obligations would the lawyers have had when Wilson confessed to them?
3. Logan's jury split 10 to 2 in favor of execution. Unanimity was required for a death sentence, so he was sentenced to life. Would it change your answer if Logan were on death row?
4. What should a jurisdiction's rule say on these facts? Should there be an express exception permitting disclosure to prevent an unjust incarceration? Requiring disclosure? Should the length of a prison sentence matter?
5. What might have happened to Wilson if the lawyers had disclosed Wilson's confession to Logan's lawyer and the prosecutor? How does that affect your analysis?

"Lori Is on Opioids"

"I have a longtime client I'll call Roland. He runs a family company, founded by his great-grandfather. He has two children. The older one is 19. I'll call her Lori. She's a sophomore at a top university. She got arrested for drunk driving. She crossed the center line and sideswiped an oncoming car. She had been drinking. This was her second driving under the influence charge in six months. She faced the loss of her license.

"Lori called her father to help get a lawyer. Roland called me. We have an office in the city where Lori is at school and one of my partners, Neera, is a defense lawyer. In fact, she was once the local U.S. Attorney. This is not the kind of case Neera handles, but Roland said he'd feel better if we took it so we did. He's paying the fee.

"Last night Neera called me with some hard news. 'In addition to being intoxicated,' Neera said, 'Lori was on opioids. I'm not sure which ones. The cops missed it because the alcohol masked the effects.' Lori told Neera she runs track. She started with a prescription after a bad fall, and didn't stop.

"Neera said, 'Dorothy, you better tell her parents. I don't think she'll kick this without help, although she said she will. I don't think she realizes the risk. I didn't ask how she got her supply. This could lead to a disaster for Lori and her family.'

"I've since learned that opioids cause more than 48,000 deaths in the U.S. yearly, a number that has been rising steadily. One medical site says: 'Opioids can make your brain and body believe the drug is necessary for survival. As you learn to tolerate the dose you've been prescribed, you may find that you need even more medication to relieve the pain or achieve well-being, which can lead to dependency. Addiction takes hold of our brains in several ways—and is far more complex and less forgiving than many people realize.'

"When I next talk to Roland about his company's legal matters, he may ask how it's going with Lori's case. What can and should I tell him about the opioids?"

How Does *Your Garden*™ Grow?

"We have long represented Your Garden™, a family company that sells gardening products. Six months ago we helped it apply for a substantial increase in its bank line of credit, for which it had to submit certified profit and loss statements for the last two fiscal years, which it did. We negotiated the loan terms with the bank and submitted the statements on Your Garden's behalf. The bank approved the increase. Last week we got information suggesting that the statements were materially false. We confronted Emmett Blank, the CEO, and he admitted that the statements were indeed false. He said he needed the cash to get through a rough patch caused by unexpected expenses and the failure of sales projections to materialize. He said things were looking better now although he was not yet out of the woods.

"Our firm's work helped Your Garden defraud the bank, although of course did not then know it. Some of us want to alert the bank if Emmett won't. Others think we cannot because what we know is privileged and confidential. Yet others just want to wait, hoping that the market will rebound and Your Garden will make its payments. Advise us."

Short though it is, and decades old, the following valuable opinion surfaces themes that appear in this chapter and beyond it. They are addressed in the note following.

PEREZ v. KIRK & CARRIGAN
822 S.W.2d 261 (Tex. App. 1991)

DORSEY, JUSTICE.

Ruben Perez appeals a summary judgment rendered against him on his causes of action against the law firm of Kirk & Carrigan, and against Dana Kirk and Steve Carrigan individually (henceforth all three will be collectively referred to as "Kirk & Carrigan"). We reverse the summary judgment and remand this case for trial.

The present suit arises from a school bus accident on September 21, 1989, in Alton, Texas. Ruben Perez was employed by Valley Coca-Cola Bottling Company as a truck driver. On the morning of the accident, Perez attempted to stop his truck at a stop sign along his route, but the truck's brakes failed to stop the truck, which collided with the school bus. The loaded bus was knocked into a pond and 21 children died. Perez suffered injuries from the collision and was taken to a local hospital to be treated.

The day after the accident, Kirk & Carrigan, lawyers who had been hired to represent Valley Coca-Cola Bottling Company, visited Perez in the hospital for the purpose of taking his statement. Perez claims that the lawyers told him they were his lawyers too and that anything he told them would be kept confidential. With this understanding, Perez gave them a sworn statement concerning the accident. However, after taking Perez' statement, Kirk & Carrigan had no further contact with him. Instead, Kirk & Carrigan made arrangements for criminal defense attorney Joseph Connors to represent Perez. Connors was paid by National Union Fire Insurance Company which covered both Valley Coca-Cola and Perez for liability in connection with the accident.

Some time after Connors began representing Perez, Kirk & Carrigan, without telling either Perez or Connors, turned Perez' statement over to the Hildalgo County District Attorney's Office. Kirk & Carrigan contend that Perez' statement was provided in a good faith attempt to fully comply with a request of the district attorney's office and under threat of subpoena if they did not voluntarily comply. Partly on the basis of this statement, the district attorney was able to obtain a grand jury indictment of Perez for involuntary manslaughter for his actions in connection with the accident. . . .

By his sole point of error, Perez complains simply that the trial court erred in granting Kirk & Carrigan's motion for summary judgment. . . .

With regard to Perez' cause of action for breach of the fiduciary duty of good faith and fair dealing, Kirk & Carrigan contend that no attorney-client relationship existed and no fiduciary duty arose, because Perez never sought legal advice from them.

An agreement to form an attorney-client relationship may be implied from the conduct of the parties. Moreover, the relationship does not depend upon the payment of a fee, but may exist as a result of rendering services gratuitously.[4]

In the present case, viewing the summary judgment evidence in the light most favorable to Perez, Kirk & Carrigan told him that, in addition to representing Valley Coca-Cola, they were also Perez' lawyers and that they were going to help him. Perez did not challenge this assertion, and he cooperated with the lawyers in giving his statement to them, even though he did

---

4. An attorney's fiduciary responsibilities may arise even during preliminary consultations regarding the attorney's possible retention if the attorney enters into discussion of the client's legal problems with a view toward undertaking representation.

not offer, nor was he asked, to pay the lawyers' fees. We hold that this was sufficient to imply the creation of an attorney-client relationship at the time Perez gave his statement to Kirk & Carrigan.

The existence of this relationship encouraged Perez to trust Kirk & Carrigan and gave rise to a corresponding duty on the part of the attorneys not to violate this position of trust. Accordingly, the relation between attorney and client is highly fiduciary in nature, and their dealings with each other are subject to the same scrutiny as a transaction between trustee and beneficiary. Specifically, the relationship between attorney and client has been described as one of *uberrima fides*, which means, "most abundant good faith," requiring absolute and perfect candor, openness and honesty, and the absence of any concealment or deception. In addition, because of the openness and candor within this relationship, certain communications between attorney and client are privileged from disclosure in either civil or criminal proceedings. . . .[5]

There is evidence that Kirk & Carrigan represented to Perez that his statement would be kept confidential. Later, however, without telling either Perez or his subsequently-retained criminal defense attorney, Kirk & Carrigan voluntarily disclosed Perez' statement to the district attorney. Perez asserts in the present suit that this course of conduct amounted, among other things, to a breach of fiduciary duty.

Kirk & Carrigan seek to avoid this claim of breach, on the ground that the attorney-client privilege did not apply to the present statement, because unnecessary third parties were present at the time it was given. However, whether or not the . . . attorney-client privilege extended to Perez' statement, Kirk & Carrigan initially obtained the statement from Perez on the understanding that it would be kept confidential. Thus, regardless of whether from an evidentiary standpoint the privilege attached, Kirk & Carrigan breached their fiduciary duty to Perez either by wrongfully disclosing a privileged statement or by wrongfully representing that an unprivileged statement would be kept confidential. Either characterization shows a clear lack of honesty toward, and a deception of, Perez by his own attorneys regarding the degree of confidentiality with which they intended to treat the statement. . . .

In addition, however, even assuming a breach of fiduciary duty, Kirk & Carrigan also contend that summary judgment may be sustained on the ground that Perez could show no damages resulting from the breach. Kirk & Carrigan contend that their dissemination of Perez' statement could not have caused him any damages in the way of emotional distress, because the

5. Disclosure of confidential communications by an attorney, whether privileged or not under the rules of evidence, is generally prohibited by the disciplinary rules governing attorneys' conduct in Texas. [The court cited the Texas equivalent to Rule 1.6.] In addition, the general rule is that confidential information received during the course of any fiduciary relationship may not be used or disclosed to the detriment of the one from whom the information is obtained.

statement merely revealed Perez' own version of what happened. We do not agree. Mental anguish consists of the emotional response of the plaintiff caused by the tortfeasor's conduct. It includes, among other things, the mental sensation of pain resulting from public humiliation.

Regardless of the fact that Perez himself made the present statement, he did not necessarily intend it to be a public response as Kirk & Carrigan contend, but only a private and confidential discussion with his attorneys. Perez alleged that the publicity caused by his indictment, resulting from the revelation of the statement to the district attorney in breach of that confidentiality, caused him to suffer emotional distress and mental anguish. We hold that Perez has made a valid claim for such damages. . . .

[Reversed]

―――――――――

Perez inspired a fine novel, *The Sweet Hereafter* by Russell Banks. An equally fine movie, directed by Atom Egoyan, followed. The main character is a lawyer who wants to represent the families of the children on the school bus. Unlike some lawyer novels, the portrayals ring true.

In May 1993, more than three and a half years after the accident, Perez was tried on 21 counts of involuntary manslaughter. The jury acquitted him on all counts after less than four hours of deliberation. Coca-Cola paid the survivors and the families of the victims $133 million to settle liability claims. The bus company, whose bus had windows that were difficult to open and only one emergency exit, settled for $23 million. Maggie Rivas, Dallas Morning News, May 6, 1993.

It didn't matter that Kirk & Carrigan had only a preliminary meeting with Perez. The attorney-client privilege and the duty of confidentiality (each of which is explained below) protect information gained from a potential client even if no retention ensues. See Model Rule 1.18 and Disciplinary Counsel v. Cicero, 982 N.E.2d 650 (Ohio 2012) (one-year suspension of lawyer who disclosed confidential information of potential client). Why protect a lawyer's *potential* clients, i.e., those who don't become actual clients either because the lawyer declines the matter or the potential client hires someone else?

Here are four questions *Perez* raises:

- What was the legal basis for Perez's claim? That is, what law gave him a right to sue for damages? As we will see later, the Rules do not create a right to sue, although a violation of the Rules may be admissible as some evidence of a violation of a legal duty.
- Assume Kirk & Carrigan had said only that "the company hired us because of the accident." You represent Perez. What do you argue?
- How could the lawyers have protected themselves, if at all? See Rule 4.3.
- How can the court characterize Perez's communications with Kirk & Carrigan as "confidential" if the presence of a third person in the hospital room would have destroyed the attorney-client privilege?

Civil claims against lawyers for improper disclosure of a client's confidential information are rare, but the doctrinal basis for them is clear. Rebecca Parkinson sued her former divorce lawyer James Bevis. She alleged that he had shared her confidential communications with the lawyer for her former husband. The Idaho Supreme Court held that Parkinson's complaint stated a valid claim for breach of fiduciary duty for which the remedy could be disgorgement of some or all of the fees Parkinson paid Bevis. Parkinson v. Bevis, 448 P.3d 1027 (Idaho 2019).

Bye, a lawyer, had represented Thiery in a personal injury action. Before the matter ended, Bye asked Thiery if his nurse-investigator could use Thiery's medical records to teach a class at a technical college. Bye said Thiery would be paid $500 and that all identifying information would be removed. Thiery agreed. Thiery then claimed that Bye had failed to remove some identifying information and sued for malpractice. Citing Wisconsin's version of Rule 1.6, the agreement, and the law of agency, the court reversed summary judgment for Bye. Bye had an obligation to maintain Thiery's confidential information during and after the relationship. Nor did Thiery need an expert witness to prove her case. "A layperson would have little difficulty understanding the duty Bye accepted in his letter to Thiery or determining whether Bye's failure to assure the redaction was completed was a breach of his obligation to his client. We have concluded as a matter of law that Bye owed a duty to maintain the confidentiality of Thiery's records." Thiery v. Bye, 597 N.W.2d 449 (Wis. Ct. App. 1999).

The most notorious recent instance of unauthorized disclosure of a confidence may be the outing of *Harry Potter* author J.K. Rowling as the author of *The Cuckoo's Calling*, written under the pseudonym Robert Galbraith. Chris Gossage, a partner at Russells, Rowling's U.K. law firm, disclosed her identity to a friend. The friend then revealed the pseudonym to a journalist via Twitter and the story appeared in the Sunday Times. Russells then informed Rowling's agent that its own lawyer had been the source of the revelation. Rowling sued and the firm made a "substantial" charitable donation to settle. Matilda Battersby, The Independent, July 31, 2013. Following disclosure, the book went from nowhere to bestseller. The Solicitors Regulation Authority later rebuked Gossage and fined him £1,000.

Email and the transmission of documents over the internet pose threats to the secrecy of attorney-client communications. While that threat may not *ordinarily* require heightened protection, it may for particularly sensitive information. ABA Opinion 477 (2017) ("[I]f client information is of sufficient sensitivity, a lawyer should encrypt the transmission and determine how to do so to sufficiently protect it, and consider the use of password protection for any attachments. Alternatively, lawyers can consider the use of a well vetted and secure third-party cloud based file storage system to exchange documents normally attached to emails.").

Privileged Communications and Confidential Information: What Is the Difference?

These two distinct categories differ in what they do, but they are often confused. It's easy to see why. A goal of each is to protect information and often the very same information. But they have different legal pedigrees and different (if overlapping) exceptions, and they create different rights and duties. It is important to understand these differences.

Privileged Information. The *law of evidence* is the source of the attorney-client privilege. The privilege protects communications between a lawyer (or his agent) and a client (or its agent). The definition of the privilege may appear in case law, statutory law, or both. Unenacted Federal Rule of Evidence 503 has a good description of the privilege. It is influential even though Congress chose not to adopt specific privilege provisions, instead telling federal courts to construe privileges "in the light of reason and experience." Fed. R. Evid. 501. Many states adopted the unenacted rule anyway. It provides in part:

> A client has a privilege to refuse to disclose and to prevent any other person from disclosing confidential communications made for the purpose of facilitating the rendition of professional legal services to the client, (1) between himself or his representative and his lawyer or his lawyer's representative, or (2) between his lawyer and the lawyer's representative, or (3) by him or his lawyer to a lawyer representing another in a matter of common interest,* or (4) between representatives of the client or between the client and a representative of the client, or (5) between lawyers representing the client.

The three conditions to note here are the required identities of the parties to the communications, the required reason for the communications, and the requirement that the communications be "confidential." If a third person is present who is not an agent of the lawyer or client and not necessary to facilitate the representation (like an interpreter), the communication is not privileged. The client's identity and fee arrangement are not ordinarily considered privileged except in the "limited and rarely available" situation where disclosure will reveal "the confidential purpose for which the client sought legal advice." Taylor Lohmeyer Law Firm v. United States, 957 F.3d 505 (5th Cir. 2020).

Confidential Information. A lawyer's confidentiality duties derive from *agency and fiduciary duty law* as well as the professional conduct rules. See, e.g., Rules 1.6, 1.8(b), and 1.9(c). As we will see shortly, lawyers are agents of their clients and all agents owe their principals fiduciary duties.

---

* The common interest doctrine is discussed in chapter 5B3.

Rule 1.6(a) defines a category of information (described as "information relating to the representation of a client") that a lawyer may not *reveal* unless there is an exception (as in, e.g., Rules 1.6(b), 1.13(c), and 3.3(c), all of which we will study) or the client has given consent, which may be implied. Nor may the lawyer *use* such information about a current client to the client's "disadvantage" (Rule 1.8(b)); *reveal* such information about a former client unless there is an exception (Rule 1.9(c)(2)); or *use* such information about a former client to the client's "disadvantage" unless there is an exception or the information is "generally known" (Rule 1.9(c)(1)).

Information is confidential whether the source is the client (and therefore also privileged) or a person not described in unenacted Rule 503 (and therefore not privileged). For example, a conversation with an eyewitness to an intersection accident is confidential, but it is not privileged because the client was not the source. Communications from the client about the accident are both privileged and confidential.

Some Further Reflections on Privilege and Confidentiality. It should now be obvious that much information that is confidential will not be privileged because *the source* of the information is not the client or its agents. On the other hand, all privileged communications will be confidential. Think of the two categories as concentric circles. One category is nested in the other. The inner (smaller) circle contains privileged information only. The outer circle comprises all information within the inner circle *plus* all other information "relating to the representation of a client," regardless of source.

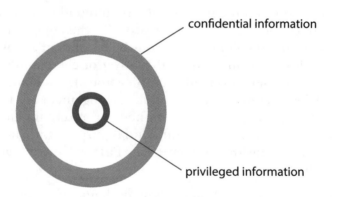

confidential information

privileged information

Because the category of confidential information includes all privileged communications (and more), why do we even need the privilege? Does it do any extra work?

Yes, it does. Here is an important difference between the two concepts, which many lawyers may overlook. When a court orders a person to answer a question, she must do so or risk contempt. But if a question calls for information protected by the attorney-client (or other) privilege, unenacted Rule

503 tells us that both a lawyer and a client can "refuse to disclose" it. Their refusal is not contempt. Nothing can happen to them.

By contrast, a court order can require disclosure of confidential information that is *not* also privileged. In re Original Grand Jury Investigation, 733 N.E.2d 1135 (Ohio 2000) (incriminating letter discovered by lawyer's investigator subject to grand jury subpoena because it is not privileged under Ohio rules). If the lawyer had *voluntarily* revealed the letter (i.e., without a court order or subpoena), he could face civil liability as in *Perez*.

In addition to civil liability, a lawyer's use or disclosure of confidential information can lead to discipline. After her client replaced her with other counsel, Donna Tonderum revealed confidential information to the prosecutor to ensure a conviction. (I'm not making this up.) She was suspended for at least three years. In re Tonderum, 840 N.W.2d 487 (Neb. 2013). (Was this sanction too light?) Disclosing a client's confidences on a consumer website in response to the client's negative evaluation of the lawyer merits discipline. In re Skinner, 740 S.E.2d 171 (Ga. 2013). Careless disposal of client files can get a lawyer into trouble. In re Litz, 950 N.E.2d 291 (Ind. 2010) (leaving closed client files next to town dump's recycling bin violates Rule 1.6; shredding recommended).

Does the motive for the lawyer's disclosure matter? It could if the lawyer relies on an exception to confidentiality, which we study later. But not otherwise. Thomas Tamm, a Justice Department lawyer, gave The New York Times confidential client information about what he perceived to be the government's illegal conduct in its applications for electronic surveillance warrants. Tamm accepted a public censure to settle a disciplinary complaint alleging violation of D.C. Rule 1.6. In support of the mild discipline, the D.C. disciplinary board cited among other factors that Tamm's "sole intent was to further government compliance with the law." In re Tamm, 145 A.3d 1022 (D.C. 2016). The Times went on to win a Pulitzer Prize for its reporting on electronic surveillance by the George W. Bush administration.

Misuse of confidential information can be a crime. United States v. O'Hagan, 521 U.S. 642 (1997), upheld the securities fraud conviction of a major law firm partner who used nonpublic information of a firm client to purchase options in the target of the client's expected tender offer.

Questions*

Lynn's law firm represents Ned in a dispute with his landlord over inadequate heat to his apartment.

> **1.** Is what Ned told Lynn about the dispute privileged? Confidential? Both?
> **2.** When deposed, can Ned properly refuse to answer the question "What did you tell Lynn about the claim?" Why or why not?

* Answers to these questions appear in a few pages.

3. Can Lynn refuse to answer the question "What did Ned tell you?" Why or why not?

4. Can Lynn tell her husband what Ned told her?

5. Lynn interviews other tenants to prepare Ned's case. Is what they told her privileged? Confidential? Both?

6. If subpoenaed, can Lynn cite Rule 1.6(a) to refuse to disclose what other tenants told her?

7. Can Lynn tell her husband what the other tenants told her?

8. If Lynn convenes a meeting among Ned and three other tenants as part of her investigation, are the communications at that meeting privileged? Confidential? Both?

9. In his answer to a deposition question, Ned describes the heat problem in his apartment. The landlord's lawyer then asks, "Is what you told Lynn any different from your testimony here?" Can Ned refuse to answer? Why or why not?

10. Can Lynn tell her law partner what Ned and the other tenants told her?

The Effect of Death.   Unless there is an exception, the *confidentiality duty* in the Model Rules continues forever, even after the client's death. California Opinion 2016-195 agrees. What about the demands of history? Imagine that in the hours after he killed John F. Kennedy, Lee Harvey Oswald met with a lawyer and provided a detailed description of the plot, naming others who helped him. Now, nearly six decades later, should the lawyer (or his firm) be free to disclose the nearly verbatim notes of what Oswald said?

Whether the *privilege* survives death depends on the jurisdiction but in most places it does. Swidler & Berlin v. United States, 524 U.S. 399 (1998) (rejecting Whitewater prosecutor Kenneth Starr's effort, after Deputy White House Counsel Vince Foster's suicide, to discover Foster's communications with his lawyer). Should there be an exception to benefit the historical record? Should a court in 2100 be empowered, after balancing privacy against the public interest, to let historians see notes of the personal lawyers for Bill Clinton or Donald Trump while they were president? While they were in public life?

Policies Behind the Privilege and the Confidentiality Rules.   What policies do the privilege and the confidentiality rules serve? After all, in *The Case of the Innocent Lifer,* the lawyers could anticipate serious harm (prison and illness) to an innocent man. What is the social value of protecting clients who are willing to inflict such harm?

Two values are often advanced. The *first* is empirical. "By assuring confidentiality, the privilege encourages clients to make 'full and frank' disclosures to their attorneys, who are then better able to provide candid advice and effective representation. This, in turn, serves 'broader public interests in the observance of law and administration of justice.'" Mohawk Indus. v. Carpenter, 558 U.S. 100 (2009).

This empirical prediction relies on an intuition—some would say common sense—about how people behave. But we have no test of this prediction. Will clients really conceal information from or lie to lawyers if communications are not protected as fully as they are now? Will they do so even knowing that an ignorant lawyer is likely to be less effective? As it happens, no communications are absolutely protected. Both the confidentiality duty and the privilege have exceptions, discussed presently, yet there is no evidence, even in jurisdictions with the broadest confidentiality exceptions, that clients trust lawyers less or are less candid.

A further problem with the empirical argument is that it does not work well for (unprivileged) confidential communications from third parties whom the lawyer discovers on his own. For example, an eyewitness to a construction site accident, who was just walking by, will not be less or more forthcoming with the lawyer depending on the breadth of the lawyer's confidentiality duty to his client.

The *second* reason to protect client information is normative. Regardless of the effect on a client's willingness to be candid, protecting a client's confidences respects the client's dignity and personhood. A client should be in control of all information the lawyer learns about her. The reason the lawyer knows this information is because she represents the client. The dignity and personhood argument is strong when the client is a biological person. It seems a bit of a stretch to talk about protecting the dignity and personhood of Google or Facebook.

Recognizing the normative policy, however, does not end the inquiry. How much should it count in deciding the breadth of the confidentiality obligation and the privilege? For example, should respect for Andrew Wilson's dignity and personhood mean that Dale Coventry and Jamie Kunz must remain silent while the innocent Alton Logan sits in prison for life?

Answers to the Questions on Pages 33–34

1. Both.
2. Yes, because the communication is privileged.
3. Yes, for the same reason.
4. No. Rule 1.6(a).
5. Confidential only. They are not clients.
6. No, because the communications are not privileged.
7. No. Rule 1.6(a).
8. Communications from other tenants are confidential but not privileged because they are not clients. Ned's communications are confidential but not privileged because the presence of third persons destroys the privilege.
9. Ned can refuse to answer because the question asks for privileged communications.
10. Yes, because as the question says, Lynn's firm represents Ned. That would be true even if the retainer agreement named only Lynn. Lawyers are "impliedly authorized" within the meaning of Rule 1.6(a) to share client information within their law offices in order to represent clients. Rule 1.6 cmt. [5].

Organizational Clients

Slip and Fall (Part I)

Edith Walton, shopping in Tracy's Department Store, slipped in the third-floor timepiece department and broke her hip. She sued, alleging that the floor was excessively waxed. Under store policy, the general counsel's office oversees investigations of any injury in the store. A half-hour after the fall, Jeanine Parr, an assistant GC, asked Mike Todd in security to investigate. Todd interviewed (a) Max Burkow, head of maintenance; (b) Tim Morse, who last waxed the floor; (c) Tina Sandstrom, a salesperson in men's furnishings who was returning from lunch; (d) Rex McCormick, a buyer in the rug department who was doing personal shopping on his day off; (e) Delia Corcoran, Burkow's predecessor as head of maintenance, since retired, who had established the store's floor waxing protocols; (f) Ed Rivera, president of the company that supplies wax to Tracy's; and (g) Angie Kuhn, who was buying a watch for her father.

Only Sandstrom, McCormick, and Kuhn saw Walton fall. Todd wrote up the interviews and gave his reports to Parr. Cora Lundquist, Walton's lawyer, deposed each of the seven people Todd interviewed and Todd himself. She asked Burkow about maintenance procedures. She asked Morse about the waxing on this occasion. She asked Corcoran about the floor waxing protocols she had established. She asked Rivera about instructions his company gave Tracy's on the use of the wax. She asked the others what they saw when Walton fell. Each witness had some memory failure so she asked Todd what they told him and demanded his interview notes. In rejecting Lundquist's demand, Parr asserted attorney-client privilege and her duty of confidentiality under Rule 1.6. Is she correct?

———————

A lawyer has the same confidentiality obligations whether the client is a biological person or an organization, like a corporation, a labor union, the government, or a partnership. (For convenience, I'll assume the client is a company.) Those duties are owed to the company, not to its constituents (e.g., employees, officers, and board members), not even to constituents who are the source of a communication, unless the lawyer represents the constituent, too. We discuss that situation in chapter 10B, which also describes a distinct confidentiality exception when a client is an organization. Rule 1.13(c).

Harder questions emerge when we turn to privilege. Companies, of course, cannot speak; their constituents speak for them. The privilege, which belongs to the company, protects communications between the company's constituents and its inside and outside counsel. Rossi v. Blue Cross & Blue

Shield, 540 N.E.2d 703 (N.Y. 1989).* But which constituents? This question sounds technical, but the answer has weighty consequences given the power of large organizations. The larger the group of constituents whose communications with counsel are privileged, the greater will be a company's ability to keep secrets and to deny information to a court, information that might be relevant to the fair resolution of a case.

One test, the *least* protective, says that the privilege protects only communications with those persons who actually run the company, called the *control group.* A more generous test looks not at the identity of the constituent, but at the subject and purpose of the communication. This is the *subject matter* test. Under it, communications with the CFO or a clerk can both be privileged.

In Upjohn Co. v. United States, Upjohn had reason to believe that its subsidiaries had made illegal payments to foreign government officials. It needed legal advice. Its attorneys sent a questionnaire to employees worldwide seeking "detailed information concerning such payments." They also conducted interviews. The Internal Revenue Service (IRS) subpoenaed the answers to the questionnaires and the records of the interviews. Upjohn resisted, citing attorney-client privilege and the work-product doctrine. Only the former concerns us here. If communications with the employees were privileged, the court could not order Upjohn to reveal them to the IRS.

Under Fed. R. Evid. 501, federal courts are authorized to define the scope of federal evidentiary privileges using common law principles. The Sixth Circuit, applying a control group test, said the privilege did not apply to "communications . . . by officers and agents not responsible for directing Upjohn's actions in response to legal advice . . . for the simple reason that the communications were not the 'client's.'" These individuals were not high enough in the company. The Supreme Court reversed.

UPJOHN CO. v. UNITED STATES
449 U.S. 383 (1981)

REHNQUIST, JUSTICE . . .

The attorney-client privilege is the oldest of the privileges for confidential communications known to the common law. Its purpose is to encourage full and frank communication between attorneys and their clients and thereby promote broader public interests in the observance of law and administration of justice. The privilege recognizes that sound legal advice or advocacy

---

* But see Akzo Nobel Chemicals v. Commission, 2010 E.C.R. 791, where the European Court of Justice rejected privilege for communications with inside counsel. It wrote: "An in-house lawyer cannot, whatever guarantees he has in the exercise of his profession, be treated in the same way as an external lawyer, because he occupies the position of an employee which, by its very nature, does not allow him to ignore the commercial strategies pursued by his employer, and thereby affects his ability to exercise professional independence."

serves public ends and that such advice or advocacy depends upon the lawyer's being fully informed by the client. . . .

The Court of Appeals, however, considered the application of the privilege in the corporate context to present a "different problem," since the client was an inanimate entity and "only the senior management, guiding and integrating the several operations, . . . can be said to possess an identity analogous to the corporation as a whole." . . .

Such a view, we think, overlooks the fact that the privilege exists to protect not only the giving of professional advice to those who can act on it but also the giving of information to the lawyer to enable him to give sound and informed advice. The first step in the resolution of any legal problem is ascertaining the factual background and sifting through the facts with an eye to the legally relevant. . . .

In the case of the individual client the provider of information and the person who acts on the lawyer's advice are one and the same. In the corporate context, however, it will frequently be employees beyond the control group as defined by the court below—"officers and agents . . . responsible for directing [the company's] actions in response to legal advice"—who will possess the information needed by the corporation's lawyers. Middle-level—and indeed lower-level—employees can, by actions within the scope of their employment, embroil the corporation in serious legal difficulties, and it is only natural that these employees would have the relevant information needed by corporate counsel if he is adequately to advise the client with respect to such actual or potential difficulties. . . .

The control group test adopted by the court below thus frustrates the very purpose of the privilege by discouraging the communication of relevant information by employees of the client to attorneys seeking to render legal advice to the client corporation. The attorney's advice will also frequently be more significant to noncontrol group members than to those who officially sanction the advice, and the control group test makes it more difficult to convey full and frank legal advice to the employees who will put into effect the client corporation's policy.

The narrow scope given the attorney-client privilege by the court below not only makes it difficult for corporate attorneys to formulate sound advice when their client is faced with a specific legal problem but also threatens to limit the valuable efforts of corporate counsel to ensure their client's compliance with the law. In light of the vast and complicated array of regulatory legislation confronting the modern corporation, corporations, unlike most individuals, "constantly go to lawyers to find out how to obey the law." . . .[2]

---

2. The Government argues that the risk of civil or criminal liability suffices to ensure that corporations will seek legal advice in the absence of the protection of the privilege. This response ignores the fact that the depth and quality of any investigations to ensure compliance with the law would suffer, even were they undertaken. The response also proves too much, since it applies to all communications covered by the privilege: an individual trying to

The test adopted by the court below is difficult to apply in practice, though no abstractly formulated and unvarying "test" will necessarily enable courts to decide questions such as this with mathematical precision. But if the purpose of the attorney-client privilege is to be served, the attorney and client must be able to predict with some degree of certainty whether particular discussions will be protected. An uncertain privilege, or one which purports to be certain but results in widely varying applications by the courts, is little better than no privilege at all. The very terms of the test adopted by the court below suggest the unpredictability of its application. The test restricts the availability of the privilege to those officers who play a "substantial role" in deciding and directing a corporation's legal response. Disparate decisions in cases applying this test illustrate its unpredictability.

The communications at issue were made by Upjohn employees to counsel for Upjohn acting as such, at the direction of corporate superiors in order to secure legal advice from counsel. . . . Information, not available from upper-echelon management, was needed to supply a basis for legal advice concerning compliance with securities and tax laws, foreign laws, currency regulations, duties to shareholders, and potential litigation in each of these areas. The communications concerned matters within the scope of the employees' corporate duties, and the employees themselves were sufficiently aware that they were being questioned in order that the corporation could obtain legal advice. . . .

The Court of Appeals declined to extend the attorney-client privilege beyond the limits of the control group test for fear that doing so would entail severe burdens on discovery and create a broad "zone of silence" over corporate affairs. Application of the attorney-client privilege to communications such as those involved here, however, puts the adversary in no worse position than if the communications had never taken place. The privilege only protects disclosure of communications; it does not protect disclosure of the underlying facts by those who communicated with the attorney. . . . Here the Government was free to question the employees who communicated with [inside] and outside counsel. Upjohn has provided the IRS with a list of such employees, and the IRS has already interviewed some 25 of them. While it would probably be more convenient for the Government to secure the results of petitioner's internal investigation by simply subpoenaing the questionnaires and notes taken by petitioner's attorneys, such considerations of convenience do not overcome the policies served by the attorney-client privilege. . . .

[Chief Justice Burger concurred in part and concurred in the judgment.]

---

comply with the law or faced with a legal problem also has strong incentive to disclose information to his lawyer, yet the common law has recognized the value of the privilege in further facilitating communications.

What does the Court mean by this sentence: "The privilege only protects disclosure of communications; it does not protect disclosure of the underlying facts by those who communicated with the attorney"? How does that sentence help the IRS?

Whether or not intended, *Upjohn* appears to describe two tests. The Court first wrote: "The communications at issue were made by Upjohn employees to counsel for Upjohn acting as such, at the direction of corporate superiors in order to secure legal advice from counsel." Then in the same paragraph it wrote: "The communications *concerned matters within the scope of the employees' corporate duties*, and the employees themselves were sufficiently aware that they were being questioned in order that the corporation could obtain legal advice." (Emphasis added.) The italicized words further limit the scope of the privilege. Depending on which test we use, the answers to Slip and Fall (Part I) may differ for Sandstrom and McCormick, right?

Keefe v. Bernard, 774 N.W.2d 663 (Iowa 2009), restated and narrowed the *Upjohn* holding this way: "If an employee of a corporation or entity discusses his or her own actions relating to potential liability of the corporation, such communications are protected by the attorney-client privilege. If, on the other hand, a corporate employee is interviewed as a 'witness' to the actions of others, the communication should not be protected by the corporation's attorney-client privilege." Under this test, are the communications with McCormick and Sandstrom privileged?

Restatement §73 opts for the most protective test of all. It privileges all communications between an agent or employee of the company and its lawyer so long as the communication "concerns a legal matter of interest" to the company. There is no requirement that it concern a matter within the scope of the agent's duties. Under this test, would any constituent's communications with Todd *not* be privileged?

Upjohn is good for companies, but it is also good for lawyers. A company is encouraged to place internal investigations under the authority of a lawyer, as Upjohn did, thereby enabling it to assert privilege for what the investigation uncovers so long as the company can show that counsel's purpose was "to render legal advice or services to the client." Spectrum Sys. Int'l Corp. v. Chemical Bank, 581 N.E.2d 1055 (N.Y. 1991) (privilege protects internal investigation by outside counsel). The lawyer need not conduct the interviews herself. In re Kellogg Brown & Root, Inc., 756 F.3d 754 (D.C. Cir. 2014) ("[C]ommunications made by and to non-attorneys serving as agents of attorneys in internal investigations are routinely protected by the attorney-client privilege.").

Citing *Upjohn*, courts have upheld claims of privilege for purely factual investigations. "[C]lients often do retain lawyers to perform investigative work because they want the benefit of a lawyer's expertise and judgment. . . . [I]f a client retains an attorney to use her legal expertise to conduct an investigation, that lawyer is indeed performing legal work." In re Allen, 106 F.3d 582 (4th Cir. 1997); Costco Wholesale Corp. v. Superior Ct., 219 P.3d 736 (Cal.

2009) (recognizing privilege for lawyer's factual investigation prior to giving a legal opinion).

Citing *Kellogg*, F.T.C. v. Boehringer Ingelheim Pharmaceuticals, 892 F.3d 1264 (D.C. Cir. 2018), held that "where a communication has multiple purposes, courts apply the primary purpose test to determine whether the communication is privileged. . . . [C]ourts applying the primary purpose test should not try "to find *the* one primary purpose" of a communication. Attempting to do so "can be an inherently impossible task" when the "communications have overlapping purposes (one legal and one business, for example)." (Internal quotes omitted.)

In re Allen also applied the privilege to communications with a company's *former* employees. In Newman v. Highland School District No. 203, 381 P.3d 1188 (Wash. 2016) (collecting cases), a bare majority disagreed over a strong dissent. Which court is correct? On one hand, a former employee (like Delia Corcoran in Slip and Fall (Part I)) has information she learned because of her employment. Does it make sense to change her *Upjohn* status the day after she retires? On the other hand, she is no longer an agent of Tracy's. More important, large companies can have hundreds or thousands of former employees. If their communications with company counsel are privileged, it could hinder the truth-seeking purpose of a trial.

Upjohn construed the privilege under federal law. States are free to define the privilege under state law. Even federal judges must apply state privileges in federal cases that are governed by state law. Fed. R. Evid. 501. Some states have rejected a broad reading of *Upjohn*, opting for a narrower test, as Iowa did in Keefe v. Bernard, supra. Texas retains the control group test. Nat'l Tank Co. v. 30th Jud. Dist. Court, 851 S.W.2d 193 (Tex. 1993) (also citing Illinois' adherence to the control group test).

Should There Even Be an Attorney-Client Privilege for Corporations?

This provocative question is fanciful. The privilege for companies (and other organizations) is not about to disappear. Only its scope is debated. But the question deserves serious consideration, at least in an academic setting, because it forces us to reexamine the justifications for the privilege and because of the societal consequences of granting the privilege (and attendant secrecy) to corporations, especially very large ones.

Recall that we identified two justifications for the privilege: Empirically, it encourages clients to be candid with lawyers, which enables lawyers to do a better job for them. And it respects the dignity and personhood of clients by giving them control over their information. It makes little sense to talk about the dignity and personhood of all but very small organizations that are indistinguishable from their stakeholders. The empirical justification is also less convincing when the client is a company. Communications from a constituent enable the lawyer to do a better job *for the company*, not the constituent, who has no control over how the information is used. The company can choose to disclose it even if doing so exposes the constituent to civil or criminal liability, loss of a career, or public humiliation. At the very least, do you think a company lawyer should be required to give constituents they interview an *Upjohn* warning, formerly called a *Miranda* warning, if the constituent's answers may put him at risk? See Rule 1.13(f). We address that issue in chapter 10.

Exceptions to Privilege and Confidentiality

Lawyer: *Our communications are privileged and confidential. Anything my firm learns in representing you will not be disclosed without your permission except for your benefit.*

If you were given ten dollars each time a lawyer said something like this to a client, you'd be on your way to membership in the one percent. (Well, not quite.) Sure, it puts clients at ease and encourages candor. But it's wrong, wrong, wrong. And yet, does the statement make sense anyway? Explaining the precise scope of the privilege and the duty of confidentiality, with all of their nuances and exceptions that permit or require disclosure, would seem nearly impossible. Truth be told, most lawyers have only a general idea of these things. Whatever rules they learned in law school, even if recalled, may have changed.

An alternative is to say nothing. That might discourage candor from some clients. And what if a client asks, "What I tell you, you can't tell anyone else, right?" Any answer other than "right"—perhaps "well, it depends"—may lead to further questioning and a reluctant client. But "right" is wrong. How about: "Well, there are very limited circumstances where I could, or would have to, disclose what you tell me. For example, if I learned that you were using me to commit a crime or fraud or that you lied in court. But of course that won't happen."

In several circumstances, lawyers may choose or be required to reveal information clients wish to hide. Here are a few common exceptions to (or exclusions from) either the privilege or the duty of confidentiality or both. Would any of them allow disclosure of confidential information in the problems at the beginning of this part?

Self-Defense and Legal Claims

A lawyer "may reveal [confidential] information . . . to the extent the lawyer reasonably believes necessary . . . to establish a claim or defense on behalf of the lawyer in a controversy between the lawyer and the client, to establish a defense to a criminal charge or civil claim against the lawyer based upon conduct in which the client was involved, or to respond to allegations in any proceeding concerning the lawyer's representation of the client." Rule 1.6(b)(5). But the self-defense route is not available to respond to public criticism of the lawyer, even if it is from the client and even if it is on social media for the world to see. See Rule 1.6 cmt. [10]. Maybe as social media becomes even more pervasive (is that possible?) this will change, but so far it has not.

Consider David Bryan. He had a romantic relationship with a current client (a bad idea and often unethical, see Rule 1.8(j)). After it ended and she had new counsel, Bryan continued to pursue her. When he learned that she "had told others that [Bryan] was stalking her, that he was dangerous, and that he was in need of mental health care," he revealed embarrassing confidential information to third parties (including her employer) that "exceeded that which was reasonably necessary for him to defend against [the client's] allegations." The court held that the self-defense exception in Rule 1.6(b)(5) "requires that the [client's] disclosure be made in some type of legal forum. . . . The rule does not permit disclosure of information relating to the representation in any other setting." In re Bryan, 61 P.3d 641 (Kan. 2003), publicly censured Bryan in a lengthy opinion that reads like a soap opera.

Meyerhofer v. Empire Fire & Marine Insurance Co., 497 F.2d 1190 (2d Cir. 1974), is an old but leading case on self-defense. Goldberg had been an associate in a law firm when the firm handled an SEC registration statement for a client. The firm rejected Goldberg's view that information omitted from the statement had to be revealed. Goldberg quit and gave the SEC a detailed affidavit, with supporting documents. Three months later Goldberg was named as one of several defendants in a civil action arising out of the registration statement. In a successful effort to extricate himself, he gave the affidavit to the plaintiff's lawyers. In ruling on a defense motion to disqualify those lawyers for receiving confidential information, the Second Circuit found Goldberg's conduct proper. He had not provided information to the lawyers in order to enable them to bring the case, the court said. He was a victim, not an instigator. The complaint against Goldberg alleged civil and criminal misconduct and sought more than $4 million.

> The cost in money of simply defending such an action might be very substantial. The damage to [Goldberg's] professional reputation which might be occasioned by the mere pendency of such a charge was an even greater cause for concern.
>
> Under these circumstances Goldberg had the right to make an appropriate disclosure with respect to his role in the public offering. Concomitantly, he had the right to support his version of the facts with suitable evidence.

See also People v. Robnett, 859 P.2d 872 (Colo. 1993) (rule's authority to reveal is not restricted to proceedings initiated by a former client); In re Robeson, 652 P.2d 336 (Or. 1982) (lawyer facing charge filed with disciplinary committee by third party may reveal client confidences).

Goldberg did not have to wait until the trial to defend himself. In fact, had Goldberg known he was about to be sued, he could have revealed the information before the action was filed. In In re Friend, 411 F. Supp. 776 (S.D.N.Y. 1975), the court applied *Meyerhofer* where a lawyer and his former client were both under criminal investigation. To avoid indictment, the lawyer wanted to give the grand jury documents that (he thought) would tend to exonerate him but which the client claimed were privileged. The court approved. "Although, as yet, no formal accusation has been made against Mr. Friend, it would be senseless to require the stigma of an indictment to attach prior to allowing Mr. Friend to invoke the exception . . . in his own defense."

In-house counsel may use client confidences to prove claims against employers for retaliatory discharge and unlawful discrimination under Title VII, Kachmar v. SunGard Data Sys., 109 F.3d 173 (3d Cir. 1997), and for retaliatory discharge under 18 U.S.C. §1514A, adopted as part of the Sarbanes-Oxley Act, Van Asdale v. Int'l Game Tech., 577 F.3d 989 (9th Cir. 2009).

Waiver (or Consent)[*]

With "informed consent," a defined term, clients can waive confidentiality. Rules 1.0(e), 1.6(a), 1.8(b), and 1.9(c). The more interesting debates are about privilege. Waiver of privilege may be explicit or implicit. A defendant in a securities fraud case who testified to his "good faith" belief in the "lawfulness" of his conduct waived the privilege for communications with his former counsel that tended to undermine that claim. This is about fairness. A client cannot selectively cite counsel's advice in defense of a position and then deny his opponent access to other parts of the advice that may refute the defense. United States v. Bilzerian, 926 F.2d 1285 (2d Cir. 1991) ("[T]he attorney-client privilege cannot at once be used as a shield and a sword."). But a client who opens himself up this way only waives "the privilege with respect to what has been put 'at issue.'" The client does not waive privilege for all communications with his lawyer. Clair v. Clair, 982 N.E.2d 32 (Mass. 2013) (also holding that under state law the party asserting an "at issue" waiver must show that the privileged information is "not available from any other source"). But "asserting a claim to which privileged material is merely relevant does not waive the privilege. Instead, the client "must *rely* on privileged advice from his counsel to make his claim or defense." In re Schlumberger Tech. Corp., 2020 WL 3026316 (5th Cir. 2020) (emphasis in original; internal quotes omitted).

Clients will waive the protection of the attorney-client privilege by revelation of all or part of a communication to a third person. For example, if Jed says to his friend Isabel, "I told my lawyer I was speeding," he has waived the privilege for that statement to his lawyer (and maybe more broadly). The law will not grant privilege to communications that the client himself discloses to outsiders. Clients should be warned not to do what Jed did.

More often, a client risks waiver when it chooses, for what may be sound reasons, to disclose privileged information from one matter to protect its

---

[*] Consent means that the client has knowingly agreed to disclosure of confidential information. Waiver means that the client has done or not done something, the effect of which is to lose confidentiality whether or not the client intended it. However, the word "waiver" is often used interchangeably with "consent."

legal rights in another matter. Having made that choice, though, it must live with the consequences. Martin Marietta Corp. gave the U.S. attorney a position paper describing why it should not be indicted. Later, a former employee of Martin Marietta was indicted for fraud and sought to subpoena the paper in his defense. The court held that "the Position Paper as well as the underlying details are no longer within the attorney-client privilege." In re Martin Marietta Corp., 856 F.2d 619 (4th Cir. 1988).

One circuit court has long recognized a "limited waiver" when a company shares privileged information with the SEC but then seeks to protect the same information in private litigation. Diversified Indus. v. Meredith, 572 F.2d 596 (8th Cir. 1978) (en banc) ("To hold otherwise may have the effect of thwarting the developing procedure of corporations to employ independent outside counsel to investigate and advise them in order to protect stockholders, potential stockholders and customers."). Every other circuit court to consider the question has rejected this view, concluding that recognition of a limited waiver is not necessary to encourage communications with counsel—the goal of the privilege in the first place—and might be used for manipulative or tactical ends. In re Pac. Pictures Corp., 679 F.3d 1121 (9th Cir. 2012) (collecting cases).

The Crime-Fraud Exception to the Privilege

Communications between a client and counsel are not privileged when the client has consulted the lawyer in order to further a crime or fraud, regardless of whether the crime or fraud is accomplished and even though the lawyer is unaware of the client's purpose (as we must presume) and has done nothing to advance it. See United States v. Doe, 429 F.3d 450 (3d Cir. 2005); In re Grand Jury Proceedings, 87 F.3d 377 (9th Cir. 1996). The privilege exists to enable clients to get legal advice in order to act lawfully. We want to encourage that behavior. If the professional relationship is abused to facilitate a crime or fraud, the reason for the privilege is gone.

Every litigator must be aware of this exception to privilege and the dangers and advantages it carries. If the exception applies, you may get many of an opponent's unguarded communications made while believing they were protected. Or the opponent may get yours. But the communication must be meant to further a fraud or crime:

> In delineating the connection required between the advice sought and the crime or fraud, we have repeatedly stated that the legal advice must be used "in furtherance" of the alleged crime or fraud. We have rejected a more relaxed "related to" standard. . . . Most recently . . . we observed, "[a]ll that is necessary is that the client misuse or intend to misuse the attorney's advice in furtherance of an improper purpose." It is therefore clear from prior precedent that for advice to be used "in furtherance" of a crime or fraud, the advice must advance, or the client must intend the advice to advance, the client's criminal or fraudulent purpose. The advice cannot merely relate to the crime or fraud.

In re Grand Jury Subpoena, 745 F.3d 681 (3d Cir. 2014). Moreover, only those communications intended to further the crime or fraud lose privilege, not every communication between a lawyer and a client. In re Grand Jury Investigation, 810 F.3d 1110 (9th Cir. 2016).

Applying the Exception. Describing the crime-fraud exception is easy. Unpacking the procedures for deciding when the exception applies is more difficult.

This is a bit technical, but a lot may ride on it. Say in a civil litigation (Boe v. Joe), Joe asserts the attorney-client privilege in response to a discovery request, and Boe wants to contest the assertion on the ground of the crime-fraud exception. Must Boe actually prove a crime or fraud to discover the allegedly privileged information? Often, the ultimate issue in the litigation will be whether Joe committed the very same crime or fraud that Boe now alleges to defeat the privilege. Unless something is done, we risk creating a "chicken and egg" problem, in which Boe has to prove her case to get the information that will help her prove her case. Courts have avoided this problem by establishing a second (lower) burden of proof than the burden at trial in order to invoke the crime-fraud exception. Although this lower burden is variously phrased, the differences are not significant. Here is one description:

> The party invoking the crime-fraud exception "must make a prima facie show-ing: (1) that the client was engaged in (or was planning) criminal or fraudu-lent activity when the attorney-client communications took place; *and* (2) that the communications were intended by the client to facilitate or conceal the criminal or fraudulent activity." By prima facie showing, we mean "a reason-able basis to believe that the lawyer's services were used by the client to foster a crime or fraud." This standard may be met by "something less than a math-ematical (more likely than not) probability that the client intended to use the attorney in furtherance of a crime or fraud." However, it requires more than "speculation [or] evidence that shows only a distant likelihood of corruption."

United States v. Gorski, 807 F.3d 451 (1st Cir. 2015).*

In Camera Review. The Supreme Court has told us that the trial court may review the allegedly privileged information in camera (judge's eyes only) when deciding if the opponent of the privilege (i.e., Boe) has met the (lower) burden for proving the crime-fraud exception. United States v. Zolin, 491 U.S. 554 (1989). *Zolin* went on to create an even lower burden of proof for Boe to get that in camera review in the first place:

---

* In re Napster Copyright Litigation, 479 F.3d 1078 (9th Cir. 2007), identified a higher burden in civil cases. The party challenging the privilege must prove a crime or fraud by a preponderance of the evidence. A lower burden, such as the First Circuit's prima facie test, was deemed insufficiently respectful of the privilege. *Napster* was "abrogated" on the issue of interlocutory appellate jurisdiction in Mohawk Indus. v. Carpenter, 558 U.S. 100 (2009).

Before engaging in *in camera* review to determine the applicability of the crime-fraud exception, "the judge should require a showing of a factual basis adequate to support a good faith belief by a reasonable person" that *in camera* review of the materials may reveal evidence to establish the claim that the crime-fraud exception applies.

Finally, what evidence may a trial judge consider in determining whether the *Zolin* burden has been met? (This has now become a "chicken and egg and chicken and egg" problem, *et cetera*.) The *Zolin* Court wrote that "the threshold showing to obtain *in camera* review may be met by using any relevant evidence, lawfully obtained, that has not been adjudicated to be privileged."

The Crime-Fraud Privilege Exception Applied

This can all seem very abstract. So let's apply these rules to Boe v. Joe.

Scene 1: Boe seeks Joe's emails to his lawyer.

Scene 2: Joe asserts privilege.

Scene 3: Boe offers proof that Joe was using the lawyer's services to commit a crime or fraud. Hence, she says, no privilege. She seeks those emails that were in furtherance of the crime or fraud.

Scene 4A: The judge holds that Boe's evidence amounts to prima facie proof of a crime or fraud. The privilege is lost.

Scene 4B: Alternatively, Boe's proof is inadequate to apply the exception. So Boe asks the judge to review the emails in camera and add them to her proof.

Scene 5: The judge can do so if Boe can satisfy the *Zolin* burden, quoted above. In deciding whether the *Zolin* burden is met, the judge may consider any relevant unprivileged evidence lawfully obtained.

Scene 6: The judge reads the emails in camera and decides that the exception is or is not proved.

The Confidentiality Exceptions for Crimes and Frauds and to Prevent Death and Bodily Harm

Distinct from the crime-fraud exception to the *privilege* (but easily confused with it) is an exception to the *duty of confidentiality* that may permit (or in some states require) a lawyer to reveal confidential information to prevent future financial crimes or frauds, or to avoid or mitigate "substantial" financial injury from a completed crime or fraud, if the client has used the lawyer's services to commit the crime or fraud. Rule 1.6(b)(2) and (b)(3) describes the scope of this exception.

The focus of Rule 1.6(b)(2) and (b)(3) is financial harm. Rule 1.6(b)(1) is different. It permits lawyers to reveal confidences "to the extent the lawyer reasonably believes necessary to prevent reasonably certain death or substantial bodily harm." The threatening conduct need not be the client's and the conduct need not be a crime or fraud. For example, a lawyer may learn in a confidential communication that a company (whether or not a client) is selling a defective product that can cause death or serious injury. This exception would apply to GM lawyers who learned about the defective ignition switches on GM cars, which had already resulted in accidents and deaths. See chapter 10A.

A small number of states *require* (not merely permit) lawyers to reveal confidential information to prevent serious violence or, in a few places, to prevent or remedy substantial financial harm. New Jersey, which is among the states least protective of client confidences, provides in Rule 1.6:

> (b) A lawyer *shall* reveal [confidential] information to the proper authorities, as soon as, and to the extent the lawyer reasonably believes necessary, to prevent the client or another person:
>
>> (1) from committing a criminal, illegal or fraudulent act that the lawyer reasonably believes is likely to result in death or substantial bodily harm or substantial injury to the financial interest or property of another. (Emphasis added.)

Because confidentiality exceptions vary, if you find yourself facing this dilemma, you need to figure out which jurisdiction's rules apply and check the language.

The Difference Between the Crime-Fraud and Physical Harm Exceptions to Privilege and to Confidentiality Pithily Stated

Confidentiality: Lawyer Decides.   If the conditions in Rule 1.6(b)(1), (2), or (3) are satisfied, the lawyer decides whether to disclose confidential information. No judge is involved. The matter may not even be in court. (This is also true about the confidentiality exception in Rules 1.13(c), studied in chapter 10. Rule 3.3(c), studied in chapter 7, mandates disclosure of certain confidential communications.)

Privilege: Judge Decides.   If a party challenges an opponent's claim of privilege in court on the ground of the crime-fraud exception, she must prove a reasonable basis to believe that the client intended the allegedly privileged communication to further a crime or fraud. As part of this proof, the challenger can ask the judge to review the allegedly privileged communication in chambers if the *Zolin* conditions are met. Only judges, not lawyers, decide if the crime-fraud exception to the privilege is present.

The Effect of the Confidentiality Exceptions on Privilege

Let's say a confidentiality exception permits you to disclose certain information. But you worry that doing so will result in a waiver of the attorney-client privilege. Will your voluntary disclosure of the information waive the privilege for that information?

This dilemma confronted Jeffrey Purcell, a legal services lawyer in Boston. His client, Joseph Tyree, had been discharged as a maintenance worker at an apartment building and ordered to vacate his apartment. While Tyree was meeting with Purcell to get advice, he threatened to burn down the building. The Massachusetts rule permitted Purcell to alert the police, which he did. The police found incendiary materials in Tyree's home. When Tyree was indicted, Purcell was subpoenaed to testify against him. He challenged the subpoena, citing the privilege. The prosecutor argued that the privilege was waived because Purcell had already revealed the information under a confidentiality exception. The cat was out of the bag.

Purcell acted properly in revealing Tyree's intention to commit a crime, the court held, but by doing so he did not waive the privilege. The crime-fraud privilege exception would only apply if Tyree had sought to use Purcell's assistance to further the crime, which he did not. There was a good reason *not* to deem the privilege waived, the court said. "[A]n informed lawyer may be able to dissuade the client from improper future conduct and, if not, under the ethical rules may elect in the public interest to make a limited disclosure of the client's threatened conduct." But lawyers "will be reluctant to come forward if they know that the information that they disclose may lead to adverse consequences to their clients." Purcell v. Dist. Atty. for Suffolk Dist., 676 N.E.2d 436 (Mass. 1997).

Although it makes sense that a lawyer should be able to reveal confidences to prevent harm to others without thereby waiving the privilege, we might ask why Tyree's threat was within the privilege at all. Wasn't it just a gratuitous rant having nothing to do with Tyree's need for legal advice? The same court answered that question in In re Grand Jury Investigation, 902 N.E.2d 929 (Mass. 2009). A client made threats against a judge. His lawyer warned the judge, then asserted privilege when called before the grand jury to testify to the threats. The court upheld the lawyer's claim of privilege. Clients should have

> breathing room to express frustration and dissatisfaction with the legal system and its participants. The expression of such sentiments is a not uncommon incident of the attorney-client relationship, particularly in an adversarial context, and may serve as a springboard for further discussion regarding a client's legal options. . . .
>
> [We] reaffirm that a client's communications to his lawyer threatening harm are privileged unless the crime-fraud exception applies.

The exception did not apply because the client did not seek the lawyer's help in harming the judge.

The emphasis on "breathing room" is important. In a Kansas case that quotes In re Grand Jury Investigation, a client had threatened in a communication with his lawyer to kill his former fiancée. The lawyer told the sheriff's office and the threat was used to prosecute the client. The state argued that the threat was not privileged, but the court rejected what it called "the piecemealing of attorney-client communications. . . . Although [the client's] comment is jarring in isolation, the expression of such frustrations is not an uncommon occurrence in the course of an attorney-client relationship, 'particularly in an adversarial context, and may serve as a springboard' for discussion and attempts to dissuade the client on the part of the attorney." State v. Boatwright, 401 P.3d 657 (Kan. Ct. App. 2017). The court cited Elihu Root's dictum, quoted at the beginning of part B1, that "half of the practice of a decent lawyer is telling would-be clients that they are damned fools and should stop."

The "Fiduciary" Exception

Many courts hold that a beneficiary is entitled, on a proper showing, to communications between a fiduciary (like a trustee) and counsel for the fiduciary because the lawyer's ultimate client is the beneficiary, not the fiduciary. The English and American antecedents of this exception are traced in United States v. Jicarilla Apache Nation, 564 U.S. 162 (2011).

This issue arises in shareholder derivative actions. Plaintiff shareholders may seek otherwise privileged information between company counsel and management, claiming that they are the ultimate beneficiaries of counsel's work. The leading case here, Garner v. Wolfinbarger, 430 F.2d 1093 (5th Cir. 1970), held that the shareholders might prevail but must show why the privilege "should not be invoked in the particular instance." Among the factors to consider were the following (with brackets added for convenience):

> [1] the number of shareholders and the percentage of stock they represent; [2] the bona fides of the shareholders; [3] the nature of the shareholders' claim and whether it is obviously colorable; [4] the apparent necessity or desirability of the shareholders having the information and the availability of it from other sources; [5] whether, if the shareholders' claim is of wrongful action by the corporation, it is of action criminal, or illegal but not criminal, or of doubtful legality; [6] whether the communication related to past or to prospective actions; [7] whether the communication is of advice concerning the litigation itself; [8] the extent to which the communication is identified versus the extent to which the shareholders are blindly fishing; [9] the risk of revelation of trade secrets or other information in whose confidentiality the corporation has an interest for independent reasons.

Garner got a big boost when the Supreme Court of Delaware, the state where many large U.S. companies are incorporated, adopted it in Wal-Mart Stores v. Ind. Elec. Workers Pension Trust Fund IBEW, 95 A.3d 1264 (Del. 2014).

Although Garner has been broadly followed, endorsement has not been unanimous. See the discussion in Jicarilla Apache Nation, supra, and Pittsburgh History & Landmarks Foundation v. Zeigler, 200 A.3d 58 (Pa. 2019), where the court was able to discern the following dire consequences of adopting the Garner rule—and a similar rule in Restatement §85—in corporate derivative actions:

> The reality is that this weighing of the [Garner] factors would result in current managers and the corporation's attorneys having no meaningful way of determining whether their otherwise privileged communications would be later

divulged in derivative litigation discovery. As a result, corporate management would be less willing to discuss issues with corporate counsel, and corporate counsel would caution corporate management not to speak with her candidly. As a matter of simple logic, this will result in corporate managers being forced to act without necessary legal guidance in an already complicated legal environment. We conclude that this is inconsistent with the revered nature of the attorney-client privilege in Pennsylvania, and the clarity of it, which has been codified by our legislature and applied continuously by our courts.

In the half-century since *Garner* was decided, such ominous consequences do not seem to have emerged in the many jurisdictions that follow it, which may explain why, in a footnote, the court left open the possibility that *Garner* may yet be useful in other fiduciary settings.

Noisy Withdrawal

When a lawyer must withdraw from representing a client because of its criminal or fraudulent behavior, and she is either not permitted or does not wish to reveal confidential information to alert the victim as she exits, she may want to retract her own oral or written representations that the client may be using or have used for the illegal purpose. The retraction makes the withdrawal a "noisy" one. A noisy withdrawal is not a full-blown exception to confidentiality because the lawyer says only that she retracts something, not why. Noisy withdrawals are recognized in Rules 1.2 cmt. [10] and 4.1 cmt. [3] and are further discussed in chapter 9B1 on negotiation.

Lawyers and Social Media: Risks, Benefits, and Best Practices[*]

The turn of the century brought new ways to communicate, which lawyers eyed with suspicion. Clarence Seward, managing partner of a law firm that later became Cravath, Swaine & Moore, believed the telephone and typewriter were "destroying the simplicity of American life." He refused to answer the telephone, which was confined to a "telephone closet." When the young John Foster Dulles, a future Secretary of State, joined Sullivan & Cromwell in 1911, "many of the attorneys believed that the only proper form of communication was through the use of letters delivered by hand." The telephone was "in a separate office and . . . clerks [did not] use [it] unless it rang." Jan Jacobowitz & Danielle Singer, The Social Media Frontier: Exploring a New Mandate for Competence in the Practice of Law, 68 U. Miami L. Rev. 445 (2014). Eventually, of course, lawyers embraced the telephone.

More than a century later, the technology is new, but the need to figure out how safely to use it—and how not to use it—remains. Social media sites—both general ones, like Facebook, Twitter, and LinkedIn, and

---

[*] This cautionary note could appear in several chapters of the book but this chapter, which addresses confidentiality, competence, and the formation of the professional relationship, is most apt.

law-specific ones, like law blogs—offer lawyers new opportunities but also pose dangers. Done right, lawyers and legal organizations can use social media to attract clients and promote their reputations. Done wrong or mindlessly, it can bring grief.

Young lawyers, for whom use of social media may be as automatic as breathing, are especially at risk.

A court vacated the convictions of New Orleans police officers without "a showing of actual prejudice" because while their trial was in progress, federal prosecutors (although not those trying the case) posted anonymous accusatory blog comments on a website accessible to the jury, which was not sequestered. United States v. Bowen, 969 F. Supp. 2d 546 (E.D. La. 2013), aff'd, 799 F.3d 336 (5th Cir. 2015). The officers were charged with civil rights violations, including use of excessive force, in the aftermath of Hurricane Katrina.

Although a lawyer is permitted to seek information about potential or current jurors on publicly available social media posts, a lawyer may not send access requests to jurors in an effort to view nonpublic content. Nor may a lawyer seek to "friend" a witness by misrepresenting her purpose. NYC Opinion 2010-2. But "[t]he mere act of observing that which is open to the public would not constitute a communicative act that violates Rule 3.5(b)." ABA Opinion 466 (2014).

On the first day of trial, a federal judge in Florida referred the lawyer for the plaintiff—a cruise ship passenger—to a disciplinary panel. The lawyer had posted information about the case on Facebook, which the defendant company claimed was false or in violation of a court order. The court asked the panel to determine whether the posts violated two of its orders. Joyce Hanson, "Carnival Injury Atty's Facebook Posts Go To Conduct Panel," Law 360, June 3, 2016.

"Lawyers for Child Welfare and Legal Aid Under Scrutiny for Facebook Posts" read a New York Times headline on August 30, 2017, over a story by Nikita Stewart. Four lawyers—three at the Administration for Children's Services, a child welfare agency, and one at the Legal Aid Society—allegedly photographed Family Court litigants and then added crass or disparaging comments about their appearance. "Bra tops n butt cheeks! Somebody come look at this!!" was the caption above one of the photographs. It was not clear whether the subjects of the pictures were the lawyers' clients. Photography is forbidden in Family Court. The child welfare agency filed disciplinary charges against its three lawyers. It demoted two of them, who were supervisors, pending further investigation. The Legal Aid Society said that "appropriate action" had been taken. The news story included the names of each of the four lawyers, which means that their names may come up in computer searches forever.

Even if their actions don't violate any rules, lawyers can lose their jobs or prejudice cases through improper use of social media. One prosecutor, posing as an ex-girlfriend of an alleged murderer, used Facebook to contact two women who were the defendant's alibi witnesses. He claimed to have had the accused's child. Both women then recanted, one saying, according to the prosecutor, "This is bogus, I'm not going to lie for [the accused]." The prosecutor was fired. James McCarty, The Plain Dealer, June 6, 2013. He was also disciplined.

A senior federal prosecutor in New Orleans was demoted and sued for defamation after she posted anonymous online comments about the subject of an investigation, who was able to identify her through her use of "superfluous spacing," "ellipses without spacing," and "an obscure term, 'fender lizard.'" Debra Cassens Weiss, A.B.A. J., Nov. 12, 2012.

A public defender lost her job over a social media mishap. The family of an accused murderer, who was incarcerated, brought him clothes to wear to court, including a pair of leopard print boxer briefs. His lawyer snapped a picture of the briefs and posted the picture and a disparaging caption on her Facebook page, which was visible only to her friends. Someone told the judge, who declared a mistrial, and the defense lawyer was fired. Martha Neil, A.B.A. J., Sept. 13, 2012. A Houston prosecutor resigned after she shared a Facebook post that compared demonstrators against police brutality and racial inequality to Nazis who "banned free speech." Jack Queen, "Texas Prosecutor Resigns after Facebook Post About Nazis," Law360, June 29, 2020.

After a mass shooting at a Las Vegas country music festival killed 58 and injured hundreds, an in-house lawyer at CBS posted on Facebook: "If they wouldn't do anything when children were murdered I have no hope that Repugs will ever do the right thing. I'm actually not even sympathetic [because] country music fans are often republican gun toters." Daniel Holloway, Variety, Oct. 2, 2017. She was fired. Apparently, it was the second sentence that did her in.

John Browning, "Don't Take Heat for That Tweet: Avoiding Ethical Pitfalls in the Use of Social Media," Fed. Lawyer (Sept./Oct. 2019), collects several instances of excessive sharing, this one among them:

> In December 2017, Andrew Leonie, a top aide to Texas Attorney General Ken Paxton, wrote a Facebook post critical of the #MeToo movement, stating "Aren't you also tired of all of the pathetic 'me too' victim claims? If every woman is a 'victim,' so is every man. If everyone is a victim, no one is. Victim means nothing anymore." He also linked to an article about how women purportedly "ask" to be objectified. The response from members of the public and the media was swift, condemning the remarks. The Texas Attorney General's Office responded quickly as well. A spokeswoman for the office announced within several hours of the media reports that Leonie had resigned "effective immediately" and that the "views he expressed on social media do not reflect our values."

What about the client's social media? Destroying social media content can be the obstruction of justice and spoliation of evidence, which can lead to trial sanctions. A lawyer who instructed his client to do just that was fined $522,000 and his client was fined $200,000. The lawyer then agreed to a five-year suspension. Martha Neil, A.B.A. J., Nov. 16, 2011, and Debra Cassens Weiss, A.B.A. J., Aug. 7, 2013.

3. Lawyers Are Agents

Lawyers are their clients' agents. The law of agency therefore applies to the client-lawyer relationship. As attorneys at law (compared to attorneys in *fact*), lawyers have certain authority and certain duties within the *scope* of their agency (i.e., what they are retained to do). Agents are also fiduciaries. Restatement (Third) of Agency §1.01. In the next section, we shall discuss some of the duties imposed by agency and fiduciary status. Here we review the authority agency status confers. Not surprisingly, it is an authority to act and speak on the client's behalf in legal matters.

Acting for the client means that the lawyer's conduct may be attributed to the client, even if the lawyer is negligent, willfully misbehaves, or acts contrary to the client's instructions in the many decisions lawyers are legally and ethically authorized to make. (See part C on which decisions those are.) Speaking for the client means that what the lawyer says within the scope of the retainer will be attributed to the client. In litigation, courts say that a "litigant chooses counsel at his peril." Boogaerts v. Bank of Bradley, 961 F.2d 765 (8th Cir. 1992). See also Link v. Wabash R.R. Co., 370 U.S. 626 (1962) ("Petitioner voluntarily chose this attorney as his representative in the action, and he cannot now avoid the consequences of the acts or omissions of this freely selected agent."). A sloppy lawyer can really mess up your life. Is that disturbing? Isn't the same true when choosing a doctor?

The next two cases illustrate just how consequential a lawyer's actions can be.

TAYLOR v. ILLINOIS
484 U.S. 400 (1988)

[The charge against Taylor was attempted murder. His lawyer, in order to gain "a tactical advantage," willfully failed to reveal the identity of a defense witness, Wormley, as Illinois discovery rules required. The trial court refused to let Wormley testify. Taylor, who was not a party to his lawyer's tactic, claimed that the refusal violated his rights under the Sixth Amendment's Compulsory Process Clause. Following are excerpts from the majority opinion of Justice Stevens and the dissent of Justice Brennan (in which Justices Marshall and Blackmun joined).]

It is elementary, of course, that a trial court may not ignore the fundamental character of the defendant's right to offer the testimony of witnesses in his favor. But the mere invocation of that right cannot automatically and invariably outweigh countervailing public interests. The integrity of the adversary process, which depends both on the presentation of reliable evidence and the rejection of unreliable evidence, the interest in the fair and efficient administration of justice, and the potential prejudice to the truth-determining function of the trial process must also weigh in the balance.

A trial judge may certainly insist on an explanation for a party's failure to comply with a request to identify his or her witnesses in advance of trial. If that explanation reveals that the omission was willful and motivated by a desire to obtain a tactical advantage that would minimize the effectiveness of cross-examination and the ability to adduce rebuttal evidence, it would be entirely consistent with the purposes of the Compulsory Process Clause simply to exclude the witness' testimony. . . .

The argument that the client should not be held responsible for his lawyer's misconduct strikes at the heart of the attorney-client relationship. Although there are basic rights that the attorney cannot waive without the fully informed and publicly acknowledged consent of the client,[24] the lawyer has—and must have—full authority to manage the conduct of the trial. The adversary process could not function effectively if every tactical decision required client approval. Moreover, given the protections afforded by the attorney-client privilege and the fact that extreme cases may involve unscrupulous conduct by both the client and the lawyer, it would be highly impracticable to require an investigation into their relative responsibilities before applying the sanction of preclusion. In responding to discovery, the client has a duty to be candid and forthcoming with the lawyer, and when the lawyer responds, he or she speaks for the client. Putting to one side the exceptional cases in which counsel is ineffective, the client must accept the consequences of the lawyer's decision to forgo cross-examination, to decide not to put certain witnesses on the stand, or to decide not to disclose the identity of certain witnesses in advance of trial. In this case, petitioner has no greater right to disavow his lawyer's decision to conceal Wormley's identity until after the trial had commenced than he has to disavow the decision to refrain from adducing testimony from the eyewitnesses who were identified [by the state]. . . .

JUSTICE BRENNAN, dissenting. . . .

Although we have sometimes held a defendant bound by tactical errors his attorney makes that fall short of ineffective assistance of counsel, we have not previously suggested that a client can be punished for an attorney's *misconduct*. There are fundamental differences between attorney misconduct and tactical errors. Tactical errors are products of a legitimate choice among

---

24. See, e.g., Brookhart v. Janis, 384 U.S. 1 (1966) (defendant's constitutional right to plead not guilty and to have a trial where he could confront and cross-examine adversary witness could not be waived by his counsel without defendant's consent); Doughty v. State, 470 N.E.2d 69 (Ind. 1984) (record must show "personal communication of the defendant to the court that he chooses to relinquish the right [to a jury trial]"); Cross v. United States, 325 F.2d 629 (1963) (waiver of right to be present during trial).

tactical options. Such tactical decisions must be made within the adversary system, and the system requires attorneys to make them, operating under the presumption that the attorney will choose the course most likely to benefit the defendant. Although some of these decisions may later appear erroneous, penalizing attorneys for such miscalculations is generally an exercise in futility because the error is usually visible only in hindsight—at the time the tactical decision was made there was no obvious "incorrect" choice, and no prohibited one. . . .

The rationales for binding defendants to attorneys' routine tactical errors do not apply to attorney misconduct. An attorney is never faced with a legitimate choice that includes misconduct as an option. Although it may be that "[t]he adversary process could not function effectively if every tactical decision required client approval," that concern is irrelevant here because a client has no authority to approve misconduct. Further, misconduct is not visible only with hindsight, as are many tactical errors. Consequently, misconduct is amenable to direct punitive sanctions against attorneys as a deterrent that can prevent attorneys from systemically engaging in misconduct that would disrupt the trial process. There is no need to take steps that will inflict the punishment on the defendant. . . .

———————————

Look at this from Taylor's perspective. He was likely in jail awaiting trial with an appointed lawyer. He had no real ability to control how his lawyer represented him (as you will see in Jones v. Barnes in part C below). And he surely did not know the state's criminal procedure rules or that his lawyer had willfully violated them. He did nothing wrong but the lawyer the state assigned him did, and Taylor must now pay the price.

Would the result seem less unfair if Taylor were out on bail and had hired his own lawyer? Hardly. Defendants who manage to hire a lawyer—perhaps with financial help from friends and family—are not much better off. They will also be unaware of criminal procedure rules and unable to supervise compliance with them. Rarely will they be able to change lawyers. They will not get a refund of their retainer, at least not in time, and they will be unable to raise more money to hire a new lawyer.

And yet criminal discovery rules are a good thing. In fact, they demand more of prosecutors than defendants. They promote accurate verdicts by reducing surprise. But they will be useless if violations are cost-free.

Taylor went on to hold that preclusion will not *always* be an appropriate remedy. Other sanctions may suffice. But because Taylor's defense lawyer acted willfully and tactically, preclusion was allowed even if prejudice to the prosecution was avoidable with a less harsh remedy (such as suspending the trial for a day or two). Justice Brennan says discipline the lawyer; don't punish the client. Other cases have responded in diverse ways. Michigan v. Lucas, 500 U.S. 145 (1991), reversed a holding that preclusion is *never* allowed when a defendant in a sexual abuse case, who did not give the required pretrial notice, offers at trial to prove a prior sexual relationship with the victim. Noble v. Kelly, 246 F.3d 93 (2d Cir. 2001), held that absent a finding of defense counsel's willfulness in failing to give the required pretrial notice of an alibi witness, preclusion violated the Sixth Amendment. And in State v. Bradshaw, 950 A.2d 889 (N.J. 2008), the New Jersey Supreme Court ruled that preclusion was improper under state law where a defense lawyer misread the rule and failed to identify the defendant as his own alibi witness.

Prosecution witnesses can be precluded if a prosecutor violates a disclosure rule, but where the violation is not in "bad faith," and instead the product of "inattention," preclusion was held an abuse of discretion in United States v. Ivory, 131 Fed. Appx. 628 (10th Cir. 2005).

CHOICE HOTELS INTERNATIONAL v. GROVER
792 F.3d 753 (7th Cir. 2015)

EASTERBROOK, CIRCUIT JUDGE.

Choice Hotels sued SBQI, Inc., plus several of its managers and investors, seeking damages for a breach of a franchise agreement. The defendants did not answer the complaint, and the clerk of court entered a default. One of the defendants, Tarranpaul Chawla, an attorney admitted to practice in Illinois, represented the others but did so poorly, which led to the default. Three of the defendants—Anuj Grover, Arjun Grover, and Dharam Punwani (collectively the Investors)—asked Chawla to find a new attorney. They assert that until this suit was filed they had been unaware that their signatures were on the franchise agreement as parties, which could make them personally liable, and they insist that the signatures are forgeries. Chawla told the Investors that Elton Johnson had agreed to represent their interests by trying to vacate the default, negotiate a settlement, and if necessary defend against Choice Hotels' demand for damages.

Johnson filed an appearance and took some steps in the litigation. . . . But he did not answer the complaint or file a motion to vacate the default, engage in discovery concerning damages, respond to Choice Hotels' request for admissions, or reply to its motion for summary judgment on damages. In response to email requests from Anuj Grover, Johnson insisted that he was trying to settle the litigation. But he did not say what he was doing or share with the Investors any documents he filed in the suit. He did not return phone calls. Eventually the district court set damages at $430,286.75, and on June 26, 2013, the court entered a final judgment in that amount.

The default judgment led the Investors to hire a new lawyer, who filed a motion seeking to set aside the judgment. Because it was filed more than a year after the judgment, however, it fell into Fed. R. Civ. P. 60(b)(6). . . . A motion under Rule 60(b)(6) is addressed to the district court's discretion, and appellate review is correspondingly deferential. [R]elief under Rule 60(b)(6) requires the movant to establish that "extraordinary circumstances" justify upsetting a final decision.

The district court thought these circumstances to be short of "extraordinary." Lawyers sometimes fail to protect their clients' interests, and the district judge observed that the remedy for legal neglect lies in a malpractice suit against the lawyer, rather than continuing the original litigation and upsetting the adversary's legitimate expectations based on a final judgment. Litigants who choose a poor lawyer may bear the costs themselves, or shift them to the lawyer, but cannot shift them to an adversary . . .

[Circuit precedent] explains why it is important to visit the consequences on the bad lawyer rather than the innocent adversary:

> Holding the client responsible for the lawyer's deeds ensures that both clients and lawyers take care to comply. If the lawyer's neglect protected the client from ill consequences, neglect would become all too common. It would be a free good—the neglect would protect the client, and because the client could not suffer the lawyer would not suffer either. The court's power to dismiss a case is designed both to elicit action from the parties in the case at hand and to induce litigants and lawyers in other cases to adhere to timetables. A court cannot lightly excuse a litigant because of the lawyer's neglect without abandoning the pursuit of these objectives. . . .

[The court rejected comparison to two Supreme Court cases—*Holland* and *Maples,* discussed in the following note—where capital defendants were held *not* to be bound by their lawyer's inaction because the lawyers had abandoned them, thereby ending the agency relationship with their clients.]

The Investors recognized that Chawla was not protecting their interests, and they sensibly insisted that he find someone who would. When they began to suspect that Johnson likewise was not protecting their interests, they did not replace him. Sending him emails, and making unreturned phone calls, is no substitute for action. They readily could have consulted the docket in the litigation and learned that Johnson was not filing essential documents, but they didn't. Johnson did not abandon the investors; he performed some legal tasks, though not enough, and responded to three of Anuj Grover's inquiries. Unlike the attorneys in *Holland* and *Maples,* he had not cut off all communication with his clients and walked away from the litigation. But even if we were to treat the Investors as abandoned by Johnson, still they must bear the consequences of their own inaction. They were sued and did not defend the litigation, personally or by counsel. They were able to monitor the proceedings yet did not follow through. . . .

Affirmed.

———————

Is it reasonable to expect unsophisticated clients, especially from immigrant communities, to challenge a lawyer's assurance that all is well or to check the docket and know how to do so? But what alternative would be fair to the opponent, who played by the rules? For the meaning of "extraordinary circumstances" warranting relief from a judgment under Rule 60(b)(6), see S.E.C. v. McNulty, 137 F.3d 732 (2d Cir. 1998) (the client's "diligence" in supervising the lawyer could suffice but was absent here).

In light of cases like *Choice Hotels International*, would you support a rule that required all lawyers to carry malpractice insurance? Oregon and Idaho do so now. How about a rule requiring lawyers to advise new clients whether or not they have malpractice insurance? Some U.S. jurisdictions do so now. Lawyers have strongly opposed both rules.

When a Lawyer Abandons a Client the Agency Ends

Judge Easterbrook distinguished Holland v. Florida, 560 U.S. 631 (2010), and Maples v. Thomas, 565 U.S. 266 (2012), where the lawyers abandoned their clients:

> *Holland* holds that abandonment by counsel can justify tolling of the statute of limitations for filing a federal collateral attack on a state conviction, and *Maples* holds that abandonment by counsel during a state collateral attack can constitute a justification for a procedural default, and thus permit federal review of an issue that was not properly presented in the state proceeding.
>
> Both *Holland* and *Maples* were capital cases. Being put to death is a disproportionate penalty for having a bad lawyer—especially when as a practical matter persons on death row (and for that matter other prisoners) have only limited opportunity to choose their own counsel. They must accept volunteers, and if they fire a volunteer they cannot be sure that someone else will step in, for they lack funds to hire counsel. . . . Abandonment severs the agency relation, so that counsel's (in)action is not imputed to the client. In normal civil litigation a litigant whose lawyer has left him in the lurch can hire a new one, or represent himself, but people on death row can't replace their lawyers so easily.
>
> Although *Maples* and *Holland* were capital cases, we do not doubt that their holdings apply to all collateral litigation under 28 U.S.C. §2254 or §2255. All prisoners face difficulties in obtaining and monitoring the performance of counsel and damages for malpractice are a poor substitute for time in prison, just as they are no substitute for one's life. But these considerations are inapplicable to normal civil litigation, and the Supreme Court has not suggested that *Holland* or *Maples* has any bearing on suits about torts, contracts, and other economic matters.

Judge Easterbrook wrote that "[a]ll prisoners face difficulties in obtaining and monitoring the performance of counsel." How should that observation have affected the ruling in Taylor v. Illinois, where Taylor's counsel violated a discovery rule leading to exclusion of a defense witness?

Vicarious Admissions

A lawyer's statements may be used against her client. They are called vicarious admissions. Fed. R. Evid. 801(d)(2)(C) and (D) (vicarious admissions are nonhearsay and admissible in evidence if made by an agent or employee of a party during and within the scope of the agency or employment). These rules apply whether the statement is made in a litigation or negotiation.[*]

A lawyer's vicarious admissions may be used against the client at trial, but they don't *bind* the client. That means that the client may seek to disprove or discredit them (probably with a new lawyer). The factfinder will then decide what to believe. However, some admissions a lawyer makes *do* bind the client. The client will not be allowed to disprove or discredit them. Even though these binding admissions are also vicarious (because they are made by one person, a lawyer, but used against another person, a client), we have a special term for them. They are called *judicial admissions*. To be a judicial admission, the statement must be made in the course of a case then on trial—either in open court or in a pleading or other document that has *not* been superseded. See Carle v. Steyh, 353 P.3d 488 (Mont. 2015) ("In order to constitute a judicial admission, a party's statement must meet the following criteria: 1) There must be a statement made to the court. 2) The statement must be made by a party, or the party's attorney. 3) The statement must be a statement of fact, and not a statement of opinion or law.").

4. Lawyers Are Fiduciaries

Lawyers have a fiduciary relationship with clients. What does that mean? Lawyers must place their clients' interests above other interests in the area of the representation. Words like "honor," "integrity," and "trust" appear often in discussions of fiduciary duty. The "essence of a claim for breach of fiduciary duty involves the 'integrity and fidelity' of an attorney. An attorney breaches his fiduciary duty when he benefits improperly from the attorney-client relationship by, among other things, subordinating his client's interest to his own, retaining the client's funds, engaging in self-dealing, improperly using client confidences, failing to disclose conflicts of interest, or making misrepresentations to achieve these ends." K&L Gates LLP v. Quantum Materials Corp., 2020 WL 1313733 (Tex. App. 2020). Loyalty and diligence are also part of the equation and are the focus of the next section.

Lawyers are in fact super-fiduciaries, according to some courts. They occupy a "unique position of trust and confidence" toward clients. Milbank, Tweed, Hadley & McCloy v. Boon, 13 F.3d 537 (2d Cir. 1994). The "unique fiduciary reliance, stemming from people hiring attorneys to exercise

---

[*] Statements made in the context of settlement discussions may, however, be inadmissible as a matter of policy, whether made by the lawyer or the client. See Fed. R. Evid. 408.

professional judgment on a client's behalf . . . is imbued with ultimate trust and confidence." In re Cooperman, 633 N.E.2d 1069 (N.Y. 1994).

In Parkinson v. Bevis, 448 P.3d 1027 (Idaho 2019), the Idaho Supreme Court said that "[a] breach of fiduciary claim is an equitable claim for which a defendant may have to disgorge compensation received during the time the breach occurred, even if the plaintiff cannot show actual damages." It breaches fiduciary duty, the court wrote, "if an attorney violates special (elevated) duties of trust and confidence of his client by disclosure of secrets or confidential information."

At least four reasons support imposing strict fiduciary obligations on a lawyer after the professional relationship begins. First, the client expects it. She will have begun to trust the lawyer's integrity, fairness, skill, and judgment, which the lawyer is likely to encourage, suspending the usual caution when dealing with others on important matters. Second, most clients lack the legal acumen required to monitor a lawyer's actions and the distance needed to evaluate decisions objectively. Third, the lawyer may have acquired information about the client that affords an unfair advantage in dealings with her. Last, many clients will not be in a position to change lawyers, but rather will be financially or psychologically dependent on a lawyer's continued representation. In short, during (and possibly even after) a representation, the client is dependent on her lawyer and vulnerable to overreaching. We rely on the lawyer's fiduciary duty to prevent taking advantage.

5. Loyalty and Diligence

The duties of loyalty and diligence may be considered together because they overlap. The duty of loyalty (a part of fiduciary duty) requires a lawyer to pursue, and to be free to pursue, the client's objectives unfettered by conflicting responsibilities or interests. The duties of loyalty and confidentiality are the basis for the conflict-of-interest rules discussed in chapters 5 and 6. As we shall see, loyalty (like the duty of confidentiality) survives the end of the attorney-client relationship and prevents a lawyer from acting "adversely" to a former client's interests in matters "substantially related" to the former representation. Diligence requires that a lawyer pursue the client's interests without undue delay. Divided loyalties may undermine the lawyer's diligence as well as threaten the lawyer's fiduciary obligations. An undivided loyalty will not, however, assure diligence.

The Rules say "[a] lawyer shall act with reasonable diligence and promptness in representing a client." Rule 1.3. Among the most frequent grounds for complaints to disciplinary committees is the failure to pursue a client's interests. (This failure generally goes hand in hand with the related failure, discussed next, to keep the client informed about the status of a matter.) Sometimes the failure to act diligently will actually prejudice a client's rights, as when a lawyer permits a statute of limitations to expire or misses a court's filing deadline. If so, the client will have a malpractice claim against the lawyer. Even if not, the lawyer may still be disciplined. In an astonishing example of a lack of diligence, a California lawyer was ordered to show cause why he should not be held in contempt where he had asked for, and received, 19 extensions of time to file a brief for a capital defendant, but had failed to do so. The court found that the lawyer "had the ability to comply" with its orders and that the failure was therefore willful. He was sentenced to five days in jail. In re Young, 892 P.2d 148 (Cal. 1995).

6. The Duty to Inform and Advise

The next case is both old and very current. Its lesson, which might not be intuitive and apparently was not intuitive to Fulfer and Keller, is as true today as in 1993 and earlier. Its simplicity makes the lesson easy to understand. Although the case is about lawyers in one specialized area of practice, the ruling applies to all law work.

NICHOLS v. KELLER
15 Cal. App. 4th 1672, 19 Cal. Rptr. 2d 601 (Ct. App. 1993)

[Nichols was injured on the job. He hired attorneys Fulfer and Keller, who successfully pursued a workers' compensation claim against Nichols' employer. They did not tell Nichols that he might also have civil tort claims against third parties, which the firm would not pursue. Nichols learned of that possibility after the tort statute of limitations had run. He sued the lawyers for malpractice. The trial court granted summary judgment for the lawyers. The court of appeal, per Martin, J., reversed.]

A significant area of exposure for the workers' compensation attorney concerns that attorney's responsibility for counseling regarding a potential third party action. One of an attorney's basic functions is to advise. Liability can exist because the attorney failed to provide advice. Not only should an attorney furnish advice when requested, but he or she should also volunteer opinions when necessary to further the client's objectives. The attorney need not advise and caution of every possible alternative, but only of those that may result in adverse consequences if not considered. Generally speaking, a workers' compensation attorney should be able to limit the retention to the compensation claim if the client is cautioned (1) there may be other remedies which the attorney will not investigate, and (2) other counsel should be consulted on such matters. However, even when a retention is expressly limited, the attorney may still have a duty to alert the client to legal problems which are reasonably apparent, even though they fall outside the scope of the retention. The rationale is that, as between the lay client and the attorney, the latter is more qualified to recognize and analyze the client's legal needs. The attorney need not represent the client on such matters. Nevertheless, the attorney should inform the client of the limitations of the attorney's representation and of the possible need for other counsel. . . .

In the context of personal injury consultations between lawyer and layperson, it is reasonably foreseeable the latter will offer a selective or incomplete recitation of the facts underlying the claim; request legal assistance by employing such everyday terms as "workers' compensation," "disability," and "unemployment"; and rely upon the consulting lawyer to describe the array of legal remedies available, alert the layperson to any apparent legal problems, and, if appropriate, indicate limitations on the retention of counsel and the need for other counsel. In the event the lawyer fails to so advise the layperson, it is also reasonably foreseeable the layperson will fail to ask relevant questions regarding the existence of other remedies and be deprived of relief through a combination of ignorance and lack or failure of understanding. And, if counsel elects to limit or prescribe his representation of the client, i.e., to a workers' compensation claim only without reference or regard to any third party or collateral claims which the client might pursue if adequately advised, then counsel must make such limitations in representation very clear to his client. Thus, a lawyer who signs an application for adjudication of a workers' compensation claim and a lawyer who accepts a referral to prosecute the claim owe the claimant a duty of care to advise on available remedies, including third party actions.

[Reversed.]

Look at it through Nichols' eyes. He wanted his lawyers to get him the compensation to which he was legally entitled. He was not likely thinking about legal categories—tort vs. workers' compensation. On the other hand, the lawyers did exactly what they said they would do and, when sued, may have wondered why they should be liable for not doing what they never agreed to do.

A law firm, representing a class, recovered $90 million because for three years the defendant had failed to pay overtime, as required by the Labor Code. Two members of the class then brought a new class action against the law firm for failure to assert a claim for overtime under the state's Unfair Competition Law as well. That law, they claimed, would have permitted overtime recovery for a fourth year. The firm argued that the court's class certification specified only the Labor Code and that the "obligations of class counsel under a class certification order should be analogized to the obligations that an attorney assumes under a retainer agreement" and read no more broadly. The court agreed, but it ruled that the analogy worked to the firm's disadvantage. Janik v. Rudy, Exelrod & Zeiff, 14 Cal. Rptr. 3d 751 (Ct. App. 2004). After citing Nichols v. Keller, the court wrote:

> If prudence dictates that a claim beyond the scope of the retention agreement be pursued, the client can then consider whether to expand the retention or pursue the additional claim in some other manner. In the context of a class action, both the representative plaintiffs and the absent class members similarly are entitled to assume that their attorneys will consider

and bring to the attention of at least the class representatives additional or greater claims that may exist arising out of the circumstances underlying the certified claims that class members will be unable to raise if not asserted in the pending action.

The Client's Right to Know

An obligation to inform a client is found in Rule 1.4, the law of agency and fiduciary duty, and the Sixth Amendment, which means that failure can lead to discipline, civil liability, and reversal of a conviction.

Civil Liability. A lawyer representing a plaintiff in a personal injury action did not relay a $90,000 settlement offer. He considered it too skimpy. The case went to trial. The jury was more skimpy. It found for the defendant. The client learned of the offer and sued the lawyer. The client testified that he would have accepted the offer (of course), and the jury believed him. On appeal, the court said it "need not decide . . . whether a lawyer has an obligation to transmit a patently unreasonable offer to his client" because the jury could reasonably have decided that competent counsel would have presented the $90,000 offer. Moores v. Greenberg, 834 F.2d 1105 (1st Cir. 1987). The lawyer in First National Bank v. Lowrey, 872 N.E.2d 447 (Ill. App. Ct. 2007), had to pay his client $1 million after he failed to convey a settlement offer, then lost at trial.

Ineffective Assistance of Counsel. Both Padilla v. Kentucky, 559 U.S. 356 (2010) and Jae Lee v. United States, 582 U.S. _____ (2017), ruled that defense counsel for a lawful immigrant who failed to inform him that a guilty plea could mean deportation was constitutionally ineffective. Missouri v. Frye, 566 U.S. 134 (2012), held that a lawyer who failed to inform his client of a plea offer that included a recommended sentence was constitutionally ineffective. Frye later pled guilty without a sentence recommendation and received a significantly longer sentence.

Discipline. Discipline for violating Rule 1.4 is unusual but does occur. In re Letourneau, 792 N.W.2d 444 (Minn. 2011) (discipline for failure to keep clients informed of "significant events in their litigation"); In re Shaughnessy, 467 N.W.2d 620 (Minn. 1991) (failures to communicate are "intensely frustrating to the client, reflect adversely on the bar, and are destructive of public confidence in the legal profession") (30-day suspension).

Monetary Sanctions. When a lawyer fails to convey an offer to settle a pending litigation on terms the client would have accepted, the litigation will continue unnecessarily. That runs up the costs for the opposing party. 28 U.S.C. §1927 authorizes federal courts to impose monetary sanctions on a lawyer who "multiplies the proceedings . . . unreasonably and vexatiously." Blowers v. Lerner, 2016 WL 4575315 (E.D. Va. 2016), relied on this provision in ordering a lawyer who had failed to inform his client of a settlement offer to pay the opponent's legal fees of more than $84,000. (The court later gave the lawyer an opportunity to challenge the amount of the fees. 2017 WL 10897300.)

Thank You for Sharing.   In the course of a representation, a lawyer will learn a great deal of information bearing on the client's matter. How much of it must she share? The answer cannot be "all" because much will be technical or trivial. Time is also a factor. Yet the answer cannot be "none" because the lawyer is the client's agent. It is the client who must live with the result. So where do we draw the line?

Rule 1.2(a) tells us that in civil matters, whether to settle is a decision for the client, and in criminal matters, the client has the right to decide whether to testify, accept a plea, and waive a jury trial. Lawyers must provide the information the client needs to intelligently make these decisions. Rule 1.4(a). Conversely, lawyers are impliedly authorized to choose the means (strategies, legal theories) they will employ to achieve the client's goals. That much is easy. But comment [2] to Rule 1.2 and Rule 1.4 ("Communication") recognize that clients have an interest in participating in questions of strategy too, and in any event may wish to know how the matter is going. In a wide gray area, it's not possible definitively to say that a particular event or decision should or should not be shared with a client. Much must be left to the lawyer's judgment after considering the nature of the information, time constraints, the legal complexity, the lawyer's history with the client, and the client's expressed expectations.

The conflict-of-interest rules also contain duties to inform. They require a client's "informed consent" (defined in Rule 1.0(e)) before a lawyer with a conflict can proceed. The consent must be "confirmed in writing" (defined in Rule 1.0(b)). Rule 1.8(a) has stricter disclosure and consent requirements when lawyers engage in financial transactions with clients.

Sometimes the duty to inform can run smack into the duty of confidentiality, leaving a lawyer . . .

In a Box

"My name is Martin Chin. I do general corporate work in Seattle. One of my partners, Cherise Zagott, represents Jennie Marsh, an independent investor. Marsh is planning a joint venture with a dozen others, including Endicott Press. Marsh and the others would put up a total of about $30 million. Endicott will manage the venture, which will be in online publishing. Although Cherise is taking the lead, I met with Marsh twice and am helping Cherise with corporate issues. The deal will be signed in the next month. Until then, it must remain strictly confidential for competitive reasons.

"Last week, one of my clients, Font & Blue, a stationery wholesaler, got a visit from an investigator from the state Attorney General's office. The investigator told Mort Green, the F&B president, that the AG was investigating a kickback scheme to get state business. Wisely, Mort refused to talk without counsel. Then he called me. Mort told me that the investigator's questions suggested that F&B and Endicott (among others) are suspects. Jennie Marsh has no interest in F&B. And F&B has no interest in Jennie Marsh or her joint venture, which it is not aware of.

"What Mort told me is information that Rule 1.4 and our fiduciary duty would ordinarily require us to give Marsh. It is highly material. It might cause Marsh to abandon her plans because she would not relish the prospect of investing $2 million in an Endicott-managed venture and then see Endicott indicted. At the very least, she would share the information with the other investors and they might demand an explanation from Endicott. Maybe they would delay the deal until things get resolved. Or find someone to replace Endicott.

"At the same time, F&B would not want me to disclose the fact that it or even Endicott is the subject of a criminal investigation for kickbacks, which may come to nothing. Is there a way I can get the informed consents I need to tell Marsh that Endicott is under criminal investigation? If not, may we represent Marsh on the deal anyway? After all, if we withdraw from Marsh, her new lawyer won't know about Endicott either."

C. AUTONOMY OF ATTORNEYS AND CLIENTS

Autonomy is an idea distinct from, although entwined with, the duty to inform and advise. We can think of autonomy as the right to live one's life as one chooses (within the law) even if others find the choices imprudent or morally dubious. Clients hire lawyers when they require legal help to pursue their autonomous choices. A lawyer necessarily cedes some of her own autonomy when she agrees to represent a client. The client may expect her to employ the strategy that the client believes is best able to achieve his goal even if the lawyer disagrees with it or has moral qualms. Short of declining the matter or withdrawing from it if permitted, is there any "space" here for the lawyer to refuse? No autonomy issue arises if both client and lawyer agree. When they don't, respecting the autonomy of one may mean denying the autonomy of the other.

1. Criminal Cases

Lesser Included Offenses

Duckrath is a defendant in a homicide prosecution. When both sides have rested, Cramer, the defense lawyer, tells Duckrath that while the evidence can support a murder conviction, it can also support convictions for two lesser included offenses—manslaughter one and manslaughter two, each of which carries a lower maximum sentence than murder. He explains that the difference depends on the mental state of the accused at the time of the offense. Murder requires an intention to cause death. Manslaughter one requires an act intended to cause serious bodily harm but resulting in death. Both murder and manslaughter one will be reduced to manslaughter two if the jury is persuaded that the defendant acted under extreme emotional disturbance. Murder is punishable by 25 years to life in prison. Manslaughter one carries a sentence of 15 to 25 years, and manslaughter two carries a sentence of 10 to 15 years. Whatever the judge charges, the jury always has the option to acquit.

Cramer recommends that Duckrath ask the judge to charge both lesser included offenses. If he does ask, the judge must do so. Cramer believes that the jury, faced with the binary choice of murder or acquittal, will choose murder given the strength of the evidence, whereas it would choose one of the lesser offenses if given the choice. He thinks the prospect of acquittal is quite slim. Duckrath disagrees. He thinks that if the jury has only the option of convicting him of murder or acquitting him, it will view a murder conviction as too harsh and acquit. And Duckrath adds, "And I don't want you to argue that I was extremely emotional whatever it's called. It makes me sound wacko."

Cramer presents his disagreement with Duckrath to Judge Nielsen, who says:

> "Well, Mr. Cramer, it's a question of who gets to decide: you or Mr. Duckrath, isn't it? If the decision belongs to Mr. Duckrath and I don't charge the lesser included offenses, and he's convicted of murder, he can't really complain, can he? So maybe I should listen to him. On the other hand, if the appeals court later decides that the decision was yours, not his, he can claim he would have been convicted of a lesser crime if I had listened to you instead of him. So maybe I should listen to you. But if I do that, and he's convicted of a lesser offense, it necessarily means that the jury rejected murder. The appeals court might later rule that the decision belonged to him and that without the lesser offenses available to it, the jury might have rejected murder and acquitted.
>
> "On the one hand, Mr. Duckrath has to live with the consequences, so perhaps he should get to decide. But on the other hand, you've tried dozens of homicide cases and certainly have better insight than your client into what this very jury will do. So perhaps I should listen to you. Whatever I choose, I can be reversed if your client is convicted and the appeals court later tells me I let the wrong person choose. So I'll just do what I think is right and eventually the state supreme court will tell me if it was right or not."

What should the judge do?

"Long Black Veil"

"Long Black Veil" is a 1959 country ballad first recorded by Lefty Frizzell and later by Johnny Cash, Joan Baez, and others. In 2019, the Library of Congress selected it for the National Recording Registry.

The person speaking in the ballad tells us that he was charged with homicide ten years ago. Eyewitnesses described a man who resembled him. He had an alibi. He was in the arms of the wife of his best friend. He chose not to reveal his alibi and was convicted and executed. He is speaking to us from the grave. His lover visits the cemetery each night wearing a long black veil to disguise her identity.

Imagine that you were assigned to represent the defendant. He tells you his alibi and asks if you can tell the judge confidentially, but no one else. You tell him that it is not possible. Either he or his lover—probably both—would need to testify at trial. In that case, he says, he does not want you to use the alibi to defend him. Who gets to make that decision? If it's you, what do you do? If it's your client, what do you do?

"I Want to Die"

A judge on Thursday ordered the execution of Scott Dozier, securing a path to imminent death for the two-time convicted murderer who has spent the last year trying to persuade the state to kill him.

"It's been a long time, your honor. I'm ready to go," Dozier, 46, said during a brief court hearing. The warrant of execution, signed Thursday by Clark County District Judge Jennifer Togliatti, requires that Dozier be put to death during the week of Oct. 16.

—Las Vegas Review-Journal, July 27, 2017

"I represent Malcolm Voss, who as you probably know is on death row for two convenience store homicides 12 years ago when he was 19. Voss has had his execution delayed four times, twice when it was hours away. He's been living in a 6-by-9-foot cell since his conviction. He gets out an hour a day to exercise alone in a yard with 22-foot-high brick walls. Sometimes, they forget to give him the hour.

"Voss has always maintained his innocence. I got his case after conviction when the Death Penalty Project at the Lawyers' Human Rights Committee asked me to take it. Voss had very poor representation at trial—an appointed lawyer who did almost no investigation, hardly talked with Voss before the trial, and introduced almost no evidence in mitigation at the penalty phase.

"We've been through the state and federal systems on ineffectiveness claims, but no luck. The courts say the trial lawyer adopted a 'low profile' strategy so he wasn't ineffective. That's a very generous assessment. *Gideon*'s guarantee of free counsel for indigent defendants is a mirage in my state.

"I keep looking for new claims, but it gets harder. Voss is scheduled for execution in five weeks. I've been putting a petition together that makes some new arguments based on recent Confrontation Clause cases and some additional facts I've been able to uncover, including serious improprieties by the state crime lab chemist who testified on DNA identification. I don't know if the courts will hear me, but this is the best chance we've ever had to upset the sentence and maybe the conviction. I believe this guy is innocent, at least of the crimes that put him on death row. He's no angel, but he's not a murderer. I've represented other death row inmates and knew very well what I was dealing with.

"Two weeks ago, I told Voss about my discoveries and showed him papers in draft. He said don't file. 'Let's get it done, Emily,' he said. 'I want to die rather than live on death row or spend the rest of my life in prison.' I let it pass, but each time I went back or talked to him on the phone, he was adamant. He wrote me a letter saying I was not to file any more papers and that he was 'psychologically ready to go.' I told him I had a problem with that. He said he would fire me if it made my problem easier. I'm telling you this because I don't know what to do next. Must I accept his decision? Should I do so in any event?"

Rule 1.2(a), as we've seen, allocates authority for decisions between lawyer and client in both civil and criminal matters. The Constitution does the same in criminal cases. The Supreme Court has explained the considerations that influence its rulings:

> Numerous choices affecting conduct of the trial, including the objections to make, the witnesses to call, and the arguments to advance, depend not only upon what is permissible under the rules of evidence and procedure but also upon tactical considerations of the moment and the larger strategic plan for the trial. These matters can be difficult to explain to a layperson; and to require in all instances that they be approved by the client could risk compromising the efficiencies and fairness that the trial process is designed to promote. In exercising professional judgment, moreover, the attorney draws upon the expertise and experience that members of the bar should bring to the trial process. In most instances the attorney will have a better understanding of the procedural choices than the client; or at least the law should so assume. Gonzalez v. United States, 553 U.S. 242 (2008).

The Court went on to say that some "basic trial choices are so important that an attorney must seek the client's consent." Among these were the decision whether to plead guilty, waive a jury, testify, and appeal. *Gonzalez* held that the decision to let a federal magistrate judge conduct jury voir dire in a felony case is for counsel, not the defendant. Counsel is also authorized to waive a defendant's statutory speedy trial rights. New York v. Hill, 528 U.S. 110 (2000). More recently, the Court reaffirmed the defendant's right to decide to appeal even where, as part of a plea bargain, he had waived that right. Garza v. Idaho, _____ U.S. _____ (2019) (defense lawyer ineffective for failing to appeal when defendant stated wish to appeal). Even if the appeal waiver foreclosed the defendant from making some claims, it did not foreclose all claims, including whether the waiver itself was constitutionally effective.

JONES v. BARNES
463 U.S. 745 (1983)

CHIEF JUSTICE BURGER delivered the opinion of the Court.

We granted certiorari to consider whether defense counsel assigned to prosecute an appeal from a criminal conviction has a constitutional duty to raise every nonfrivolous issue requested by the defendant.

I

[Barnes was convicted of assault and robbery in state court. Melinger was assigned to represent him on appeal. Barnes asked Melinger to raise certain claims and gave him a brief Barnes had written. Melinger agreed to raise some of Barnes's claims but rejected most of them. Melinger told Barnes the claims he was considering and invited a response, but Barnes did not respond. Melinger's brief eventually focused on three arguments but he also submitted Barnes's pro se brief and Barnes himself submitted two more pro se briefs. At oral argument, Melinger addressed only the three claims in his brief. The state appeals court affirmed the conviction, but the Second Circuit, relying on Anders v. California, 386 U.S. 738 (1967), granted Barnes's habeas corpus petition.]

In *Anders,* this Court held that an appointed attorney must advocate his client's cause vigorously, and may not withdraw from a nonfrivolous appeal. The Court of Appeals majority held that, since *Anders* bars counsel from abandoning a nonfrivolous appeal, it also bars counsel from abandoning a nonfrivolous issue on appeal. . . .

II

In announcing a new *per se* rule that appellate counsel must raise every nonfrivolous issue requested by the client, the Court of Appeals relied primarily upon Anders v. California, supra. There is, of course, no constitutional right to an appeal, but in Griffin v. Illinois, 351 U.S. 12, 18 (1956), and Douglas v. California, 372 U.S. 353 (1963), the Court held that if an appeal is open to those who can pay for it, an appeal must be provided for an indigent. It is also recognized that the accused has the ultimate authority to make certain fundamental decisions regarding the case, as to whether to plead guilty, waive a jury, testify in his or her own behalf, or take an appeal. In addition, we have held that, with some limitations, a defendant may elect to act as his or her own advocate, Faretta v. California, 422 U.S. 806 (1975). Neither *Anders* nor any other decision of this Court suggests, however, that the indigent defendant has a constitutional right to compel appointed counsel to press nonfrivolous points requested by the client, if counsel, as a matter of professional judgment, decides not to present those points.

This Court, in holding that a state must provide counsel for an indigent appellant on his first appeal as of right, recognized the superior ability of trained counsel in the "examination into the record, research of the law, and marshalling of arguments on [the appellant's] behalf." Yet by promulgating a *per se* rule that the client, not the professional advocate, must be allowed to decide what issues are to be pressed, the Court of Appeals seriously undermines the ability of counsel to present the client's case in accord with counsel's professional evaluation.

Experienced advocates since time beyond memory have emphasized the importance of winnowing out weaker arguments on appeal and focusing on one central issue if possible, or at most on a few key issues. . . .

This Court's decision in *Anders*, far from giving support to the new *per se* rule announced by the Court of Appeals, is to the contrary. *Anders* recognized that the role of the advocate "requires that he support his client's appeal to the best of his ability." Here the appointed counsel did just that. For judges to second-guess reasonable professional judgments and impose on appointed counsel a duty to raise every "colorable" claim suggested by a client would disserve the very goal of vigorous and effective advocacy that underlies *Anders*. Nothing in the Constitution or our interpretation of that document requires such a standard. The judgment of the Court of Appeals is accordingly reversed.

[Justice Blackmun, concurring in the judgment, thought that "as an *ethical* matter, an attorney should argue on appeal all nonfrivolous claims upon which his client insists." However, Justice Blackmun did not believe that his view on the "ideal allocation of decisionmaking authority between client and lawyer necessarily assumes constitutional status." The client's "remedy, of course, is a writ of habeas corpus."]

Justice Brennan, with whom Justice Marshall joins, dissenting . . .

I believe the right to "the assistance of counsel" carries with it a right, personal to the defendant, to [decide which nonfrivolous issues should be raised on appeal] against the advice of counsel if he chooses. . . .

It is no secret that indigent clients often mistrust the lawyers appointed to represent them. There are many reasons for this, some perhaps unavoidable even under perfect conditions—differences in education, disposition, and socio-economic class—and some that should (but may not always) be zealously avoided. A lawyer and his client do not always have the same interests. Even with paying clients, a lawyer may have a strong interest in having judges and prosecutors think well of him, and, if he is working for a flat fee—a common arrangement for criminal defense attorneys—or if his fees for court appointments are lower than he would receive for other work, he has an obvious financial incentive to conclude cases on his criminal docket swiftly. Good lawyers undoubtedly recognize these temptations and resist them, and they endeavor to convince their clients that they will. It would be naive, however, to suggest that they always succeed in either task. A constitutional rule that encourages lawyers to disregard their clients' wishes without compelling need can only exacerbate the clients' suspicion of their lawyers. As in *Faretta*, to force a lawyer's *decisions* on a defendant "can only lead him to believe that the law contrives against him." In the end, what the Court hopes to gain in effectiveness of appellate representation by the rule it imposes today may well be lost to decreased effectiveness in other areas of representation. . . .

Finally, today's ruling denigrates the values of individual autonomy and dignity central to many constitutional rights, especially those Fifth and Sixth Amendment rights that come into play in the criminal process. Certainly a person's life changes when he is charged with a crime and brought to trial. He must, if he harbors any hope of success, defend himself on terms—often technical and hard to understand—that are the State's, not his own. As a practical matter, the assistance of counsel is necessary to that defense. Yet, until his conviction becomes final and he has had an opportunity to appeal, any restrictions on individual autonomy and dignity should be limited to the minimum necessary to vindicate the State's interest in a speedy, effective prosecution. The role of the defense lawyer should be above all to function as the instrument and defender of the client's autonomy and dignity in all phases of the criminal process. . . .

Since Barnes's points were not frivolous and he will do the time if the appeal fails, perhaps Melinger should have deferred. Barnes is an adult. He deserves to be able to make important decisions that affect only him. On the other hand, would we say the same if Barnes, for whatever reason, instructed Melinger *not* to include his strongest argument as Melinger saw it? True, Barnes could have chosen not to appeal, but having appealed, didn't he delegate the strategic decisions to Melinger?

Barnes apparently did not protest Melinger's decision to exclude Barnes's appeal points from the brief and submit them under Barnes's name pro se. The Court could have treated Barnes's silence as a waiver, but it may have preferred to make clear its disapproval of the lower court's reasoning.

The Constitution aside, Justice Blackmun believes the lawyer acted unethically. Do you agree? What if the lawyer was confident that inclusion of the client's nonfrivolous claims would undermine the effectiveness of the brief? What if the lawyer would be professionally embarrassed to assert them? In the final paragraph of his dissent, Justice Brennan went on to write that a client's choices "should be respected unless they would require lawyers to violate their consciences, the law, or their duties to the court." Doesn't the word "consciences" leave little to Justice Brennan's position?

Client autonomy is directly tied to the client's power in the legal services market. If a client is a source of ongoing business or the lawyer hopes it will be, the means/ends distinction in Rule 1.2(a) for allocating authority between lawyer and client would not likely arise. The firm will eagerly consult the client on all but the most mundane decisions. Barnes had no market power, so Melinger could (properly) refuse his instructions confident that the courts would support him. How likely is it that an American law firm would disobey the instructions of a lucrative client?

CASE NOTE: McCOY v. LOUISIANA

The Court again addressed the constitutional allocation of authority in criminal cases in McCoy v. Louisiana, ____ U.S.____ (2018). McCoy was charged with murdering three of his family members. The state sought the death penalty. McCoy told his lawyer, Larry English, that "he was out of State at the time of the killings and that corrupt police killed the victims when a drug deal went wrong." No evidence supported this claim (or McCoy's further belief that his lawyer and the trial judge were part of the plot). English thought that because proof of guilt was "overwhelming[,] absent a concession at the guilt stage that McCoy was the killer, a death sentence would be impossible to avoid at the penalty phase." So in an effort to avoid a death sentence, English told McCoy that he would admit that McCoy did kill the victims but lacked the mental state required for first degree murder. The problem was that McCoy denied killing the victims and "vociferously" instructed English not to concede otherwise. He also protested to the judge. English asked the judge to let him withdraw, but trial was imminent and the judge refused. English ignored McCoy's instruction, conceded the killings, and argued that the facts proved a lower degree of homicide. McCoy was convicted and sentenced to death. On appeal, he argued that he did not get the effective assistance of counsel because the decision whether to admit to the killings was his to make.

In her opinion for herself and five other Justices, reversing McCoy's conviction on ineffective assistance of counsel grounds, Justice Ginsburg wrote:

> Trial management is the lawyer's province: Counsel provides his or her assistance by making decisions such as "what arguments to pursue, what evidentiary objections to raise, and what agreements to conclude regarding the admission of evidence." Some decisions, however, are reserved for the client—notably, whether to plead guilty, waive the right to a jury trial, testify in one's own behalf, and forgo an appeal. [Citing Jones v. Barnes.]
>
> Autonomy to decide that the objective of the defense is to assert innocence belongs in this latter category. Just as a defendant may steadfastly refuse to plead guilty in the face of overwhelming evidence against her, or reject the assistance of legal counsel despite the defendant's own inexperience and lack of professional qualifications, so may she insist on maintaining her innocence at the guilt phase of a capital trial. These are not strategic choices about how best to *achieve* a client's objectives; they are choices about what the client's objectives in fact *are*.
>
> Counsel may reasonably assess a concession of guilt as best suited to avoiding the death penalty, as English did in this case. But the client may not share that objective. He may wish to avoid, above all else, the opprobrium that comes with admitting he killed family members. Or he may hold life in prison not worth living and prefer to risk death for any hope, however small, of exoneration. . . .

In this case, the court had determined that McCoy was competent to stand trial, *i.e.,* that McCoy had "sufficient present ability to consult with his lawyer with a reasonable degree of rational understanding." If, after consultations with English concerning the management of the defense, McCoy disagreed with English's proposal to concede McCoy committed three murders, it was not open to English to override McCoy's objection. English could not interfere with McCoy's telling the jury "I was not the murderer," although counsel could, if consistent with providing effective assistance, focus his own collaboration on urging that McCoy's mental state weighed against conviction.

Justice Alito dissented, joined by Justices Thomas and Gorsuch. He several times posed a challenging question: What exactly should English have done? Justice Alito wrote that English had told McCoy "some eight months" before trial that he could not argue McCoy's conspiracy claim without undermining his own credibility and that the only way to try to avoid a death penalty was to admit the killing. McCoy did not then object.

> The weekend before trial, however, petitioner changed his mind. He asked the trial court to replace English, and English asked for permission to withdraw. Petitioner stated that he had secured substitute counsel, but he was unable to provide the name of this new counsel, and no new attorney ever appeared. The court refused these requests and also denied petitioner's last-minute request to represent himself. (Petitioner does not challenge these decisions here.) So petitioner and English were stuck with each other, and petitioner availed himself of his right to take the stand to tell his wild story. Under those circumstances, what was English supposed to do?
>
> [T]he result of mounting petitioner's conspiracy defense almost certainly would have been disastrous. That approach stood no chance of winning an acquittal and would have severely damaged English's credibility in the eyes of the jury, thus undermining his ability to argue effectively against the imposition of a death sentence at the penalty phase of the trial. As English observed, taking that path would have only "help[ed] the District Attorney send [petitioner] to the death chamber." So, again, what was English supposed to do?
>
> When pressed at oral argument before this Court, petitioner's current counsel* eventually provided an answer: English was not required to take any affirmative steps to support petitioner's bizarre defense, but instead of conceding that petitioner shot the victims, English should have ignored that element entirely. So the fundamental right supposedly violated in this case comes down to the difference between the two statements set out below.
>
> > *Constitutional:* "First-degree murder requires proof both that the accused killed the victim and that he acted with the intent to kill. I submit to you that my client did not have the intent required for conviction for that offense."
> >
> > *Unconstitutional:* "First-degree murder requires proof both that the accused killed the victim and that he acted with the intent to kill. I admit

---

* McCoy's Supreme Court advocate was Seth Waxman, an experienced Supreme Court practitioner. — Ed.

that my client shot and killed the victims, but I submit to you that he did not have the intent required for conviction for that offense."

The practical difference between these two statements is negligible. If English had conspicuously refrained from endorsing petitioner's story and had based his defense solely on petitioner's dubious mental condition, the jury would surely have gotten the message that English was essentially conceding that petitioner killed the victims. But according to petitioner's current attorney, the difference is fundamental. The first formulation, he admits, is perfectly fine. The latter, on the other hand, is a violation so egregious that the defendant's conviction must be reversed even if there is no chance that the misstep caused any harm. It is no wonder that the Court declines to embrace this argument and instead turns to an issue that the case at hand does not actually present.

Whether or not you agree with the majority, does it not trouble you that McCoy's next lawyer (if the case is retried) will be obligated to assist her client in a strategy that is near certain to fail? The majority dismisses the autonomy of the lawyer, who may wonder how it could possibly be that in the name of client autonomy, professional duty requires her to assist in the judicial equivalent of suicide. Or maybe it does trouble you, but you think that a client's right to make this choice is more important and overriding his instruction more troubling. We have two bad options. The Court said client autonomy wins. McCoy did not have to prove *any* chance of acquittal if English had followed his instruction. The dissent says English got to decide, his choice was reasonable, and McCoy could not prove prejudice.

Separately, do Jones v. Barnes and McCoy v. Louisiana help you address the two problems at the top of this part?

2. Civil Cases

"It's the Right and Decent Thing to Do"

"I represent a defendant in a civil antitrust case. We have exchanged the names of expert witness economists. The plaintiff's expert, Dr. Garrick Wills, is a principal at a financial services firm. He has a Ph.D. from a top university and an impressive publication and work history, including a stint on the staff of the Senate Banking Committee.

"It is common to look into the past of opposing experts. We rarely find anything because the firms that hire them will have eliminated anyone problematic, as do we. However, our client learned (entirely properly) that Dr. Wills was the subject of academic discipline in graduate school ten years ago. He had copied, with small changes, nearly two pages in a 25-page paper and did not cite the source. Wills and the school reached a settlement. He had to rewrite the paper and his grade for the class was reduced. The school would seal the file and not report the incident to prospective employers or academic institutions.

"Under the rules of evidence, I am allowed to ask Wills on cross: 'Isn't it true that you were disciplined for plagiarism in graduate school?' If he denies it, I won't be allowed to prove otherwise or argue that it's true. But the jury will likely believe it because why would the judge let me ask unless it's true? Besides, he'll likely admit it because denial would be perjury and he doesn't know what I can prove. Also, because he won't anticipate the question, it could fluster him. The financial services industry and the financial press are watching this case. So my question and his answer may show up in a trade publication. His current employer may or may not know about the discipline.

"Now, this incident is not the basis for our credibility challenge, which relies instead on what we claim are errors of omission and commission in his expert report and inconsistent statements in his publications. I don't doubt that Wills believes that his analysis is correct. He's not lying. He's just wrong (as we see it). We're challenging his methodology, not his character.

"Because the harm it could do Wills professionally is significantly disproportionate to its value for us, I told our client that I would not ask him about the incident. I said that there is no chance that school discipline a decade ago will lead the jury to believe he's lying in court today. The client agrees but sees another purpose. I got this email from its general counsel: 'Oliver, we think there will be something to gain from springing the question on Wills right out of the box. It will ruffle him and make his testimony less effective. We want you to do it.'

"I know how to conduct what the media likes to call a withering cross-examination. But this cross seems like character assassination for little gain, if any. I don't want to be part of it. I could give a strategic reason for not asking. I could say that it will look to the jury like browbeating and boomerang. But I don't believe that. I think it might be marginally beneficial for the reason the client gives.

"My question is: Can I omit the cross when my reason is not strategic, but because I believe that it's the right and decent thing to do?"

"Accept the Offer"

"I do matrimonial work. Aside from child custody and visitation, my main objective is money. Look, I don't mean to be crass, but after 26 years at this business, I know that the one thing my clients regret, if they regret anything, is that they didn't get enough in the property settlement or support or they agreed to give away too much. Whatever they think at the time, if there's disappointment later, it's about money. Take that on faith because it's true.

"The client I wanted to ask you about is someone I'll call Chloe, who was married to Russell for 14 years and then fell out of love or decided she was never in it and had married too young at 23. Russell was 24 and had just started his second year at NYU Law School. Chloe's income was their main source of support until Russell graduated.

"Chloe told Russell she wanted a divorce. He thought they had a great marriage. He'd take her back in a heartbeat. I've seen this before. You learn a lot about people doing matrimonial work. Usually, the spouse leaving has a lover, or someone they hope will become a lover, but I'm pretty sure that's not so here. Chloe just wants her life back while she's still fairly young.

"Chloe and Russell have three children, aged three, five, and eight. Before the oldest one was born, Chloe taught high school history, but she has since stayed home and hasn't worked outside the home.

"Anyway, Russell is now a partner and rising star at an international law firm. His lawyer made a low-ball offer, in the ballpark for first offers but low in light of his income and earning prospects and obviously an invitation for a counteroffer. It's what I might do if I had Russell. I presented it to Chloe, because I have to, but told her not to be offended that it's so low, because first offers are always low and this one isn't any lower than many. Chloe will have custody.

"What she said next blew me away. 'Greg, accept the offer.' She doesn't want to negotiate, not even if she assumes—as I told her based on my experience she absolutely should—that I can get about 30 percent more on the property division and half again as much yearly on support, with cost of living escalators, for her and the children. I could do this with one phone call to Russell's lawyer, maybe two, and a little haggling. And Chloe would *still* be getting too little. I told her this. Two things more: Russell will have no financial obligations to a child, except college tuition, after that child reaches 21; and the property division in Russell's offer does not include Chloe's interest in the economic value of his law degree even though our courts recognize that interest.

"Chloe said she feels bad enough about what she's doing to Russell. She feels that his offer is an amount she can live with, and she doesn't want to bargain or do anything to create further ill feeling. She says Russell is a good person and will do right by her and the children. I've been back to her several times, but she insists. I'm certain that she's going to regret it within a year, when it'll be too late. Her quality of life, while comfortable, will change noticeably from what it is today, while his will continue to rise. He'll have a new wife, maybe more kids. They'll be living in a different universe from Chloe and the children.

"I've had this happen before—one client wants little or nothing, a second client wants to give away the store, both operating from guilt—but always I've been able to talk them out of it. Don't get me wrong. I understand and often advise taking less or giving more for the sake of harmony. These people have to cooperate about their kids for another 20 years or more. You don't push for every dollar. Life is about more than money. But this settlement would be a catastrophe for Chloe. What should I do?"

OLFE v. GORDON
93 Wis. 2d 173, 286 N.W.2d 573 (1980)

CALLOW, JUDGE . . .

[Olfe hired Gordon to handle the sale of her home to Demman. She told Gordon that she was willing to take back a first mortgage but only a first mortgage. Taking back a mortgage would make it easier for Olfe to sell her home because a buyer would not have to seek a loan from a bank. But it would also mean that Olfe would be accepting an IOU as part of the purchase price. The IOU would, however, be secured by the equity in the house. If her buyer defaulted, Olfe could rely on that equity to recoup her loan. A *first* mortgage would mean that Olfe would be preferred over any other lenders in case of default.

Gordon negotiated a contract that provided for a second mortgage. Olfe claimed that Gordon and his partner encouraged her to believe that it was a first mortgage. After the buyer defaulted and the first mortgage was foreclosed, nothing remained for Olfe, who lost more than $25,000. Olfe sued Gordon alleging negligence. The trial court dismissed the case because of insufficiency of evidence and "a lack of expert testimony relating to the standard of care required of attorneys in similar circumstances."]

Since Olfe did not present expert testimony to establish the standard of care and a departure from that standard, we must determine whether Gordon's actions fall within the exception to the rule requiring expert testimony. Olfe's first two allegations, that Gordon failed to provide in the offer to purchase that Olfe's security interest would be a first mortgage and that he failed to draft or cause to be drafted a mortgage that would be senior to any other Demman would obtain on the premises of sale, are contentions that Gordon is liable for damages caused by his negligent disregard of Olfe's instructions. The legal theory on which these allegations are premised is well established:

> It has generally been recognized that an attorney may be liable for all losses caused by his failure to follow with reasonable promptness and care the explicit instructions of his client. Moreover, an attorney's honest belief that the instructions were not in the best interests of his client provides no defense to a suit for malpractice.

The attorney-client relationship in such contexts is one of agent to principal, and as an agent the attorney "must act in conformity with his authority and instructions and is responsible to his principal if he violates this duty." While actions for disregard of instructions can be based upon fiduciary and contractual principles, the principal's cause of action for an agent's breach of duty may also lie in tort. "[I]f a paid agent does something wrongful, either knowing it to be wrong, or acting negligently, the principal may have either an action of tort or an action of contract." See also [precedent], where this court stated, "It is elementary that a principal has a cause of action sounding in tort against his agent when the latter violates a duty that he owes to the former." Expert testimony is not required to show that the agent (attorney) has violated his duty.

[Reversed.]

The Scope of the Client's Autonomy

Here's a riddle: Gordon failed to follow Olfe's instructions. Melinger refused to follow Barnes's instructions. Barnes lost. Olfe won. Why? Was it simply because one action depended on the Sixth Amendment and the other was governed by state law? Or is the explanation the kind of decision? Both, actually.

Olfe's employment of Gordon did not authorize him to make the decision he did in the face of her contrary instruction. In the language of Rule 1.2(a), the decision concerned "the objectives of representation" and belonged to her. Not only did Olfe not have to present expert evidence, she won as a matter of law. But in *Barnes*, the decision how to argue an appeal belonged to the lawyer under the Sixth Amendment.

If Olfe said only that she was willing to "take back a mortgage," could Gordon have accepted a second mortgage without informing Olfe? No. The decision was hers. Gordon had a duty to explain that she was getting a second mortgage and what that meant. Rule 1.4(b).

Clients with Diminished Capacity

The allocation of decisionmaking authority is difficult enough when a client is a competent adult. When a client has diminished capacity because of a mental disability, or because the client is a minor, the issue becomes even harder. Read Rule 1.14. Justice Pollock relied on it in In re M.R., 638 A.2d 1274 (N.J. 1994). M.R. was "a twenty-one-year-old woman with Down's Syndrome." Her parents were divorced. She had been living with her mother since 1979. Her father had visitation rights at his home. M.R. "expressed a desire to move from her mother's to her father's home." In order to prevent that move, M.R.'s mother filed a guardianship proceeding. The "trial court appointed [a lawyer] to act as M.R.'s attorney." On appeal, Justice Pollock held that M.R.'s mother had the burden of proving by clear and convincing evidence that M.R. was not competent to choose to live with her father. Because the trial court had placed the burden of proof on M.R.'s father, the case was remanded. The court then turned to the role of M.R.'s lawyer. It distinguished between a guardian ad litem and counsel. Counsel "is a zealous advocate for the wishes of the client. The guardian *ad litem* evaluates for himself or herself what is in the best interests of his or her client-ward and then represent[s] the client-ward in accordance with that judgment." The court continued:

> An adversarial role for the attorney recognizes that even if the client's incompetency is uncontested, the client may want to contest other issues, such as the identity of the guardian or, as here, the client's place of residence. With proper advice and assistance, the developmentally-disabled client may be able to participate in such a decision. From this perspective, the role of an attorney for a developmentally-disabled person is like that of an attorney representing any other client.
>
> Advocacy that is diluted by excessive concern for the client's best interests would raise troubling questions for attorneys in an adversarial system. An attorney proceeds without well-defined standards if he or she forsakes a client's instructions for the attorney's perception of the client's best interests. Further, "if counsel has already concluded that his client needs 'help,'" he is more likely to provide only procedural formality, rather than vigorous representation. Finally, the attorney who undertakes to act according to a best-interest standard may be forced to make decisions concerning the client's mental capacity that the attorney is unqualified to make. . . .
>
> [W]e offer the following guidelines to assist the attorney for an incompetent. First, a declaration of incompetency does not deprive a developmentally-disabled person of the right to make all decisions. The primary duty of the attorney for such a person is to protect that person's rights, including the right to make decisions on specific matters. Generally, the attorney should advocate any decision made by the developmentally-disabled person. On perceiving a conflict between that person's preferences and best interests, the attorney may inform the court of the possible need for a guardian *ad litem.*

D. TERMINATING THE RELATIONSHIP

The Rules describe the circumstances under which lawyers may withdraw from a representation. Case law describes the client's authority to discharge a lawyer.

1. *Termination by the Client*

Clients, it is said, may fire their lawyers for any reason or no reason. Harrill & Sutter, PLLC v. Kosin, 378 S.W.3d 135 (Ark. 2011) ("Attorney-client contracts contain an implied provision that the client may discharge the attorney at any time, either with or without cause."). One court has held that a client may even fire a retained lawyer because he wants to be represented by a lawyer of a different race. Giaimo & Vreeburg v. Smith, 599 N.Y.S.2d 841 (2d Dept. 1993) (construing state and federal civil rights laws). On the other hand, laws that protect employees against discrimination or retaliatory discharge also protect *employed* lawyers. An employed lawyer can invoke the Rule 1.6(b)(5) exception to confidentiality to prove her case. Kachmar v. SunGard Data Sys., 109 F.3d 173 (3d Cir. 1997).

Indigent criminal defendants cannot fire the lawyers appointed to represent them, although they may ask the court to assign a new lawyer or may be allowed to represent themselves. Even a litigant with a retained lawyer may not be able to change counsel if it will delay the trial. By then, the interests of others—the courts, witnesses, the opponent—will be given substantial, even decisive, weight. Courts also suspect that efforts to fire counsel may be intended to delay the trial.

When a professional relationship ends, whether terminated by the lawyer or the client or simply at the end of the matter, the client is "presumptive[ly]" entitled to the lawyer's "entire file on the represented matter." However, "narrow exceptions" will entitle the lawyer to keep "firm documents intended for internal law office review and use." Sage Realty Corp. v. Proskauer Rose Goetz & Mendelsohn LLP, 689 N.E.2d 879 (N.Y. 1997) (presenting this as the majority view, collecting cases, and acknowledging that a valid lien may supersede the client's right to the file). Iowa Supreme Court Attorney Disciplinary Board v. Gottschalk, 729 N.W.2d 812 (Iowa 2007), also holds that the client is presumptively entitled to the entire file.

2. Termination by the Lawyer

The lawyer's ability to terminate a professional relationship is circumscribed by Rule 1.16, which tells us when a lawyer may or must withdraw. Leaving a client without a good reason can be characterized as abandonment, which is disloyal and has consequences. Consider Augustson v. Linea Aerea Nacional-Chile, 76 F.3d 658 (5th Cir. 1996). Plaintiff's law firm requested and received permission to withdraw after plaintiff rejected a settlement offer against the firm's advice. The case arose out of an air crash, and other clients of the law firm had accepted the offer. With new counsel, the plaintiff got a substantially higher settlement. The firm then sought a fee for its work. In Texas, whose law applied, and elsewhere, a lawyer who abandons a client loses all right to compensation. The firm cited the court's permission to withdraw as proof that it had not abandoned the client, but the Fifth Circuit rejected this argument. The decision whether to settle belonged to the client, not the law firm. Permission to withdraw merely reflected the court's evaluation of what was in the "best interests of the client" at the time, not a determination that the firm acted correctly. In agreement is Lofton v. Fairmont Specialty Insurance Managers, 367 S.W.3d 593 (Ky. 2012).

Courts will allow lawyers to withdraw if a client is seriously delinquent in paying fees. King v. NAIAD Inflatables of Newport, 11 A.3d 64 (R.I. 2010) (civil case).

3. Termination by Drift

Some representations end for reasons other than lawyers or clients explicitly ending them. Some, probably most, end because the work ends. But does the end of the work always mean the end of the relationship? The answer can be important. If the relationship is not truly over, the lawyer may have a duty to continue to advise the client and protect its legal interests on the subject of the work. Lama Holding Co. v. Shearman & Sterling, 758 F. Supp. 159 (S.D.N.Y. 1991) (denying motion to dismiss malpractice claim where following completion of work, firm allegedly failed to advise client of relevant tax law changes after promising to do so); Barnes v. Turner, 606 S.E.2d 849 (Ga. 2004) (lawyer had duty to renew client's security interest five years after representation ended where lawyer had not warned client of the need to do so in order to protect that interest). If the client is a current, not a former, client, stricter conflicts of interest rules govern the lawyer, as we see in chapters 5 and 6.

Going rather far in finding a current client relationship is Jones v. Rabanco, Ltd., 2006 WL 2237708 (W.D. Wash. 2006). A firm that had not done work for a client for more than three years was deemed still to be its current counsel because (a) it stored many files from the matter; (b) it had not marked the matter closed in its own records; and (c) it was listed on settlement documents to receive a copy of any notice to the client. Consequently, it was disqualified when it then appeared against the client's parent.

4. Episodic Clients

Lawyers might believe that a client is no longer a client if they are doing no work for it at the moment and haven't for a while. This is not necessarily true. Courts recognize what we might call an episodic client. For example, a firm may have done a particular kind of work for a client—trademark registration, for example—two or three times a year for the past three years, a month each time. That can create a reasonable client expectation that the professional relationship continues during the intervals and that the lawyer will be available the next time the client needs a trademark registered. If I ask you, "Who's your dentist?," you might answer "Dr. Goodsmile," even if you haven't seen her in eight months, because she's the dentist you see if your teeth need care. She's your dentist even when you're not in the chair. Clients can feel the same way about lawyers.

Obviously, this is a question of fact that looks at the frequency with which the client has called on the firm and over what period of time. RAK had served as patent counsel to Adobe intermittently between 2006 and February 2012. In July 2012, when RAK was doing no work for Adobe, it sued Adobe, which moved to disqualify RAK on the ground that RAK was suing a current client. (That's forbidden without informed consent. See chapter 5B3.) Was Adobe a current client? The court said yes.

> It is true that RAK would have been free to reject any Adobe request for further opinion letters. RAK, however, had never refused work from Adobe in the past, which strengthens the reasonableness of Adobe's belief that RAK would take further work and the relationship was ongoing. Moreover, RAK's freedom to reject additional work from Adobe is not dispositive. . . . The fact that [RAK] may freely choose to end the relationship and refuse further business does not mean it is free to sue its client prior to making it clear that the relationship is over. It is the law firm's responsibility to ensure there are no questions regarding the status of its current client relationships. It would have been a simple enough task for RAK to notify Adobe that it would no longer be available as opinion counsel.

Parallel Iron, LLC v. Adobe Sys., 2013 WL 789207 (D. Del. 2013).

Given the consequences, it makes good sense to clarify any ambiguity. A firm could send a "Dear Former Client" letter saying that "our representation of you on the X matter is now concluded and you are now our former client." When I suggest this liberating option to lawyers, they don't like it. They have a reason. What do you imagine it is?

Self-Assessment Questions*

1. Lem Clarick represents Sheelah Boyd in a personal injury action. The complaint seeks $3.5 million. Lem's experience tells him that a jury will award at least $2.8 million, probably more, but of course no one can know for sure. Lem is working on a one-third contingency. Six months before trial, the defendant offers $450,000. He tells Sheelah and recommends that she reject the offer "because we'll likely get more than seven times that at trial. Maybe five times." Sheelah says she wants to accept the offer, which would net Lem a fee of $150,000. But he's been keeping time records and he already has $250,000 of time invested in the case. "I also have an interest in the size of the recovery." Lem says. "Can I tell Sheelah that if she accepts, she has to pay my time charges of $250,000?"

2. Corey Shack sued her former matrimonial lawyer, Tina Holly, alleging that Holly failed to advise her that the law was unsettled on whether certain property was part of the marital estate in divorce entitling her to half of it. As a result, Shack said, she made no claim for a portion of

---

* Most chapters conclude with self-assessment questions. Answers appear at the end of the book. Consult the table of contents. The answers represent one way to analyze the questions but don't exclude the possibility of other defensible approaches.

that property and settled for less than she could have received. Holly moved for summary judgment. She agreed that the law was unsettled when she represented Shack and in fact has remained unsettled. But she argued that her conclusion that the property was not part of the marital estate was nonetheless reasonable. She disclosed her copious legal research notes and a file memo laying out the reasoning for her conclusion. She argued that well-established case law holds that lawyers are not liable if their predictions made after reasonable legal and factual investigation turn out to be wrong. In fact, Holly argued, her decision may not even turn out to be wrong depending on what the courts eventually hold. Shack does not question the thoroughness of Holly's research or the reasonableness of her conclusion. Does Shack have any argument that nonetheless Holly's motion for summary judgment should be denied?

3. Clyde Snoot is representing Edie Santos in a federal claim against Morkett Sales, whose lawyer is Luis Caspone. After the action is filed, Snoot notices the depositions of four current and former Morkett employees. He also subpoenas any internal memos written by Caspone and his associates and that contain the substance of interviews with those four employees on the subject of Santos's claim. To what extent if at all does the attorney-client privilege apply to the subject of the subpoenas? To questions Snoot asks at the deposition of current and former Morkett employees? (Ignore the work product doctrine.)

III

Protecting the Attorney-Client Relationship Against Outside Interference

The theme of this chapter is the legal ethics equivalent of espionage.

Ethics rules and case law protect the client-lawyer relationship against spies, at least when the spies are other lawyers. That should not be surprising given the many ways that the rules protect clients from their own lawyers. If we're going to hammer home the sanctity of the lawyer-client relationship, we should expect rules that prevent adversaries from interfering with it. Exhibit One is Rule 4.2. It forbids a lawyer to communicate with another lawyer's client under certain circumstances. This "no-contact" (or "anti-contact") rule, examined in part A, applies to both civil matters (litigation and transactional; see part A1) and criminal law enforcement (where an exception may swallow the rule; see part A2). Prohibited contact with an opposing client is not, however, the only way in which an outsider may intercept confidential communications or otherwise undermine a client-lawyer relationship. See part B.

A. COMMUNICATING WITH ANOTHER LAWYER'S CLIENTS

Rule 4.2 says that "[i]n representing a client, a lawyer shall not communicate about the subject of the representation with a person the lawyer knows to be represented by another lawyer in the matter, unless the lawyer has the consent of the other lawyer or is authorized to do so by law or a court order."*

---

* "The origin of the no-contact rule can be traced to an 1836 treatise, which declared 'I will never enter into any conversation with my opponent's client, relative to his claim or defence, except with the consent, *and* in the presence of his counsel.' 2 D. Hoffman, A Course of Legal Study Addressed to Students and the Profession Generally 771 (2d ed. Baltimore 1836) (emphasis in original), *as quoted in* John Leubsdorf, Communicating With Another Lawyer's Client: The Lawyer's Veto and the Client's Interest, 127 U. Pa. L. Rev. 683, 684 (1979)." State v. Miller, 600 N.W.2d 457 (Minn. 1999).

The rule applies in litigation and transactional matters. The rule applies even if the "represented" person is not the client's *direct* opponent, but, e.g., a co-defendant or another party to a transaction who shares most of a client's objectives. The no-contact rule has quite a few conditions:

- The communication must occur while a lawyer is herself "representing a client" on the matter in which the contacted person is represented. If she is not representing a client in the matter, she may talk to the other lawyer's client about it. This allows a client to get a second opinion. Iowa Sup. Ct. Bd. of Prof'l Ethics & Conduct v. Herrera, 626 N.W.2d 107 (Iowa 2001).

- Does Rule 4.2 restrain a party who happens to be a lawyer, whether acting pro se or with counsel? Authorities are divided. In re Lucas, 789 N.W.2d 73 (N.D. 2010), reviews the cases and concludes that the rule should apply to a pro se lawyer, and by implication a lawyer who is a represented party, "to prevent lawyers from taking advantage of laypersons." Restatement §99, comment *e*, disagrees.

- The communicating lawyer must *know* that the person with whom she is communicating is represented on the subject of the communication. Comment [8] to Rule 4.2 warns that knowledge "may be inferred from the circumstances" and that a "lawyer cannot evade the requirement . . . by closing eyes to the obvious." If a lawyer does not "know" that the contacted person is represented, the rule does not impose a duty to find out. Nevertheless, it makes sense to inquire because a tribunal might later say that the lawyer did know or consciously avoided knowledge.

- Members of an uncertified class are not "represented" by counsel for the named class members, so the lawyers on either side of the matter may contact them consistent with rules on advertising and solicitation unless the court orders otherwise. ABA Opinion 07-445.

- The communicating lawyer is only forbidden to communicate with a represented party on the "subject" of the representation. She may communicate about anything else, like politics or sports. Rule 4.2 cmt. [4].

- The prohibition does not apply if the other lawyer consents to the communication or if it is "authorized . . . by law or a court order." A represented client may not waive the protection of this rule without counsel's consent. Iowa Supreme Court Attorney Disciplinary Board v. Box, 715 N.W.2d 758 (Iowa 2006) collects the cases. And if a represented person claims that his lawyer does consent or that he has fired his lawyer, it's best to get confirmation from the lawyer. Highly paternalistic, don't you think? Or is there a good reason to require that a client get the advice of counsel before he can choose to forego the advice of counsel?*

---

* Paradoxically perhaps, in response to police questioning, a person may waive the Sixth Amendment right to counsel without the advice of appointed counsel. "[T]he decision to waive [the Sixth Amendment right] need not itself be counseled." Montejo v. Louisiana, 556 U.S. 778 (2009) (5-4 decision) (lawyer had been appointed at arraignment without Montejo's request; the Court distinguished cases where appointment follows defendant's request).

- Forbidden is "communication." Videotaping employees of a represented company "going about their activities in what those employees believe is the normal course" is allowed. Hill v. Shell Oil Co., 209 F. Supp. 2d 876 (N.D. Ill. 2002) (not a violation to videotape behavior of gas station attendants to gather evidence of racial discrimination in their treatment of customers).
- A violation can occur if a lawyer engages in forbidden communication through a third party, like an investigator or even the lawyer's own client (but see the next two paragraphs). Rule 8.4(a).

Clients are free to talk to each other. Clients may be able to get past a problem when lawyers cannot. That can be beneficial. But sometimes it is ill-advised because one client may be more adept at learning the other client's strategic or confidential information.

How far can a lawyer go in aiding client-to-client communications? Rule 4.2 cmt. [4] says "a lawyer is not prohibited from advising a client concerning a communication that the client is legally entitled to make." "Advising" is not a precise term; nor is "assisting" in Restatement §99(2) (rule "does not prohibit the lawyer from assisting the client in otherwise proper communication by the lawyer's client with a represented nonclient"). ABA Opinion 11-461 concludes that "a lawyer may give substantial assistance to a client regarding a substantive communication with a represented adversary. That advice could include, for example, the subjects or topics to be addressed, issues to be raised and strategies to be used. Such advice may be given regardless of who—the lawyer or the client—conceives of the idea of having the communication." The opinion cautions against "overreaching," as by "assisting the client in securing from the represented person an enforceable obligation, disclosure of confidential information, or admissions . . . without the opportunity to seek the advice of counsel." But then it allows that very assistance if the adverse client is first "encourage[d] . . . to consult with counsel before entering into obligations, making admissions or disclosing confidential information."

The Competing Interests. What interests does this rule protect? The rule prevents a lawyer from

- getting a damaging admission from the represented person;
- learning a fact or getting a document that may be protected by the attorney-client privilege or another rule and which she might not learn or get if counsel were present;
- learning the client's true position in negotiation;
- learning the client's strategy;
- weakening the represented person's resolve by casting doubt on the strength of his position; and
- driving a wedge between the represented person and his lawyer.

Countervailing interests that the rule may impede include the interest in

- informal and inexpensive access to information—interviews rather than costly, formal discovery. Also, if the deponent is an employee of an adverse organization, her employer's lawyer's presence at the deposition may be inhibiting;
- facilitating compliance with rules (like Fed. R. Civ. P. 11) that obligate lawyers to do factual investigations *before* filing complaints or other papers; and
- solving, prosecuting, and preventing crimes. Although the rule does not bind law enforcement agents or the police, it does apply to prosecutors who may supervise their work.

1. Civil Matters

If the represented client is a biological person, there should be no difficulty identifying the client. See Inorganic Coatings v. Falberg, 926 F. Supp. 517 (E.D. Pa. 1995) (plaintiff's lawyer disqualified after he accepted a telephone call from a represented defendant).

That's not so easy if the represented person is a corporation, the government, a partnership, or another legal entity. Take corporations. Recall *Upjohn* (chapter 2B2). The Court held that communications of Upjohn lawyers with Upjohn employees about matters within the scope of their employment were within the company's privilege. It assumed that the government would be free to speak to the same employees. The underlying information was not privileged, the Court said. Only communications with counsel were privileged.

But what about Rule 4.2? Will it prohibit government lawyers from contacting Upjohn's employees without consent of the company's lawyers on the ground that the employees are "represented persons"? In other words, if some employees are deemed clients of the company's lawyers for purposes of the attorney-client privilege under *Upjohn*, are they not also "represented persons" for purposes of Rule 4.2? *Upjohn* was a criminal investigation, where other policy considerations may favor law enforcement (see part A2). So let's ask how *Upjohn*'s assumption would fare in a civil matter against a corporation.

If no company constituents are considered to be represented persons, Rule 4.2 does the company no good. On the other hand, if all or most constituents are deemed represented persons with whom contact is forbidden, we expand corporate secrecy exponentially and seriously restrict avenues of informal information-gathering. Some companies have tens of thousands of employees.

Slip and Fall (Part II)

"Slip and Fall (Part I)" in chapter 2B2 asked you to say whether memoranda from the interviews that Mike Todd, Tracy's investigator, conducted were subject to the attorney-client privilege. Assume instead that Cora Lundquist, the plaintiff's lawyer, wants to talk informally to each person Todd interviewed, and Todd himself, without Jeanine Parr's presence or permission. She wants to avoid the expense of depositions. She also fears that Tracy's employees, Rivera, and Corcoran will all be more guarded at a deposition, where Parr will be present. And she needs the interviews to decide if her client has a claim and to frame a complaint. Can she do what she wants?

"We Want to Know What Reach Tekkno Is Saying"

"Our client was a highly paid executive at Reach Tekkno. He was fired a few months after he protested certain business practices that he claimed, justifiably, were illegal. We've sued for retaliatory discharge but that's not why I'm talking to you. Our client, I'll call him Cooper, has been unable to find new work and he has strong suspicions that Reach Tekkno is giving him a bad reference. But no one he applies to will say so. When Cooper left, the Reach HR chief promised to support his search and of course it's in Reach's interest to do so to mitigate possible damages. But there are officials at Reach who don't feel kindly toward Cooper.

"There's a service, Verify Reference, Ltd., that will pose as our client's prospective employer and call for a reference. They use a person knowledgeable about Cooper's line of work. In this state, one party to a phone call can record it without telling the other party, and that's what Verify will do. If Reach's reference is good, there's no problem. If not, we'll get the evidence and we may amend our complaint to allege defamation and business tort theories. Even if we don't amend, it will help us in proving actual and punitive damages.

"One of our young lawyers thinks maybe we can't do that because we know Reach has counsel in the matter and because we'd be asking Verify to misrepresent itself. But we're not looking for strategic information or secrets. We want to know what Reach Tekkno is saying to the rest of the world. Can we do it? We know that Cooper can hire Verify himself and leave us out of it, but he rightly feels that it will go better if we're there to direct things."

The following opinion construed the Code equivalent to Rule 4.2, which is substantively the same although it referred to a represented "party," not "person." Previously, some courts had held that the same persons whose communications with an organization's lawyers were privileged under *Upjohn* were also those a lawyer could not contact under Rule 4.2. As Judge Kaye explains, however, these cases failed to recognize that *Upjohn* and Rule 4.2 protect different interests. An employee whose communications with counsel are privileged will not *necessarily* be a "person" within the no-contact rule. In decoupling *Upjohn* from Rule 4.2, *Niesig* influenced courts nationally. The ABA then changed the comment to Rule 4.2 to incorporate *Niesig*'s holding in somewhat different language.

NIESIG v. TEAM I

76 N.Y.2d 363, 558 N.E.2d 1030, 559 N.Y.S.2d 493 (1990)

KAYE, JUDGE.

Plaintiff in this personal injury litigation, wishing to have his counsel privately interview a corporate defendant's employees who witnessed the accident, puts before us a question that has generated wide interest: are the employees of a corporate party also considered "parties" under Disciplinary Rule 7-104(A)(1) of the Code of Professional Responsibility [now Rule 4.2], which prohibits a lawyer from communicating directly with a "party" known to have counsel in the matter?

[Niesig was working for DeTrae Enterprises when he fell from scaffolding at a construction site. He sued the general contractor at the site and Team I, the property owner. He had a separate workers' compensation claim, not at issue here, against DeTrae. His lawyers asked the court for permission to conduct ex parte interviews of other DeTrae employees who witnessed the events. The lower court held that all current (but not former) DeTrae employees were "parties" within the meaning of DR 7-104(A)(1) and denied the motion.]

In the main we disagree with the Appellate Division's conclusions. However, because we agree with the holding that DR 7-104(A)(1) applies only to current employees, not to former employees, we modify rather than reverse its order, and grant plaintiff's motion to allow the interviews. . . .

The difficulty is not in whether DR 7-104(A)(1) applies to corporations. It unquestionably covers corporate parties, who are as much served by the rule's fundamental principles of fairness as individual parties. But the rule does not define "party," and its reach in this context is unclear. In litigation only the entity, not its employee, is the actual named party; on the other hand, corporations act solely through natural persons, and unless some employees are also considered parties, corporations are effectively read out of the rule. The issue therefore distills to *which* corporate employees should be deemed parties for purposes of DR 7-104(A)(1), and that choice is one of policy. The broader the definition of "party" in the interests of fairness to the corporation, the greater the cost in terms of foreclosing vital informal access to facts.

The many courts, bar associations and commentators that have balanced the competing considerations have evolved various tests, each claiming some adherents, each with some imperfection. At one extreme is the blanket rule adopted by the Appellate Division and urged by defendants, and at the other is the "control group" test—both of which we reject. The first is too broad and the second too narrow.

Defendants' principal argument for the blanket rule—correlating the corporate "party" and all of its employees—rests on Upjohn v. United States. As the Supreme Court recognized, a corporation's attorney-client privilege includes communications with low- and mid-level employees; defendants argue that the existence of an attorney-client *privilege* also signifies an attorney-client *relationship* for purposes of DR 7-104(A)(1).

Upjohn, however, addresses an entirely different subject, with policy objectives that have little relation to the question whether a corporate employee should be considered a "party" for purposes of the disciplinary rule. First, the privilege applies only to *confidential communications* with counsel, it does not immunize the underlying factual information—which is in issue here—from disclosure to an adversary. Second, the attorney-client privilege serves the societal objective of encouraging open communication between client and counsel, a benefit not present in denying informal access to factual information. Thus, a corporate employee who may be a "client" for purposes of the attorney-client privilege is not necessarily a "party" for purposes of DR 7-104(A)(1).

The single indisputable advantage of a blanket preclusion—as with every absolute rule—is that it is clear. No lawyer need ever risk disqualification or discipline because of uncertainty as to which employees are covered by the rule and which are not. The problem, however, is that a ban of this nature exacts a high price in terms of other values, and is unnecessary to achieve the objectives of DR 7-104(A)(1).

Most significantly, the Appellate Division's blanket rule closes off avenues of informal discovery of information that may serve both the litigants and the entire justice system by uncovering relevant facts, thus promoting the expeditious resolution of disputes. Foreclosing all direct, informal interviews of employees of the corporate party unnecessarily sacrifices the long-recognized potential value of such sessions. "A lawyer talks to a witness to ascertain what, if any, information the witness may have relevant to his theory of the case, and to explore the witness' knowledge, memory and opinion—frequently in light of information counsel may have developed from other sources. This is part of an attorney's so-called work product." Costly formal depositions that may deter litigants with limited resources, or even somewhat less formal and costly interviews attended by adversary counsel, are no substitute for such off-the-record private efforts to learn and assemble, rather than perpetuate, information.

Nor, in our view, is it necessary to shield all employees from informal interviews in order to safeguard the corporation's interest. Informal encounters between a lawyer and an employee-witness are not—as a blanket ban assumes—invariably calculated to elicit unwitting admissions; they serve long-recognized values in the litigation process. Moreover, the corporate party has significant protection at hand. It has possession of its own information and unique access to its documents and employees; the corporation's lawyer thus has the earliest and best opportunity to gather the facts, to elicit information from employees, and to counsel and prepare them so that they will not make the feared improvident disclosures that engendered the rule.

We fully recognize that, as the Appellate Division observed, every rule short of the absolute poses practical difficulties as to where to draw the line, and leaves some uncertainty as to which employees fall on either side of it. Nonetheless, we conclude that the values served by permitting access to relevant information require that an effort be made to strike a balance, and that uncertainty can be minimized if not eliminated by a clear test that will become even clearer in practice.

We are not persuaded, however, that the "control group" test—defining "party" to include only the most senior management exercising substantial control over the corporation—achieves that goal. Unquestionably, that narrow (though still uncertain) definition of corporate "party" better serves the policy of promoting open access to relevant information. But that test gives insufficient regard to the principles motivating DR 7-104(A)(1), and wholly overlooks the fact that corporate employees other than senior management also can bind the corporation. The "control group" test all but "nullifies the benefits of the disciplinary rule to corporations." Given the practical and theoretical problems posed by the "control group" test, it is hardly surprising that few courts or bar associations have ever embraced it. . . .

The test that best balances the competing interests, and incorporates the most desirable elements of the other approaches, is one that defines "party" to include corporate employees whose acts or omissions in the matter under inquiry are binding on the corporation (in effect, the corporation's "alter egos") or imputed to the corporation for purposes of its liability, or employees implementing the advice of counsel. All other employees may be interviewed informally.

Unlike a blanket ban or a "control group" test, this solution is specifically targeted at the problem addressed by DR 7-104(A)(1). The potential unfair advantage of extracting concessions and admissions from those who will bind the corporation is negated when employees with "speaking authority" for the corporation, and employees who are so closely identified with the interests of the corporate party as to be indistinguishable from it, are deemed "parties" for purposes of DR 7-104(A)(1). Concern for the protection of the attorney-client privilege prompts us also to include in the definition of "party" the corporate employees responsible for actually effectuating the advice of counsel in the matter. . . .

Apart from striking the correct balance, this test should also become relatively clear in application. It is rooted in developed concepts of the law of evidence and the law of agency, thereby minimizing the uncertainty facing lawyers about to embark on employee interviews. A similar test, moreover, is the one overwhelmingly adopted by courts and bar associations throughout the country, whose long practical experience persuades us that—in day-to-day operation—it is workable. . . .

Today's decision resolves the present controversy by allowing ex parte interviews with nonmanagerial witnesses employed by a corporate defendant; even in that limited context, we recognize that there are undoubtedly questions not raised by the parties that will yet have to be answered. Defendants' assertions that ex parte interviews should not be permitted because of the dangers of overreaching, moreover, impel us to add the cautionary note that, while we have not been called upon to consider questions relating to the actual conduct of such interviews, it is of course assumed that attorneys would make their identity and interest known to interviewees and comport themselves ethically. . . .

[Judge Bellacosa, concurring, would have adopted the control group test.]

How Large Is the Circle of Secrecy?

After *Niesig*, comment [7] of Rule 4.2 was revised to adopt substantially the same position when another lawyer's client is an organization.

Rule 3.4(f) permits a company's lawyer to request (but not require) employees and agents to "refrain from voluntarily giving relevant information to another party" so long as the "lawyer reasonably believes that [that] person's interests will not be adversely affected." One tactic is not available. The "[r]ule does not contemplate that a lawyer representing the entity can invoke the rule's prohibition to cover all employees of the entity, by asserting a blanket representation of all of them. So, for example, if in-house counsel for the XYZ corporation announces that no one may talk to any XYZ employee without obtaining in-house counsel's permission, the communicating lawyer is not barred from communicating with all employees." ABA Opinion 95-396.

Niesig assumed that lawyers (or their investigators) will reveal their "identity and interest" when interviewing unrepresented persons. Rule 4.2 does not say the same. Rule 4.3, however, does require a lawyer to correct an unrepresented person who misunderstands the lawyer's role.

Rule 4.2 and much other authority also allow a lawyer to contact *former* employees of a represented organization so long as they do not have their own counsel. But the lawyer must not seek "to elicit privileged or confidential information from an opponent's former employee." Muriel Siebert & Co. v. Intuit, Inc., 868 N.E.2d 208 (N.Y. 2007) (collecting cases). Clark v. Beverly Health and Rehabilitation Services, 797 N.E.2d 905 (Mass. 2003), citing an "abundance of authority," held that "counsel must also be careful to avoid violating applicable privileges or matters subject to appropriate confidences or protections."

Those seem like sensible limits but consider the challenge. While interviewers can frame questions with care—so they won't, for example, ask a current or a former employee about communications with the organization's lawyer—an entirely innocent question can unwittingly elicit "confidential information." The interviewer can warn the interviewee not to disclose "privileged or confidential information," but it's doubtful that an interviewee will know exactly what that means and may just say nothing.

Some companies require employees to sign agreements that make everything about the company confidential. If everything is confidential, *Niesig*'s categories are irrelevant. The Restatement rejects the view that information is confidential for purposes of Rule 4.2 simply because of a confidentiality agreement. Confidentiality must come from law, not a contract. The Restatement says that a lawyer "may not seek to obtain information that the lawyer reasonably should know the nonclient may not reveal without violating a duty of confidentiality to another *imposed by law*." Restatement §102. (Emphasis added.)

Sometimes a lawyer, unable to get anywhere with the company's outside counsel, will want to speak to someone within its general counsel's office. May she bypass outside counsel? On one hand, this is a direct contact with an employee of the opposing client without permission. On the other hand, the contact is with a *lawyer*, who presumably does not need the rule's protection. Bar opinions have allowed the contact unless specifically instructed otherwise. ABA Opinion 06-443; D.C. Opinion 331 (2005).

When Government Is the "Represented Person"

When in a civil case a government body is the "represented person" — most often as a party — two values clash. The government has the same interest as any litigant in preventing communications with constituents in the *Niesig* categories. On the other hand, there is a First Amendment right to petition the government. Which interest prevails? The comment to Rule 4.2 says that "communications by a lawyer on behalf of a client who is exercising a constitutional or other legal right to communicate with the government" are allowed. Restatement §101 says the rule only applies to the "negotiation or litigation . . . of a specific claim of a client against a governmental agency or against a governmental officer in the officer's official capacity." Requiring contact with the government to go through the government's lawyer more broadly, it says, would "compromise the public interest in facilitating direct communication between representatives of citizens and government officials." Comment *b*.

ABA Opinion 97-408 goes even further. It permits contact with officials "who have authority to take or to recommend action in the matter, provided that the sole purpose of the lawyer's communication is to address a policy issue, including settling the controversy." The lawyer must, however, "give government counsel reasonable advance notice of his intent to communicate with such officials, to afford an opportunity for consultation between government counsel and the officials on the advisability of their entertaining the communication." The no-contact rule continues to apply where the official lacks the described authority or the lawyer's goal is to "develop evidence" or learn information that would be useful in the matter.

The government is the opposing party in criminal prosecutions. Who may defense counsel not contact? Who is the prosecutor's client? The answer is that the client is the United States, or the State, or the People, not the prosecutor's witnesses, not the arresting officers, not the victim. Defense counsel do not need permission to interview any of them unless they are known to have personal counsel. Prosecutors must not interfere. See

Stearnes v. Clinton, 780 S.W.2d 216 (Tex. Crim. App. 1989) (writ of mandamus issued against trial judge who disqualified appointed counsel after counsel had attempted to interview the state's witnesses without permission of the prosecutor).

Testers

You work at a public interest law firm that brings housing discrimination cases. You've settled a dispute with a landlord, but you get reliable information that it is continuing to discriminate. You want to send in "testers" to find out. A "tester" is someone who pretends to be what she is not. The two tester couples will pretend to want an apartment. One couple will be white and the other will be persons of color. Their financial and employment status will be the same. You want to see if they are treated differently. You know that the landlord has a lawyer on the matter. May you use the testers? Courts say that you may. See, e.g., In re Curry, 880 N.E.2d 388 (Mass. 2008).

Like discrimination cases, intellectual property cases are also ripe for the use of testers. Say a lawyer for a manufacturer believes that a seller is "passing off" someone else's product as her client's product. If you look at the text of the no-contact rule, it would seem that the lawyer may not use a tester to speak to employees of the seller, at least not those employees in the *Niesig* and comment [7] categories, if she knows that the seller has a lawyer in the matter. On the other hand, the tester will only pretend to be a member of the public seeking information that the seller offers anyone. So perhaps we should say that the abuses the no-contact rule is meant to prevent are absent.

That was the conclusion in Gidatex, S.r.L. v. Campaniello Imports, 82 F. Supp. 2d 119 (S.D.N.Y. 1999) (collecting other authority). A law firm had sent testers to the business establishment of a represented furniture wholesaler, which the firm believed was guilty of violating its client's trademark. Posing as interior decorators, they talked with the sales clerks and recorded some of the conversations. The court addressed claims that this tactic violated both the no-contact rule and the rule forbidding lawyers to engage in misrepresentation (through another). Rule 8.4(c). The court wrote that

> hiring investigators to pose as consumers is an accepted investigative technique, not a misrepresentation. The policy interests behind forbidding misrepresentations by attorneys are to protect parties from being tricked into making statements in the absence of their counsel and to protect clients from misrepresentations by their own attorneys. The presence of investigators posing as interior decorators did not cause the sales clerks to make any statements they otherwise would not have made. There is no evidence to indicate that the sales clerks were tricked or duped by the investigators' simple questions such as "is the quality the same?" or "so there is no place to get their furniture?"

It is important in *Gidatex* and like cases that the wrongdoing was ongoing and that the testers elicited the same responses that the sales clerks would give any interior decorator. To reach the result it did, however, the court had to ignore the literal language of the no-contact rule, whose prohibition, it acknowledged, may "technically" have been violated. In the alternative, the court held that suppression was not required even if there was a violation.

It is not possible to predict whether this *implicit* "testers" exception to the no-contact rule will be available beyond intellectual property and discrimination cases. The exception will in any event be narrow. In *In re Curry*, supra, the court identified the following categories:

> "Testing" involves deception of a particular kind: investigators pose as members of the public interested in procuring housing or employment, in order to determine whether they are being treated differently based on their race or sex. Their aim is to reproduce an existing pattern of illegal conduct. Some private investigators whose aim is to uncover other civil wrongdoing, such as trademark infringement or breach of contract, similarly disguise their identity and purpose without running afoul of ethical rules.

The question here goes beyond the no-contact rule because lawyers are also forbidden to engage in "deceit" or "misrepresentation," personally or "through the acts of another." Rules 4.1(a) and 8.4(a) and (c). That is true whether or not the target has a lawyer. Using testers is one example of what is sometimes called "pretexting," developing a false story to get information. Two deceit cases that would be beyond belief if they weren't true—and are hard to believe anyway—are the disbarment opinions in In re Crossen, 880 N.E.2d 352 (Mass. 2008) and In re Curry, supra. Two lawyers (one a former high-ranking assistant U.S. attorney and partner in a large law firm) employed an elaborate ruse to get a judge's law clerk to disclose information they hoped to use (unsuccessfully as it turned out) to challenge a judge's ruling and force her recusal.

Another pretexting case, also hard to believe, is Leysock v. Forest Laboratories, 2017 WL 1591833 (D. Mass. 2017), where the district court dismissed a *qui tam* case because the relator's law firm used pretexting to gather information for its complaint.[*] The court wrote:

> The investigation [based on "falsehoods, misrepresentations, and deceptive conduct"] was designed to appear as if it were a medical research study; its only purpose, however, was to obtain otherwise-confidential information from busy medical professionals for use in litigation. To accomplish that end, Dr. Godec [working for the law firm] falsely stated, and repeatedly implied, that the study had a benign research purpose. Indeed, the survey invitation explicitly said so.
>
> Dr. Godec also falsely stated that the information obtained from the physicians would be kept confidential.

---

[*] In a *qui tam* case, a private person, called a "relator," sues in the name of the government to recover money allegedly owed the government because of the defendant's fraud. If successful, the relator can earn huge rewards.

For years, the ABA has struggled unsuccessfully to write a rule that would identify when a lawyer may use deception to gather information. Oregon has such a rule. Oregon Rule 8.4(b) provides that

> it shall not be professional misconduct for a lawyer to advise clients or others about or to supervise lawful covert activity in the investigation of violations of civil or criminal law or constitutional rights, provided the lawyer's conduct is otherwise in compliance with these Rules of Professional Conduct. "Covert activity," as used in this rule, means an effort to obtain information on unlawful activity through the use of misrepresentations or other subterfuge. "Covert activity" may be commenced by a lawyer or involve a lawyer as an advisor or supervisor only when the lawyer in good faith believes there is a reasonable possibility that unlawful activity has taken place, is taking place or will take place in the foreseeable future.

This rule gives private lawyers some of the same authority courts give prosecutors. Virginia Rule 8.4(c) forbids deception that "reflects adversely on the lawyer's fitness to practice law."

"The Adverse Client . . ."

(a) The adverse client, whom you know to be represented in the matter, calls you to discuss settlement or negotiate a deal directly. She tells you it's okay because she has fired her lawyer. What do you do?

(b) The adverse client, whom you know to have counsel in the matter, is a personal injury plaintiff who claims that your client's negligence left him without full use of his left arm. Can you hire an investigator to join the plaintiff's gym and secretly photograph him making full use of his left arm?

(c) The adverse client, whom you know to have counsel in the matter, is in negotiation to sell a company to your client. Its CFO is prominent on social media sites. Can you ask your paralegal to frequent those sites and watch for statements that will assist your client's negotiation strategy?

2. Criminal Matters

The Case of the Cooperating Target

United States Attorney Nelly Werker is investigating commercial bribery by companies in the local building trades. Among the dozens of "persons of interest" are Letitia Wall and Mort Blakely, executives at Newtonian Construction, Inc., which is also under investigation. Wall is believed to be the ringleader. While the investigation is in progress, Blanche Menendez, a lawyer for Blakely, asks Werker for a meeting. At it, Blakely offers to cooperate with Werker's investigation.

Werker says she is prepared to let Blakely plead to a 5-year felony count (he could have faced a 20-year count) with a promise that the government would recommend a sentence of not more than 18 months. In exchange, Blakely must secretly record conversations with Wall. Blakely must do the same with top Newtonian officers who are not under investigation (and do not have lawyers), but who, in Werker's view, have not been fully candid. The conversations are meant to identify past bribes and ongoing concealment efforts. Werker's office will conduct mock conversations to prepare Blakely and will instruct him on how to steer the conversation to get admissions. Blakely has two days to accept Werker's offer.

The next morning, coincidentally, Werker receives a letter from Barry Hu, who says that "Wall has retained me in connection with the building trades investigation." The same day, Marta Russo emails Werker and says, "Newtonian has retained me in the building trades investigation." A day later Blakely accepts the deal. May Werker implement her plan?

Rule 4.2 applies in both civil and criminal matters, as its comment recognizes. The Sixth Amendment right to counsel also applies in criminal matters and prohibits the government from questioning an accused person outside the presence of his counsel after "judicial proceedings have been initiated." Rothgery v. Gillespie Cty., 554 U.S. 191 (2008) ("[A] criminal defendant's initial appearance before a judicial officer, where he learns the charge against him and his liberty is subject to restriction, marks the start of adversary judicial proceedings that trigger attachment of the Sixth Amendment right to counsel."). But even where the Sixth Amendment right has not yet attached, what about the no-contact rule? What if a person under investigation but uncharged is known to be represented by counsel in the matter? This is Werker's dilemma. In the last three decades, this simple question has prompted a debate, not only about Rule 4.2, but also about federalism and separation of powers.

Construing DR 7-104(A)(1) of the Code (equivalent to Model Rule 4.2), the court in United States v. Hammad, 858 F.2d 834 (2d Cir. 1988), stunned federal prosecutors by holding that the rule *did* apply to them, even before judicial proceedings have begun. The prosecutor had sent a cooperating informant to speak to Hammad at a time when the government knew that Hammad had counsel. To bolster the informant's credibility, the prosecutor armed him with a fake grand jury subpoena. Hammad made incriminating statements on tape, which he moved to suppress. The court found a violation of the no-contact rule but declined to suppress because the question was novel.

> The principal question presented to us herein is: to what extent does DR 7-104(A)(1) restrict the use of informants by government prosecutors prior to indictment, but after a suspect has retained counsel in connection with the subject matter of a criminal investigation? . . .

. . . As we see it, under DR 7-104(A)(1), a prosecutor is "authorized by law" to employ legitimate investigative techniques in conducting or supervising criminal investigations, and the use of informants to gather evidence against a suspect will frequently fall within the ambit of such authorization.

Notwithstanding this holding, however, we recognize that in some instances a government prosecutor may overstep the already broad powers of his office, and in so doing, violate the ethical precepts of DR 7-104(A)(1). In the present case, the prosecutor issued a subpoena for the informant, not to secure his attendance before the grand jury, but to create a pretense that might help the informant elicit admissions from a represented suspect. Though we have no occasion to consider the use of this technique in relation to unrepresented suspects, we believe that use of the technique under the circumstances of this case contributed to the informant's becoming the alter ego of the prosecutor. Consequently, the informant was engaging in communications proscribed by DR 7-104(A)(1).

Although the *Hammad* ruling may not have helped Hammad personally, it loomed as a warning to federal prosecutors, especially in the Second Circuit. But only briefly, as it turned out. Almost from the day it was decided, *Hammad* has been on life support. Other circuit courts have refused to follow it. Cases are collected in United States v. Balter, 91 F.3d 427 (3d Cir. 1996) and United States v. Carona, below.

Hammad alarmed the Justice Department, not least of all because its boundaries were unclear. Two successive attorneys general purported to issue rules meant to limit its reach. They then argued that so long as a federal prosecutor followed their rules, the conduct would be "authorized by law" within the exception to the no-contact rule. That effort came to naught when United States ex rel. O'Keefe v. McDonnell Douglas Corp., 132 F.3d 1252 (8th Cir. 1998), held that the department did not have "valid statutory authority" for its rules.

Then, in 1998, Congress passed what has come to be known as the "McDade Amendment." The lesson here is to be careful whom you mess with or, as in this case, whom you indict. Joseph McDade, a powerful Republican congressman, was acquitted in 1996 of federal conspiracy and racketeering charges. Enlightened by the unhappy experience of being a federal defendant, McDade sponsored a bill that added Section 530B to Title 28 of the United States Code. The section says that lawyers for the federal government "shall be subject to State laws and rules, and local Federal court rules, governing attorneys in each State where such attorney engages in that attorney's duties to the same extent and in the same manner as other attorneys in that State." The attorney general was directed to "make and amend rules . . . to assure compliance with this section." Those rules can be found at 28 C.F.R. Part 77. The key provision (§77.3) states:

In all criminal investigations and prosecutions, in all civil investigations and litigation (affirmative and defensive), and in all civil law enforcement investigations and proceedings, attorneys for the government shall conform their conduct and activities to the state rules and laws, and federal local court rules, governing attorneys in each State where such attorney engages in that attorney's duties, to the same extent and in the same manner as other attorneys in that State, as these terms are defined in §77.2 of this part.

As befits a C.F.R. provision, many phrases and nouns in this sentence are defined.

Even though the McDade amendment now binds Justice Department lawyers, the question remains: Is contact with a represented person whose Sixth Amendment right to counsel has *not* yet attached "authorized by law" within the meaning of Rule 4.2? Attorney general rulemaking cannot answer this question but courts can because, after all, Rule 4.2 is a court's own rule. The Ninth Circuit, which had favorably cited but distinguished *Hammad* in United States v. Talao, 222 F.3d 1133 (9th Cir. 2000), considered that question in the next case.

UNITED STATES v. CARONA
660 F.3d 360 (9th Cir. 2011)

CLIFTON, CIRCUIT JUDGE: . . .

Carona served as Sheriff of Orange County, an elected position, from January 1999 until early 2008, when he resigned following his indictment. During his initial campaign for sheriff in 1998, Carona received financial support from Donald Haidl. Haidl testified at trial that Carona "offered [him] the complete power of the sheriff's department for raising money and supporting him."

After Carona took office, Haidl testified that he continued to make payments to Carona. He became concerned that Carona was jeopardizing his position and Haidl's arrangement by accepting small amounts from other people. Haidl testified that he offered Carona and Assistant Sheriff George Jamarillo each a "bribe not to take bribes" in the amount of $1000 per month, which they accepted. Haidl also testified that he gave Carona a speedboat in 2001, which they concealed through a sham transaction.

In 2004, the federal government began an investigation. In early 2007, Haidl admitted his own criminal misconduct and signed a cooperation plea agreement with the government. Following this plea agreement, government attorneys instructed Haidl to meet with Carona and to make surreptitious recordings of their meetings. At this time, Carona was represented by attorney Dean Stewart, who had notified the government that he was representing Carona.

Haidl met with Carona on July 7, 2007, and July 15, 2007, but these meetings did not provide enough evidence to satisfy the prosecutors. In preparation for a subsequent meeting, the government equipped Haidl with two fake "subpoena attachments" that identified certain records that Haidl was to tell Carona he had been subpoenaed to produce. These documents referred to cash payments Haidl provided to Carona and to the sham transaction they used to conceal the gift of the speedboat. Haidl and Carona met again on

August 13, 2007, and in their conversation, Carona made statements that suggested both that he had received payments and gifts from Haidl and that he wanted Haidl to lie to the grand jury about these transactions. . . .

[Carona was convicted of witness tampering. On appeal he argued that the prosecution had violated California Rule 2-100, the then counterpart to Model Rule 4.2. Rule 2-100 had an exception for contact "authorized by law." The district court ruled that the prosecution had violated Rule 2-100 but it declined to suppress, leaving any sanction to disciplinary authorities.]

We disagree with the conclusion that the prosecutors violated Rule 2-100. To determine whether "pre-indictment, non-custodial communications by federal prosecutors and investigators with represented parties" violated Rule 2-100, we have adopted a "case-by-case adjudication" approach rather than a bright line rule. [*Talao.*] We have recognized the possibility that such conversations could violate the rule and "declined to announce a categorical rule excusing all such communications from ethical inquiry." Nonetheless, our cases have more often than not held that specific instances of contact between undercover agents or cooperating witnesses and represented suspects did not violate Rule 2-100.

The only relevant factual difference between [precedent] and the current case is that here the prosecutors provided the informant with fake subpoena attachments to use in getting Carona to incriminate himself. In *Hammad*, the Second Circuit held that issuing a false subpoena to an informant to "create a pretense that might help the informant elicit admissions . . . contributed to the informant's becoming that alter ego of the prosecutor." Relying on *Hammad*, the district court held that the use of the fake subpoena attachments made Haidl the alter ego of the prosecutor, causing Haidl's communication with Carona to violate Rule 2-100.

While in *Talao* we held *Hammad*'s "case-by-case" approach to be the proper one, *Talao* did not involve the use of a fake subpoena or any other falsified documents, and we did not adopt *Hammad*'s holding on that subject. . . .

We have not previously needed to consider the question of whether providing fake court papers to an informant to use during a conversation with a represented party is conduct that violates Rule 2-100. Under the facts presented here, we conclude that it does not.

The use of a false subpoena attachment did not cause the cooperating witness, Haidl, to be any more an alter ego of the prosecutor than he already was by agreeing to work with the prosecutor. Haidl was acting at the direction of the prosecutor in his interactions with Carona, yet no precedent from our court or from any other circuit, with the exception of *Hammad*, has held such indirect contacts to violate Rule 2-100 or similar rules.

The false documents were props used by government to bolster the ability of the cooperating witness to elicit incriminating statements from a suspect. The district court appears to have been concerned that by allowing such conduct a suspect could be " 'tricked' into giving his case away by opposing counsel's artful questions," but it has long been established that the government may use deception in its investigations in order to induce suspects into making incriminating statements. See, e.g., Sorrells v. United States, 287 U.S. 435, 441 (1932) ("Artifice and stratagem may be employed to catch those engaged in criminal enterprises."). The use of fake documents here was just such a stratagem. The reasoning of the Third Circuit in United States v. Martino, 825 F.2d 754 (3d Cir. 1987), rejecting a claim of a prosecutorial ethical violation based on a fake subpoena, seems to us particularly persuasive:

> If government officials may pose as non-existent sheiks in an elaborately concocted scheme, supply a necessary ingredient for a drug operation, and utilize landing strips, docking facilities, and other accouterments of an organized smuggling operation, all in order to catch criminals, then their use of a subpoena in the name of an undercover agent to enable him to retain his credibility with suspected criminals seems innocuous by comparison.

Additionally, the concern that a suspect might be tricked by counsel's artful examination is inapplicable here, since Carona was not subject to any interrogation, let alone one by the prosecutor. Rather he was engaging in a conversation with an individual he believed to be his ally against the prosecution.

It would be antithetical to the administration of justice to allow a wrongdoer to immunize himself against such undercover operations simply by letting it be known that he has retained counsel. Particularly here, where the undercover investigation revealed Carona encouraging Haidl to lie, to hold otherwise would be contrary to our observation in *Talao* that "it would be a perversion of the rule against *ex parte* contacts to extend it to protect [individuals] who would suborn perjury by [others]."

There were no direct communications here between the prosecutors and Carona. The indirect communications did not resemble an interrogation. Nor did the use of fake subpoena attachments make the informant the alter ego of the prosecutor. On the facts presented in this case, we conclude that there was no violation of Rule 2-100. For this reason, we affirm the district court's decision not to suppress evidence obtained through the use of the fake subpoena attachments. . . .

———

Carona not only permitted prosecutors to use an intermediary armed with a fake subpoena to contact a represented defendant despite Rule 4.2, it also permitted deceit. Rule 8.4(c), as noted, forbids "conduct involving dishonesty, fraud, deceit or misrepresentation." Investigators are not subject to the professional conduct rules, but lawyers may not use them to do what the lawyers may not. Rule 8.4(a). If, however, *supervising* deception is allowed, as *Carona* held, may a prosecutor choose to skip the intermediary and do the same thing herself? Maybe not. Disciplinary Counsel v. Brockler, 48 N.E.3d 557 (Ohio 2016), issued a stayed one-year suspension of the prosecutor who created a fake Facebook page in an effort to get two alibi witnesses to recant. See page 52. He had reason to believe they were planning to lie at trial. And in In re Pautler, 47 P.3d 1175 (Colo. 2002), the court sanctioned a prosecutor who pretended to be a public defender after a dangerous murder suspect, holed up in an apartment, demanded to talk to a lawyer before surrendering. Both cases cite Rule 8.4(c) among other rules.

Hammad has fared little better in the Second Circuit than elsewhere. In United States v. Binday, 804 F.3d 558 (2d Cir. 2015), co-defendant Resnick, charged with conspiracy to obstruct justice and other crimes, cited *Hammad* to suppress pre-indictment recordings in which he admitted to a "cooperating witness" that he was "stupid" and "wrong" to have deleted a hard drive. The court rejected the challenge.

> In *Hammad*, we held that a prosecutor's eliciting statements from a represented defendant prior to his indictment through the use of a sham grand jury subpoena fell outside of the "authorized by law" exception. "The court in *Hammad* was very careful, however, to urge restraint in applying the Rule in the pre-indictment context so as not to unduly hamper legitimate law enforcement investigations. . . ." Since *Hammad,* this Court, in considering an alleged violation of Rule 4.2, has not found government conduct to fall outside the "authorized by law" exception. [Precedent] makes clear that a pre-indictment undercover communication with a represented person does not *ipso facto* violate the rule. . . .
>
> Resnick argues that the government conduct was impermissible because "the goal of the investigation was not ongoing criminal and/or obstructive activity, but rather a discussion of . . . past conduct." But as we explained in *Hammad,* the "use of informants by government prosecutors in a preindictment, non-custodial situation . . . will generally fall within the 'authorized by law' exception. . . ." The limitation that Resnick proposes is not supported by our case law, and would swallow the rule generally permitting use of informants, as "past conduct" will often be the focus of such investigations.

Notice the word "non-custodial," meaning that Resnick was not under arrest or incarcerated. *Carona* also cited the fact that Carona was not in custody when he made his statement. Hammad himself was not in custody. Why do you suppose courts stress this fact?

Even though *Hammad* has precious little influence today, prosecutors, especially within the Second Circuit, would be remiss if they ignore it. It has never been overruled. Courts may expansively define "authorized by law," but the exception is not a license to pay Rule 4.2 no mind. See, e.g., State v. Miller, 600 N.W.2d 457 (Minn. 1999) (suppressing statements citing *Hammad*).

In light of these cases, how should Nelly Werker proceed? What should Barry Hu and Marta Russo do to protect Letitia Wall and Newtonian Construction?

Are criminal defense lawyers, like prosecutors, "authorized by law" to use investigators who misrepresent themselves? The lawyer in In re McCormick,

819 N.W.2d 442 (Minn. 2012), argued that his conduct in sending an investigator to talk to a represented co-defendant was authorized by law within the meaning of Rule 4.2. The court disagreed and suspended him for 60 days. The authorized by law exception applied to "law enforcement agencies, not defense attorneys." McCormick could have asked permission from the co-defendant's lawyer. He could also "have sought authorization from the court."

B. IMPROPER OR ACCIDENTAL ACQUISITION OF CONFIDENTIAL INFORMATION

At the direction of the deputy attorney in Oakland, California, jail authorities taped a conversation between a defendant and his expert. When this was discovered, the prosecutor was put on administrative leave.[*]

"It's the Discovery Wellmost Suppressed"

"I got a surprise visit at my office yesterday from a woman who didn't reveal her name. She told the receptionist it was about Wellmost, a big pharma company I am suing on behalf of a class of patients who claim that a Wellmost drug had undisclosed side effects. So I met with her and she told me she was formerly a paralegal at the law firm defending Wellmost. I remembered enough from my legal ethics class to say 'You have to leave right away. Please don't say anything about the case.' 'I won't,' she said. Then she put a large envelope a half-inch thick on my desk and turned to leave. 'What are you giving me?' I asked, then said, 'No, don't tell me. I don't want it, whatever it is. Please take it with you.'

" 'It's the discovery Wellmost suppressed,' she said, and walked out.

"So now I have this envelope and I don't know what to do with it. Read the contents? Shred it unopened? Mail it back to Wellmost anonymously? What if it is suppressed discovery? There were gaps in the company's document production."

Courts have dismissed claims where a client or lawyer (or both) have invaded an opponent's confidential relationship other than through a Rule 4.2 violation. Joan Lipin brought a sexual harassment claim against her former employer and supervisor. During a pretrial proceeding, she surreptitiously read a confidential memorandum of the opposing party's law firm. "At a break, [she] slipped the documents into a Redweld file 'for [her] own

---

* Paul Rosynsky, Contra Costa Times, May 4, 2012.

protection.'" When she told her lawyer what she had done, he first declined to look at the papers but then, after concluding "that any claim of privilege as to the documents had been lost as a result of [his opponent's] careless handling of them . . . he read through them." After the trial judge granted protective orders, with which the plaintiff only partly complied, the case was dismissed. The New York Court of Appeals affirmed the dismissal. Lipin v. Bender, 644 N.E.2d 1300 (N.Y. 1994):

> The trial court, and the Appellate Division, could hardly have been clearer in their conclusions, characterizing plaintiff's conduct—as well as that of her attorney—as "heinous" and "egregious," a threat to the attorney-client privilege, to the concept of civilized, orderly conduct among attorneys, and even to the rule of law. . . .
>
> While the Appellate Division made plain that it would reach the same result whether or not the documents were actually privileged, in fact both courts agreed as to the protected nature of the documents. . . . Similarly lacking any basis in the record . . . is plaintiff's claim that defendants waived the privilege by leaving the documents on the hearing room table during argument.

Lipin's lawyer was later suspended from practice for two years for this and other conduct. In re Wisehart, 721 N.Y.S.2d 356 (1st Dept. 2001). In a divorce case, "Husband improperly accessed Wife's personal email account and obtained the list of direct examination questions [her lawyer planned to ask and her] payroll information." He gave these items to Eisenstein, his lawyer, who knew the source but used them. Eisenstein was suspended indefinitely. In re Eisenstein, 485 S.W.3d 759 (Mo. 2016).

I have a special category called "What Were They Thinking?", a question that makes a factual assumption—that is, thinking. One case in this category is In re Winkler, 834 N.E.2d 85 (Ind. 2005). Two prosecutors, Goode and Winkler, attended a deposition in connection with a criminal case. Apparently, depositions are allowed in criminal cases in Indiana. The court describes what happened after the defendant and his lawyer left the room:

> Goode seized notes the defendant had written and shared with his attorney. Goode tore the notes from a legal pad that had been turned face down on a table before the defendant and his counsel left the room to confer. Goode gave the notes to Winkler who concealed them by placing the notes among a stack of files she had before her on the table. Respondents wanted to use the notes as a handwriting exemplar to compare with other evidence in the case. When defendant and his counsel returned to the room neither respondent advised them that they had seized the notes. When counsel and the defendant began looking for the notes, Winkler went so far as to shuffle through her files as if looking for the notes. Only when defendant saw the edge of a yellow piece of paper protruding from Winkler's files, did she acknowledge having the notes and return them to defendant.

Both prosecutors were suspended.

Inadvertent Disclosure and Metadata

Modern technology has made it increasingly likely that even careful lawyers will slip up and provide privileged or other protected information to an opponent. Dial the wrong number on a fax machine. Click "Reply All" on a screen. Include a privileged document among thousands delivered (or electronically transmitted) in discovery. It can happen to anyone. And because it can, we have a rule to avoid inadvertent waiver.

Rule 4.4(b) requires a lawyer to give prompt notice to an opponent when the lawyer "knows or reasonably should know that [a] document or electronically stored information was inadvertently sent." The rule then leaves to substantive law whether the lawyer must comply with the opponent's instructions to return it. The Arizona Supreme Court has held that delivering the inadvertently disclosed documents to the court is appropriate. The lawyers can then work out whether the documents must be returned. If they can't agree, the judge can decide. Lund v. Myers, 305 P.3d 374 (Ariz. 2013).

A 2008 amendment to the Federal Rules of Evidence adds Rule 502: "When made in a federal proceeding or to a federal office or agency, the disclosure does not operate as a waiver in a federal or state proceeding if: (1) the disclosure is inadvertent; (2) the holder of the privilege or [work-product] protection took reasonable steps to prevent disclosure; and (3) the holder promptly took reasonable steps to rectify the error, including (if applicable) following [Fed. R. Civ. P.] 26(b)(5)(B)." Rule 26(b)(5)(B) provides:

> If information produced in discovery is subject to a claim of privilege or of protection as trial-preparation material, the party making the claim may notify any party that received the information of the claim and the basis for it. After being notified, a party must promptly return, sequester, or destroy the specified information and any copies it has; must not use or disclose the information until the claim is resolved; must take reasonable steps to retrieve the information if the party disclosed it before being notified; and may promptly present the information to the court under seal for a determination of the claim. The producing party must preserve the information until the claim is resolved.

Consider Rico v. Mitsubishi Motors Corp., 171 P.3d 1092 (Cal. 2007). After a deposition at their offices, plaintiffs' counsel "somehow" found themselves in possession of the defense lawyers' notes. It is unclear how that happened. For a time, plaintiffs' lawyers were alone in a conference room with defense counsel's case file, which had contained the notes. The benign explanation is that defense counsel mistakenly left the notes behind when the deposition ended. A less charitable explanation is also possible. Either way, without alerting their opponents, plaintiffs' counsel made strategic use of the notes, including by sharing them with their own experts. When defense counsel realized what had happened, they moved for return of the notes and to disqualify plaintiffs' counsel and their experts. The court agreed:

> When a lawyer who receives materials that obviously appear to be subject to an attorney-client privilege or otherwise clearly appear to be confidential and

privileged and where it is reasonably apparent that the materials were provided or made available through inadvertence, the lawyer receiving such materials should refrain from examining the materials any more than is essential to ascertain if the materials are privileged, and shall immediately notify the sender that he or she possesses material that appears to be privileged. The parties may then proceed to resolve the situation by agreement or may resort to the court for guidance with the benefit of protective orders and other judicial intervention as may be justified.

Metadata. Metadata is information in an electronic document that is not visible on the screen, but can be restored, often with a few keystrokes. A lawyer may unintentionally include metadata in documents she produces. Bar ethics opinions diverge in describing a recipient lawyer's responsibility when a document that was intentionally produced contains metadata of which the sender may be unaware. ABA Opinion 06-442 concluded that the recipient lawyer "generally" may review and use the metadata. It took no position on whether the sending lawyer must be notified. However, a 2012 amendment to comment [2] to Rule 4.4 identifies metadata as within the scope of Rule 4.4(b)'s notice requirements. A lawyer who knows or reasonably should know that metadata was inadvertently sent must "promptly notify the sender."

New York Opinion 749 (2001) concludes that *even searching* for a document's metadata is dishonest and prejudicial to the administration of justice. D.C. Opinion 341 (2007) takes a middle view. It says that reviewing metadata in a document is unethical only if the lawyer "knows" that the metadata was inadvertently sent. The D.C. opinion makes the important point that different rules apply when the metadata is contained in documents produced in discovery or via subpoena as part of the history of the case. Then, the receiving lawyer may have a right to it, and obstruction of justice statutes may forbid the sending lawyer from stripping documents of metadata. When a document becomes the subject of discovery or relevant to a foreseeable litigation, it cannot be altered.

Self-Assessment Questions

1. Prosecutors believe that an investment advisory company with an international presence is assisting some of the company's wealthy clients to launder money. The company gets wind of the investigation as a result of a story in the financial press. It hires a lawyer who notifies the prosecutors that he has been retained to represent the company. The prosecutors want to proceed with planned undercover work, in which two current clients of the company will ask about money laundering (although in a subtle way). In a jurisdiction that has adopted the Model Rules and its comments, how should the prosecutors proceed with the investigation of the company?

2. You work for a criminal reform public interest law firm. It has concluded after study that the quality of indigent legal services in state X is too low to ensure compliance with Gideon v. Wainwright. The state provides legal services through a statewide office of defender services that oversees the work of five regional offices. Your office sues state X, which will be defended by the attorney general of the state. Some officials in the statewide office and some lawyers who are not officials of the organizations but defend clients in court call your office and offer to provide it with more leads to prove its case. How do you respond?

3. This is a variation on a self-assessment question in chapter 2. Edie Santos is planning to sue her former employer, Morkett Sales, for discrimination based on ethnic identity and sex. Clyde Snoot is her lawyer. Snoot has not yet filed a complaint but he has sent the general counsel of Morkett a draft complaint as a way to prompt settlement talks. And Snoot has discussed the claim with Morkett's outside counsel, Luis Caspone. Santos has given Snoot the names of eight current and former co-workers who can substantiate her claims. Can Snoot attempt to interview them?

IV

Lawyers, Money, and the Ethics of Legal Fees

Kent: This is nothing, Fool.

Fool: Then 'tis like the breath of an unfee'd lawyer. You gave me nothing for't.

—Shakespeare, *King Lear*, 1.04.132-134

There can be no equal justice where the kind of trial a man gets depends on the amount of money he has.

—Justice Hugo Black, in Griffin v. Illinois, 351 U.S. 12 (1956)

If the bar is to become merely a mode of making money, making it in the most convenient way possible, but making it at all hazards, then the bar is degraded.

—Samuel J. Tilden, on formation of the Association of the Bar of the City of New York, 1869

Years ago, when I was the resident guru in legal ethics at Washington and Lee University, in the little mountain town of Lexington, Virginia, a reporter from the daily newspaper in Roanoke asked me to identify the most serious ethical issue for American lawyers. My answer: "Money."

—Thomas Shaffer, Jews, Christians, Lawyers, and Money, 25 Vt. L. Rev. 451 (2001)

Most lawyers get paid by their clients. Lawyers in firms charge fees. Other lawyers, like those who work for corporations or a government, are salaried. Fees, in turn, can be structured in many ways: a flat fee for a specified service, an hourly fee, a fee contingent on success, a general or special retainer,* or some combination of these. Some law firms may request a "performance fee"

---

* General retainers are rare today. A client may pay a law firm a retainer to be generally available for all of its needs, whatever they might be. Actual work, when it arises, may be separately billed. The general retainer buys availability for all needs and the assurance that the firm will not appear adverse to the client. A special retainer also assures availability but,

in addition to the agreed fee for highly favorable results. So far as I know, firms don't return fees when the result is unfavorable.

The client is usually the source of the fee, but not always. A lawyer may represent a client but be paid by her parents. An insurance company may retain counsel to represent an insured. The state may pay a lawyer to represent an indigent criminal defendant to comply with Gideon v. Wainwright, 372 U.S. 335 (1963). States may pay lawyers for indigent clients in civil matters even though not constitutionally obligated to do so. Employers may pay the legal costs of employees who are sued for conduct within the scope of their employment.

Sometimes a client's opponent will pay its lawyer. This can happen by agreement, as when a person who obtains a loan pays the lender's lawyer. It can also happen when a statute authorizes a court to order one litigant to pay the fees of a prevailing adverse party. Such fee-shifting statutes appear in civil liberties and civil rights cases and also in antitrust, copyright, and patent litigation, among other places.

Legal services need not be financed with the payment of money at all. A lawyer may work pro bono publico ("for the public good"). When she does, it is the lawyer herself who "finances" the arrangement. Many lawyers do pro bono work voluntarily. Some have argued that lawyers should be required to perform pro bono work or contribute to legal services organizations. According to one estimate, 86 percent of the civil legal needs of the poor go unmet. Legal Services Corporation, The Justice Gap: Measuring the Unmet Civil Legal Needs of Low-Income Americans (June 2017). That gap fluctuates depending on the nature of the service and the resources of clients, but it is routinely reported to be above 50 percent.

Beyond the various ways of financing legal services are questions about the nature and amount of legal fees. How are they controlled? Most prominent are market forces of supply and demand. Ethical and legal rules, however, also restrict the nature and size of fees. It is not a wholly laissez-faire system.

The *median* lawyer income in 2019 according to the Bureau of Labor Statistics was $122,960. But that figure disguises a large variation. Partners in big law firms earn millions of dollars yearly, whereas the *average* annual income for lawyers in Montana (ranked lowest in lawyer salary) was $88,600 and in California (ranked highest) was $171,550.

IOLTA.   In the last several decades, one of the most successful innovations to help fund legal services goes by the awkward name IOLTA. Its arrival was not without opposition.

Lawyers may not put client money and their own money in the same account. That's called comingling and it can lead to disciplinary action.

---

unlike a general retainer, does so only for a specific category of work, for example, all of the client's trademark or labor work. Special retainers have appeared in the world of mergers and acquisitions and takeovers if a company does not want to see a powerful law firm representing an opponent.

Instead, lawyers are required to hold client money in separate accounts, usually called escrow or special accounts. These accounts often pay interest. States require or permit lawyers whose clients do not direct otherwise to pool all client money in a single account and to contribute the interest to a trust that is then used to fund legal help for individuals who cannot afford it. IOLA and IOLTA, acronyms for Interest on Lawyer (Trust) Accounts, are the terms used to describe these programs. They have generated millions of dollars to support legal services for those who could not afford them.

The Supreme Court held, 5-4, that interest on client funds in Texas's Mandatory IOLTA Program constituted client "property" within the meaning of the Fifth Amendment's takings clause, which threatened to kill the idea. But even if the interest was "property," three legal issues remained: Did the program effect a *taking* of the property, for *public use*, without *just compensation*? Phillips v. Wash. Legal Found., 524 U.S. 156 (1998). Brown v. Legal Foundation of Washington, 538 U.S. 216 (2003), legitimized IOLTA programs. Justice Stevens first cited "the overall, dramatic success of these programs in serving the compelling interest in providing legal services to literally millions of needy Americans." That success established the public use of the IOLTA programs, a requirement of the takings clause. The Court then assumed that the state's use of IOLTA money was a taking of private property. The Fifth Amendment therefore required just compensation, which the Court said is "measured by the property owner's loss rather than the government's gain." Did clients suffer a loss?

Washington's program required lawyers "to deposit client funds in non-IOLTA accounts whenever those funds could generate net earnings for the client." Only if the client's funds were too small to generate net earnings for the client did IOLTA apply. Justice Stevens cited an example from a dissenting opinion below: $2,000 held for two days in an account paying 5 percent would yield 55 cents interest. But the administrative cost of computing the interest and mailing a check to the client would be higher than 55 cents. "The fair market value of a right to receive $.55 by spending perhaps $5.00 to receive it would be nothing," he wrote. Justice Scalia dissented in an opinion in which Chief Justice Rehnquist and Justices Kennedy and Thomas joined. IOLTA survived—barely.

A. THE ROLE OF THE MARKETPLACE

BROBECK, PHLEGER & HARRISON v. TELEX CORP.
602 F.2d 866 (9th Cir.) (1979), cert. denied, 444 U.S. 981

Per Curiam.

This is a diversity action in which the plaintiff, the San Francisco law firm of Brobeck, Phleger & Harrison ("Brobeck"), sued the Telex Corporation and Telex Computer Products, Inc. ("Telex") to recover $1,000,000 in attorney's fees. Telex had engaged Brobeck on a contingency fee basis to prepare a petition for certiorari after the Tenth Circuit reversed a $259.5 million judgment in Telex's favor against International Business Machines Corporation ("IBM") and affirmed an $18.5 million counterclaim judgment for IBM against Telex. Brobeck prepared and filed the petition, and after Telex entered a "wash settlement" with IBM in which both parties released their claims against the other, Brobeck sent Telex a bill for $1,000,000, that it claimed Telex owed it under their written contingency fee agreement. When Telex refused to pay, Brobeck brought this action. Both parties filed motions for summary judgment. The district court granted Brobeck's motion, awarding Brobeck $1,000,000 plus interest. Telex now appeals. . . .

Having had reversed one of the largest antitrust judgments in history, Telex officials decided to press the Tenth Circuit's decision to the United States Supreme Court. To maximize Telex's chances for having its petition for certiorari granted, they decided to search for the best available lawyer. They compiled a list of the preeminent antitrust and Supreme Court lawyers in the country, and Roger Wheeler, Telex's Chairman of the Board, settled on Moses Lasky of the Brobeck firm as the best possibility.

Wheeler and his assistant made preliminary phone calls to Lasky on February 3, 4, and 13, 1975 to determine whether Lasky was willing to prepare the petition for certiorari. Lasky stated he would be interested if he was able to rearrange his workload. When asked about a fee, Lasky stated that, although he would want a retainer, it was the policy of the Brobeck firm to determine fees after the services were performed. Wheeler, however, wanted an agreement fixing fees in advance and arranged for Lasky to meet in San Francisco on February 10th to discuss the matter further with Telex's president, Stephen Jatras, and Floyd Walker, its attorney in the IBM litigation.

[When the parties met, Telex officials wanted a contingent fee with a ceiling. Lasky said there should then be a floor. Drafts were exchanged and the following is part of a much more detailed agreement that was eventually signed.]

Memorandum

1. Retainer of $25,000.00 to be paid. If Writ of Certiorari is denied and no settlement has been effected in excess of the Counterclaim, then the $25,000.00 retainer shall be the total fee paid; provided however, that
2. If the case should be settled before a Petition for Writ of Certiorari is actually filed with the Clerk of the Supreme Court, then the Brobeck firm would bill for its services to the date of settlement at an hourly rate of $125.00 per hour for the lawyers who have worked on the case; the total amount of such billing will be limited to not more than $100,000.00, against which the $25,000.00 retainer will be applied, but no portion of the retainer will be returned in any event.

3. Once a Petition for Writ of Certiorari has been filed with the Clerk of the United States Supreme Court then Brobeck will be entitled to the payment of an additional fee in the event of a recovery by Telex from IBM by way of settlement or judgment of its claims against IBM; and, such additional fee will be five percent (5%) of the first $100,000,000.00 gross of such recovery, undiminished by any recovery by IBM on its counterclaims or cross-claims. The maximum contingent fee to be paid is $5,000,000.00, provided that if recovery by Telex from IBM is less than $40,000,000.00 gross, the five percent (5%) shall be based on the net recovery, i.e., the recovery after deducting the credit to IBM by virtue of IBM's recovery on counterclaims or cross-claims, but the contingent fee shall not then be less than $1,000,000.00.

4. Once a Writ of Certiorari has been granted, then Brobeck will receive an additional $15,000.00 retainer to cover briefing and arguing in the Supreme Court.

5. Telex will pay, in addition to the fees stated, all of the costs incurred with respect to the prosecution of the case in the United States Supreme Court.

Jatras signed Lasky's proposed agreement, and on February 28 returned it to Lasky with a letter and a check for $25,000 as the agreed retainer. To "clarify" his thinking on the operation of the fee agreement, Jatras attached a set of hypothetical examples to the letter. This "attachment" stated the amount of the fee that would be paid to Brobeck assuming judgment or settlements in eight different amounts. In the first hypothetical, which assumed a settlement of $18.5 million and a counterclaim judgment of $18.5 million, Jatras listed a "net recovery" by Telex of "$0" and a Brobeck contingency fee of "$0."

Lasky received the letter and attachment on March 3. Later that same day he replied:

Your attachment of examples of our compensation in various contingencies is correct, it being understood that the first example is applicable only to a situation where the petition for certiorari has been denied, as stated in paragraph 1 of the memorandum.

No Telex official responded to Lasky's letter. . . .

On October 2 IBM officials became aware that the Supreme Court's decision on the petition was imminent. They contacted Telex and the parties agreed that IBM would release its counterclaim judgment against Telex in exchange for Telex's dismissal of its petition for certiorari. On October 3, at the request of Wheeler and Jatras, Lasky had the petition for certiorari withdrawn. Thereafter, he sent a bill to Telex for $1,000,000. When Telex refused to pay, Brobeck filed its complaint. On the basis of depositions and exhibits, the district court granted Brobeck's motion for summary judgment. . . .

Telex contends that the $1 million fee was so excessive as to render the contract unenforceable. Alternatively it argues that unconscionability depends on the contract's reasonableness, a question of fact that should be submitted to the jury.

Preliminarily, we note that whether a contract is fair or works an unconscionable hardship is determined with reference to the time when the contract was made and cannot be resolved by hindsight.

There is no dispute about the facts leading to Telex's engagement of the Brobeck firm. Telex was an enterprise threatened with bankruptcy. It had won one of the largest money judgments in history, but that judgment had been reversed in its entirety by the Tenth Circuit. In order to maximize its chances of gaining review by the United States Supreme Court, it sought to hire the most experienced and capable lawyer it could possibly find. After compiling a list of highly qualified lawyers, it settled on Lasky as the most able. Lasky was interested but wanted to bill Telex on an hourly basis. After Telex insisted on a contingent fee arrangement, Lasky made it clear that he would consent to such an arrangement only if he would receive a sizable contingent fee in the event of success.

In these circumstances, the contract between Telex and Brobeck was not so unconscionable that "no man in his senses and not under a delusion would make on the one hand, and as no honest and fair man would accept on the other." [Citing a 1944 California intermediate appellate opinion on an attorney-client fee dispute.] This is not a case where one party took advantage of another's ignorance, exerted superior bargaining power, or disguised unfair terms in small print. Rather, Telex, a multi-million [dollar] corporation, represented by able counsel, sought to secure the best attorney it could find to prepare its petition for certiorari, insisting on a contingent fee contract. Brobeck fulfilled its obligation to gain a stay of judgment and to prepare and file the petition for certiorari. Although the minimum fee was clearly high, Telex received substantial value from Brobeck's services. For, as Telex acknowledged, Brobeck's petition provided Telex with the leverage to secure a discharge of its counterclaim judgment, thereby saving it from possible bankruptcy in the event the Supreme Court denied its petition for certiorari. We conclude that such a contract was not unconscionable.

The judgment of the district court is affirmed.

Telex was in trouble. Moses Lasky was among the nation's most prominent antitrust lawyers. Telex had other lawyers to advise it on the negotiation with Lasky. It's hard to imagine how a fee agreement could be more "arm's length" than this one. Lasky's petition for certiorari provided "leverage" for a settlement that eliminated the threat of Telex's bankruptcy. We should not weep for Telex. The court refused to save the company from its own (sensible) business judgment. And Lasky did take a risk. What would his contingent fee have been if the Supreme Court had granted review but then affirmed the Tenth Circuit decision? Zero. Or if the Court had denied certiorari? Zero. Yet Telex must have been pretty angry. It hired other lawyers to fight the fee ($1 million in 1975, when Brobeck was hired, equals about $4.8 million in 2020) all the way to the Supreme Court.

Rule 1.5 forbids an "unreasonable" fee. This is a stricter requirement than the unconscionability test *Brobeck* used. Assume Lasky spent 120 hours on the certiorari petition. Is the fee reasonable? We ask that question again in part B.

In re Lawrence, 23 N.E.3d 965 (N.Y. 2014), also declined to review the fairness of a contingent fee retroactively. It upheld a $44 million partially contingent legal fee for five months of work. "Absent incompetence, deception or overreaching," the court wrote, "contingent fee agreements that are not void at the time of inception should be enforced as written." Apparently, this is true without regard to how disproportionate the fee is to the work or, depending on the meaning of "overreaching," the client's sophistication.

Not all courts agree. The City of Detroit settled a police brutality complaint for $5.25 million within a month after the incident and three weeks after the complaint was filed, in part because of a public outcry over the event. The court refused to enforce an agreement for one-third of the recovery, a common contingent fee in personal injury cases, even though there was no finding that the plaintiffs' lawyers did anything wrong or took advantage of their client. Green v. Nevers, 111 F.3d 1295 (6th Cir. 1997) ("Courts have broad authority to refuse to enforce contingent fee arrangements that award excessive fees. A fee can be unreasonable and subject to reduction without being so 'clearly excessive' as to justify a finding of breach of ethical rules."). See also In re Powell, 953 N.E.2d 1060 (Ind. 2011), which suspended a lawyer for four months for taking a contingent fee that, although "reasonable . . . at the time entered into," was rendered "unreasonable" by "subsequent developments."

As a practical matter, the *Brobeck* and *Lawrence* tests would seem to impose no limits at all. Perhaps they are correct for contingent fees. Or for any fee if the client is as sophisticated as Telex. Perhaps we should say that when dealing with sophisticated clients, Rule 1.5 is irrelevant. The market is the only test. In some places, that seems to be true.

Time or Value? Or Does Value = Time?

If we omit personal injury cases, where contingent fees are the norm, flat rates and hourly billing are the most common ways lawyers charge for their services. A client might prefer a flat fee because "I know what it will cost me." A lawyer may offer a flat fee for an estate plan, a home purchase, or the defense of a misdemeanor. But flat fees are really hourly rates in disguise. A lawyer predicts how many hours the work will require and multiplies it by an hourly rate. The lawyer will predict high to compensate for situations when the work takes longer than predicted.

In the third decade of the twenty-first century, hourly rates for American lawyers range from less than $200 to $1,500 or more, the latter for a very few specialists in big cities. Much depends on location, the lawyer's experience and reputation, the nature and sophistication of the service, and the gravity and urgency of the client's need.

Some clients (and even some lawyers) question the wisdom of hourly billing. They protest that it encourages inefficiency, even dishonesty. They support "value billing." At the end of the matter, lawyer and client sit down and evaluate what the lawyer has done for the client and agree on a fee commensurate with the value achieved.

The "value billing" question may surface when courts award fees to prevailing parties under fee-shifting statutes. Courts then often use a multiple of time and a reasonable hourly rate (called the "lodestar") to determine a fee. But this can result in a fee far in excess of the client's recovery, which in turn leads some critics to question the logic of the policy. City of Riverside v. Rivera, 477 U.S. 561 (1986), was a controversial early example. Two young lawyers sued the city of Riverside, California, in federal court on behalf of eight Chicano individuals, alleging that Riverside police used unnecessary physical force in breaking up a party. At a 1980 trial, the lawyers recovered $13,300 (or about $41,600 in 2020 dollars) for violation of plaintiffs' federal civil rights. The court ordered the defendants to pay the plaintiffs' lawyers more than $245,000 (or about $767,000 in 2020 dollars) under 42 U.S.C. §1988. This is the federal fee-shifting statute that authorizes federal judges to award "reasonable" fees to parties who prevail on certain federal civil rights claims.

Now, the private market will not support fees of this magnitude for such modest recoveries. Should that be relevant in fee-shifting cases under civil rights and antidiscrimination laws? It depends on how we define value. The value produced by a victory in these cases is not solely the benefit conferred on the successful plaintiff. See Blanchard v. Bergeron, 489 U.S. 87 (1989) ("[A] civil rights plaintiff seeks to vindicate important civil and constitutional rights that cannot be valued solely in monetary terms.") (quoting Rivera).* By paying market rates if the lawyers win, we encourage them to take these cases.

We began by putting contingent fees to the side, but contingent fees are the quintessential example of value billing, aren't they? The lawyer says, "You win, I win; you lose, I lose." In fact, the main difference between evaluating the lawyer's work at the end of the matter, which proponents of value billing favor, and a contingent fee is that the latter is determined by a formula that the lawyer and client accept at the outset, then arithmetically apply at the end. So the risk of misunderstanding should be nearly nil and there is no need to negotiate the value of the lawyer's success. (See Rule 1.5(c) for the level of detail required in a contingent fee agreement.) Yet even as the

* Sometimes a recovery is so low measured against the claim that a court will award no fee. See Aponte v. City of Chicago, 728 F.3d 724 (7th Cir. 2013) (plaintiff sought $25,000 in compensatory damages and $100,000 in punitive damages; jury awarded $100; court denied all fees).

arguments *for* value billing—and *against* hourly rates, which take no account of value—have become more common, contingent fees remain a constant focus of criticism, including on the editorial pages of the Wall Street Journal (but not only there). How do we explain that paradox?

B. UNETHICAL FEES AND BILLING PRACTICES

California Rule 1.5(a) forbids an "unconscionable" fee. Model Rule 1.5(a) requires a "reasonable" fee. (Can there be an unreasonable but conscionable fee?) Whatever the test, should it matter whether the question arises in an action to collect fees (*Brobeck*) or in discipline?

"Sparrow Owes Robin a Refund"

Chantal Robin, a successful stock trader, received letters from the Justice Department and the SEC saying that she was the subject of a civil and criminal investigation. She went right out and hired Claire Sparrow, the best defense lawyer in town for these matters. Sparrow's "minimum fee" is $50,000 if the matter is resolved before charges are filed. If charges are filed, the fee goes up. The $50,000 fee is reasonable at the time given Sparrow's prominence and the gravity of the threat to Robin. Two days later, after Sparrow's associate did three hours of research but before she notified the government that she was retained, a binding court decision no one expected construed the law to give Robin a complete defense to any claim of civil or criminal liability. The government dropped the investigations. Robin's new lawyer, Ayelet Swann, sued Sparrow after she refused to discuss a refund. In court, Swann wrote that "intervening events made the fee unreasonable and a violation of Rule 1.5(a) unless most of it is returned. Sparrow owes Robin a refund." The court, she said, should decide how much using the criteria in the rule. Marcus Stork, Sparrow's lawyer, replied that because the fee was reasonable when paid, it satisfied Rule 1.5(a). "It doesn't become unreasonable retroactively." You're on the state supreme court. There is no precedent. How do you vote?

"What Are You Worth?"

Edward Porgby has grown rich running a San Francisco hedge fund. He is indicted for hiring two men to kill his partner, whose body is found one morning floating in Lake Tahoe. Out on bail, he calls Clarice Darrow, who at 58 is acknowledged by many to be the best homicide defense lawyer in the country. Porgby leaves four messages with Darrow's assistant, but Darrow never responds. Unaccustomed to being ignored, Porgby confronts Darrow at the entrance to the Yale

Club. "I'm Edward Porgby," he says. "Congratulations," Darrow says, not slowing her pace and proceeding to walk around him.

"I've been trying to get an appointment with you," Porgby says to Darrow's receding back, trying to disguise his annoyance.

"I'm aware of that," Darrow says without turning around. "I'm not interested in your case."

"You don't know anything about my case," Porgby shouts after her, drawing stares.

Darrow turns. "You got to be kidding. Your face has been on the front page of the Journal, the Times, and the Chronicle. Besides, I don't think we'd get along, from all I've read."

"We don't have to get along. This is business. I'm not looking for a friend."

Porgby follows Darrow into the club. "Just consider it," Porgby says a little too loud, drawing more stares. Darrow stops and studies Porgby.

"All right. I'll consider it," Darrow says to avoid a scene. "Call me tomorrow."

"What are you worth?" Darrow asks when Porgby calls the next day.

"Twenty-five billion. About."

"Okay. Tell you what. I'll do it through trial for 2 percent of your net worth, that's half a billion. Win or lose, of course. Pay in advance. Contingent fees aren't allowed in criminal cases."

Darrow had expected Porgby to hang up, but instead he asks, "What would you charge if I were, you know, just ordinary rich?"

"Oh. Ordinary rich? Maybe $10 million and expenses. I hear that Jeffrey Skilling of Enron fame paid Dan Petrocelli of O'Melveny $40 million and owed him another $30 million before he got sentenced to 24 years, since reduced to 14," Darrow says. "Don't know if Petrocelli ever got the balance. And I read that NBA star Kevin Durant got $54.3 million for a two-year contract with the Golden State Warriors. Defending you will take two years at least with no break. No opportunity for product endorsements, either."

"That's sports," Porgby says.

"What you mean is that's *only* sports. While this is your life. So shouldn't I be worth more? Anyway, I have enough business and from all I've heard, you're not a nice guy even if you're not a killer, which, out of professional courtesy, I will assume you're not. Also, I've got plans to play golf with friends in Scotland next month, which I'd hate to miss. With half a billion, I can get my alma mater to become the RBG School of Law. Scalia, O'Connor, Cardozo, Brandeis, and both Marshalls—John and Thurgood—have law schools named for them. So should Ruth. And I'll have enough left over for a big contribution to the Equal Justice Initiative and Doctors Without Borders. Besides, how old are you?"

"Forty-five."

"There you go. If I win, you've got 25 more high-earning years at least. Anyway, you'll recoup my fee before the trial is over. I understand you work miracles in the market."

"What if you lose?"

"Lose?" Darrow says, as if hearing that word for the first time. "Lose," she repeats. "Yes, I could . . . lose. I think the last time I lost was in 2014. The client insisted on testifying against my advice. Anyway, so what if I lose? What would you do with the money anyway? You can't spend it in prison. Besides, you can hire Paul Clement or Miguel Estrada for the appeal. They're Republicans, you know."

"I don't like your sense of humor, counselor," Porgby says.

"At my age and in my position, Eddie—can I call you Eddie?—I don't care. You called me."

Porgby confers with other prominent homicide counsel, none of whom would charge more than $10 million for the work. After thinking about it for a few more days, he hires Darrow and is acquitted after a six-week trial. Porgby then challenges the fee as unconscionable, illegal, and unethical. The evidence shows that Darrow worked full time for 27 months, for a total of 4,000 hours. So her recovery is $125,000 per hour.

Porgby's lawyer, Caleb Sodd, argues:

> Imagine if Darrow were a great brain surgeon and Porgby needed a difficult operation to avoid profound disability. Dr. Darrow usually charged $500,000, but because of Porgby's wealth she demands $25 million, 50 times as much. Because that's what lawyer Darrow wants here, your Honor, 50 times as much as she'd usually charge. Would a court enforce that fee agreement with Dr. Darrow? We say no. Neither should it enforce this one.

"And your Honor," Sodd continues, "professionals agree, in exchange for their monopoly power and state licenses, to limit their fees. That's what Rule 1.5 does. If this fee is reasonable, why do we bother with Rule 1.5? Let's just say it's a market like any other."

Assume Rule 1.5 governs. Who wins? If you think lawyer Darrow wins, how do you answer the medical analogy? Or perhaps you think Dr. Darrow should win, too. And if your case is in Massachusetts, how would you distinguish *Fordham*, which follows? Or maybe you would ask the court to overrule it.

CASE NOTE: IN RE FORDHAM

Discipline for violating Rule 1.5 is rare but it happens. Laurence Fordham worked all the hours for which he billed, the client knew his hourly rate, which was fair, and the result was excellent. Yet Fordham was censured. The opinion offers a convenient contrast with *Brobeck*. In re Fordham, 668 N.E.2d

816 (Mass. 1996), was decided under the old Code. Today, Massachusetts has the ABA Rule except that at the time (and still) Massachusetts prohibited a "clearly excessive fee," whereas Rule 1.5(a) requires a "reasonable" fee.

Timothy Clark was charged with drunk driving (DUI) after the police found "a partially full quart of vodka" in his car and he failed a sobriety and two breathalyzer tests. Laurence Clark ("Clark"), his father, asked Laurence Fordham about representing Timothy. Clark knew Fordham because he had serviced an alarm system in Fordham's home. Fordham told Clark that he billed hourly (not a flat fee) and that he was a civil litigator without DUI experience. Fordham said, however, that he was "efficient and economic in the use of his time." Clark interviewed other lawyers, who had quoted flat fees of $3,000 to $10,000. He chose Fordham.

Fordham sent Clark bills across six months. They showed the mounting fees and eventually totaled $50,000.

Fordham succeed in having the breathalyzer tests suppressed with a "creative, if not novel, approach," according to a hearing committee and Timothy was acquitted. The committee found that although the fee was "much higher than the fee charged by many attorneys with more experience litigating [DUI] cases . . . it was not clearly excessive because Clark went into the relationship with Fordham with open eyes." Furthermore, it said, "Clark acquiesced in Fordham's fee by not strenuously objecting to his bills." The Supreme Judicial Court rejected this conclusion.

> The finding that Clark had entered into the fee agreement "with open eyes" was based on the finding that Clark hired Fordham after being fully apprised that he lacked any type of experience in defending [a DUI] charge and after interviewing other lawyers who were experts in defending [DUI] charges. Furthermore, the hearing committee and the board relied on testimony which revealed that the fee arrangement had been fully disclosed to Clark including the fact that Fordham "would have to become familiar with the law in that area." It is also significant, however, that the hearing committee found that "despite Fordham's disclaimers concerning his experience, Clark did not appear to have understood in any real sense the implications of choosing Fordham to represent Timothy. Fordham did not give Clark any estimate of the total expected fee or the number of $200 hours that would be required." The express finding of the hearing committee that Clark "did not appear to have understood in any real sense the implications of choosing Fordham to represent Timothy" directly militates against the finding that Clark entered into the agreement "with open eyes." . . .
>
> Finally, bar counsel challenges the hearing committee's finding that "if Clark objected to the numbers of hours being spent by Fordham, he could have spoken up with some force when he began receiving bills." Bar counsel notes, and we agree, that "the test . . . is whether the fee 'charged' is clearly excessive, not whether the fee is accepted as valid or acquiesced in by the client." Therefore, we conclude that the hearing committee and the board erred in not concluding that Fordham's fee was clearly excessive.

———————

Are *Fordham* and *Brobeck* Compatible?

In constant dollars, Moses Lasky earned a lot more per hour than Fordham. Fordham reached his agreement in 1989. Lasky was hired in 1975. In 1989 dollars, Lasky's fee would equal $2.3 million. Assuming Lasky and his firm spent as many as 120 hours—three weeks—on the certiorari petition (a generous assumption), his hourly fee would be $19,000 in 1989 dollars, whereas the blended fee for Fordham and his associates yielded $220 hourly.* (In 2020 dollars, again assuming 120 hours for the certiorari petition, Lasky earned about $40,000 hourly and Fordham earned about $460 hourly.)

The client of each attorney knew the score. Fordham's client received monthly bills showing the accumulating fee. Yet Brobeck wins the civil dispute and Fordham loses the discipline case. How can that be? What are Lasky's best arguments if he were before the *Fordham* court? What are Clarice Darrow's?

Inflating Bills and Other Abuses

Time and again, when lawyers get into trouble, money is the reason. Billing is one place this happens. The system relies on honor, which explains why billing abuse is (or should be) seriously punished. Honor in billing begins before law school—in your work as a paralegal, in part-time work while in law school, or as a summer associate. But the system does not rely only on honor. The time is recorded (and so is your image) when you enter and leave an office building, when you use an electronic key, when you're on the phone, and when you're doing computer research. What you're researching is also recorded. If you're suspected, your recorded time and the substance of your research may be monitored without your knowing it, until you're confronted with discrepancies.

Donald Hess had a difficult client. He was a good client in one sense: He produced a lot of work. But he paid his bills very late. What's more, he insisted on a discount. Hess's firm orally agreed to a 15-percent discount if bills were timely paid. But the client continued to pay late. So, employing a kind of self-help and without telling the client, Hess began "inflating the bills to offset the discount for prompt payment." This went on for more than two years and involved hundreds of matters. Hess eventually confessed, but the client was not sympathetic. The firm repaid more than $470,000. Hess was suspended for three years. Atty. Griev. Comm'n. of Md. v. Hess, 722 A.2d 905 (Md. 1999) (court cited other cases of lawyers who inflated bills "where there was no offsetting purported discount" and where the lawyers were disbarred).

---

* A blended rate is the total fee divided by the total number of hours for all attorneys.

Inflating expenses and creating fictitious expenses will also support discipline. In re Lerner, 973 N.Y.S.2d 218 (1st Dept. 2013) (one-year suspension of lawyer who charged client $50,000 across ten years for personal car service).

Kristin Stahlbush took cases on court assignment. After a matter ended, she would submit her voucher for services. She claimed time she had not worked, including "numerous" 24-hour days, 90 hours in a 96-hour period, and 139 hours in a 144-hour period. What was she thinking? An audit would inevitably detect her conduct. What's the right sanction? Toledo Bar Ass'n v. Stahlbush, 933 N.E.2d 1091 (Ohio 2010) (two-year suspension with one year stayed).

In one way, Hess, Stahlbush, and the others got off easy. Lying on a bill is a form of theft. Prosecution, although rare, happens. A state judge sentenced Mark McCombs, a former Greenberg Traurig partner, to six years in prison after he pled guilty to billing Calumet Park, Illinois for work he never performed. Erin Meyer, Chicago Tribune, Sept. 12, 2011. The overbilling reportedly exceeded $1 million, which the firm repaid.

A Tennessee discipline case would likely take the prize for billing abuse if one existed. In addition to other misconduct leading to a one-year suspension, a lawyer billed for "many hours" watching the television show *48 Hours.* Sallee v. Tennessee Board of Professional Responsibility, 469 S.W.3d 18 (Tenn. 2015), citing the requirement that work performed be "reasonable," held that while "a lawyer who represents criminal clients may be interested in watching *Perry Mason* or *Breaking Bad* on television, and may even pick up a useful tidbit or two from doing so . . . [t]he lawyer may not . . . equate that to research for which he or she may charge a client."

Courts and Billing Guidelines Make Lawyers Defend Every Dollar

> Judges trust lawyers. They expect that lawyers will provide the
> court the accurate and complete information that is necessary to
> decide matters properly. . . . [T]his case demonstrates that not all
> lawyers can be trusted when they are seeking millions of dollars
> in attorneys' fees and face no real risk that the usual adversary
> process will expose misrepresentations that they make.
> —Judge Mark Wolf in Arkansas Teacher Retirement System v.
>   State Street Bank & Trust Co. (D. Mass. Feb. 27, 2020)
>   (ruling on a fee application after settlement of a class action)

Courts must approve fees in class actions, where the plaintiff is a minor, in derivative actions, and under fee-shifting statutes like those in civil rights cases. The lawyers submit a request, which the court will examine. The lawyers must be ready to defend every dollar. What a difference! In all other cases, the client must protect himself. Relatively few clients have the power and experience to do what judges do before approving a fee or to demand what corporate clients (or their in-house lawyers) demand in billing guidelines.

These guidelines may require outside lawyers to itemize every task and the time spent doing it. "Work on case, 7 hours" will not suffice. What exactly was the work? Guidelines may limit to one or two the number of lawyers who can bill for a court appearance. Corporate clients may refuse to pay for educating first-year associates. If a time charge seems too high for the task, the lawyer may have to explain.

An example of what a judge may do in ruling on a fee application is found in Houston v. Cotter, 234 F.Supp.3d 392 (E.D.N.Y. 2017). Houston, who was incarcerated, filed a pro se civil rights claim against two individual corrections officers. He alleged that the officers used excessive force in an altercation and then placed him on suicide watch for two weeks as punishment. Apparently seeing some merit in the complaint, the court asked Cleary Gottlieb to represent Houston, which to its credit it did. It filed an amended complaint, which added a due process claim against Suffolk County. A jury awarded the plaintiff $30,000 in compensatory and punitive damages. The victory entitled Cleary to seek fees from the defendants. It asked for more than $685,000. The court awarded $345,000. In a lengthy opinion, Judge Bianco (now on the Second Circuit) explained why he would not credit Cleary for all hours its lawyers worked.

> First, the matter was overstaffed. . . .
> Second, and relatedly, the Court does not find the Due Process claim to have involved such thorny and unusual legal issues to warrant so many attorneys. . . .
> Third, the Court concludes that a reduction in hours is appropriate based on vague and block-billed time entries. . . .
> Finally, that [Cleary] decided to apportion an identical amount of time to the excessive force and the Due Process claims during the trial phase demonstrates that [it] did not adequately distinguish between work product on the two causes of action in its time entries. . . .

You get the picture, but read the full opinion to see the court's extraordinary attention to detail. Well, at least Cleary got paid. On rare occasions, a court may be so offended by a fee request that it denies all fees, even for work that could properly be compensated. Clemens v. New York Central Mutual Fire Insurance Co., 903 F.3d 396 (3rd Cir. 2018), is an example. The fee request was deemed "outrageously excessive." But was the firm entitled to anything at all for its work? It was not, said the court, because "if courts did not possess this kind of discretion, 'claimants would be encouraged to make unreasonable demands, knowing that the only unfavorable consequences of such conduct would be reduction of their fee to what they should have asked for in the first place.' . . . [A] fee petition . . . is not the 'opening bid in the quest for an award.'" See also Chen v. Chen Qualified Settlement Fund, 552 F.3d 218 (2d Cir. 2009) (all fees denied where firm requested a fee higher than allowed by statute).

A lawyer's failure to keep contemporaneous time records can also lead to denial of court-awarded fees, except for time spent in court if corroborated by court records, even when it is apparent that the lawyer did a great deal of work on the matter. Scott v. City of New York, 643 F.3d 56 (2d Cir. 2011).

Billing Judgment

Perhaps Fordham can be faulted for not exercising billing judgment, notwithstanding that he did what the fee agreement allowed. Rule 1.5 does not use the term "billing judgment," but the rule does require that fees be reasonable. The Wyoming Supreme Court held that a failure to exercise billing judgment can make a fee unreasonable even if the fee would be reasonable in other circumstances. Stacy Casper's fee agreement said she would bill her hourly rate in 15-minute increments. (Billing in six-minute increments is far more common.) That meant that a discrete task requiring five minutes to complete would be billed at 15 minutes or three times her hourly rate. The court did not say that this provision was invariably unreasonable, but as applied here it was. Reasonableness of attorneys' fees

> requires the application of "billing judgment," which usually is demonstrated by the attorney writing off unproductive, excessive, or redundant hours. Billing for legal services . . . should not be a merely mechanical exercise. . . . A reasonable fee can only be fixed by the exercise of judgment, using the mechanical computations simply as a starting point. . . .
>
> Respondent in this case billed in fifteen-minute increments, in accordance with the contractual terms, times a reasonable rate. However, her practice of billing fifteen minutes for such tasks as signing subpoenas, stipulated orders, and one-page letters demonstrated a complete failure to exercise business judgment, which would have required her to write off unproductive, excessive, or redundant hours.

Bd. of Prof'l Resp. v. Casper, 318 P.3d 790 (Wyo. 2014).

Post-Retainer Fee Agreements

In some courts, a fee agreement reached during the professional relationship can be characterized as a type of financial arrangement between lawyer and client subject to the rather strict requirements of Rule 1.8(a). (See chapter 5A1.) After retainer, the client may not be able to pay another retainer. The client may have begun to rely on and confide in the lawyer, especially in personal legal matters. This puts the lawyer in a far superior negotiating position.

In In re Krasnoff, 78 N.E.3d 657 (Ind. 2017), Krasnoff was found to have violated Rule 1.8(a) "by renegotiating his fee agreement with [his client] on terms more advantageous to [Krasnoff] without adhering to the safeguards required by the rule, including the need to advise the client in writing of the desirability of seeking independent counsel and to give the client a reasonable opportunity to do so. . . . The relevant inquiry [is] whether the terms of a renegotiated fee agreement are more advantageous to the attorney than the terms of the original fee agreement." A lawyer for an estate who switched from an hourly to a contingent fee after he learned that the estate would recover substantial assets was suspended for six months. The renegotiated fee agreement violated Rule 1.8(a). In re Hefron, 771 N.E.2d 1157 (Ind. 2002).

For an especially egregious example of a post-retainer fee agreement that significantly disfavored the client, and that was signed while the client was in a hurry to catch a plane, see Mar Oil v. Morrissey, 982 F.2d 830 (2d Cir. 1993) (Morrissey "buried" critical fee information in papers he asked client to sign). For this conduct, Morrissey was suspended from practice for two years. In re Morrissey, 634 N.Y.S.2d 51 (1st Dept. 1995). Morrissey was later disbarred following his conviction for a scheme to defraud and other crimes in stealing from his client Brooke Astor, who was suffering from dementia. In re Morrissey, 898 N.Y.S.2d 1 (1st Dept. 2010).

Even in courts where Rule 1.8(a)'s requirements do not apply to a post-retainer fee agreement, much case law agrees with the following approach to all lawyer-client fee agreements: "While, in the law generally, equivocal contracts will be construed against the drafters, courts as a matter of public policy give particular scrutiny to fee arrangements between attorneys and clients, casting the burden on attorneys who have drafted the retainer agreements to show that the contracts are fair, reasonable, and fully known and understood by their clients." Shaw v. Mfrs. Hanover Trust, 499 N.E.2d 864 (N.Y. 1986). ABA Opinion 11-458 lays out the obligations of lawyers who wish to change a fee arrangement during the representation.

Should a Lawyer Be Required to Put Fee Agreements in Writing?

The January 1980 draft of the Model Rules proposed:

> The basis or rate of a lawyer's fee shall be put in writing before the lawyer has rendered substantial services in the matter, except when (1) [a]n agreement as to the fees is implied by the fact that the lawyer's services are of the same general kind as previously rendered to and paid for by the client; or (2) [t]he services are rendered in an emergency where a writing is impracticable.

As finally adopted, Rule 1.5(b) simply says that the fee "shall be communicated to the client, preferably in writing, before or within a reasonable time after commencing the representation." The Ethics 2000 Commission also said lawyers should be required to have a written fee agreement with some exceptions. The ABA again rejected the idea. A contingent fee, however, "shall be in a writing." Rule 1.5(c). Do you think the Rules should require written fee agreements, at least when the lawyer has not regularly represented the client? How does it affect your answer to know that fees are a frequent source of client complaints or bitterness? The New Jersey, Pennsylvania, and Washington, D.C. rules contain a writing requirement where the lawyer has not regularly represented the client. See also Cal. Bus. & Prof. Code §6148 (writing generally required) and N.Y.C.R.R. part 1215 (same). At least ten jurisdictions require a written agreement for new clients.

C. CONTINGENT FEES

In a contingent fee agreement, a lawyer's fee depends on the occurrence or nonoccurrence of an event. Usually, the event is recovery of a sum of money, and the fee is a percentage of the recovery. These fees are prevalent in personal injury or property damage actions, whether based in negligence or strict liability, but they also (and increasingly) appear in a variety of commercial cases seeking money damages. A lawyer may charge a fee composed of a reduced hourly rate, thereby assuring cash flow, and a reduced contingent fee, thereby participating in any recovery.

There are other possibilities. A lawyer may agree that she will be entitled to a fee only if she achieves a particular result for a client (for example, a mortgage commitment). Or a lawyer may agree to a percentage of the amount of money he *saves* the client. For example, the IRS may demand $100,000 in back taxes. A fee may be 25 percent of the difference between the demand and what the client ends up paying. Such "reverse" contingent fees have been approved. See ABA Opinion 93-373. Contingent fees are conceptually possible in all representations that produce a fund or have a definable objective, but they are forbidden in criminal and (nearly everywhere) in matrimonial cases.

One of the most unusual (and most rewarding) contingent fees in U.S. history was the 1932 agreement between Greenbaum, Wolff & Ernst, a now defunct New York firm specializing in publishing and the First Amendment, and Random House, then a new publisher started by two young men, Bennett Cerf and Donald Klopfer. Random House retained the firm to enable it to publish James Joyce's *Ulysses* in the United States without risk of an obscenity prosecution. (It was published in Paris in 1922.) Random House could not afford Greenbaum's hourly rates, or, more accurately, the rate of its prominent partner Morris Ernst. So beyond a modest advance, Ernst agreed to a fee, contingent on publication, of 5 percent of the price of the trade edition of the book, 2 percent of any reprint edition, and 5 percent from book club sales, apparently for the duration of the copyright (it is still in copyright) although some sources say that it was only for the balance of Ernst's life. Ernst died in 1976. Ernst succeeded and Random House published *Ulysses* in the United States in 1934. For a history of obscenity law, from its nineteenth century English roots through the Second Circuit decision that affirmed that the book was not obscene, and a description of Ernst's brilliant litigation strategy and the women[*] who put themselves at financial and personal risk by publishing the book or parts of it, see Stephen Gillers, A Tendency to Deprave and Corrupt: The Transformation of American Obscenity Law from *Hicklin* to *Ulysses II*, 85 Wash. U. L. Rev. 215 (2007).

---

[*] Among them was Sylvia Beach, an expatriate American in Paris who founded the original Shakespeare and Company bookstore on rue de l'Odéon in Paris in 1919 and published the first English version of *Ulysses* on February 2, 1922, Joyce's fortieth birthday.

A lawyer may be entitled to a contingent fee that would be unconscionably high if it were a guaranteed fee. See In re Brown & Williamson Tobacco Corp., 777 N.Y.S.2d 82 (1st Dept. 2004) (upholding arbitrators' award of $1.25 billion in tobacco class action). Perhaps the largest contingent fee of all time occurred in a common fund litigation. In Americas Mining Corp. v. Theriault, 51 A.3d 1213 (Del. 2012), the Delaware Supreme Court affirmed a lower court's fee of $304 million after the plaintiff's lawyers won a judgment of $2.0316 billion (including prejudgment interest) for minority shareholders of a company whose majority shareholder had caused it to overpay for shares in a company the majority shareholder owned. The lawyers worked on the case for about eight years, spending 8,597 hours. Had they lost, they would have recovered nothing. The fee worked out to an hourly rate of about $35,000.

A Lawyer's Advantage When Negotiating a Contingent Fee

For lawyers, whether a contingent fee is worth the risk of getting nothing depends on five factors. Try to list them before reading on.

Take your time. Really.

The factors are: (i) the likelihood of the occurrence of the contingency, (ii) when it is likely to occur, (iii) the size of the likely recovery, (iv) the effort required to get it, and (v) the lawyer's percentage. The first four factors require predictions, which in turn will influence the fifth factor. The less likely the contingency, the greater the percentage the lawyer will want because of the greater risk of no recovery. Lawyers are usually better able than clients to make these predictions. This puts clients at a disadvantage when negotiating the final factor and in deciding whether to opt for a contingent fee at all (assuming they can pay a noncontingent fee).

From a client's perspective, a contingent fee gives a lawyer incentive. It is the most common example of "value billing." From the perspective of critics of contingent fees, however, the lawyer's financial interest in the client's recovery warps the lawyer's independent judgment on behalf of the client and encourages frivolous litigation, meaning the case has no basis in law. Can the second be true? If a case is frivolous, it will lose in court, generate no fee, and may even result in sanctions. Lawyers who bring frivolous cases for a contingent fee won't be long in business.

Contingent Fees and Conflicts of Interest

What about the other claim—i.e., contingent fees can warp a lawyer's independent judgment on behalf of the client? A contingent fee arrangement can indeed lead to a conflict between what is good for the lawyer and what is good for the client.

Assume Lawyer (*L*), based on years of experience, estimates that a personal injury case is worth $600,000 to $750,000 in damages *if* the jury finds that the defendant was at fault. Assume an 80 percent chance that the jury will find fault. *L*'s experienced opponent will make the same estimates. Assume a contingent fee of one-third.

Scenario A: With 100 hours of work, *L* gets an offer of $330,000, yielding a contingent fee of $110,000 or $1,100 hourly. The client would get $220,000.

Scenario B: If *L* puts in another 100 hours of pretrial work, experience tells him he could increase the settlement offer to $450,000 because he will strengthen his case, because the opponent realizes he is serious, and because settlement offers tend to rise as trial looms. *L* then gets $750 for each hour worked (a $150,000 fee divided by 200 hours). The client would get $300,000 instead of $220,000. That's much worse for *L* on an hourly basis, but better for the client (putting aside the longer wait).

Scenario C: To go to trial would increase the time requirement to a total of 400 hours (because trials are labor intensive) with the prospect of a fee of up to $250,000 if the client wins the $750,000 maximum *L* figures the claim may be worth. This yields an hourly rate of $625 ($250,000 divided by 400 hours). The client would get $500,000. If the client wins $600,000, the lawyer's hourly rate is $500 and the client gets $400,000. But there's a 20 percent chance the client will lose and the lawyer and client will get nothing.

The Lesson: So while going to trial carries a risk of loss for both lawyer and client, the upside to the client is substantial, but the lawyer's hourly compensation shrinks. Or to put it another way, it will often be better for the lawyer to accept an early offer and go on to the next matter because doing so maximizes hourly compensation with no risk. For the client, settling closer to trial may be more remunerative than an early settlement, but less rewarding for the lawyer. Even going to trial may be worth the risk for the client if the case is strong enough and the upside is great enough.

True, these numbers "prove" my point only because I got to choose the numbers. It won't always play out this way. But when it will or looks like it will, you can see the dramatic decline in the lawyer's fee on an hourly basis, making an early low settlement preferable to a higher later one and both preferable to a still higher trial verdict. The time saved can be spent settling other cases for a higher net fee. And yet the client's source of advice on whether to accept a settlement offer will be the very lawyer who may benefit if she does.

Is this an argument against contingent fees? Not at all. Settlement will often be in the best interest of clients, who may be overly optimistic about their trial chances despite little experience on which to predict. And as a nation we've decided that contingent fees are a socially valid way to pay counsel, especially for plaintiffs who might otherwise be unable to get a lawyer. We should, however, recognize the conflicting incentives. As important, lawyers who advise on whether to settle should be aware of their own biases. Here we can learn from work in behavioral legal ethics, cited in chapters 1 and 5B.

Prohibitions on Contingent Fees in Criminal and Matrimonial Cases

The Model Rules forbid a contingent fee in a criminal case and impose substantial limits on contingent fees "in a domestic relations matter." Rule 1.5(d).

Why are contingent fees limited in domestic relations matters? Here are some reasons often given:

1. The state has an interest in seeing that as much money stays with the family as possible (especially for children and nonworking spouses).
2. Because the law empowers the judge to order a wealthier spouse to pay the other spouse's counsel fees, the less wealthy spouse does not need a contingent fee to attract a lawyer.
3. A contingent fee gives the lawyer a stake in the outcome that might lead to recommendation of a course of action not in the client's best interests. This is true for all contingent cases, as we saw above. But society, it is said, has a special concern for families. In this view, a fee contingent on a divorce might prevent the lawyer from encouraging reconciliation. A fee that is a percentage of alimony or the property that goes to the client might cause the lawyer to litigate aggressively—with attendant acrimony—when settlement ought to be encouraged.

Do any of these reasons persuade you? All of them together? Is it unseemly to give a lawyer a contingent interest in divorce, alimony, and marital property? Or does the rule interfere with freedom of contract? The rule is the product of an era when divorce was unusual and comparatively few women worked outside the home. That's changed.

The reasons for prohibiting contingent fees in criminal cases are easy to understand. A fee contingent on acquittal could, for example, prompt a lawyer to encourage the client to reject a favorable plea offer and go to trial in order to give the lawyer a chance to win acquittal—and the fee. Every once in a while a convicted person will seek to have his conviction overturned on the ground that his lawyer had been working for a contingent fee. These efforts usually fail. The fact that contingent fees are banned in criminal matters because of the risk of disloyalty does not mean that a conflict actually affected performance. That mere possibility is not enough to prompt a reversal. See Winkler v. Keane, 7 F.3d 304 (2d Cir. 1993), and People v. Winkler, 523 N.E.2d 485 (N.Y. 1988).

A Radical Proposal or Client Protection?

Contingent fees are controversial. For some reason (what might it be?), the debate seems to fall along a left/right axis. Conservatives argue that the fees lead to frivolous litigation, which one would expect liberals to oppose as well. Liberals argue that they give ordinary people access to the courts for legitimate claims, which one would expect conservatives to support as well. So what's this debate about?

The prospect of prohibiting contingent fees is nil. But some voices have spoken in favor of further limiting contingent fees in personal injury actions—beyond current limits, commonly between one-third and 40 percent. Rethinking Contingency Fees (Manhattan Inst. 1994), authored by law professors Lester Brickman and Jeffrey O'Connell (whose work led to no-fault insurance) and Michael Horowitz, then of the Hudson Institute, proposed a new way to cap these fees. Many lawyers hate their proposal. Is it because it's bad for clients or bad for them?

Consider that we permit contingent fees to be larger than what would constitute a reasonable hourly fee because if the contingency does not occur, the lawyer gets nothing for her work. But most personal injury cases—certainly most cases that lawyers are willing to accept—have *some* value. Why should the plaintiff's lawyer get a full contingent fee for "recovering" this sum? She need do little or nothing to secure it.

The following rule is similar to one posed in a 1996 California voter referendum inspired by the Brickman-O'Connell-Horowitz proposal. It failed by less than two percentage points.

> A plaintiff's lawyer in individual (*i.e.*, non-class) tort cases must make a settlement demand within 60 days of being retained. The defendant may respond with an offer. If it does not, this rule is inapplicable. If the defendant does make an offer and it is accepted, the contingent fee is limited to 15 percent of the settlement, with the balance going to the client. If the offer is not accepted, the contingent fee for any eventual recovery, by settlement or trial, is 15 percent of the amount of the rejected offer and the lawyer's usual percentage for any excess, with the balance going to the client.

Here's an example. Green is injured by XYZ Corp.'s truck. He hires Smith to represent him. Within 60 days, Smith demands $300,000. XYZ immediately offers to settle for $100,000. (Or maybe XYZ has offered Green $100,000 before he even hires Smith.) If Green accepts this early offer, Smith's fee is limited to $15,000. Green gets $85,000. If Green rejects the offer and Green later recovers $250,000 in trial or settlement, Smith's fee is limited to 15 percent of the first $100,000 ($15,000) and her usual contingent rate for the excess ($150,000). So if that rate is one-third, Smith's gross fee will be $65,000 instead of $83,333 (one-third of the total). Green walks away with $18,333 more than if Smith's one-third contingent fee were applied to the full recovery. Good for Green, right? Not good for Smith.

Proponents argue that the rule will lead to early settlements. Defendants will be encouraged to make high early offers because plaintiffs, who will get more of the money, will be more inclined to accept. Eighty-five cents of every dollar will go to the plaintiff. Because Smith did not take a risk in eliciting the early offer and would not have done much work to get and evaluate it, she has no fair claim to a one-third contingent fee on this amount. Fifteen percent is enough.

If you view the situation through the eyes of a lawyer engaged in Smith's line of work, self-interest may cause you to reject the proposal. But if we say that rules governing legal fees should be fair to clients, that they don't exist to enrich lawyers, and if we forget for a minute that we are or will soon be lawyers, can we defend giving to Smith (*and taking from Green*) one-third of the money that XYZ was willing to pay Green within weeks of Smith's appearance, perhaps even before Green hired Smith?

Here's another complication, or maybe it simplifies things. In a competitive market, we might expect some plaintiffs' lawyers to charge a lower percentage of an early offer. That is, we might expect competition among personal injury lawyers to lead some of them to offer Green the same fee arrangement as in the proposal, without need for a rule. But it has not. A personal injury plaintiff is likely to discover that no one will lower the contingent percentage for early offers. The fee is one-third or even 40 percent from every lawyer she consults. Is there some reason to distrust the market for legal services, at least in the world of personal injury contingent fees?

As I say, lawyers hate this proposal and, in my experience, so do most law students. ABA Opinion 94-389, responding to it, said that a full contingent fee was permitted even where "liability is clear and some recovery is anticipated." But why? A lower contingent fee cap on early offers is better for clients, isn't it? Lawyers do profess support for consumer protection rules, but they are less enthusiastic when the consumer is a client and the rule will limit fees. Maybe you think the proposal is wrong. But can you explain why? Or maybe you agree with it.

D. MINIMUM FEE SCHEDULES

Canon 12 of the 1908 Canons of Ethics deemed it "proper" for a lawyer determining his fee "to consider a schedule of minimum fees adopted by a Bar Association," but added that "no lawyer should permit himself to be controlled thereby or to follow it as his sole guide in determining the amount of his fee." Some disciplinary authorities viewed it as unprofessional for a lawyer consistently to charge less than the minimum fee schedule. In their view, doing so led to price competition, which was seen as inconsistent with a learned profession. Of course, enforcement of minimum fee schedules through threat of discipline could be viewed less charitably—as price fixing in violation of antitrust laws. However, a state may authorize conduct that would otherwise violate antitrust laws. This state action defense arose in *Goldfarb*, a case that dramatically reveals the effect of a fee schedule on the cost of a routine legal service.

Bar-imposed minimum fee schedules, now forbidden, were one of the ways that rules regulating the profession impeded access to legal services. Another was the prohibition on almost all lawyer advertising, which suppressed price competition and the public's awareness of its legal rights (chapter 16). Yet others—like broad unauthorized practice rules that limit who can give advice deemed "legal" (see chapter 12C) and the prohibition against helping a needy client with living expenses so she can hold out until trial or for an acceptable settlement offer (chapter 5A3)—remain.

GOLDFARB v. VIRGINIA STATE BAR
421 U.S. 773 (1975)

CHIEF JUSTICE BURGER delivered the opinion of the Court. . . .

I

In 1971 petitioners, husband and wife, contracted to buy a home in Fairfax County, Va. The financing agency required them to secure title insurance; this required a title examination, and only a member of the Virginia State Bar could legally perform that service. Petitioners therefore contacted a lawyer who quoted them the precise fee suggested in a minimum-fee schedule published by respondent Fairfax County Bar Association; the lawyer told them that it was his policy to keep his charges in line with the minimum-fee schedule which provided for a fee of 1% of the value of the property involved. Petitioners then tried to find a lawyer who would examine the title for less than the fee fixed by the schedule. They sent letters to 36 other Fairfax County lawyers requesting their fees. Nineteen replied, and none indicated that he would charge less than the rate fixed by the schedule; several stated that they knew of no attorney who would do so. . . .

Because petitioners could not find a lawyer willing to charge a fee lower than the schedule dictated, they had their title examined by the lawyer they had first contacted. They then brought this class action against the State Bar and the County Bar alleging that the operation of the minimum-fee schedule, as applied to fees for legal services relating to residential real estate transactions, constitutes price fixing in violation of §1 of the Sherman Act. Petitioners sought both injunctive relief and damages. . . .

II

Our inquiry can be divided into four steps: did respondents engage in price fixing? If so, are their activities in interstate commerce or do they affect interstate commerce? If so, are the activities exempt from the Sherman Act because they involve a "learned profession"? If not, are the activities "state action" . . . and therefore exempt from the Sherman Act?

A . . .

A purely advisory fee schedule issued to provide guidelines, or an exchange of price information without a showing of an actual restraint on trade, would present us with a different question. The record here, however, reveals a situation quite different from what would occur under a purely advisory fee schedule. Here a fixed, rigid price floor arose from respondents' activities: every lawyer who responded to petitioners' inquiries adhered to the fee schedule, and no lawyer asked for additional information in order to set an individualized fee. The price information disseminated did not concern past standards, but rather minimum fees to be charged in future transactions, and those minimum rates were increased over time. The fee schedule was enforced through the prospect of professional discipline from the State Bar, and the desire of attorneys to comply with announced professional norms; the motivation to conform was reinforced by the assurance that other lawyers would not compete by underbidding. . . .

Moreover, in terms of restraining competition and harming consumers like petitioners the price-fixing activities found here are unusually damaging. A title examination is indispensable in the process of financing a real estate purchase, and since only an attorney licensed to practice in Virginia may legally examine a title, consumers could not turn to alternative sources for the necessary service. All attorneys, of course, were practicing under the constraint of the fee schedule. . . .

B

[The Court concluded that the services at issue affected interstate commerce and were therefore within the ambit of the antitrust laws.]

C . . .

In arguing that learned professions are not "trade or commerce" the County Bar seeks a total exclusion from antitrust regulation. Whether state regulation is active or dormant, real or theoretical, lawyers would be able to adopt anticompetitive practices with impunity. We cannot find support for the proposition that Congress intended any such sweeping exclusion. The nature of an occupation, standing alone, does not provide sanctuary from the Sherman Act, nor is the public-service aspect of professional practice controlling in determining whether §1 includes professions. Congress intended to strike as broadly as it could in §1 of the Sherman Act, and to read into it so wide an exemption as that urged on us would be at odds with that purpose. . . .

In the modern world it cannot be denied that the activities of lawyers play an important part in commercial intercourse, and that anticompetitive activities by lawyers may exert a restraint on commerce.

D

In Parker v. Brown, 317 U.S. 341 (1943), the Court held that an anticompetitive marketing program which "derived its authority and its efficacy from the legislative command of the state" was not a violation of the Sherman Act because the Act was intended to regulate private practices and not to prohibit a State from imposing a restraint as an act of government. Respondent

State Bar and respondent County Bar both seek to avail themselves of this so-called state-action exemption. . . .

The threshold inquiry in determining if an anticompetitive activity is state action of the type the Sherman Act was not meant to proscribe is whether the activity is required by the State acting as sovereign. Here we need not inquire further into the state-action question because it cannot fairly be said that the State of Virginia through its Supreme Court Rules required the anticompetitive activities of either respondent. . . .

III

We recognize that the States have a compelling interest in the practice of professions within their boundaries, and that as part of their power to protect the public health, safety, and other valid interests they have broad power to establish standards for licensing practitioners and regulating the practice of professions. We also recognize that in some instances the State may decide that "forms of competition usual in the business world may be demoralizing to the ethical standards of a profession." The interest of the States in regulating lawyers is especially great since lawyers are essential to the primary governmental function of administering justice, and have historically been "officers of the courts." In holding that certain anticompetitive conduct by lawyers is within the reach of the Sherman Act we intend no diminution of the authority of the State to regulate its professions. . . .

Reversed and remanded.

JUSTICE POWELL took no part in the consideration or decision of this case.

The State Bar argued that the Sherman Act did not apply. It wrote that "competition is inconsistent with the practice of a profession because enhancing profit is not the goal of professional activities." Rather, "the goal is to provide services necessary to the community." The Court shot that down: "The reason for adopting the fee schedule does not appear to have been wholly altruistic," it wrote. "The first sentence in respondent State Bar's 1962 Minimum Fee Schedule Report states: 'The lawyers have slowly, but surely, been committing economic suicide as a profession.'"

CASE NOTE: NORTH CAROLINA STATE BOARD OF DENTAL EXAMINERS v. FEDERAL TRADE COMMISSION

The profession in North Carolina State Board of Dental Examiners v. F.T.C., 574 U.S. 494 (2015), was dentistry, not law, but the decision carries implications for all professional regulation. We see again the Court's rejection of a state action defense where the state action was illusory. The decision was 6 to 3, with Justices Scalia and Thomas joining Justice Alito's dissent.

North Carolina had created a Board of Dental Examiners to regulate dentistry in the state. Six of its members were practicing dentists, one was a dental hygienist, and one was a consumer. Justice Kennedy wrote the majority opinion.

In the 1990's, dentists in North Carolina started whitening teeth. Many of those who did so, including 8 of the Board's 10 members during the period at issue in this case, earned substantial fees for that service. By 2003, nondentists arrived on the scene. They charged lower prices for their services than the dentists did. Dentists soon began to complain to the Board about their new competitors. Few complaints warned of possible harm to consumers. Most expressed a principal concern with the low prices charged by nondentists.

Responding to these filings, the Board opened an investigation into nondentist teeth whitening. A dentist member was placed in charge of the inquiry. Neither the Board's hygienist member nor its consumer member participated in this undertaking. The Board's chief operations officer remarked that the Board was "going forth to do battle" with nondentists. . . .

Starting in 2006, the Board issued at least 47 cease-and-desist letters on its official letterhead to nondentist teeth whitening service providers and product manufacturers. Many of those letters directed the recipient to cease "all activity constituting the practice of dentistry"; warned that the unlicensed practice of dentistry is a crime; and strongly implied (or expressly stated) that teeth whitening constitutes "the practice of dentistry." . . .

These actions had the intended result. Nondentists ceased offering teeth whitening services in North Carolina.

The Federal Trade Commission (FTC) challenged the Board's actions as "an anticompetitive and unfair method of competition" and eventually ordered the Board to stop sending cease-and-desist letters and to send certain notices to prior recipients. The Fourth Circuit ruled for the FTC and the Board appealed. Justice Kennedy's opinion affirmed, concluding that there was too little state action to exempt the Board from the antitrust laws.

The similarities between agencies controlled by active market participants and private trade associations are not eliminated simply because the former are given a formal designation by the State, vested with a measure of government power, and required to follow some procedural rules. *Parker* immunity does not derive from nomenclature alone. When a State empowers a group of active market participants to decide who can participate in its market, and on what terms, the need for supervision is manifest. The Court holds today that a state board on which a controlling number of decisionmakers are active market participants in the occupation the board regulates must satisfy [the] active supervision requirement [of California Retail Liquor Dealers Ass'n v. Midcal Aluminum, 445 U.S. 97 (1980)] . . .

The Court has identified only a few constant requirements of active supervision: The supervisor must review the substance of the anticompetitive decision, not merely the procedures followed to produce it; the supervisor must have the power to veto or modify particular decisions to ensure they accord with state policy; and the "mere potential for state supervision is not an adequate substitute for a decision by the State." Further, the state supervisor may not itself be an active market participant. In general, however, the adequacy of supervision otherwise will depend on all the circumstances of a case.

The Sherman Act protects competition while also respecting federalism. It does not authorize the States to abandon markets to the unsupervised control of active market participants, whether trade associations or hybrid agencies. If a State wants to rely on active market participants as regulators, it must provide active supervision if state-action immunity under *Parker* is to be invoked.

E. COURT-AWARDED FEES

1. *What's the Right Amount?*

With the advent of fee-shifting statutes in civil rights, discrimination, and environmental cases, and the concomitant growth of common fund cases and derivative claims (in which a lawyer brings an action on behalf of stake-holders in an entity, usually shareholders in a corporation), courts must often decide the size of the lawyer's fee if the plaintiff prevails. This trend has engendered a slew of judicial opinions and law review articles that seek to identify how fees should be determined. To the extent that courts are more generous, more lawyers will be willing to bring these cases. And if less generous, less willing. A critical difference between court-ordered fees in fee-shifting cases, whether on behalf of an individual or a class, and court-ordered fees in common fund and derivative cases is that in the former the opponent pays the fee (it does not come out of the client's recovery), whereas in the latter the client pays. Courts closely scrutinize these fee petitions.

Fee-Shifting Cases

In federal fee-shifting cases, the Supreme Court created a strong presumption in favor of a fee that reflects "the number of hours reasonably expended on the litigation multiplied by a reasonable hourly rate." (That number is today called the "lodestar.") Hensley v. Eckerhart, 461 U.S. 424 (1983). The result can yield a fee far above the client's recovery.

In a case under the Solid Waste Disposal Act and the Clean Water Act, the Supreme Court refused to permit percentage fee *enhancements* based on the results achieved. It rejected the argument that the lodestar does not adequately compensate lawyers for the risk that a case will fail and the lawyers will get nothing. City of Burlington v. Dague, 505 U.S. 557 (1992). This is the flip side of awarding large fees for small victories. Do lawyers want a fee bonus for good outcomes, but no fee reduction for modest ones? Probably they do. But Justice Scalia rejected that result. To "engraft this [enhancement] feature onto the lodestar model would be to concoct a hybrid scheme that resorts to the contingent-fee model to increase a fee award but not to reduce it."

That's right, isn't it? Traditional contingent fee lawyers get a percentage of the recovery if they win, which can be far greater than their lodestar, but it may also be far less or nothing if the recovery is small or they lose. Fee-shifting lawyers are in a different position. If they win they get a lodestar that can far exceed a modest recovery because they will have vindicated an important public policy, such as nondiscrimination or protection of a constitutional right. We pay them more than the market would pay in order to attract them to this important work. And like contingent fee lawyers, they get nothing if they lose. Each "business model" has an advantage and a disadvantage that the other does not.

Enhancement is not categorically forbidden in all fee-shifting cases. In Perdue v. Kenny A., 559 U.S. 542 (2010), a class of children challenged Georgia's foster care systems. They won and sought counsel fees. The Court held that "there is a 'strong presumption' that the lodestar figure is reasonable, but that presumption may be overcome in those rare circumstances in which the lodestar does not adequately take into account a factor that may properly be considered in determining a reasonable fee." The Court then noted that it "has never sustained an enhancement of a lodestar amount for performance" and cited various factors (e.g., "the novelty and complexity of a case," "the quality of an attorney's performance") that would *not* overcome the presumption. These factors should already be reflected in the lodestar. The import of the decision is that enhancement is possible in theory but highly remote in practice.

Common Fund and Derivative Cases

If a case is not brought under a fee-shifting statute, the fee is deducted from the fund the lawyer will have created for the client. In Americas Mining Corp. v. Theriault, 51 A.3d 1213 (Del. 2012), the Delaware Supreme Court explained how these fees are computed.

> Typically, successful derivative or class action suits which result in the recovery of money or property wrongfully diverted from the corporation . . . are viewed as fund creating actions. . . .
>
> In the United States, there are two methods of calculating fee awards in common fund cases: the percentage of the fund method and the lodestar method. . . .
>
> Today, after several years of experimentation with the lodestar method, the vast majority of courts of appeals now permit or direct courts to use the percentage method in common-fund cases.

Some federal courts have insisted on use of the percentage method for fixing fees in common fund and derivative cases. See Swedish Hosp. Corp. v. Shalala, 1 F.3d 1261 (D.C. Cir. 1993). Others leave it to the discretion of the trial judge. See Goldberger v. Integrated Res., 209 F.3d 43 (2d Cir. 2000) (recognizing that two circuits require the percentage method but holding, along with six other circuits, that district courts have discretion to use either the lodestar or the percentage method so long as the fee awarded is "reasonable").

Depending on the size of the client's recovery, awarding a lawyer her entire lodestar may eat up all or most of the recovery in a common fund or derivative case, leaving the client with little or nothing. By contrast, a fee based on a percentage of the recovery—say one-third or 40 percent—will leave most of the money to the plaintiffs. So a court using the lodestar method may award a lawyer less than the full lodestar to ensure that a reasonable amount remains for the client. The advantage for the lawyer is that the court can also award more than the lodestar to recognize skilled work and good results so long as enough remains for the client.

2. Settlement Conditioned on Fee Waiver

CASE NOTE: EVANS v. JEFF D.

In August 1980 the Idaho Legal Aid Society filed a class action challenging "the educational programs and the healthcare services" available to children in the care of the state "who suffer from emotional and mental handicaps." The Society quickly settled the educational claims, waiving its legal fees, but the healthcare claims remained. In March 1983, a week before trial, the defendants "offered virtually all of the injunctive relief [the class] had sought in their complaint." But the offer had a catch. It "included a provision for a waiver . . . of any claim to fees or costs," including those under §1988 ("the Civil Rights Attorney's Fees Award Act" or "Fees Act"). Charles Johnson, a Legal Aid attorney, "determined that his ethical obligation to his clients mandated acceptance of the proposal. The parties conditioned the waiver on approval by the District Court," which would have to approve the class settlement in any event.

The district court denied Johnson's motion for fees, but the Ninth Circuit reversed, holding that "the strong federal policy embodied in the Fees Act normally requires an award of fees to prevailing plaintiffs in civil rights actions, including those who have prevailed through settlement." When "attorney's fees are negotiated as part of a class action settlement, a conflict frequently exists between the class lawyers' interest in compensation and the class members' interest in relief." The circuit court therefore "disapproved simultaneous negotiation of settlements and attorney's fees" absent "unusual circumstances," not present here. In effect, its decision forced defendants to negotiate fees after negotiating settlement. Until then, the defendant would not know the full cost of the settlement.

The issues in Evans v. Jeff D., 475 U.S. 717 (1986), were challenging. They still are. Several interests are at play: those of the plaintiffs; the lawyers for the plaintiffs; the defendants; and future plaintiffs in being able to attract lawyers. Also to be considered was the congressional policy behind fee-shifting statutes. Often, those lawyers work for public interest law firms that do not (or legally cannot) take fees from their clients and whose budgets rely on court-awarded fees. Lawyers in private firms may decline civil rights cases if the defendant can avoid paying fees simply by making a conditional settlement offer that the plaintiff accepts.

Justice Stevens began his opinion (for himself and five others) by rejecting the argument that a settlement offer conditioned on fee waiver created an "ethical dilemma" for Johnson.

> Although respondents contend that Johnson, as counsel for the class, was faced with an "ethical dilemma" when petitioners offered him relief greater than that which he could reasonably have expected to obtain for his clients at trial (if only he would stipulate to a waiver of the statutory fee award), and although we recognize Johnson's conflicting interests between pursuing relief for the class and a fee for the Idaho Legal Aid Society, we do not believe that the "dilemma" was an "ethical" one in the sense that Johnson had to choose between conflicting duties under the prevailing norms of professional conduct. Plainly, Johnson had no *ethical* obligation to seek a statutory fee award. His ethical duty was to serve his clients loyally and competently. Since the proposal to settle the merits was more favorable than the probable outcome of the trial, Johnson's decision to recommend acceptance was consistent with the highest standards of our profession. The District Court, therefore, correctly concluded that approval of the settlement involved no breach of ethics in this case.

Justice Stevens then turned to an interpretation of the Fees Act. He concluded that the right to a fee belonged to the client, not the lawyer, and the client was free to waive it.

> The text of the Fees Act provides no support for the proposition that Congress intended to ban all fee waivers offered in connection with substantial relief on the merits. On the contrary, the language of the Act, as well as its legislative history, indicates that Congress bestowed on the "prevailing *party*" (generally plaintiffs) a statutory eligibility for a discretionary award of attorney's fees in specified civil rights actions. It did not prevent the party from waiving this eligibility any more than it legislated against assignment of this right to an attorney, such as effectively occurred here. Instead, Congress enacted the fee-shifting provision as "an integral part of the remedies necessary to obtain" compliance with civil rights laws, to further the same general purpose — promotion of respect for civil rights — that led it to provide damages and injunctive relief. The statute and its legislative history nowhere suggest that Congress intended to forbid *all* waivers of attorney's fees — even those insisted upon by a civil rights plaintiff in exchange for some other relief to which he is indisputably not entitled[20] — anymore than it intended to bar a concession on damages to secure broader injunctive relief. Thus, while it is undoubtedly true that Congress expected fee-shifting to attract competent counsel to represent

---

20. Judge Wald has described the use of attorney's fees as a "bargaining chip" useful to plaintiffs as well as defendants. . . .

citizens deprived of their civil rights, it neither bestowed fee awards upon attorneys nor rendered them nonwaivable or nonnegotiable; instead, it added them to the arsenal of remedies available to combat violations of civil rights, a goal not invariably inconsistent with conditioning settlement on the merits on a waiver of statutory attorney's fees.

Forbidding fee waivers as part of a settlement agreement would impede settlements, Stevens explained.

> Most defendants are unlikely to settle unless the cost of the predicted judgment, discounted by its probability, plus the transaction costs of further litigation, are greater than the cost of the settlement package. If fee waivers cannot be negotiated, the settlement package must either contain an attorney's fee component of potentially large and typically uncertain magnitude, or else the parties must agree to have the fee fixed by the court. Although either of these alternatives may well be acceptable in many cases, there surely is a significant number in which neither alternative will be as satisfactory as a decision to try the entire case.

Next, Stevens took up the argument that permitting fee waivers would frustrate the purpose of the Fees Act, which held out the prospect of fees to encourage lawyers to take civil rights cases.

> The Court of Appeals, respondents, and various *amici* supporting their position suggest . . . that the court's authority to pass on settlements, typically invoked to ensure fair treatment of class members, must be exercised in accordance with the Fees Act to promote the availability of attorneys in civil rights cases. Specifically, respondents assert that the State of Idaho could not pass a valid statute precluding the payment of attorney's fees in settlements of civil rights cases to which the Fees Act applies. From this they reason that the Fees Act must equally preclude the adoption of a uniform state-wide policy that serves the same end, and accordingly contend that a consistent practice of insisting on a fee waiver as a condition of settlement in civil rights litigation is in conflict with the federal statute authorizing fees for prevailing parties, including those who prevail by way of settlement. . . .
>
> We find it unnecessary to evaluate this argument, however, because the record in this case does not indicate that Idaho has adopted such a statute, policy, or practice. Nor does the record support the narrower proposition that petitioners' request to waive fees was a vindictive effort to deter attorneys from representing plaintiffs in civil rights suits against Idaho. It is true that a fee waiver was requested and obtained as a part of the early settlement of the education claims, but we do not understand respondents to be challenging that waiver . . . and they have not offered to prove that the petitioners' tactics in this case merely implemented a routine state policy designed to frustrate the objectives of the Fees Act. Our own examination of the record reveals no such policy. . . .
>
> What the outcome of this settlement illustrates is that the Fees Act has given the victims of civil rights violations a powerful weapon that improves their ability to employ counsel, to obtain access to the courts, and thereafter to vindicate their rights by means of settlement or trial. For aught that appears, it was the "coercive" effect of respondents' statutory right to seek a fee award

that motivated petitioners' exceptionally generous offer. Whether this weapon might be even more powerful if fee waivers were prohibited in cases like this is another question, but it is in any event a question that Congress is best equipped to answer. Thus far, the Legislature has not commanded that fees be paid whenever a case is settled. . . .

The judgment of the Court of Appeals is reversed.

Justice Brennan (for himself and Justices Marshall and Blackmun) dissented. As he saw it, allowing settlement offers conditioned on a fee waiver would inevitably frustrate the goals of the Fees Act.

It seems obvious that allowing defendants in civil rights cases to condition settlement of the merits on a waiver of statutory attorney's fees will diminish lawyers' expectations of receiving fees and decrease the willingness of lawyers to accept civil rights cases. . . .

[I]t does not require a sociological study to see that permitting fee waivers will make it more difficult for civil rights plaintiffs to obtain legal assistance. It requires only common sense. Assume that a civil rights defendant makes a settlement offer that includes a demand for waiver of statutory attorney's fees. The decision whether to accept or reject the offer is the plaintiff's alone, and the lawyer must abide by the plaintiff's decision. As a formal matter, of course, the statutory fee belongs to the plaintiff and thus technically the decision to waive entails a sacrifice only by the plaintiff. As a practical matter, however, waiver affects only the lawyer. Because "a vast majority of the victims of civil rights violations" have no resources to pay attorney's fees, lawyers cannot hope to recover fees from the plaintiff and must depend entirely on the Fees Act for compensation.[10] The plaintiff thus has no real stake in the statutory fee and is unaffected by its waiver. Consequently, plaintiffs will readily agree to waive fees if this will help them to obtain other relief they desire.[11] . . .

Of course, from the lawyer's standpoint, things could scarcely have turned out worse. He or she invested considerable time and effort in the case, won, and has exactly nothing to show for it. Is the Court really serious in suggesting that it takes a study to prove that this lawyer will be reluctant when, the following week, another civil rights plaintiff enters his office and asks for representation? Does it truly require that somebody conduct a test to see that legal aid services, having invested scarce resources on a case, will feel the pinch when they do not recover a statutory fee?

---

10. Nor can attorneys protect themselves by requiring plaintiffs to sign contingency agreements or retainers at the outset of the representation. *Amici* legal aid societies inform us that they are prohibited by statute, court rule, or Internal Revenue Service regulation from entering into fee agreements with their clients. Moreover, even if such agreements could be negotiated, the possibility of obtaining protection through contingency fee arrangements is unavailable in the very large proportion of civil rights cases which, like this case, seek only injunctive relief. . . .

11. This result is virtually inevitable in class action suits where, even if the class representative feels sympathy for the lawyer's plight, the obligation to represent the interests of absent class members precludes altruistic sacrifice. In class action suits on behalf of incompetents, like this one, it is the lawyer himself who must agree to sacrifice his own interests for those of the class he represents.

And, of course, once fee waivers are permitted, defendants will seek them as a matter of course, since this is a logical way to minimize liability. Indeed, defense counsel would be remiss *not* to demand that the plaintiff waive statutory attorney's fees. A lawyer who proposes to have his client pay more than is necessary to end litigation has failed to fulfill his fundamental duty zealously to represent the best interests of his client. Because waiver of fees does not affect the plaintiff, a settlement offer is not made less attractive to the plaintiff if it includes a demand that statutory fees be waived. Thus, in the future, we must expect settlement offers routinely to contain demands for waivers of statutory fees.

[Brennan's solution was to "permit simultaneous negotiation of fees and merits claims," but forbid plaintiffs to waive fees.]

The Effect of Evans v. Jeff D. on Civil Rights Class Actions

Stevens and Brennan predicted different consequences if civil rights defendants could make settlement offers conditioned on attorney fee waivers. A recent study investigated these predictions. It looked at civil rights cases filed in federal courts across the 30 years after Evans v. Jeff D. It concluded that the overall number of civil rights *cases* filed, which were in decline even before the opinion, did not further decline significantly. But the number of civil rights *class actions* did.

> *[O]verall* civil rights filings do not tell the full story of *Jeff D.* The case immediately preceded a collapse in new private civil rights *class action* filings, a collapse from which the civil rights class action bar has yet to fully recover. While, prior to *Jeff D.* the number of civil rights class actions filed annually in federal court had been trending steadily downward from its peak of 2022 new cases in 1976, with an average 9.2% annual decline from 1977 to 1986, the drop in new private filings after *Jeff D.* was nothing short of precipitous. . . . Not until 2003 did the civil rights class action filing rate reach pre-*Jeff D.* levels—and it did not stay there! Despite the passage of new civil rights legislation in the 1990s, including the Americans with Disabilities Act, since *Jeff D.* the annual filing rate for civil rights class actions has only equaled or exceeded the 1986 filing rate in only four out of thirty years.

William Fedullo, Classless and Uncivil: The Three-Decade Legacy of Evans v. Jeff D., 21 U. Pa. J. Const. L. 1349 (2019) (emphasis in original).

Questions and Comments About *Jeff D.*

Evans v. Jeff D. presents dilemmas for public interest law firms to this day. Did the Court reach the right result? It's complicated. The case turned on statutory interpretation and statutes can be amended.

1. By saying the fee belongs to the client, who can waive it, has Justice Stevens put the immediate interests of an individual plaintiff over the interests of future civil rights plaintiffs in being able to attract

competent counsel? Well, yes, he has, because the decision can affect the willingness of lawyers to take new civil rights cases. Lawyers will be out of luck if the defendant offers the client all she wants, but only if she waives a fee. Indeed, in a part of the opinion not included here, the majority acknowledged that a "tyranny of small decisions" could operate to shrink the pool of available civil rights lawyers but finds no "reason or documentation to support such a concern at the present time."

2. The anti-*Jeff D.* view is not without problems. If the client cannot waive the fee, the plaintiff's lawyer can impede a settlement the client finds attractive by refusing to accept the defendant's fee offer. She may demand more or refuse even to negotiate her fee until the client's claim is settled. Or she may offer to let the court decide. A defendant who wants to settle and who cares only how much it will cost, not where the money goes, might then be inclined to reduce the relief to the plaintiff (monetary or equitable) to fund a fee that it thinks the plaintiff's lawyer will accept or that the court may later award. The dissent's approach, in other words, can pit the lawyer's fee demand against the client's interest in the settlement and its size.

3. What about prohibiting simultaneous negotiation of the lawyer's fees and the plaintiff's claim? The court unanimously rejected that solution. In any event, it could lead the defendant who cares only about total cost to the same strategy as in the prior paragraph. The defendant will hold back enough to pay the anticipated fee demand or court order, probably erring on the high side.

4. In part of the dissent not included, Justice Brennan wrote that "it may be that civil rights attorneys can obtain agreements from their clients not to waive attorney's fees." Can the client *irrevocably* assign her fee rights to the lawyer? Clients get to make settlement decisions under Rule 1.2(a). While they can delegate that authority, they can also withdraw it. Consider Pony v. County of Los Angeles, 433 F.3d 1138 (9th Cir. 2006) (California law forbids an irrevocable assignment of §1988 fees). Of course, this strategy, even where allowed, may not help the legal services offices that are prohibited from entering fee agreements with clients.

5. Elsewhere, Justice Brennan wrote that the "Court's decision in no way limits the power of state and local bar associations to regulate the ethical conduct of lawyers," including by forbidding defense lawyers to demand fee waivers. This is true. In New Jersey, a defendant in a *state* law fee-shifting case may not demand a fee waiver by a public interest law firm as a condition of settlement, whether the relief offered the plaintiff is equitable or monetary. Pinto v. Spectrum Chems. & Lab. Prods., 985 A.2d 1239 (N.J. 2010) (citing the Brennan dissent in *Jeff D.*). But what would that accomplish if, as Justice Stevens held for federal cases, the fee belongs to the client, not the lawyer? Wouldn't a plaintiff's lawyer then be obliged to tell her clients that if they offer to waive

fees, which they may do, the defendant may be willing to sweeten its offer?

6. Justice Stevens rejected the argument that Johnson, the Legal Aid lawyer, faced an "ethical dilemma" when presented with a settlement offer conditioned on fee waiver. He wrote that Johnson's "ethical duty was to serve his clients loyally and competently." Well, of course, but that's too easy. Johnson had a conflict between his fee interest and his clients' goals. He had no "dilemma," however, because he had only one ethical way to respond to the conflict. Many conflicts are not as obvious and the dilemmas they create not as easy to resolve.

F. MANDATORY PRO BONO PLANS

"Should We Adopt Mandatory Pro Bono?"

The chief justice of your state's supreme court appoints you to chair a committee to study whether the court should adopt a mandatory pro bono rule for lawyers in the state. Right now, your state has Model Rule 6.1. Everything is on the table.

- Should the court require lawyers to do pro bono work?
- If not, should it follow the Florida and Illinois schemes, described next, which require lawyers to report their pro bono work in a publicly available form?
- If the committee does recommend mandatory pro bono or mandatory reporting, how should the court define "pro bono" work?
- Should a lawyer be able to satisfy the requirement with a cash payment?
- May a firm satisfy the requirement cumulatively or should the obligation be personal to each lawyer in the firm?

For as long as anyone can remember, tens of millions of Americans, both below and well above the poverty line, have been unable to afford a lawyer when confronted with civil legal problems. As stated at the start of this chapter, the Legal Services Corporation estimates that 86 percent of civil legal needs are unmet because people cannot afford lawyers. An indigent criminal defendant is guaranteed free counsel, although the quality ranges from poor to excellent. Civil litigants with low incomes may be able to find a lawyer in a legal services office, but these offices are underfunded and understaffed.

An ABA survey of self-help centers (August 2014) offers one picture of the problem. A self-help center is a place to which persons who will represent themselves in court can go for advice. The advice may come from lawyers, paralegals, or trained volunteers. Some states, including California and Illinois, have many centers relative to population. Some have none. One question on the ABA survey asked for the percentage of litigants who could pay the going rate for a lawyer in the center's community. The 68 percent of the 114 centers that answered this question said between 0 and 25 percent of persons in their community could pay the going rate.

The Model Rules address pro bono work in two interlocking ways. Rule 6.1 encourages but does not require lawyers to provide pro bono legal services and describes the work that will satisfy this aspiration. Rules 6.3 through 6.5 ease the conflict-of-interest rules for certain kinds of public interest work. The effect is to enable a lawyer to take on this work without thereby preventing the lawyer or her firm from accepting certain paying work. As a result, lawyers may be more willing to help at a legal services organization (Rule 6.3) or with law reform work (Rule 6.4).

In your research for the chief justice, you learn that Florida and Illinois have *voluntary* pro bono plans, which, however, require lawyers to report their pro bono activities. In Florida, lawyers may satisfy this voluntary provision each year by giving "twenty hours of pro bono legal service to the poor; or . . . contribut[ing] at least $350 to a legal aid organization." The annual report is mandatory and available to the public. Two judges dissented from the reporting requirements. Two other judges would have made the pro bono obligation mandatory. One judge dissented from the "buy-out" option. In re Amendments to Rules Regulating the Fla. Bar, 630 So. 2d 501 (Fla. 1993).

A federal challenge to the Florida scheme on due process grounds failed in Schwarz v. Kogan, 132 F.3d 1387 (11th Cir. 1998). Among other arguments, plaintiffs claimed that the mandatory reporting obligation converted the aspirational goals of the rule into a mandatory obligation because "private lawyers are implicitly coerced into satisfying the Rule's aspirations in order to preserve their professional 'honor' and ability to climb the professional and political ladder." In response, the court held that "even assuming that the reporting requirement may have some implicit coercive effect, and thereby motivates otherwise reluctant lawyers to honor their professional responsibility, this result justifiably furthers the Rule's legitimate purpose."

You find many articles arguing the virtues or vices of different pro bono plans. Following are excerpts from two of them, which can only touch on the authors' broader arguments. Professor Rhode challenges opponents' moral objection to mandatory pro bono and their separate claim that implementation of a pro bono plan with a mandatory component would be unworkable. Professor Macey predicts that mandatory pro bono will favor large law firms and wealthy lawyers over small firms and solo practitioners, and, perversely, may make pro bono clients even worse off. He rejects the argument that the bar's monopoly on the provision of legal services, which increases cost, justifies a rule requiring lawyers to do free work for those priced out of the market.

Deborah L. Rhode
CULTURES OF COMMITMENT: PRO BONO FOR
LAWYERS AND LAW STUDENTS

67 Fordham L. Rev. 2415 (1999)

The bar's response to inadequate access alternates between confession and avoidance. Some lawyers simply deny the data. Unburdened by factual support, they insist that no worthy cause goes unassisted, thanks to voluntary pro bono efforts, legal-aid programs, and contingent fee representation. A more common approach is to acknowledge the problem of unmet needs but to deny that mandatory pro bono service is the solution. In one representative survey, about sixty percent of California attorneys believed that poor people's access to legal assistance would continue to decline, but an equal number opposed minimum pro bono requirements.

Opponents raise both moral and practical objections. As a matter of principle, some lawyers insist that compulsory charity is a contradiction in terms. From their perspective, requiring service would undermine its moral significance and compromise altruistic commitments.

There are several problems with this claim, beginning with its assumption that pro bono service is "charity." As the preceding discussion suggested, pro bono work is not simply a philanthropic exercise; it is also a professional responsibility. Moreover, in the small number of jurisdictions where courts now appoint lawyers to provide uncompensated representation, no evidence indicates that voluntary assistance has declined as a result. Nor is it self-evident that most lawyers who currently make public-service contributions would cease to do so simply because others were required to join them. As to lawyers who do not volunteer but claim that required service would lack moral value, David Luban has it right: "You can't appeal to the moral significance of a gift you have no intention of giving." . . .

The stronger arguments against pro bono obligations involve pragmatic rather than moral concerns. Many opponents who support such obligations in principle worry that they would prove ineffective in practice. A threshold problem involves defining the services that would satisfy a pro bono requirement. If the definition is broad, and encompasses any charitable work for a nonprofit organization or needy individual, then experience suggests that poor people will not be the major beneficiaries. Most lawyers have targeted their pro bono efforts at friends, relatives, or matters designed to attract or accommodate paying clients. A loosely defined requirement is likely to assist predominately middle-class individuals and organizations such as hospitals, museums, and churches. By contrast, limiting a pro bono requirement to low-income clients who have been given preferred status in the ABA's current rule would exclude many crucial public-interest contributions, such as work for environmental, women's rights, or civil rights organizations. Any compromise effort to permit some but not all charitable groups to qualify for pro bono credit would bump up against charges of political bias.

A related objection to mandatory pro bono requirements is that lawyers who lack expertise or motivation to serve under-represented groups will not provide cost-effective assistance. In opponents' view, having corporate lawyers dabble in poverty cases will provide unduly expensive, often incompetent services. The performance of attorneys required to accept uncompensated appointments in criminal cases does not inspire confidence that unwillingly conscripted practitioners would provide acceptable representation. Critics also worry that some lawyers' inexperience and insensitivity in dealing with low-income clients will compromise the objectives that pro bono requirements seek to advance.

Requiring all attorneys to contribute minimal services of largely unverifiable quality cannot begin to satisfy this nation's unmet legal needs. Worse still, opponents argue, token responses to unequal access may deflect public attention from the fundamental problems that remain and from more productive ways of addressing them. Preferable strategies might include simplification of legal procedures, expanded subsidies for poverty law programs, and elimination of the professional monopoly over routine legal services.

Those arguments have considerable force, but they are not as conclusive as critics often assume. It is certainly true that some practitioners lack the skills and motivation necessary to serve those most in need of assistance. As Michael Millemann notes, however, the current alternative is scarcely preferable:

> Assume that after four years of college, three years of law school, and varying periods of law practice, some lawyers are "incompetent" to help the poor. . . . All this despairing assumption tells us is that the poor are far less competent to represent themselves, and do not have the readily available access to attaining competency that lawyers have. . . .

Moreover, mandatory pro bono programs could address concerns of cost-effectiveness through various strategies. One option is to allow lawyers to buy out of their required service by making a specified financial contribution to a legal-aid program. Another possibility is to give credit for time spent in training. Many voluntary pro bono projects have effectively equipped participants to provide limited poverty-law services through relatively brief educational workshops, coupled with well-designed manuals and accessible backup assistance.

A final objection to pro bono requirements involves the costs of enforcing them. Opponents often worry about the "Burgeoning Bureaucratic Boondoggle" that they assume would be necessary to monitor compliance. Even with a substantial expenditure of resources, it would be extremely difficult to verify the amount of time that practitioners reported for pro bono work or the quality of assistance that they provided.

Supporters of mandatory pro bono programs have responded with low-cost enforcement proposals that would rely heavily on the honor system. In the absence of experience with such proposals, their effectiveness is difficult to assess. There is, however, a strong argument for attempting to impose pro bono requirements even if they cannot be fully enforced. At the very least, such requirements would support lawyers who want to participate in public-interest projects but work in organizations that have failed to provide adequate resources or credit for these efforts. Many of the nation's most profitable law firms and leading corporate employers fall into that category. They could readily afford a greater pro bono commitment and a formal requirement might nudge them in that direction. As to lawyers who have no interest in public-interest work, a rule that allowed financial contributions to substitute for direct service could materially assist underfunded legal aid organizations.

Jonathan R. Macey
MANDATORY PRO BONO: COMFORT FOR THE POOR OR WELFARE FOR THE RICH?
77 Cornell L. Rev. 1115 (1992)

The reason lawyers ought not to be obliged to help the poor — indeed the reason forcing lawyers to serve the poor is odious and unethical — is that we can make both lawyers *and* the poor better off by abandoning mandatory pro bono and providing the poor with lump sum transfers of cash. In other words, if the rationale for mandatory pro bono is to help the poor, then it is a peculiarly bad way to provide assistance. Alternatively, mandatory pro bono may really be designed to serve some other purpose besides helping the poor. In fact, I will argue that the real effect of a mandatory pro bono system will be to transfer wealth from solo practitioners and lawyers in small- and medium-sized firms to lawyers in large firms.

I

MANDATORY PRO BONO AND THE POOR

Contrary to popular belief, mandatory pro bono will not help the poor. To understand why this is so, one must first understand that the real reason why the poor do not presently consume more legal services is because they are rational. Given their limited wealth, the poor simply would rather spend their money on other things. In other words, legal services are very, very low on a poor person's shopping list. Food is higher. Shelter is higher. Clothing is higher. And even after all of those expenses are covered, lawyers should not be surprised to learn that a poor person might choose to allocate his resources in ways other than hiring a lawyer — like buying a car or obtaining an education. . . .

Given a choice between $2500 in cash and twenty billable hours of legal services provided by a partner at a Wall Street law firm (valued at around $10,000), most people — middle class or poor — would take the $2500 in cash. . . .

Ironically, the increased consumption of legal services by the poor may actually harm the indigent rather than help them. For example, among the primary justifications for a regime of mandatory pro bono is that poor people need representation in landlord-tenant and matrimonial disputes.

Lawyers forced to do pro bono work will spend much of their time representing people involved in matrimonial disputes who are unable or unwilling to pay for legal representation. People getting divorced may decline to hire lawyers to represent them for a variety of reasons. The most plausible explanation for the failure of indigent people to hire lawyers in matrimonial disputes is that there are not enough assets in the matrimonial estate to justify the expense. A recent study by Marsha Garrison shows that 31 percent of divorcing couples in New York State had a net worth of less than $5000 and 18 percent of divorcing couples had a *negative* net worth. . . . With the possible exception of matrimonial work, lawsuits against landlords are expected to occupy the lion's share of the time that lawyers compelled to provide legal services for the poor would spend on mandatory pro bono. If more marginal lawsuits are brought against landlords because lawyers need something to do to fulfill their mandatory pro bono obligations, the landlords' costs of providing housing to the indigent inevitably will go up. As the cost of providing housing goes up, rents will increase, and the supply of housing for the poor will go down. The benefit that some poor people derive from having representation in landlord-tenant disputes must be weighed against the increased costs to tenants that will result from a regime of mandatory pro bono in which lawsuits are brought against landlords regardless of whether the expected benefits to the tenants outweigh the costs of the suit. . . .

II

MANDATORY PRO BONO AND TRANSFERS OF WEALTH WITHIN THE LEGAL PROFESSION . . .

Mandatory pro bono programs will help large law firms by increasing the demand for lawyers to defend suits brought under such programs. Lawyers forced to bring cases on behalf of poor people will usually be bringing them against defendants who must pay to hire lawyers to defend those suits. In other words, mandatory pro bono programs artificially expand society's demand for paid legal services. In particular, the demand for the services of lawyers at large firms who specialize in representing defendants will increase. As one commentator presciently has observed, "[W]henever clients who cannot pay get more legal services, clients who can pay need more legal services. This results in new business for the bar."

A mandatory pro bono requirement will increase the demand for lawyers in large law firms in other, subtler ways. First, under the New York plan [never adopted], lawyers at large law firms could credit the excess pro bono hours of some lawyers in the firm to meet the obligation of other lawyers in the firm. This flexibility will benefit large firms far more than small firms, because large firms can more easily afford to hire lawyers to specialize in pro bono work. In large firms the pro bono activities of these lawyers can be amortized over a large number of lawyers. In addition, at any given time, large firms predictably will have excess capacity in certain practice areas and no room for additional work in others. These large firms can ameliorate this problem by shifting the burden of pro bono work onto the shoulders of the lawyers with extra time in their schedules. This is a luxury that smaller, more specialized firms lack because all of the lawyers in such firms are likely to have slack times and busy times simultaneously.

Even if lawyers in large law firms were prohibited from assigning the burden of their pro bono obligations to other, more junior lawyers in the firm, satisfying the burdens of a mandatory pro bono obligation would still be easier for a large firm. Suppose, for example, that a solo practitioner is scheduled to make a court appearance on a particular day for a pro bono client. During that day the solo practitioner will be unable to represent any of his paying clients. By contrast, a large law firm simply can reassign personnel (many of whom will have expertise in the relevant area of law) to handle the work of the absent lawyer. . . .

Mandatory pro bono programs also benefit large firms at the expense of smaller firms because under some pro bono plans, large firms can fulfill their obligations by doing work for foundations and other low-pay/high-prestige clients that such firms normally represent. Similarly, unlike small firms and solo practitioners, large firms can use mandatory pro bono programs as vehicles for training associates because younger lawyers working for large firms that deal almost exclusively with very high stakes legal issues understandably do not get as much courtroom experience or contact with paying clients as lawyers at smaller firms that litigate smaller stakes issues.

III

THE GOOD OLD DAYS: THE LEGAL PROFESSION AS SOMETIME MONOPOLY

A final argument in favor of mandatory pro bono is that lawyers are professionals, and as such, their license to practice law comes with certain societal obligations. In less prosaic terms, the licensing requirements of the bar have created barriers to entry that permit lawyers to earn supercompetitive profits. According to this argument, lawyers are under an obligation to perform legal services for the poor in order to compensate society for the social losses associated with their monopoly position. Since the legal profession's monopoly allows it to charge above-market prices, this monopoly status permits lawyers to transfer wealth from the rest of society to themselves. Mandatory pro bono requirements merely effectuate a retransfer back to society of this initial wealth transfer. But this argument is completely flawed.

If at any time in history the legal profession was a monopoly, it is not any longer. If one hundred years ago lawyers erected barriers to entry that enabled them to obtain monopoly profits, those were short-term gains that are not presently being enjoyed by members of the profession. This is because nonlawyers, observing the economic rents earned by a cartelized legal profession, would begin expending the resources and developing the human capital necessary to enter the profession and obtain these rents. Thus any gains from cartelizing the legal profession were lost long ago by competition from new entrants.

Despite arguments that mandatory pro bono requirements would violate the Thirteenth Amendment ("involuntary servitude") or constitute a taking of property without just compensation, courts have upheld judicial power to order a lawyer to work for free on a particular matter. This is not about a mandatory pro bono *plan*. Rather it is about a court assignment in narrow circumstances. Naranjo v. Thompson, 809 F.3d 793 (5th Cir. 2015), a Section 1983 civil rights case, concerned one of those circumstances. After stating the courts' "inherent power to appoint counsel . . . at least in the criminal defense context," the court held that the power was broader.

> So too with the power to compel attorneys to represent indigent civil rights plaintiffs. The possibility of such an appointment arises only when an indigent plaintiff has colorable claims that will not receive a meaningful hearing without counsel (i.e. exceptional circumstances exist) and when all other options for making an appointment have failed. Under such conditions, a court cannot carry out its duties without ordering an attorney to take the case. "Even the most dedicated trial judges are bound to overlook meritorious cases without the benefit of an adversary presentation."
>
> The inherent power to make a compulsory appointment is also rooted in courts' duty to maintain the functioning of the civil justice system as a whole. "[T]he bar's monopoly over legal services entails obligations to court and society." These obligations often take the form of ethical duties to the profession as opposed to legally enforceable requirements, but some bar associations give force to those ethical duties by mandating that attorneys perform a certain quantity of *pro bono* work for indigents each year, and the Supreme Court has approved of such arrangements. Courts have a critical role to play as well. Inherent powers exist where necessary to serve the proper administration of justice. "The court's responsibility for the administration of justice would be frustrated were it unable to enlist or require the services of those who have, by virtue of their license, a monopoly on the provision of such services."
>
> Some courts and commentators have raised constitutional concerns with compelled *pro bono* appointments, particularly under the Fifth Amendment Takings Clause and the Thirteenth Amendment prohibition of involuntary servitude. This circuit has expressly rejected these concerns.

Self-Assessment Questions

1. Tony Rozenzwei is representing Muriel Villenova in a commercial litigation. Muriel is the plaintiff. She claims that Micah Button, the defendant, underpaid her for her share of the profits in a limited partnership. Micah was the general partner. She claims $600,000. Tony's retainer agreement with Muriel provides that he will charge $375 hourly. Muriel paid him a $10,000 retainer. Tony has so far spent 42 hours on the matter for total time charges of $15,750. Tony figures that taking the case up to but not including trial will require a total of 100 hours. Trial will require another 100 hours. So Tony's total anticipated fee through trial is $75,000. Unexpectedly, discovery turns up evidence that Muriel is owed, conservatively, $1.5 million. Tony wants to switch from an hourly rate to a contingent fee of 25 percent, although he recognizes that if the case goes to trial, Muriel may lose. How can Tony properly change the terms of the fee agreement if he wants to take that risk?

2. You've been appointed by the court to study and advise on whether lawyers in the state who bill for services based on time should be required to bill in tenths of an hour increments rather than quarter of an hour increments. What do you advise? And if the court decides not to impose that restriction, what if any restriction should it impose on lawyers who bill in quarter-hour increments?

3. You work for the chairperson of the state legislature's judiciary committee. The committee is about to pass a law that gives employees who inform the state of employer fraud against the state (whistleblowers) a claim if they suffer retaliation in employment as a result. The statute will require the defendant (employer) to pay the legal fees of the whistleblower if he or she prevails in a retaliation claim. Your boss has read Evans v. Jeff D., which dealt with federal law. The state can adopt the same rules as in *Jeff D.* or different rules with regard to the timing of the negotiation of the amount of a prevailing plaintiff's right to a legal fee. What do you recommend?

PART TWO

CONFLICTS OF INTEREST

V

Concurrent Conflicts of Interest

No man can serve two masters: for either he will hate the one, and love the other; or else he will hold to the one, and despise the other. Ye cannot serve God and mammon.
> —Matthew 6:24, King James Bible, sometimes quoted by plaintiffs' lawyers in actions against law firms based on conflicts of interest

Loyalty and independent judgment are essential elements in the lawyer's relationship to a client.
> —Model Rule 1.7 cmt. [1]

I never had a conflict. I did what was best for me.
> —Possibly apocryphal comment of a disbarred lawyer

Conflicts of Interest: Definition and Context

Even if in your legal career you confront no other rule, you will almost certainly confront the conflict rules. They will appear occasionally or often, depending on the nature of your practice. They will arise in your own work or the work of colleagues. They will surface in the behavior of your opponents. You need to understand these rules not only to protect yourself, but also to protect your clients from the conflicts of their other former or current lawyers. You (or your law office) will also need a system for monitoring and avoiding conflicts, including the ability to recognize them when they arise. For any but the simplest offices, detailed electronic recordkeeping is essential.

Conflicts come in many shapes and sizes. The next few pages give you a road map for the balance of this chapter and chapter 6. Their lessons will be repeated, but an initial view from 1,000 feet up can aid understanding when we move to ground level.

Despite the variety of conflicts, general definitions are possible. Here is the one for *concurrent* conflicts from Restatement §121:

> A conflict of interest is involved if there is a *substantial* risk that the lawyer's representation of the client would be *materially and adversely* affected by the lawyer's own interests or by the *lawyer's duties* to another current client, a former client, or a third person. (Italics added.)

The sentence talks about a *risk* to the representation. A finding of a conflict does not mean that the lawyer *will* succumb to the conflict and harm the client in fact, only that the risk that she will do so, perhaps unwittingly, is *substantial.* Later, we will see that often a client can give informed consent to a conflict and run this risk, trusting that the lawyer will act properly.

There's something biblical about conflicts. Or, if you prefer, behavioral. We're trying to quantify temptation. How much risk is too much? It depends on how we define "substantial," "materially," and "adversely." Critical, too, is what we recognize to be the "lawyer's duties" in the particular matter. The sentence has a lot packed into it. It is also written at a high level of generality. If I gave you only a set of facts and that sentence, you might find it difficult or impossible to say if the situation presented a conflict of interest.

The same is true for Rule 1.7(a)(2), which tells us that a current client conflict exists if

> there is a *significant risk* that the representation of one or more clients will be *materially limited* by the lawyer's *responsibilities* to another client, a former client or a third person or by a personal interest of the lawyer. (Italics added.)

Rule 1.7(a)(1) is narrower. It says a lawyer has a conflict if "the representation of one client will be *directly adverse* to another client." (Italics added.) But "directly adverse" is not defined in the rule.

These definitions state objective tests. They say nothing about an individual lawyer's integrity or her ability to resist conflicting interests. They simply state risks that are forbidden without informed client consent when allowed.

You might wonder why we try to outlaw temptation. Why not, instead, punish lawyers who succumb to it and actually betray a client, which we also do? There are two reasons:

- Sometimes it is better to have a prophylactic rule that reduces the risk of misbehavior rather than try to discover and prove the misbehavior later. True, a prophylactic rule may result in false positives (prohibiting work even though nothing bad would have occurred). But with no rule, a lawyer's transgression may escape detection. Because most conflicts can be eliminated with informed client consent, we opt for a prophylactic rule that reduces risk as the default and allow lawyers and clients to displace it.
- The second aim of conflict rules is to encourage client trust and candor. Clients may withhold both if they know that their lawyers may, without telling them, accept conflicting work, either while representing them or later.

In this chapter we review varieties of *concurrent* conflicts—interests that conflict with a client's interests during the representation. In chapter 6, we turn to *successive* conflicts. The difference is *temporal*. Ethics rules protect against different risks to a former client's interests than they do to those of a current client. Former clients get less protection. Complicating matters, as we'll see, it is not always evident whether a client is a former client or still a client.

A lawyer caught in a conflict faces a number of unhappy possibilities. Discipline is one, although disciplinary committees seem to recognize that the technical nature of many (but not all) conflicts makes them inappropriate candidates for discipline, especially given the availability of other remedies. Conflicts can lead to disqualification from a representation, with attendant embarrassment and cost, delay of a client's cause, negative publicity, fee forfeiture, and civil liability. In a rare case, failure to reveal a conflict can be a crime. United States v. Gellene, 182 F.3d 578 (7th Cir. 1999) (upholding perjury conviction of large law firm partner whose sworn declaration and oral testimony to bankruptcy court failed to reveal firm's representation of clients with conflicting interests).

As if all this were not daunting enough, most conflict rules have no mens rea requirement. They seem to be absolute liability rules. At least, that's how they read. A lawyer may violate them believing, in good faith, that she had no conflict. One important exception concerns *imputed* conflicts—a conflict that arises only because the conflict of one lawyer is deemed also to be a conflict for her office colleagues. In other words, partner *A* may have a conflict only because her partner *B* has a conflict. Rule 1.10(a) forbids a lawyer "knowingly" to accept certain client work that a conflicted colleague would have to decline. Without such knowledge, the lawyer is spared discipline, but her firm still risks disqualification, loss of a fee, and civil liability.

Here are nine perspectives from which to view conflict rules.

First: Current Client Conflicts. A lawyer may find her loyalties divided between two or more current clients. For example, a lawyer for co-defendants in a civil or criminal case may discover that one wants to blame the other. Or the prosecutor may tell a lawyer that she is prepared to offer one of two clients a generous plea bargain in exchange for testimony against the other. A lawyer representing two clients wishing to form a business may find that she cannot draft a partnership agreement or bylaw provisions without disadvantaging one of them. A lawyer may be asked to represent Joe in litigation against Sue, but a conflicts check reveals that Sue is a client of the lawyer's firm on other matters.

Concurrent conflicts need not be between or among clients. A lawyer may have personal interests that pose a loyalty threat. A lawyer whose wife has a large stock investment in a company or who is on its board may not be able to represent a plaintiff wishing to sue the company. A lawyer whose client wishes to challenge a tax regulation that gives the lawyer's daughter a generous benefit may be conflicted.

These examples all raise issues about the lawyer's ability to be loyal to one or more clients and, to a lesser extent, about danger to client confidences. Comment [1] to Rule 1.7 uses the word "loyalty." Whereas Rule 1.7(a) offers a generic definition of concurrent lawyer-client conflicts, Rule 1.8 addresses specific concurrent conflicts that experience tells us recur.

Second: Former (or Successive) Client Conflicts. The term "successive conflicts" may sound like a self-contradiction. Do you really have a duty to former clients to avoid conflicts after the work is done? Yes. Maybe long after. Consider a lawyer who successfully represented client *A* in securing a patent. Later, client *B* retains the lawyer to challenge the patent's validity. The duty of loyalty to client *A* prevents the lawyer from seeking to invalidate the patent that she secured for *A*. Rule 1.9(a). In addition, the lawyer will likely have gained confidential information about the patent that could help *B* in its challenge. If the lawyer reveals or uses this information, she will violate Rule 1.9(c). On the other hand, if client *B* seeks to sue former client *A* for violating a commercial lease, there should be no problem because the two matters—securing the patent and the lease claim—are entirely unrelated. As we see in chapter 6, "unrelated" has a specific meaning in the world of former client conflicts.

Third: Imputed Conflicts. If we conclude that a lawyer is prevented from representing a client because of a current or former client conflict, should we nevertheless permit her partner to accept the representation? Or should we instead *impute* the lawyer's conflicted status to partners, associates, and office colleagues? The Rules do impute client conflicts within a law firm. Rule 1.10(a). "Law firm" is defined in Rule 1.0(c).

Matters become more complicated, however, if a lawyer represented a former client while in a different law firm and has since changed firms (a *lateral* lawyer). Will her conflict *travel* with her? Yes. But will it also be imputed to her new colleagues? Under the Model Rules, the answer is no *if* the new firm timely screens the new lawyer and provides certain notices. Rule 1.10(a)(2). Rules in some jurisdictions do not recognize screens to avoid imputation of lateral lawyer conflicts or do so in limited circumstances.

Fourth: Government-Lawyer Conflicts. Lawyers who work for government and move to the private sector and those who leave the private sector to work for government introduce us to "the revolving door." Rule 1.11's screening provisions enable former government lawyers to work in the private sector without imputing their conflicts to their new colleagues.

Fifth: Lawyer-Witness Conflicts. A problem arises when a lawyer for a litigation client will or should be a witness, for either the client or the opposing side. See Rule 3.7. This *advocate-witness* rule seeks to avoid a conflict between the lawyer's interest in being an advocate and the interest of the client, the adversary, or the system of justice in having the lawyer testify. With narrow exceptions, a lawyer cannot occupy both roles. However, the advocate-witness conflict is not necessarily imputed to the lawyer's colleagues.

Sixth: Organizational Lawyer Conflicts.   The same conflict rules that apply when the client is a biological person apply when the client is an organization. But organizational clients pose additional issues. A lawyer for an organization must work through its constituents—board members, officers, and other employees. Conflicts can develop if the lawyer represents both the company and a constituent. Even if the company is the sole client, its officers decide an in-house lawyer's status (salary, title). They may have interests that are adverse to the company, creating a lawyer-client conflict. See Rule 1.13 and chapter 10.

Seventh: Conflicts in Conflict Rules.   Conflict rules vary among American jurisdictions. When a dispute touches more than one jurisdiction and their conflicts rules (or indeed any other rules) differ, a court may need to decide which rules apply. See Rule 8.5, which we can think of as a "conflict of rules" rule. Further, federal courts need not apply the conflict rules of the states in which they sit. The Fifth Circuit has held that "[m]otions to disqualify are substantive motions. Therefore, they are decided under federal law." The court would look to "norms embodied in the Model Rules and the Model Code" as well as local rules, which may differ. FDIC v. U.S. Fire Ins. Co., 50 F.3d 1304 (5th Cir. 1995).

Eighth: Conflict Rules as Default Rules.   Despite all the ink and labor that has gone into fashioning and interpreting the conflict rules, it turns out that lawyers and clients may remove nearly all of them in civil matters if the client gives *informed consent,* as defined in Rule 1.0(e). But the door swings both ways. A client may demand *more* protection than the Rules provide. Why would lawyers agree to greater restrictions on their autonomy? Money. A firm that is offered a big piece of Apple's legal work, for example, might happily agree to Apple's demand that the firm not represent Apple's competitors while Apple is a client. In criminal matters, informed consent can remove many conflicts, subject, however, to the Sixth Amendment. See part B1, below.

Ninth: The Competing Interests.   As you think about the issues raised in this and the next chapter, keep in mind how the scope of these rules, especially those dealing with client conflicts, can affect lawyers and clients.

- The greater the number of matters that a lawyer or firm is forbidden to accept, the greater the number of clients who will be denied counsel of choice and the greater the disincentive for lawyers to specialize in a narrow area of law or the problems of a specific industry (because the client base will be smaller).
- Conflict rules encourage firms to venture beyond their historical office locations in search of new clients who do not present conflicts.
- If the rules do not allow screening of lateral lawyers to avoid imputation of conflicts, or permit screening only in limited circumstances, law firms may be reluctant to hire laterally.
- The narrower the conflict rules, on the other hand, the less protection they will afford clients or former clients, who may suffer (or may believe they will suffer) from a breach of confidentiality or an act of disloyalty.

If clients begin to fear the loyalty of their lawyers or the sanctity of their communications, we risk weakening the trust on which the lawyer-client relationship depends.

As in much of law, the trick is to find the right balance between too broad and too narrow a definition of conflicts. Complicating that effort is the fact that the conflict rules may be abused for strategic advantage. A person who wants to deny a particular firm's expertise to an anticipated future adversary might retain the firm with that goal in mind. The broader the scope of the eventual disqualification, the easier it will be to do this. Stories go around about a husband or wife who, secretly planning a divorce, consults the five most prominent matrimonial lawyers in town, thereby hoping to prevent their spouse from retaining them. The film *Marriage Story* dramatized the tactic. (A judge who finds that a litigant has done this can refuse to disqualify the consulted lawyers.) For an approach to these and other policy issues from an economic perspective, see Jonathan Macey & Geoffrey Miller, An Economic Analysis of Conflict of Interest Regulation, 82 Iowa L. Rev. 965 (1997).

A. CLIENT-LAWYER CONFLICTS

1. A Lawyer's Business and Financial Interests

Lawyer. Realtor. Any Problem?

"Dear Ethics Advisory Committee:

"I request an opinion on the following facts. Can I do what I plan to do and if so, under what circumstances? I used to be a real-estate broker. I made good money. But the real estate market slowed during the financial crisis. I was only four years out of college, so I went to law school. For the last six years I've had a general practice, representing individuals on personal matters and advising small business people. Meanwhile, the real estate market has picked up, and the realtors are just raking it in as brokers for buyers or sellers. I did a closing yesterday on a $500,000 house. My fee was $5,000, and the two brokers divided $30,000. Can you believe it?

"I still have my real estate license so I figure why not do some brokering along with the lawyering. If I hear that one of my law clients wishes to sell or buy a house, I can agree to be her broker and then be her lawyer on the sale or purchase. The way I see it, we have the same goal. Get the house bought or sold. I can also offer to be the broker for buyers or sellers who are not clients and then offer to become their lawyer if they make a deal. Before I go ahead, I wanted to get your opinion.

"Sincerely yours,

"Melanie Winterbottom, Esq."

The following case and note material will help you advise Melanie Winterbottom. Melanie's business plan for current clients who may hire her as their broker and then as their lawyer is governed by Rules 1.8(a) and 1.7(a)(2), respectively. Her work for buyers or sellers who hire her first as a broker and then as their lawyer is governed by Rule 1.7(a)(2). You should be able to identify how each rule operates in each circumstance. How can Melanie satisfy Rule 1.8(a)? What are the conflict risks under Rule 1.7(a)(2)?

In re Neville is based on DR 5-104(A) of the former Code. Arizona now has Rule 1.8(a), which is even more demanding. The case has perfect facts for illustrating the risks of lawyer-client business deals and how easy it can be to violate the rule with what might be the best of intentions.

IN RE NEVILLE

147 Ariz. 106, 708 P.2d 1297 (1985)

FELDMAN, JUSTICE.

[Attorney Neville represented Bly in real estate deals but not the one at issue here. Bly was "a licensed real estate broker" and "a knowledgeable and sophisticated real estate investor." Neville purchased options in one of Bly's properties. Thereafter, Neville, Bly, and a third party entered into a contract, drafted by Neville, whereby the Bly property in which Neville had an option would go to the third party, the third party's property would go to Neville, and Neville would give Bly a promissory note. "Bly created the substantive terms [for these transfers], and respondent [Neville] accepted these terms with no negotiation."]

A.

WAS BLY RESPONDENT'S "CLIENT?" . . .

We think it quite likely that Bly was told or at least knew that respondent, the buyer, was not also undertaking to act as Bly's attorney [in these real estate transactions].

However, Bly's knowledge does not resolve the question of whether respondent was engaged in a business transaction in which his interests were adverse to those of his "client." The rule does not expressly limit its applicability to situations in which the lawyer represents the client in the very transaction in which their interests differ. We believe that the rule should not be so limited for several reasons. First, the rule is grounded in the fiduciary duty owed by an attorney to his client. That duty continues beyond the completion of any particular matter which the attorney undertakes for the client. The fiduciary duty arises when the attorney-client relationship is established and continues until it is abandoned. Abandonment is found when the lawyer's influence over the client has dissipated. Thus, DR 5-104 is applicable "as long as the influence arising from an attorney-client relationship continues." Second, the policy expressed by DR 5-104 is based on the realization that those who consider themselves clients come to depend upon the confidentiality and fairness arising from their relationships with their attorneys. They do not take a transactional approach to these relationships, turning their confidence on and off at the end of each transaction. Clients can be expected to assume that one whom they have come to look upon as "their lawyer" will protect them or, at least, not harm them. A lawyer's analytical training may permit expansion or limitation of professional obligations as circumstances warrant, but clients are usually neither required nor trained to make so careful an analysis. In any event, the profession prefers that its clients continue to repose confidence in their lawyers even after the immediate case has been finished, partly, no doubt, in the expectation that when the next case arises the clients will return. A third objective served by the rule is the hope that clients will obtain full disclosure on which to base their decision in all transactions. This objective is not served by a narrow, transactional application of the rule to situations in which the attorney is formally acting as counsel for the client. . . .

It is appropriate to note at this point that the evidence does not permit a finding that respondent intended to defraud his client. We do not believe this to be of consequence. The rule contains no words which limit its applicability to cases where scienter is shown. The rule is not intended to deter and punish actual fraud alone. . . .

B.

DID BLY EXPECT RESPONDENT TO EXERCISE HIS PROFESSIONAL JUDGMENT FOR BLY'S PROTECTION?

The resolution of this question is substantially controlled by the determination of the existence of the attorney-client relationship. It is natural and proper for a client with a longstanding business relationship with a lawyer to feel that the lawyer is to be trusted, will not act unfairly, and will protect him against danger. This is true even though he knows that the lawyer is not representing him in the particular transaction and the lawyer is drawing papers for the use of both parties. . . .

C.

DID RESPONDENT MAKE FULL DISCLOSURE AND OBTAIN BLY'S KNOWING AND VOLUNTARY CONSENT?

We assume that respondent actually did tell Bly—or Bly realized—that respondent was not acting as Bly's attorney in the transaction in question, and that Bly should get independent counsel. Is this the "full disclosure" required by the rule? We think not. The words "I am not representing you in this matter" may convey a great deal to another lawyer, but their full legal import will escape most laymen. The lay person may realize that the lawyer is not representing him and that he will not have to pay for legal services, but he may not recognize that he is in a situation where he must protect himself from his own lawyer. Justifiably, he may continue to repose confidence in the person who usually acts as "his lawyer" and feel that he can be trusted to do nothing unfair or harmful. In short, the confidence which lawyers wish to engender in their clients may still exist and the consequent influence may extend to the transaction. We believe, therefore, that the requirement of "full disclosure" means much more than advising the client that he is not being represented in the particular transaction.

Thus, even accepting respondent's version of the disclosure, he failed to make full disclosure as required by the Disciplinary Rule. We adopt the view of the cases which hold that full disclosure requires not only that the lawyer make proper disclosure of non-representation, but that he also must disclose every circumstance and fact "which the client should know to make an intelligent decision concerning the wisdom of entering the agreement." The rule is strict. The lawyer must give the client that information which he would have been obliged to give if he had been counsel rather than interested party, and the transaction must be as beneficial to the client as it would have been had the client been dealing with a stranger rather than with his lawyer. Thus, "full disclosure" requires not only a full explanation of the divergence in interest between the lawyer and the client and an explanation about the need to seek independent legal advice, but also "a detailed explanation of the risks and disadvantages to the client which flow from the agreement." The "consent" after "full disclosure" required by DR 5-104(A) must be the client's consent, after full explanation, to all terms that are either advantageous to the lawyer or disadvantageous to the client.

We believe . . . the agreement drawn by respondent contained terms that were, to say the least, disadvantageous to Bly. These should have been called to his attention, explained and removed from the agreement unless Bly had some reason for wanting the terms to be included. [The court here outlines noneconomic terms of Neville's promissory note and concludes that "no respectable practitioner would have allowed a seller to accept." For example, speaking of Neville's obligations on a promissory note he gave Bly, the court wrote:

> [Neville] is to pay 8% interest in semi-annual payments, but there are no provisions for remedies in the event of default. [Bly] is not given the right to accelerate the due date of the principal, nor increase the rate of interest after default. Thus, if [Neville] should default on an interest payment, [Bly's] only remedy is consecutive suits and recoveries for each payment of delinquent interest as it comes due.]

We believe that respondent should have called such problems to Bly's attention and should have explained why they were adverse to Bly's interests. Respondent argues, however, that the terms of the transaction were set by Bly and that he should not be subject to discipline for mere acquiescence.

We disagree. First, although Bly may have outlined the transaction (including the concept of precomputed interest, payment of principal on sale and the like), respondent drafted the actual agreement between himself and a client with whom he had an ongoing relationship; he was obligated to be fair to and protect his client. The client had no duty to foresee all the dangers inherent in the deal which he had outlined. Respondent's fiduciary duty required that he take no advantage except with his client's "consent" after "full disclosure." . . .

Respondent is censured.

A Lawyer's Financial Interests

A lawyer's financial deals with a current client must comply with the substantive and procedural requirements of Rule 1.8(a). This is true, as in *Neville,* even if the lawyer is not representing the client on that very deal and the client knows it. Separately, apart from Rule 1.8(a), a lawyer's own interests in a matter may conflict with the interests of the client who the lawyer is representing in that matter. Rule 1.7(a)(2). These rules operate independently. Some situations will trigger one or the other; some will implicate both. Rule 1.8(a) alone would govern the facts in *Neville* because Bly was not Neville's client on the land swap. If Neville were also representing Bly on the land swap, then both Rule 1.8(a) *and* Rule 1.7(a)(2) would govern his behavior. Let's take the two rules seriatim.

Deals with Clients

Rule 1.8(a) applies whenever lawyers "knowingly acquire an ownership, possessory, security or other pecuniary interest adverse to a client." Neville did that. It also includes taking a lien in a client's property, which lawyers sometimes do to protect their fee. ABA Opinion 02-427. It includes loans to (or more often from) clients. In re Torre, 127 A.3d 690 (N.J. 2015) (one-year suspension of lawyer who borrowed $89,250 from an "elderly, unsophisticated client" without complying with Rule 1.8(a)). And, as discussed in chapter 4B, the rule is broad enough to encompass fee agreements first entered or revised *after* creation of the professional relationship, which is probably the most common example of a lawyer-client financial arrangement.

Bly's real-estate sophistication—and Neville's lack of it—did not help Neville. Nor did it matter that Neville accepted without objection the economic terms Bly dictated. The court stressed that the deal's nonfinancial terms were entirely one-sided, including the terms of Bly's promissory note.

Neville was not representing Bly on the land swap and Bly knew it. Let's assume that Neville was not doing any other work for Bly at the time and had done no work for him for several months. Rule 1.8(a) could still apply. Why?

Interests Adverse to Clients

A lawyer's financial or other interests in a client matter may create conflicts with the client's interests in that matter. Rule 1.7(a)(2). Informed consent can avoid this conflict. The lawyers in the two cases following not only failed to get informed consent, they hid the conflicting interests. Their conflicts are less obvious (and so more important to study) than the one Melanie Winterbottom would have if she acted as both broker and lawyer for the buyer or seller of a home.

In In re Hager, 812 A.2d 904 (D.C. 2002), the respondent (a law professor) and his co-counsel cut a deal with the opposing client for a confidential payment as part of the settlement of their clients' claim. The court described Hager's conflict this way:

> In early 1997, Debra Duke and Erika Littlewood, both health care professionals, contacted respondent. They discussed with him pursuing legal action against Warner-Lambert Co. with respect to its head-lice shampoo Nix. According to Duke and Littlewood, Nix was ineffective in eradicating head lice because a Nix-resistant strain of lice had evolved. . . .
>
> The evidence showed that during negotiations Warner-Lambert offered $225,000 to [respondent and his co-counsel] as long as they promised to keep the fact and amount of payment confidential. If respondent had rejected the confidentiality requirement and had waived his fee instead, his clients still would have received the relief provided by the Settlement Agreement. Nevertheless, respondent agreed to the secret fee payment.
>
> Respondent faced a classic conflict of interest—his interest in maximizing his fee versus his clients' interest in maximizing the amount paid to them. That it occurred in the midst of secret settlement negotiations meant the conflict was even more pronounced.
>
>> Any settlement represents a total value figure that one party is willing to pay to end the controversy. Attorneys' fees, even though they may not be technically deducted from the amount paid to the litigants, represent an integral part of the overall amount that the settling party is willing to pay, and as such, they have a direct effect on the net amount that will ultimately be paid to the litigants [quoting precedent].

Hager argued that there was no conflict because the clients got everything they wanted and would not have been entitled to the secret fee in any event. The court held that Hager's theory

> rests on two unsupportable foundations. First, the Board [of Professional Responsibility] explicitly refused to say that respondent had obtained full relief, and we see nothing in the evidentiary record that would compel us to say otherwise. As the Board observed, "disciplinary proceedings are ill-suited to be mini-trials on the merits of the clients' potential claims."
>
> More importantly, even if respondent's clients did receive full relief in some objective sense through his actions, such a result is irrelevant in deciding whether respondent violated [the D.C. rules]. . . .

This is indeed the fundamental fallacy in respondent's position. It is the client, not the attorney, who decides whether full or acceptable relief has been obtained. The conflict of interest rule in the circumstances here is designed to assure that the attorney pursues the client's objectives as the client views them, unaffected by any personal interest of the attorney in the outcome. Of course an attorney is entitled to obtain reasonable compensation as a result of negotiations, but this must be done within the boundaries of undivided loyalty to client interests.

The court concluded that Hager's "own . . . financial interest" would reasonably have affected his "professional judgment." If the clients got everything they wanted, how exactly could concealing the side payment adversely affect Hager's judgment? What could the clients have done with the information? Or does it not matter? What did Warner-Lambert think it was buying?

Hager was suspended for one year. Compared to Charles Hausmann, he got off easy. Hausmann was a personal injury lawyer in Wisconsin. He worked for a contingent fee of about one-third of the client's recovery prior to deduction of the expenses of litigation. He referred certain clients to Scott Rise, a chiropractor. Payments to Rise came from the client's portion of a settlement, which was appropriate. But Rise *secretly* gave 20 percent of his fees from the referrals to third parties who Hausmann identified, like people who had provided personal services to Hausmann or his relatives. A kickback. So, in effect, Hausmann got more than a third of the recovery, notwithstanding his fee agreement.

Stop for a second. What interest did Hausmann have that was in conflict with the interests of his clients? What could the clients have done if they knew about the kickback?

Hausmann and Rise were convicted of conspiracy to commit mail and wire fraud. United States v. Hausmann, 345 F.3d 952 (7th Cir. 2003) (citing Wisconsin's version of Rule 1.7(a)(2)). The theory behind Hausmann's conviction was simple. He used the mails to deprive his clients of his honest services in violation of his fiduciary duty. The indictment, which the circuit said "clearly and correctly stated the fiduciary relationship between Hausmann and his clients," alleged:

> During the time period of the scheme . . . Hausmann . . . owed a fiduciary duty to the clients of the law firm, . . . [including] the obligation . . . to disclose to the client any financial interest that the law firm may have involving the representation; to advise the client in a conflict-free manner; . . . to negotiate in the best interest of the client[; and] *to provide accurate and complete information to the clients regarding the financial terms of personal injury case settlements, as well as the amount of compensation taken by the lawyers involved in the case.* (Emphasis in the opinion.)

Hausmann had a conflict between his duty to inform his clients of the extra compensation and his own interest in hiding and keeping it. The court wrote:

> [Hausmann and Rise] maintain that Hausmann's clients had no right to the settlement funds paid to Rise nor, consequently, to the allocation of twenty

percent of those funds to expenditures designated by Hausmann. In this sense, reason Appellants, no harm resulted to Hausmann's clients, who were deprived of nothing to which they were entitled. This reasoning ignores the reality that Hausmann deprived his clients of their right to know the truth about his compensation: In addition to one third of any settlement proceeds he negotiated on their behalf, every dollar of Rise's effective twenty percent fee discount went to Hausmann's benefit. Insofar as Hausmann misrepresented this compensation, that discount should have inured to the benefit of his clients.

The analysis here moves from (i) the conflict, to (ii) a breach of common law fiduciary duty, to (iii) the theft of honest services, to (iv) a federal crime because the defendants used the mails. Does this mean that every conflict of interest (or breach of fiduciary duty) that deprives the client of honest services may be mail fraud? No. Most won't. But if the conflict involves a bribe or kickback (as here), the honest services law remains a risk for lawyers. Skilling v. United States, 561 U.S. 358 (2010).

2. Media Rights

Maybe you have dreams of writing novels, true-crime books, and scripts for movies and TV shows like *The Lincoln Lawyer, The Verdict,* and *Law & Order.* You figure that your work as a lawyer will give you good plot lines. You're right. There are great stories in the law. Every court case is a story. Some of them can be riveting if told dramatically.

Rule 1.8(d) forbids lawyers to acquire literary or media rights to the client's matter before it concludes. Why should acquisition of media rights during a representation create a conflict between client and lawyer? Consider a lawyer retained to represent a defendant in a criminal case as celebrated as the murder trial of O.J. Simpson. Suppose the lawyer agrees that all or part of his fee will be the exclusive rights to the defendant's story, which the lawyer plans to write and sell to Hollywood after the case is over. If the case is truly over, and if the lawyer never uses or reveals confidential information, what's the problem?

The problem is that the media rights will be more valuable to the lawyer if there is a trial (whatever the verdict) than if the client cuts a deal. Trials are dramatic. Guilty pleas are boring. Celebrity trials especially get publicity, which sells books, which become movies, which sell more books. So the lawyer will want to go to trial, which means he may urge his client to reject an attractive plea offer or, worse, not even seek to secure one in the first place.*

---

* Apart from the conflict, a lawyer who wants to use a client's matter as fodder for a story, fiction or not, must be conscious of his Rule 1.6 duty to protect the client's confidences even after the matter is closed. Nor could the lawyer cast the client in a bad light even without revealing confidential information because the public will infer that the lawyer has a basis for the unkind treatment.

Clients who may wish to assign media rights to their lawyers are usually criminal defendants. If the defendant is convicted, she may seek to vacate the conviction on the ground that the lawyer's media rights created an impermissible conflict leading to denial of the Sixth Amendment guarantee of the effective assistance of counsel. Notice the overlap between the conflict rules and the amendment. Later in this chapter we'll see that a conflict may render counsel constitutionally ineffective. However, as stated in chapter 4, a conflict is not enough. Courts hold that even if a lawyer had a conflict between the client's interest and lawyer's desire to exploit the media rights, the client must still prove that the conflict led to ineffective representation. Clients are rarely able to do that. The lawyer is subject to discipline, however.

Denying a client the right to "pay" a lawyer she cannot afford with publicity rights to her story interferes with the client's autonomy. Why not allow a properly informed client to decide to take her chances? We let clients consent to most other conflicts. The justification given for not allowing it is that there is a superior interest at play. The ethics rules (and as we see in part B1, constitutional law) recognize that the state also has an interest in accurate criminal verdicts. A conflicted defense lawyer may undermine that confidence.

3. Financial Assistance

Becca Dionne Is Puzzled

Falling bricks injured Mary O'Meara, 33, as she walked past a building site. She lost her waitress job. She has medical bills. She will face eviction when her savings run out. Becca Dionne is O'Meara's experienced lawyer, working on contingency. She tells O'Meara that the evidence of liability is strong and that her claim is worth at least two million dollars. But it could take two years or longer before the defendant (or its insurer) makes a serious settlement offer and, because of calendar delays, longer still for the case to go to trial. The defendant and its insurer are aware of O'Meara's plight and will seek, through discovery and motions, to delay the case as long as possible. As O'Meara's needs become more acute, she will be receptive to settling for less.

Dionne wants to help O'Meara pay for food, rent, transportation, and medical expenses while the case proceeds. She figures that whatever she gives O'Meara will be a pittance compared to the investment of her time and the time of an associate, not to mention the $25,000 that she expects to (and may ethically) advance for expert witnesses, discovery, and investigators. Enabling O'Meara to tolerate delay is good for both O'Meara and Dionne.

Dionne (re)reads Rule 1.8(e). It says that in a litigation, she can advance court costs and other expenses required to prepare the case for trial, with repayment contingent on the outcome. But the rule does not have what Dionne learns is informally called a humanitarian exception that would allow her to help O'Meara pay for food or rent. Connecticut Opinion 1990-3 declares that there is no "humanitarian exception" to the prohibition against advancing living expenses. New York Opinion 2019-6 (same). Even small sums are forbidden. The Alaska Supreme Court held that a lawyer who lent $6,000 to a wrongful death client, who had been evicted and was living in her car with her children, violated Rule 1.8(e). The money helped the client hold out for a $665,000 settlement. In re K.A.H., 967 P.2d 91 (Alaska 1998). But see The Fla. Bar v. Taylor, 648 So. 2d 1190 (Fla. 1994) (recognizing humanitarian exception where lawyer gave client $200 for "basic necessities" with no expectation of repayment).*

Becca Dionne is puzzled. If O'Meara were a client on a business deal, not litigation, the prohibition would not apply. What is it about litigation that calls for a different rule? Dionne started her career as a Big Law associate and knows that the partners had five-figure entertainment budgets to take clients to expensive restaurants, concerts, the theater, and sports events. It was called client development and it did not matter whether the client was a litigation client. Further research reveals that eleven states do have a humanitarian exception of one kind or another. But her state does not. It has the Model Rule.

Dionne asks you: "What am I missing here?"

———————

The Oklahoma Supreme Court rejected a constitutional challenge to Rule 1.8(e). It suspended a lawyer for 60 days for making a $1,200 loan to a workers' compensation client whose home had been destroyed by fire. The court said that the rule's purpose was to prevent clients from "selecting a lawyer based on improper factors" and to avoid "conflicts of interests, including compromising a lawyer's independent judgment in the case." State ex rel. Okla. Bar Ass'n v. Smolen, 17 P.3d 456 (Okla. 2000).

Really? Let us examine *Smolen*'s two reasons. Conflicts first. The argument is that allowing lawyers to provide living expenses, even small loans of a few hundred dollars, will compromise their judgment. They might recommend an imprudent settlement to ensure that the client is able to repay the money they advanced. But that argument would also prohibit the lawyers from advancing the costs of litigation, which they can and which will usually far exceed living expenses, with repayment conditioned on a recovery. In

---

* In 2020, the ABA debated whether to add a narrow exception to Rule 1.8(e) to allow a lawyer working pro bono to make a gift (not a loan) to an "indigent" client to help pay for food, transportation, housing, and the like. At the ABA Annual Meeting in August 2020, the House of Delegates voted to add the exception. It is available only to lawyers working without fee and allows only "modest" gifts.

fact, the argument casts doubt on the legitimacy of contingent fees, which as we have seen can also create conflicts.

Smolen's second justification for the rule was to ensure that clients choose a lawyer not based on who will pay more toward living expenses, but on quality. We don't want lawyers to compete with other lawyers in this way. Why is that? We have no problem if clients choose lawyers based on whose fees are lower or who will invest more in experts and investigators. In fact, clients are encouraged to compare these items. In any event, a rule containing a humanitarian exception can limit its availability to current (not prospective) clients, as the California rule does. See below.

The Model Rules give a third reason for the rule. Allowing lawyers to provide financial assistance "would enable clients to pursue lawsuits that might not otherwise be brought." Rule 1.8 cmt. [10]. Doesn't the comment have it backwards? This is a reason to *permit* the help. A change will enable people like O'Meara to get their day in court, a social good. The Supreme Court has recognized the importance of court access.*

Perhaps what the comment means is that without Rule 1.8(e) people will be motivated to bring cases that aren't worth much, may even be frivolous, to get financial help from their lawyers. But why would a lawyer invest her time in a contingent fee case that wasn't worth much and then invest more by financially helping the client? And if the case *is* worth much, as O'Meara's is, allowing Dionne to help her while the case moves through the courts won't "encourage" her to bring the case in the first place. It empowers her to withstand financial duress and hold out for a fair settlement or a trial.

California is one of the jurisdictions that do allow a lawyer to provide living expenses under various circumstances. California Rule 1.8.5(a)(2) says that "after the lawyer is retained by the client," the lawyer may "agree to lend money to the client based on the client's written promise to repay the loan, provided the lawyer complies with [conflict rules] before making the loan or agreeing to do so." By forbidding preretainer promises, the rule means to eliminate the second *Smolen* risk—i.e., that clients will

---

* In response to the argument that restrictions on lawyer advertising had the beneficial purpose of not "stirring up litigation," Justice White wrote for the Court:

> But we cannot endorse the proposition that a lawsuit, as such, is an evil. Over the course of centuries, our society has settled upon civil litigation as a means for redressing grievances, resolving disputes, and vindicating rights when other means fail. There is no cause for consternation when a person who believes in good faith and on the basis of accurate information regarding his legal rights that he has suffered a legally cognizable injury turns to the courts for a remedy: "we cannot accept the notion that it is always better for a person to suffer a wrong silently than to redress it by legal action." That our citizens have access to their civil courts is not an evil to be regretted; rather, it is an attribute of our system of justice in which we ought to take pride.

Zauderer v. Off. of Disciplinary Counsel (1985) (see chapter 16B).

choose lawyers based on who offers the most generous help. See also North Dakota Rule 1.8(e)(3).

The District of Columbia's rule allows a lawyer to "pay or otherwise provide . . . financial assistance which is reasonably necessary to permit the client to institute or maintain" a case. D.C. Rule 1.8(d)(2). The comment to the rule says the permission is limited to expenses that are "strictly necessary to sustain the client during" the matter in order "to avoid situations in which a client is compelled by exigent financial circumstances to settle a claim on unfavorable terms. . . . Regardless of the types of payments involved . . . client reimbursement of the lawyer is not required."

Note that the D.C. rule envisions that the lawyer's help may be in the form of a gift. If one reason for a rule prohibiting financial assistance is to avoid conflicts—the first of *Smolen*'s two justifications—a gift can do that because the lawyer's judgment will not be affected by the prospect of repayment. In his article surveying American jurisdictions, Professor John Sahl quotes D.C. bar counsel's comments that the rule has been in place for a "long time and has not produced any official complaints." John Sahl, Helping Clients with Living Expenses: "No Good Deed Goes Unpunished," 13 Prof. Law. 1 (Winter 2002).

The market may yet rescue Mary O'Meara, and also others who, although not financially needy, may wish to sell an investor an interest in a claim to hedge their bets or because they have a better use for the money. This new type of investor advances funds with repayment contingent on recovery. The amount of the repayment is much higher than interest on a loan because the investor gets nothing if there is no recovery. The industry is still relatively young but growing quickly. See generally Maya Steinitz, Whose Claim Is This Anyway? Third Party Litigation Funding, 95 Minn. L. Rev. 1268 (2011), and Maya Steinitz & Abigail Field, A Model Litigation Finance Contract, 99 Iowa L. Rev. 711 (2014).[*]

4. Fee-Payer Interests

Sometimes, lawyers get paid by one person to represent another person. Liability insurance policies generally obligate the insurer to defend the insured if a claim against the insured is wholly or partly within the policy's coverage. Or a company might provide counsel for its employees if alleged wrongdoing is within the scope of employment. A father may pay his son's lawyer. Rules 1.8(f) and 5.4(c) permit these payments. The client must consent to the arrangement, the payer must not interfere with the lawyer's

---

[*] Loans to persons like O'Meara are sometimes referred to as *consumer* financing to distinguish them from money that a finance company might invest in one or more of a law firm's cases, with repayment contingent on success. The firm is the borrower. In that situation, no money goes to the client or comes out of her recovery. See chapter 14B.

"independence of professional judgment or with the client-lawyer relationship," and the lawyer must protect the client's confidences. Deferring to the instructions of, and without permission discussing the matter with, the person paying the fee, can lead to discipline. In re Gorokhovsky, 824 N.W.2d 804 (Wis. 2012).

This "triangular" relationship can create conflicts between the interests of the source of the fee and the client, which is why the lawyer is instructed that the source is not a client. In criminal cases, those conflicts can result in the ineffective assistance of counsel. In Wood v. Georgia, 450 U.S. 261 (1981), the petitioners were sentenced to jail after they failed to pay fines following obscenity convictions. The petitioners' lawyer was hired and paid by their employer. Although certiorari had been granted to review the constitutionality of incarcerating persons unable to pay a fine, the Court declined to pass on this issue after it became apparent that the employer's interest in litigating the constitutional question may have conflicted with the defendants' interests in avoiding assessment of the huge fines. The Court said:

> Courts and commentators have recognized the inherent dangers that arise when a criminal defendant is represented by a lawyer hired and paid by a third party, particularly when the third party is the operator of the alleged criminal enterprise. One risk is that the lawyer will prevent his client from obtaining leniency by preventing the client from offering testimony against his former employer or from taking other actions contrary to the employer's interest. Another kind of risk is present where, as here, the party paying the fees may have had a long-range interest in establishing a legal precedent and could do so only if the interests of the defendants themselves were sacrificed.

The Court remanded for determination of whether a conflict of interest "actually existed."

5. Related Lawyers, Significant Others, and Friends

As we will see in part B3, Rule 1.10(a) imputes the client conflicts of one lawyer to other lawyers within her firm. Partner Jones cannot accept a matter that her partner Smith cannot accept because of a former or current client conflict. What if Smith and Jones are partners in life, not in practice? Spouses, say. One may have confidential information from her legal work that would assist the other in his legal work. Should we impute conflicts within a family or domestic partnership? After all, family members, spouses, and domestic partners are in many ways much closer than office colleagues, and success for one may directly benefit the other. Many families contain two or more lawyers, which means whatever we decide can have significant consequences.

The Model Rules require informed client consent when each of certain related lawyers are *personally* representing two clients in the same or a substantially related matter. But where Jones is representing a client against

Smith's *firm*, not Smith personally, we allow it without need for consent. Rule 1.7 cmt. [11] provides:

> When lawyers representing different clients in the same matter or in substantially related matters are closely related by blood or marriage, there may be a significant risk that client confidences will be revealed and that the lawyer's family relationship will interfere with both loyalty and independent professional judgment. As a result, each client is entitled to know of the existence and implications of the relationship between the lawyers before the lawyer agrees to undertake the representation. Thus, a lawyer related to another lawyer, e.g., as parent, child, sibling or spouse, ordinarily may not represent a client in a matter where that lawyer is representing another party, unless each client gives informed consent. The disqualification arising from a close family relationship is personal and ordinarily is not imputed to members of firms with whom the lawyers are associated. See Rule 1.10.

6. Can a Lawyer's Gender, Religion, or Race Create a Conflict?

> I felt it was important to have a woman on the team.
> —Harvey Weinstein, explaining to a reporter why he changed lawyers for his New York sex crimes trial

Implicit Bias in the Jury Room

Karen

"My name is Karen Horowitz. I'm a 30-year-old fifth-year litigation associate at a large midwestern law firm. I went to law school at Berkeley, clerked for a Ninth Circuit judge, then started at my current firm. Because it is relevant to what I'm about to raise, you also have to know that I'm Jewish. I'm married and have two kids. My husband's a chemist.

"I have learned a lot at my job. I have always been treated with respect and courtesy. I work with all the litigation partners. That is not to say I like everyone here equally, but that's another matter.

"Two years ago I began working on a very complicated civil case brought in a state court in the south. The defendant is a bank holding company that our firm represents on many matters. I worked on the pleadings, discovery, evidentiary issues, motions to dismiss and for partial summary judgment, and on a challenge on federal preemption grounds to the constitutionality of the statute under which our client is sued. We won some, and we lost some.

"The case was filed in a diverse, progressive city, but last month it was moved to a rural county that according to polls and voting does not embrace difference, a category that apparently includes me, and is suspicious of northerners, which I am.

"Last week, Blair Thomas, the head of our litigation department, told me that I would not be in the courtroom as part of the defense team. The reason: They think a Jewish woman lawyer could prejudice the jury against our client. I was told that the client concurred in this decision. They said it was bad enough that some of the lawyers are northerners—we also have local counsel—we couldn't afford to complicate matters by bringing me into the courtroom. I must say, Blair was quite candid. He could have made some excuse—they needed me elsewhere, for instance. I appreciate that, I guess. He said I was a valuable associate whose work was appreciated and would be recognized at bonus time and with other important assignments. But the firm had a responsibility to its client, which came first.

"I think the firm has a responsibility to me too, and that's a responsibility not to exclude me from an important case—on which I've already been working for two years—because of my sex or religion. If clients don't like it, the firm shouldn't represent them. It used to be that businesses justified discrimination against this group or that by pointing to their customers. 'It's not us,' they'd say, 'we're not prejudiced. But our customers won't work with you-name-it, so what can we do?'

"Well, if you ask me, this is no different. The firm tells me it's not prejudiced, even its clients aren't prejudiced, it says, but someone else is and so my career gets sidetracked.

"I don't know what I'm going to do about this. I don't know what I can do. But I don't buy the 'our client comes first' explanation. Bias should have no excuses."

Blair

"I know how Karen feels. It stinks. No question about it. We would never tolerate such treatment for any other reason but this one—our responsibility to our client. Make no mistake about it. It's not the firm that wants to exclude Karen, or the client, which has worked with Karen on this matter and other matters for years. But we can't ignore where we're going to try this case. The demographics of this county are astonishing. Our polling of the probable jury venire shows bias against people of color, women working outside the home, religious minorities, members of the LGBTQ community, and immigrants. State, local, and national voting patterns in the county confirm these attitudes.

"I'm not saying the jury will be composed of sexists and bigots. I don't think that. But we've learned a lot lately about implicit biases—biases that a person is not even aware of but which may influence his or her behavior. On voir dire, jurors will disclaim all biases and even believe what they say, but their true attitudes may affect how they vote. And we'll never know.

"I think Karen has to be reasonable. This case can cost our client more than $500 million if it goes the wrong way. The fact is there are situations—other cases, other courts—where we'd *want* her in the courtroom because we'd expect to do better if we had a woman or a Jewish lawyer on our team. The same goes for members of other groups—racial, religious, you name it. Some cases, I want a minority right up there. Other cases, I want a woman. Sometimes, I want a younger lawyer or an older lawyer, depending.

"A trial is a performance and a convincing performance relies on good casting. Lawyers choose their trial team to appeal to the jury, or at least not alienate it. Identity is not the dominant consideration, of course, but you do have to think about the kind of lawyer the jury is most likely to believe. You know it's the same thing when a firm hires local counsel. Those guys just sit around, smile at the jurors, and talk in the local idiom a couple of minutes a day. Why do we—why does anyone—hire them? And we all do. It's not because they know the law. It's to curry favor with the locals. We all say we want verdicts based on reason alone, unaffected by the identities of parties and lawyers. I know I do. Someday that may be true, but it is not true today.

"The judge and jury are going to decide this case. We have to appeal to them whether we like their biases or not. I'm a lawyer with a client who is at serious risk. My client is my only concern, whether it's a bank or a death-row inmate. Karen has to understand that. Her day will come in other matters. Her career hasn't been sidetracked at all. We owe her one and we'll make it up to her."

Does Karen's story raise a lawyer-client conflict? I think so (obviously, it's in the book). Karen's conflict is between her understandable wish to participate in the trial, on one hand, and on the other hand, the possibility, as Blair sees it, that doing so may harm her client. This issue does not get talked about much in the profession, yet it's very real.

So we need to pose a remarkable and uncomfortable question: Can it be that despite persistent efforts since World War II to eliminate bias in American life, one place we may be helpless to do so is the jury trial? Unless a juror makes overtly racist (or perhaps other kinds of biased) statements on voir dire or in deliberations,* litigants will not be able to discover and correct for biased verdicts after trial. So lawyers do their best before trial to minimize bias against them and maximize biases that may work in their favor. They do so in selecting the members of their trial team and in picking the jurors most likely to favor their client's position. If a client has the money, its lawyers will hire consultants to help choose optimal jurors by age, race, marital status, religion, education, job, ethnicity, and gender. (Google "Jury Consultants.") Karen's situation is unusual only because she has been *removed* from the trial team when the case is unexpectedly moved to a rural

---

* Pena-Rodriguez v. Colorado, ____ U.S. ____ (2017) (when in deliberations "a juror makes a clear statement that indicates he or she relied on racial stereotypes or animus to convict a criminal defendant, the Sixth Amendment requires . . . [the] trial court to consider the evidence of the juror's statement and any resulting denial of the jury trial guarantee").

county. If the case had been filed in the rural county at the outset, Karen might never have been assigned to it and never know why.

At a bar event about this issue some years ago, a lawyer in the audience said he represented plaintiffs injured in motorcycle accidents. (We do live in an age of specialization.) The defendant in a case he tried was a manufacturer of motorcycles. On the first day of jury selection, an older Korean-American woman was chosen. The next day, the defense showed up with a male Korean-American associate at counsel's table. This associate (and the lawyer telling the story said he assumed he was an associate, not a paralegal or an actor) had never appeared in any of the pretrial work, nor was his name on any papers, for the two years the case had been pending. The lawyer believed that the defense brought him in just to sit at counsel table, as close to the Korean-American juror as possible, which in fact is all he did.

Should the plaintiff's lawyer have objected to this apparent effort to appeal to a juror as "conduct prejudicial to the administration of justice" and cite Rule 8.4(d)? Would you? What would you expect the trial judge to do?

Film producer Harvey Weinstein, more knowledgeable than most of us about casting a credible performance, seemed to have had no doubt that his sex crimes trial required a woman to lead his defense. But the fact that identity can work to a lawyer's advantage cannot be the answer, can it? The solution for bias cannot be more bias. And yet the risk of bias, however deplorable, is also real. If a firm is casting its trial team with an eye on how juror bias may help or hurt, it will be difficult for the opposing firm to resist doing the same.

Read Rule 8.4(g), which broadly prohibits bias in law practice. Do decisions like Blair's violate it? Or can Blair rightly say in defense that the firm is not biased? Rather it fears the jury is biased and must protect its client.

Following are two historical events that may or may not enlighten this debate. They arose at another time in America. Would a contemporary Roger Baldwin or Bernard Wolfman say and do the same today?

How Roger Baldwin Picked a Lawyer

Consider the perspective of Roger Baldwin, founder of the American Civil Liberties Union (ACLU), an organization committed to elimination of bias. (This information comes to us in a portrait of Baldwin by Peggy Lamson.*) Baldwin was arrested in a labor demonstration in Patterson, New Jersey in the fall of 1924. Citing a 1796 statute, the indictment charged that Baldwin "unlawfully, riotously and tumultuously did make and utter great and loud noises and threatenings" with the intent to "commit assault and battery upon the police officers and . . . to break, injure, damage and destroy

---

* Peggy Lamson, Roger Baldwin, *Founder of the American Civil Liberties Union: A Portrait* 160-162 (1976).

and wreck the city hall." Baldwin was convicted by the trial judge and sentenced to six months in jail. New York lawyer Samuel Untermyer handled the appeal without fee, but lost. Baldwin told Lamson:

One more possible appeal remained, to the Court of Errors, the highest tribunal in the state. At this point Roger and all the ACLU lawyers came to a conclusion that Mr. Untermyer would have to be replaced. "They all said, including our Jewish lawyers, that a New Yorker, a rich Jew like Untermyer, would certainly get licked pleading before the Court of Errors in New Jersey."

Lamson then pursued the issue with Baldwin:

"Does that mean you can't conceive of a situation in which a black lawyer would defend, let's say, a Mormon who was prevented from holding a public meeting?"

"No, I can't conceive of such a situation."

"Then do you think Mr. Redding [an ACLU cooperating lawyer] or any other black lawyer would be less effective in such a case *just because* he was black?"

"Yes, of course, that's what I think. He'd be less effective unless he was extraordinarily good. Because he'd have to be extraordinarily good to overcome a jury's prejudice."

"Whereas a white lawyer would just have to be average good, is that it?"

"Not necessarily," Roger said calmly. "It depends on the prejudice. For instance, we wouldn't use a New York lawyer in Alabama, and we wouldn't use a southern lawyer, particularly one with a strong accent, in a northern court. In New Jersey we all decided not to use a Jewish lawyer when we knew prejudice against him existed. And you have to remember that because of that tactic we won the Patterson, New Jersey case, which was far more of a victory than just keeping me out of jail."

The Schempp Case

Here's another example. School District of Abington Township v. Schempp, 374 U.S. 203 (1963), was an important Supreme Court opinion on the constitutionality of school prayer. Ellory Schempp was a high school student in Abington Township, a Philadelphia suburb. In 1957, he wrote to the ACLU's Philadelphia chapter. As a Unitarian, he felt uncomfortable when the Lord's Prayer and the Bible were read each day in school.

According to U.S. District Judge Louis Pollak, Bernard Wolfman, a partner at a Philadelphia firm and a member of the ACLU, interviewed Ellory and urged the ACLU to take the case. It agreed. But as Judge Pollak wrote in a memorial to Henry Sawyer, Wolfman (later a Harvard law professor) did not argue the case. Instead, the work fell to Sawyer, then a young partner at another Philadelphia firm.

The Board's decision to provide counsel for the Schempps, however, did not mean that Wolfman would be that counsel. Wolfman decided that for him, as a

Jew, to represent the Schempps in a challenge to Bible reading and recitation of the Lord's Prayer merely would add unnecessary and probably detrimental baggage to what clearly would be a controversial and, in many quarters, an unpopular cause.

Louis Pollak, Lawyer Sawyer, 148 U. Pa. L. Rev. 25 (1999). The Supreme Court found the prayer and mandatory Bible reading unconstitutional.

B. CLIENT-CLIENT CONFLICTS

1. Criminal Cases (Defense Lawyers)

Murder One, Murder Two

Andy Simon was retained to represent Tommy "Pinball" Dash and Malcolm "Reb" Snyder in a murder case arising out of an alleged turf battle between two gangs, both engaged in drug sales in Culver City. Dash is 51. Snyder is 23. Dash allegedly ran one gang's drug trade and has three prior felony convictions. Snyder has no record. The indictment charged that Snyder, claiming to be interested in a major purchase, lured Vincent "Little Man" Mallen to a vacant lot, where Dash shot him. The indictment charged murder one, which carries a life sentence without possibility of parole. Dash and Snyder told Simon they were 180 miles away in Dorchester when Mallen was shot. They produced alibi witnesses whose credibility Simon seriously doubted, but he could not say that he knew that the alibi was false.

The prosecutor, Tina Rand, offered to accept pleas to murder two, which carries a sentence of life with parole eligibility after 20 years. Dash figured whether he was convicted of murder one or murder two, he would never get paroled given his record, even if he lived 20 years, which he doubted he would. So he wanted to go to trial and take his chances. Snyder wanted to take the plea, but not if he had to testify against Dash. While maintaining his alibi to Simon, Snyder (whom Simon thought was a little slow) also implied that he thought Dash only wanted to scare Mallen.

Simon told Rand that Snyder wanted to accept the deal but only if he didn't have to testify against Dash and that Dash insisted on a trial.

"It's both or neither, Andy. It's only a deal if it frees resources. If Dash doesn't plead, I've got to try it anyway."

"But this way you get one sure conviction."

"My proof on Snyder is stronger than on Dash. And the alibi is bull. I've got two credible eyewitnesses who saw Snyder with Mallen near the murder scene ten minutes before he was killed. Snyder wasn't in Dorchester."

"A lot can happen in ten minutes, Tina."

"Snyder is history, Andy. His best chance is, because of his age, the jury convicts him of murder two as a lesser included. So I get that anyway. You're not giving me anything."

"I think Snyder needs another lawyer," Simon said. "I've got a conflict."

"Between what and what, tell me. You've got no conflict because there's only one thing you or anyone can do. Go to trial. Snyder can get ten lawyers. Story ends the same way. If Dash goes to trial, Snyder goes to trial, and you're saying Dash is going to trial. So Snyder is too. The offer stays open only until Tuesday noon."

Simon talked to his clients, but Dash was adamant about going to trial, which both did. Neither testified. They were convicted of murder one and sentenced to life without parole. Snyder's new lawyer, Nadia Perlov, seeks a new trial based on Cuyler v. Sullivan (set out below). She argues that Simon had a conflict that affected his performance, depriving Snyder of his Sixth Amendment right to the effective assistance of counsel. Rand responds that given her position, Simon and any other lawyer for Snyder had only one option, so there was no conflict. "Any conflict was between Dash, who wanted a trial, and Snyder, who wanted to plead. Not between Simon and either of them," Rand argues.

Did Simon have a conflict? If so, how would you describe it? If so, did it deprive Snyder of his Sixth Amendment right to counsel? Make the argument to the court on behalf of Snyder.

Did Officer Schwarz Get the Effective Assistance of Counsel?

A headline federal case featuring a defense lawyer's concurrent client and personal conflicts arose from the brutal police station assault on Brooklyn resident Abner Louima in 1997. Several New York City police officers, including Justin Volpe, Charles Schwarz, and Thomas Wiese, were jointly tried in 1999. Before the case went to the jury, Volpe pled guilty and received a 30-year sentence. The jury was instructed that Volpe's plea could not be used as evidence against Schwarz.

An open question was whether Volpe acted alone or whether, as Louima and other witnesses testified, a second officer was present in the police precinct bathroom where the assault occurred. The government claimed that there was a second officer and that it was Schwarz. The jury convicted him of conspiracy to violate Louima's civil rights and of violating them. He was sentenced to more than 15 years in prison. On appeal, citing Cuyler v. Sullivan, Schwarz argued that Stephen Worth, his lawyer, had a conflict that rendered him ineffective. Here are the facts.

- Worth and his firm had a $10 million contract with the PBA, the police union, to represent it, including in all civil matters. The PBA could terminate the contract on 30 days' notice. It was up for renewal in 2000.

- Louima had a suit pending against the PBA and its president. The complaint claimed that they "participated in a conspiracy to injure Louima and cover it up." Neither Worth nor his firm represented the defendants in that civil action.
- The government introduced proof from Louima and others tending to prove that there was a second officer in the bathroom and that it was Schwarz.
- Worth had some proof that a second officer was in the bathroom with Volpe and that it was Wiese, not Schwarz. Wiese resembles Schwarz. Worth had no relationship with Wiese.
- Volpe, when entering his guilty plea, said that there was a second officer in the bathroom. The press prominently reported this statement. After Volpe pleaded guilty, Stuart London, Volpe's lawyer, told Worth in private, "my guy [Volpe] can take your guy [Schwarz] out of the bathroom." The jury was not sequestered.
- Worth argued to the jury that Volpe acted alone. That is, he chose not to credit the government's proof that another officer was in the bathroom but then argue that it was Wiese, not Schwarz.
- At a hearing, Schwarz acknowledged and waived all conflicts on the record, after being advised by court-appointed independent counsel. That counsel told the court that "he had advised Schwarz of all these conflicts and believed Schwarz understood them." The judge accepted the waiver and permitted Worth to continue to represent Schwarz.[*]

You represent Schwarz on appeal. Make your argument to the Second Circuit.[†]

Issues of concurrent client conflicts in a criminal representation arise when a single lawyer or firm represents two or more defendants. Representation can occur during the investigation of the matter (including before the grand jury), in plea negotiations, at trial, or on appeal. Sometimes two partners will each represent one of two defendants. Burger v. Kemp, 483 U.S. 776 (1987) (assumes partners are one lawyer for conflicts purposes as does Rule 1.10(a)). The conflict issue may emerge, among other ways, if a client is convicted and challenges the lawyer's performance as constitutionally ineffective, as Officer Schwarz did.

As we will see in Wheat v. United States, below, the conflict issue can arise in an inverted way when a defendant wants to hire a lawyer and the judge

---

[*] United States v. Schwarz, 283 F.3d 76 (2d Cir. 2002).

[†] Skills training tip: Try framing your argument by citing the facts and using this summary sentence: "On the one hand, Worth could have argued that _____. On the other hand, Worth had a conflict that prevented him from making that argument because_____."

refuses to allow it (usually in response to an objection from the prosecutor) on the ground that the lawyer has a disqualifying conflict. The defendant may offer to waive any conflict, after getting advice from an independent lawyer, and argue that denying him his desired lawyer violates his Sixth Amendment right to counsel of choice. Schwarz did that, too. The prosecutor may respond that the conflicted lawyer will not be able to provide constitutionally effective representation. "She's a walking Sixth Amendment violation, your Honor. You can't always get what you want."

Why is this any of the prosecutor's business? Read on.

In addition to the constitutional and ethical questions that swirl around this issue, Rule 44(c) of the Federal Rules of Criminal Procedure applies in federal criminal trials. Adopted in 1979, it is set out in relevant part in *Wheat* and in draft form in note 10 of the next case.

As you read Cuyler v. Sullivan, try to identity the conflict that confronted lawyers DiBona and Peruto in their representation of John Sullivan. Again, try to state it in a sentence.

CUYLER v. SULLIVAN
446 U.S. 335 (1980)

JUSTICE POWELL delivered the opinion of the Court.

The question presented is whether a state prisoner may obtain a federal writ of habeas corpus by showing that his retained defense counsel represented potentially conflicting interests.

I

Respondent John Sullivan was indicted with Gregory Carchidi and Anthony DiPasquale for the first-degree murders of John Gorey and Rita Janda. . . .

Two privately retained lawyers, G. Fred DiBona and A. Charles Peruto, represented all three defendants throughout the state proceedings that followed the indictment. Sullivan . . . could not afford to pay his own lawyer. At no time did Sullivan or his lawyers object to the multiple representation. Sullivan was the first defendant to come to trial. The evidence against him was entirely circumstantial, consisting primarily of [a Mr.] McGrath's testimony. At the close of the Commonwealth's case, the defense rested without presenting any evidence. The jury found Sullivan guilty and fixed his penalty at life imprisonment. Sullivan's post-trial motions failed, and the Pennsylvania Supreme Court affirmed his conviction by an equally divided vote. Sullivan's codefendants, Carchidi and DiPasquale, were acquitted at separate trials. . . .

DiBona and Peruto . . . gave conflicting accounts of the decision to rest Sullivan's defense. DiBona said he had encouraged Sullivan to testify even though the Commonwealth had presented a very weak case. Peruto remembered that he had not "want[ed] the defense to go on because I thought we would only be exposing the [defense] witnesses for the other two trials that were coming up." Sullivan testified that he had deferred to his lawyers' decision not to present evidence for the defense. But other testimony suggested that Sullivan preferred not to take the stand because cross-examination might have disclosed an extramarital affair. Finally, Carchidi claimed he would have appeared at Sullivan's trial to rebut McGrath's testimony about Carchidi's statement at the time of the murders. . . .

[Sullivan sought release in habeas corpus. The Third Circuit ruled in his favor and the state petitioned for certiorari.]

IV

We come at last to Sullivan's claim that he was denied the effective assistance of counsel guaranteed by the Sixth Amendment because his lawyers had a conflict of interest. The claim raises two issues expressly reserved in Holloway v. Arkansas, [435 U.S. 475, 483-484 (1978)]. The first is whether a state trial judge must inquire into the propriety of multiple representation even though no party lodges an objection. The second is whether the mere possibility of a conflict of interest warrants the conclusion that the defendant was deprived of his right to counsel.

A

In *Holloway*, a single public defender represented three defendants at the same trial. The trial court refused to consider the appointment of separate counsel despite the defense lawyer's timely and repeated assertions that the interests of his clients conflicted. This Court recognized that a lawyer forced to represent codefendants whose interests conflict cannot provide the adequate legal assistance required by the Sixth Amendment. Given the trial court's failure to respond to timely objections, however, the Court did not consider whether the alleged conflict actually existed. It simply held that the trial court's error unconstitutionally endangered the right to counsel.

Holloway requires state trial courts to investigate timely objections to multiple representation. But nothing in our precedents suggests that the Sixth Amendment requires state courts themselves to initiate inquiries into the propriety of multiple representation in every case.[10] Defense counsel have an ethical obligation to avoid conflicting representations and to advise the court promptly when a conflict of interest arises during the course of trial. Absent special circumstances, therefore, trial courts may assume either that

10. In certain cases, proposed Federal Rule of Criminal Procedure 44(c) provides that the federal district courts "shall promptly inquire with respect to . . . joint representation and shall personally advise each defendant of his right to the effective assistance of counsel, including separate representation." See also ABA Project on Standards for Criminal Justice, Function of the Trial Judge §3.4(b) (App. Draft 1972). . . .

multiple representation entails no conflict or that the lawyer and his clients knowingly accept such risk of conflict as may exist. . . .

Nothing in the circumstances of this case indicates that the trial court had a duty to inquire whether there was a conflict of interest. . . .

B

Holloway reaffirmed that multiple representation does not violate the Sixth Amendment unless it gives rise to a conflict of interest. Since a possible conflict inheres in almost every instance of multiple representation, a defendant who objects to multiple representation must have the opportunity to show that potential conflicts impermissibly imperil his right to a fair trial. But unless the trial court fails to afford such an opportunity, a reviewing court cannot presume that the possibility for conflict has resulted in ineffective assistance of counsel. Such a presumption would preclude multiple representation even in cases where "[a] common defense . . . gives strength against a common attack."

In order to establish a violation of the Sixth Amendment, a defendant who raised no objection at trial must demonstrate that an actual conflict of interest adversely affected his lawyer's performance. In Glasser v. United States, for example, the record showed that defense counsel failed to cross-examine a prosecution witness whose testimony linked Glasser with the crime and failed to resist the presentation of arguably inadmissible evidence. The Court found that both omissions resulted from counsel's desire to diminish the jury's perception of a codefendant's guilt. Indeed, the evidence of counsel's "struggle to serve two masters [could not] seriously be doubted." Since this actual conflict of interest impaired Glasser's defense, the Court reversed his conviction. . . .

Glasser established that unconstitutional multiple representation is never harmless error. Once the Court concluded that Glasser's lawyer had an actual conflict of interest, it refused "to indulge in nice calculations as to the amount of prejudice" attributable to the conflict. The conflict itself demonstrated a denial of the "right to have the effective assistance of counsel." Thus, a defendant who shows that a conflict of interest actually affected the adequacy of his representation need not demonstrate prejudice in order to obtain relief. But until a defendant shows that his counsel actively represented conflicting interests, he has not established the constitutional predicate for his claim of ineffective assistance.

C

The Court of Appeals granted Sullivan relief because he had shown that the multiple representation in this case involved a possible conflict of interest. We hold that the possibility of conflict is insufficient to impugn a criminal conviction. In order to demonstrate a violation of his Sixth Amendment rights, a defendant must establish that an actual conflict of interest adversely affected his lawyer's performance. Sullivan believes he should prevail even under this standard. He emphasizes Peruto's admission that the decision to rest Sullivan's defense reflected a reluctance to expose witnesses who later might have testified for the other defendants. The petitioner, on the other hand, points to DiBona's contrary testimony and to evidence that Sullivan himself wished to avoid taking the stand. Since the Court of Appeals did not weigh these conflicting contentions under the proper legal standard, its judgment is vacated and the case is remanded for further proceedings consistent with this opinion.

So ordered.

JUSTICE BRENNAN, concurring [in part and in the result]. . . .

"[A] possible conflict inheres in almost every instance of multiple representation." Therefore, upon discovery of joint representation, the duty of the trial court is to ensure that the defendants have not unwittingly given up their constitutional right to effective counsel. This is necessary since it is usually the case that defendants will not know what their rights are or how to raise them. This is surely true of the defendant who may not be receiving the effective assistance of counsel as a result of conflicting duties owed to other defendants. Therefore, the trial court cannot safely assume that silence indicates a knowledgeable choice to proceed jointly. The court must at least affirmatively advise the defendants that joint representation creates potential hazards which the defendants should consider before proceeding with the representation.

Had the trial record in the present case shown that respondent made a knowing and intelligent choice of joint representation, I could accept the Court's standard for a postconviction determination as to whether respondent in fact was denied effective assistance. Where it is clear that a defendant has voluntarily chosen to proceed with joint representation, it is fair, if he later alleges ineffective assistance growing out of a conflict, to require that he demonstrate "that a conflict of interest actually affected the adequacy of his representation." Here, however, where there is no evidence that the court advised respondent about the potential for conflict or that respondent made a knowing and intelligent choice to forgo his right to separate counsel, I believe that respondent, who has shown a significant possibility of conflict, is entitled to a presumption that his representation in fact suffered. Therefore, I would remand the case to allow the petitioners an opportunity to rebut this presumption by demonstrating that respondent's representation was not actually affected by the possibility of conflict.

JUSTICE MARSHALL, concurring in part and dissenting in part. . . .

I believe . . . that whenever two or more defendants are represented by the same attorney the trial judge must make a preliminary determination that the joint representation is the product of the defendants' informed choice. I therefore agree with Mr. Justice Brennan that the trial court has a duty to inquire whether there is multiple representation, to warn defendants of the possible risks of such representation, and to ascertain that the representation is the result of the defendants' informed choice.

I dissent from the Court's formulation of the proper standard for determining whether multiple representation has violated the defendant's right to the effective assistance of counsel. The Court holds that in the absence of an objection at trial, the defendant must show "that an actual conflict of interest adversely affected his lawyer's performance." . . . The appropriate question under the Sixth Amendment is whether an actual, relevant conflict of interests existed during the proceedings. If it did, the conviction must be reversed. Since such a conflict was present in this case, I would affirm the judgment of the Court of Appeals. . . .

Turning Conflicts into Sixth Amendment Claims After Cuyler v. Sullivan

Cuyler v. Sullivan asked whether an actual conflict of interested affected the lawyer's performance. It was decided in 1980, before Strickland v. Washington, 466 U.S. 668 (1984), stated the test for ineffectiveness when the defendant does *not* rely on his lawyer's conflict. See chapter 13E. In *Strickland,* the defendant cited the lawyer's failure to call certain witnesses at the sentencing stage of a capital case. A defendant may also cite a lawyer's failure to make a suppression motion or to do an investigation. The *Strickland* Court said that the test in these *nonconflict* cases was whether counsel's performance "was reasonable considering all the circumstances." If not, the "defendant must show that there is a reasonable probability that, but for counsel's unprofessional errors, the result of the proceeding would have been different." In Burger v. Kemp, supra, the Court recognized that the defendant's burden when her ineffectiveness claim relies on a defense lawyer conflict, as in Cuyler v. Sullivan, is less demanding than under *Strickland*. Why should that be? (The answer appears presently.)

Sullivan's travels continued for three years. Ultimately, the Third Circuit affirmed a judgment finding ineffective assistance of counsel. Counsel's conflict led them to fail to call Carchidi, one of their other clients awaiting trial. The court quoted lawyer Peruto, who helpfully explained the reason for his failure, and therefore his conflict and its effect on performance, with great brevity:

> Carchidi took the position of, hey, don't hurt me. If it's going to help John, yes, I'm willing to help John; but not if it's going to hurt me. So on the one hand I have to listen to John Sullivan, on the other hand I have to listen to Carchidi.

Sullivan v. Cuyler, 723 F.2d 1077 (3d Cir. 1983).

Pennsylvania made a kind of proximate cause argument: If Carchidi had had different counsel, he or she would have advised him to assert his privilege against self-incrimination and not testify at Sullivan's trial. Consequently, Sullivan was not prejudiced because an unconflicted lawyer would not have allowed Carchidi, facing his own murder trial, to testify anyway. The court responded: "But, as we noted earlier, a defendant need not demonstrate actual prejudice to make out a violation of his sixth amendment rights where he has already established an actual conflict of interest adversely affecting counsel's performance." What was the adverse effect on performance? Perhaps it was Peruto's failure even to try to persuade Carchidi to testify for Sullivan.

Holloway Error

Holloway v. Arkansas, 435 U.S. 475 (1978), cited in Cuyler v. Sullivan, is a dramatic opinion because it reversed a conviction without the need to show any effect on counsel's performance at all. The trial court had appointed a public defender to represent three defendants in the same trial. The lawyer repeatedly requested separate counsel, citing conflicts of interest, but the trial judge refused to consider the request. The Supreme Court held that the trial court's failure to investigate the alleged conflicts required reversal with no need to prove prejudice.

Why would the Court adopt this generous remedy? Look at it from the perspective of judicial economy. If the trial judge ignores the defense lawyer's conflict claim, the courts must expect Cuyler v. Sullivan claims on appeal of any conviction and in collateral attacks. It's far better to investigate and resolve the conflict question at the start. An automatic reversal rule encourages trial judges to do so. If they don't and there's a conviction, all their work will be for naught. Viewed this way, *Holloway*'s remedy is not so much for the benefit of the defendant as it is for the efficient administration of justice.

Relying on language in Wood v. Georgia, 450 U.S. 261 (1981), some lower courts then applied *Holloway*'s automatic reversal rule even where the defense lawyer did *not* call a conflict to the court's attention, so long as the trial judge knew or should have known of it. The Supreme Court rejected that view in Mickens v. Taylor, 535 U.S. 162 (2002) (5-4), where in dicta the Court also cast doubt on the breadth, though not the holding, of Cuyler v. Sullivan itself.

Mickens was charged with killing Hall. Saunders had been representing Hall on an unrelated charge at the time of his death. Four days after a trial judge relieved Saunders from representing the now-dead Hall, she appointed Saunders to represent Mickens for allegedly killing Hall. So the murder victim's former lawyer was now representing his accused murderer. Mickens was convicted and sentenced to death. Years after his conviction, Mickens's new lawyer asked to see Hall's court file. Hall had been a juvenile and the file was under seal, but a court clerk mistakenly gave it to Mickens's counsel. It revealed the entire history.

Mickens argued that the trial judge's failure to inquire into Saunders's conflict warranted automatic reversal under *Holloway* because the judge knew or should have known about the conflict. After all, the same judge had relieved Saunders from representing Hall and then, days later, had appointed him to represent Mickens at a trial for killing Hall. But Justice Scalia's opinion for the Court held that *Holloway* did not apply. Why not?

The automatic reversal rule operates "only where defense counsel is forced to represent codefendants over his timely objection, unless the trial court has determined that there is no conflict." What the trial judge knew did not matter. The defense lawyer made no objection, so *Holloway* did not apply.* As a result, under *Sullivan*, Mickens had to prove that Saunders had a conflict that actually affected his performance and could not. He was sentenced to death and executed.

Beyond limiting *Holloway*, the *Mickens* Court (in dicta) questioned whether the Cuyler v. Sullivan test for ineffectiveness (more generous to defendants than the *Strickland* test) should even apply to someone in Mickens's position. The lawyers in *Sullivan* had a conflict between *current* clients. Saunders's conflict was between his duty of confidentiality to Hall, a *former* client, and his duty to Mickens, a current client whose defense might have benefitted from disclosure of Hall's confidential information. The Court left open the possibility that the more demanding *Strickland* test might govern conflicts that are not between current clients as in *Sullivan*. Since then, lower federal courts have considered the question open.

> In the sixteen years since *Mickens* was decided, circuit courts have been hesitant to apply *Sullivan*'s presumption outside the multiple- or serial-representation context. [Citing cases from the First, Second, Fifth, Sixth, Eighth, Tenth, and Eleventh Circuits.] Weighing further against the extension of *Sullivan* here is the rationale behind it: in cases of multiple representation, "it is difficult to measure the precise effect on the defense of representation corrupted by conflicting interests."

McRae v. United States, 734 Fed. Appx. 978 (6th Cir. 2018) (declining to apply *Sullivan* where defendant alleged that his lawyer's performance was affected by the lawyer's financial interest in wishing to avoid a retrial).

Why Do We Have Two Ineffectiveness Tests? Does the distinction in *Mickens*'s dicta and some lower court decisions make sense? To answer that question, we have to ask why *Sullivan* imposes a lower burden than *Strickland* in the first place, a question we left open a few pages back.

Sullivan is premised on the difficulty of predicting how a case would have gone with an unconflicted lawyer. That is, once the conflict is shown to have

---

* Why didn't Saunders raise the conflict or at least tell Mickens? Could it have been because of yet another conflict? If he had raised the conflict, the judge might have removed him from the case. But his duty to Mickens required him to raise the conflict even so. *That* conflict was not explored, nor were its implications.

actually affected the lawyer's performance—how she tried the case—the courts are not in a position to know whether the verdict would have differed if the lawyer's performance had not been affected. Too speculative. Why then should the kind of conflict make it any less speculative? A *former* client conflict or, indeed, a current *lawyer*-client conflict, can be as debilitating to a lawyer's actual performance as a conflict between two current clients, as in *Sullivan,* and prediction of how the case would have gone with an unconflicted lawyer equally conjectural. Or is a current client conflict somehow more worrisome, and if so, why? Eventually, the Supreme Court will have to decide whether to turn its *Mickens* dicta into a holding. Most likely, it will limit *Sullivan* to current client conflicts and require proof of the *Strickland* test for all other conflicts.

Whatever the federal rule, state courts may offer defendants greater protection against conflicted counsel under their state constitutions. State v. Cottle, 946 A.2d 550 (N.J. 2008) (prejudice presumed where lawyer was under indictment in same county as case he was defending); Taylor v. State, 51 A.3d 655 (Md. 2012) ("We recognize that, particularly since *Mickens,* there is no clear rule across jurisdictions. . . . We join those states continuing to apply *Sullivan* to various types of conflicts . . . whether the right is rooted in the Sixth Amendment [or] the Maryland Declaration of Rights."). *Taylor* went on to "hold . . . that the *Sullivan* analysis and presumption of prejudice applies when a defendant alleges ineffective assistance of counsel based on an attorney's personal conflict of interest due to the attorney's filing suit against the client before trial for unpaid legal fees arising from the very action where the attorney is representing the client, creating an adversarial relationship during the course of representation."

Disqualification of Defense Counsel

The *Sullivan* inquiry occurs after conviction. It is retrospective. Did defense counsel labor under an actual conflict that adversely affected her performance? A similar question can arise prospectively: Does the defense have a conflict that could affect her performance? A judge and prosecutor won't relish holding a trial if the convicted defendant can then mount a *Sullivan* challenge. But isn't it hard to predict whether an alleged conflict *will* adversely affect a lawyer's performance? Yes, it's hard. In fact, it's almost always impossible. But sometimes a judge will view that likelihood as so great that she will be disposed to disqualify defense counsel. The defendant may then cite his Sixth Amendment right to counsel of choice and offer to waive the conflict, thereby purporting to remove the possibility of a challenge to any conviction. When if ever should predictions of what will happen at trial defeat a constitutional right and an accompanying waiver?

Murder at the Ballgame

These are the events that led to State v. Joe Potero.

In 2019, Shari LaGuardia was found dead in a toilet stall during the seventh-inning stretch at an afternoon baseball game at Reynoso Park. A 30-pound piece of scrap metal had been dropped on her head from the adjacent stall.

Shari was estranged from her husband Pete LaGuardia, whose threats against her had caused Shari to get an order of protection four months earlier. Pete denied any culpability in Shari's death. Asked for an alibi, Pete said he slept days because he worked the midnight to 8 A.M. shift at a factory. The police confirmed that Pete worked that shift, but no one could support Pete's claim that he was asleep at home when Shari was killed because he lived alone. No forensic or other evidence pointed to Pete. No one at the game saw Pete or his car there. Pete claimed that he had not seen Shari nor gone near her home or workplace since she got the order of protection and that he was over her. "I'm not sorry the bitch is dead," he told one detective. "But I didn't kill her."

Working with tape from video surveillance cameras, a partial shoe print on the floor of the bathroom, and interviews, the police arrested Joe Potero, a short-order cook at Reynoso Park. In court papers, the prosecutor alleged that Potero's motive was to steal LaGuardia's pocketbook, but he panicked and fled when he realized that he might have killed her. No evidence connected Potero, who was an avid weightlifter, with the scrap metal that killed Shari LaGuardia. D.A. Ingrid Chadha announced that she would seek the death penalty. Potero's family and friends put up the money to hire Lydia Hinojosa, a prominent defense lawyer whose resume included ten years as an assistant district attorney in the county (the last three as head of the homicide bureau), followed by 12 years in practice.

At the time of Shari's death, Pete was facing charges for breaking into vending machines. The charges are still pending.

Two months after Lydia noted her appearance and filed her first set of discovery motions, assistant D.A. Paul Chen moved to disqualify her, citing the fact that one of Lydia's partners, Virgil Pajyk, then represented Pete LaGuardia on the vending machine charges and had earlier represented Pete in a felony assault case.

"What's that got to do with anything?" an angry Lydia asked Paul when she received the motion.

"It means your defenses are limited by one. You can't argue that Pete may have done it. You don't have to prove he did. You only have to create a reasonable doubt whether he did, which you can't do because he's your own client."

"Pete's not the killer, Paul. You don't think he's the killer. I don't think he's the killer. Why would anyone even for a second consider that strategy?"

"Doesn't matter what *we* think. You can't even get the jury to wonder if we got the wrong guy. And you've got the proof: Pete threatened Shari in the past and pushed her down at least once. She got an order of protection. He's strong and could easily lift and toss a 30-pound weight. He has no confirmed alibi. He works in a factory with a lot of junk metal around. He was pleased when the detectives told him she was murdered. It's an obvious strategy. The police considered him a serious suspect in the first place. So would a jury."

"It would be the dumbest defense in the world to blame Pete when no one can place him or his car at the park. You showed Pete's picture to everyone. He's not on any video. He had no contact with Shari in four months. No calls. No visits. The lab guys don't say that the scrap metal came from Pete's factory. A Pete-did-it defense would be so transparent, as your summation would no doubt take pains to emphasize. I mean it's like saying look how pathetic we are. You're trying to knock me out because I can't do — assuming you're even right that I can't — what I wouldn't do anyway, and no competent defense lawyer we know would do. Besides, I've got a lot better than that."

"Like what?"

"Like what? Keep dreaming. 'Like what' is what you'll find out at trial."

"But not from you. I don't want to win and then face a *Sullivan* challenge."

"Potero will waive that. We'll get independent counsel."

"If the judge lets him. If he's convicted, his next lawyer will claim the waiver's no good, as would you."

Paul's motion seeks to disqualify Lydia and her firm. You are the trial judge. How do you rule and why? What if anything further would you wish to know and how would the information affect your ruling?

WHEAT v. UNITED STATES

486 U.S. 153 (1988)

Chief Justice Rehnquist delivered the opinion of the Court.

The issue in this case is whether the District Court erred in declining petitioner's waiver of his right to conflict-free counsel and by refusing to permit petitioner's proposed substitution of attorneys.

I

Petitioner Mark Wheat, along with numerous codefendants, was charged with participating in a far-flung drug distribution conspiracy. Over a period of several years, many thousands of pounds of marijuana were transported from Mexico and other locations to southern California. Petitioner acted primarily as an intermediary in the distribution ring; he received and stored large shipments of marijuana at his home, then distributed the marijuana to customers in the region.

Also charged in the conspiracy were Juvenal Gomez-Barajas and Javier Bravo, who were represented in their criminal proceedings by attorney Eugene Iredale. Gomez-Barajas was tried first and was acquitted on drug charges overlapping with those against petitioner. To avoid a second trial on other charges, however, Gomez-Barajas offered to plead guilty to tax evasion and illegal importation of merchandise. At the commencement of petitioner's trial, the District Court had not accepted the plea; Gomez-Barajas was thus free to withdraw his guilty plea and proceed to trial.

Bravo, evidently a lesser player in the conspiracy, decided to forgo trial and plead guilty to one count of transporting approximately 2400 pounds of marijuana from Los Angeles to a residence controlled by Victor Vidal. At the conclusion of Bravo's guilty plea proceedings on August 22, 1985, Iredale notified the District Court that he had been contacted by petitioner and had been asked to try petitioner's case as well. . . .

[T]he Government objected to petitioner's proposed substitution on the ground that Iredale's representation of Gomez-Barajas and Bravo created a serious conflict of interest. The Government's position was premised on two possible conflicts. First, the District Court had not yet accepted the plea and sentencing arrangement negotiated between Gomez-Barajas and the Government; in the event that arrangement were rejected by the court, Gomez-Barajas would be free to withdraw the plea and stand trial. He would then be faced with the prospect of representation by Iredale, who in the meantime would have acted as petitioner's attorney. Petitioner, through his participation in the drug distribution scheme, was familiar with the sources and size of Gomez-Barajas' income, and was thus likely to be called as a witness for the Government at any subsequent trial of Gomez-Barajas. This scenario would pose a conflict of interest for Iredale, who would be prevented from cross-examining petitioner and thereby from effectively representing Gomez-Barajas.

Second, and of more immediate concern, Iredale's representation of Bravo would directly affect his ability to act as counsel for petitioner. The Government believed that a portion of the marijuana delivered by Bravo to Vidal's residence eventually was transferred to petitioner. In this regard, the Government contacted Iredale and asked that Bravo be made available as a witness to testify against petitioner, and agreed in exchange to modify its position at the time of Bravo's sentencing. In the likely event that Bravo were called to testify, Iredale's position in representing both men would become untenable, for ethical proscriptions would forbid him to cross-examine Bravo in any meaningful way. By failing to do so, he would also fail to provide petitioner with effective assistance of counsel. Thus, because of

Iredale's prior representation of Gomez-Barajas and Bravo and the potential for serious conflict of interest, the Government urged the District Court to reject the substitution of attorneys.

In response, petitioner emphasized his right to have counsel of his own choosing and the willingness of Gomez-Barajas, Bravo, and petitioner to waive the right to conflict-free counsel. . . .

[The District Court disqualified Iredale and Wheat was convicted with other counsel.]

II

The Sixth Amendment to the Constitution guarantees that "in all criminal prosecutions, the accused shall enjoy the right . . . to have the Assistance of Counsel for his defence." . . .

The Sixth Amendment right to choose one's own counsel is circumscribed in several important respects. . . . The question raised in this case is the extent to which a criminal defendant's right under the Sixth Amendment to his chosen attorney is qualified by the fact that the attorney has represented other defendants charged in the same criminal conspiracy. In previous cases, we have recognized that multiple representation of criminal defendants engenders special dangers of which a court must be aware. . . .

Petitioner insists that the provision of waivers by all affected defendants cures any problems created by the multiple representation. But no such flat rule can be deduced from the Sixth Amendment presumption in favor of counsel of choice. Federal courts have an independent interest in ensuring that criminal trials are conducted within the ethical standards of the profession and that legal proceedings appear fair to all who observe them. Both the American Bar Association's Model Code of Professional Responsibility and its Model Rules of Professional Conduct, as well as the rules of the California Bar Association (which governed the attorneys in this case), impose limitations on multiple representation of clients. Not only the interest of a criminal defendant but the institutional interest in the rendition of just verdicts in criminal cases may be jeopardized by unregulated multiple representation.

For this reason, the Federal Rules of Criminal Procedure direct trial judges to investigate specially cases involving joint representation. In pertinent part, Rule 44(c) provides:

> "The court shall promptly inquire with respect to such joint representation and shall personally advise each defendant of his right to the effective assistance of counsel, including separate representation. Unless it appears that there is good cause to believe no conflict of interest is likely to arise, the court shall take such measures as may be appropriate to protect each defendant's right to counsel."

Although Rule 44(c) does not specify what particular measures may be taken by a district court, one option suggested by the Notes of the Advisory

Committee is an order by the court that the defendants be separately represented in subsequent proceedings in the case. . . .

To be sure, this need to investigate potential conflicts arises in part from the legitimate wish of district courts that their judgments remain intact on appeal. As the Court of Appeals accurately pointed out, trial courts confronted with multiple representations face the prospect of being "whipsawed" by assertions of error no matter which way they rule. If a district court agrees to the multiple representation, and the advocacy of counsel is thereafter impaired as a result, the defendant may well claim that he did not receive effective assistance. On the other hand, a district court's refusal to accede to the multiple representation may result in a challenge such as petitioner's in this case. Nor does a waiver by the defendant necessarily solve the problem, for we note, without passing judgment on, the apparent willingness of Courts of Appeals to entertain ineffective-assistance claims from defendants who have specifically waived the right to conflict-free counsel.

Thus, where a court justifiably finds an actual conflict of interest, there can be no doubt that it may decline a proffer of waiver, and insist that defendants be separately represented. . . .

Unfortunately for all concerned, a district court must pass on the issue of whether or not to allow a waiver of a conflict of interest by a criminal defendant not with the wisdom of hindsight after the trial has taken place, but in the murkier pretrial context when relationships between parties are seen through a glass, darkly. . . .

Here the District Court was confronted not simply with an attorney who wished to represent two coequal defendants in a straightforward criminal prosecution; rather, Iredale proposed to defend three conspirators of varying stature in a complex drug distribution scheme. The Government intended to call Bravo as a witness for the prosecution at petitioner's trial.[4] The Government might readily have tied certain deliveries of marijuana by Bravo to petitioner, necessitating vigorous cross-examination of Bravo by petitioner's counsel. Iredale, because of his prior representation of Bravo, would have been unable ethically to provide that cross-examination.

Iredale had also represented Gomez-Barajas, one of the alleged kingpins of the distribution ring, and had succeeded in obtaining a verdict of acquittal for him. Gomez-Barajas had agreed with the Government to plead guilty to other charges, but the District Court had not yet accepted the plea arrangement. If the agreement were rejected, petitioner's probable testimony at the resulting trial of Gomez-Barajas would create an ethical dilemma for Iredale from which one or the other of his clients would likely suffer.

Viewing the situation as it did before trial, we hold that the District Court's refusal to permit the substitution of counsel in this case was within its

---

4. Bravo was in fact called as a witness at petitioner's trial. His testimony was elicited to demonstrate the transportation of drugs that the prosecution hoped to link to petitioner.

discretion and did not violate petitioner's Sixth Amendment rights. Other district courts might have reached differing or opposite conclusions with equal justification, but that does not mean that one conclusion was "right" and the other "wrong." The District Court must recognize a presumption in favor of petitioner's counsel of choice, but that presumption may be overcome not only by a demonstration of actual conflict but by a showing of a serious potential for conflict. The evaluation of the facts and circumstances of each case under this standard must be left primarily to the informed judgment of the trial court.

The judgment of the Court of Appeals is accordingly [a]ffirmed.

JUSTICE MARSHALL, with whom JUSTICE BRENNAN joins, dissenting. . . .

The Court's resolution of the instant case flows from its deferential approach to the District Court's denial of petitioner's motion to add or substitute counsel; absent deference, a decision upholding the District Court's ruling would be inconceivable. Indeed, I believe that even under the Court's deferential standard, reversal is in order. . . .

At the time of petitioner's trial, Iredale's representation of Gomez-Barajas was effectively completed. As the Court notes, Iredale had obtained an acquittal for Gomez-Barajas on charges relating to a conspiracy to distribute marijuana. Iredale also had negotiated an agreement with the Government under which Gomez-Barajas would plead guilty to charges of tax evasion and illegal importation of merchandise, although the trial court had not yet accepted this plea arrangement. Gomez-Barajas was not scheduled to appear as a witness at petitioner's trial; thus, Iredale's conduct of that trial would not require him to question his former client. The only possible conflict this Court can divine from Iredale's representation of both petitioner and Gomez-Barajas rests on the premise that the trial court would reject the negotiated plea agreement and that Gomez-Barajas then would decide to go to trial. In this event, the Court tells us, "petitioner's probable testimony at the resulting trial of Gomez-Barajas would create an ethical dilemma for Iredale."

This argument rests on speculation of the most dubious kind. The Court offers no reason to think that the trial court would have rejected Gomez-Barajas' plea agreement; neither did the Government posit any such reason in its argument or brief before this Court. The most likely occurrence at the time petitioner moved to retain Iredale as his defense counsel was that the trial court would accept Gomez-Barajas' plea agreement, as the court in fact later did. Moreover, even if Gomez-Barajas had gone to trial, petitioner probably would not have testified. The record contains no indication that petitioner had any involvement in or information about crimes for which Gomez-Barajas might yet have stood trial. The only alleged connection between petitioner and Gomez-Barajas sprang from the conspiracy to distribute marijuana, and a jury already had acquitted Gomez-Barajas of that charge. It is therefore disingenuous to say that representation of both petitioner and Gomez-Barajas posed a serious potential for a conflict of interest.

Similarly, Iredale's prior representation of Bravo was not a cause for concern. The Court notes that the prosecution intended to call Bravo to the stand at petitioner's trial and asserts that Bravo's testimony could well have "necessitat[ed] vigorous cross-examination . . . by petitioner's counsel." The facts, however, belie the claim that Bravo's anticipated testimony created a serious potential for conflict. Contrary to the Court's inference, Bravo could not have testified about petitioner's involvement in the alleged marijuana distribution scheme. As all parties were aware at the time, Bravo did not know and could not identify petitioner; indeed, prior to the commencement of legal proceedings, the two men never had heard of each other. Bravo's eventual testimony at petitioner's trial related to a shipment of marijuana in which petitioner was not involved; the testimony contained not a single reference to petitioner. Petitioner's counsel did not cross-examine Bravo, and neither petitioner's counsel nor the prosecutor mentioned Bravo's testimony in closing argument. All of these developments were predictable when the District Court ruled on petitioner's request that Iredale serve as trial counsel; the contours of Bravo's testimony were clear at that time. Given the insignificance of this testimony to any matter that petitioner's counsel would dispute, the proposed joint representation of petitioner and Bravo did not threaten a conflict of interest.[3]

Moreover, even assuming that Bravo's testimony might have "necessitat[ed] vigorous cross-examination," the District Court could have insured against the possibility of any conflict of interest without wholly depriving petitioner of his constitutional right to the counsel of his choice. Petitioner's motion requested that Iredale either be substituted for petitioner's current counsel or be added to petitioner's defense team. Had the District Court allowed the addition of Iredale and then ordered that he take no part in the cross-examination of Bravo, any possibility of a conflict would have been removed. Especially in light of the availability of this precautionary measure, the notion that Iredale's prior representation of Bravo might well

3. The very insignificance of Bravo's testimony, combined with the timing of the prosecutor's decision to call Bravo as a witness, raises a serious concern that the prosecutor attempted to manufacture a conflict in this case. The prosecutor's decision to use Bravo as a witness was an 11th-hour development. Throughout the course of plea negotiations with Bravo, the prosecutor never had suggested that Bravo testify at petitioner's trial. At Bravo's guilty-plea proceedings, when Iredale notified the District Court of petitioner's substitution motion, the prosecutor conceded that he had made no plans to call Bravo as a witness. Only after the prosecutor learned of the substitution motion and decided to oppose it did he arrange for Bravo's testimony by agreeing to recommend to the trial court a reduction in Bravo's sentence. Especially in light of the scarce value of Bravo's testimony, this prosecutorial behavior very plausibly may be viewed as a maneuver to prevent Iredale from representing petitioner at trial. Iredale had proved to be a formidable adversary; he previously had gained an acquittal for the alleged kingpin of the marijuana distribution scheme. . . .

have caused a conflict of interest at petitioner's trial is nothing short of ludicrous. . . .

JUSTICE STEVENS, with whom JUSTICE BLACKMUN joins, dissenting. . . .

As Justice Marshall demonstrates, the Court exaggerates the significance of the potential conflict. Of greater importance, the Court gives inadequate weight to the informed and voluntary character of the clients' waiver of their right to conflict-free representation. Particularly, the Court virtually ignores the fact that additional counsel representing petitioner had provided him with sound advice concerning the wisdom of a waiver and would have remained available during the trial to assist in the defense. . . .

Wheat's Harvest

Wheat has provided fertile soil for prosecutors asking judges to disqualify defense lawyers. Unless courts carefully evaluate government claims of defense lawyer conflicts, defendants may lose their chosen counsel even though the purported conflict is speculative. Also, we cannot entirely reject the danger that prosecutors will use the *Wheat* rationale to remove a formidable opponent, as Justice Marshall implied was true in *Wheat* itself. See his footnote 3. The majority acknowledged but dismissed that danger. Wheat, it wrote, "of course rightly points out that the Government may seek to 'manufacture' a conflict in order to prevent a defendant from having a particularly able defense counsel at his side; but trial courts are undoubtedly aware of this possibility, and must take it into consideration along with all of the other factors which inform this sort of a decision."

State courts are not bound by *Wheat* and some have been more protective of the right to counsel of choice. See, e.g., State v. Smith, 761 N.W.2d 63 (Iowa 2009) (court refused to disqualify a defense lawyer whose partner was representing a prosecution witness in another case; court cites the defendant's waiver of the conflict, screening, availability of unconflicted co-counsel to cross-examine the witness, and the speculative nature of the witness's testimony).

Compare United States v. Campbell, 491 F.3d 1306 (11th Cir. 2007). Campbell, a former mayor of Atlanta charged with RICO violations and other crimes, retained Gillen as one of his defense lawyers. Parker is Gillen's partner and previously represented Greene "on corruption charges related to those Campbell faced." Greene, who had pled guilty, would be a witness against Campbell. Parker could not himself represent Campbell because he would then be in the position of having to cross-examine Greene, his former client on a related matter. See chapter 6A. But could Gillen do so? Campbell offered to waive any conflict, but Greene would not. Citing *Wheat*, the Eleventh Circuit affirmed disqualification of Gillen. It said that by disqualifying Gillen, "the district court chose to avoid a situation in which the fairness of Campbell's trial undoubtedly and quite legitimately would have been called into account, whether by Campbell or by Greene." It added that "[w]hile it is true that Campbell was free to waive the conflict, the district court was not required to accept his waiver" in light of Greene's nonwaiver.

There was no proof that Gillen had received Greene's confidential information from Parker. So why should Greene's refusal to waive any conflict related to him defeat Campbell's Sixth Amendment right to counsel of choice if, as the court wrote, "Campbell was free to waive the conflict"?*

Shadow Counsel.   Wheat tried to avoid the conflict by having another lawyer substitute for Iredale in cross-examining Bravo. Courts have allowed the use of so-called "shadow counsel" to avoid a conflict if their task is limited. Rehnquist ignored Wheat's offer; Marshall did not. If Bravo's direct testimony posed significant harm to Wheat, which it did not, denial of shadow counsel might be proper. It would not then be so easy to compartmentalize summations, with Iredale summing up on most of the testimony, leaving Bravo to shadow counsel. A judge might worry about jury confusion and doubt that the defense, if cannibalized this way, could provide the effective assistance of counsel. That should not have been a concern in *Wheat*, but shadow counsel could not as a practical matter so neatly remedy the conflict in Murder at the Ballgame. Why not?

Criminal Case Disqualification and the "Automatic Reversal" Debate

Flanagan v. United States, 465 U.S. 259 (1984), unanimously held that pretrial orders disqualifying criminal defense counsel are not subject to immediate appeal under 28 U.S.C. §1291. If defense counsel is disqualified and interlocutory review is not otherwise available (as through a certified question or mandamus), the defendant will have to proceed with another lawyer, as Wheat did. If the defendant is convicted, he will be able to raise the disqualification order on appeal. If the appellate court finds that disqualification was in error, should it reverse automatically? Or should the defendant have to show that the lawyer he got was constitutionally ineffective? If he does have to prove ineffectiveness, the erroneous disqualification is irrelevant because the conviction would be reversed for ineffectiveness anyway. Maybe there's a middle position. Perhaps the defendant need only show that the lawyer he lost was more skilled than the one he got and that he could have (would have? should have?) won with the former lawyer. But how in the world does one prove that?

Lower courts struggled with these questions and reached different conclusions. Then in 2006, the Supreme Court ended the debate. In a 5-4 decision, it said that an erroneous denial of counsel of choice warrants automatic

---

* These facts form the basis for one of the self-assessment questions (and answers) at the end of this chapter.

reversal, even if the defendant can show no other error. The defendant was represented by a California lawyer who was admitted to the federal court in Missouri pro hac vice (i.e., for that case only). The trial judge later erroneously concluded that the lawyer had violated the no-contact rule and revoked his admission. After conviction, the government agreed that the trial judge erred but argued that the trial was fair anyway. Over four dissents, Justice Scalia responded that the Sixth Amendment

> commands, not that a trial be fair, but that a particular guarantee of fairness be provided—to wit, that the accused be defended by the counsel he believes to be best. "The Constitution guarantees a fair trial through the Due Process Clauses, but it defines the basic elements of a fair trial largely through the several provisions of the Sixth Amendment, including the Counsel Clause." [Quoting *Strickland.*] In sum, the right at stake here is the right to counsel of choice, not the right to a fair trial; and that right was violated because the deprivation of counsel was erroneous. No additional showing of prejudice is required to make the violation "complete."

United States v. Gonzalez-Lopez, 548 U.S. 140 (2006).

Can a Conflicted Lawyer Advise a Current Client on Whether to Waive Her Conflict?

In "Murder at the Ballgame," defense lawyer Lydia tells prosecutor Paul that Joe Potero will waive any conflict arising from her partner's representation of the victim's estranged husband, just as Wheat offered to waive Iredale's conflicts. Can Lydia impartially advise Potero on whether to do so? After all, Lydia has an interest. She wants the case or so we must assume. And consider what Potero will be offering to waive—the right if convicted to complain that Lydia's conflict actually affected her performance in a trial that has yet to occur. (He would not be waiving the right to claim that Lydia was ineffective for other reasons.)

In recent years, lessons from behavioral economics have suggested that a lawyer in Lydia's position may not be able impartially to advise her client. No matter how scrupulous she is, she will discount the conflict's effect on her performance. She will downplay risks because she believes in her own integrity. This is why judges will often require that an independent lawyer advise an accused who wants to waive defense counsel's conflict. Then the court will schedule a hearing—called a *Curcio* hearing in the Second Circuit after a case of the same name —at which the judge can closely question the defendant to ensure he or she understands the risks. That is what the trial judge did in the prosecution of Officer Schwarz.

Behavioral economics, an established academic subject, has found a friend in the Kentucky Supreme Court. In an ethics opinion, the Kentucky Bar Association had addressed the following questions:

> (1) May a criminal defense lawyer advise a client with regard to a plea agreement that waives the client's right to pursue a claim of ineffective assistance of

counsel [IAC] as part of the waiver of the right to collaterally attack a conviction covered by the plea agreement?

(2) May a prosecutor propose a plea agreement that requires a waiver of the defendant's or potential defendant's right to pursue a claim of [IAC] relating to the matter that is the subject of the plea agreement?

The association said no to both questions. The two U.S. Attorneys in the state challenged that conclusion. (Not all states permit court review of bar ethics opinions, but some do.) The U.S. Attorneys first argued that the state's rule could not bind federal prosecutors under the Supremacy Clause.[*] The court rejected this claim and proceeded to approve the state bar's answers.

[P]sychological studies have "uncovered psychological biases that make it extremely difficult for professionals, even those who are acting in good faith and whose only limitation is unconscious, to appreciate the deleterious consequences of conflicts of interest." Sure, the "venal lawyer may, from time to time, intentionally seek to obscure evidence of a conflict of interest, or the harmful effects that a conflict had during representation"; but "psychological research demonstrates that most lawyers — even those who are acting with the best intentions — are unable consciously to identify many conflicts that exist or to appreciate the corrosive effects that such conflicts may have on decision[-]making." . . .

As a result, even an attorney acting in good faith, diligently attempting to provide the best advice for a client, is at risk of unconsciously painting an ethical gloss over his or her decision. In fact, "the decision-maker uses rational thought to search for arguments that support an already-made judgment through moral intuition"; and, furthermore, studies have indicated "people tend to overestimate their ability to act ethically, both prospectively when asked to consider how ethical they will be in the future and in hindsight when asked to evaluate how ethical they have been in the past." Perhaps consistent with intuition, "[r]esearch demonstrates that situations where discretion is permitted, and bright lines do not exist, are where psychological biases that skew judgment are most likely to operate." [The bar's opinion] is both useful and necessary.

United States v. Ky. Bar Ass'n, 439 S.W.3d 136 (Ky. 2014). For nearly all of this part of its analysis, the court relied on Tigran Eldred, The Psychology of Conflicts of Interest in Criminal Cases, 58 U. Kan. L. Rev. 43 (2009). The Justice Department has since announced that it will not require waiver of ineffectiveness claims in plea offers. Adopting a narrower version of the same principle is Sanders v. State, 773 S.E.2d 580 (S.C. 2015) ("[W]e agree with the wealth of federal jurisprudence which allows for ineffective assistance of counsel claims to proceed despite a previous waiver of collateral review *where the challenge directly attacks the effectiveness of the advice to agree to that waiver.*") (emphasis added).

---

[*] We encountered the same issue in connection with application of state no-contact rules to federal prosecutors. Chapter 3A2.

What about civil case consents? Should the lawyer who needs consent to keep a case be the sole source of advice for the client? The lawyer may have the same financial or reputational incentives to secure consent as a criminal defense lawyer. That incentive may (entirely in good faith) affect how she sees and describes the risks and advises the client. So far, behavioral economics has not led to a requirement of "conflicts counsel" in civil cases. It probably should not because of the added expense if civil litigants, who are not constitutionally guaranteed effective assistance, are required to hire conflicts counsel. Nonetheless, civil lawyers who want to be confident that a client's waiver will stand in the face of a later challenge might advise the client to get independent advice and allow time to do so. And in high-stakes matters, the civil lawyer may insist on it, even offer to pay for it.

2. *Criminal Cases (Prosecutors)*

Forfeiture Plus Prosecution

Indiana, like other states, enables the state to take a person's property (called "forfeiture") if the property was used in or is a product of drug-dealing. Delaware County, Indiana has an elected prosecutor and part-time deputy prosecutors. The deputies also have private law practices. Josiah Melville is a part-time prosecutor. County prosecutors handle forfeiture claims for crimes in their counties. Sherry Forsh, the elected prosecutor, wants Melville to prosecute drug cases for the county and also, through his private firm, to seek forfeiture. Melville gets a salary as a part-time prosecutor. For his forfeiture work, Melville is paid 25 percent of the value of any forfeited property. The balance goes to the county for use in law enforcement activities. Forfeiture can be ordered as part of a plea bargain or in a civil claim following conviction. Can Melville hold both positions?

YOUNG v. UNITED STATES EX REL. VUITTON ET FILS S.A.
481 U.S. 787 (1987)

[Vuitton, a leather goods manufacturer, had settled a trademark dispute with the defendants. The settlement enjoined the defendants from further trademark violations. When the defendants violated the injunction, Vuitton's lawyers secured an order to show cause why the defendants should not be held in criminal contempt. The court appointed those lawyers to prosecute the contempt. Young and others were convicted and received prison sentences. The Second Circuit affirmed. The Supreme Court upheld a district court's power to appoint private counsel to prosecute a contempt of court. It then considered whether Vuitton's own lawyers could be so appointed. Young argued that they could not be appointed because of a conflict between the duties of a prosecutor, on one hand, and the interests of Vuitton, their client, on the other. Part III-A of Justice Brennan's opinion for the Court follows.]

In Berger v. United States, 295 U.S. 78, 88 (1935), this Court declared:

> "The United States Attorney is the representative not of an ordinary party to a controversy, but of a sovereignty whose obligation to govern impartially is as compelling as its obligation to govern at all; and whose interest, therefore, in a criminal prosecution is not that it shall win a case, but that justice shall be done. As such, he is in a peculiar and very definite sense the servant of the law, the twofold aim of which is that guilt shall not escape nor innocence suffer."

This distinctive role of the prosecutor is expressed in Ethical Consideration (EC) 7-13 of Canon 7 of the American Bar Association (ABA) Model Code of Professional Responsibility (1982): "The responsibility of a public prosecutor differs from that of the usual advocate; his duty is to seek justice, not merely to convict."

Because of this unique responsibility, federal prosecutors are prohibited from representing the Government in any matter in which they, their family, or their business associates have any interest. 18 U.S.C. §208(a). Furthermore, the Justice Department has applied to its attorneys the ABA Model Code of Professional Responsibility, 28 C.F.R. §45.735-1(b) (1986), which contains numerous provisions relating to conflicts of interest. The concern that representation of other clients may compromise the prosecutor's pursuit of the Government's interest rests on recognition that a prosecutor would owe an ethical duty to those other clients. "Indeed, it is the highest claim on the most noble advocate which causes the problem— fidelity, unquestioned, continuing fidelity to the client."

Private attorneys appointed to prosecute a criminal contempt action represent the United States, not the party that is the beneficiary of the court order allegedly violated. . . . The prosecutor is appointed solely to pursue the public interest in vindication of the court's authority. A private attorney appointed to prosecute a criminal contempt therefore certainly should be as disinterested as a public prosecutor who undertakes such a prosecution.

If a Justice Department attorney pursued a contempt prosecution for violation of an injunction benefitting any client of that attorney involved in the underlying civil litigation, that attorney would be open to a charge of committing a felony under §208(a). Furthermore, such conduct would violate the ABA ethical provisions, since the attorney could not discharge the obligation of undivided loyalty to both clients where both have a direct interest. The Government's interest is in dispassionate assessment of the propriety of criminal charges for affronts to the Judiciary. The private party's interest is in obtaining the benefits of the court's order. While these concerns sometimes may be congruent, sometimes they may not. A prosecutor may be tempted to bring a tenuously supported prosecution if such a course promises financial or legal rewards for the private client. Conversely, a prosecutor may be tempted to abandon a meritorious prosecution if a settlement providing benefits to the private client is conditioned on a recommendation against criminal charges.

Regardless of whether the appointment of private counsel in this case resulted in any prosecutorial impropriety (an issue on which we express no opinion), that appointment illustrates the *potential* for private interest to influence the discharge of public duty. Vuitton's California litigation had culminated in a permanent injunction and consent decree in favor of Vuitton against petitioner Young relating to various trademark infringement activities. This decree contained a liquidated damages provision of $750,000 for violation of the injunction. The prospect of such a damages award had the potential to influence whether Young was selected as a target of investigation, whether he might be offered a plea bargain, or whether he might be offered immunity in return for his testimony. In addition, Bainton [Vuitton's lawyer] was the defendant in a defamation action filed by Klayminc [one of the petitioners] arising out of Bainton's involvement in the litigation resulting in the injunction whose violation was at issue in this case. This created the possibility that the investigation of Klayminc might be shaped in part by a desire to obtain information useful in the defense of the defamation suit. Furthermore, Vuitton had various civil claims pending against some of the petitioners. These claims theoretically could have created temptation to use the criminal investigation to gather information of use in those suits, and could have served as bargaining leverage in obtaining pleas in the criminal prosecution. In short, as will generally be the case, the appointment of counsel for an interested party to bring the contempt prosecution in this case at a minimum created *opportunities* for conflicts to arise, and created at least the *appearance* of impropriety.

As should be apparent, the fact that the judge makes the initial decision that a contempt prosecution should proceed is not sufficient to quell concern that prosecution by an interested party may be influenced by improper motives. A prosecutor exercises considerable discretion in matters such as the determination of which persons should be targets of investigation, what methods of investigation should be used, what information will be sought as evidence, which persons should be charged with what offenses, which persons should be utilized as witnesses, whether to enter into plea bargains and the terms on which they will be established, and whether any individuals should be granted immunity. These decisions, critical to the conduct of a prosecution, are all made outside the supervision of the court. . . .

The use of this Court's supervisory authority has played a prominent role in ensuring that contempt proceedings are conducted in a manner consistent with basic notions of fairness. The exercise of supervisory authority is especially appropriate in the determination of the procedures to be employed by courts to enforce their orders, a subject that directly concerns the functioning of the Judiciary. We rely today on that authority to hold that counsel for a party that is the beneficiary of a court order may not be appointed as prosecutor in a contempt action alleging a violation of that order. . . .

Prosecutors Avec Deux Chapeaux

May prosecutors wear two hats? The Court was divided in *Young*. Although seven Justices chose to rely on the Court's supervisory powers, only four (Brennan, Marshall, Blackmun, and Stevens) agreed that "harmless-error analysis is inappropriate in reviewing the appointment of an interested prosecutor in a case such as this." Justice Blackmun wrote that due process also forbids appointment of any "interested party's counsel" to prosecute for criminal contempt. Justice Scalia concluded that the appointment of a private prosecutor was not an exercise of the "judicial power of the United States" within the meaning of Article III, §§1, 2 of the Constitution. "Since that is the only grant of power that has been advanced as authorizing these appointments, they were void." Justice White dissented. He found no due process violation and would not have invoked the Court's supervisory powers to overturn the appointment of Vuitton's lawyer. Because the court did not rely on the Due Process Clause, its decision does not bind state courts.

The danger in *Young* was that Vuitton's lawyer would make prosecutorial decisions that were in the best interest of Vuitton or himself and not because of a "dispassionate assessment of the propriety of criminal charges for affronts to the Judiciary."

Consider this variation. A county district attorney hires lawyers in private practice to assist her as "special assistant prosecutors" in seeking civil penalties against various companies for violation of the state's Unfair Competition Law (UCL). The lawyers will advance all costs of the litigation, will have "the authority and responsibility to control and direct the performance and details of their work," and will sue in the name of the state. The district attorney would retain "final authority over all aspects of the litigation, including settlement." The lawyers would get 30 percent of any recovery and repayment of their costs.

Unlike *Young*, this will be a civil case with no possibility of incarceration. Also, the private lawyers have no client (like Vuitton) whose interests might threaten a "dispassionate assessment" of the state's interests. But they do have an interest in their fee. The greater the civil penalty, the greater the fee. Might not that interest lead them to seek to maximize the recovery regardless of what is fair? We would not allow government lawyers privately to profit from fines in cases they bring.

On facts like these, the Ninth Circuit rejected a challenge to the county's use of private lawyers. Am. Bankers Mgmt. Co. v. Heryford, 885 F.3d 629 (9th Cir. 2018). The court compared the arrangement to False Claims Act (FCA) cases, where a party (called a relator) sues in the name of the sovereign (the state or the United States) to vindicate a claim that belongs to it. (The sovereign can take control of the case or leave it to the relator's lawyers.) If victorious, the lawyers will get a portion of the recovery, which can amount to millions of dollars. The circuit had previously upheld this arrangement. United States ex rel. Kelly v. Boeing Co., 9 F.3d 743 (9th Cir. 1993). In *American Bankers*, it wrote that

> nothing meaningfully distinguishes the Law Firms' pursuit of civil penalties under the UCL from private relators' pursuit of civil penalties under the qui tam provisions of the False Claims Act. Indeed, nothing meaningfully distinguishes the situation here from a hypothetical one in which California has amended the UCL to allow private plaintiffs to pursue civil penalties—and *Kelly* leaves no doubt that California could, consistent with federal due process, do just that. Because *Kelly* held that the qui tam provisions of the False Claims Act do not offend due process, and because the contingency-fee arrangement here is not meaningfully different from qui tam litigation in terms of the incentives it creates or the powers it confers, we hold that the contingency-fee arrangement at issue here does not offend due process either.

Was it important to the *American Bankers* court that the district attorney maintained final control over the litigation? He thought so. He argued "that because he supervises the Law Firms and maintains ultimate authority over the litigation, and because he is a government attorney with no personal financial stake in the outcome of the litigation, there is not even the potential for a due process problem here." The court responded: "Our holding does not turn on [the district attorney's] exercise of control, however, because *Kelly* dictates the result in this case regardless of how much actual day-to-day supervision [the district attorney] exerts."

The upshot, which may seem puzzling, is that while the presence of another client's interests (Vuitton's) may be sufficient to cast doubt on the independence of its lawyer's judgment when she is acting as a public prosecutor, that concern disappears when a lawyer, who anticipates compensation for herself, not a client, sues civilly on behalf of the sovereign. The difference may turn on the fact that FCA and UCL cases are civil, not criminal. Yet civil fines can be as large as criminal fines or larger.

PEOPLE v. ADAMS

20 N.Y.3d 608, 987 N.E.2d 272, 964 N.Y.S.2d 495 (N.Y. 2013)

Pigott, J.

On September 20, 2009, complainant, a sitting Rochester City Court Judge, accused defendant, her neighbor and ex-paramour, of committing a crime by sending her three offensive text messages by cell phone earlier that day. The messages were vulgar and personal in nature, and unrelated to complainant's judicial duties. Defendant was charged, by way of an information/complaint filed in Rochester City Court, with two misdemeanor counts of aggravated harassment in the second degree. . . .

[The defense counsel originally assigned asked to withdraw and defense counsel from another county was assigned. He] spoke with the District Attorney's office regarding a possible settlement of the case, in which defendant would plead guilty to harassment in the second degree, a violation, in return for a sentence that would include 40 hours community service and psychiatric treatment. As defense counsel later recalled their conversation, the prosecutor told him that, while in most cases this would be an adequate resolution, he was rejecting the offer "due to the position of the victim." Defense counsel then spoke with complainant herself, who told him that she was "not willing to reduce the charges" and "wanted to go to trial." No plea offers were extended to defendant.

In February 2010, defendant [moved to disqualify the district attorney's office]. Defendant contended "that the District Attorney's office is in a conflict of interest position; to wit: By giving undue weight to the wishes of the victim in screening their case, the District Attorney's office is no longer acting as a fair and impartial official."

Counsel recounted the communications he had with the District Attorney's office in which the prosecutor stated, in essence, that complainant was unwilling to accept a reduced charge. In an accompanying affidavit, defendant's original counsel from the Public Defender's office stated that, in his view, the District Attorney's office was treating complainant's wishes much differently than it would any other victim's. The original defense counsel pointed out that the District Attorney's office, like his own office, appears before the complainant judge frequently each day and "would prefer not to engender any hostility from her." . . .

In response, though generally denying the allegation that defendant was being singled out for harsh treatment, the District Attorney's office did not specifically rebut the allegation that it consistently offered to accept pleas to a reduced charge in comparable cases. Nor did it offer an example of any other circumstance when it had refused to offer a plea to a violation or agree to dispose of the case by [adjournment in contemplation of dismissal (ACD)] in a comparable misdemeanor case. . . .

In general, "[t]he objector [to a prosecutor] should demonstrate actual prejudice or so substantial a risk thereof as could not be ignored."

However, in rare situations, the appearance of impropriety itself is a ground for disqualification, as our case law recognizes, when the appearance is such as to "discourage . . . public confidence in our government and the system of law to which it is dedicated." In a case of that nature, "defendants, and indeed the public at large, are entitled to protection against the appearance of impropriety." We are persuaded by the unique circumstances that this is such a case.

Although no constitutional right to a plea bargain exists, an appearance of impropriety may arise when the record provides an objective basis to question whether the prosecutor is exercising pretrial prosecutorial discretion in an evenhanded manner, based on the merits of the case or other legitimate prosecutorial concerns. Here, while we do not find that any actual impropriety occurred, there is an unacceptably great appearance of impropriety—the appearance that the District Attorney's office refused to accept a reduced charge because the complainant was a sitting judge who demanded that the matter go to trial, rather than because a trial was, in its own disinterested judgment, appropriate.

The complainant was a City Court Judge who had the authority to preside over cases involving this District Attorney's office, and the criminal charges were unrelated to her official position, so that her status as a judge should not have been a factor in the resolution of the case. Nor was there anything unique or unusual about the charges, since they involved communications between two people who had formerly been in an intimate relationship—a scenario frequently seen in harassment cases. However, despite protracted and repeated plea negotiations, the District Attorney's office did not offer defendant a reduced charge or agree to a plea that included a favorable sentence, such as an ACD, community service, or the like. While this alone would not be enough to raise an appearance of impropriety, there are other aspects of the record that do. Defendant's original counsel from the Public Defender's office, who had represented defendants in cases involving this District Attorney's office for more than a decade, averred that he had never before seen the office take such a hard-line position in a case involving comparable charges and a similar defendant. Although provided ample opportunity to respond, the District Attorney's office replied with nothing more than conclusory denials, failing to rebut the allegations with even a single example of a comparable case it had similarly refused to resolve with an ACD or a plea to a violation. Because the District Attorney's office failed to take steps to dispel the appearance of inappropriate disparate treatment, we conclude that this is one of those rare cases in which a significant appearance of impropriety was created, requiring disqualification.

Accordingly, the order of County Court should be reversed. . . .

———————

Do you get the sense, reading between the lines, or maybe the lines themselves, that the court was not happy about having to write this opinion but felt compelled to do so (which it certainly was)? Perhaps it feared a tidal wave of motions to disqualify prosecutors. So it called the facts "rare" and "unique." The court also seemed unwilling to criticize the prosecutors, but unless it did, it could not reverse. The court wrote that a defendant must show either "actual prejudice or so substantial a risk thereof as could not be ignored" *or* in "rare situations, the appearance of impropriety." Because the defendant did not get the business-as-usual plea deal others get because the victim, a judge, would not go along and the prosecutors appeared daily before her, it sure sounds like "actual prejudice." But the court chose not to go that far. It fell back on appearances and a failure in the burden of proof—"the District Attorney's office failed to take steps to dispel the appearance of inappropriate disparate treatment"—which allowed the court to say that the prosecutor's conduct only *looked* prejudicial, not that it actually was.

Two men were charged with trespass and one of them was charged with burglary of a vehicle. The victim happened to be the district attorney, Brett

Ligon, whose office brought the charges against the men. Ligon could not himself prosecute the men, but could his subordinates do so? The answer might seem obvious, but this happened in Texas, where apparently it was not obvious, at least not to Ligon. The defendants moved to disqualify Ligon's entire office and the trial judge agreed and appointed a special prosecutor. Ligon sought a writ of mandamus to overturn the decision. He lost. The appellate court's opinion contains an extensive review of authorities on prosecutorial disqualification in many jurisdictions. In re Ligon, 408 S.W.3d 888 (Tex. Ct. App. 2013).

3. Civil Cases

"Will You Represent Us Both?"

"As the Supreme Court has made it harder to bring Title VII actions for employment discrimination, and harder for plaintiffs' lawyers to collect reasonable counsel fees, my colleagues and I have gotten more requests for help. We work at the Deadwood Fair Employment Resource Center, a nonprofit firm. The other day two guys, Miguel Nunez and William Joseph—who are Hispanic and African-American, respectively—came in to see me. They were both passed over for a supervisory promotion. Instead, their employer, Beware Industries, a manufacturer of security devices, gave the job to a white guy with substantially less seniority. Miguel and William believe they were the victims of discrimination. They have pretty much the same qualifications, training, and experience. 'Sheila,' they told me, 'we went to five lawyers, but we can't afford to pay, and the lawyers say the judges here are stingy with fees, which they get only if we win. Will you represent us both?' No one else at Beware is in Miguel and William's position. There's no class here. How could we represent both Miguel and William?"

"My Birthday Poodle"

"I have a small practice in a small city. I do work for small companies. Tax. Corporate. Employment. Basil, my partner, is a T&E and real estate guy. Together we're Masuda & Simonetti. I'm Penelope Masuda.

"One thing I really enjoy is startups, young people usually with an idea and a lot of energy and determination but not so much money. They want advice—how to get started, should they incorporate or form a partnership, taxes, negotiate a lease, raise capital, trade name. I love this. They really believe in themselves, figure they'll be the next Bill Gates, whatever. I try to help, don't charge a whole lot. I figure if they survive, and many do, I have a good client, who will use me for other work and eventually they hire Basil for a will or to buy a house. So all in all it's a good business plan, don't you think?

"Yesterday, I read an article in the state bar journal about conflicts. Written by some law professor who probably never had a client. But it got me worried. Some of the startups are two, three, four people. The professor says this sort of thing can be 'rife' with conflicts and a 'minefield' for malpractice. Those were her words—'rife' and 'minefield.' And meanwhile, a day earlier, some new clients came in who want to start a business that will run birthday parties for children. One's a magician. One's a baker and bakes the cake with the children. One does a thing with puppets. And they each play a musical instrument. They hope eventually to hire others and offer different packages.

"They've divided the responsibility. The magician said she is going to put up most of the money. The baker has been baking for children's parties for eight years and gets many referrals. His trade name is 'My Birthday Poodle,' which the clients plan to keep. The puppeteer, she has an MBA and is going to handle the management.

"Way I see it, they're all on the same page. They all want this business to thrive. I don't see the conflict. What do you think?"

"If You're Adverse to Gyro, You're Adverse to Us"

Mercury Cycle is a leading manufacturer of custom built racing bikes that sell for many thousands of dollars. While it makes most of the parts for its bikes in house, it buys the gear assembly for three-quarters of its bikes from Gyro Equipment, an independent supplier. Specifically, Mercury buys the gear assembly that Gyro markets under the trade name Swift Gear. One of Mercury's outside law firms is Shmerlov, Usher & Pekoe ("SUP").

A company called BikeTech retained SUP to bring a patent infringement action against Gyro. Gyro has never been an SUP client. BikeTech claims that Gyro's Swift Gear violates its patent. It seeks an injunction against sales of Swift Gear unless Gyro and BikeTech can reach a licensing arrangement. When Fabian Crumm, the in-house lawyer at Mercury, reads about the lawsuit in the trade press and learns that SUP is representing BikeTech, he complains to Lori Vanilla, SUP's relationship partner for Mercury.

"If you're adverse to Gyro, you're adverse to us," Crumm says. "You're adverse to your own client." Crumm cites Rule 1.7(a)(1). "The rule says we can't be *directly* adverse to you and we're not," Vanilla counters. "We didn't sue you. We won't sue you. That is what the rule forbids. If we win, it might affect you marketwise. Maybe you'll need to find a new supplier or maybe Swift Gear will cost you more because Gyro will have to pay a royalty, which you can pass on to customers. Economic adversity is not direct adversity.

"Economic adversity is when you represent a competing bike maker," Crumm says. "That's not what you're doing. A victory for BikeTech will disrupt our supply of a critical component that cannot readily be replaced. That's different."

Who's right? Should the answer be the same as the answer to the next problem? Should Mercury also have cited Rule 1.7(a)(2)?

"Significant and Direct Financial Harm"

Borra, Axum & Hirsh (BAH) is representing its client Carson Electric in the Eleventh Circuit, where it will argue for a particular interpretation of the antitrust law. Xylon, a current BAH client on employment and labor matters, is defending itself against an antitrust claim in federal district court in Florida. Florida is within the Eleventh Circuit. BAH is not representing Xylon in the district court and has never represented Xylon on any antitrust or trade regulation matter. However, victory for Carson Electric in the Eleventh Circuit will eliminate Xylon's only viable defense in the Florida district court and result in millions of dollars in damages. Xylon is not a party in the Eleventh Circuit case, but it intervenes and moves to disqualify BAH from representing Carson Electric. It argues that the firm's representation of Carson Electric is "directly adverse" to it under Rule 1.7(a)(1) because of the "significant and immediate financial harm" to it if BAH wins.

What result? Should the answer be the same as the answer to the prior problem? Should Xylon also have cited Rule 1.7(a)(2)?

———————

The next case, Fiandaca v. Cunningham, although atypical in some ways, well illustrates client conflicts in civil litigation. The clients were two classes. The lawyers worked for New Hampshire Legal Assistance (NHLA). Using the text of the current version of Rule 1.7, did NHLA have a conflict under Rule 1.7(a)(1) or (a)(2) or both? How would you fill in the blanks in this sentence: "On one hand, NHLA_____, but on the other hand it _____." At the time, New Hampshire's version of Rule 1.7 had a different numbering system. I have inserted the current rule number in brackets where helpful.

FIANDACA v. CUNNINGHAM
827 F.2d 825 (1st Cir. 1987)

COFFIN, JUDGE.

[In the *Fiandaca* class action, 23 female New Hampshire prisoners alleged that opportunities for women inmates were inferior to those afforded to men. New Hampshire Legal Assistance (NHLA) was lead counsel for the class. In another litigation (the *Garrity* class action), NHLA represented "mentally retarded citizens" at Laconia State School in a challenge to conditions there.]

I . . .

The state extended a second offer of judgment to [the *Fiandaca* class] on October 21, 1986. This offer proposed to establish an in-state facility for the incarceration of female inmates at an existing state building by June 1, 1987. Although the formal offer of judgment did not specify a particular location for this facility, the state informed NHLA that it planned to use the Speare Cottage at the Laconia State School. NHLA, which also represented the plaintiff class in the ongoing *Garrity* litigation, rejected the offer on November 10, stating in part that "plaintiffs do not want to agree to an offer which is against the stated interests of the plaintiffs in the *Garrity* class." The state countered by moving immediately for the disqualification of NHLA as class counsel in the case at bar due to the unresolvable conflict of interest inherent in NHLA's representation of two classes with directly adverse interests. The court, despite recognizing that a conflict of interest probably existed, denied the state's motion on November 20 because NHLA's disqualification would further delay the trial of an important matter that had been pending for over three years. It began to try the case four days later.

[The trial judge then issued a decision, which found that "the conditions of confinement, programs, and services available to New Hampshire female prisoners are not on par with the conditions, programs, and services afforded male inmates." He ordered the state to build a permanent facility that "shall not be located at the Laconia State School or its environs."]

II . . .

[T]he state challenges the district court's decision on two independent grounds. First, it claims that the court should have disqualified NHLA as plaintiffs' class counsel prior to the commencement of the trial. Second, it contends that the court's proscription of the use of a site at the Laconia State School is unsupported either by relevant findings of fact or by evidence contained in the record. Because we find in favor of the state on its first claim and remand for a new trial on the issue of an appropriate remedy, we confine ourselves to an analysis of the disqualification issue.

A. REFUSAL TO DISQUALIFY FOR CONFLICT OF INTEREST

The state's first argument is that the district court erred in permitting NHLA to represent the plaintiff class at trial after its conflict of interest had become apparent. . . .

The state's theory is that NHLA faced an unresolvable conflict because the interests of two of its clients were directly adverse after the state extended its second offer of judgment on October 21, 1986. [The court quoted N.H. Rule 1.7(b), which is now Rule 1.7(a)(2), and its comment.] In this case, it is the state's contention that the court should have disqualified NHLA as class counsel pursuant to Rule 1.7 because . . . NHLA's representation of the plaintiff class in this litigation was materially limited by its responsibilities to the *Garrity* class.

We find considerable merit in this argument. The state's offer to establish a facility for the incarceration of female inmates at the Laconia State School, and to use its "best efforts" to make such a facility available for occupancy by June 1, 1987, presented plaintiffs with a legitimate opportunity to settle a protracted legal dispute on highly favorable terms. As class counsel, NHLA owed plaintiffs a duty of undivided loyalty: it was obligated to present the offer to plaintiffs, to explain its costs and benefits, and to ensure that the offer received full and fair consideration by the members of the class. Beyond all else, NHLA had an ethical duty to prevent its loyalties to other clients from coloring its representation of the plaintiffs in this action and from infringing upon the exercise of its professional judgment and responsibilities.

NHLA, however, also represents the residents of the Laconia State School who are members of the plaintiff class in *Garrity*. Quite understandably, this group vehemently opposes the idea of establishing a correctional facility for female inmates anywhere on the grounds of LSS. As counsel for the *Garrity* class, NHLA had an ethical duty to advance the interests of the class to the fullest possible extent and to oppose any settlement of the instant case that would compromise those interests. In short, the combination of clients and circumstances placed NHLA in the untenable position of being simultaneously obligated to represent vigorously the interests of two conflicting clients. It is inconceivable that NHLA, or any other counsel, could have properly performed the role of "advocate" for both plaintiffs and the *Garrity* class, regardless of its good faith or high intentions. Indeed, this is precisely the sort of situation that Rule 1.7 is designed to prevent.

Plaintiffs argue on appeal that there really was no conflict of interest for NHLA because the state's second offer of judgment was unlikely to lead to a completed settlement for reasons other than NHLA's loyalties to the *Garrity* class. We acknowledge that the record contains strong indications that settlement would not have occurred even if plaintiffs had been represented by another counsel. . . . The question, however, is not whether the state's second offer of judgment would have resulted in a settlement had plaintiffs' counsel not been encumbered by a conflict of interest. Rather, the inquiry we must make is whether plaintiffs' counsel was able to represent the plaintiff class unaffected by divided loyalties, or as stated in Rule 1.7(b) [Rule 1.7(a)(2)], whether NHLA could have reasonably believed that its representation would not be adversely affected by the conflict. Our review of the record and the history of this litigation—especially NHLA's response to the state's second offer, in which it stated that "plaintiffs do not want to agree to an offer which is against the stated interests of plaintiffs in the *Garrity* case"—persuade us that NHLA's representation of plaintiffs could not escape the adverse effects of NHLA's loyalties to the *Garrity* class. . . .

As we are unable to identify a reasoned basis for the district court's denial of the state's pre-trial motion to disqualify NHLA from serving as plaintiffs' class counsel, we hold that its order amounts to an abuse of discretion and must be reversed.

B. PROPER REMEDY

In light of the district court's error in ignoring NHLA's conflict of interest, we believe it necessary to remand the case for further proceedings. We must consider a further question, however: must the district court now start from scratch in resolving this dispute? The state argues that the court's failure to disqualify NHLA is plain reversible error, and therefore requires the court to try the matter anew. We subscribe to the view, however, that merely "conducting [a] trial with counsel that should have been disqualified does not 'indelibly stamp or taint' the proceedings." With this in mind, we look to the actual adverse effects caused by the court's error in refusing to disqualify NHLA as class counsel to determine the nature of the proceedings on remand.

We do not doubt that NHLA's conflict of interest potentially influenced the course of the proceedings in at least one regard: NHLA could not fairly advocate the remedial option—namely, the alternative of settling for a site at the Laconia State School—offered by the state prior to trial. The conflict, therefore, had the potential to ensure that the case would go to trial, a route the state likely wished to avoid by achieving an acceptable settlement. Nevertheless, we do not see how a trial on the merits could have been avoided given the manner in which the case developed below. Judge Loughlin stated on the record that he would not approve a settlement infringing on the rights of LSS residents, and under Rule 23(e), any settlement of this class action required his approval to be effective. It seems to us, therefore, that even if some other counsel had advised plaintiffs to accept the state's offer for a building at LSS, a trial on the merits would have been inevitable. . . .

The situation is different, however, with respect to the remedy designed by the district court. We believe that it would be inappropriate to permit the court's remedial order—which includes a specific prohibition on the use of LSS—to stand in light of the court's refusal to disqualify NHLA. The ban on the use of buildings located on the grounds of LSS is exactly the sort of remedy preferred by NHLA's *other* clients, the members of the *Garrity* class, and therefore has at least the appearance of having been tainted by NHLA's conflict of interest. Consequently, we hold that the district court's remedial order must be vacated and the case remanded for a new trial on the issue of the proper remedy for this constitutional deprivation.

What was NHLA's conflict? In what way was its representation of either class "materially limited" at the remedy stage? And why did the appellate court limit its relief to vacating the "remedial order of the district court"? Why wasn't the entire judgment reversed?

You could get the wrong impression from *Fiandaca* that appellate courts will reverse civil judgments because a lawyer had a conflict. Rarely is that so. The remedy may instead be a civil suit against a loser's conflicted firm. See chapter 13A and 13B. True, new trials are ordered in criminal cases where a defense lawyer's conflict violates the Sixth Amendment guarantee of the effective assistance of counsel, but the Sixth Amendment does not protect civil litigants. The new trial in *Fiandaca,* on remedy only, is best explained by the unusual public interest in the case. Three facts are important: Class members are less able to protect themselves than are individual clients; the members of the *Fiandaca* class (prisoners) were especially under a disability; and the conflict harmed the state by taking Speare Cottage off the table.

"Directly Adverse" Conflicts

The *Garrity* class, with independent counsel, had moved to intervene in *Fiandaca* "ten days after the conclusion of the trial on the merits. The group alleged that it had only recently learned of the state's proposal to develop a correctional facility for women at the Laconia State School. The members of the class were concerned that the establishment of this facility at the school's Speare Cottage, which they understood to be the primary building under consideration, would displace 28 residents of the school and violate the remedial orders issued [in the *Garrity* litigation]." The trial court denied the motion to intervene, but the First Circuit reversed.

The circuit disqualified NHLA under (what is today) Rule 1.7(a)(2). NHLA could not advise the *Fiandaca* class on whether to accept a settlement that included Speare Cottage because the *Garrity* class, its other client (albeit on another matter), opposed use of Speare Cottage. That created a "significant risk" that NHLA's representation of the *Fiandaca* class would be "materially limited" by its "responsibilities" to the *Garrity* class. After the *Garrity* class intervened, NHLA would also be disqualified under Rule 1.7(a)(1), which forbids a representation "directly adverse" to a current client, namely the *Garrity* class as a party.[*]

What makes a representation "*directly* adverse"? The phrase is not defined in the rule. Maybe someone thought the meaning was self-evident. It's not. The comment says the rule is an aspect of the duty of loyalty. It then adds: "The client as to whom the representation is directly adverse is likely to feel betrayed, and the resulting damage to the client-lawyer relationship is likely to impair the lawyer's ability to represent the client effectively." Rule 1.7 cmt. [6]. Opposing a client who is a *party* to a negotiation or litigation is surely encompassed by the words "directly adverse," even if the client is represented by a different firm. And *that* describes NHLA's position after the

---

[*] We might ask whether Rule 1.7(a)(1) is merely a specific application of Rule 1.7(a)(2) and therefore redundant. The difference between the two parts of Rule 1.7(a) is further explained in the hypothetical at page 216 involving Luís Calderon and Micro Used Autos.

Garrity class intervened, with new counsel, and became a party. But should "directly adverse" be broader?

Two of the problems set out above—"If You're Adverse to Gyro, You're Adverse to Us" (which is based on a real case) and "Significant and Direct Financial Harm" (which is not, not yet anyway)—pose that question. Should the lawyers in each be deemed directly adverse to a current client, which, although not a party to a litigation, would face financial harm if the lawyers win it? Should the answer be the same for each problem?

Imputed Conflicts

Assume (surely counterfactually) that NHLA had 100 lawyers in five New Hampshire cities. Wouldn't it then be plausible to screen the *Garrity* team (in, say, Concord) from the *Fiandaca* team (in Manchester) so that neither communicated with the other and had no access to the other team's files? Why didn't the court consider this solution? Why didn't the lawyers suggest it?

With exceptions for lawyers who join a firm from another firm or from a government office (see chapter 6B and 6C) and lawyers who meet with prospective clients (Rule 1.18), the Rules impute client conflicts among all firm lawyers. Read Rule 1.10(a). It treats a firm of 3,000 lawyers as one lawyer. Lawyers are affiliated for imputation purposes if they work in the same law firm, even if they are located in different cities or nations. The definition of "firm" includes private firms, public interest firms, and corporate law offices, but not government law offices. Rule 1.0(c). A partner's or associate's conflicts are imputed to other partners and associates. Lawyers with titles like "Senior Counsel," "Special Counsel," and "Of Counsel" are ordinarily deemed part of the same firm for conflicts purposes. All are presumed to have a significant relationship with their firm. See, e.g., People v. Speedee Oil Change Sys., 980 P.2d 371 (Cal. 1999). But not always. Hempstead Video v. Inc. Vill. of Valley Stream, 409 F.3d 127 (2d Cir. 2005) ("We believe the better approach for deciding whether to impute an 'of counsel' attorney's conflict to his firm for purposes of ordering disqualification in a suit in federal court is to examine the substance of the relationship under review and the procedures in place.").

Some courts refuse *automatically* to impute conflicts within a public defender's office, even if they would do so on the same facts for a private firm. Wyoming conclusively presumes prejudice when lawyers at the same private firm represent co-defendants in a criminal case, but not when the firm is a public defender's office. Among its reasons: A public defender's office, unlike a private firm, will have no reason to favor one client over another; the lawyers themselves have no financial incentive to prefer one client over another; indigent clients are likely to get better counsel from the defender than from appointed counsel; and "[p]aying outside counsel . . . would, no doubt, be quite an expense for the taxpayers of the state." Asch v. State, 62 P.3d 945 (Wyo. 2003). What do you make of this last reason? Is the court saying that conflict risks faced by poor people must bow to state fiscal constraints? And if a goal of the Rules is to encourage client trust and confidence, what difference should it make that the public defenders have no financial interest in their cases? All lawyers have an interest in winning.

Georgia, by contrast, has refused to relax the imputation rule for Georgia public defenders. In re Formal Advisory Opinion 10-1, 744 S.E.2d 798 (Ga. 2013). See also State v. McKinley, 860 N.W.2d 874 (Iowa 2015) (collecting authorities on both sides of the question).

Imputation has its limits. Rule 1.10(a), which imputes Rule 1.7 and Rule 1.9 client-client conflicts firmwide, was amended in 2002 to exclude imputation when one lawyer's conflict is based on that lawyer's personal interests if, in addition, there is no "significant risk" that the representation will be "materially" limited. So if, for example, a lawyer is conscientiously opposed to representing big tobacco or abortion providers, other firm lawyers may still do so. But if a lawyer who is powerful in the firm has a large personal investment in a company that is adverse to a firm client and therefore could not herself represent that client against the company, her conflict might be imputed to other firm lawyers who depend on the lawyer's good opinion.

Standing to Object

Another interesting aspect of *Fiandaca* is that state officials, not the NHLA's clients, raised the conflicts issue. Since conflict rules mean to protect clients, why did the adversary have standing? And once raised, why didn't the court ask NHLA's clients if *they* objected? One explanation, although unstated, may be the fact that the clients, two classes under some disadvantage, were not viewed as freely able to assert their rights. The *Garrity* class claimed to be unaware of the *Fiandaca* case. Another explanation may be the public interest in the correct resolution of these class actions. Recall that courts let the government raise the issue of criminal defense lawyer conflicts and may disqualify counsel even if defendants are prepared to consent. More broadly, however, the First Circuit has recognized nonclient standing to raise an opposing lawyer's conflict. See Kevlik v. Goldstein, 724 F.2d 844 (1st Cir. 1984), which views it as the duty of every lawyer to call a court's attention to another lawyer's violation of conflict rules.

The First Circuit is in the minority on the standing issue. Some courts suggest that only a client or former client has standing to complain. In re Yarn Processing Patent Validity Litig., 530 F.2d 83 (5th Cir. 1976). Other courts grant nonclients standing in limited circumstances. Foley-Ciccantelli v. Bishop's Grove Condo. Ass'n, 797 N.W.2d 789 (Wis. 2011) (nonclient has standing "when the prior representation is so connected with the current litigation that the prior representation is likely to affect the just and law-ful determination of the nonclient party's position"). Xcentric Ventures v. Stanley, 2007 WL 2177323 (D. Ariz. 2007) rejects *Kevlik* and collects authorities.

Should the Rules Let a Lawyer Act Adversely to a Current Firm Client on a Matter That Is *Unrelated* to the Representation of That Client?

The conflict in *Fiandaca* appeared because NHLA's advice on whether to accept the Laconia State School site in settlement was "materially limited." NHLA also represented the school's residents, who opposed the plan (or their guardians did). The clients' interests were in conflict on a question *related* to each representation—the use of the school grounds. Of course, it may be that the clients' interests were not inconsistent at all, that it was actually in the best interest of neither class to use the school as a site for female prisoners. Or maybe it was in the interest of the *Fiandaca* class but not the *Garrity* class. NHLA had to be in a position to give each class its best judgment without regard to the interests of the other class and it was not.

Now consider these alternatives.

Luís Calderon is suing Micro Used Autos for breach of warranty. The com-plaint says that Micro sold him a lemon. Barry Schmidt's firm represents nei-ther party in this dispute. But Schmidt is doing Calderon's estate plan, and Schmidt's partner, Delia Mickeljohn, is handling a zoning matter for Micro. The same firm represents two clients on *unrelated* matters, which means that the two matters have nothing to do with each other. As it happens, though, the two clients are adversaries in a third matter where the firm represents neither. Any problem? No, because the fact that they are adversaries in another matter will not affect the firm's work for either client and the firm's work will not affect the adverse matter. Micro may not want *its* firm to have anything to do with Calderon and vice versa, but that's not an interest that conflict rules recognize. Fremont Indem. Co. v. Fremont Gen. Corp., 49 Cal. Rptr. 3d 82 (Ct. App. 2006).

Suppose instead that Schmidt agrees to represent Calderon on the breach of warranty claim against Micro while his partner, Mickeljohn, con-tinues to handle Micro's zoning problem. Assume that the two matters— Calderon's warranty claim and Micro's zoning matter—are unrelated, which means nothing the lawyers do or learn in either matter can have any bearing on the other matter. But now the firm *is* conflicted. The Micro conflict falls under Rule 1.7(a)(1) and the Calderon conflict falls under Rule 1.7(a)(2). The firm is "directly adverse" to its client Micro, which may find it rather difficult to trust and confide in it. That trust is some-thing the Rules aim to protect. Calderon, in turn, may worry that the firm will not pursue his claim against Micro with ardor so as to avoid antago-nizing another firm client. Both clients must give informed consent. See Rule 1.7 cmt. [6].

Case law recognizes the validity of these interests. In Cinema 5, Ltd. v. Cinerama, Inc., 528 F.2d 1384 (2d Cir. 1976), as seminal a case in the modern world of legal ethics as you are ever going to find (it helps to be among the first to decide an issue), an order disqualifying the plaintiff's lawyer was affirmed because his partner was representing the defendant in another matter. The firm was adverse to its own client. The court wrote that "adverse representation is prima facie improper, and the attorney must be prepared to show, at the very least, that there will be no actual or *apparent* conflict in loyalties or diminution in the vigor of his representation. We think that appellants have failed to meet this heavy burden."

Or consider IBM v. Levin, 579 F.2d 271 (3d Cir. 1978), another early and prominent case. CBM represented Levin in an antitrust action against IBM. Before and during the prosecution of that action, certain partners at CBM, not involved in the antitrust action, were representing IBM on various unrelated matters (labor disputes, a replevin action). IBM moved to disqualify CBM from representing Levin in the antitrust action. CBM argued that DR 5-105 (the precursor to Rule 1.7) did not foreclose the representation since "no effect adverse to IBM resulted from CBM's concurrent representation . . . and no adverse effect on CBM's exercise of its independent professional judgment on behalf of IBM was likely to result." The court disagreed. It held that it is "likely that some 'adverse effect' on an attorney's exercise of his independent judgment on behalf of a client may result from the attorney's adversary posture toward that client in another legal matter."

Cinema 5 and IBM v. Levin are frequently cited (or cases citing them are). Yet are you able, from the excerpts, to discern the precise client interests we protect by prohibiting a lawyer from acting adversely to a current firm client on a matter wholly unrelated to the matter on which her firm is representing that client?

Many Big Law firms argue that the prohibition against representing a client against a second client in an unrelated matter is too harsh given the imputation rule and the size of some modern law firms. And they have a point. Imagine a firm with eight worldwide offices and 1,500 lawyers. On behalf of a long-standing client, a lawyer in the firm's Chicago office is asked to accept a matter adverse to company X. A conflicts check reveals that a partner in the firm's London office is currently handling an unrelated corporate matter for company X. This is the only work company X has ever given the firm and, relatively speaking, it is "very small potatoes." Yet, because client conflicts are imputed firmwide, the status of company X as a current client of the firm in London will prevent the Chicago partner from accepting a matter adverse to it in Chicago if company X does not consent.

Imagine that company X is a sophisticated global entity. Should the policies behind the imputed prohibition on adverse *unrelated* representation really apply here? Surely not as forcefully as they would if clients are individuals or small businesses, with little market power and unsophisticated in the use of lawyers. But can we have different conflict regimes depending on whether the client is or is not sophisticated? On the other hand, under the current rule, large companies can try to hire powerful law firms for small potatoes matters and thereby ensure that the firm cannot be adverse to them. Law firms are, however, aware of this risk and may reject small potatoes matters to avoid a later conflict.

One argument in favor of the current rule is that it can readily be displaced by agreement. The firm may ask company X, before accepting its small potatoes work, to give its consent in advance to adverse representation on unrelated matters should any arise. Many large firms do just that and many clients do consent. These advance consents are often upheld (see below). Of course, the opposite is also true. If the "default" rule instead *permitted* unrelated adverse representations, then a client like company X could insist on a stricter conflict rule. In fact, that happens even today. Verizon may insist that its firms never represent AT&T on anything at all as long as Verizon is a client, even if the conflict rules would otherwise allow it. If Verizon's business is sufficiently rewarding, a law firm may be willing to agree.

Confidentiality and Privilege in Multiple Client Representations

Joint Representations and Privilege.   Two criminal defendants (or subjects of an investigation) may decide to hire the same lawyer. If their interests do not conflict, or if they can and do consent to any conflict that may exist, they have a couple of good reasons to use one firm: It can save money and it will enable them to present a unified position. As Justice Powell wrote in Cuyler v. Sullivan, quoting Justice Frankfurter, "[a] common defense . . . gives strength against a common attack."

Joint representations as they're commonly called are not limited to criminal defendants or subjects of investigation. They apply equally to clients who are or can anticipate becoming civil litigants, whether as plaintiffs or defendants. Efficiency and cost may encourage employment of a single lawyer in transactional matters, too. Think of two individuals who want to start a business. They have similar goals and they will not likely want to pay two lawyers. But their interests may not be exactly aligned. Penelope Masuda's clients in "They're All on the Same Page" above had overlapping but not identical interests. So consent to any conflict would be needed.

Communications between one common lawyer and her two (or more) clients retain their privileged status so long as they would have been privileged in the first place. The fact that the communications between client *A* and the lawyer are shared with client *B* (who may be present at the time or informed later) will not sacrifice the privilege, as it would if a stranger were given access to the communication, because, very simply, client *B* is not a stranger. See generally Restatement §75. However, in the event of a dispute between the two clients, neither client will be able to assert privilege for communications with the common lawyer. See, e.g., In re Teleglobe Commc'ns Corp., 493 F.3d 345 (3rd Cir. 2007); unenacted Rule 503(d)(5), Fed. R. Evid. The clients must be so warned. They also need to understand that the lawyer's communications with either client may be shared with the other one. Rule 1.7 cmts. [30] and [31].

What language should Penelope Masuda include in her retainer agreement?

The Common Interest Rule. Let us now alter the example and imagine that our two clients decide to hire separate counsel. They still have interests in common, but the interests are not identical and a single lawyer would need a conflict waiver, which one or both of them are unwilling to give. Or it may simply be a matter of personal preference. If we are prepared to afford the protection of the privilege when two clients hire the same lawyer, must they sacrifice that protection for information they share with the other client's lawyer, even if all other facts remain unchanged?

No. If we were to say that a client loses the privilege by sharing her privileged information with the lawyer for another client with a common interest, we would be exacting a rather high price for what may be the perfectly sensible decision to hire separate counsel. We would also discourage cooperation. This seems a little harsh. On the other hand, we must remember that the privilege, for all its virtues, limits access to information.

The issue of privilege in multiple-lawyer situations arises most often in criminal matters, which explains why the courts began to talk about a "joint defense privilege" when holding that otherwise privileged information will not lose that status if two or more defense lawyers and two or more defendants (or suspects) exchange information. But it should not matter whether the two clients are criminal defendants or plaintiffs or defendants in civil matters. So perhaps a better phrase is "joint litigant privilege." That term, however, would seem to limit the doctrine to litigation. Clients may also have legitimate confidentiality interests when cooperating in transactional matters. What then about using the term "common interest privilege," a phrase that can extend the doctrine to nonlitigation matters, assuming for the moment that it *should* apply outside pending or impending litigation? (Some jurisdictions do not do so. See below.)

But that label still uses the word "privilege." We are not really discussing a privilege as such, are we, but rather an *exception* to the rule that an existing privilege is waived when a lawyer-client communication is shared with a third party. Other clients who have a common interest (and their lawyers) are not viewed as third parties. So in the end the best term may be the "common interest rule." That is the conclusion and reasoning of United States v. Schwimmer, 892 F.2d 237 (2d Cir. 1989), a leading case. It is also recognized in unenacted Rule 503(b)(3), Fed. R. Evid. The rule avoids loss of privilege for communications between lawyers or between any client and any lawyer in the common interest arrangement.* Communications between

---

* One of my students perceptively pointed out that this is really a matter of definition. Is the glass half full or half empty? One might equally well call the common interest privilege a new and distinct privilege for communications among lawyers and clients with a common interest. But the courts have instead chosen to say that the privilege is the original privilege and the common interest rule prevents its loss.

the clients (in the absence of a lawyer) are not privileged, which is why lawyers tell their clients not to discuss the matter among themselves.

In some courts, the common interest rule may be available only for pending or impending litigation. In re Santa Fe Int'l Corp., 272 F.3d 705 (5th Cir. 2001) ("[I]n this circuit . . . there must be a palpable threat of litigation at the time of the communication, rather than a mere awareness that one's questionable conduct might some day result in litigation."). Ambac Assur. Corp. v. Countrywide Home Loans, 57 N.E.3d 30 (N.Y. 2016), refused to extend the common interest rule to transactional matters. Other courts, however, have disagreed, as does Restatement §76(1). See, e.g., Schaeffler v. United States, 806 F.3d 34 (2d Cir. 2015) and Hanover Ins. Co. v. Rapo & Jepsen Ins. Servs., 870 N.E.2d 1105 (Mass. 2007).

How common must the common interest be? Can the clients also have some divergent interests or must their interests be identical? Some courts insist on a near-identity of interests. Santa Fe Pac. Gold Corp. v. United Nuclear Corp., 175 P.3d 309 (N.M. 2007). Others do not. "The common interest need not be identical, and even where the parties might have some adverse motives, the common interest doctrine can apply. However, the overall interests of the parties who assert the common interest doctrine must be aligned to the extent that they are 'maintaining substantially the same cause.'" Shenwick v. Twitter, Inc., 2019 WL 3815717 (N.D. Cal. 2019).

Some Other Issues.   What should a lawyer do if one of two joint clients gives her information about the joint matter but instructs her not to tell the other client? The lawyer may be trapped between her duty of confidentiality and her duty to inform. Restatement §60 comment *l* and Johnson v. Superior Court, 45 Cal. Rptr. 2d 312 (Ct. App. 1995), uphold the lawyer's duty or power to inform the other client. By hiring a single lawyer, clients should expect that their lawyer may share all information relevant to the lawyer's work with each of them. In any event, the lawyer can and should avoid the problem by making clear at the outset that information from either client may be shared with the other client. A. v. B., 726 A.2d 924 (N.J. 1999) ("[A]n attorney, on commencing joint representation of co-clients, should agree explicitly with the clients on the sharing of confidential information. . . . Such a prior agreement will clarify the expectations of the clients and the lawyer and diminish the need for future litigation."). Giving this warning can smoke out conflict situations that argue against the joint representation in the first place. See also Rule 1.7 cmt. [31].

A second repetitive issue concerns waiver. Does either (or any) joint client, or either (or any) of the clients in a common interest arrangement, have the right to waive the protection for otherwise privileged information? When one lawyer represents two or more clients, California purports to resolve this issue by statute. Section 912(b) of the California Evidence Code provides that when "two or more persons are joint holders of a privilege . . . a waiver of the right of a particular joint holder of the privilege to claim the privilege does not affect the right of another joint holder to claim the privilege." The Restatement gives both co-clients and clients in a common-interest arrangement the right to waive the privilege only for their own communications to counsel, absent contrary agreement. See §§75 and 76. If a document contains communications from two or more co-clients or members of the common interest arrangement, waiver is effective only if all the clients agree, unless a nonwaiving client's communications "can be redacted." Section 75 comment *e*; §76 comment *g*. See also United States v. Gonzalez, 669 F.3d 974 (9th Cir. 2012).

A final important question, which arises only in a common interest arrangement, asks what, if any, duties lawyer *A* owes to client *B*? Remember, client *B* is the client of lawyer *B*, not of lawyer *A*, so the gamut of duties that lawyers owe clients would seem to be inapplicable. But absent agreement to the contrary, a court might read the common interest agreement to give lawyer *A* a *fiduciary* duty to client *B*. That duty may prevent lawyer *A* from using or revealing client *B*'s information to client *B*'s disadvantage even if it would advantage her own client. Nat'l Med. Enters. v. Godbey, 924 S.W.2d 123 (Tex. 1996). Courts have even inferred an attorney-client relationship between lawyer *A* and client *B*, as happened in re Gabapentin Patent Litig., 407 F. Supp. 2d 607 (D.N.J. 2005), which should especially concern lawyers. The Restatement concludes that lawyer *A* could not act adversely to client *B* in a later matter if information *B* shared with *A* is "material and relevant" to the adverse matter. Restatement §132, comment *g*. Roosevelt Irrigation District v. Salt River Project Agricultural Improvement & Power District, 810 F. Supp. 2d 929 (D. Ariz. 2011), collects numerous cases. Lawyers can eliminate these disabling consequences by putting the scope of the common interest agreement in writing.

Put It in Writing. A common interest agreement need not be written or, in the view of some courts, even explicit. It "may be implied from conduct and situation, such as attorneys exchanging confidential communications from clients who are or potentially may be codefendants or have common interests in litigation." United States v. Gonzalez, supra. This is a generous conclusion. Not all courts may agree, which is why lawyers in a common interest arrangement should put it in a writing that defines its scope, including the common interest. And, given the uncertainty about the duties one lawyer owes to another lawyer's common interest client, the writing should (if that is desired) explicitly negate an attorney-client or fiduciary relationship with the clients of other lawyers and any confidentiality duty to them. Last, the agreement should, if desired, prohibit each client from using it to disqualify another client's lawyer in the event of a later dispute between or among the clients.

Appealability of Civil Disqualification Orders

An order granting or denying a motion to disqualify civil counsel is not subject to immediate appeal as of right in federal court. Richardson-Merrell,

Inc. v. Koller, 472 U.S. 424 (1985) (disqualification order); Firestone Tire & Rubber Co. v. Risjord, 449 U.S. 368 (1981) (refusal to disqualify). The Ninth Circuit has refused to entertain an appeal by permission (under 28 U.S.C. §1292(b)) from a refusal to disqualify counsel because to do so "would greatly enhance [the] usefulness [of such motions] as a tactical ploy." Shurance v. Planning Control Int'l, Inc., 839 F.2d 1347 (9th Cir. 1988). Mandamus remains a possible route to review a disqualification order, but the scope of review on mandamus is narrow. In re Kellogg Brown & Root, 756 F.3d 754 (D.C. Cir. 2014). A consequence of these rulings is that the law of lawyer disqualification in federal civil cases is largely the province of trial judges with no higher court available to reconcile their decisions.

Malpractice and Fee Forfeiture Based on Conflicts

Sometimes the remedy for a conflict of interest will be disqualification, as in *Fiandaca*. Sometimes it will be discipline, especially when the conflict was flagrant, as in Iowa Supreme Court Attorney Disciplinary Board v. Clauss, 711 N.W.2d 1 (Iowa 2006) (attorney suspended six months for representing creditor against debtor while representing debtor on unrelated matter). Conflicts can also lead to malpractice liability and forfeiture of the right to a fee. These remedies are not mutually exclusive. We discuss malpractice and fee forfeiture in greater detail in chapter 13. Here, we view civil liability through the conflicts prism. The obvious conflicts in the next case occurred in two rather ordinary transactions. As you read the opinion, ask yourself: What was the *legal* basis for Sheila Simpson's claim? What role did the *ethical* conflicts have in the case?

SIMPSON v. JAMES
903 F.2d 372 (5th Cir. 1990)

WISDOM, CIRCUIT JUDGE.

This appeal concerns a malpractice suit brought by the sellers of corporate assets against the partners of a law firm that represented both the buyers and the sellers in the transaction. The plaintiffs alleged two incidents of negligence on the part of the attorneys: the handling of the original sale and the subsequent restructuring of the buyers' note in favor of the plaintiffs. After a jury trial, the court rendered judgment in favor of the plaintiffs, awarding the sellers $100,000 for each act of negligence. We affirm.

STATEMENT OF THE CASE

The plaintiffs, Sheila Simpson and Lovie and Morelle Jones, were the sole stockholders in H.P. Enterprises Corporation. The business of H.P. Enterprises was operating and franchising catfish restaurants. Sheila Simpson's late husband, Buck Simpson, handled most of the business affairs of the corporation until his death. Mrs. Simpson then took over operation of the company, but she later decided to sell the corporation to devote more time to her children.

Mrs. Simpson turned to Ed Oliver for help in selling the corporation. Since 1968, Oliver practiced in Texarkana, Texas, with the firm now known as Keeney, Anderson & James. He had represented Mr. Simpson for many years in matters relating to H.P. Enterprises and in personal matters. In November 1983 a group of investors approached Oliver to inquire into purchasing H.P. Enterprises. Oliver formed a corporation for the investors, Tide Creek, and drew up the legal documents to transfer the assets of H.P. Enterprises to Tide Creek. Oliver was the sole source of legal advice for both parties.

The price agreed upon was $500,000, of which $100,000 was paid at the execution of the sale. As security for the sellers, Oliver provided for a lien on the stock of Tide Creek, personal guarantees of the buyers on the corporation's $400,000 note to the sellers, and certain restrictions on operation of the business. The sale took place on November 18, 1983. After the transaction, Mr. Oliver's firm continued to represent Mrs. Simpson in estate and tax matters. During this time, all of her business records were kept at the firm's office.

Thereafter, two significant events occurred. In April 1984 a fire destroyed Tide Creek's commissary, which contained its inventory. David James, a partner in Oliver's firm, represented Tide Creek in recovering over $200,000 in insurance proceeds. In October 1984, Oliver left the firm to practice in Houston. The firm was renamed Keeney, Anderson & James. An associate in the firm, Fred Norton, took over tax and estate work for Mrs. Simpson.

Under the original terms of the sale arranged by Oliver, a $200,000 note by Tide Creek in favor of the plaintiffs became due on November 18, 1984. Tide Creek did not meet this obligation. On January 29, 1985, the plaintiffs visited David James at his office. James told them that Tide Creek was having financial difficulties, and that the company could pay them only $50,000 at that time. James restructured the note between the parties. At that meeting, Mrs. Simpson asked James what he would do if her interests and those of Tide Creek diverged. James replied: "We would have to support you."

In the Fall of 1985, Mrs. Simpson became concerned when she heard rumors of Tide Creek's impending bankruptcy. She called Fred Norton, an associate at the firm, and Norton arranged a meeting for her with David James. James advised Mrs. Simpson that her interests were in conflict with those of Tide Creek. He told her that she should find another lawyer to represent her; James was representing Tide Creek.

The plaintiffs received their last payment from Tide Creek on October 1, 1985. Tide Creek then filed for bankruptcy. The plaintiffs filed a claim in bankruptcy court, but received nothing. Their efforts to enforce the personal guarantees proved fruitless; the guarantors filed for personal bankruptcy.

Mrs. Simpson filed suit against the three partners of Keeney, Anderson & James on January 16, 1987. The suit alleged that acts of negligence by Oliver and James proximately damaged the plaintiffs. The plaintiffs alleged that the defendants had a conflict of interest that prevented them from acting in the plaintiffs' best interests. The jury found that Ed Oliver was negligent in his representation of Mrs. Simpson and the Joneses and awarded them $100,000 damages. It also found David James liable for negligence for his role in restructuring the delinquent note and awarded $100,000 damages to Simpson. . . .

Discussion . . .

2. Evidence to Satisfy the Elements of the Cause of Action

In Texas, an attorney malpractice claim is based on negligence. A plaintiff in a malpractice action must prove four elements to recover: that 1) the defendant owed a duty to the plaintiff; 2) the defendant breached that duty; 3) the breach proximately caused the plaintiff injury; and 4) damages resulted. The defendants challenge the existence of a number of these elements.

A. Attorney-Client Relationship: James and Simpson

The defendants argue that no attorney-client relationship existed between David James and Sheila Simpson, and consequently, James owed no duty to her that could form the basis of malpractice liability. . . .

The evidence adduced at trial indicated that Ed Oliver represented the plaintiffs' business interests in H.P. Enterprises before and at the time of the sale of its assets to Tide Creek. After Oliver left, the firm represented Mrs. Simpson in tax and estate matters and continued to maintain all of her business records. Mrs. Simpson testified that on January 29, 1985, at the time the note was restructured, and on a subsequent occasion, James encouraged her about Tide Creek's future economic viability. She added that she relied on those assurances. Significantly, Simpson stated that James advised her that she was entering into a good deal in agreeing to the restructuring. At the same meeting, James assured Simpson that he would stand by her in the event of a conflict of interest between Simpson and Tide Creek. James stated that at no time did Mrs. Simpson specifically ask him to represent her interests against Tide Creek. He testified that he never gave any advice to Mrs. Simpson and never charged her for his time. Nevertheless, the evidence was sufficient for a reasonable jury to conclude that an attorney-client relationship existed, as manifested through the parties' conduct.

B. Negligence

Under Texas law, an attorney "is held to the standard of care which would be exercised by a reasonably prudent attorney." This is not a result-oriented analysis; an attorney will not be liable for undesirable effects of a decision that was reasonable at the time it was made.

The plaintiffs alleged negligent acts that arose out of the defendants' conflicts of interest in representing both sides of a transaction. Liability may not be premised solely on the fact that an attorney represented both buyer and seller; after full disclosure by the attorney, it may be proper in some circumstances for an attorney to represent both sides in a real estate transaction.

Both sides in this case presented expert testimony on the propriety of Oliver's representing both the plaintiffs and the investors from Tide Creek. Of course, in case of conflicting expert testimony, the jury is entitled to make credibility determinations and to believe the witness it considers more trustworthy. Although the defense maintains that Oliver merely reduced a settled agreement to writing, the plaintiffs presented evidence suggesting that Oliver negotiated the sale price for the assets of H.P. Enterprises and determined the "mechanics" of the sale. Moreover, the plaintiffs' expert witness, John Ament, testified that Oliver did not adequately protect Simpson against the possibility that Tide Creek would fail financially. For example, he stated that instead of a lien on Tide Creek stock, Oliver should have provided for a lien on the assets. Oliver also might have named the plaintiffs as beneficiaries of insurance policies. Ament added that the interests of the plaintiffs and buyers varied significantly from the beginning. Although the evidence of Oliver's negligence is not overwhelming, we are not persuaded that the jury's conclusion is unreasonable.

David James prepared the instrument whereby Tide Creek's note in favor of Simpson and Jones was restructured. Simpson argues that James did not disclose Tide Creek's desperate financial condition, did not explain other options to her, and did not pursue over $200,000 insurance money for her benefit. The plaintiffs' expert also testified that it was improper for James to represent parties with such divergent interests: a creditor seeking recovery and a debtor in default. We believe that this evidence is sufficient to uphold the jury's finding of negligence.

C. Whether Attorney Negligence Proximately Caused the Plaintiffs' Damages

The plaintiffs have the burden to prove that but for the defendants' negligence, they would have recovered the payments due. The jury found that Oliver and James, by their individual acts of negligence, each caused the plaintiffs $100,000 damages. We review the record to determine whether the plaintiffs proved that amount of damages.

It is apparent that proper conduct on the part of Oliver could have averted the loss of at least $100,000. The plaintiff's expert accountant testified that the sellers of the corporate assets were not adequately protected. Protection could have been provided by a lien on the conveyed assets or by naming the plaintiffs as beneficiaries of property insurance. The evidence is sufficient on this issue.

Whether the plaintiffs proved damages as a result of James's conduct is a closer question. The plaintiff's expert accountant testified that as of March 1985, Tide Creek had combined equity of over $368,000. His estimate was based on internal corporation figures that were not verified. Had the plaintiffs foreclosed on Tide Creek, however, they would have taken it back with over $477,000 in worthless accounts receivable. Moreover, it is undisputed that as of September 30, 1985, Tide Creek had equity of −$483,427.

However, the plaintiffs presented evidence that James was involved in recovering over $200,000 in insurance proceeds after a fire destroyed the restaurant's commissary. As argued by the plaintiff and admitted by the defendants' expert witness, James could have seized the insurance proceeds to satisfy the delinquent note. Perhaps because of a conflict of interest, James did not mention this possibility to the plaintiffs. We conclude that the plaintiffs proved damages caused by James. . . .

What Did Oliver and James Do Wrong?

This simple case churns up several intriguing questions that may arise when lawyers are sued for malpractice or breach of fiduciary duty. One is why the firm's conflicts even mattered. We know that the Rules do not themselves create legal liability. Scope cmt. [20]. Greene v. Frost Brown Todd, LLC 2017 WL 6210784 (6th Cir. 2017) (in negligence action against law firm, summary judgment for defendant; plaintiff failed to show that "conflict of interest caused any harm"). Yet conflicts are routinely alleged in civil actions against lawyers.

If Oliver and James had acted differently, Simpson might have been protected. Fine. But then wouldn't any lawyer who failed to protect them in the same way also be liable? Or could it be that the lawyers' conflicts transformed *non*actionable behavior into an actionable claim? Another way of asking this question is: Why were the lawyers' conflicts relevant to liability?

Oliver and James had dual loyalties. Without the conflict, Oliver could have argued that he had tried to get the best deal possible for Simpson. The conflict allowed Simpson to argue that Oliver's divided loyalties explain why he did not get her a better deal. The more he got for her, the worse it would be for the buyers, his other clients. Yet Oliver did insist on the buyers' personal guarantees. He got something for each client. May the buyers now sue on the ground that an unconflicted lawyer would have protected them from promises that led to bankruptcy?

We can say similar things about James's work. Any effort he made to favor Simpson on the terms of the restructured note or on control of the insurance proceeds would disfavor the buyers. James's conflict may explain why he didn't do more to protect Simpson.

This case presents two other riddles. The first is the causation issue. The court says that James's conduct presents "a closer question" on causation than does Oliver's conduct. The opposite may be true. Oliver could at least argue that an unconflicted lawyer could not have negotiated a better deal. Negotiation entails compromise. Simpson had the burden to prove otherwise. But James cannot say the same. Another lawyer could have gone to court to preserve the insurance money before the buyers could get their hands on it. No negotiation would be required.

The second riddle asks why the court talked about negligence as the basis for liability. Isn't it obvious that both lawyers acted intentionally, not negligently? Simpson is claiming that they intentionally failed to get a better deal for her to give something of value to the buyers. In fact, Simpson might have argued that both lawyers favored the buyers over her because chances for future work were greater from a going business than from Simpson personally.

Consent and Waiver

Would Oliver and James have been safe if they had gotten conflicts consents from each set of clients? Rule 1.7 lets a client consent to work that would otherwise be forbidden. (But not all work. See Rule 1.7(b).) Courts and the Rules require lawyers to explain the conflict to a client before accepting consent. Rule 1.7 requires "informed consent" that is "confirmed in writing." Both phrases are defined in Rule 1.0. The Restatement and numerous courts recognize that a client's sophistication is a significant consideration in determining whether consent is informed. See Restatement §122 and comment *d*. The greater the client's sophistication, the less detail the lawyer will be expected to provide.

What should the lawyers have asked Simpson or the buyers to consent to? The multiple representation? Freedom to prefer another client? Malpractice? No on malpractice, unless the client is independently represented. See Rule 1.8(h)(1). Nor does consent allow the lawyer to disserve the consenting client. See Van Kirk v. Miller, 869 N.E.2d 534 (Ind. Ct. App. 2007), where a lawyer represented both the buyer and the seller of a business. The court wrote that "by holding that Van Kirk knowingly signed the conflict waiver, we are *not* holding that he was not entitled to competent, diligent representation," which the court held Miller provided. Proof of informed consent could have changed the dynamics in the courtroom and put Oliver and James in a somewhat better light. It would not, however, have allowed them to favor one client over the other, which is what Simpson said they in fact did.

Advance Consents. Clients may consent to conflicts before they arise. For example, a firm may ask a client to agree that the firm can be adverse to the client on unrelated litigation even while it is representing the client on a different matter. At the time, no adverse litigation may be foreseen. But then, how can the consent be informed? If the consent comes before the conflict arises, it may not be possible to know the full scope of the conflict to which the client is consenting.

The comment to Rule 1.7 recognizes that even a blanket advance consent (i.e., little or no detail) can stand if the "client is an experienced user of the legal services involved and is reasonably informed regarding the risk that a conflict may arise . . . particularly if . . . the client is independently represented by other counsel in giving consent and the consent is limited to future conflicts unrelated to the subject of the representation." The Restatement also calibrates the need for specificity by looking to the sophistication of the client. "Client consent to conflicts that might arise in the future is subject to special scrutiny, particularly if the consent is general. A client's open-ended agreement to consent to all conflicts normally should be ineffective unless the client possesses sophistication in the matter in question and has had the opportunity to receive independent legal advice about the consent." §122 comment *d.*

Caution: Despite this generous authority, some courts have been more skeptical about the enforceability of open-ended consents than the comment to the Rules and the Restatement envision. With less detail, it is less likely that the court will consider the consent informed. Lennar Mare Island, LLC v. Steadfast Ins. Co., 105 F. Supp. 3d 1100 (E.D. Cal. 2015) (applying California rules and rejecting an advance waiver even though the client had been represented by its in-house counsel on its terms).

4. *The Insurance Triangle*

Ed's Daughter Was Driving

"My name is Carmella Vicks. I do insurance defense work in a north-western city. A half-dozen insurance companies hire me to represent policyholders who get sued after auto accidents or for injuries covered by a homeowner's policy. Almost always the insured couldn't care less about the case because the company is paying. They just care about premiums going up. The policies require the insureds to cooperate, however, and they do.

"An insured I'll call Ed had an accident. His car hit a parked car, unfortunately, a high-end BMW, at about 10 P.M. one evening. No one was hurt. Ed left a note with his name and contact information. Ed's insurer lets its customers report an accident online, and Ed did. A few days later, the BMW owner sent Ed an estimate for the cost of repairing the car—about $10,500. Ed's policy covers property damage up to $50,000. Ed sent the estimate to the insurer. The insurer sent me Ed's online notice and the estimate along with Ed's policy. This particular insurer has used me a half-dozen times a year for the last seven or eight years.

"When I contacted Ed, he told me that his daughter Erin was driving. He was in the car with her. The thing is Erin has only a learner's permit, which does not allow her to drive at night. I pointed out to

Ed that under the policy, the insurance company is not liable 'if the insured permits an unlicensed person to drive the vehicle.' This apparently was news to him. Ed's online notice to the insurer begins: 'I wish to report an accident in which my car hit a parked car.' It does not identify the driver. Ed said he didn't intend to conceal that information. He didn't think it mattered. He also said couldn't Erin's permit be a license depending on how you defined 'unlicensed.' Although that argument isn't foreclosed, I'm pretty sure Ed would lose.

"Ed asked if I could settle the claim, so that the company pays, without revealing that Erin was driving, which might cause the company to refuse payment. What should I do?"

Client Identity and the Obligation to Defend

Three overlapping questions may arise in insurance defense work. *First:* Who is the lawyer's client: the insurer, the insured, or both? If in "Ed's Daughter Was Driving," Ed is the only client, your solution will be different than if the insurer is also Carmella's client and owed the same duties as she owes Ed. *Second,* assuming that the insurer is not a client, what are Carmella's obligations to it? And *third,* what does it mean to say (as cases do) that an insurer's obligation to defend is "broader than" the obligation to indemnify?

The *first* question will be of only academic interest if the entire claim against the insured is covered by the insurance. Then, the interests of insurer and insured are aligned. Nevertheless, sometimes their interests will diverge. Then we need to identify the client. There is a diversity of opinion on whether the lawyer represents the insured alone or the insurer, too. Finley v. Home Insurance Co., 975 P.2d 1145 (Haw. 1998), says "the modern view" is that "the sole client of the attorney is the insured." Remodeling Dimensions v. Integrity Mut. Ins. Co., 819 N.W.2d 602 (Minn. 2012), agrees but adds that "a law firm representing an insurance company could also represent the insured in the same matter [where] there was no apparent conflict of interest . . . the insured consulted with an independent attorney . . . and the insured had expressly consented to the dual representation."

Another view, whose adherents probably consider it equally modern, says that the insurer is also a client. State Farm Mut. Auto. Ins. Co. v. Hansen, 357 P.3d 338 (Nev. 2015). Sometimes the insured is referred to as the "primary" client, which would make the insurer a "secondary" client. Exactly how these imprecise terms affect the lawyer's duties is unclear. What is clear, though, is that if the interests of the insured and insurer conflict, the same lawyer cannot represent them both without *informed* consents, which may be impossible to get.

Authority on the "who is the client?" question can be found in Restatement §134 comment *f* and the Reporter's Notes to that comment. The Restatement takes no position, probably because the ALI membership was divided.

As for the *second* question: The interests of the insured and insurer diverge if the insurer has a basis to claim that a loss was caused by an event or conduct that is not within the policy. This is called a coverage dispute. If the insurer is aware that there is such a basis, it might bring a declaratory judgment action to establish nonliability. Meanwhile, it will have to provide a defense if the complaint alleges an event or conduct within the policy. It will do so under a *reservation of rights*, which means that by defending, it is not conceding that it will be responsible to pay any judgment.

In "Ed's Daughter Was Driving," Carmella Vicks, the lawyer, realizes that the insurance company has a basis to resist coverage and does not know it. Ed's contrary argument is weak but not frivolous. If the insurer is also considered her client, Carmella would have a duty to inform it that Ed's daughter was driving. But that certainly harms Ed, her other client. So Carmella might need to withdraw without saying why. But that also harms Ed because it alerts the insurer to a problem. Or Carmella could tell the insurer that she cannot represent both it *and* Ed without saying why, but that hurts Ed for the same reason. This is why it makes sense to recognize Ed as the only client.

Assuming Carmella is in a jurisdiction where the insured is the only client, what can she do for Ed without violating any obligation to the insurer? Many American lawyers earn their living when insurers hire them to represent people like Ed, which makes this an important question as well as an interesting one. Carmella's challenge would be to find an ethical way to get the insurer to pay. She could not lie or mislead the insurer, so she has to be careful in what she says, but she would have no duty to disclose a basis to challenge coverage, a fact she knows confidentially. The insurer is not defenseless. It can ask Ed who was driving. Both a refusal to answer and the true answer will reveal the coverage issue.

The *third* question asks what it means to say that an insurer's obligation to defend is broader than the obligation to indemnify. A complaint may allege conduct and injuries that may or may not be covered, depending on what the jury decides are the facts. Then, "the question of insurance coverage" and "the question of the insured's liability" are "intertwined." Pub. Serv. Mut. Ins. Co. v. Goldfarb, 425 N.E.2d 810 (N.Y. 1981). We will eventually learn whether what the insured is alleged to have done or not done is covered by the policy because the jury can be asked to tell us in a special verdict. In *Goldfarb*, for example, a dentist was sued for molesting a patient. She alleged either that he intended to cause her injury or that his intentional act caused an unintended injury. Under New York law at the time, the insurer would not have to indemnify on the first theory, but it would on the second. Depending on what the jury decided, then, the insurer would or would not have to pay the judgment. Because we cannot know the answer until the jury tells us the dentist's intentions, the insurer was required to defend because the complaint contained theories of recovery that were both within and outside the policy's coverage.

A plaintiff can eliminate the insurer's duty to defend by asserting only claims not within the policy. Why might it choose *not* to do that? Indeed, why might it choose to assert only claims certainly within the policy? This question reappears in Greycas, Inc. v. Proud (page 411).

C. THE ADVOCATE-WITNESS RULE

A special conflict confronts attorneys who are or ought to be called as witnesses in a litigation in which they represent one of the parties. It may be that the attorney ought to be a witness for the party her firm represents or for an opponent. Model Rule 3.7 does not distinguish between testimony for or against a client. Unless one of its narrow exceptions applies, it simply prohibits lawyers from acting "as advocate at a trial [if] the lawyer is likely to be a necessary witness." FDIC v. U.S. Fire Ins. Co., 50 F.3d 1304 (5th Cir. 1995) (thorough review of application of Rule 3.7). Notice the several limitations the quoted words imply. The disqualification runs only to advocacy at trial, not to pretrial work. A lawyer will not be disqualified simply because his testimony would "likely" be "relevant" or even "highly useful." It must be "necessary." Macheca Transp. Co. v. Phila. Indem. Ins. Co., 463 F.3d 827 (8th Cir. 2006).

Rule 3.7(a) disqualifies the lawyer personally but not her firm. Other firm lawyers may appear as advocates "unless precluded from doing so by Rule 1.7 or Rule 1.9." In other words, there must be another kind of conflict — other than one under the advocate-witness rule — in order to require imputation. Can you think of an example in which the entire firm of a lawyer-witness should be disqualified? What if in *P* v. *D*, *D* calls *W*, a partner in the firm representing *P*, and *W*'s (necessary) testimony is expected to be highly damaging to *P*'s case? What will *P*'s trial lawyer, who is *W's* partner, wish to do if free to do it?

Rule 3.7 has been used to disqualify criminal defense counsel, notwithstanding that the defendant is willing to waive counsel's testimony in order to keep her as an advocate. Gonzalez v. State, 117 S.W.3d 831 (Tex. Crim. App. 2003) (5-4 decision, citing *Wheat,* upholding disqualification of defense lawyer on state's motion, despite defendant's willingness to forego counsel's purportedly favorable testimony); United States v. Evanson, 584 F.3d 904 (10th Cir. 2009) (same).

Policies Behind the Advocate-Witness Rule

In Murray v. Metropolitan Life Insurance Co., 583 F.3d 173 (2d Cir. 2009), the plaintiffs planned to call four lawyers from the Debevoise firm to testify against defendant Metropolitan Life, which other Debevoise lawyers planned to represent at trial. The four lawyers would not themselves be on the trial team, but plaintiff claimed that their conflict should be imputed to the firm. The court disagreed.

> [The party moving for disqualification] "bears the burden of demonstrating specifically how and as to what issues in the case the prejudice may occur and that the likelihood of prejudice occurring [to the witness-advocate's client] is substantial." "Prejudice" in this context means testimony that is "sufficiently adverse to the factual assertions or account of events offered on behalf of the client, such that the bar or the client might have an interest in the lawyer's independence in discrediting that testimony."
>
> As this definition suggests, the showing of prejudice is required as a means of proving the ultimate reason for disqualification: harm to the integrity of the judicial system. We have identified four risks that Rule 3.7(a) is designed to alleviate: (1) the lawyer might appear to vouch for his own credibility; (2) the lawyer's testimony might place opposing counsel in a difficult position when she has to cross-examine her lawyer-adversary and attempt to impeach his credibility; (3) some may fear that the testifying attorney is distorting the truth as a result of bias in favor of his client; and (4) when an individual assumes the role of advocate and witness both, the line between argument and evidence may be blurred, and the jury confused. These concerns matter because, if they materialize, they could undermine the integrity of the judicial process. . . .
>
> Therefore, we now hold that a law firm can be disqualified by imputation only if the movant proves by clear and convincing evidence that [A] the witness will provide testimony prejudicial to the client, and [B] the integrity of the judicial system will suffer as a result. . . .
>
> The parties dispute whether the Debevoise lawyer-witnesses will give testimony so prejudicial to MetLife that the integrity of the judicial system may be threatened and disqualification warranted. Our review of the record suggests that the Debevoise witnesses will do little more than authenticate documents and confirm facts that do not appear to be in dispute.

Giuffre v. Dershowitz

Compared to Rules 1.7 through 1.10, Rule 3.7(a) is rarely a basis to disqualify a lawyer, and Rule 3.7(b) is even more rarely a basis for disqualifying the witness-lawyer's entire firm. That issue did, however, arise in the libel case brought by Virginia Giuffre against Alan Dershowitz, an entirely ordinary dispute but for the identity of the players and the facts. Giuffre v. Dershowitz, 410 F. Supp. 3d 564 (S.D.N.Y. 2019).

In 2014, Virginia Giuffre alleged in a Florida court that she was forced by convicted pedophile Jeffrey Epstein to have sex with Harvard law professor Alan Dershowitz among others when she was underage. Dershowitz has publicly and vehemently denied Giuffre's charge, called Giuffre a "serial perjurer" and a "serial prostitute," and alleged that Giuffre and her lawyers at Boies Schiller Flexner LLP (BSF) had "fabricated the assertion [against him] in order to get money from other powerful, wealthy people." In response, Giuffre, represented by BSF but not David Boies personally, sued Dershowitz for libel. Dershowitz moved to disqualify the entire firm under Rule 3.7.

Years earlier, after Giuffre first made her allegation against him, Dershowitz secretly recorded a conversation between himself and Boies. Dershowitz claims that Boies said on the tape that he did not believe Giuffre. Dershowitz told the court that he planned to call BSF lawyers, including Boies, to testify that his accusation against BSF and Giuffre was true. Because Boies himself would be a necessary witness, Rule 3.7 disqualified him from representing Giuffre in court. The issue for Judge Preska was whether BSF was also disqualified by imputation. She held that it was:

> Here, Dershowitz offers tape-recorded evidence of the [Boies] statements which he contends support the truth of his extortion statement. For example, the preliminary transcript prepared by defense counsel quotes Boies as proposing that he and [BSF partner] McCawley say to Giuffre, "[W]e have reviewed the documentary evidence and we are convinced that your belief [that you had relations with Dershowitz] is wrong and we would like to explore with you how you could have come to this conclusion that is wrong." . . .
>
> The discussions between Boies and Dershowitz are not the only facts . . . that raise the issue of the witness-advocate rule — they are simply the most developed at this stage. Dershowitz has also announced his intention to take the depositions of several BSF lawyers to help prove the truth of his extortion assertion. Again, it is essential to follow the litigation jujitsu at work here: Giuffre says Dershowitz defamed her by falsely saying she and BSF engaged in an extortion scheme; Dershowitz says he said it and it is true. Giuffre's burden is to prove it is false in the face of Dershowitz's vehement claim that it is true. Truth, of course, is a complete defense. Dershowitz stated that "if testifying truthfully, these witnesses will offer testimony adverse and prejudicial to their own client, Giuffre," because their testimony will tend to prove what Dershowitz said is true. Thus, it is plain that several of the Firm's lawyers will be essential trial witnesses on a major claim in the Complaint, likely to be called by both parties and not merely called to identify documents. . . . Even if each of those lawyers denied participation in such a plot . . . some or all of the concerns raised by the Court of Appeals in *Murray* are present, particularly that "some may fear that the testifying attorney is distorting the truth as a result of bias in favor of his client." Accordingly, the Firm must be disqualified to "preserve the integrity of the adversary process" and avoid "taint[ing] the underlying trial." Dershowitz has carried his burden of imputation under Rule 3.7(b). He has shown that at the very least Boies "is likely to be called as a witness on a significant issue," i.e., whether Dershowitz's extortion claims (which the Complaint says are false) are true. Dershowitz has also shown that "the testimony may be prejudicial to the client" based on the recorded conversations.

Self-Assessment Questions

1. Recall this case from the note following Wheat v. United States in part B1 of this chapter.

> Campbell, a former mayor of Atlanta charged with RICO violations and other crimes, retained Gillen as one of his defense lawyers. Parker is Gillen's partner and previously represented Greene "on corruption charges related to those Campbell faced." Greene, who had pled guilty, would be a witness against Campbell. Parker could not himself represent Campbell because he would then be in the position of having to cross-examine Greene, his former client on a related matter. But could Gillen do so? Campbell offered to waive any conflict, but Greene would not. Citing *Wheat*, the Eleventh Circuit affirmed disqualification of Gillen. United States v. Campbell, 491 F.3d 1306 (11th Cir. 2007). It said only that by disqualifying Gillen, "the district court chose to avoid a situation in which the fairness of Campbell's trial undoubtedly and quite legitimately would have been called into account, whether by Campbell or by Greene." It added that "[w]hile it is true that Campbell was free to waive the conflict, the district court was not required to accept his waiver" in light of Greene's nonwaiver.

   You represent Campbell and will ask the circuit court to rehear your appeal en banc. What will you argue is wrong with the court's analysis?

2. "We represent a major maker of light fixtures, company A. We do collection work, draft contracts, handle litigation over warranties, tax planning, some employment. Another client, company B, a homebuilder, has asked us whether certain pricing policies of a different maker of light fixtures (company C) violate the antitrust laws. We have never done work for company C. It happens that C's pricing policies are nearly the same as A's policies. We have never advised A on any of its pricing policies or, indeed, any antitrust matters. Can we advise company B? Any advice we give that casts doubt on the legality of C's policies will make the rounds among homebuilders including those who buy from company A. Separately, would we be free to represent company B in court challenging company C's policies when we know that success could threaten company A's pricing policies and lead to litigation against it?"

3. Vera DeQuesto has been indicted for theft. Specifically, the charge is that she operated a Madoff-style Ponzi scheme that, when it collapsed, caused 17 companies and individuals to lose a total of $21 million. Two of those companies are Credentia and Pashion. DeQuesto wishes to retain Chiara Mirapoli. Mirapoli is an experienced criminal defense lawyer but her firm is small—just Mirapoli, one partner, and two associates. The case against DeQuesto will require complex pretrial motions and analysis of vast quantities of financial data. Mirapoli tells

DeQuesto she can take the case only if DeQuesto is also willing to retain co-counsel who will help with the data analysis and legal research and arguments. She recommends Wishon & Bonderant, a midsize firm with expertise in financial crimes. DeQuesto agrees. When Wishon notes its appearance, the prosecutors move to disqualify it on the ground that Credentia and Pashion are two of its clients. Wishon was aware of that. It arranged its work so that none of the lawyers who will work on DeQuesto's matter will have worked, or will work during the prosecution, for Credentia or Pashion. Also, Wishon will not analyze the financial harm to those clients. And Mirapoli alone will do all the questioning of witnesses and the opening and closing. Wishon lawyers may argue generic legal issues unrelated to the identity of the alleged victims, including Credentia and Pashion. What should the judge do?

VI

Successive Conflicts of Interest

A. PRIVATE PRACTICE

Divorce and Default

In late 2018, Clarissa Rasmussen represented Patrick Roth in a divorce from his wife, Leila, after a 28-year marriage. Representation took eight months, during which time Clarissa negotiated with Leila's lawyer over the economic terms of the divorce, which required her to evaluate Patrick's net worth and income. Their three children were grown and quite self-sufficient, so there were no custody or child support issues. Leila had not worked outside the home for 24 years, while Patrick had built a substantial business, Slipshod, Inc., a maker of casual footwear. Slipshod was a closely held corporation. Patrick was its president and majority shareholder. Eight investors, all but one employees of the company, had small stock interests. Patrick and Leila signed a separation agreement dividing their property and giving Leila lifetime support payments.

In 2021, Slipshod was having trouble meeting its payments to Wumco Bank on its line of revolving credit. After several months, Wumco sent Patrick Roth a letter threatening to invoke the acceleration clause of the credit agreement, which would obligate Slipshod to pay the outstanding balance immediately, something Slipshod could not do. The inevitable result would be bankruptcy.

Patrick alleged duress and other actionable conduct that violated Wumco's lender obligations to Slipshod. He requested a meeting with his counsel, Lincoln Grey, present. On the meeting date, Wumco appeared with its counsel, Kevin DeVries. The negotiating session was not productive, but the parties planned a second meeting a week later. When they exchanged business cards, Patrick realized for the first time that Kevin was a partner in the same firm as Clarissa Rasmussen, his former divorce lawyer. Lincoln then wrote to Kevin, asserting that neither Kevin nor anyone from his firm could represent Wumco in the negotiations with Slipshod because the firm previously represented Patrick in the divorce. Kevin replied:

The Roths were divorced two years ago. That was purely a personal law issue. It was between Patrick and Leila Roth. It's over. The current financial matter is between Wumco Bank, my client, and Slipshod, Inc., two different parties. Not only are the parties different, but the issues are different, the areas of law are different, and our professional duties are different. There is no conflict.

Who is right?[*]

"What Do I Owe Haywood Tallman?"

Jane Lopez has developed a practice representing retail startups in New York City. She has represented dozens of restaurants, dress shops, bakeries, and shoe stores. Jane is retained by Haywood Tallman to help him with the legal work required to open a store dedicated to the cultural heritage of indigenous peoples, mostly in developing countries. Lopez incorporates the store, negotiates and reviews the terms of the lease, works out financing arrangements with banks and suppliers of sheet music, musical instruments, CDs, DVDs, and even LPs (making a comeback), and helps Tallman get a registered trade name for the store. At Tallman's request, Lopez successfully petitions the zoning board to permit retailers on his street to place merchandise bins on the sidewalk in front of their stores. Six months after Lopez's work is done and she has billed for her services and been paid, she asks you, "What do I owe Haywood Tallman?" Specifically, she asks:

1. "May I represent the landlord in an action to evict Tallman? The landlord claims that music from speakers in the store is interfering with the building's other commercial and residential tenants, in violation of a lease term forbidding excessive noise affecting quiet enjoyment."

---

[*] This problem has been in many editions of the book. The facts might seem unrealistic, the product of an overactive imagination, but they nicely illustrate the reach of Rule 1.9(a). Then, a few years ago, a district court judge in Arizona was faced with a disqualification motion in a Title VII case with strikingly similar facts.

> Thomas Longfellow is an attorney at Burch & Cracchiolo, P.A. [which represents] Plaintiff in this matter; however, Mr. Longfellow has not appeared in this case. Nonetheless, Mr. Longfellow represented E.B. Chester in his 2011–12 marital dissolution. Mr. Chester is not a party to this action, but he owns approximately a one-third interest in Chester Group, LLC. Chester Group is the parent company that owns Defendant Chester Cycles. . . . During the former representation, Mr. Chester communicated "confidential information about the business and assets of Chester Group, LLC" to Mr. Longfellow as part of a property settlement related to the divorce proceedings. Defendant now seeks the imputed disqualification of Plaintiff's Counsel pursuant to [Rules 1.9 and 1.10] due to Mr. Longfellow's former representation of Mr. Chester in his divorce.

Plotts v. Chester Cycles LLC, 2016 WL 614023 (D. Ariz. 2016).

2. "May I represent a community group in an effort to repeal the rezoning? Not only do the retail bins narrow pedestrian space, but shoppers congregate around them, resulting in further congestion. Pedestrians are then forced to walk in the gutter, creating particular challenges for seniors and people with disabilities. But Tallman's bins have produced significant revenue for the store."

3. "May I represent Elspeth Dundee, who wants to hire me to open the same kind of store across the street from Tallman's store?"

"Stop the High Rise"

Sherwood Forrest Properties has acquired a square block of land in Canal St. Cloud, a gentrifying neighborhood of Kingston. Much of the neighborhood consists of single-family homes. Four-story loft buildings are nearby. Artists have moved into the lofts, and restaurants and clothing stores soon followed. Now Sherwood Forrest plans to build a 27-story residential condominium with a health club, a Whole Foods, and a Uniqlo clothing store as commercial tenants. It needs various city approvals, which will be a challenge because of the size of the project in relation to the neighborhood.

The company hires George Dauphine, a lawyer at Allbright & Sterne, a leading Kingston firm. His views will carry much weight with the city. George, who happens to live in the Canal St. Cloud neighborhood, studies the company's plans and makes suggestions for alterations to increase its chance of winning approvals. After a year, with most of the difficult work completed, George recommends that Sherwood Forrest retain a different, less costly firm to handle the balance, which was likely to be largely ministerial, and the company does so.

Six months later, Sherwood Forrest has received all of the required authorizations but one. The final step is city council approval. Meanwhile, for quite some time George has been having second thoughts about the effect of the project on the quality of life in the neighborhood—increased density, increased vehicular traffic, and overcrowding in the local schools. Also, the project changed. Whereas all apartments were originally going to have two or three bedrooms, now a third will have one bedroom, which will mean increased turnover and less stability as families outgrow their space. George believes that one of the virtues of Canal St. Cloud is the deep roots his neighbors have in the community.

So George and his wife join their neighbors in soliciting signatures on a petition to the city council to stop the high rise and, if the council does not, to put it to a popular vote. The petition eventually garners 1,433 signatures, more than the 1,000 signatures needed to put the question on the ballot if the city council approves the project. George and his wife collected 47 of the signatures. George speaks in opposition to the project at the city council meeting. However, the council approves the project. Some of the opponents, including George, then distribute leaflets urging voters to reject the project, but it is approved.

Sherwood Forrest then sues George and Allbright & Sterne. The complaint charges breach of fiduciary duty and cites Rule 1.9 of the jurisdiction's professional conduct rules (same as the ABA's). In a motion to dismiss, the defendants argue that there is no claim that Sherwood Forrest's confidential information was revealed. In opposing the project, George did not tell anyone that he had anything to do with it. He did not reveal his affiliation with Allbright & Sterne or that he was a lawyer. Nor does the complaint assert otherwise. George's position is that he did not violate Rule 1.9(a) or his fiduciary duty. Even if he did, he argues, professional conduct rules and state fiduciary duty law are subordinate to his First Amendment right to voice his opposition to the plan and to petition the government. What result?

The materials that follow comprise issues that arise when applying the successive conflict-of-interest rules and will help address the three problems above.

ANALYTICA, INC. v. NPD RESEARCH
708 F.2d 1263 (7th Cir. 1983)

POSNER, CIRCUIT JUDGE.

Two law firms, Schwartz & Freeman and Pressman and Hartunian, appeal from orders disqualifying them from representing Analytica, Inc. in an antitrust suit against NPD, Inc. . . .

[Malec was an employee of NPD between 1972 and 1977. Malec had two shares, or 10 percent, of NPD's stock. During the course of his employment, his two co-owners wished to give him an additional two shares of stock as compensation for his services. They told him to find "a lawyer who would structure the transaction in the least costly way." Malec hired Richard Fine, a partner in Schwartz & Freeman, and Fine devised a plan for the transfer of the stock. Since Malec had to pay income tax on the stock, it was necessary to evaluate it. NPD gave Fine information on its financial condition, sales trends, and management, after which Fine fixed a value for the stock, which the corporation adopted. NPD paid Fine's bill for the services. Eventually, Malec and his wife, who was also employed at NPD, left their jobs. Mrs. Malec thereafter incorporated Analytica to compete with NPD in the market-research business.

[In October 1977, several months after the Malecs had left NPD, Analytica retained Schwartz & Freeman to represent it in connection with its claim of anticompetitive behavior against NPD. After complaints to the Federal Trade Commission proved unavailing, Analytica authorized Schwartz & Freeman to hire Pressman and Hartunian as trial counsel. An antitrust suit was brought against NPD in 1979. The defendant moved to disqualify both of the plaintiff's law firms. The district judge disqualified both firms and ordered Schwartz & Freeman to pay NPD $25,000 for resisting the disqualification motion. Both firms appealed but the Pressman firm's appeal was judged moot.]

For rather obvious reasons a lawyer is prohibited from using confidential information that he has obtained from a client against that client on behalf of another one. But this prohibition has not seemed enough by itself to make clients feel secure about reposing confidences in lawyers, so a further prohibition has evolved: a lawyer may not represent an adversary of his former client if the subject matter of the two representations is "substantially related," which means: if the lawyer could have obtained confidential information in the first representation that would have been relevant in the second. It is irrelevant whether he actually obtained such information and used it against his former client, or whether—if the lawyer is a firm rather than an individual practitioner—different people in the firm handled the two matters and scrupulously avoided discussing them.

There is an exception for the case where a member or associate of a law firm (or government legal department) changes jobs, and later he or his new firm is retained by an adversary of a client of his former firm. In such a case, even if there is a substantial relationship between the two matters, the lawyer can avoid disqualification by showing that effective measures were taken to prevent confidences from being received by whichever lawyers in the new firm are handling the new matter.* The exception is inapplicable here; the firm itself changed sides.

Schwartz & Freeman's Mr. Fine not only had access to but received confidential financial and operating data of NPD in 1976 and early 1977 when he was putting together the deal to transfer stock to Mr. Malec. Within a few months, Schwartz & Freeman popped up as counsel to an adversary of NPD's before the FTC, and in that proceeding and later in the antitrust lawsuit advanced contentions to which the data Fine received might have been relevant. Those data concerned NPD's profitability, sales prospects, and general market strength—all matters potentially germane to both the liability and damage phases of an antitrust suit charging NPD with monopolization. The two representations are thus substantially related, even though we do not know whether any of the information Fine received would be useful in Analytica's lawsuit (it might just duplicate information in Malec's possession, but we do not know his role in Analytica's suit), or if so whether he conveyed any of it to his partners and associates who were actually handling the suit. If the "substantial relationship" test applies, however, "it is not appropriate for

---

* This is a reference to the utility of screening against imputed disqualification where a conflicted lawyer changes firms and her new firm wants to avoid disqualification. Authorities are divided on whether screening can prevent imputation. See part B. Screening would, in any event, be inadequate here because of the next sentence in Judge Posner's opinion.—Ed.

the court to inquire into whether actual confidences were disclosed," unless the exception noted above for cases where the law firm itself did not switch sides is applicable, as it is not here. . . .

Schwartz & Freeman argues, it is true, that Malec rather than NPD retained it to structure the stock transfer, but this is both erroneous and irrelevant. NPD's three co-owners retained Schwartz & Freeman to work out a deal beneficial to all of them. All agreed that Mr. Malec should be given two more shares of the stock; the only question was the cheapest way of doing it; the right answer would benefit them all. . . . As is common in closely held corporations, Fine was counsel to the firm, as well as to all of its principals, for the transaction. If the position taken by Schwartz & Freeman prevailed, a corporation that used only one lawyer to counsel it on matters of shareholder compensation would run the risk of the lawyer's later being deemed to have represented a single shareholder rather than the whole firm, and the corporation would lose the protection of the lawyer-client relationship. Schwartz & Freeman's position thus could force up the legal expenses of owners of closely held corporations.

But it does not even matter whether NPD or Malec was the client. In Westinghouse's antitrust suit against Kerr-McGee and other uranium producers, Kerr-McGee moved to disqualify Westinghouse's counsel, Kirkland & Ellis, because of a project that the law firm had done for the American Petroleum Institute, of which Kerr-McGee was a member, on competition in the energy industries. Kirkland & Ellis's client had been the Institute rather than Kerr-McGee but we held that this did not matter; what mattered was that Kerr-McGee had furnished confidential information to Kirkland & Ellis in connection with the law firm's work for the Institute. Westinghouse Elec. Corp. v. Kerr-McGee Corp., [580 F.2d 1311 (7th Cir. (1978))]. As in this case, it was not shown that the information had actually been used in the antitrust litigation. The work for the Institute had been done almost entirely by Kirkland & Ellis's Washington office, the antitrust litigation was being handled in the Chicago office, and Kirkland & Ellis is a big firm. The connection between the representation of a trade association of which Kerr-McGee happened to be a member and the representation of its adversary thus was rather tenuous; one may doubt whether Kerr-McGee really thought its confidences had been abused by Kirkland & Ellis. If there is any aspect of the Kerr-McGee decision that is subject to criticism, it is this. The present case is a much stronger one for disqualification. If NPD did not retain Schwartz & Freeman—though we think it did—still it supplied Schwartz & Freeman with just the kind of confidential data that it would have furnished a lawyer that it had retained; and it had a right not to see Schwartz & Freeman reappear within months on the opposite side of a litigation to which that data might be highly pertinent.

We acknowledge the growing dissatisfaction . . . with the use of disqualification as a remedy for unethical conduct by lawyers. The dissatisfaction is based partly on the effect of disqualification proceedings in delaying the underlying litigation and partly on a sense that current conflict of interest standards, in legal representation as in government employment, are too stringent, particularly as applied to large law firms—though there is no indication that Schwartz & Freeman is a large firm. But we cannot find any authority for withholding the remedy in a case like this, even if we assume contrary to fact that Schwartz & Freeman is as large as Kirkland & Ellis. NPD thought Schwartz & Freeman was its counsel and supplied it without reserve with the sort of data—data about profits and sales and marketing plans—that play a key role in a monopolization suit—and lo and behold, within months Schwartz & Freeman had been hired by a competitor of NPD's to try to get the Federal Trade Commission to sue NPD; and later that competitor, still represented by Schwartz & Freeman, brought its own suit against NPD. We doubt that anyone would argue that Schwartz & Freeman could resist disqualification if it were still representing NPD, even if no confidences were revealed, and we do not think that an interval of a few months ought to make a critical difference.

The "substantial relationship" test has its problems, but conducting a factual inquiry in every case into whether confidences had actually been revealed would not be a satisfactory alternative, particularly in a case such as this where the issue is not just whether they have been revealed but also whether they will be revealed during a pending litigation. Apart from the difficulty of taking evidence on the question without compromising the confidences themselves, the only witnesses would be the very lawyers whose firm was sought to be disqualified (unlike a case where the issue is what confidences a lawyer received while at a former law firm), and their interest not only in retaining a client but in denying a serious breach of professional ethics might outweigh any felt obligation to "come clean." While "appearance of impropriety"* as a principle of professional ethics invites and maybe has undergone uncritical expansion because of its vague and open-ended character, in this case it has meaning and weight. For a law firm to represent one client today, and the client's adversary tomorrow in a closely related matter, creates an unsavory appearance of conflict of interest that is difficult to dispel in the eyes of the lay public—or for that matter the bench and bar—by filing of affidavits, difficult to verify objectively, denying that improper communication has taken place or will take place between the lawyers in the firm handling the two sides. Clients will not repose confidences in lawyers whom they distrust and will not trust firms that switch sides as nimbly as Schwartz & Freeman.

[The court affirmed the disqualification and the $25,000 payment. Judge Coffey dissented on the ground that the presumption of shared confidential information should be rebuttable.]

---

* The Model Rules do not include an "appearance of impropriety" as a basis for lawyer regulation. See the notes following this case.—ED.

The "Substantial Relationship" Test

Schwartz & Freeman argued that NPD was never its client. We saw this tactic (unsuccessfully) employed in Simpson v. James (chapter 5B3) and will again in Togstad v. Vesely, Otto, Miller & Keefe (chapter 13A). The court offered two reasons for quickly disposing of this formalistic argument: Forcing NPD and Malec to hire separate counsel would have been inefficient (i.e., costly), and even if NPD was not a client (although the court thought it was) it gave the firm confidential information to enable it to perform a legal service from which NPD would directly benefit. It had a right not to see the firm later oppose it in a matter where it could use that information against it.

The modern articulation of the substantial relationship test, preserved in Rule 1.9(a) and Restatement §132, is credited to Judge Edward Weinfeld's opinion in T.C. Theatre Corp. v. Warner Bros. Pictures, 113 F. Supp. 265 (S.D.N.Y. 1953). Judge Weinfeld, a renowned district court judge during his long tenure (1950-1988), wrote:

> [W]here any substantial relationship can be shown between the subject matter of a former representation and that of a subsequent adverse representation, the latter will be prohibited. . . .
>
> [T]he former client need show no more than that the matters embraced within the pending suit wherein his former attorney appears on behalf of his adversary are substantially related to the matters or cause of action wherein the attorney previously represented him, the former client. The Court will assume that during the course of the former representation confidences were disclosed to the attorney bearing on the subject matter of the representation.

Others have traced the substantial relationship test to substantive law doctrines, including fiduciary duty and agency. In re Am. Airlines, 972 F.2d 605 (5th Cir. 1992); Maritrans GP, Inc. v. Pepper, Hamilton & Scheetz, 602 A.2d 1277 (Pa. 1992).

The substantial relationship test aims to tell *when* a lawyer may and may not be adverse to a former client. The answer is not *never*. "Certainly, a client does not own a lawyer for all time. In appropriate circumstances our rules allow lawyers to take positions adverse to former clients and even to bring suit against them." In re Carey, 89 S.W.3d 477 (Mo. 2002). And that is pretty much the question: When are circumstances "appropriate"? In *Analytica*, Judge Posner wrote that the lawyer will be disqualified if the "subject matter of the two representations is 'substantially related,'" and then immediately stated this to mean: "if the lawyer *could have obtained* confidential information in the first representation that would have been relevant in the second." (Emphasis added.)* Although Schwartz & Freeman was hired to give two different kinds of advice—tax first, antitrust second—it was now in a position

---

* While Posner focused on threats to confidential information, loyalty to a former client may separately forbid a representation, as we will shortly see.

to use NPD financial information that it "could have obtained" in its tax work against NPD in the antitrust case.

Why say "could have obtained," as Posner did, and not "did obtain"? Why not ask whether it is really true, not merely whether it could be true, that a lawyer has relevant confidential information?

Asking whether the *two matters* are related *in substance* is a proxy (or substitute) for having the court actually inspect the information from the prior matter, a solution that is rejected for four reasons. First, requiring the former client to reveal the very information it wants to protect is inconsistent with the client's legitimate wish to keep the information confidential. Second, as we see below, while protection of confidential information is the dominant reason for the rule, the prohibition against subsequent adverse representation also protects a lawyer's loyalty to a former client. Third, it would require much time for courts actually to inspect the files in a prior representation and then predict the relevance of what they contain to the current matter. Fourth, it would be difficult even to attempt that prediction. The current matter will be in its early stages. How it might evolve will be uncertain. In short, we need a proxy, because there is no other efficient test that will work. The Sixth Circuit recognized as much in Bowers v. Ophthalmology Group, 733 F.3d 647 (6th Cir. 2013). It described what a court must do in deciding whether a substantial relationship is present:

> [T]he court must look to the general type of information that the potentially conflicted lawyer would have been exposed to in a normal or typical representation of the type that occurred with the now-adverse client. Admittedly, this approach has its difficulties, most notably that reconstructing a representation using generalities is less exact than examining what actually happened. Nonetheless, this method presents a necessary alternative to engaging with the specific—perhaps confidential—facts surrounding a potentially conflicted attorney's prior representation of a now-adverse client.

Much is at stake here. The more broadly we define "substantially related," the greater the scope of disqualification and interference with the new client's choice of counsel. Remember, too, that the lawyer's conflict will be imputed to other lawyers in the office. Rule 1.10(a). On the other hand, if we define the test to demand too close a connection between the prior and later matters, we risk undermining trust in the professional relationship. Clients will soon realize that lawyers may later oppose them in matters that, to clients, look very much like side switching in (nearly) the same matter.

We must also be cognizant of the risk of error. Because the test is a proxy, it gives us only an approximation of what is true. We will get false negatives (i.e., where the test *mistakenly* reveals no threat to confidential information) and false positives (i.e., where the test *mistakenly* identifies a threat that does not exist).

The danger of false positives and false negatives requires that we acknowledge another aspect of the test. The answer it yields is conclusive. So a disqualified law firm can't say, "But, Judge, please, we can prove we don't know anything that would help us here if you would just give us the chance." Firms don't get the chance. If the former client can show that the new (adverse) matter is substantially related to the former matter, the court will conclusively presume that the lawyer gained confidential information in the prior matter that can now be used against the former client. Conversely, if the court concludes that the matters are not substantially related, the court will conclusively presume that the former firm has no relevant confidences of its former client.*

Could Schwartz & Freeman have argued: "Even if we have relevant financial information, we promise not to use it. We will screen the lawyers who worked on the Malec matter from those representing Analytica here." No, it could not, not even if it were a firm of 2,000 lawyers and the two sets of lawyers worked on opposite coasts or in different nations. For one thing, the promise is difficult to police. For another, we don't ask clients to accept such a promise on faith (unless they want to do so via consent).

But there is an exception for *lateral lawyers*—i.e., lawyers who are conflicted because of work they did at a prior firm. (There is an exception as well for former government lawyers. See part C, below.) This is the import of the *Analytica* footnote. The Rules and most courts now allow a firm to screen a lateral lawyer to prevent imputation of her conflict. Won't the former client be as concerned and won't the screen be as difficult to police? Yes. But the Rules allow it in order to make it easier for lawyers to change jobs. The ABA, which had rejected screening of lateral lawyers for decades, reversed itself when the 2008 Great Recession left many lawyers unemployed. By permitting screening, the change assured firms that hiring a lateral lawyer would not disqualify firms from current or new matters.

For Schwartz & Freeman, however, screening was not an option. There was no lateral lawyer. The firm itself changed sides.

Can *Playbook* Create a Substantial Relationship?

The information threatened in Watkins v. Trans Union, LLC, 869 F.3d 514 (7th Cir. 2017) comprised what has come to be known as *playbook* information, although the court did not use that term. Playbook information is not specifically about a matter, as was NPD's financial information in *Analytica*, but rather general information about a former client that could give its former lawyer an advantage. *Trans Union* described the information in that case as "internal policies and practices or legal strategy," and held that this information could not support disqualification. Rule 1.9 cmt. [3] makes the same distinction. "In the case of an organizational client, general knowledge of

---

* On rare occasion, a court might let a party seek to rebut a false negative by disclosing the confidential information to the judge ex parte. Decora v. DW Wallcovering, 901 F. Supp. 161 (S.D.N.Y. 1995).

the client's policies and practices ordinarily will not preclude a subsequent representation."

But sometimes it might. Consider Rosalyn.

For nine years, Rosalyn was associate general counsel at Clarity, which she represented in cases alleging harm from its skin care products. She has since resigned and entered private practice. A year later, can she accept a new client who wishes to sue Clarity alleging harm from its shampoo? The suit is certainly "adverse" to Clarity, but is it "substantially related" to the matters in which Rosalyn previously represented it? The facts will be different, won't they: skin care v. hair care. Another way to put this question is: Can a matter be "substantially related" to *an area of law* in which the lawyer previously represented the client? Here, that area is products liability. The products differ. Yet both are for personal care.

Comment [2] to Rule 1.9 can be read to allow the lawyer to accept the new matter: "[A] lawyer who recurrently handled a type of problem for a former client is not precluded from later representing another client in a factually distinct problem of that type even though the subsequent representation involves a position adverse to the prior client." See also cmt. [3], supra. Two matters are not "substantially related . . . just because they involve . . . claims under the same statute." Khani v. Ford Motor Co., 155 Cal. Rptr. 3d 532 (Ct. App. 2013).

On the other hand, Clarity's argument for disqualifying Rosalyn is more focused. She is benefited by knowing Clarity's strategy in products liability cases. What's more, she may have other deep background information about Clarity's manufacturing and testing policies, its settlement positions, and other shampoo cases it quietly settled with confidentiality promises even if Rosalyn did not work on them. This all gives Rosalyn an advantage. So maybe she should be disqualified.

Courts have recognized that a lawyer may have an advantage based on significant familiarity with the operations and strategies of a former client in an area of law, even though the subsequent adverse matter involves different facts from those in matters where the lawyer previously represented the client. The cases are not easy to reconcile, and there aren't all that many of them. Of relevance are the number of matters on which the lawyer had represented the client, for how long and how long ago, and the degree of similarity between the lawyer's prior work and the current adverse matter. The issue is important because to the extent we recognize that some degree of playbook information (i.e., not too general) can conflict a lawyer, we expand the potential reach of the substantial relationship test beyond *matter-specific* facts and sideline more firms. Which is not to say we shouldn't do it, only that we should be aware of what we're doing. So the question remains.

Sometimes the decision is painfully easy. Chrysler sued two young lawyers who, while working as associates at their former firm, "did a significant amount of work" defending Chrysler in class actions alleging product defects. "After leaving the firm, the two attorneys formed their own firm and agreed to serve as plaintiff's counsel in a putative class action against Chrysler albeit involving an alleged defect different from the defects claimed to exist in the cases on which they had worked while at their former firm. Claiming that the conduct of the attorneys was not only unethical but also tortious, Chrysler filed the instant suit." The court, in denying the lawyers' summary judgment motion, wrote that

> a reasonable juror could find or not find that defendants breached their duty of loyalty to Chrysler. The undisputed facts in this case show that Carey and Danis elected to prosecute a class action product liability lawsuit against Chrysler within a year after leaving a firm where they had performed significant work defending Chrysler in product liability class actions. Given their intimate familiarity with Chrysler's approach to vehicular defect class actions, a reasonable juror could find that it was a breach of loyalty for them to turn around and bring such a lawsuit against Chrysler.

Chrysler Corp. v. Carey, 5 F. Supp. 2d 1023 (E.D. Mo. 1998). See also Franzoni v. Hart Schaffner & Marx, 726 N.E.2d 719 (Ill. App. Ct. 2000) ("Stein's involvement in defending hundreds of discrimination claims against HC and its subsidiaries and in setting the companies' human resources policies is sufficient to compel disqualification" in an employment-related case against HC).

At the other end of the spectrum, a "general representation . . . that gave the attorney insight into or access to litigation strategies or similar information, is insufficient to establish a substantial relationship between the former representation and the present matter." Giambrone v. Meritplan Ins. Co., 117 F. Supp. 3d 259 (E.D.N.Y. 2015). The court then added that "disqualification may be warranted in rare cases where an attorney had extensive access to and insight into the client's strategies on issues of a similar subject matter to the legal issues in question." Obviously, although the line between the two situations will sometimes be clear, it will often be hazy and require a lawyer to make her best educated guess. That would seem to describe Rosalyn's relationship with Clarity.*

The Loyalty Duty to Former Clients (*or* It's Not Only About Confidences)

Analytica used the substantial relationship test as a proxy for determining whether confidences from a prior matter would be relevant in a later matter. But confidentiality is not the only goal of successive conflict rules. The word "confidential" or variants of it do not appear in Rule 1.9(a). Although often overlooked, because it is rarely at stake, loyalty to a former client is a

---

* The playbook issue reappears in the problem "You Don't Know Anything" in part B, below.

separate value the rule protects. Trone v. Smith, 621 F.2d 994 (9th Cir. 1980), early on identified this interest:

> Both the lawyer and the client should expect that the lawyer will use every skill, expend every energy, and tap every legitimate resource in the exercise of independent professional judgment on behalf of the client and in undertaking representation on the client's behalf. That professional commitment is not furthered, but endangered, if the possibility exists that the lawyer will change sides later in a substantially related matter. Both the fact and the appearance of total professional commitment are endangered by adverse representation in related cases. From this standpoint it matters not whether confidences were in fact imparted to the lawyer by the client. The substantial relationship between the two representations is itself sufficient to disqualify.

In agreement are Sullivan County Regional Refuse Disposal District v. Town of Acworth, 686 A.2d 755 (N.H. 1996) ("[E]ven in the absence of any confidences, an attorney owes a duty of loyalty to a former client that prevents that attorney from attacking, or interpreting, work she performed, or supervised, for the former client.") and the oft-cited early decision in Brennan's, Inc. v. Brennan's Restaurants, Inc., 590 F.2d 168 (5th Cir. 1979).

But what does it mean to be loyal to a *former* client? What would disloyalty look like? Let's play a little mind game. It's a mind game because it would never happen. (I hope.) Ashley gets a $10 million judgment against Zelda. Zelda then hires famed appellate lawyer Daniela Webster to appeal to the state's intermediate appellate court. Daniela has had no previous relationship with either party. Zelda says, "All I want you to do is argue that the statute under which Ashley got her judgment violates the state constitution. Pure question of law. All you need is the trial record, a public document." Daniela wins and charges a bundle. She never got confidential information. Can Ashley now hire Daniela to represent *her* in a further appeal to the state's highest court, in an effort to reinstate the judgment? No. Why not? Because it would be disloyal to Zelda, who hired Daniela to achieve one specific objective: reverse the trial court. Daniela cannot help Ashley undo precisely what Zelda hired her to do. (Nor would Daniela Webster ever do such a thing.)

"What do I owe Haywood Tallman?," above, includes a pure former client loyalty issue — i.e., where no confidences are at risk.

Who Counts as a *Client* Under the Former Client Conflict Rule?

We encountered the client identity issue in chapters 1 and 5. It is a question that often arises in the conflicts world because with no client there can be no conflict. In the area of successive conflicts, the issue is more complex. We must first ask whether a person or entity ever was a client, and second, if so, whether it is now a former or still a current client (the subject of the next discussion). In *Analytica*, NPD had either been a firm client or was treated as one because it had provided "just the kind of confidential data that it would have furnished a lawyer that it had retained." In *Westinghouse*, cited in *Analytica*, Kerr-McGee certainly had not been a Kirkland & Ellis client, but it had given the firm relevant confidential information to enable it to represent its trade association and that was sufficient to require disqualification. A lawyer may also be disqualified from opposing a former "prospective client," someone who after consulting the lawyer and providing confidential information does not retain her. Sturdivant v. Sturdivant, 241 S.W.3d 740 (Ark. 2006) (applying Rule 1.18).

"Like a Hot Potato": Is the Client Former or Current?

A client who wishes to disqualify a lawyer would prefer to be her current client, but the lawyer would prefer to say that she is a former client, if ever a client at all. You can see why. The current client conflicts rules give clients significantly more protection. We saw in chapter 2D that unless something is done, it may not be so clear if a representation has ended. Now we consider one way in which a current client cannot be converted to a former client.

Smith Knight represents Corkskroo Ltd. on a small matter that will be resolved in six months. One day Smith Knight receives a visit from Marie Shelton. Shelton has a claim against Corkskroo for $50 million and wants the firm to take it. Shelton's claim is factually unrelated to the matter the firm currently handles for Corkskroo. If Shelton had come in six months later, representation of Corkskroo would have ended, and the firm could have accepted her factually unrelated claim. But Shelton won't wait.

The problem for Smith Knight is that it cannot accept Shelton's case and sue Corkskroo while continuing to represent Corkskroo, even on an unrelated matter. How nice if Corkskroo would just disappear. Poof! So Smith Knight "fires" Corkskroo (by withdrawing), returns all files, waits what it believes is a respectable 24 hours, and then accepts Shelton's retainer. Corkskroo moves to disqualify the firm, which defends by arguing that Corkskroo, (now) a *former* client, can disqualify it only on substantially related matters, which Shelton's claim is not. Further, the firm argues, Corkskroo suffered not one penny's worth of injury. The matter was simple and Corkskroo's new firm (which Smith Knight had offered to assist and even pay for) got up to speed in two seconds flat.

Assuming that Corkskroo's matter has not been harmed, what interest might Corkskroo have (if any) that the court should protect and how should it do so? Should the court balance Corkskroo's interests against Smith Knight's interest in accepting a new case and Marie Shelton's interest in counsel of her choice?

In a footnote in Unified Sewerage Agency v. Jelco, Inc., 646 F.2d 1339 (9th Cir. 1981), Judge Goodwin wrote that law firms could not escape the stricter current client conflict rules simply by withdrawing from a representation and converting a current client into a former one. The court would apply the current client conflict rules anyway. Why? If the second matter is truly unrelated, who is hurt? Certainly the now "former" client may encounter some additional expense, but assume the firm is prepared to pay it. What the *Jelco* footnote honors is a client's interest in uninterrupted representation to the conclusion of a matter. Think of it as an attribute of loyalty. It is disloyal for a lawyer to drop a client in the midst of the work because a financially more lucrative client happens along. Judge Goodwin's footnote acquired a simile in Picker International v. Varian Associates, 670 F. Supp. 1363 (N.D. Ohio 1987), aff'd, 869 F.2d 578 (Fed. Cir. 1989). There, Judge Aldrich wrote that Jones Day (which was in a position like Smith Knight's) had dropped a client "like a hot potato" in order to be free to continue work for another client. She disqualified the firm under the current client conflict rules. Today the "hot potato rule" is broadly recognized.*

"Thrust Upon" Conflicts

Just as poetic as "hot potato" is the phrase "thrust upon." A firm represents P against D in court when either (a) D acquires T, another client of the law firm, or (b) T acquires D. The firm wants to continue to represent P but now the firm, through no fault of its own, finds itself adverse to its own client, who won't consent to the conflict. The conflict has been thrust upon it. May the firm withdraw from representing the defendant despite the hot potato rule? Yes. See Gould, Inc. v. Mitsui Mining & Smelting Co., 738 F. Supp. 1121 (N.D. Ohio 1990); Pennwalt Corp. v. Plough, Inc., 85 F.R.D. 264 (D. Del. 1980). It must extricate itself from the conflict. If it can't get both clients' informed consent, it must drop one of them. And if it must do so, it would hardly be fair to say that it violated the hot potato rule when it does. The firm might choose to withdraw from P's representation. If so, it will need the court's approval. Rule 1.16(c).

Standing and Waiver

As we saw, in civil cases, concurrent conflicts may usually be waived (chapter 5B3). Successive conflicts may always be waived. Rule 1.9(a). Should nonclients ever have standing to seek disqualification in successive conflict situations? Some courts have said yes because of the court's interest in ethical conduct. See Tessier v. Plastic Surgery Specialists, 731 F. Supp. 724 (E.D. Va. 1990) (collecting cases). Others have said no because the rule is meant to protect the former client, not a stranger. In re Yarn Processing Patent Validity Litig., 530 F.2d 83 (5th Cir. 1976).

---

* Rule 1.16(c)(1) allows a lawyer to withdraw if "withdrawal can be accomplished without material adverse effect on the interests of the client." (If the matter is in court, the judge would have to approve.) If given full force, this language would eliminate the hot potato rule in situations it describes. So far, that does not seem to have happened.

The Appearance of Impropriety

Neither the Canons of Professional Ethics nor the Code of Professional Responsibility contained a direct equivalent to Rule 1.9(a). Courts fashioned one, relying on the duty of loyalty, the duty of confidentiality, and, under Canon 9 of the Code, the direction to "avoid even the appearance of professional impropriety." Pretty soon the appearance-of-impropriety standard was overused and the object of criticism, not least of all because of its unpredictability. The Second Circuit in Board of Education v. Nyquist, 590 F.2d 1241 (2d Cir. 1979), deemed it "too slender a reed" on which to base disqualification. The Restatement and the Model Rules do not contain it. Some courts reject it as a basis for disqualification. See Marcum v. Scorsone, 457 S.W.3d 710 (Ky. 2015): "Before a lawyer is disqualified based on a relationship with a former client or existing clients, the complaining party should be required to show an actual conflict, not just a vague and possibly deceiving appearance of impropriety. And that conflict should be established with facts, not just vague assertions of discomfort with the representation."

Still, we cannot archive the appearance test. The legal education of many thousands of (now aging) lawyers and judges stressed the need to avoid the "appearance of impropriety." Some courts continue to cite it in disqualifying a lawyer. In Continental Resources v. Schmalenberger, 656 N.W.2d 730 (N.D. 2003), the court said the appearance "standard has not been wholly abandoned in spirit." It would view the question "from the perspective of a reasonable layperson." That's not a lot of guidance. How does a lawyer play it safe in North Dakota?

The "appearance of impropriety" standard will continue to have a role in evaluating the conduct of public officials—including government lawyers and judges—because the public's perception of the fair administration of justice is almost as important (some would say as important) as its reality.

Conflicts in Class Actions

The application of traditional successive disqualification doctrine to class actions can work great hardship, sometimes for little gain. The Second Circuit had to confront this problem in In re "Agent Orange" Product Liability Litigation, 800 F.2d 14 (2d Cir. 1986). Class counsel switched from representing class members supporting a settlement to those opposing it. In an influential opinion rejecting disqualification, Judge Kearse wrote:

> Automatic application of the traditional principles governing disqualification of attorneys on grounds of conflict of interest would seemingly dictate that whenever a rift arises in the class, with one branch favoring a settlement or a course of action that another branch resists, the attorney who has represented the class should withdraw entirely and take no position. Were he to take a position, either favoring or opposing the proposed course of action, he would be opposing the interests of some of his former clients in the very matter in which he has represented them . . . .

[A]lthough automatic disqualification might "promote the salutary ends of confidentiality and loyalty, it would have a serious adverse effect on class actions." When many individuals have modest claims against a single entity or group of entities, the class action may be the only practical means of vindicating their rights, since otherwise the expenses of litigation could exceed the value of the claim. In such class actions, often only the attorneys who have represented the class, rather than any of the class members themselves, have substantial familiarity with the prior proceedings, the fruits of discovery, the actual potential of the litigation. And when an action has continued over the course of many years, the prospect of having those most familiar with its course and status be automatically disqualified whenever class members have conflicting interests would substantially diminish the efficacy of class actions as a method of dispute resolution. This is so both because the quality of the information available to the court would likely be impaired and because even if a class member were familiar with all the prior proceedings, the amount of his stake in the litigation might well make it unattractive for him to participate actively, either on his own or through new counsel.

B. IMPUTED DISQUALIFICATION AND MIGRATORY LAWYERS

"You Don't Know Anything"

Sherry Lakoff was an associate at Penbauer, Rich, Ivanhoe & Mora (PRIM) for three years, eight months, and eight days. PRIM, based in Chicago, represented AxiMartin Carburetor (which made other auto parts too) on transactional and litigation matters, sometimes working with AxiMartin's three inside lawyers. Lakoff worked on the litigation side, helping to defend AxiMartin in a mix of matters, including breach of contract, breach of warranty, and tort. Occasionally, AxiMartin got involved in employment issues, including union issues, ERISA, labor law, OSHA, and Equal Pay Act claims. Lakoff worked on some of them. AxiMartin was twice sued for age discrimination and Lakoff worked on both cases, which settled. After leaving PRIM, Lakoff went to another Chicago firm, Cross, Cudlup & Charles. C3, as it was known, styled itself a "litigation boutique," which so far as Lakoff could tell, meant that it was small (nine lawyers, counting Lakoff), which is why she chose it.

Two years after Lakoff went to C3, she was asked to assist Cudlup in representing Arianna Stile in a sex discrimination case against AxiMartin. Stile joined AxiMartin as a mechanical engineer *after* Lakoff left PRIM. Stile claims that AxiMartin constructively discharged her because, although she had complained to management, the company did nothing to protect her from the sexist comments and conduct of the other engineers, all men.

"Can I do this?" Lakoff asked Cudlup. "I used to work at PRIM defending AxiMartin, including in two age discrimination cases. PRIM will probably defend this one too."

"You didn't work on this case," Cudlup said. "Stile started at Axi after you left PRIM. And you never worked on a sex case. What do you know about it? You don't know anything. No rule says you may never sue a former client. Also, PRIM isn't representing Axi here."

May Lakoff work on Stile v. AxiMartin? If not, or if it is unclear, can C3 take the case and avoid disqualification by screening Lakoff? What is a screen?

"Can We Hire Taylor Monk?"

Kane, Grossman & Russo (KGR) handles the products liability defense work for Admiral Industries, a nationwide manufacturer of consumer products. The firm has 1,400 lawyers, about two-thirds of them associates. Admiral is the defendant in some 40 lawsuits nationwide, brought by consumers who say they suffered injuries as a result of malfunctions in various Admiral products. Taylor Monk graduated from UCLA Law School in 2017 and has since been working as an associate at Horton, Israel & Pinto (HIP), a plaintiff's firm in Providence, R.I., where her wife, a physician, was doing her ophthalmology residency. She is now about to pursue postresidency study at Weill Cornell Medical School in Manhattan, where KGR has its main office. Monk, who is also a member of the New York bar, writes to KGR about employment.

Before Monk is hired, KGR's general counsel, Addison Collar, does a conflicts check, as he does for all lateral hires. He discovers that HIP is currently representing the plaintiff in Crickett v. Admiral, pending in federal court in Providence based on diversity jurisdiction. The Cricketts seek damages after their son Jimmy was injured while using an Admiral toaster oven. When asked, Monk tells Collar that her only work on *Crickett* was research on federal preemption and industry wiring standards, for a total of 19 hours.

Collar knows that HIP is part of an informal group of eight law firms representing plaintiffs with toaster-oven claims. The group discusses strategies and shares legal research and information from investigations and laboratory tests pursuant to a written common interest agreement (chapter 5B3). Monk has occasionally participated in the group's discussions to take notes and has reviewed shared research. KGR is eager to hire Monk, depending on whether it will be able to avoid disqualification from Admiral toaster-oven cases including the Cricketts' case because of Monk's work. Collar asks you, "Can we hire Taylor Monk? If so, what can she work on?" In answering, you need to consider Rule 8.5(b)(1) as well as Rule 1.10(a).

A Conflict Bouquet

After Red Rose Importers sued the Marigold Company for $100 million for constructive fraud and breach of contract, Elvira Lilly, the Marigold general counsel, called Tyrell Aster, a partner at Cosmos Clover, to discuss representing Marigold. Lilly sent Aster the complaint and she met with Aster and his associate, Daphne Heather, for two hours to discuss the theories of liability. Cosmos Clover had never represented either Red Rose or Marigold.

Lilly interviewed two other firms, too, and ultimately opted to go with Thistle & Weed LLP. She informed Aster and told him to bill her for his time, but he never did. Seven months into the litigation, Red Rose, the plaintiff, became dissatisfied with its lawyers. Its general counsel, Dahlia Jasmine, called Daisy Holly, a Cosmos partner she met at a conference, about representing Red Rose in the case. Because of an embarrassing oversight four years earlier, Cosmos kept records of all prospective clients. So Holly discovered the meeting between Lilly and Aster. Can Cosmos Clover represent Red Rose against the Marigold Company? Can Tyrell Aster and Daphne Heather? What else do you want to know?

In *Analytica*, the Seventh Circuit wrote that "the firm itself changed sides." It distinguished the situation where a personally conflicted lawyer moves from one private firm to a second one. (A lawyer is personally conflicted because of her own work or exposure to information, not simply because a colleague's conflict is imputed to her.) When are a lateral lawyer's personal conflicts imputed to her new firm? The following opinion, also from the Seventh Circuit, identifies the two presumptions courts use when faced with this question. (Rule 1.9(b) and comments [4]-[6] and Rule 1.10(a)(2) incorporate the same presumptions.) Former government lawyers who return to the private sector are the subject of part C of this chapter and governed by a different rule. Incidentally, the next case ignores two conflict issues suggested by its facts. See if you can figure out what they are. Perhaps the plaintiff's lawyer didn't argue them. But wouldn't you?

CROMLEY v. BOARD OF EDUCATION
17 F.3d 1059 (7th Cir. (1999)), cert. denied, 513 U.S. 816

RIPPLE, CIRCUIT JUDGE.

Marcella Ann Cromley, a high school teacher, brought an action under 42 U.S.C. §1983. She claimed that she had been denied various administrative positions because she had exercised her right to free speech as guaranteed by the First Amendment and made applicable to the states by the Fourteenth Amendment. The district court granted summary judgment to the defendants Board of Education of Lockport Township High School District 205 and its superintendent, assistant superintendent, principal, and one teacher (the "defendants"). It also denied Ms. Cromley's motion to disqualify defendants' attorneys. She now appeals the judgment of the district court. For the reasons that follow, we affirm.

[Cromley alleged that the defendants "had retaliated against her because she had complained to [a state agency] about the sexual misconduct of [a co-worker toward two students], a complaint which she asserted was protected speech." After two years of pretrial litigation, Cromley's attorney, Larry Weiner, accepted a partnership in the Scariano law firm, which was representing the defendants. Weiner withdrew as Cromley's lawyer. The district court denied Cromley's motion to disqualify the Scariano firm.]

The approach taken by this circuit for determining whether an attorney should be disqualified is a three-step analysis.

> First, we must determine whether a substantial relationship exists between the subject matter of the prior and present representations. If we conclude a substantial relationship does exist, we must next ascertain whether the presumption of shared confidences with respect to the prior representation has been rebutted. If we conclude this presumption has not been rebutted, we must then determine whether the presumption of shared confidences has been rebutted with respect to the present representation. Failure to rebut this presumption would also make the disqualification proper.

Schiessle v. Stephens, 717 F.2d 417, 420 (7th Cir. 1983).

The "substantial relationship" test is easily met in this case. It is undisputed that the subject matter under scrutiny both before and after Mr. Weiner changed law firms was the litigation brought by Ms. Cromley against the School Board. The only change made was attorney Weiner's shift from the firm of Schwartz & Freeman, the firm representing Ms. Cromley, to . . . the firm representing the School Board. Because Mr. Weiner's representation of Ms. Cromley before he moved to the Scariano firm is substantially related to his new firm's relationship to the School Board, a "presumption of shared confidences" arises:

> Implicit in a finding of substantial relationship is a presumption that particular individuals in a law firm freely share their clients' confidences with one another. . . . [However, we have] recognized that the presumption that an attorney has knowledge of the confidences and secrets of his firm's clients is rebuttable.

As a first step in deciding whether that presumption has been rebutted, "we must determine whether the attorney whose change of employment created the disqualification issue was actually privy to any confidential information his prior law firm received from the party now seeking disqualification of his present firm."[3] The rebuttal can be established either by proof that

---

3. In Analytica, Inc. v. NPD Research Inc., 708 F.2d 1263 (7th Cir. 1983), this court held that the presumption of shared confidences was irrebuttable when an entire law firm changed sides. We acknowledged in *Analytica*, however, that a lawyer who changes jobs and moves to a

"the attorney in question had no knowledge of the information, confidences and/or secrets related by the client in the prior representation," or by proof that screening procedures were timely employed in the new law firm to prevent the disclosure of information and secrets. Uncontroverted affidavits are sufficient rebuttal evidence.

Because Mr. Weiner, Ms. Cromley's attorney for two years, clearly had confidential information from his client when he moved to the firm representing the defendant School Board, we must focus on whether the Scariano law firm that Mr. Weiner later joined has demonstrated that it had established an effective screening procedure to block the disclosure of Ms. Cromley's confidences within the "new" firm. "[T]he presumption of shared confidences should be rebutted by demonstrating that 'specific institutional mechanisms' . . . had been implemented to effectively insulate against any flow of confidential information from the 'infected' attorney to any other member of his present firm."

The types of institutional mechanisms that have been determined to protect successfully the confidentiality of the attorney-client relationship include: (1) instructions, given to all members of the new firm, of the attorney's recusal and of the ban on exchange of information; (2) prohibited access to the files and other information on the case; (3) locked case files with keys distributed to a select few; (4) secret codes necessary to access pertinent information on electronic hardware; and (5) prohibited sharing in the fees derived from such litigation. Moreover, the screening devices must be employed "as soon as the 'disqualifying event occurred.'" . . .

In this case, the defendants have rebutted the presumption of shared confidences by describing the timely establishment of a screening process. When Mr. Weiner joined the firm he was denied access to the relevant files, which were located in a different office, under the control of David Kula, the partner handling the case. Mr. Weiner and all employees of the firm were admonished not to discuss any aspect of the case, and all were subject to discipline. In addition, Mr. Weiner was not allowed to share in the fees derived from this case. . . . We conclude, as did the district court, that the Scariano law firm successfully rebutted the presumption of shared confidences by proving that the screening procedures were timely employed and fully implemented. . . .

---

firm retained by an adversary "can avoid disqualification by showing that effective measures were taken to prevent confidences from being received by whichever lawyers in the new firm are handling the new matter." In the case now before us, one attorney changed employment from the firm representing the plaintiff to a firm representing the defendants. This circumstance falls within the exception recognized in *Analytica*; therefore our analysis does not conflict with that decision.

Why Didn't *Cromley* Ask . . . ?

Before we unpack the rules governing imputation of lateral lawyer conflicts, our reason for reading *Cromley*, let's detour to two issues the court did not address. Weiner had been representing Cromley for two years, as her lead lawyer, when he informed her that he was leaving Schwartz & Freeman (coincidentally, the same firm that figured in *Analytica*) to join the law firm opposing her. What issues does this suggest?

1. **Why didn't the *Cromley* court ask whether it was proper for Weiner to negotiate his partnership with the Scariano firm while he was representing Cromley *against* the Scariano firm's clients?** For a time at least Weiner was both Cromley's advocate against the Scariano firm and negotiating with it in his own interests. That creates a conflict under Rule 1.7(a)(2). The court recounts an affidavit from Kula, the Scariano attorney opposing Weiner. It "stated that, as soon as [Kula] was informed that his law firm was discussing with Mr. Weiner the possibility of Mr. Weiner's joining the law firm, he and Mr. Weiner 'agreed that absolutely nothing of a substantive nature regarding the instant lawsuit would occur' until decisions were made and the clients were made aware of them." So the lawyers recognized the issue, but is the remedy sufficient? Was a standstill agreement in Cromley's interest or only the lawyers' interest? When was *she* told about the negotiations or that her matter was on ice? ABA Opinion 96-400 concludes that once a lawyer's negotiations with an opposing law firm reach a critical stage, which can happen in a single conversation, the lawyer must obtain client consent to the conflict between the client's and lawyer's interests. The opinion cites (what is now) Rule 1.7(a)(2). It also concludes that the opposing firm may need the consent of *its* client as well. Can you explain why? What was the risk to Cromley's opponent?

2. **Why didn't the *Cromley* court ask whether it was proper for Weiner to drop a client in the middle of a representation in order to further his own career?** Did Weiner's obligations to Cromley require him to put her interests in uninterrupted and diligent representation above his own professional and financial interest in becoming a partner at the Scariano firm? Weiner's situation should remind you of the hot potato issue in Picker International v. Varian Associates (part A). There, Jones Day, which was representing Picker, merged with a patent boutique, MH&S, which was then representing Varian in unrelated matters. As a result, postmerger Jones Day was adverse to its own client, which would not consent. To eliminate the conflict, the firm dropped Varian. The court held that by doing so, it had violated the hot potato rule, a term (but not a concept) that it coined, and disqualified Jones Day. Is Weiner's wish for a professional realignment any different from Jones Day's wish to acquire MH&S?

Presumptions in Imputed Disqualification

Consider this diagram.

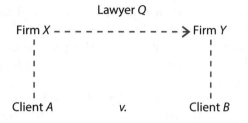

The diagram schematically depicts the *Cromley* facts. Firm *X* has represented client *A*. Lawyer *Q* has worked at firm *X* as a partner or an associate. *Q* moves to firm *Y*. When *Q* changes firms, client *A* is in the middle of a litigation against client *B*, represented by firm *Y*. In *Cromley*, Weiner, the equivalent of lawyer *Q*, was working on Cromley's matter when he left Schwartz & Freeman and joined the Scariano firm.

Variations are possible:

- Unlike Weiner, the lateral lawyer may have had nothing to do with the matter at his former firm and may not even know about it. He is not, in other words, *personally conflicted.*
- The matter may be a negotiation.
- Firm *Y* may not be handling the same or a substantially related matter when lawyer *Q* arrives, but gets one later.

The fundamental question remains the same: Will the lateral lawyer's new firm be disqualified by imputation once he arrives?

Cromley answered this question *yes* if these three things are all true:

(i) firm *X*'s representation of client *A* was on a matter that has a "substantial relationship" to (or is the same as) firm *Y*'s representation of client *B* against client *A*; *and*

(ii) lawyer *Q* received confidences of *A* on the matter while he was at firm *X*; *and*

(iii) the other lawyers at firm *Y* have received (or are likely to receive) those confidences from *Q* after he arrives at firm *Y*.

The Rules and cases create *two rebuttable* presumptions. If (i) is true, then it is presumed that (ii) is true. If (ii) is true, then it is presumed that (iii) is true. (*Cromley* combined the two presumptions into one.) Only if one of these two presumptions is rebutted will the Scariano firm avoid disqualification. In *Cromley,* (i) was true because the two firms were opponents on *the very same* matter. Therefore (ii) was presumed true and could not be rebutted because Weiner personally represented Ms. Cromley while at Schwartz & Freeman. So the question for the court was whether Weiner had rebutted the presumption in (iii) that he has shared or would share Cromley's confidential information with his new firm. The Scariano firm tried to do that with a screen.

Rebutting the First Presumption. There is universal agreement that the first presumption is rebuttable. Billing records and affidavits can show that the lawyer did not work on any matter for the particular client or otherwise learn its confidential information, as for example at a firm event or working on a firm committee.

Silver Chrysler Plymouth v. Chrysler Motors Corp., 518 F.2d 751 (2d Cir. 1975), is an early and influential decision that nicely illustrates this point.* The plaintiff was represented by a small firm, one of whose partners, Schreiber, formerly worked as an associate at Kelley Drye, which represented Chrysler, the current defendant. Kelley Drye sought to disqualify Schreiber's new firm because Schreiber had been an associate at Kelley Drye while it represented Chrysler. The Second Circuit rejected this effort as insufficient.

> It is unquestionably true that in the course of their work at large law firms, associates are entrusted with the confidences of some of their clients. But it would be absurd to conclude that immediately upon their entry on duty they become the recipients of knowledge as to the names of all the firm's clients, the contents of all files relating to such clients, and all confidential disclosures by client officers or employees to any lawyer in the firm. . . .
>
> Thus, while this Circuit has recognized that an inference may arise that an attorney formerly associated with a firm himself received confidential information transmitted by a client to the firm, that inference is a rebuttable one. . . . The importance of not unnecessarily constricting the careers of lawyers who started their practice of law at large firms simply on the basis of their former association underscores the significance of [not making "the standard of proof for rebuttal unattainably high"].

Schreiber's conflict while he remained at Kelley Drye was imputed to him because of the work of others, not because of work he personally did. The imputation ended when he departed, freeing his new firm and even Schreiber himself to oppose Chrysler. See Rule 1.9(b) and cmts. [4] and [5].

Rebutting the Second Presumption. Should the second presumption be rebuttable? The first presumption is *retrospective*. It presumes that the lateral lawyer did get relevant confidences at her former firm. It can be rebutted with contrary proof. The second presumption is *prospective*. It presumes that if the lawyer did get relevant confidential information at her former firm, she will now share it with her new colleagues, who will be able to use it against the client of the former firm.

---

* *Silver Chrysler*, like other interlocutory appeals of disqualification motions, has been overruled on the issue of appellate jurisdiction. That hasn't diminished its influence.

How does our lateral lawyer rebut a prediction about what she will do? The Rules' answer is with a *timely* screen, like the one in *Cromley,* between the lateral lawyer and colleagues at her new firm who represent her former client's adversary. See Rule 1.10(a)(2). Rule 1.10(a)(2) also provides for notices and certifications regarding the screen. The idea that a timely screen can rebut the second presumption first arose at a time when documents were on paper and files were in cabinets. In effect, the solution was to lock the cabinets to all but those entitled to open them. In a digital age, the lock is a password and construction of the screen is more elaborate.

If the second presumption were not rebuttable, firms would hesitate to hire lawyers who create a high risk of disqualification in current or future matters because of work elsewhere. This danger will be greater in smaller communities or in specialized areas of practice, where the client pool is smaller. And it will most harm younger lawyers who do not (yet) have a client list large enough to take a risk. The screen must be erected before the lawyer arrives to negate the inference that confidences were already shared.

But look at it from the client's point of view. A client (like Cromley) may find herself opposed by a law firm one of whose members knows everything about her matter. Can she be comfortable that a purported screen will be honored? Should the profession ask clients to "just trust us"? Rule 1.10 says yes. But that view is not unanimous. Rules in some U.S. states do not allow lateral screening of lawyers from another private law office or do so but limit those who can be screened.[*]

California and some other states adopt such a limit. California Rule 1.10(a) allows screening only if a lateral lawyer "did not substantially participate in the same or substantially related matter." If *Cromley* arose in California today, Weiner could not be screened because his participation in the case was substantial. He ran it. But sometimes that won't be clear. In an ambiguous situation, a prospective new firm must decide whether to take a chance on whether, in the event of a disqualification motion, a court will find its screen adequate to rebut the second presumption, or will reject it because of a screened lawyer's substantial participation in the matter at his prior firm.

A firm needs to know about a lawyer's prior work to know whether a screen, where allowed, is needed. KGR can ask Taylor Monk about her work at her prior firm. But what is she allowed to say without disclosing confidential information? In 2012, the ABA added an exception to Rule 1.6 to permit a prospective lateral lawyer like Monk (or firms contemplating a merger) to reveal client confidences to "detect and resolve conflicts of interest." Rule 1.6(b)(7). Disclosures must not "compromise the attorney-client privilege or otherwise prejudice the client." Although this rule would permit Monk's

---

[*] Lawyers who move from government to private practice may be screened everywhere. See Rule 1.11 and part C, below.

disclosure of her work on *Crickett,* the person at KGR to whom Monk made it should not be among the KGR lawyers opposing the Cricketts.

Removing Conflicts from a Former Firm

The Model Rules and case law also speak to the situation where a lawyer terminates an association with a firm and the firm then wishes to represent a new client on a substantially related matter whose interests are materially adverse to those of its former client who had been represented by the departed lawyer. Does the departed lawyer take her conflicts with her when she leaves? Yes. Rule 1.10(b) permits the firm to represent the new client so long as the can show that no lawyer remaining in the firm has protected information that could be used to the disadvantage of the former client. Thus, just as a personally conflicted lawyer may "infect" every lawyer at her new firm if screening is not allowed or not timely implemented, so too, when a personally conflicted lawyer departs and none remains, other firm lawyers are "cured" of the imputed conflict.

C. GOVERNMENT SERVICE

Investigating Landlords

After the local press reported abuses by landlords in the city—charging excessive rents, failure to provide services, and the like—the mayor decided she had to respond. She had recently won office by pledging to reduce inequality and homelessness. "But we can't afford to hire more inspectors," she told the city attorney. "No problem," the city attorney said. "The private bar will do it with the right financial incentives." He asked his first assistant, Adisa Okori, to conduct an investigation and propose a law.

Using subpoena power, Okori conducted a six-month investigation, followed by three months of hearings before a city council committee. She then spent two months writing a law giving tenants treble-damage claims and counsel fees for violations. The real estate industry lobbied to defeat or water down the law, but it passed the council 27-6.

A few months later, Okori entered private practice. May she or others at her firm represent (1) a tenant who is suing a landlord under the new law, or (2) a landlord sued under the new law? To the extent that Okori can represent a landlord sued under the law, can she argue for an interpretation of its terms that would limit its effectiveness? What other facts do you want to know? In answering these questions, recognize that Rule 1.9(a) and (b) do not apply but Rule 1.9(c) does. See Rule 1.11(a)(1).

The prospect of remunerative employment after leaving government (but not only that) makes working there attractive to many lawyers, even if the pay is (much) lower than they can earn in private practice. Nothing wrong there. It enables government to attract talented lawyers without paying market salaries.

If the government were no different from any other former client, Rules 1.9 and 1.10 would define the limits on postgovernment work. (They do apply if the government hires a lawyer in private practice.) Why do we need a special rule for government lawyers who leave their government jobs? What broader or different issues does their postdeparture (or pre-arrival) employment raise?

The following case was decided under the Model Code but we can use its facts and reasoning to examine the reach of Rule 1.11. We can do the same for the *General Motors* case cited in note 24 and the subsequent discussion.

ARMSTRONG v. McALPIN

625 F.2d 433 (2d Cir. 1980) (en banc), vacated on other
grounds, 449 U.S. 1106 (1981)

FEINBERG, CIRCUIT JUDGE . . .

[Altman, while a lawyer at the SEC, supervised an investigation and litigation against certain of the defendants, including McAlpin. The SEC litigation alleged that McAlpin and others had looted millions of dollars from the Capital Growth companies. McAlpin and other defendants defaulted, and the trial judge appointed Armstrong as receiver of the Capital Growth companies.

[Armstrong was charged with recovering all misappropriated property. He retained the law firm Gordon Hurwitz to represent him. Before Gordon Hurwitz appeared as counsel, Altman ended a nine-year tenure with the SEC and became associated with the firm. In the last three years of his tenure, Altman was assistant director of the SEC's Enforcement Division, with responsibility over numerous cases including the Capital Growth investigation and litigation. Although Altman "was not involved on a daily basis, he was generally aware of the facts of the case and the status of the litigation. . . . Altman's name appeared on the SEC complaint, although he did not sign it."

[Gordon Hurwitz and Armstrong concluded that Altman "should not participate in the Gordon firm's representation of the receiver, but that the firm would not be disqualified if Altman was properly screened from the case." Thereafter Gordon Hurwitz "asked the SEC if it had any objection to the retention, and was advised in writing that it did not, so long as Altman was screened from participation." After Armstrong began this action, McAlpin and others moved to disqualify Gordon Hurwitz. Judge Werker denied the motion but a Second Circuit panel reversed. The case then came before the circuit en banc.

[Judge Feinberg first held that the denial of disqualification was not immediately appealable, but nevertheless concluded that there were "strong reasons in the unusual context of this case to reach the merits of the appeal rather than to dismiss it." He viewed the court's role as deciding whether disqualification was an appropriate remedy. That inquiry turned on assessing the risk that Altman's presence at the Gordon firm would taint the integrity of the trial. That was the court's sole concern. Consistent with circuit precedent, any ethical issues would be left to the disciplinary process. Ultimately the Supreme Court vacated the Second Circuit's decision in *Armstrong* on the ground of nonappealability, but the case remains influential.]

It is apparent from a close reading of Judge Werker's opinion that he saw no threat of taint of the trial by the Gordon firm's continued representation of the receiver. Nor did the panel opinion in this case challenge that view. Although appellants assert that the trial will be tainted by the use of information from Altman, we see no basis on the record before us for overruling the district court's rejection of that claim. . . . [T]here is certainly no reason to fear any lack of "vigor" by the Gordon firm in representing the receiver; this is not a case where a law firm, by use of a "Chinese wall," is attempting to justify representation of conflicting interests at the same time. Nor is the Gordon firm "potentially in a position to use privileged information" obtained through prior representation of the other side. And finally, the receiver will not be making unfair use of information obtained by Altman as a government official, since the SEC files were turned over to the receiver long before he retained the Gordon firm and Altman has been entirely screened from all participation in the case, to the satisfaction of the district court and the SEC.[24] Nor is there any reason to believe that the receiver retained the Gordon firm because Altman was connected with it or that Altman had anything to do with the retention. If anything, the presence of Altman as an associate at that time was a problem, not a benefit, for the Gordon firm, as the district court, the receiver and the Gordon firm all apparently recognized.

Thus, because the district court justifiably held that the Gordon firm's representation of the receiver posed no threat to the integrity of the trial process, disqualification of the firm can only be based on the possible appearance of impropriety stemming from Altman's association with the firm. However, as previously noted, reasonable minds may and do differ on the ethical propriety of screening in this context. But there can be no doubt that disqualification of the Gordon firm will have serious consequences for this litigation; separating the receiver from his counsel at this late date will

24. The case therefore is entirely distinguishable from General Motors Corp. v. City of New York, 501 F.2d 639 (2d Cir. 1974), where an attorney who had substantial responsibility over an antitrust litigation against General Motors Corporation while he was employed by the Antitrust Division of the Justice Department later accepted employment as plaintiff's attorney in a private antitrust action against the same defendant for substantially the same conduct.

seriously delay and impede, and perhaps altogether thwart, his attempt to obtain redress for defendants' alleged frauds. Under the circumstances, the possible "appearance of impropriety is simply too slender a reed on which to rest a disqualification order . . . particularly . . . where . . . the appearance of impropriety is not very clear." Thus, we need not resolve the ethical propriety of the screening procedure used here at this time as long as the district court justifiably regarded it as effective in isolating Altman from the litigation. . . .

Accordingly, we vacate the panel opinion in this case and affirm the judgment of the district court.

[Two other judges concurred with the majority on the merits but disagreed on the appealability issue. Another judge would have dismissed the appeal for lack of jurisdiction. A final judge agreed with the majority on the appealability issue but disagreed on the merits.]

The Revolving Door in the Model Rules: The Two Issues

In *Armstrong*, the successive conflict risks were not the traditional ones that arise when a lawyer opposes a former client on a substantially related matter because the Gordon firm was not opposing Altman's former client (the SEC or even the government). The concern was different. The Gordon firm and its client, Armstrong as receiver, stood to benefit from information Altman presumably learned about the defendants while at the SEC. We don't want lawyers to exploit information learned in government service to benefit private clients, at the expense of the subjects of that information, unless the information is generally available. We can call this the *confidential government information concern*.

In *General Motors*, cited in footnote 24 of *Armstrong*, New York City brought an antitrust action against GM charging monopolization in the manufacture and sale of city buses. The city's private lawyer, George Reycraft, had previously worked at the Department of Justice on a case against GM for monopolizing the manufacture and sale of buses. Resisting GM's motion to disqualify Reycraft, the city argued that he had not "switched sides" but was continuing to represent a government entity, although a different one, against the same company, GM. I always found that a clever argument. The Second Circuit did not. It wrote:

> We believe, moreover, that [disqualification is required] for there lurks great potential for lucrative returns in following into private practice the course already charted with the aid of governmental resources. And, with such a large contingent fee at stake, we could hardly accept "pro bono publico" as a proper characterization of Reycraft's work, simply because the keeper of the purse is the City of New York. . . .

Disqualification ensured that government lawyers would not be tempted to choose subjects of an investigation in order to improve their employment prospects when they return to the private sector. We can call this the *agenda setting concern*.

The Model Rules address both the agenda setting and the confidential government information concerns.

Agenda Setting.   Rule 1.11(a) allows a lawyer to represent a private "client in connection with a matter in which the lawyer participated personally and substantially as a public officer or employee"—not necessarily as a lawyer—but *only if* the "appropriate government agency gives its informed consent, confirmed in writing." Consent will allow the work whether the lawyer remains on the same "side," as the city unsuccessfully claimed that Reycraft had, or appears on the other "side," for example, if Reycraft had appeared *for* GM. This rule aims to discourage government lawyers, who have much discretion, from choosing to work on matters in anticipation of continuing to work on them in private practice. They cannot be confident that their agency will permit it.

Confidential Government Information.   Rule 1.11(c) created a new category called "confidential government information," to be distinguished from the confidential information described in Rule 1.6. Rule 1.11(c) contemplates that while in government a lawyer will gain information about individuals and companies to which only the government has access or which it is particularly within its power to compel. Think tax returns, trade secrets, and grand jury testimony. The rule prevents a private client (like NYC) from hiring a former government lawyer (like Reycraft) to exploit such information about its opponent (like GM). Government consent will not avoid the conflict. The Rule protects GM. Rule 1.11(c) would not, however, prevent Reycraft from representing GM instead because the information is GM's own information. It is not being used against GM. But the agenda-setting concern would remain and Reycraft would need government consent.

Screening Allowed.   If the former government lawyer cannot get the consent contemplated by Rule 1.11(a), or is disqualified because she possesses "confidential government information" under Rule 1.11(c), the Rules permit her firm to accept the representation so long as the lawyer is screened and receives no portion of the fee. Rule 1.11(b) requires notice of the screen to the government if a former government lawyer is conflicted under paragraph (a). Permission to screen means a lawyer thinking about taking a government job need not worry that she will find it hard to get a private job after leaving. Private employers can screen them to avoid imputation of the lawyer's conflict. The Second Circuit in *Armstrong* was not prepared to approve screening to avoid all former government lawyer conflicts, but did allow it on the facts before it. Rule 1.11 goes further and permits screening whenever the former government lawyer is disqualified.

Many jurisdictions have statutes controlling the postdeparture work of government employees, including lawyers. In the federal system, 18 U.S.C. §207 imposes postdeparture restrictions on former government employees. These include permanent restrictions on certain work and two-year and one-year restrictions on a variety of activities before the employee's former department or agency. The duration of the disability depends on the nature of the employee's work and his or her status. Violation of the section is a crime and can also lead to civil liability. See 18 U.S.C. §216.

Self-Assessment Questions

1. Baker & Bly's client, the City of Greenwood, has sued MMM Company. It alleges that MMM's trucks transport chemicals through city streets creating a public nuisance. After acrimonious pre-trial skirmishing, the parties settle. As part of the settlement, MMM agrees that thereafter its trucks will use only Second Avenue. But then property owners on Second Avenue hire Baker & Bly to sue MMM on the ground that its trucks create a private nuisance. They seek substantial money damages but no injunction. The City of Greenwood is not a party to the lawsuit. It intervenes and moves to disqualify Baker & Bly citing Rule 1.9(a). What are the City's and Baker & Bly's best arguments?

2. Moss & Michael is asked to represent BBB Company in its negotiations with QQQ Company under which BBB will supply concrete for QQQ's construction project. Moss & Michael has never represented QQQ but Kara, a midlevel associate, previously worked at Adams & Quincy, which did do work for QQQ. How should Moss & Michael decide whether and how it is able to accept BBB's work?

3. Your firm is considering an offer to Lois, a senior SEC lawyer. But she is personally and substantially involved in two matters where your firm's client is opposing the SEC itself. And in a third matter, she investigated JJJ Company, which is a litigation opponent of your firm in a private civil case. Can Lois personally work on any of the matters? Can she join your firm without conflicting it out of these matters? How?

PART THREE

SPECIAL LAWYER ROLES

VII

Ethics in Advocacy

Bassanio: So may the outward shows be least themselves—
          The world is still deceiv'd with ornament.
          In law, what plea so tainted and corrupt
          But, being season'd with a gracious voice,
          Obscures the show of evil? In religion,
          What damned error but some sober brow
          Will bless it, and approve it with a text,
          Hiding the grossness with fair ornament?
                    —Shakespeare, *The Merchant of Venice*, 3.02.73-80

Tranio: Sir, I shall not be slack: in sign whereof,
          Please ye we may contrive this afternoon,
          And quaff carouses to our mistress' health,
          And do as adversaries do in law,
          Strive mightily, but eat and drink as friends.
                    —Shakespeare, *The Taming of the Shrew*, 1.02.271-275

[The plaintiff] brought an action against a neighbor for
borrowing and breaking a cooking pot. Advice of counsel was
that the defendant should plead that he never borrowed the pot;
and that he used it carefully and returned it whole; also, that the
pot was broken and useless when he borrowed it; also, that he
borrowed the pot from someone not the plaintiff; also, that the
pot in question was defendant's own pot; also that the plaintiff
never owned a pot, cooking or other; also that—and so on,
and so on.
                    —James Gould Cozzens, *The Just and the Unjust*

And yet, while we should never prosecute the innocent,
we need not have scruples against undertaking on occasion
the defence of a guilty person, provided he be not infamously
depraved and wicked. For people expect it; custom sanctions it;
humanity also accepts it. It is always the business of the judge in
a trial to find out the truth; it is sometimes the business of the
advocate to maintain what is plausible, even if it be not strictly
true, though I should not venture to say this, especially in an

ethical treatise, if it were not also the position of Panaetius, that strictest of Stoics. Then, too, briefs for the defence are most likely to bring glory and popularity to the pleader, and all the more so, if ever it falls to him to lend his aid to one who seems to be oppressed and persecuted by the influence of someone in power. This I have done on many other occasions; and once in particular, in my younger days, I defended Sextus Roscius of Ameria against the power of Lucius Sulla when he was acting the tyrant. The speech is published, as you know.

—Cicero, *De Officiis*

The only real lawyers are trial lawyers, and trial lawyers try cases to juries.

—Clarence Darrow

I could fill many pages of this book with pithy comments about lawyers as advocates, some complimentary, most not. Nonlawyers wrote nearly all those that are not.

Popular culture's appetite for tales about trial lawyers, in books, in film, and on television, is insatiable. In January 2020 alone, three prominent films, playing simultaneously, had lawyers as central players. Two of the films—*Just Mercy* and *Richard Jewell*—are based on real events. They depict lawyers as heroes. In the third film—*Marriage Story*—the divorce lawyers are not admirable. They increase acrimony and costs (and therefore fees). In March 2020, before COVID-19 forced Broadway to close, a play based on Harper Lee's novel *To Kill a Mockingbird,* featuring Atticus Finch, the most famous fictional lawyer in American history, had been playing eight times a week for more than a year, without a single empty seat at any performance (the producers say). It looked like it would go on forever.

We can appreciate popular culture's focus on trials and trial lawyers. The role of the courtroom advocate raises controversial ethical and moral issues, for both the public and the bar. In this chapter, we look at some of the issues that confront trial lawyers and litigators (the latter being lawyers whose cases rarely go to trial and whom Clarence Darrow would therefore not honor with the label "trial lawyers").

Why are trial lawyers so fascinating? Many people think of the advocate as amoral. A gun for hire. True, the advocate may respond, if that means she does not judge her client. But she would insist that the moral thing to do is to remain true to your assigned role in the adversary system. In the advocate's world, whatever result the adversary system reaches is just by definition. If a result seems unjust, possibly even to the lawyer who achieved it, that's the concern of those empowered to change the law or the rules of advocacy. The advocate simply does her job under the rules as they are, one case at a time. To fail to do so because the lawyer believes her client is "wrong" betrays the client and her oath.

An advocate may concede that she means to win all or as much as possible for her client, regardless of who is "right." But she may deny that it is even possible to talk about "right" in the conventional sense. That will not, however, stop her from trying, before the court and the jury, to get as much mileage as possible from conventional notions of "good" and "bad" or "fair" and "unfair." She views herself as the agent of her client in a highly structured, artificial combat system called litigation, a system the client may only dimly understand but which can play havoc with the client's life. In this system, you are "right" if you win; you don't necessarily win because you are "right." As Samuel Johnson is said to have told James Boswell, "[Y]ou do not know [a cause] to be good or bad till the judge determines it." So far as the advocate is concerned, the loser is wrong by definition.

The advocate adopts this perspective only after a client retains her. She may, of course, reflect on the rightness of a matter *before* accepting it and decline cases she finds objectionable. In choice of client, lawyers have much autonomy. Or do they? Some lawyers—law firm associates, employed corporate lawyers, lawyers in government and public defender offices—may have little choice. They do what they are assigned. Enlightened law offices will allow for some conscientious objection, but not much. There must be a limit.

A lawyer may also be able to withdraw from a matter (with a court's consent when required) if a client "insists upon taking action" with which the lawyer has a "fundamental disagreement" or that she finds "repugnant." Rule 1.16(b)(4). But usually the lawyer will know the score at the outset and can choose to decline the matter. And again, employed lawyers may lack this option.

Let's say a lawyer accepts or is assigned a case that she comes to find morally dubious or, worse, odious. Professionally, she must forget her reservations. Once she's in, she's in unless Rule 1.16 lets her out. If it does not, she must act as though the client's cause were her own. Trial lawyers delight in quoting Lord Brougham (1778-1868), the lawyer for Queen Caroline in her criminal trial for adultery. Brougham apparently had some evidence that would embarrass the King, but would he use it to defend the Queen? Indeed he would. As quoted in the introduction to chapter 2, Brougham told the judges: "[A]n advocate, in the discharge of his duty, knows but one person in all the world, and that person is his client." He then added, lest there be any doubt about his intentions, that the "hazards and costs to other persons" are of no concern to the advocate, that the advocate "must not regard the alarm, the torments, the destruction which he may bring upon others. . . . [H]e must go on reckless of consequences, though it should be his unhappy fate to involve his country in confusion."

For many people outside the legal community (and for some in it), Lord Brougham's view is offensive. (To be fair, we must remember that he was making a threat. We don't know if he would have done those things.) Popular suspicion of this attitude encourages cynicism about lawyers, especially criminal defense lawyers, and often leads to that common question: "How can you defend a guilty person?" (Don't think you won't be asked that question even if you specialize in corporate law.)

For lawyers, this question is nonsense. Guilt is a legal conclusion. By definition no one is guilty until declared so after a due process trial with the assistance of counsel, if desired. The response may then be: "Don't quibble. You know what I mean. How can you defend someone *who you know did it?*" In reply, the advocate will invoke her historical role in the Anglo-American criminal justice system and patiently explain that it could not work as envisioned unless she or another lawyer took the defense. She might quote the Sixth Amendment's guarantee of counsel and tell you to read *Gideon's Trumpet,* Anthony Lewis's classic retelling of the events that led to the Supreme Court's 1963 Gideon v. Wainwright decision.

To many members of the public, this sounds like "lawyer talk" or dissembling. To lawyers it is a sacred truth, a hallmark of a civilized people, essential to liberty and the rule of law. Cue the trumpets.

Things get more complicated when the focus shifts from the (perhaps) morally dubious, if nonetheless legal, goals of the advocate's client in a civil or criminal case, goals she is helping him achieve, to the means she uses to reach them. Those means, although legal and ethical, might appear unfair to the public. It is easier to blame the advocate for unfair means because, while clients choose the goals, chapter 2 taught us that lawyers ordinarily choose the means to achieve them and have the specialized knowledge required to do so.

But just as the words "right" and "wrong" do not have the same meaning in Lawyerland as they do in real life, neither does the word "unfair" retain its conventional meaning. For many lawyers, any strategy the rules permit is fair by definition. Utility is the only issue: Will it work? Is it worth the time and expense? An example is the well-funded defendant who prolongs a litigation with creative but plausible procedural motions, thereby forcing a needy plaintiff to compromise for much less than the value of his claim. Another example is the lawyer who pummels a witness, who the lawyer knows is telling the truth, with vigorous but permissible cross-examination intended to persuade the jury (as the lawyer then argues in summation) that the witness is a liar. If the tactic is "unfair," lawyers say, blame the rules, not us. We're doing our job, obeying our oath.

The public, however, appears to blame lawyers. In 2013, the Pew Research Center asked Americans to say whether certain groups contributed "'a lot' to society's well-being." Between 63 and 78 percent of respondents put the military, teachers, doctors, scientists, and engineers in this category. Lawyers came in last: Only 18 percent said lawyers contributed "a lot," down from 23 percent in 2009. An astonishing 34 percent said lawyers contributed "nothing" or "not very much" to society's well-being. By comparison, for others in the top five professional groups, only 5 to 9 percent said "nothing" or "not very much."

Gallup routinely asks Americans to rate the "honesty and ethical standards" of various groups. In recent surveys, nurses were rated very high or high in 85 percent of responses. Only one percent rated nurses low or very low. The numbers for doctors were 65 percent and 8 percent, respectively.

Toward the bottom of the list, the ratings for real estate agents were 25 percent and 19 percent, respectively. Lawyers did worse. They were rated high or very high for honesty and ethical standards by 22 percent of respondents and low or very low by 28 percent. They did better than members of Congress, however — 12 percent rated members of Congress high or very high for these qualities and 55 percent said low or very low.

What rules should a justice system adopt to govern the behavior of trial lawyers? Answers to this question have filled libraries. Even to begin to answer it, we need a satisfactory theory of justice. Common law nations need a satisfactory theory of adversary justice. Our theory must be sufficiently flexible to change. We don't have the same adversary system as 50 years ago. The foundation is the same but details differ and details count. The next half-century will bring new changes.

We must also remember that a justice system, however beautiful in design, is not self-executing. Legal theorists do not always dwell on that fact. That's fine. Their job is to think big thoughts, not necessarily to be practical. But theories must accommodate a political and historical tradition. They must take account of human error, malevolence, and institutional incompetence. They must ask how wealth or lack of it will distort the operation of the theory (a great deal, as it happens). One side may be able to afford better lawyers or lawyers with more time to prepare; have more money to pay investigators, to hire jury consultants, to "try" a case before a mock jury, and for high-tech videos that tell a compelling story in court; and have a greater tolerance for the law's delay. An imperfect system of justice might be as close to the "most perfect" system that a society's traditions, politics, and institutions are capable of at the time. And, we must ask, "perfect compared to what?" Is another nation's method for resolving questions of liability and guilt better? What does "better" actually mean in this context?

The rule of unintended consequences intrudes here as elsewhere. Humility is demanded. Because we are dealing with a system of great complexity, with many participants in different roles and serving a diverse society, we must be aware that structural changes we might make in one place to advance a perceived good can have harmful effects elsewhere in the system, effects we might not anticipate. This is not an argument against change. It is an argument for caution in making systemic change.

Systems aside, at the individual level, lawyers are forbidden to act outside their given role to achieve what they might honestly perceive to be "justice" in the particular situation (although the popular culture loves to play with that narrative). Lacking omniscience, they may be wrong about what justice requires and actually work injustice as a result. Beyond that, the system operates on the assumption that across the vast run of cases, justice will be best served when lawyers stick to their assigned job, which they will have sworn to do, and if clients can trust that they will.

We begin this chapter with selections from the vast literature defending and criticizing the adversary system in the United States. It is not possible to provide a representative survey. I can, however, give you a feel for the debate from four highly articulate authors writing from diverse perspectives. In turn, you should be able to begin to form your own conclusions as you assess the information in the succeeding material.

A. FOUR VIEWS OF ADVERSARY JUSTICE*

Simon Rifkind was a district judge in the Southern District of New York from 1941 to 1950, when he resigned to join Paul, Weiss, Rifkind, Wharton & Garrison (as it was then renamed). Marvin Frankel, formerly a Columbia law professor, was a judge on the same court (1965-1978) and then a partner in Kramer Levin Naftalis & Frankel. Robert Post was dean of Yale Law School. Anthony Trollope (1815-1882), the author of *Orley Farm,* was a prominent English novelist, as productive and accomplished as his contemporary Charles Dickens.

Simon Rifkind and Marvin Frankel: Two Views on the Role of Truth in the Adversary System

Simon H. Rifkind
THE LAWYER'S ROLE AND RESPONSIBILITY IN MODERN SOCIETY
30 The Record 534 (1975)

The adversary process is . . . seen as a form of organized and institution-alized confrontation. Because organized confrontations also occur in many forms of sport, some have seized upon the superficial similarity to down-grade the adversary process as socially trivial. This contemnation would be appropriate if the object of the adversary process were to select the more skillful lawyer, as it is, for instance, to select the better boxer or tennis player. In the courtroom contest, the judge does not award prizes for skill. He uses the adversary process for illumination. And it is, I believe, the teaching of experience that the incentives generated by the adversary system do, indeed, tend to bring about a more thorough search for and evaluation of both the facts and the law. . . .

From some of my philosophically oriented brethren I hear murmurs that the Anglo-American reliance on the adversary process may have exceeded the limits of its utility and that re-examination is now in order. Re-examination of a major premise is always in order. Most logical errors are imbedded in major premises uncritically accepted. I have no doubt that to the logician, the adversary process will present many flaws. The inequality of resources

---

* Plus Shakespeare's lesson on emotion in performance.

between the contestants, the disparity in talent, are but two of many. But I should recall the sage words of the Yankee from Olympus, "The life of the law has not been logic; it has been experience."

Experience tells me that the adversary system has been good for liberty, good for peaceful progress and good enough to have the public accept that system's capacity to resolve controversies and, generally, to acquiesce in the results.

And it has also accomplished something else. It has tended to reward most highly those lawyers who are best suited to the adversary process. In consequence, such lawyers have established the norms of performance. Anyone who has worked with lawyers around the globe knows that those brought up in the Anglo-American tradition of the adversary process devote themselves more comprehensively, more passionately, to the solution of their clients' problems than the lawyers reared under any other system.

Recent events surrounding the whole epoch called Watergate have caused an unflattering light to shine upon quite a number of lawyers. Some laymen have suggested that the very function the attorney presumes to discharge involves a conflict of interest between his duty to his client and his duty to society.

Those who have voiced such views have not taken account of the operation of the adversary process. The utility of that process is that it relieves the lawyer of the need, or indeed the right, to be his client's judge and thereby frees him to be the more effective advocate and champion. Since the same is true of his adversary, it should follow that the judge who will decide will be aided by greater illumination than otherwise would be available.

Lord MacMillan in his famous address on the ethics of advocacy delivered in 1916 quotes this exchange:

Boswell: But what do you think of supporting a cause which you know to be bad?

Johnson: Sir, you do not know it to be good or bad till the judge determines it. You are to state facts clearly; so that your *thinking*, or what you call *knowing*, a cause to be bad must be from reasoning, must be from supposing your arguments to be weak and inconclusive. But, sir, that is not enough. An argument which does not convince yourself may convince the judge to whom you urge it; and if it does convince him, why then, sir, you are wrong and he is right. It is his business to judge; and you are not to be confident in your opinion that a cause is bad, but to say all you can for your client, and then hear the judge's opinion.

Of course the process I have described is subject to human frailty. Sometimes the poorer cause prevails. That is a price worth paying for the long-range benefits of the system. It is comparable to the price we are willing to pay for democracy in the acceptance of the mistakes of the majority. We pay a price for the jury system. We pay these in return for values which we believe exceed the costs.

Even when the poorer cause prevails at the end of the adversary process, it is not necessarily a total loss. Sometimes it flags an error in the law. Sometimes it stokes the fires of reform and produces corrective legislative action.

What I have said thus far would have sounded orthodox twenty years ago. Today I think it is radical doctrine. It is radical because it rejects the notion which has gained considerable ground at the bar and very widespread allegiance on the campus that the lawyer should not be client-oriented but cause oriented. . . .

With some trepidation I should like to tender the suggestion that in actual practice the ascertainment of the truth is not necessarily the target of the trial, that values other than truth frequently take precedence, and that, indeed, courtroom truth is a unique species of the genus truth, and that it is not necessarily congruent with objective or absolute truth, whatever that may be.

When I once casually expressed this notion to a group of laymen, they expressed shock and dismay as if I were a monk uttering some unutterable heresy to a Tenth Century congregation of bishops. But that reaction has not deterred me. On reflection, I have framed the hypothesis that courtroom truth is one of several varieties of truth and I have discovered that, consciously or unconsciously, the practicing trial lawyer behaves in a way compatible with that hypothesis. I have also formulated the conclusion that the object of a trial is not the ascertainment of truth but the resolution of a controversy by the principled application of the rules of the game. In a civilized society these rules should be designed to favor the just resolution of controversy; and in a progressive society they should change as the perception of justice evolves in response to greater ethical sophistication. . . .

I believe, the courtroom has developed its own version of truth.

The reception of information in most court proceedings is conducted through a complex filtering process. The filtering is designed in large measure to exclude information which is suspect or which experience has adjudged generally untrustworthy. In addition, there are baffles which exclude information, without reference to its truthbearing quality. These exclusions have been established to serve policies and to recognize values totally unrelated to truth.

It seems inescapable to me that the so-called truth which the trier of the facts, judge or jury, will discover at the end of the trial may, likely will, differ materially from the truth it might have found had no such barriers to information been in place. I make no assessment whether, measured by some standard not yet invented, such truth is of higher or lesser quality than courtroom truth. All I assert is that it may very well, and likely will, be different.

Marvin E. Frankel
PARTISAN JUSTICE
Pages 11-19 (1980)

Our leading religions may teach about loving our neighbors, about the expectancies of the meek, and about forbearance, gentleness, and other fond virtues. In our arena for secular justice, however, we enthrone combat as a paramount good. The "adversary system," as we call it, is not merely borne as a supposedly necessary evil. It is cherished as an ideal of constitutional proportions, not only because it embodies the fundamental right to be heard, but because it is thought (often) to be the best assurance of truth and sound results. Decisions of the Supreme Court give repeated voice to this concept. We are taught to presume as a vital premise the belief that "partisan advocacy on both sides," according to rules often countenancing partial truths and concealment, will best assure the discovery of truth in the end. We are not so much as slightly rocked in this assumption by the fact that other seekers after truth have not emulated us. Ours is, after all, a special world of special cases. Even we who made and run that world would fear for our lives if physicians, disagreeing about the cause of our chest pains, sought to resolve the issue by our forms of interrogation, badgering, and other forensics. But for the defendant whose life is at stake—and for the public concerned whether the defendant is a homicidal menace—this is thought to be the most perfect form of inquiry. We live, at any rate, as if we believe this.

Like any sweeping proposition, the claim that our adversary process is best for truth seeking has qualifications and limits recognized by its staunchest proponents. While it would not be essential, we have again the high authority of Supreme Court pronouncements noting that lawyers in the process are often expected, with all propriety, to help block or conceal rather than pursue the truth. These endeavors are commonly justified in the service of interests that outweigh truth finding—interests in privacy, personal dignity, security, autonomy, and other cherished values. The problem of how to weigh the competing values is, obviously, at the heart of the concerns to be addressed in these chapters. Nobody doubts that there are ends of diverse kinds, at diverse times and places, more worthy than the accurate discovery or statement of facts; that there are even occasions, not easily defined with unanimity, when a lie is to be preferred. One way to state the thesis of this book is to say, recognizing the complex relativities of life, that the American version of the adversary process places too low a value on truth telling; that we have allowed ourselves too often to sacrifice truth to other values that are inferior, or even illusory. But the elaboration of the position is best postponed until after we have described how the process works and how its actors perform.

The quality of private initiative and private control is, in its degree, the hallmark of the American judicial process. While the administration of justice is designated as the public's business and the decision-makers are public people (whether full-time judges or the lay judges who sit in jury boxes), the process is initiated, shaped, and managed by the private contestants in civil matters and by the government and non-government lawyer-contestants in criminal matters. The deciders, though commissioned to discover the truth, are passive recipients, not active explorers. They take what they are given. They consider the questions raised by counsel, rarely any others. Issues not joined are not resolved, though they might have led to wiser, fairer dispositions than those reached. The parties, almost always the lawyers or those under their direction, investigate the facts, interview possible witnesses, consult potential experts to find opinions most agreeable to their causes, decide what will be told and what will not be told. The judges and jurors almost never make inquiries on their own, and are not staffed or otherwise equipped to do so. The reconstructions of the past to be given in the courtroom are likely to be the sharply divergent stories told by partisans, divergent from each other and from the actual events supposed to be portrayed. If history can never reproduce the past with total fidelity, one wonders often whether we could not miss by margins much narrower than those marked in courtrooms. . . .

The system rests, we must always remember, on the assumption that we can accurately re-create the facts so that our rules of law, democratically evolved, will work just results. If the rule is that the signer of the note must pay, it works acceptably only if we correctly identify the signer. If we fail to make the identification, or, worse yet, falsely identify one who really did not sign, the result will be an injustice. It is no answer that some of our laws are no good. Nobody who thinks the society good enough to preserve, and improve, argues seriously that the cure for bad laws is feckless decisions about facts.

The simple point to be stressed, here and throughout, is that many of us trained in the learned profession of the law spend much of our time subverting the law by blocking the way to the truth. The subversion is not for the most part viewed as a pathology; rather, if somewhat paradoxically, it follows from the assigned roles of counsel in the very system of law which thus finds its purposes thwarted.

The games we play about fact finding are, of course, an old story and an old source of professional worry and efforts toward reform. During the last half-century or so, much has been done through rules of "discovery" to cut down on concealment and surprises at trial. The idea is to allow demands for information before trial and to require responses from the adverse party. The device has on the whole worked substantial improvements. Predictably, however, it has been turned—and twisted—to adversary uses. Lawyers react characteristically by demanding as much as possible and giving as little as possible. What is not demanded is not given. It remains as true as ever that if a lawyer fails to ask the right question, the adversary will cheerfully refrain from disclosing what might be vital or decisive information. The discovery process itself, with rules that frequently are (or are made to be) intricate and abstruse, becomes the occasion for expensive contests, producing libraries full of opinions. Where the object always is to beat every plowshare into a sword, the discovery procedure is employed variously as weaponry. A powerful litigant in a complex case may impose costly, even crushing, burdens by demands for files, pretrial testimony of witnesses, and other forms of discovery. An approximately converse ploy has also been evolved to make the procedure a morass rather than the revelatory blessing it was meant to be. A litigant may contrive to dump truckloads of [unsorted] files on the party demanding discovery, hoping, often not in vain, that the searcher will be so exhausted that the damaging items will be overlooked or never reached.

The key point at every stage, which will bear recalling from time to time, is that the single uniformity is always adversariness. There are other goods, but the greatest is winning. There are other evils, but scarcely any worse than losing. Every step of the process, and any attempt to reform it, must be viewed in this light until or unless the adversary ethic comes to be changed or subordinated. The lawyer's response to a tax is how to avoid or minimize its impact on the client. Every law is probed for its loopholes—unless the lawyer has done the job in advance by being placed strategically to sew them in during the legislative process. Every idea for improved procedures must be imaginatively pretested to foresee its evolving shapes under the fires of adversary zeal.

Because the route of a lawsuit is marked by a running battle all the way, the outcome is nothing like the assuredly right result imagined in our dream that "justice will out." In that dream, neither eloquence nor lawyers' techniques nor cunning has much place. The person who is "right" should win. But that is very far from assured in the kind of contest we've been considering. Where skill and trickery are so much involved, it must inevitably happen that the respective qualities of the professional champions will make a decisive difference. Where sheer power and endurance may count, the relative resources of clients become vital. Describing the tendency of the enterprise as the major forces propel it, two students of the American legal system were led to conclude: "In an ideal adversary system, the less skillful antagonist is expected to lose, which under the laissez-faire notion is the proper outcome."

If that is, fortunately, an exaggeration, it describes a probability high and uncertain enough to be harrowing. One of the nation's greatest judges, Learned Hand, paid grim tribute to the uncertainty in a famous utterance: "I must say that, as a litigant, I should dread a lawsuit beyond almost anything else short of sickness and of death." Hand's distinguished colleague for a number of years, Jerome Frank [once] focused . . . on the utter chanciness of factual determinations as the main reason why lawsuits are gambles too often and routes to justice more seldom than they should be.

Faking It: Lawyers and Actors, Lawyers As Actors

At Hamlet's request, an itinerant player enacted Hecuba's turmoil when Pyrrhus slew her husband Priam in the Trojan War. In his ensuing soliloquy, reprinted in part below, Hamlet contrasts the player's passion "but in a fiction" with his own failure to avenge his father's death despite in fact having "the motive and the cue for passion." Dean Post, drawing on the work of Erving Goffman and others, writes that "unlike the actor . . . the lawyer's job requires that he totally conceal his performance" and present a false self, which may explain "the special hatred that popular culture holds for the lawyer." In part D, below, you will see that ethics rules forbid false statements. But a courtroom performance, like an actor's, can be false in other ways yet proper. Is that a contradiction, a premise of the adversary system, or both?

William Shakespeare
HAMLET
2.02.545-560

Hamlet: O, what a rogue and peasant slave am I!
Is it not monstrous that this player here,
But in a fiction, in a dream of passion,
Could force his soul so to his own conceit
That from her working all his visage wann'd,
Tears in his eyes, distraction in's aspect,
A broken voice, and his whole function suiting
With forms to his conceit? and all for nothing!
For Hecuba!
What's Hecuba to him, or he to Hecuba,
That he should weep for her? What would he do,
Had he the motive and the cue for passion
That I have? He would drown the stage with tears
And cleave the general ear with horrid speech,
Make mad the guilty and appal the free,
Confound the ignorant, and amaze indeed
The very faculties of eyes and ears. Yet I,
A dull and muddy-mettled rascal, peak,
Like John-a-dreams, unpregnant of my cause,
And can say nothing; no, not for a king,
Upon whose property and most dear life
A damn'd defeat was made.

Robert C. Post
ON THE POPULAR IMAGE OF THE LAWYER:
REFLECTIONS IN A DARK GLASS
75 Calif. L. Rev. 379 (1987)

We owe especially to the sociologist Erving Goffman the insight that the self in modern society can be understood not as something of substance that actually exists, but rather as a series of performances. The character attributed by others to an individual is the result of these performances. Goffman tells us:

> In our society the character one performs and one's self are somewhat equated, and this self-as-character is usually seen as something housed within the body of its possessor. . . . I suggest that this view is . . . a bad analysis of the presentation. In this [book] the performed self was seen as some kind of image, usually creditable, which the individual on stage and in character effectively attempts to induce others to hold in regard to him. While this image is entertained *concerning* the individual, so that a self is imputed to him, this self does not derive from its possessor, but from the whole scene of his action, being generated by that attribute of local events which renders them interpretable by witnesses.

It is of immense importance for us as a society, however, to deny this insight. We get queasy when we view the personality of others to be constituted merely by a series of staged performances. Sartre makes a similar point in his famous analysis in *Being and Nothingness*:

> A grocer who dreams is offensive to the buyer, because such a grocer is not wholly a grocer. Society demands that he limit himself to his function as a grocer, just as the soldier at attention makes himself into a soldier-thing with a direct regard which does not see at all. . . . There are indeed many precautions to imprison a man in what he is, as if we lived in perpetual fear that he might escape from it, that he might break away and suddenly elude his condition.

This perpetual fear of the self escaping its concrete and given substance is in some measure behind the centuries of abuse and loathing that the premodern era poured onto actors, for actors are the living embodiment of the performing, protean self. Jean-Jacques Rousseau, for example, thought actors "dishonorable" because the talent of the actor lies in "the art of counterfeiting himself, of putting on another character than his own, of appearing different than he is, . . . of forgetting his own place by dint of taking another's." Rousseau contrasted the actor to the orator:

> When the orator appears in public, it is to speak and not to show himself off; he represents only himself; he fills only his own role, speaks only in his own name, says, or ought to say, only what he thinks; the man and the role being the same, he is in his place; he is in the situation of any citizen who fulfills the functions of his estate. But an actor on the stage, displaying other sentiments than his own, saying only what he is made to say, often representing a chimerical being, annihilates himself, as it were, and is lost in his hero.

Actors, however, lie directly: we all know that Olivier is only pretending to be King Lear, and that it is just a performance. But consider, in this light, the trial lawyer making a summary to the jury. In that case we know both (1) that the lawyer must be representing the interests of his client, so that his speech does not sincerely represent his "personal" views; and (2) that if the lawyer distinguishes between his personal views and those of his client, his client will suffer, so that the lawyer can perform his job only if he "appears" to be and in fact convinces us that he is sincere. Unlike the actor, then, the lawyer's job requires that he totally conceal his performance. And he must do this about issues of public importance, where the integrity of the self as a constituted member of the community is most at stake. To paraphrase Rousseau, the lawyer must convince us that he is an orator, exercising his highest function as a citizen, when in reality he is simply a secret actor, "lost" in the identity of his client.

This is extraordinarily disturbing. And so in popular culture we say of the lawyer, as the old adage goes, "A good lawyer must be a great liar." Or we say, with Jonathan Swift, that lawyers are a "society of men . . . bred up from their youth in the art of proving by words multiplied for the purpose, that white is black and black is white, according as they are paid."

These hostile characterizations of the lawyer put her at a distance, as though her performances were something specially devious and different from the rest of us. If our acceptance of the acting profession demonstrates that we have come to acknowledge that role-playing is an integral aspect of modern experience, our excoriation of lawyers illustrates that this acceptance has definite limits. The performances of the lawyer are hidden, and hence they obliterate the distinction between the performing self and the true or innate self. But in this the lawyer is merely representative of the concealed performances we must all undertake every day. We would like to believe that we are the master of our many roles, rather than the reverse, but the persistent and unsettling example of the lawyer will not let us rest easy in this belief. If Goffman is correct, and if we are in fact constituted by our performances, the intensity of the animosity we bear toward lawyers may come precisely from the fact that they are so very threatening to our need to believe that we possess stable and coherent selves.

The Advocate in Literature

Anthony Trollope
ORLEY FARM*

[Moulder, a traveling salesman, worldly wise by his own estimation, is explaining to his unworldly brother-in-law, John Kenneby, what Kenneby should expect when he testifies when called as a witness at an upcoming criminal trial.]

"All right," said Moulder. "And now, John, I'll just tell you what it is. You've no more chance of being allowed to speak freely there than — than — than — no more than if you was in church. What are them fellows paid for if you're to say whatever you pleases out in your own way?"

"He only wants to say the truth, M.," said Mrs. Moulder, who probably knew less than her husband of the general usages of courts of law.

"Truth be —," said Moulder.

* www.gutenberg.org.

"Mr. Moulder!" said Mrs. Smiley. "There's ladies by, if you'll please to remember."

"To hear such nonsense sets one past oneself," continued he; "as if all those lawyers were brought together there—the cleverest and sharpest fellows in the kingdom, mind you—to listen to a man like John here telling his own story in his own way. You'll have to tell your story in their way; that is, in two different ways. There'll be one fellow'll make you tell it his way first, and another fellow'll make you tell it again his way afterwards; and its odds but what the first'll be at you again after that, till you won't know whether you stand on your heels or your head."

"That can't be right," said Mrs. Moulder.

"And why can't it be right?" said Moulder. "They're paid for it; it's their duties; just as it's my duty to sell Hubbles and Grease's sugar. It's not for me to say the sugar's bad, or the sample's not equal to the last. My duty is to sell, and I sell;—and it's their duty to get a verdict."

"But the truth, Moulder—!" said Kenneby.

"Gammon!" said Moulder. "Begging your pardon, Mrs. Smiley, for making use of the expression. Look you here, John; if you're paid to bring a man off not guilty, won't you bring him off if you can? I've been at trials times upon times, and listened till I've wished from the bottom of my heart that I'd been brought up a barrister. Not that I think much of myself, and I mean of course with education and all that accordingly. It's beautiful to hear them. You'll see a little fellow in a wig, and he'll get up; and there'll be a man in the box before him,—some swell dressed up to his eyes, who thinks no end of strong beer of himself; and in about ten minutes he'll be as flabby as wet paper, and he'll say—on his oath, mind you,—just anything that that little fellow wants him to say. That's power, mind you, and I call it beautiful."

"But it ain't justice," said Mrs. Smiley.

"Why not? I say it is justice. You can have it if you choose to pay for it, and so can I. If I buy a greatcoat against the winter, and you go out at night without having one, is it injustice because you're perished by the cold while I'm as warm as a toast. I say it's a grand thing to live in a country where one can buy a greatcoat."

"Adversary Justice Is Good for Lawyers But Bad for Justice"

"The ability to get justice should not depend on how rich you are. We at the non-profit organization Justice As Fairness are working to establish a cooperative civil law system. No one can deny that the adversary system favors the rich. That's good for lawyers, who are the suppliers of the product in this laissez-faire litigation world, and it's good for wealthy clients, who are its favored consumers. But it's bad for society and it's bad for everyone else. The adversary system is a product of the same historical forces that have long benefitted the one percent. Adversary justice is good for lawyers but bad for justice.

"In the cooperative civil law system that we support, lawyers for both sides will have responsibility to share *all factual information about the dispute that tends to prove or disprove an element of a claim or defense.* This language draws on the current duties of prosecutors in Rule 3.8(d). Reports of investigators and experts are included. While no client and no lawyer is obligated to search for facts or find authority useful to his opponent, if in preparing his case a lawyer happens to come upon such facts or authorities, he must reveal them. There is no work-product protection for facts, although there is for a lawyer's thought processes. In effect, the facts in each lawyer's file also belong to the opponent. Or should I say, to the institution of justice? It costs money to find facts, so today wealthy litigants have an advantage, sometimes a sizeable one. This should not be.

"Liberal discovery rules, while welcome, go only part way toward ameliorating disparities of wealth. Discovery is expensive. And I might remind you that there were vociferous objections to liberal discovery rules, with dire predictions of widespread disobedience, which has not come to pass.

"In our proposal, the attorney-client privilege survives. Lawyers and clients may not be forced to reveal their communications. Also lawyers would remain free to argue different inferences from the facts, to introduce any admissible evidence they choose, to challenge the credibility of witnesses, and to argue different theories of what the law is (or should be). We agree with Judge Frankel when he wrote: 'Where skill and trickery are so much involved, it must inevitably happen that the respective qualities of the professional champions will make a decisive difference. Where sheer power and endurance may count, the relative resources of clients become vital.' That should not be. We're talking about justice, not luxuries.

"The cooperative system will provide greater accuracy in fact-finding; reduce unfairness due to disparities in wealth; and lead to swifter and cheaper resolution of civil disputes. It gives real content to the idea that lawyers are 'officers of the court.' But these changes will not come from lawyers. The more combative the adversary system, the more services lawyers have to sell and the greater will be their income. The changes must come from the people whom the justice system is meant to serve. Imagine that you're not (going to be) either a lawyer or wealthy. Which system do you prefer?

"The trend favors us. In 2017, the Federal Judicial Center began a three-year mandatory pilot program in Arizona and Illinois whereby litigants are obligated early in the case to disclose substantial information without request. The judiciary is promoting the value of truth over power and gamesmanship. Google *Mandatory Initial Discovery Pilot (MIDP) Project* to learn more.[*]

"We think courtroom truth should be closer to historical truth. We recognize that other values may impede the search for truth. Privileges are an example. None of our goals should be controversial. Lawyers in civil matters should have duties closer to those the *Brady* rule has long required of prosecutors. Is that so revolutionary?"

B. ARE LAWYERS MORALLY ACCOUNTABLE FOR THEIR CHOICE OF CLIENTS OR WHAT THEY DO FOR THEM?

Model Rule 1.2(b) states: "A lawyer's representation of a client, including representation by appointment, does not constitute an endorsement of the client's political, economic, social or moral views or activities." What is a sentence like that doing in a legal ethics document? It's not a rule a lawyer can violate, is it? Well, it's there, so what does it mean? Does it mean that lawyers should not publicly criticize other lawyers because of the clients they have chosen to represent, perhaps over a lifetime, but should instead come to their defense, however despised the client? Let's say a lawyer's clients have routinely been large-quantity drug conspirators, organized crime defendants, purveyors of pornography demeaning to women, brutal dictators, tobacco companies in product liability cases, or manufacturers of Saturday Night Specials. What about the lawyers who for decades after Brown v. Board of Education helped state and local governments avoid school integration? Was their help immoral, even if ethical?

Many lawyers would say that making any moral judgments about lawyers based on the identity or goals of their clients or the nature of their work will impede the availability of counsel, including counsel for political dissidents, minorities, capital defendants, and others most in need of the law's protection. So think what you want privately, but don't criticize publicly. The powerful will always be able to get good lawyers. It is others who will suffer if lawyers become targets of public hostility because of whom they represent. Are they right?

Consider lawyers for tobacco companies. Some defended class actions in which former smokers (or their estates) sought damages for tobacco-related illnesses. Others helped with all of the mundane transactional work required to market any consumer product. Yet others helped hide evidence of tobacco's health hazards behind weak claims of privilege. Let's assume that none of the lawyers violated any ethical or legal rule. Can we morally

---

[*] For the Model Order describing the scope of the enhanced obligations, see https://www.fjc.gov/sites/default/files/2017/MIDPP%20Model%20Standing%20Order.pdf.

criticize them? Does it matter if, when they did their work, they (a) knew or (b) had good reason to believe that tobacco kills? Are the lawyers immune to moral criticism (at least from other lawyers) precisely because they were acting as lawyers, in the role our justice system assigns, and should therefore be defended so as to encourage the bar to represent unpopular clients? Would you extend the same immunity to other professionals who helped bring tobacco to market, say the creative teams that designed print (and, until the ban, electronic) advertisements depicting smoking as sophisticated, glamorous, and sexy? Like them, the tobacco lawyers freely chose how they wished to use their talents and free choice carries moral responsibility. Or does it not for lawyers?

Consider the criticism of Ronald Sullivan and King & Spalding in the following two incidents. Do you agree with it?

Ronald S. Sullivan, Jr., Defends Harvey Weinstein

The prominent film producer Harvey Weinstein was indicted in New York in May 2018 for rape and sexual assault. Many women sued him civilly. In February 2020 he was found guilty of both crimes and in March 2020 he was sentenced to 23 years in prison. Weinstein has appealed.

Ronald S. Sullivan, Jr. is a clinical law professor at Harvard. He also directs the law school's criminal law clinic. Sullivan and his wife, Stephanie Robinson, served for ten years as faculty deans of Winthrop House, one of the undergraduate residences where about 400 students lived.

In January 2019, Sullivan joined Weinstein's defense team. "The move set off protests and intense debate" on campus, Jan Ransom and Michael Gold reported in the New York Times. "[A] small, but vocal, group of students have called for [Sullivan's] resignation as dean of Winthrop House." Some Winthrop House residents said that they felt "unsafe."

The Harvard College Dean, Rakesh Khurana, announced a "climate review" to see how students at Winthrop House felt and to "take action as appropriate." Sullivan responded: "It is not lost on me that I'm the first African-American to hold this position. Never in the history of the faculty dean position has the dean been subjected to a 'climate review' in the middle of some controversy."

In May, Khurana said efforts "to improve the climate have been ineffective." He said the situation was "untenable." He removed Sullivan and Robinson from their positions at Winthrop House. Sullivan responded in a New York Times op-ed: "I am willing to believe that some students felt unsafe. But feelings alone should not drive university policy. Administrators must help students distinguish between feelings that have a rational basis and those that do not."

In the Times, columnist Nicholas Kristof described his and his daughter's different reactions. To Kristof, removing Sullivan was a "violation of hard-won liberal values, a troubling example of a university monoculture nurturing liberal intolerance." To his daughter, "a house dean should not defend a notorious alleged rapist . . . while caring for undergraduates." Although Kristof acknowledged that his daughter "has a point," he added that her point had to be weighed "against the right of a law professor to take on a despised client."

In May, Sullivan withdrew from representing Weinstein because a new trial schedule conflicted with his teaching obligations.

Was Dean Khurana right to remove Sullivan and Robinson from their faculty dean positions? Will the criticism of Sullivan make it harder for lawyers to represent unpopular clients for fear of community hostility, as sometimes does happen? Does it affect your judgment that Sullivan has done much work on behalf of sexual assault victims and to overturn wrongful convictions? Did the Winthrop House undergraduates overreact? Do you agree with Nicholas Kristof or with his daughter?

At Harvard Law School, 52 faculty members signed a petition defending Sullivan and urging the school not to remove him as Winthrop House dean. If you were on that faculty, would you sign the petition? The school has more than 100 faculty members, so many did not sign, but we don't know why.

Lawyers for Opponents of Marriage Equality

In 2011, Paul Clement, a former Solicitor General and then a partner at King & Spalding LLP, agreed to represent the House of Representatives in defending the constitutionality of the Defense of Marriage Act (DOMA). Plaintiffs had challenged the part of DOMA that prohibited the federal government from recognizing same-sex marriages performed in states that permitted them. The Obama Administration had been defending DOMA but declared that it no longer would do so. The House then hired Clement to represent the interests of the United States in upholding DOMA, and the firm noted its appearance in court. Within weeks of accepting the matter, King & Spalding withdrew. Its chairman, Robert Hays, issued a short statement saying that the case had been accepted without going through the firm's usual "vetting" process, but offered no further explanation. Another partner later said that the appropriate firm committee had not signed off on taking the case. One firm lawyer was quoted as saying, "The firm did not back out. We never agreed to take it." Some questioned that explanation.

The firm dropped the case (or clarified that it had never taken it) only after various constituencies, but especially LGBTQ rights groups, criticized the firm for accepting it. Some firm lawyers were reportedly surprised and dismayed to learn of the representation. Press stories centered on the firm's possible concern about reactions of clients, its own lawyers, and potential new hires. But some clients criticized the firm for *dropping* the House. A Wall Street Journal editorial entitled "Knave and Spalding" speculated that the firm feared a client backlash. The Journal noted that after the firm had accepted the case, the Human Rights Campaign announced that it would proceed to "educate" firm clients "about King and Spalding's decision to promote discrimination." Wall Street Journal, April 26, 2011. Others, however, congratulated the firm for giving up the case rather than lending its name and prestige to the defense of DOMA. Dropping the House was not cost-free. Two clients, the National Rifle Association (NRA) and the Commonwealth of Virginia, withdrew their business. (Virginia may have reconsidered after the Democrats regained control of state government.) The general counsel of the NRA wrote in part:

> We believe King & Spalding's decision is indefensible and raises serious concerns about its ability to be a reliable and effective advocate for any client facing potentially controversial litigation. . . . We are . . . often involved in controversial issues on which emotions can run high. This is as true in the legal arena as it is in the legislative. It goes without saying that in situations in which we retain outside counsel, we expect them to zealously advocate for our interests and not abandon the representation due to pressure from those who may disagree with us.

In a publicly released letter, Paul Clement resigned from the firm and took the defense of DOMA to another firm. He wrote that he was not resigning because of his views on DOMA, which he claimed were irrelevant.

> Instead, I resign out of the firmly-held belief that a representation should not be abandoned because the client's legal position is extremely unpopular in certain quarters. Defending unpopular positions is what lawyers do. The adversary system of justice depends on it, especially in cases where the passions run high. Efforts to delegitimize any representation for one side of a legal controversy are a profound threat to the rule of law. Much has been said about being on the wrong side of history. But being on the right or wrong side of history on the merits is a question for the clients. When it comes to the lawyers, the surest way to be on the wrong side of history is to abandon a client in the face of hostile criticism.

Clement further wrote that "having undertaken the representation, I believe there is no honorable course for me but to complete it. If there were problems with the firm's vetting process, we should fix the vetting process, not drop the representation."

The law firm had no obligation to accept the case in the first place and its decision to withdraw is proper under the permissive provisions of Rule 1.16. But having accepted the client (which is how the client saw it), even if it did so without going through its usual intake procedures, was it wrong to withdraw?

Perhaps causation cannot be proved, but the inference seems strong that the firm's departure from the case was at least in part a reaction to the negative publicity, which would likely grow if it remained. If that is true, does the firm deserve the criticism in Clement's resignation letter? In the Wall Street Journal editorial? Or should the firm be congratulated for choosing, if belatedly, not to defend DOMA? The House would have no trouble finding new counsel and, as it turned out, kept Clement at his new firm. Should the validity of criticism turn on the ability of the client to find equally competent new counsel? Or does it not matter?

C. (COURTROOM) TRUTH AND CONFIDENCES

Truth loves open dealing.
—Queen Katherine to Cardinal Wolsey in Shakespeare,
Henry VIII, 3.01.39

Attorney Andrew Beckett (played by Tom Hanks): "It's that every now and again—not often, but occasionally—you get to be a part of justice being done. That really is quite a thrill when that happens."
—From the film *Philadelphia* (1993)

A lawyer will do anything to win a case, sometimes he will even tell the truth.
—Patrick Murray, British actor

Vinny Gambini [in opening statement]: "Uh. Everything that guy just said is bullshit. Thank you."
    DA Jim Trotter: "Objection. Counsel's entire opening statement is argumentative."
    Judge Chamberlain Haller: "Sustained. Counselor's entire opening statement, with the exception of 'thank you,' will be stricken from the record."
—From the film *My Cousin Vinny* (1992)

"Out Carousing with Mikey"

"I'm sorry to disturb you with this email on Friday of the July Fourth weekend, but my friend Slade, who used to work with you, Slade Catterson, said, 'Tanya, your problem is beyond my casual knowledge of the ethics rules.' Given the dangers in guessing wrong, he told me to email you. I would have waited until Monday, but I think I have to act quickly. Or anyway make a decision.

"I'm defending a man named Carlo on a manslaughter charge. He's indigent and I'm court-appointed. The whole case comes down to identity. The crime took place at two in the morning last August 4 on a street corner. Poor lighting. There are two eyewitnesses, one of whom had had a lot to drink. Both picked Carlo in a lineup. Nothing else connects Carlo with the victim. They were strangers. All in all, not a strong case. No DNA, no prints. The state's theory is that it was a robbery gone wrong. The victim resisted, the robber hit him, the victim fell and banged his head on a steel pipe in the street. Of course, the state doesn't have to prove motive to win.

"Carlo says it wasn't him; he says he was out carousing with Mikey, his best friend. He can't say exactly where this carousing put them at two in the morning August 4. During the night, they drank four six-packs between them. They started in the park, then they walked over to the docks, then went to the financial district, then back to the docks, getting and staying drunk and being boisterous. It was a warm night.

"So of course I talked to Mikey, who has a demeanor you associate with a punch-drunk ex-boxer, which in fact he is. Not very bright. But very sweet. He does odd jobs. Cutting grass. Chopping wood. He has some injury from the first Gulf War that seems to have made concentration a bit of a challenge. Mostly, he lives on disability.

"This was not an easy conversation, getting Mikey to focus. He keeps losing the thread. But he says he and Carlo hang together a lot, buy beer, get drunk, vomit, buy more beer. They're friends from the service. He says they were doing that August 4, the morning of the crime, actually from late on the third until daylight on the fourth. Basically he confirms Carlo's story—the beer, the park, the docks.

"I put Carlo on the stand to testify to how he was out carousing with Mikey. Of course, it helps greatly to confirm a defendant's story, so I also called Mikey, who is very credible, open, a ready smile. He supports Carlo's testimony and, to my amazement, he does well on cross. Not evasive or defensive. I've seen this before. Aggressive cross-examination cannot touch a truly guileless witness. It only backfires.

"This was two days ago, and I rested yesterday morning. The state has some rebuttal after the July Fourth weekend. Then we'll sum up. We had off yesterday afternoon, and when I get to my office, there's Mikey.

"This is where I have my problem. He says it wasn't August 3-4 when he and Carlo went carousing. He thought it was, he said, because 'after Carlo reminded me when it was, I remembered when it was.' I have no doubt he testified to what he believed was the truth.

"So why now all of a sudden does he not believe it was true? Yesterday, July 3, he called his sister who lives in Fort Wayne to wish his niece a happy birthday, and his sister says he's got the wrong month. Her birthday is not July 3, it's August 3, and doesn't he remember because last year he came to her sweet sixteen in Fort Wayne, which is 600 miles from here, and he gave her an iPod. Suddenly, he does remember and realizes that he must have gone carousing with Carlo a different night last August. Or maybe July. Or maybe September. He's really mixed up now. But he's sure it wasn't August 3-4.

"One of the things about Mikey is he's a pack rat. He saves everything. He pulls out his bus ticket stub and receipt showing a roundtrip to Fort Wayne last August 2, returning the afternoon of August 4. And the iPod receipt from Walmart on Apple Glen Road in Fort Wayne, dated August 3 at 6:44 P.M. And an ATM receipt for $20 from a bank in Fort Wayne stamped 9:14 A.M. August 4 so he could buy lunch for the trip home. I confirmed online that Mikey's debit card was used for each transaction. He feels really bad about this, he says, and thought he should tell me. He hasn't told anyone else.

"So don't I now know that Mikey's testimony is false, even if he didn't lie, and that Carlo's is false and maybe that he lied? I don't know what I should do but I'm hoping you do."

What may or must Tanya do under the Model Rules? Do the Rules properly balance the interests of the courts in accurate verdicts with the interests of Carlo? While most American courts follow the Rules' resolution of these questions, not all do. Compare Model Rule 3.3 with California Rule 3.3.

To advise Tanya, a threshold question is whether she *knows* that testimony she introduced is false. If so, a second question might be whether Carlo lied or is just mistaken. (We can assume that Mikey did not lie.) A lie would be perjury, which is a fraud on the court. As we'll see, however, Tanya's obligations under Rule 3.3 will be the same whether or not a witness's false answer is also a lie. (Rule 3.3(a)(3) refers to "false" evidence.) But we begin with lies and look at false evidence later.

Chapter 2B2 showed us that outside litigation, a lawyer may have the authority, or in some jurisdictions an obligation, to reveal a future crime or fraud, or even a concluded one if the harm can still be prevented or remedied, where the lawyer's services were used to commit the crime or fraud. Rule 1.6(b). Now we focus on fraudulent conduct directed toward a *tribunal*, a word defined in Rule 1.0(m) and which will usually be a court. A fraud on the court may take several forms, but the most common is a lie under oath at a trial or deposition. What should a lawyer do if she learns that a client has committed, is committing, or plans to commit a fraud on a court, personally or through others? How certain should the lawyer be before doing anything?

A lawyer's authority or duty to reveal a client's fraudulent behavior toward a court has been the subject of much debate. It still is. The attention we pay to this issue is surely disproportionate to the frequency with which lawyers encounter it. Why do we spend the time? Perhaps because the issue raises fundamental questions about what it means to be an American lawyer. Paradoxically, lawyers feel they have a lot riding on the answers—professional identity itself—even if it is highly unlikely that any lawyer will encounter the dilemma.

We need to recognize several variables.* A court contest may be civil or criminal. The fraud may come in the form of a false document that the lawyer has unwittingly introduced in evidence. Or it may come via client perjury or the perjury of a witness whom the lawyer has called. The lie may come on

---

* The variables are set out in an outline at the end of this part.

direct or cross-examination of the lawyer's witness. The fraud may be prospective (e.g., the lawyer knows the witness will lie if called to testify) or the lawyer may learn of the lie after the testimony. The lawyer's knowledge may be based on a client communication (and therefore privileged) or it may be confidential but not privileged.

Despite these variables, the paradigmatic example of fraud on a court has been perjury by a criminal defendant. If we answer the questions posed here *against* the interests of the accused, we should be able to answer them for all other witnesses. That is because only a criminal defendant has a constitutional right to testify. A lawyer exercising independent professional judgment has the authority, even over her client's objection, to call or not call any other witness (including the client) in any case because this is a "means" decision (see Rule 1.2(a) and chapter 2C). But a lawyer may not refuse to call a criminal defendant who insists on exercising his constitutional right to testify, even if the lawyer thinks that testifying would be a foolish mistake, so long as the lawyer does not *know* that the defendant will lie. Obviously, then, a lot rides on the meaning of "know," which Rule 1.0(f) defines this way:

> "Knowingly," "known," or "knows" denotes actual knowledge of the fact in question. A person's knowledge may be inferred from circumstances.

When the rules were adopted in 1983, uncertainty existed over whether a criminal defense lawyer who alerts (or threatens to alert) the judge that her client will commit or has committed perjury has thereby rendered ineffective assistance. A unanimous Supreme Court responded to that uncertainty as a matter of constitutional law in 1986, but its answers, as we shall see, have sparked more questions. Nix v. Whiteside is among the most important Supreme Court efforts to reconcile a lawyer's duty to a tribunal with the duty to her client. Two sources of rules—the Sixth Amendment guarantee of the effective assistance of counsel (where the Supreme Court has final say) and a state's ethical rules for lawyers (where the Court has no say)—are both in play here. That partly explains the difference between how the majority and concurring opinions see things in *Nix*.

NIX v. WHITESIDE
475 U.S. 157 (1986)

CHIEF JUSTICE BURGER delivered the opinion of the Court.

We granted certiorari to decide whether the Sixth Amendment right of a criminal defendant to assistance of counsel is violated when an attorney refuses to cooperate with the defendant in presenting perjured testimony at his trial.[1]

---

1. Although courts universally condemn an attorney's assisting in presenting perjury, Courts of Appeals have taken varying approaches on how to deal with a client's insistence on presenting perjured testimony. The Seventh Circuit, for example, has held that an attorney's

I

A

Whiteside was convicted of second-degree murder by a jury verdict which was affirmed by the Iowa courts. The killing took place on February 8, 1977, in Cedar Rapids, Iowa. Whiteside and two others went to one Calvin Love's apartment late that night, seeking marihuana. Love was in bed when Whiteside and his companions arrived; an argument between Whiteside and Love over the marihuana ensued. At one point, Love directed his girlfriend to get his "piece," and at another point got up, then returned to his bed. According to Whiteside's testimony, Love then started to reach under his pillow and moved toward Whiteside. Whiteside stabbed Love in the chest, inflicting a fatal wound.

Whiteside was charged with murder, and when counsel was appointed he objected to the lawyer initially appointed, claiming that he felt uncomfortable with a lawyer who had formerly been a prosecutor. Gary L. Robinson was then appointed and immediately began an investigation. . . .

Until shortly before trial, Whiteside consistently stated to Robinson that he had not actually seen a gun, but that he was convinced that Love had a gun in his hand. About a week before trial, during preparation for direct examination, Whiteside for the first time told Robinson and his associate Donna Paulsen that he had seen something "metallic" in Love's hand. When asked about this, Whiteside responded:

"[I]n Howard Cook's case there was a gun. If I don't say I saw a gun, I'm dead."

Robinson told Whiteside that such testimony would be perjury and repeated that it was not necessary to prove that a gun was available but only that Whiteside reasonably believed that he was in danger. On Whiteside's insisting that he would testify that he saw "something metallic" Robinson told him, according to Robinson's testimony,

> [We] could not allow him to [testify falsely] because that would be perjury, and as officers of the court we would be suborning perjury if we allowed him to do it; . . . I advised him that if he did do that it would be my duty to advise the Court of what he was doing and that I felt he was committing perjury; also, that I probably would be allowed to attempt to impeach that particular testimony.

---

refusal to call the defendant as a witness did not render the conviction constitutionally infirm where the refusal to call the defendant was based on the attorney's belief that the defendant would commit perjury. United States v. Curtis, 742 F.2d 1070 (CA7 1984). The Third Circuit found a violation of the Sixth Amendment where the attorney could not state any basis for her belief that the defendant's proposed alibi testimony was perjured. United States ex rel. Wilcox v. Johnson, 555 F.2d 115 (CA3 1977). See also Lowery v. Cardwell, 575 F.2d 727 (CA9 1978) (withdrawal request in the middle of a bench trial, immediately following defendant's testimony).

Robinson also indicated he would seek to withdraw from the representation if Whiteside insisted on committing perjury.[2]

Whiteside testified in his own defense at trial and stated that he "knew" that Love had a gun and that he believed Love was reaching for a gun and he had acted swiftly in self-defense. On cross-examination, he admitted that he had not actually seen a gun in Love's hand. Robinson presented evidence that Love had been seen with a sawed-off shotgun on other occasions, that the police search of the apartment may have been careless, and that the victim's family had removed everything from the apartment shortly after the crime. Robinson presented this evidence to show a basis for Whiteside's asserted fear that Love had a gun.

The jury returned a verdict of second-degree murder, and Whiteside moved for a new trial, claiming that he had been deprived of a fair trial by Robinson's admonitions not to state that he saw a gun or "something metallic." The trial court held a hearing, heard testimony by Whiteside and Robinson, and denied the motion. The trial court made specific findings that the facts were as related by Robinson.

[The Iowa Supreme Court affirmed, holding that Robinson's actions were not only "permissible, but were required." The Eighth Circuit directed that Whiteside be granted a writ of habeas corpus.]

II . . .

B

In Strickland v. Washington, [466 U.S. 668 (1984)], we held that to obtain relief by way of federal habeas corpus on a claim of a deprivation of effective assistance of counsel under the Sixth Amendment, the movant must establish both serious attorney error and prejudice. To show such error, it must be established that the assistance rendered by counsel was constitutionally deficient in that "counsel made errors so serious that counsel was not functioning as 'counsel' guaranteed the defendant by the Sixth Amendment." To show prejudice, it must be established that the claimed lapses in counsel's performance rendered the trial unfair so as to "undermine confidence in the outcome" of the trial. . . .

C

We turn next to the question presented: the definition of the range of "reasonable professional" responses to a criminal defendant client who

---

2. Whiteside's version of the events at this pretrial meeting is considerably more cryptic:

> "Q. And as you went over the questions, did the two of you come into conflict with regard to whether or not there was a weapon?
>
> "A. I couldn't—I couldn't say a conflict. But I got the impression at one time that maybe if I didn't go along with—with what was happening, that it was no gun being involved, maybe that he will pull out of my trial."

informs counsel that he will perjure himself on the stand. We must determine whether, in this setting, Robinson's conduct fell within the wide range of professional responses to threatened client perjury acceptable under the Sixth Amendment.

In *Strickland,* we recognized counsel's duty of loyalty and his "overarching duty to advocate the defendant's cause." Plainly, that duty is limited to legitimate, lawful conduct compatible with the very nature of a trial as a search for truth. Although counsel must take all reasonable lawful means to attain the objectives of the client, counsel is precluded from taking steps or in any way assisting the client in presenting false evidence or otherwise violating the law. This principle has consistently been recognized in most unequivocal terms by expositors of the norms of professional conduct since the first Canons of Professional Ethics were adopted by the American Bar Association in 1908. . . .

It is universally agreed that at a minimum the attorney's first duty when confronted with a proposal for perjurious testimony is to attempt to dissuade the client from the unlawful course of conduct. Wolfram, Client Perjury, 50 S. Cal. L. Rev. 809, 846 (1977). A statement directly in point is found in the commentary to [Rule 3.3] under the heading "False Evidence." . . .

The commentary [] also suggests that an attorney's revelation of his client's perjury to the court is a professionally responsible and acceptable response to the conduct of a client who has actually given perjured testimony. Similarly, the Model Rules and the commentary, as well as the Code of Professional Responsibility adopted in Iowa, expressly permit withdrawal from representation as an appropriate response of an attorney when the client threatens to commit perjury. Withdrawal of counsel when this situation arises at trial gives rise to many difficult questions including possible mistrial and claims of double jeopardy.[6] . . .

---

6. In the evolution of the contemporary standards promulgated by the American Bar Association, an early draft reflects a compromise suggesting that when the disclosure of intended perjury is made during the course of trial, when withdrawal of counsel would raise difficult questions of a mistrial holding, counsel had the option to let the defendant take the stand but decline to affirmatively assist the presentation of perjury by traditional direct examination. Instead, counsel would stand mute while the defendant undertook to present the false version in narrative form in his own words unaided by any direct examination. This conduct was thought to be a signal at least to the presiding judge that the attorney considered the testimony to be false and was seeking to disassociate himself from that course. Additionally, counsel would not be permitted to discuss the known false testimony in closing arguments. See ABA Standards for Criminal Justice Proposed Standard 4-7.7 (2d ed. 1980). Most courts treating the subject rejected this approach and insisted on a more rigorous standard. . . . The Eighth Circuit in this case and the Ninth Circuit have expressed approval of the "free narrative" standards. The Rule finally promulgated in the current Model Rules of Professional Conduct rejects any participation or passive role whatever by counsel in allowing perjury to be presented without challenge.

D

Considering Robinson's representation of respondent in light of these accepted norms of professional conduct, we discern no failure to adhere to reasonable professional standards that would in any sense make out a deprivation of the Sixth Amendment right to counsel. Whether Robinson's conduct is seen as a successful attempt to dissuade his client from committing the crime of perjury, or whether seen as a "threat" to withdraw from representation and disclose the illegal scheme, Robinson's representation of Whiteside falls well within accepted standards of professional conduct and the range of reasonable professional conduct acceptable under *Strickland.* . . .

The Court of Appeals' holding that Robinson's "action deprived [Whiteside] of due process and effective assistance of counsel" is not supported by the record since Robinson's action, at most, deprived Whiteside of his contemplated perjury. Nothing counsel did in any way undermined Whiteside's claim that he believed the victim was reaching for a gun. Similarly, the record gives no support for holding that Robinson's action "also impermissibly compromised [Whiteside's] right to testify in his own defense by conditioning continued representation . . . and confidentiality upon [Whiteside's] *restricted* testimony." The record in fact shows the contrary: (a) that Whiteside did testify, and (b) he was "restricted" or restrained only from testifying falsely and was aided by Robinson in developing the basis for the fear that Love was reaching for a gun. Robinson divulged no client communications until he was compelled to do so in response to Whiteside's post-trial challenge to the quality of his performance. We see this as a case in which the attorney successfully dissuaded the client from committing the crime of perjury.

Paradoxically, even while accepting the conclusion of the Iowa trial court that Whiteside's proposed testimony would have been a criminal act, the Court of Appeals held that Robinson's efforts to persuade Whiteside not to commit that crime were improper, *first,* as forcing an impermissible choice between the right to counsel and the right to testify; and, *second,* as compromising client confidences because of Robinson's threat to disclose the contemplated perjury. . . .

Robinson's admonitions to his client can in no sense be said to have forced respondent into an *impermissible* choice between his right to counsel and his right to testify as he proposed for there was no *permissible* choice to testify falsely. For defense counsel to take steps to persuade a criminal defendant to testify truthfully, or to withdraw, deprives the defendant of neither his right to counsel nor the right to testify truthfully. . . . When an accused proposes to resort to perjury or to produce false evidence, one consequence is the risk of withdrawal of counsel.

On this record, the accused enjoyed continued representation within the bounds of reasonable professional conduct and did in fact exercise his right to testify; at most he was denied the right to have the assistance of counsel in the presentation of false testimony. Similarly, we can discern no breach of professional duty in Robinson's admonition to respondent that he would disclose respondent's perjury to the court. The crime of perjury in this setting is indistinguishable in substance from the crime of threatening or tampering with a witness or a juror. A defendant who informed his counsel that he was arranging to bribe or threaten witnesses or members of the jury would have no "right" to insist on counsel's assistance or silence. Counsel would not be limited to advising against that conduct. . . .

E

We hold that, as a matter of law, counsel's conduct complained of here cannot establish the prejudice required for relief under the second strand of the *Strickland* inquiry. Although a defendant need not establish that the attorney's deficient performance more likely than not altered the outcome in order to establish prejudice under *Strickland,* a defendant must show that "there is a reasonable probability that, but for counsel's unprofessional errors, the result of the proceeding would have been different." According to *Strickland,* "[a] reasonable probability is a probability sufficient to undermine confidence in the outcome." The *Strickland* Court noted that the "benchmark" of an ineffective-assistance claim is the fairness of the adversary proceeding, and that in judging prejudice and the likelihood of a different outcome, "[a] defendant has no entitlement to the luck of a lawless decisionmaker."

Whether he was persuaded or compelled to desist from perjury, Whiteside has no valid claim that confidence in the result of his trial has been diminished by his desisting from the contemplated perjury. Even if we were to assume that the jury might have believed his perjury, it does not follow that Whiteside was prejudiced. . . .

Reversed.

JUSTICE BRENNAN, concurring in the judgment.

This Court has no constitutional authority to establish rules of ethical conduct for lawyers practicing in the state courts. Nor does the Court enjoy any statutory grant of jurisdiction over legal ethics. . . .

JUSTICE BLACKMUN, with whom JUSTICE BRENNAN, JUSTICE MARSHALL, and JUSTICE STEVENS join, concurring in the judgment.

How a defense attorney ought to act when faced with a client who intends to commit perjury at trial has long been a controversial issue. But I do not believe that a federal habeas corpus case challenging a state criminal conviction is an appropriate vehicle for attempting to resolve this thorny problem. When a defendant argues that he was denied effective assistance of counsel because his lawyer dissuaded him from committing perjury, the only question properly presented to this Court is whether the lawyer's actions deprived the defendant of the fair trial which the Sixth Amendment is meant to guarantee. Since I believe that the respondent in this case suffered no injury justifying federal habeas relief, I concur in the Court's judgment. . . .

II . . .

B

The Court approaches this case as if the performance-and-prejudice standard requires us in every case to determine "the perimeters of [the] range of reasonable professional assistance," but *Strickland v. Washington* explicitly contemplates a different course:

> Although we have discussed the performance component of an ineffectiveness claim prior to the prejudice component, there is no reason for a court deciding an ineffective assistance claim to approach the inquiry in the same order, or even to address both components of the inquiry if the defendant makes an insufficient showing on one. In particular, a court need not determine whether counsel's performance was deficient before examining the prejudice suffered by the defendant as a result of the alleged deficiencies. . . . If it is easier to dispose of an ineffectiveness claim on the ground of lack of sufficient prejudice, which we expect will often be so, that course should be followed. . . .

C

In light of respondent's failure to show any cognizable prejudice, I see no need to "grade counsel's performance." The only federal issue in this case is whether Robinson's behavior deprived Whiteside of the effective assistance of counsel; it is not whether Robinson's behavior conformed to any particular code of legal ethics. . . .

I therefore am troubled by the Court's implicit adoption of a set of standards of professional responsibility for attorneys in state criminal proceedings. The States, of course, do have a compelling interest in the integrity of their criminal trials that can justify regulating the length to which an attorney may go in seeking his client's acquittal. But the American Bar Association's implicit suggestion in its brief *amicus curiae* that the Court find that the Association's Model Rules of Professional Conduct should govern an attorney's responsibilities is addressed to the wrong audience. It is for the States to decide how attorneys should conduct themselves in state criminal proceedings, and this Court's responsibility extends only to ensuring that the restrictions a State enacts do not infringe a defendant's federal constitutional rights. . . .

JUSTICE STEVENS, concurring in the judgment.

Justice Holmes taught us that a word is but the skin of a living thought. A "fact" may also have a life of its own. From the perspective of an appellate judge, after a case has been tried and the evidence has been sifted by another judge, a particular fact may be as clear and certain as a piece of crystal or a small diamond. A trial lawyer, however, must often deal with mixtures of sand and clay. Even a pebble that seems clear enough at first glance may take on a different hue in a handful of gravel.

As we view this case, it appears perfectly clear that respondent intended to commit perjury, that his lawyer knew it, and that the lawyer had a duty—both to the court and to his client, for perjured testimony can ruin an otherwise meritorious case—to take extreme measures to prevent the perjury from occurring. The lawyer was successful and, from our unanimous and remote perspective, it is now pellucidly clear that the client suffered no "legally cognizable prejudice."

Nevertheless, beneath the surface of this case there are areas of uncertainty that cannot be resolved today. A lawyer's certainty that a change in his client's recollection is a harbinger of intended perjury—as well as judicial review of such apparent certainty—should be tempered by the realization that, after reflection, the most honest witness may recall (or sincerely believe he recalls) details that he previously overlooked. Similarly, the post-trial review of a lawyer's pretrial threat to expose perjury that had not yet been committed—and, indeed, may have been prevented by the threat—is by no means the same as review of the way in which such a threat may actually have been carried out. Thus, one can be convinced—as I am—that this lawyer's actions were a proper way to provide his client with effective representation without confronting the much more difficult questions of what a lawyer must, should, or may do after his client has given testimony that the lawyer does not believe. The answer to such questions may well be colored by the particular circumstances attending the actual event and its aftermath.

Elsewhere in his opinion, Justice Blackmun cited Monroe Freedman, Professional Responsibility of the Criminal Defense Lawyer: The Three Hardest Questions, 64 Mich. L. Rev. 1469 (1966). Freedman was a leading legal ethics scholar and, at his death in 2015, a faculty member (and former dean) at Hofstra University School of Law. His article, which began as a speech, created much controversy. Criminal defense lawyers, judges, and law teachers continue to debate it more than a half-century later. Freedman argued that if a criminal defense lawyer knows that the defendant intended to lie under oath and cannot dissuade the client from doing so, he should call the client as a witness, conduct a direct examination, and argue the testimony in summation. That conduct would ordinarily be subornation of perjury, a crime. Many criminal defense lawyers have reluctantly supported the idea as the least bad of the several options available to a defense lawyer faced with the situation, which Freedman labeled a "trilemma." Other options are further discussed below. No court has ever accepted Freedman's argument.

There is a backstory to Chief Justice Burger's willingness (or perhaps eagerness) to address the legal ethics question in *Nix* even though the Court lacked jurisdiction to supply the answer. Freedman's New York Times obituary tells us that after Freedman, then a law professor in Washington, D.C., gave a speech that later became the Michigan Law Review article, "[s]everal prominent jurists, including Warren E. Burger, then a federal appellate judge and later the United States chief justice, called, without success, for Professor Freedman's disbarment." Margalit Fox, N.Y. Times, Mar. 2, 2015. Incredibly, the judges accused Freedman of contributing to client perjury even though he had no client and was merely advocating an academic view about how best to resolve what was and still is a difficult issue. A disciplinary committee opened an investigation of Freedman, but did not pursue it.*

The discussion so far has concerned criminal defense lawyers trying a case in court. But the issues here can arise in an entirely different context. Consider the next problem. Does Rule 3.3 govern the lawyers' responsibilities? Or does Rule 3.9? The answer, which turns out to be circular, depends on whether the City Council is a "tribunal" within the meaning of Rule 3.3. It likely is not a tribunal because in passing legislation the Council does not act in an "adjudicative capacity" as that phrase is defined in Rule 1.0(m). So Rule 3.9 will apply, but it refers us back to Rule 3.3.

"Streets for Bikes Not Trucks"

A bill has been introduced in the Glover City Council to allow trucks and private buses on 27 city streets and avenues where they are now banned. It is supported by a trucking trade association and by intercity and tour bus companies. The supporters are represented by Quigley, Undermill & Ellis (QUE), the trade association's outside law firm. The change is opposed by four citizen groups and by Transportation Alternatives (TA), which supports bicycle lanes and other nonmechanized forms of transportation.

The city council held a hearing on the bill. Each side offered live testimony and written submissions. Among the spectators were opponents of the bill, who wore forest green T-shirts imprinted with "STREETS FOR BIKES NOT TRUCKS" in sky blue lettering.

QUE submitted a report performed for the trucking association by two urban planning faculty members at a prominent university. It is based on experience in seven other cities of comparable size and purports to show that the change will not increase traffic congestion or vehicular accidents. Marla Lewisohn, the president of the trucking association, testified before the council and summarized the findings

---

* I disagree with the conclusion in Freedman's Michigan article. For our debate, see Stephen Gillers, Monroe Freedman's Solution to the Criminal Defense Lawyer's Trilemma Is Wrong as a Matter of Policy and Constitutional Law, 34 Hofstra L. Rev. 821 (2006), and Monroe Freedman's rebuttals, Getting Honest About Client Perjury, 21 Geo. J. Legal Ethics 133 (2008), and Lawyer-Client Confidentiality: Rethinking The Trilemma, 43 Hofstra L. Rev. 1025 (2015).

of the report. The council took no action while its staff reviewed the testimony and submissions.

A day after the council hearing, QUE asked its associate Leonora Saroyan to research possible court remedies should the council reject the bill. In addition to a law degree, Saroyan has a Ph.D. in statistics. She read the trade association report and other sources and identified substantial errors in the report's analysis. She told the assigning partner that the data actually prove the opposite of Lewisohn's testimony. QUE has now asked you what it may or must do.

After *Nix*, Open Questions?

The Best Ethical Solution. *Nix* may answer some constitutional questions, and Rule 3.3 may answer some ethical ones, but questions remain, including questions about the answers. Both the Court and the ABA have rejected the narrative solution (described in note 6 of *Nix*), but state courts are free to adopt it anyway. Both before and after *Nix*, a few state courts endorsed narrative when a criminal defendant wishes to testify and her lawyer knows (or thinks he knows or even "suspects") that she will lie. (How certain should the lawyer be? We discuss that below.) Here are the options a jurisdiction might give a lawyer in Robinson's position, taken from People v. Johnson, 72 Cal. Rptr. 2d 805 (Ct. App. 1998), a California opinion as pertinent as if it were written yesterday. The court addressed situations where an "attorney knows or suspects the defendant will give perjured testimony."

1. *Full Cooperation with Presenting Defendant's Testimony even when Defendant Intends to Commit Perjury.* This is Freedman's view. The court rejected it, finding that no tribunal has ever endorsed it and concluding that it could result in disciplinary action. It would also be subornation of perjury.
2. *Persuading the Client Not to Commit Perjury.* The court said that "when it succeeds," this was the "ideal solution."
3. *Withdrawal from Representation.* "This approach, while it protects the attorney's interest in not presenting perjured testimony, does not solve the problem. The court may deny the motion to withdraw. Even if the motion to withdraw is granted, the problem remains." The next lawyer may have the same dilemma or the client may deceive the next lawyer about his intentions.
4. *Disclosure to the Court.* This approach "has been criticized because it compromises the attorney's ethical duty to keep client communications confidential. . . . Additionally, until the defendant actually takes the stand and testifies falsely, there is always a chance the defendant will change his mind and testify truthfully."
5. *Refusing to Permit the Defendant to Testify.* "Preclusion of the testimony as a solution has been criticized because it essentially substitutes defense counsel for the jury as the judge of witness credibility. . . . Further,

a determination of whether the defendant will commit perjury may result in a mini-trial, with the attorney essentially 'testifying' against the defendant. Finally, this approach, while safeguarding the attorney's ethical obligations not to participate in presenting perjured testimony, results in a complete denial of the defendant's right to testify."

6. *The Narrative Approach Represents the Best Accommodation of the Competing Interests.*

Johnson gave the following reasons for choosing number 6:

We disagree with those commentators who have found the narrative approach necessarily communicates to the jury that defense counsel believes the defendant is lying. As was pointed out in [precedent], the jury may surmise the "defendant desired to testify unhampered by the traditional question and answer format." . . . We do not believe the possibility of a negative inference the defendant is lying should preclude the use of the narrative approach since the alternative would be worse, i.e., the attorney's active participation in presenting the perjured testimony or exclusion of the defendant's testimony, neither of which strikes a balance between the competing interests involved. . . .

The narrative approach also avoids having a pre-perjury hearing, a mini-trial on whether the defendant might commit perjury if called to the stand; a hearing which could result in the attorney testifying against the client and which would require the court to be able to see into the future and determine that an individual who has stated only an intention to testify falsely (at least as according to his attorney) will actually testify falsely once on the witness stand.

The narrative approach may or may not be the best option, but the court's exuberance is excessive. Even if narrative does not "necessarily" telegraph that the defendant may be lying, it certainly creates a high risk of doing so. So, too, will the lawyer's failure even to argue the client's narrative in summation to avoid aiding the perjury. The defendant will be the only witness whose testimony is not elicited in the usual way and the only witness whose testimony is ignored by her own lawyer on summation, but not by the prosecutor. What will a juror think when the defendant's lawyer does not ask the jury to believe his client?

"What of it?" may be the response. "Why worry about a lying defendant?" But if the defendant is lying, *Nix* tells us she has no right to testify at all (at least not about the lies). There is no right to lie under oath. So why give her half a loaf (a narrative) when she's entitled to no loaf? On the other hand, if the lawyer does not *know* that the defendant will lie, she is entitled to the full loaf, not a narrative.

The *Johnson* court rejected the solution of not letting the defendant testify falsely because that substitutes the lawyer "for the jury as the judge of witness credibility." But the lawyer must make that very credibility determination before settling on the narrative approach.

Last, the court says that a narrative avoids a "mini-trial" to determine whether in fact the lawyer really does "know" that the defendant will lie.

Does it? What should a court do when a client, whose lawyer wishes to invoke narrative because he thinks he knows his client will lie, insists that her testimony will be true and protests that a narrative will deny her constitutional right to testify with the "effective assistance of counsel"? Does the court just accept the lawyer's word for it or do we get that mini-trial anyway?

Or maybe the defendant doesn't even get a right to be heard before the lawyer and the judge agree that the lawyer will proceed in a narrative fashion. Can that be true? In People v. Andrades, 828 N.E.2d 599 (N.Y. 2005), a client planned to testify at a suppression hearing where the judge would be the factfinder. The court held that the defendant did not have a constitutional right to be present when his lawyer told the judge that because of "an ethical conflict"—code for "my client will lie"—the lawyer would use narrative. The Court of Appeals said that "a colloquy of this nature involves procedural matters at which a defendant can offer no meaningful input." No meaningful "input" on the accuracy of the lawyer's implication about the defendant's own intentions?

Addressing problems with narrative is Professor L. Timothy Perrin, The Perplexing Problem of Client Perjury, 76 Fordham L. Rev. 1707 (2007) (part of a symposium on ethics and evidence). Professor Perrin writes:

> Narrative testimony is certainly no panacea, but are there viable alternatives? Two very basic principles should guide lawyers, courts, and drafters of the ethics rules in addressing this ethical dilemma. The first principle is that lawyers should not be required to participate, even passively, in the presentation of evidence that they know is false. To do otherwise undermines the truth-seeking purpose of the trial. As recognized by the 2002 draft of the Model Rules, the defense lawyer's position as an officer of the court means that he must be able to exercise control over false evidence.
>
> The second principle, which is a matter of procedural necessity, is that defendants must have some opportunity to be heard before the court decides to exclude their allegedly false testimony. This is a fundamental aspect of due process and comports with the process followed in deciding preliminary questions of fact under Rule 104(a) of the Federal Rules of Evidence. Here, of course, is where things turn particularly perplexing. The defendant and the defendant's lawyer are placed in the position of opposing each other before the trial judge. The defense lawyer must reveal communications from the client and must argue against the defendant's expressed desire to testify. The "cure" of attempting to adjudicate the defendant's right to testify may be worse than the disease, though the disease is nothing less than an affront to the system's search for the truth.

The Epistemology Problem. *Nix* moved the focus of the inquiry back a few squares. While we continue to debate defense counsel's obligations when a defendant testifies falsely or intends to do so, when does a lawyer *know* that the defendant is lying or will lie? All agree that a defense lawyer does not act improperly by calling a witness (defendant or not) who the lawyer merely *believes* will lie. See People v. Riel, 998 P.2d 969 (Cal. 2000):

> Although attorneys may not present evidence they know to be false or assist in perpetrating known frauds on the court, they may ethically present evidence that they suspect, but do not personally know, is false. Criminal defense attorneys sometimes have to present evidence that is incredible and that, not being naive, they might personally disbelieve. Presenting incredible evidence may raise difficult tactical decisions—if counsel finds evidence incredible, the fact finder may also—but, as long as counsel has no specific undisclosed factual knowledge of its falsity, it does not raise an ethical problem.*

In *Nix*, Justice Stevens recognized that the Supreme Court was in the luxurious position of being able to assume that Whiteside planned to lie. Lower courts so found as a fact. But a trial lawyer may face ambiguous facts. In Commonwealth v. Mitchell, 781 N.E.2d 1237 (Mass. 2003), the court identified various tests that courts have used in deciding when a lawyer's level of confidence is the equivalent of knowledge: "good cause to believe," "compelling support," "knowledge beyond a reasonable doubt," "firm factual basis," "good-faith determination," and "actual knowledge." The court adopted "firm factual basis." The Idaho Supreme Court has agreed.

> We hold that the firm factual basis standard is appropriate to determine whether counsel knows his client will testify falsely. The firm factual basis standard "satisfies constitutional concerns because it requires more than mere suspicion or conjecture on the part of counsel, more than a belief and more information than inconsistencies in statements by the defendant or in the evidence." This standard also permits counsel to "act on the information he or she possesses" and does not "impose an independent duty on the part of counsel to investigate," which would be "incompatible" with the fiduciary nature of the attorney-client relationship and "is unnecessary when an attorney relies, in significant part, on incriminating admissions made by the client." . . . The firm factual basis standard strikes a balance between the competing interests of the defendant's constitutional right to testify and the attorney's ethical obligation as an officer of the court.

State v. Abdullah, 348 P.3d 1 (Idaho 2015).

Not to quibble, but nowhere does the Idaho court define "firm." Yet the adjective (a metaphor) is essential. A mere "factual basis" is not enough. And "firm factual basis" says nothing about the lawyer's own state of mind. Is it purely an objective test? It seems the court has substituted one ambiguous test for another. What do you make of the statement that it would be *incompatible* with fiduciary duty for the lawyer to investigate before concluding that she has a firm factual basis, based only on the client's statements? Isn't the opposite true?

---

* For the *Johnson* court narrative was acceptable where a lawyer merely "suspects" that her client will lie. We could call this a sloppy use of language except that later cases have agreed. People v. Hayes, 238 Cal. Rptr. 3d 120 (Cal. Ct. 2018) (unpublished opinion) (reaffirming Johnson's use of the word "suspects" while also attempting to distinguish *Riel*).

After reviewing cases from several jurisdictions and secondary authorities, State v. Chambers, 994 A.2d 1248 (Conn. 2010), chose "actual knowledge" as the test. How is "actual knowledge" different from "knowledge"? Wisconsin also rejected "firm factual basis" in favor of the most stringent and specific test of all. State v. McDowell, 681 N.W.2d 500 (Wis. 2004) ("Absent the most extraordinary circumstances, [the defense lawyer's] knowledge must be based on the client's expressed admission of intent to testify untruthfully." It "must be unambiguous and directly made to the attorney.").

Why isn't the right test "knows beyond a reasonable doubt," which the Idaho court rejected? Should a lawyer be able to deny an accused's wish to testify in the usual way, as he has a constitutional right to do, if all she can say is that she has a "firm factual basis" to believe the client will lie but cannot say that she knows beyond a reasonable doubt? If so, a lower standard of confidence will permit a defendant's own lawyer to deprive him of the Sixth Amendment right to testify than the level of confidence the Constitution requires for conviction.

Criminal defense lawyers have been heard to argue that lawyers never "know" anything. Lawyers are trained skeptics. Even when a client confesses, the lawyer doesn't *know* that the client is telling the truth. He may be delusional or protecting someone. False confessions happen all too frequently. Is this a fair solution to the lawyer's "trilemma"? Or is it too cute? May lawyers use the words "know" and "knowledge" in their ethics rules and then claim that knowledge can never exist (at least not for lawyers)? My vote: too cute.

Avoiding Knowledge.   Assuming knowledge can exist, is it ethical for a lawyer to avoid getting it? Without knowledge, a lawyer might be able to call a witness and introduce a document that she could not if she "knew" that either was false. A lawyer might avoid knowledge by not doing an investigation, by not even asking for the client's story. But then the lawyer would find it rather difficult to represent the client competently. "[T]he lawyer should know all the facts, everything," William Faulkner instructed in his novel *Sanctuary*. Good advice. Is it possible to learn the facts but not "know" them? This is not a riddle. Consider the following solution attributed to one prominent lawyer (although others also claim credit for it and some defense lawyers will admit to a similar strategy—off the record):

> I never ask the client what it is that he contends are the facts from his point of view in the initial interview. . . . The thing to do is to ask him what he suspects the other side might claim.

Alternatively, is there anything wrong with telling a client the elements of a defense before asking the client for his side of the story? Or is that just a more subtle way to avoid knowledge by discouraging the client from telling you what you don't want to hear? Here's an example.

"Maybe I Was Insane"

Before John Grisham, before Scott Turow, before Lisa Scottoline, there was Robert Traver. Traver, a pseudonym for former Michigan Supreme Court Justice John D. Voelker, wrote the novel *Anatomy of a Murder* (1958). It is slower paced than modern courtroom dramas, but it does an excellent job of capturing the details of law practice and the intellectual content of the law, at least the law of homicide and insanity.

Paul Biegler, a former prosecutor and now a defense lawyer in rural Michigan, is retained to represent Lt. Frederic Manion, who is charged with murdering Barney Quill. Quill raped Manion's wife in a bar. Manion, who was not present, went to the bar and shot Quill about an hour later. The most discussed scene in the book (at least for lawyers) occurs when Biegler visits Manion in jail and gives him what Biegler's mentor earlier called "The Lecture." Biegler starts by describing the defenses to a murder charge. "For all the elaborate hemorrhage of words in the law books about the legal defenses to murder, there are only about three basic defenses: one, that it didn't happen but was instead a suicide or accident or what not; two, that whether it happened or not, you didn't do it, such as alibi, mistaken identity, and so forth; and three, that even if it happened and you did it, your action was legally justified or excusable." Biegler explained that justification would not work because Manion did not shoot Quill in the act, but an hour later. Biegler lists and dismisses other defenses, including intoxication. The Lecture and novel then continue:

> "Where do I fit in that rosy picture?" Manion asks.
>
> "Since a whole barroom full of people saw you shoot down Barney Quill in apparent cold blood, you scarcely fit in the first two classes of defenses. I'm afraid we needn't waste time on those."
>
> "Then finally there's the defense of insanity." I paused and spoke abruptly, airily: "Well, that just about winds it up." I arose as though making ready to leave.
>
> "Tell me more."
>
> "There is no more." I slowly paced up and down the room.
>
> "I mean about this insanity."
>
> "Oh, insanity," I said, elaborately surprised. It was like luring a trained seal with a herring. "Well, insanity, where proven, is a complete defense to murder. It does not legally justify the killing, like self-defense, say, but rather excuses it." The lecturer was hitting his stride. He was also on the home stretch. . . . "If a man is insane, legally insane, the act of homicide may still be murder but the law excuses the perpetrator. . . . So the man who successfully invokes the defense of insanity is taking a calculated risk. . . ."
>
> I paused and knocked out my pipe. The Lecture was about over. The rest was up to the student. The Lieutenant looked out the window. . . . I sat very still. Then he looked at me.

"Maybe," he said, "maybe I was insane."

Very casually: "Maybe you were insane when?" I said. . . .

"You know what I mean. When I shot Barney Quill."

Thoughtfully: "Hm. . . . Why do you say that?"

"Well, I can't really say," he went on slowly. "I—I guess I blacked out. I can't remember a thing after I saw him standing behind the bar that night until I got back to my trailer."

"You mean—you mean you don't remember shooting him?" I shook my head in wonderment.

"Yes, that's what I mean."

"You don't even remember driving home?"

"No."

"You don't even remember threatening Barney's bartender when he followed you outside after the shooting—as the newspaper says you did?" I paused and held my breath. "You don't remember telling him, 'Do you want some, too, Buster?'"

The smoldering dark eyes flickered ever so little. "No, not a thing."

"My, my," I said, blinking my eyes, contemplating the wonder of it all. "Maybe you've got something there."

The Lecture was over; I had told my man the law; and now he had told me things that might possibly invoke the defense of insanity. It had all been done with mirrors.

Did Biegler act ethically? Was there any legitimate reason for this little exercise with mirrors other than to steer Manion toward telling Biegler the story he needed to hear, and away from the one he did not want to hear, so that Biegler would be ethically free to mount the only plausible defense?

Video Tip. The novel went to Hollywood. Like the book, the 1959 film (Otto Preminger, director) is a classic in the genre called trial movies, along with *Witness for the Prosecution, The Verdict, Twelve Angry Men,* and (yes, really) *My Cousin Vinny.* Jimmy Stewart plays Biegler. Ben Gazzara plays Manion. Lee Remick plays Mrs. Manion. Watch "The Lecture" scene carefully. It shows what non-verbal communication (and good acting) can convey. Notice Stewart's expressions, body language, and phrasing in response to Gazzara's questions and statements. Notice Stewart's use of silence. It's all done to impart a meaning that a transcript (and the novel) could never convey. Furthermore, the dialogue is better because a professional screenwriter (Wendell Mayes) wrote it. See if your answers to the questions posed above change.[*]

---

[*] **Trivia note:** The man who plays the judge in the movie is Joseph Welch, who is not an actor but was a partner at Hale and Dorr in Boston (since merged into Wilmer Hale). Welch had been the lawyer for the Army in the 1954 Army-McCarthy hearings. His question to Senator McCarthy ("Have you no sense of decency, sir? At long last, have you left no sense of decency?") is considered to be the beginning of the end of the senator's career. You can see

Giving the Problem to the Judge.   Imagine a criminal defense lawyer who, honoring his Rule 3.3 obligation, tells a judge that his client has lied on the stand. The client denies it. What should the judge do? If the judge instructs the jury to ignore the testimony, isn't there a risk that the lawyer will turn out *not* to have *known* that the testimony was false (even though the lawyer believed he did know)? One possibility is for the judge to do nothing. Judges and trial lawyers like to say that the jury is the lie detector in the courtroom. So why not just let the jury do its job? But if *that's* the solution, why should we require defense counsel to reveal concluded perjury in the first place? Just to negate any inference of the lawyer's complicity?

Consider the following segment from the television series *L.A. Law* (1986-1994). The show was television's first attempt to present legal ethics issues seriously and in all their complexity, so far as the needs of network television might allow. See Stephen Gillers, Taking *L.A. Law* More Seriously, 98 Yale L.J. 1607 (1989). In the 1980s and 1990s some law graduates—most prominently David E. Kelley, who found fame with *L.A. Law*—reinvented themselves as screenwriters. A couple of the lessons in this chapter draw on clever *L.A. Law* episodes. Here's one.

Michael Kuzak is representing a man named Sears, who is accused of leaving the scene of an accident while driving a car owned by his aunt. Kuzak calls the aunt as a witness to explain how others may have gotten access to her car. Kuzak expects her to testify, truthfully, that she hangs the key to the car on a nail in her open garage. Kuzak would then argue in summation the possibility that someone else could have entered the garage, taken the key, and used the car. That might create a reasonable doubt. But then, in the middle of her testimony and to Kuzak's surprise, the aunt testifies that she and Sears were at the beach when the accident occurred. Kuzak knows (as a result of a prior discussion with Sears) that Sears was the hit-and-run driver. His aunt lied, and very credibly, too. What should Kuzak do?

What he did was ask to speak with the judge alone in chambers. This could only happen with the prosecutor's agreement. *L.A. Law* contained ex parte contacts with judges for dramatic purposes. Good as the show was on legal ethics issues, it still had to pull an audience. In chambers, Kuzak moves to withdraw. The judge denies the withdrawal motion after a discussion that might have enlightened the Supreme Court in Nix v. Whiteside:

Judge: What's to prevent him [the defendant] from playing the same time- and money-wasting game with his next lawyer and the one after that? No, Mr. Kuzak, withdrawing is not the answer to your dilemma.

---

it all in the riveting documentary *Point of Order.* How did Otto Preminger come to cast Boston lawyer Joseph Welch as the judge in *Anatomy of a Murder*? A Life Magazine article reports that a Preminger press aide proposed Welch, who was famous from the Army-McCarthy hearings. The first choice, Burl Ives, was not available. Ernest Havemann, Joe Welch in Juicy New Role, Life Magazine, May 11, 1959. Welch was nominated for a Golden Globe award for his supporting role.

> The answer is to let the system work. You do your job, let the D.A. do her job, and the jury will do their job of sorting out the truth, the falsity, of the testimony.
>
> *Kuzak:*   That's a comforting homily, Your Honor. But you know as well as I that Sears will be acquitted. That sweet little old lady had the jury eating out of the palm of her hand. . . .
>
> *Judge:*   Witnesses lie on the stand every day, Mr. Kuzak. You want to debate the ethical conundrum, we'll have dinner after this thing is over. In the meantime, let's just do our jobs.

Noble Kuzak, confused and distraught, returns to court, tries to resume questioning, cannot, announces that he withdraws from the case without permission, and is jailed for contempt. The judge tells the defendant to get a new lawyer and return for a new trial. What has been gained? Who was right? (Kuzak might not be the Boy Scout he claims to be. We return to this episode in part D4.)

Life follows Hollywood. In United States v. Litchfield, 959 F.2d 1514 (10th Cir. 1992), defense counsel had advised the trial judge ex parte that the defendant wished to testify but that counsel worried that the testimony "would include untruths." The judge responded:

> Well, you're not in a position that seems to me to decide—not in the best position, let's put it that way, to decide what is true and not true. Certainly, there may be things that he testifies to that are contradictory. Nor am I in a good position even based upon what I've heard from you because I don't hear a declaration from you that I believe that my client will speak untruthfully or that a fraud will be perpetrated upon the Court, and so I'm not making up my mind or making any decision in that regard and would prefer to let the jury listen to the evidence, weigh it and arrive at its own conclusions.[*]

Astonishing, isn't it, the similarity between what the television judge said and what the real judge said?

Robert Bennett's Letter to Judge Susan Webber Wright

Kenneth Starr's investigation of Bill and Hillary Clinton produced many issues in the world of lawyer regulation, some of which appear in this chapter. Robert Bennett of Skadden Arps was Bill Clinton's lawyer in Paula Jones's sexual harassment lawsuit against Clinton. Clinton was deposed in Washington, D.C. on January 17, 1998. U.S. District Judge Susan Webber Wright (appointed by Clinton) presided at the deposition in person. Lawyers

---

[*] The defendant argued on appeal that counsel was ineffective because he revealed his qualms to the judge to protect his reputation even though he did not *know* that the defendant would lie. The circuit court affirmed without endorsing the behavior: "This situation presented counsel with a difficult dilemma, and we cannot say that his ex parte discussion with the district court was a violation of his ethical duty or evidence of a conflict of interest."

for Jones asked many pointed questions about Clinton's relationship with White House intern Monica Lewinsky. As we later learned, the night before the deposition these lawyers had received information about the Clinton-Lewinsky affair from Linda Tripp. Lewinsky had confided in Tripp, thinking her a friend. She was an enemy. Tripp recorded their conversations without Lewinsky's knowledge and shared them with Jones's lawyers.

Prior to his deposition, Lewinsky had submitted an affidavit denying "a sexual relationship with the President." Lewinsky's recorded conversation with Tripp directly contradicted the affidavit.

Bennett was unaware that Clinton and Lewinsky did have a sexual relationship. He introduced Lewinsky's affidavit at Clinton's deposition. Later, under grant of immunity, Lewinsky testified to a federal grand jury that she and Clinton had a sexual relationship. Bennett concluded that he now knew that the Lewinsky affidavit was false. The Jones v. Clinton lawsuit was pending in federal court in Arkansas, where Bennett, a Washington, D.C., lawyer, was admitted pro hac vice. The court's rules incorporated the Arkansas professional conduct rules, including Rule 3.3. That rule required Bennett to rectify material false evidence that he may have unwittingly introduced, namely Lewinsky's affidavit. This Bennett did in the following letter:

> Dear Judge Wright,
>
> As you are aware, Ms. Monica Lewinsky submitted an affidavit dated January 7, 1998 in the above-captioned case in support of her motion to quash the subpoena for her testimony. This affidavit was made part of the record of President Clinton's deposition on January 17, 1998.
>
> It has recently been made public in the Starr Report that Ms. Lewinsky testified before a federal grand jury in August 1998 that portions of her affidavit were misleading and not true. Therefore, pursuant to our professional responsibility, we wanted to advise you that the Court should not rely on Ms. Lewinsky's affidavit or remarks of counsel characterizing that affidavit.
>
> Very truly yours,
> Bob Bennett

This letter may go down in the legal ethics archives as the most famous example of a lawyer's remedial obligation under Rule 3.3.

Summary: Variables in Analyzing Issues Concerning Witness Perjury and False Testimony

The focus so far has been on criminal cases and in particular on the testimony of the accused. But as we see presently the same issues can arise with any witness in any case. This summary identifies the variables.

1. Timing
   a. Prospective perjury or false testimony
   b. Concluded perjury or false testimony

2. Nature of the case
   a. Criminal
      i. The defendant as witness
      ii. Other witnesses
   b. Civil (court or other tribunal)
3. Lawyer's state of mind
   a. Knowledge
   b. Reasonable belief
   c. A firm factual basis, etc.
4. Remedies
   a. Remonstrate with client and correct
   b. Reveal to tribunal
   c. Withdraw if allowed
   d. Let criminal defendant testify falsely in narrative and refrain from arguing in summation
   e. Refuse to call client or other witness
   f. Let criminal defendant testify falsely, question client, argue testimony (Monroe Freedman's proposal)
5. Legal considerations
   a. Text of jurisdiction's rule
   b. Constitutional right of criminal defendants to testify and to assistance of counsel
   c. Client autonomy
   d. Duty of confidentiality
   e. Duty of competence
   f. Criminal law prohibitions against suborning perjury (and like crimes)

D. FOSTERING FALSITY OR ADVANCING TRUTH?

> I know you lawyers can with ease
> Twist words and meanings as you please;
> That language, by your skill made pliant,
> Will bend to favour every client;
> That 'tis the fee directs the sense,
> To make out either side's pretence.
> —John Gay, *The Dog and the Fox*

> They had stopped shouting at each other and put their faith in
> legal counsel. With the result that how things could be made to
> look was what counted, not how they actually were.
> —William Maxwell, *So Long, See You Tomorrow*

Here we discover a variety of strategies that a lawyer may employ in civil or criminal cases, often quite properly, sometimes not, to increase the chances of victory, at the risk (or often with the intention) of misleading the judge or jury. A trial, we learn, may be a search for truth, but the path has many roadblocks. Some are doctrinal and aim to serve values deemed more important than truth. In this category are the attorney-client and other privileges, the work-product doctrine, suppression of evidence illegally obtained, and the criminal law standard of proof beyond a reasonable doubt, which impedes conviction of the innocent even if it may lead to acquittal of the guilty. To these doctrines we add the tactics of lawyers, whose job description requires them to present evidence that benefits their clients, so long as they do not know it is false, and if possible to exclude or discredit evidence that harms their clients, even if they know it is true. (We omit prosecutors from this description. They are a special case, as later explained.) From the perspective of the adversary system, a verdict does justice simply by being the verdict.

Truth seems to have a different meaning for lawyers (only, we may hope, when acting as lawyers) than for other varieties of humankind. Other professions—scientists, journalists, and historians—also value truth. For them, a fact is true if it is true. But in litigation, a fact can be true so long as it could (possibly) be true whether or not, in some omniscient sense, it is true. Lawyers do not find truth as scientists do; they construct truth, which requires imagination and storytelling skills. If litigation language games—or let's call them creative interpretation—occur in discovery to conceal harmful information, as they often do, the judge and opponent may never learn of it. And if somehow it comes to light, what's the worst that can happen? The judge will order disclosure. Sometimes, however, the worst that can happen is a hefty sanction (or even, as in Jones v. Clinton, infra, a finding of contempt). For an extreme example of a law firm's fancy dancing to avoid discovery obligations, and the financial penalty it and the client had to pay, see Washington State Physicians Insurance Exchange & Ass'n v. Fisons Corp., 858 P.2d 1054 (Wash. 1993).

Lawyers also produce and direct a nonverbal performance, where there seems to be little in the way of discernable limits. Think of it as a kind of staging, as Johnnie Cochran literally did in his defense of O.J. Simpson. See page 382. A trial is often likened to a play. The jurors are the audience (also the critics). The "actors" dress the part. Telling clients to wear a suit and tie or a conservative dress (including the style, fabric, and color) is meant to present an image to the jury. Telling the client to get a haircut, to change hairstyles, to wear or not wear jewelry, to keep his or her hands where the jury can see them, to take notes, to appear vulnerable, not angry or threatening—these are all signaling devices. Indeed, experts will, for a fee, help a client (and even a lawyer) dress for court. I was once an expert for a very successful trial lawyer (*very*) who each day wore the same off-the-rack sport coat with a torn lining. He left it unbuttoned so the jury could see the torn lining. "Juries don't give money to clients with rich lawyers," he explained. "Like me," he might have added. I have no idea if that is universally true, but it worked for him. And there's this about glasses: "Defense Lawyers Swear by Gimmick of Having Defendants Wearing Glasses at Trial" read one Daily News story by Kevin Deutsch (Feb. 13, 2011):

> The most famous murder suspect to sway a jury with the help of eyewear was Larry Davis, who was charged with executing four men in 1986, then shooting six cops as they tried to arrest him.
>
> At trial, Davis looked nothing like the gold chain-clad thug police had portrayed. He dressed like a college student, sporting horn-rimmed glasses and sweaters. Separate Bronx juries found him not guilty of quadruple murder and the cop shootings.

New Yorker writer Janet Malcolm was found, at a first trial, to have libeled the plaintiff. In her essay "A Second Chance," she recounts how professional advice on how to speak, what to wear, and even how to sit when testifying then helped her to win the retrial. N.Y. Review of Books (Sept. 24, 2020).

Few if any rules limit *how* lawyers present (or is the better word "direct"?) their "characters," including their client, themselves, and their witnesses, on the stage set we call a courtroom. This is a gap worth noting. In court, rules mainly govern what can be said, the content. They do not govern how something is said or various methods of nonverbal messaging. As anyone who has studied theater knows, the content of the lines is only part of the performance and sometimes not the most important one.*

1. Literal Truth

If we are going to give lawyers certain duties that turn on the truth or falsity of information, we might be expected to know what we mean by "true" and "false." Linguists and philosophers of language would tell us that this is actually more complicated than might first appear. In a New York Times op-ed on October 3, 1998, Harvard linguist Steven Pinker explained that we don't read words literally in daily life. The shampoo bottle may say "Lather, Rinse, Repeat," he wrote, but we understand that "repeat" means "repeat once," not endlessly. Through cooperation and context, we create meaning.

Litigation seems to operate from the postulate that lawyers should be as uncooperative as possible. That can lead to literal interpretation of language. This is why discovery demands for "documents" spend paragraphs defining document. When I was a young lawyer, a witness was asked if there was "correspondence" between him and Jack on a particular subject. It was an important question. This was before computers, before faxes. No, said the witness. It transpired, however, that there was a very relevant telegram. The witness had decided, probably instructed by counsel, that "correspondence" meant mail and did not include telegrams. Now, you can look at this as really clever lawyering. But if your best friend or your sweetheart asked

---

* For a dramatic example of how identical lines can convey different meanings depending on how they are spoken, see *Mulholland Drive*, generally regarded as director David Lynch's best film.

the same question and you said no using the same secret definition, they would probably call it a lie, as would you. Friends and lovers rightly bring different expectations of honesty to their conversations. (We test that assumption shortly.) Just how slippery can a lawyer be and not cross "the line" that trial lawyers proudly proclaim they will "go right up to" for their clients?

a. The Parable of Billy and the Cookies

His parents come home before dinner and find ten-year-old Billy in the kitchen and crumbs around the cookie jar. "Are you eating the cookies?" his mother asks. "No," says Billy, taking umbrage. When Billy later admits that he did in fact enjoy just a single cookie, his parents lecture him about lying. "I didn't lie," he insists. "You asked me the wrong question. First, I only ate one cookie, and you said 'cookies.' Second, when you asked '*Are* you eating the cookies?' I had already finished. You should have asked 'Have you eaten one or more cookies?'" Was Billy's answer false? Was it a lie? Does it depend on what the meaning of "are" is and whether the plural includes the singular? Or is it false and a lie regardless? And if your answer is that it is not false because it is literally true, can it also be a lie? As we'll see, the answer is yes.

b. The Romance of Annie and Bill

Billy grew up and now calls himself Bill. He went to law school (naturally), where he met Annie. A romance blossomed and in their 3L year, they discussed moving in together after graduation, when each would become a litigation associate at different firms. One Sunday, six months into their relationship, Annie had to stay home to write a paper on Model Rule 3.3. Bill went out around six o'clock for a dinner of pizza and Ben & Jerry's chocolate fudge brownie ice cream, taking his MPRE review book for some quick studying. Wouldn't you know it, but whom should he run into but their classmate Jana. Sweet Jana. One thing led to another and then another and another—a walk in the park, a cappuccino, a beer, another beer, a third beer, and Bill wound up at Jana's place, where they streamed *Fleabag* and *High Fidelity* and by then it was very late. Too late for Bill to go home, although home was one street away. So Bill spent the night and part of the morning. The next day, Annie and Bill had the following conversation:

Annie: Did you go out last night?
Bill: I ran out for some ice cream and pizza.
Annie: I tried calling.
Bill: I didn't hear the phone. It might have been while I was out.
Annie: It was after eleven.
Bill: Oh, I must have been in the shower. ("Not a lie," Bill thinks. "I *was* in the shower around then, just not mine and not alone.")
Annie: What did you do?

Bill: Watched *Fleabag* and *High Fidelity* and went to bed. ("Well, that's also true," thinks Bill. "This is pretty easy. I seem to have a knack for it.")

A week later, after Jana paid a return visit to Bill's apartment, Annie discovered Jana's legal ethics casebook under Bill's bed, opened to the very page you are now reading. "How did this get here?" Annie asked. Bill confessed all and asked Annie to forgive him. "You lied to me," she said.

"I didn't lie," Bill said. ("It's like the cookies," he thinks.) "Everything I said was true. You asked the wrong questions. If you had asked the right questions, I would have admitted it." Seeing Annie's (sweet Annie's) incredulous expression, Bill added, and then regretted adding, "I mean, we're in law school, right? We've chosen litigation."

Did Bill tell the truth? Did he lie?

c. In the Matter of William Jefferson Clinton

Bill (formerly Billy) became a successful trial lawyer. We return to him shortly. Bill did *not* become president of the United States. But another Bill did. Recall that President Clinton was deposed on Saturday, January 17, 1998, in Paula Jones's sexual harassment case against him for conduct when he was governor of Arkansas. Hours earlier, unknown to Clinton, Jones's lawyers had received information from Linda Tripp about Clinton's intimate sexual relationship with White House intern Monica Lewinsky. Many of the deposition questions focused on that relationship, which Clinton emphatically denied. See pages 311-312.

Seven months later, on August 17, 1998, after Lewinsky had testified before a grand jury and admitted a sexual relationship with the president and after physical evidence (the semen-stained blue dress that Lewinsky never brought to the cleaners) made it impossible for Clinton to continue to deny one, Clinton was himself questioned before the grand jury.

Q: [by prosecutor, quoting statement that Bob Bennett, Clinton's lawyer, had made at Clinton's deposition] "Counsel is fully aware that Ms. Lewinsky has filed, has an affidavit . . . saying that there *is* absolutely no sex of any kind in any manner, shape or form, with President Clinton." (Emphasis added.) That statement is made by your attorney in front of Judge Susan Webber Wright, correct?

A: That's correct.

Q: That statement is a completely false statement. Whether or not Mr. Bennett knew of your relationship with Ms. Lewinsky, the statement that there *was* "no sex of any kind in any manner, shape or form, with President Clinton," was an utterly false statement. Is that correct? (Emphasis added.)

A: It depends on what the meaning of the word "is" is. If the — if he — if "is" means is and never has been that is not — that is one thing. If it means there is none, that was a completely true statement.

Is (was) the president right?*

The second subject on which Clinton seems to have lied at his deposition was whether he and Lewinsky were ever "alone" in the White House. He testified:

> *Q:* At any time were you and Monica Lewinsky alone together in the Oval Office?
>
> *A:* I don't recall, but as I said, when she worked at the legislative affairs office, they always had somebody there on the weekends. I typically worked some on the weekends. . . .
>
> *Q:* So I understand, your testimony is that it was possible then, that you were alone with her, but you have no specific recollection of that ever happening?
>
> *A:* Yes, that's correct. It's possible that she, in, while she was working there, brought something to me and that at the time she brought it to me, she was the only person there. That's possible. . . .
>
> *Q:* At any time were you and Monica Lewinsky alone in the hallway between the Oval Office and this kitchen area?
>
> *A:* I don't believe so, unless we were walking back to the dining room with the pizza. I just, I don't remember. I don't believe we were alone in the hallway, no . . . .
>
> *Q:* At any time have you and Monica Lewinsky ever been alone together in any room in the White House?
>
> *A:* I think I testified to that earlier. I think that there is a, it is—I have no specific recollection . . . .

In August, the first sentence of the president's prepared statement to the grand jury, before questioning, was: "When I was *alone* with Ms. Lewinsky on certain occasions in early 1996, and once in early 1997, I engaged in conduct that was wrong." Emphasis added. Did Clinton and his lawyers forget what he said back in January? The prosecutor didn't. He asked:

> *Q:* Let me ask you, Mr. President, you indicate in your statement that you were alone with Ms. Lewinsky. Is that right?
>
> *A:* Yes, sir.
>
> *Q:* How many times were you alone with Ms. Lewinsky?

---

* Clinton should have cited Shakespeare in his defense. In *As You Like It*, 3.4.20-29, Rosalind is complaining to her cousin Celia that Orlando, whom she loves, has missed their appointment.

> *Celia:* Nay, certainly, there is no truth in him.
> *Rosalind:* Do you think so?
> *Celia:* Yes. . . .
> *Rosalind:* Not true in love?
> *Celia:* Yes, when he is in, but I think he is not in.
> *Rosalind:* You have heard him swear downright he was.
> *Celia:* "Was" is not "is."

A: Let me begin with the correct answer. I don't know for sure. . . .

Q: You were alone with her on December 28, 1997, is that [right] —

A: Yes, sir . . . I was . . . .

Q: Do you agree with me that [your January 17, 1998, deposition] state-ment "I was never alone with her," is incorrect? You were alone with Monica Lewinsky, weren't you? *[We might assume that at this point Clinton realized his mistake and needed to backpedal.]*

A: Well, again, it depends on how you define "alone." Yes, we were alone from time to time, even during 1997, even when there was absolutely no improper conduct occurring. Yes, that is accurate. But there were also a lot of times when, even though no one could see us, the doors were open to the halls, on both ends of the halls, people could hear. The Navy stewards could come in and out at will, if they were around. Other things could be happening. So, there were a lot of times when we were alone, but I never really thought we were.

Did the president lie at the deposition? Were his answers false? Are the answers to these questions different in Lawyerland than in Real Life?

On his last day in office in 2000, Clinton settled all possible criminal and bar disciplinary charges against him by accepting a five-year suspen-sion of his Arkansas bar license (as of mid-2020 he has not requested reinstatement) and by making certain admissions. He admitted that he had given false answers under oath, but he insisted that he did not lie. How can that be? The president's exceptionally talented lawyer, David Kendall of Williams & Connolly, maintained that it was never the pres-ident's *intention* to give false answers, but some of his answers turned out to be false anyway despite his good intention. Judge Wright was not impressed. See below.

d. The Law of Perjury (and Rules Governing "False" Statements)

Because ethics rules give lawyers certain duties to correct not only lies but also "false" statements that are not lies because they are not know-ingly false, we must define "false." Can a literally true statement be false? Billy's answer to his parents and Bill's answers to Annie's questions were (let us be generous here) literally true. Clinton also claimed that his statements were literally true. Even so, were any of these statements false? Were they lies? Whatever your answer when the context is a familial or intimate relationship or a friendship, law is a parallel universe with its own interpretive standards and tests for meaning. Lawyers need clarity about that universe, not only to decide whether correction is required, but also to guide their answers to interrogatories and to prepare witness testimony.

The Legal Backdrop. We begin with Bronston v. United States, 409 U.S. 352 (1973), a famous and gratifying case for litigators. A company of which

Bronston was sole owner had filed a petition under the Bankruptcy Act. At a hearing to trace his assets, Bronston testified under oath as follows:

Q: Do you have any bank accounts in Swiss banks, Mr. Bronston?
A: No, sir.
Q: Have you ever?
A: The company had an account there for about six months, in Zurich.
Q: Have you any nominees who have bank accounts in Swiss banks?
A: No, sir.
Q: Have you ever?
A: No, sir.

At the time, Bronston did not have a Swiss bank account in his own name, but he had once had one. Did Bronston lie? (Reread the dialogue.) The government alleged that Bronston (falsely) implied that the answer to the second question was no, although he did not actually say no. He was convicted of perjury.

The Supreme Court unanimously reversed. Bronston's answer was "true and complete on its face." It did not matter that Bronston may have intended to evade the question and mislead the questioner. Protection against non-responsive answers lay in effective cross-examination.

> It is the responsibility of the lawyer to probe; testimonial interrogation, and cross-examination in particular, is a probing, prying, pressing form of inquiry. If a witness evades, it is the lawyer's responsibility to recognize the evasion and to bring the witness back to the mark, to flush out the whole truth with the tools of adversary examination.

Lawyers love *Bronston*. It allows evasive but true answers intended to conceal harmful but true information. And indeed appellate courts have reversed convictions citing *Bronston*. But they reject the *Bronston* defense when the witness tries to mislead not through a non-responsive answer that ignores the question, as Bronston did, but by taking advantage of an ambiguity (or what the witness hopes is an ambiguity) in the question. The defendant in United States v. Sarwari, 669 F.3d 401 (4th Cir. 2012), stated under oath (on passport applications) that he was the "father" of the applicants. He was not. He was their stepfather. He was convicted of perjury and appealed. After a review of cases construing *Bronston*, the court affirmed the guilty verdict:

> *Bronston's* literal truth defense does not apply . . . to an answer [that] would be true on one construction of an arguably ambiguous question but false on another. For these reasons, Sarwari's claim to the *Bronston* literal truth defense must fail. The truth or falsity of Sarwari's answer — that he, the children's stepfather, was their father — depends entirely on the arguable ambiguity of the question asked. . . .
>
> When a question is . . . susceptible to multiple interpretations, and a defendant's answer is true under one understanding of the question but false under

another, the fact finder determines whether the defendant knew his statement was false. An appellate court's only role in this situation is to assess the sufficiency of the evidence offered to support the conviction.

Bronston evaded the question. He did not answer it. That should have been obvious to the questioner, as it was to you. Sarwari answered the question but took advantage of (what he claimed was) an ambiguity. Even if his answer could be true as he interpreted the question, the jury found that he knew what the question was asking and intended to mislead.

Doesn't the court's holding mean that it behooves a witness to detect a question's possible ambiguity and clarify it before answering? And her lawyer, if she has one, must do the same. Otherwise, a trier of fact may later find that the witness intended to lie, even if her answer was true as the witness (perhaps honestly) interpreted the question. *Sarwari* and other cases make the witness (and especially her lawyer) the opponent's partner in fashioning a precise question. Lawyers routinely assume that it's not their problem if an opposing lawyer asks an ambiguous question and as a result does not learn important information. That may often be so, but it's not the whole story.

This brings us to United States v. DeZarn, 157 F.3d 1042 (6th Cir. 1998). Think of *DeZarn* as the anti-*Bronston*. It was cited, along with *Bronston,* during Clinton's House impeachment and Senate trial. Lawyers do not love *DeZarn.* Lawyers hate *DeZarn.*

The Inspector General of the Army was investigating whether contributions to a Kentucky gubernatorial campaign improperly influenced subsequent appointments to the Kentucky National Guard. Suspected fundraising had allegedly occurred at a 1990 party at the home of Billy Wellman, a former Guard officer. Sixty people, including the candidate, the then-Lieutenant Governor, attended this party, which had been billed as a "Preakness Party" because it was scheduled to occur during the Preakness Stakes, a prominent annual horse race in the state. The investigation of the 1990 party was headline news in Kentucky. Various witnesses were questioned under oath. Robert DeZarn was one of them. Following are some of the questions and answers:

Q: Okay. In 1991, and I recognize this is in the period that you were retired, [Wellman] held the Preakness Party at his home. Were you aware of that?

A: Yes.

Q: Did you attend?

A: Yes.

Q: Okay. Sir, was that a political fundraising activity?

A: Absolutely not.

Q: Okay. Did then Lieutenant Governor Jones, was he in attendance at the party?

A: I knew he was invited. I don't remember if he made an appearance or not.

As you can see, the questioner misspoke. He said "1991," not 1990. DeZarn was indicted for perjury. The government proved that DeZarn *had* attended a 1990 political fundraiser at Wellman's home. The jury convicted him. On appeal, DeZarn argued that Wellman also had a dinner party at the time of the 1991 Preakness, which was not a fundraiser but could (he claimed) be characterized as a "Preakness Party." Consequently, his answer was literally true and not perjury. He cited *Bronston*.

The Sixth Circuit affirmed DeZarn's conviction. It distinguished *Bronston* on the ground that Bronston gave literally true answers that were "nonresponsive," thereby alerting the questioner. By contrast, Judge Rosen wrote, DeZarn gave responsive and "categorical answers to questions" intending to mislead (as the jury found).

> [A] perjury inquiry which focuses only upon the precision of the question and ignores what the Defendant knew about the subject matter of the question at the time it was asked, misses the very point of perjury: that is, the Defendant's intent to testify falsely and, thereby, mislead his interrogators. Such a limited inquiry would not only undermine the perjury laws, it would undermine the rule of law as a whole. . . .
>
> Even if the questioning was not perfectly precise, the context in which the questions were asked made the object of the questioning clear and, more importantly, it is clear that DeZarn knew exactly the party to which Colonel Tripp [the questioner] was referring. The evidence at trial clearly established that Billy Wellman held only one Preakness Party and that was in 1990. No Preakness Party was held in 1991.

Recent cases distinguish between questions that are "fundamentally ambiguous," essentially inept, and questions that are "arguably ambiguous." If a question is in the first category, no perjury prosecution can be based on it as a matter of law. If it is in the second category, the jury decides if the defendant understood what the questioner was asking and intended to mislead by taking advantage of the ambiguity. Here is how two courts explain the difference.

1. "Challenges to the clarity of a question are typically left to the jury, which has the responsibility of determining whether the defendant understood the question to be confusing or subject to many interpretations. Moreover, consistent with our standard of review, we will not disturb a jury's determination that a response under oath constitutes perjury unless it is entirely unreasonable to expect that the defendant understood the question posed to him." United States v. Hird, 913 F.3d 332 (3d Cir. 2019).

2. "[A]nswers to fundamentally ambiguous questions cannot support a perjury conviction. . . . Several factors affect fundamental ambiguity, including:

   > "(1) the inherent vagueness—or, conversely, the inherent clarity—of certain words and phrases, (2) the compound character of a question,

(3) the existence of defects in syntax or grammar in a question, (4) the context of the question and answer, and (5) the defendant's own responses to allegedly ambiguous questions.

"However, fundamental ambiguity is the exception, not the rule. A question is not fundamentally ambiguous when it is entirely reasonable to expect a defendant to have understood the terms used in the questions. Put differently, when a question is merely susceptible to multiple interpretations, and a defendant's answer is true under one understanding of the question but false under another, the fact finder determines whether the defendant knew his statement was false." United States v. Chujoy, 207 F. Supp. 3d 626 (W.D. Va. 2016).

Hird illustrates the point. In a prosecution for fixing traffic tickets for political friends and others, a traffic court judge was asked at the grand jury whether his "personal assistant" had "received any *calls* [related to ticket fixing] from other judges, other ward leaders . . . saying so and so has called about this case?" He answered, "If she did, she didn't convey them to me." The witness was indicted for perjury because his assistant had received index cards with such requests. At trial, he claimed that if he had been asked about index cards, not calls, his answer would have differed. The circuit rejected this defense. Context mattered. "The transcript makes it obvious," the court wrote, "that [the defendant's] singular reliance on the reference to a 'call' ignores the thrust of the Government's line of questions. The questions focus on the substance of the communications between [the defendant's] personal assistant and himself, rather than the mode of those communications."

The Ethical Backdrop. Rule 3.3(a) tells lawyers they may have a duty to correct "false" statements, even if they are not knowingly false. Rule 8.4(c) is broader. It forbids deceit, dishonesty, and misrepresentation. As we've seen, a literally true answer to an ambiguous question can be perjury. Can a literally true statement also violate Rule 8.4? Yes. In re Shorter, 570 A.2d 760 (D.C. 1990), disbarred Shorter, who (among other things) had given "technically true" answers to IRS agents who were trying to locate his assets. Although the agents asked about many asset categories (bank accounts, cars), they did not ask about Shorter's law partnership interest, and he didn't volunteer. The court "decline[d] to describe [Shorter's] . . . parsimonious dissemination of information as either fraudulent, deceitful, or misrepresentative" within the meaning of the predecessor to Rule 8.4(c). But it ruled that the answers "evinc[ed] a lack of integrity and straightforwardness, and [were] therefore dishonest. . . . As long as the IRS did not ask just the right questions, respondent was prepared to deprive it of the right answers. This conduct was of a dishonest character" and unethical. Shorter would have been better off not talking.

Intolerance for literally true statements is also found in opinions applying Rule 11. In re Taylor, 655 F.3d 274 (3d Cir. 2011), upheld sanctions under

Rule 9011 of the Federal Rules of Bankruptcy Procedure (the counterpart to Rule 11). "[W]e are aware of [no authority] which permits statements under Rule 9011 that are literally true but actually misleading. If the reasonably foreseeable effect of [statements] to the bankruptcy court was to mislead the court, [the makers of the statements] cannot be said to have complied with Rule 9011." In *Taylor*, the court held that a lawyer's statement that a debtor in bankruptcy "had failed to make regular mortgage payments," even if "literally accurate," was misleading and warranted Rule 11 sanctions, where "at least partial payments had been made and . . . the failure to make some of the rest of the payments was due to a bona fide dispute over the amount due, not simple default."

e. The Law of Contempt

We have seen that in deciding whether a literally true statement might be considered "false," or otherwise forbidden, we must evaluate it in context under the law of perjury and rules of legal ethics. Discovery rules and the law of contempt also count. Clinton was never prosecuted for perjury. But Judge Wright, who presided at his deposition, cited the president for civil contempt. She relied solely on his testimony denying that he was ever "alone" with Monica Lewinsky in any room in the White House and that he and Lewinsky had "sexual relations." She rejected the claim by Clinton's lawyer that he did not intend to make a false statement even if, as it happened, the answers turned out to be false.

> Simply put, the President's deposition testimony regarding whether he had ever been alone with Ms. Lewinsky was intentionally false, and his statements regarding whether he had ever engaged in sexual relations with Ms. Lewinsky likewise were intentionally false, notwithstanding tortured definitions and interpretations of the term "sexual relations."

Jones v. Clinton, 36 F. Supp. 2d 1118 (E.D. Ark. 1999). Judge Wright ordered the president to pay Jones's lawyers $89,484.05 to compensate them for their fees and expenses arising out of the president's civil contempt of court. She also ordered the president to pay the court $1,202.00 for the judge's expenses in attending the deposition. Jones v. Clinton, 57 F. Supp. 2d 719 (E.D. Ark. 1999). The president sensibly did not appeal, thereby avoiding a possibly harsher opinion from the Eighth Circuit.

The next problem requires you to decide whether particular statements are "false" or perjurious in Lawyerland and a lawyer's options if they are either. Pay attention to questions and answers in bold.

"Did You Talk to Cassie?"

Bill (formerly Billy) and Annie broke up. Jana dumped him. He married Natasha Freud-Jung, a psychiatrist, who warned him that she could read his mind, which he believed. He joined a litigation boutique. He started to earn a lot of money. He was a natural trial lawyer. He exuded charm and credibility. He had a talent for appearing sincere when talking to juries because he truly believed what he was saying while he was saying it. Juries loved him and he loved juries.

One day, Bill was retained by Pierre Monnier, who had been sued for stock fraud. The plaintiffs claimed that on April 4, 2019, a few days after getting inside information, Pierre sold them his stock in Zizzlet, Ltd. After Zizzlet issued its first quarter report on April 18, 2019, its stock sank 37 percent. Lucia Beach, the plaintiffs' lawyer, alleged in her complaint that Pierre had received an advance warning about Zizzlet's finances from Cassandra Beaumont, its CFO, whereabouts unknown. The following transcript is from Pierre's deposition in September 2019.

> *Q:* Do you know Cassandra Beaumont?
> *A:* Sure. I know Cassie.
> *Q:* How do you know her?
> *A:* I invested in Zizzlet. She was CFO.
> *Q:* **Did you ever date Cassie?**
> *A:* **I'm married with kids.**
> *Q:* **Is that a no?**
> *A:* **I never dated Cassie.**
> *Q:* When, prior to April 18, 2019, did you last communicate with Ms. Beaumont?
> *A:* Let's see. I dropped in on their holiday party in mid-December 2018. We talked.
> *Q:* **Did Cassandra Beaumont ever provide you with Zizzlet financial information?**
> *A:* **A few times in 2018.**
> *Q:* **Did you talk to Cassie about Zizzlet financial information in 2019 — before April 18?**
> *A:* **No.**

A few days later, Lucia reduced her settlement offer from $6 million to $3 million. Bill said he'd confer with Pierre and get back to her. At their meeting, Pierre said, "Bill, you know, Lucia asked if I had talked to Cassie in 2019 before April 18."

"And you said no."

"Right, and that's true."

"Okay. I'm glad to hear it."

"But I did hear from her a few days before I sold the stock."

Bill sat down. "You did hear from her," he repeated.

"She left a voicemail. I didn't talk to her. Technically, she didn't talk to me either. She left a voicemail. If Lucia Beach had asked '*Did you hear* from Cassie in 2019?' I would have told her. Wasn't it her job to be precise? She messed up. I told the truth."

Bill said nothing.

"Bill, you told me not to volunteer," Pierre said.

"Where is the voicemail now?"

"Deleted."

"Did she say anything about the financial condition of Zizzlet on the voicemail?"

"Not really."

"Not *really*. What does that mean?"

"I mean Lucia would probably see it in a different light. But no, not really."

Bill said nothing.

"Nothing you couldn't explain," Pierre added.

Silence.

"You told me just answer the question, listen to the question and just answer it. Don't volunteer. That's what you told me."

Silence.

"And one more thing. I never dated Cassie, like I said."

"Why am I expecting a 'but?'"

"But we did have a couple of spontaneous, you know, spontaneous, unplanned . . . ."

"Hookups?"

"They were unplanned. No dates. Just happened. Hey, this is confidential. I can't let it get out."

"A couple is two."

"Well, a few then. How many is a few?"

Bill remembered his parents' question about eating the cookies. He remembered sweet Annie (yet again). He remembered his legal ethics teacher whose name he forgot and whose classes he mostly missed. He wondered if he could call for advice. (Yes, Bill, you can.) He thought about the outstanding settlement offer. He thought maybe he should have gone into politics.

What may or must Bill do now? Is accepting Lucia's offer a way out?

2. Cross-Examining the Truthful Witness

Max Steuer was a renowned criminal defense lawyer in New York City in the early 1900s. He represented the defendants in the criminal case arising out of the infamous Triangle Shirtwaist Company fire of 1911, where 146 people, mostly immigrant women, died. In the excerpt below, New York lawyer Daniel Kornstein praises Steuer's skills in that case, as do many lawyers today. A critical response to Kornstein and his reply follow. If you want to learn more about the legendary Max Steuer (and other notable cross-examiners) read Francis Wellman's classic book, *The Art of Cross-Examination*.

Daniel J. Kornstein
A TRAGIC FIRE—A GREAT CROSS-EXAMINATION
N.Y. L.J., Mar. 28, 1986, at 2

We remember events for different reasons. For example, March 25 was the seventy-fifth anniversary of the terrible Triangle Shirtwaist Fire, which killed 146 sweatshop workers, mostly young immigrant women barred by locked doors from escaping the blaze in their New York City factory. The fire in 1911 stands as a turning point in the history of labor because it led to significant labor reforms in workplace health and safety laws. Important as those reforms are, however, they are not the only reason for lawyers to remember the Triangle Shirtwaist Fire.

Lawyers should remember the fire for another reason, unmentioned in the anniversary accounts. Lawyers should remember it because it was the subject of one of the all-time great cross-examinations in American courtroom history.

The memorable cross-examination grew out of the criminal case that followed the fire. Within a month after the fire, the government indicted the two owners of the Triangle Shirtwaist Company on manslaughter charges. The indictment was based on a New York State law providing that factory doors "shall be so constructed as to open outwardly, where practicable, and shall not be locked, bolted or fastened during working hours." For their defense counsel, the proprietors chose Max D. Steuer. . . .

The trial lasted several weeks. Just before it rested, the prosecution called a final witness to supply a missing piece of crucial evidence. This final witness was supposed to testify that Rose Schwartz, one of the fire's victims named in the indictment, was in fact the same person who lost her life in the fire. Up to that point in the trial, the testimony had uniformly been that the bodies discovered in the building were so charred that identification was impossible.

The prosecution had built suspense. It had kept its final witness in Philadelphia, beyond reach of defense counsel who knew neither her identity nor her location. There, the prosecutor and his staff met with her several times in preparation for her testimony. When the government's final witness appeared, everyone in the courtroom felt that something important was about to happen. They were not disappointed.

First, the key witness testified to preliminary details. She said that she had been an employee at the factory and was there when the fire broke out and that she knew Rose Schwartz. Then the prosecutor asked her: "Now tell everything that you saw and did on the ninth floor of those premises from the time the fire broke out." The response was heartrending.

The witness told how she first saw the flames. She described how the girls scattered from one floor and ran to another. She testified that many of them ran to the windows and began to jump out and that she herself had decided to follow their example.

While at the window ready to jump, the witness said she looked around the room in a last-ditch effort to escape. She then saw Rose Schwartz, the witness said, with both hands on the knob of the door desperately turning and pushing, but the door would not give.

Watching Rose, the witness was mesmerized. She saw the flames envelop Rose's hands, saw her fall to the floor and then saw her once more struggle to her feet, again grab the knob of the door and turn it one way and then another, pull and then push, but the door would not give. Once more the flames enveloped Rose and again she had to withdraw her hands from the door knob and she fell to the floor; the flames were now coming very close to the witness; she turned once more toward the door and there for the third time, was Rose Schwartz, on her knees, screaming and praying, with both hands on the door knob, turning it first one way, then the other, and pulling and pushing, but the door would not give, and finally she was completely covered by the flames, and fell to the floor within a foot of the door. At the end of her direct testimony, tears ran down the cheeks of the jurors.

Steuer began his cross-examination slowly. He spent the first half hour on preliminaries. At the end of the half hour, using the exact words employed by the prosecutor, he asked the witness to state all she did herself and all that she saw done on the ninth floor from the moment she first saw the fire.

There was something odd about the witness's answer. She started her narrative with exactly the same word that she had used when telling her story the first time. She went on in precisely the same words that she had used when answering the same question put to her by the prosecutor.

Steuer changed the subject for a while and asked the witness to describe what happened for the third time. The witness again started with the same word and continued to narrate the story in precisely the same words that she had used twice before. The only difference was that this time she omitted one word. Steuer asked her if she had omitted a word, naming the word.

Her lips began to move and start the narrative to herself all over again, and when she reached the position where that word belonged she said: "Yes, I made a mistake; I left that word out." [*Question:*] "But otherwise your answer was correct?" She again began to move her lips, obviously reciting to herself what she had previously said, and then said, "Yes, otherwise my answer is correct."

When Steuer asked her the same question a third time, the prosecutor objected but was overruled. After twenty minutes on other subjects, Steuer asked, for the fourth time: "Will you please tell the jury what you saw and what you did after you first observed any sign of the flames?"

She started with the same word, and continued her narrative, but again left out one word, this time a different word. Asked whether she had not now omitted a word, naming it, she went through the same lip performance and replied that she had, and upon being asked to place the word where it belonged, she proceeded to do so.

Neither Steuer nor the prosecutor had any further questions of that witness. The tears in the jury box had dried. The situation had entirely changed. The witness had not hurt, but had very materially helped, the defense; she had succeeded in casting grave suspicion on the testimony of many of the girls who had previously testified; her carefully prepared story had aroused the suspicion of the jury regarding the entire case of the prosecution.

The jury acquitted the two defendants.

Ann Ruben & Emily Ruben
LETTER TO THE EDITOR
N.Y. L.J., Apr. 14, 1986, at 2

In 1911, one hundred forty-six sweatshop workers, mostly young immigrant women, were incinerated as a result of the sweatshop's owners' efforts to ensure maximization of profit. When fire broke out at the Triangle Shirtwaist Factory, workers were unable to escape because the owners had bolted exits shut. The men charged with responsibility were acquitted after trial.

Daniel Kornstein's eulogy of Max Steuer's role in this acquittal underscores the moral vacuum in which many lawyers operate. Kornstein asks us to "celebrate" Max Steuer's cross-examination of Kate Alterman, one of the young immigrant women who managed to survive the fire. We cannot.

Mr. Kornstein's facile assumption that this young woman's testimony was perjured leads him to extol the virtues of Steuer's cross-examination. Mr. Kornstein exhibits all of the narrow-mindedness of the men (judge, jury, and lawyers) who exonerated those responsible for the results of this tragic fire. He fails even to consider the very obvious and likely possibility that the testimony was not perjured. To equate Kate Alterman's possibly rehearsed testimony with premeditated dishonesty represents an enormous leap of faith and completely ignores the socioeconomic and historic context of that testimony. The women who testified at the trial spoke little English. Approximately half of them spoke no English at all, and many of those who did were illiterate. They had barely survived a traumatic fire in which many of their friends and co-workers had burned to death. The notorious conditions under which they had worked in this country provided no basis for them to believe that their own words could sway the power structure the legal system represented. Unfortunately, the judge's narrow jury instructions, Steuer's technique, and the jury results underscored the powerlessness of young immigrant women.

Mr. Kornstein has used the anniversary of the Triangle Shirtwaist Factory Fire to applaud the technique of Max Steuer and to belittle the courage of women like Kate Alterman who came forward to testify. It would be more appropriate for lawyers to remember those who lost their lives in the fire and to explore ways to combat the oppressive working conditions that still exist throughout this country.

I asked Daniel Kornstein for his response to the Rubens' charge that his eulogy reveals the "moral vacuum in which many lawyers operate." He wrote in part:

> The Rubens movingly make telling points that, in retrospect, I wish I had expressly taken into consideration. First, they are absolutely correct in saying that I neglected to distinguish between outright perjury and overly rehearsed, overly memorized but essentially truthful testimony. I should have drawn that distinction, and I regret not having done so. But even that distinction in no way lessens Steuer's tactical achievement in neutralizing and offsetting the natural sympathy the jury must have had for the witness. For, in light of the obvious coaching, the fact remains that we simply do not know if the witness's testimony was or was not truthful and accurate.
>
> Second, as the Rubens point out, the class struggle aspects of the cross-examination and the whole trial are obvious. But that economic overhang is not the end of the story. Unless we have come to the point where representing unpopular clients (such as sweatshop owners, landlords, large corporations, defendants accused of heinous crimes, or persons with controversial political, social, or moral beliefs) is itself unethical, I do not see how Steuer overstepped his professional responsibility. We have not yet so abandoned the presumption of innocence of the adversary process, so that we know who will win or lose a trial before the evidence is in.
>
> The Rubens rightly press for a closer moral study of Steuer's trial tactics and their impact on the trial outcome. That is quite different from broadside attacks on the "power structure the legal system represented." It may be that, in some cosmic sense, the wrong side prevailed in the *Triangle Shirtwaist Factory* case; but it was not because Steuer did anything inappropriate. He did precisely what he should have done—and what any good lawyer should have done. I don't think Steuer acted irresponsibly or in a "moral vacuum" by cross-examining the witness as he did. He took advantage of an adversary's blunder, which happens all the time.

This exchange exposes what many nonlawyers, and some lawyers, view as the morally compromised behavior of the bar. Can all the theory about adversary justice possibly justify Steuer's effort to make it appear that the truthful Kate Alterman was a liar in order to exonerate sweatshop owners who were responsible for the deaths of 146 factory workers? Should we say that Steuer was both a good trial lawyer and a bad man? Or is that question fundamentally incoherent?

Of course, maybe Kate Alterman was a liar, for all we know, or carefully rehearsed by the prosecution and mistaken, although neither explanation seems likely. In any event, the profession owes it to the public to explain why Steuer, and the rules that enabled him, should not be questioned. So let's ask: Is Kornstein right to praise Steuer? If he is right, are the rules that permitted Steuer's strategy wrong, even if Steuer did his duty? Does your answer change if you assume that Steuer had incontrovertible proof (i.e., he knew) that Kate Alterman was telling the truth? Would your answer change if Steuer had instead been the prosecutor and had employed the same tactic in cross-examining a defense witness who he knew to be telling the truth?

There is another question lurking here. Does the moral vacuum the Rubens discern take a toll on the lawyers who work within it? Thankfully, most legal work does not present such a dilemma, but some does. When that is so—and recognizing that different lawyers will have different moral sensibilities and tolerances—can lawyers take comfort in the moral imperative to honor one's oath and fulfill their assigned role in the justice system?

3. Appeals to Bias

The rules of many jurisdictions forbid lawyers to exhibit bias in their professional activities. In addition, the ABA Code of Judicial Conduct obligates judges to require "lawyers in proceedings before the court to refrain from manifesting bias or prejudice, or engaging in harassment, based upon attributes including but not limited to race, sex, gender, religion, national origin, ethnicity, disability, age, sexual orientation, marital status, socioeconomic status, or political affiliation, against parties, witnesses, lawyers, or others." The prohibition does "not preclude . . . lawyers from making legitimate reference to the listed factors, or similar factors, when they are relevant to an issue in a proceeding." Rule 2.3(C) and (D).

Rule 8.4(g) of the Rules of Professional Conduct, adopted in 2016, forbids lawyers to "engage in conduct that the lawyer knows or reasonably should know is harassment or discrimination on the basis of race, sex, religion, national origin, ethnicity, disability, age, sexual orientation, gender identity, marital status or socioeconomic status in conduct related to the practice of law." This rule has engendered much debate in academic and professional circles, some of it heated. It has been challenged as a violation of the First Amendment's speech and religion clauses. The rule and the constitutional arguments are addressed in chapter 13D5f.

PEOPLE v. MARSHALL
995 N.E.2d 1045 (Ill. App. Ct. 2013)

JUSTICE GOLDENHERSH:

[Murder trial. Two government witnesses, Lacy and Blye, implicated Marshall in statements they gave the police. But they later gave exculpatory statements to Marshall's lawyer. Then they recanted the statements to the lawyer and testified against Marshall at trial. The prosecutor's challenge was to explain why the jury should accept their court testimony as true despite their exculpatory statements to Marshall's lawyer. How he tried to meet that challenge creates the issue on appeal. Marshall was convicted and sentenced to 85 years in prison.]

The issues in this appeal concern the prosecutor's opening statement and closing argument regarding the witnesses, Lacy and Blye. In his opening statement, the prosecutor, apparently in an effort to explain why both Lacy and Blye gave statements to police, then recanted those statements, and agreed to testify for the State at trial, stated the following:

> "And you will see, ladies and gentlemen, that there are some, not all—there are many good people in the black community, but basically you will see that there are a few in the black community who refuse to cooperate with the police even when a murder happens right under their nose, and those people have a habit of intimidating, harassing, sometimes threatening anybody who they think is cooperating with the police. That's what makes this case so difficult, ladies and gentlemen."

In his closing argument, the prosecutor stated the following:

> "But I think what is most crucial in deciding this case, in deciding the credibility of Jodie Lacy and Crystal Blye, and in deciding most of the other issues in this case, is to understand the culture of the black community here in Marion.
>
> Please, you have to keep in the back of your mind how many people in that community feel about law enforcement. You have to understand and keep in mind how they react to the police and to the prosecutors. Sometimes for people like us, that's hard to understand. People were brought up to believe that the police were their friends; that when something happens, when we are in trouble, that the police are our friends. And that's where we go to get help from is the police when bad things happen.
>
> But in the black community here in Marion, it's just the opposite. Most—for whatever reasons, most of these people were raised to believe that the police and prosecutors are the enemy; that for some reason, we are always out to get them. In their mindset, the biggest sin that you could—that you can commit is to be a snitch in the community. The biggest sin that you could commit is to ever cooperate with the police on anything. It's a sin to even cooperate when one of your own people gets brutally gunned down and is left to bleed to death.
>
> And I am not saying that the whole black community is like that, ladies and gentlemen. There are some very good law[-]abiding citizens in that community here in Marion. But the evidence has shown that again, for whatever reasons, there is an intense dislike and even hatred for the police. And this group of people who feel that way make it extremely hard on the people who are law-abiding and want to do what is right and who are willing to come forward and give information that they have when a crime has been committed."

The other notable statement the prosecutor made during closing argument was as follows:

> "Now, in our white world, ladies and gentlemen, our automatic reaction in that type of situation, if somebody gives a statement to the police and then later on changes their story, the automatic response would be that that person is not truthful and that there is a problem with their credibility.

> But again, please look at their testimony and what they did and what they didn't do through the eyes of the people who are raised, again, to feel that the police are always against them and that they cannot trust the police."

[Defense counsel did not object but the court ruled that the prosecutor's statements were "plain error" and warranted appellate review anyway.]

[T]he errors committed constituted a fundamental violation that affected the fairness of the trial. . . . The prosecutor's remarks were not an isolated event in this case. It was a consistent theme in the presentation of the State's theory of the case. The introduction of race was arbitrary—the elements of the charge of first-degree murder do not require any showing of the racial makeup of the community in which the crime took place. Nor does race bear on the credibility of the State's witnesses. The prosecutor urged the jurors to keep in the back of their minds how the "black community" felt about law enforcement, that "understand[ing] the culture of the black community here in Marion" would decide "most of the other issues in this case" along with the witnesses' credibility. We cannot say that the jury did not consider these improper and inflammatory remarks when reaching its verdict. This error was substantial, and we have found plain error for less-flagrant remarks from a prosecutor.

Next, a prosecutor has wide latitude in closing argument and may argue fair and reasonable inferences drawn from the evidence presented at trial. However, a prosecutor may not argue facts not based in evidence in the record. Here, the prosecutor did not introduce any evidence about the makeup of the community in which the crime took place, yet he did argue supposed "facts" about the community during the presentation of the case, such as the "culture of the black community" and "how many people in that community feel about law enforcement." These "facts" had no basis in the evidence and lacked any sort of foundation. His "facts" were naked prejudice.

Finally, the prosecutor improperly aligned himself with the jury when he contrasted the "black community" with "our white world." Ignoring, for a moment, the extremely racially prejudicial comparison that the prosecutor introduced when he said that statement, the prosecutor cannot create an "us versus them" argument during closing argument and effectively make himself a thirteenth member of the jury.

The State's use of race was an egregious and consistent theme throughout the trial. Even if the prosecutor had made only one reference to race, such reference would fall within a category that our courts have previously found to be plain error. That there were multiple instances of such racial prejudice is all the more reason to warrant a new trial for Marshall. These errors were so substantial that Marshall was denied the right to a fair trial.

[Reversed and remanded.]

What is astonishing about this case, apart from the prosecutor's argument, is that the defense lawyer did not object and the judge did not intervene even without an objection. Did they think the argument was okay? And while the appellate court was properly critical of the prosecutor, what do you make of this sentence in the opinion: "Here, the prosecutor did not introduce any evidence about the makeup of the community in which the crime took place, yet he did argue supposed 'facts' about the community during the presentation of the case, such as the 'culture of the black community' and 'how many people in that community feel about law enforcement.'" Did the court mean to suggest that if a prosecutor had claimed to have such evidence about "the black community"—perhaps from a sociological study—it would have been appropriate to introduce it and then ask the jury to draw an inference about Lacy and Blye's own motives from it because they are members of that community? The rules of evidence would not allow that.

Here is what a prosecutor told the sentencing judge after Peter David was convicted of murder in Hawai'i. (The facts are taken from the decision of the intermediate appellate court. State v. David, 339 P.3d 1090 (Haw. Ct. App. 2014).)

> The prosecutor made David's ethnicity and national origin a central part of his sentencing recommendation. Early in his sentencing argument, the prosecutor specifically drew attention to David's ethnicity and national origin by telling the Circuit Court, "You know he comes from Micronesia, from Chuuk[.]" The comment suggested that David's status as a Micronesian from Chuuk was relevant to the punishment he should receive. As the prosecutor continued with his sentencing argument, he repeatedly made inappropriate references to David's status as a Micronesian male and the need to send a message to the Micronesian community:
>
>> And when I talk about, perhaps, a sentence like this could save lives, I'm talking about sending a message to the Micronesian community.
>> Even more so than just a community, but I say this, by no means mean to be a racist about anything, but in my experience, and I believe in the Court's experience, as well as [defense counsel's] experience, over the past few years, we have had a number of cases that have come in involving Chuukese, Micronesian males drinking. . . .
>> But we're talking Micronesians who get inebriated on alcohol, then become violent with their own family members, their own friends and they involve knives.

The intermediate appellate court had held that the sentencing judge "did not go far enough to make its repudiation of the prosecutor's improper arguments clear on the record." It affirmed David's conviction, but remanded for resentencing before a different judge. On appeal, the Hawai'i Supreme Court reversed the conviction, too, after finding evidentiary errors, but it agreed that the prosecutor's argument was out of line. It wrote:

> We concur with the [lower court] that comments made during the sentencing hearing were improper. See [State v.] Rogan, 984 P.2d [1231], 1240-41

[Haw. 1999] ("[A]rguments by the prosecution contrived to stimulate racial prejudice . . . threaten[ ] our multicultural society and constitutional values. . . . [A]ppeals to racial prejudice lack the professionalism and decorum required of attorneys who practice before the bar of the courts of Hawai'i and will not be tolerated."). The [lower court] also correctly concluded that the circuit court did not meet its burden to repudiate the improper remarks made by the prosecutor when he appealed to race in arguing for a sentence that would "send a message to the Micronesian community."

State v. David, 409 P.3d 719 (Haw. 2017).

Appeals to bias, racial and otherwise, may be rare (so far as we know), but they are also too common. One appeal would be too common. Disturbing too is the willingness of some courts to construe them as not so serious, or merely as overzealous advocacy, thereby encouraging more of the same. That's what happened in Johnny Bennett's case. Bennett, a Black man who was 6′6″ and weighed 300 pounds, was convicted of murdering a man who was 5′7″ and weighed 135 pounds. A mixed-race jury sentenced Bennett to death but a state court ordered resentencing. In the Fourth Circuit, Judge Wilkinson tells what then happened.

> The second sentencing proceeding was held in 2000. As in the first trial, [Donald] Myers led the prosecution and the jury sentenced Bennett to death. But this time, the jury was composed of white jurors only. And before this all-white jury, Myers chose to use racially charged language from the first sentence of his opening argument to his final soliloquy, casting aside the race-neutral presentation he had employed with the mixed-race jury.
>
> The most egregious appeals to racial prejudice came in his closing argument, in which he referred to Bennett using a slew of derogatory terms. Myers admonished the jury, "Meeting [Bennett] again will be like meeting King Kong on a bad day." He also labeled Bennett a "caveman," a "mountain man," a "monster," a "big old tiger," and "[t]he beast of burden." In addition, Myers intentionally elicited irrelevant, inflammatory testimony from one of the state's witnesses, who recounted a dream in which he was chased by murderous, black Indians. While cross-examining a defense witness, Myers alluded to Bennett's sexual partner as "the blonde-headed lady," alerting the jury to the interracial nature of the relationship. . . .
>
> The South Carolina Supreme Court affirmed the death sentence, holding that the comments "did not improperly inject racial issues into the trial." The court observed that the "King Kong" label "could have racial connotations" but found that Myers's use of the term "was not an appeal to the passions or prejudices of the jury." Instead, the reference conveyed Bennett's "size and strength as they related to his past crimes" and was an invited response. The court found the "caveman" comment "merely descriptive" of testimony that Bennett had twice pulled someone else by the hair.

Judge Wilkinson was having none of this. He wrote in part:

> With all respect, these were unreasonable findings of fact. The prosecutor's comments were poorly disguised appeals to racial prejudice. It is impossible to divorce the prosecutor's "King Kong" remark, "caveman" label, and other

descriptions of a black capital defendant from their odious historical context. And in context, the prosecutor's comments mined a vein of historical prejudice against African-Americans, who have been appallingly disparaged as primates or members of a subhuman species in some lesser state of evolution. We are mindful that courts "should not lightly infer that a prosecutor intends an ambiguous remark to have its most damaging meaning." But here, "the prosecutor's remarks were quite focused, unambiguous, and strong." The comments plugged into potent symbols of racial prejudice, encouraging the jury to fear Bennett or regard him as less human on account of his race.

The "King Kong" comment especially drew on longtime staples of racial denigration. That comment was "not just humiliating, but degrading and humiliating in the extreme." Likening Bennett to King Kong in particular stoked race-based fears by conjuring the image of a gargantuan, black ape who goes on a killing spree and proceeds to swing the frail, white, blonde Fay Wray at the top of the Empire State Building. Petitioner is right to note that the film is regarded by many critics as "a racist cautionary tale about interracial romance."

Bennett v. Stirling, 842 F.3d 319 (4th Cir. 2016).

In the first two of the three prior cases, the courts did not name the prosecutor. In the third, it did. Should courts name lawyers who commit serious violations of procedural or ethical rules? What if the lawyer is a prosecutor? Prosecutors rarely face discipline even if a court has identified unethical behavior. A court may view naming as a necessary deterrent. United States v. Farinella, 558 F.3d 695 (7th Cir. 2009).

4. The Boundaries of Proper Argument

> And yet as [Mr. Furnival] sat down [after his summation] he knew that [his client] had been guilty! To his ear her guilt had never been confessed; but yet he knew that it was so, and, knowing that, he had been able to speak as though her innocence were a thing of course. That those witnesses [against her] had spoken truth he also knew, and yet he had been able to hold them up to the execration of all around them as though they had committed the worst of crimes from the foulest of motives! And more than this, stranger than this, worse than this,—when the legal world knew—as the legal world soon did know—that all this had been so, the legal world found no fault with Mr. Furnival, conceiving that he had done his duty by his client in a manner becoming an English barrister and an English gentleman.
>
> —Anthony Trollope, *Orley Farm*

Many trial lawyers will tell you that summations separate truly great advocates from the merely excellent ones. The rules governing summation are easy to state. A lawyer's argument may not ask the jury to find facts that are neither supported by the evidence nor reasonable inferences from it. Whittenburg v. Werner Enter., 561 F.3d 1122 (10th Cir. 2009); Rule 3.4(e).

Inevitably, however, there are subtle (and less subtle) appeals to emotion and sometimes a dose of histrionics. Much is tolerated. Maybe too much. True, the opposing lawyer gets to sum up, too, and is given the same leeway, but that would only seem to aggravate the threat to rational decision-making. There are limits, however. *Whittenburg* reversed a $3.2 million jury verdict for the plaintiff because his lawyer "spent the bulk of his argument placing before the jury fictitious admissions never uttered by defendants and launching vituperative and unprovoked attacks on defendants and their counsel." The court stressed that a closing argument "need not, nor should, be a sterile exercise devoid of passion. . . . Arguments may be forceful, colorful, or dramatic, without constituting reversible error. Counsel may resort to poetry, cite history, fiction, personal experiences, anecdotes, biblical stories, or tell jokes." That's a pretty generous license. It rewards performance skills that may detract from rational deliberation and the search for truth. And it underscores the advantage of being the final lawyer to sum up.

"I Hang a Key on a Nail"

Return to the *L.A. Law* episode in which Michael Kuzak, defending Barney Sears in a hit-and-run case, called Sears's aunt to testify. (See page 310.) In response to Kuzak's question, the aunt truthfully testified: "I hang a key on a nail" in an open garage. Kuzak then planned to argue that "anyone" could have taken the car key and gone for a joyride. Yet Kuzak knew that Sears was the driver. He planned to argue for a false inference from true evidence to create a reasonable doubt. Do the Rules allow that? Should they?

The Eyewitness (Part I)

"My name is Guy Goody and I am a criminal defense lawyer. My client is charged with robbing the First Federal Bank. He has confessed his guilt to me, and I have no doubt he is telling me the truth because we have successfully suppressed a detailed confession to the police and the bank money and a gun seized in an unlawful search of his home. He was wearing a ski mask at the time, so no one at the bank will be able to identify him. However, after he left the bank, he ran into the metro station and removed his ski mask. A woman saw him do this. The prosecutor will call her to identify my client. I have evidence that last year this witness pled guilty to a misdemeanor of lying on a mortgage application and received a sentence of two years' probation. She is still on probation. Can I use this evidence to impeach her credibility and argue to the jury that she is lying even though I know she is telling the truth?

"I have a second question. I plan to call a witness who will testify that she saw my client in a Burger King five blocks from the bank ten minutes before the robbery. A time-stamped videotape from the restaurant's camera confirms her testimony. I will then call another witness who will testify to the level of street congestion and traffic density on the day and at the time the bank was robbed. He will testify that he attempted to get from the restaurant to the bank in ten minutes and succeeded on only two of 15 tries. We will show videos of each effort taken from a camera mounted on a helmet he wore. Can I do this?"

The Eyewitness (Part II)

"My name is Charlotte Daring. I am an assistant U.S. Attorney. I am about to try a case in which a man is charged with armed robbery of the First Federal Bank. We know he is guilty because he confessed and his confession led us to the gun and stolen money, but the confession and the money and gun were suppressed. So we are going to trial. The defense has an eyewitness who can place the defendant in a Burger King five blocks away about ten minutes before the robbery. The defendant told us the same thing in his suppressed confession. It is further corroborated by the time-stamped videotape from a camera in the Burger King, which shows a person who strongly resembles the defendant leaving the Burger King ten minutes before the robbery. I have no reason to doubt that it is the defendant. The picture is blurry, however. I plan to call a facial recognition expert who will point out differences between the face in the video and the defendant's face, but he will not give an opinion on whether the man in the video is the defendant. I will then argue that the video is of someone else. Can I do that?

"Now, even with the defendant in the Burger King ten minutes before the robbery, he could still have done it. However, he would have had to move quickly in heavy pedestrian and vehicular traffic. I am worried that the defense lawyer will use his eyewitness to argue reasonable doubt, even though he knows his client did it. May I impeach the credibility of the witness with a two-year-old misdemeanor conviction? She provided a false alibi to the police to help a friend facing a drug charge."

ZAPATA v. VASQUEZ
788 F.3d 1106 (9th Cir. 2015)

FISHER, CIRCUIT JUDGE:. . .

In May 2001, shortly after placing a call on a pay phone, a 19-year-old student named Juan Trigueros was shot and killed in a 7-Eleven parking lot on Leavesley Road in Gilroy, California. At the time of the shooting, which took place around 2 a.m., Trigueros was wearing a basketball jersey emblazoned with the number 8, for Los Angeles Lakers star Kobe Bryant. The area in which the shooting took place was controlled by the Norteños street gang, of which there were several subgroups, or "cliques." One such clique, of which Zapata was a member, was Outside Posse, or "OSP." As an OSP member, Zapata had participated in attacks on Eighth Street gang members and Mexican nationals.

The Norteños' rivals were a subset of the Sureños street gang known as Eighth Street, whose identifying symbol was the number 8. Sureños tended to be first-generation Mexican immigrants who spoke limited English, whereas Norteños tended to be established U.S. residents who spoke English rather than Spanish. According to an expert on gang activity in the area, by wearing the number 8 in Norteño territory, Trigueros, a first-generation Mexican immigrant, was a "marked man." There was no evidence Trigueros was affiliated with the Sureños. . . .

Critical to the issue before us, at the end of the trial during the prosecution's closing rebuttal argument, [Prosecutor Stuart] Scott wove out of whole cloth, with no evidentiary support, a fictional and highly emotional account of the last words Trigueros heard Zapata shout as Zapata supposedly shot him. The prosecutor ascribed to Zapata several despicable, inflammatory ethnic slurs:

> Picture, if you will, the last words that Juan Trigueros heard before the defendant shot him in the back and to make sure he was dead shot him in the chest. What were the last things he heard? What's the reasonable inference of what was going on that precise moment the second before he's mortally wounded? Fuckin' scrap. You fuckin' wetback. Can you imagine the terror and the fear Juan Trigueros must have felt as he's cowering into the phone. . . . Fuckin' scrap. Wetback.

The prosecutor repeated these inflammatory remarks twice more, including just before the jury retired to begin deliberations.

These slurs were invoked deliberately. In his opening statement, the prosecutor had told the jury the word "scrap" is "a derogatory term—it's like using the N word—for Mexican nationals. It's very derogatory. Mojado [wetback] is another derogatory term." The prosecution's expert witness testified "scrap" means "piece of shit," and that although Mexican nationals "might not realize exactly what it means as far as the significance of it . . . it's taken as an insult" and would be "fighting words" to a Sureño gang member.

Zapata's counsel neither objected to the fictional, inflammatory statements in the closing argument nor asked the trial court to issue a curative instruction. The jury was then sent to deliberate. After three hours, it found Zapata guilty of first-degree murder. . . .

[B]y urging the jurors to base their decision on an experience of the victim the state court labeled "pure fiction," the prosecutor improperly encouraged them to convict Zapata out of sympathy for Trigueros and animus towards the killer. Second, by falsely saying the victim heard hateful ethnic slurs in the moments before his death, the prosecutor manipulated and misstated the evidence. As the state court explained, the only eyewitness to the murder, Brian Puphal, testified that he could not hear what the killer was yelling in the moments before Trigueros' death. Yet the prosecutor presented this fictional scenario as though it was fact. And just before concluding his rebuttal argument, he invited the jurors to "remember those last words" Trigueros heard as though Zapata had uttered them. The fabrication was especially pernicious because of the extensive evidence of Zapata's gang-related criminal history. By concocting the details of the victim's dying experience in this manner, the prosecutor purposefully blurred the distinction between Zapata's past convictions and the crime for which he was standing trial.[6]

Finally, the statements were improperly designed to appeal to the passions of the jury. That the slurs were directed at a specific ethnic group particularly risked sparking visceral outrage among members of the jury and encouraged them to convict based on emotion rather than evidence. . . .

That the prosecutor's comments were not a reasonable inference from the record also magnifies their prejudicial impact. As the state court declared, they were "pure fiction." Although the evidence showed Zapata was involved in another incident in which OSP members used such epithets, there was no evidence to even suggest such comments were made here. Additionally, the failure of either defense counsel or the court to question the prosecutor's repeated, albeit fictitious, version of the victim's last minutes would have led the jurors either to assume the statements were accurate or, at least, that the rank speculation was permissible. This case thus stands apart from others concluding that prosecutorial misconduct was not prejudicial. . . .

Defense counsel's failure to object to the prosecutor's inflammatory, fabricated and ethnically charged epithets, delivered in the moments before the jury was sent to deliberate Zapata's case, constituted ineffective assistance of counsel. The California Court of Appeal's failure to so conclude was based on unreasonable factual determinations and was an unreasonable application of controlling Supreme Court law. [Reversed and remanded.]

Why precisely was Zapata's conviction overturned? It wasn't only because the summation asked the jury to draw a false inference, was it? It wasn't only because his lawyer was ineffective for not objecting. So what was it?

Courts are especially vigilant when a prosecutor asks a jury to draw inferences that the evidence does not support. United States v. Wilson, 135 F.3d 291 (4th Cir. 1998), held that a defendant who had been convicted of drug and firearm offenses was denied a fair trial because the prosecutor argued that the evidence showed that he had committed murder when he shot

---

6. Nor can the prosecutor's statements be characterized as reasonable inferences that could be drawn from the evidence. Although there was evidence that OSP members had shouted these words in an unrelated attack that occurred seven weeks after the Trigueros shooting, there was not a shred of evidence in the record that the shooter uttered these words to Trigueros. Although a prosecutor "may strike hard blows, he is not at liberty to strike foul ones."

at a moving car. At most, the court said, the evidence showed that defendant's "gunfire hit the car, or perhaps that a shot struck the driver, [but the evidence was] not enough to suggest that the driver *died* as a result of any gunshot from [the defendant]." In United States v. Farinella, supra, the court expressed surprise that the local U.S. Attorney's office intended no sanction, beyond a "talking-to," of a prosecutor who far exceeded the limits of permissible summation. It placed her name in an opinion critical of her conduct, where it will be available in a database search forever. Defense lawyer summations, by contrast, are unlikely to be the subject of an appellate ruling. If the defendant is acquitted, there will be no appeal, and if convicted, the defendant can hardly complain about his lawyer's excess of passion.

Reversals for civil case summations are infrequent but they do happen. Hopson v. Riverbay Corp., 190 F.R.D. 114 (S.D.N.Y. 1999), granted the plaintiff a new trial when the defense lawyer, in an otherwise routine civil rights case, misstated the record to the jury in her summation. (The court found other professional misconduct as well.)

In any event, there are other ways to defeat the truth without resorting to impermissible summation inferences. May a lawyer ask the jury to infer a false fact from the truthful evidence that she introduced, as Michael Kuzak planned to do in "I Hang a Key on a Nail"? Yes. May she do so even if she believes but does not know that the fact she introduced is false? Yes. If an opponent's evidence is ambiguous, may a lawyer ask the jury to draw the inference most favorable to her client even if she knows it is not true? Yes. And earlier we saw that a lawyer may impeach a witness who she knows is telling the truth and then ask the jury to disbelieve the witness.

But how can these tactics be allowed if a trial is a search for the truth, as we also say? That assurance encourages the public to trust verdicts. Where would that trust go if the public were aware of the legitimate ways available to lawyers to impede that search?

Lawyers may not knowingly introduce evidence they know is false. Shouldn't it follow that lawyers may not ask a jury to infer the truth of a fact they know is false — the very same fact they are forbidden to prove with testimony? Is there a difference? Truth is truth.* The conventional justification for the difference is that jury arguments are only arguments. They are not evidence (as the judge will instruct). They are not under oath. Do you buy that? Does your friend with a degree in science, philosophy, or religion buy that?

---

* Or maybe not. Rudolph Giuliani, Donald Trump's personal lawyer and a former New York City mayor and U.S. Attorney for the Southern District of New York, was mocked after he told Chuck Todd of NBC News in August 2018 that "truth isn't truth," by way of explaining why his client would not submit to an interview with Special Counsel Robert Mueller.

The Subin-Mitchell Debate

Professor Harry Subin, my former faculty colleague, envisioned a role for criminal defense lawyers sharply less adversarial than the present conception. He would forbid defense lawyers to present "a false case" using the techniques described below. The right to present a defense, he argued, is "not absolute." Witness the prohibition on the use of perjured testimony. Professor Subin criticized "the utterly arbitrary line we have drawn" between the use of perjured testimony (disallowed) and the presentation of what he calls a "false case" (allowed).[*]

After Professor Subin's article appeared, John Mitchell, an experienced criminal defense lawyer whose work Professor Subin had cited, challenged Subin's conception with a fact pattern and the jury argument he would make based on it. Subin then replied to Mitchell's critique. Excerpts from all three articles follow. Who do you think is right? Whomever you choose, try to make the opposing argument.

Harry Subin
THE CRIMINAL LAWYER'S "DIFFERENT MISSION": REFLECTIONS ON THE "RIGHT" TO PRESENT A FALSE CASE
1 Geo. J. Legal Ethics 125 (1987)

The question is not, however, whether a "guilty" person has a right to a defense, but what kind of defense can be advanced on behalf of anyone, whether known to be guilty or not, or even if known to be innocent. Here what the defense attorney knows should be crucial to what he or she does.

It may help to explain this position by positing the defense function as consisting of two separate roles, usually intertwined but theoretically distinct. One enlists the attorney as the "monitor" of the state's case, whose task it is to assure that a conviction is based on an adequate amount of competent and admissible evidence. The lawyer as monitor is a kind of quality inspector, with no responsibility for developing a different product, if you will, to "sell" to the jury. The other attorney role involves the attorney as the client's "advocate," whose task is to present that different product, by undermining the state's version of the facts or presenting a competing version sufficient at least to establish a reasonable doubt about the defendant's guilt. The monitor's role is to assure that the state has the facts to support a conviction. The advocate attempts to demonstrate that the state's evidence is not fact at all. Where, as in most cases, the facts are in doubt, or where the state's case is believed or known to be based upon mistaken perceptions or lies, the defense attorney quite properly plays both roles. Having monitored the state's case and found it factually and legally sound, however, should he

---

[*] Subin's focus was criminal defense, but his argument would apply in civil cases, too.

or she be permitted to act as advocate and attempt to undermine it? I submit that the answer to that is no, and that the defendant's rights in cases of this kind extend only as far as the monitoring role takes the attorney. The right in question, to have the state prove guilt beyond a reasonable doubt, can be vindicated if the attorney is limited to good faith challenges to the state's case; to persuading the jury that there are legitimate reasons to doubt the state's evidence. It may on occasion be more effective for the attorney to use his or her imagination to create doubts; but surely there cannot be a right to gain an acquittal whenever the imagination of one's attorney is good enough to produce one. . . .

I propose a system in which the defense attorney would operate not with the right to assert defenses known to be untrue, but under the following rule:

> It shall be improper for an attorney who knows beyond a reasonable doubt the truth of a fact established in the state's case to attempt to refute that fact through the introduction of evidence, impeachment of evidence, or argument.

In the face of this rule, the attorney who knew there were no facts to contest would be limited to the "monitoring" role. Assuming that a defendant . . . wanted to assert his right to contest the evidence against him, the attorney would work to assure that all of the elements of the crime were proven beyond a reasonable doubt, on the basis of competent and admissible evidence. This would include enforcing the defendant's rights to have privileged or illegally obtained evidence excluded: The goal sought here is not the elimination of all rules that result in the suppression of truth, but only those not supported by sound policy. It would also be appropriate for the attorney to argue to the jury that the available evidence is not sufficient to sustain the burden of proof. It would not, however, be proper for the attorney to use any of the presently available devices to refute testimony known to be truthful. I wish to make clear, however, that this rule would not prevent the attorney from challenging *inaccurate* testimony, even though the attorney knew that the defendant was guilty. Again, the truth-seeking goal is not applicable when a valid policy reason exists for ignoring it. Forcing the state to prove its case is such a reason.

John Mitchell
REASONABLE DOUBTS ARE WHERE YOU FIND THEM: A RESPONSE TO PROFESSOR SUBIN'S POSITION ON THE CRIMINAL LAWYER'S "DIFFERENT MISSION"
1 Geo. J. Legal Ethics 339 (1987)

[I]magine I am defending a young woman accused of shoplifting a star one places on top of Christmas trees. I interview the store manager and find that he stopped my client when he saw her walk straight through the store, star in hand, and out the door. When he stopped her and asked why she had taken the star without paying, she made no reply and burst into tears. He was then about to take her inside to the security office when an employee called out, "There's a fire!" The manager rushed inside and dealt with a small blaze in the camera section. Five minutes later he came out to find my client sitting where he left her. He then took her back to the security room and asked if she would be willing to empty her pockets so that he could see if she had taken anything else. Without a word, she complied. She had a few items not belonging to the store and a ten-dollar bill. The star was priced at $1.79.

In an interview with my client, she admitted trying to steal the star: "It was so pretty, and would have looked so nice on the tree. I would have bought it, but I also wanted to make a special Christmas dinner for Mama and didn't have enough money to do both. I've been saving for that dinner and I know it will make her so happy. But that star. . . . I could just see the look in Mama's eyes if she saw that lovely thing on our tree."

At trial, the manager tells the same story he told me, except he *leaves out* the part about her waiting during the fire and having a ten-dollar bill. If I bring out these two facts on cross-examination and argue for an acquittal based upon my client "accidentally" walking out of the store with the star, surely Professor Subin will accuse me of raising a "false defense." I have brought out testimony, not itself false, to accredit a false theory and have argued to the jury based on this act. But I am not really arguing a false theory in Professor Subin's sense.

My defense is not that the defendant accidentally walked out, but rather that the prosecution cannot prove the element of intent to permanently deprive beyond a reasonable doubt. Through this theory, I am raising "doubt" in the prosecution's case, and therefore questioning the legitimacy of the government's lawsuit for control over the defendant. In my effort to carry out this legal theory, I will *not assert* that facts known by me to be true are false or those known to be false are true. As a defense attorney, I do not have to prove what *in fact* happened. That is an advantage in the process I would not willingly give up. Under our constitutional system, I do not need to try to convince the factfinder about the truth of any factual propositions. I need only try to convince the factfinder that the prosecution has not met its burden. Again, I will not argue that particular facts are true or false. Thus, in this case I will not claim that my client walked out of the store with innocent intent. . . .

Is this a "false defense" for Professor Subin? Admittedly, I am trying to raise a doubt by persuading the jury to appreciate "possibilities" other than my client's guilt. Perhaps Professor Subin would say it is "false" because I know the possibilities are untrue. But if that is so, Professor Subin will have taken a leap from defining "false defense" as the assertion that true things are false and false things are true, for I am doing neither of those things here. The fact that one cannot know how Subin will reach this "pure" reasonable doubt case only reinforces my initial statement that Professor Subin's categories are imprecise.

Another perspective from which to look at the function of a defense attorney involves understanding that function in the context of the nature of evidence at trial. Professor Subin speaks of facts and the impropriety of try-ing to make "true facts" look false and "false facts" look true. But in a trial there are no such things as facts. There is only information, lack of infor-mation, and chains of inferences therefrom. In the courtroom there will be no crime, no store, no young girl with a star in her hand. All there will be is a collection of witnesses who are strangers to the jury, giving information which may include physical evidence and documents. For example, most people would acknowledge the existence of eyewitness identifications; how-ever, in an evidentiary sense they do not exist. Rather, a particular person with particular perceptual abilities and motives and biases will recount an observation made under particular circumstances and will utter particular words on the witness stand (e.g., "That's the man"). From this mass of infor-mation, the prosecution will argue, in story form, in favor of the inference that the defendant is their man (e.g., "The victim was on her way home, when . . ."). The defense will not then argue that the defendant is the wrong man in a *factual sense,* but instead will attack the persuasiveness of the crimi-nal inference and resulting story (e.g., "The sun was in the witness' eyes; she was on drugs").

In our shoplifting example, the prosecution will elicit that the defendant burst into tears when stopped by the manager. From this information will run a chain of inferences: defendant burst into tears; people without a guilty conscience would explain their innocence, not cry; defendant has a guilty conscience; her guilty conscience is likely motivated by having committed a theft. Conversely, if the defense brings out that the manager was shaking a lead pipe in his hand when he stopped the defendant, defense counsel is *not asserting* that defendant did not have a guilty conscience when stopped. Counsel is merely *weakening* the persuasiveness of the prosecution's infer-ence by raising the "possibility" that she was crying not from guilt, but from fear. By raising such "possibilities," the defense is making arguments against the ability of the prosecution's inferences to meet their burden of "beyond a reasonable doubt." The defense is not arguing what are true or false facts (i.e., that the tears were from fear as opposed to guilt). Whatever Professor Subin cares to call it, this commentary on the prosecution's case, complete with raising possibilities which weaken the persuasiveness of central infer-ences in that case, is in no ethical sense a "false case." "False case" is plainly a misnomer. In a system where factual guilt is not at issue, Professor Subin's "falsehoods" are, in fact, "reasonable doubts."

Harry Subin
IS THIS LIE NECESSARY? FURTHER REFLECTIONS ON THE RIGHT TO PRESENT A FALSE DEFENSE
1 Geo. J. Legal Ethics 689 (1988)

[Subin notes Mitchell's statement that he will not "claim that my cli-ent walked out of the store with innocent intent (a fact which I know is false)," but will instead make what Mitchell calls a "pure" reasonable doubt argument.]

I applaud this apparent concession that presenting a false defense might be ethically wrong. (Why else would Mitchell go to the trouble of making the argument?) I believe, moreover, that if defense attorneys were required to give this kind of closing argument in "reasonable doubt" cases, it would help to reconcile the goals of assuring a truthful verdict and putting the state to its proof. Mitchell's presentation is, however, flawed in two respects. In the first place, the closing argument which he offers, with its intimations that the defense theory is not dependent upon the facts, is much more forthright than those which most attorneys would give. . . .

Moreover, even if Mitchell's sanitized closing was given, it still is designed to persuade the jury of the existence of facts he knows not to be true: here, that the woman in fact left the store accidentally (i.e., "maybe she did (leave accidentally). None of us was there."). That is not a lie, but it certainly creates a false impression, which amounts to the same thing.

Consider another example of "not arguing what are true or false facts" which Mitchell draws from his hypothetical: the woman bursts into tears after being caught stealing the ornament. The lawyer knows that she did so as a result of her guilty conscience. The store manager, however, was shaking a lead pipe in his hand when he stopped the woman. Mitchell says that if he brings out that fact, he is not "asserting" that the defendant did not have a guilty conscience; he is merely "weakening the persuasiveness of the prosecutor's inferences." It is perfectly clear, however, that he is attempting to do this by suggesting to the jury that this woman was in fact frightened by this lead pipe. Mitchell would, moreover, make this argument even if his client swore to him that she never even *saw* the lead pipe.

Questions

1. Let's ask again: Who wins this debate? Mitchell, you say? Then how do you answer Subin's argument that it is "utterly arbitrary" to draw the line at perjurious testimony while permitting a "false case"? If the latter is acceptable, why not the former? If the former is unacceptable, why do we permit the latter? False is false in the search for truth. Can you state an intellectually credible defense for the different treatment?

2. Mitchell says that his "defense is not that the defendant accidentally walked out, but rather that the prosecution cannot prove the element of intent to permanently deprive beyond a reasonable doubt." Does Mitchell concede too much? Using Mitchell's hypothetical, could the defense lawyer ask the jury to find *as a fact* that his client did not knowingly take the ornament? That *in fact* the defendant's tears were caused by the lead pipe? Could he make these arguments even though he knew both were false? True, the defense lawyer does not have the burden to prove these facts, but it would likely be more effective to argue

innocence in fact, not merely the state's failure to prove guilt. We can ask the same questions about "I Hang a Key on a Nail." Could Kuzak argue that someone else was driving the car, not merely that there's a reasonable doubt about it? Defense lawyers would not, of course, state their own belief, which is forbidden. They would frame the summation by identifying inferences (with phrases like "I submit" or "I ask you to find") that support their argument.

3. Do any of your answers change if the lawyer arguing for the false inference is a prosecutor? A government lawyer in a civil case? United States v. Reyes, 577 F.3d 1069 (9th Cir. 2009):

> In representing the United States, a federal prosecutor has a special duty not to impede the truth. The United States Department of Justice's Mission Statement describes the government's duty as one "to ensure fair and impartial administration of justice for all Americans."
>
> There is good reason for such a high standard. A "prosecutor's opinion carries with it the imprimatur of the Government and may induce the jury to trust the Government's judgment rather than its own view of the evidence." For this reason, it is improper for the government to present to the jury statements or inferences it knows to be false or has very strong reason to doubt.

4. If prosecutors have less freedom to argue reasonable but false inferences in summation because of what they know is true, aren't they at a serious disadvantage? Jurors are unlikely to realize that prosecutors have greater duties of candor than other lawyers or what those duties are. (Did you know the differences before law school?) How can we tolerate juror ignorance? Why not explain these differences in the jury instructions?

5. The unnamed prosecutor in Fortune v. State, 837 S.E.2d 37 (S.C. 2019), surely felt disadvantaged by the differences between the rules governing his behavior and those that apply to defense counsel.

> [I]n his closing argument to the jury in Oscar Fortune's murder trial, [the prosecutor] claimed, "My job is to present the truth," and said, "if you look in the . . . Code of Laws . . . [, I] have to say what the truth is." "On the other hand," the prosecutor told the jury, "the defense attorneys' jobs are to manipulate the truth. Their job is to shroud the truth. Their job is [to] confuse jurors. Their job is to do whatever they have to—without regard for the truth." The prosecutor explained that if he—the prosecutor—believes "somebody else did the crime," then he must "dismiss it." "And [if] I know the person has done something that I think the facts show they're guilty of, then I can't [dismiss] it. I have to go forward with it."

Putting aside the hyperbole, there's a grain of truth to these comments, isn't there? But juries are encouraged (or at least allowed) to believe that all lawyers play by the same rules when they don't. Or at least juries are not told otherwise. The South Carolina Supreme Court called these comments "blatantly improper." It wrote that "the prosecutor's improper remarks violated the defendant's rights under the Due Process Clause. We reverse the denial of post-conviction relief, and remand to the court of general sessions for a new trial."

6. Whenever we discuss the Subin-Mitchell debate in class, Subin gets creamed, to put it mildly. (But it's not unanimous.) I do my best to defend him. Doesn't he have a point somewhere in there? I suspect that Subin's views would fare better among the public. But not among lawyers.

7. Let me make it a little harder for Mitchell (and maybe for you). Mitchell's argument is based on his claim that the defense lawyer is merely exposing a weakness in the state's proof: Was the conduct intentional or accidental? This argument depends on the fact that the state has the burden to prove mental state and all elements of the charge. The defendant has no burden. But what if the defense lawyer is seeking to establish the truth of facts that provide an affirmative defense, say self-defense, where the defendant does have the burden in some jurisdictions? Or what about a lawyer who must prove the elements of a claim or defense in a civil case? Does Mitchell's argument then run into trouble? The lawyer would be introducing true evidence (or evidence she does not know is false) and from it asking the jury to infer as true a fact she must prove but knows is false. Mitchell's reasonable doubt argument won't work there. Consider the next problem.

"Maxwell's Silver-Handled .38"

Calvin is charged with shooting Maxwell. Next to Maxwell's body is a silver-handled .38. Calvin admitted to Otto, his lawyer, that he shot Maxwell because Maxwell was encroaching on his drug territory. Calvin was unaware that Maxwell was carrying a gun. Calvin was also unaware that the day before he shot Maxwell, Maxwell told Porky and Juvie that he was going to "snuff" Calvin because Calvin was interfering with Maxwell's drug business. And Maxwell showed Porky and Juvie his silver-handled .38 to make it clear he had the means to do it. But Calvin shot Maxwell before Maxwell ever had a chance to carry out his threat. Only after Calvin shot him did Maxwell reach for his gun, but he collapsed and died before he could return fire, which is how the .38 wound up next to his body.

In the jurisdiction, self-defense is an affirmative defense, which means Calvin must prove by a preponderance of the evidence that he had a reasonable basis to believe that he was at risk of death or serious bodily harm. Otto wants to argue that Calvin shot Maxwell to defend himself against Maxwell's imminent use of deadly force. Can Otto call Porky and Juvie to testify to what Maxwell told them a day earlier and identify the gun Maxwell showed them? Can he then argue that the jury should find as a fact that Maxwell was the initial aggressor, thereby establishing self-defense? Calvin can't testify that Maxwell was the initial aggressor because that's not true. Besides, if Calvin testifies, the jury will learn about his felony convictions.

If your answer is that Otto can do this because criminal cases are somehow "different"—but are they different?—would your answer change if a lawyer wanted to use the same strategy for a tort plaintiff or defendant—that is, ask the jury to infer the truth of a fact he knew to be false and on which he has the burden of proof?

Phantom Profits

MJB Pleasure Craft, based in Miami, makes and sells yachts. It has a contract to deliver five yachts to Oceana Inc., a company in Naples, Italy that leases yachts for group travel on the Amalfi coast. The deal will net MJB $5 million in profits. MJB contracted to buy engines for the yachts from Mechano Limited. Mechano fails to deliver on time so MJB cannot fulfill its contract with Oceana. It sues Mechano for lost profits. MJB's lawyer is Miki Saito. While the case is headed for trial, Saito learns from a friend in finance that Oceana is in financial distress and would not have had the cash to pay for the yachts had MJB been able to deliver them. This information is not public. MJB has the burden of proving Mechano's breach and MJB's lost profits.

Saito wants to introduce (a) MJB's contract with Mechano, (b) proof of MJB's costs to make and deliver the yachts, and (c) MJB's contract with Oceana. She will then ask the jury to infer lost profits of $5 million (what Oceana agreed to pay less MJB's costs). In reality, MJB would not have reaped those profits because the buyer, Oceana, could not have paid. Saito asks you, "Can I do this? All my evidence is true but the inference is not."

5. Spoliation

We've seen some strategies a lawyer may properly employ to encourage a jury or judge to find that a fact, which she knows is false, is true. Here's one that she cannot use.

Spoliation (also called fraudulent concealment) describes the alteration, concealment, or destruction of evidence that a litigant has a legal obligation to disclose or preserve because of its possible relevance to the resolution of a pending or impending case. Courts have a range of sanctions if spoliation is discovered while the case remains pending. See, e.g., Gentex Corp. v. Sutter, 827 F. Supp. 2d 384 (M.D. Pa. 2011), where the court said that "[p]otential sanctions for spoliation include: dismissal of a claim or granting judgment in favor of a prejudiced party; suppression of evidence; an adverse inference, referred to as the spoliation inference;* fines; and attorneys' fees and costs." Destruction or alteration of evidence may also be the crime of obstruction of justice. See chapter 8A.

Imagine, though, that it is only after the case is over that a civil litigant concludes that her opponent, aided by counsel, had destroyed evidence that could possibly have helped her. Can she now bring a new lawsuit against the former opponent and its law firm claiming that absent the spoliation, she would have won rather than lost, or won more or lost less, or reached a better settlement? The Third Circuit has said she can. Williams v. BASF Catalysts LLC, 765 F.3d 306 (3d Cir. 2014).

Williams is a story in four acts and an epilogue. In Act One, a plaintiff named David Westfall sued BASF's predecessor ("BASF") in 1979 claiming that its talc contained asbestos that caused a relative's death. Westfall apparently had the proof because BASF settled with a confidentiality agreement, meaning Westfall could not disclose what he knew. (The use of such agreements to hide dangers in consumer products still for sale raises profound moral questions, which we consider in chapter 10.)

In Act Two, many other plaintiffs later sued individually for the same harm, but unlike Westfall, they lacked the proof and either settled for small sums or abandoned their cases.

In Act Three, pretrial discovery in another case fortuitously revealed that BASF may have destroyed evidence between Acts One and Two to avoid a repeat of the Westfall case.

In Act Four, a putative class of plaintiffs from Act Two, relying on the information produced in Act Three, sued BASF and its law firm, Cahill Gordon, alleging both fraud and spoliation (or fraudulent concealment) in connection with the Act Two cases. Among other things, the plaintiffs alleged:

> As early as 1979, BASF faced actual or threatened litigation over asbestos injuries caused by its products. BASF, and its lawyers at Cahill, anticipated additional lawsuits in the future. BASF possessed evidence that its talc products contained asbestos, including assays, lab notes, and testimony. . . . [R]ather than maintain the evidence, BASF and Cahill concealed or destroyed it. Taken together, these facts, if proven, establish that BASF and Cahill intentionally destroyed or withheld material evidence that they were duty-bound to disclose and that their adversaries could not otherwise access.

The court said these facts stated a claim under New Jersey law. It defined spoliation as follows:

> (1) The defendant had a legal obligation to disclose evidence in connection with an existing or pending litigation; (2) the evidence was material to the litigation; (3) the plaintiff could not reasonably have obtained access to the

---

* The judge calls the jury's attention to the availability of an inference that the evidence would have been harmful to the party that failed to produce it. —ED.

evidence from another source; (4) the defendant intentionally withheld, altered, or destroyed the evidence with purpose to disrupt the litigation; and (5) the plaintiff was damaged in the underlying action by having to rely on an evidential record that did not contain the evidence defendant concealed.*

Important for lawyers is the court's holding that the complaint stated a claim against the law firm, not only its client. The lesson to draw is not that lawyers must refrain from spoliation, but that prudence requires that they monitor a client's conduct—and for an entity, the conduct of constituents. Even if a lawyer can claim ignorance, no one will relish a lawsuit in which the defense will be "I didn't know." And a jury, of course, may find that the lawyer did know or consciously looked the other way.

The Epilogue: In July 2020, Cahill and BNSF agreed to pay $72.5 million, exclusive of legal fees and costs, to settle the case. The report of the settlement did not identify the amount each would contribute.

E. HARDBALL AND INCIVILITY

> "To opposing parties and their counsel, I pledge fairness, integrity, and civility, not only in court, but also in all written and oral communications; I will abstain from all offensive personality and advance no fact prejudicial to the honor or reputation of a party or witness, unless required by the justice of the cause with which I am charged. . . ."
> —From the Oath of Admission to the Florida Bar

> "As officers of the court with responsibilities to the administration of justice, attorneys have an obligation to be professional with clients, other parties and counsel, the courts and the public. This obligation includes civility, professional integrity, personal dignity, candor, diligence, respect, courtesy, and cooperation, all of which are essential to the fair administration of justice and conflict resolution."
> —From the California Attorney Guidelines of Civility and Professionalism

> A DeKalb County State Court judge has slapped Sutherland, Asbill & Brennan with more than $175,000 in sanctions after finding its attorney tried to "litigate [the] plaintiff to death" in a contract dispute.
> —Daily Report, Aug. 22, 2014

"Hardball," also known as "Rambo tactics," in litigation and elsewhere is seen to betoken a decline in professionalism. The opposite of "hardball," apparently, is not "softball" or "no ball," but "civility." Hardball, then, might be defined as incivility, or perhaps extreme incivility. Committees and commissions nationwide have called for a "return" to civility, the assumption

---

* These remedies may be available even if the matter is not pending but only foreseeable.—ED.

being that it was once prevalent. Lawyers can be disciplined for lack of civil-ity. In re White, 707 S.E.2d 411 (S.C. 2011) (violation of Rules 4.4(a) and 8.4(e) — equivalent to Model Rule 8.4(d) — where in a letter lawyer referred to Town Manager as having "no brains," appearing to have no "soul," and as "insane" and "pigheaded") (suspension ordered).

The *Mullaney* opinion below imposes monetary sanctions for gender-biased comments at a deposition. Racially biased behavior has also led to discipline. See In re Thomsen, 837 N.E.2d 1011 (Ind. 2005) (discipline of lawyer for husband in divorce and custody case who repeatedly referred to the man living with the wife as "the black guy" or "the black man" where race was irrelevant to the issues before the court); Thomas v. Tenneco Packaging Co., 293 F.3d 1306 (11th Cir. 2002) (lawyer censured for filing documents "strewn with generalizations and conclusory comments that paint opposing counsel as a racist bigot and thus impugn his character").

Behavior need not be sexist or racist to invite judicial criticism. In Para-mount Communications v. QVC Network, 637 A.2d 34 (Del. 1994), the court chastised famed Texas lawyer Joe Jamail for the manner in which he defended a deposition, held in Texas but incident to a Delaware court contest for con-trol of Paramount. One example of Jamail's deposition statements: "Don't 'Joe' me, asshole. You can ask some questions, but get off of that. I'm tired of you. You could gag a maggot off a meat wagon." (The meaning of the last comment has always escaped me. It must be a Texas thing.[*]) Jamail was not a member of the Delaware bar, so the court invited him to come to Delaware and explain his conduct. Jamail responded: "I'd rather have a nose on my ass than go to Delaware for any reason." Tex. Law., Feb. 14, 1994, at 11. If Jamail appears rather independent, recall that he was the lawyer who won a $10 billion judgment against Texaco for his client Pennzoil and settled for $3 billion. Jamail was representing Pennzoil for a contingent fee.

Incivility can be toward the court as well as counsel. In my "What Got Into Them?" file is Taboada v. Daly Seven, Inc., 636 S.E.2d 889 (Va. 2006). After losing an appeal, lawyer Barnhill's petition to rehear "described this Court's opinion as 'irrational and discriminatory' and 'irrational at its core.' [He wrote that] 'George Orwell's fertile imagination could not supply a clearer distortion of the plain meaning of language to reach such an absurd result.'" (He didn't say "Kafkaesque" or invoke Kafka, but others do.) For reasons that escape me, Barnhill included the following line: "'[I]f you attack the King, kill the King; otherwise, the King will kill

---

[*] A former student, after reading this sentence in an earlier edition, sought to educate me:

> Being from Texas, I thought I might offer this explanation: I believe Mr. Jamail is saying that opposing counsel makes him sick and/or is generally sickening. That is to say that opposing counsel would ruin the appetite of even a maggot on a wagon full of meat. One might say the same thing of a year-old, rotting cucumber found in a dark corner of one's refrigerator. A common, shorter version of this idiom is that something would "gag a maggot."

you.'" Obviously, Barnhill was very angry. He forgot Ambrose Bierce's advice: "Speak when you are angry and you will make the best speech you will ever regret." When the court told Barnhill to explain why he should not be sanctioned, he sensibly hired a lawyer and expressed "his apology and sincere regret." The episode was aberrational. He would not file any more briefs until another lawyer reviewed them. The court said the conduct was "very serious" and suspended Barnhill's right to practice before it for one year.

I could fill quite a few of this book's pages with examples of male lawyers behaving badly toward female lawyers, witnesses, opposing clients, judges, and even their own clients. Why does this happen? Possibilities include (a) it's strategic — the aggressors believe that it will rattle the women; (b) it's instinctive — this is just the way these men treat women, nothing personal; (c) it's generational — the offenders are often older lawyers who are threatened by women professionals; (d) it's a product of confusion — the offenders don't know how to talk to women as equals; or (e) something else. (We return to this conduct as a basis for discipline in chapter 13D5f.) How do you explain Allan Harris's comments in the next case?

MULLANEY v. AUDE
126 Md. App. 639, 730 A.2d 759 (Ct. Spec. App. 1999)

ADKINS, JUDGE.

This case involves the adversarial use of gender bias in the discovery process. James L. Mullaney, Esq. and [Alan] E. Harris, Esq., appellants, appeal from the imposition . . . of attorneys' fees incurred in obtaining a protective order against them. . . .

FACTS AND PROCEDURAL BACKGROUND

Betty Sue Aude, appellee, brought a tort action for fraud, negligence, intentional infliction of emotional distress, and battery against Mr. Mullaney, alleging that he infected her with genital herpes. Susan R. Green, Esq. and Gary S. Bernstein, Esq., represented Ms. Aude. Mr. Mullaney was represented by Mr. Harris and Benjamin Lipsitz, Esq. After a trial, the jury found that Mr. Mullaney negligently infected Ms. Aude with genital herpes, but that Ms. Aude was contributorily negligent. Accordingly, judgment was entered in favor of Mr. Mullaney on December 10, 1996.

APPELLANTS' DEPOSITION CONDUCT

During the course of pre-trial discovery, Ms. Aude was deposed. At the deposition, she was asked about a document that she failed to bring with her. As Ms. Aude was leaving the room to retrieve that document, Mr. Harris remarked that she was going to meet "another boyfriend" at the car. Ms. Green and Mr. Bernstein quickly told Mr. Harris that his comment was in poor taste and asked him to refrain from making further derogatory comments. The following ensued:

> *Mr. Mullaney:* It's going to be a fun trial.
>
> *Mr. Harris:* It must have been in poor taste if Miss Green says it was in poor taste. It must have really been in poor taste.
>
> *Ms. Green:* You got a problem with me?
>
> *Mr. Harris:* No, I don't have any problem with you, babe.
>
> *Ms. Green:* Babe? You called me babe? What generation are you from?
>
> *Mr. Harris:* At least I didn't call you a bimbo.
>
> *Mr. Lipsitz:* Cut it out.
>
> *Ms. Green:* The committee will enjoy hearing about that.
>
> *Mr. Bernstein:* Alan, you ought to stay out of the gutter. . . .

Appellants next contend that Mr. Harris's comments to Ms. Green at Ms. Aude's deposition were not sexist behavior or disruptive to the discovery process. We unequivocally reject this assertion, and with this decision hope to make it crystal clear how this Court views the exhibition of gender bias by lawyers in the litigation process.

A.

STRATEGIC NAME CALLING AND BIAS

The absence of civility and respect exhibited by lawyers towards one another has been for years the subject of significant concern for bar and bench leaders. In the words of Judge Paul L. Friedman of the United States District Court for the District of Columbia:

> Although the "modern age" of the legal profession has witnessed progress in opening its doors wider to women and minorities and others who were previously excluded, this age has also opened its doors to the "Rambo litigator" which has spawned a generation of lawyers, too many of whom think they are more effective when they are more abrasive. . . .

Some attorneys engage in actively undermining another attorney's case by using gender. . . .

Mr. Harris's behavior with respect to Ms. Aude and her counsel at the deposition was a crass attempt to gain an unfair advantage through the use of demeaning language, a blatant example of "sexual [deposition] tactics." With respect to the effect on the profession, we think Judge Waldron stated it well when he said: "These actions . . . have no place in our system of justice and when attorneys engage in such actions they do not merely reflect on their own lack of professionalism but they disgrace the entire legal profession and the system of justice that provides a stage for such oppressive actors."

Appellants refused to acknowledge, in their brief or at oral argument, that it was derogatory for Mr. Harris to address Ms. Green as "babe," during a deposition. They unblushingly ask this Court to construe Mr. Harris's use of the term "babe" as a term of endearment because it is "a nickname for 'Babe' Ruth, a towering athletic figure and an American folk hero, and 'Babe' Didrickson, an outstanding and multi-talented female athlete. . . ." They contend that the term "indicates approval, [and] is a sign of approbation." Thus, they say, Mr. Harris's "calling someone 'babe' would to him not in any way be a derogatory act, but would at least imply a commendatory opinion of the person so addressed." We find this argument singularly unpersuasive. If Ms. Green, when up to bat at the annual Bar Association softball tournament, hit a home run, and in that context Mr. Harris chose to call her "Babe," this argument *might* be plausible. In the context of this case, however, we can only characterize the argument as disingenuous.

Lest there be any doubt about Mr. Harris's intended meaning when he addressed Ms. Green as "babe," we need look no further than the transcript of the deposition. When Ms. Green asked him to refrain from the use of that term, Mr. Harris responded: "At least I didn't call you a bimbo." To our knowledge, neither Babe Ruth nor Babe Didrickson was endearingly addressed as "bimbo." . . .

If Mr. Harris, by the use of such tactics, can evoke in Ms. Green any emotional response that puts her off-balance, makes her defensive, makes her feel inadequate, or just plain angry and distracted, he has succeeded with his strategy. In so doing, he likely has interfered with the discovery process. While strategy and tactics are part of litigation, and throwing your adversary off-balance may well be a legitimate tactic, it is not legitimate to do so by the use of gender-based insults.

Mr. Harris defends his action by including in the record copies of advertisements in which Ms. Green held herself out to be a "hardball" attorney. At oral argument, counsel suggested that if she advertises herself as "hardball," she should expect some "rough and tumble"[7] experiences during the course of litigation. This incident, he posits, was simply that. Mr. Harris and his counsel widely miss the mark with this argument. There is no doubt that with our adversarial system of justice, lawyers who choose to litigate must withstand pressure, adversity, and the strategic maneuvers of their opponent. Fortunately, however, we have long passed the era when bias relating to sex, race, religion, or other specified groups is considered acceptable as a litigation strategy. The Maryland Code of Judicial Conduct mandates that "[a] judge shall require lawyers in proceedings before the judge to refrain from manifesting, by words or conduct, bias or prejudice based upon race, sex, religion, national origin, disability, age, sexual orientation or socioeconomic status, against parties, witnesses, counsel or others."* . . .

7. The term "rough and tumble" is a paraphrase of the words used by counsel at argument.
* Today, the ABA's Code of Judicial Conduct is broader. See Rule 2.3(C) and (D). — ED.

We think that the trial court, in finding that Mr. Harris's conduct exhibited gender bias in a deposition, acted in a manner consistent with the directives of this Canon. . . .

The imposition of sanctions under these circumstances reinforces the commitment of the judicial system to impartiality.

Lawyers may respond to accusations of offensive behavior by citing their duty to "zealously represent" their clients. "You might not like my tactics," they may say, "I myself may be unhappy about them. But as a lawyer my duty to represent my client zealously left me no choice. Litigation is not a tea party." (Incivility is not confined to litigation but most often arises there.) Harris's behavior is toward the milder end of the offensiveness spectrum. I could have chosen instances where the sexist comments were egregious, of which there are many. But they would be too easy to dismiss as obvious. (An example is In re Jordan Schiff in chapter 13D5f.) The pedagogical value of *Mullaney* is that it shows a court's intolerance for what many lawyers might once have viewed (and some still view) as just good-natured banter. "Hey, why are you so sensitive?"

Sex can be used tactically in other ways than through epithets like "babe" and "bimbo." Consider the following events.

She Had to Explain "Slut Shaming"

This story of how the Boies Schiller law firm litigated against novelist Emma Cline (*The Girls*) draws on two pieces of journalism, both published on December 1, 2017. Sheelah Kolhatkar, "How the Lawyer David Boies Turned a Young Novelist's Sexual Past Against Her," published digitally by the New Yorker; and Alexandra Alter, "Sex, Plagiarism and Spyware. This Is Not Your Average Copyright Complaint," which appeared on page one of the New York Times. Why was this story so prominent? There are three reasons. First, David Boies has a leading role and he's a magnet for the press. Second, Cline's novel (her first) earned a $2 million advance, was a bestseller, and was optioned to the movies. Third, the events tell a #MeToo story. All that would have sufficed to make the story newsworthy, but Boies had the added misfortune of appearing unfavorably in #MeToo stories arising out of his work for Harvey Weinstein.

You decide if the Boies firm did nothing more than represent its client, albeit aggressively, or whether instead it violated Rule 4.4(a) and New York Rule 8.4(h), which provides: "A lawyer or law firm shall not engage in . . . conduct that adversely reflects on the lawyer's fitness as a lawyer."

Cline and Chaz Reetz-Laiolo started dating when she was 20 and he was 33. After they broke up, she sold him her used laptop. Big mistake.

Representing Reetz-Laiolo, the Boies firm relied on the laptop's contents to claim that Cline had stolen ideas from Reetz-Laiolo and had invaded his privacy by installing spyware on the laptop, which he also used when they were together. Cline responded that Reetz-Laiolo "had been emotionally and physically abusive toward her, that he had cheated on her, and that she had installed the spyware in order to monitor his behavior and protect herself, not to steal his writing." Reetz-Laiolo denied her allegations.

None of this need concern us. What does concern us is the draft complaint the Boies firm sent to Cline and which it threatened to file unless she settled. In the New Yorker, Kolhatkar tells us:

> Reading through the allegations, Cline was stunned to find a section titled "Cline's History of Manipulating Older Men," which purported to illustrate how Boies Schiller would easily discredit her arguments about her former boyfriend's treatment of her before a jury. . . . What followed were thirteen pages containing screenshots of explicit chat conversations with lovers, including one in which Cline had sent a naked photo of herself (the photo was blacked out in the letter) to a boyfriend, explicit banter with people she'd met online, and snippets of her most intimate diary entries. All of this material had been recorded by the spyware and remained on Cline's old laptop, which Reetz-Laiolo now had in his possession.
>
> A letter that Boies Schiller sent along with the draft complaint included even more graphic sexual details and screenshots pertaining to Cline's romantic relationships. Cline had "engaged in random sexual encounters with strangers she met on Craigslist"; "frequently participated in sexual chat groups in which she, inter alia, posted pornographic 'selfies'"; and "authored pornographic 'stories,'" the letter stated, including images showing exchanges and erotic writings in excruciating detail, all of which also came from Cline's old computer.

In the New Yorker article, the Boies firm did not cite a duty of zealous representation—not, that is, explicitly. It claimed that Cline's sexual history was relevant because she had herself raised the issue of sexual conduct in defending her use of spyware. A firm lawyer told the New Yorker that Cline's "lawyer tried to excuse the inexcusable by raising aspects of the parties' sexual history. Only then did we respond, *as lawyers must*, describing why her claimed defense was inconsistent with the relevant facts." (Emphasis added.) In other words, we had no choice but to inform her that the most intimate details of her sex life would be revealed if she did not settle.

Carrie Goldberg, Cline's lawyer, told the New Yorker: "I'm not going to speculate about their motives, but it was content that was completely inappropriate and ludicrous, just based on how sexually graphic it was, to put in a complaint. Legal complaints are public record, and, basically, they're saying, 'Hey, if you don't give us what our client wants, we're going to put this very personal information out into the open, and the whole world is going to know the inner workings of your sex life and your sexual history and every proclivity that you have.'"

Goldberg said she "explained the concept of 'slut-shaming' to David Boies, who, according to Goldberg, claimed to be unfamiliar with it."

After the Times and New Yorker stories appeared, the firm stripped the complaint of references to Cline's sexual history—"as a gesture of good faith," it explained. For more on the legal issues, see Cline v. Reetz-Laiolo, 329 F. Supp. 3d 1000 (N.D. Cal. 2018). In 2019, the parties stipulated to dismiss all claims with prejudice.

Here are the questions: Did lawyers at the Boies firm (or the firm itself in the case of New York Rule 1.8(h), which applies to both lawyers and law firms) act unethically? If a complaint were filed against lawyers and the firm itself, and the case came before you as a member of the disciplinary committee, what would you do? (We don't know of any complaint. There has been no public discipline.) Does it affect your analysis to know that, in an effort to settle a claim, lawyers routinely send a prospective defendant a draft complaint containing harmful information that will become public on filing? That can be beneficial. See, e.g., Sussman ex rel. Guilden v. Bank of Isr., 56 F.3d 450 (2d Cir. 1995) (construing Rule 11) ("It is hardly unusual for a would-be plaintiff to seek to resolve disputes without resorting to legal action; prelitigation letters airing grievances and threatening litigation if they are not resolved are commonplace, sometimes with salutary results, and do not suffice to show an improper purpose if nonfrivolous litigation is eventually commenced."). What else would you like to know?

A final word about "zealously." Canon 7 of the superseded Code of Professional Responsibility said: "A Lawyer Should Represent A Client Zealously Within The Bounds Of The Law." But the Rules themselves do not contain the word "zealously" or variations (Rule 1.3 cmt. [1] tells lawyers to "act . . . with zeal in advocacy upon the client's behalf."). The trend has been toward reducing the kind of behavior that the word "zealously" was routinely invoked to justify. Rule 4.4(a) (entitled "Respect for the Rights of Third Persons"), which has no Code equivalent, forbids a lawyer to "use means that have no *substantial* purpose other than to embarrass, delay, or burden a third person." (Emphasis added.) But a lawyer also has a duty to pursue the client's goals diligently. In an adversary system, that may entail conduct that others (even some lawyers) find offensive. I've heard lawyers compare themselves to "junkyard dogs." They mean it as a compliment.

F. MISSTATING FACTS, PRECEDENT, OR THE RECORD

Whatever tolerance courts may have when lawyers engage in the artful use of language with each other, expectations are higher when lawyers talk to judges. Justice Department lawyer Mikki Graves Walser learned that lesson the hard way. Her experience is especially instructive because although her omissions were relatively minor, the court was not inclined to accept fine distinctions.

The Court of International Trade had given Walser a deadline of May 5 to file a response to a summary judgment motion in a customs case. On May 4, not having started work on the response, she requested an extension. On May 10, the court denied the extension and ordered her to file "forthwith." What should she have done next? What would you do?

Take a minute.

What Walser did was wait until May 22 to file her response. The court struck it as untimely. The government moved for reconsideration. Its argument, which Walser wrote, claimed that the delay from May 10 to May 22 was "forthwith" as case law had construed that word. Walser cited or quoted several sources. For two of them, she omitted language from her quotations.

First, in the body of her memo, she wrote the following:

See City of New York v. McAllister Brothers, Inc., 278 F.2d 708 (1960) ("'Forthwith' means immediately, without delay, *or as soon as the object may be* accomplished by reasonable exertion." Emphasis added.)

She omitted the following additional sentence in the court's opinion:

The Supreme Court has said of the word that "in matters of practice and pleading it is usually construed, and sometimes defined by rule of court, as within twenty-four hours."

Next, in a footnote, Walser wrote:

While we did not review the Supreme Court's decision in Henderson v. United States, 517 U.S. 654, 680 (1996) in interpreting the meaning of "forthwith," it is noteworthy that in his dissenting opinion, Justice Thomas, with whom the Chief Justice and Justice O'Connor joined, citing Amella v. United States, 732 F.2d 711, 713 (C.A. 1984), stated that "although we have never undertaken to define 'forthwith' . . . , *it is clear that the term 'connotes action which is immediate, without delay, prompt, and with reasonable dispatch.'*"

The ellipsis replaced the words "as used in the SAA," a reference to actions under the Suits in Admiralty Act, which hers was not. Nor did Walser reveal that the emphasis in the footnote was hers, not the court's. Both opinions from which Walser quoted cited a 1900 Supreme Court case that supported the harmful language she omitted, but Walser did not cite it.

The lower court issued a Rule 11 reprimand in an unpublished opinion. The Federal Circuit affirmed.

> The effect of Walser's editing of this material and ignoring the [1900] Supreme Court decision that dealt with the issue—a decision that seriously weakened her argument—was to give the Court of International Trade a misleading impression of the state of the law on the point. She eliminated material that indicated that her delay in filing the motion for reconsideration had not met the court's requirement that she file "forthwith," and presented the remaining material in a way that overstated the basis for her claim that a "forthwith" filing requirement meant she could take whatever time would be reasonable in the circumstances. This distortion of the law was inconsistent with and violated the standards of Rule 11.

Precision Specialty Metals v. United States, 315 F.3d 1346 (Fed. Cir. 2003).

The First Circuit cited *Precision Metals* in upholding a sanction under Bankruptcy Rule 9011 (the counterpart to Rule 11 of the Federal Rules of Civil Procedure) against David Baker, "a very experienced bankruptcy practitioner" who "fashioned support for an otherwise unsupported position by materially mischaracterizing what [a] statute says, and by leaving out the most relevant, and to his argument, the most discrediting, portion of it." Baker was ordered to take a three-credit legal ethics class at an ABA-approved law school. In re Hoover, 827 F.3d 191 (1st Cir. 2016).

The Ninth Circuit ordered two prominent national law firms to explain themselves in Swinomish Indian Tribal Community v. BNSF Ry. Co., 2019 WL 3074050 (9th Cir. 2019). The underlying substantive law is complicated and, for our purposes, not important. Essentially, the question was whether the firms' client, BNSF, had a right of way across Swinomish land. The firms made certain questionable statements in an appeal to the circuit. Here are three of them. In each, the firms omitted text that weakened their argument and the court demanded explanations. These excerpts are taken directly from the order (emphasis in original).

1. On page 15, Appellant's Opening Brief states:

> The Easement provides that BNSF may run, **at a minimum**, "one eastern bound train, and one western bound train, (of twenty-five (25) cars or less)" across the rail line each day.

The text of the easement reads:

> Burlington Northern agrees that, unless otherwise agreed in writing, **only** one eastern bound train, and one western bound train, (of twenty-five (25) cars or less) shall cross the Reservation each day.

Please explain how the substitution, without comment, of "at a minimum" for "only" candidly represents the terms of the easement.

2. On page 28, Appellant's Opening Brief states:

> Consistent with the statutory text, "[e]very court that has examined [Section 10501(b)] has concluded that [its] preemptive effect . . . is

> broad and sweeping," **forbidding** "impinge[ment] on the [STB]'s juris-
> diction or a railroad's ability to conduct its rail operations." [Citing CSX
> Transportation]

The text of CSX Transportation reads:

> Every court that has examined the statutory language has concluded that
> the preemptive effect of section 10501(b) is broad and sweeping, **and
> that it blocks actions by states or localities** that would impinge on the
> Board's jurisdiction or a railroad's ability to conduct its rail operations.

Please explain how the omission of the qualifying language referring to
"actions by states or localities," without comment, candidly represents
the Order in CSX Transportation.

3. On pages 28–29, Appellant's Opening Brief states:

> This Court, too, has held that ICCTA squarely preempts **remedies** that
> "may reasonably be said to have the effect of managing or governing
> rail transportation." Ass'n of Am. Railroads v. S. Coast Air Quality Mgmt.
> Dist. . . .

The text of Association of American Railroads reads:

> As stated by our sister circuits, ICCTA "preempts **all 'state laws** that may
> reasonably be said to have the effect of managing or governing rail trans-
> portation, while permitting the continued application of laws having a
> more remote or incidental effect on rail transportation.'"

Please explain how the omission of the qualifying language referring
to "state laws," without comment, candidly represents the opinion in
Association of American Railroads.

Relevant here are several provisions of the Rules that forbid lawyers to
make false statements of fact or law. Rule 4.1(a) contains a prohibition
against making "a false statement of material fact or law to a third person."
Rule 8.4(c) forbids a lawyer to "engage in conduct involving dishonesty,
fraud, deceit or misrepresentation." Rule 3.3(a)(1) provides that a lawyer
"shall not knowingly make a false statement of fact or law to a tribunal."

United States v. Williams, 952 F.2d 418 (D.C. Cir. 1991), relied on Rule
3.3(a)(1) in issuing a public reprimand to a prosecutor for making five misstatements of material fact in the government's brief. The prosecutor was
either "irresponsibly careless [or] deliberately misleading." The prosecutor
had a duty to "assert facts only if, after a reasonably diligent inquiry, he
believes those facts to be true."

Mischaracterizing a cited case also violates Rule 3.3(a)(1). Chan v.
Wellington Mgmt. Co., 424 F. Supp. 3d 148 (D. Mass. 2019) ("The Court is
disturbed by the apparent lack of candor shown by counsel for Wellington
and Argyle in citing *Taylor* for the unqualified proposition that 'there is a
presumption against the application of Massachusetts statutes outside the
United States,' while omitting without comment the preceding words of the
Taylor Court that it was '[a]ssuming without deciding' the issue . . . . The Court

harbors serious concerns that these misleading descriptions . . . amount to 'a false statement of . . . law to a tribunal.'") (citing Rule 3.3(a)(1)).

G. THE OBLIGATION TO REVEAL ADVERSE LEGAL AUTHORITY

THUL v. ONEWEST BANK, FSB
2013 WL 212926 (N.D. Ill. 2013)

MATTHEW F. KENNELLY, DISTRICT JUDGE.

The Court entered an order directing defendants' attorneys to show cause why they should not be sanctioned in connection with their failure to bring adverse Seventh Circuit precedent to the Court's attention in their brief supporting their motion to dismiss plaintiffs' complaint. The attorneys are John Beisner and Jessica Miller of the Washington, D.C. office of Skadden, Arps, Meagher & Flom, and Andrew Fuchs of the Skadden firm's Chicago office. The attorneys filed a written response and also appeared in court yesterday, as directed. The Court made comments on the record and now enters this order to summarize its findings and resolve the issue of sanctions.

First of all, the Court vacates the order to show cause as to Mr. Fuchs. In the attorneys' written response, they stated that Mr. Fuchs "was neither the principal drafter of the briefs nor tasked with conducting research related to the briefs"; he relied on the other two attorneys concerning the legal content of the briefing; and he was not personally aware of the Seventh Circuit decision in question, Wigod v. Wells Fargo Bank, N.A., 673 F.3d 547 (7th Cir. 2012). Mr. Fuchs is an associate, and the other lawyers are senior to him. The Court accepts the attorneys' statement and vacates the show cause order as it relates to Mr. Fuchs.

In the written response, the other two attorneys, Mr. Beisner and Ms. Miller, took responsibility for filing the brief in question. They apologized for their failure to cite Wigod and explained why they did not do so. The attorneys also reported that in the interim, the parties had reached a settlement of the case (including a related state court case), to which the attorney's law firm will contribute "in order to personally redress plaintiffs' counsel for responding to the motion to dismiss."

The attorneys' written response indicated that Ms. Miller, the principal drafter of the brief, and Mr. Beisner, who took ultimate responsibility for filing the brief, were aware of Wigod and did not cite it because they considered it distinguishable. They reaffirmed this orally in court and repeated what the Court found to be a sincere apology to plaintiffs' counsel and to the Court.

The Court acknowledges counsel's contention that Wigod was distinguishable but respectfully disagrees. . . .

There is no appreciable difference between the argument that the Seventh Circuit rejected in Wigod and the argument that the attorneys for OneWest made here. Because Mr. Beisner and Ms. Miller were aware of *Wigod* and because it was "directly adverse to the position of the[ir] client," Ill. RPC 3.3(a)(2), they should have cited it. The fact that they cited, on the general contract-law issue involved, both older Seventh Circuit cases and non-binding precedent from trial courts, underscores the inappropriateness of their failure to cite *Wigod.*. . .

Enough said about that. The question now before the Court is what further action it should take with regard to Mr. Beisner and Ms. Miller's conduct. Determination of this issue turns on not just what counsel did that got them into this position in the first place, but what has happened since then. First of all, the Court's prior ruling, which like this one identified Mr. Beisner and Ms. Miller by name, is a matter of public record. That is of no small consequence to a professional whose reputation "is his or her bread and butter." Second, Mr. Beisner and Ms. Miller took full responsibility for their actions, apologized sincerely, and took Mr. Fuchs off the hook. Third, OneWest promptly settled the case; the attorneys' law firm has contributed financially to the settlement; and the settlement takes into account the additional expense plaintiffs' counsel incurred due to the filing of the motion to dismiss.

The Court fully understands the impact that a finding of misconduct can have upon an attorney even without the imposition of additional sanctions. This impact was brought home to the Court by counsel's demeanor when they spoke in the courtroom and when they listened to the oral admonition that the Court rendered. Given all the circumstances, the Court's issuance of the earlier decision and this one as well as the oral admonition amounts to a sufficient remedy. The Court trusts that Mr. Beisner and Ms. Miller will be more cautious in the future. The Court will impose no further sanction.

Rule 3.3(a)(2) is narrow. The precedent must be both controlling and "directly adverse." Controlling means *binding*. "Directly adverse" means not distinguishable or as lawyers like to say, "on all fours." The lawyers in *Thul* decided that *Wigod* could be distinguished. The court thought not. The rule has a third condition. Disclosure is required only if no other party has cited the authority. These conditions mean that the rule will rarely apply. But it does happen.

Self-Assessment Questions

1. One evening, you receive the following urgent question in an email from a colleague who is in the midst of a trial.

   "I'll try to present the issue concisely because the details are not so important. As you know, we represent one of six companies that are defendants in a large civil litigation currently on trial. Our client is company *ABC*. I'm also asking you the question here on behalf of the lawyer ('Jo') for company *DEF*, a co-defendant.

"Today, the CFO ('Selma') of another co-defendant testified to a fact ('fact *X*') that is quite helpful to all defendants. Jo and I happen to know that fact *X* is not true. We have no reason to believe that the lawyer for the co-defendant who called Selma, or Selma herself, knows this. Cross-examination of Selma did little to weaken her credibility. Of course, Jo and I prefer not to say anything about what we know and then rely on Selma's testimony in our summations.

"So you can see what I'm asking. Can we do that? This is time sensitive so please could you get back to me tomorrow?"

2. In 2004, Crawford was legally stopped and searched in New York City when he was discovered on the street late at night in violation of his parole conditions. As later described in court:

> The officers then began to search Crawford, and in his pocket they discovered a tin containing a small amount of marijuana. The officers placed Crawford under arrest for possessing marijuana and violating his curfew. At that point, one officer began to search a black gym bag that Crawford had with him. That search was interrupted, however, when Crawford began to flee and the searching officer dropped the bag to chase after him. The bag was picked up by another officer and was later searched when the officers arrived at the police precinct station. The search revealed a .45 caliber semi-automatic pistol and a box containing 15 rounds of ammunition.
>
> Crawford testified in the defense case. He stated that he was arrested for violating his curfew, but denied resisting arrest. He testified that at his arrest the officers searched his bag and his person and found nothing. He denied possessing a gun or marijuana. In closing arguments, his counsel emphasized that the gun was not found at the scene of the arrest, that no fingerprints were taken to match the gun to Crawford, and that no testimony was presented concerning a trace report for the gun.

The sole factual question for the jury was: Was the gun in the bag Crawford was carrying or did the police frame him? The government did do a "trace report" on the gun, which is meant to identify its chain of ownership, and it had given a copy of the report to defense counsel before trial. The report showed that the gun was last legally purchased in 1996, eight years before Crawford's arrest. The government said it would introduce the report but then did not do so because, it claimed, of an oversight. It may not have seemed all that important to the factual question either.

But the jury seemed to think otherwise. During the second day of deliberation, the jury asked: "Why wasn't the gun traced to the original owner?" The judge then allowed the government to reopen the case and call a witness who introduced the trace report and who also testified that the defense counsel had been given a copy. This testimony damaged the defense counsel's credibility with the jury because his summation had cited the absence of a trace report as a reason to question the prosecutor's proof. When the defense lawyer objected, the trial judge said: "You've left an erroneous impression with the jury. They picked up on it and I don't know why it can't be corrected. It's one thing to put the government to its burden of proof. It's another to play games here."

Crawford was convicted of being a felon in possession of a firearm and appealed. Was the defense lawyer's summation improper?

3. A student posed this problem in a class discussion of *Anatomy of a Murder.* Assume an undocumented immigrant is facing deportation. Assume that her chance to stay in the country is very good if her illegal entry occurred before 2011, but remote if she entered in 2011 or thereafter. Her lawyer has two options. He can ask her when she entered the country, without first revealing the effect of the year of entry on her chances. Or he can tell her that her ability to avoid deportation is much better if she entered before 2011 and then ask her when she entered the country. The student said that it is easier to defend Biegler on the facts of *Anatomy of a Murder* than it is to defend the second option. It is, isn't it? Is the second option permissible anyway? Analyze this problem and compare it to *Anatomy of a Murder.*

VIII

Special Issues in Criminal Prosecutions

A. REAL EVIDENCE

The Client's Loaded .45 (Part I)

A man walks into his lawyer's office, takes a loaded .45 from his pocket, and puts it on her desk. Visibly distressed, he says, "I shot Lenny," and points to the gun. "He's dead." Or maybe it happens this way: The man walks into the office and says, "I shot Lenny. He's dead. His body is near the abandoned mill covered with leaves. I tossed the gun in a trash bin near the Oak Street playground. It's loaded." Or this way: The man is arrested for homicide. He tells his wife the gun is under a floorboard in the shed behind their home. She brings it to his lawyer. It's loaded.* What may or must the lawyer in each instance do about the gun?

Lawyers and Real Evidence: An Introduction

What is a lawyer's responsibility for physical objects—weapons, stolen property, drugs, contraband—that come into her possession and are relevant to a pending or foreseeable court case? What if instead the item is an incriminating document or flash drive file? Sometimes the very possession of the object may itself be criminal—e.g., an unlicensed gun or stolen property—as well as probative of guilt. Other times, the object may be probative of guilt but not unlawful to possess, like a diary or surveillance pictures of a bank. These questions create serious dilemmas for lawyers. Answers may require us to reconcile as many as eight interests:

- The client's right to the loyalty and confidential advice of counsel.
- The attorney-client privilege.

---

* This problem and the introductory note are drawn from Stephen Gillers, Guns, Fruits, Drugs, and Documents: A Criminal Defense Lawyer's Responsibility for Real Evidence, 63 Stan. L. Rev. 813 (2011).

- The client's Fifth Amendment privilege against self-incrimination.
- The client's Sixth Amendment right to the effective assistance of counsel.
- The lawyer's need to avoid criminal prosecution and professional discipline.
- The state's interest in prosecuting crime.
- The right of the owner of stolen property to its return.
- Public safety.

Lawyers who represent clients in civil or criminal cases may come into possession of what the law of evidence calls "real evidence." Certainly, the most famous (and surely the most consequential) item of real evidence in U.S. history are Richard Nixon's White House tapes. These were secret recordings that Nixon made in the Oval Office. The tapes became an issue during the 1973-1974 investigations of the burglary of the Democratic National Headquarters in Washington's Watergate Hotel prior to the 1972 presidential election. In July 1973, White House aide Alex Butterfield revealed the existence of the tapes in response to a question from the Senate Watergate Committee chaired by Sam Ervin of North Carolina. In the next few days, before the Committee subpoenaed the tapes, Nixon and his advisers discussed whether Nixon could lawfully destroy them. That discussion will concern us presently. Imagine being among the lawyers asked to give this advice.

As it happened, the tapes were not destroyed, and eventually a federal district court in Washington, D.C., subpoenaed them upon motion of a special prosecutor investigating the burglary. Nixon challenged the subpoena but the Supreme Court upheld it in United States v. Nixon, 418 U.S. 683 (1974). Transcripts of the tapes were released on August 5, 1974. The president announced his resignation August 8, effective August 9, 1974. Nixon had recorded his own criminal conduct. He was never prosecuted, although others were, because Gerald Ford, his successor, pardoned him.

Doctrinally, real evidence questions occupy at least four untidy and interconnected categories.

- *First* are the *ethical* obligations of a lawyer when dealing with real evidence. What is she obligated to do and not do? What is permitted?
- *Second* are obligations under the *criminal law*, especially obstruction of justice or "tampering" statutes (by whatever name). As we will see, at the federal level, the reach of these laws is quite broad and was broadened further by the Sarbanes-Oxley legislation passed in the wake of the U.S. corporate scandals of the 1990s and thereafter.
- *Third* is the interplay between real evidence and the attorney-client *privilege*. To what extent can lawyers legitimately claim that their knowledge of the existence of an item of real evidence or the identity of its source or location — even the evidence itself — is privileged?
- *Fourth* is spoliation of evidence, a cousin of obstruction of justice, which occurs when litigants or lawyers destroy, conceal, or alter evidence that

is (or would have been) helpful to the opponent. Spoliation, discussed in chapter 7D5, can lead to judicial sanctions, even dismissal of a claim or defense, and also to the civil liability of both clients and lawyers.

These categories are untidy because their boundaries overlap—a situation can implicate one or more of them—and because court opinions give unclear or inconsistent answers. The rules governing real evidence are the same for criminal and civil matters but (except for spoliation) usually arise in criminal cases.

1. Real Evidence and Legal Ethics

The facts and ruling in In re Ryder, decided more than 50 years ago, continue to offer an ideal introduction to the ethical duties of lawyers who come into (or take) possession of real evidence. As explained in the note following the case, the issues aren't as straightforward as they appeared to this and other courts.

IN RE RYDER
263 F. Supp. 360 (E.D. Va. 1967)

PER CURIAM.

This proceeding was instituted to determine whether Richard R. Ryder should be removed from the roll of attorneys qualified to practice before this court. Ryder was admitted to this bar in 1953. He formerly served five years as an Assistant United States Attorney. He has an active trial practice, including both civil and criminal cases. . . .

On August 24, 1966 a man armed with a sawed-off shotgun robbed the Varina Branch of the Bank of Virginia of $7,583. Included in the currency taken were $10 bills known as "bait money," the serial numbers of which had been recorded.

On August 26, 1966 Charles Richard Cook rented safety deposit box 14 at a branch of the Richmond National Bank. Later in the day Cook was interviewed at his home by agents of the Federal Bureau of Investigation, who obtained $348 from him. Cook telephoned Ryder, who had represented him in civil litigation. Ryder came to the house and advised the agents that he represented Cook. He said that if Cook were not to be placed under arrest, he intended to take him to his office for an interview. The agents left. Cook insisted to Ryder that he had not robbed the bank. He told Ryder that he had won the money, which the agents had taken from him, in a crap game. At this time Ryder believed Cook.

Later that afternoon Ryder telephoned one of the agents and asked whether any of the bills obtained from Cook had been identified as a part of the money taken in the bank robbery. The agent told him that some bills had been identified. Ryder made inquiries about the number of bills taken and their denominations. The agent declined to give him specific information but indicated that several of the bills were recorded as bait money.

The next morning, Saturday, August 27, 1966, Ryder conferred with Cook again. He urged Cook to tell the truth, and Cook answered that a man, whose name he would not divulge, offered him $500 on the day of the robbery to put a package in a bank lockbox. Ryder did not believe this story. Ryder told Cook that if the government could trace the money in the box to him, it would be almost conclusive evidence of his guilt. He knew that Cook was under surveillance and he suspected that Cook might try to dispose of the money. . . .

On Monday morning Ryder asked Cook to come by his office. He prepared a power of attorney, which Cook signed. . . .

Ryder took the power of attorney which Cook had signed to the Richmond National Bank. He rented box 13 in his name with his office address, presented the power of attorney, entered Cook's box, took both boxes into a booth, where he found a bag of money and a sawed-off shotgun in Cook's box. The box also contained miscellaneous items which are not pertinent to this proceeding. He transferred the contents of Cook's box to his own and returned the boxes to the vault. He left the bank, and neither he nor Cook returned. . . .

On September 7, 1966 Cook was indicted for robbing the Varina Branch of the Bank of Virginia. A bench warrant was issued and the next day Ryder represented Cook at a bond hearing. Cook was identified as the robber by employees of the bank. He was released on bond. Cook was arraigned on a plea of not guilty on September 9, 1966.

On September 12, 1966 F.B.I. agents procured search warrants for Cook's and Ryder's safety deposit boxes in the Richmond National Bank. They found Cook's box empty. In Ryder's box they discovered $5,920 of the $7,583 taken in the bank robbery and the sawed-off shotgun used in the robbery. . . .

On October 14, 1966 the three judges of this court removed Ryder as an attorney for Cook; suspended him from practice before the court until further order; referred the matter to the United States Attorney, who was requested to file charges within five days; set the matter for hearing November 11, 1966; and granted Ryder leave to move for vacation or modification of its order pending hearing. . . .

At the outset, we reject the suggestion that Ryder did not know the money, which he transferred from Cook's box to his was stolen. We find that on August 29 when Ryder opened Cook's box and saw a bag of money and a sawed-off shotgun, he then knew Cook was involved in the bank robbery and that the money was stolen. The evidence clearly establishes this. Ryder knew that the man who had robbed the bank used a sawed-off shotgun. He disbelieved Cook's story about the source of the money in the lockbox. He knew that some of the bills in Cook's possession were bait money. . . .

We also find that Ryder was not motivated solely by certain expectation the government would discover the contents of his lockbox. He believed discovery was probable. In this event he intended to argue to the court that the contents of his box could not be revealed, and even if the contents were identified, his possession made the stolen money and the shotgun inadmissible against his client. He also recognized that discovery was not inevitable. His intention in this event, we find, was to assist Cook by keeping the stolen money and the shotgun concealed in his lockbox until after the trial. . . .

We accept his statement that he intended eventually to return the money to its rightful owner, but we pause to say that no attorney should ever place himself in such a position. Matters involving the possible termination of an attorney-client relationship, or possible subsequent proceedings in the event of an acquittal, are too delicate to permit such a practice.

We reject the argument that Ryder's conduct was no more than the exercise of the attorney-client privilege. The fact that Cook had not been arrested or indicted at the time Ryder took possession of the gun and money is immaterial. Cook was Ryder's client and was entitled to the protection of the lawyer-client privilege.

Regardless of Cook's status, however, Ryder's conduct was not encompassed by the attorney-client privilege. . . .

It was Ryder, not his client, who took the initiative in transferring the incriminating possession of the stolen money and the shotgun from Cook. Ryder's conduct went far beyond the receipt and retention of a confidential communication from his client. Counsel for Ryder conceded, at the time of argument, that the acts of Ryder were not within the attorney-client privilege. . . .

The money in Cook's box belonged to the Bank of Virginia. The law did not authorize Cook to conceal this money or withhold it from the bank. His larceny was a continuing offense. Cook had no title or property interest in the money that he lawfully could pass to Ryder. . . .

No canon of ethics or law permitted Ryder to conceal from the Bank of Virginia its money to gain his client's acquittal.

Cook's possession of the sawed-off shotgun was illegal. 26 U.S.C. §5851. Ryder could not lawfully receive the gun from Cook to assist Cook to avoid conviction of robbery. Cook had never mentioned the shotgun to Ryder. When Ryder discovered it in Cook's box, he took possession of it to hinder the government in the prosecution of its case, and he intended not to reveal it pending trial unless the government discovered it and a court compelled its production. No statute or canon of ethics authorized Ryder to take possession of the gun for this purpose. . . .

In helping Cook to conceal the shotgun and stolen money, Ryder acted without the bounds of law. He allowed the office of attorney to be used in violation of law. The scheme which he devised was a deceptive, legalistic subterfuge — rightfully denounced by the canon as chicane. . . .

[Ryder was suspended for 18 months.]

The Fourth Circuit affirmed Ryder's suspension. In re Ryder, 381 F.2d 713 (4th Cir. 1967). In some ways, *Ryder* is an easy case. The money and gun were illegal for Ryder to possess. The money belonged to the bank. It was stolen property. Possession was a crime. Possession of a sawed-off shotgun was also a crime. Although these facts aggravated Ryder's transgression, they were unnecessary to the opinion. Other courts have held that a lawyer may not retain evidence that, although *not* independently illegal to possess, tend to incriminate the client, a diary for example. People v. Sanchez, 30 Cal. Rptr. 2d 111 (Ct. App. 1994) (lawyer who received incriminating documents in client's own handwriting from another lawyer, who had received them from jailed client's sister, acted properly when he gave them to the court, which gave them to the prosecutor). In this view, Ryder had no duty to help the prosecutor, but neither could he hinder it by moving evidence to his lockbox, where discovery was a bit less likely.

But not so fast. Thinking about Ryder's dilemma across successive editions of this book, I began to realize that the court's decision is not obviously correct. Or that it is too narrowly focused. Here's why. If Ryder must turn over the money and gun, future lawyers in his position will leave such items where they found them. Their incriminating value is apparent (through their location and fingerprints, for example). Cook was still at large and, even if he was under surveillance, he might have been able to retrieve both items. By taking possession, Ryder at least ensured that the money would not be spent and the gun would not be used. Do we really want to encourage lawyers to let weapons and stolen property remain available to clients like Cook? Do we want the lawyer in "The Client's Loaded .45 (Part I)" to let his distressed client leave his office with the loaded gun? Or to leave it in a trash bin near a playground? Yet if we give lawyers a turnover duty, we encourage just that because lawyers are not going to help convict their clients.

What about the state's interest? A paper trail at the bank led from Cook's lockbox to Ryder's so the FBI found the gun and money anyway, as was likely. Then again, there will be situations where the lawyer's possession of physical evidence of a crime will impede an investigation because there will be no trail, paper or otherwise, for the authorities to follow. If lawyers don't have a turnover obligation, clients will be encouraged to stash incriminating items (weapons, stolen property, contraband) at law offices. If prosecutors manage to identify the law office and have probable cause, they may seek a warrant to search it, not an attractive prospect. If the prosecutor does not know the lawyers' identity, they may never find the items, at least not in time to use them in a prosecution. Our challenge is to find a way to recognize everyone's legitimate interests, which is what the Stanford article cited on the first page of this chapter tried to do.

What do the Model Rules say? They are entirely unhelpful. Rule 3.4(a) simply forbids a lawyer "unlawfully [to] alter, destroy or conceal a document or other material having potential evidentiary value." Nor can a lawyer assist another person in doing so. In other words, it depends on the criminal law. The Rules add nothing. (Washington, D.C. Rule 3.4 offers more guidance.)

So we turn to the criminal law.

2. Real Evidence and Criminal Law

The Client's Loaded .45 (Part II)

The lawyer in Part I of this problem takes the client's gun from the client or his wife and puts it in her office safe, taking care not to leave or remove fingerprints or alter it in any way. Or she retrieves the gun from the trash bin and puts it in her safe with the same care. Has she committed a crime?

———

It turns out that the criminal law is pretty demanding. State statutes on obstruction of justice or tampering with evidence (or like crimes) vary, so we'll focus on federal crimes. Its provisions are broad and overlapping. A minor attempt at interference with the work of the courts, grand juries, or enforcement agencies can lead to years in prison, even if the attempt fails.

Return to Richard Nixon and the White House tapes that led to his downfall but that he never attempted to destroy. Could Nixon legally have destroyed the tapes? Could his lawyers have advised him to do so? Did they? Therein lies a tale.

Mr. Nixon thought he could destroy the tapes. He said that one reason he did not was bad advice from well-meaning lawyers who had decided that destroying the tapes would obstruct justice even when no subpoena had been served for their production. Who were those lawyers?

In a New York Times op-ed (August 18, 1988), journalist Henry Brandon quoted the late and renowned Edward Bennett Williams (the Williams of Williams & Connolly) as saying that Nixon had no duty to retain the tapes. According to Brandon, Williams thought Nixon could have destroyed the tapes and then explain that he did it to protect secret communications with other nations. Really? Could Williams have given Nixon this advice if protecting secrets was never Nixon's motive? Williams invented a false story. May a lawyer advise a client to lie to the public? It would seem so. If the lie is not otherwise illegal, then, so far as I can tell, the advice is allowed. Even Williams, as Nixon's lawyer, could have lied to the public. How often do you see a criminal defense lawyer proclaiming that his indicted client is innocent and looks forward to his day in court? The lawyer may have already told the client that he has no defense and will eventually have to negotiate a guilty plea.

Back to 1973: Who were the well-intentioned lawyers who told Nixon that he could not destroy the tapes? Brandon tells us that Nixon had received this advice from his legal counsel, Leonard Garment. Although a subpoena had not been served, all knew it would be. Destroying the tapes despite that knowledge would be obstruction of justice, in Garment's view. In 1985, Brandon told Garment that Williams had the contrary opinion. Garment replied (correctly) with a "1956 decision by the Federal District Court in New York City," discussed below, which held that obstruction can occur even though no subpoena had yet been served. Later, according to Brandon, even Garment conceded that Williams's pragmatic advice "was probably right and that Nixon could have got away with the destruction of the tapes." That, of course, means Nixon would likely have completed his term, which in turn means that a lot of national politics may have happened differently. Nixon would have nominated Justice Douglas's successor in 1975 and it would not likely have been John Paul Stevens. Would Vice President Gerald Ford, whose pardon of Nixon is said to have contributed to Jimmy Carter's victory in 1976, instead have won?

The 1956 case Garment had in mind was United States v. Solow, 138 F. Supp. 812 (S.D.N.Y. 1956), which refused to dismiss the indictment of a man who allegedly destroyed documents he knew were wanted by a sitting grand jury, even though neither the man nor the documents were yet under subpoena. The defendant was charged under 18 U.S.C. §1503, which applies when a person obstructs a *pending* court or grand jury proceeding. Today, the obstruction statutes have exponentially expanded. No pending proceeding may be needed. And redundancy reigns. The same act can be obstruction under multiple statutes that provide for periods of incarceration from five to 20 years. Further, the list of synonyms used to describe how obstruction can occur (alters, conceals, destroys, mutilates, impedes) suggests reliance on a thesaurus.

Obstruction and related laws were headlined in the prosecutions of Big Five accounting firm Arthur Andersen for destruction of documents in anticipation of and during an SEC investigation; of investment banker Frank Quattrone of Credit Suisse for sending one email urging deletion of files during an SEC investigation (following reversal of a conviction in 2006, he was acquitted); and of Martha Stewart, convicted of attempting to conceal stock trades allegedly made on inside information. The underlying trades were not criminal, as it turns out, which makes the point, a paradox for many, that a person can be guilty of obstructing the investigation of an innocent act. Arthur Andersen was convicted, but a unanimous Supreme Court reversed because of errors in the judge's jury charge. Arthur Andersen LLP v. United States, 544 U.S. 696 (2005). The government did not retry Andersen, whose fate (corporate death) was sealed the day it was indicted, reminiscent of the precedent set by the Red Queen in *Alice in Wonderland*: "Sentence first, trial after."

Here's just one example of the breadth of the obstruction statutes, taken from 18 U.S.C. §1512. Paragraph (b) was used in the prosecutions of Arthur Andersen and stock trader Frank Quattrone. United States v. Quattrone, 441 F.3d 153 (2d Cir. 2006) (vacating conviction). Paragraph (c) was added by the Sarbanes-Oxley Act in 2002 in response to the wave of corporate scandals.

> (b) Whoever knowingly . . . corruptly persuades another person, or attempts to do so, or engages in misleading conduct toward another person, with intent to . . .
>> (2) cause or induce any person to—
>>> (B) alter, destroy, mutilate, or conceal an object with intent to impair the object's integrity or availability for use in an official proceeding . . . shall be fined under this title or imprisoned not more than 20 years, or both.
>> (c) Whoever corruptly—
>>> (1) alters, destroys, mutilates, or conceals a record, document, or other object, or attempts to do so, with the intent to impair the object's integrity or availability for use in an official proceeding; or
>>> (2) otherwise obstructs, influences, or impedes any official proceeding, or attempts to do so, shall be fined under this title or imprisoned not more than 20 years, or both.

Appreciate the breadth of these provisions. Paragraph (b) makes it a crime for one person to "knowingly . . . corruptly persuade" another person (or to attempt to do so) to act as described in the section. This is sometimes called witness tampering. Paragraph (c) makes it a crime for the first person to do these acts herself. Then, just in case paragraph (c)(1) is insufficiently broad to catch all obstructionist conduct, paragraph (c)(2) fills the gap. *Arthur Andersen*, supra, defined "knowingly . . . corruptly":

> "Knowledge" and "knowingly" are normally associated with awareness, understanding, or consciousness. "Corrupt" and "corruptly" are normally associated with wrongful, immoral, depraved, or evil. Joining these meanings together here makes sense both linguistically and in the statutory scheme. Only persons conscious of wrongdoing can be said to "knowingly . . . corruptly persuade." And limiting criminality to persuaders conscious of their wrongdoing sensibly allows §1512(b) to reach only those with the level of "culpability . . . we usually require in order to impose criminal liability."

An "official proceeding," moreover, need not be pending or even impending for this section to apply, §1512(f)(1), so long as the defendant "expected a grand jury investigation and/or a trial in the foreseeable future." United States v. Frankhauser, 80 F.3d 641 (1st Cir. 1996). And the term "official proceeding" includes not only court cases but also congressional hearings and a "proceeding before a Federal Government agency which is authorized by law." §1515(a)(1)(C). But what if the destroyed or altered item would have been inadmissible at trial because, for example, of a privilege or as irrelevant? It doesn't matter. It's still obstruction. §1512(f)(2). So depending on your state of mind, asking one person to shred or backdate one document or to delete one email, or doing either yourself, may send you to prison for up to 20 years, even if the person refuses or your own attempt fails.

The temptation to destroy or to have someone else destroy a document that may be harmful in court can be rather strong, especially if (one thinks) it's the only copy and the consequences of losing a court case are dire. Destruction is private. Who's looking? And documents can be destroyed without a trace—shredded, burned, sent to the bottom of the ocean. But, of course, often copies surface, especially electronically.

Section 1512 is not limited to destruction or alteration of evidence. It also uses the verbs "impedes" and "conceals." Ryder did not alter or destroy the money or gun. But he did conceal them in his own safety deposit box, which would impede their discovery if only briefly. Even if these items had not been illegal to possess, relocating them to his lockbox would today violate §1512(c). Ryder would be better off leaving them where they were despite their accessibility to this client. Today, §1512 would make it a crime for a person, with the forbidden intent, to advise Nixon to destroy the tapes in order to keep them from a foreseeable grand jury, court, or legislative proceeding, even if the tapes had not yet been subpoenaed. Nor could Nixon do it himself.

Lawyers are not immune to obstruction charges arising out of the representation of a client. United States v. Kellington, 217 F.3d 1084 (9th Cir. 2000), and United States v. Kloess, 251 F.3d 941 (11th Cir. 2001), were both §1512 prosecutions of lawyers. Both appeals—one from a conviction, which the court reversed and remanded; the other from dismissal of an indictment, which the court reinstated—construed §1515(c). That opaque section creates a safe harbor for lawyers who "provid[e] lawful, bona fide, legal representation services in connection with or anticipation of an official proceeding."

And how did Leonard Garment, in retirement, look back on this episode in his life? When I interviewed him for the law review article cited on the first page of this chapter, he said he did not believe that Nixon would have destroyed the tapes even if his lawyers had told him he could. They had great historical and financial value. Garment also told me that in any event, Nixon could not have done it alone. They were the old reel-to-reel acetate tapes, he said, not today's digital recordings, and there were too many of them. Nixon would have needed a lot of help, which Garment doubted he would have been able to get. The Watergate burglary had already produced indictments and more were expected.

3. Real Evidence and the Attorney-Client Privilege

The Client's Loaded .45 (Part III)

The lawyer in Part I of this problem took the loaded gun from her client or her client's wife and gave it to the authorities to avoid any charge that she unlawfully concealed it. Or she retrieved it from the trash bin and turned it over. The gun may be incriminatory even

> without knowing the lawyer's source. Fingerprints may connect it to
> the client and ballistics tests may connect it to the homicide. But what
> if they don't? The government wants to prove that the lawyer got the
> gun from her client, her client's wife, or a location her client gave her.
> Will the court require the lawyer to reveal the source? Or is the source's
> identity privileged?

People v. Meredith is a law teacher's dream opinion. If it weren't semi-famous, it would be a great exam question for those with the imagination to invent it. The court confronted hard policy choices. Did it choose correctly? *Meredith* cites the *Belge* case from New York, sometimes called "The Buried Bodies Case," which is even more famous.

PEOPLE v. MEREDITH
29 Cal. 3d 682, 631 P.2d 46, 175 Cal. Rptr. 612 (1981)

TOBRINER, JUSTICE.

[Scott and Meredith were implicated in the murder of Wade. While in jail, Scott told his then-lawyer, Schenk, that he had retrieved Wade's wallet at the murder scene, removed $100, tried unsuccessfully to burn it, and left it in the burn barrel behind his home. Schenk sent his investigator, Frick, to retrieve the wallet, which he did. Schenk examined it and gave it to the police.]

At trial Frick, called by the prosecution, identified the wallet and testified that he found it in a garbage can behind Scott's residence. . . .

Defendant Scott concedes, and we agree, that the wallet itself was admissible in evidence. Scott maintains, however, that [the attorney-client privilege] bars the testimony of the investigator concerning the location of the wallet. We consider, first, whether the California attorney-client privilege . . . extends to observations which are the product of privileged communications.

[The court concluded that California law protected as privileged the defendant's statements to his lawyer regarding the location of the wallet. Furthermore, the information retained its protection even though the lawyer disclosed the substance of the communication to the investigator, since the purpose of this disclosure was to aid in the representation.]

The statutes codifying the attorney-client privilege do not, however, indicate whether that privilege protects facts viewed and observed as a direct result of confidential communication. To resolve that issue, we turn first to the policies which underlie the attorney-client privilege, and then to the cases which apply those policies to observations arising from a protected communication. . . .

In a venerable decision involving facts analogous to those in the instant case, the Supreme Court of West Virginia held that the trial court erred in admitting an attorney's testimony as to the location of a pistol which he had discovered as the result of a privileged communication from his client. That the attorney had observed the pistol, the court pointed out, did not nullify the privilege:

> All that the said attorney knew about this pistol, or where it was to be found, he knew only from the communications which had been made to him by his client confidentially and professionally, as counsel in this case. And it ought, therefore, to have been entirely excluded from the jury. It may be, that in this particular case this evidence tended to the promotion of right and justice, but [citing precedent]: "Truth like all other good things may be loved unwisely, may be pursued too keenly, may cost too much."

State of West Virginia v. Douglass, 20 W. Va. 770, 783 (1882). . . .

More recent decisions reach similar conclusions. In State v. Olwell, 64 Wash. 2d 828, 394 P.2d 681 (1964), the court reviewed contempt charges against an attorney who refused to produce a knife he obtained from his client. The court first observed that "[t]o be protected as a privileged communication . . . the securing of the knife . . . must have been *the direct result of information* given to Mr. Olwell by his client." (Italics added.) The court concluded that defense counsel, after examining the physical evidence, should deliver it to the prosecution, but should not reveal the source of the evidence; "[b]y thus allowing the prosecution to recover such evidence, the public interest is served, and by refusing the prosecution an opportunity to disclose the source of the evidence, the client's privilege is preserved and a balance reached between these conflicting interests."

Finally, we note the decisions of the New York courts in People v. Belge [372 N.Y.S.2d 798 (Sup. Ct.), aff'd 376 N.Y.S.2d 771 (4th Dept. 1975)]. Defendant, charged with one murder, revealed to counsel that he had committed three others. Counsel, following defendant's directions, located one of the bodies. Counsel did not reveal the location of the body until trial, 10 months later, when he exposed the other murders to support an insanity defense.

Counsel was then indicted for violating two sections of the New York Public Health Law for failing to report the existence of the body to proper authorities in order that they could give it a decent burial. The trial court dismissed the indictment; the appellate division affirmed, holding that the attorney-client privilege shielded counsel from prosecution for actions which would otherwise violate the Public Health Law.[5]

The foregoing decisions demonstrate that the attorney-client privilege is not strictly limited to communications, but extends to protect observations

---

5. In each of the cases discussed in text, a crucial element in the court's analysis is that the attorney's observations were the direct product of information communicated to him by his client. Two decisions, People v. Lee, 3 Cal. App. 3d 514, 83 Cal. Rptr. 715 (1970), and Morrell v. State, 575 P.2d 1200 (Alaska 1978), held that an attorney must not only turn over evidence given him by *third parties*, but also testify as to the source of that evidence. Both decisions emphasized that the attorney-client privilege was inapplicable because the third party was not acting as an agent of the attorney or the client.

made as a consequence of protected communications. We turn therefore to the question of whether that privilege encompasses a case in which the defense, by removing or altering evidence, interferes with the prosecution's opportunity to discover that evidence.[7]

In some of the cases extending the privilege to observations arising from protected communications the defense counsel had obtained the evidence from his client or in some other fashion removed it from its original location; in others the attorney did not remove or alter the evidence. None of the decisions, however, confronts directly the question whether such removal or alteration should affect the defendant's right to assert the attorney-client privilege as a bar to testimony concerning the original location or condition of the evidence.

When defense counsel alters or removes physical evidence, he necessarily deprives the prosecution of the opportunity to observe that evidence in its original condition or location. As the amicus Appellate Committee of the California District Attorney Association points out, to bar admission of testimony concerning the original condition and location of the evidence in such a case permits the defense in effect to "destroy" critical information; it is as if, he explains, the wallet in this case bore a tag bearing the words "located in the trash can by Scott's residence," and the defense, by taking the wallet, destroyed this tag. To extend the attorney-client privilege to a case in which the defense removed evidence might encourage defense counsel to race the police to seize critical evidence. (See In re Ryder, 263 F. Supp. 360, 369 (E.D. Va. 1967)).

We therefore conclude that courts must craft an exception to the protection extended by the attorney-client privilege in cases in which counsel has removed or altered evidence. Indeed, at oral argument defense counsel acknowledged that such an exception might be necessary in a case in which the police would have inevitably discovered the evidence in its original location if counsel had not removed it. Counsel argued, however, that the attorney-client privilege should protect observations of evidence, despite subsequent defense removal, unless the prosecution could prove that the police probably would have eventually discovered the evidence in the original site.

---

7. We agree with the parties' suggestion that an attorney in Schenk's position often may best fulfill conflicting obligations to preserve the confidentiality of client confidences, investigate his case, and act as an officer of the court if he does not remove evidence located as the result of a privileged communication. We must recognize, however, that in some cases an examination of evidence may reveal information critical to the defense of a client accused of crime. If the usefulness of the evidence cannot be gauged without taking possession of it, as, for example, when a ballistics or fingerprint test is required, the attorney may properly take it for a reasonable time before turning it over to the prosecution. Similarly, in the present case the defense counsel could not be certain the burnt wallet belonged in fact to the victim: in taking the wallet to examine it for identification, he violated no ethical duty to his client or to the prosecution.

We have seriously considered counsel's proposal, but have concluded that a test based upon the probability of eventual discovery is unworkably speculative. Evidence turns up not only because the police deliberately search for it, but also because it comes to the attention of policemen or bystanders engaged in other business. In the present case, for example, the wallet might have been found by the trash collector. Moreover, once physical evidence (the wallet) is turned over to the police, they will obviously stop looking for it; to ask where, how long, and how carefully they would have looked is obviously to compel speculation as to theoretical future conduct of the police.

We therefore conclude that whenever defense counsel removes or alters evidence, the statutory privilege does not bar revelation of the original location or condition of the evidence in question. We thus view the defense decision to remove evidence as a tactical choice. If defense counsel leaves the evidence where he discovers it, his observations derived from privileged communications are insulated from revelation. If, however, counsel chooses to remove evidence to examine or test it, the original location and condition of that evidence lose the protection of the privilege. Applying this analysis to the present case, we hold that the trial court did not err in admitting the investigator's testimony concerning the location of the wallet. . . .

The Turnover Duty

Attorney Schenk gave the wallet to the police. Did he have to? Yes. That's one lesson of In re Ryder and other cases.* But a lawyer can escape the turnover obligation simply by not taking possession. Wemark v. State, 602 N.W.2d 810 (Iowa 1999), put it starkly:

> [I]f defense counsel leaves the evidence alone, the only matter possessed is the communication which remains insulated from disclosure by the attorney-client privilege. Thus, a defense lawyer has no legal obligation to disclose information about the location of an instrument of a crime when possession of the instrument is not taken. Instead, a defense lawyer has a duty to preserve the confidences of the client.

Meredith cites Morrell v. State in note 5. The facts of that case are intriguing and its holding ambiguous. Stephen Cline, a public defender in Alaska, was appointed to represent Clayton Morrell, who was charged with kidnapping. While Morrell was in jail, his friend, John Wagner, used his car and residence with his permission. Wagner discovered a plan for the kidnapping in Morrell's car, in Morrell's handwriting. He gave it to Cline.

What should Cline do? What would you do?

---

* Every case I read for the article cited on the first page of this chapter required a lawyer either to return the evidence to the source or give it to authorities. A few did not even allow return to the source.

What Cline did was attempt to return it to Wagner, who refused it, and then, after seeking ethics advice, arranged with Wagner to give the plan to the state, which used it to convict Morrell. Morrell claimed that Cline's conduct violated his Sixth Amendment right to the effective assistance of counsel. Cline should not have given the plan to the authorities, he argued.

The obstruction statute in Alaska made it a crime to willfully destroy, alter, or conceal evidence of a crime "which is being sought for production during an investigation, inquiry or trial, with the intent to prevent the evidence from being discovered or produced." Remember, the question for the court was whether Cline's representation was constitutionally ineffective. Did the Sixth Amendment forbid him to do what he did? At one point, the court concluded that Cline "would have been obligated to see that the evidence reached the prosecutor in this case even if he had obtained the evidence from Morrell" himself, not from Wagner. That's a remarkable statement, though dicta. (Other courts reject it. See below.) It seems to say that Cline would be forbidden even to return the plan to Morrell after having taken it to read and evaluate. Yet failure to read and evaluate it would be incompetence. At another point, the court says only that Cline could "have reasonably concluded" that he was required to "reveal the existence of the evidence." Those are two very different conclusions, aren't they? In any event, whichever is correct, the court found that handing over the notes that Wagner gave Cline did not make Cline ineffective.

Does the Source Matter?

In *Meredith*, would Schenk have had to reveal the source of the wallet if the immediate source had been Scott personally, not his "burn barrel"? Analytically the answer would seem to be yes. By taking the wallet from Scott, Schenk would have made it impossible for the authorities to find it in Scott's possession. The evidentiary value of the wallet depended on its location, whether that was the defendant personally or his burn barrel. On the other hand, *Meredith* cited *Olwell*, which would not allow the prosecutor to elicit that the client was personally the source of the evidence. People v. Nash, 341 N.W.2d 439 (Mich. 1983), and Hitch v. Pima County Superior Court, 708 P.2d 72 (Ariz. 1985), agree with *Olwell*.* Does it make sense to distinguish between receipt of the item directly from the client as in *Olwell* and recovery from a location the client reveals as in *Meredith*?

Or as in *Ryder*. Like Frick, Ryder destroyed evidence by destroying a location when he moved the money and gun from Cook's safe deposit box to his own box. (He also provided a service by keeping both from Cook.) Unlike

---

* Should you encounter this issue in your work on a journal or in practice, you should know that *Nash* is easily misread. The lead opinion of Justice Brickley looks like an opinion for the court on all issues and it rejects *Olwell*. But on that issue, Brickley's opinion is in the minority. Four of seven justices wrote or joined concurring opinions that said the prosecutor could not prove that the lawyer was the source of the evidence to support an inference that the client was the lawyer's source.

Meredith, the government did not need to prove that the money and gun were initially in Cook's box because forensic evidence and bank records did that job. Nevertheless, the proof would have been stronger if an FBI agent could testify to finding these items in Cook's box.

Tampering is a crime if the item tampered with is "an object" within the meaning of an obstruction statute like 18 U.S.C. §1512. Does that include redecorating your home?

"The White Women on the Walls Have to Go"

In his review of Lawrence Schiller's *American Tragedy,* a book on the prosecution of O.J. Simpson on a charge of murdering his ex-wife Nicole Brown Simpson and her friend Ronald Goldman, Jeffrey Rosen calls defense lawyer Johnnie Cochran "an applied critical race theorist" and writes that Cochran "insisted from the beginning that the facts of the Simpson case were less important to the defense than the social meaning that might be attached to the protagonists." Schiller quotes Cochran as saying: "Our theory was based not only on the facts before us but also on what our experience suggested to us about their meaning." (This is an unvarnished example of law as performance. See pages 282 and 314-315.) Many trial lawyers would agree. In court, truth is not the sum of the facts, but facts refracted through performance to yield meaning. Jeffrey Rosen, "The Bloods and the Crits," The New Republic, Dec. 9, 1996, p. 27. Rosen continues:

> So how, precisely, did Cochran construct a story that transformed a wealthy shill for white corporations into an oppressed tribune of the underclass? Among other things, by interior decoration. Perhaps the most shameful of Cochran's many shameful exercises in racial storytelling was his redecoration of Simpson's home, in preparation for the look-see visit of the black jurors. All day on Saturday, according to Schiller, members of the defense team were hard at work "establishing O.J.'s African-American identity." The lawyers found Simpson's walls lined with pictures of white people: girlfriends, celebrities, corporate sponsors. "The faces were overwhelmingly white," Schiller notes. "That's not the way to please a jury dominated by African American women." On Cochran's orders, "The white women on the walls have to go, and the black people have to come in." Down went a nude portrait of Paula Barbieri that had been hanging near the fireplace, and up went pictures of Simpson's family—"his black family," in Cochran's words. Kardashian had the photographs enlarged at Kinko's, and nicely framed. "The jurors won't notice that they are color photocopies," Schiller notes cheerfully.
>
> But homey Xeroxed pictures of Simpson and his mother weren't enough for Cochran. As Schiller reports: "Cochran wants something depicting African-American history. 'What about that framed poster from my office of the little girl trying to get to school?' he asks. Johnnie

means Norman Rockwell's famous 1963 painting, *The Problem We All Live With,* in which a black grade school girl walks to school surrounded by federal marshals." And so Cochran's framed picture was hung at the top of the stairs, where the jury couldn't miss it as they trooped up to Simpson's bedroom. "Everyone," Schiller reports, "is pleased."

The prosecutors were outmaneuvered here. In her own book, Marcia Clark, the lead prosecutor, wrote that the state had argued against a visit to Simpson's house, which was not the crime scene. But the defense insisted on it, citing the jury's visit to the home of Nicole Brown Simpson. Plus, bloody socks had been discovered in Simpson's home. Before the jury entered the home, the lawyers did a walk-through, and Clark saw the changes for the first time. "I'd gotten no farther than the foyer when I realized something was very wrong here. . . . [T]he most dramatic transformation was that collection of photographs. The Wall of Fat Cats had been cleansed of Caucasians. Gone were the golfing buddies and shots of Nicole in Aspen. Every single shot contained a black face. Simpson's mother, his sister, their husbands, their kids. Upstairs there was even a Norman Rockwell reproduction. . . . But the piece de resistance was the master bedroom. On the mantel above the fireplace sat books on philosophy and religion. On the nightstand, next to a Holy Bible, stood a photo of defendant's mother, Eunice." Marcia Clark, *Without a Doubt* 302 (1997).

Did the defense lawyers act ethically? Did they tamper with evidence? Rosen is a law professor, so we might expect a greater understanding of the issues from him than from a nonlawyer book reviewer. Is his criticism correct?

Copycats. The Simpson defense lawyers' strategy was later attempted in the prosecution of NFL star Aaron Hernandez, who was charged with killing semi-pro Odin Lloyd. The defense lawyers added "religious items" and NFL memorabilia to Hernandez's home, the scene of the crime, in advance of a jury visit. The prosecutor objected and the defense agreed to remove the items. Michelle Smith, "Hernandez Prosecutor Cites OJ Simpson Case in Judge Request," Associated Press, Feb. 5, 2015. Hernandez was convicted and sentenced to life without parole. Before the murder, he had a $40 million contract with the New England Patriots.[*]

---

[*] Hernandez died by suicide in prison at age 27. His conviction was vacated because he died before his appeal was heard. An autopsy revealed a degenerative brain disease ordinarily found in the elderly.

The Rules Today (So Far as Can Be Known)

It's not possible to speak for every jurisdiction, but my review suggests that, subject to local variations, these are the rules for criminal cases:

- A lawyer can hold an item of real evidence to examine it but then must either return it to the source or the original location or give it to the authorities. This is true whoever may be the source of the item or whatever the location.
- Some courts, however, forbid return of the item to the source, even if it's the client, and require the lawyer to give it to authorities, which encourages lawyers to say "Don't give me that" or "Don't leave it here."
- If a lawyer receives real evidence from the client personally, the state cannot require her to reveal the client as the source.
- If a lawyer gets real evidence, or information about location, from a third person, the state can require the lawyer to identify the third person or the location.
- The privilege protects the client's *communications,* including about the location of real evidence, and the lawyer's confirmation of it in that location, but not the item itself.
- But if the lawyer "destroys" evidence of the location, as happened in *Ryder* and *Meredith,* the lawyer can be required to disclose the location despite a claim of privilege.

B. SOME ISSUES CONCERNING PROSECUTORS

> [A prosecutor's duties are] not of an ordinary party to a controversy, but of a sovereignty whose obligation to govern impartially is as compelling as its obligation to govern at all; and whose interest, therefore, in a criminal prosecution is not that it shall win a case, but that justice shall be done.
> —Berger v. United States (U.S. Supreme Court 1935)

> A prosecutor has the responsibility of a minister of justice and not simply that of an advocate. This responsibility carries with it specific obligations to see that the defendant is accorded procedural justice, that guilt is decided upon the basis of sufficient evidence, and that special precautions are taken to prevent and to rectify the conviction of innocent persons.
> —Model Rule 3.8 cmt. [1]

> The primary duty of the prosecutor is to seek justice within the bounds of the law, not merely to convict. The prosecutor serves the public interest and should act with integrity and balanced judgment to increase public safety both by pursuing

> appropriate criminal charges of appropriate severity, and by exercising discretion to not pursue criminal charges in appropriate circumstances. The prosecutor should seek to protect the innocent and convict the guilty, consider the interests of victims and witnesses, and respect the constitutional and legal rights of all persons, including suspects and defendants.
>
> —Standard 3-1.2(b), ABA Criminal Justice Standards

Prosecutors have broad powers that are almost always beyond review. These include deciding who to investigate, which crimes to charge, and whether to offer a plea bargain and its terms. Prosecutors are absolutely immune from liability for conduct "intimately associated with the judicial phase of the criminal process," which includes "initiating and pursuing a criminal prosecution." Imbler v. Pachtman, 424 U.S. 409 (1976). But that does not include their "administrative duties and those investigatory functions that do not relate to an advocate's preparation for the initiation and prosecution or for judicial proceedings." Buckley v. Fitzsimmons, 509 U.S. 259 (1993). The Fifth Circuit denied absolute immunity where a complaint alleged that the New Orleans District Attorney's Office and named prosecutors within it "used fake 'subpoenas' to pressure crime victims and witnesses to meet with them," in violation of the Constitution and state law. Singleton v. Cannizzaro, 956 F.3d 773 (5th Cir. 2020).

There is the trial, of course. A trial is where a prosecutor's work and charging decision will be tested. Judges and juries will examine the prosecutor's proof under the rules of evidence and procedure and the Constitution. The evidence must prove guilt of all elements of the offense beyond a reasonable doubt and satisfy other safeguards meant to ensure fairness, protect constitutional rights, and avoid convicting the innocent. But many critical prosecutorial decisions are made long before trial. And the vast majority of cases are resolved without trial. At trial, furthermore, a prosecutor has resources far greater than nearly all defendants.

1. Constitutional and Ethical Disclosure Obligations

"[T]he investigation and prosecution of Senator [Ted] Stevens [by the Justice Department] were 'permeated by the systematic concealment of significant exculpatory evidence which would have independently corroborated his defense and his testimony, and seriously damaged the testimony and credibility of the government's key witness.'"[*]

---

[*] From Nov. 21, 2011 order of Judge Emmet Sullivan summarizing findings of court-appointed special prosecutors in In re Special Proceedings. Stevens's conviction was vacated. In re Special Proceedings, 825 F. Supp. 2d 203 (D.D.C. 2011).

"We Can Make No Promises But . . ."

Ilana Mallow is in an Omaha jail awaiting trial for killing her former boyfriend, Ashton Boyle. The police interview Millie Koppel, who does not know Mallow or Boyle but was an eyewitness. She gives the police a description of the killer that matches Mallow and picks her in a lineup. There is other evidence against Mallow, including threatening text messages to Boyle and a partial confession, which Mallow recanted. A second eyewitness was unable to identify Mallow and a third identified someone else. Koppel says she won't testify, even if a judge orders her to do so, "unless there's something in it for me." She's currently under indictment for forgery. "Can you reduce that," she asks the detective questioning her, "or make it go away?" The detective responds that "we can make no promises, but the D.A.'s office here will always take a witness's *helpful* cooperation into consideration when dealing with the witness's own case and the judges give that a lot of weight. What they'll do is up to them." There is no further discussion along these lines. Koppel testifies at trial and Mallow is convicted. The defense first learns of the detective's conversation with Koppel after the conviction is affirmed on appeal. Was there a *Brady* violation? A violation of Rule 3.8(d)? Are the two answers the same? What more do you want to know?

One prominent set of constitutional rules regulating prosecutors derives from the landmark *Brady* decision. Brady v. Maryland, 373 U.S. 83 (1963). In Strickler v. Greene, 527 U.S. 263 (1999), the Court described the *Brady* obligation this way:

In *Brady* this Court held "that the suppression by the prosecution of evidence favorable to an accused upon request violates due process where the evidence is material either to guilt or to punishment, irrespective of the good faith or bad faith of the prosecution." We have since held that the duty to disclose such evidence is applicable even though there has been no request by the accused, and that the duty encompasses impeachment evidence as well as exculpatory evidence. Such evidence is material "if there is a reasonable probability that, had the evidence been disclosed to the defense, the result of the proceeding would have been different." Moreover, the rule encompasses evidence "known only to police investigators and not to the prosecutor." In order to comply with *Brady,* therefore, "the individual prosecutor has a duty to learn of any favorable evidence known to the others acting on the government's behalf in this case, including the police." . . .

This special status explains both the basis for the prosecution's broad duty of disclosure and our conclusion that not every violation of that duty necessarily establishes that the outcome was unjust. Thus the term "*Brady* violation" is sometimes used to refer to any breach of the broad obligation to disclose exculpatory evidence—that is, to any suppression of so-called "*Brady* material"—although, strictly speaking, there is never a real "*Brady* violation" unless the nondisclosure was so serious that there is a reasonable probability that the suppressed evidence would have produced a different verdict. There are three components of a true *Brady* violation: The evidence at issue must be favorable to the accused, either because it is exculpatory, or because it is impeaching; that evidence must have been suppressed by the State, either willfully or inadvertently; and prejudice must have ensued.

Evaluation of a *Brady* claim is addressed after conviction. This is because the defense may not know what the prosecutor withheld until then and because the prejudice component—a "reasonable probability" of a different outcome—is retrospective.* "A reasonable probability does not mean that the defendant 'would more likely than not have received a different verdict with the evidence,' only that the likelihood of a different result is great enough to 'undermine [] confidence in the outcome of the trial.'" Smith v. Cain, 565 U.S. 73 (2012). You need to know all the evidence to know if there's prejudice. As the Second Circuit explained in United States v. Certified Environmental Services, 753 F.3d 72 (2d Cir. 2014):

> "Although the government's obligations under *Brady* may be thought of as a constitutional duty arising before or during the trial of a defendant, the scope of the government's constitutional duty . . . is ultimately defined retrospectively, by reference to the likely effect that the suppression of particular evidence had on the outcome of the trial." . . . This aspect of *Brady* affects not only what the Government is obligated to disclose, but when it is required to do so. Temporally, "the timing of a disclosure required by *Brady* is . . . dependent upon the anticipated remedy for a violation of the obligation to disclose: the prosecutor must disclose . . . exculpatory and impeachment information no later than the point at which a reasonable probability will exist that the outcome would have been different if an earlier disclosure had been made."

The fact that the *Brady* inquiry is retrospective may tempt a prosecutor who is thinking like an advocate, not like the "minister of justice" she is, to withhold disclosure. "After all," she might think, "if I get a conviction, the defendant may never learn about the evidence, in which case no court will ever review my decision. If the evidence is discovered, the court may find a lack of prejudice. Even if the court does find prejudice, it will order a retrial. I don't have to worry about discipline because prosecutors are rarely disciplined.† If I disclose the exculpatory or impeaching evidence, however, this clever defense lawyer will use it to create a reasonable doubt and get the

---

* It is conceivable for a *Brady* issue to arise during or before trial if the prosecutor's turnover is too late to enable the defendant to make adequate use of the information. United States v. Lee, 573 F.3d 155 (3d Cir. 2009).

† Emily Bazelon, "She Was Convicted of Killing Her Mother. Prosecutors Withheld the Evidence That Would Have Freed Her," N.Y. Times Magazine, Aug. 1, 2017, is one among the occasional media stories that describes a miscarriage of justice due to *Brady* violations and the consequences (or lack of them) for the prosecutors.

acquittal of an obviously guilty defendant. Why is that justice? Why take the chance?"

In a dissent from a decision not to hear an appeal en banc, five Ninth Circuit judges analyzed these and other disincentives for a prosecutor to honor *Brady* obligations. United States v. Olsen, 737 F.3d 625 (9th Cir. 2013) (Kozinski, J., dissenting). Olsen had been convicted of "knowingly developing a biological agent for use as a weapon." The dissenters wrote:

> A robust and rigorously enforced *Brady* rule is imperative because all the incentives prosecutors confront encourage them not to discover or disclose exculpatory evidence. Due to the nature of a *Brady* violation, it's highly unlikely wrongdoing will ever come to light in the first place. This creates a serious moral hazard for those prosecutors who are more interested in winning a conviction than serving justice. In the rare event that the suppressed evidence does surface, the consequences usually leave the prosecution no worse than had it complied with *Brady* from the outset. Professional discipline is rare, and violations seldom give rise to liability for money damages. Criminal liability for causing an innocent man to lose decades of his life behind bars is practically unheard of. . . . If the violation is found to be material (a standard that will almost never be met under the panel's construction), the prosecution gets a do-over, making it no worse off than if it had disclosed the evidence in the first place.

"There is an epidemic of *Brady* violations abroad in the land," the dissenters added. "Only judges can put a stop to it." They cited as examples 29 federal and state cases finding *Brady* violations since 1998. The majority agreed that the withheld information—which would have undermined the credibility of a witness who testified that pills in Olsen's possession contained the poison ricin—should have been disclosed. But the majority found no reasonable probability that disclosure would have led to a different outcome.

A *Brady* violation may be found and a conviction overturned after many years of incarceration. If the accused is innocent, he will have lost years of his life. If guilty, the state may find it hard or impossible to retry him. A person whose conviction is overturned because a prosecutor has violated *Brady* or another constitutional right might seek monetary compensation for his incarceration. He can sue the prosecutor, of course, but must expect an immunity defense. Further, it's the city or county that will be able to pay significant damages. These entities are not vicariously liable for the misconduct of prosecutors. Instead, the plaintiff will have to prove that the prosecutor's conduct was the "policy" of the city or county. A policy may be proved by showing that, formally or not, a policymaker in the office (like the elected D.A. or other high officials) authorized or approved the conduct. But of course an office will never have an explicit policy to violate *Brady*. Policy may also be proved by showing conscious disregard of a risk of misconduct through failure to train prosecutors in their professional obligations or to punish prosecutors who have committed *Brady* violations. A "municipality's failure to train its employees in a relevant respect must amount to 'deliberate indifference to the rights of persons with whom the [untrained employees] come into contact'" in order to be an office policy. Connick v. Thompson, 563 U.S 51 (2011), quoting City of Canton v. Harris, 489 U.S. 378 (1989).

Connick itself reversed a $14 million verdict in favor of a man who spent 18 years in prison, 14 of them on death row. He was released following discovery of *Brady* violations and sued the office of the New Orleans District Attorney. In a 5-4 decision Justice Thomas held that the failure to train prosecutors on their *Brady* obligations did not reveal deliberate indifference because D.A. Connick could assume that his prosecutors knew their obligations, or at least knew enough to know to research close questions. The fact that in the decade before Thompson's trial, state courts had overturned four convictions from Connick's office for *Brady* violations did not count, Justice Thomas wrote, because those cases involved different kinds of *Brady* violations.

A year after *Connick*, the Supreme Court (8-1, Thomas dissenting) overturned a conviction from the same New Orleans District Attorney's office based on *Brady* violations. Smith v. Cain, 565 U.S. 73 (2012). The undisclosed evidence consisted of the contradictory statements of prosecution witness Boatner, the only eyewitness to the crime. At oral argument, the state's lawyer seemed to maintain that although it would have been "prudent" to do so, *Brady* did not require turnover. Justice Sotomayor was surprised: "[I]t is somewhat disconcerting that your office is still answering equivocally on [as] basic [an] obligation as one that requires you to have turned these materials over." In his opinion for the Court, the Chief Justice wrote:

> Boatner's undisclosed statements directly contradict his testimony: Boatner told the jury that he had "[n]o doubt" that Smith was the gunman he stood "face to face" with on the night of the crime, but [a detective's] notes show Boatner saying that he "could not ID anyone because [he] couldn't see faces" and "would not know them if [he] saw them." Boatner's undisclosed statements were plainly material.

Connick sparked a good bit of discussion in the profession, mostly critical. One reaction was a 2014 opinion from the ABA Standing Committee on Ethics and Professional Responsibility, addressing the ethical, as opposed to the constitutional, duties of supervisors and managers in prosecutorial offices. ABA Opinion 467 (2014) recognizes that no single set of rules can apply to all prosecutorial agencies regardless of size and structure. The opinion offers detailed guidance on how managers and supervisors can fulfill their duties under Rules 5.1 and 5.3.

Is the Rule 3.8(d) Turnover Duty Broader Than *Brady*?

You would think so after reading Rule 3.8(d), wouldn't you?

As we've seen, the *Brady* inquiry occurs after conviction. The defendant must prove a "reasonable probability" of a different trial outcome. Rule 3.8(d), by contrast, requires a prosecutor to "timely" disclose certain information, which means when the defense can still use it at trial. It has no prejudice component, only a turnover duty. Because prosecutors do not know the defense case, they are not in a position to say how the information the rule describes (i.e., information that "tends to negate the guilt of the accused or mitigates the offense") may help the defense or, conversely, whether a failure to provide it will cause prejudice. Evaluating prejudice after conviction substitutes judges for defense lawyers, who would otherwise have assessed the usefulness of the information, and for jurors, who would otherwise have decided what weight to give it. When followed, Rule 3.8(d) should avoid the need for a judge to decide years or decades later whether exculpatory information would have helped. No need to guess. The evidence would have been disclosed before trial.*

Even though the text of the rule is explicitly broader than *Brady*, courts are divided on whether or not to read it that way. The question arises in discipline or judicial review of a bar ethics opinion (where allowed), not in an appeal from a conviction. In re Riek, 834 N.W.2d 384 (Wis. 2013), failed to see how the two rules worked in tandem and held that Rule 3.8(d) was not broader than *Brady*.

> Under conflicting standards, prosecutors would face uncertainty as to how to proceed and could face professional discipline for failing to disclose evidence even when applicable constitutional law does not require disclosure of the same evidence. The practical effect—disclosing evidence to avoid disciplinary sanctions—could effectively expand the scope of discovery currently required of prosecutors in criminal cases. A broader interpretation also invites the use of the ethics rule as a tactical weapon in litigation, contrary to our stated intent in [the Preamble to the state's rules]. What better way to interfere with law enforcement efforts than to threaten a prosecutor with a bar complaint? Prosecutors should not be subjected to disciplinary proceedings for complying with legal disclosure obligations. We thus construe the ethical mandate of [the state equivalent to Rule 3.8(d)] in a manner consistent with the scope of disclosure required by the United States Constitution, federal or Wisconsin statutes, and court rules of procedure.

In agreement are State ex rel. Oklahoma Bar Ass'n v. Ward, 353 P.3d 509 (Okla. 2015) (collecting cases), and In re Petition to Stay the Effectiveness of Ethics Opinion, 582 S.W.3d 200 (Tenn. 2019), and other cases.

The District of Columbia Court of Appeals disagrees. In In re Kline, 113 A.3d 202 (D.C. 2015), the court rejected the claim that a broad reading of Rule 3.8(d) "will give rise to any confusion among local prosecutors as to what

---

* For an example of the demanding record review required to adequately evaluate a claim of prejudice, see Juniper v. Zook, 876 F.3d 551 (4th Cir. 2017) (Wynn, J.) (reversing a trial court's finding of no prejudice in a capital case after an extensive review of the trial transcript).

they are obligated to disclose." It cited and rebutted *Riek* and explained what it saw as the need for a broad reading of the rule:

> Retrospective analysis [of a turnover failure], while it necessarily comports with appellate review, is wholly inapplicable in pretrial prospective determinations. Specifically, in [precedent], this court recognized that *Brady* and its progeny were retrospective evaluations that were difficult to apply in a pretrial context. "While it is therefore true that the constitutional question commonly comes up retrospectively, the due process underpinning of [*Brady*] is a command for disclosure [b]efore an accused has to defend himself." . . .
>
> In short, although significant overlaps exist in a pretrial versus post-trial ethical analysis, it makes little common sense to premise a violation of an ethical rule on the effect compliance with that rule may have on the outcome of the underlying trial, because there can be "no objective, ad hoc way" for a prosecutor "to evaluate before trial whether [evidence or information] will be material to the outcome." For that reason, it is important not to use *Brady* as a "canon of prosecutorial ethics." . . .
>
> Further, adopting an ethical rule that errs in favor of disclosure will better ensure that criminal defendants in the District of Columbia receive a fair trial. All too often we are asked to decide whether information withheld by the government was exculpatory and whether that information undermined the fairness of the criminal trial in that case. Often, the call is a close one, with the court making the best judgments it can about the impact the exculpatory evidence would have had on a jury's verdict or whether the information would have led to other potentially exculpatory information that might have impacted the jury's verdict. These are judgment calls that can undermine the public's trust and confidence in the courts because they are not being made by a jury of one's peers but by a court that is sitting and reviewing a cold record.

In agreement is In re Feland, 820 N.W.2d 672 (N.D. 2012). The ABA has also construed the rule, which the ABA itself promulgated, as broader than *Brady*. ABA Opinion 09-454. And, remarkably, so has the Supreme Court! Kyles v. Whitley, 514 U.S. 419 (1995), observed that *Brady* "requires less of the prosecution than the ABA Standards for Criminal Justice," citing *both* the Standards and Rule 3.8(d). But state courts are not bound by the Supreme Court's reading of Rule 3.8(d) when they construe their own version of that rule, even if their version is identical to the rule the Supreme Court cited. State high courts are the final arbiters of the meaning of state ethics rules.*

---

* In one way, the *Brady* obligation is broader than Rule 3.8(d). *Brady* is violated even when a prosecutor is ignorant of exculpatory information known to law enforcement. Rule 3.8(d) requires that the prosecutor personally know the information. However, as the Court wrote in Strickler v. Greene, supra, "'the individual prosecutor has a duty to learn of any favorable evidence known to the others acting on the government's behalf in this case, including the police.'"

2. *Ethical Issues in Making the Charging Decision*

Prosecutors have no client in the ordinary sense. Yes, their client is the State, or the People, or the United States. But practically speaking, the prosecutor is both the representative of the client and its lawyer. She (or her supervisors) make the decisions that ordinarily belong to the client.

Rule 3.8(a) requires a prosecutor to "refrain from prosecuting a charge that the prosecutor knows is not supported by probable cause." That's not much of a rule. First, who could possibly argue with it? Prosecutors can't prosecute a person who is legally innocent even if they think the person is factually guilty. Second, why would a prosecutor waste resources prosecuting someone likely to be acquitted or whose conviction is likely to be overturned for lack of evidence? Perhaps because the charge itself will win cooperation in the investigation of others. Or it might lead to a plea bargain because the defendant will not know what evidence the prosecutor has (or does not have) and may not want to risk trial. Rule 3.8(a) implicitly rejects the legitimacy of those motives. Third, the rule applies only when the prosecutor "knows" the charges are not supported by probable cause. It would seem practically impossible to prove a violation of the rule. Sure, charges may turn out to lack probable cause, but that doesn't mean the prosecutor knew it. You would need a smoking-gun confession, which is most unlikely.

The interesting ethical issue here is not whether, before proceeding, the prosecutor must have probable cause to charge or, as some describe it, whether she must or should have evidence sufficient to support a finding of proof beyond a reasonable doubt, a higher burden. Let's say she has that proof. Then, she may charge or not, and if she charges, she can often select from a menu of crimes. Because no rule constrains her decision when she has the proof, her choices truly are ethical in the everyday meaning of the word. What is the *right* thing to do? What is the right thing to do in the case against Anita Winslow and Abel Mertz?

The People of the State of Montana v. Anita Winslow and Abel Mertz

The major industries in Skyler, Montana, population 27,300, are ranching and farming. It gets a bit of tourism, mostly people on their way to Yellowstone or Grand Teton National Parks. It's a typical rural Western town in just about every way, including one way its citizens regret. In the last five years, opioids have come to Skyler.

At first, Sheriff Baxter Lovell and D.A. Sue Kochin had to deal with small sellers in rural parts of the county. They thought they had put an end to it. But lately they learned that large quantities were coming through Montana from Denver and Chicago for sale locally and in the west. Skyler was becoming a distribution hub. Lovell and Kochin have witnessed the drug's effects. Victims include infants and children whose parents neglect them, whole families when a user withdraws savings or pawns valuables, targets of violent crimes, and burglarized pharmacies. Lovell and Kochin are part of a group of regional law enforcement officials addressing the problem.

Anita Winslow is the daughter of a single mother. Her father disappeared when she was six. Her mother works two jobs to support the family, which includes Winslow's brother Andy, 15. Winslow, 20, is a student at Skyler Community College.

To discover the drug's distributors, Lovell has been trying to arrange a controlled buy for nearly a year. Over Thanksgiving weekend, he got lucky. One of his deputies arranged to make a $10,000 buy in the parking lot of a big box store. At dusk, a car pulled up and Anita Winslow exited the passenger side and walked to the undercover car with a paper bag. She passed it through the window and received $10,000 in marked money. The bag contained fentanyl, a synthetic opioid 30 to 50 times more powerful than heroin. The driver of Winslow's car appeared to be a male in his 30s, whose face was obscured by a wide-brimmed hat and oversized sunglasses. He apparently suspected a setup and sped away leaving Winslow, who was arrested. The car, found abandoned in Bend, Oregon a day later, had been stolen in Duluth, Minnesota. Fingerprints and eyewitnesses enabled the police to connect Abel Mertz with the car and they arrested him.

The case against Winslow is strong. The entire event was videotaped, and Winslow made recorded statements showing that she knew the contents of the bag. In a valid search of her home, police found a quantity of opioids with a street value of $20,000 and nearly $14,000 in cash hidden in a hollowed-out copy of *The Girl with the Dragon Tattoo*.

Winslow was released to the custody of her mother but required to wear an ankle bracelet. A lawyer, Beth Wooten, was appointed to represent her. Kochin told Wooten that she was prepared to charge Winslow with the lowest-grade drug felony. In light of Winslow's age, this will permit a diversionary sentence of treatment and eventual expungement of the conviction. But as part of the deal, Winslow had to plead guilty, tell Kochin everything she knows, and accept two years supervised probation, to testify against Mertz and others.

Winslow repeatedly refused to talk to either Kochin or even Wooten. Wooten told her that absent a deal, the quantity Winslow sold and possessed would permit Kochin to prosecute under the top felony drug charge, which carries a mandatory sentence of 20 years to life. The judge won't have a choice. While Winslow would likely get out in 20 years, at age 40, there would be no guarantee. Wooten explained in great and unpleasant detail the conditions of confinement at the women's prison in Billings, which is a six-hour drive from Winslow's home. But Winslow remained adamant.

Kochin, Lewis Tan, her senior deputy, Cody Miller, Montana's criminal justice coordinator, and Taya Whitehorse, the first assistant attorney general of the state, meet to discuss Winslow and Mertz. All have been working on the opioid problem, which has grown worse since the arrests two months ago. It was apparent that the distribution ring had found replacements for Mertz and Winslow. A week earlier the police discovered three children under five, one an infant, dehydrated and hungry. Their parents were passed out in the bedroom.

Whitehorse wants Kochin to charge Winslow with the top drug felony. "Conviction is certain," she says. "She'll come around pretty fast after a few months at Billings. We then ask the court to vacate the convictions and let her plead down. Courts have never refused when we can show cooperation."

"And if she doesn't come around," Miller says, "her life is ruined."

Whitehorse says, "How about the children who are suffering in this epidemic? I include the teenage users, as well as the children of parents who are too strung out to take care of them. Aren't their lives ruined? They're Winslow's victims. We owe all of them, and future victims, an effort to turn her. We don't owe Anita Winslow anything if she refuses to help us help them."

"Maybe whatever she knows won't help us anyway," Tan says.

"We're only asking her to tell us what she does know," Kochin says. "We do know that in the last half year she disappeared several times and then lied to her mother about where she was. A Greyhound driver remembers her going to Yakima about two months before the arrest. We got video confirmation from the bus depot. She stayed three days. The feds say Yakima is a distribution point for Portland, Eugene, Seattle, and Spokane. It looks like she was more than just a local dealer in Skyler. Why else would a 20-year-old spend three days in Yakima?"

"What would we charge without regard to whether she helped us?" Miller asks.

"There is no 'without regard,'" Whitehorse says. "It's all part of the moral equation. Helping us is a factor in deciding the appropriate charge. Judges do that all the time at sentencing, just as they consider whether the defendant has taken responsibility and pled guilty. You're not saying that cooperation can never be a factor."

Miller says, "Well, that's really the question, Taya, isn't it? Some defendants have no information to trade."

"Flip it," Kochin says. "Let's say hypothetically, charging a five-year felony would be appropriate given that she's dealing, not just using, and because we believe she has no information. We offer five but then her lawyer tells us that she does have information to trade and tries to plea bargain down. Would we reject that?"

"Of course, not," Miller says. "But Taya wants us to charge higher, then offer to plead down for cooperation. That's different. Isn't it?"

"Not here, Cody. Because contrary to the assumptions in Sue's question, we know that Winslow has information that could help us, at least about Mertz and the Yakima people and probably more. Besides I hope you're not saying that cooperation can get a reduction from some 'appropriate' benchmark, if there even is such a thing, but a refusal to help can't justify a higher charge. A one-way street?"

The conversation turned to Mertz. "Mertz was convicted of opioid sales five years ago and served 39 months in Ohio," Tan reported. "Informants tell us he was second in charge of distribution in the Northwest. He'll know others that Winslow doesn't. He's 33. We think Mertz and Winslow have been intimate. Mertz is married, which Winslow may not know. If she did, she might not be willing to protect him. It looks like he groomed her for the work. Showed her a lot of attention. Made her feel special."

"We should charge him with a 20 to life felony, too," Whitehorse says, "and offer 10 to 20 if he pleads and cooperates. If Winslow agrees to testify and helps us, our case against him will be stronger."

Miller says, "What kind of case do we have against Mertz without Winslow? Ironic, isn't it. He's a ringleader, but our case against her is stronger. We have the video of the buy, the bag of opioids, the marked money, the undercover's testimony, her statements, and the contents from her room search. For him, the video of the buy won't help much. There's a man generally matching his description, but his face is hidden. We can tie him to the car and the car to the buy. But putting him *in the car at the buy*? I don't know. He ditched the hat and sunglasses. We have enough to get to the jury, but just barely."

They all turn to Kochin. Miller says, "Sue, it's your call. You're the elected D.A. We will support whatever you decide." Kochin says she wants to do "the right thing." She's worried about her community and future fentanyl victims. She also wants to be fair. No rule tells her what to do. What should she do?

3. The Victim's Interest in How a Prosecutor Decides

Although a crime victim is not the prosecutor's client and cannot make decisions that a client is entitled to make, victims do have an interest in whether a case is brought, in any plea offer, and at sentence, where victims are allowed to speak. Prosecutors may and often do discuss these questions with victims. Yet the prosecutor alone has the power and responsibility to answer them. So then, what can victims reasonably expect? What does society owe them? Consultation? Information? Anything else?

Contributions to Justice

"I've been the elected D.A. in Clarendon County for 14 years. Last two times I ran, I had no opposition. I run a nonpolitical office. I hire on merit and that's also how I make my decisions. The county seat is Ralston, where I have my office. It's a city of about 122,000, half of the county's population. A lot of what I do is management, not law. I have 27 assistant prosecutors. We're stretched. Our budget, which we get from the state, is inadequate for the job I'd like to do. I don't think there's a D.A. in my state (or maybe any other) who doesn't say the same. But we do our best.

"One of the biggest employers in the county is Extant Technologies, which makes computer chips and other components. Extant came into the county a dozen years ago, starting small, but it grew as the demand for computers grew. It has a specialty niche I don't understand but it's special enough to insulate it from Silicon Valley competition. It pays good salaries and augments the tax base, so all in all it's been a real blessing.

"Two months ago, Sally Hendricks, who's a partner at a leading firm in the state and a lawyer for Extant, made an appointment to see me because, she said, Extant believed that certain former employees had stolen secret technology. Our penal law was amended five years ago to cover such things. Sally gave me a four-inch-thick file, the product of her firm's investigation. Tell you the truth, this is not what we're used to dealing with. It's not fingerprints, ballistics, and lineups. We've just gotten comfortable with DNA.

"I tried to read the file but I didn't understand the half of it. A couple of my assistants, the younger ones, understand more than I do. But not enough more. The bottom line is we haven't got the resources to prosecute this case. We don't have the money to hire the experts who can help us understand what happened and guide our investigation or the experts to testify if it goes to trial. Extant's former employees do have the money and expertise and they'd run rings around us.

"I had another meeting with Sally and told her just that. She said Extant realized this might be so and was prepared to do one of two things, whichever we choose. It would make its personnel available to walk us through the technology and testify at trial. Or it would give us a budget to hire any qualified experts we picked to do the same. Extant was quite concerned that failure to prosecute would only invite additional thefts. Of course, I understand that. I said, 'Let's call the Feds.' Sally said she went to them first, which I could understand. The feds said they would look at it when they could get to it. We know what that means.

"'Aren't you in effect looking to privatize my office?' I asked Sally. I've known her a long time. She used to work for me.

" 'No, Bonnie, not at all,' she said. You'll make all the decisions—no matter the help we give you. You'll decide whether to charge at all, what to charge, whether to offer a plea. We'll just provide the knowledge base. We don't want you to reject this case because you don't understand the technology or can't afford the experts. Those would be the wrong reasons.' I said I'd get back.

"That brings me to my question. Can I accept either of Sally's offers?"

Whose Reasonable Doubt?

At 11 P.M. on a Sunday in June, Patsy Prasad, a young actress, was robbed while on her way home from a theater party. The incident left a small scar on her chin. She stayed calm enough to study the face of her assailant, who said, "Give it up. Your cell phone, too." A passerby saw the face of the assailant as he ran off. The police discovered a footprint in the mud, with an unusual pattern, a half block away in the direction the assailant fled.

Following days of looking at mug shot photos, Prasad and the passerby, Anthony Munoz, independently picked the same photo and then each separately identified the same man in a lineup. The man is Morris Charles. A search of his home produced a pair of sneakers with caked mud and a footprint that is "consistent with" the one found near the scene of the robbery, according to the police lab. Prasad is "totally sure he's the guy who hurt me," and Munoz is "very sure."

Charles, 28, has two misdemeanor convictions for street robberies when he was 23 and 25. One was a plea bargain from a felony. Asher McEvoy, his appointed lawyer, has asserted an alibi defense. Charles will testify that he was miles away drinking with three friends at the time of the robbery. The two misdemeanors cannot be used to impeach his credibility.

The case is assigned to Viveka Montrose, an assistant D.A. who heads the street crimes unit. She indicted Charles on a class C felony, carrying a potential sentence of seven to 15 years. Montrose believes she has a strong case. She believes she will successfully cross-examine Charles and his three alibi witnesses. Two of them were vague when questioned by the police and in fact contradicted each other on some details. One of the witnesses is distantly related to Charles. And Charles said nothing about an alibi when first questioned at his home before his arrest. Also, Prasad has been highly cooperative, which has not always been Montrose's experience with victims, especially as cases drag on.

Prasad is prominent. She played "Honey" in a revival of Edward Albee's "Who's Afraid of Virginia Woolf?" and was nominated for an Academy Award for her portrayal of Ariella Sue Fishbein in Woody Allen's film *The Hungarian Herring Heist*. The news media will cover the trial.

In an effort to resolve the case before trial, Montrose offered Charles an E felony with a sentence recommendation of two years. Charles rejected it.

At trial, Montrose's case begins to fall apart. Munoz is now only "pretty sure" when he identifies Charles in court. On cross, McEvoy gets him to say that he "isn't certain it wasn't someone else, but I'm pretty sure it was him," pointing to Charles. "I mean it was dark." Prasad gets confused on cross-examination and has to correct herself on minor details. McEvoy spends 20 minutes reviewing the precise number, times, and types of drinks Prasad had at her party and whether she is an experienced drinker ("not very"). Charles and his three alibi witnesses testify more credibly than expected despite some inconsistencies. A manager of the company that made Charles's sneakers testifies that more than 400 pairs were sold in the city before the line was discontinued.

As the evidence draws to a close after six days of trial, Montrose realizes that she now has a reasonable doubt about Charles's guilt. If she were on the jury, she would vote to acquit. At the same time, Montrose knows that the evidence amply supports a finding of guilt beyond a reasonable doubt if the jury credits it. She is also confident that she can make an effective argument on summation.

Prasad has no doubts at all. She is more certain than ever. "I remember him like it was yesterday," she tells Montrose after Charles testifies. "This is the guy that cut me. No question. I recognized his face and I recognized his voice when he testified. You did a great cross. The jury didn't believe him either. I watched their faces. He'll do it again if he's not locked up."

Montrose takes her concerns to her boss, Burton Morgenstern, the elected D.A. Summations are scheduled for the following Monday, after Montrose calls one rebuttal witness on the footprint evidence. She asks Morgenstern what she should do given her own doubt. "What if anything at this stage do I or the office owe to Prasad? To Charles? To the public? To the jurors who sat through the trial? This case has been in the news every day because of Prasad."

Morgenstern says, "Look, Viveka, you've been here a dozen years. You've tried, what, 32, 33, felony cases, four in the last year. You head the street crimes unit. You have excellent judgment. You know the case. I know only its outline. I trust your judgment, which is why I picked you to head the unit. All I can tell you is, as far as the office is concerned, it's okay to let it go to the jury despite your doubt, and it's okay to drop it. You decide what's right."

Later in the day, while Montrose is reviewing the evidence and trying to decide what to do, McEvoy, the defense lawyer, calls. "Charles is willing to plead to an E felony with a recommendation of two years," he says. "Is the offer still open?"

You are someone whose judgment Montrose trusts. "What's the right thing to do?" she asks. "I know I can let this go to the jury, but my personal standard has been not to prosecute where I have a reasonable doubt."

Self-Assessment Questions

1. Brickstone is a large private equity firm. It buys and sells companies. Tony, the president of Brickstone, has learned that private plaintiffs may sue Brickstone and other private equity companies, including K.K.R., alleging that they had agreed not to bid against each other for target companies. That would violate antitrust laws. Tony consults you. He brings copies of two emails. In one, he wrote to others at Brickstone to say that George, a principal of K.K.R., "just called to say congratulations and that they were standing down [i.e., choosing not to bid for a company Brickstone wanted] because he had told me before they would not jump a signed deal of ours." In an email to George, Tony wrote that "[w]e would much rather work with you guys than against you. Together we can be unstoppable but in opposition we can cost each other a lot of money." George replied, "Agreed."

   What advice do you give Tony about the emails? What else do you do?*

2. In the prosecution of Kiplinger for selling opioids, the government calls a scientist who testifies that a substance found in the defendant's home was an opioid. Unfortunately, the substance was destroyed in testing so it was not possible for the defense to conduct its own test. The scientist worked in a state crime laboratory. A year earlier, he had been dismissed from a job in a different state's crime laboratory because in three cases his testimony about the composition of a controlled substance was shown to be inaccurate. The defense lawyer knows this. An investigation in that other state later concluded that the scientist was not merely sloppy, but had lied, and this further conclusion is contained in a written report. However, the report was not yet public when the case was on trial and Kiplinger's defense lawyer was unaware of it. Kiplinger is convicted. He moves to overturn his conviction citing the *Brady* line of cases. Meanwhile, the state disciplinary committee opens an investigation into whether the prosecutor violated Rule 3.8(d). Analyze the issues in Kiplinger's motion and the issues before the disciplinary committee.

---

* Although the consultation described in this problem is hypothetical, the lawsuit and the quotes are real. "K.K.R., Blackstone and TPG Private Equity Firms Agree to Settle Lawsuit on Collusion," N.Y. Times, Aug. 7, 2014.

IX

Negotiation and Transactional Matters

He recalled what his favorite professor, Leonard Leech, once told him about getting ahead in law. Leech said that, just as a good airplane pilot should always be looking for places to land, so should a lawyer be looking for situations where large amounts of money were about to change hands.

"In every big transaction," said Leech, "there is a magic moment during which a man has surrendered a treasure, and during which the man who is due to receive it has not yet done so. An alert lawyer will make that moment his own, possessing the treasure for a magic microsecond, taking a little of it, passing it on. If the man who is to receive the treasure is unused to wealth, has an inferiority complex and shapeless feelings of guilt, as most people do, the lawyer can often take as much as half the bundle, and still receive the recipient's blubbering thanks."

—Kurt Vonnegut, Jr., *God Bless You, Mr. Rosewater*

Discourage litigation. Persuade your neighbors to compromise whenever you can. . . . As a peacemaker, the lawyer has superior opportunity of being a good man. There will still be business enough.

—Abraham Lincoln

I realized the true function of a lawyer was to unite parties riven asunder. The lesson was so indelibly burnt into me that a large part of my time during the twenty years of my practice as a lawyer was occupied in bringing about private compromises of hundreds of cases. I lost nothing thereby—not even money, certainly not my soul.

—Mahatma Gandhi (himself a lawyer)

When the final result is expected to be a compromise, it is often prudent to start from an extreme position.

—John Maynard Keynes

> Man is an animal that makes bargains: no other animal does this—no dog exchanges bones with another.
>
> —Adam Smith

A. LAWYERS AS NEGOTIATORS: AN INTRODUCTION

Negotiating is not an intrinsically legal service. Persons who are not members of the bar frequently negotiate for their clients without fear that they are engaging in unauthorized law practice. Agents of various kinds—real estate, literary, business, sports, talent, theatrical—negotiate large deals. Most are not lawyers and do not have to be, unless they also want to draft the client's contract.

Although not every negotiator is a lawyer, virtually every lawyer is, at one time or another, a negotiator. It is nearly impossible to have a legal career without some need to negotiate. Some lawyers negotiate rarely, others do daily. Litigators negotiate settlements and pleas much more often than they try cases. How is it that lawyers have so large a share of the negotiating market even though negotiation is not, for the most part,* the practice of law, and anyone can do it? The answer seems clear enough for litigators negotiating settlements. They negotiate against the backdrop of the risks at trial, whose assessment requires legal judgment. But what about transactional matters? In part, the answer is circumstantial. Many clients who need services that only lawyers can lawfully provide under unauthorized practice of law rules—for example, writing contracts, preparing instruments for filing in real estate transactions, establishing security for a loan, effecting a merger—must also negotiate incident to their need for the legal service. The lawyer can do both.

As with litigation, negotiation is built on the premises of the adversary system. In negotiation, as in litigation, each party is responsible for its own legal and factual research and, ordinarily, has no duty to share what it learns. Information imbalance can be greater in negotiation than in litigation because there is no formal discovery. If lawyer A (or her client) is a more thorough researcher than lawyer B (or her client), she can exploit her greater knowledge to her client's advantage. If lawyer C is not as informed on the law as lawyer D and does not appreciate the implications of a particular contract provision or its omission, that's no concern of lawyer D, whose client will benefit.

But it is not an unalloyed adversary system. Chapter 7 introduced us to the limits in litigation. Negotiation also has limits. A lawyer may not lie, assist fraud, deceive, or remain silent if substantive law imposes a duty to speak. See Rules 1.2(d), 4.1, and 8.4(a) and (c). The law may impose disclosure obligations for some transactions (e.g., in securities or home sales). If that were all, this chapter could end here, but it is not all. There are uncertainties that carry risk for lawyers.

---

* Negotiation that requires contract interpretation may be considered law practice. See chapter 12C.

The scope of a lawyer's responsibility to other parties to a negotiation raises some daunting issues in "big ticket" transactional matters. The term "transactional," as applied to a lawyer's work, came increasingly into vogue somewhere between the first and seventh editions of this book, at about the time male Wall Street lawyers started to copy the Gordon Gekko look. As played by Michael Douglas in *Wall Street*, the money men wore suspenders, had slicked-back hair, rarely smiled, perfected intimidating stares, and rode in stretch limos. The term has no precise meaning. It is sometimes used to mean "not litigation." But often it is used to describe the work of lawyers who do eight-, nine-, and ten-figure deals.

Negotiation risks for lawyers mainly arise in one of three ways.

- *First* is what we can call the "bad client" problem. You've been representing Kendra Karpit on a deal and you learn, at some point—maybe during the negotiation, maybe after the deal closes—that she's a fraudster and that, unwittingly, you've assisted her fraud. Maybe she concealed information the law required her to disclose or has made materially false statements. ("Materially" is a word lawyers use a lot. We define it soon. For the moment, consider that a statement is material if it could reasonably have mattered.) Or maybe Kendra is honest but unintentionally made a material false statement and now won't correct it. What can and should you do?

- *Second* is the risk of liability for your own statements where the client may or may not have done wrong. What you say (or fail to say) may violate a rule. It may also create civil liability even if you tried to be perfectly accurate and believed you were.

- *Third,* the opposing lawyer may be laboring under an erroneous factual or legal assumption that neither you nor your client created. Or he may have made an error, harmful to his client, in preparing the draft of a contract after you and he have agreed on its terms. May you exploit these errors? Must or may you correct your opponent?

B. NEGOTIATION: THE RISKS TO LAWYERS

1. The "Bad Client" Problem

The Bad Builder's Good Lawyer

MEMORANDUM
To: New Business Committee
From: Alicia Hariri

We've been asked to take a new case. The clients are the Sonibels, who purchased a second home in the Fair Mountain development. You recall the ads: high-end homes on three acres, lots of amenities, lakefront, tennis courts, golf, hiking trails. It has 52 homes in all, and the

Sonibels, an older couple approaching retirement, bought one of the most expensive three years ago. Assume we can prove the following facts, though we'll have to make a separate determination of that. The question for the new business committee is whether the Sonibels would have a case against Lucy McIntosh.

The builder is a guy named Howard Kluny. He'd been a home-builder for 30 years. He started Fair Mountain more than four years ago after he bought the Gerontin farm from Sam's estate. Lucy is—or was—Kluny's lawyer. She had worked for him in-house for six years when these events occurred.

Lucy's job included preparing or reviewing various documents: She wrote the master contract for the sales, which then became a form with the sales force filling in the blanks (price, home, financing, closing, etc.). She reviewed and approved the promotional materials, including brochures. Each of these documents represented that all systems in the homes would be above code. In fact, given the prices (the Sonibels paid about $2.8 million), each document specified particular brands and qualities for appliances and materials. For the plumbing, the documents specified Arrow Point as the supplier, and the top of its line specifically, known as the A-X line. Lucy's name is on the contracts as Kluny's lawyer.

Lucy also handled the negotiation of the legal terms of the contracts and went to the closings with the buyers' lawyers. Kluny or his sales chief negotiated the economic terms of the contract price up to a point, whether Kluny would put in an extra window, a cook's stove, whatever. The Sonibels' lawyer and Lucy spent about an hour on a few small changes, not relevant here.

Well, it seems that shortly after the Sonibels showed up to buy, there was a strike at Arrow Point, and Kluny couldn't get what he needed. Meanwhile, he was paying the scheduled plumbers, but he had to suspend work on the homes that were ready for the plumbing installation. When houses are ready for the plumbers, there's not much else you can do. Or so I'm told. Kluny could have terminated the plumbing subcontractors for a penalty, and stopped the meter that way, but then he might not be able to get them back as soon as the strike ended. He needed to finish the houses so he could sell them. He needed to sell them to show his lender the purchase contracts before it would let him continue to draw down on his line of credit. Kluny was being squeezed pretty bad. He waited for a while. But the strike showed no sign of ending, and he was looking at mounting bills, and maybe thinking about bankruptcy if he couldn't finish the houses and get them to market. He tried to get equivalent quality elsewhere, but other builders had the same idea and nothing was immediately available.

So Kluny ordered inferior plumbing, up to code but barely. It was the best he could get at the time but far inferior to what he promised.

This stuff went into seven of the 52 homes before the strike ended. When I say "into," I mean *into*. In the walls, under the floors, in the ground. And these are really big homes.

The next thing that happened was that Lucy learned by accident what Kluny had done. She learned this several months after the strike had ended in casual conversation with one of the subcontractors. She questioned Kluny, who confessed but refused to rip out the marginal stuff and replace it with what he had promised. The seven homes were done or nearly done. One had since been sold and closed, three were in contract, and three were on the market. One of those in contract was the Sonibel home. Lucy suggested telling the buyers the situation and reducing the price, letting them out of the contract, buying back the house that had closed, or making some other concessions. Kluny, a crusty old guy, wouldn't do it. He said the pipes he put in were good enough. And they were buried in the walls and floor. No one would ever know.

Lucy quit her job the next day. I imagine she got advice from someone. But she said nothing about the plumbing to anyone, probably based on advice that what she knew was confidential. A couple of months later, the Sonibels closed on their house. Kluny got a new lawyer to handle the work Lucy used to do, and I'm sure told him nothing about the plumbing. He never changed the promotional materials.

So just to be clear on the sequence: When Lucy confronted Kluny, he had already put the inferior plumbing in the home that the Sonibels had contracted to buy. They had not yet closed. The contract and all advertising specified Arrow Point A-X. Lucy had negotiated its legal terms with the Sonibels' lawyer. Her name is in the contract as Kluny's lawyer.

Jump ahead about a year. Two months ago, the pipes in the Sonibel house burst while they were abroad celebrating their fortieth anniversary and—I'll spare you the details—the house is unlivable. The pipes burst around midnight on Thursday, January 3. The guy who checks the house twice weekly had just been by and all seemed fine. He didn't come by again until Monday, January 7. It is going to cost approaching $250,000 to rip out the plumbing, repair the damage, and put the house back in shape. But that's not all. The Sonibels had paintings, rugs, antiques, and a carload of stuff with sentimental value, all destroyed or seriously damaged. And, of course, they can't use the house for up to a year (not much work can get done in the winter). So their losses could reach $500,000 apart from any punitive damages.

The Sonibels want to sue everyone. So would I. Kluny, the real bad guy here, is unfortunately broke or claims he is. If we sue at all, we'll add him but I'm not sure what we'd get. That leaves Lucy McIntosh, who has significant personal assets and may have a malpractice policy.

The other six homes with inferior plumbing (all of which have now closed) haven't had a flood, but the buyers are now on notice and maybe they'll sue, too.

We've already concluded that Kluny's conduct is fraud under state law. My questions are about Lucy. Did her quiet withdrawal without warning violate the professional conduct rules? Do the Sonibels have a case against her?

"Come to the Cabaret"

Lenny Max retained Cindy Oranger to help him get a cabaret license in New York City. A cabaret is defined as: "Any room, place, or space in which patron dancing is permitted in connection with the restaurant business or a business that sells food and/or beverages to the public." Lenny owns a barbecue restaurant. A trio plays country music on weekends. Lenny wants to allow patron dancing.

The application for a cabaret license asks whether the applicant has ever been convicted of a crime. Eight years ago, in another state, Lenny pled guilty to a misdemeanor. He permitted illegal gambling in a restaurant he managed and was fined $5,000. Lenny did not tell Cindy about the conviction. The application, which Cindy prepared and submitted and Lenny signed under oath, omitted it. The Department of Consumer Affairs inspected Lenny's restaurant to ensure compliance with various requirements (electrical, sound insulation, fire safety). Lenny put a tasteful neon blue sign in the front window:

COME TO THE
CABARET
DINE AND DANCE
LIVE MUSIC

Lenny's reservations increased nearly 20 percent. He was reviewed in New York Magazine and Lonely Planet. He was rated the fifth best barbecue restaurant in New York City on TripAdvisor. Then, several months later, he told Cindy about his misdemeanor conviction.

Cindy reads Rules 1.0(m), 3.3, 3.9 and its comments [3] and [4], and 4.1. But she's unsure of her obligations and seeks your advice. Assume New York has the Model Rules (it doesn't).

The bad client problem weighs loyalty and confidentiality against the interest in avoiding or minimizing harm to innocent victims of a client's illegal conduct or to courts and other tribunals. Which interest prevails in the event of a clash? Compare Rule 4.1(b) with Rule 3.3. A lawyer may have to correct fraud or a false statement in a matter before a tribunal even if that means revealing confidences protected by Rule 1.6. But what if there is no tribunal? What if the issue arises in a negotiation? A lawyer, Rule 4.1(b) tells us, "shall not knowingly . . . fail to disclose a material fact to a third person" when it is "necessary" to avoid assisting a client's "criminal or fraudulent act . . . *unless disclosure is prohibited by Rule 1.6.*" (Emphasis added.) On a casual reading, it looks like Rule 4.1 has flipped the priorities when compared with Rule 3.3. Now confidentiality seems to prevail. This appears to be true even if the client's crime or fraud will be financially devastating to third parties, even if revelation can stop the crime or fraud before it is concluded or can at least minimize the damage, and even though the lawyer may have been an unwitting enabler of the unlawful conduct.

Of course, a lawyer who discovers that a client is perpetrating a fraud or a crime cannot assist the client (risking civil and criminal liability and discipline if she does) and will have to withdraw from the particular representation. Rules 1.2(d), 1.16(a)(1). But if the lawyer withdraws without alerting the former client's intended victim before the fraud or crime is accomplished, or when harm from it can still be avoided or reversed, isn't there a risk that the victim will later sue the lawyer for failure to warn, as happened in the famous *O.P.M.* case discussed in the note on noisy withdrawal on the next page? While the lawyer may defend by pointing to her confidentiality duty, the court may hold that an ethics rule does not displace tort liability, especially where the lawyer had unwittingly aided the harm. Can she just walk away, saying nothing, like Lucy McIntosh did in "The Bad Builder's Good Lawyer"?

What's more, Rule 4.1 may not, on closer examination, make the confidentiality duty superior to the disclosure duty in jurisdictions that have adopted Rule 4.1(b) — most have — particularly in light of two exceptions introduced by the 2003 amendments to Rule 1.6. This analysis is a bit technical, requiring close parsing of the text. But lawyers who negotiate can be at risk of personal liability (as well as discipline) if they are unfortunate enough to find that their client is up to no good, they say nothing, and a third party is harmed. So understanding the interplay between Rules 1.6 and 4.1 and between those rules and the substantive law is essential.

Rule 4.1(b) says that confidentiality prevails *only* when disclosure is "prohibited" by Rule 1.6. But four confidentiality exceptions may *permit* disclosure in these circumstances. When one of these exceptions is available, Rule 1.6 does not "prohibit" disclosure and Rule 4.1's mandate — "shall not knowingly . . . fail to disclose" — is left standing.* Whether a client's conduct is a crime or fraud and whether a lawyer's silence would constitute assisting it are questions of law. Assume both. The confidentiality exceptions are:

- Rule 1.6(b)(2), which permits a lawyer to reveal confidential information to prevent a client's crime or fraud that is reasonably certain to cause substantial financial injury to a third person if the client has used the lawyer's services in committing the misconduct.

---

* The wording of the rule is odd. Would the rule work better if "not fail to" were omitted and the rule simply said "shall disclose"?

- Rule 1.6(b)(3), which permits the disclosure even if the fraud is completed but the injury can still be prevented, mitigated, or rectified. Rectification envisions retroactive correction.
- Rule 1.6(b)(6), which permits disclosure to "comply with other law or a court order." Like Rule 1.6(b)(2) and (b)(3), Rule 1.6(b)(6) is widely adopted.
- Rule 1.13(c), which permits a lawyer for an organization to disclose confidential information outside the organization to protect the organization from certain harms from constituent misconduct.

Rule 1.6(b)(2) and (b)(3) may have permitted Lucy McIntosh to disclose Kluny's conduct to the Sonibels. Assume it did. How would that help answer Alicia Hariri's question? What about Cindy Oranger? Lenny's lie about his misdemeanor conviction did not cause financial harm to anyone. Rule 4.1(b) would seem to block disclosure. If, however, the Consumer Affairs Department is a "nonadjudicative tribunal" within the meaning of Rule 3.9, Cindy would have the same remedial obligations to it that Rule 3.3(a) through (c) imposes on lawyers who appear in tribunals. We studied these in chapter 7. But maybe the department is not a tribunal at all. See Rule 3.9 cmt. [3]. Then, Cindy's authority (even a duty) to disclose Lenny's lie would have to come from elsewhere—perhaps Rule 1.6(b)(6) together with Rule 4.1(b). What else do you need to know before advising Cindy?

The Noisy Withdrawal

This is the place to reintroduce the noisy withdrawal, briefly mentioned in chapter 2. It is an idea that was once as novel as it was controversial, but which has become less prominent (but still relevant) in light of the exceptions to confidentiality in Rule 1.6(b)(2) and (b)(3) and Rule 1.13. Think of a noisy withdrawal as halfway between quietly slinking away when a lawyer discovers a client's fraudulent or criminal conduct, on one hand, and invoking the authority of a confidentiality exception to warn the client's victim, on the other hand. But how can you go halfway?

Long ago and far away . . . well, actually, in New York City in the 1970s and 1980s, a law firm called Singer Hutner represented a company called O.P.M. Without the firm's knowledge, O.P.M. officers used fictitious collateral (forged leases that purported to show a cash flow) as security for big bank loans. Believing that the collateral existed, the law firm had prepared documents that aided the client in getting the loans and made certain representations to the banks. The lawyers eventually discovered the ruse and confronted the client's officers, who confessed.

The lawyers sought advice from a local law dean, who consulted an adjunct faculty member who taught legal ethics. They advised that the lawyers' confidentiality duty under the former Code of Professional Responsibility prevented disclosure to the banks and that the firm should stop representing the client unless the client promised not to do it again.

The client promised not to do it again. The firm continued to represent it. But the promise was as false as the leases. When the firm realized that the client was still up to no good, it withdrew. Quietly. The client went to a new lawyer. The new lawyer called the former lawyer to find out why he had let such an attractive client get away. (It paid its bills.) The former lawyer said something vague about a breakdown in the relationship and the new lawyer accepted the client. (*Lesson*: When a new client is changing lawyers, insist that it free the former lawyer to reveal the true story. If it won't, that's a danger sign.) Soon enough, O.P.M. collapsed. Its officers went to prison. And a joke went around that O.P.M. stood for Other People's Money.

Next came the lawsuits. The banks wanted their money. The client was toast. So the banks sued Singer Hutner, which was insured, among others. The firm's insurance company paid up (purportedly $20 million), revealing its lack of confidence in the law dean's advice and a defense based on the firm's duty of confidentiality. But that wasn't the end of it. Lawyers everywhere worried. What if it happened again? (To *us*?) How should lawyers reconcile the confidentiality duty with the strong desire not to be sitting on the wrong side of a multimillion-dollar lawsuit brought by a client's victims? The solution was the noisy withdrawal authority, which now appears in Rules 1.2 comment [10] and 4.1 comment [3].

The idea is simple. Of course, a lawyer must withdraw from a representation when he learns that the client is engaged in a crime or fraud and won't reform. The O.P.M. lawyers (eventually) did that, but they got sued anyway. So now, the comments say, when lawyers withdraw, they can also "disaffirm an opinion, document, affirmation or the like" that they may have given to the client's victim. That's the noisy part. The option is not always discretionary. If under the substantive law the only way to avoid "assisting" the client's crime or fraud is by disaffirming something, then a *noisy* withdrawal (at least) is mandatory. The conversation with opposing counsel might go like this:

> "Hi, Eloise. I just wanted you to know I'm no longer representing Crooked and Sly."
>
> "Sorry to hear it, Sherlock. I've enjoyed working with you and Watson."
>
> "And I have to tell you something else, Eloise. Remember that letter I sent you last March 5, where I gave you certain information about the deal?"
>
> "Sure do. Very useful."
>
> "Well, I take it back. Don't rely on anything I said there. For anything. Whatsoever. At all. Email notice to follow."
>
> "What? Why, Sherlock?"
>
> "I can't say any more. Bye." Click.

Thus may a lawyer warn and perhaps prevent the harm or at least hope to avoid liability. But Sherlock did not literally reveal the client's confidences. The ABA was certainly ambivalent about this compromise. It placed it in a comment. New York, home to O.P.M., went further. It put its differently worded version in its Code of Professional Responsibility and retained it when it moved to a rules format. See New York Rule 1.6(b)(3).

What if there is no document or opinion for a lawyer to disaffirm? Then, there is nothing to withdraw and this option won't work.

Rule 1.6(b)(2) and (b)(3) expands the confidentiality exceptions and diminishes the importance of the noisy withdrawals comments. It allows full-blown revelation. But the noisy withdrawal alternative remains available in jurisdictions (like New York) that have not adopted these exceptions or when they don't apply (for example, if the financial injury will not be "substantial"). Even where Rule 1.6(b)(2) and (b)(3) is in force, noisy withdrawal offers an alternative that lawyers may find as effective and less traumatic than revealing confidential information.

Court opinions dealing with these issues in negotiation are few, but one is In re Potts, 158 P.3d 418 (Mont. 2007) (in will contest, lawyer disciplined for failure to correct misimpression created by client's statement about the size of the estate).

For more on the *O.P.M.* saga, see Susan Koniak, When the Hurlyburly's Done: The Bar's Struggle with the SEC, 103 Colum. L. Rev. 1236 (2003).

2. *The Lawyer's Own Statements*

Rule 8.4(c) forbids "conduct involving dishonesty, fraud, deceit, or misrepresentation" even if not while representing a client.* Rule 4.1(a) tells us that in representing a client "a lawyer shall not knowingly make a false statement of material fact or law to a third person." This prohibition does not depend on whether the false statement assists (or is) a fraud or crime. Lawyers cannot speak falsely to a third person, at least not *materially* falsely, when representing a client. The prohibition sounds right, doesn't it? But when exactly is a statement false? Materially false? We saw in chapter 7 how the words "true" and "false" seem to have different meanings in the part of Lawyerland called Litigation than they do in Real Life. What is false in the part called Negotiation? What is dishonest?

True or False in Negotiation Land

Are the following statements "true" or "false" within the meaning of Rules 4.1 and 8.4(c)?

a. "My client won't take less than $200,000." In fact, the client has authorized the lawyer to settle for half that amount. Or the statement might be rephrased as "My client wants $200,000," which is true. Then the other lawyer asks, "Will he take $100,000?"

---

* This rule must be read to apply only in professional or commercial endeavors, not to a lawyer's lies in his or her private life.

b. "If you don't lower your price, my client will get a new supplier." The client has told the lawyer that no one else can supply the particular product.

c. "We have documentary proof of the claim." None exists.

d. "We have an eyewitness who will (identify) (exonerate) the accused." None exists.

e. "If you don't reduce your demand by half, my client will declare bankruptcy," said to the client's creditor. The client is not legally eligible to declare bankruptcy.

What Does "Material" Mean?

Lawyers use the word a lot. It appears in statutes, case law, agency regulations, and the Model Rules, including Rule 4.1. What does it mean when used in the Rules? Ausherman v. Bank of America Corp., 212 F. Supp. 2d 435 (D. Md. 2002), referred a lawyer for discipline based on a false statement in negotiation. The lawyer argued that his lie was merely "bluster." No dice. The magistrate judge wrote a thoughtful analysis of Rule 4.1, collecting much case law and secondary authority and offering this definition of *material fact*:

> While the term "material" is not defined in Rule 4.1 or its commentary, it is not a difficult concept to comprehend. A fact is material to a negotiation if it reasonably may be viewed as important to a fair understanding of what is being given up and, in return, gained by the settlement. While the legal journals engage in some hand-wringing about the vagueness of this aspect of Rule 4.1, in reality, it seldom is a difficult task to determine whether a fact is material to a particular negotiation. In cases of real doubt, disciplinary committees and ultimately the courts will decide.[*]

Can Others Rely on an Opposing Lawyer's Representations of Fact?

GREYCAS, INC. v. PROUD
826 F.2d 1560 (7th Cir. 1987)

POSNER, CIRCUIT JUDGE.[†]

Theodore S. Proud, Jr. . . . appeals from a judgment against him for $833,760, entered after a bench trial. The tale of malpractice and

---

[*] The opinion quotes at length John W. Cooley, Mediation Magic: Its Use and Abuse, 29 Loy. U. Chi. L.J. 1, 42 (1997).

[†] Clarity in expression is essential in litigation as elsewhere. So is reader engagement. You want judges to read your brief, not just turn the pages. So you must make it easy to follow your statement of facts and argument. Appreciate how Posner describes and analyzes the facts and applies the law. The opinion flows. It's conversational. You can hear his voice as he works through the issues. Unlike many opinions, it can be read aloud and understood. That's a good test of clarity. There are detours and asides, to be sure. It's not linear. But you know where you are. Signal words ("but," "however," "so," "therefore") are the opinion's road signs. Sentence length varies. No word requires a dictionary. A judge I know wanted his opinions to "read well." He and his clerks would gather periodically and read drafts aloud to each other.

misrepresentation that led to the judgment begins with Proud's brother-in-law, Wayne Crawford, like Proud a lawyer but one who devoted most of his attention to a large farm that he owned in downstate Illinois. The farm fell on hard times and by 1981 Crawford was in dire financial straits. He had pledged most of his farm machinery to lenders, yet now desperately needed more money. He approached Greycas, Inc., the plaintiff in this case, a large financial company headquartered in Arizona, seeking a large loan that he offered to secure with the farm machinery. He did not tell Greycas about his financial difficulties or that he had pledged the machinery to other lenders, but he did make clear that he needed the loan in a hurry. Greycas obtained several appraisals of Crawford's farm machinery but did not investigate Crawford's financial position or discover that he had pledged the collateral to other lenders, who had perfected their liens in the collateral. Greycas agreed to lend Crawford $1,367,966.50, which was less than the appraised value of the machinery.

The loan was subject, however, to an important condition, which is at the heart of this case: Crawford was required to submit a letter to Greycas, from counsel whom he would retain, assuring Greycas that there were no prior liens on the machinery that was to secure the loan. Crawford asked Proud to prepare the letter, and he did so, and mailed it to Greycas, and within 20 days of the first contact between Crawford and Greycas the loan closed and the money was disbursed. A year later Crawford defaulted on the loan. . . . Greycas then learned that most of the farm machinery that Crawford had pledged to it had previously been pledged to other lenders. . . .

[Proud wrote the letter that Greycas demanded as a condition of making the loan.] Typed on the stationery of Proud's firm and addressed to Greycas, it identifies Proud as Crawford's lawyer and states that, "in such capacity, I have been asked to render my opinion in connection with" the proposed loan to Crawford. It also states that "this opinion is being delivered in accordance with the requirements of the Loan Agreement" and that

> I have conducted a U.C.C., tax, and judgment search with respect to the Company [i.e., Crawford's farm] as of March 19, 1981, and . . . all units listed on the attached Exhibit A ("Equipment") are free and clear of all liens or encumbrances other than [Greycas's] perfected security interest therein. . . .

Proud never conducted a search for prior liens on the machinery listed in Exhibit A. His brother-in-law gave him the list and told him there were no liens. . . . Proud made no effort to verify Crawford's statement. The theory of the complaint is that Proud was negligent in representing that there were no prior liens, merely on his brother-in-law's say-so. No doubt Proud *was* negligent in failing to conduct a search, but we are not clear why the *misrepresentation* is alleged to be negligent rather than deliberate and hence fraudulent, in which event Greycas's alleged contributory negligence would not be an issue (as it is, we shall see), since there is no defense of contributory or comparative negligence to a deliberate tort, such as fraud. Proud did not merely say, "There are no liens"; he said, "I have conducted a U.C.C., tax, and judgment search"; and not only is this statement, too, a false one, but its falsehood cannot have been inadvertent, for Proud knew he had not conducted such a search. The concealment of his relationship with Crawford might also support a charge of fraud. But Greycas decided, for whatever reason, to argue negligent misrepresentation rather than fraud. It may have feared that Proud's insurance policy for professional malpractice excluded deliberate wrongdoing from its coverage, or may not have wanted to bear the higher burden of proving fraud, or may have feared that an accusation of fraud would make it harder to settle the case — for most cases, of course, are settled, though this one has not been. In any event, Proud does not argue that either he is liable for fraud or he is liable for nothing.

He also does not, and could not, deny or justify the misrepresentation; but he argues that it is not actionable under the tort law of Illinois, because he had no duty of care to Greycas. (This is a diversity case and the parties agree that Illinois tort law governs the substantive issues.) He argues that Greycas had an adversarial relationship with Proud's client, Crawford, and that a lawyer has no duty of straight dealing to an adversary, at least none enforceable by a tort suit. In so arguing, Proud is characterizing Greycas's suit as one for professional malpractice rather than negligent misrepresentation, yet elsewhere in his briefs he insists that the suit was solely for negligent misrepresentation — while Greycas insists that its suit charges both torts. Legal malpractice based on a false representation, and negligent misrepresentation by a lawyer, are such similar legal concepts, however, that we have great difficulty both in holding them apart in our minds and in understanding why the parties are quarreling over the exact characterization. . . .

[The court cited an Illinois case, *Pelham*, that held that a *non*-client could sue for legal malpractice but only if it could "prove that the primary purpose and intent of the attorney-client relationship itself was to benefit or influence" the non-client, as was true here. The court then discussed negligent misrepresentation.]

The claim of negligent misrepresentation might seem utterly straightforward. It might seem that by addressing a letter to Greycas intended (as Proud's counsel admitted at argument) to induce reliance on the statements in it, Proud made himself prima facie liable for any material misrepresentations, careless or deliberate, in the letter, whether or not Proud was Crawford's lawyer or for that matter anyone's lawyer. Knowing that Greycas was relying on him to determine whether the collateral for the loan was encumbered and to advise Greycas of the results of his determination, Proud negligently misrepresented the situation, to Greycas's detriment. But merely labeling a suit as one for negligent misrepresentation rather than professional malpractice will not make the problem of indefinite and perhaps excessive liability, which induced the court in *Pelham* to place limitations on the duty of care, go away. So one is not surprised to find that courts have placed similar limitations on suits for negligent misrepresentation. . . .

[More recent Illinois decisions] hold that "one who in the course of his business or profession supplies information for the guidance of others in their business transactions" is liable for negligent misrepresentations that induce detrimental reliance. . . . Proud, in the practice of his profession, supplied information (or rather misinformation) to Greycas that was intended to guide Greycas in commercial dealings with Crawford. Proud therefore had a duty to use due care to see that the information was correct. He used no care. . . .

There is no serious doubt about the existence of a causal relationship between the misrepresentation and the loan. Greycas would not have made the loan without Proud's letter. Nor would it have made the loan had Proud advised it that the collateral was so heavily encumbered that the loan was as if unsecured, for then Greycas would have known that the probability of repayment was slight. . . .

Proud argues, however, that his damages should be reduced in recognition of Greycas's own contributory negligence, which, though no longer a complete defense in Illinois, is a partial defense, renamed "comparative negligence." It is as much a defense to negligent misrepresentation as to any other tort of negligence. . . .

But we think it too clear to require a remand for further proceedings that Proud failed to prove a want of due care by Greycas. Due care is the care that is optimal given that the other party is exercising due care. It is not the higher level of care that would be optimal if potential tort victims were required to assume that the rest of the world was negligent. . . .

So we must ask whether Greycas would have been careless not to conduct its own UCC search had Proud done what he had said he did—conduct his own UCC search. The answer is no. The law normally does not require duplicative precautions unless one is likely to fail or the consequences of failure (slight though the likelihood may be) would be catastrophic. One UCC search is enough to disclose prior liens, and Greycas acted reasonably in relying on Proud to conduct it. Although Greycas had much warning that Crawford was in financial trouble and that the loan might not be repaid, that was a reason for charging a hefty interest rate and insisting that the loan be secured; it was not a reason for duplicating Proud's work. It is not hard to conduct a UCC lien search; it just requires checking the records in the recorder's office for the county where the debtor lives. So the only reason to backstop Proud was if Greycas should have assumed he was careless or dishonest; and we have just said that the duty of care does not require such an assumption. Had Proud disclosed that he was Crawford's brother-in-law this might have been a warning signal that Greycas could ignore only at its peril. To go forward in the face of a known danger is to assume the risk. But Proud did not disclose his relationship to Crawford.

[The discussion of damages is omitted. The court affirmed the lower court's judgment.]

Lessons for Lawyers: Watch What You Say

1. Proud misrepresented his search in his letter to Greycas. He said he did the search. He did not. Why did Greycas sue for negligent misrepresentation rather than fraud? There are advantages and disadvantages to each theory of liability. Greycas made a tactical decision here. Why?

2. If Greycas was contributorily negligent, Proud would have had a partial defense. Why wasn't Greycas negligent? It just took Proud's word that the assets were not encumbered. It did not verify. Would the issue of Greycas's negligence have been resolved differently if Proud told Greycas he was Crawford's brother-in-law?

3. As the *Greycas* court implied and as Fire Insurance Exchange v. Bell, 643 N.E.2d 310 (Ind. 1994), explicitly held, the word of a lawyer (still) carries special weight. It invites reliance because of the speaker's status. In *Fire Insurance*, Scaletta, a lawyer for an insured defendant, misstated the limits on the defendant's insurance policy (he said $100,000 but it was $300,000). Because the defendant had meager assets, plaintiff settled for the lower sum. When his lawyer later learned the truth, plaintiff sued Scaletta and his firm, Ice Miller, for fraudulent misrepresentation. In defense, they argued that the plaintiff, as the adverse party, "had no right to rely on" what was said. The court disagreed:

> We decline to require attorneys to burden unnecessarily the courts and litigation process with discovery to verify the truthfulness of material representations made by opposing counsel. The reliability of lawyers' representations is an integral component of the fair and efficient administration of justice. The law should promote lawyers' care in making statements that are accurate and trustworthy and should foster the reliance upon such statements by others.
>
> We therefore reject the assertion of Ice Miller and Scaletta that Bell's attorney was, as a matter of law, not entitled to rely upon their representations. . . . [W]e hold that Bell's attorney's right to rely upon any material misrepresentations that may have been made by opposing counsel is established as a matter of law.

4. A nonclient sued Jones Day for "fraud based on nondisclosure" in the course of a financial transaction. Vega v. Jones, Day, Reavis & Pogue, 17 Cal. Rptr. 3d 26 (Ct. App. 2004).

> Vega's allegations may be summarized as follows. Jones Day hid the existence of the "toxic" stock provisions [in connection with a merger] with the intent to induce Vega to give up his valuable stock in Monsterbook in exchange for Transmedia's "toxic" and worthless stock. Jones Day knew about the "toxic" stock provisions, and knew the acquisition would not occur if Monsterbook, Vega and their lawyers discovered them. Jones Day deliberately concealed the "toxic" stock provisions by telling [Vega's lawyers] the transaction was "standard" and "nothing unusual," by failing to provide the proper written disclosure it prepared [for others],

and by instead providing a different, sanitized version of the disclosure. Vega did not know, and had no reason to suspect, that the financing contained "toxic" provisions, and would not have given up his valuable stock in Monsterbook had he known. As a result of Jones Day's concealment of the "toxic" terms of the financing, Vega lost his $3.45 million interest in Monsterbook.

Jones Day argued that it had no duty to Vega, the adverse party. So whatever it might have said "is entirely irrelevant." The court:

> We disagree. Jones Day specifically undertook to disclose the transaction and, having done so, is not at liberty to conceal a material term. Even where no duty to disclose would otherwise exist, "where one does speak he must speak the whole truth to the end that he does not conceal any facts which materially qualify those stated. One who is asked for or volunteers information must be truthful, and the telling of a half-truth calculated to deceive is fraud."

5. The Florida Supreme Court suspended for three years a lawyer who (among other things) told a negotiation opponent of his client that his client was an "honest man" even though he knew but did not disclose public information inconsistent with honesty. His motive was to protect his expected fees. The lawyer's statement "triggered a duty on his part to also reveal . . . the negative information . . . that could have impacted [the opponent's] decision to go into business with" the client. Fla. Bar v. Scott, 39 So.3d 309 (Fla. 2010). Would the ruling differ if the undisclosed information had not been public, but rather confidential? It shouldn't. It is no defense to telling a lie that telling the truth would have disclosed confidential information.

6. Despite these and other cases, in some states an opponent would be wise *not* to trust the factual representations of an opposing lawyer—to assume falsity—or to trust but verify. That of course creates extra work (and fees). Ironshore Europe DAC v. Schiff Hardin, L.L.P., 912 F.3d 759 (5th Cir. 2019) (based on lower state court cases, court predicts that the Texas Supreme Court would hold that "Texas law shields an attorney against claims by a non-client based on negligent misrepresentation made in the course of counsel's representation of his clients.").

7. Another line of cases has upheld claims by lawyers against lawyers. They arise when a client sues his own lawyer for malpractice for failing to protect him from an opposing lawyer's misrepresentation and the defendant then seeks indemnification from the opposing lawyer for any damages she is required to pay. See, e.g., Hansen v. Anderson, Wilmarth & Van Der Maaten, 630 N.W.2d 818 (Iowa 2001):

> We hold that once a lawyer responds to a request for information in an arm's-length transaction and undertakes to give that information, the lawyer has a duty to the lawyer requesting the information to give it truthfully. Such a duty is an independent one imposed for the benefit

of a particular person or class of persons. We further hold that a breach of that duty supports a claim of equitable indemnity by the defrauded lawyer against the defrauding lawyer.

8. In federal law, a lawyer's material misstatements *or omissions* can support securities law liability. Thompson v. Paul, 547 F.3d 1055 (9th Cir. 2008) (with citations to other circuits).

Can Others Rely on an Opposing Lawyer's Legal Opinions?

In treating the "what is false?" issue, we must distinguish between legal opinions and facts. Rule 4.1(a) forbids a lawyer knowingly to make a "false statement of material fact or law to a third person." But what if a lawyer merely ventures an opinion about the law but makes no representation of fact? Does that eliminate a claim for negligent representation? Error in a legal opinion may create malpractice liability to a client. But lawyers have no malpractice exposure to non-clients for an inaccurate legal opinion unless they have accepted (or are held to have accepted) that responsibility. See, e.g., Linegar v. DLA Piper, LLP, 495 S.W.3d 276 (Tex. 2016) (although a lawyer for a company or a trust has no liability to a shareholder or beneficiary for an incorrect legal opinion, if she gives that opinion directly to the shareholder or beneficiary who relies on it, the lawyer may thereby have created an attorney-client relationship and be liable in the event of error). An opposing party must look to her own lawyer for the meaning of the law. As we see from the next case, however, even a legal opinion can support liability because of the *facts* that the opinion implies are true.

HOYT PROPERTIES v. PRODUCTION RESOURCE GROUP
736 N.W.2d 313 (Minn. 2007)

PAGE, JUSTICE: . . .

[Hoyt Properties brought an eviction action against Production Resource Group (PRG) and Entolo, its subsidiary. Hoyt settled with Entolo and released PRG. Before he agreed to release PRG, Steve Hoyt, who owned and operated the plaintiff, alleged that he had had a conversation with PRG's lawyer in which Hoyt said, "I don't know of any reason how we could pierce the [corporate] veil, do you?" Hoyt claims that PRG's lawyer replied, "There isn't anything. PRG and Entolo are totally separate." Later, Hoyt learned that a complaint in another action contradicted that statement. He sought to rescind the settlement so he could sue PRG, claiming that PRG's lawyer's reply was a fraudulent misrepresentation.

[To succeed, Hoyt would have to prove that the reply was (a) knowingly (b) false and that (c) he relied on it. PRG's position was that the statement was one of legal opinion, not fact, and therefore not false, and that in any event it was not knowingly false. PRG won summary judgment in the trial court, lost in the intermediate appellate court, and appealed to the supreme court. That court discussed when a legal opinion can be actionable as false because of *facts it implies*. It then addressed what it means to be *knowingly* false. Notice the two legal theories the court cites in the third paragraph as sufficient to prove knowledge. The part of the opinion dealing with reliance is omitted.]

Here, the question allegedly asked by Steve Hoyt was, "I don't know of any reason how we could pierce the veil, do you?" Hoyt alleges that the response was "There isn't anything." When viewed in the light most favorable to Hoyt, as is required under the summary judgment standard, the representation "There isn't anything" is a representation that no facts exist that would support a piercing claim against PRG—for example, no facts indicating that Entolo did not maintain corporate formalities. Even if we assume, as appellants argue, that the alleged statement made by PRG's attorney was an expression of his legal opinion, that representation implies that the attorney was aware of facts supporting that opinion, namely, that there were no facts to support a claim to pierce the corporate veil. Because the representation was not an expression of pure legal opinion (for example, "I do not think someone could pierce the veil but I am not sure"), but rather a statement implying that facts existed that supported a legal opinion, we conclude that the representation is actionable.

We conclude that the second alleged representation, "PRG and Entolo are totally separate," is also actionable. Again viewed in the light most favorable to Hoyt, the second representation constitutes a direct factual assertion that the relationship between PRG and Entolo is such that no facts exist that would allow the corporate veil to be pierced; for example, that no facts existed that would demonstrate that Entolo was a facade for PRG's own dealings. As such, it is the kind of representation that we have traditionally held to be actionable.

Having determined that the representations are actionable, we must next determine whether they create a genuine issue for trial. We have explained that, in order for the representation to be fraudulent, it must be "made with knowledge of the falsity of the representation or made as of the party's own knowledge without knowing whether it was true or false." For the purposes of summary judgment, we must determine whether PRG's attorney either: (1) knew of some facts that would support a piercing claim such that his representations to the effect that there were no facts supporting a piercing claim were knowingly false; or (2) made the representations without knowing whether there were facts that would support a piercing claim.

Appellants assert that the representations allegedly made by PRG's attorney were not false, much less knowingly false. Hoyt alleges that they were known or should have been known to be false when made. At this stage of the proceedings, the record as to whether the representations were knowingly false when made consists solely of the parties' assertions. Accordingly, the only way for the district court to have concluded that the representations were not knowingly false was to have weighed the evidence and assessed the credibility of the parties. Weighing the evidence and assessing credibility on summary judgment is error. Absent evidence in the record establishing, as a matter of law, that the representations were not knowingly false when made, we conclude that there is a genuine issue of material fact for trial on that issue.

The record is sufficient for us to conclude that there are also genuine issues of material fact for trial as to whether PRG's attorney made the representations at issue without knowing whether they were true or false. In his deposition, the attorney admitted that before he made the representations at issue he "knew what was contained in" the complaint brought by the third party. The complaint alleges a number of facts that, if true, would support the conclusion that PRG and Entolo did not maintain corporate formalities and that PRG would, therefore, be susceptible to a piercing claim. In his deposition, PRG's attorney also admitted that when he made the alleged representations at issue he had not yet formed an opinion, one way or the other, about the facts alleged in the complaint. Given these admissions, a finder of fact could conclude that when PRG's attorney responded to Steve Hoyt's question he did not know whether his representations were true. As such, there is a genuine issue of material fact for trial as to whether he made the representations "without knowing whether [they were] true or false."

On remand, Hoyt would have a chance to prove knowing falsity of the implied facts. Although the remedy sought was to rescind the settlement, the opinion could also support damages. What should Entolo's lawyer have said in response to Steve Hoyt's question? How about, "Don't ask me, Steve. I'm not your lawyer. Ask her."

3. Exploiting an Opponent's Mistake

The Case of the Dead Witness

Mira Rakov is prosecuting Chris Parenti, who is charged with robbing Beth Hentzel. Beth picked him out of a lineup and will make a good witness, as Chris's defense lawyer, Josh Mbaka, realizes. A month ago, Mira offered to let Chris plead to a felony carrying a three-year term. Conviction after trial could result in a sentence of up to nine years. Chris agreed and is scheduled to plead in two weeks. Before he enters the plea, Mira learns that Beth has died of unrelated causes. Without Beth's testimony, the case against Chris would be weak at best. A judge might even direct a verdict of acquittal. If Josh knew of Beth's death, he would advise Chris to withdraw his acceptance of the plea offer, which he has a right to do until he enters the plea in court. Does Mira have a duty to tell Josh that Beth died? Could Mira have made her plea offer *after* she learned that Beth had died and without informing the defendant?

Negotiation Mistakes (Part I)

In January 2021, Advika Banerjee represented Ginger Towers in the sale of her florist shop, Towers Flowers, to Declan O'Neil. O'Neil's lawyer was Bryce Parrott. O'Neil wanted a non-compete clause in the sales contract. Parrott raised that issue with Banerjee, who said she'd discuss it with Towers.

After the economic terms were ironed out, Parrott offered to do the first draft of the contract. Not having heard back from Banerjee on a non-compete clause, he included one that defined the temporal and geographic scope of the covenant broadly—until January 2024 and within 25 miles of Towers Flowers. When she read the draft, Banerjee immediately realized that the courts would not enforce so broad a covenant, nor would they narrow it. The effect would be that Towers would be free to compete. Does Banerjee have a duty to present this information to Towers? Can or must she inform Parrott of his error even if her client objects?

Negotiation Mistakes (Part II)

Same as Part I except that Banerjee told Parrott that "Towers will agree to a non-compete for 16 months within a three-mile radius of Towers Flowers." The courts will enforce that agreement. Parrott then sent a draft agreement that said that Towers will not "operate" a florist within this time period or location. Banerjee realized that "operate" is ambiguous and that Towers would have a good argument that it would not forbid her to "consult" with area florists or even authorize a competing florist to use the name "Flowers by Ginger Towers," so long as she did not "operate" a florist. Does Banerjee have a duty to present this information to Towers? Can or must she inform Parrott of his error even if her client objects?

Negotiation Mistakes (Part III)

Same as Part II except Parrott wrote a draft agreement with enforceable restrictions broader than "operate." But instead of saying that the covenant will remain in effect "through May 2022," which would be the 16 months to which Banerjee had orally agreed, he mistakenly wrote "through May 2021," an obvious typographical error. Does Banerjee have a duty to present this information to Towers? Can or must she inform Parrott of his error even if her client objects?

MOK v. 21 MOTT ST. RESTAURANT CORP.

2017 WL 3981308 (S.D.N.Y. 2017)

P. KEVIN CASTEL, J.

In this Memorandum and Order, the Court concludes that [Brandon Sherr] the attorney for the plaintiff in this action should be sanctioned under the inherent power of the Court and 28 U.S.C. §1927. The attorney did not disclose to the Court or to opposing counsel that his client had died until eight months after the client's death and four months after he says he learned of it. The death of the client was highly material to the value of this wage and hour action because his client never testified at a deposition and, thus, proving the claim would have been exceedingly difficult. Instead, he obtained adjournments from the Court on the premise that he was negotiating a settlement with defendants on behalf [of] his client. The adjournments had the effect of delaying the filing of a Joint Pretrial Order that would have disclosed that his client would not be a witness at trial. He did not disclose the death to the defendants or the Court until after he announced that an agreement-in-principle had been reached to settle the case. Even then, he only disclosed the date of the death under a Court Order to do so. . . .

The Court now sets forth its findings of fact and conclusions of law:

[T]he N.Y. Rules [of Professional Conduct] govern the conduct of attorneys appearing in this Court. The fact that an attorney has violated one of the N.Y. Rules does not necessarily mean that his or her conduct is sanctionable under either the inherent powers of the Court or 28 U.S.C. §1927. The N.Y. Rules however are relevant and useful norms that this Court may take account of in assessing whether the lawyer acted in bad faith or unreasonably and vexatiously.

Rule 3.3(a)(1) provides that "A lawyer shall not knowingly: (1) make a false statement of fact or law to a tribunal or fail to correct a false statement of material fact or law previously made to the tribunal by the lawyer. . . ." As Sherr knew, his statements to the Court that he was the lawyer for Mok after Mok had died were false statements of fact.

Rule 3.3(e) provides that "In presenting a matter to a tribunal, a lawyer shall disclose, unless privileged or irrelevant, the identities of the clients the lawyer represents and of the persons who employed the lawyer." Sherr did not disclose that he had no client in this action and instead stated that his client was the then-deceased Mok.

Rule 3.4 addresses "Fairness to Opposing Party and Counsel." Rule 3.4(a)(3) provides that "A lawyer shall not: (a)(3) conceal or knowingly fail to disclose that which the lawyer is required by law to reveal. . . ." Sherr knowingly failed to disclose his client's death, which he was obliged to reveal. . . .

The record before this Court establishes with clarity that Sherr acted in subjective bad faith and that he unreasonably and vexatiously prolonged the proceedings. . . .

Sherr unnecessarily caused defendants to incur attorneys' fees in negotiating with him. Also, his conduct has taken precious judicial time away from other deserving litigants in other cases who seek judicial rulings on habeas corpus petitions, naturalization petitions, criminal cases, personal injury cases, civil rights cases, social security appeals and all other manner of cases . . . .

Sherr was admitted to the bar in 2011 and has been practicing for six years, a relatively short period of time. He has never been the subject of professional discipline. . . .

Based upon the inherent power of the Court, the Court imposes a monetary sanction of $3,000 to be paid into the Registry of the Court within 90 days. As a sanction under 28 U.S.C. §1927, the Court will require Sherr to pay defendants' legal fees . . . from the date of the misconduct, i.e. when Sherr had a duty to disclose but did not. . . .

Section 1927 and the court's inherent power both authorize judges to impose sanctions in circumstances like those before Judge Castel. They get less attention than does Federal Rule of Civil Procedure 11, but they are potent judicial remedies when lawyers misbehave.

Harren and Connell's client, the plaintiff, died in January, after losing in the district court. The lawyers appealed but did not inform the circuit court of their client's death or seek to substitute the estate for the plaintiff for more than 11 months. (The defendants had informed the court of the plaintiff's death within a month.) The circuit said Harren and Connell's failure was "inexcusable" and appeared to reveal "a lack of candor." It dismissed the appeal with prejudice and referred the lawyers to the court's grievance panel. Marentette v. City of Canandaigua, 799 Fed. Appx. 48 (2d Cir. 2020).

What Does *Mok* Stand For?

That a lawyer must always reveal the death of a client? The death of a client who is a party to the settlement of a litigation? All facts that may be important to the other side when negotiating settlement of a case in litigation? Does *Mok* control the answer to "The Case of the Dead Witness"? Or are the situations different?

Imagine that Sherr (the lawyer in *Mok*) was negotiating a settlement with the defendant but had not yet filed the case. We eliminate the court—and duties to a tribunal—from the story. Could Sherr then have properly negotiated a settlement without disclosing Mok's death? Two rules that would likely have required disclosure even if no action were pending are Rule 4.1(a), which forbids lawyers to make a "false statement of material fact," and Rule 8.4(c), which forbids "deceit" and "misrepresentation." Sherr would have violated both rules if despite Mok's death, he uttered the words "my client." He had no client. In fact, he probably would have violated both rules if he merely implied that he had a client, which he would do simply by negotiating.

Courts have consistently upheld discipline of lawyers who conceal the death of their litigation clients citing, as the court here did, ethics rules and the court's own procedural rules. See, e.g., In re Forrest, 730 A.2d 340 (N.J. 1999) (failure to reveal client's death violated N.J. Rule 3.3(a)(5) (duty to provide tribunal with certain material facts) and Rule 8.4(c), despite the absence of any affirmative statement that client was still alive).

By contrast, courts do not otherwise impose a disclosure duty when a lawyer's (or his client's) factual ignorance results in an unjust agreement in some cosmic sense. This can be seen as a bow to the premises of the adversary system. It is ordinarily not unjust (but rather a duty) for a lawyer to take advantage of her superior factual or legal knowledge.

Brown alleged that the county had failed to hire her in violation of a law protecting people with disabilities. Eventually plaintiff was hired, and the case was tentatively settled for lost pay. Plaintiff's lawyer demanded the pay that plaintiff would have received had she been properly hired and submitted a written settlement offer designating the pay at level "C." The county accepted the offer. Plaintiff's lawyer then learned that plaintiff's starting salary would have been level "D," which was higher. The county's lawyer did not know, but thought it likely, that plaintiff's counsel had mistakenly assumed that level "C" was the highest pay level. After discovering his error, plaintiff's lawyer moved to change the settlement terms, citing the defense lawyer's failure to correct the error. Brown v. County of Genesee, 872 F.2d 169 (6th Cir. 1989), denied the motion, concluding that "absent some misrepresentation or fraudulent conduct, the appellant had no duty to advise the appellee of any . . . factual error, whether unknown or suspected. . . . We need only cite the well-settled rule that the mere nondisclosure to an adverse party and to the court of facts pertinent to a controversy before the court does not add up to 'fraud upon the court' for purposes of vacating a judgment." The mistake could have been avoided with proper investigation.

Some Special Situations

Transactions with Unrepresented Persons.   Sometimes the opposing party has no lawyer. Then a lawyer may have to clarify her role in the matter if she knows or should know that the opponent misunderstands it. She cannot create the impression that she is disinterested and she may not give the opponent advice (except to get a lawyer) if his interests may conflict with those of the lawyer's client. See Rule 4.3.

Threatening Criminal Prosecution or Discipline.   The former Code said a lawyer could not threaten criminal prosecution "solely" to gain an advantage in a civil matter. The Rules omit this provision. Consider these two statements in a business matter:

1. "If you don't pay my client the $10,000 you embezzled, we're going to the D.A."
2. "If you don't pay my client the $10,000 you embezzled, we're going to disclose your extramarital affair."

ABA Opinion 92-363 concluded that a lawyer can raise the possibility of criminal charges in negotiating a civil claim so long as the civil and criminal matters are related and the lawyer does not claim an improper influence over the criminal process. That means that statement 1 is proper and statement 2 is not. The law of extortion may reach the same result. See, e.g., N.Y. Penal Law §155.15(2). If the law permits, the lawyer can also agree to refrain from presenting the criminal charges in exchange for a favorable settlement. State ex rel. Oklahoma Bar Ass'n v. Worsham, 957 P.2d 549 (Okla. 1998), cites the ABA opinion in declining to discipline a lawyer who said that, absent a settlement of her client's claims, the client "will contact the District Attorney concerning the filing of criminal charges."

Some states have retained the Code provision. The District of Columbia, expanding it, forbids a lawyer to "[s]eek or threaten to seek criminal charges or disciplinary charges solely to obtain an advantage in a civil matter." D.C. Rule 8.4(g). In reasoning that is a bit of a stretch, the ABA has concluded that even though the Model Rules do not "expressly" forbid threatening to file a disciplinary charge against opposing counsel, "there will frequently be circumstances in which such a threat will violate Model Rule 8.3" or other rules. ABA Opinion 94-383. Lawyers have been disciplined for conditioning settlement of a civil case (here, against the lawyer personally) on an agreement to dismiss a disciplinary charge even though no specific rule forbids it. Disciplinary Counsel v. Chambers, 928 N.E.2d 1061 (Ohio 2010).

Threatening to Report an Undocumented Immigrant. Washington State adds the following comment [4] to its version of Rule 4.4.

> The duty imposed by paragraph (a) of this Rule [which forbids the use of "means that have no substantial purpose other than to embarrass, delay, or burden a third person"] includes a lawyer's assertion or inquiry about a third person's immigration status when the lawyer's purpose is to intimidate, coerce, or obstruct that person from participating in a civil matter. Issues involving immigration status carry a significant danger of interfering with the proper functioning of the justice system. When a lawyer is representing a client in a civil matter, a lawyer's communication to a party or a witness that the lawyer will report that person to immigration authorities, or a lawyer's report of that person to immigration authorities, furthers no substantial purpose of the civil adjudicative system if the lawyer's purpose is to intimidate, coerce, or obstruct that person. A communication in violation of this Rule can also occur by an implied assertion that is the equivalent of an express assertion prohibited by paragraph (a).

Self-Assessment Questions

1. "My name is Michelle LeBlanc, and I represent a man named Chester in a divorce from his wife Phoebe. The couple has no children, but they do have substantial property acquired before and during the marriage, including a valuable art and wine collection.

   "Chester and Phoebe have decided how to divide their property, but we've had prolonged negotiations over how to evaluate the items each will receive and the amount of any payments that the recipient of a particular piece of property will have to make to the other spouse in exchange for his or her interest.

   "Kate, Phoebe's lawyer, proposed a rather complex formula for making this evaluation. I spoke with Chester about it, and we asked Phoebe to send us a written proposal that describes and applies the formula and identifies a bottom line. Then, we would decide whether or not the proposal was acceptable.

   "Kate did that, and I got her materials yesterday. In going over them, I realized that she made an arithmetic mistake in applying the formula to certain pieces of the art collection that the couple had decided would go to Chester. As a result, Kate underestimated the amount that Chester should pay Phoebe for these pieces. The upshot is that when this error is factored into the final number, Chester (who's getting a majority of the pieces) will have to pay Phoebe $515,000. But if Kate had not made the error, her formula would require Chester to pay Phoebe $721,000. Now, as I said, Chester and I have never bought into the formula. And we would not accept the $721,000 figure in any event. But we like the lower number.

   "My questions are: Must or may I alert Kate to her error without consulting Chester, or is this a decision Chester has a right to make? Do I even have to tell him? If I don't have to tell Kate, or can't if Chester tells me not to, how can I exploit her error? I don't want to say anything that may prompt her to check her arithmetic. But I also want to comply with the rules and take care that any agreement is not subject to challenge in court."

2. You have long represented Equips, Ltd., a closely held company whose majority shareholder is Chandra Gold. Gold is planning to retire and is negotiating to sell Equips to Planit, Inc. Equips rents equipment for a week or two at a time to do-it-yourself home renovators and small contractors. Equips buys or leases its inventory of equipment from various suppliers with which it has long-term contracts. At a meeting with the buyers, Chandra says that the contract with Mekanics, Equips' most important supplier, has four years to run and that the contract terms, which she summarizes, are very favorable to Equips. This was true when she said it. However, days later, before the deal closes, you

learn over lunch with a friend in the industry that Mekanics is about to be acquired by another company, which is not an Equips supplier but rather a supplier to one of Equips' competitors, and that Mekanics will soon terminate its contract with Equips on 30 days' notice, as the contract permits it to do in the event of an acquisition. What do you do?

X

Lawyers for Companies and Other Organizations

Introduction: "Who's Your Client?"

Lawyers for an entity or organization—for example, a corporation, the government, a union, or a limited or general partnership—confront especially thorny professional issues. The material on confidentiality and privilege introduced some of them. (See chapter 2B.) These problems often flow from the fact that while the lawyer's client is the organization, the lawyer must represent it through its officers, employees, and agents, who ordinarily are not clients and who may on occasion have interests or act in ways that are adverse to the client.

In a single sentence, Rule 1.13(a) attempts to sort this out. It says that a lawyer, whether employed or retained, "represents the organization acting through its duly authorized constituents."

Many of the issues that arise when a lawyer represents a company (and for convenience let us talk of companies) are the same as those that confront all lawyers: issues of loyalty, conflicts, client identity, confidentiality and privilege, authority, and the duty not to aid a client's crimes and frauds. The conflict rules studied in chapters 5 and 6 protect all clients.

When a client is represented "through" others and is itself a legal fiction, however, the issues can become more complex. The situation is further complicated when a lawyer is employed, rather than retained, by the company-client.* An in-house lawyer is in an especially vulnerable position. Management will decide her title, salary, bonus, benefits, work assignments, office space, expense account, promotion, support staff, and even whether to continue to employ her. Put her in a small city with a mortgage and two children headed for college, and we can envision the threat to professional

---

* This is why the European Court of Justice, as noted in chapter 2B2, and many nations do not recognize privilege for communications between employed lawyers and company constituents and why in some nations, when a lawyer goes in-house, he or she ceases to be a member of the bar.

independence. Yet her job, of course, is to protect her client, even as against the possibly bad behavior of the managers who have so much control over her professional life. Although such facts are supposed to be irrelevant, they may be hard to ignore if the lawyer is faced with a duty to her client that the CEO suggests she overlook. The threat need not be explicit.

Retained lawyers can be more independent, but not by much if the company is an important client, producing much of their income.

An employed lawyer who is fired or demoted and believes that it was because of her refusal to act unethically, her insistence that the company act lawfully, or for some other reason that may deserve judicial protection can bring a retaliatory discharge claim in jurisdictions that recognize such claims. Not all do. See, e.g., Karstetter v. King Cty. Corr. Guild, 444 P.3d 1185 (Wash. 2019) (collecting cases); Crews v. Buckman Labs. Int'l, 78 S.W.3d 852 (Tenn. 2002) (same). In an opinion that has faced much criticism, the Illinois Supreme Court rejected retaliation claims when brought by employed lawyers even though it recognizes them for other employees. Balla v. Gambro, Inc., 584 N.E.2d 104 (Ill. 1991) (allowing such claims would undermine a client's trust and confidence in counsel and they are not needed to ensure that lawyers act ethically). *Crews* and other cases have refused to follow *Balla.*

Federal law recognizes certain claims by employees for discrimination (race, religion, sex, etc.) and for retaliation. An in-house lawyer will be able to use confidential information to prove her federal claim, even in states like Illinois, because federal, not state, law controls. Kachmar v. SunGard Data Sys., 109 F.3d 173 (3d Cir. 1997) (Title VII claim); Van Asdale v. Int'l Game Tech., 577 F.3d 989 (9th Cir. 2009) (retaliatory discharge claim under Sarbanes-Oxley) (18 U.S.C. §1514A).

A. COMPANIES BEHAVING BADLY: "WHERE WERE THE LAWYERS?"

In recent years, we have witnessed serious wrongdoing at many of the nation's largest banks, leading to fines and settlements of billions of dollars. See, e.g., Matthew Goldstein, "Deutsche Bank Settles Over Ignored Red Flags on Jeffrey Epstein," N.Y. Times, July 13, 2020. The bank paid $150 million after it failed to prevent Epstein, a sex crime offender, from engaging in suspicious cash transactions. Its motive was the prospect of "millions of dollars" in bank fees and "leads for other lucrative clients," according to New York State's Department of Financial Services. See also Christina Rexrode & Andrew Grossman, "Bank of America Reaches $16.65 Billion Settlement Over Mortgage Bonds," Wall St. J., Aug. 21, 2014, reporting that Bank of America settled accusations that it sold flawed mortgage securities in what is said to be the largest settlement between the United States and a single company. Bank of America was not the sole offender in the mortgage scandal. "Citigroup Settles Mortgage Inquiry for $7 Billion" reads a New York Times headline of July 14, 2014, in a story by Michael Corkery. JPMorgan Chase, Citigroup, Barclays, UBS, and the Royal Bank of Scotland pled guilty to foreign exchange and LIBOR manipulations and collectively paid more than $5 billion, about half of which were criminal fines. Peter Henning, "Guilty Pleas and Heavy Fines Seem to Be Cost of Business for Wall St.," N.Y. Times, May 20, 2015.

"More than 800,000 people who took out car loans from Wells Fargo were charged for auto insurance they did not need, and some of them are still paying for it, according to an internal report prepared for the bank's executives," reports the New York Times of July 27, 2017 in an article by Gretchen Morgenson. The bank vowed to make its customers whole.

Mortgage fraud and exchange rate manipulation cause financial harm. Defective products kill. In 2014, we learned that employees of General Motors (G.M.) were aware for years of a faulty ignition switch, but did not warn drivers despite more than two dozen deaths. Hilary Stout, Bill Vlasic, Danielle Ivory, & Rebecca Ruiz, "General Motors Misled Grieving Families on a Lethal Flaw," N.Y. Times, Mar. 24, 2014. G.M. lawyers were implicated. According to an internal investigation at G.M. by former U.S. Attorney Anton R. Valukas, then a partner at Jenner & Block, employees were discouraged from taking notes at meetings. In-house lawyers concealed what they learned about the defects from their boss, the company's general counsel. Emails were periodically reviewed for incriminating information. Bill Vlasic, "G.M. Lawyers Hid Fatal Flaw from Critics and One Another," N.Y. Times, June 6, 2014. G.M. allegedly stonewalled federal regulators when they asked for information that might help explain crashes. Rebecca Ruiz & Danielle Ivory, "Documents Show General Motors Kept Silent on Fatal Crashes," N.Y. Times, July 15, 2014. At a Senate subcommittee hearing, Senator Claire McCaskill said it was "clear that the culture of lawyering up and Whac-a-Mole to minimize liabilities in individual lawsuits killed customers of General Motors." Bill Vlasic & Aaron Kessler, "At Hearing on G.M. Recall, [G.M. Chief] Mary Barra Gives Little Ground," N.Y. Times, July 17, 2014.

Volkswagen pled guilty to three felony charges and paid $4.3 billon in fines and penalties for illegally importing nearly 600,000 vehicles equipped to circumvent emission standards. Bill Vlasic, "VW Moves Beyond Criminal Case, but Not Without a Scolding," N.Y. Times, April 22, 2017. The trial judge cited VW's "corporate greed" and its "deliberate and massive fraud."

Takata, a maker of airbags, knew for a decade that its airbags could malfunction and cause serious injury or death. But it did not alert federal regulators to the danger and instead deleted test results. Fourteen million cars have since been recalled. Hiroko Tabuchi, "Takata Saw and Hid Risks in Airbags in 2004, Former Workers Say," N.Y. Times, Nov. 6, 2014. Takata eventually pled guilty and paid a $1 billion fine. Jonathan Soble, "With Guilty Plea, Takata Clears Way for a Likely Global Rescue," N.Y. Times, Jan. 15, 2017.

Food companies also cheat and it sometimes proves fatal. Dole knew that products in one of its salad plants tested positive for listeria nine times but said nothing until the FDA inspected. Then Dole closed the plant, but not before four people died and 33 more went to the hospital. Stephanie Strom, "Dole Knew About Listeria Problem at Salad Plant, F.D.A. Report Says," N.Y. Times, Apr. 29, 2016. The same article reports on listeria problems at Blue Bell Creameries and Chipotle. Blue Bell did not report the problem. Three customers died, and ten fell ill. Chipotle waited to warn. Two hundred customers fell ill. Georgia ConAgra was fined $11.2 million to settle criminal charges for shipping Peter Pan peanut butter tainted with salmonella. N.Y. Times, May 20, 2015.

Drug companies have their own hall of shame. A "federal judge sentenced John Kapoor, the founder of the opioid manufacturer Insys Therapeutics, to five and a half years in prison Thursday for his role in a racketeering scheme that bribed doctors to prescribe a highly addictive opioid and misled insurers." Katie Thomas, N.Y. Times, Jan. 23, 2020. Other executives were also sentenced. "Federal prosecutors have said that Insys, based in Arizona, embarked on an intensive marketing plan—including paying doctors for sham educational talks and luring others with lap dances—to sell its under-the-tongue fentanyl spray . . . for a much wider pool of patients [than were FDA approved], and to mislead insurance companies so they would pay for the expensive medication." In 2015, the company's market value had reached $3.2 billion.

In 2007, Merck agreed to pay $4.85 billion to settle civil claims arising from use of its drug Vioxx. In 2011, the company pled guilty to a misdemeanor and agreed to pay another $950 million to settle Vioxx-related civil and criminal claims. Duff Wilson, "Merck to Pay $950 Million Over Vioxx," N.Y. Times, Nov. 22, 2011. SmithKline fought for 11 years to conceal evidence that its diabetes drug Avandia caused heart problems. Gardiner Harris, "Diabetes Drug Maker Hid Test Data, Files Indicate," N.Y. Times, July 13, 2010.

And there is also this about opioids:

> To resolve criminal and civil charges related to the drug's "misbranding," the parent of Purdue Pharma, the company that markets OxyContin, agreed to pay some $600 million in fines and other payments, one of the largest amounts ever paid by a drug company in such a case.
>
> Also, in a rare move, three executives of Purdue Pharma, including its president and its top lawyer, pleaded guilty today as individuals to misbranding, a criminal violation. They agreed to pay a total of $34.5 million in fines.

Barry Meier, "In Guilty Plea, Oxycontin Maker to Pay $600 Million," N.Y. Times, May 10, 2007.

Are criminal prosecutions and large fines just a cost of doing business, tolerable so long as executives are not charged? Here are two more examples. The first describes an opioid investigation.

> Federal prosecutors in Brooklyn have opened a criminal investigation into whether several large drug companies intentionally skirted regulations in

order to promote the sale of addictive opioids, according to corporate filings and a person familiar with the matter.

The investigation is part of a heightened law enforcement scrutiny around the country into companies that make and distribute prescription painkillers. Drug companies have faced criminal probes and multibillion-dollar lawsuits for their alleged role in the opioid epidemic.

This year, federal prosecutors in Manhattan and Cincinnati have brought novel cases against companies that distributed opioids to pharmacies, using criminal conspiracy charges typically deployed against drug dealers.

At least six companies disclosed in recent regulatory filings that they received grand jury subpoenas from federal prosecutors in Brooklyn[.]

Nicole Hong, "6 Drug Companies' Role in Opioid Epidemic Scrutinized by Prosecutors," N.Y. Times, Nov. 27, 2019. The second example describes alleged money laundering.

[Angola] is rich in oil and diamonds but hobbled by corruption, with grinding poverty, widespread illiteracy and a high infant mortality rate. . . . Now, a trove of more than 700,000 documents obtained by the International Consortium of Investigative Journalists, and shared with The New York Times, shows how a global network of consultants, lawyers, bankers and accountants helped [Isabel dos Santos, daughter of a former president, amass $2 billion] and park it abroad. Some of the world's leading professional service firms—including the Boston Consulting Group, McKinsey & Company and PwC—facilitated her efforts to profit from her country's wealth while lending their legitimacy.

What do the "professional service firms" say in their defense? They're shocked.

PwC, based in London, said it was investigating its dealings with Ms. dos Santos and would stop working with her family. Boston Consulting said it took steps, when hired, "to ensure compliance with established policies and avoid corruption and other risks." McKinsey called the allegations against Ms. dos Santos "concerning," and said it wasn't doing any work now with her or her companies.

Michael Forsythe, Kyra Gurney, Scilla Alecci & Ben Hallman, "How U.S. Firms Helped Africa's Richest Woman Exploit Her Country's Wealth," N.Y. Times, Jan. 19, 2020.

Our interest is law firms. Where were the lawyers while all of this malfeasance and criminal conduct was going on?

Judge Sporkin's Four Questions. District Judge Stanley Sporkin famously asked the "Where were the lawyers?" question following an earlier financial scandal in which many of America's savings and loan institutions in the 1980s and early 1990s defaulted. You don't need a lawyer to rob a bank. But you do need a lawyer, or more likely many lawyers, to run a bank. One would expect those lawyers to be able to recognize signs that the bank was robbing others.

In Lincoln Savings & Loan Ass'n v. Wall, 743 F. Supp. 901 (D.D.C. 1990), Judge Sporkin upheld the decision of a federal agency to assume control of

Lincoln Savings and Loan, run by Charles Keating. Lincoln's collapse due to executive malfeasance is estimated to have cost the government billions of dollars in federal deposit insurance. That led Judge Sporkin (a former SEC enforcement official) to end his opinion with some rhetorical questions that have since become well-known in legal circles. Indeed, they get dusted off and quoted in successive scandals. Sporkin wrote:

> Keating testified that he was so bent on doing the "right thing" that he surrounded himself with literally scores of accountants and lawyers to make sure all the transactions were legal. The questions that must be asked are:
>
> Where were these professionals, a number of whom are now asserting their rights under the Fifth Amendment, when these clearly improper transactions were being consummated?
>
> Why didn't any of them speak up or disassociate themselves from the transactions?
>
> Where also were the outside accountants and attorneys when these transactions were effectuated?
>
> What is difficult to understand is that with all the professional talent involved (both accounting and legal), why at least one professional would not have blown the whistle to stop the overreaching that took place in this case.

We can let accountants worry about themselves. What were the responsibilities of Lincoln's law firms, both to the victims and their own client? Some law firms were later sued by the government, as successor in interest to Lincoln, and by bondholders of Lincoln's parent company. Prominent law firms settled these claims for tens of millions of (mostly insured) dollars. The district court decision rejecting the law firms' motions for summary judgment is In re American Continental Corp./Lincoln Savings & Loan Securities Litigation, 794 F. Supp. 1424 (D. Ariz. 1992).

Lawyers are uniquely positioned to stop corporate frauds and crimes at their inception and no doubt many do. In the highly regulated world of big U.S. financial institutions and companies (or foreign ones with a U.S. presence), it is nearly impossible to engage in any but the simplest financial transactions, marketing schemes, and product promotion without expert legal advice, usually from a team of lawyers, each with her or his own specialty. When officers and employees cause the company to misbehave, lawyers in the general counsel's office will be especially close to the action and will either know about it or be on notice. Many regulators therefore see lawyers as a sort of early warning system against corporate wrongdoing, expect them to protect their clients and innocent victims, and insist on compliance with regulatory requirements even at the expense of their bosses' ire and perhaps their own job security. That perspective, in fact, is partly behind the Sarbanes-Oxley and Dodd-Frank legislation and the 2003 amendments to Rule 1.13. See part C.

Many lawyers and corporate officers protest that while it is true that counsel's loyalty runs solely to the company, "deputizing" them to be the eyes and ears of regulators in this way will lead to less, not more, compliance. How so?

The company's officers, they say, so as not to be restrained in the implementation of unlawful plans, will exclude lawyers from learning about them. The lawyers will not then discover the bad behavior in time to stop it. To which opponents respond that it is simply not possible to wall off the lawyers. The big stuff requires their help.

Should We Forbid Secret Settlements That Conceal Danger?

In 1999, Richard Zitrin of the Hastings College of Law proposed to add paragraph (B) to Rule 3.2 and amend its comment. The idea resurfaced after the disclosure that G.M.'s settlements of wrongful death cases were conditioned on promises of confidentiality. Richard Zitrin, The Case Against Secret Settlements (or What You Don't Know *Can* Hurt You), 2 J. Inst. for Study Legal Ethics 115 (1999). Zitrin refined the language of his proposed rule in Why Lawyers Keep Secrets About Public Harm, 12 Prof. Law. 1 (Summer 2001). Is the Zitrin proposal a good idea? The bracketed options below require *either* that the lawyer reasonably believes there is a danger (a subjective and objective inquiry) *or* that a reasonable lawyer would believe it (an objective option).

Proposed Rule 3.2(B)
(B) A lawyer shall not participate in offering or making an agreement among parties to a dispute, whether in connection with a lawsuit or otherwise, to prevent or restrict the availability to the public of information that [the lawyer reasonably believes] [a reasonable lawyer would believe] directly concerns a substantial danger to the public health or safety, or to the health or safety of any particular individual(s).

Comment
Some settlements have been facilitated by agreements to limit the public's access to information obtained both by investigation and through the discovery process. However, the public's interest in being free from substantial dangers to health and safety requires that no agreement that prevents disclosure to the public of information that directly affects that health and safety may be permitted. This includes agreements or stipulations to protective orders that would prevent the disclosure of such information. It also precludes a lawyer seeking discovery from concurring in efforts to seek such orders where the discovery sought is reasonably likely to include information covered by subsection (B) of the rule. However, in the event a court enters a lawful and final protective order without the parties' agreement thereto, subsection (B) shall not require the disclosure of the information subject to that order. . . .

Zitrin's proposal has gone . . . nowhere. But why? What *legitimate* interest does a company have in hiding behavior that could cause future harm, even death? G.M. cars with faulty ignition switches were on the road when company lawyers conditioned settlement of wrongful death claims on confidentiality agreements. The Zitrin proposal would forbid the condition.

B. CONFLICTS AND CONFIDENTIALITY IN ENTITY REPRESENTATION

In this part, we look at the operation of loyalty, privilege, and other rules when lawyers represent organizations. We begin with internal investigations and mergers and acquisitions, two common areas of legal work. We then examine conflicts and privilege when a lawyer represents one member of a corporate family, say a parent but not its subsidiaries, or a subsidiary but not the parent. What are her duties to other companies in the corporate family? We next turn to representation of (very) small companies to see if rules for big companies make sense there. Although the factual settings of the cases that follow differ, a common question is client identity, resolution of which may in turn bear on questions of privilege, confidentiality, conflicts, and civil liability.

1. Internal Investigations

"Please Just Find Out What Happened"

"I'm in-house at UPress. We're a listed company in the book, magazine, and online entertainment fields. The SEC has asked our general counsel about discrepancies in our filings. My boss, the GC, said I should investigate—'interview people, do a memo, so we're prepared,' she said. 'Eleanor, just talk to everyone who had any role in the filing or in compiling the information and tell me what you learn. Please just find out what happened.'

"I've since reviewed documents and there are maybe seven or eight people I should talk to from the CFO down to middle managers. I've read about corporate *Miranda* warnings, or *Upjohn* warnings I guess they're called now, but I've never done an investigation before and I don't know exactly what I should say or not say to the people I interview. What should I worry about? I also don't know what to answer if people ask me if they need a lawyer, if I can be their lawyer, too, or if they should or must talk to me. Can you help? Maybe you can pretend to be me and I can pretend to be the CFO."

Clients under suspicion often hire an outside, and presumably independent, law firm to conduct an internal investigation. (To be seen as independent, it's best that the company has never been the firm's client.) Recall *Upjohn* in chapter 2B2. The advantages are several: The client can say that it too wants to get to the bottom of it, which is also good for public relations; the client can stay ahead of, or at least keep up with, whatever prosecutors or regulators are learning in their investigations; and the client will be able to keep the lawyers' work secret because of the privilege. That's what happened in *Upjohn*. As noted, General Motors hired former U.S. Attorney Anton Valukas of Jenner & Block when it got caught in a scandal. "As Scandal Unfolds, G.M. Calls in the Lawyers," is the March 15, 2014 New York Times headline above a story by Matthew Goldstein and Barry Meier. When New Jersey Governor Chris Christie came under fire for an apparently politically motivated decision to close access lanes to the George Washington Bridge, he hired former New York City Deputy Mayor Randy Mastro of Gibson Dunn to do an internal investigation. Mastro was instructed to cooperate with the U.S. Attorney, who was doing his own investigation. Kate Zernike, "A Hiring by Christie Raises Questions Over Cooperation," N.Y. Times, Jan. 16, 2014. Mastro exonerated Christie. (Do you think the U.S. Attorney needed Mastro's help?)

Another benefit of hiring a law firm to investigate is that the company can choose to waive confidentiality and offer the results to the government, in an effort to show cooperation and avoid indictment. But it cannot do that if the constituents the firm interviewed are also the firm's clients and can assert privilege. The next case, *In re Grand Jury Subpoena*, arose out of an internal investigation at AOL. The lawyers conducting the investigation (eventually) gave the officers they interviewed what the court calls "*Upjohn* warnings," and what some once called "corporate *Miranda* warnings." In an effort to prevent AOL from disclosing the content of their interviews to a grand jury, the officers claimed privilege. Yes, the interviews were privileged, but who owned the privilege? The officers argued that they did (along with AOL) because they and AOL were part of a joint representation. One of them also claimed protection under the common interest doctrine. (See pages 218-221 for these arrangements.) Recall that a joint representation occurs when a lawyer or firm represents two or more clients in a single matter. A common interest arrangement occurs when each of two or more lawyers or firms (lawyer *A*, lawyer *B*, etc.) *separately* represents a client (client *A*, client *B*, etc.) on a matter of common interest.

IN RE GRAND JURY SUBPOENA UNDER SEAL
415 F.3d 333 (4th Cir. 2005)

WILSON, DISTRICT JUDGE: . . .

I.

In March of 2001, AOL began an internal investigation into its relationship with PurchasePro, Inc. AOL retained the law firm of Wilmer, Cutler & Pickering ("Wilmer Cutler") to assist in the investigation. Over the next several months, AOL's general counsel and counsel from Wilmer Cutler (collectively referred to herein as "AOL's attorneys" or the "investigating attorneys") interviewed appellants, AOL employees Kent Wakeford, John Doe 1, and John Doe 2.

The investigating attorneys interviewed Wakeford, a manager in the company's Business Affairs division, on six occasions. At their third interview, and the first one in which Wilmer Cutler attorneys were present, Randall Boe, AOL's General Counsel, informed Wakeford, "We represent the company. These conversations are privileged, but the privilege belongs to the company and the company decides whether to waive it. If there is a conflict, the attorney-client privilege belongs to the company." Memoranda from that meeting also indicate that the attorneys explained to Wakeford that they represented AOL but that they "could" represent him as well, "as long as no conflict appeared." The attorneys interviewed Wakeford again three days later and, at the beginning of the interview, reiterated that they represented AOL, that the privilege belonged to AOL, and that Wakeford could retain personal counsel at company expense.

The investigating attorneys interviewed John Doe 1 three times. Before the first interview, Boe told him, "We represent the company. These conversations are privileged, but the privilege belongs to the company and the company decides whether to waive it. You are free to consult with your own lawyer at any time." Memoranda from that interview indicate that the attorneys also told him, "We can represent [you] until such time as there appears to be a conflict of interest, [but] . . . the attorney-client privilege belongs to AOL and AOL can decide whether to keep it or waive it." At the end of the interview, John Doe 1 asked if he needed personal counsel. A Wilmer Cutler attorney responded that he did not recommend it, but that he would tell the company not to be concerned if Doe retained counsel.

AOL's attorneys interviewed John Doe 2 twice and followed essentially the same protocol they had followed with the other appellants. They noted, "We represent AOL, and can represent [you] too if there is not a conflict." In addition, the attorneys told him that, "the attorney-client privilege is AOL's and AOL can choose to waive it." . . .

[Thereafter, in December 2001, "AOL and Wakeford, through counsel, entered into an oral 'common interest agreement,' which they memorialized in writing in January 2002." In February 2002, the SEC sought to question Wakeford and John Doe I about their conversations with the AOL attorneys but each claimed attorney-client privilege.]

On February 26, 2004, a grand jury in the Eastern District of Virginia issued a subpoena commanding AOL to provide "written memoranda and other written records reflecting interviews conducted by attorneys for [AOL]" of the appellants between March 15 and June 30, 2001. While AOL agreed to waive the attorney-client privilege and produce the subpoenaed documents, counsel for the appellants moved to quash the subpoena on the grounds that each appellant had an individual attorney-client relationship with the investigating attorneys, that his interviews were individually privileged, and that he had not waived the privilege. Wakeford also claimed that the information he disclosed to the investigating attorneys was privileged under the common interest doctrine. . . .

II.

Appellants argue that because they believed that the investigating attorneys who conducted the interviews were representing them personally, their communications are privileged. However, we agree with the district court that essential touchstones for the formation of an attorney-client relationship between the investigating attorneys and the appellants were missing at the time of the interviews. There is no evidence of an objectively reasonable, mutual understanding that the appellants were seeking legal advice from the investigating attorneys or that the investigating attorneys were rendering personal legal advice. Nor, in light of the investigating attorneys' disclosure that they represented AOL and that the privilege and the right to waive it were AOL's alone, do we find investigating counsel's hypothetical pronouncement that they *could* represent appellants sufficient to establish the reasonable understanding that they *were* representing appellants. Accordingly, we find no fault with the district court's opinion that no individual attorney-client privilege attached to the appellants' communications with AOL's attorneys. . . .

The person seeking to invoke the attorney-client privilege must prove that he is a client or that he affirmatively sought to become a client. "The professional relationship . . . hinges upon the client's belief that he is consulting a lawyer in that capacity and his manifested intention to seek professional legal advice." An individual's subjective belief that he is represented is not alone sufficient to create an attorney-client relationship. Rather, the putative client must show that his subjective belief that an attorney-client relationship existed was reasonable under the circumstances.

With these precepts in mind, we conclude that appellants could not have reasonably believed that the investigating attorneys represented them personally during the time frame covered by the subpoena. First, there is no evidence that the investigating attorneys told the appellants that they represented them, nor is there evidence that the appellants asked the investigating attorneys to represent them. To the contrary, there is evidence that the investigating attorneys relayed to Wakeford the company's offer to retain personal counsel for him at the company's expense, and that they told John Doe 1 that he was free to retain personal counsel. Second, there is no evidence that the appellants ever sought personal legal advice from the investigating attorneys, nor is there any evidence that the investigating attorneys rendered personal legal advice. Third, when the appellants spoke with the investigating attorneys, they were fully apprised that the information they were giving could be disclosed at the company's discretion. Under these circumstances, appellants could not have reasonably believed that the investigating attorneys represented them personally. Therefore, the district court's finding that appellants had no attorney-client relationship with the investigating attorneys is not clearly erroneous.

The appellants argue that the phrase "we *can* represent you as long as no conflict appears," manifested an agreement by the investigating attorneys to represent them. They claim that, "it is hard to imagine a more straight-forward assurance of an attorney-client relationship than 'we can represent you.'" We disagree. As the district court noted, "we *can* represent you" is distinct from "we *do* represent you." If there was any evidence that the investigating attorneys had said, "we *do* represent you," then the outcome of this appeal might be different. Furthermore, the statement actually made, "we *can* represent you," must be interpreted within the context of the entire warning. The investigating attorneys' statements to the appellants, read in their entirety, demonstrate that the attorneys' loyalty was to the company. That loyalty was never implicitly or explicitly divided. In addition to noting at the outset that they had been retained to represent AOL, the investigating attorneys warned the appellants that the content of their communications during the interview "belonged" to AOL. This protocol put the appellants on notice that, while their communications with the attorneys were considered confidential, the company could choose to reveal the content of those communications at any time, without the appellants' consent.

We note, however, that our opinion should not be read as an implicit acceptance of the watered-down "*Upjohn* warnings" the investigating attorneys gave the appellants. It is a potential legal and ethical mine field. Had the investigating attorneys, in fact, entered into an attorney-client relationship with appellants, as their statements to the appellants professed they could, they would not have been free to waive the appellants' privilege when a conflict arose. It should have seemed obvious that they could not have jettisoned one client in favor of another. Rather, they would have had to withdraw from all representation and to maintain all confidences. Indeed, the court would be hard pressed to identify how investigating counsel could robustly investigate and report to management or the board of directors of a publicly-traded corporation with the necessary candor if counsel were constrained by ethical obligations to individual employees. However, because we agree with the district court that the appellants never entered into an attorney-client relationship with the investigating attorneys, they averted these troubling issues.

III.

Wakeford also claims that the documents in question are protected by the joint defense privilege because of his common interest agreement with AOL. However, the district court found that no common interest agreement existed at the time of the interviews in March-June 2001. This finding was not clearly erroneous. . . .

Because there is no evidence that Wakeford and AOL shared a common interest before December 2001, we find no error in the district court's conclusion that Wakeford had no joint defense privilege before that time. . . .

"Who's Your Client?" (Reprise)

A corporate officer or employee will have a privilege, along with the company, for what he says in an interview if he can establish that his communications with the company's lawyer were part of a joint representation in which the lawyer represented him, too. These efforts almost always fail absent an explicit commitment. United States v. Graf, 610 F.3d 1148 (9th Cir. 2010) (corporate employee not entitled to assert privilege to prevent the company's lawyer from disclosing communications). The court relied on the influential five-part test of In re Bevill, Bresler & Schulman Asset Management Corp., 805 F.2d 120 (3d Cir. 1986), to identify when an organization's constituents can claim a personal privilege for communications with corporate counsel:

> *First*, they must show they approached counsel for the purpose of seeking legal advice. *Second*, they must demonstrate that when they approached counsel they made it clear that they were seeking legal advice in their individual rather than in their representative capacities. *Third*, they must demonstrate that the counsel saw fit to communicate with them in their individual capacities, knowing that a possible conflict could arise. *Fourth*, they must prove that their conversations with counsel were confidential. And *fifth*, they must show that the substance of their conversations with counsel did not concern matters within the company or the general affairs of the company.

In joining other circuit and district courts that have adopted the *Bevill* test, *Graf* wrote:

> There are strong policy reasons to adopt the *Bevill* test. As noted above, any time a corporation retains counsel, counsel will have to talk to individual employees to represent the company effectively. The *Bevill* test responds to this reality by ensuring that a corporation is free to obtain information from its officers, employees, and consultants about company matters and then control the attorney-client privilege, waiving it when necessary to serve corporate interests. The test also preserves the individual's ability to claim a personal attorney-client privilege when the individual makes clear he or she is seeking personal legal advice and the communications relate to personal legal affairs, not to the company's business. Moreover, there are reasons to look to other circuits when contemplating the proper standard in this arena. As the Supreme Court cautioned in *Upjohn*, "[a]n uncertain privilege, or one which purports to be certain but results in widely varying applications by the courts, is little better than no privilege at all."

A finding that a company's lawyer also represented a company constituent on the same matter can create real headaches for the company and the lawyer if the two clients later take different positions, as the AOL opinion takes pains to point out. See the paragraph immediately preceding part III of the opinion. The lawyer may have to withdraw from working for either client and his conflicts may be imputed to other lawyers in his firm or general counsel's office.

Of course, sometimes a company will want to have a single lawyer represent both it and a constituent, as when the company and one of its officers or employees are sued for discrimination. Using a single lawyer will save money and facilitate coordination of the defense. In deciding whether to do so, however, the parties must consider whether a conflict between the interests of the company and its constituent is likely to emerge. And a lawyer asked to represent both the organization and a constituent must determine whether the joint representation satisfies Rule 1.7 and whether the informed consent of each client is needed.

Apart from the risk of forming an implicit attorney-client relationship with a company constituent, as nearly happened in the AOL investigation, lawyers must also comply with ethical rules that obligate them to clarify their role when talking to an unrepresented person. Rule 4.3 addresses the situation generally. Rule 1.13(f)'s particular focus is company constituents. That rule instructs lawyers to "explain the identity of the client when the lawyer knows or reasonably should know that the organization's interests are adverse to those of the constituents with whom the lawyer is dealing." This is about fairness. A corporate officer, for example, may fail to appreciate that the company's lawyer owes her loyalty and confidentiality duties solely to the company and that whatever the constituent tells the lawyer can be disclosed to law enforcement agencies or lead to job loss.

In the Fourth Circuit's AOL case, Wakeford separately argued that his communications were privileged because of a common interest agreement. That could have worked *if* there really was one, but the court concluded that none was in place during the interviews. The lack of an agreement also facilitated the conviction of the defendant in United States v. Weissman, 195 F.3d 96 (2d Cir. 1999). Every lawyer who represents a corporate constituent during an internal investigation should remember what happened to Jerry Weissman. Amid a federal investigation of a company where he was CFO, Weissman participated in two meetings with the company's lawyer, his own lawyer, and a company officer. The company waived the privilege for what was said at the meetings and the government used this evidence to convict Weissman. Weissman claimed that the meetings were held pursuant to a common interest agreement and *he* had not waived the privilege. His problem was that none of the participants at the first of the two meetings had bothered to say that it was held pursuant to a common interest agreement, much less to put the agreement in writing (highly advisable but generally not required). The court was not prepared to infer an agreement from the circumstances, especially as it could discern no common interest. (At the second meeting, a day later, the parties did agree to a common interest arrangement, but the harm had already been done.)

What About Government Lawyers?

Special Counsel Robert Mueller was appointed to investigate possible Russian influence during the 2016 presidential campaign. Congressional committees were investigating the same thing. President Trump and many White House staff members hired private lawyers to represent them. That's costly. Why not use lawyers from the Justice Department or the White House Counsel's office instead? Because a court might find that the government, not the official, controls the attorney-client privilege for communications with a government lawyer and that the government has no valid interest in concealing these from a grand jury or other investigative body.

In re Grand Jury Subpoena, 828 F.3d 1083 (9th Cir. 2016), addressed a claim by John Kitzhaber, a former Oregon Governor.

> Kitzhaber . . . claims the privilege protects . . . specific communications with government attorneys regarding [Kitzhaber's] potential conflicts of interest. . . .
>
> Much uncertainty surrounds the reach of the attorney-client privilege in the context of investigations into public officials. That uncertainty, however, has concerned cases in which an attorney-client privilege with a government lawyer was invoked by a governmental entity, or by an individual in his or her official capacity. Where courts have acknowledged the attorney-client privilege to apply to conversations between government officials and government lawyers, they have construed the privilege to mean that "*the Government* may invoke the attorney-client privilege," not that officeholders in their personal capacity may invoke the privilege. In no instance, as far as we are aware, has a former officeholder successfully claimed that a government staff lawyer discussing a matter relating to official business was representing the officeholder personally during a conversation had while both were government employees. . . .
>
> Further, Kitzhaber could have hired his own lawyer for consultation about his conflict-of-interest concerns, and indeed did hire his own lawyer to represent him in an ethics inquiry. Generally, "[a]n official who fears he or she may have violated the criminal law and wishes to speak with an attorney in confidence should speak with a private attorney, not a government attorney." As to any communications with a private lawyer, Kitzhaber must "receive[] the full protection of the attorney-client and work product privileges in his dealings with personal counsel."

The subpoena in this case was from a federal grand jury investigating criminal conduct by a former state official. Courts have also enforced federal grand jury subpoenas when the subject of an investigation is a federal official, even the president. In re Lindsey, 148 F.3d 1100 (D.C. Cir. 1998) (requiring deputy White House counsel to disclose communications with President Clinton). Collecting cases that rule both ways on these questions, without taking a position because the facts did not require one, is In re Grand Jury Subpoena, 909 F.3d 26 (1st Cir. 2018). In civil cases, the government may properly claim privilege. United States v. Jicarilla Apache Nation, 564 U.S. 162 (2011).

2. Change of Corporate Control

"We're Still on the Same Side"

"My firm is outside counsel for the Matterick family of companies. In addition to Matterick, Ltd., the parent, there are 10 to 15 wholly owned subsidiaries, which we also represent. Their identity and number change because subs are bought and sold every so often. Matterick and its subs are vintners, importers, exporters, and retailers of fine wines and liquors. One of its subs was Vasco Castilian Wines, Inc. ("Vasco").

Last year, Matterick sold Vasco. The buyer was a shell company called Prime Acquisition, formed by Cortina Foods Ltd. ("Cortina") for the sole purpose of acquiring Vasco. After it did, Cortina dissolved Vasco and Prime Acquisition changed its name to Prime Wines ("Prime"). It's the same business with a new name and new owner. My firm represented Vasco for the five years that Matterick owned it, and I represented Matterick and Vasco on negotiation of the sale of Vasco to Prime Acquisition, the shell company.

Matterick made certain warranties about the size of two vineyards Vasco owned in Spain. Cortina and Prime now say that these warranties were false, and they have sued Matterick for breach of warranty. They say that one of the vineyards is actually smaller by 600 acres (out of 7,000 acres) than Matterick represented. When my partner appeared for Matterick, the plaintiffs said we were disqualified because we represented Vasco when it bought the two vineyards from its former owners three years ago and we were now opposing Vasco's buyer, Prime Wines, in a substantially related matter. They cited Rule 1.9(a).

Are we disqualified? As I see it, we're still on the same side — Matterick's side — and all work we did for Vasco was only on behalf of its parent, Matterick, when Matterick wholly owned it. Vasco is now defunct. We never represented Prime Wines. How can we owe it anything?

Sincerely,

Angus E. Mackenzie"

Tom Y.C. Tang had a great business, Tekni-Plex. It packaged products for drug companies and others. It was a closely held company, with never more than 18 shareholders. In 1994, when Tang was the sole owner, he decided to sell. The buyers created a company called Acquisition. The plan was for Tekni-Plex to merge into Acquisition, which would then change its name back to Tekni-Plex. This happened. The purchase price was $43 million (about $75 million in 2020 dollars). To avoid confusion, the court's opinion calls the company when Tang owned it "old Tekni-Plex" and the postmerger company "new Tekni-Plex."

Meyner and Landis (M&L) represented old Tekni-Plex for more than 20 years. It also did work for Tang personally. Two of its assignments are important here. First, in the 1980s, M&L helped the company get an environmental permit to operate a laminator in Somerville, New Jersey and generally advised it on environmental compliance. Second, on behalf of Tang, M&L negotiated the agreement that merged old Tekni-Plex into Acquisition.

Tang gave his personal warranty that the company was in compliance with environmental laws. Following the merger, new Tekni-Plex claimed that the Somerville laminator did not comply with those laws. It demanded arbitration. M&L appeared for Tang. New Tekni-Plex challenged the firm's right to do so. It said that M&L was *its* former lawyer and was now adverse to it on a matter substantially related to the very environmental advice M&L previously provided to old Tekni-Plex. New Tekni-Plex also demanded all of M&L's files from its representation of old Tekni-Plex, including on the Somerville laminator, and its files on the merger negotiations.

These issues raised questions about client identity, confidences, and conflicts. New York law required a court to resolve them. So the arbitration was put on hold while the parties went to court. The court had to answer three questions: Did M&L formerly represent *new* Tekni-Plex in the work on the Somerville laminator? M&L naturally argued that it did not because new Tekni-Plex did not even exist at that time and M&L's then-client, old Tekni-Plex, existed no longer. However, if the court answered this question affirmatively, it would next have to decide whether the former client conflict rule (today Rule 1.9(a)) disqualified M&L. Last, the court had to decide who as between Tang and new Tekni-Plex was entitled to the law firm's files on both its pre-merger work and on the merger itself.

TEKNI-PLEX, INC. v. MEYNER & LANDIS[*]
89 N.Y.2d 123, 674 N.E.2d 663, 651 N.Y.S.2d 954 (1996)

KAYE, CHIEF JUDGE . . .

Acquisition was a shell corporation created by the purchasers solely for the acquisition of Tekni-Plex. Under the Merger Agreement, Tekni-Plex merged into Acquisition, with Acquisition the surviving corporation, and Tekni-Plex ceased its separate existence. Tekni-Plex conveyed to Acquisition all of its tangible and intangible assets, rights and liabilities. Acquisition in return paid Tang the purchase price "in complete liquidation of Tekni-Plex,"

---

[*] *Tekni-Plex* is a complicated case and the full opinion is dense. If your professional life leads you to the world of mergers and acquisitions, you should read all of it. It has influenced other courts. Here, however, we are concerned only with certain issues of client identity when the client is an organization, so I have done serious editing and offer pre- and post-case notes by way of explanation. — ED.

and all of Tang's shares in Tekni-Plex—the only shares outstanding—were canceled. . . .

C. Disqualification of Counsel . . .

1. is new tekni-plex a "former client" of m&l? . . .

When ownership of a corporation changes hands, whether the attorney-client relationship transfers as well to the new owners turns on the practical consequences rather than the formalities of the particular transaction. In Commodity Futures Trading Commn. v. Weintraub, 471 U.S. 343 [1985], the Supreme Court held that power to exercise the attorney-client privilege of an insolvent corporation passed to the bankruptcy trustee, who assumed managerial responsibility for operating the debtor company's business. In reaching this conclusion, the Court noted with regard to solvent corporations that

> "when control of a corporation passes to new management, the authority to assert and waive the corporation's attorney-client privilege passes as well. New managers installed as a result of a takeover, merger, loss of confidence by shareholders, or simply normal succession, may waive the attorney-client privilege with respect to communications made by former officers and directors."

Weintraub establishes that, where efforts are made to run the preexisting business entity and manage its affairs, successor management stands in the shoes of prior management and controls the attorney-client privilege with respect to matters concerning the company's operations. It follows that, under such circumstances, the prior attorney-client relationship continues with the newly formed entity.

By contrast, the mere transfer of assets with no attempt to continue the pre-existing operation generally does not transfer the attorney-client relationship. . . .

Here, appellants [Tang and M&L] emphasize that old Tekni-Plex merged into Acquisition and ceased to exist as a separate legal entity. That Acquisition, rather than old Tekni-Plex, was designated the surviving corporation, however, is not dispositive. Acquisition was a mere shell corporation, created solely for the purpose of acquiring old Tekni-Plex. Following the merger, the business of old Tekni-Plex remained unchanged, with the same products, clients, suppliers and non-managerial personnel. Indeed, under the Merger Agreement, new Tekni-Plex possessed all of the rights, privileges, liabilities and obligations of old Tekni-Plex, in addition to its assets. Certainly, new Tekni-Plex is entitled to access to any relevant pre-merger legal advice rendered to old Tekni-Plex that it might need to defend against these liabilities or pursue any of these rights.

As a practical matter, then, old Tekni-Plex did not die. To the contrary, the business operations of old Tekni-Plex continued under the new managers. Consequently, control of the attorney-client privilege with respect to any confidential communications between M&L and corporate actors of old Tekni-Plex concerning these operations passed to the management of new Tekni-Plex. An attorney-client relationship between M&L and new Tekni-Plex necessarily exists.

Thus, the first of the three prongs for disqualification is established: new Tekni-Plex is a "former client" of M&L.

2. IS THERE A SUBSTANTIAL RELATIONSHIP BETWEEN THE CURRENT AND FORMER REPRESENTATIONS?

[The court concluded that there was one, first, because the current dispute concerned the merger agreement on which the law firm had represented old Tekni-Plex; and, second, because the plaintiff was alleging misrepresentation in connection with the Somerville permit and environmental law compliance generally, where the firm had also represented the company.]

3. ARE THE INTERESTS OF M&L'S PRESENT CLIENT MATERIALLY ADVERSE TO THE INTERESTS OF ITS FORMER CLIENT?

The arbitration claims pit Acquisition's interest as purchaser against Tang's interest as the selling shareholder. Furthermore, the Merger Agreement provides that Tang is responsible for indemnifying Acquisition for any misrepresentation or breach of warranty made by either Tang *or old Tekni-Plex*. Plainly the parties contemplated a unity of interest between old Tekni-Plex and Tang should a dispute arise between the buyer and seller regarding the representations and warranties. Thus, to the extent the arbitration relates to the merger negotiations—as opposed to corporate operations—Tang and old Tekni-Plex remain on the same side of the table. The interest of M&L's former client old Tekni-Plex is aligned with the interest of the law firm's present client Tang—both in opposition to the buyer. . . .

The dispute here, however, . . . goes beyond the merger negotiations. It also involves issues relating to the law firm's long-standing representation of the acquired corporation on matters arising out of the company's business operations—namely, M&L's separate representation of old Tekni-Plex prior to the merger on environmental compliance matters. Any environmental violations will negatively affect not only the purchasers but also the business interests of the merged corporation. In this regard, the interests of M&L's current client Tang are adverse to the interests that new Tekni-Plex assumed from old Tekni-Plex.

Indeed, M&L's earlier representation of old Tekni-Plex provided the firm with access to confidential information conveyed by old Tekni-Plex concerning the very environmental compliance matters at issue in the arbitration. M&L's duty of confidentiality with respect to these communications passed to new Tekni-Plex; yet its current representation of Tang creates the potential for the law firm to use these confidences against new Tekni-Plex in the arbitration.

Under the circumstances, the appearance of impropriety is manifest and the potential conflict of interest apparent. M&L should therefore be disqualified from representing Tang in the arbitration.

D. Confidential Communications

As a final matter, we must determine whether M&L was properly enjoined from revealing to Tang any confidential communications obtained from old Tekni-Plex and whether new Tekni-Plex owns the confidences created during the law firm's prior representation of old Tekni-Plex. For analytical purposes, the attorney-client communications must be separated into two categories: general business communications and those relating to the merger negotiations.

1. General Business Communications

As explained above, the management of new Tekni-Plex continues the business operations of the pre-merger entity. Control of the attorney-client privilege with regard to confidential communications arising out of those operations — including any pre-merger communications between old Tekni-Plex and M&L relating to the company's environmental compliance — thus passed to the management of new Tekni-Plex. As a result, new Tekni-Plex now has the authority to assert the attorney-client privilege to preclude M&L from disclosing the contents of these confidential communications to Tang. Likewise, ownership of the law firm's files regarding its pre-merger representation of old Tekni-Plex on environmental compliance matters passed to the management of new Tekni-Plex. This conclusion comports with new Tekni-Plex's right to invoke the pre-merger attorney-client relationship should it have to prosecute or defend against third-party suits involving the assets, rights or liabilities that it assumed from old Tekni-Plex. . . .

2. Communications Relating to the Merger Negotiations

As to the other category of attorney-client communications between old Tekni-Plex and M&L — those relating to the merger transaction — new Tekni-Plex did not succeed to old Tekni-Plex's right to control the attorney-client privilege. New Tekni-Plex's misrepresentation and breach of warranty claims do not derive from the rights it inherited from old Tekni-Plex but from the rights retained by the buyer, Acquisition, with respect to the transaction. . . .

This conclusion is especially compelling here, where at the time of the acquisition the seller corporation was solely owned and managed by one individual, Tang. "As corporate stock ownership is concentrated into fewer and fewer hands, the distinction between corporate entity and shareholders begins to blur" and "[i]n the case of a sole-owner corporation, they may merge." To allow new Tekni-Plex access to the confidences conveyed by the seller company to its counsel during the negotiations would, in the circumstances presented, be the equivalent of turning over to the buyer all of the privileged communications of the seller concerning the very transaction at issue. The parties here, moreover, recognized the community between the selling shareholder and his corporation and expressly provided that it be preserved in any subsequent dispute regarding the acquisition.

Indeed, to grant new Tekni-Plex control over the attorney-client privilege as to communications concerning the merger transaction would thwart, rather than promote, the purposes underlying the privilege. The attorney-client privilege encourages "full and frank communication between attorneys and their clients and thereby promote[s] broader public interests in the observance of law and administration of justice." Where the parties to a corporate acquisition agree that in any subsequent dispute arising out of the transaction the interests of the buyer will be pitted against the interests of the sold corporation, corporate actors should not have to worry that their privileged communications with counsel concerning the negotiations might be available to the buyer for use against the sold corporation in any ensuing litigation. Such concern would significantly chill attorney-client communication during the transaction.

Thus, while generally "parties who negotiate a corporate acquisition should expect that the privileges of the acquired corporation would be incidents of the sale," the agreement between the parties here contemplated that, in any dispute arising from the merger transaction, the rights of the acquired corporation, old Tekni-Plex, relating to the transaction would remain independent from and adverse to the rights of new Tekni-Plex. . . .

––––––––––––––

Although this opinion might seem technical, because it is, the consequences to Tang were anything but. He lost his trusted lawyers and control of their pre-merger files. And we now know that this result could have been avoided.

To address the conflict issue, the court had to interpret the contract. It had to discern the parties' intentions from the language they used. It concluded:

- New Tekni-Plex was the former client of M&L on all business-related matters, including environmental advice, that M&L provided prior to the merger itself. Former client status traveled to new Tekni-Plex because the merger documents were read to say so. "Intangible rights" were part of the deal and they included the lawyers' professional duties to old Tekni-Plex.

- M&L was now appearing adverse to new Tekni-Plex in a substantially related matter and was disqualified.

- As M&L's former client on pre-merger work, new Tekni-Plex was entitled to all law firm files on that work and had "[c]ontrol of the attorney-client privilege with regard to confidential communications arising out of those operations."

- But in the work on the merger itself, unlike the pre-merger work, Tang and old Tekni-Plex (the sellers) were opposed to Acquisition (the buyer). As the "adverse" party in the merger negotiations, Acquisition could not now claim to have been M&L's client, as it could for pre-merger work. And new Tekni-Plex's claims derived from Acquisition.

There is a valuable lesson here for lawyers representing parties in merger negotiations. Acquisition bought more than the business itself. The contract also conveyed M&L's obligations arising from 20 years of work. These were the "intangible rights" of old Tekni-Plex and the "incidents of the sale." In effect, the firm's ethical and fiduciary obligations were property that could be (and were) sold. It surprises some lawyers to learn this. After all, we like to stress the personal (noncommercial) nature of the attorney-client relationship. Clients are not customers, we say.

If Tang had contracted to keep the "incidents" of the attorney-client relationship, he could have kept his lawyers and M&L could have kept its client. Acquisition might have agreed to that, perhaps for something in return. Because the court's opinion interprets the language of the contract, either party could have tried to negotiate different language to achieve a different result.

Agreeing with *Tekni-Plex* is Goodrich v. Goodrich, 960 A.2d 1275 (N.H. 2008) ("If . . . an entity acquires control of [a] corporation's business operations, rights and liabilities, it . . . also acquires authority over the attorney-client privilege.") and Girl Scouts-Western Oklahoma v. Barringer-Thomson, 252 P.3d 844 (Okla. 2011).

3. Conflict and Privilege Issues in Representing a Member of a Corporate Family

"We Have Never Done Work for the Parent"

"For as long as I can recall, certainly more than a decade, our firm has done work for Federal General (FG). It's not a major client and we're not its only firm, but it's been a steady source of work including currently. FG is a wholly owned subsidiary of United Marine (UM). UM has about 50 subsidiaries. UM has brought a patent infringement case against seven small tech startups, including our client Zink Data (ZD). ZD has asked us to take the defense and it seemed to us that there was no reason not to because we have never done work for UM. Or indeed for any of UM's other subs. Can we defend ZD against UM, the parent of one of our clients but never itself a client? Anything else you need to know?

Thanks,
Maeve"

Corporate Family Conflicts

Many corporate families are remarkably large (and their membership may change often). There may be hundreds of wholly owned subsidiaries, some of which may have subsidiaries of their own. The companies may be in different industries and nations. A law firm that represents one corporate family member, even the parent, does not for that reason alone have an attorney-client relationship with any other corporate family member. More is needed. What more? Obviously, the answer to that question can have a dramatic effect on the law firm's ability to accept new clients. Remember, client conflicts are imputed firmwide.

ABA Opinion 95-390 concluded that the representation of one company may forbid the law firm from acting adversely to an affiliate if

- the law firm and the client agree that the client's affiliates will be deemed clients of the law firm. The agreement may be express or implied;
- the two companies operate as alter egos, meaning they behave as one;
- the operations and management personnel of the two companies substantially overlap;
- the same in-house legal staff does the legal work for both the affiliate and the client; or
- representation of the client provided the law firm with confidential information relevant to the matter in which it now wished to appear adverse to the affiliate.

The Restatement of Law Governing Lawyers added yet another test to those in ABA Opinion 95-390, a test the ABA rejected. Section 121 comment *d* first states the general rule that when a lawyer represents Corporation A, the company "is ordinarily the lawyer's client; neither individual officers of Corporation A nor other corporations in which Corporation A has an ownership interest, that hold an ownership interest in Corporation A, or in which a major shareholder in Corporation A has an ownership interest, are thereby considered to be the lawyer's client." So far, so good. But the comment then goes on to say that in some situations this will not be true, and gives as one such instance "where financial loss or benefit to the nonclient person or entity will have a direct, adverse impact on the client." The comment offers this example:

> Lawyer represents Corporation A in local real-estate transactions. Lawyer has been asked to represent Plaintiff in a products-liability action against Corporation B claiming substantial damages. Corporation B is a wholly owned subsidiary of Corporation A; any judgment obtained against Corporation B will have a material adverse impact on the value of Corporation B's assets and on the value of the assets of Corporation A. Just as Lawyer could not file suit against Corporation A on behalf of another client, even in a matter unrelated to the subject of Lawyer's representation of Corporation A, Lawyer may not represent Plaintiff in the suit against Corporation B without the consent of both Plaintiff and Corporation A. . . .

JP Morgan Chase Bank ex rel. Mahonia Ltd. v. Liberty Mutual Insurance Co., 189 F. Supp. 2d 20 (S.D.N.Y. 2002), cited a potentially huge economic impact in disqualifying Davis Polk from pursuing a $183 million claim against Federal, 95 percent of which was owned by Chubb, a firm client. Federal accounted for 90 percent of Chubb's business. The case would seem to endorse the Restatement view except that there were other factors supporting the same result. Also, the percentages are so dramatic that it might not be necessary to accept the Restatement view to defend the holding. As a practical matter, Chubb was Federal.

In federal court, a district judge's disqualification rulings are usually the end of the matter because interlocutory appeals are unavailable and mandamus jurisdiction is narrow. But the Second Circuit got a rare chance to address corporate family conflicts in GSI Commerce Solutions v. BabyCenter, L.L.C., 618 F.3d 204 (2d Cir. 2010). The district judge had refused to order arbitration because he concluded that the law firm representing the party seeking arbitration had a corporate family conflict. That made the decision final and appealable. The Second Circuit affirmed.

> We agree that representation adverse to a client's affiliate can, in certain circumstances, conflict with the lawyer's duty of loyalty owed to a client, a situation that we shall refer to as "a corporate affiliate conflict."
>
> The factors relevant to whether a corporate affiliate conflict exists are of a general nature. Courts have generally focused on: (i) the degree of operational commonality between affiliated entities, and (ii) the extent to which one depends financially on the other. As to operational commonality, courts have considered the extent to which entities rely on a common infrastructure. Courts have also focused on the extent to which the affiliated entities rely on or otherwise share common personnel such as managers, officers, and directors. . . . This focus on shared or dependent control over legal and management issues reflects the view that neither management nor in-house legal counsel should, without their consent, have to place their trust in outside counsel in one matter while opposing the same counsel in another.
>
> As to financial interdependence, several courts have considered the extent to which an adverse outcome in the matter at issue would result in substantial and measurable loss to the client or its affiliate. Courts have also inquired into the entities' ownership structure. Some have even suggested that an affiliate's status as a wholly-owned subsidiary of the client may suffice to establish a corporate affiliate conflict. However, we agree with the ABA that affiliates should not be considered a single entity for conflicts purposes based solely on the fact that one entity is a wholly-owned subsidiary of the other, at least when the subsidiary is not otherwise operationally integrated with the parent company.

The last paragraph, although not crystal clear, seems to reject financial harm as alone sufficient to pose a conflict.

Following the Second Circuit is Dr. Falk Pharma GMBH v. Generico, LLC, 916 F.3d 975 (Fed. Cir. 2019) (predicting that four circuits "would agree that shared or dependent control over operations and legal matters between [corporate] affiliates is significant" on the question of client identity).

4. Closely Held Entities

Rule 1.13(a)'s distinctions work less well when the entity is small. Does it make sense to say that counsel to a corporation whose officers, directors, and shareholders total only three people "represents the organization acting through its duly authorized constituents"? The owners are likely to think of themselves as the clients or clients along with the company. But sometimes it will make sense. If one of the three is found stealing from the company, we won't have a problem if its lawyer sues him. Or if one of the shareholders sues the company, its lawyer will be allowed to defend it. Bobbitt v. Victorian House, Inc., 545 F. Supp. 1124 (N.D. Ill. 1982) (company counsel can defend dissolution and accounting action brought by 50-percent shareholder against company and other shareholder). By contrast, in a battle among shareholders for control of the company, the company's lawyer should not choose sides but instead take her instructions from whomever the company's bylaws and resolutions purport to recognize as authorized to give them.

Or else! The following opinion was delivered in open court on June 6, 1994, following a bench trial before Judge Roush of the Fairfax County (Virginia) Circuit Court. Afterward, the parties settled with no appeal.

Here's what you should know for background. Murphy & Demory was a corporation with a three-person board and two co-owners, Admiral Murphy and Mr. Demory. Its business was lobbying, and its law firm was Pillsbury Madison (now Pillsbury Winthrop). The company sued Admiral Murphy, Pillsbury, and two Pillsbury lawyers, Deanne Siemer and Keith Mendelson. Essentially, it charged that Murphy, aided by Pillsbury and the two lawyers, attempted either to take control of the company (ousting Demory) or secretly to start a competing company, even though Murphy owed fiduciary duties to Murphy & Demory. Judge Roush found against Murphy and then proceeded to consider the liability of Pillsbury and the two lawyers. Note her findings on the firm's failure to heed the warnings of junior associates (some of which were discovered in email) and her criticism of the firm's procedures for monitoring compliance with ethics rules. Why were those procedures inadequate?

MURPHY & DEMORY, LTD., ET AL. v. ADMIRAL DANIEL J. MURPHY, U.S.N. (RET.)

Circuit Court of Fairfax County (Virginia) Chancery No. 128219
June 6, 1994

Roush, Judge . . .*

On count VI of the bill of complaint, Murphy & Demory alleges a cause of action against the Defendants [Pillsbury and its lawyers], Deanne Siemer []

---

* The reporter's transcript has been reparagraphed for easier reading. Bracketed numbers are added.

and Keith Mendelson, for legal malpractice. I will refer to those Defendants collectively as the Pillsbury Defendants. All parties agree that the law of the District of Columbia applies. . . .

In rendering my decision on count VI, I've considered and carefully reviewed the Rules of Professional Conduct of the District of Columbia . . . as well as the testimony of the Plaintiff's expert witness, Mr. David Epstein.

I find Murphy & Demory has proven by a preponderance of the evidence that the Pillsbury Defendants have committed legal malpractice [1] by violating the standard of care for attorneys practicing in the District of Columbia; [2] by accepting representation of Admiral Murphy in his efforts either to take control of Murphy & Demory or to form, prior to his resignation from Murphy & Demory, a new corporation to compete with Murphy & Demory, [as a result of which] the exercise of their professional judgment on behalf of the corporation would likely be adversely affected; [3] by simultaneously representing Admiral Murphy in matters adverse to their client, Murphy & Demory, without disclosing to the corporation or to Admiral Murphy the fact of the dual representation in obtaining the corporation's consent of such representation; [4] by meeting with the director of the corporation, Margot Bester, for the purpose of enlisting her support in Admiral Murphy's plans to take over control of the corporation; [5] by inducing or attempting to induce employees of Murphy & Demory to resign from Murphy & Demory and to join Murphy & Associates and by assisting Murphy & Demory employees in drafting their letters of resignation from the company; [6] by generally assisting Admiral Murphy in his plans to either take control of Murphy & Demory or to divert business from Murphy & Demory in favor of his new competing company, Murphy & Associates, while at the same time representing Murphy & Demory without the corporation's consent to the dual representation after full disclosure of all material facts; [7] by drafting the restructuring or takeover proposal for Admiral Murphy; [8] by drafting letters for Murphy & Demory clients to send, terminating their relationship with Murphy & Demory and directing that their files be transferred to Murphy & Associates; [9] by assisting Admiral Murphy while still counsel to Murphy & Demory in preparing his remarks to be delivered to the Murphy & Demory employees on August 30, 1992, in which, among other things, Admiral Murphy in effect invited employees to join him in his new company if the board of Murphy & Demory did not accede to his demands for control of the corporation; [10] by calling and/or attending meetings with Mr. Demory and other Murphy & Demory employees in the Pillsbury Defendants' capacity as the corporation's counsel; [11] in using confidential information obtained at such meetings for the benefit of Admiral Murphy; [12] by failing to disclose to Murphy & Demory material information known to the Pillsbury Defendants that might affect how the board of directors of Murphy & Demory might act; [13] by filing on behalf of Murphy & Demory a lawsuit seeking judicial dissolution of their by-then former client, Murphy & Demory, based in part on the confidential information obtained from

Murphy & Demory employees during the course of their representation of Murphy & Demory. . . .

I was struck and disturbed by the fact that every inquiry by an associate into the propriety of the firm's actions was referred back to Ms. Siemer for resolution. Clearly, Pillsbury, Madison & Sutro's internal mechanisms for resolution of ethical issues are seriously deficient. The partner in charge of the client relationship affected by the issue, who is least likely to be objective, is the ultimate arbiter of whether the firm has a conflict of interest. I found Ms. Siemer's testimony to lack credibility when she stated that she wrestled with the ethical issues posed by the joint representation of Murphy & Demory and Admiral Murphy and concluded that there was no conflict because both clients had an identical interest in ensuring that Admiral Murphy had the best information possible as to what his options were, even if one option was to divert business from Murphy & Demory and let the company wither. As Mr. Epstein aptly noted in his expert testimony, Murphy & Demory had no interest in Admiral Murphy's knowledge of how to undermine the company.

I find that Ms. Siemer willfully ignored the District of Columbia Rules of Professional Conduct with which she was well familiar, having written a treatise on legal ethics. I find that Pillsbury, Madison & Sutro is equally responsible for Ms. Siemer's lapses in this regard, particularly because in the face of warning bells from the associates, the firm allowed Ms. Siemer to be the final determiner of whether the firm had a conflict of interest.

Although I'm not unsympathetic to Mr. Mendelson's difficult position at the time of most of the activities complained of, I find that he too was equally responsible for the legal malpractice. Simply put, Mr. Mendelson was senior enough that he should have put a stop to the undisclosed dual representation of Admiral Murphy and Murphy & Demory by disclosing the conflict to Admiral Murphy and Murphy & Demory's board in obtaining their consent, or failing that, by withdrawing from the representation. . . .

I find that as a direct and proximate result of the Pillsbury Defendants' legal malpractice, Murphy & Demory suffered compensatory damages in the amount of $500,000. . . .

Three "incredible but true" lessons from this case are:

- *First,* Judge Roush's description of Siemer's conduct and the firm's failure to intercede are examples in how *not* to run a law firm. Concerns from an associate were "referred back to" Siemer, whose conduct prompted those concerns.
- *Second,* why didn't the firm settle before trial? Liability was clear. A public trial could harm the reputation of the firm and the two lawyer defendants. Indeed, the verdict led to a story in the national legal press, which is how others and I learned about this unreported opinion and are able to use it in class.

- *Third,* how could it happen that a lawyer who had written a book about legal ethics also did what the court described? One reason lawyers err is because of a demanding client whose work accounts for much of a lawyer's income. Perhaps that happened here.

C. SARBANES-OXLEY, DODD-FRANK, AND THE RULE 1.13 AMENDMENTS

On July 25, 2002, Congress passed what has come to be known as the Sarbanes-Oxley Act (SOX). The House vote was 423 to 3 and the Senate vote was 99 to 0. The President signed the law on July 30, 2002. Sarbanes-Oxley was the most significant federal legislative response to corporate scandals in the United States, beginning with the collapse of Enron, followed by the indictment, conviction (later reversed), and demise of accounting firm Arthur Andersen, and financial machinations at Imclone, Tyco, WorldCom, and HealthSouth, among others.

Section 307 of the Act (15 U.S.C. §7245) was submitted as an amendment by Senators Edwards, Enzi, and Corzine on July 10, 2002. It passed unanimously. It provides:

RULES OF PROFESSIONAL RESPONSIBILITY FOR ATTORNEYS

Not later than 180 days after [July 30, 2002], the [SEC] shall issue rules, in the public interest and for the protection of investors, setting forth minimum standards of professional conduct for attorneys appearing and practicing before the Commission in any way in the representation of issuers, including a rule—

(1) requiring an attorney to report evidence of a material violation of securities law or breach of fiduciary duty or similar violation by the company or any agent thereof, to the chief legal counsel or the chief executive officer of the company (or the equivalent thereof); and

(2) if the counsel or officer does not appropriately respond to the evidence (adopting, as necessary, appropriate remedial measures or sanctions with respect to the violation), requiring the attorney to report the evidence to the audit committee of the board of directors of the issuer or to another committee of the board of directors comprised solely of directors not employed directly or indirectly by the issuer, or to the board of directors.

The premise here is that lawyers who work for companies are likely to know early on if something is amiss. Since the company is the client, the import of §307 is to compel the lawyer to act to protect the client against the misconduct of its agents. Critics of §307 (and the SEC rules it spawned) and (to a lesser extent) of the contemporaneous amendments to Rule 1.13 contend that they micromanage how lawyers should protect their corporate clients. Even lawyers who have no principled quarrel with the content of the SEC rules may object to their source—the federal government—in the belief that the tradition of state regulation of lawyers should not be breached.

The SEC rules implementing §307 can be found at 17 C.F.R. Part 205. In substance, they impose very specific *reporting-up* requirements for certain lawyers. "Reporting up" is shorthand for a duty to go up the corporate chain of command to correct certain perceived illegalities by corporate constituents. The SEC rules impose the reporting-up duty on lawyers "appearing and practicing before the Commission." That group is *not* limited to lawyers who personally submit documents to or appear before the Commission. Rather, the rules expansively include lawyers "[t]ransacting any business with the Commission"; representing "an issuer . . . in connection with any Commission investigation [or] inquiry"; providing advice regarding any document if the lawyer "has notice" that it will be filed with the Commission or incorporated in another filed document; and advising on whether information is required to be filed with the Commission. A first-year associate can fall within the definition even though the SEC does not know she exists.

Further, the reporting-up obligation is *not* limited to securities law violations. It extends to "any breach of fiduciary or similar duty to the issuer recognized under an applicable Federal or State statute or at common law, including but not limited to misfeasance, nonfeasance, abdication of duty, abuse of trust, and approval of unlawful transactions."

The Commission's rules are detailed, with various triggers requiring lawyers to act and react. Here, it suffices to focus on the larger picture. Lawyers who become "aware of evidence of a material violation" of securities law or of a fiduciary or similar duty to the issuer, whether federal or state, must report what they know to the company's chief legal officer or its chief executive officer. The term "evidence of a material violation" is defined, awkwardly, to mean "credible evidence, based upon which it would be *un*reasonable, under the circumstances, for a prudent and competent attorney *not* to conclude that it is reasonably likely that a material violation has occurred, is ongoing, or is about to occur." (Emphasis added.) The Commission was criticized for adopting a definition containing a double negative, which in the view of some made reporting up too easy to avoid.

In any event, once a report is made, the reporting lawyer and the chief legal officer or chief executive officer have various duties depending upon what a further inquiry, which is mandatory, reveals. The expectation is that once the top officials, especially independent directors, learn of a serious problem, action will follow because inaction can mean substantial personal liability.

The Commission's rules also permit, but do not require, lawyers appearing and practicing before it to disclose to the Commission a client's confidential information related to the representation under certain conditions.

This is called "reporting out." See 17 C.F.R. §205.3(d)(2), set out in the note.*

The conditions that permit a lawyer to report out overlap, but are not identical to, the Model Rules confidentiality exceptions and differ significantly from the rules in many states, creating the *potential* for a clash between the scope of a lawyer's disclosure authority under SOX and the scope under state confidentiality rules. The SEC reporting-out provisions took on much greater importance after the Dodd-Frank legislation discussed below.

Activity, meanwhile, was proceeding on a parallel track. Anticipating congressional action in light of the corporate scandals, in March 2002 the ABA created a Task Force on Corporate Responsibility. If the ABA and then state courts modified their own rules of professional conduct in a way the SEC approved, the bar could hope that the agency would take a minimalist approach to the authority Congress conferred in §307. Indeed, the Task Force's recommendations to amend Rules 1.6 and 1.13, which the ABA House of Delegates accepted in August 2003, likely explains the SEC's decision not to adopt a *mandatory* reporting-out obligation.

As stated in chapter 2, the amendments to Rule 1.6 expand the exceptions under which a lawyer is permitted to reveal client confidential information to third persons. The amendments to Rule 1.13 are also significant. First, they strengthen the reporting-up obligation in Rule 1.13(b). Although reporting up is not always obligatory, it is now presumptively required "[u]nless the lawyer reasonably believes that it is not necessary in the best interest of the organization to do so." Previously, reporting up was simply one option available to the lawyer. Of greater consequence, Rule 1.13 now contains its own exception to confidentiality. It permits, but does not require, reporting out if, after reporting up, "the highest authority . . . insists upon or fails to address in a timely and appropriate manner an action, or a refusal to act, that is clearly a violation of law," and if, in addition, "the lawyer reasonably believes that the violation is reasonably certain to result

---

* An attorney appearing and practicing before the Commission in the representation of an issuer may reveal to the Commission, without the issuer's consent, confidential information related to the representation to the extent the attorney reasonably believes necessary:

(i) To prevent the issuer from committing a material violation that is likely to cause substantial injury to the financial interest or property of the issuer or investors;

(ii) To prevent the issuer, in a Commission investigation or administrative proceeding from committing perjury, proscribed in 18 U.S.C. 1621; suborning perjury, proscribed in 18 U.S.C. 1622; or committing any act proscribed in 18 U.S.C. 1001 that is likely to perpetrate a fraud upon the Commission; or

(iii) To rectify the consequences of a material violation by the issuer that caused, or may cause, substantial injury to the financial interest or property of the issuer or investors in the furtherance of which the attorney's services were used.

17 C.F.R. §205.3(d)(2).

in substantial injury to the organization." Rule 1.13 applies to lawyers for all organizational clients, even if the client is not a public company within the jurisdiction of the SEC.

Cash for Confidences

What if we paid lawyers to tattle on their clients? Really. What if we paid lawyers to reveal client wrongdoing that has harmed or will harm others? Paid them to report out. Hard to imagine? The post-Civil War False Claims Act, authorizing qui tam lawsuits,* and the 2010 Dodd-Frank legislation hold out the promise of rewards, which can amount to tens of millions of dollars, for information revealing (respectively) fraud against the United States or certain illegal conduct by public companies. Both laws envision that a lawyer can be a whistleblower (or in the language of the FCA, a "relator") regarding her own client. So does Rule 1.13(c). Yes, but can a lawyer collect a reward for it?

Take Dodd-Frank, which was passed in the wake of the financial crisis that hit the United States in 2008. The part of the law germane here, as implemented by the SEC, promises generous rewards for disclosure of information that reveals violation of securities laws, breach of fiduciary duty, or "similar" violations of federal or state law. Lawyers can be among the whistleblowers, even by disclosing client confidences, if their information is within an exception to confidentiality or privilege. But *whose* exceptions? The SEC's exceptions or those in the lawyer's licensing jurisdiction? 17 C.F.R. §240:21F-4(b)(4) purports to answer that question (take note of the "unless" clauses and the word "or" which I've italicized):

> The Commission will not consider information to be derived from your independent knowledge or independent analysis in any of the following circumstances [and therefore the information is not a basis for a reward]:
>
> (i) If you obtained the information through a communication that was subject to the attorney-client privilege, *unless* disclosure of that information would otherwise be permitted by an attorney pursuant to §205.3(d)(2) of this chapter, the applicable state attorney conduct rules, *or* otherwise . . . .

So a lawyer can get a Dodd-Frank reward even if she discloses privileged information so long as the disclosure is permitted by the rules in the lawyer's jurisdiction (rules like Rule 1.6 and 1.13). But what if it is not? The reward may still be available if the disclosure is permitted by the SEC's own rule—i.e., §205.3(d)(2), quoted in the footnote on page 456. If the exceptions to confidentiality in the lawyer's licensing jurisdiction are more restrictive than the

---

* "*Qui tam* is short for '*qui tam pro domino rege quam pro se ipso in hac parte sequitur,*' which means 'who pursues this action on our Lord the King's behalf as well as his own.'" United States v. Quest Diagnostics, 734 F.3d 154 (2d Cir. 2013).

SEC's exceptions, a federal agency, with congressional authorization, will have offered the possibility of monetary rewards to lawyers willing to violate their own state's rules. If the state exceptions are the same as or broader than those the SEC adopted, we won't have that problem. But we will have added large financial incentives to encourage lawyers to invoke those exceptions and report their clients' (allegedly) bad behavior.[*]

The public policy and professional regulation questions here are formidable and will likely demand the attention of judges and lawyers for some time. It's one thing to create a permissive confidentiality exception and leave it to each individual lawyer, in the exercise of his or her conscience and moral judgment, to decide whether to invoke it. It is quite different, however, to hold out the promise of a large reward (potentially many millions of dollars) to tempt a lawyer to make the decision in favor of disclosure. The difference is between disclosure because it's the right thing to do and disclosure to get the money. A lawyer might persuade herself that she would have disclosed anyway, so why not take the money. Maybe so. But surely the reward is likely to influence the lawyer's judgment.

Conversely, however, the absence of a reward will discourage disclosure. If we want to encourage whistleblowing to prevent or mitigate the harms that the FCA and SOX identify, why not make it worthwhile or at least not economic suicide to do so? Rewards just compensate for the harm that disclosure may inflict on a lawyer's career.

In the first federal appellate case to confront some of these questions directly, a former in-house lawyer sought (unsuccessfully) to become a whistleblower against a client under the False Claims Act. United States v. Quest Diagnostics, 734 F.3d 154 (2d Cir. 2013) (lawyer's participation in the case violated state confidentiality rules; his conduct was imputed to nonlawyer co-plaintiffs and the law firm representing them, effectively ending the case). The district court opinion in the same case, which was affirmed, also found violations of conflict rules that the circuit decided it did not need to reach. 2011 WL 1330542 (S.D.N.Y. 2011). See also United States ex rel. Holmes v. Northrop Grumman Corp., 642 Fed. Appx 373 (5th Cir. 2016) (disqualifying lawyer relator in False Claims Act case because of ethical violations).

Neither Rule 1.13 nor the SEC's rules, it should be added, permit lawyers to rush to the SEC's cash-for-confidences window as soon as they detect wrongdoing. Both require the lawyer to seek amelioration by first reporting up within the company. Rule 1.13(c) is explicit about that. The SEC rules authorize reporting out only "to the extent the attorney reasonably believes

---

[*] The SEC rules are broader than Rule 1.6 in one significant way. Paragraph (d)(2)(i), unlike its analogue in Rule 1.6(b)(2), does not require that the lawyer's services have been used in connection with the violation. And they are much broader than the rules in some states like New York and California. Unlike the Dodd-Frank regulations, the Civil War-era False Claims Act says nothing about whether a lawyer may disclose confidential or privileged information to get a reward, probably because those doctrines were not developed at the time.

necessary." The lawyer's client is the company, not any wrongdoing constituent. So until the highest authority that can speak for the company acquiesces in the conduct, after it has a chance to remedy it, we cannot say that it is the *client* who misbehaved.

Addressing many of these issues is Kathleen Clark and Nancy Moore, Financial Rewards for Whistleblowing Lawyers, 56 B.C. L. Rev. 1697 (2015).

Self-Assessment Questions

1. Dorsey & Whitney represented Discotrade adverse to defendant "WAII," a second-tier, wholly owned subsidiary of Wyeth. The firm also represented a division of Wyeth Pharmaceuticals, which was another second-tier Wyeth subsidiary. What questions will you ask in deciding whether the firm is disqualified? Discotrade Ltd. v. Wyeth-Ayerst Int'l, 200 F. Supp. 2d 355 (S.D.N.Y. 2002). A second-tier subsidiary is one that is owned by a subsidiary of the parent.

2. "I have been retained by an in-house lawyer who says she has confidential information about her company that, if disclosed to the SEC, could yield tens of millions of dollars of Dodd-Frank reward money but subject her client to many millions of dollars in fines and possibly criminal liability. How should I advise her? What else do I need to know?"

XI

Judges

The judge should not be young; he should have learned to know evil, not from his own soul, but from late and long observation of the nature of evil in others; knowledge should be his guide, not personal experience.

—Plato, *The Republic*

Isabella: Yet show some pity.
Angelo: I show it most of all when I show justice
   For then I pity those I do not know,
   Which a dismissed offense would after gall
   And do him right that, answering one foul wrong,
   Lives not to act another. Be satisfied:
   Your brother dies tomorrow; be content.
Isabella: So you must be the first that gives this sentence,
   And he that suffers. O, it is excellent
   To have a giant's strength but it is tyrannous
   To use it like a giant.

—Shakespeare, *Measure for Measure*, 2.02.127-137

Justice should not only be done, but should manifestly and undoubtedly be seen to be done.

—Lord Hewart (1870-1943), in **Rex v. Sussex Justices**

There is in each of us a stream of tendency, whether you choose to call it philosophy or not, which gives coherence and direction to thought and action. Judges cannot escape that current any more than other mortals. All their lives, forces which they do not recognize and cannot name, have been tugging at them—inherited instincts, traditional beliefs, acquired convictions; and the resultant is an outlook on life, a conception of social needs. . . . In this mental background every problem finds its setting. We may try to see things as objectively as we please. None the less, we can never see them with any eyes except our own.

—Benjamin Cardozo, *The Nature of the Judicial Process* (1921)

> I remember once I was with [Justice Holmes]; it was a Saturday
> when the Court was to confer. . . . When we got to the Capitol,
> I wanted to provoke a response, so as he walked off, I said to him,
> "Well, sir, goodbye. Do justice!" He turned quite sharply and he
> said: "Come here. Come here." I answered: "Oh, I know, I know."
> He replied: "That is not my job. My job is to play the game
> according to the rules."
> —Learned Hand, A Personal Confession, in *The Spirit of Liberty*

Introduction to Judicial Ethics

As it does for lawyers, the ABA promulgates a model code of conduct for judges. The ABA adopted the Canons of Judicial Ethics in 1924 and replaced it in 1972 with the Code of Judicial Conduct. The Code itself was substantially amended in 1990 and again in 2007. The states, the District of Columbia, and the U.S. Judicial Conference have adopted judicial conduct codes based largely on the ABA models. All jurisdictions also have a mechanism for judicial discipline. Sanctions for violations can range from a private reprimand to removal. Discipline cannot, however, be used to remove federal judges appointed under Article III of the Constitution. Impeachment and conviction by Congress is constitutionally required. Nevertheless, discipline short of removal is statutorily contemplated for "conduct prejudicial to the effective and expeditious administration of the business of the courts." 28 U.S.C. §351 et seq.

Two circuit courts have held that the Code of Conduct for United States Judges "cannot be the standard for judicial discipline [under §351]. The Canons are aspirational goals, voluntarily adopted by the judiciary itself. . . . Congress imposed a standard for discipline that is significantly lower than, and conceptually different from, the ideals embodied in the Canons." In re Charge of Judicial Misconduct, 62 F.3d 320 (9th Cir. 1995). See also In re Charge of Judicial Misconduct, 91 F.3d 1416 (10th Cir. 1996). Compare In re Charge of Judicial Misconduct or Disability, 85 F.3d 701 (D.C. Cir. 1996), which, while generally subscribing to this proposition, concludes: "Still, there is some indication that judicial councils should be guided in part by the Canons in determining whether a [statutory] violation occurred." And the Judicial Conference of the United States has also written that the Code "may have informational value" on the meaning of §351. Comment, Rule 3, Rules for Judicial Conduct and Judicial Disability Proceedings.

Nine American judges are *not* governed by any ethics code. They are the Justices of the U.S. Supreme Court. The explanation is simple. The committee of the Judicial Conference of the United States, which adopted the Code of Conduct for U.S. Judges, is composed of lower court judges who lack (or believe they lack) authority to adopt ethical rules that bind the Justices. Nor have the Justices imposed ethical rules on themselves. In his 2011 Year-End Report on the Federal Judiciary, Chief Justice Roberts wrote that "[i]n 1991, the Members of the Court adopted an internal resolution in which they agreed to follow the Judicial Conference regulations as a matter of internal practice." Justice Thomas was appointed in 1991. The other Justices arrived later. It is unclear whether a majority of the Court has the power to impose ethical rules on a current or future Justice who disagrees with them. Do the eight Justices not on the Court in 1991 subscribe to the "internal resolution"? Nor is it clear whether Congress, under separation of powers principles, has that power. Occasionally, individual Justices say they will comply with the Code of Conduct for U.S. Judges but there is no mechanism for enforcing any such decision short of impeachment. The conduct of lower court judges is subject to the review of a council of federal judges established in each circuit and by the Judicial Conference of the United States. 28 U.S.C. §351 et seq. There is no equivalent process for the Justices.

The federal recusal statute, 28 U.S.C. §455, which is addressed below and whose focus is solely the circumstances in which a judge must stay out of a case, *does* apply to the Justices.* The statute, like state recusal provisions, draws heavily on the ABA Code of Judicial Conduct. But the statute is limited to recusal while the Code of Conduct for U.S. Judges and state judicial conduct codes cover much else, including fundraising for advocacy groups, gifts, political activity, and the misuse of judicial office to assist others. No such provisions constrain the Justices.

Beyond codes and statutes, the Due Process Clause of the Constitution offers a third basis for judicial disqualification of any judge. Its requirements are, however, harder to meet than those in the codes and legislation. Due process challenges most often arise in criminal cases. See, e.g., Tumey v. Ohio, 273 U.S. 510 (1927) (judicial income may not depend on fines from convicted persons). But sometimes, as in *Caperton*, excerpted below, the clause is applied in a civil case.

Whereas the Model Rules reject "appearance of impropriety" as a standard for evaluating a private lawyer's conduct, judicial codes are sensitive to appearances. One test in Canon 2 for disqualifying a judge is that the judge's "impartiality might reasonably be questioned." See also Canon 1 ("A Judge Shall . . . Avoid . . . the Appearance of Impropriety"). That does not mean the judge is partial in fact but rather that she might reasonably appear so. Where a judge at sentencing said that his "object in this case from day one has always been to get back to the public that which was taken from it as a result of the fraudulent activities of this defendant and others," his impartiality was reasonably in question. The judge appeared to have an agenda "from day one." The case was remanded for retrial before a different judge. United States v. Antar, 53 F.3d 568 (3d Cir. 1995), overruled on another issue

---

* In his 2011 year-end report, the Chief Justice emphasized that although the Justices do comply with the recusal statute, "the limits of Congress's power to require recusal have never been tested." He said the same with regard to the duty to report outside income. This language has been read as a veiled warning to Congress not to adopt ethical rules for the Justices, who will have the last word on whether Congress has the power to do so.

in Smith v. Berg, 247 F.3d 532 (3d Cir. 2001). Why does it make sense, for surely it does, to retain an appearance standard for judges (and government lawyers) but not for private lawyers?

Ex Parte Communications

A bedrock premise of the adversary system is that all parties get to see information that other parties give the court—judge or jury—and to reply. The ABA Code of Judicial Conduct is quite stern about this. Rule 2.9A forbids a judge, without party consent, to "initiate, permit, or consider ex parte communications, or consider other communications made to the judge outside the presence of the parties or their lawyers" unless one of several narrow exceptions applies. Lawyers are separately forbidden to communicate ex parte with the judge absent one of the narrow exceptions. Model Rule 3.5(b).

A famous instance of (highly improper) ex parte communication arose in one of the most famous federal criminal trials. In 1951, Julius and Ethel Rosenberg were tried and convicted of conspiracy to engage in espionage. They allegedly passed secrets to the Soviet Union. Irving Kaufman, the trial judge, sentenced them to death. They were executed in 1953. Roy Cohn, later an aide to Senator Joseph McCarthy, was one of the prosecutors. Two Cohn biographies report that he had ex parte contacts with Kaufman during the trial.[*] Kaufman later became Chief Judge of the Second Circuit. Tony Kushner "reincarnated" Cohn (who died in 1986) as a character in his play (and then film) *Angels in America*. Shortly before he died, Cohn was disbarred for cheating private clients. Matter of Cohn, 503 N.Y.S.2d 759 (1st Dept. 1986). More about Cohn can be learned in the fascinating (and streaming) documentary *Where's My Roy Cohn?* The film takes its title from a quote by Donald Trump, whose business interests Cohn once represented, when as president Trump apparently longed for a lawyer like Roy Cohn.

Whatever one thinks of the Rosenbergs—and recent revelations now seem to confirm that Julius was guilty of something but Ethel was not[†]—the perception is widespread that their trial, and certainly their death sentences, fell far below the requirements of due process and that the sentence was far harsher than the conduct warranted. Years later, Irving Kaufman was said to bemoan that despite all of his enlightened rulings following his appointment to the Second Circuit, and there were many, the New York Times would cite the Rosenberg case in the second sentence of his obituary. He was wrong

---

[*] See Sidney Zion, *The Autobiography of Roy Cohn* (1988), and Nicholas von Hoffman, *Citizen Cohn* (1988).

[†] Sam Roberts, "Rosenbergs' Sons Accept Conclusion That Father Was a Spy," N.Y. Times, Sept. 17, 2008.

about that. It was in the first sentence, which also recognized Kaufman's "landmark" opinions on the First Amendment and civil rights. Kaufman was 81 years old. Marilyn Berger, N.Y. Times, Feb. 3, 1992.

It is rare for a judgment to be overturned because of ex parte communications, but it happened in United States v. Atwood, 941 F.3d 883 (7th Cir. 2019), where the judge's communications were with the prosecutors' office although not about Atwood's case. After conviction and sentencing, it "came to light that while Atwood's case was pending, Judge Bruce engaged in extensive ex parte communication with the prosecuting U.S. Attorney's Office about other cases." The judge, who formerly worked in that office, had "communicated ex parte with the Office over 100 times since taking the bench." Citing 28 U.S.C. §455(a), the court concluded that Bruce's impartiality in Atwood's case might reasonably be questioned and sent the case to a new judge for resentencing.

A. CONFLICTS AND DISQUALIFICATION

Unlike some of its legal ancestors, English common law assumed that judges could maintain impartiality in the face of most connections to a case. It did not follow the path of Roman or Jewish law, both of which disqualified judges for a variety of reasons. *See* THE CODE OF JUSTINIAN 3.1.14 (S.P. Scott trans., 1932) (allowing litigants to "reject judges appointed to hear a case . . . [e]ven when the judge was appointed by the Emperor, for the reason that We have set our hearts upon all suits being conducted without any suspicion of unfairness"); THE CODE OF MAIMONIDES, BOOK FOURTEEN: THE BOOK OF JUDGES, ch. 23, at 68–69 (Abraham M. Hershman, trans., Yale Univ. Press 1949) (requiring disqualification even when a party performed minor tasks for the judge such as removing a bird's feather from the judge's mantle or helping the judge get out of a boat when it reached shore).
—Judge Gregg Costa, Caliste v. Cantrell (5th Cir. 2019)

Abortion on Appeal

Narrowly interpreting Supreme Court cases that protect the right to terminate a pregnancy, several states have passed laws that impose severe restrictions on the procedure without banning it outright. The laws carry criminal penalties of up to life in prison for women and doctors who violate them. The ACLU and Planned Parenthood challenged the laws in each state that has passed one and won preliminary injunctions in federal district courts.

State L is the first state to appeal an injunction to a federal circuit court. The ruling is expected to be influential. On the three-judge panel that will hear the appeal are:

Judge Sherri-Lynn Endo, whose husband Josiah, a doctor, is on the board of a local pro-life organization that had filed an amicus brief in the district court (but not the circuit court) on the side of the law's supporters;

Judge Norbert Wishner, who as a law professor before his appointment to the bench seven years ago wrote two influential law review articles, cited in Supreme Court majority and dissenting opinions. They lay out a basis for an expansive constitutional right to abortion; and

Judge Valencia Rose-Deepra, who, as a district court judge before her appointment to the circuit court six months ago, had preliminarily enjoined State T from enforcing its substantially identical law.

A motion to recuse each judge has been made, based on the Due Process Clause and also on 28 U.S.C. §455(a), which disqualifies judges from sitting on cases in which their "impartiality might reasonably be questioned" and which is discussed below. What rulings?

"My Daughter Abby Is a Lawyer"

"My name is Selena Moreau. I am a judge on our state supreme court. My daughter Abby is a lawyer and a partner in a prominent law firm in the state. One of the firm's biggest corporate clients is Beanstalk, Ltd., which sells gardening supplies nationwide and landscape services locally. It lost a contract case in our trial court. Damages were set at $32 million, nearly as much as Beanstalk's net annual profit. Beanstalk has appealed to our court. Abby had no role in the case or in the events leading to the dispute. She is not a litigator but she does do corporate work for Beanstalk on matters unrelated to the case before us. It is common knowledge among lawyers in our state that Abby is my daughter. In any event, I will remind the lawyers of that fact as I do whenever Abby's firm is before me. I expect the plaintiff may seek my recusal based on the Due Process Clause and also on our state version of 28 U.S.C. §455(a) and §455(b)(5)(iii). It will cite my relationship to Abby. The real reason may be a perception that I will not be receptive to its arguments on the merits. In truth, I am not familiar with the record and have no view on the merits. Can I sit?"

"The City Gets the Money, Not the Judge"

Doraville (population 22,500), like other Georgia "home rule" municipalities, passes its own ordinances and tries violations in its municipal court. Doraville's police department issues thousands of citations every year, mostly for such quality-of-life transgressions as overgrown lawns, excessive noise, and violation of trash disposal rules. Those cited appear in Doraville's municipal court.

At municipal court hearings, the city attorney acts as prosecutor. The presiding judge is appointed by the city council and holds office at its pleasure. The judge is authorized to impose fines of up to $1,000. The money goes to the city's treasury. The judge has no authority over how city revenues, including those from fines, are spent.

> The city generates $3 million or more annually from the fines. This amounts to 17 to 30 percent of the city's yearly budget. The city council includes projected revenue from fines in its budget.
>
> A federal class action, citing *Caperton* (which follows) and cases in it, alleges that the Due Process Clause forbids this arrangement. The city responds that the cases are distinguishable because the city gets the money, not the judge.
>
> What is the best argument for the class?

What Judicial Conflicts Violate the Due Process Clause?

CAPERTON v. A.T. MASSEY COAL CO.
556 U.S. 868 (2009)

JUSTICE KENNEDY delivered the opinion of the Court.

In this case the Supreme Court of Appeals of West Virginia reversed a trial court judgment, which had entered a jury verdict of $50 million. Five justices heard the case, and the vote to reverse was 3 to 2. The question presented is whether the Due Process Clause of the Fourteenth Amendment was violated when one of the justices in the majority denied a recusal motion. The basis for the motion was that the justice had received campaign contributions in an extraordinary amount from, and through the efforts of, the board chairman and principal officer of the corporation found liable for the damages.

Under our precedents there are objective standards that require recusal when "the probability of actual bias on the part of the judge or decision-maker is too high to be constitutionally tolerable." Applying those precedents, we find that, in all the circumstances of this case, due process requires recusal.

I.

In August 2002 a West Virginia jury returned a verdict that found respondents A. T. Massey Coal Co. and its affiliates (hereinafter Massey) liable for fraudulent misrepresentation, concealment, and tortious interference with existing contractual relations. The jury awarded petitioners Hugh Caperton, Harman Development Corp., Harman Mining Corp., and Sovereign Coal Sales (hereinafter Caperton) the sum of $50 million in compensatory and punitive damages. . . .

Don Blankenship is Massey's chairman, chief executive officer, and president. After the verdict but before the appeal, West Virginia held its 2004 judicial elections. Knowing the Supreme Court of Appeals of West Virginia would consider the appeal in the case, Blankenship decided to support an attorney who sought to replace Justice McGraw. Justice McGraw was a candidate for reelection to that court. The attorney who sought to replace him was Brent Benjamin.

In addition to contributing the $1,000 statutory maximum to Benjamin's campaign committee, Blankenship donated almost $2.5 million to "And For

The Sake Of The Kids," a political organization formed under 26 U.S.C. §527. The §527 organization opposed McGraw and supported Benjamin. Blankenship's donations accounted for more than two-thirds of the total funds it raised. This was not all. Blankenship spent, in addition, just over $500,000 on independent expenditures—for direct mailings and letters soliciting donations as well as television and newspaper advertisements—" 'to support . . . Brent Benjamin.' "

To provide some perspective, Blankenship's $3 million in contributions were more than the total amount spent by all other Benjamin supporters and three times the amount spent by Benjamin's own committee. Caperton contends that Blankenship spent $1 million more than the total amount spent by the campaign committees of both candidates combined.

Benjamin won. He received 382,036 votes (53.3%), and McGraw received 334,301 votes (46.7%).

In October 2005, before Massey filed its petition for appeal in West Virginia's highest court, Caperton moved to disqualify now-Justice Benjamin under the Due Process Clause and the West Virginia Code of Judicial Conduct, based on the conflict caused by Blankenship's campaign involvement. Justice Benjamin denied the motion in April 2006. . . .

In November 2007 that court reversed the $50 million verdict against Massey. . . .

II.

It is axiomatic that "[a] fair trial in a fair tribunal is a basic requirement of due process." As the Court has recognized, however, "most matters relating to judicial disqualification [do] not rise to a constitutional level." The early and leading case on the subject is Tumey v. Ohio, 273 U.S. 510 (1927). There, the Court stated that "matters of kinship, personal bias, state policy, remoteness of interest, would seem generally to be matters merely of legislative discretion."

The *Tumey* Court concluded that the Due Process Clause incorporated the common-law rule that a judge must recuse himself when he has "a direct, personal, substantial, pecuniary interest" in a case. . . .

As new problems have emerged that were not discussed at common law, however, the Court has identified additional instances which, as an objective matter, require recusal. These are circumstances "in which experience teaches that the probability of actual bias on the part of the judge or decisionmaker is too high to be constitutionally tolerable." To place the present case in proper context, two instances where the Court has required recusal merit further discussion.

A.

The first involved the emergence of local tribunals where a judge had a financial interest in the outcome of a case, although the interest was less than what would have been considered personal or direct at common law.

This was the problem addressed in *Tumey*. There, the mayor of a village had the authority to sit as a judge (with no jury) to try those accused of violating a state law prohibiting the possession of alcoholic beverages. Inherent in this structure were two potential conflicts. First, the mayor received a salary supplement for performing judicial duties, and the funds for that compensation derived from the fines assessed in a case. No fines were assessed upon acquittal. The mayor-judge thus received a salary supplement only if he convicted the defendant. Second, sums from the criminal fines were deposited to the village's general treasury fund for village improvements and repairs.

The Court held that the Due Process Clause required disqualification "both because of [the mayor-judge's] direct pecuniary interest in the outcome, and because of his official motive to convict and to graduate the fine to help the financial needs of the village." It so held despite observing that "[t]here are doubtless mayors who would not allow such a consideration as $12 costs in each case to affect their judgment in it." The Court articulated the controlling principle:

> "Every procedure which would offer a possible temptation to the average man as a judge to forget the burden of proof required to convict the defendant, or which might lead him not to hold the balance nice, clear and true between the State and the accused, denies the latter due process of law."

The Court was thus concerned with more than the traditional common-law prohibition on direct pecuniary interest. It was also concerned with a more general concept of interests that tempt adjudicators to disregard neutrality.

This concern with conflicts resulting from financial incentives was elaborated in Ward v. Monroeville, 409 U.S. 57 (1972), which invalidated a conviction in another mayor's court. In *Monroeville*, unlike in *Tumey*, the mayor received no money; instead, the fines the mayor assessed went to the town's general fisc. The Court held that "[t]he fact that the mayor [in *Tumey*] shared directly in the fees and costs did not define the limits of the principle." The principle, instead, turned on the "'possible temptation'" the mayor might face; the mayor's "executive responsibilities for village finances may make him partisan to maintain the high level of contribution [to those finances] from the mayor's court." As the Court reiterated in another case that Term, "the [judge's] financial stake need not be as direct or positive as it appeared to be in *Tumey*." Gibson v. Berryhill, 411 U.S. 564 (1973) (an administrative board composed of optometrists had a pecuniary interest of "sufficient substance" so that it could not preside over a hearing against competing optometrists).

The Court in [Aetna Life Ins. Co. v.] Lavoie [475 U.S. 813 (1986)] further clarified the reach of the Due Process Clause regarding a judge's financial interest in a case. There, a justice had cast the deciding vote on the Alabama Supreme Court to uphold a punitive damages award against an insurance company for bad-faith refusal to pay a claim. At the time of his vote, the justice was the lead plaintiff in a nearly identical lawsuit pending in Alabama's lower courts. His deciding vote, this Court surmised, "undoubtedly 'raised the stakes'" for the insurance defendant in the justice's suit.

The Court stressed that it was "not required to decide whether in fact [the justice] was influenced." The proper constitutional inquiry is "whether sitting on the case then before the Supreme Court of Alabama would offer a possible temptation to the average . . . judge to . . . lead him not to hold the balance nice, clear and true." The Court underscored that "what degree or kind of interest is sufficient to disqualify a judge from sitting cannot be defined with precision.'" In the Court's view, however, it was important that the test have an objective component. . . .

B.

The second instance requiring recusal that was not discussed at common law emerged in the criminal contempt context, where a judge had no pecuniary interest in the case but was challenged because of a conflict arising from his participation in an earlier proceeding. [The Court discussed In re Murchison, 349 U.S. 133 (1955), and Mayberry v. Pennsylvania, 400 U.S. 455 (1971). In *Murchison,* a judge who had investigated criminal conduct and issued charges then proceeded to try the defendants and convict them. In *Mayberry,* a judge presided over the trial of a defendant for contempt where the allegation was that the defendant had "vilified" the same judge. In each case, the Court held a different judge had to preside.]

III. . . .

Caperton contends that Blankenship's pivotal role in getting Justice Benjamin elected created a constitutionally intolerable probability of actual bias. Though not a bribe or criminal influence, Justice Benjamin would nevertheless feel a debt of gratitude to Blankenship for his extraordinary efforts to get him elected. That temptation, Caperton claims, is as strong and inherent in human nature as was the conflict the Court confronted in *Tumey* and *Monroeville* when a mayor-judge (or the city) benefited financially from a defendant's conviction, as well as the conflict identified in *Murchison* and *Mayberry* when a judge was the object of a defendant's contempt. . . .

[B]ased on the facts presented by Caperton, Justice Benjamin conducted a probing search into his actual motives and inclinations; and he found none to be improper. We do not question his subjective findings of impartiality and propriety. Nor do we determine whether there was actual bias. . . .

We turn to the influence at issue in this case. Not every campaign contribution by a litigant or attorney creates a probability of bias that requires a judge's recusal, but this is an exceptional case. We conclude that there is a serious risk of actual bias—based on objective and reasonable perceptions—when a person with a personal stake in a particular case had a significant and disproportionate influence in placing the judge on the case by raising funds or directing the judge's election campaign when the case was pending or imminent. The inquiry centers on the contribution's relative size in comparison to the total amount of money contributed to the campaign, the total amount spent in the election, and the apparent effect such contribution had on the outcome of the election.

Applying this principle, we conclude that Blankenship's campaign efforts had a significant and disproportionate influence in placing Justice Benjamin on the case. Blankenship contributed some $3 million to unseat the incumbent and replace him with Benjamin. His contributions eclipsed the total amount spent by all other Benjamin supporters and exceeded by 300% the amount spent by Benjamin's campaign committee. Caperton claims Blankenship spent $1 million more than the total amount spent by the campaign committees of both candidates combined. . . .

Whether Blankenship's campaign contributions were a necessary and sufficient cause of Benjamin's victory is not the proper inquiry. Much like determining whether a judge is actually biased, proving what ultimately drives the electorate to choose a particular candidate is a difficult endeavor, not likely to lend itself to a certain conclusion. This is particularly true where, as here, there is no procedure for judicial factfinding and the sole trier of fact is the one accused of bias. Due process requires an objective inquiry into whether the contributor's influence on the election under all the circumstances "would offer a possible temptation to the average . . . judge to . . . lead him not to hold the balance nice, clear and true." In an election decided by fewer than 50,000 votes (382,036 to 334,301), Blankenship's campaign contributions—in comparison to the total amount contributed to the campaign, as well as the total amount spent in the election—had a significant and disproportionate influence on the electoral outcome. And the risk that Blankenship's influence engendered actual bias is sufficiently substantial that it "must be forbidden if the guarantee of due process is to be adequately implemented."

The temporal relationship between the campaign contributions, the justice's election, and the pendency of the case is also critical. It was reasonably foreseeable, when the campaign contributions were made, that the pending case would be before the newly elected justice. The $50 million adverse jury verdict had been entered before the election, and the Supreme Court of Appeals was the next step once the state trial court dealt with posttrial motions. So it became at once apparent that, absent recusal, Justice Benjamin would review a judgment that cost his biggest donor's company $50 million. Although there is no allegation of a *quid pro quo* agreement, the fact remains that Blankenship's extraordinary contributions were made at a time when he had a vested stake in the outcome. Just as no man is allowed to be a judge in his own cause, similar fears of bias can arise when—without the consent of the other parties—a man chooses the judge in his own cause. And applying this principle to the judicial election process, there was here a serious, objective risk of actual bias that required Justice Benjamin's recusal. . . .

IV.

Our decision today addresses an extraordinary situation where the Constitution requires recusal. . . .

"The Due Process Clause demarks only the outer boundaries of judicial disqualifications. Congress and the states, of course, remain free to impose more rigorous standards for judicial disqualification than those we find mandated here today." Because the codes of judicial conduct provide more protection than due process requires, most disputes over disqualification will be resolved without resort to the Constitution. Application of the constitutional standard implicated in this case will thus be confined to rare instances.

[Reversed and remanded.]

CHIEF JUSTICE ROBERTS, with whom JUSTICES SCALIA, THOMAS, and ALITO join, dissenting. . . .

Unlike the established grounds for disqualification, a "probability of bias" cannot be defined in any limited way. The Court's new "rule" provides no guidance to judges and litigants about when recusal will be constitutionally required. This will inevitably lead to an increase in allegations that judges are biased, however groundless those charges may be. The end result will do far more to erode public confidence in judicial impartiality than an isolated failure to recuse in a particular case. . . .

III. . . .

B.

[W]hy is the Court so convinced that this is an extreme case? It is true that Don Blankenship spent a large amount of money in connection with this election. But this point cannot be emphasized strongly enough: Other than a $1,000 direct contribution from Blankenship, *Justice Benjamin and his campaign had no control over how this money was spent.* Campaigns go to great lengths to develop precise messages and strategies. An insensitive or ham-handed ad campaign by an independent third party might distort the campaign's message or cause a backlash against the candidate, even though the candidate was not responsible for the ads. The majority repeatedly characterizes Blankenship's spending as "contributions" or "campaign contributions," but it is more accurate to refer to them as "independent expenditures." Blankenship only "contributed" $1,000 to the Benjamin campaign.

Moreover, Blankenship's independent expenditures do not appear "grossly disproportionate" compared to other such expenditures in this very election. "And for the Sake of the Kids"—an independent group that received approximately two-thirds of its funding from Blankenship—spent $3,623,500 in connection with the election. But large independent expenditures were also made in support of Justice Benjamin's opponent. "Consumers for Justice"—an independent group that received large contributions from the plaintiffs' bar—spent approximately $2 million in this race. And Blankenship has made large expenditures in connection with several previous West Virginia elections, which undercuts any notion that his involvement in this election was "intended to influence the outcome" of particular pending litigation.

It is also far from clear that Blankenship's expenditures affected the outcome of this election. Justice Benjamin won by a comfortable 7-point margin (53.3% to 46.7%). Many observers believed that Justice Benjamin's opponent doomed his candidacy by giving a well-publicized speech that made several curious allegations; this speech was described in the local media as "deeply disturbing" and worse. Justice Benjamin's opponent also refused to give interviews or participate in debates. All but one of the major West Virginia newspapers endorsed Justice Benjamin. Justice Benjamin just might have won because the voters of West Virginia thought he would be a better judge than his opponent. Unlike the majority, I cannot say with any degree of certainty that Blankenship "cho[se] the judge in his own cause." I would give the voters of West Virginia more credit than that. . . .

I respectfully dissent.

JUSTICE SCALIA, dissenting.

The principal purpose of this Court's exercise of its certiorari jurisdiction is to clarify the law. As The Chief Justice's dissent makes painfully clear, the principal consequence of today's decision is to create vast uncertainty with respect to a point of law that can be raised in all litigated cases in (at least) those 39 States that elect their judges. . . .*

John Roberts's 40 Socratic Questions and Andrew Frey's Strategic Decision

By adopting a test based on "probability of bias" in fact, the Court avoided constitutionalizing the ABA's "appearance of impropriety" test. A probability of bias test means that it is probable that the judge is actually biased without calling a judge biased for certain. The fact that Justice Benjamin "conducted a probing search into his actual motives" and found no bias was not controlling because the test is objective. That seems to be another way of saying that on these "extreme" facts, Benjamin may not have known his own mind. Although Justice Kennedy did not rely on behavioral legal ethics—referenced in chapters 1 and 5B1—scholarship on the subject supports that very possibility.

In his dissent, the Chief Justice played 1L law teacher and asked 40 Socratic questions about the reach of the phrase "probability of bias." I imagine that

---

* On remand, the West Virginia court again voted to reverse (6-1). Caperton v. A.T. Massey Coal Co., 690 S.E.2d 322 (W. Va. 2009). —ED.

he and his law clerks had great fun writing the questions, which are intended to reveal that the majority's "probability of bias" test "fails to provide clear, workable guidance for future cases." It will be hard for lawyers, Chief Justice Roberts is saying, to know if they have a *Caperton* claim should they confront the facts described in his 40 questions. And it will lead to many certiorari petitions alleging *Caperton* violations. Since the Court will routinely reject these petitions, enforcement of the *Caperton* test will in reality fall to state high courts in those states that elect judges.*

Here are four of the Chief Justice's 40 questions (actually, groups of questions). Do they prove the unworkability of the "probability of bias" test? How would you answer them?

- What if the case involves a social or ideological issue rather than a financial one? Must a judge recuse from cases involving, say, abortion rights if he has received "disproportionate" support from individuals who feel strongly about either side of that issue? If the supporter wants to help elect judges who are "tough on crime," must the judge recuse in all criminal cases?
- What if the candidate draws "disproportionate" support from a particular racial, religious, ethnic, or other group, and the case involves an issue of particular importance to that group?
- Should we assume that elected judges feel a "debt of hostility" towards major *opponents* of their candidacies? Must the judge recuse in cases involving individuals or groups who spent large amounts of money trying unsuccessfully to defeat him?
- Does it matter whether the campaign expenditures come from a party or the party's attorney? If from a lawyer, must the judge recuse in every case involving that attorney?

In *Caperton*, Massey's experienced Supreme Court advocate, Andrew Frey, faced a strategic challenge. He could argue that the Due Process Clause has no role at all to play when a recusal motion is based on a litigant's campaign

---

* *Caperton* claims will likely arise only in civil cases because the government, one of the parties in a criminal case, does not make campaign contributions. A wealthy criminal defendant could choose to spend money on behalf of a judicial candidate (or have done so in past elections), but the government is not likely to seek recusal, nor does the Due Process Clause protect it. It is conceivable that a crime victim's expenditures on behalf of a judicial candidate will give the defendant a *Caperton* claim, but that is highly remote. The flood of certiorari petitions that so troubled the dissenters would more likely come in civil cases, but that does not seem to have happened. Yet it is true that *Caperton* created the opportunity for recusal motions (and appeals of denial) in the many states that elect judges. One bright line antidote is a rule requiring recusal when a party has provided campaign help to a judicial candidate of more than a certain dollar amount. Only a few states have done this. See Charles Raley, Judicial Independence in the Age of Runaway Campaign Spending: How More Vigilant Court Action and Stronger Recusal Statutes Can Reclaim the Perception of an Independent Judiciary, 62 Case W. Reserve L. Rev. 175 (2011).

contributions, a position that could lead to the question: What about a $100 million contribution in a race where all other expenditures combined equal $1 million? Or he could argue that in any event the Blankenship-inspired contributions were not great enough to offend the clause, a position that could lead to the question: How much is great enough?

Which strategy would you choose? Would you argue both? No, of course, you would not argue both.

Frey chose the first. Due process had no role to play.

Williams v. Pennsylvania

In *Caperton*, a conflicted judge cast the deciding vote. What if a conflicted judge's vote is not dispositive? That question got bounced around for decades until Williams v. Pennsylvania, ___ U.S. ____ (2016). Williams was on death row for a 1984 murder. On collateral review, he alleged *Brady* violations and a lower state court stayed his execution. Pennsylvania then asked the state supreme court to vacate the lower court stay and reinstate the death sentence. Williams asked Chief Justice Castille to recuse himself from participating in that decision because as Philadelphia's district attorney, Castille had approved the decision to seek the death sentence against Williams. Castille refused to recuse. A unanimous court ruled against Williams.

Justice Kennedy, writing for the Court, held that under *Caperton*'s "objective standard," Castille could not sit. (Chief Justice Roberts and Justices Alito and Thomas thought Castille could sit.) But shouldn't it matter that even if Castille had recused, it would not have changed the result? Kennedy answered no.

> [I]t does not matter whether the disqualified judge's vote was necessary to the disposition of the case. The fact that the interested judge's vote was not dispositive may mean only that the judge was successful in persuading most members of the court to accept his or her position. That outcome does not lessen the unfairness to the affected party. . . .
>
> The Commonwealth points out that ordering a rehearing before the Pennsylvania Supreme Court may not provide complete relief to Williams because judges who were exposed to a disqualified judge may still be influenced by their colleague's views when they rehear the case. An inability to guarantee complete relief for a constitutional violation, however, does not justify withholding a remedy altogether. Allowing an appellate panel to reconsider a case without the participation of the interested member will permit judges to probe lines of analysis or engage in discussions they may have felt constrained to avoid in their first deliberations.

Campaign Contributions and (the Appearance of) Partiality

One benefit of *Caperton*, even if its boundaries are unclear, is that it encouraged a dialogue about the rules, if any, that should limit campaign contributions to or on behalf of judicial candidates. Whether viewed through a constitutional lens or left to statutes and judicial conduct codes, campaign contributions to judicial candidates are increasingly viewed as a problem.

As *Caperton* headed to the Supreme Court, an April 15, 2008 New York Times editorial quoted former Supreme Court Justice Sandra Day O'Connor as saying at a Fordham Law School conference, "We put cash in the courtrooms, and it's just wrong."

Why is it "just wrong"?

State high court judges face election or a retention election in 38 states. They have campaign committees that seek contributions. Contributors are often lawyers but often, too, they are individuals and businesses that have an interest in how state high courts rule. The cost of running a state high court election, once rather cheap and sleepy affairs, has escalated as corporate interests have attempted to influence the composition of these courts and thereby to affect the development of legal doctrines important to their businesses. Often these doctrines concern tort and products liability law, burden of proof requirements, standards for dispositive motions, and the measure (and availability) of damages.

The Brennan Center for Justice at New York University School of Law periodically studies spending in state high court elections. Its report for the 2017-2018 cycle, available on its website, reaches these conclusions among others:[*]

- **Special interest groups maintained their outsize role in supreme court elections.** Spending by interest groups, rather than by the candidates or political parties, accounted for 27 percent of all supreme court election spending. By comparison, over the last 20 years, congressional elections have never seen interest groups account for more than 19 percent of all spending in a cycle. The share of outside spending in this cycle's supreme court races was down from a high of 40 percent in 2015–16, but it continued to far outstrip any cycle prior to the U.S. Supreme Court's 2010 *Citizens United* decision [558 U.S. 310 (2010)], which set the stage for the rapid growth of interest group spending.

- **In some states, interest groups vastly outspent the candidates they supported.** In Arkansas and West Virginia, groups accounted for at least two-thirds of every dollar spent. This is consistent with other recent cycles, where a handful of states saw interest groups take over their supreme court races in a similar way.

- **Interest group spending was almost entirely nontransparent.** Eight of the ten biggest spenders did not disclose the true sources of their funds in a way that would allow voters to know who was trying to influence the election and future court decisions. This is in line with our 2015–16 analysis, which found that 82 percent of all outside spending that cycle was nontransparent.

---

[*] Douglas Keith with Patrick Berry and Eric Velasco, The Politics of Judicial Elections: How Dark Money, Interest Groups, and Big Donors Shape State High Courts.

The report reveals that in 46 high court contests in 21 states "outside spending by special interest groups" equaled $10.8 million in independent expenditures, out of a total of $39.7 million spent.

Apart from making all state (or state supreme court) positions appointive rather than elective, which is not about to happen, there seems to be no good solution to this problem, short of seriously limiting the amount of campaign contributions, a strategy that could pose constitutional problems in itself. See Randall v. Sorrell, 548 U.S. 230 (2006) (contribution limit of $400 in gubernatorial contests and lower limit in other state contests violates First Amendment); Thompson v. Hebdon, ____ U.S. ____ (2019) (remand to Ninth Circuit "for that court to revisit whether Alaska's [$500 annual] contribution limits are consistent with our First Amendment precedents").

Besides, does the problem go away, or merely get buried, if the executive appoints judges? At least, with elections, legislation can require judicial candidates and others to report contributions or expenditures. Will that money now go to the governors who appoint judges?

But wait. Is there even a problem here? Critics (like the Times) claim that campaign contributions are at bottom a form of legal bribery. Judges know they will have to run for reelection or retention (some as frequently as every six years), and they know that they may need a big war chest to beat back challengers. So, critics argue, judges will tilt toward favoring the interests that have the money to contribute to their future campaigns. Defenders reply that this argument confuses cause and effect. Judges don't favor the views of donors to increase fundraising. Rather, donors favor candidates whose policy preferences—and judging does involve policy preferences; see the Cardozo quote at the beginning of this chapter—that they like. Whatever you think about judicial elections, the defenders say, so long as we have them, everyone is entitled to spend money or time to help candidates who they believe share their views.

Who's right?

Ethical and Statutory Disqualification

Caperton was a due process case. It's also an outlier. Due process disqualifications are rare. Disqualification under statutes and judicial conduct codes are less rare but still infrequent. Rule 7.6, adopted in 2000, weakly limits a lawyer's and law firm's ability to accept a "government legal engagement or an appointment by a judge," if the lawyer or law firm has made a political contribution, or solicited contributions, for the judge "*for the purpose of* obtaining or being considered for that type of legal engagement or appointment." (Emphasis added.) How do you prove the "purpose"? Some states have a more demanding rule. See, e.g., the New York rule at 22 NYCRR §151.1.

The federal statute, 28 U.S.C. §455(a), and the judicial conduct codes require a judge to step aside if, among other reasons, his or her "impartiality might reasonably be questioned." This test, broadly adopted, is based on the ABA's Code of Judicial Conduct. Proof of actual partiality is not needed. Section 455(a) "is to be evaluated on an *objective* basis, so that what matters is not the reality of bias or prejudice but its appearance. The question . . . is whether an objective, disinterested observer fully informed of the underlying facts, [would] entertain significant doubt that justice would be done absent recusal." ISC Holding AG v. Nobel Biocare Fin. AG, 688 F.3d 98 (2d Cir. 2012). Section 455(b)(1), by contrast, requires recusal if a judge is actually biased.

The difference between the Due Process Clause and the statute and code language surfaced in the *Caperton* argument. Following up on a question from Justice Stevens, Justice Souter asked Andrew Frey, Massey's lawyer, whether the case "implicated" the code standard in the ABA rules. Justice Souter recognized that his question was hypothetical. The Court cannot review a state court's application of its own recusal provision. That is a matter of state law. Here is part of the colloquy:

> *Justice Souter:* I understood you to imply in response to Justice Stevens that there would be no appearance problem that would ever justify a constitutional standard.
> *Mr. Frey:* Appearance is a standard for recusal, a nonconstitutional statutory standard for recusal in virtually every State, so we already have—and in the Federal system, so—
> *Justice Souter:* Yes. And we have—and we have an appearance standard under the ABA Canons, but I think it would be difficult to make a very convincing argument that that standard was effective in this case.
> *Mr. Frey:* Well, that—that's a matter of opinion.
> *Justice Souter:* Well, it's—it's the matter of opinion that brings the case before us. And would you agree—I am not—I am not asking you to agree that the ABA standard was violated. That's not what you're here for. But would you agree that the ABA standard is certainly implicated by the facts of this case, whatever the ultimate recusal decision should have been?
> *Mr. Frey:* I think I would agree that reasonable people could have a different view one way or the other about whether there is an appearance of impropriety for Justice Benjamin sitting. I would agree with that. I don't think I would go further than that because my personal view is that there was no impropriety, that it was reasonable, and if you read his opinion I think you'll see a—a fair, balanced, thoughtful statement of the reasons why he feels he could sit.

Caperton turned on the Due Process Clause. *Liljeberg* interpreted several provisions in section 455.

CASE NOTE: LILJEBERG v. HEALTH SERVICES ACQUISITION CORP.

John Liljeberg formed a company called St. Jude to seek a certificate of need from Louisiana to build a hospital in Kenner, Louisiana. The certificate was required for the hospital to qualify for Medicare and Medicaid payments. At the same time, Liljeberg was negotiating to buy land from Loyola University as a site for the hospital. If Liljeberg's plans succeeded, Loyola would profit both from the land sale and from the increased value of its adjacent property.

Liljeberg was also negotiating with HAI, the predecessor to plaintiff Health Services Acquisition Corp., to build a hospital on other land. Eventually Liljeberg and HAI entered a contract whose meaning became the subject of the current litigation. In essence, the question before Judge Robert Collins was whether, under their contract, Liljeberg or HAI owned St. Jude. This was important because, in the interim, St. Jude had received the certificate of need. If Liljeberg owned St. Jude, he now intended to buy Loyola's land and build the hospital there. Apparently, that option became financially more attractive than continuing with HAI. So Loyola, although not a party to the dispute between Liljeberg and HAI, had a financial interest in seeing Liljeberg win control of St. Jude. Judge Collins was on Loyola's board of trustees. If he knew of Loyola's interest when he tried the case, he, as a Loyola fiduciary, would be disqualified from sitting. Section 455(b)(4). But he said he didn't know.

The dates are important. On November 30, 1981, HAI sued for a declaratory judgment that it, not Liljeberg, controlled St. Jude. Judge Collins tried the case without a jury on January 21 and 22, 1982, and immediately announced his intention to rule for Liljeberg. That was good for Loyola. On March 16, he issued that ruling. The Fifth Circuit affirmed. Ten months later, HAI moved to vacate the judgment after discovering Collins's Loyola connection. Collins denied the motion but the circuit reversed. Justice Stevens, for a majority of five Justices, affirmed. 486 U.S. 847 (1988). He wrote:

> During the period between November 30, 1981, and March 16, 1982, Judge Collins was a trustee of Loyola University, but was not conscious of the fact that the University and Liljeberg were then engaged in serious negotiations concerning the Kenner hospital project, or of the further fact that the success of those negotiations depended upon his conclusion that Liljeberg controlled the certificate of need. To determine whether Judge Collins' impartiality in the Liljeberg litigation "might reasonably be questioned," it is appropriate to consider the state of his knowledge immediately before the lawsuit was filed, what happened while the case was pending before him, and what he did when he learned of the University's interest in the litigation.
>
> After the certificate of need was issued, and Liljeberg and HAI became embroiled in their dispute, Liljeberg reopened his negotiations with the University. On October 29, 1981, the [Loyola] Real Estate Committee sent a written report to each of the trustees, including Judge Collins, advising them of "a significant change" concerning the proposed hospital in Kenner and stating specifically that Loyola's property had "again become a prime location." The Committee submitted a draft of a resolution authorizing a University vice-president "to continue negotiations with the developers of the St. Jude Hospital." At the Board meeting on November 12, 1981, which Judge Collins attended, the trustees discussed the connection between the rezoning of

Loyola's land in Kenner and the St. Jude project and adopted the Real Estate Committee's proposed resolution. Thus, Judge Collins had actual knowledge of the University's potential interest in the St. Jude hospital project in Kenner just a few days before the complaint was filed.

While the case was pending before Judge Collins, the University agreed to sell 80 acres of its land in Kenner to Liljeberg for $6,694,000. The progress of negotiations was discussed at a Board meeting on January 28, 1982. Judge Collins did not attend that meeting, but the Real Estate Committee advised the trustees that "the federal courts have determined that the certificate of need will be awarded to the St. Jude Corporation [i.e., Liljeberg]." Presumably this advice was based on Judge Collins' comment at the close of the hearing a week earlier, when he announced his intended ruling because he thought "it would be unfair to keep the parties in doubt as to how I feel about the case."

The formal agreement between Liljeberg and the University was apparently executed on March 19th. . . . Thus, the University continued to have an active interest in the outcome of the litigation because it was unlikely that Liljeberg could build the hospital if he lost control of the certificate of need. . . .

The details of the transaction were discussed in three letters to the trustees dated March 12, 15, and 19, 1982, but Judge Collins did not examine any of those letters until shortly before the Board meeting on March 25, 1982. Thus, he acquired actual knowledge of Loyola's interest in the litigation on March 24, 1982. . . .

In considering whether the Court of Appeals properly vacated the declaratory relief judgment, we . . . must . . . determine whether §455(a) can be violated based on an appearance of partiality, even though the judge was not conscious of the circumstances creating the appearance of impropriety. . . .

The Court quoted the following provisions in 28 U.S.C. §455:

(a) Any justice, judge, or magistrate of the United States shall disqualify himself in any proceeding in which his impartiality might reasonably be questioned.

(b) He shall also disqualify himself in the following circumstances: . . .

(4) He knows that he, individually or as a fiduciary, or his spouse or minor child residing in his household, has a financial interest in the subject matter in controversy or in a party to the proceeding, or any other interest that could be substantially affected by the outcome of the proceeding. . . .

(c) A judge should inform himself about his personal and fiduciary financial interests, and make a reasonable effort to inform himself about the personal financial interests of his spouse and minor children residing in his household.

The Court then turned to the question of whether Judge Collins's impartiality might reasonably be questioned based on facts of which he was unaware when he tried and decided the case. It said it could.

Scienter is not an element of a violation of §455(a). The judge's lack of knowledge of a disqualifying circumstance may bear on the question of remedy, but it does not eliminate the risk that "his impartiality might reasonably be questioned" by other persons. To read §455(a) to provide that the judge must know of the disqualifying facts, requires not simply ignoring the language of the provision—which makes no mention of knowledge—but further requires concluding that the language in subsection (b)(4)—which expressly provides that the judge must *know* of his or her interest—is extraneous. A careful reading of the respective subsections makes clear that Congress intended to require knowledge under subsection (b)(4) and not to require knowledge under subsection (a). Moreover, advancement of the purpose of the provision—to promote public confidence in the integrity of the judicial process—does not depend upon whether or not the judge actually knew facts creating an appearance of impropriety, so long as the public might reasonably believe that he or she knew. . . .

Contrary to petitioner's contentions, this reading of the statute does not call upon judges to perform the impossible—to disqualify themselves based on facts they do not know. If, as petitioner argues, §455(a) should only be applied prospectively, then requiring disqualification based on facts the judge does not know would of course be absurd; a judge could never be expected to disqualify himself based on some fact he does not know, even though the fact is one that perhaps he should know or one that people might reasonably suspect that he does know. But to the extent the provision can also, in proper cases, be applied retroactively, the judge is not called upon to perform an impossible feat. Rather, he is called upon to rectify an oversight and to take the steps necessary to maintain public confidence in the impartiality of the judiciary. If he concludes that "his impartiality might reasonably be questioned," then he should also find that the statute has been violated. This is certainly not an impossible task. No one questions that Judge Collins could have disqualified himself and vacated his judgment when he finally realized that Loyola had an interest in the litigation. . . .

In this case . . . the Court of Appeals found an ample basis in the record for concluding that an objective observer would have questioned Judge Collins' impartiality. Accordingly, even though his failure to disqualify himself was the product of a temporary lapse of memory, it was nevertheless a plain violation of the terms of the statute. . . .

Last, the Court turned to remedy. Section 455 does not give courts discretion to open a judgment. But Federal Rule of Civil Procedure 60(b)(6) empowers a district court to grant relief from a judgment for "any . . . reason that justifies relief." The court of appeals granted that relief, and the Supreme Court explained its reasons for affirming.

Like the Court of Appeals, we accept the District Court's finding that while the case was actually being tried Judge Collins did not have actual knowledge of Loyola's interest in the dispute over the ownership of St. Jude and its precious certificate of need. When a busy federal judge concentrates his or her full attention on a pending case, personal concerns are easily forgotten. The problem, however, is that people who have not served on the bench are often all too willing to indulge suspicions and doubts concerning the integrity of judges. The very purpose of §455(a) is to promote confidence in the judiciary by avoiding even the appearance of impropriety whenever possible. Thus, it is critically important in a case of this kind to identify the facts that might reasonably cause an objective observer to question Judge Collins' impartiality. There are at least four such facts.

First, it is remarkable that the judge, who had regularly attended the meetings of the Board of Trustees since 1977, completely forgot about the University's interest in having a hospital constructed on its property in Kenner. The importance of the project to the University is indicated by the fact that the 80-acre parcel, which represented only about 40% of the entire tract owned by the University, was sold for $6,694,000 and that the rezoning would substantially increase the value of the remaining 60%. The "negotiations with the developers of the St. Jude Hospital" were the subject of discussion and formal action by the trustees at a meeting attended by Judge Collins only a few days before the lawsuit was filed.

Second, it is an unfortunate coincidence that although the judge regularly attended the meetings of the Board of Trustees, he was not present at the January 28, 1982, meeting, a week after the 2-day trial and while the case was still under advisement. The minutes of that meeting record that representatives of the University monitored the progress of the trial, but did not see fit to call to the judge's attention the obvious conflict of interest that resulted from having a University trustee preside over that trial. These minutes were mailed to Judge Collins on March 12, 1982. If the Judge had opened that envelope when he received it on March 14th or 15th, he would have been under a duty to recuse himself *before* he entered judgment on March 16.

Third, it is remarkable—and quite inexcusable—that Judge Collins failed to recuse himself on March 24, 1982. A full disclosure at that time would have completely removed any basis for questioning the Judge's impartiality and would have made it possible for a different judge to decide whether the interests—and appearance—of justice would have been served by a retrial. Another 2-day evidentiary hearing would surely have been less burdensome and less embarrassing than the protracted proceedings that resulted from Judge Collins' nonrecusal and nondisclosure. Moreover, as the Court of Appeals correctly noted, Judge Collins' failure to disqualify himself on March 24, 1982, also constituted a violation of §455(b)(4), which disqualifies a judge if he "knows that he, individually or as a fiduciary, . . . has a financial interest in the subject matter in controversy or in a party to the proceeding, or any other interest that could be substantially affected by the outcome of the proceeding." This separate violation of §455 further compels the conclusion that vacatur was an appropriate remedy; by his silence, Judge Collins deprived respondent of a basis for making a timely motion for a new trial and also deprived it of an issue on direct appeal.

Fourth, when respondent filed its motion to vacate, Judge Collins gave three reasons for denying the motion, but still did not acknowledge that he had known about the University's interest both shortly before and shortly after the trial. Nor did he indicate any awareness of a duty to recuse himself in March of 1982.

These facts create precisely the kind of appearance of impropriety that §455(a) was intended to prevent. The violation is neither insubstantial nor excusable. Although Judge Collins did not know of his fiduciary interest in the litigation, he certainly should have known. In fact, his failure to stay informed of this fiduciary interest may well constitute a separate violation of §455. See §455(c).

Chief Justice Rehnquist, joined by Justices White and Scalia, dissented.

The Court here holds, as did the Court of Appeals below, that a judge must recuse himself under §455(a) if he *should have known* of the circumstances requiring disqualification, even though in fact he did not know of them. I do not believe this is a tenable construction of subsection (a). . . .

[T]he Court nevertheless concludes that "public confidence in the impartiality of the judiciary" compels retroactive disqualification of Judge Collins under §455(a). This conclusion interprets §455(a) in a manner which Congress never intended. As the Court of Appeals noted, in drafting §455(a) Congress was concerned with the "appearance" of impropriety, and to that end changed the previous subjective standard for disqualification to an objective one; no longer was disqualification to be decided on the basis of the opinion of the judge in question, but by the standard of what a reasonable person would think. But the facts and circumstances which this reasonable person would consider must be the facts and circumstances *known* to the judge at the time. . . .

Justice O'Connor dissented separately.

President Carter had nominated Judge Collins in 1978. In 1991, Collins was convicted of bribery, conspiracy, and obstruction of justice in connection with his judicial duties unrelated to the *Liljeberg* case. He was sentenced to nearly seven years in prison. He remained a federal judge and continued to draw his salary while in prison. In 1993, to avoid impeachment (and the loss of a pension), he resigned his judgeship. He was disbarred in November 1994. New Orleans Times-Picayune, Nov. 22, 1994.

Liljeberg is as critical of a district court judge as one can imagine. Did Justice Stevens believe Judge Collins's assertion that, while trying the case, he did not know of Loyola's interest? The majority wrote that "we accept" the finding in this regard. Are you convinced? But if Judge Collins did not know of Loyola's interest, what then is the harm that the Court's remedy — opening the judgment — is meant to address? Section 455(a) asks us to imagine a fully informed objective observer. That includes the fact that Collins lacked knowledge of Loyola's interest when he tried the case. Why would an observer lose confidence in the courts if she assumed that Collins did not know of Loyola's interest? This is the basis for the Rehnquist dissent.

The response may lie in this sentence from the majority opinion and those that follow it: "The problem, however, is that people who have not served on the bench are often all too willing to indulge suspicions and doubts concerning the integrity of judges." In other words, even though the Court purports to accept Collins's claim of ignorance, the disqualification rule is meant to encourage *public* trust in the courts. The public may doubt the truth of Collins's claim of ignorance for the reasons Stevens goes on to describe.

Justice Stevens identified four actual or possible violations of §455:

- violation of subsection (a);
- violation of subsection (b)(4);
- failure to reveal a possible basis for recusal when, after trial, Judge Collins discovered it; and
- possible violation of subsection (c).

Each section is quoted in the majority opinion. How was each violated?

Who Decides?

A higher court can review a lower court judge's denial of a recusal motion. But what if a U.S. Supreme Court Justice declines to recuse himself or herself under §455? Who reviews that? No one. Each Justice decides if he or she can sit. This may not be ideal, but who else could do it? Perhaps the full court or three Justices randomly chosen. But that solution creates problems of its own. Justices Gorsuch and Sotomayor often disagree. Should either have the power to decide that the other should not sit in a case likely to be decided by a narrow majority?

A Judge's Personal Relationships or Interests

In Cheney v. United States District Court, 542 U.S. 367 (2004), the Supreme Court turned back an effort to require the vice president to reveal the names of members of an energy task force he headed in the early days of the second Bush Administration. The identity of the members (some of whom may later have been caught up in the scandal surrounding Enron, or so some suspected) became an issue in the 2004 presidential campaign. The trial court had ordered the vice president to reveal the names, and the court of appeals said it lacked jurisdiction to review the order.

Certiorari in the vice president's case was granted on December 15, 2003. On January 17, 2004, David Savage of the Los Angeles Times reported that Justice Scalia and Vice President Cheney had traveled together to hunt ducks at a private camp in southern Louisiana. Their trip occurred three weeks after the Supreme Court had agreed to review Cheney's appeal from the lower court decision. The national press was all over the story. Late-night comics lampooned Scalia. Editorials criticized the trip. The Sierra Club, one of the two organizations that brought the case, asked Scalia to recuse himself, citing 28 U.S.C §455(a). It came to light that Scalia was accompanied on the trip by his son and son-in-law and that the three flew to Louisiana as guests on the vice president's plane (but flew home commercially on a round-trip ticket). In responding to the Sierra Club's recusal motion, Justice Scalia wrote:

> We departed from Andrews Air Force Base at about 10 A.M. on Monday, January 5, flying in a Gulfstream jet owned by the Government. We landed in Patterson, Louisiana, and went by car to a dock where Mr. Carline met us, to take us on the 20-minute boat trip to his hunting camp. We arrived at about 2 P.M., the 5 of us joining about 8 other hunters, making about 13 hunters in all; also present during our time there were about 3 members of Mr. Carline's staff, and, of course, the Vice President's staff and security detail. It was not an intimate setting. The group hunted that afternoon and Tuesday and Wednesday mornings; it fished (in two boats) Tuesday afternoon. All meals were in common. Sleeping was in rooms of two or three, except for the Vice President, who had his own quarters. Hunting was in two- or three-man blinds. As it turned out, I never hunted in the same blind with the Vice President. Nor was I alone with him at any time during the trip, except, perhaps, for instances so brief and unintentional that I would not recall them—walking to or from a boat, perhaps, or going to or from dinner. Of course we said not a word about the present case. The Vice President left the camp Wednesday afternoon, about two days after our arrival. I stayed on to hunt (with my son and son-in-law) until late Friday morning, when the three of us returned to Washington on a commercial flight from New Orleans.

In rejecting recusal, Scalia said the vice president was sued only in his official, not his personal, capacity and that friendship should not "affect impartiality in official-action suits." The Sierra Club argued that the vice president's reputation and integrity were on the line in the lawsuit, but Justice Scalia rejected that argument. The only issues before the Court, he wrote, were "what powers the District Court possessed under [the Federal Advisory Committee Act], and whether the Court of Appeals should have asserted mandamus or appellate jurisdiction over the District Court. Nothing this Court says on those subjects will have any bearing upon the reputation and integrity of Richard Cheney." He went on to conclude that even if the vice president lost the case and was forced to disclose the names of the task force members, it still would not affect his reputation and integrity.

> To be sure, there could be political consequences from disclosure of the fact (if it be so) that the Vice President favored business interests, and especially a sector of business with which he was formerly connected. But political consequences are not my concern, and the possibility of them does not convert an official suit into a private one. That possibility exists to a greater or lesser degree in virtually all suits involving agency action.

Justice Scalia supported his ruling by citing a trip Justice Jackson took with President Roosevelt in 1942 and a trip Justice White took with Attorney General Robert Kennedy in 1963. However, the statute the Sierra Club cited as the basis for recusal was passed in 1974. No equivalent statutory language restricted Jackson or White. Also, unlike the case against Cheney in an election year, the cases before the earlier Justices would not affect the reputations or political standing of the officials with whom they traveled. Those cases dealt with the power of the Executive Branch generally and not the behavior of Roosevelt or Kennedy.

Justice Scalia also rejected the allegation that the trip to Louisiana on the vice president's plane, for himself and two family members, constituted a gift requiring recusal. Cheney v. U.S. Dist. Court, 541 U.S. 913 (2004).

Few judges know the vice president. How about ordinary friendships between judges and lawyers who appear before them? Dan Webb, the U.S. Attorney in Chicago, personally prosecuted the defendant in United States v. Murphy, 768 F.2d 1518 (7th Cir. 1985). Webb and his family and the trial judge, Charles Kocoras, and his family had planned a joint vacation immediately following the trial. The Webbs and the Kocorases had vacationed together before, as the defense lawyer knew, although he did not know about this particular posttrial vacation. After Murphy was sentenced, he moved to vacate the conviction citing the joint vacation. While the Seventh Circuit rejected the motion because defense counsel's awareness of prior vacations should have led him to inquire about future ones,* it said the trip was improper. Judge Easterbrook first addressed the broader question of friendships between judges and lawyers and the duty to disclose them.

> Neither the close friendship between Kocoras and Webb nor either of the vacations was disclosed on the record. Yet the statute places on the judge a personal duty to disclose on the record any circumstances that may give rise to a reasonable question about his impartiality. Although a judge may accept a waiver of disqualification under §455(a), the "waiver may be accepted [only if] it is preceded by a full disclosure on the record of the basis of the disqualification." . . .
>
> In today's legal culture friendships among judges and lawyers are common. They are more than common; they are desirable. A judge need not cut himself off from the rest of the legal community. Social as well as official communications among judges and lawyers may improve the quality of legal decisions. Social interactions also make service on the bench, quite isolated as a rule, more tolerable to judges. Many well-qualified people would hesitate to become judges if they knew that wearing the robe meant either discharging one's friends or risking disqualification in substantial numbers of cases. Many courts therefore have held that a judge need not disqualify himself just because a friend—even a close friend—appears as a lawyer.

Easterbrook then considered the particular friendship before the court.

> [W]e conclude that an objective observer reasonably would doubt the ability of a judge to act with utter disinterest and aloofness when he was such a close

---

* Placing the burden on defense counsel to ask about the judge's posttrial vacation plans, rather than requiring the judge to reveal them unasked, seems wrong. That view appears to have been rejected in *Liljeberg* and when the question of a judge's affirmative disclosure obligations arose in Liteky v. United States, 510 U.S. 540 (1994).

friend of the prosecutor that the families of both were just about to take a joint vacation. A social relation of this sort implies extensive personal contacts between judge and prosecutor, perhaps a special willingness of the judge to accept and rely on the prosecutor's representations. The U.S. Attorney lays his own prestige, and that of his office, on the line in a special way when he elects to try a case himself. By acting as trial counsel he indicates the importance of the case and of a conviction, along with his belief in the strength of the Government's case. It is a particular blow for the U.S. Attorney personally to try a highly visible case such as this and lose. A judge could be concerned about handing his friend a galling defeat on the eve of a joint vacation. A defendant especially might perceive partiality on learning of such close ties between prosecutor and judge.

Can judges "friend" a lawyer on Facebook or other social media sites (or the lawyer "friend" the judge) without thereby requiring the judge to recuse when the lawyer appears before her? Yes. The word "friend"—both online and otherwise—is vague. What matters is the closeness of the relationship wherever it is formed. ABA Opinion 488 (2019).

Source of Knowledge: The Extrajudicial Source Doctrine (or Factor)

Section 455(b)(1) requires a judge to disqualify herself if the judge "has a personal bias or prejudice concerning a party." This provision covers *actual* bias. But §455(a) would require disqualification if the judge's impartiality might reasonably be questioned because of *apparent* bias—in other words, people will reasonably believe that the judge is biased, even if the judge is not biased. That's partly what *Liljeberg* was about. One question that has arisen is whether §455(a) can require recusal for apparent bias if the apparent bias is based only on information the judge learns in his judicial capacity—that is, while sitting as a judge.

Subsection (b)(1) has long been read to require an extrajudicial source for actual bias. This has been called the "extrajudicial source doctrine." A judge who becomes disposed against a party because of what she learns in doing her job—like hearing evidence—will not trigger the statute's actual bias standard. Judges are supposed to form opinions based on what they learn while judging. That's what judging is all about. Disqualification for actual bias, in this view, requires that the source of the judge's bias be something that happened outside of court (i.e., extrajudicially).

Lower courts were divided on whether the extrajudicial source doctrine also limited recusal motions under §455(a). Even if a judge cannot be disqualified under §455(b)(1) unless the source of bias is extrajudicial, might she be disqualified under subsection (a) if the source of her *apparent* bias is only "intrajudicial"—what she hears while judging—on the theory that subsection (a) is more demanding than subsection (b)? Or to put the question in the language of the statute: Is a judge recused based on what she learns while judging if a fair-minded, objective person knowing all the facts would question the judge's impartiality?

This question arose in Liteky v. United States, 510 U.S. 540 (1994), where the answer was yes. Although the extrajudicial source doctrine did apply to subsection (a), "there is not much doctrine to the doctrine" because the presence of an extrajudicial source for a judge's bias is neither a necessary nor a sufficient cause for disqualification. Justice Scalia's majority opinion relabeled the doctrine the "extrajudicial source factor" and described how it works:

> [O]pinions formed by the judge on the basis of facts introduced or events occurring in the course of the current proceedings, or of prior proceedings, do not constitute a basis for a bias or partiality motion unless they display a deep-seated favoritism or antagonism that would make fair judgment impossible. Thus, judicial remarks during the course of a trial that are critical or disapproving of, or even hostile to, counsel, the parties, or their cases, ordinarily do not support a bias or partiality challenge. They *may* do so if they reveal an opinion that derives from an extrajudicial source; and they *will* do so if they reveal such a high degree of favoritism or antagonism as to make fair judgment impossible. An example of the latter (and perhaps of the former as well) is the statement that was alleged to have been made by the District Judge in Berger v. United States, 255 U.S. 22 (1921), a World War I espionage case against German-American defendants: "One must have a very judicial mind, indeed, not [to be] prejudiced against the German Americans" because their "hearts are reeking with disloyalty." *Not* establishing bias or partiality, however, are expressions of impatience, dissatisfaction, annoyance, and even anger, that are within the bounds of what imperfect men and women, even after having been confirmed as federal judges, sometimes display. A judge's ordinary efforts at courtroom administration—even a stern and short-tempered judge's ordinary efforts at courtroom administration—remain immune.

Justice Kennedy concurred in the judgment in an opinion for himself and three others.

Law Clerks

A law clerk's career may also lead to disqualification. In Hall v. Small Business Administration, 695 F.2d 175 (5th Cir. 1983), the court (citing §455(a)) reversed a judgment for the plaintiffs in a Title VII sex discrimination case tried before a magistrate, because his "sole law clerk was initially a member of the plaintiff class in this suit, had before her employment with the magistrate expressed herself as convinced of the correctness of its contentions, and accepted employment with its counsel before judgment was rendered." It was "immaterial" that the magistrate asserted he had made up his mind "immediately after hearing the case" and before the law clerk worked on it.

But in Hunt v. American Bank & Trust Co., 783 F.2d 1011 (11th Cir. 1986), recusal was denied where a law clerk did not work on a case in which his prospective employer was counsel, nor did he "even talk[] with the judge about it to any significant extent." In In re Allied-Signal, Inc., 891 F.2d 967 (1st Cir. 1989), disqualification was likewise rejected where siblings of two clerks represented litigants. The proper remedy, said the court, was not disqualification of the judge but exclusion of the clerks from the matter.

Law clerks have to be careful what they say to the parties or indeed publicly, including on social media. Doe v. Cabrera, 134 F. Supp. 3d 439 (D.D.C. 2015), shows what can happen if they're not.

> The motion [to recuse a district judge was] primarily based on comments made by one of the Court's law clerks . . . who [in text messages] insinuated in jest to members of defense counsel's law firm, including an attorney who has made an appearance in this matter on behalf of the defendant, that she influenced the Court's decisionmaking process with respect to certain discovery rulings in this case. To be sure, the Court does not condone these comments even though they were made in jest. There was no factual basis for them, and they should not have been made. For the reasons that follow, however, the ill-advised conduct by the law clerk provides no basis for the Court to recuse itself.

When the law clerk realized "the impropriety of the text messages, she informed the Court about them that same night." We would hope so. "The following day . . . the Court contacted the parties to schedule an emergency conference to disclose what [the law clerk] had told the Court." The clerk had not in fact worked on the case. She was conflicted from doing so because of her relationship to one of the law firms. Recusal was denied.

It should not escape notice that the law clerk's mistake occurred in a text. The speed of electronic communications interferes with reflection and can lead to embarrassment or worse in all areas of a lawyer's work. "I sent it without thinking" is not an excuse you want to offer. News reports and court opinions are increasingly populated with such stories. At a panel I was on in the early days of social media, a circuit judge told of her chagrin on learning that her law clerk had blogged that he was drafting a court opinion on a controversial legal issue. He didn't name the case or the judge. But he had revealed just enough information about the issue for anyone knowing his employer (easy to discover), cases in which she had recently heard oral arguments, and her views on issues in them to anticipate how the court was likely to rule. Lesson: Never rely on an assumption of anonymity unless you would make the same statement publicly.

A Judge's Duty to Reveal

How can a lawyer know facts of a judge's life that might support a disqualification motion? Some facts may be a matter of public record, like the judge's prior professional affiliations and information contained in financial disclosure forms. But other facts—like the financial, employment, or other interests of close relatives—may not be. A comment to Rule 2.11 of the ABA Code requires judges to "disclose on the record information that the judge believes the parties or their lawyers might reasonably consider relevant to a possible motion for disqualification, even if the judge believes there is no basis for disqualification." Recall the Court's criticism of Judge Collins for failure to disclose Loyola's interest in the litigation before him after he learned of it following trial and before expiration of the deadline for a new trial motion. In United States v. Murphy, supra, the court said that Judge Korocas should have disclosed his family's posttrial vacation plans with prosecutor Webb and his family.

Section 455(b) says that a judge *shall* disqualify herself in certain circumstances. It is "self-executing." Aronson v. Brown, 14 F.3d 1578 (Fed. Cir. 1994). In Liteky v. United States, supra, which construed §455(a) — which also says "shall" — and by implication subsection (b), the Court placed "the obligation to identify the existence of [disqualifying] grounds upon the judge himself, rather than requiring recusal only in response to a party affidavit."

B. EXPRESSIONS OF GENDER, RACIAL, AND OTHER BIAS

The Judge and the Boy Scouts

State trial judge Wilbur Claremont III, 54, is a lifetime member of the Boy Scouts, which he has supported with contributions and time. He has helped run the local Boy Scouts troop in Sunnyvale, where he lives, has gone on scouting overnights, and has encouraged his two sons, Homer and Wilbur IV, to be active in the Scouts.

At one time, the Scouts did not permit gay men to serve as scoutmasters, and this exclusion was upheld by the Supreme Court. Boy Scouts of Am. v. Dale, 530 U.S. 640 (2000) (First Amendment right of expressive association prevents state from using public accommodations law to require Boy Scouts to admit gay man as assistant scoutmaster). In 2015, the Scouts' policy changed. Now, openly gay men may be Scout leaders, but chapters affiliated with religious institutions can opt out. In 2017, the organization allowed transgender boys to become Scouts.

On one occasion, during the debate over the Scouts' policy of excluding openly gay men as leaders, Judge Claremont wrote a letter to his local newspaper in which he mentioned his lifelong work with the Scouts, did not identify himself as a judge, and endorsed the exclusionary policy. "Understandably, many parents might not let their sons participate in the Scouts if gay men were permitted to serve as scoutmasters, which task can include supervision on overnight camping excursions," he wrote. When the exclusionary policy was changed except for church-affiliated chapters, Judge Claremont was active in starting a chapter at his church, in which he enrolled his sons. His church adheres to a reading of the Bible that treats same-sex intimate relationships as a sin and will not allow gay men to be scoutmasters.

These facts raise several questions.

First, did Judge Claremont's participation in the Boy Scouts, before the exclusionary policy changed, violate his obligations under the ABA Code of Judicial Conduct rule 3.6(A), which has been adopted in Claremont's state and which forbids "membership in any organization that practices invidious discrimination on the basis of . . . sexual orientation"?* Does participation in the church troop do so now? The comment to the rule states that whether an organization practices "invidious discrimination is a complex question," dependent on a number of factors, identified below.

Second, Judge Claremont was randomly selected to preside over a lawsuit challenging his state's refusal to allow gay men and lesbians, whether single or married, to act as foster parents for children who the state's Department of Children and Families has removed from their homes during investigations of abuse or neglect. The lawsuit, which will be decided without a jury, seeks an injunction. Plaintiffs moved to disqualify Judge Claremont under the Due Process Clause as construed in *Caperton* and because his "impartiality might reasonably be questioned." In opposing the motion, the state argued that Judge Claremont's support of an exclusionary policy and his decision to move his sons to the church chapter were motivated not by animus toward gay men and lesbians but solely by parental concern. The state cited these paragraphs from Mike Baker, "Boy Scouts Seek Bankruptcy to Survive a Deluge of Sex-Abuse Claims," N.Y. Times, Feb. 18, 2020, as evidence that Judge Claremont had a good faith basis for concern.

> Hoping to contain a deluge of sexual-abuse lawsuits, the Boy Scouts of America took shelter in bankruptcy court on Tuesday, filing for Chapter 11 protection that will let the group keep operating while it grapples with questions about the future of the century-old Scouting movement.
>
> The bankruptcy filing was made by the national organization, and does not involve the local councils that run day-to-day programs. Even so, the case sets up what may be one of the most complex financial restructurings in American history. Thousands of people have already come forward with allegations that they were abused as scouts, and many more are expected to do so.

In declining to recuse himself, Judge Claremont wrote: "I understand my job to be to decide the issues according to law without regard to my religious views, about which plaintiffs speculate and which are irrelevant. I can and will do that. If I am disqualified here, so too would

---

* The Code of Conduct for U.S. Judges, by contrast, does not list sexual orientation in Canon 2C, its equivalent provision. But the Commentary says that "a judge's membership in an organization that engages in any invidiously discriminatory membership practices prohibited by applicable law violates Canons 2 and 2A and gives the appearance of impropriety."

be an openly gay judge. Or a Muslim judge in a case challenging immigration policies as biased against Muslims."

Is Judge Claremont disqualified?

"Where You Live, Not Who You Are"

Mariana Shute, a state high court judge, and her family live in Lakeside, population 18,000, which as its name implies borders a lake, a rather large lake, attractive to boaters (no motors allowed) and swimmers. The Lakeside Country Club has choice property abutting the lake, and the Shutes are longtime members. Membership is restricted to residents of Lakeside. Also, the number of members is capped at 375 families, a common restriction to ensure that a club's facilities can be fully enjoyed. About 30 family memberships open yearly. There's a waiting list. The club's membership is entirely white because Lakeside is 92 percent white and no non-white Lakesider has ever applied for membership.

The contiguous and nearly as affluent town of Ellington, population 25,000, is not on the lake and does not have a country club. A walker who crossed Huckleberry Farm Lane would not realize that he had gone from one town to the other. Half the residents of Ellington live within three miles of the club, whereas a third of the residents of Lakeside live more than three miles from it. Residents of each town routinely shop in the other.

Ellington is 66 percent white. Americans of Japanese, Korean, Chinese, Hispanic, and African descent comprise 31 percent of the Ellington population. Average family income is 12 percent lower in Ellington than in Lakeside. An Ellington home will cost on average 15 percent less than a comparable Lakeside home.

From time to time, Ellington residents, including its white residents, have applied for club membership and been rejected because of the restriction of membership to Lakeside residents.

Some club members have tried to open membership to residents of Ellington, but have met arguments that the club should be "a local place where neighbors can get to know neighbors and talk about common concerns," and that "it would be wrong" to deny membership to Lakeside residents in favor of Ellington residents. And they question why the proponents of change stop at Ellington and don't seek to open membership to residents of non-contiguous towns with larger populations of persons of color. "Why not open membership to anyone? Why not New Yorkers?" one opponent of a rule change asked rhetorically. And answered: "Because then it's not a local club anymore." Another opponent asked if the supporters "would still favor change if Ellington was 100 percent white. I don't think so. This is some politically correct thing."

Opponents of a rule change have said their position would change if membership fell below 375 and the waiting list of Lakesiders could not meet the shortfall, which no one believes will ever happen. The waiting list has never dipped below 126.

Three times at membership meetings, Judge Shute has spoken against a rule change when the issue came to a vote—once before she was appointed to the bench and twice thereafter. Each time she stressed the importance of the local nature of the club. "Lakeside," she said, "is local in many ways. We share interests in the town government, zoning rules, land use, parks, schools, and taxes. The club is a place where we can have conversations about these and other matters that are unique to us."

A complaint is filed against Judge Shute alleging that she is a member of an organization that engages in invidious discrimination in violation of the state's judicial conduct code. It alleges that bias against non-whites was the reason for the club's refusal to admit Ellingtonians. A few club members have indeed made comments at membership meetings, reported in the local press, that strongly imply bias against people of color. A few members have used words like "people like us" and "different cultural traditions" in defending their opposition to a rule change. Judge Shute was at meetings where these comments were made. She did not criticize them but others did. There is no claim that Judge Shute is personally biased and in fact there is evidence otherwise.

In her reply, Judge Shute argues that her membership is not unethical, that no non-white Lakeside resident has ever been turned down because none has applied, and that the club's all-white membership is a result of "where you live, not who you are." She points to her own efforts to persuade a Korean-American Lakeside family living two houses away from her to apply for club membership. She contends that the residential rule has a perfectly legitimate neutral purpose

Does Judge Shute's membership in the club violate the judicial conduct rule that forbids a judge to be a member of an organization that practices "invidious discrimination"? If you think it does not, should it?

———————

In 1990 the ABA amended the Code of Judicial Conduct and rewrote or introduced new sections intended to address judicial and courtroom bias. These were expanded in the 2007 Code. See Rules 2.3 and 3.6 and their comments, summarized below but worth reading in full. Following are decisions addressing allegations of bias in or out of the courtroom and the consequences thereof (discipline or overturning a judgment).

Courtroom Bias

The 1990 Code imposed obligations on a judge to prevent bias in the courtroom. Canon 3(B)(6) said that a judge shall "require lawyers in proceedings before the judge to refrain from manifesting, by words or conduct, bias or prejudice based upon race, sex, religion, national origin, disability, age, sexual orientation or socioeconomic status, against parties, witnesses, counsel or others." The 2007 Code makes a few non-substantive changes; adds gender, ethnicity, marital status, and political affiliation to the list; says that the list is not exclusive; and further forbids "harassment" based on these characteristics. Rule 2.3(C). The same requirements apply to the conduct of judges. Rule 2.3(B). Rule 2.3(D) states that "[t]he restrictions of paragraphs (B) and (C) do not preclude judges or lawyers from making legitimate reference to the listed factors, or similar factors, when they are relevant to an issue in a proceeding."

Discriminatory Organizations

Canon 2(C) of the 1990 Code stated: "A judge shall not hold membership in any organization that practices *invidious* discrimination on the basis of race, sex, religion or national origin." (Emphasis added.) The 2007 Code expands the list to include gender, ethnicity, and sexual orientation. A comment requires judges who learn they are members of such organizations to "resign immediately." Rule 3.6(A). Notice that even as expanded this list remains shorter than the one in ABA Rule 2.3 dealing with courtroom bias. Absent, for example, are disability, socioeconomic status, and political affiliation.

The reach of Rule 3.6(A) depends on how we define "invidious discrimination." New York State Club Ass'n v. City of New York, 487 U.S. 1 (1988), tells us that the Constitution's guarantee of freedom of association will sometimes override a jurisdiction's antidiscrimination laws. Say a judge is nominated for membership in a club whose discrimination based on national origin or race is constitutionally protected. Can such a club nonetheless be said to engage in "invidious" discrimination? The comment to the rule says to ask whether the club "arbitrarily" excludes members and says that a "relevant" factor is whether the exclusion is constitutionally protected:

> Whether an organization practices invidious discrimination is a complex question to which judges should be attentive. The answer cannot be determined from a mere examination of an organization's current membership rolls, but rather, depends upon how the organization selects members, as well as other relevant factors, such as whether the organization is dedicated to the preservation of religious, ethnic, or cultural values of legitimate common interest to its members, or whether it is an intimate, purely private organization whose membership limitations could not constitutionally be prohibited.

Is a judge's constitutionally protected freedom of association more important than encouraging the perception of an unbiased judiciary? A person who agrees to become a judge must expect to give up some rights she has as a private citizen. A comment to Rule 1.2 makes this point generally: "A judge should expect to be the subject of public scrutiny that might be viewed as burdensome if applied to other citizens, and must accept the restrictions imposed by the Code." This is a difficult balance. Would we forbid a judge to belong to a club whose membership is limited to Irish Catholic men? Should a female judge be able to join a women-only lawyer group that meets quarterly to network and discuss career issues confronting women judges and lawyers?

Bankruptcy Judge George Paine belonged to the Belle-Meade Country Club near Nashville, Tennessee, for 15 years. The club had never had a woman or an African-American as a voting member in its 110-year history. Women could join as nonvoting members. The club had one non-voting African-American member, a nonresident of the area. The club's exclusionary rules were *not* constitutionally protected.

Judge Paine had tried over the years to gain admission of a Black applicant. Evidence showed that Black applicants were placed in a holding category for years and never voted on, up or down. A disciplinary complaint was filed against Paine for remaining a member of the club. In a bitterly divided decision, the Sixth Circuit Judicial Council rejected discipline 10-8. It concluded that the club did not engage in invidious discrimination. It did not address the then-Code requirement that judges who cannot change the policies of a discriminatory club should resign within two years, except to imply that this requirement was merely aspirational.* The majority further concluded that even if the membership violated the Code of Conduct for U.S. Judges because the club's policies constituted "invidious discrimination," it would not warrant discipline. The dissenters found invidious discrimination, marshaling abundant supporting evidence, and wrote that Judge Paine was obligated to resign once his efforts to integrate the club proved fruitless. In re Complaint of Judicial Misconduct, No. 06-08-90031 (6th Cir. Apr. 8, 2011).

A committee of the Judicial Conference of the United States, in its first decision applying Canon 2C, overturned the Sixth Circuit Judicial Council. It wrote:

> [O]n the present record, the conclusion that Belle Meade engages in invidious discrimination against women and African Americans is inescapable and, to the extent the Sixth Circuit Judicial Council reached a different conclusion, that conclusion is clearly erroneous. Therefore, Judge Paine's membership in Belle Meade while sitting as a judge violates Canons 2A and 2C and thus constitutes misconduct under the Act.

The conference initially imposed no discipline, but ten days later it reversed itself and reprimanded Judge Paine. But it apparently reached that conclusion with reluctance. It expressed its "unreserved sincerity that our decision is not intended to impugn Judge Paine's good faith, of which there is much evidence. . . . Thus, in our view, Judge Paine is retiring from the judiciary with his reputation for devoted service to his country

---

* Today, a comment in the Code requires the judge to "resign immediately."

intact." In re Complaint of Judicial Misconduct, 664 F.3d 332 (U.S. Jud. Conf. 2011).

The Tenth Circuit Judicial Counsel reprimanded Kansas District Judge Carlos Murguia. It wrote:

> Judge Murguia committed judicial misconduct by: (1) sexually harassing Judiciary employees; (2) engaging in an extramarital sexual relationship with an individual who had been convicted of felonies in state court and was then on probation; and (3) demonstrating habitual tardiness for court engagements. . . .

On the first charge, the Council wrote:

> Judge Murguia gave preferential treatment and unwanted attention to female employees of the Judiciary in the form of sexually suggestive comments, inappropriate text messages, and excessive, non-work-related contact, much of which occurred after work hours and often late at night. All of the harassed employees stated that they were reluctant to tell Judge Murguia to cease his behavior because of the power he held as a federal judge. One of the employees eventually told him explicitly to stop his harassing conduct, but he continued.
>
> This type of behavior violates several provisions of the Code of Conduct for United States Judges. *See* Code of Conduct for U.S. Judges, Canon 3B(4) (providing that "[a] judge should not engage in any form of harassment of court personnel"); Canon 3 cmt. to 3A(3) (advising that "[t]he duty to be respectful includes the responsibility to avoid comment or behavior that could reasonably be interpreted as harassment"); Canon 3 cmt. to 3B(4) (advising that "harassment encompasses a range of conduct having no legitimate role in the workplace"). Further, the Rules include "[a]busive or [h]arassing behavior" in the definition of misconduct, which, in turn, includes "engaging in unwanted, offensive, or abusive sexual conduct, including sexual harassment." Rule 4(a)(2) & 4(a)(2)(A).

In Re: Complaint Under the Judicial Conduct and Disability Act (10th Cir. 2019).*

Self-Assessment Questions

1. In 2011, under Scott Walker, then the newly elected (now the former) Republican governor of Wisconsin, the legislature eliminated the collective bargaining rights of most public employees.

   Wisconsin also held elections for its state supreme court in 2011. One race pitted David Prosser, who had been on the court for 12 years, against JoAnne Kloppenburg, an assistant attorney general. Prosser was seen as part of the conservative wing of a closely divided court, where

---

* https://www.ca10.uscourts.gov/sites/default/files/misconduct/10-18-90022.J.pdf

the validity of the collective bargaining law would ultimately be challenged. Huge amounts of money, much of it from outside Wisconsin and much of it spent independently of the two campaigns, poured in on behalf of each candidate. The race became, in effect, a referendum on Governor Walker's policies, the new collective bargaining law, and the direction in which the Republican-controlled legislature was leading the state.

According to the Associated Press, Prosser's campaign spent $406,283 and Kloppenburg's spent $351,259. Outside groups supporting Prosser independently spent $2.7 million and those supporting Kloppenburg spent $1.8 million. Assume the groups spending for Prosser did so because they expected that he would uphold the legislation eliminating collective bargaining for public employees and that those spending for Kloppenburg did so because they expected her to rule against the legislation. Also, assume that many public employees opposed to the legislation actively campaigned for Kloppenburg and against Prosser.

Prosser won by about 7,000 votes out of 1.5 million votes cast.

If a motion were made to recuse Prosser from deciding the challenge to the collective bargaining legislation, should it be granted?[*] Assume the motion cites both the Due Process Clause of the U.S. Constitution (discussed in *Caperton*) and Wisconsin's code of judicial conduct. Assume that that code has the same language as §455(a), the federal recusal statute cited in *Liljeberg*.

2. Fanta Kaba was an immigrant to the United States from Guinea who had established a successful restaurant in New York. She was convicted of a federal drug offense. At the sentencing hearing, the prosecutor said:

> Agent Grey has spent the better part of several years investigating the West African community that is involved in international heroin smuggling into the United States.
>
> It is a very difficult community to infiltrate because of language barriers. It is a very close-knit community, and too often people in this community, like in other drug organizations, get pretty small sentences and they're deported and Agent Grey informs me his information is that they will come back and it will start all over again.
>
> I think that word of your Honor's sentence today is going to get out very quickly, and I think it is important that the message sent is one of deterrence because our investigation in this case demonstrated that there are many people involved in this activity in New York and elsewhere in the United States and in the world and that they are aware of one another's criminal cases, and word will get out probably by this afternoon.

---

[*] The legislation was upheld 5-2. Madison Teachers, Inc. v. Walker, 851 N.W.2d 337 (Wis. 2014). Prosser was in the majority.

The district judge then explained his 72-month sentence:

> What I am hearing, I don't often say that deterrence is a major factor, sometimes it is, but rarer than we might wish, but from what I hear from the prosecutor, it is entirely reasonable to assume that people from the Guinea community are going to say "Gee, did you hear what happened to Kaba? I don't want that to happen to me."
>
> I hope that that has some effect here that will deter other people from that background from doing what you've done here, and you certainly had the brains not to do it to start with. The sentence is one that I don't think people coming here from Guinea are going to want to say "I want to put in that kind of time being stupid about American laws."

Does the judge's reference to Kaba's national origin mean his impartiality might reasonably be questioned? Should the appeals court remand the case to a different judge for resentencing if so?

PART FOUR

AVOIDING AND REDRESSING PROFESSIONAL FAILURE

XII

Control of Quality: Reducing the Likelihood of Professional Failure

A state may try to reduce the risk of professional failures, such as malpractice, breach of fiduciary duty, or neglect of client matters, in several ways. When one nevertheless occurs, various remedies are possible. In this chapter, we look at ways to reduce the likelihood of professional failure. Chapter 13 addresses remedial measures. This division is a bit arbitrary. A remedial measure—for example, discipline or a civil action against the lawyer for malpractice—can have a preventive effect (it can deter others) as well as a curative one.

One issue with regard to preventive measures is the relationship between a particular, possibly onerous, rule and the likelihood that it will reduce the risk of professional failure. For example, do bar examinations, character investigations, or educational prerequisites to bar membership reduce the likelihood of error or misconduct or improve the quality of the work? If so, what is the benefit compared with the cost of the requirement? A requirement that bar applicants graduate from ABA-approved law schools after three years of study is costly—in time, money, and lost income, not to mention anxiety. Is the cost justified by a higher quality of work than if law school were one or two years? How should we balance the costs and benefits of bar character committees, which can exclude applicants based on questions about their honesty? Do they really exclude the bad apples and only them? A related issue is epistemological. Is there even data that will help us answer these questions? Do we simply accept the value of education requirements, bar examinations, and character committees because they make intuitive sense? Because *we*—those who get to decide—had to endure them?

In the pages that follow, courts weigh the costs of a particular rule against the interests of the jurisdiction that wishes to impose it. How do they do that? What level of constitutional scrutiny do they apply?

Certainly, bar applicants cannot be excluded because of race, national origin, sex, sexual orientation, ethnicity, religion, or other such attributes. This was not always so. An infamous Supreme Court decision, for example, upheld Illinois's refusal to admit a married woman to its bar. See Bradwell v. State, 83 U.S. 130 (1873). Just over a century later, the Supreme Court held that Connecticut could not limit bar admission to United States citizens. In re Griffiths, 413 U.S. 717 (1973) (applicant had permanent residence status). However, the Fifth Circuit allowed Louisiana to exclude foreigners legally in the United States but not permanent residents. LeClerc v. Webb, 419 F.3d 405 (5th Cir. 2005). The plaintiffs were not a suspect class and the rule was rationally related to the state's interest in continuity and accountability in legal services. Rehearing en banc was denied over seven dissents. LeClerc v. Webb, 444 F.3d 428 (5th Cir. 2006). The Second Circuit disagreed when it addressed the same question for a pharmacist. Dandamudi v. Tisch, 686 F.3d 66 (2d Cir. 2012). California and New York, by contrast, will admit undocumented immigrants. In re Garcia, 315 P.3d 117 (Cal. 2014) (federal law forbidding undocumented immigrants from receiving "any State or local public benefit" did not prevent bar admission); In re Vargas, 10 N.Y.S.3d 579 (2nd Dept. 2015) (applicant was brought to the U.S. at age five and was now authorized to be in the U.S. under the DACA policy).

Nor should we ignore competitive motives. A subtext to any discussion of rules that limit the supply of lawyers is the economic consequences: The smaller the lawyer population, the fewer the competitors.

Two other ways for a state to reduce competition are through the definition of law practice and the exclusion of lawyers licensed elsewhere from working for clients in the state. A person who is not admitted to the state's bar but who practices law there risks civil and criminal liability. But what is "the practice of law"? A broad definition prevents nonlawyers from providing even simple advice that does not require three years of law school. A rule that makes it hard for lawyers licensed in (say) Arizona to join the Texas bar, or to represent Texans virtually from Arizona or while temporarily in Texas, reduces competition for Texas lawyers. Is economic protectionism the motive for these rules or is the motive an interest in ensuring quality legal work, performed by honest lawyers trained in the law of the state? Or is it both? To what extent should the courts be influenced by economic motives in analyzing these barriers?

A. ADMISSION TO THE BAR

The United States has a federal system, but there is no general federal bar examination. States (and Washington, D.C.) license lawyers. In the nineteenth and most of the twentieth century, this made much sense. Law firms had their offices in one state. Many client matters did not cross state lines or if they did, not often, and when they did, clients could hire a local firm. Trial lawyers had recourse to pro hac vice admission – i.e., court rules that allow lawyers to try a case in a court in which they are not otherwise admitted.

But a system of local licensure is incompatible with twenty-first-century communications technology, easy travel, and the needs of clients, especially clients with national or international interests. Clients may require legal advice in a dozen or more states and several nations. Today, large firms have offices in every region of the country and abroad, the better to serve clients whose needs do not stop at state or national borders. Even a very small firm with one office may attract a distant client because of its expertise.

Technology makes cross-border practice easy, as does the ready accessibility of online law libraries and the increasing national uniformity of much commercial law. Federal law is the same in Michigan and New Mexico. So is international law. Like law libraries, file rooms are becoming quaint. A lawyer's documents can be accessed online from anywhere, making it easier for her to be anywhere. Specialization is also a factor. A lawyer from State A who specializes in criminal defense will be better able to defend a State B client than can a State B copyright lawyer. These developments suggest that the "brick and mortar" law office is likely to shrink in importance (and size) and virtual practice to grow. By forcing lawyers to work at home, the COVID-19 pandemic accelerated the experience with remote work and its benefits. A smaller physical footprint can increase profits by reducing the need for space in high-rent business districts.

In the modern world, it makes increasingly less sense to define a lawyer's authority as coterminous with the geographic borders of her licensing state. Yet a Wisconsin lawyer is not a lawyer in Texas, and a British or Japanese lawyer is not a lawyer anywhere in the United States. If a lawyer does legal work where she is not admitted, she risks violating rules against the unauthorized practice of law (UPL), which can be a crime in some places, unless we create exceptions to UPL rules specifically for lawyers, as we do. Unauthorized presence may even occur through a lawyer's *virtual* presence in another state (sometimes called a host state). In the *Birbrower* case, set out later in this chapter, the California Supreme Court said that even a lawyer who never leaves home can be guilty of UPL in California, leading to a loss of fees, if he spends too much *virtual* time in California. But how much is too much? The court did not say.

Without adjustment, the nineteenth-century geocentric licensing system could not serve our twenty-first-century legal economy, and, indeed, it survives only by overlooking how lawyers really behave and by making small doctrinal adjustments along the way, which we discuss in this chapter. More changes are likely in ensuing decades, though prediction of what they might be is difficult. Young lawyers are especially likely to see their career trajectories affected. This is not solely an American problem either. Globalization is affecting law practice and lawyers everywhere. Be that as it may, we proceed to decipher the system we have now (and will likely have for a while) and to learn how we got where we are and perhaps where we should go.

1. Geographical Exclusion

May a state prohibit a lawyer who lives outside its borders from joining its bar? The fact that many states once did (and that some even required residence for a year or more before a lawyer from elsewhere could apply) tells you something about how parochial (and anticompetitive) admission rules once were. New Hampshire's rule was tested in Supreme Court of New Hampshire v. Piper, 470 U.S. 274 (1985). Piper passed the state bar examination, but she lived in Vermont, 400 yards from the New Hampshire border, and New Hampshire restricted admission to its bar to state residents. Piper challenged the requirement under Article IV, §2 of the Constitution, which guarantees that the "Citizens of each State shall be entitled to all Privileges and Immunities of Citizens in the several States." The Court held that this guarantee included the right to practice law. But the guarantee "is not an absolute." The state sought to justify its rule by arguing "that nonresident members would be less likely (i) to become, and remain, familiar with local rules and procedures; (ii) to behave ethically; (iii) to be available for court proceedings; and (iv) to do *pro bono* and other volunteer work in the state." The Court held "that none of these reasons" was adequate and further "that the means chosen do not bear the necessary relationship to the State's objectives." The ruling did not turn on the fact that Piper lived so close to New Hampshire. Justice Rehnquist dissented. Today, a resident of any state can seek admission through examination to the bar of any state.

2. Geographical Restriction

A Virginia rule granted motion admission to lawyers admitted elsewhere but only if they lived and worked full-time in Virginia. Motion admission, which many states recognize, allows lawyers admitted elsewhere to gain admission to a state's bar without taking its bar examination if they have practiced, for example, for five of the prior seven (or three of the prior five) years. Myrna Friedman worked full-time in Virginia but she lived in Maryland. Her application for motion admission was denied. The Court (7-2) held that the denial violated her rights under the Privileges and Immunities Clause, citing *Piper*. Supreme Court of Virginia v. Friedman, 487 U.S. 59 (1988). Virginia discriminated against non-Virginians. The state relied on its interest in assuring that admitted lawyers "have the same commitment to service and familiarity with Virginia law that is possessed by applicants securing admission upon examination." It also argued that the rule assured that admitted lawyers would practice full-time in the state. The Court rejected both arguments. It stated that Friedman

> has a substantial stake in the practice of law in Virginia. . . .
>
> Further, to the extent that the State is justifiably concerned with ensuring that its attorneys keep abreast of legal developments, it can protect these

interests through other equally or more effective means that do not themselves infringe constitutional protections. . . . The Supreme Court of Virginia could, for example, require mandatory attendance at periodic continuing legal education courses. The same is true with respect to the State's interest that the nonresident bar member does his or her share of volunteer and *pro bono* work.

Piper won because she passed the New Hampshire bar examination and the state could not treat her differently from how it treated its own residents. Friedman won because her full-time job in Virginia entitled her to the same rights as resident Virginia lawyers with full-time Virginia jobs. A third permutation is revealed in Goldfarb v. Supreme Court of Virginia, 766 F.2d 859 (4th Cir. 1985), decided before *Friedman*. Whereas Friedman lived in Maryland and worked in Virginia, Goldfarb lived in Virginia and worked in Washington, D.C. The Fourth Circuit upheld Virginia's in-state work requirement as a condition of motion admission when applied to a Virginia resident. Is that because, this time, Virginia wasn't treating an out-of-stater differently? It was discriminating against its own citizens.

3. Education and Examination

If there is one institution that has resisted all efforts to end it, it is the bar examination. No one seriously believes that a bar examination is even a near-perfect way to test knowledge or competence to practice law. Even those charged with examining bar applicants probably recognize the rough justice the examination delivers. The trouble is, no one has advanced a persuasive substitute or been able to convince state courts and legislatures to do away with it altogether. Wisconsin will admit and Montana once admitted graduates of law schools in the state without examination. The practice (called a "diploma privilege") has been upheld. Huffman v. Montana Supreme Court, 372 F. Supp. 1175 (D. Mont. 1974), aff'd, 419 U.S. 955. The fact that these graduates appear to enter the profession and practice law as uneventfully as much-examined bar applicants elsewhere would seem to provide a "control group" that could be used to study the predictive value of the bar examination. However, no such study is likely to lead to repeal of the examination or to persuade a court to declare it unconstitutional.*

Wiesmueller v. Kosobucki, 571 F.3d 699 (7th Cir. 2009), identified Wisconsin as the only state to admit graduates of in-state law schools without examination. The circuit reinstated a challenge to this rule with instructions to determine whether "Wisconsin law occupies a larger place in the curriculum of the Wisconsin law schools than of law schools elsewhere," thereby

---

* What no study can accomplish the COVID-19 pandemic might. In the spring and summer of 2020, courts nationwide had to weigh whether to admit law graduates without examination rather than risk spreading the virus or requiring law graduates to go many months unable to practice law. Some did so.

possibly justifying the diploma privilege. The parties thereafter settled. The Wisconsin Law Journal of March 29, 2010 quotes the plaintiff: "[I]t is clear that Marquette and the University of Wisconsin teach some Wisconsin law; so you get into the increasingly difficult question of how much Wisconsin law is enough to justify the privilege. Resolving the case at this point seemed the right thing to do."

Bar examinations have been challenged without success on nearly every ground imaginable. Plaintiffs have charged that methods of grading were improper, that particular questions were improper, and that the exams have a discriminatory impact.

For statistics on jurisdictions that limit the number of times an applicant can sit for the bar, Google "Comprehensive Guide to Bar Admission Requirements," published yearly.

4. Character Inquiries

Borrowing from the Moot Court Account

J.M. and L.B. were co-chairs of their law school's moot court program during their 3L year. As such, they had access to the program's funds. Across half a year, J.M. wrote checks to himself totaling more than $5,000 for personal expenses. When L.B. discovered this, he confronted J.M., who admitted the withdrawals. Two weeks later, L.B. disclosed J.M.'s conduct to the dean, and on the same day J.M. disclosed his conduct to a professor and to the state bar admissions committee. J.M. made full restitution before graduating and agreed to accept a letter of censure and to inform the law firm where he planned to work following graduation. The firm did not withdraw its offer. J.M. applied for bar membership. Two professors and three partners at his law firm wrote letters of support to the bar admissions committee. J.M. argued that his transgression did not predict that he would behave dishonestly as a lawyer. What should the committee do? What else do you want to know?

The Racist Bar Applicant

M.H. is an avowed racist. A character committee of the state supreme court rejected M.H.'s application for admission to the state bar on the ground that his white supremacist views were "diametrically opposed to the letter and spirit" of the Rules of Professional Conduct. Although M.H. has never been charged with a crime, an associate of his in a white supremacist organization killed two people and wounded nine others. All were people of color. M.H. has publicly called for a racial "holy war" of whites against people of color.

> M.H. appealed his rejection to the state supreme court. He cited the First Amendment and further argued that if an admitted lawyer were to make the same racist statements and hold the same views, he would not and could not be disbarred. Should the court admit M.H.? If you think it should not, do you support disbarring lawyers who do exactly the same? If not, can you reconcile the two positions?

In addition to testing for knowledge, all jurisdictions test for what may loosely be called "character." Character committees have a disreputable history. They were once used to exclude bar applicants who were "different from," or not members of the same religious or ethnic groups as, those who dominated the bar. See Jerold Auerbach, *Unequal Justice* 94-101 (1976) for an eye-opening account. We saw the same exclusionary behavior in large law firms. Jews were once excluded from leading U.S. law firms. They formed their own, some of which are now Big Law leaders. See Eli Wald, The Rise of the Jewish Law Firm or Is the Jewish Law Firm Generic?, 76 UMKC L. Rev. 885 (2008). Lawyers of color have long faced, and still face, impediments to becoming Big Law partners.

Today, the role of the admission committees is narrow. They may investigate four aspects of an applicant's life. First is a narrow inquiry about the applicant's mental health. Second is the applicant's honesty and integrity, which includes academic misconduct and any criminal acts whether or not leading to conviction. Third is financial responsibility. Finally, character committees may ask about support for the Constitution.

Criticism of the work of character committees has taken many forms. Many agree that the areas of inquiry are appropriate if the focus is narrow. Others question the underlying premise of character inquiries, namely that it is possible, based on past conduct, to predict future behavior. See generally Deborah Rhode, Moral Character as a Professional Credential, 94 Yale L.J. 491 (1985). Is the only reason to conduct a character inquiry to determine how the applicant will behave as a lawyer? Or are there other reasons? For example, may a state exclude some applicants on the ground that their admission would undermine confidence in the bar? Public confidence might suffer if a state admitted, for example, an applicant who had been convicted of embezzling from his employer or running a Ponzi scheme.

Alternatively, might it be argued that when a state licenses a person to be a lawyer, it is implicitly representing that person to the public as a person of honesty and integrity? If so, doesn't it then have a duty to assure itself that he or she fits and will likely continue to fit that description? The tricky word is "likely." How confident must a state be in its prediction? Who should bear the risk of error? Remember, clients considering whether to hire a lawyer will not know the lawyer's past, but will see the court's certificate of admission on her office wall and reasonably believe that the state has deemed her worthy of trust.

A state might also conclude that the very prospect of a character inquiry will screen out people who might otherwise have pursued a legal career but lack the character for admission. But the converse is also possible: The prospect of a character inquiry may deter people who would not in the end have been excluded but assumed they would be and chose not to make the investment.

Bar applicants rarely attract media attention. But Stephen Glass's effort to join the New York and California bars was headline news for reasons that will become apparent. Previous editions of this book presented Glass's story as a problem and asked whether Glass should be admitted to the bar. Now, the California Supreme Court has spoken. But there has been debate about its answer, so the new question is: Was the court right?*

IN RE GLASS
316 P.3d 1199 (Cal. 2014)

THE COURT:

Stephen Randall Glass made himself infamous as a dishonest journalist by fabricating material for more than 40 articles for The New Republic magazine and other publications. He also carefully fabricated supporting materials to delude The New Republic's fact checkers. The articles appeared between June 1996 and May 1998, and included falsehoods that reflected negatively on individuals, political groups, and ethnic minorities. During the same period, starting in September 1997, he was also an evening law student at Georgetown University's law school. Glass made every effort to avoid detection once suspicions were aroused, lobbied strenuously to keep his job at The New Republic, and, in the aftermath of his exposure, did not fully cooperate with the publications to identify his fabrication.

Glass applied to become a member of the New York bar in 2002, but withdrew his application after he was informally notified in 2004 that his moral character application would be rejected. In the New York bar application materials, he exaggerated his cooperation with the journals that had published his work and failed to supply a complete list of the fabricated articles that had injured others.

Glass passed the California bar examination in 2006 and filed an application for determination of moral character in 2007. It was not until the California State Bar moral character proceedings that Glass reviewed all of his articles, as well as the editorials The New Republic and other journals published to identify his fabrications, and ultimately identified fabrications

---

* The Stephen Glass story became a riveting film — *Shattered Glass* — which is as much about journalism as about law. And Glass wrote a novel, *The Fabulist*, after his lies were revealed.

that he previously had denied or failed to disclose. In the California proceedings, Glass was not forthright in acknowledging the defects in his New York bar application. . . .

Glass testified at the State Bar Court hearing that he "wrote nasty, mean-spirited, horrible" things about people: "My articles hurt, and they were cruel. . . ." He testified that the fabrications gave him "A-plus" stories that afforded him status in staff meetings and also gave particular enjoyment to his colleagues. He said: "Overwhelmingly, what everyone remembers about my pieces are the fake things."

A notable 1996 article was entitled *Taxis and the Meaning of Work*. It was Glass's first cover article and one he viewed as "key" to his successful period of writing for The New Republic. Its theme was that Americans, and in particular, African-Americans, were no longer willing to work hard or to take on employment they consider menial. The article falsely recounted as factual a supposed encounter between Glass and three entirely fabricated characters, one a limousine driver, one a taxicab driver, and one a criminal. The limousine driver was depicted as an African-American man who had driven a cab at one time, but now drove a limousine instead because he was "sick of those curry people" and found that limousines attracted beautiful women, or, in the purported words of the driver, gave him "the woo quotient." The author went on to say that he had been permitted to ride along for journalistic purposes with a taxi driver of Middle Eastern descent. The article recounted that the driver stopped for a young African-American passenger — "the type of fare Imran would normally refuse" but felt he had to accept because of nearby police observation. The article describes the pounding music audible from the young fare's headphones, and claims that as they neared his destination, the young African-American man threatened the driver with a knife, hurled coarse abuse at him, and took his wallet. According to the article: " 'These things happen,' Imran said coldly on the drive back downtown. 'I give them whatever they want. I just want my life.' " . . .

[After reviewing other false articles, the court continued:]

In another example, Glass wrote an article entitled *The Vernon Question* for George magazine. The lengthy article, published in April 1998, concerned Vernon Jordan, an advisor to then President Clinton during the then-emerging Monica Lewinsky scandal. In two paragraphs, Glass used nonexistent sources to describe Jordan's supposed reputation as a "boor" and attributed various fictitious statements to "political operatives," "socialites," "political hostesses" and officials. These persons assertedly stated that Jordan was well known for sexually explicit comments, unwanted sexual advances, and crude stares, and added that he was known in their circles as "Vern the Worm" or "Pussyman," and that young women needed protection against him. Another paragraph attributed to a fictional "watchdog" group contained certain claims about Jordan's asserted conflicts of interest and questionable corporate ethics along with statements attributed to fictional "senior officials" at companies on whose boards Jordan sat, saying that

Jordan is "totally unaware of the issues" but "we get what we want, access, and he gets what he wants, cash." These were all fabrications. . . .

[Charles Lane was then the editor of The New Republic.] Lane's suspicions were aroused in May 1998 when a journalist employed by Forbes Digital Tool telephoned to warn him that factual assertions in Glass's recent article for The New Republic magazine, *Hack Heaven*, did not seem to be true. The article had described a teenager hacking a California software company and extorting money to stop the intrusion. The article described a convention in Bethesda, Maryland, where some of the events occurred, and when Lane challenged Glass, the latter journeyed with Lane to Bethesda, purporting to identify the building where the convention had been held. A person working in the building denied such a convention had occurred, and Lane became persuaded that Glass was lying. Lane pressed Glass about the factual basis for the article, and although Glass was evasive, he insisted the article was accurate. Glass spent the night at home fabricating what he would assert were his reporter's notes from interviews, fake business cards, a voicemail box, a Web site, and newsletters. He also induced his brother to impersonate a source.

Upon their return to the office from Bethesda, Glass lobbied the executive editor and others to intervene on his behalf with Lane, urging that he was being treated unfairly. Lane, now suspecting that other fabrications may have occurred, wanted to fire him, but in response to the lobbying, suspended him. The next day, a Saturday, Lane was surprised to discover Glass at the office. Thinking Glass had been told not to return, Lane suspected he had altered his computer files. He confronted Glass with evidence that Glass had used his brother as a false source in the *Hack Heaven* piece. Ultimately, during this exchange Glass admitted the article was fabricated, and Lane fired him.

[The court extensively reviewed additional evidence including Glass's many character witnesses, among them Martin Peretz, who owned The New Republic at the time, and Glass's claim, by way of explanation for his conduct, that "during his childhood and young adulthood his parents exerted extremely intense and cruel pressure upon him to succeed academically and socially."]

II. DISCUSSION

A. APPLICABLE LAW . . .

Good moral character includes "qualities of honesty, fairness, candor, trustworthiness, observance of fiduciary responsibility, respect for and obedience to the law, and respect for the rights of others and the judicial process." "Persons of good character . . . do not commit acts or crimes involving moral turpitude — a concept that embraces a wide range of deceitful and depraved behavior." A lawyer's good moral character is essential for the protection of clients and for the proper functioning of the judicial system itself. . . .

B. ANALYSIS . . .

Glass's conduct as a journalist exhibited moral turpitude sustained over an extended period. As the Review Department dissent emphasized, he engaged in "fraud of staggering proportions" and he "use[d] . . . his exceptional writing skills to publicly and falsely malign people and organizations for actions they did not do and faults they did not have." As the dissent further commented, for two years he "engaged in a multi-layered, complex, and harmful course of public dishonesty." Glass's journalistic dishonesty was not a single lapse of judgment, which we have sometimes excused, but involved significant deceit sustained unremittingly for a period of years. Glass's deceit also was motivated by professional ambition, betrayed a vicious, mean spirit and a complete lack of compassion for others, along with arrogance and prejudice against various ethnic groups. In all these respects, his misconduct bore directly on his character in matters that are critical to the practice of law.

Glass not only spent two years producing damaging articles containing or entirely made up of fabrications, thereby deluding the public, maligning individuals, and disparaging ethnic minorities, he also routinely expended considerable efforts to fabricate background materials to dupe the fact checkers assigned to vet his work. When exposure threatened, he redoubled his efforts to hide his misconduct, going so far as to create a phony Web site and business cards and to recruit his brother to pose as a source. In addition, to retain his position, he engaged in a spirited campaign among the leadership at The New Republic to characterize Lane's obviously well-founded concerns as unfair and to retain his position.

Glass's conduct during this two-year period violated ethical strictures governing his profession. Believing that "public enlightenment is the forerunner of justice and the foundation of democracy," the Code of Ethics of the Society of Professional Journalists provides that "[t]he duty of the journalist is to further those ends by seeking truth and providing a fair and comprehensive account of events and issues[,] . . . striv[ing] to serve the public with thoroughness and honesty. . . . Deliberate distortion is never permissible." Glass's behavior fell so far short of this standard that Lane recounted seeing Glass featured in an exhibit in the Newseum, a Washington, D.C. museum dedicated to journalism, as embodying one of the worst episodes of deceit in journalistic history.

Glass's misconduct was also reprehensible because it took place while he was pursuing a law degree and license to practice law, when the importance of honesty should have gained new meaning and significance for him. . . .

Honesty is absolutely fundamental in the practice of law; without it, "the profession is worse than valueless in the place it holds in the administration of justice." "[M]anifest dishonesty . . . provide[s] a reasonable basis for the conclusion that the applicant or attorney cannot be relied upon to fulfill the moral obligations incumbent upon members of the legal profession."

As the dissent in the Review Department pointed out, "if Glass were to fabricate evidence in legal matters as readily and effectively as he falsified material for magazine articles, the harm to the public and profession would be immeasurable."

We also observe that instead of directing his efforts at serving others in the community, much of Glass's energy since the end of his journalistic career seems to have been directed at advancing his own career and financial and emotional well-being. . . .

Glass and the witnesses who supported his application stress his talent in the law and his commitment to the profession, and they argue that he has already paid a high enough price for his misdeeds to warrant admission to the bar. They emphasize his personal redemption, but we must recall that what is at stake is not compassion for Glass, who wishes to advance from being a supervised law clerk to enjoying a license to engage in the practice of law on an independent basis. Given our duty to protect the public and maintain the integrity and high standards of the profession, our focus is on the applicant's moral fitness to practice law. On this record, the applicant failed to carry his heavy burden of establishing his rehabilitation and current fitness. . . .

Glass proffered one defense that is unique in my reading of admission and discipline cases. He partly blamed his parents, at least psychologically. "According to Glass," the court wrote, "during his childhood and young adulthood his parents exerted extremely intense and cruel pressure upon him to succeed academically and socially." That may be true, but was saying so a good strategy? It could be read as an effort to diminish personal responsibility.

Journalists and lawyers have much in common, including a professional commitment to honesty. While the Glass case was pending, a New York Times columnist wrote about the importance of redemption. Glass did "terrible things as a journalist," he wrote, but he hoped that Glass would get admitted. Would you, I asked him, hire Glass to write for the Times? His answer: Glass's "notoriety in journalism is much more profound than his notoriety as a-journalist-who-is-now-working-as-a-law-clerk, so the switch to a different profession seems to me a way to lessen the curse of who he is and what he did. I realize that is not the kind of logic that works in your classroom, but it makes sense to me." Does it make sense to you?

Stanford Law professor Deborah Rhode, whose article "Moral Character as a Professional Credential" is cited above, was critical of the court's opinion. She told the L.A. Times that it was a poor signal to future applicants who wished to turn their lives around. Although we can never be certain, it is extremely unlikely that Glass would misbehave as a lawyer. Does that make Rhode right? Or would you agree that how Glass will behave as a lawyer is not the only consideration? Another commentator observed: "Admitting someone with Glass's extensive record of deception and fabrication, willingness to harm others for personal advancement, and lack of candor in the bar admission process of two states will harm the public's trust in the courts and the bar, which is a social good worthy of protection regardless of how he would later behave as a lawyer." With whichever position you agree, what about the applicants in the two problems above?

Frequently Cited Grounds for Delaying or Denying Admission to the Bar

Criminal Conduct.   Criminal conduct has traditionally excluded applicants to the bar, whether or not it has led to conviction. Even an acquittal will not prevent the alleged conduct from being weighed in the admission process. In In re Prager, 661 N.E.2d 84 (Mass. 1996), the applicant certainly turned his life around. Over a period of six years, he had "organized and led a large-scale international drug smuggling operation" (marijuana). That ended in 1981, but Prager continued to sell marijuana in the United States until he was indicted in 1983. He was a fugitive abroad until 1987. He pled guilty and received a suspended sentence plus probation, which he satisfactorily completed in 1993. He graduated from law school in 1994, clerked for a supreme court justice in Maine (where he had attended law school), and applied to the Massachusetts bar. In a lengthy opinion, the court concluded that Prager had failed to show that his "admission would not be detrimental to the integrity of the bar or the public interest." What does "integrity of the bar" mean? Should the only question be what Prager would or would not do as a lawyer? The court gave him leave to reapply in five years.

According to the annual Comprehensive Guide to Bar Admission Requirements, no state makes every felony a conclusive basis for excluding a bar applicant for all time. In re Manville, 538 A.2d 1128 (D.C. 1988), admitted three applicants who had been convicted, respectively, of manslaughter, attempted armed robbery, and the sale of narcotics. See also In re Polin, 630 A.2d 1140 (D.C. 1993) (applicant who had been convicted of cocaine conspiracy in 1984 and released from incarceration in 1987 was denied admission to the bar in 1991 but admitted two years later). But do not conclude that felony convictions are at most a minor impediment. Not so. And those involving dishonesty or breach of trust (lying on a bank loan, fraud, or embezzlement, for example) will be difficult to overcome.

Some states will admit applicants on the condition that for a designated period they practice under the supervision of an admitted lawyer. In re McMillian, 617 S.E.2d 824 (W. Va. 2005). McMillian, a deputy sheriff, had been discharged from his position for misconduct and later pled guilty to the federal felony of illegal wiretapping, committed while he was working as a private investigator.

Lack of Candor in the Application Process or Misconduct on the Bar Exam. This can be deadly. Pre-application conduct that would not result in exclusion can lead to exclusion or delay if the applicant consciously omits it or lies about it on the bar application. Strigler v. Bd. of Bar Examiners, 864

N.E.2d 8 (Mass. 2007) ("An applicant's failure to answer all of the board's questions candidly, both on the application and at any hearing, is a powerful indication that the applicant lacks the good character required for admission to the bar."). In re Parker, 985 N.E.2d 476 (Ohio 2013), denied admission with permission to reapply where the applicant continued to write at the bar examination despite being told that time had expired. See also Radtke v. Bd. of Bar Examiners, 601 N.W.2d 642 (Wis. 1999) (admission delayed where applicant "omitted a material fact [and] thereby minimized his culpability and responsibility for the termination" from his job as a university lecturer); and In re Knight, 211 A.3d 265 (Md. 2019) (misleading answers on bar application). The fact that a criminal conviction has been expunged or sealed does *not* justify omitting it from an application that asks about criminal convictions unless the application says otherwise. Kentucky Bar Ass'n v. Guidugli, 967 S.W.2d 587 (Ky. 1998). That's also true for law school applications. The lesson: If there is any ambiguity in what a bar or law school admission question asks, either get a clarification or resolve it in favor of disclosure.

Dishonesty or Lack of Integrity in Legal Academic Settings. No excuses. By the time you're in law school, expect little sympathy. You can't plead your youth and inexperience. Cheating on LSAT or law school examinations can result in delay or even denial of admission. Radtke v. Board of Bar Examiners, supra, delayed admission where the applicant was guilty of plagiarizing a scholarly article submitted for publication. Maryland rejected an applicant who had falsified her resume during law school. In re Brown, 144 A.3d 1188 (Md. 2016) (she had also failed to reveal a criminal charge on her bar application). Lying on a law school application can lead to delay or exclusion. If your bar application reveals academic discipline in college, you may be asked whether you revealed it on your law school application. If it reveals a conviction, even an expunged conviction, the same. If you did not, you may be required to have the school certify that disclosure would not have prevented your admission.

Mental Health. The Americans with Disabilities Act (ADA) appears to have changed the rules here. In Clark v. Virginia Board of Bar Examiners, 880 F. Supp. 430 (E.D. Va. 1995) (citing the ADA), Judge Cacheris collected the cases and identified the "mental health" inquiry in every American jurisdiction's bar admission process. (Only seven states, according to *Clark*, made no inquiry into mental health at the time.) With applications to the Virginia bar then running at about 2,000 yearly, only 47 bar applicants in the prior five years disclosed mental health treatment. Yet experts testified that about one-fifth of the population "suffers from some form of mental or emotional disorder." The opinion also reveals that, as of that date, no Virginia bar applicant had been denied admission based on such treatment.

In 2020, New York and New Hampshire dropped the mental health question from their bar applications. New Hampshire authorities cited a 2014 study that reported that 42 percent of law students said they needed help with a mental health or emotional issue in the prior year, but only half sought it. Chief Judge DiFiore of the New York Court of Appeals said the bar application would drop "intrusive" questions about mental health or treatment. Law 360, June 22, 2020.

Financial Probity. Think repaying student loans and paying bills and taxes. Admission committees and courts inquire about financial irregularities in the applicant's life. Dishonesty, financial irresponsibility, or abuse of trust in business or personal matters may predict lack of probity as a lawyer. In re Anonymous, 549 N.E.2d 472 (N.Y. 1989), held that an application may be rejected because of an inability to handle personal finances, as long as filing for bankruptcy, a federal right, is not the sole reason for the rejection. In re C.R.W., 481 S.E.2d 511 (Ga. 1997) (application denied in part because applicant failed to show a satisfactory payment history on two student loans totaling over $35,000). See also In re Fla. Bd. of Bar Examiners, 124 So. 3d 172 (Fla. 2013) (admission denied; applicant failed to pay state and local taxes, student loans, and creditors and gave false answers on application).

Unauthorized Practice of Law. In re Jordan, 85 So. 3d 683 (La. 2012), refused admission to an applicant who had engaged in law practice (among other reasons). See also In re Phillips, 175 A.3d 824 (Md. 2017) (admission denied where applicant practiced law before admission and failed to update application). These cases reveal an important lesson for law students and law graduates. It can be tempting to help friends and relatives with their legal problems prior to admission, but it is important to resist. Most (perhaps all) bar applications ask about unauthorized law practice. All law work should be done under the supervision of a lawyer or a student practice order. While free and isolated advice is unlikely to result in delay or denial of admission — in *Jordan* the work was compensated and lasted seven years — it is best to refrain.

5. Admission in a Federal System

Federal trial courts routinely admit applicants who are members of the bar of the highest court of the state in which that federal court is located. Many federal trial courts will admit lawyers who are admitted in other states. Federal courts also have their own pro hac vice (or temporary) admission rules. They reserve the right to conduct character inquiries and in rare cases decline to admit a lawyer who has been admitted in the state in which the federal court sits. In re G.L.S., 745 F.2d 856 (4th Cir. 1984).

B. TRANSIENT LAWYERS AND MULTIJURISDICTIONAL FIRMS: LOCAL INTERESTS CONFRONT A NATIONAL BAR

A client's legal problems do not always stop at a state border. Even when they do, the client may have good reason for seeking the advice of an out-of-state specialist. Does a lawyer admitted in Oregon have a right to assist a client with legal problems in Nevada if the lawyer is not admitted to practice there? Whether or not the lawyer has that right, does the client have the right to the lawyer's assistance? Think about a criminal defendant in Ohio who wants to hire a prominent New York defense lawyer and cites his Sixth Amendment right to counsel. Can Ohio forbid it?

There are several variables. The lawyer may perform services in connection with a litigation or a transaction or simply advise. The litigation or the advice may encompass federal law, the law of the lawyer's home state, or the law of a state in which the lawyer is not admitted. If the lawyer is helping the client in connection with a litigation, it may be pending (i) in a federal or state court in the lawyer's home state, yet require the lawyer to depose or interview witnesses or conduct an investigation in another state; (ii) in the client's home state; or (iii) somewhere else. Or litigation might not yet be filed, only expected. The lawyer's work may not require her to leave her home state physically. Can she participate virtually in another state? Remember, if a lawyer serves a client in a jurisdiction in which she is not admitted, she may be guilty of the unauthorized practice of law (UPL), unless a rule permits the work. Some rules do. Discipline is rare because the UPL prohibition is rarely enforced against lawyers unless the conduct is egregious. The more worrisome risk is the loss of fees for the work (as has happened) or a critical court opinion.

The question of when an out-of-state lawyer is guilty of unauthorized law practice in another state captured the bar's attention after the California Supreme Court's disappointing 1998 decision in Birbrower, Montalbano, Condon & Frank, P.C. v. Superior Court, set out below. The Birbrower firm's work in California was in connection with an impending arbitration in the state. Lawyers who engage in transactional work or appear in arbitrations are at greater risk of UPL claims than are lawyers who litigate in court. This is because litigators can request a judge to grant them temporary (or pro hac vice) admission to try a particular case. Pro hac vice admission translates to "for this turn." Lawyers who arbitrate, like the *Birbrower* lawyers, may be stymied because arbitrators have not traditionally been authorized to grant pro hac vice admission. (That's changing.) But even litigators have a problem. The legal work they do in a state may precede filing an action (which may never occur). Then, there is no judge who can authorize the work. Also, lawyers may do legal work in one state for a case elsewhere.

One rule is clear. If lawyers stay home, they can advise local clients on the law of any jurisdiction in the world if competent to do so. Problems arise only when lawyers do work *in* a jurisdiction in which they are not admitted. But what does it mean to serve a client *in* a jurisdiction? It turns out that a lawyer need not travel to the other jurisdiction to practice "in" it. *Virtual* presence through technology may violate UPL rules, the same as physical presence. Rule 5.5 cmt. [4]. Further complications—or does it simplify things?—arise because the laws of U.S. and many foreign jurisdictions are accessible to lawyers anywhere via computer databases, a good deal of the law of U.S. jurisdictions is uniform (or nearly so), and federal and international law is the same everywhere. When a lawyer is advising on (substantially) uniform state law, national, or international law, shouldn't the UPL problem dissolve?

In recent decades, the decentralized American system for regulating lawyers has had to confront the reality of a national legal economy and the cross-border needs of clients. Both trends support a move toward a centralized regulator, but that is not about to happen. State courts show no interest in yielding control of their bar, although those that adopt the Uniform Bar Exam do so to that extent. The next best solution is for state rules and state courts to facilitate cross-border work and lawyer mobility through changes to unauthorized practice laws and rules as applied to lawyers licensed elsewhere. The last 25 years have seen such changes, some significant, but they have been slow in coming. Meanwhile, the nature of law practice continues to change. To put it another way, our licensing system recognizes borders. Law practice resists them.

1. Admissions Pro Hac Vice

LEIS v. FLYNT
439 U.S. 438 (1979)

PER CURIAM.

[The Sixth Circuit] upheld a Federal District Court injunction that forbids further prosecution of respondents Larry Flynt and Hustler Magazine, Inc., until respondents Herald Fahringer and Paul Cambria are tendered a hearing on their applications to appear *pro hac vice* in the Court of Common Pleas on behalf of Flynt and Hustler Magazine. Petitioners contend that the asserted right of an out-of-state lawyer to appear *pro hac vice* in an Ohio court does not fall among those interests protected by the Due Process Clause of the Fourteenth Amendment. Because we agree with this contention, we grant the petition for certiorari and reverse the judgment of the Sixth Circuit.

Flynt and Hustler Magazine were indicted on February 8, 1977, for multiple violations of [a state law that] prohibits the dissemination of harmful material to minors. . . .

As this Court has observed on numerous occasions, the Constitution does not create property interests. Rather it extends various procedural safeguards to certain interests "that stem from an independent source such as state law." The Court of Appeals evidently believed that an out-of-state lawyer's interest in appearing *pro hac vice* in an Ohio court stems from some such independent source. It cited no state-law authority for this proposition, however, and indeed noted that "Ohio has no specific standards regarding *pro hac vice* admissions. . . ." Rather the court referred to the prevalence of *pro hac vice* practice in American courts and instances in our history where counsel appearing *pro hac vice* have rendered distinguished service. We do not question that the practice of courts in most States is to allow an out-of-state lawyer the privilege of appearing upon motion, especially when he is associated with a member of the local bar. In view of the high mobility of the bar, and also the trend toward specialization, perhaps this is a practice to be encouraged. But it is not a right granted either by statute or the Constitution. Since the founding of the Republic, the licensing and regulation of lawyers has been left exclusively to the States and the District of Columbia within their respective jurisdictions. The States prescribe the qualifications for admission to practice and the standards of professional conduct. They also are responsible for the discipline of lawyers.

A claim of entitlement under state law, to be enforceable, must be derived from statute or legal rule or through a mutually explicit understanding. The record here is devoid of any indication that an out-of-state lawyer may claim such an entitlement in Ohio, where the rules of the Ohio Supreme Court expressly consign the authority to approve a *pro hac vice* appearance to the discretion of the trial court. Even if, as the Court of Appeals believed, respondents Fahringer and Cambria had "reasonable expectations of professional service," they have not shown the requisite *mutual* understanding that they would be permitted to represent their clients in any particular case in the Ohio courts. The speculative claim that Fahringer's and Cambria's reputation might suffer as the result of the denial of their asserted right cannot by itself make out an injury to a constitutionally protected interest. There simply was no deprivation here of some right previously held under state law.

Nor is there a basis for the argument that the interest in appearing *pro hac vice* has its source in federal law. There is no right of federal origin that permits such lawyers to appear in state courts without meeting that State's bar admission requirements. . . .

It is so ordered.

JUSTICE WHITE would grant certiorari and set the case for oral argument.

JUSTICE STEVENS, with whom JUSTICE BRENNAN and JUSTICE MARSHALL join, dissenting.

A lawyer's interest in pursuing his calling is protected by the Due Process Clause of the Fourteenth Amendment. The question presented by this case is whether a lawyer abandons that protection when he crosses the border of the State which issued his license to practice. . . .

The premises for [the Court's] holding can be briefly stated. A nonresident lawyer has no right, as a matter of either state or federal law, to appear in an Ohio court. Absent any such enforceable entitlement, based on an explicit rule or mutual understanding, the lawyer's interest in making a *pro hac vice* appearance is a mere "privilege" that Ohio may grant or withhold in the unrestrained discretion of individual judges. The conclusion that a lawyer has no constitutional protection against a capricious exclusion seems so obvious to the majority that argument of the question is unnecessary. Summary reversal is the order of the day. . . .

I

The notion that a state trial judge has arbitrary and unlimited power to refuse a nonresident lawyer permission to appear in his courtroom is nothing but a remnant of a bygone era. . . .

History attests to the importance of *pro hac vice* appearances. As Judge Merritt, writing for the Court of Appeals, explained:

> Nonresident lawyers have appeared in many of our most celebrated cases. For example, Andrew Hamilton, a leader of the Philadelphia bar, defended John Peter Zenger in New York in 1735 in colonial America's most famous freedom-of-speech case. Clarence Darrow appeared in many states to plead the cause of an unpopular client, including the famous *Scopes* trial in Tennessee where he opposed another well-known, out-of-state lawyer, William Jennings Bryan. Great lawyers from Alexander Hamilton and Daniel Webster to Charles Evans Hughes and John W. Davis were specially admitted for the trial of important cases in other states. A small group of lawyers appearing *pro hac vice* inspired and initiated the civil rights movement in its early stages. In a series of cases brought in courts throughout the South, out-of-state lawyers Thurgood Marshall, Constance Motley and Spottswood Robinson, before their appointments to the federal bench, developed the legal principles which gave rise to the civil rights movement. . . .

The modern examples identified by Judge Merritt, though more illustrious than the typical *pro hac vice* appearance, are not rare exceptions to a general custom of excluding nonresident lawyers from local practice. On the contrary, appearances by out-of-state counsel have been routine throughout the country for at least a quarter of a century. The custom is so well recognized that, as Judge Friendly observed in 1966, there "is not the slightest reason to suppose" that a qualified lawyer's *pro hac vice* request will be denied.

This case involves a *pro hac vice* application by qualified legal specialists; no legitimate reason for denying their request is suggested by the record. They had been retained to defend an unpopular litigant in a trial that might be affected by local prejudices and attitudes. It is the classic situation in which the interests of justice would be served by allowing the defendant to be represented by counsel of his choice.

The interest these lawyers seek to vindicate is not merely the pecuniary goal that motivates every individual's attempt to pursue his calling. It is the profession's interest in discharging its responsibility for the fair administration of justice in our adversary system. The nature of that interest is surely worthy of the protection afforded by the Due Process Clause of the Fourteenth Amendment.

II

In the past, Ohio has implicitly assured out-of-state practitioners that they are welcome in Ohio's courts unless there is a valid, articulable reason for excluding them. Although the Ohio Supreme Court dismissed respondents' petition for an extraordinary writ of mandamus in this case, it has not dispelled that assurance because it did not purport to pass on the merits of their claim. In my opinion the State's assurance is adequate to create an interest that qualifies as "property" within the meaning of the Due Process Clause.

The District Court found as a fact that Ohio trial judges routinely permit out-of-state counsel to appear *pro hac vice*. This regular practice is conducted pursuant to the Rules of the Supreme Court of Ohio, Ohio's Code of Professional Responsibility, rules of each local court, and a leading opinion of the Ohio Court of Appeals identifying criteria that should inform a trial judge's discretion in acting on *pro hac vice* applications. While it is unquestionably true that an Ohio trial judge has broad discretion in determining whether or not to allow nonresident lawyers to appear in his court, it is also true that the Ohio rules, precedents, and practice give out-of-state lawyers an unequivocal expectation that the exercise of that discretion will be based on permissible reasons. . . .

III

Either the "nature" of the interest in *pro hac vice* admissions or the "implicit promise" inhering in Ohio custom with respect to those admissions is sufficient to create an interest protected by the Due Process Clause. Moreover, each of these conclusions reinforces the other. . . .

Justice and the Traveling Lawyer

The dissent cites Judge Merritt's observation that out-of-state lawyers "gave rise to the civil rights movement" through their work in the South. The courage of Black lawyers in the 1940s and 1950s, including Thurgood Marshall, Constance Baker Motley (later a district judge in New York), and Robert Carter (the same), cannot be overstated. They labored in the Jim Crow South where many hotels and restaurants refused to serve them. In the rural areas to which their cases took them, their presence at night (or even during the day) invited danger. The Klan effectively controlled the law, such as it was, in many counties, with police officers and even judges among its members. For a riveting account of the work of Marshall and others, read Gilbert King, *Devil in the Grove* (2012), which won a Pulitzer Prize. For a visual account, see the film *Thurgood*. Judge Motley's autobiography, *Equal Justice Under Law* (1998), details the risks she faced working as a civil rights lawyer in the South in the 1950s and 1960s. Judge Motley was appointed to the Southern District of New York in 1964. She was the first woman on that bench and the first African-American female federal judge.

In the 1960s, northern lawyers continued to go south to do civil rights work. One was Richard Sobol, whose story is told in Sobol v. Perez, 289 F. Supp. 392 (E.D. La. 1968), cited in an omitted portion of the Stevens dissent. Here's a snapshot. Sobol was a young Arnold & Porter associate who was admitted to practice in New York and Washington, D.C. During his vacation in the summer of 1965, he went to Louisiana as a volunteer with the Lawyers Constitutional Defense Committee and worked alongside local lawyers. This was shortly after Michael Schwerner, Andrew Goodman, and James Chaney, two northerners and a southerner, were murdered doing voting rights work in and around Philadelphia, Mississippi, as recounted in the film *Mississippi Burning*. The need for lawyers like Sobol to go south was great, but so were the dangers.

Leander Perez was the powerful, racist district attorney of Plaquemines Parish, Louisiana, where Sobol was doing some of his work. Perez did not appreciate the presence of northern lawyers in his parish (i.e., county) and he set out to make an example. Sobol was about to appear in state court for Gary Duncan, who was charged with assault. Eugene Leon, the state judge hearing Duncan's case, told Daryl Bubrig, an assistant district attorney, of Sobol's imminent court appearance. Bubrig alerted Perez, who "signed a bill of information charging Sobol with practicing law without a license." When Sobol appeared, Judge Leon "issued a bench warrant for [his] arrest." In other words, the judge and the prosecutors cooperated to impede Sobol's representation of Duncan.

As a federal court later described the situation in its ruling on Sobol's successful request for an injunction against his prosecution:

> Shortly after leaving the Judge's chambers and while still in the courthouse Sobol was arrested and charged with practicing law without a license. Sobol was incarcerated in the Plaquemines Parish Prison for approximately four hours. He was fingerprinted and photographed several times, his belt and tie were taken away, and his brief case containing all the Duncan case papers was taken over his objection. Bail was set at $1500.00, without his ever appearing before the Judge in regard to it, and Sobol was released upon posting that bond later in the day. . . .

In enjoining the prosecution, the court concluded:

> The circumstances surrounding the arrest and charge against Sobol, and the course of the Duncan case, convince us that Sobol was prosecuted only

because he was a civil rights lawyer forcefully representing a Negro in a case growing out of the desegregation of the Plaquemines Parish school system. . . .

This prosecution was meant to show Sobol that civil rights lawyers were not welcome in the parish, and that their defense of the Negroes involved in cases growing out of civil rights efforts would not be tolerated. It was meant also as a warning to other civil rights lawyers and to Negroes in the parish who might consider retaining civil rights lawyers to advance their rights to equal opportunity and equal treatment under the Equal Protection Clause of the Fourteenth Amendment.

Sobol went on to argue and win Gary Duncan's case in the Supreme Court. The decision applied the Sixth Amendment's right to a jury trial to the states. Duncan v. Louisiana, 391 U.S. 145 (1968).* Sobol practiced in Louisiana and Washington, D.C., for the rest of his life. In 2017, in an essay about his Louisiana work, he wrote: "I saw the impact one lawyer, familiar with federal litigation practice, could have." He died March 24, 2020. Katharine Seelye, "Richard Sobol, 82, Who Defended Civil Rights in South, Dies," N.Y. Times, Apr. 25, 2020.

What About the Defendant's Interests?

Leis v. Flynt addressed the rights of the lawyers. The defendants could not themselves seek federal relief because of the *Younger* abstention doctrine in federal court. They would have to go to state court, which was not promising. *Leis* notwithstanding, courts nationwide routinely admit out-of-state lawyers pro hac vice in both civil and criminal matters.

2. *Services Other Than Litigation*

Food Pantry Law

"My name is Alejandra Blanche-Ciarra. I work for a nonprofit in Washington, D.C., called Feed the Nation. Its focus is implementation of policies that ensure that no one goes hungry. We work with the Department of Agriculture to define a balanced diet. We promote the use of food stamps, now called SNAP. We do educational outreach.

"I focus on food pantries around the nation. Food pantries (or food banks) feed people who are food insecure. Food insecurity is defined as a lack of consistent access to enough food for an active, healthy life. About 37 million people in the United States, including 11 million children, are food insecure. I love my work.

"For health reasons, food is heavily regulated at the local level and federally. I advise on those regulations. I connect food pantries with

---

* Sobol gave an oral history of his experience that summer. Google "Richard Sobol oral history."

food producers and restaurants in their area to get free food and I negotiate their relationship. I help organize food pantries as non-profits and get funding from public and private sources. I don't go to court. I do most of my work in D.C. on various online platforms and by phone. But I'm on the road about a quarter of my time, especially when a food pantry is getting started. I'm admitted only in D.C. and Arizona.

"Last week I got a letter from a lawyer discipline agency in State X, where I've been advising food banks both virtually and in person. The agency had received a complaint from a trade group for fast food restaurants—the kind that sell fries, sugary soft drinks, sweet desserts—saying I was practicing law but was not admitted in State X. Apparently, the group's members see food pantries as competition. The private bar isn't interested in doing what I do. It doesn't pay. And it's a bit of a specialty. Few lawyers have the knowledge and experience for my practice. I have to respond to the complaint. What should I say? What else do you need to know?"

Employment Law Professor

"I'm an employment law professor at a U.S. law school on the West Coast. You might recognize my name if you've taken employment law, but let's just call me Cecily. A global company based in the Midwest wants to pay me a monthly retainer to advise its inside and outside counsel and its executives on employment law issues, as needed. The company has consulted me in the past but now it wants a formal relationship. It anticipates ten hours monthly, but we'd revisit the arrangement after six months. Most of my work would be responding to telephone questions and periodically informing the company's lawyers electronically of developments in the field. The company would also like me to visit its offices two or three days every six months to discuss labor policies with company lawyers and executives. I'm admitted to practice where I teach but not where the company is headquartered. Rule 5.5 applies. Can I do it?"

Appearing in a court where a lawyer is not admitted to practice permanently or pro hac vice is unambiguously unauthorized practice (and may be a crime). In New York ex rel. Stephen B. Diamond, P.C. v. My Pillow, 119 N.Y.S.3d 439 (1st Dept. 2020), a firm lost its fees where its unadmitted lawyers

> drafted the complaint that was ultimately filed in New York Supreme Court, conducted research, prepared the memorandum for the New York Attorney General and assisted with settlement negotiations. [N]one of the attorneys working on this matter were admitted in New York. Because the attorneys were engaged in the unauthorized practice of law, the fees incurred by them were unlawful. The fact that plaintiff hired New York counsel to assist in some of the

legal work does not alter the analysis or cure his failure to seek pro hac vice admission in New York.

The lawyers could have protected themselves with pro hac vice admission, usually a quick and simple process, and did not. The plaintiff also had a New York lawyer for "some of the legal work," but not all of it. Association with a local lawyer who "actively participates" in the matter can be a defense to unauthorized practice as we see shortly. Rule 5.5(c)(1). This decision should not be controversial.

The next case *is* controversial. We might say that the implications of the *Birbrower* decision were so uncertain and threatening that it turned out to be a good thing. It startled the bar and brought about changes that would not have occurred as soon, if at all. Yet for all that, the decision and the aftermath left much unclear, in California and nationally. The fact that it turned on the meaning of just one word — *in* — made prediction a challenge. Think about it. What does it mean, in an age when cyberspace can be as or more important to law practice than physical space, to talk about being "in" a place? *Birbrower*'s implications have been *partly* muted in California by adoption of new rules that give out-of-state lawyers greater freedom to practice there and in other states with even more permissive rules modeled after Rule 5.5.[*]

BIRBROWER, MONTALBANO, CONDON & FRANK, P.C. v. SUPERIOR COURT

17 Cal. 4th 119, 949 P.2d 1, 70 Cal. Rptr. 2d 304 (1998),
cert. denied, 525 U.S. 920

CHIN, J.

Business and Professions Code section 6125 states: "No person shall practice law in California unless the person is an active member of the State Bar." We must decide whether an out-of-state law firm, not licensed to practice law in this state, violated section 6125 when it performed legal services in California for a California-based client under a fee agreement stipulating that California law would govern all matters in the representation.

Although we are aware of the interstate nature of modern law practice and mindful of the reality that large firms often conduct activities and serve clients in several states, we do not believe these facts excuse law firms from complying with section 6125. . . . [We] conclude that Birbrower's fee agreement with real party in interest ESQ Business Services, Inc. (ESQ), is invalid to the extent it authorizes payment for the substantial legal services

---

[*] I expected *Birbrower* to quickly become a historical curiosity, a subject for historians of the profession, without continuing influence. I was wrong. Its influence has surely diminished because of the reforms it inspired, but its basic approach to cross-border practice and local control survives, even as changes in the profession continue to make that approach impractical and unnecessary to protect clients.

Birbrower performed in California. If, however, Birbrower can show it generated fees under its agreement for limited services it performed in New York, and it earned those fees under the otherwise invalid fee agreement, it may, on remand, present to the trial court evidence justifying its recovery of fees for those New York services. . . .

I. Background . . .

Birbrower is a professional law corporation incorporated in New York, with its principal place of business in New York. During 1992 and 1993, Birbrower attorneys [Hobbs and Condon] performed substantial work in California relating to the law firm's representation of ESQ. Neither Hobbs nor Condon has ever been licensed to practice law in California. None of Birbrower's attorneys were licensed to practice law in California during Birbrower's ESQ representation.

ESQ is a California corporation with its principal place of business in Santa Clara County. In July 1992, the parties negotiated and executed the fee agreement in New York, providing that Birbrower would perform legal services for ESQ, including "All matters pertaining to the investigation of and prosecution of all claims and causes of action against Tandem Computers Incorporated [Tandem]." The "claims and causes of action" against Tandem, a Delaware corporation with its principal place of business in Santa Clara County, California, related to a software development and marketing contract between Tandem and ESQ dated March 16, 1990 (Tandem Agreement). The Tandem Agreement stated that "The internal laws of the State of California (irrespective of its choice of law principles) shall govern the validity of this Agreement, the construction of its terms, and the interpretation and enforcement of the rights and duties of the parties hereto." Birbrower asserts, and ESQ disputes, that ESQ knew Birbrower was not licensed to practice law in California.

While representing ESQ, Hobbs and Condon traveled to California on several occasions [in 1992 and 1993].

Around March or April 1993, Hobbs, Condon, and another Birbrower attorney visited California to interview potential arbitrators and to meet again with ESQ and its accountants. Birbrower had previously filed a demand for arbitration against Tandem with the San Francisco offices of the American Arbitration Association (AAA). In August 1993, Hobbs returned to California to assist ESQ in settling the Tandem matter. . . .

ESQ eventually settled the Tandem dispute, and the matter never went to arbitration.

[ESQ and Birbrower had a falling out, with the client alleging malpractice and the firm suing for its fee. ESQ claimed that the firm could not collect a fee because of its unauthorized practice. The trial court refused to enforce the fee agreement but left open the possibility that the firm could collect in quantum meruit without specifying the work that could be so compensated. The court of appeal agreed.]

II. Discussion

A. THE UNAUTHORIZED PRACTICE OF LAW . . .

Although [section 6125] did not define the term "practice law," case law explained it as "'the doing and performing services in a court of justice in any matter depending therein throughout its various stages and in conformity with the adopted rules of procedure.'" [Precedent] included in its definition legal advice and legal instrument and contract preparation, whether or not these subjects were rendered in the course of litigation. . . .

Section 6125 has generated numerous opinions on the meaning of "practice law" but none on the meaning of "in California." In our view, the practice of law "in California" entails sufficient contact with the California client to render the nature of the legal service a clear legal representation. In addition to a quantitative analysis, we must consider the nature of the unlicensed lawyer's activities in the state. Mere fortuitous or attenuated contacts will not sustain a finding that the unlicensed lawyer practiced law "in California." The primary inquiry is whether the unlicensed lawyer engaged in sufficient activities in the state, or created a continuing relationship with the California client that included legal duties and obligations.

Our definition does not necessarily depend on or require the unlicensed lawyer's physical presence in the state. Physical presence here is one factor we may consider in deciding whether the unlicensed lawyer has violated section 6125, but it is by no means exclusive. For example, one may practice law in the state in violation of section 6125 although not physically present here by advising a California client on California law in connection with a California legal dispute by telephone, fax, computer, or other modern technological means. Conversely, although we decline to provide a comprehensive list of what activities constitute sufficient contact with the state, we do reject the notion that a person automatically practices law "in California" whenever that person practices California law anywhere, or "virtually" enters the state by telephone, fax, e-mail, or satellite. . . .

This interpretation acknowledges the tension that exists between interjurisdictional practice and the need to have a state-regulated bar. . . .

B. THE PRESENT CASE

[The court characterized Birbrower's conduct as "extensive practice in this state." In a footnote, it rejected the appeals court's observation that the UPL statute would not apply if an out-of-state lawyer associated with a California lawyer. This statement was dicta because Birbrower had not done so.] As noted, in 1992 and 1993, Birbrower attorneys traveled to California to discuss with ESQ and others various matters pertaining to the dispute between ESQ and Tandem. Hobbs and Condon discussed strategy for resolving the dispute and advised ESQ on this strategy. Furthermore, during California meetings with Tandem representatives in August 1992, Hobbs demanded Tandem pay $15 million, and Condon told Tandem he believed damages in the matter would exceed that amount if the parties proceeded to litigation. Also in California, Hobbs met with ESQ for the stated purpose of helping to reach a settlement agreement and to discuss the agreement that was eventually proposed. Birbrower attorneys also traveled to California to initiate arbitration proceedings before the matter was settled. . . .

Assuming that section 6125 does apply to out-of-state attorneys not licensed here, Birbrower alternatively asks us to create an exception to section 6125 for work incidental to private arbitration or other alternative dispute resolution proceedings. . . . [A]t least one court has decided that an out-of-state attorney could recover fees for services rendered in an arbitration proceeding. (See Williamson v. John D. Quinn Const. Corp. (S.D.N.Y. 1982) 537 F. Supp. 613, 616). . . .

We decline Birbrower's invitation to craft an arbitration exception to section 6125's prohibition of the unlicensed practice of law in this state. Any exception for arbitration is best left to the Legislature, which has the authority to determine qualifications for admission to the State Bar and to decide what constitutes the practice of law. . . . [In a footnote, the court explained that an arbitration exception would not apply anyway because there never was an arbitration, only preparation for one.]

C. COMPENSATION FOR LEGAL SERVICES . . .

We agree with Birbrower that it may be able to recover fees under the fee agreement for the limited legal services it performed for ESQ in New York to the extent they did not constitute practicing law in California, even though those services were performed for a California client. Because section 6125 applies to the practice of law in California, it does not, in general, regulate law practice in other states. . . .

Thus, the portion of the fee agreement between Birbrower and ESQ that includes payment for services rendered in New York may be enforceable to the extent that the illegal compensation can be severed from the rest of the agreement. . . .

[The court remanded for a determination of services performed physically in New York and not "virtually" in California.]

KENNARD, J., dissenting . . .

[U]nder this court's decisions, arbitration proceedings are not governed or constrained by the rule of law; therefore, representation of another in an arbitration proceeding, including the activities necessary to prepare for the arbitration hearing, does not necessarily require a trained legal mind. . . .

The majority gives no adequate justification for its decision to deprive parties of their freedom of contract and to make it a crime for anyone but California lawyers to represent others in arbitrations in California. . . .

The majority's attempt to distinguish *Williamson* from this case is unpersuasive. The majority points out that in *Williamson*, the lawyers of the New Jersey firm actually rendered services at the New York arbitration hearing, whereas here the New York lawyers never actually appeared at an arbitration hearing in California. The majority distinguishes *Williamson* on the ground that in this case no arbitration hearing occurred. Does the majority mean that an actual appearance at an arbitration hearing is not the practice of law, but that preparation for arbitration proceedings is? . . .

Why Is *Birbrower* a Problem and What Is the Solution?

Birbrower has not won favor. Most caustic has been the Ninth Circuit, which noted that "[a]dmissions rules and procedure for federal court are independent of those that govern admission to practice in state courts." In granting fees to an out-of-state lawyer, it wrote:

> Even at a time when the largest law firms in the United States were composed of not many more than one hundred lawyers, Judge Friendly observed that we live in an "age of increased specialization and high mobility of the bar." Spanos v. Skouras, 364 F.2d 161, 170 (2d Cir. 1966). But in 1966, there were no personal computers, no Internet, no Blackberries, no teleconferencing, no emails, and the only person who had a two-way wrist radio was cartoon character Dick Tracy. Today, largely because of the benefits of modern technology, hundreds of U.S.-based law firms are composed of many hundreds, or even thousands, of lawyers and support personnel contemporaneously doing business in many states and throughout the world. Lawyers throughout the United States regularly participate in teleconferences and group email sessions with other lawyers in other states, and lawyers and paralegals from one or more firms participate in massive discovery projects arising out of a single case concerning papers and data located in several states. In many such instances, only a small fraction of the lawyers involved in a case are members of the bar of the state where the presiding court sits. Current law does not compel us to be judicial Luddites, and we may properly accommodate many of the realities of modern law practice, while still securing to federal courts the ability to control and discipline those who practice before them.

Winterrowd v. Am. Gen. Annuity Ins. Co., 556 F.3d 815 (9th Cir. 2009).

The *Winterrowd* court discussed *Birbrower* at length, distinguished it, and rejected it, but its opinion does not bind state courts. Despite criticism from the Ninth Circuit and other courts, the *Birbrower* issues and the court's limited perspective remain alive and will grow more acute as technology makes cross-border practice easy and appealing, even irresistible, including to small firms. Indeed, firms with only one office have more to gain from permissive rules than do large firms with offices in many U.S. jurisdictions. Even lawyers who don't travel much physically may travel virtually through their phones and computers.

A challenge for lawyers who don't want to transgress the UPL barrier is figuring out where it is. In *Birbrower* there were the following California connections but the court does not tell us how to weigh them: The lawyers made three trips to the state of a few days each; the client was a California company; the arbitration was to occur in California; the arbitrator was to apply

California law; and California law governed the fee agreement. Would the result have changed if the arbitration were to occur in Washington, D.C., or under New York law, or if the client were a Delaware company? The court offered no guidance on how to avoid the risks it created except perhaps never to agree to arbitrate in California. In a national legal economy, that would be an unfortunate lesson. The opinion was bad for California. Out-of-state lawyers would advise their clients not to include California as a venue for arbitration. Californians who might have been able to arbitrate at home would now have to travel. With legislative prodding, the California Supreme Court eventually adopted UPL exceptions for lawyers (many times more wordy and less generous than Rule 5.5). See California Rules of Court 9.45 through 9.48.

The national bar responded to *Birbrower* with shock and awe, first, because what the lawyers there did was (and is) so very common in this highly mobile age; second, because while it appears that the lawyer regulators in California were unconcerned with the firm's conduct, the client was nonetheless permitted to use an unauthorized law practice claim to avoid paying a fee; third, because the court held, contrary to what many lawyers believed, that the Birbrower lawyers could not have protected themselves by associating with local counsel; and fourth, perhaps most alarming, because the court said that the lawyers would be guilty of UPL "in" California through "virtual" presence there via phone, fax, email, or satellite, even while they remained in New York.

Perhaps because lawyers everywhere realized that the Birbrower lawyers' fate could easily befall them, the ABA appointed a commission—the Multijurisdictional Practice (MJP) Commission—to study the question and propose solutions. The MJP Commission made nine recommendations, all of which were approved. The most important were amendments to Rule 5.5 to create four safe harbors for lawyers who temporarily cross state lines (physically or virtually) to serve clients in host states. A further change, since expanded, makes it easier for in-house lawyers to relocate to a new jurisdiction. See Rule 5.5(d). As of mid-2020, 48 U.S. jurisdictions have adopted the amendments in the same or substantially similar form. (Not all adoptions are as generous.) The New York courts initially rejected the amendments, which led Connecticut to adopt a reciprocity provision that denied New York lawyers the benefits of Connecticut's Rule 5.5. New York has since adopted a version of Rule 5.5 in the rules of the New York Court of Appeals. 22 NYCRR Parts 522 and 523.

Consider the converse situation. A lawyer lives and works in a jurisdiction where she is not admitted but serves only those clients who retain her in her home jurisdiction. She does not hold herself out as a lawyer where she lives. Sound farfetched? A Washington, D.C. lawyer needed to renew her membership in the Maryland federal district court. Membership required that she "maintain [her] principal law office" in her place of admission, namely D.C. Her law firm was in D.C., she got her mail there, her letterhead had a D.C. address, her computer server was in D.C., and phone calls went to a D.C. area code. But she lived and worked in Massachusetts, where she was not admitted. The court concluded nonetheless that her office was in D.C. In re Carlton, 708 F. Supp. 2d 524 (D. Md. 2010). The court stressed that it would not tolerate a "mere 'mail drop'" in D.C., a term lacking a precise definition. Why not? Indeed, why must the lawyer have any physical presence anywhere? Why can't she practice virtually? Pennsylvania Opinion 2010-200, California Opinion 2012-184, and NYC Opinion 2014-2 allow virtual law practice under described conditions.

A question left open in *Carlton* is whether Massachusetts has any reason for concern. True, Carlton was physically in Massachusetts, but she was not *professionally* visible there. I would think Massachusetts would have no concern. In fact, why shouldn't a lawyer admitted in any state be able visibly to practice anywhere if she limits her practice to federal and international law and the law of her own jurisdiction? Arizona and Minnesota allow just that if clients are informed that the lawyer is not admitted there.

Although rules like Rule 5.5 bespeak greater openness to cross-border practice, courts can be obstinate. Imagine that you are a Colorado lawyer. Your in-laws live in Minnesota. Their condominium association has obtained a judgment against them for $2,400 and the association's lawyer has been pressing them to pay. It's a lot of money for your in-laws, so they ask you to help. You have an email exchange with the association's lawyer in an effort to settle the claim. Have you engaged in unauthorized practice in Minnesota? You're not getting paid. You didn't troll for Minnesota clients. You did not physically enter Minnesota. The legal issues are not complicated, and all you really want to do is find room to compromise. You were trying to be a good son- or daughter-in-law. On the other hand, the judgment is from a Minnesota court, is based on Minnesota law, and the opposing party and lawyer are from Minnesota. So did you cross a line?

I regret to tell you that in a 4-3 opinion, the state supreme court upheld an admonition against you (well, not *you*) on very similar facts. In re Charges of Unprofessional Conduct, 884 N.W.2d 661 (Minn. 2016). In a rather picky deconstruction of Rule 5.5, the court disciplined the Colorado lawyer. The best that can be said for this decision is that it protects Minnesota's justice system against mischief by out-of-state lawyers, although the record before the court disclosed no mischief, and the clients sought help from their own son-in-law. Less charitably, we might say that the effect, if not the purpose, of the decision is to force clients like the lawyer's in-laws to pay a Minnesota lawyer, to negotiate themselves, or to just give up. In 2019, perhaps to make amends for a myopic opinion, the Minnesota Supreme Court amended its rules to allow out-of-state lawyers to advise their family members in the state.

The View from Canada and the European Union

The EU has 27 nations (post-Brexit) with different legal systems and traditions. While U.S. states fret about the appropriate level of tolerance for lawyers from other U.S. *states*, the EU members have opened their doors to lawyers from other *nations*.

In two ways, an EU lawyer can permanently relocate to another EU state:

One is establishment as a home state lawyer. For example, a French avocat can relocate to England while retaining his or her status as an avocat and, as such, he or she can practice French law, English law, and European law without limit. It is important to recognize that, pursuant to the [Establishment Directive], a migrant lawyer can simply establish under his or her home state title, and practice host state law without joining the host state legal profession. Currently, there are over 250 Registered European Lawyers with the Law Society of England and Wales. Overall, it is estimated that just under 4,000 [European Economic Area] lawyers are registered outside their own jurisdiction.

The other mode . . . is to transform oneself into a host state lawyer, a new entry route to membership of bars and law societies. Fully qualified lawyers from other [European Economic Area] Member States can practice and join a host state bar or law society with no prior examination of their competence. They can become local lawyers after three years of relevant legal practice in the host state, with no formal examination to complete. Bars and law societies rely on the integrity of their members as lawyers to limit their practice to areas in which they are competent. . . .

Julian Lonbay, Assessing the European Market for Legal Services: Developments in the Free Movement of Lawyers in the European Union, 33 Fordham Int'l L.J. 1629 (2010). European lawyers may also practice temporarily in a member state.

Canadian provinces and territories have adopted a National Mobility Agreement that makes it easy for lawyers to practice up to 100 days a year in another Canadian province or to relocate their practice from one place to another. Google "Canada and National Mobility Agreement" to see how it works. A separate agreement addresses Quebec, whose law is based on the civil law system.

C. UNAUTHORIZED PRACTICE OF LAW

"The Landlords' Lawyers Are a Mean Bunch"

"For the last four years, my colleagues Diarmuid and Grainne and I have been working for a tenants' rights organization. We organize tenants, including rent strikes in extreme cases, and we help them report problems to government agencies (no heat, vermin, broken appliances, and the like). We picket landlords where they live (very effective, by the way). Now we have come up with two other ways to help.

"More than 96 percent of tenants who are sued in housing court have no lawyer. Landlords mostly do. The tenants have to represent themselves. We're not lawyers, so we know we can't represent them in housing court even though they'd be better off with us than with no one. We know the local housing laws and the housing court rules better than most lawyers. We wrote and self-published in Spanish, Chinese, Korean, Filipino, and English a free guide to the legal rights of tenants, with citations to statutes, cases, regulations, and forms. We also put the text on our website. Our first question is, is that allowed?

"We have a second question. On our website, we want to invite tenants who have been sued for eviction or nonpayment of rent to send us the court papers and their side of the story. At no charge, we will then send them the relevant housing code sections and court opinions and sketch out the arguments they should make pro se. We're not taking business from lawyers because these tenants cannot afford lawyers. (And so what if they could? Why should that matter?) The landlords' lawyers are a mean bunch (I may be biased but it doesn't mean I'm wrong) and will not hesitate to report us for unauthorized law practice when they learn what we're doing, which they inevitably will. Can we do it? Thank you for helping us. Min."

States license lawyers to ensure competence and honesty, both of which are examined. Nonlawyers cannot practice law. Remedies should they do so include injunctions and even criminal prosecution. As a result, we should expect the cost (as well as the quality) of a legal service to be higher than if anyone could provide it. But what if the service demands little discretion, or if the knowledge required is well within the competence of others, like the tenant advisers in the problem above, so that the threat to quality is low and the person advised is better off with the advice than if she had to go it alone?

In two ways, the bar's monopoly on the sale of legal services might be diluted or expanded. First, we could create an exception for certain nonlawyers or certain work. Even though a particular service is considered "legal," we could allow others to perform it. And sometimes we do. Tax accountants, for example, interpret a complex statute, the Internal Revenue Code. Second, we could adopt a narrow definition of what constitutes the practice of law. If a service is not defined as legal, a person who is not a lawyer may perform it, even though, paradoxically, when a lawyer does the same work, it may be law practice. (That's important in order to maintain privilege for communications.) Negotiation of a contract's economic terms, for example, is a nonlegal service that nonlawyer agents can do, but which can be law practice when lawyers do it as part of their practice. The work of compliance officers and consultants also resembles legal work. After all, compliance with what? Law. See Tanina Rostain, The Emergence of "Law Consultants," 75 Fordham L. Rev. 1397 (2006) ("Although compliance consultants do not hold themselves out to be practicing law, some of their services bear more than a passing resemblance to activities traditionally considered law practice and, in particular, the provision of legal advice."). When lawyers do the same work, it will usually be law practice.

Who decides whether to create an exception? Who decides how to define the practice of law? The answer to each question is the courts, although some courts will tolerate or even welcome legislative participation. Recall the inherent powers doctrine discussed in chapter 1. Whether particular conduct is law practice is a question of law, not ethics. Rule 5.5 forbids lawyers to engage in unauthorized practice or to help another to do so, but it does not define "law practice." *Birbrower* offered one definition of "law practice" in the first paragraph of part IIA of the opinion.

LINDER v. INSURANCE CLAIMS CONSULTANTS
348 S.C. 477, 560 S.E.2d 612 (2002)

WALLER, JUSTICE . . .

Petitioners ("the Linders") suffered property loss due to a fire at their home in February 1996. While their claim was being adjusted by the insurance company, the Linders had many concerns about how the repairs to their home were being handled. One of the repairmen recommended respondent Insurance Claims Consultants, Inc. ("ICC") to Mrs. Linder. Mrs. Linder called ICC and met with respondent Gerald Moore.

In that initial meeting with Moore, the Linders discussed the fact that the insurance company had rejected their claim for the full value of Mr. Linder's gun collection. According to Mrs. Linder, Moore advised them the guns should be covered under their policy. Moore indicated that he advised the Linders to read their insurance policy and that he and Mr. Linder read the policy together. Respondent Jeffrey Raines [of ICC] states in an affidavit that they "were successful in obtaining payment for Mr. Linder's guns which was originally and erroneously denied by the company."

The Linders entered into a contract with ICC and agreed to pay ICC 10% of the total amount adjusted or otherwise recovered. . . .

ICC communicated directly with the insurance company's adjuster both orally and in writing, as well as with the insurance company's attorney. The majority of the communications reflect that the adjusters concentrated on cost-related issues, such as completing the contents inventory and the sworn statement of proof of loss, as well as discussions on the extent and amount of repairs. Indeed, Raines stated that ICC spent over 300 man hours preparing the detailed inventory of the damaged household contents. According to Raines, ICC was able to obtain an almost $12,000 increase in what the insurance company originally agreed to cover. The Linders approved the claim, but the insurance company delayed payment. Raines stated that he then recommended to Mrs. Linder that she get an attorney. When the attorney settled the claim, the Linders executed a release of all claims.

[The Linders refused to pay ICC its 10%. ICC sued. The Linders then brought this action in the state supreme court, which had exclusive jurisdiction to define the practice of law, to declare the contract void.]

The practice of law "is not confined to litigation, but extends to activities in other fields which entail specialized legal knowledge and ability. Often, the line between such activities and permissible business conduct by non-attorneys is unclear." Indeed, we have recognized "it is neither practicable nor wise" to attempt to formulate a comprehensive definition of what constitutes the practice of law. Because of this ambiguity, what is, and what is not, the unauthorized practice of law is best decided in the context of an actual case or controversy. Moreover, it is this Court that has the final word on what constitutes the practice of law.

The issue of whether insurance adjusters engage in the unauthorized practice of law is a novel one in South Carolina, but has been entertained by many courts in other jurisdictions. [The court surveyed cases from other states.]

In our opinion, the business of public insurance adjusting does not *per se* constitute the practice of law. We note the parties agree that public adjusters may act as appraisers. Since a public adjuster may use his expertise to determine a value, we simply do not see why it would be beyond his expertise to discuss that value, and the insurer's competing value, with the client and the insurer's adjuster. This type of negotiation activity—as long as it is limited to valuations of property and repairs—does not require legal skill and knowledge. . . .

Specifically, we find there is no problem with a public adjuster measuring and documenting insurance claims, and then presenting those valuations to the insurance company. Therefore, we declare the following practices permissible:

A. Providing an estimate of property damage and repair costs, i.e., any purely appraisal-oriented activities by the public adjuster.
B. Preparing the contents inventory and/or sworn statements on proof of loss.
C. Presenting the claim to the insurance company, i.e., delivering the necessary paperwork and data to the insurer.
D. Negotiating with the insurance company, as long as the discussions only involve competing property-damage valuations.

As to what activities are prohibited, we declare that public adjusters shall not:

A. Advise clients of their rights, duties, or privileges under an insurance policy regarding matters requiring legal skill or knowledge, i.e., interpret the policy for clients.
B. Advise clients on whether to accept a settlement offer from an insurance company.
C. Become involved, in any way, with a coverage dispute between the client and the insurance company.
D. Utilize advertising that would lead clients to believe that public adjusters provide services which require legal skill. . . .

The question remains whether respondents engaged in the unauthorized practice of law. Although they certainly did not have the benefit of the guidelines we announce today, we nevertheless must decide whether respondents crossed the line into the unauthorized practice of law. Because they advised the Linders on their rights under the insurance policy and became involved with a known coverage dispute, we conclude that they did. . . .

Their involvement went beyond an evaluation on the vital question of "how much" the gun collection was worth, and transgressed into an evaluation of whether, and to what extent, the guns should be covered pursuant to the policy language. . . .

[T]he majority of respondents' work appears to have *not* entailed the unauthorized practice of law. We therefore hold that the most appropriate manner in which to sanction respondents for their transgressions is for the trial court . . . to determine the value of respondents' work which did not constitute the unauthorized practice of law. Respondents are entitled to that amount, but are not to be compensated for any amount attributable to their unauthorized activities.

Justice Pleicones [joined by Chief Justice Toal, dissenting] . . .

I would permit licensed public adjusters to interpret insurance contracts to the extent necessary to adjust their clients['] claim, to negotiate coverage disputes, and to advise their clients whether to accept settlement offers. Public adjusters are hired for their expertise in the handling of insurance claims, and I would permit them to use their specialized knowledge in aid of their clients' claims.

For example, the majority concludes that ICC engaged in the unauthorized practice of law when it assisted the Linders in recovering the full value of their gun collection. I would not deny the Linders the benefit of the very expertise which led them to hire ICC in the first place, nor would I require ICC to remain silent when it perceived a coverage issue not apparent to the client. I would, however, require the public adjuster to refrain from advising the client at the point where the insurance company involves an attorney in the matter or when the legal process is invoked. . . .

Unlike *Linder,* some state high courts hold that even *negotiating* the amount of a loss with an insurer is the practice of law. This is odd because nonlawyer agents routinely negotiate for clients and because public adjusters are likely to be more knowledgeable in evaluating a loss than are lawyers. The explanation may be that, as these courts see it, in order to negotiate, the adjuster must interpret the contract, which may require some legal knowledge.

In states that forbid negotiation, a public adjuster may only evaluate the loss and provide its evaluation to the insured, who can then negotiate for himself or hire a lawyer. See, e.g., Bergantzel v. Mlynarik, 619 N.W.2d 309

(Iowa 2000); Prof'l Adjusters v. Tandon, 433 N.E.2d 779 (Ind. 1982). The *Tandon* decision is particularly restrictive because the insurer accepted Professional Adjusters' evaluation without any negotiation. But the court wrote that the company *might* have wanted to negotiate, which the adjuster could not do, and that possibility was enough to make the work unauthorized law practice.

The *Linder* majority explained the distinction between the work that a public adjuster could and could not do. The disallowed work required interpretation of the contract. The allowed work was limited to evaluating the loss and negotiating its value.

If a jurisdiction is not willing to interpret its unauthorized practice rules to allow the tenant advisors in "The Landlords' Lawyers Are a Mean Bunch" to do what they wish, perhaps it would be willing to license them to do it without requiring three years of law school. Is one way to increase access to justice for those unable to afford lawyers to allow nonlawyers, properly trained and tested, to give legal advice in uncomplicated areas of law where the need is great but the potential clients lack funds to pay the going legal rates? Medicine has created the nurse-practitioner. How about law? See chapter 14B.

Jailhouse Lawyering. Courts have carved out an exception to UPL rules for prisoners who help other prisoners prepare legal papers. In In re Morales, 151 A.3d 333 (Vt. 2016), the Vermont Supreme Court summarized the United States Supreme Court's precedent and expanded it to the somewhat different facts before it. The state had filed a criminal complaint against Morales. It alleged that she had violated unauthorized practice rules by helping other prisoners do legal research and by drafting motions.

> In [Johnson v. Avery, 393 U.S. 483 (1969)], the U.S. Supreme Court recognized that barring nonlawyer inmates from helping their peers with legal matters may raise constitutional issues in some cases. In that case, the U.S. Supreme Court invalidated a Tennessee prison regulation that prohibited inmates from assisting other inmates in the preparation of "Writs or other legal matters." The Court held inmates had a fundamental right of access to the courts "for the purpose of presenting their complaints," and that this right could not "be denied or obstructed." The Court noted that it was common practice for trial courts to appoint counsel in post-conviction relief cases only after an inmate has filed a pro se petition "with such help as he [or she] can obtain within the prison walls or the prison system." Accordingly, the Court struck down the Tennessee regulation because it limited inmates' ability to file habeas corpus petitions. Unless some "reasonable alternative to assist inmates in the preparation of petitions for post-conviction relief" was provided by the state, the regulation could not stand. . . .
>
> Although the Supreme Court's constitutional ruling does not directly apply in this case because the inmates Morales assisted were represented by lawyers in connection with the matters in which Morales gave them advice, the policy considerations that animated the Court's analysis have broader application.

Incarcerated prisoners are not only disproportionately undereducated; their access to a range of legal resources and information is severely limited, and their need may be great. As Justice William Douglas recognized, in addition to a host of issues relating to the underlying conviction and parole, an incarcerated offender may have civil matters such as divorce and custody issues, or social security, workers' compensation, or veterans' claims. In addition, "litigation is one of the few means by which prisoners can bring public attention to serious health and safety risks, including inadequate health care, widespread violence, sexual assault, and unsafe environmental conditions." In contrast to a layperson who is not incarcerated, many inmates cannot seek a second opinion from another lawyer, research a legal question online, or visit a law library.

Three Limitations on State UPL Rules: The Supremacy Clause, the First Amendment, and Antitrust Laws

Despite the claim of inherent judicial power to define "law practice," constraints exist. Two are constitutional.

The Supremacy Clause.   Sperry v. State ex rel. Florida Bar, 373 U.S. 379 (1963), ruled that state power to regulate the practice of law had to yield to incompatible federal legislation that authorized lay representation in cases before the U.S. Patent Office. By virtue of the Supremacy Clause, Congress could authorize lay agents to provide legal services "reasonably necessary and incident to the preparation and prosecution of patent applications." The Court ruled that the "State maintains control over the practice of law within its borders except to the limited extent necessary for the accomplishment of the federal objectives." Furthermore, the Patent Office "safeguards [citizens from unskilled and unethical practitioners] by testing applicants for registration" and by authorizing practice only before the Patent Office.

The First Amendment.   Efforts to stop publication of books or materials that enable purchasers to represent themselves have generally failed, on the theory that the author is offering only general legal information and is not addressing the reader's or user's particular situation. In New York County Lawyers' Ass'n v. Dacey, 234 N.E.2d 459 (N.Y. 1967), the plaintiff bar association tried to stop nonlawyer Norman Dacey from selling his book, *How to Avoid Probate!* The book purported to instruct readers on how they might go about organizing their assets during their lifetime so that upon death these assets would pass to others without having to be administered under the supervision of a probate court. Probate is a lucrative area of practice for lawyers, including general practitioners, possibly explaining the motivation for the lawsuit. The Court of Appeals ruled that Dacey was not practicing law simply by selling a book containing information about law. It relied on a dissent from the lower court that had in turn relied in part on the First Amendment.

The following tale is not a spoof from The Onion. Unauthorized Practice of Law Committee v. Parsons Technology, 1999 WL 47235 (N.D. Tex. 1999), offers a pitch-perfect parody of state bar efforts to deny consumers self-help legal material. Plaintiff sought to enjoin the sale of Quicken Family Lawyer (QFL) in Texas. As the court described it,

> QFL offers over 100 different legal forms (such as employment agreements, real estate leases, premarital agreements, and seven different will forms) along with instructions on how to fill out these forms. QFL's packaging represents that the product is "valid in 49 states including the District of Columbia;" is "developed and reviewed by expert attorneys;" and is "updated to reflect recent legislative formats." The packaging also indicates that QFL will have the user "answer a few questions to determine which estate planning and health care documents best meet [the user's] needs;" and that QFL will "interview you in a logical order, tailoring documents to your situation." Finally, the packaging reassures the user that "handy hints and comprehensive legal help topics are always available."

The court went on to explain in some detail the volume of information available on QFL and the methodology for interactive use. Distinguishing *Dacey* and rejecting Parsons's First Amendment arguments, the court concluded that QFL violated the Texas UPL statute and enjoined its sale. "QFL is far more than a static form with instructions on how to fill in the blanks. For instance, QFL adapts the content of the form to the responses given by the user. QFL purports to select the appropriate health care document for an individual based upon the state in which she lives. The packaging of QFL makes various representations as to the accuracy and specificity of the forms." The Texas legislature then amended the state UPL statute to provide that the practice of law "does not include the design, creation, publication, distribution, display, or sale . . . [of] computer software, or similar products if the products clearly and conspicuously state that the products are not a substitute for the advice of an attorney." Thereafter, the Fifth Circuit vacated the lower court's injunction. Unauthorized Practice of Law Comm. v. Parsons Tech., 179 F.3d 956 (5th Cir. 1999).

The growth in the powers of technology in the years since *Parsons* has made it dramatically clear that interactive programs that also generate documents can be formidable competitors to human sources of legal advice, although, of course, humans (possibly including lawyers) create the programs. LegalZoom and others have aggressively sought to exploit this business model. They enable consumers to create and download jurisdiction-specific documents intended to satisfy business and personal needs. Many of the services that small law firms offer respond to the same needs, setting up an interesting competition. As inspection of their websites reveals, the online ventures are offering increasingly sophisticated services, promising (or threatening) even greater competition with traditional firms. Whether they will prosper and how the courts finally respond to any efforts to restrict or stop them remain open questions.

Some companies that offer computer-assisted, interactive legal forms may employ lawyers (whether or not licensed in the relevant jurisdiction) who sign off on and are responsible for the forms the company generates, even though the customer may never know who they are. Nevertheless, it is unauthorized law practice, as traditionally understood, because the *entity* providing the service is not a law firm. Lawyers may offer their services to the public only through law firms, whether organized as partnerships or in corporate form. See Rule 5.4(b) and (d). There is an exception if the organization offering legal help is nonprofit. That exception is what makes public interest law firms possible. See chapter 14A.

How companies like LegalZoom will fare—whether they will enjoy the same First Amendment rights for an algorithm (and freedom from UPL regulation) as Norman Dacey did for his simple book—remains a question. Unlike Dacey's book, these companies use artificial intelligence to produce a bespoke document that will address a user's specific need.

Antitrust Laws. LegalZoom faced legal threats to its operations in North Carolina. It alleged that the threats violated the antitrust laws and cited North Carolina State Board of Dental Examiners v. F.T.C. (chapter 4D), where the same state lost. As part of a settlement, the state legislature authorized companies like LegalZoom to sell to customers in the state subject to certain protections. These may become influential nationwide. Here is what North Carolina Gen. Stat. §84-2.2 provides. Does it protect clients?

> (a) The practice of law, including the giving of legal advice . . . does not include the operation of a Web site by a provider that offers consumers access to interactive software that generates a legal document based on the consumer's answers to questions presented by the software, provided that all of the following are satisfied:
>
> (1) The consumer is provided a means to see the blank template or the final, completed document before finalizing a purchase of that document.
>
> (2) An attorney licensed to practice law in the State of North Carolina has reviewed each blank template offered to North Carolina consumers, including each and every potential part thereof that may appear in the completed document. The name and address of each reviewing attorney must be kept on file by the provider and provided to the consumer upon written request.
>
> (3) The provider must communicate to the consumer that the forms or templates are not a substitute for the advice or services of an attorney.
>
> (4) The provider discloses its legal name and physical location and address to the consumer.
>
> (5) The provider does not disclaim any warranties or liability and does not limit the recovery of damages or other remedies by the consumer.
>
> (6) The provider does not require the consumer to agree to jurisdiction or venue in any state other than North Carolina for the resolution of disputes between the provider and the consumer. . . .

Self-Assessment Questions

1. Flooding damaged the foundation of Elmer Cluett's house and destroyed many pieces of furniture on the first floor, including antiques. Luckily, he was insured. Unluckily, the insurance company was difficult. It said that Cluett's policy might not cover a loss due to flooding, in which case it would owe nothing. Even if the policy did cover Cluett's loss, the insurer disputed the cost of repair and the value of the destroyed property.

   Cluett consults Yolanda Flores, a lawyer. She offers to negotiate with the insurer for a contingency fee of 25 percent of the recovery. The fee will be higher if the matter goes to court. Cluett asks Flores how she will evaluate the loss. Flores says that the insurer's no-coverage claim is simply a matter of contract interpretation, which is what lawyers do. As for the value of the loss, she says she will retain experts whom Cluett will have to pay. Cluett says he'll think it over.

   Then someone tells Cluett that there are people who will do it all (except go to court) for a contingent fee of 10 to 15 percent of the recovery. They are called public adjusters. They are not lawyers. Cluett learns that insurance companies have nonlawyer adjusters on staff to do the same work for them.

   What can public adjusters do for someone like Elmer Cluett without engaging in unauthorized law practice?

2. Because of your reputation in the area of international trade law, a company in Atlanta wants to retain you, for a fixed quarterly sum, as a special outside counsel whom it can consult on international trade issues. Although you practice in New York, there will rarely be need for you to go to Atlanta. All advice can be provided by phone, express mail, email, and videoconferencing. But the client envisions quarterly trips to Atlanta for important meetings. You are not admitted in Georgia. Can you do it? Assume the Model Rules apply.

3. *The following facts are taken verbatim from a decision of the Maryland Court of Appeals. Mr. Stern was seeking admission to the bar. The character committee turned him down. The question for you is this: If you were representing Stern, what would you argue in an effort to gain admission?*

   The Committee found that in 1993, Mr. Stern opened a credit account with Discover Card in order to meet his regular living expenses while attending Frostburg State University and to obtain cash advances to finance the startup of his business, Priority Plus, which provided various services to law firms including service of private process. As of May of 2001, the unpaid balance on the Discover Card account, the Committee found, was $11,190.00. Eventually, the Discover Card balance was sold to NCO Financial Systems, Inc., a debt collector. The Committee found that in 2006, after Mr. Stern had submitted his Bar application, he had negotiated a settlement with NCO. Just 33 days before the Committee hearing, on August 15, 2006, Mr. Stern's mother submitted a check to NCO for $6,000.00 in settlement of the debt.

In 1996, Mr. Stern applied for and received a credit card from Home Depot. The record does not reflect the amount of the unpaid account balance, but subsequently, the delinquent account was sold to Monogram Credit Card Bank of Georgia, which filed suit against Mr. Stern. In July of 2001, Mr. Stern tendered $705.00 to Monogram in settlement. In 1997, Mr. Stern obtained a credit account from First USA Bank to pay for living expenses and also to finance Priority Plus. The delinquent balance rose to $8,375.73, and subsequently, was sold to Asset Acceptance LLC, which filed suit against Mr. Stern in February of 2003. In March, a judgment was entered against Mr. Stern in the amount of the unpaid balance and two separate writs of garnishment were issued in July of 2004 and April of 2005. Thereafter, following Mr. Stern's submission of his Bar application, he agreed to a settlement.

In 1999, Mr. Stern took out a loan to purchase a car. The past due loan amount grew to $4,476.91, and subsequently, the unpaid balance was purchased by American General Finance. The account was then sold to Debt One, and then, again, to American Coradius International, which, in 2000, obtained a judgment against Mr. Stern. Again, after he had submitted his Bar application, Mr. Stern settled the dispute by remitting $2,638.00 in satisfaction in October of 2005.

Mr. Stern also obtained a credit card from Citibank Visa in 1999. The account's unpaid balance rose to $3,833.07, and thereafter, the Committee found, the account was sold to Unifund, which obtained a judgment in October of 2002. Mr. Stern satisfied the judgment in November of 2005, again, after he had submitted the Bar application.

The Committee further found that, in 2007, Mr. Stern had a student loan payment of approximately $260.00 a month, [which] was in good standing; his only other outstanding debts were a Capital One credit card that had a balance of $479.00 and a PayPal account with a $50.00 balance. According to a Personal Financial Statement prepared with the help of a financial advisor, Mr. Stern also had savings of $21,500.00, two cars valued at $16,000.00, a bicycle worth $5,000.00, personal effects valued at $15,000.00, and $10,000.00 worth of artwork.

The Committee further found that Mr. Stern, when he was 26 or 27, had had an inappropriate relationship with a 15-year old female. The relationship, which became sexual after the female turned 16, lasted for approximately seven or eight years and ended in 2006; other allegations included in the young woman's testimony before the Committee were not relied upon.

In response, before the Committee, Mr. Stern proffered that he did not pay his outstanding debts because they became overwhelming, and he believed that making the required minimum payments would be pointless. He also claimed that he had recognized the error of his ways and had sought the assistance of a certified financial advisor.

Mr. Stern admitted that his relationship with the [15-year-old] female was unwise, but contended that he had maintained his relationship with the female because she saw him as a "father figure," and because she had threatened on numerous occasions to report him to the Character Committee.

XIII

Control of Quality: Remedies for Professional Failure

A. MALPRACTICE AND BREACH OF FIDUCIARY DUTY

An attorney's negligence is based on an objective standard, and whether the attorney acted in good faith in representing a client has no bearing on liability. Although an attorney is not liable for every mistake that may occur in practice, and an error in judgment does not necessarily constitute a basis for liability, a subjective good faith exercise of judgment or an honest belief will not protect an attorney from an otherwise negligent act or omission.

> —Meyer v. Wagner (Mass. Sup. Jud. Ct. 1999)

Maybe an unscrupulous lawyer could have thrown enough sand in the jury's eyes to avert a judgment for the Weekleys, or at least an award of punitive damages, but unwillingness to do so is not evidence of malpractice. Refusal to violate professional ethics—or even to approach as near to the line as humanly possible—is not professional misconduct. A scrupulous lawyer, a lawyer who takes Law Day rhetoric seriously, who sincerely believes that he has a dual duty, to his client and to the law, and acts on his belief, may lose some clients to his less scrupulous competitors but he should not be deemed to be courting a tort judgment.

> —Transcraft, Inc. v. Galvin, Stalmack, Kirschner & Clark (7th Cir. 1994)

The Sixth Amendment guarantees reasonable competence, not perfect advocacy judged with the benefit of hindsight. To recall the words of Justice (and former Solicitor General) Jackson: "I made three arguments of every case. First came the one that I planned—as I thought, logical, coherent, complete. Second was the one actually presented—interrupted, incoherent, disjointed, disappointing. The third was the utterly devastating argument that I thought of after going to bed that night." . . . To be sure, Gentry's [criminal defense] lawyer was no Aristotle or even Clarence Darrow. But the Ninth Circuit's conclusion [that counsel's performance was deficient] gives too little deference to the state courts that have primary responsibility for supervising defense counsel in state criminal trials.

—Yarborough v. Gentry (U.S. Supreme Court 2003)

1. Liability to Clients

The next problem introduces you to legal malpractice and also enables you to review doctrines in the conflicts chapters.

When Sally Left Ari . . .

MEMORANDUM

To: New Business Committee

From: Emily Adichie

Adam Rosini represented Sally Kostas nearly three years ago when she told her husband, Ari Kovair, she wanted a divorce. You know Ari Kovair from the business pages—bald with a close beard, skinny as a string bean. Anyway, Adam is a partner in Rosini, Wattenberg & Yossarian LLP, a nine-lawyer firm that does general civil representation. Sally's divorce ended the way most do—with a settlement agreement. In fact, going to court was pro forma since the couple had agreed on everything beforehand.

Sally came to see me last Tuesday because she was beginning to have doubts about Adam's work. It seems she was at a party down at the beach last month and a woman there told her that when *she* got divorced two years ago, the settlement included nearly half the increase in the value of property her husband inherited during their marriage, which apparently was a lot. That got Sally thinking.

In our state, as you know, property you inherit during the marriage and hold in your own name is not subject to division in the event of divorce. Of that there is no doubt. But for quite some time, it was unclear whether the same exclusion applied to any increase in the value of that property. Say you inherit stock worth $10,000 and two years later, when you divorce, it's worth $12,000. Does your spouse have a claim against the $2,000 gain? That was the question in Sally's case.

When Sally left Ari, nobody knew the answer for sure. Two years before Sally hired Adam, in a case called Rojinski v. Rojinski, a trial judge in another county of the state had ruled that the increase was *not* part of the marital estate. The intermediate appeals court affirmed. *Rojinski* is not binding in our county (where Sally and Ari lived) because we're in a different judicial district. But it was likely to be influential. *Rojinski* settled without going to the state supreme court.

Cases from other state high courts have gone both ways, but most disagreed with *Rojinski*. Most secondary authorities, including a leading law review article, also disagreed. That was the state of things when Sally hired Adam.

I don't know how much of this Adam knew or what research he did, except that I do know that he was intimately familiar with *Rojinski* because he represented the successful spouse, the wife. The increase in the value of her inheritance was not subject to division. When Adam negotiated Sally's separation agreement, he did not seek half of the increased value of the real estate Ari inherited during their marriage. That increase totaled about $3 million. Now Sally wants to know why she didn't get some of the $3 million, like the woman at the beach.

The other thing I learned since I met with Sally is that while Adam was her lawyer on the divorce, his partner Gretchen Baxindell was representing a limited real-estate partnership that was negotiating for a large parcel of land on which to build a shopping center. Ari had a 25 percent interest in the partnership. (Sally did get her share of Ari's interest.) Sally knew that Gretchen was Adam's partner but she would have had no reason to know that Gretchen was the lawyer for the real-estate partnership. So you see where I'm going. Adam represents Sally against Ari while Adam's partner Gretchen is representing a real estate partnership in which Ari has a 25 percent interest.

Last year, our state supreme court finally addressed the appreciated value question and unanimously agreed with *Rojinski*. Four months later, the legislature overturned that ruling prospectively. So we know that if Sally got divorced today, she'd get half of the $3 million increment. But we also know that at the time of her divorce, she would have lost before the supreme court, whose membership hasn't changed in six years, assuming as we must that the judges would have voted the same way.

Sally is coming by to see me tomorrow to find out if she has a case against Adam and, if so, whether we're willing to take it. So I would first like to know what you think about that. What would be the theory of liability? Was Adam guilty of malpractice? Was he conflicted because of Gretchen's work or his work on *Rojinski*? Does the fact that Sally would have lost before the state high court mean she has no damages?

If we decide not to take the case for whatever reason, what do I tell Sally, if anything, about what my preliminary research shows with respect to Adam's (and vicariously his firm's) liability? The statute of limitations on lawyer malpractice and breach of fiduciary duty claims in this jurisdiction is three years, which means Sally has seven weeks and three days to bring any claim or she's sunk.

Once again we ask, "Who is a client?" As you know by now, in our new Einsteinian universe of lawyer regulation, this question can no longer be answered with good old Newtonian certainty. Very often, of course, there will be no room to quibble, especially if the purported client has a retainer agreement, monthly statements, and a pile of canceled checks. Occasionally, however, the issue will be fuzzier, as we see in the wonderful *Togstad* case and the note following. *Togstad* has been in the book since the first edition. Periodically, I look for a more recent substitute. But none packs so many issues into so small a space.

As you read *Togstad*, think about the following questions:

1. What was the court's basis for concluding that an attorney-client relationship existed for each of Mr. and Mrs. Togstad? How did each of the parties characterize their conversation so as to encourage the conclusion that there was or was not a professional relationship?
2. Precisely what did Miller do or fail to do that subjected him to liability? What could he have done to avoid liability for either of the two reasons the Togstads claim?
3. Does *Togstad* mean that law firms that decline to accept a matter must always advise on the statute of limitations? That advice may require research, including into when the statute started to run and tolling provisions. Sometimes the answer won't be clear.
4. What were the Togstads' damages and what did they have to prove in order to win?

TOGSTAD v. VESELY, OTTO, MILLER & KEEFE
291 N.W.2d 686 (Minn. 1980)

PER CURIAM. . . .

In August 1971, John Togstad began to experience severe headaches and on August 16, 1971, was admitted to Methodist Hospital where tests disclosed that the headaches were caused by a large aneurysm on the left internal carotid artery. The attending physician, Dr. Paul Blake, a neurological surgeon, treated the problem by applying a Selverstone clamp to the left common carotid artery. The clamp was surgically implanted on August 27, 1971, in Togstad's neck to allow the gradual closure of the artery over a period of days. . . .

In the early morning hours of August 29, 1971, a nurse observed that Togstad was unable to speak or move. At the time, the clamp was one-half (50%) closed. Upon discovering Togstad's condition, the nurse called a resident physician, who did not adjust the clamp. Dr. Blake was also immediately informed of Togstad's condition and arrived about an hour later, at which time he opened the clamp. Togstad is now severely paralyzed in his right arm and leg, and is unable to speak.

Plaintiffs' expert, Dr. Ward Woods, testified that Togstad's paralysis and loss of speech was due to a lack of blood supply to his brain. . . .

About 14 months after her husband's hospitalization began, plaintiff Joan Togstad met with attorney Jerre Miller regarding her husband's condition. Neither she nor her husband was personally acquainted with Miller or his law firm prior to that time. John Togstad's former work supervisor, Ted Bucholz, made the appointment and accompanied Mrs. Togstad to Miller's office. Bucholz was present when Mrs. Togstad and Miller discussed the case.[3]

Mrs. Togstad had become suspicious of the circumstances surrounding her husband's tragic condition due to the conduct and statements of the hospital nurses shortly after the paralysis occurred. One nurse told Mrs. Togstad that she had checked Mr. Togstad at 2 A.M. and he was fine; that when she returned at 3 A.M., by mistake, to give him someone else's medication, he was unable to move or speak; and that if she hadn't accidentally entered the room no one would have discovered his condition until morning. Mrs. Togstad also noticed that the other nurses were upset and crying, and that Mr. Togstad's condition was a topic of conversation.

Mrs. Togstad testified that she told Miller "everything that happened at the hospital," including the nurses' statements and conduct which had raised a question in her mind. She stated that she "believed" she had told Miller "about the procedure and what was undertaken, what was done, and what happened." She brought no records with her. Miller took notes and asked questions during the meeting, which lasted 45 minutes to an hour. At its conclusion, according to Mrs. Togstad, Miller said that "he did not think we had a legal case, however, he was going to discuss this with his partner." She understood that if Miller changed his mind after talking to his partner, he would call her. Mrs. Togstad "gave it" a few days and, since she did not hear from Miller, decided "that they had come to the conclusion that there wasn't a case." No fee arrangements were discussed, no medical authorizations were requested, nor was Mrs. Togstad billed for the interview.

Mrs. Togstad denied that Miller had told her his firm did not have expertise in the medical malpractice field, urged her to see another attorney, or related to her that the statute of limitations for medical malpractice actions was two years. She did not consult another attorney until one year after she talked to Miller. Mrs. Togstad indicated that she did not confer with another attorney earlier because of her reliance on Miller's "legal advice" that they "did not have a case."

On cross-examination, Mrs. Togstad was asked whether she went to Miller's office "to see if he would take the case of [her] husband. . . ." She replied, "Well, I guess it was to go for legal advice, what to do, where shall we go from here? That is what we went for." Again in response to defense counsel's questions, Mrs. Togstad testified as follows:

Q. And it was clear to you, was it not, that what was taking place was a preliminary discussion between a prospective client and lawyer

3. Bucholz, who knew Miller through a local luncheon club, died prior to the trial of the instant action.

as to whether or not they wanted to enter into an attorney-client relationship?

A. I am not sure how to answer that. It was for legal advice as to what to do.

Q. And Mr. Miller was discussing with you your problem and indicating whether he, as a lawyer, wished to take the case, isn't that true?

A. Yes.

On redirect examination, Mrs. Togstad acknowledged that when she left Miller's office she understood that she had been given a "qualified, quality legal opinion that [she and her husband] did not have a malpractice case."

Miller's testimony was different in some respects from that of Mrs. Togstad. Like Mrs. Togstad, Miller testified that Mr. Bucholz arranged and was present at the meeting, which lasted about 45 minutes. According to Miller, Mrs. Togstad described the hospital incident, including the conduct of the nurses. He asked her questions, to which she responded. Miller testified that "the only thing I told her [Mrs. Togstad] after we had pretty much finished the conversation was that there was nothing related in her factual circumstances that told me that she had a case that our firm would be interested in undertaking."

Miller also claimed he related to Mrs. Togstad "that because of the grievous nature of the injuries sustained by her husband, that this was only my opinion and she was encouraged to ask another attorney if she wished for another opinion" and "she ought to do so promptly." He testified that he informed Mrs. Togstad that his firm "was not engaged as experts" in the area of medical malpractice, and that they associated with the Charles Hvass firm in cases of that nature. Miller stated that at the end of the conference he told Mrs. Togstad that he would consult with Charles Hvass and if Hvass's opinion differed from his, Miller would so inform her. Miller recollected that he called Hvass a "couple days" later and discussed the case with him. It was Miller's impression that Hvass thought there was no liability for malpractice in the case. Consequently, Miller did not communicate with Mrs. Togstad further.

On cross-examination, Miller testified as follows:

Q. Now, so there is no misunderstanding, and I am reading from your deposition, you understood that she was consulting with you as a lawyer, isn't that correct?

A. That's correct.

Q. That she was seeking legal advice from a professional attorney licensed to practice in this state and in this community?

A. I think you and I did have another interpretation or use of the term "Advice." She was there to see whether or not she had a case and whether the firm would accept it.

Q. We have two aspects; number one, your legal opinion concerning liability of a case for malpractice; number two, whether there was or wasn't liability, whether you would accept it, your firm, two separate elements, right?

A. I would say so.

Q. Were you asked on page 6 in the deposition, folio 14, "And you understood that she was seeking legal advice at the time that she was in your office, that is correct also, isn't it?" And did you give this answer, "I don't want to engage in semantics with you, but my impression was that she and Mr. Bucholz were asking my opinion after having related the incident that I referred to." The next question, "Your legal opinion?" Your answer, "Yes." Were those questions asked and were [those answers] given?

Mr. Collins: Objection to this, Your Honor. It is not impeachment.

The Court: Overruled.

The Witness: Yes, I gave those answers. Certainly, she was seeking my opinion as an attorney in the sense of whether or not there was a case that the firm would be interested in undertaking.

Kenneth Green, a Minneapolis attorney, was called as an expert by plaintiffs. He stated that in rendering legal advice regarding a claim of medical malpractice, the "minimum" an attorney should do would be to request medical authorizations from the client, review the hospital records, and consult with an expert in the field. John McNulty, a Minneapolis attorney, and Charles Hvass testified as experts on behalf of the defendants. McNulty stated that when an attorney is consulted as to whether he will take a case, the lawyer's only responsibility in refusing it is to so inform the party. He testified, however, that when a lawyer is asked his legal opinion on the merits of a medical malpractice claim, community standards require that the attorney check hospital records and consult with an expert before rendering his opinion.

Hvass stated that he had no recollection of Miller's calling him in October 1972 relative to the Togstad matter. . . .

In addition, Hvass acknowledged that if he were consulted for a "legal opinion" regarding medical malpractice and 14 months had expired since the incident in question, "ordinary care and diligence" would require him to inform the party of the two-year statute of limitations applicable to that type of action.

This case was submitted to the jury by way of a special verdict form. The jury found that Dr. Blake and the hospital were negligent and that Dr. Blake's negligence (but not the hospital's) was a direct cause of the injuries sustained by John Togstad; that there was an attorney-client contractual relationship between Mrs. Togstad and Miller; that Miller was negligent in rendering advice regarding the possible claims of Mr. and Mrs. Togstad; that, but for Miller's negligence, plaintiffs would have been successful in the prosecution of a legal action against Dr. Blake; and that neither Mr. nor Mrs. Togstad was negligent in pursuing their claims against Dr. Blake. The jury awarded damages to Mr. Togstad of $610,500 and to Mrs. Togstad of $39,000. . . .

In a legal malpractice action of the type involved here, four elements must be shown: (1) that an attorney-client relationship existed; (2) that defendant acted negligently or in breach of contract; (3) that such acts were the proximate cause of the plaintiffs' damages; (4) that but for defendant's conduct the plaintiffs would have been successful in the prosecution of their medical malpractice claim. . . .

We believe it is unnecessary to decide whether a tort or contract theory is preferable for resolving the attorney-client relationship question raised by this appeal. The tort and contract analyses are very similar in a case such as the instant one, and we conclude that under either theory the evidence shows that a lawyer-client relationship is present here. . . .

Defendants argue that even if an attorney-client relationship was established the evidence fails to show that Miller acted negligently in assessing the merits of the Togstads' case. They appear to contend that, at most, Miller was guilty of an error in judgment which does not give rise to legal malpractice. However, this case does not involve a mere error of judgment. The gist of plaintiffs' claim is that Miller failed to perform the minimal research that an ordinarily prudent attorney would do before rendering legal advice in a case of this nature. The record, through the testimony of Kenneth Green and John McNulty, contains sufficient evidence to support plaintiffs' position.

In a related contention, defendants assert that a new trial should be awarded on the ground that the trial court erred by refusing to instruct the jury that Miller's failure to inform Mrs. Togstad of the two-year statute of limitations for medical malpractice could not constitute negligence. The argument continues that since it is unclear from the record on what theory or theories of negligence the jury based its decision, a new trial must be granted.

The defect in defendants' reasoning is that there is adequate evidence supporting the claim that Miller was also negligent in failing to advise Mrs. Togstad of the two-year medical malpractice limitations period and thus the trial court acted properly in refusing to instruct the jury in the manner urged by defendants. One of defendants' expert witnesses, Charles Hvass, testified:

> *Q.* Now, Mr. Hvass, where you are consulted for a legal opinion and advice concerning malpractice and 14 months have elapsed [since the incident in question], wouldn't—and you hold yourself out as competent to give a legal opinion and advice to these people concerning their rights, wouldn't ordinary care and diligence require that you inform them that there is a two-year statute of limitations within which they have to act or lose their rights?
>
> *A.* Yes. I believe I would have advised someone of the two-year period of limitation, yes.

Consequently, based on the testimony of Mrs. Togstad, *i.e.*, that she requested and received legal advice from Miller concerning the malpractice claim, and the above testimony of Hvass, we must reject the defendants' contention, as it was reasonable for a jury to determine that Miller acted negligently in failing to inform Mrs. Togstad of the applicable limitations period. . . .

There is also sufficient evidence in the record establishing that, but for Miller's negligence, plaintiffs would have been successful in prosecuting their medical malpractice claim. Dr. Woods, in no uncertain terms, concluded that Mr. Togstad's injuries were caused by the medical malpractice of Dr. Blake. Defendants' expert testimony to the contrary was obviously not believed by the jury. Thus, the jury reasonably found that had plaintiffs' medical malpractice action been properly brought, plaintiffs would have recovered.*

Based on the foregoing, we hold that the jury's findings are adequately supported by the record. Accordingly we uphold the trial court's denial of defendants' motion for judgment notwithstanding the jury verdict. . . .

Was Miller Just a Nice Guy?

I sometimes try to understand why *Togstad* ever happened. Why did Miller slip up? The answer I keep returning to is that he slipped up because he was a nice guy. As I imagine it, Miller agreed, at the request of a friend (now deceased), to meet with Mrs. Togstad to allay her nagging concern that she was not doing right by her husband. Her visit would give her peace of mind. I accept that Miller believed his advice was correct. Perhaps many lawyers would do the same out of compassion. But if I'm right—and maybe I'm not; I'm just trying to channel Miller and understand why this sort of thing happens—is there a lesson here?

Every lawyer can find herself in a social setting (or now on social media) where someone says, "Can I ask you about something? Just off the top of your head?" (Or the less pleasant "head" image: "Can I pick your brain?") Do you say no, at the risk of being rude? Do you answer the best you can at the risk of being wrong? If you're careful, you equivocate: "Well, it would depend on knowing more and some legal research. I don't want to mislead you."

What Is the Required Standard of Care?

Togstad said that a "mere error of judgment" following legal and factual research is not malpractice. Other courts agree. One court wrote that a lawyer is obligated to exercise "that degree of care, skill, diligence and knowledge commonly possessed and exercised by a reasonable, careful and prudent lawyer in the practice of law in this jurisdiction." Cook, Flanagan & Berst v. Clausing, 438 P.2d 865 (Wash. 1968). An old opinion but the law hasn't changed. Forty-eight years later, the Connecticut Supreme Court said

---

* The causation requirement in legal malpractice cases is further discussed in part B2 below. — ED.

the same: "Malpractice is commonly defined as the failure of one rendering professional services to exercise that degree of skill and learning commonly applied under all the circumstances in the community by the average prudent reputable member of the profession." Bozelko v. Papastavros, 147 A.3d 1023 (Conn. 2016). The standard of care is the same for all lawyers in the state. Chapman v. Bearfield, 207 S.W.3d 736 (Tenn. 2006) ("We also believe the adoption of a statewide professional standard of care for attorneys who practice law in Tennessee is good policy.").

Judgmental Immunity. Justice Holmes said that the law "is what the courts will do in fact." Lawyers are hired to make these predictions. A reasonable but mistaken opinion reached after appropriate legal and factual research may be immune to liability because not every misjudgment is malpractice. In *Togstad*, Miller argued that at most he was guilty of "an error in judgment." Miller's problem, however, was that he did no legal and factual research before reaching his judgment.

Seed Co. sued its former lawyers for failing to include a translation of certain documents in a patent application, as required. As a result, someone else got the patent. In a summary judgment motion, the lawyers claimed judgmental immunity, but failed to show that they had exercised any judgment at all.

> To fall under the judgmental-immunity doctrine, the lawyer must "undertak[e] reasonable research of the relevant legal princip[les] and facts of the given case." It is not enough to "characteriz[e] an act or omission as a matter of judgment."
>
> The Westerman defendants have introduced no evidence of their deliberative process in reaching the decision not to file the translation. They have produced no research, memoranda, or other internal correspondence. . . . Nor have they submitted any affidavits about their consideration of such questions. Although the absence of evidence is not necessarily dispositive, it at least permits a factfinder to draw an inference that the Westerman defendants did not exercise reasonable care. That sort of reasonable inference makes summary judgment for the defendants inappropriate in this case.

Seed Co. v. Westerman, 832 F.3d 325 (D.C. Cir. 2016).

The duty of care includes a duty to attempt to settle if settlement is the most reasonable way to reach the client's goals. Mutuelles Unies v. Kroll & Linstrom, 957 F.2d 707 (9th Cir. 1992) (applying California law). Settlement may yield a better outcome than trial. Jonathan Glater, "Study Finds Settling Is Better Than Going to Trial," N.Y. Times, Aug. 7, 2008. When a lawyer does recommend a settlement, he must do the legal and factual research necessary to ensure its adequacy. Meyer v. Wagner, 709 N.E.2d 784 (Mass. 1999) (collecting cases).

Lesson: Save your research.

Breach of Fiduciary Duty or Malpractice?

Civil liability can also be based on violation of a duty the lawyer owes the client as a fiduciary. (See chapter 2B4.) For example, a fiduciary's duty of loyalty requires that he avoid conflicts of interest. (Ethics rules require the same.) As a matter of doctrinal purity, we should realize that only professionals can commit malpractice (as we use the word). A bus driver may be negligent, but we do not say she is guilty of malpractice. The same for a carpenter who builds a wobbly desk. We reserve the word for lawyers, doctors, architects, and accountants, among other professionals. Why this should be so—and the criteria for designation as a professional—is partly a product of history, interest group politics, and the pursuit of status.

The Restatement says that a lawyer's fiduciary status creates a duty to "comply with obligations concerning the client's confidences and property, avoid impermissible conflicting interests, deal honestly with the client, and not employ advantages arising from the client-lawyer relationship in a manner adverse to the client." Sections 16(3) and 49.

Malpractice and breach of fiduciary duty are not hermetically distinct categories in practice. Courts and lawyers often use the former label to subsume any act that would fall within the latter one. Weil, Gotshal & Manges, LLP v. Fashion Boutique of Short Hills, 780 N.Y.S.2d 593 (1st Dept. 2004) (malpractice charge encompasses allegations of fiduciary breach). Complaints against lawyers may cite both theories to cover all bases. Because state law defines fiduciary duty and malpractice claims, if you find yourself prosecuting or defending either one, you need to check the definitions in the jurisdiction whose law applies. The next case, while factually unusual, highlights the difference between the two.

TANTE v. HERRING
264 Ga. 694, 453 S.E.2d 686 (1994)

HUNT, CHIEF JUSTICE . . .

The Herrings retained Tante to pursue a claim for social security disability benefits for Mrs. Herring before the Social Security Administration. During his representation of Mrs. Herring, Tante appeared with her at a hearing before an administrative law judge and wrote a letter brief on her behalf. Thereafter, the administrative law judge issued a favorable award to Mrs. Herring. Tante's subsequent request for attorney fees for his work in representing Mrs. Herring, which request had been approved by both the Herrings, was approved by the administrative law judge.

The issues underlying this appeal involve the Herrings' action against Tante for legal malpractice, breach of fiduciary duty and breach of contract, all pertaining to Tante's adulterous relationship with Mrs. Herring during the period in which he was pursuing the disability claim on her behalf. The Herrings allege that Tante caused physical and mental harm to Mrs. Herring by taking advantage of confidential information regarding her emotional and mental condition to convince her to have an affair with him. The Herrings also allege Tante violated rules and standards of the State Bar of Georgia, violated his fiduciary duty, and breached his contract with the Herrings. . . .

There is no evidence that Tante's conduct of which the Herrings complain had any effect on his performance of legal services under his agreement with the Herrings. Indeed, Tante obtained for Mrs. Herring precisely the results for which he was retained, the recovery of social security disability benefits. . . .

However . . . the Herrings have a claim against Tante for damages for breach of fiduciary duty. That claim is not one for professional malpractice based on negligence involving Tante's performance of legal services, and, therefore, no expert affidavit is required in support of it. The fiduciary duty in this context arises from the attorney-client relationship. Tante was a fiduciary with regard to the confidential information provided him by his client just as he would have been a fiduciary with regard to money or other property entrusted to him by a client. Thus, the Herrings' claim is based on Tante's alleged misuse, to his own advantage, of confidential information in medical and psychological reports concerning Mrs. Herring obtained in and solely because of Tante's representation of her. Tante did not controvert the allegations that he took advantage of information contained in Mrs. Herring's confidential medical and psychological reports about her impaired emotional and mental condition, that Tante took advantage of that condition, convincing her to have an affair with him, resulting in physical and mental harm to the Herrings. The Court of Appeals correctly noted that, as a fiduciary with regard to information shared with him by his client, Tante owed his client the utmost good faith and loyalty. By using information available to him solely because of the attorney client relationship to his advantage and to the Herrings' disadvantage, he breached that fiduciary duty. Accordingly, the Herrings may pursue their claim for damages resulting from that breach.[7]

As described by the lower court, Mrs. Herring's unrebutted affidavit stated "that Tante received her psychological evaluations which stated she had organic brain damage, was depressed and anxious with feelings of insecurity, inadequacy, and inferiority, and suffered from impairment of judgment and difficulty with interpersonal relationships . . . that Tante was given medical reports showing she had a severe decrease in her desire for sex [and] that shortly after their first meeting, Tante advised her that she would be less depressed and would feel better if she would enter into a sexual relationship with him." Tante v. Herring, 439 S.E.2d 5 (Ga. Ct. App. 1993).

---

7. [Either plaintiff] also may have a claim against Tante for some other tort, e.g., assault or battery, intentional infliction of emotional distress, or negligent transmission of an infectious disease (based on the Herrings' allegation that Tante infected Mrs. Herring with venereal disease which she then unknowingly transmitted to Mr. Herring).

For the same conduct, Tante was suspended for 18 months. In re Tante, 453 S.E.2d 688 (Ga. 1994). See part 4D5c below and Rule 1.8(j) on the risk of discipline when a lawyer begins a sexual relationship with a current client.

Lawyer-client intimate relationships almost always occur in divorce cases, when a client may be especially vulnerable to imposition and her lawyer is in a position to ask highly personal questions about her marriage. The power imbalance in attorney-client relationships, especially in divorce and criminal matters, may be compared with the one between a therapist or doctor and a patient, where the impropriety of a sexual relationship is indisputable.

2. Liability to Third Parties for Professional Negligence

Reggie retained Vincent Starcross to draft a will leaving his autographed first edition of *The Great Gatsby* to his dear friend Carmella. Reggie died two years later. Starcross neglected to include the bequest. Carmella does not get the book. She sues Starcross, who responds that he owed nonclient Carmella no duty.

Many courts have upheld professional liability to third parties on similar facts on the ground that the plaintiff was the intended beneficiary of the lawyer's services. These courts see the claim as an unremarkable application of the third-party beneficiary doctrine in the law of contracts, albeit as applied to the work of a lawyer. Blair v. Ing, 21 P.3d 452 (Haw. 2001) (recognizing recovery under negligence or third-party beneficiary theories and citing numerous cases); Thorsen v. Richmond S.P.C.A., 786 S.E.2d 453 (Va. 2016). A "handful" of jurisdictions reject liability to a disappointed legatee, according to Estate of Schneider v. Finmann, 933 N.E.2d 718 (N.Y. 2010).

Nor is liability limited to will cases. In In re Estate of Powell, 12 N.E.3d 14 (Ill. 2014), the court held that a minor had a claim against lawyers hired by the personal representative of his father's estate. The lawyers had failed to seek a guardian to protect the minor's share of a wrongful death settlement. Instead, they gave his share to his mother, who spent most of it.

> Our starting point is the traditional, general rule that an attorney is liable only to his client, not to third persons. However, if a nonclient is an intended third-party beneficiary of the relationship between the client and the attorney, the attorney's duty to the client may extend to the nonclient as well. The key consideration is whether the attorney is acting at the direction of or on behalf of the client to benefit or influence a third party. We concluded in [precedent] that "for a nonclient to succeed in a negligence action against an attorney, he must prove that the primary purpose and intent of the attorney-client relationship itself was to benefit or influence the third party." This is referred to as the "intent to directly benefit" test.

Courts that resist creating client-like duties to third parties often cite the danger to the lawyer-client relationship if the lawyer must also protect the interests of someone else, someone whose interests may not be identical to the client's interests. Baker v. Wood, Ris & Hames, 364 P.3d 872 (Colo. 2016). In *Estate of Schneider*, supra, the New York Court of Appeals said giving a will beneficiary the right to sue the decedent's lawyer "would produce undesirable results—uncertainty and limitless liability." Why is that? The liability is neither uncertain nor limitless. It is solely to the intended beneficiary for the amount of a bequest lost because of a lawyer's negligence in following a client's instructions. And the risk of conflicting duties is nil. Both client and beneficiary want the same thing, but unfortunately the client is no longer alive to complain.

3. Vicarious Liability

Law partners, like other partners, are responsible for each other's professional failures within the scope of the partnership. Kansallis Fin. v. Fern, 659 N.E.2d 731 (Mass. 1996) (vicarious liability imposed if law firm partner acted at least in part to benefit the partnership or if partner "has apparent authority to do the act" alleged).

Does this sound scary? Many lawyers think so. Especially when firms have many offices, nationally and globally, a partner in one city may not like the idea of being vicariously liable for the misdeeds of a partner half the world away, over whom she has no practical control and whom she may never have met. Large settlements against big law firms that are accused of aiding a client's financial shenanigans prompted lawyer-inspired legislation permitting firms to practice as limited liability partnerships (LLPs or, if you prefer, L.L.P.s). These work like ordinary partnerships except that partners are personally liable only for their own conduct and possibly those of lawyers they supervise. The partnership, *as an entity*, remains liable for the actionable conduct of its lawyers. The advantage of a limited liability partnership is that in the event of catastrophe, after depletion of insurance and the firm's own assets (which includes future income), only the personal assets of the responsible lawyers will be at risk.

B. PROVING LAWYER LIABILITY

1. Use of Ethics Rules and Expert Testimony

A former client, whether suing in tort or contract, must prove that the defendant lawyer either violated a duty of care or breached a fiduciary or other duty. How will she do that? As in actions against other professionals, very often the plaintiff will call another lawyer as an expert witness. If the claim is that the lawyer did not perform competently (even if well-meaning), the expert will be someone familiar with the area of practice. She will be prepared to say that the defendant failed to exercise the reasonable degree of care, skill, and judgment that lawyers in the jurisdiction exercise in that area of practice. And she will explain exactly what the defendant failed to do or did wrong. This is what Kenneth Green did as an expert in *Togstad.*

On the other hand, some defaults are so obviously careless or wrong that even a lay juror can say so. That is true when a lawyer fails to communicate a settlement offer. Rizzo v. Haines, 555 A.2d 58 (Pa. 1989). In Olfe v. Gordon, chapter 2C2, no expert was needed where lawyers negotiated for a second mortgage, not the first mortgage the client wanted, and did not inform the client. And in Wagenmann v. Adams, 829 F.2d 196 (1st Cir. 1987), a lawyer did virtually nothing to secure the release of a client after his arrest. The court held that the lawyer "committed malpractice 'so gross or obvious' that expert testimony was not required to prove it."

A malpractice plaintiff might also (or instead) wish to introduce evidence of the jurisdiction's ethics rules (and expert testimony to explain the meaning of those rules) where the plaintiff claims that the lawyer's conduct violated rules meant to protect her.

SMITH v. HAYNSWORTH, MARION, MCKAY & GEURARD
322 S.C. 433, 472 S.E.2d 612 (1996)

WALLER, JUSTICE . . .

This case arises out of respondent, Haynsworth, Marion, McKay & Geurard's (Haynsworth) representation of appellants, Smith and Murray, in a real estate development scheme. Smith and Murray contracted with a developer, Bill Bashor, to purchase lots on Wild Dunes. Bashor planned to develop the lots, then sell them for a profit. Two of the investors in the scheme were partners in the Haynsworth firm. Haynsworth represented Bashor in his acquisition and sale of the lots, as well as in various other legal matters. Haynsworth also represented Smith and Murray in the transaction, with Bashor paying their attorney's fees.

The development scheme fell through and the lots were ultimately foreclosed by the bank. Smith and Murray sued Haynsworth for malpractice. The jury returned a verdict for respondents. . . .

Respondents moved to exclude the testimony of appellant's expert, Professor Gregory Adams, contending his testimony concerning the Rules of Professional Conduct (RPC) . . . was inadmissible, and claiming that Adams was not qualified to give an expert opinion as he was neither a real estate lawyer nor licensed to practice law in South Carolina. The trial court agreed and excluded Professor Adams' testimony. This was error.

A plaintiff in a legal malpractice action must generally establish the standard of care by expert testimony. The parameters of such testimony have, however, been the subject of much debate.

The preamble to the RPC states that "violation of a Rule should not give rise to a cause of action nor should it create any presumption that a legal duty has been breached." The RPC are silent, however, as to whether or not they are relevant in assessing the duty of care, or whether an expert may base his opinions in reliance thereon.* Courts in other jurisdictions are divided.

A majority of courts permit discussion of such a violation at trial as some evidence of the common law duty of care.[4] These courts generally rule that the expert must address his or her testimony to the breach of a legal duty of care and not simply to breach of [a] disciplinary rule. Other Courts have held that ethical standards conclusively establish the duty of care and that any violation is negligence *per se.* A minority find that violation of an ethical rule establishes a rebuttable presumption of legal malpractice. And, finally, a few courts hold that ethical standards are inadmissible in a legal malpractice action.

We concur with the majority of jurisdictions and hold that, in appropriate cases, the RPC may be relevant and admissible in assessing the legal duty of an attorney in a malpractice action. However, we adopt the view taken by the Supreme Court of Georgia in Allen v. Lefkoff, Duncan, Grimes & Dermer, 453 S.E.2d 719 (Ga. 1995), as follows:

> This is not to say, however, that all of the Bar Rules would necessarily be relevant in every legal malpractice action. In order to relate to the standard of care in a particular case, we hold that a Bar Rule must be intended to protect a person in the plaintiff's position or be addressed to the particular harm. . . .

Further, the fact that Adams is not licensed to practice law in this state does not disqualify him as an expert. Likewise, the fact that Adams is not a real estate lawyer does not prohibit his testimony concerning those ethical obligations which are relevant to appellants' claims.

Accordingly, in light of our holding the matter must be reversed and remanded for a new trial. . . .

In 2002, paragraph [20] of the Scope, cited in *Smith,* was amended to make clear what *Smith* held. The final sentence of the paragraph now says that "since the Rules do establish standards of conduct by lawyers, a lawyer's violation of a Rule may be evidence of a breach of the applicable standard of conduct." This is what most courts, as in *Smith,* had held anyway although some courts reject any use of the rules to prove civil liability. Cases are collected in Stender v. Blessum, 897 N.W.2d 491 (Iowa 2017) (following the majority view). The claim itself, however, must be based on a legal duty, not the Rules.

---

* This is a reference to paragraph [20] of the Scope as it then read. —ED.

4. The theory behind this view is that, since the ethical rules set the minimum standard of competency to be displayed by all attorneys, a violation thereof may be considered as evidence of a breach of the standard of care. Other courts admit this evidence in an analogous manner of admitting statutes, ordinances, or practice codes in defining the duty of care.

Because the *Smith* court's focus was whether the proffered testimony was properly excluded, it did not describe the plaintiffs' theories of liability. The facts suggest at least two conflicts. See if you can identify them. One of them might also have harmed Bashor, the other client.

Fee Forfeiture Due to Rule Violations

The next case is not a traditional malpractice case, but as in *Smith*, the court looks to conflict rules to guide its decision. However, unlike in *Smith*, the question before the court was not whether the law firm was liable for damages. Instead, it was whether the firm's violation of conflict rules forfeited its right to a fee from the recovery it achieved for a class. The alleged conflict is not as clear as it was in *Smith*. But once you see it, it should become—and for class action lawyers should have been—obvious.

RODRIGUEZ v. DISNER
688 F.3d 645 (9th Cir. 2012)

IKUTA, CIRCUIT JUDGE:

[A firm that later merged into McGuireWoods (hereafter McGuireWoods) brought an antitrust class action against West Publishing. The named class members entered "incentive agreements" with McGuireWoods under which each would receive a payment, the amount of which would depend on the amount of the class recovery. A recovery of $10 million or more would yield $75,000, the maximum. A court-approved settlement then created a common fund of $49 million, 25 percent of which was set aside for counsel fees, in an amount to be determined by the court. Other class members then objected to any fee at all on the ground that McGuireWoods had a conflict of interest arising out of the incentive agreements. The district court awarded fees of $7 million but in *Rodriguez I* the Ninth Circuit reversed, instructing the district court to reconsider the fees in light of the alleged conflict. On remand, the district court awarded no fees and the law firm appealed, leading to the following decision (*Rodriguez II*). The governing conflict rule at the time was California Rule 3-310(C), the counterpart to Rule 1.7(a)(2). It provides that a lawyer "shall not, without the informed written consent of each client, [a]ccept representation of more than one client in a matter in which the interests of the clients potentially conflict."]

III

A . . .

In determining what fees are reasonable, a district court may consider a lawyer's misconduct, which affects the value of the lawyer's services. . . .

Our sister circuits are in accord. . . .

Although the application of the common fund doctrine is a matter of federal courts' equitable powers, we have frequently looked to state law for guidance in determining when an ethical violation affects an attorney's entitlement to fees. California courts have affirmed a trial court's decision to deny fees to attorneys laboring under an actual conflict of interest, such as where an attorney represented two entities with adverse interests entering a business deal without informed consent, a law firm represented both wife and husband in marital dissolution proceedings, and an attorney undertook to represent a client in a proxy fight with a corporation for which the attorney had been general counsel. By contrast, where the ethical violation is less severe, for example where the attorney represented clients with only a potential conflict of interest, California courts have affirmed decisions to award attorneys some fees depending on the equities. In [precedent], the state court held that a trial court may consider " 'the gravity and timing of the violation, its willfulness, its effect on the value of the lawyer's work for the client, any other threatened or actual harm to the client, and the adequacy of other remedies' " in determining whether and to what extent fee forfeiture is appropriate. . . .

We apply these equitable principles even more assiduously in common fund class action cases, such as this one, because "the district court has a special duty to protect the interests of the class" and must "act with a jealous regard to the rights of those who are interested in the fund in determining what a proper fee award is." In serving this "fiduciary role for the class," the district court must consider whether class counsel has properly discharged its duty of loyalty to absent class members. As we noted in *Rodriguez I,* " '[t]he responsibility of class counsel to absent class members whose control over their attorneys is limited does not permit even the appearance of divided loyalties of counsel.' " This general principle has exceptions; we have acknowledged that "conflicts of interest among class members are not uncommon and arise for many different reasons," and a court may tolerate certain technical conflicts in order to permit attorneys who are familiar with the litigation to continue to represent the class. But a court may appropriately determine that a conflict of interest affects class counsel's entitlement to fees where the conflict was not one "that developed beyond the control or perception of class counsel," and where the conflict was never disclosed to the district court "so that it could take steps to protect the interests of absentee class members."

In sum, under long-standing equitable principles, a district court has broad discretion to deny fees to an attorney who commits an ethical violation. In making such a ruling, the district court may consider the extent of the misconduct, including its gravity, timing, willfulness, and effect on the various services performed by the lawyer, and other threatened or actual harm to the client. See Restatement (Third) of Law Governing Lawyers §37 (2000). The representation of clients with conflicting interests and without informed consent is a particularly egregious ethical violation that may be a proper basis for complete denial of fees. . . .

B

Applying these principles here, we first confirm the district court's conclusion that McGuireWoods committed an ethical violation. Indeed, McGuireWoods does not dispute that its representation of conflicting interests constituted an ethical violation. Nor could it. . . .

In *Rodriguez I* we indicated that the incentive agreements created an actual conflict of interest between the named members and class counsel, on the one hand, and the other members of the class, on the other. We explained that the incentive agreements "put class counsel and the contracting class representatives into a conflict position from day one" because "[b]y tying their compensation—in advance—to a sliding scale based on the amount recovered, the incentive agreements disjoined the contingency financial interests of the contracting representatives from the class." This meant that "once the threshold cash settlement was met, the agreements created a disincentive to go to trial; going to trial would put their $75,000 at risk in return for only a marginal individual gain even if the verdict were significantly greater than the settlement." We then noted that under California law, "[s]imultaneous representation of clients with conflicting interests (and without written informed consent) is an automatic ethics violation in California and grounds for disqualification" and faulted the district court for not considering "the effect on the award of attorney's fees of the conflict of interest that resulted from the incentive agreements."

[Denial of all counsel fees was affirmed.]

Fee Forfeiture (and Disgorgement)

Exactly what was the conflict—and between or among whom—that led to the denial of all fees despite a significant victory? Is there any basis to conclude that the conflict harmed the class? No. But fee forfeiture does not depend on proof of harm. Or, more precisely, the harm is the fiduciary duty breach itself.

Forfeiture occurs when the lawyer loses the right to collect the fee. Disgorgement occurs when the lawyer has to return fees. Because both are available where the lawyer violated an ethical duty to the client, even absent any basis for civil liability or other harm, forfeiture and disgorgement can be powerful remedies. Parkinson v. Bevis, 448 P.3d 1027 (Idaho 2019) (disgorgement recognized, despite absence of claim for damages, where lawyer allegedly breached fiduciary duty by disclosing client confidences). Claims for forfeiture or disgorgement are often added to a former client's civil complaint, for good reason. The amounts may be large. And the claim provides leverage in settlement talks, especially if the claim is for disgorgement.

While the law firm may not want to forego a fee, human nature is such that it may find the prospect of returning money especially unattractive.

Rodriguez says that the "appropriate" amount of any forfeiture depends on multiple factors. While older cases do not recognize partial forfeiture, see In re Clarke's Estate, 188 N.E.2d 128 (N.Y. 1962) (denying all compensation, even absent harm, because "the vice is placing oneself in a position where self interest presents a second master to serve"), later cases do. Bertelsen v. Harris, 537 F.3d 1047 (9th Cir. 2008) (affirming as within his discretion a district judge's refusal to order any fee disgorgement where even assuming multiple ethical violations and breach of fiduciary duty, the fee was reasonable for the results achieved) (2-1 decision); Burrow v. Arce, 997 S.W.2d 229 (Tex. 1999) (establishing criteria for determining the amount, if any, of appropriate forfeiture). Restatement §37, on which *Rodriguez* and *Burrow* rely, also opts for calibration but recognizes the possibility of total forfeiture in cases of "clear and serious violation of duty to a client."

Some jurisdictions do not calibrate even today. New York is apparently among them. "New York courts have consistently held that 'an attorney who engages in misconduct by violating the Disciplinary Rules is not entitled to legal fees for any services rendered.'" Chen v. Chen Qualified Settlement Fund, 552 F.3d 218 (2d Cir. 2009) (in applying for fees in connection with the settlement of an infant's medical malpractice claim lawyer was denied all fees because he knowingly requested $20,000 more than the $388,000 fee statutorily allowed). See also Phansalkar v. Andersen Weinroth & Co., 344 F.3d 184 (2d Cir. 2003), which, while focusing on New York law, contains an extensive discussion of the "faithless servant doctrine" and the items subject to forfeiture or disgorgement under it.

2. Causation and Defenses

Traditionally, a tort or contract plaintiff must prove that the tort or breach caused damages and their amount. Where a lawyer's negligence occurs in connection with litigation, the plaintiff must ordinarily prove (in what is called the "outer" case) that "but for" the lawyer's negligence, she would have won or done better in the underlying (or "inner") case. The Togstads proved that they would have won their medical malpractice case and the amount but for Miller's malpractice. In the problem at the start of this chapter, should Sally have to prove that but for Adam Rosini's alleged malpractice, she would have won half the incremental value of Ari's inheritance in the state supreme court? If so, she loses. Looking back, we know that the state supreme court would have ruled against her. So Sally must find another way to prove that Rosini's alleged negligence caused damages. Imagine that you are Sally's lawyer. What would you argue?

Where the negligence arises in a transactional matter, as in Simpson v. James (chapter 5B3) and Viner v. Sweet, two questions arise: Is "but for" still the right test for causation, or should the burden of proof be less onerous, as the Viners argued? In *Viner*, the lower court's causation charge is described in note 2. Whatever the burden of proof, how does a lawyer meet it in transactional matters, which, unlike litigations, have no clear winners and losers?

VINER v. SWEET

30 Cal. 4th 1232, 70 P.3d 1046 (Cal. 2003)

KENNARD, J.

In a client's action against an attorney for legal malpractice, the client must prove, among other things, that the attorney's negligent acts or omissions caused the client to suffer some financial harm or loss. When the alleged malpractice occurred in the performance of transactional work (giving advice or preparing documents for a business transaction), must the client prove this causation element according to the "but for" test, meaning that the harm or loss would not have occurred without the attorney's malpractice? The answer is yes.

I

In 1984, plaintiffs Michael Viner and his wife, Deborah Raffin Viner, founded Dove Audio, Inc. (Dove). The company produced audio versions of books read by the authors or by celebrities, and it did television and movie projects.

In 1994, Dove went public by issuing stock at $10 a share. In 1995, the Viners and Dove entered into long-term employment contracts guaranteeing the Viners, among other things, a certain level of salaries, and containing indemnification provisions favorable to the Viners. The Viners received a large share of Dove's common stock and all of its preferred cumulative dividend series "A" stock. . . .

[In 1997, the Viners, represented by Charles Sweet of Williams & Connolly, agreed to sell their business to Media Equities International (MEI). Following the sale, the Viners disputed certain provisions of the agreement and these could not be resolved in arbitration.]

On June 3, 1998, the Viners brought a malpractice action against Attorney Sweet and the law firm of Williams & Connolly. [The Viners described seven ways in which Sweet's alleged negligence failed to protect them. The jury awarded the Viners $13,291,532 in damages. The Court of Appeal reduced the award to $8,085,732.]

We granted defendants' petition for review, and thereafter limited the issues to whether the plaintiff in a transactional legal malpractice action must prove that a more favorable result would have been obtained *but for* the alleged negligence.[2]

II

Defendants contend that in a transactional malpractice action, the plaintiff must show that *but for* the alleged malpractice, a more favorable result would have been obtained. Thus, defendants argue, the Viners had to show that without defendants' negligence (1) they would have had a more advantageous agreement (the "better deal" scenario), or (2) they would not have entered into the transaction with MEI and therefore would have been better off (the "no deal" scenario). . . .

The Court of Appeal here held that a plaintiff suing an attorney for transactional malpractice need not show that the harm would not have occurred in the absence of the attorney's negligence. We disagree. We see nothing distinctive about transactional malpractice that would justify a relaxation of, or departure from, the well-established requirement in negligence cases that the plaintiff establish causation by showing either (1) *but for* the negligence, the harm would not have occurred, or (2) the negligence was a concurrent independent cause of the harm. . . .

In a litigation malpractice action, the plaintiff must establish that *but for* the alleged negligence of the defendant attorney, the plaintiff would have obtained a more favorable judgment or settlement in the action in which the malpractice allegedly occurred. The purpose of this requirement, which has been in use for more than 120 years, is to safeguard against speculative and conjectural claims. It serves the essential purpose of ensuring that damages awarded for the attorney's malpractice actually have been caused by the malpractice.

The Court of Appeal here attempted to distinguish litigation malpractice from transactional malpractice in order to justify a relaxation of the "but for" test of causation in transactional malpractice cases. One of the distinguishing features, according to the court, was that in litigation a gain for one side necessarily entails a corresponding loss for the other, whereas in transactional representation a gain for one side does not necessarily result in a loss for the other. We question both the accuracy and the relevance of this generalization. In litigation, as in transactional work, a gain for one side does not necessarily result in a loss for the other side. Litigation may involve multiple claims and issues arising from complaints and cross-complaints, and parties in such litigation may prevail on some issues and not others, so that

---

2. The trial court refused defendants' requested instruction on "but for" causation. The court did instruct the jury that a cause of an injury "is something that is a substantial factor in bringing about" the harm. Because the Court of Appeal addressed this case as presenting the "pure question of law" of whether the legal requirement of showing "but for" causation applies at all to transactional malpractice cases, and because we limited our review to that issue, we have not framed our discussion in terms of instructional error.

in the end there is no clear winner or loser and no exact correlation between one side's gains and the other side's losses. In addition, an attorney's representation of a client often combines litigation and transactional work, as when the attorney effects a settlement of pending litigation. The "but for" test of causation applies to a claim of legal malpractice in the settlement of litigation, even though the settlement is itself a form of business transaction.

Nor do we agree with the Court of Appeal that litigation is inherently or necessarily less complex than transactional work. Some litigation, such as many lawsuits involving car accidents, is relatively uncomplicated, but so too is much transactional work, such as the negotiation of a simple lease or a purchase and sale agreement. But some litigation, such as a beneficiary's action against a trustee challenging the trustee's management of trust property over a period of decades, is as complex as most transactional work.

It is true, as the Court of Appeal pointed out, that litigation generally involves an examination of past events whereas transactional work involves anticipating and guiding the course of future events. But this distinction makes little difference for purposes of selecting an appropriate test of causation. Determining causation always requires evaluation of hypothetical situations concerning what might have happened, but did not. In both litigation and transactional malpractice cases, the crucial causation inquiry is *what would have happened* if the defendant attorney had not been negligent. This is so because the very idea of causation necessarily involves comparing historical events to a hypothetical alternative.

The Viners also contend that the "but for" test of causation should not apply to transactional malpractice cases because it is too difficult to obtain the evidence needed to satisfy this standard of proof. In particular, they argue that proving causation under the "but for" test would require them to obtain the testimony of the other parties to the transaction, who have since become their adversaries, to the effect that they would have given the Viners more favorable terms had the Viners' attorneys not performed negligently. Not so. In transactional malpractice cases, as in other cases, the plaintiff may use circumstantial evidence to satisfy his or her burden. An express concession by the other parties to the negotiation that they would have accepted other or additional terms is not necessary. And the plaintiff need not prove causation with absolute certainty. Rather, the plaintiff need only " 'introduce evidence which affords a reasonable basis for the conclusion that it is more likely than not that the conduct of the defendant was a cause in fact of the result.' " In any event, difficulties of proof cannot justify imposing liability for injuries that the attorney could not have prevented by performing according to the required standard of care. . . .

For the reasons given above, we conclude that, just as in litigation malpractice actions, a plaintiff in a transactional malpractice action must show that *but for* the alleged malpractice, it is more likely than not that the plaintiff would have obtained a more favorable result. . . .

On remand, the lower court concluded that on five of their seven claims the Viners' trial evidence failed to prove "but for" causation as a matter of law. A dissent said the Viners were entitled to a new trial so a jury could make this determination as a matter of fact and, in addition, to give the Viners a chance to introduce additional evidence to satisfy the court's new causation requirement. Viner v. Sweet, 12 Cal. Rptr. 3d 533 (Ct. App. 2004).

The "But For" Test in Malpractice and Fiduciary Duty Claims: Additional Issues

In Transactional Matters.   Just how might a lawyer go about proving circumstantially that absent the defendant lawyer's negligence or breach of fiduciary duty, the former client would have gotten better contract terms or would have been better off rejecting the deal it did get? (The *Viner* court calls these the "better deal" and the "no deal" scenarios.) Imagine that you were the Viners' lawyer on remand (assuming that they were allowed a second chance, which they were not). What evidence would you introduce?

Here's a pared-down example of the challenge that would have faced the Viners. Say Max represented Abel in negotiating the sale of a business to Clara. Abel asked Max to negotiate for a clause giving him three percent of the gross receipts of the business above a certain threshold in the first year after the sale. Max forgot to do so and never disclosed the absence of the provision to Abel. Abel has hired you to sue Max. Assume negligence. You must prove the dollar value of the omitted term. Easy. It's three percent of an identifiable sum. But how would you go about proving that Clara would have agreed to it? If Max had requested the term, Clara would either have rejected it or asked for value in return. Negotiation is give and take. *Viner* says you can prove the "better deal" option circumstantially, but how? Re-creating the dynamics of a negotiation will be difficult at best and maybe impossible.

You might instead choose to pursue the "no deal" option. Abel could testify that had he known that the agreement did not give him three percent of gross sales, he would have walked away. But that strategy can work only if he would have been better off with no deal than with the deal he got. Similarly, the Viners (if allowed on remand) might have tried to satisfy the "but for" test by trying to prove that they would have walked away better off with no deal than the one they got. What would that proof look like?

In Litigation.   As *Viner* recognizes, the "but for" test is relatively straightforward where malpractice occurs in litigation. But the test has also been criticized there. First, when the legal malpractice (or outer) case actually goes to trial, substantial time will have elapsed since the original event, making proof of the inner case (the one the defendant lawyer mishandled) more difficult. Second, Rule 1.6(b)(5) will permit the former lawyer to use the plaintiff's confidential (including privileged) information in defense, an advantage the original opponent would not have had. Third, a malpractice plaintiff who was a plaintiff in the inner case will have to prove that she would have been able to collect a favorable money judgment in that case. Otherwise, she will have no damages.

To make things easier, a malpractice plaintiff may want to prove *not* that she would have won or done better at trial of the inner case but that she would have been able to settle it on more favorable terms absent her lawyer's negligence. Consider a personal injury plaintiff who lost her day in court because her lawyer filed too late. The malpractice is clear. The only issue is causation and damages. Rather than prove what she would have recovered at the trial that never was, which may now be harder to do, she may instead wish to show that the inner case would have settled. She will call an expert witness to testify that 96 percent of personal injury cases in the jurisdiction (at least of her type) do settle and to tell the jury the range of settlements for persons in her demographic who have injuries like hers. May she do that?

A few courts have said she may. Labair v. Carey, 383 P.3d 226 (Mont. 2016) ("The Labairs must prove two elements to recover for the lost opportunity to settle with Dr. Baumgartner: (1) that they more probably than not would have recovered a settlement with Dr. Baumgartner, and (2) the likely range of value of the lost settlement."). The Restatement of Law Governing Lawyers, §53 comment *b*, says the same. Garcia v. Kozlov, Seaton, Romanini & Brooks, P.C., 845 A.2d 602 (N.J. 2004), agrees. It has a good discussion of the "but for" burden in litigation malpractice cases and possible mitigating devices.

In Fiduciary Duty Cases. Courts also use the "but for" test when a lawyer is charged with breach of fiduciary duty. Garrett v. Bryan Cave LLP, 211 F.3d 1278 (10th Cir. 2000) (applying Oklahoma and Missouri law). But some courts relax that burden in certain fiduciary duty cases. These courts apply a less demanding "substantial factor" test of causation when the former client seeks *not* the value of the lost claim—i.e., what she would have won from the opponent—but the fiduciary's profits from the breach. American Federal Group v. Rothenberg, 136 F.3d 897 (2d Cir. 1998), identified two lines of fiduciary duty cases in New York. One imposed the traditional causation requirement ("but for"), and the other applied the "less stringent, 'substantial factor' causation requirement." The court reconciled these cases by reference to the remedy the plaintiff sought. Where the remedy is compensation for a loss (as in Simpson v. James, the catfish restaurant case in chapter 5B3), the stricter ("but for") causation rule applied, but when the remedy "being sought is a restitutionary one to prevent the fiduciary's unjust enrichment as measured by his ill-gotten gain," the "substantial factor" standard "may be more appropriate." See also Gibbs v. Breed, Abbott & Morgan, 710 N.Y.S.2d 578 (1st Dept. 2000) ("[T]he purpose of this type of action is not merely to *compensate* the plaintiff for wrongs committed . . . [but also] to *prevent* them, by removing from agents and trustees all inducement to attempt dealing for their own benefit in matters which they have undertaken for others, or to which their agency or trust relates."). In *Gibbs,* the lawyer defendants breached their fiduciary duty when they provided their new law firm with their former firm's "confidential firm data."

In Claims of Organizational Clients. When shareholders of a company, the company itself, or a bankruptcy trustee charge the company's outside lawyers (or accountants) with professional negligence in failing to prevent wrongdoing by corporate officers, the causation issue has an extra hurdle. The misbehaving corporate officers may have acted unlawfully *toward the company*, in which case the company was a victim, or they may have caused the company to act unlawfully *toward others*, in which case it was the (unwitting) wrongdoer because the company is vicariously liable for its officers' misconduct. Victim or vicarious wrongdoer. Does it matter?

Cenco, Inc. v. Seidman & Seidman, 686 F.2d 449 (7th Cir. 1982), said it does matter. The court wrote that "[f]raud on behalf of a corporation is not the same thing as fraud against it." When "top management" causes a company to defraud others, the company is a "participant" in, not a "victim" of, the fraud. As a result, the auditor defendants in that case had a complete defense in a class action shareholder derivative suit charging the auditors with negligence. This is called an "in pari delicto" defense. The company is deemed more culpable than the malpractice defendants because fraud is more blameworthy than negligence. So it can't complain. See also Eastern Trading Co. v. Refco, Inc., 229 F.3d 617 (7th Cir. 2000). Does calling the company a "participant" to the fraud presume, probably counterfactually, that shareholders know what management was up to? Or is the aim to encourage shareholder vigilance? *Cenco* says it is the second.

Other circuits have agreed and so too has the New York Court of Appeals in a 4-3 ruling, also arising from Refco's collapse. The defendants were outside lawyers, financial advisers, and accountants who allegedly either "assisted or [did] not detec[t], at all or soon enough," the "financial fraud" of Refco's management toward the company's creditors. The plaintiffs were the shareholders and the trustee of the now-bankrupt company. The court imputed management's creditor fraud to the company on whose behalf the plaintiffs were suing, thereby putting the company in pari delicto and defeating its recovery.

> Traditional agency principles play an important role in an in pari delicto analysis. Of particular importance is a fundamental principle that has informed the law of agency and corporations for centuries; namely, the acts of agents, and the knowledge they acquire while acting within the scope of their authority are presumptively imputed to their principals. Corporations are not natural persons. "[O]f necessity, [they] must act solely through the instrumentality of their officers or other duly authorized agents." A corporation must, therefore, be responsible for the acts of its authorized agents even if particular acts were unauthorized. "The risk of loss from the unauthorized acts of a dishonest agent falls on the principal that selected the agent." After all, the principal is generally better suited than a third party to control the agent's conduct, which

at least in part explains why the common law has traditionally placed the risk on the principal.

Agency law presumes imputation even where the agent acts less than admirably, exhibits poor business judgment, or commits fraud.

To avoid imputation, the court wrote, an agent "must have *totally abandoned* his principal's interests and be acting entirely for his own or another's purposes, not the corporation's. So long as the corporate wrongdoer's fraudulent conduct enables the business to survive . . . this test is not met." Plaintiffs argued that this rule sacrifices the interests of the company's innocent shareholders to the stakeholders (partners and shareholders) of the negligent professional firms (and let's focus on law firms) that allegedly assisted or failed to stop the fraud. The court countered: "[T]he equities are [not] so obvious. In particular, why should the interests of innocent stakeholders of corporate fraudsters trump those of innocent stakeholders of the outside professionals who are the defendants in these cases?" Of course, a law firm's stakeholders are the firm's own lawyers, not the investing public. But the court, quoting the First Circuit, explained that the broader public would be harmed because money judgments against outside professionals would inevitably be passed on to the public. Perhaps, but that would simply make a law firm less competitive as a result of having to pay for what we are assuming was its lawyers' negligence. The upshot is that innocent people will be harmed and the court said they should be the client's shareholders, not the law firm's lawyers. The New York case collects authorities including inconsistent decisions in New Jersey and Pennsylvania. Kirschner v. KPMG LLP, 938 N.E.2d 941 (N.Y. 2010).

Causation in Criminal Cases

We come now to a difficult question because the right answer requires us to balance public policy and traditional doctrine, cases disagree, and there are at least four options available to a jurisdiction.

Arenns v. Dobbins

Arenns is charged with two homicides. He is indigent, so the judge appoints Dobbins to represent him. Arenns (who knows a bit of law from prior incarcerations) urges Dobbins to move to dismiss the charges on speedy trial grounds, and Dobbins does so but loses. Arenns is then convicted in separate trials and sentenced to two concurrent life terms. Dobbins appeals both convictions, but makes the speedy trial argument in only one of them. It wins. But the other conviction is affirmed. Arenns gets a new lawyer and goes to a higher court, which refuses to consider the speedy trial claim on the affirmed conviction because it had not been raised below and is deemed waived. Arenns is in jail for life. He sues Dobbins for malpractice. It is stipulated that both charges should have been dismissed on speedy trial grounds and that Dobbins was negligent in omitting that ground in the second appeal. Now what? Is Dobbins liable? And for what? Arenns argues that Dobbins is liable because if Dobbins had acted competently, Arenns would be free.

Your options include:

1. Make no distinction between criminal and civil malpractice. Because Arenns can prove that but for Dobbins's negligence his conviction would have been reversed, Dobbins must compensate Arenns for his life in prison. "If this were a civil malpractice case," argues Arenns's lawyer, "and Dobbins had negligently failed to assert a defense that would have relieved Arenns of all liability, Dobbins would be responsible for the judgment against Arenns. This case should be no different."

2. Treat criminal case malpractice differently as a matter of policy. Insist that Arenns prove his factual innocence by a preponderance of the evidence as part of his malpractice case. In this view, his factual guilt, as determined by his conviction, not his lawyer's negligence, is the *legal* cause of his incarceration. "Arenns is locked up because of his crimes," Dobbins's lawyer argues. "Dobbins's negligence didn't put him in prison. Arenns wants Dobbins to pay for Arenns's crimes."

3. Require that Arenns have his conviction overturned on appeal or in a postconviction challenge before he can bring a malpractice case. This is sometimes called "exoneration." In this view, so long as Arenns remains *legally guilty*, he has no malpractice claim. "The guilty judgment is a legal impediment to the malpractice claim," Dobbins's lawyer argues.

4. Require that Arenns meet the hurdles in paragraph two *and* paragraph three. They are not the same. A person who is factually guilty—that is, he did it—may still be able to have a conviction overturned. And a person who is factually innocent may be unable to do so.

The issues here are intertwined with broader criminal justice policies. As you might imagine, state high courts disagree, with the majority choosing 2 or 3, a few choosing 4, and fewer choosing 1. If you were on your state high court and there were no state precedent, how would you rule?

It may be tempting to choose option 1. Most law students do initially. It seems the fairest on first look—but that's where policy intrudes. We would be making the defense lawyer "pay" for a (legally and presumed factually) guilty person's punishment and thereby easing the punishment to the extent of the damages awarded. Faced with this issue in Levine v. Kling, 123 F.3d 580 (7th Cir. 1997), Judge Posner wrote that the plaintiff was seeking damages "to compensate him for the loss of his liberty during the period of his rightful imprisonment." Is "rightful" the right word? Doesn't it beg the question?* He continued:

> Not only would this be a paradoxical result, depreciating and in some cases wholly offsetting the plaintiff's criminal punishment, but it would be contrary to fundamental principles of both tort and criminal law. Tort law provides damages only for harms to the plaintiff's legally protected interests and the liberty of a guilty criminal is not one of them. The guilty criminal may be able to obtain an acquittal if he is skillfully represented, but he has no *right* to that result (just as he has no right to have the jury nullify the law, though juries sometimes do that), and the law provides no relief if the "right" is denied him.

Posner's statement of the issue is characteristically concise, but is he correct? In Mashaney v. Board of Indigents' Defense Services, 355 P.3d 667 (Kan. 2015), the court quoted from and approved Judge Atcheson's contrary view in his dissent below:

> A criminal defendant successfully suing his or her lawyer for negligence based on a conviction and the resulting incarceration isn't profiting from his or her underlying crime. He or she is being compensated for a legal injury—a loss of liberty—directly resulting from the lawyer's malpractice in failing to obtain a favorable result for the client in the criminal prosecution. That's not profiting any more than a person injured in a motor vehicle collision 'profits' from a damage award for the harm he or she has suffered

Mashaney held that the client must first win exoneration (option 3) but need not prove actual innocence (option 2). For further discussion of these issues, see Barker v. Capotosto, 875 N.W.2d 157 (Iowa 2016) (collecting cases), and Adkins v. Dixon, 482 S.E.2d 797 (Va. 1997), on which Arenns v. Dobbins is based. But first address the problem in Arenns v. Dobbins. How will you rule?

C. LAWYER LIABILITY TO THIRD PERSONS

> Though we certainly do not suggest that a lawyer by rendering services becomes a partner in his client's misdeeds, membership in the legal profession is not a shield against liability for conduct in excess of professional right or duty.
> —Hartford Accident & Indemnity Co. v. Sullivan,
> (7th Cir. 1988)

Hartford Accident cites Wahlgren v. Bausch & Lomb Optical Co., 68 F.2d 660 (7th Cir. 1934) ("One may not use his license to practice law as a shield to

---

* According to the website the Grammarist, the phrase "begs the question" describes "a logical fallacy in which the writer or speaker assumes the statement under examination to be true. In other words, begging the question involves using a premise to support itself."

protect himself from the consequences of his participation in an unlawful or illegal conspiracy.")

In chapter 9B2, we saw various ways in which a party to a negotiation may have a claim against the opposing lawyer because of what that lawyer says or does. The legal labels vary: fraud, fraudulent concealment, constructive fraud, negligent misrepresentation. Jurisdictions differ in their recognition of one or more of these theories. Lawyers are ordinarily not liable to an opposing party for an error of law unless he or she represents that law in an opinion letter that invites reliance. Following are a few prominent theories for holding lawyers accountable to non-clients.

Negligent Misrepresentation

As with the *Greycas* case in chapter 9B2, non-clients may be able to sue for malpractice or for negligent misrepresentation of facts on which the non-client was invited to and did rely. Each claim depends on negligence.

Banco Popular North America v. Gandi, 876 A.2d 253 (N.J. 2005), explained when a lawyer will be liable for negligent misrepresentation (citing *Wahlgren*, supra):

> If the attorney's actions are intended to induce a specific non-client's reasonable reliance on his or her representations, then there is a relationship between the attorney and the third party. Contrariwise, if the attorney does absolutely nothing to induce reasonable reliance by a third party, there is no relationship to substitute for the privity requirement [in malpractice]. Indeed, in [precedent], we noted that "when courts relax the privity requirement, they typically limit a lawyer's duty to situations in which the lawyer intended or should have foreseen that the third party would rely on the lawyer's work." Put differently, the invitation to rely and reliance are the linchpins of attorney liability to third parties.

Consumer Protection Laws

The Fair Debt Collection Practices Act applies to a lawyer who "regularly," through litigation, tries to collect consumer debts. Heintz v. Jenkins, 514 U.S. 291 (1995). In Garrett v. Derbes, 110 F.3d 317 (5th Cir. 1997), the defendant was hired by a local phone company to collect delinquent telephone bills. In nine months, he mailed about 639 demand letters to individual customers of the company. Although this work accounted for only one-half of one percent of Derbes's entire law practice, the court held that, given the number of demand letters sent, Derbes "regularly" attempted to collect consumer debts within the meaning of the Act and was subject to it.

As it happens, consumer protection laws protect clients, too. In Crowe v. Tull, 126 P.3d 196 (Colo. 2006), a former client claimed that the defendant law firm used extensive advertising, primarily on television, portraying the firm "as highly skilled at negotiating with insurance companies and promised the firm would obtain full value for its clients' personal injury claims." In fact, the plaintiff alleged, the firm was nothing more than a settlement "mill" that "relies for its profitability on quick settlements of cases with minimal expenditure of effort." The plaintiff claimed that the firm mishandled his case. The court held that attorneys are liable under the consumer protection law, not only for deceptive advertising but also for the manner in which they represented the plaintiff.

Criminal Law

A lawyer who performs otherwise mundane legal services for a client may be guilty of conspiracy or other crimes in connection with the client's misconduct if the lawyer knows that the services advance the client's criminal goals. In United States v. Ross, 190 F.3d 446 (6th Cir. 1999), attorney Mark Ross was found guilty of drug and money-laundering conspiracies. In part, the evidence against him showed that he had assisted his clients in transferring real property and in posting a cash bond, unremarkable legal tasks. But both acts advanced the client's crimes and the court found "ample evidence to support a finding that [Ross] knew of and joined in both conspiracies by engaging in money laundering in connection with the [real] property" and "from which the jury could find that Mark Ross knew that drug proceeds would be used to post the bond for [his client] with the hope that he would not cooperate with the government."

The legal profession has become increasingly aware of the danger that a client may try to use a lawyer's (one hopes unwitting) help to launder money. For an introduction to the warning signs and a lawyer's due diligence or "gatekeeper" responsibilities to prevent the activity, go to americanbar.org and search for the paper "Voluntary Good Practices Guidance for Lawyers to Detect and Combat Money Laundering and Terrorist Financing." ABA Opinion 491 (2020) addressing Rule 1.2(d) in general and money laundering in particular concludes that "a lawyer who has knowledge of facts that create a high probability that a client is seeking the lawyer's services in a transaction to further criminal or fraudulent activity has a duty to inquire further to avoid assisting that activity under Rule 1.2(d). Failure to make a reasonable inquiry is willful blindness punishable under the actual knowledge standard of the Rule."

Violation of Escrow Agreements

When a lawyer agrees to act as an escrow agent—to hold property under an agreement between two or more parties, one of whom is usually the lawyer's client—she may assume certain obligations to the parties to the agreement that are superior to the responsibilities she owes her client. If she violates those obligations, she may be liable to the other party to the escrow agreement even if the violation benefited her client.

In Wasmann v. Seidenberg, 248 Cal. Rptr. 744 (Ct. App. 1988), Seidenberg had represented a wife in negotiating a settlement agreement. The lawyer for Wasmann, the husband, sent Seidenberg a final draft of the agreement with a deed conveying realty from the husband to the wife. The agreement contemplated that in return the wife would pay Wasmann $70,000 for his share of the value of the realty. Wasmann's lawyer instructed Seidenberg that he (Seidenberg) could record the deed "only upon obtaining" the money for Wasmann. Without getting the money, Seidenberg allowed the wife to get the deed. She recorded it. Wasmann then sued the wife and Seidenberg. The court held that Seidenberg owed Wasmann "no professional duty," but that "his acceptance of [the] deed would give rise to a duty of care. The wellspring of this duty is the fiduciary role of an escrow holder."

D. DISCIPLINE

1. Why Do Lawyers Violate the Rules?

After investing much time and money to get a J.D. and a law license, why do some lawyers engage in conduct that risks career-ending discipline and civil liability? Circumstances differ so there is no one reason. In any event, therapists, not lawyers or law professors, will be better able to answer this question for any particular lawyer. My experience reading thousands of discipline cases suggests eight answers that, while not explaining every case, may help explain many.

  a. *Venality.* A lawyer knows the conduct is wrong and can lead to professional sanctions, even disbarment, but he figures (or hopes) he can get away with it. Often, the temptation is money, often a lot of money. Lawyers who steal from their escrow account or don't pay or underpay taxes are in this category. See part D5a.
  b. *Bad mentoring.* A lawyer, usually young, copies the bad behavior of his seniors. In re Jordan Schiff in part D5f is an example.
  c. *Demanding bosses or clients.* A lawyer is unable to resist the demands of a (perhaps important) client or a boss. In re Austern, 524 A.2d 680 (D.C. 1987), offers an example. The lawyer allowed a client to close a deal with a check for which the lawyer knew there were insufficient funds on deposit. Donald Trump's lawyer Michael Cohen pled guilty to, among other crimes, making illegal campaign contributions. Cohen said he did this "at the direction of the candidate" to buy the silence of both a model and a pornographic film actress about alleged affairs with Trump. (While president, Trump could not be prosecuted.)
  d. *Rationalization.* The lawyer convinces herself that the conduct is allowed, often through tortuous reasoning. In re Hager in chapter 5A1 and *Siderits* in part D5a are examples. See also Murphy & Demory, Ltd. v. Murphy in chapter 10B4.

e. *Financial exigency.* The lawyer has an urgent and legitimate need for cash, which he borrows from, and means to return to, his client escrow account. (Even if he does return it, and quickly, it is still improper.) In re Warhaftig in part D5a is an example.

f. *The clueless lawyer.* The lawyer is unaware that the behavior is or may be forbidden and does no research. This is a particular danger if the disciplinary rule can be violated because of what the lawyer should have known, not what she actually knew. In re Fordham in chapter 4B and In re Ryder in chapter 8A1 seem to be examples.

g. *Too much work.* The lawyer is overburdened and fails to do the work, perhaps missing a deadline. Lawyers may accept more clients than they can diligently represent or their bosses may assign them more work than it is possible for them to handle competently. See chapter 2B1.

h. *Substance abuse and depression.* Lawyers, studies show, are prone to abuse alcohol and controlled substances and are at greater risk of depression. One prominent study of American lawyers concluded:

> Substantial rates of behavioral health problems were found, with 20.6% screening positive for hazardous, harmful, and potentially alcohol-dependent drinking. Men had a higher proportion of positive screens, and also younger participants and those working in the field for a shorter duration. Age group predicted Alcohol Use Disorders Identification Test scores; respondents 30 years of age or younger were more likely to have a higher score than their older peers. Levels of depression, anxiety, and stress among attorneys were significant, with 28%, 19%, and 23% experiencing symptoms of depression, anxiety, and stress, respectively.[*]

As summarized in part D6, courts are disinclined to accept addiction and mental health defenses, not because they disbelieve them but because a (if not the) goal of discipline is to protect the public.

2. Purposes of Discipline

The ABA's Standards for Imposing Lawyer Sanctions describes the goals of discipline this way: "The purpose of lawyer discipline proceedings is to protect the public and the administration of justice from lawyers who have not discharged, will not discharge, or are unlikely properly to discharge their professional duties to clients, the public, the legal system, and the legal profession."

[*] Patrick Krill, Ryan Johnson, & Linda Albert, The Prevalence of Substance Abuse and Other Mental Health Concerns Among American Attorneys, 10 J. Addict. Med. 46 (Feb. 2016). A heartbreaking story about one successful lawyer, which also cites empirical research, is told in Eilene Zimmerman, "The Lawyer, the Addict," N.Y. Times, July 15, 2017.

Unlike malpractice and other civil remedies, discipline serves the public interest. Discipline is not intended to afford a legal remedy to persons injured by a lawyer's misconduct. See In re Robertson, 612 A.2d 1236 (D.C. 1992) (restitution can be a disciplinary remedy, but only to the extent of ordering the return of money or property that the client has paid or entrusted to the lawyer, not as a substitute for a malpractice action); Iowa Supreme Court Bd. of Prof'l Ethics & Conduct v. Erbes, 604 N.W.2d 656 (Iowa 2000) (ethics rules "are chiefly intended to provide protection to the public").

Another distinction between discipline and civil liability lies in the nature of the conduct that can serve as a basis for either. An act that violates the Rules (e.g., improper advertising) may bring discipline but will not support a civil claim. Similarly, a negligent act may bring civil liability even though it could not (or as a practical matter would not) support discipline. Of course, there is still a wide area of overlap in which the same conduct may subject a lawyer to both damages and discipline—and sometimes a criminal conviction.

3. Sanctions

While some terms are uniform, there is no national consistency in the labels attached to the escalating types of discipline. "Disbarment" generally refers to indefinite or permanent exclusion from the bar. In a few jurisdictions, such as New Jersey, disbarment is permanent. In others, the court may elect permanent disbarment as the maximum sanction. Of course, the right to reapply by no means guarantees readmission. Jurisdictions use "suspension" to refer to the less harsh sanction of allowing a lawyer to continue as a member of the bar while her right to practice is suspended for a period of time, which can range from a few months to five or more years. Censure (or public reprimand) is a near-universal punishment. Like disbarment and suspension, the fact of censure is public, although many jurisdictions also provide for private censure (or reprimand). Although the censured lawyer is not removed or suspended from practice, publicity attached to a public censure can hurt business, but that assumes that future clients will discover it. The censure will be considered in determining the sanction should the lawyer again be guilty of a professional transgression.

The nomenclature becomes less uniform at this point. Words like "admonition" are among those used in various jurisdictions. They do not carry a consistent import. But whatever words are used, grievance bodies seek to have gradations of responses at their disposal. Some jurisdictions have used "warnings" or similar words to caution a lawyer where discipline is not called for because no rule has been violated, but where the lawyer appears ignorant of the riskiness of the conduct.

4. Disciplinary Systems

Jurisdictions have various ways to provide the staff necessary to run their disciplinary systems. Needed are investigators, lawyers, and judges, in addition to support personnel. Many states use employed investigators and employed lawyers to gather evidence and prosecute disciplinary violations. Some of these states may supplement paid staff with volunteer lawyers. A few states are predominantly dependent on volunteer lawyers to investigate and prosecute cases.

Once a finding of probable cause is made, at least 40 states open the disciplinary process to the public, whether or not the lawyer consents. A few states, including New York, mandate secrecy unless and until a court imposes public discipline. N.Y. Judiciary Law §90(10). Since most sanctions are private, there is often no way in these states for a prospective client to learn a lawyer's disciplinary history except by asking. Rules forbidding the complainant publicly to reveal the fact or content of her complaint or the result violate the First Amendment. R.M. v. Supreme Court, 883 A.2d 369 (N.J. 2005) (also holding that an ethics complaint and statements made in the disciplinary process enjoy absolute immunity); Doe v. Doe, 127 S.W.3d 728 (Tenn. 2004).

The majority view is that the disciplining body has the burden of proving the facts justifying discipline by clear and convincing evidence, although the precise articulation of the standard varies. The minority view is that the burden is only a fair preponderance of the evidence. In re Capoccia, 453 N.E.2d 497 (N.Y. 1983).

5. Acts Justifying Discipline*

Much of this book describes conduct that could support professional discipline. Here we highlight some of the frequent reasons for discipline and some others.

a. Dishonesty

The Defense Sting

Monroe Chalk has been hired to defend Analisa Wells, who is charged with a drug offense. A successful prosecution will depend on the testimony of Bo Bjork, an informant with outstanding drug charges. Chalk believes that Bjork is continuing to sell drugs even while acting as an informant. He searches for proof of his suspicion in order to impeach

---

* For an examination of the mens rea requirements in lawyer discipline, especially for violations of the conflict rules that lack any mens rea element, see Nancy Moore, Mens Rea Standards in Lawyer Disciplinary Codes, 23 Geo. J. Legal Ethics 1 (2010).

Bjork at trial. Finding none to his satisfaction, Chalk has Vin Westerly, his paralegal, arrange to buy a felony quantity of marijuana from Bjork, then testify to Bjork's drug dealing. He gives Westerly $200 and a voice-activated recorder. Westerly makes the purchase and Chalk presents his evidence including the marijuana to the police. The case against Wells is dropped. But Chalk and Westerly are prosecuted for conspiracy to buy drugs, and a disciplinary complaint is filed against Chalk. "Prosecutors do stings like mine all the time," Chalk argues. "Why can't the defense? I reported everything to the authorities and gave them the proof." Should there be discipline?

A Research Shortcut

Dirk Smallwood has a brief due on appeal. His client secured a $287,000 federal judgment against MetroTech for age discrimination in employment. Smallwood is overwhelmed with deadlines. But the brief is due Tuesday. In his Point I, Smallwood wants to lay out the general requirements of the age discrimination law and something about its legislative history. Subsequent points will focus on the facts of his case. He finds a law review article on the history and policies behind the law, written by a law professor who teaches employment law. He also finds a brief filed in a court in another state by a well-regarded employment lawyer. He takes four pages from the law review article and three pages from the brief and combines them in his Point I without attribution, making modest editorial changes. The judge notices that the quality of Point I far exceeds the quality of the rest of the brief and eventually all is discovered.

Smallwood is referred for discipline. The notice of charges says that he "made a false statement of fact" in violation of Rule 3.3(a)(1) and "engaged in conduct involving dishonesty, deceit, and misrepresentation" in violation of Rule 8.4(c) by implying that the written work was his own. What result?

———————

Dishonesty in its many forms is among the most frequent reasons for discipline (neglect of client matters is repeatedly cited as the most frequent basis). The following case concerns unauthorized withdrawals from an attorney's trust or escrow account. Taking escrow money for personal use is the reason for much discipline nationwide. Lawyers are required to place funds that belong to others, or to which others have a claim even if the lawyer has a competing claim, in trust accounts. It is unethical for a lawyer to commingle those funds with her own money and, even worse, to make actual (even if just "temporary") use of them. An escrow violation may be discovered in a random audit, as in the next case. At this point in your career you should read and remember the substance of Rule 1.15 or its equivalent wherever you plan to practice.

IN RE WARHAFTIG
524 A.2d 398 (N.J. 1987)

PER CURIAM . . .

I

The charges filed against respondent were the result of a random compliance audit. . . . "The audit disclosed that respondent continually issued checks to his own order for fees in pending real estate matters. He would replace the 'advance' when the funds were received for the real estate closing. . . ."

[When Warhaftig anticipated a real estate fee from one client but had not yet received the money from which the fee would come, he would withdraw the amount of the fee from the money of other clients in his escrow account.] Respondent maintained his own lists of fees taken in advance. This list contained the names of clients and the amounts he anticipated earning from these clients in pending real estate closings. As a closing occurred and the fee was earned, respondent would delete the client's name and fee. When an anticipated closing fell through, respondent would replace the fee he had earlier advanced to himself. . . .

When respondent received notice of the audit, he contacted his accountant who advised him that if his trust account was short he should immediately replace the funds. Respondent borrowed $11,125 from accounts in the names of his two teenage sons and deposited the money into his trust account to cover the withdrawn fees. Respondent made this deposit about five days before the originally scheduled audit date of October 4, 1983.

The auditor was not able to determine which clients' monies respondent had taken because of the size of respondent's real estate practice. Money continually flowed in and out of the trust account. Respondent, at the ethics hearing, maintained that he never failed to make the proper disbursements at the closings and that no one ever lost money as a result of his practice. He discontinued this practice in September 1983 when he received notice of the audit.

At the Ethics Committee hearing, respondent explained that his withdrawal of advance fees from the trust account was necessitated by the "gigantic cash flow burden" he experienced beginning in the early 1980's. Such pressures were the result of a precipitous decline in his real estate practice. At the same time, an additional strain on respondent's finances was created by his wife's having to undergo treatment for cancer, and by his son's need for extensive psychiatric counseling. According to respondent, only a small portion of these expenses was covered by insurance.

Respondent was also questioned at the hearing as to whether he knew, at the time the advance-fee scheme was implemented, that his conduct constituted an ethical violation. Respondent stated:

> I was aware that what I was doing was wrong, and I was also aware that no one was being hurt by what I was doing. And what I was doing, especially by keeping lists like this, was making sure that nobody would get hurt by what I was doing. . . .

II

In recommending public discipline, the [Disciplinary Review Board] recognized that In re Wilson, which requires the disbarment of an attorney who knowingly misappropriates his clients' funds, controls the outcome of this case. However, the Board emphasized a perceived distinction between respondent's conduct, which it characterized as the "premature withdrawal of . . . monies to which he had a colorable interest[,]" and the knowing misappropriation described in *Wilson*, supra. Apparently, the Board was persuaded by respondent's contention that while he was aware that he was violating a Disciplinary Rule, he "didn't feel that [he] was stealing. . . ."

The distinction drawn by the DRB cannot be sustained under the *Wilson* rule. As we stated in [precedent], knowing misappropriation under *Wilson* "consists simply of a lawyer taking a client's money entrusted to him, knowing that it is the client's money and knowing that the client has not authorized the taking." We have consistently maintained that a lawyer's subjective intent, whether it be to "borrow" or to steal, is irrelevant to the determination of the appropriate discipline in a misappropriation case. . . .

It is clear that respondent's conduct constituted knowing misappropriation as contemplated by *Wilson*. Through the use of the advance-fee mechanism, he took funds from his trust account before he had any legal right to those monies. These "fees" were taken by respondent before he received any deposits in connection with the relevant real-estate closings. Thus, he was effectively borrowing monies from one group of clients in order to compensate himself, in advance, for matters being handled for other clients. Respondent made these withdrawals with full recognition that his actions had not been authorized by his clients, and that he was therefore violating the rules governing attorney conduct. Respondent's unauthorized misappropriation of clients' trust funds for his personal needs cannot be distinguished from the conduct condemned in *Wilson*, supra.

[The court concluded that various mitigating factors were insufficient to prevent disbarment.]

Noteworthy in *Warhaftig* are the relatively modest amounts, the fact that Warhaftig did the underlying work to earn the fees, the fact that no one was harmed, and the fact that he would soon be entitled to the fees when closings occurred. But the court is not sympathetic.

Intentionally taking or borrowing escrow money without authorization will usually lead to serious discipline even if no client is actually harmed. In a few jurisdictions, disbarment is nearly automatic. In re Cleland, 2 P.3d 700 (Colo. 2000) ("As we have said numerous times before, disbarment is the presumed sanction when a lawyer knowingly misappropriates funds belonging to a client or a third person."); In re Schoepfer, 687 N.E.2d 391 (Mass. 1997) (if "an attorney intended to deprive the client of funds, permanently or temporarily, or if the client was deprived of funds (no matter what the attorney intended), the standard discipline is disbarment or indefinite suspension"). A violation is ridiculously easy to prove. Nearly all it takes is a subpoena to the lawyer's bank. Banks may also have a duty to notify authorities when a lawyer bounces a check on her business or escrow account.

IN RE DISCIPLINARY PROCEEDINGS AGAINST SIDERITS
824 N.W.2d 812 (Wis. 2013)

PER CURIAM: . . .

[To earn a bonus in any one year, Siderits's law firm required shareholders to bill at least 1,800 hours in that year. Siderits billed time in 2007 and 2008 that he had never worked and that he then "wrote-down" (i.e., erased from the firm's computerized billing system) the following year. The effect was to put him over the bonus threshold for 2007 and 2008. But because of the later write-downs, clients were never charged for the phantom time. Siderits received undeserved bonuses of almost $47,000.]

[T]his case does not turn on the bare fact that Attorney Siderits wrote-down his time; if Attorney Siderits had made occasional, modest write-downs which did not affect his eligibility for a bonus, this misconduct case would not exist. At issue here is whether Attorney Siderits was manipulating his billing records for the sole purpose of achieving a bonus. The answer to this question, according to the referee, is an unequivocal yes; the referee determined that Attorney Siderits' arguments to the contrary were not credible—a determination which we will not disturb. It is obvious that with or without a written Firm policy [on write-downs], misappropriating Firm funds through billing sleight of hand is inimical to the best interests of the Firm, the public, and the profession, and, as such, constitutes misconduct.

Attorney Siderits [] argues that his due process rights have been violated by this proceeding in two respects. First, he claims that in the absence of a formal Firm policy governing write-downs, he reasonably could not have known his actions to be wrong. Second, he argues that he was unaware of [cases that hold] that a lawyer has a fiduciary duty to his law firm, or [a case] in which this court pledged to treat lawyers' misappropriation of law firm funds no differently than misappropriation of client funds.

We reject these arguments. . . . [T]his case does not turn on the bare fact that Attorney Siderits wrote-down his time; this case is about Attorney Siderits abusing his write-down discretion and lying to his law partners in order to collect almost $47,000 in bonuses to which he was not entitled.

Attorney Siderits cannot seriously contend that firms must have a written policy forbidding stealing and lying before a misconduct charge for one of these actions can be sustained. As to Attorney Siderits' ignorance-of-the-law defense, we emphatically reject it. To allow an ignorance-of-the-law excuse in lawyer ethics cases would encourage and reward indifference to the ethics code and the cases interpreting it, a pernicious outcome. In any event, the injunction against stealing from one's own law firm is not an abstract one, and this court has stated it clearly and repeatedly. Attorney Siderits should have known better.

[The court imposed a one-year suspension after considering that Siderits had lost his job and his equity interest in the firm, had repaid the firm $60,000 for the unearned bonuses and other claims, and would pay the nearly $19,000 in costs for the disciplinary proceedings.]

Deceit, Dishonesty, Et Cetera

Lawyers sometimes defraud their own partners, law firms, and employers. This can be done, for example, by seeking reimbursement for false expenses. Courts will routinely visit harsh discipline on lawyers who do so. In re Thompson, 991 P.2d 820 (Colo. 1999) (law firm associate disbarred for keeping $15,000 in client fees that should have been turned over to his firm); In re Greenberg, 714 A.2d 243 (N.J. 1998) (disbarment where "multiple acts of misappropriation" resulted in lawyer taking more than $34,000 from his firm "for his own purposes"); In re Shapiro, 644 N.Y.S.2d 894 (1st Dept. 1996) (lawyer resigned from bar while under investigation for altering receipts for expenditures, creating receipts, and sending bills to clients that contained false descriptions of disbursements).

Beth Bant worked in-house at an insurance company in Wisconsin. Her request to attend an ABA seminar in New Orleans was approved. She never went, nor did she pay the $1,115 seminar fee, but she submitted a fabricated bill for it using "computer editing software" and her employer "repaid" her. She similarly created false bills for the travel costs but she had not yet submitted them when the ruse was discovered. When confronted, she lied to her employer. Previously, she had falsely submitted (and been "repaid") for a $557 hotel stay during a legal education seminar. She had no prior discipline. What's the right sanction? In re Bant, 936 N.W.2d 152 (Wis. 2019).

Sometimes the lawyer is a high earner and the amounts in false expense reports are small. This could be the very definition of self-destructive behavior. If discovered, it will likely result in loss of a partnership or job and discipline. Further, the reporting duty described below may require the lawyer's firm to notify the disciplinary committee (as well as any defrauded client), although often they are willing to do so anyway. When firms suspect this sort of conduct they bring in the forensic accountants, who x-ray the suspected lawyer's financial life, going back years and to the penny.

Lying or misleading omissions on a resume or law school or bar application will also bring discipline following admission. (If it's discovered before admission, it can delay or prevent admission.) When he applied for a job at Williams & Connolly, Seth Nadler "falsified" his law school transcript to show a GPA of 3.825 when in reality his GPA was 3.269. For this and other resume misstatements, the New Jersey Supreme Court suspended him for one year. In re Nadler, 227 A.3d 1187 (N.J. 2020).[*] Joe McDaniel, not yet admitted to the bar, got a job at Skadden Arps using a false law school transcript. While at Skadden, he altered credit card slips to get reimbursements to which he was not entitled. Skadden discovered his misconduct, and he resigned. McDaniel then gained admission to the New York bar, but he concealed his Skadden employment, ostensibly to avoid discovery of the reason for his departure. When his misconduct was later discovered, he was disbarred. In re McDaniel, 699 N.Y.S.2d 397 (1st Dept. 1999).

Although courts are quite strict when lawyers steal law firm or client money, they are oddly lenient when a lawyer has been convicted of "stealing" the government's money through conscious failure to pay taxes or lying on returns. Even New Jersey, which will permanently disbar a lawyer who takes money from a client or law firm, shows great leniency in tax matters. In re Garcia, 574 A.2d 394 (N.J. 1990) (willful failure to file income tax returns warrants public reprimand). See also Attorney Grievance Comm'n of Md. v. Atkinson, 745 A.2d 1086 (Md. 2000) (failure to file and pay federal and state income taxes for 11 years warrants suspension with leave to reapply after one year) (three judges, dissenting, said the penalty was *too harsh*). Sanctions are light even when the lawyer has been convicted of tax crimes. In re Haugabrook, 606 S.E.2d 257 (Ga. 2004) (one-year suspension of lawyer who pled guilty to two federal tax felonies).

Dishonesty in business affairs unrelated to law practice can also support discipline. In re Herman, 348 P.3d 1125 (Or. 2015) (disbarment of lawyer for dishonest conduct in a business venture). A law professor who altered his student evaluations to increase his chances of getting a chair was suspended from practice for a minimum of three months and resigned his faculty position. Iowa Supreme Court Attorney Disc. Bd. v. Kress, 747 N.W.2d 530 (Iowa 2008).

Beth Bant, the lawyer who created a fabricated bill for a New Orleans seminar she never attended, lied about it, and had previously submitted a false bill for reimbursement was suspended for six months. Do you think that's the right sanction? Too strict? Too lenient?

b. Neglect and Lack of Candor

Neglect of client matters is a recurrent basis for client complaints and discipline. The likelihood of discipline increases as the number of neglected matters increases. In In re Snow, 530 N.Y.S.2d 886 (3d Dept. 1988), a pattern

---

[*] The facts are in Kathryn Rubino, "Lawyer Suspended After Submitting an Inflated Resume to a Biglaw Firm," Above the Law, Mar. 23, 2020.

of neglect of several legal matters resulted in a one-year suspension. The court was especially unimpressed with the lawyer's "attempt to blame his failure to respond to telephone calls or correspondence on his secretary's illness." (Is that the disciplinary equivalent of "the dog ate my homework"?) A lawyer's failure to provide a defense for a client in a personal injury case resulted in a default judgment of $221,000. Given the serious harm to the client and prior discipline, the lawyer was disbarred. In re Scott, 979 P.2d 572 (Colo. 1999). Neglect should be distinguished from negligence: Inaction is more likely to bring discipline than will negligence, which is left to the tort system to sort out.

It is in response to allegations of neglect (along with failure to file tax returns) that lawyers may offer psychological defenses, including dependency on prescribed or illegal substances, depression, and obsessive character traits. These are discussed below.

c. Sex with a Client

In the film *Jagged Edge*, the character played by Glenn Close has an affair with a man she is defending (played by Jeff Bridges) who is charged with murdering his wife. Several times during the trial, the skills of Close's character are (visibly) hampered because of information she learns about her client's relationships with other women.

For a very long time, the courts and the bar mostly ignored ethical issues that arise when lawyers become intimate with clients during a representation. Or when a lawyer says or implies that sexual favors will earn a client more of his attention. No longer. The ABA and many states have a specific rule that forbids lawyers to begin an intimate personal relationship with a current client. Rule 1.8(j). Other states have relied on conflict of interest rules to discipline this behavior. See, e.g., In re Vogel, 482 S.W.3d 520 (Tenn. 2016) (Rule 1.7(a)(2)). We are not talking about sexual assault, which would be a crime as well as a basis for discipline, but about allegedly consensual relationships.

We encountered this behavior in connection with a lawyer's civil liability (see Tante v. Herring in part A1). There, the client was claiming disability benefits. It is, however, matrimonial work that accounts for the vast majority of cases in which lawyers have begun intimate relationships with clients. In every reported case of which I am aware but one, the lawyer has been a man and the client has been a woman.[*]

The South Carolina Supreme Court, in In re Bellino, 417 S.E.2d 535 (S.C. 1992), gave the following reason, as true now as in 1992, for forbidding lawyers to initiate sexual relationships with clients. See also the explanation in Rule 1.8 cmt. [17]. Bellino was suspended after he kissed and fondled

---

[*] The exception is Allen County Bar Ass'n v. Bartels, 924 N.E.2d 833 (Ohio 2010) (public reprimand for female lawyer who had an intimate encounter with male matrimonial client).

two matrimonial clients while he was a lawyer in the Marine Corps. The court wrote:

> This case is not about sex or sex abuse. It is about power—the awesome power that comes with the license to practice law—and the abuse thereof. A certain amount of courage is required for a person to make romantic overtures to another person. The fear of rejection is legitimate, and the pain of rejection is real. Some people find ways to cheat and, thereby, avoid the possibility of rejection. One way is by the use of a prostitute. Another and even more reprehensible way is by taking advantage of a weaker person, a person either physically weaker or, as the result of circumstances, less able to say no. This is precisely what Mr. Bellino did. He took advantage of his superior position as an officer in the Marine Corps and as a lawyer. It would be difficult to imagine anyone more vulnerable or more subject to the control of another than the women on whom Mr. Bellino forced himself.

Cases that discipline lawyers for having sex with clients (or trying to[*]) often describe fairly unremarkable facts. The parties may drift into an intimate relationship. Most often the lawyer is the instigator, but sometimes the client is, or it just happens. It doesn't matter. In re Halverson, 998 P.2d 833 (Wash. 2000) (even if intimate relationship with matrimonial client was consensual, lawyer, a former state bar president, suspended for one year); In re Voss, 795 N.W.2d 415 (Wis. 2011) (lengthy sexual relationship with client "who suffered from numerous vulnerabilities"; suspension for four years and eight months). Opinions emphasize the threat to the lawyer's independent professional judgment and the danger, especially in matrimonial or custody matters, to the client's case. In re Lewis, 415 S.E.2d 173 (Ga. 1992). The privilege is also endangered, isn't it? Were they talking as lovers or as lawyer and client?

Rule 1.8(j) uses the term "sexual relations." That is broad enough to encompass relations that are not physical but nonetheless sexual in nature. The Alaska Supreme Court has held that the rule forbids sexting—an exchange of sexually explicit text messages and photos—with a client. In re Stanton, 376 P.3d 693 (Alaska 2016). An Oklahoma lawyer was suspended for three months after he asked one client to send him sexually suggestive photographs, made unwanted sexual advances toward another client, and had sex with a third client who at the time was unable to pay his fee. State ex rel. Okla. Bar Ass'n v. Stout, 451 P.3d 155 (Okla. 2019).

Comment [19] to Model Rule 1.8 also addresses relationships with client representatives. "When the client is an organization, paragraph (j) of this Rule prohibits a lawyer for the organization (whether inside counsel or outside counsel) from having a sexual relationship with a constituent of the

---

[*] A lawyer was disciplined for propositioning a client via texts "of a sexual nature." Disciplinary Counsel v. Detweiler, 989 N.E.2d 41 (Ohio 2013). Making an advance is improper even if rebuffed. Disciplinary Counsel v. Moore, 804 N.E.2d 423 (Ohio 2004).

organization who supervises, directs or regularly consults with that lawyer concerning the organization's legal matters."* This expands the prohibition beyond biological clients. What justifies it?

Some have argued that rules that forbid all consensual sexual relationships with clients are bad policy and may also violate the constitutional right of association. If the relationship was in fact voluntary, should it be a basis for discipline? Or should we say that because of the lawyer's power and the client's reliance, an intimate relationship cannot be truly voluntary?

d. The Lawyer's "Private" Life and Conduct Unrelated to Practice

To what extent should a lawyer's behavior unrelated to practice be a basis for discipline? As we saw earlier, cheating on taxes and making false statements in a business venture can result in discipline. Some other examples are:

- Leaving the scene of a fatal automobile accident warrants disbarment. In re Tidwell, 831 A.2d 953 (D.C. 2003) (lawyer previously disbarred in New York following felony conviction for same incident).
- Major drug crimes. La. State Bar Ass'n v. Bensabat, 378 So. 2d 380 (La. 1979) (disbarment for conspiracy to import cocaine).
- Drunk driving. Grievance Adm'r v. Deutch, 565 N.W.2d 369 (Mich. 1997) ("We find that the filings of judgments of conviction against respondents Deutch and Howell . . . for their respective drunk driving convictions evidenced 'misconduct' regardless of whether these convictions, on their face, reflected adversely on the attorneys' honesty, trustworthiness, or fitness as lawyers.") (remanded for hearing).
- New York mandates disbarment for all felony convictions in New York State courts or felony convictions in any court if the crime would be a felony in New York. See Mitchell v. Ass'n of the Bar of the City of N.Y., 351 N.E.2d 743 (N.Y. 1976) (disbarment of former Attorney General John Mitchell following conviction of a federal felony that would also be a felony in New York).
- Assault, increasingly including domestic violence, will bring discipline. In re Zulandt, 939 N.Y.S.2d 338 (1st Dept. 2012) (three-year suspension for assaulting girlfriend and destroying her property); People v. Musick, 960 P.2d 89 (Colo. 1998) (one year and one day suspension where respondent physically assaulted his girlfriend three times). Eli Cherkasky had been an assistant district attorney in Manhattan for nine years when, in 2015, he assaulted and choked a woman at a bar while drunk. He was fired, convicted of a misdemeanor, and suspended

---

* In In re Bergman, 382 P.3d 455 (Kan. 2016), a corporate lawyer was disciplined for, among other reasons, beginning a relationship with an outside consultant to her client who later became an officer of the client. Without explanation, the court deemed an outside consultant to be a "constituent" of the client, a conclusion that is not supported by the text of the rule or its comment.

for two months. In re Cherkasky, 120 N.Y.S.3d 325 (1st Dept. 2020). Robert Nickol was admitted to the New York bar in 2013. In 2018, a jury convicted him of misdemeanor assault. His then-girlfriend testified that in 2017 Nickol slapped her in the face following an argument. Subsequently, he whipped the victim's leg with a television cord. Both incidents resulted in physical injuries. He was suspended for six months. In re Nickol, 121 N.Y.S.3d 920 (3d Dept. 2020).

- Willful failure to make child support payments. In re Chase, 121 P.3d 1160 (Or. 2005) (30-day suspension); In re Geer, 858 N.E.2d 388 (Ohio 2006) (one-year suspension). Section 90(2-a) of New York's judiciary law requires suspension of any lawyer who has failed to pay court-ordered child or spousal support.

What is the justification for discipline when the conduct does not arise in practice and there is no reason to predict misconduct in practice? The answer would seem to be that a lawyer's disregard for the rule of law or his legal obligations adversely reflects on fitness to practice.

e. Discrimination in Choice of Clients

Laws forbid places of public accommodation to discriminate on the basis of age, sex, race, disability, and other attributes. Hotels and restaurants are covered. Is a law office? A rejected male client complained about lawyer Nathanson to the Massachusetts Commission Against Discrimination, citing her policy of not representing men in divorce. Stropnicky v. Nathanson (Feb. 25, 1997). At a hearing, Nathanson explained

> that she needs to feel a personal commitment to her client's cause in order to function effectively as an advocate, and that in family law she has only experienced this sense of personal commitment in representing women. She testified that her female divorce clients derive a specific benefit from her limited practice. They feel comfortable sharing their anxieties and concerns with an advocate whom they trust to be wholeheartedly as well as intellectually committed to their interests. Nathanson believes that her practice of advancing arguments only on behalf of women enhanced her credibility with judges she appeared before in the family law courts.
>
> Nathanson testified that all of her potential clients undergo a screening process. She does not make a final decision about whether to represent a particular client in divorce proceedings without having spoken at length to the client about the matters in controversy and conferring with her partners. She would not represent women whose positions in divorce litigation were repugnant to her personal values. She testified that in other legal proceedings, not involving controversies between men and women, she has no ethical problem with representing men.

Stropnicky, the client she rejected, testified

> that his role throughout his marriage was non-traditional. During the early years of his eighteen-year marriage, [he] worked to support himself and his

wife while she pursued a career in medicine. Once [he] and his wife had children, he stayed home serving as homemaker and caregiver for seven years. After his second child's third birthday, he returned to school and acquired a teaching degree in biology. . . . At the time of their divorce, [he] was earning one-tenth of his wife's salary.

The Commission rejected Nathanson's defense and fined her $5,000. The hearing officer wrote that Nathanson could have met with Stropnicky and decided that the issues in his divorce "were not consistent with her specialty and area of interest." But she did not meet with him but rejected him only because he was a man. "[R]ejection of a female or African-American on similar grounds . . . would appear more starkly to be a violation." Although the discrimination here was against a male, it was no less unlawful.

f. Racist and Sexist Conduct in Law Practice

Stropnicky raises a broader question: When is biased conduct or harassment in law practice a violation of ethics rules? When should it be? These seemingly simple questions have created intense debate among lawyers and legal academics, accelerated by the ABA's 2016 adoption of Rule 8.4(g). In an attenuated way, dramatic changes in the profession's demographics may partly explain the attention to these questions. The attention was not prominent when Baby Boomers entered the bar.

In the decade ending in 2019, female lawyers increased from 31 percent of the bar to 36 percent. The increase has been slow but steady. Between 1950 and 1970, women accounted for 3 percent of the bar, then 8 percent in 1980, 20 percent in 1991, and 27 percent in 2000.

Minority lawyer bar membership increased from 12 percent of the profession in 2009 to 15 percent a decade later. Black and Latinx lawyers remained at 5 percent in this period. The increase reflected inclusion of Native Americans and mixed-race lawyers.

The female population of law students increased from 9 percent in 1970 to more than 52 percent in 2018.

Minority law student enrollment increased from 25 percent in 2011 to 31 percent in 2018. The breakdown in 2018 was 63 percent white, 13 percent Latinx, 8 percent African-American, 6 percent Asian, and 10 percent race unknown or other. Forty years earlier, 9 percent of law students were members of minority groups.[*]

The following opinion is by a court disciplinary committee, which the court then approved.

---

[*] All numbers are from the 2019 ABA publication Legal Profession Statistics, available online.

IN RE JORDAN SCHIFF

Docket No. HP 22/92 (Feb. 2, 1993), Departmental Disciplinary Committee, First Judicial Department, New York State Supreme Court

REPORT AND RECOMMENDATIONS OF HEARING PANEL . . .

FACTS

The first deposition of respondent's client, Mrs. Morales, was held on August 30, 1989. . . .

Early in this deposition, a senior partner of Mr. Schiff's firm, Mr. Yankowitz, set a highly improper tone. When Mr. Schiff, after a dispute, rudely told [opposing counsel] Ms. Mark to "get out of here" and walked out of the room, Mr. Yankowitz thereupon appeared. Ms. Mark attempted on the record to protest Mr. Schiff's actions, and, after hearing Mr. Yankowitz, asked him to stop mischaracterizing what had occurred. Mr. Yankowitz replied:

Mr. Yankowitz: Don't tell me what to do. Ever. It's my office, it's my firm. This is my client. The record is clear. I have made my statement and I have recited what the judge has directed in this case. You don't make the rules, you don't wear a black robe, you are not the judge.

Ms. Mark: Excuse me, first of all, let the record reflect that Mr. Yankowitz is pointing at me, standing and shouting. In the second place, let the record reflect that the court hasn't said a thing about this deposition so you obviously don't know what you are talking about. Finally—

Mr. Yankowitz: Your statements are ludicrous.

Ms. Mark: I am not finished.

Mr. Yankowitz: You have lost your mind, young lady, continue the deposition or leave.

After this example of mentoring at Shapiro & Yankowitz, the deposition proceeded.

Respondent Schiff said to Ms. Mark:

Just do your examination and shut up. Just do your examination already. Enough with the bullshit. Do your examination or I am going to throw you out of the office. Bitch. You are the nastiest person I ever met and I am going to really be all over you during this exam, so you better watch your ass.

Ms. Mark: Mark that for a ruling as well, please. I will be seeking sanctions for all of this.

Mr. Schiff: Do whatever you want to do. Do whatever you want to do. The judge is sick of you and your firm anyway.

Ms. Mark: Mark that for a ruling.

Mr. Schiff: You give lawyers a bad name. You and your firm give attorneys a bad name, I will tell you that right now. . . .

Ms. Mark: I am not going to sit here and listen to your scatological comments all day.

Mr. Schiff: I know a scatalog when I see one.

Mr. Schiff descended further during discussions which were held off the record but in the presence of the court reporter, Mr. Harold Brown, and the Spanish interpreter, Ms. Nancy Adler, both of whom testified before us. Ms. Mark testified that Mr. Schiff referred to her as a "cunt," an "asshole," and advised her that she should "go home and have babies." This evidence was corroborated in substantial part by the other witnesses. . . .

Ms. Mark explained why she continued with the deposition after the degrading and vulgar comments had been made to her by respondent. "I had a client to protect and this case was about to be certified for trial."

[A] panel member asked, "Ms. Mark, was there a procedural advantage, to your knowledge, which Mr. Schiff was seeking to achieve by engaging in misconduct?" Her answer was:

> I have no explanation for why these events took place as they did. I felt there was an attempt here to prevent the defense from obtaining relevant information regarding an additional injury that had been alleged in a supplemental Bill of Particulars, and if I had just crawled back to my office and felt bad about what happened and not made my motion, I would not have had benefit of all the information that was uncovered at a supplemental deposition as far as the medical records that were obtained as a result of this and the continued deposition.

DISCUSSION

Not surprisingly, there is a paucity of precedent in disciplinary cases concerning sexual harassment of female attorneys by male adversaries. Possibly this is because those women so victimized are hesitant to complain, perhaps believing that if a woman aspires to have the designation "Attorney-at-Law" on her business card she must be willing to ignore obscene, explicit vulgarities directed at her anatomy and gender. Indeed, in this case, the complaint to the Disciplinary Committee did not come from the victim but rather came by referral from Judge Jane Solomon. However, women attorneys must be assured that humiliating and reprehensible sexual harassment is definitely not a "rite of passage" which must be silently endured, and that should they encounter it in the course of their practice, they must feel confident they can file a complaint, secure in the knowledge that it will be taken very seriously and investigated very thoroughly. . . .

We conclude that respondent, without provocation, chose to degrade and disparage his adversary by using dirty, discriminatory gutter language offensively directed to harass her because of her gender. Moreover, his was not an isolated comment, possibly uttered spontaneously and without intent, but was instead an ongoing calculated rudeness intended to intimidate a female colleague. . . .

In mitigation, respondent apologized to Ms. Mark by letter and at the hearing. Half of the panel gives very little weight to apologies made under pressure of a court order and the disciplinary process. The other half considers the apologies to constitute evidence of contrition.

In aggravation, the record shows that a direction by Judge Postel to apologize to Ms. Mark, which reflected the Court's opinion of respondent's conduct, and the sanctions imposed on Shapiro & Yankowitz by Judge Solomon on May 3 and September 6, 1991, were insufficient warning to convince Mr. Schiff that his conduct was in need of reform. This was evidenced by . . . the transcript of a deposition taken March 17, 1992, in yet another case, where he called Eileen Stegensky, Esq. a "cunt" and . . . a "nasty fucking bitch."

The Panel finds that on the evidence presented to us all charges are sustained. . . . The Panel unanimously finds that public censure is the appropriate sanction, because those in the profession must understand that sexual harassment is unacceptable behavior and the public must understand that the profession abhors such behavior and will not condone it. Were it not for respondent's unblemished record and his youth, 28 years, which leaves room to believe that he can mend his ways, and the consideration that he is no longer with the firm that set him such a bad example, our recommendation would be even more severe.

s/Sheldon H. Elsen, Chair for the Panel

The court censured Schiff in In re Schiff, 599 N.Y.S.2d 242 (1st Dept. 1993), writing that his conduct was "inexcusable and intolerable [and] reflects adversely on his fitness to practice law."

Schiff's facts are extreme. Most discipline for racist or sexist conduct reveals less egregious behavior. At a deposition, New York lawyer Thomas Monaghan criticized the opposing lawyer's pronunciation of certain words. A sample: "This is finished. We are not going any further. Because you, my dear, with all due respect, are not totally aware of what you are saying, and that is frightening. Because not only did you say extablish, you repeatedly said expecially." When the opposing lawyer, an African-American woman, asked Monaghan what he wanted her to do, he said: "I want you to admit on the record, you cannot pronounce two words." At a hearing on a sanction motion, Judge Mukasey cited the fact that on admission to the court lawyers promise to "abstain from all offensive personality," called Monaghan's conduct "outrageous," and fined him $500. The court referred Monaghan to the federal court's disciplinary committee, where he agreed to accept a public censure from both the federal and state courts "for his race-based abuse of opposing counsel." N.Y.L.J., Apr. 30, 2001; In re Monaghan, 743 N.Y.S.2d 519 (2d Dept. 2002).

A public reprimand and two-year probation were ordered for a lawyer who, among other things, "made demeaning facial gestures and stuck out his tongue at Ms. Berger and Ms. Figueroa . . . told Ms. Figueroa that she was a 'stupid idiot' and that she should 'go back to Puerto Rico' [and] told

Ms. Figueroa that depositions are not conducted under 'girl's rules.' The entire record is replete with evidence of Martocci's verbal assaults and sexist, racial, and ethnic insults." Fla. Bar v. Martocci, 791 So. 2d 1074 (Fla. 2001).

In Cruz-Aponte v. Caribbean Petroleum Corp., 123 F. Supp. 3d 276 (D.P.R. 2015), Mr. Salas had the following exchange with Ms. Monserrate, the opposing lawyer, during a deposition:

Mr. Nevares: The air conditioner works.

Ms. Monserrate: I don't know, but it's hot in here.

Mr. Salas: *¿Tienes calor todavía?* ["You're still warm?"] You're not getting menopause, I hope.

Ms. Monserrate: That's on the record.

Mr. Salas: No, no, no, no.

Ms. Monserrate: You know that a lawyer here got in big trouble for a comment just like that.

Mr. Salas: Really.

On a motion for sanctions, the court wrote: "Mr. Salas's comment intended to humiliate Ms. Monserrate on the basis of her age and gender. This conduct is adverse to the goals of justice and cannot be permitted to find a safe haven in the practice of law. The Court therefore finds that the following sanctions are warranted. First, to ensure that he bears some of the burden of the costs of bringing his discriminatory conduct to light, Mr. Salas should pay Ms. Monserrate reasonable attorney's fees for bringing the motion. Second, Mr. Salas should complete a continuing legal education course on attorney professionalism and professional conduct."

The Rule 8.4(g) Debate

Rule 8.4(g), added in 2016, says that a lawyer shall not

> engage in conduct that the lawyer knows or reasonably should know is harassment or discrimination on the basis of race, sex, religion, national origin, ethnicity, disability, age, sexual orientation, gender identity, marital status or socioeconomic status in conduct related to the practice of law. This paragraph does not limit the ability of a lawyer to accept, decline or withdraw from a representation in accordance with Rule 1.16. This paragraph does not preclude legitimate advice or advocacy consistent with these Rules.

Comments [3]-[5] to Rule 8.4 were also added in 2016. In July 2020, the ABA Ethics Committee issued Opinion 493, which contains hypothetical descriptions of conduct that would and would not violate the rule.

Prior to 2016, 24 states had a rule forbidding bias or harassment (or both). None was as broad as Rule 8.4(g), although rules in Minnesota and Indiana were (and still are) nearly as broad. The rules in most other states were narrower. Twelve states, like the Model Rules before Rule 8.4(g), had only a comment, not a rule.* It focused solely on conduct in representing a client that was prejudicial to the administration of justice, which usually refers to matters before a tribunal. The remaining states had nothing.

As noted in chapter 7E, Rule 2.3(C) of the ABA's Code of Judicial Conduct addresses the same conduct. It says a judge "shall require lawyers in proceedings before the court to refrain from manifesting bias or prejudice, or engaging in harassment, based upon attributes including but not limited to race, sex, gender, religion, national origin, ethnicity, disability, age, sexual orientation, marital status, socioeconomic status, or political affiliation, against parties, witnesses, lawyers, or others." This section, broad as it is, applies only in court matters whereas Rule 8.4(g) applies to all "conduct related to the practice of law."

Some critics have argued that Rule 8.4(g) violates the First Amendment's Free Speech Clause. Others have criticized it as a violation of the Amendment's Free Exercise Clause, including by requiring lawyers who oppose same-sex relationships on religious grounds to represent clients in the LGBTQ community.†

"Affirmative Action Hurts Those It Promises to Help"

Wyatt Berbach is a partner at a leading East Coast firm. In law school he published a note arguing that affirmative action policies at public and private organizations, including colleges and universities, discriminated against white men and women in favor of persons of color. In his view, those policies are counterproductive because, as he wrote, "their beneficiaries are set up for failure when they can't compete with their

---

* The comment provided:

> A lawyer who, in course of representing a client, knowingly manifests by words or conduct, bias or prejudice based upon race, sex, religion, national origin, disability, age, sexual orientation or socioeconomic status, violates paragraph (d) when such actions are prejudicial to the administration of justice. Legitimate advocacy respecting the foregoing factors does not violate paragraph (d). A trial judge's finding that peremptory challenges were exercised on a discriminatory basis does not alone establish a violation of this rule.

† The following articles are from the growing academic literature about the rule. Rebecca Aviel, Rule 8.4(g) and the First Amendment: Distinguishing Between Discrimination and Free Speech, 31 Geo. J. Legal Ethics 31 (2018); Veronica Martinez, Combatting Silence in the Profession, 105 Va. L. Rev. 805 (2019); Stephen Gillers, A Rule to Forbid Bias and Harassment in Law Practice: A Guide for State Courts Considering Model Rule 8.4(g), 30 Geo. J. Legal Ethics 195 (2017); Josh Blackman, Reply: A Pause for State Courts Considering Rule 8.4(g), 30 Geo. J. Legal Ethics 241 (2017); Robert Weiner, "Nothing to See Here": Model Rule 8.4(g) and the First Amendment, 41 Harv. J. Law & Pub. Policy 125 (2018); and Symposium, Using the Licensing Power of the Administrative State: Rule 8.4(g), 31 Regent U. L. Rev. 31 (2018-2019).

better educated peers." As a lawyer, he has said the same in the following circumstances.

1. He wrote an opinion piece for a legal newspaper criticizing affirmative action for law school admission and law firm hiring as bad policy.

2. He stated the same views as a panel member at a bar association forum on minorities in the profession. He quoted Chief Justice John Roberts's majority opinion in Parents Involved in Community Schools v. Seattle School Dist. No. 1, 551 U.S. 701 (2007) (rejecting, 5-4, an affirmative action plan for school assignments): "The way to stop discrimination on the basis of race is to stop discriminating on the basis of race."

3. As a member of his firm's hiring committee, he has argued that all offers should be race-blind and has voted accordingly.

4. Over lunch in the firm's cafeteria with associates Lydia Gutiérrez, who is Latina, and Teddy Morris and Zena Engle-Lacks, who are white, Berbach said: "Affirmative action hurts those it promises to help and has been a disaster for all concerned. That's my view. Others here disagree." He does not know whether and does not suggest that affirmative action played a role in the careers of any of the associates.

5. While questioning a deposition witness, Berbach repeatedly clashed with the opposing lawyer, who is African-American. Berbach whispered to his associate loud enough for others to hear: "This is why I oppose affirmative action. She never learned how to do this."

Assume that the First Amendment test for a facial challenge to Rule 8.4(g) asks whether it is narrowly drawn to achieve a compelling state interest. Nat'l Inst. of Family & Life Advocates v. Becerra, ____ U.S. ____ (2018). Is it? Even if it is, Berbach could still mount an "as applied" claim by arguing that application of the rule *to his conduct* in these five instances would violate his First Amendment rights.* To survive the "as applied" challenge in each instance, the government would

---

* A rule's overbreadth is not fatal.

> [T]here comes a point at which the chilling effect of an overbroad law, significant though it may be, cannot justify prohibiting all enforcement of that law—particularly a law that reflects "legitimate state interests in maintaining comprehensive controls over harmful, constitutionally unprotected conduct." For there are substantial social costs *created* by the overbreadth doctrine when it blocks application of a law to constitutionally unprotected speech, or especially to constitutionally unprotected conduct. To ensure that these costs do not swallow the social benefits of declaring a law "overbroad," we have insisted that a law's application to protected speech be "substantial," not only in an absolute sense, but also relative to the scope of the law's plainly legitimate applications before applying the "strong medicine" of overbreadth invalidation.

Virginia v. Hicks, 539 U.S. 113 (2003) (Scalia, J.) (9-0).

need to prove that applying the rule to Berbach furthers a compelling interest and is narrowly tailored to achieve that interest. Reed v. Town of Gilbert, Ariz., 576 U.S. 155 (2015).

LGBTQ Policy

Munroe & Munroe is a five-person law firm whose practice focuses on family law and estate planning. The firm consists of Gabriel Munroe, his wife Belinda, his two sons Merle and Maurice, and Merle's wife, Imogene. The following happens. In each instance, has the firm violated Rule 8.4(g)? Does the Free Exercise Clause of the First Amendment provide a defense to any such charge? Does the Religious Freedom Restoration Act (RFRA), adopted by Congress and copied in some states, do so?

Under the Free Exercise Clause, assume that the question is whether the law is a neutral law of general applicability that furthers a rational state purpose. Under the more protective RFRA, government is forbidden substantially to burden a person's exercise of religion, even with a law of general applicability, unless the burden is the least restrictive means of advancing a compelling government interest. Because RFRA is more demanding, let's analyze the firm's conduct under a state version of RFRA.[*]

1. Two women who plan to marry ask the firm to draft a prenuptial agreement, a service it routinely offers to heterosexual clients. The firm declines, citing its lawyers' honestly held religious belief that same-sex marriage and gay relationships are sins.

2. Two men, married to each other, wish to start a business renovating old homes and ask the firm to do the necessary legal work. The firm declines for the same reasons.

3. Two men, married to each other, ask the firm to represent them in connection with their desire to use an egg donor and a surrogate to become fathers. This is a specialized field that requires detailed contracts with the egg donor, the woman who bears the child, and a private agency. The firm has done this work for heterosexual couples unable to conceive. But it declines for the same reasons and also because its lawyers believe that the Bible forbids surrogacy except for married infertile heterosexual couples.

---

[*] Most states do not have a RFRA, but some of those states have court decisions that are substantially equivalent. The federal RFRA does not apply to the states. On the validity of anti-discrimination laws under the First Amendment's Speech and Religion clauses and RFRA, see Kyle Velte, All Fall Down: A Comprehensive Approach to Defeating the Religious Right's Challenges to Antidiscrimination Statutes, 49 Conn. L. Rev. 1 (2016).

Inappropriate Touching

From the court opinion in In re Hill, 144 N.E.3d 184 (Ind. 2020):

At the conclusion of the 2018 state legislative session, several legislators, lobbyists, and legislative staff attended an event at a local bar. Respondent [Curtis Hill, the State Attorney General,] also attended this event at the invitation of a lobbyist with whom Respondent had been dining and drinking that evening. While at the event, Respondent engaged in acts against four women—a state representative and three legislative assistants—that involved various forms of nonconsensual and inappropriate touching. More specifically, as summarized by the hearing officer, Respondent:

(a) "Touch[ed] [M.R.'s] bare back, rubbing his hand down her back down to or just above her buttocks without her consent. He did not accidentally or inadvertently rub [M.R.'s] back down to her mid to low back."

(b) "Rub[bed] [G.B.'s] back without her consent. He did not accidentally or inadvertently rub [G.B.'s] back."

(c) "Put[] his arm around [S.L.'s] waist and pull[ed] her toward him without her consent. He did not inadvertently touch [S.L.] and pull her to him."

(d) "Touch[ed] [N.D.'s] back, moving his hand down her back and moving [N.D.'s] hand toward her buttocks and touching her buttocks without her consent. He did not accidentally or inadvertently touch [N.D.'s] back and move his hand down her back toward her buttocks."

Hill was charged with violating Indiana Rules 8.4(b), which forbids criminal conduct that reflects adversely on a lawyer's fitness, and 8.4(d), which forbids conduct prejudicial to the administration of justice. (Hill was not prosecuted but Rule 8.4(b) does not require prosecution.) Assume that in response, Hill argued that he was inebriated and that the alleged conduct occurred at a private party unrelated to the practice of law or the work of his office and therefore is not a valid basis for discipline. You are the hearing officer charged to make a recommendation to the state supreme court. Did the respondent violate these rules? Or was his conduct, even though offensive, beyond the reach of professional discipline? If you think he violated either or both of the rules, what sanction do you recommend?

g. Failure to Report Another Lawyer's Misconduct

Rule 8.3(a) requires lawyers to report misconduct of other lawyers under certain circumstances. Lawyers sometimes call this the "squeal rule," which should tell you how popular it is. (Judges are under a similar obligation. Code of Judicial Conduct §2.15.) The rule requires reporting misconduct that raises "a substantial question as to [another] lawyer's honesty, trustworthiness or fitness as a lawyer." It excuses reporting if the basis for a lawyer's knowledge is confidential information as defined in Rule 1.6. That will almost always be so given the breadth of Rule 1.6, won't it? But not always. See In re Riehlmann, 891 So. 2d 1239 (La. 2005), which reprimanded a former prosecutor who failed for five years to report a dying colleague's confession that he had suppressed exculpatory evidence in a capital case. During those years, the defendant, later exonerated, was in solitary confinement on death row. Was a reprimand the right sanction?

6. Defenses

Lawyers often cite stress, depression, substance abuse, obsessive-compulsive disorders, or other mental illnesses to explain what they characterize as aberrant behavior. These defenses will rarely avoid discipline, but they may affect the sanction. Why should that be? If disciplinary sanctions are intended to protect the public, not punish the lawyer, shouldn't these defenses instead underscore the need for a tough sanction? Three other mitigating factors that influence sanction are a lawyer's "unblemished record" (a phrase that regularly appears in disciplinary opinions), expressions of "remorse" (a much-invoked word), and the lawyer's pro bono work.

Alcoholism and substance abuse are unlikely even to reduce the severity of a sanction in some jurisdictions. After canvassing cases nationwide, Attorney Grievance Commission v. Kenney, 664 A.2d 854 (Md. 1995), cautioned that "absent truly compelling circumstances, alcoholism will not be permitted to mitigate where an attorney commits a violation of ethical or legal rules which would ordinarily warrant disbarment." The court relied on its obligation "to protect the public from being victimized." See also In re Marshall, 762 A.2d 530 (D.C. 2000) (cocaine addiction did not prevent disbarment for misappropriation of client funds and submitting false documents) (collecting cases).

E. CONSTITUTIONAL PROTECTION IN CRIMINAL CASES

"She Didn't Call My Alibi"

Roscoe Duchamp was indicted for robbery. Katha Tomaiko was appointed to represent him. Duchamp has a felony conviction. In response to a pretrial motion, the judge ruled that the prosecutor could elicit the conviction on cross-examination if Duchamp testified. So Duchamp, on Tomaiko's advice, decided that he would not testify.

Duchamp tells Tomaiko that he was at the home of his boyfriend, Lorton Pale, at the time of the robbery. Tomaiko interviewed Pale, who confirmed Duchamp's alibi and described their evening the same way that Duchamp did. But Tomaiko was worried about how the jury would see Pale. "He'll come across to the jury—his manner, appearance—as, I don't know, odd, eccentric," Tomaiko said. "Politically, religiously, this is a very conservative county. Trump won it by 34 points. If the jury doesn't believe Pale, it'll color its view of you. Also, it'll come out that you're lovers and I'm very worried about gay bias. Half or more of the jury will believe LGBTQ identification is a lifestyle and a sin. The robbery happened at night. Lighting was poor. We're better off arguing that the state's two eyewitnesses are mistaken and we do have grounds to challenge their credibility. It's a reasonable doubt case."

Duchamp disagreed. "Why's my relationship with Lorton any of the jury's business?" he asked. "You don't have to ask about that. Only that we're friends."

"The prosecutor will discover it and be permitted to use it on cross," Tomaiko explained, "because it's relevant to Pale's credibility. The closer a relationship, the greater the room to impeach for bias."

After Duchamp is convicted, he hires a new lawyer, Maxine Spell, to challenge the conviction. "She didn't call my alibi," Duchamp complains. "I told her I wanted her to, but she said she got to make that decision, not me." Spell argues that Tomaiko was ineffective. "This wasn't a situation where Tomaiko had to choose between two inconsistent defenses," Spell tells the court. "She could have argued reasonable doubt *and* called Pale. Besides, anticipation of juror bias against a same-sex relationship should have played no role in Tomaiko's decision. If she was worried, she could have asked the judge for an instruction. She overreacted and Duchamp lost a defense."

"Tomaiko made a reasonable decision based on her experience," the prosecutor replied. "If she had deferred to Duchamp over her better judgment, and called Pale, Duchamp would be challenging *that* decision as ineffective. Duchamp wants to try the case both ways, but our system doesn't work that way. A choice was needed and the decision belonged to Tomaiko. Also, even if she was ineffective, which we don't concede, Duchamp can't show a reasonable probability of acquittal."

You're the judge. What's your ruling?

The Sixth Amendment guarantees criminal defendants "the assistance of counsel," whether counsel is appointed or retained. Cuyler v. Sullivan, 446 U.S. 335 (1980). Counsel must be "effective," not simply awake and present. McMann v. Richardson, 397 U.S. 759 (1970). The conviction of a defendant whose counsel was ineffective *and* whose defense was prejudiced as a result will be overturned. Evitts v. Lucey, 469 U.S. 387 (1985). We encountered the Sixth Amendment guarantee in Nix v. Whiteside in chapter 7C, where the Supreme Court held that the defense lawyer was not ineffective and the defendant was not prejudiced by his lawyer's threat to disclose the defendant's intended perjury. In McCoy v. Louisiana (chapter 2C1), counsel was found to be ineffective because over his client's objection he admitted guilt in the first phase of a capital trial in the hope that it would benefit the client at the penalty phase. The Court said the choice was the client's to make.

Some overlap must be expected in the standards of performance for the Sixth Amendment, the law of malpractice, and the ethical duty of competence, but these are distinct concepts. The effective assistance of counsel is a constitutional guarantee and applies uniformly nationwide. Malpractice law and ethical rules are determined by each jurisdiction. The constitutional guarantee applies only in criminal cases and protects only the defendant. Malpractice and incompetence can occur in all representations.

At one time, the test of effectiveness was very deferential, requiring little more than a person admitted to the bar who shows up and mostly stays awake. In Trapnell v. United States, 725 F.2d 149 (2d Cir. 1983), the Second Circuit wrote that for 30 years under its caselaw a "lack of effective assistance of counsel must be of such a kind as to shock the conscience of the court and make the proceedings a farce and mockery of justice." As of 1970 every circuit had adopted the "farce and mockery" standard, if indeed it can even be called a standard. But in the next decade every circuit except the Second Circuit moved to a "reasonably competent assistance" test or its equivalent. In *Trapnell*, the Second Circuit joined them.

A year later, the Supreme Court decided Strickland v. Washington, 466 U.S. 668 (1984). The defendant, who had pled guilty in Florida, challenged his death sentence on the ground that his lawyer was constitutionally ineffective at the sentencing phase of his trial, when the judge weighed aggravating and mitigating factors and decided the sentence. (In most other states with a death penalty, the jury makes this decision.) Justice O'Connor wrote that a defendant challenging counsel's effectiveness, whether at a trial or at the penalty phase of a capital case, "must identify the acts or omissions of counsel that are alleged not to have been the result of reasonable professional judgment." "Prevailing norms of practice reflected in American Bar Association [Standards for Criminal Justice] and the like are guides to determining what is reasonable, but they are only guides." Furthermore,

[j]udicial scrutiny of counsel's performance must be highly deferential. It is all too tempting for a defendant to second-guess counsel's assistance after conviction or adverse sentence, and it is all too easy for a court, examining counsel's defense after it has proved unsuccessful, to conclude that a particular act or omission of counsel was unreasonable. A fair assessment of attorney performance requires that every effort be made to eliminate the distorting effects of hindsight, to reconstruct the circumstances of counsel's challenged conduct, and to evaluate the conduct from counsel's perspective at the time. Because of the difficulties inherent in making the evaluation, a court must indulge a strong presumption that counsel's conduct falls within the wide range of reasonable professional assistance; that is, the defendant must overcome the

presumption that, under the circumstances, the challenged action "might be considered sound trial strategy." There are countless ways to provide effective assistance in any given case. Even the best criminal defense attorneys would not defend a particular client in the same way. . . .

In making that determination, the court should keep in mind that counsel's function, as elaborated in prevailing professional norms, is to make the adversarial testing process work in the particular case.

Even if a lawyer is ineffective, the defendant must also show a "reasonable probability" that the result would have differed. In *Strickland*, the Court held that the defense lawyer acted reasonably in deciding which mitigating facts to emphasize. *Strickland*'s two-part test for ineffectiveness—inquiry into the lawyer's performance and prejudice—remains the law.*

How does a court know if a lawyer's acts or omissions are unreasonable? Errors of judgment and unsuccessful strategies do not equal ineffectiveness, just as they do not equal malpractice. *Strickland* told us that courts should look to "prevailing norms reflected in" the ABA Criminal Justice Standards (you can find them online) "and the like." The meaning of "ineffective" can change over time. Padilla v. Kentucky, 559 U.S. 356 (2010), lists the kind of sources to which a court might look.† *Padilla* held that counsel was ineffective because he had failed to tell the defendant that a guilty plea could result in deportation.

Hundreds of ineffectiveness claims are asserted yearly in federal and state courts. Nearly all fail. But some succeed, including in the Supreme Court. We might expect to find the greatest receptivity to these claims in death

---

* Recall that where the claim is that counsel was ineffective because they were conflicted, the prejudice test is easier to meet. See chapter 5B1. Sometimes there is no need to show any prejudice. The *Strickland* Court wrote: "In certain Sixth Amendment contexts, prejudice is presumed. Actual or constructive denial of the assistance of counsel altogether is legally presumed to result in prejudice. So are various kinds of state interference with counsel's assistance. Prejudice in these circumstances is so likely that case-by-case inquiry into prejudice is not worth the cost. Moreover, such circumstances involve impairments of the Sixth Amendment right that are easy to identify and, for that reason and because the prosecution is directly responsible, easy for the government to prevent." All circuit courts that have addressed the question "have held that prejudice must be presumed when counsel sleeps either through a 'substantial portion of [a defendant's] trial' or at a critical time during trial." United States v. Ragin, 820 F.3d 609 (4th Cir. 2016).

† "The weight of prevailing professional norms supports the view that counsel must advise her client regarding the risk of deportation. National Legal Aid and Defender Assn., Performance Guidelines for Criminal Representation §6.2 (1995); G. Herman, Plea Bargaining §3.03, pp. 20–21 (1997); Gabriel J. Chin & Richard W. Holmes, Jr., Effective Assistance of Counsel and the Consequences of Guilty Pleas, 87 Cornell L. Rev. 697, 713–718 (2002); A. Campbell, Law of Sentencing §13:23, pp. 555, 560 (3d ed. 2004); Dept. of Justice, Office of Justice Programs, 2 Compendium of Standards for Indigent Defense Systems, Standards for Attorney Performance, pp. D10, H8–H9, J8 (2000) (providing survey of guidelines across multiple jurisdictions); ABA Standards for Criminal Justice, Prosecution Function and Defense Function 4–5.1(a), p. 197 (3d ed. 1993); ABA Standards for Criminal Justice, Pleas of Guilty 14–3.2(f), p. 116 (3d ed. 1999). . . ."

penalty cases, especially at the penalty phase, where a finding of ineffectiveness will not upset a conviction. And that seems to be true. In fact, it can appear that the effective assistance of counsel has a different meaning in capital cases. Here are three examples, in each of which the court reversed a lower federal or state court.

In Wiggins v. Smith, 539 U.S. 510 (2003), the defense lawyers did not introduce mitigating evidence — of which there was much — at the penalty phase of the case. While that decision might have been defensible if counsel knew about the evidence and then chose not to use it, here the lawyers made the decision after an inadequate investigation that left them ignorant of the extent of the mitigating evidence.

Hinton v. Alabama, 571 U.S. 263 (2014), held that a defense lawyer was constitutionally ineffective in failing to ask for funds to hire an additional expert on critical bullet evidence. The lawyer mistakenly believed that the funds were not available.

In Buck v. Davis, ____ U.S. ____ (2017), counsel was found ineffective at the sentencing phase of a capital case by inexplicably introducing the following evidence through his expert witness Dr. Quijano:

> Counsel knew that Dr. Quijano's report reflected the view that Buck's race disproportionately predisposed him to violent conduct; he also knew that the principal point of dispute during the trial's penalty phase was whether Buck was likely to act violently in the future. Counsel nevertheless (1) called Dr. Quijano to the stand; (2) specifically elicited testimony about the connection between Buck's race and the likelihood of future violence; and (3) put into evidence Dr. Quijano's expert report that stated, in reference to factors bearing on future dangerousness, "Race. Black: Increased probability."
>
> Given that the jury had to make a finding of future dangerousness before it could impose a death sentence, Dr. Quijano's report said, in effect, that the color of Buck's skin made him more deserving of execution.

Outside capital cases, the Court has found a Sixth Amendment violation where a lawyer failed to communicate a plea offer and the client was then convicted of a higher offense, Missouri v. Frye, 566 U.S. 134 (2012), and where a lawyer's advice to reject a plea bargain was based on a fundamental misunderstanding of the law. The client rejected the offer and was convicted of a higher offense. Lafler v. Cooper, 566 U.S. 156 (2012).

The Ineffectiveness Test in a System of Procedural Defaults

Chapter 2B3 told us that a lawyer's decisions, even errors, will usually bind the client. A lawyer's failure to raise a defendant's constitutional claims in state court will be a procedural default that will prevent the defendant from later raising those claims in a state or federal collateral attack. This will be true even if counsel's failure was the product of "ignorance or inadvertence," Murray v. Carrier, 477 U.S. 478 (1986), and the defendant was not responsible for it. "[T]he mere fact that counsel failed to recognize the factual or legal basis for a claim, or failed to raise the claim despite recognizing it, does not constitute cause for [excusing] a procedural default."

Self-Assessment Questions

1. A child's parents brought a medical malpractice action against the hospital in which the child was born and others, alleging that the child suffered neurological and brain damage as a result of professional negligence at his birth. During the trial, but before a verdict, the parties settled for $185,000. McGrath, the lawyer for the hospital, made certain representations to counsel for the plaintiffs. So far as can be known, he believed them to be true. On one occasion, he said that he "knew" the hospital's insurance coverage was $200,000. On another occasion, he said that this was what he had been informed. In agreeing to the settlement, the plaintiffs expressly relied on these statements. It transpired that the hospital had a separate policy for $1 million in addition to the $200,000 policy to which McGrath referred. McGrath had access to documents (of which he claimed to be unaware) revealing the excess coverage. After the settlement and after the plaintiffs learned about the additional coverage, they sued McGrath, among others. Is McGrath liable to the plaintiffs? On what theories? What could he have said to avoid this risk?

2. Ambase was part of a corporate family. In a series of complex transactions, it became an independent entity. Other parties agreed to indemnify Ambase for any tax liability it might have prior to the spinoff or as a result of it. The IRS claimed Ambase owed $20 million in taxes and Ambase asked Davis Polk & Wardwell (DPW) to defend it against the claim. Ambase gave DPW all of the documents leading up to and in the transactions that led to its independence. The retainer agreement stated that the firm was hired "to resolve the tax issues currently before the IRS." DPW represented Ambase in the tax court against the IRS and won. Ambase refused to pay the firm's fee and sued for malpractice. It claimed that the documents it gave the firm revealed another possible defense. Namely, that if anyone was primarily liable to the IRS, it was one of the other companies, not Ambase, which was only secondarily liable, and that DPW failed to recognize as much. Had it done so promptly, Ambase would not have had to pay to litigate the IRS claim—someone else would have had to do so—and, moreover, Ambase could have profitably invested the $20 million it had kept in reserve for years in case it lost. What arguments might the firm have?

3. Carl Whitten, a lawyer in his mid-30s, was having dinner with his wife Sara at an upscale restaurant in Miami, where they lived. The Whittens had been having marital problems and the dinner was intended to give

them unpressured, romantic time as a couple. They dressed up for the occasion. Sara Whitten is a model and often recognized. Carl noticed that a solitary male diner at a nearby table was staring at Sara and, it seemed to Carl, especially at her low-cut dress. He walked over to tell the man to cut it out. They exchanged words and Carl tipped over the man's chair, sending him to the floor, then kicked him repeatedly until waiters interceded. The police were called. Carl eventually entered a guilty plea to misdemeanor assault and was sentenced to six months of probation and a $5,000 fine. Should Carl be disciplined and if so what should be the sanction? What else do you want to know?

XIV

Control of Quality: Nonlawyers in the Law Business (and Related Issues)

In the mid-1920s, a group of people in Illinois organized the Motorists' Association of Illinois as a not-for-profit corporation. The association hired competent and licensed lawyers, whose only work was to represent the 50,000 members of the association, without charge, in court proceedings arising out of the operation of their automobiles. Each member paid an annual fee. The Chicago Bar Association did not like this arrangement. (Why not?) It petitioned the court to forbid the motorists' group from continuing in business. It argued that the group was practicing law without a license. True, the lawyers themselves were licensed to practice law in Illinois, but the association was not a law firm, which meant that *it* was practicing law illegally. The Illinois Supreme Court agreed. Not only did it hold that the association was practicing law without a license, it also ruled that the state legislature was without power to authorize the association's work. Only the court could decide who was, and who was not, fit to practice law. People ex rel. Chicago Bar Ass'n v. Motorists' Ass'n, 188 N.E. 827 (Ill. 1933).

Obviously, the motorists understood that their plan would reduce the cost of legal help in claims arising from driving their cars. It made economic sense to join together and hire lawyers on salary. The legal fees if the motorists had to pay their own lawyers would be much higher than their association's dues. But the plan was not good for Illinois lawyers for the same reason that it was good for the motorists. And if the idea spread, it could reduce legal fees in other circumstances where clients could pool their purchasing power. But the Illinois Supreme Court stopped it and that was that.* Here we have an

---

* Today, for-profit insurance companies do what the nonprofit Motorists' Association attempted and in many states the companies can use staff lawyers to defend an insured when the interests of insured and insurer are aligned. Unauth. Practice of Law Comm. v. Am. Home Assur. Co., 261 S.W.3d 24 (Tex. 2008). In other words, for-profit insurers today can do essentially the same thing that was forbidden to the Illinois motorists—sharing costs and risks and purchasing legal help wholesale—but for profit.

early example of how rules governing the legal services market can raise the price of legal help, even making advice too costly for many. Later in this chapter, we'll ask whether changes in governing doctrines would today (or might soon) allow a different outcome.

When and how can a lay entity or nonlawyers participate in delivery of legal services? This chapter investigates the rules from several perspectives.

First, and most important to public interest law firms, are two cases that constitutionally insulate lawyers and their nonprofit law offices from certain rules that regulate for-profit law offices and therefore from interest groups that may wish to weaken or eliminate their work. The first case, NAACP v. Button, which today may not get full treatment in constitutional law classes, enabled the growth of public interest law as we know it. The second case, In re Primus, builds on *Button* and gives constitutional protection to public interest lawyers who solicit clients to serve as plaintiffs, notwithstanding state rules that forbid the same activities by lawyers in private practice.

Second are the union cases. These constitutionally empower unions to "buy" legal services for their members more cheaply, including through the very strategy that Illinois prohibited for the motorists. There's a difference, though. The motorists had in common only their ownership of cars. Union members can build on a preexisting membership in a labor organization. Bar groups fiercely opposed the union plans. It defended its opposition as a well-intentioned effort to protect clients from bad advice. But Justice Black saw through this explanation and called it an effort to protect legal fees.

Third is another development only just emerging—state court recognition of a licensing system for law workers (legal technicians or paralegals) who are authorized to sell a limited menu of services that are traditionally reserved for lawyers. The idea was implemented in Washington State (until recently) and in mid-2020 was authorized by state high courts in Arizona and Utah. It is one response to what is sometimes called the Access to Justice Movement, which seeks solutions for the plight of poor people and people of moderate (or even greater) means who are priced out of the market for civil legal services. See chapter 12C.

A *fourth* looming trend, related to the third but distinct, would allow nonlawyers to invest in the profits of the law industry.

Although the materials in this chapter can reasonably be analyzed as raising unauthorized practice of law issues, they differ from the unauthorized practice issues studied in chapter 12C. That material addressed competency risks when those with no formal legal training or license perform work that is labeled (rightly or wrongly) the "practice of law." By contrast, the following pages describe other ways in which nonlawyers or organizations that are not law firms may legitimately seek to participate in the law industry.

In reading the balance of this chapter, keep two themes in mind. First, lay participation in the delivery of legal services for profit can have economic consequences for the cost of those services—and therefore the affordability of legal advice—and for the identity of those who share in the profits. The ramifications of changes in this area are unpredictable. But if lay interests (and private capital) can compete with traditional law firms, competition on the "supply" side is likely to grow and legal fees are likely to decline. Or, as in the union cases, if consumers can buy legal services in bulk, they will have more market power and prices should fall. Second, money aside, eliminating a clear distinction between the "law business" and "other businesses" may, in unpredictable ways, affect how lawyers think of themselves, how the public thinks of lawyers, and who decides to go or not go to law school.

A. NONPROFIT ENTITIES AND INTERMEDIARIES

1. Public Interest Organizations

The civil rights movement of the middle third of the twentieth century had to confront state laws aimed at curtailing lay influence in the attorney-client relationship. The movement included organizations run by nonlawyers and which were not traditional law firms. Some of these organizations used litigation to effect social change. A mid-1950s Virginia law frustrated that strategy for the NAACP. Although Virginia said its law was simply a neutral effort to protect clients, the timing—the law was passed soon after Brown v. Board of Education—encouraged the (nearly) irresistible inference that Virginia was seeking to impede the NAACP's efforts to implement *Brown*. *Button* identifies this timeline, but it did not rely on a finding that the state had discriminatory motives. As a result, its influence has been greater than if it had.

Button introduces you to the common law offenses of champerty, barratry, and maintenance, ill-defined doctrines that continue to have an unpredictable (and, some argue, unfortunate) influence on innovation in the delivery of legal services. These are discussed in the note following the case.

NAACP v. BUTTON
371 U.S. 415 (1963)

JUSTICE BRENNAN delivered the opinion of the Court. . . .

[The NAACP sought to enjoin enforcement of certain Virginia laws. The NAACP's Virginia chapter, or Conference, had for over ten years "concentrated upon financing litigation aimed at ending racial segregation in the public schools of the Commonwealth." To this end, the association provided attorneys, whom it paid, to represent litigants challenging segregated schooling. "The actual conduct of assisted litigation is under the control of the attorney, although the NAACP continues to be concerned that the outcome of the lawsuit should be consistent with NAACP's policies. . . . A client is free at any time to withdraw from an action."

[In 1956, the state passed laws that would make it more difficult for the NAACP to represent school desegregation plaintiffs. The laws carried criminal penalties. A federal court invalidated three chapters of these laws and ordered the NAACP to go to state court for authoritative interpretations of two remaining chapters. The state courts voided one of these chapters but upheld Chapter 33, which prohibited solicitation by "an agent for an individual or an organization which retains a lawyer in connection with an action to which it is not a party and in which it has no pecuniary right or liability." The Virginia Supreme Court of Appeals held that this amendment prohibited the NAACP's agents from soliciting persons to serve as plaintiffs in challenges to segregated education. Without plaintiffs, of course, no case could be brought. The law impeded the NAACP's ability to find plaintiffs. The Supreme Court granted review.]

II . . .

A

We meet at the outset the contention that "solicitation" is wholly outside the area of freedoms protected by the First Amendment. To this contention there are two answers. The first is that a State cannot foreclose the exercise of constitutional rights by mere labels. The second is that abstract discussion is not the only species of communication which the Constitution protects; the First Amendment also protects vigorous advocacy, certainly of lawful ends, against governmental intrusion. In the context of NAACP objectives, litigation is not a technique of resolving private differences; it is a means for achieving the lawful objectives of equality of treatment by all government, federal, state and local, for the members of the Negro community in this country. It is thus a form of political expression. Groups which find themselves unable to achieve their objectives through the ballot frequently turn to the courts. . . . And under the conditions of modern government, litigation may well be the sole practicable avenue open to a minority to petition for redress of grievances. . . .

B . . .

We read the decree of the Virginia Supreme Court of Appeals in the instant case as proscribing any arrangement by which prospective litigants are advised to seek the assistance of particular attorneys. No narrower reading is plausible. We cannot accept the reading suggested on behalf of the Attorney General of Virginia on the second oral argument that the Supreme Court of Appeals construed Chapter 33 as proscribing control only of the actual litigation by the NAACP after it is instituted. . . .

We conclude that under Chapter 33, as authoritatively construed by the Supreme Court of Appeals, a person who advises another that his legal rights have been infringed and refers him to a particular attorney or group of attorneys (for example, to the [NAACP's] Virginia Conference's legal staff) for assistance has committed a crime, as has the attorney who knowingly renders assistance under such circumstances. There thus inheres in the statute the gravest danger of smothering all discussion looking to the eventual institution of litigation on behalf of the rights of members of an unpopular minority. . . . We cannot close our eyes to the fact that the militant Negro civil rights movement has engendered the intense resentment and opposition of the politically dominant white community of Virginia; litigation assisted by the NAACP has been bitterly fought. In such circumstances, a statute broadly curtailing group activity leading to litigation may easily become a weapon of oppression, however even-handed its terms appear. Its mere existence could well freeze out of existence all such activity on behalf of the civil rights of Negro citizens. . . .

C

[Virginia contends that it] has a subordinating interest in the regulation of the legal profession, embodied in Chapter 33, which justifies limiting petitioner's First Amendment rights. Specifically, Virginia contends that the NAACP's activities in furtherance of litigation, being "improper solicitation" under the state statute, fall within the traditional purview of state regulation of professional conduct. However, the State's attempt to equate the activities of the NAACP and its lawyers with common-law barratry, maintenance and champerty, and to outlaw them accordingly, cannot obscure the serious encroachment worked by Chapter 33 upon protected freedoms of expression. The decisions of this Court have consistently held that only a compelling state interest in the regulation of a subject within the State's constitutional power to regulate can justify limiting First Amendment freedoms. . . .

However valid may be Virginia's interest in regulating the traditionally illegal practices of barratry, maintenance and champerty, that interest does not justify the prohibition of the NAACP activities disclosed by this record. Malicious intent was of the essence of the common-law offenses of fomenting or stirring up litigation. And whatever may be or may have been true of suits against government in other countries, the exercise in our own, as in this case, of First Amendment rights to enforce constitutional rights through litigation, as a matter of law, cannot be deemed malicious. Even more modern, subtler regulations of unprofessional conduct or interference with professional relations, not involving malice, would not touch the activities at bar; regulations which reflect hostility to stirring up litigation have been aimed chiefly at those who urge recourse to the courts for private gain, serving no public interest. . . .

Objection to the intervention of a lay intermediary, who may control litigation or otherwise interfere with the rendering of legal services in a confidential relationship, also derives from the element of pecuniary gain. Fearful of dangers thought to arise from that element, the courts of several States have sustained regulations aimed at these activities. We intimate no view one way or the other as to the merits of those decisions with respect to the particular arrangements against which they are directed. It is enough that the superficial resemblance in form between those arrangements and that at bar cannot obscure the vital fact that here the entire arrangement employs constitutionally privileged means of expression to secure constitutionally guaranteed civil rights. There has been no showing of a serious danger here of professionally reprehensible conflicts of interest which rules against solicitation frequently seek to prevent. This is so partly because no monetary stakes are involved, and so there is no danger that the attorney will desert or subvert the paramount interests of his client to enrich himself or an outside sponsor. And the aims and interests of NAACP have not been shown to conflict with those of its members and non-member Negro litigants. . . .

Resort to the courts to seek vindication of constitutional rights is a different matter from the oppressive, malicious, or avaricious use of the legal process for purely private gain. Lawsuits attacking racial discrimination, at least in Virginia, are neither very profitable nor very popular. They are not an object of general competition among Virginia lawyers; the problem is rather one of an apparent dearth of lawyers who are willing to undertake such litigation. There has been neither claim nor proof that any assisted Negro litigants have desired, but have been prevented from retaining, the services of other counsel. We realize that an NAACP lawyer must derive personal satisfaction from participation in litigation on behalf of Negro rights, else he would hardly be inclined to participate at the risk of financial sacrifice. But this would not seem to be the kind of interest or motive which induces criminal conduct.

We conclude that although the petitioner has amply shown that its activities fall within the First Amendment's protections, the State has failed to advance any substantial regulatory interest, in the form of substantive evils flowing from petitioner's activities, which can justify the broad prohibitions which it has imposed. . . .

Reversed.

[Justice Douglas concurred. Justice White concurred in part and dissented in part.]

JUSTICE HARLAN, joined by JUSTICES CLARK and STEWART, dissenting. . . .

III . . .

The regulation before us has its origins in the long-standing common-law prohibitions of champerty, barratry, and maintenance, the closely related prohibitions in the Canons of Ethics against solicitation and intervention by a lay intermediary, and statutory provisions forbidding the unauthorized practice of law. The Court recognizes this formidable history, but puts it aside in the present case on the grounds that there is here no element of malice or of pecuniary gain, that the interests of the NAACP are not to be regarded as substantially different from those of its members, and that we are said to be dealing here with a matter that transcends mere legal ethics—the securing of federally guaranteed rights. But these distinctions are too facile. They do not account for the full scope of the State's legitimate interest in regulating professional conduct. For although these professional standards may have been born in a desire to curb malice and self-aggrandizement by those who would use clients and the courts for their own pecuniary ends, they have acquired a far broader significance during their long development.

First, with regard to the claimed absence of the pecuniary element, it cannot well be suggested that the attorneys here are donating their services, since they are in fact compensated for their work. . . .

Underlying this impressive array of relevant precedent is the widely shared conviction that avoidance of improper pecuniary gain is not the only relevant factor in determining standards of professional conduct. Running perhaps even deeper is the desire of the profession, of courts, and of legislatures to prevent any interference with the uniquely personal relationship between lawyer and client and to maintain untrammeled by outside influences the responsibility which the lawyer owes to the courts he serves.

When an attorney is employed by an association or corporation to represent individual litigants, two problems arise, whether or not the association is organized for profit and no matter how unimpeachable its motives. The lawyer becomes subject to the control of a body that is not itself a litigant and that, unlike the lawyers it employs, is not subject to strict professional discipline as an officer of the court. In addition, the lawyer necessarily finds himself with a divided allegiance—to his employer and to his client—which may prevent full compliance with his basic professional obligations. . . .

Second, it is claimed that the interests of petitioner and its members are sufficiently identical to eliminate any "serious danger" of "professionally reprehensible conflicts of interest." . . .

The NAACP may be no more than the sum of the efforts and views infused in it by its members; but the totality of the separate interests of the members and others whose causes the petitioner champions, even in the field of race relations, may far exceed in scope and variety that body's views of policy, as embodied in litigating strategy and tactics. Thus it may be in the interest of the Association in every case to make a frontal attack on segregation, to press for an immediate breaking down of racial barriers, and to sacrifice minor points that may win a given case for the major points that may win other cases too. But in a particular litigation, it is not impossible that after authorizing action in his behalf, a Negro parent, concerned that a continued frontal attack could result in schools closed for years, might prefer to wait with his fellows a longer time for good-faith efforts by the local school board than is permitted by the centrally determined policy of the NAACP. Or he might see a greater prospect of success through discussions with local school authorities than through the litigation deemed necessary by the Association.

The parent, of course, is free to withdraw his authorization, but is his lawyer, retained and paid by petitioner and subject to its directions on matters of policy, able to advise the parent with that undivided allegiance that is the hallmark of the attorney-client relation? I am afraid not. . . .

Third, it is said that the practices involved here must stand on a different footing because the litigation that petitioner supports concerns the vindication of constitutionally guaranteed rights.

But surely state law is still the source of basic regulation of the legal profession, whether an attorney is pressing a federal or a state claim within its borders. The true question is whether the State has taken action which unreasonably obstructs the assertion of federal rights. Here, it cannot be said that the underlying state policy is inevitably inconsistent with federal interests. The State has sought to prohibit the solicitation and sponsoring of litigation by those who have no standing to initiate that litigation themselves and who are not simply coming to the assistance of indigent litigants. Thus the state policy is not unrelated to the federal rules of standing—the insistence that federal court litigants be confined to those who can demonstrate a pressing personal need for relief. . . .

Maintenance, Barratry, Champerty, and Change: What Did *Button* Decide?

The Common Law Background.   *Button's* importance to public interest law, then and now, can hardly be overstated. Virginia unsuccessfully argued that its law merely represented a traditional effort to prevent the kinds of evils condemned by the common law offenses of barratry, champerty, and maintenance. Here are some definitions:

> "**Maintenance** exists when a person without interest in a suit officiously intermeddles therein by assisting either party with money or otherwise to prosecute or defend it." Mut. of Omaha Bank v. Kassebaum, 814 N.W.2d 731 (Neb. 2012). Lord Denning said that maintenance is "improperly stirring up litigation and strife by giving aid to one party to bring or defend a claim without just cause or excuse." In re Trepca Mines, Ltd., [1963] 3 All E.R. 351 (C.A.). A person lacked just cause, according to the *Button* majority, if there was "malicious intent," which was absent if the maintaining party's motives were charitable.
>
> "**Barratry** (or barretry) is the offense of frequently exciting and stirring up quarrels and suits between other individuals." Osprey, Inc. v. Cabana Ltd. P'ship., 532 S.E.2d 269 (S.C. 2000). It is rarely invoked today.
>
> **Champerty** is the most frequently mentioned of the offenses. "Champerty has been described as the unlawful maintenance of a suit, where a person without an interest in it agrees to finance the suit, in whole or in part, in consideration for receiving a portion of the proceeds of the litigation. . . . The ancient prohibition against champerty arose in feudal England. More recently the doctrine has been viewed as a check on frivolous or unnecessary litigation, or a mechanism to encourage the settlement of disputes without recourse to litigation." Saladini v. Righellis, 687 N.E.2d 1224 (Mass. 1997). Champerty

"consists of an agreement whereby a person without interest in another's suit undertakes to carry it on at his or her own expense, in whole or in part, in consideration of receiving, in the event of success, a part of the proceeds of the litigation." *Mut. of Omaha*, supra.*

Although we can find alternate definitions for each of these doctrines, which may reveal a lack of precision, it should be apparent that maintenance and barratry are particularly ill-defined and that champerty, though less so, lacks clear boundaries. The consequence is that the three doctrines are wild cards in any efforts to change the traditional way legal services are organized and funded. Further, they rest on a view that litigation, even if not an evil, can be used abusively and, in any event, should be discouraged. Discouraging litigation means preventing outsiders from funding or encouraging it, so far as possible. In *Button,* that would stop the NAACP's strategy for implementing *Brown.* But as the *Button* majority saw it, the common law doctrines can themselves be used abusively—to deny unpopular litigants access to the courts to vindicate constitutional rights. They can also make it harder for persons with even mundane claims to seek funding for a court case.

It seems clear today that various roadblocks to litigation in rules governing lawyers often had the effect, and perhaps the purpose, of protecting those who might be sued from those who with financing would be able to sue them. Better to keep your opponent out of court entirely than to defend and risk losing. With no empirical support, proponents of the common law offenses argue that they are needed to discourage "frivolous" litigation. But frivolous litigation is bound to fail and may lead to sanctions. Who would invest in it? A similar argument—that litigation is an "evil" and should be discouraged—was made against giving First Amendment protection to legal advertising. The Supreme Court disagreed in Zauderer v. Office of Disciplinary Counsel, 471 U.S. 626 (1985), which held that "access to [the] civil courts is not an evil to be regretted; rather, it is an attribute of our system of justice in which we ought to take pride."

Several state high courts, including *Saladini* and *Osprey,* have held that champerty and the other doctrines will no longer be recognized. Some other states never recognized them at all. The *Saladini* court wrote:

> We have long abandoned the view that litigation is suspect, and have recognized that agreements to purchase an interest in an action may actually foster resolution of a dispute. . . . We also no longer are persuaded that the champerty doctrine is needed to protect against the evils once feared: speculation in lawsuits, the bringing of frivolous lawsuits, or financial overreaching by a party of superior bargaining position. There are now other devices that more effectively accomplish these ends.

---

* In re Primus, 436 U.S. 412 (1978), summarizes the three doctrines this way: "Put simply, maintenance is helping another prosecute a suit; champerty is maintaining a suit in return for a financial interest in the outcome; and barratry is a continuing practice of maintenance or champerty."

More recently, Minnesota abandoned the champerty doctrine. A funded litigant asserted a champerty defense to avoid her contractual obligation to the funder in Maslowski v. Prospect Funding Partners, 944 N.W.2d 235 (Minn. 2020). (See pages 631–632.) The court, rejecting the defense, wrote:

> Societal attitudes regarding litigation have also changed significantly. Many now see a claim as a potentially valuable asset, rather than viewing litigation as an evil to be avoided. The size of the market for litigation financing reflects this attitudinal change. Businesses often seek financing to mitigate the risks associated with litigation and maintain cash flow for their operations. It is also possible that litigation financing, like the contingency fee, may increase access to justice for both individuals and organizations.*

But champerty is much alive elsewhere. Some states have statutes that preserve the basic idea behind them so courts in those states may not see themselves as free to abolish the common law offences. For example, §489 of New York's Judiciary Law, with a few exceptions, forbids a person or entity to "solicit, buy or take an assignment of, or be in any manner interested in buying or taking an assignment of a bond, promissory note, bill of exchange, book debt, or other thing in action, or any claim or demand, with the intent and for the purpose of bringing an action or proceeding thereon." Bluebird Partners v. First Fidelity Bank, N.A., 731 N.E.2d 581 (N.Y. 2000), narrowly construes the statute to require that "intent to sue on [the] claim must at least have been the primary purpose for, if not the sole motivation behind, entering into the transaction."†

---

* The court cited eight states that regulate consumer litigation financings through legislation: Arkansas, Indiana, Maine, Nebraska, Ohio, Oklahoma, Tennessee, and Vermont.

† *Bluebird* explains the fascinating etymology of the word "champerty":

> The "champerty" concept is based on a type of French feudal tenure in land, a "champart," in which the fee for use of the land was neither in money nor ordinary service in kind. The tenant-by-champart was a partial owner of the land bound to share any rents and profits with the grantor, but the grantor took the risk that the crops might fail and that there would be no return. Anyone who then obtained a legal interest in that grant of land would also take a share of the profits in champart (see Radin, Maintenance by Champerty, 24 Cal. L. Rev. 48, 61-62 [1935]).
>
> "Champerty," as a term of art, grew out of this practice to describe the medieval situation where someone bought an interest in a claim under litigation, agreeing to bear the expenses but also to share the benefits if the suit succeeded. The most important litigation of that era was over land, and a person who bought lawsuits could acquire a partial interest in landed estates—an estimable power play. The taint on the process arose because the purchase price was usually far below the value of the potential land acquisition—a transaction suffused with speculation related to the "sin" of usury and its concomitant legal prohibitions. The champerty transaction, however, evaded the strict prohibitive laws involving usury (see, id., at 60-61, 67).
>
> Even as the feudal system faded, English law retained the word "champart" as a metaphor to indicate a disapproval of lawsuits brought "for part of the profits" of the action (see, id., at 63; see also, Winfield, The History of Maintenance and Champerty, 35 L.Q. Rev. 50 [1919]).

Even where the offenses are not statutory, courts may prefer to let the legislature decide whether to abolish them. Toste Farm Corp. v. Hadbury, Inc., 798 A.2d 901 (R.I. 2002) (upholding civil damage claim for maintenance against a law firm).

The Constitutional Context. When *Button* reached the Supreme Court, the single remaining issue was whether Virginia could prohibit the NAACP from using agents to solicit plaintiffs whom lawyers, paid by the NAACP, would then represent in school desegregation cases. But neither the majority nor the dissent was able—or apparently wished—to avoid a larger question: May NAACP lawyers, working for an organization that is not a law firm, represent plaintiffs in these cases under *any* circumstances, even if the plaintiffs had not been solicited by NAACP agents? Both opinions identify the state's interest as avoidance of conflicts between the interests of the lawyers' employer and the interests of their clients. But the majority and dissent disagree about the likelihood of an actual conflict and harm to the client. They also disagree about the scope of constitutional protection for the arrangement and the degree of deference the Court should give the state's professed interest in ensuring a lawyer's undivided loyalty. Finally, they disagree about motives—both Virginia's and the NAACP's.

The majority implies that Virginia is motivated by hostility to desegregation lawsuits, although its opinion does not rely on such a finding. The dissent, by contrast, accepts Virginia's claim that all it truly wished to do is maintain "high professional standards among those who practice law within its borders." Chapter 33 was, after all, much like antisolicitation provisions in many jurisdictions at the time, which were intended to prevent conduct sometimes disparaged as "ambulance chasing." See chapter 16. Virginia could argue it was just a coincidence that Chapter 33 was passed shortly after *Brown*.

What about the NAACP's motives? The fact that they were not monetary led Justice Brennan to conclude that there was small risk of an actual conflict with the clients. Justice Harlan was not so sure. He's right, isn't he? Doesn't history teach us that political motives can be at least as strong an influence on deeds (and misdeeds) as financial ones? Sometimes stronger. Even so, we can nevertheless defend *Button* on the ground that the First Amendment gives greater protection to political motives than to commercial ones. The amendment protects the right to petition the government, which includes the courts. It doesn't protect a right to make money.

The precise holding of In re Primus has now been superseded by later Supreme Court decisions on lawyer advertising and solicitation. These decisions would (with qualifications) protect letters like the one Edna Smith Primus sent to Mary Etta Williams even if (unlike Primus herself) the sender's motive was financial. But *Primus* makes a more important point, one that remains vital for the public interest bar: States have less power to regulate client solicitation (and by implication other activities of public interest lawyers) when the lawyer's motive is political, defined broadly, rather than financial, defined narrowly. In *Button*, the focus was on the lay status of the intermediary organization (the NAACP) and the danger of conflicts between its interests and those of the client. In *Primus*, the focus was on how a lawyer could try to get a client.

IN RE PRIMUS
436 U.S. 412 (1978)

JUSTICE POWELL delivered the opinion of the Court.

We consider on this appeal whether a State may punish a member of its Bar who, seeking to further political and ideological goals through associational activity, including litigation, advises a lay person of her legal rights and discloses in a subsequent letter that free legal assistance is available from a nonprofit organization with which the lawyer and her associates are affiliated. Appellant, a member of the Bar of South Carolina, received a public reprimand for writing such a letter. . . .

I

Appellant, Edna Smith Primus, is a lawyer practicing in Columbia, S.C. During the period in question, she was associated with the "Carolina Community Law Firm," and was an officer of and cooperating lawyer with the Columbia branch of the American Civil Liberties Union (ACLU). She received no compensation for her work on behalf of the ACLU, but was paid a retainer as a legal consultant for the South Carolina Council on Human Relations (Council), a nonprofit organization with offices in Columbia.

During the summer of 1973, local and national newspapers reported that pregnant mothers on public assistance in Aiken County, S.C., were being sterilized or threatened with sterilization as a condition of the continued receipt of medical assistance under the Medicaid program. Concerned by this development, Gary Allen, an Aiken businessman and officer of a local organization serving indigents, called the Council requesting that one of its representatives come to Aiken to address some of the women who had been sterilized. At the Council's behest, appellant, who had not known Allen previously, called him and arranged a meeting in his office in July 1973. Among those attending was Mary Etta Williams, who had been sterilized by Dr. Clovis H. Pierce after the birth of her third child. Williams and her grandmother attended the meeting because Allen, an old family friend, had invited them and because Williams wanted "[t]o see what it was all about . . ." At the meeting, appellant advised those present, including Williams and the other women who had been sterilized by Dr. Pierce, of their legal rights and suggested the possibility of a lawsuit.

Early in August 1973, the ACLU informed appellant that it was willing to provide representation for Aiken mothers who had been sterilized. Appellant testified that after being advised by Allen that Williams wished to institute suit against Dr. Pierce, she decided to inform Williams of the

ACLU's offer of free legal representation. Shortly after receiving appellant's letter, dated August 30, 1973[6] — the centerpiece of this litigation — Williams visited Dr. Pierce to discuss the progress of her third child who was ill. At the doctor's office, she encountered his lawyer and at the latter's request signed a release of liability in the doctor's favor. Williams showed appellant's letter to the doctor and his lawyer, and they retained a copy. She then called appellant from the doctor's office and announced her intention not to sue. There was no further communication between appellant and Williams. [The Supreme Court of South Carolina issued Primus a public reprimand for her letter to Mrs. Williams.]

III

[The Court reviewed *Button*.]

Subsequent decisions have interpreted *Button* as establishing the principle that "collective activity undertaken to obtain meaningful access to the courts is a fundamental right within the protection of the First Amendment." . . . Without denying the power of the State to take measures to correct the substantive evils of undue influence, overreaching, misrepresentation, invasion of privacy, conflict of interest, and lay interference that potentially are present in solicitation of prospective clients by lawyers, this Court has required that "broad rules framed to protect the public and to preserve respect for the administration of justice" must not work a significant impairment of "the value of associational freedoms."

IV

We turn now to the question whether appellant's conduct implicates interests of free expression and association sufficient to justify the level of protection recognized in *Button* and subsequent cases. . . .

Although the disciplinary panel did not permit full factual development of the aims and practices of the ACLU, the record does not support the state court's effort to draw a meaningful distinction between the ACLU and

---

6. Written on the stationery of the Carolina Community Law Firm, the letter stated: . . .

> You will probably remember me from talking with you at Mr. Allen's office in July about the sterilization performed on you. The American Civil Liberties Union would like to file a lawsuit on your behalf for money against the doctor who performed the operation. We will be coming to Aiken in the near future and would like to explain what is involved so you can understand what is going on. . . .
>
> About the lawsuit, if you are interested, let me know, and I'll let you know when we will come down to talk to you about it. We will be coming to talk to Mrs. Waters at the same time; she has already asked the American Civil Liberties Union to file a suit on her behalf.
>
> Sincerely,
> *s/Edna Smith*
> Edna Smith,
> Attorney-at-law

the NAACP. From all that appears, the ACLU and its local chapters, much like the NAACP and its local affiliates in *Button*, "[engage] in extensive educational lobbying activities" and "also [devote] much of [their] funds and energies to an extensive program of assisting certain kinds of litigation on behalf of [their] declared purposes." The court below acknowledged that "'the ACLU has only entered cases in which substantial civil liberties questions are involved. . . .'" It has engaged in the defense of unpopular causes and unpopular defendants and has represented individuals in litigation that has defined the scope of constitutional protection in areas such as political dissent, juvenile rights, prisoners' rights, military law, amnesty, and privacy. For the ACLU, as for the NAACP, "litigation is not a technique of resolving private differences"; it is "a form of political expression" and "political association."

We find equally unpersuasive any suggestion that the level of constitutional scrutiny in the case should be lowered because of a possible benefit to the ACLU. The discipline administered to appellant was premised solely on the possibility of financial benefit to the organization, rather than any possibility of pecuniary gain to herself, her associates, or the lawyers representing the plaintiffs in the Walker v. Pierce litigation[21] [another sterilization lawsuit against Dr. Pierce]. It is conceded that appellant received no compensation for any of the activities in question. It is also undisputed that neither the ACLU nor any lawyer associated with it would have shared in any monetary recovery by the plaintiffs in Walker v. Pierce. If Williams had elected to bring suit, and had been represented by staff lawyers for the ACLU, the situation would have been similar to that in *Button*, where the lawyers for the NAACP were "organized as a staff and paid by" that organization.

Contrary to appellee's suggestion, the ACLU's policy of requesting an award of counsel fees does not take the case outside of the protection of *Button*. . . . [I]n a case of this kind there are differences between counsel fees awarded by a court and traditional fee-paying arrangements which militate against a presumption that ACLU sponsorship of litigation is motivated by considerations of pecuniary gain rather than by its widely recognized goal of vindicating civil liberties. Counsel fees are awarded in the discretion of the court; awards are not drawn from the plaintiff's recovery, and are usually premised on a successful outcome; and the amounts awarded often may not correspond to fees generally obtainable in private litigation. . . .

Appellant's letter of August 30, 1973, to Mrs. Williams thus comes within the generous zone of First Amendment protection reserved for associational freedoms. The ACLU engages in litigation as a vehicle for effective political expression and association, as well as a means of communicating useful

---

21. Appellee conjectures that appellant would have received increased support from private foundations if her reputation was enhanced as a result of her efforts in the cause of the ACLU. The decision below acknowledged, however, that the evidence did not support a finding that appellant solicited Williams on her own behalf. . . .

information to the public. As *Button* indicates, and as appellant offered to prove at the disciplinary hearing, the efficacy of litigation as a means of advancing the cause of civil liberties often depends on the ability to make legal assistance available to suitable litigants. . . .

V

South Carolina's action in punishing appellant for soliciting a prospective litigant by mail, on behalf of the ACLU, must withstand the "exacting scrutiny applicable to limitations on core First Amendment rights. . . ." South Carolina must demonstrate "a subordinating interest which is compelling," and that the means employed in furtherance of that interest are "closely drawn to avoid unnecessary abridgment of associational freedoms." . . .

B . . .

Where political expression or association is at issue, this Court has not tolerated the degree of imprecision that often characterizes government regulation of the conduct of commercial affairs. The approach we adopt today in *Ohralik* [chapter 16A], that the State may proscribe in-person solicitation for pecuniary gain under circumstances likely to result in adverse consequences, cannot be applied to appellant's activity on behalf of the ACLU. Although a showing of potential danger may suffice in the former context, appellant may not be disciplined unless her activity in fact involved the type of misconduct at which South Carolina's broad prohibition is said to be directed.

The record does not support appellee's contention that undue influence, overreaching, misrepresentation, or invasion of privacy actually occurred in this case. . . .

Nor does the record permit a finding of a serious likelihood of conflict of interest or injurious lay interference with the attorney-client relationship. Admittedly, there is some potential for such conflict or interference whenever a lay organization supports any litigation. That potential was present in *Button*, in the NAACP's solicitation of non-members and its disavowal of any relief short of full integration. But the Court found that potential insufficient in the absence of proof of a "serious danger" of conflict of interest, or of organizational interference with the actual conduct of the litigation. . . .

The State's interests in preventing the "stirring up" of frivolous or vexatious litigation and minimizing commercialization of the legal profession offer no further justification for the discipline administered in this case. The *Button* Court declined to accept the proffered analogy to the common-law offenses of maintenance, champerty, and barratry, where the record would not support a finding that the litigant was solicited for a malicious purpose or "for private gain, serving no public interest." The same result follows from the facts of this case. And considerations of undue commercialization of the legal profession are of marginal force where, as here, a nonprofit organization offers its services free of charge to individuals who may be in need of legal assistance and may lack the financial means and sophistication necessary to tap alternative sources of such aid.

At bottom, the case against appellant rests on the proposition that a State may regulate in a prophylactic fashion all solicitation activities of lawyers because there may be some potential for overreaching, conflict of interest, or other substantive evils whenever a lawyer gives unsolicited advice and communicates an offer of representation to a layman. Under certain circumstances, that approach is appropriate in the case of speech that simply "[proposes] a commercial transaction." See *Ohralik.* In the context of political expression and association, however, a State must regulate with significantly greater precision.

VI

The State is free to fashion reasonable restrictions with respect to the time, place, and manner of solicitation by members of its Bar. The State's special interest in regulating members of a profession it licenses, and who serve as officers of its courts, amply justifies the application of narrowly drawn rules to proscribe solicitation that in fact is misleading, overbearing, or involves other features of deception or improper influence. As we decide today in *Ohralik,* a State also may forbid in-person solicitation for pecuniary gain under circumstances likely to result in these evils. And a State may insist that lawyers not solicit on behalf of lay organizations that exert control over the actual conduct of any ensuing litigation. Accordingly, nothing in this opinion should be read to foreclose carefully tailored regulation that does not abridge unnecessarily the associational freedom of nonprofit organizations, or their members, having characteristics like those of the NAACP or the ACLU. . . .

[Justice Rehnquist dissented.]

The Court wrote that a state can forbid solicitations like Primus's if "lay organizations" (like the ACLU) would "exert control over the actual conduct of any ensuing litigation." The organization and a client may have the same interest at the outset. But that can change. The organization may believe that the client's claim presents an ideal test case, one that can lead to an appellate ruling beneficial to many. But the client may then choose to accept the defendant's pre-trial settlement offer. The offer may be intended specifically to derail a strong case. The lawyer's duty is to the client. The lay officers and directors of public interest and nonprofit law firms must not interfere with that duty.

2. Labor Unions

In due course, and inevitably, the focus shifted from grand social and political goals to modest financial ones, from civil rights and liberties to money. It happened because of labor unions, which emerged as another "lay intermediary" between lawyers and clients. Unions, too, had to struggle to earn the constitutional right to assist their members in gaining low-cost legal help. Their opponents were state bar groups (aided by state courts), just as the opponent of the Motorists' Association of Illinois was the Chicago Bar Association. As in *Button*, the opposition was again couched in neutral terms—to protect clients, not to enrich lawyers. The opponents now were more plentiful than the single state fighting the NAACP. CBS newsman Fred Friendly used to say, "When someone says it's not about the money, it's about the money."* And so it was.

The story is told in a trilogy of Supreme Court cases. Take note of several distinctions between the union cases and *Button* and *Primus*.

- The unions were seeking to provide lawyers for their members, whereas the NAACP and the ACLU were offering help to unaffiliated persons.
- The needs of the union members were routine—mainly workers compensation or disability claims—unlike the soaring constitutional rights that the NAACP and ACLU seek to vindicate.
- The goal of the union plans was to control the cost of pursuing a claim, not to win judicial recognition of it. The legal right was clear and statutory. The only questions were whether the worker had a case and its worth.

A year after *Button*, the Supreme Court decided Brotherhood of Railroad Trainmen v. Virginia ex rel. Virginia State Bar, 377 U.S. 1 (1964). The union's Department of Legal Counsel advised injured members not to settle injury claims without consulting a lawyer. The department also recommended particular lawyers, who the union believed were "legally and morally competent to handle injury claims for members." The union president identified law firms in each of 16 regions of the country. Members were free to choose other lawyers. Virginia enjoined this practice.

The Supreme Court reversed (Justices Harlan and Clark dissenting) in an opinion by Justice Black:

> [T]he First and Fourteenth Amendments protect the right of the members through their Brotherhood to maintain and carry out their plan for advising workers who are injured to obtain legal advice and for recommending specific lawyers. . . . And, of course, lawyers accepting employment under this constitutionally protected plan have a like protection which the State cannot abridge.

It tells you something about what was at stake and the size of the opposition that the ABA and 48 state and local bar associations asked the Court to rehear the case. It refused.

---

* Professor Robert Condlin of the University of Maryland Law School wrote to tell me that he and three students, Rory Murray, Calvin Fisher, and Sara Mohavhed, have traced this quote to 1916 and Frank McKinney Hubbard, a humorist whose character Abe Martin says, "When a fellow says, 'it hain't the money, but th' principle o' the thing,' it's th' money." H. L. Mencken said it, too. I don't have a citation for Fred Friendly but I heard him say it many times.

That was chapter one of the story. Three years later the Court wrote chapter two in United Mine Workers, District 12 v. Illinois State Bar Ass'n, 389 U.S. 217 (1967). A union had now raised the monetary stakes substantially. It employed a lawyer on a salary basis to handle the workers' compensation claims of its members. (The members had previously paid individual counsel 40 or 50 percent of their recoveries.) Again Justice Black reversed a lower court opinion enjoining the practice. Citing the First Amendment, *Button*, and *Trainmen*, he wrote: "The litigation in question is, of course, not bound up with political matters of acute social moment . . . but the First Amendment does not protect speech and assembly only to the extent it can be characterized as political."

Justice Harlan again dissented:

> The union lawyer has little contact with his client. He processes the applications of injured members on a mass basis. Evidently, he negotiates with the employer's counsel about many claims at the same time. The State was entitled to conclude that, removed from ready contact with his client, insulated from interference by his actual employer, paid a salary independent of the results achieved, faced with a heavy caseload, and very possibly with other activities competing for his time, the attorney *will be tempted* to place undue emphasis upon quick disposition of each case. . . . He *might* be led, so the State *might* consider, to compromise cases for reasons unrelated to their own intrinsic merits, such as the need to "get on" with negotiations or a promise by the employer's attorney of concessions relating to other cases. The desire for quick disposition also *might* cause the attorney to forgo appeals in some cases in which the amount awarded seemed unusually low. (Emphasis added.)

Justice Harlan says "the attorney will be tempted." He uses the word "might" three times in two sentences. But he is right, isn't he? Bad things *might* happen. Then again, they might not. The question was whether the union members had asserted a constitutional right that Harlan's conjecture could not override without greater proof that bad things were going to happen.

The third and final chapter in our story was written in 1971. By this time, Justice Black is entirely fed up, as is apparent from the tone of his first, scathing paragraph. Justice Black's description of the "common thread running through our decisions" in the opinion's final paragraph did the trick. Bar efforts to prevent unions from buying legal help wholesale ended for good (so far).

UNITED TRANSPORTATION UNION v. STATE BAR OF MICHIGAN
401 U.S. 576 (1971)

JUSTICE BLACK delivered the opinion of the Court.

The Michigan State Bar brought this action in January 1959 to enjoin the members of the Brotherhood of Railroad Trainmen [later merged into the petitioner] from engaging in activities undertaken for the stated purpose of assisting their fellow workers, their widows and families, to protect themselves from excessive fees at the hands of incompetent attorneys in suits for damages under the Federal Employers' Liability Act. The complaint charged, as factors relevant to the cause of action, that the Union recommended selected attorneys to its members and their families, that it secured a commitment from those attorneys that the maximum fee charged would not exceed 25% of the recovery, and that it recommended Chicago lawyers to represent Michigan claimants. The State Bar's complaint appears to be a plea for court protection of unlimited legal fees. . . .

[The] Michigan Supreme Court gave our holding in *Trainmen* the narrowest possible reading. . . . The Michigan Supreme Court failed to follow our decisions in *Trainmen, United Mine Workers,* and NAACP v. Button, upholding the First Amendment principle that groups can unite to assert their legal rights as effectively and economically as practicable. When applied, as it must be, to the Union's activities reflected in the record of this case, the First Amendment forbids the restraints imposed by the injunction here under review for the following among other reasons.

First. The decree approved by the Michigan Supreme Court enjoins the Union from "giving or furnishing legal advice to its members or their families." Given its broadest meaning, this provision would bar the Union's members, officers, agents, or attorneys from giving any kind of advice or counsel to an injured worker or his family concerning his FELA claim. In *Trainmen* we upheld the commonsense proposition that such activity is protected by the First Amendment. Moreover, the plain meaning of this particular injunctive provision would emphatically deny the right of the Union to employ counsel to represent its members, a right explicitly upheld in *United Mine Workers* and NAACP v. Button. . . .

Second. The decree also enjoins the Union from furnishing to any attorney the names of injured members or information relating to their injuries. The investigation of accidents by Union staff for purposes of gathering evidence to assist the injured worker or his family in asserting FELA claims was part of the Union practice upheld in *Trainmen.* It would seem at least a little strange now to hold that the Union cannot communicate that information to the injured member's attorney.

Third. A provision of the decree enjoins the members of the Union from "accepting or receiving compensation of any kind, directly or indirectly, for the solicitation of legal employment for any lawyer, whether by way of salary, commission or otherwise." The Union conceded that prior to 1959, Union representatives were reimbursed for their actual time spent and out-of-pocket expenses incurred in bringing injured members or their families to the offices of the legal counsel. Since the members of a union have a First Amendment right to help and advise each other in securing effective legal representation, there can be no doubt that transportation of injured members to an attorney's office is within the scope of that protected activity.

To the extent that the injunction prohibits this practice, it is invalid under *Trainmen, United Mine Workers*, and NAACP v. Button.

Fourth. . . . Our Brother Harlan appears to concede that the State Bar has neither alleged nor proved that the Union has engaged in the past, is presently engaging, or plans to engage, in the sharing of legal fees. Nonetheless, he suggests that the injunction against such conduct is justified in order to remove any "temptation" for the Union to participate in such activities. We cannot accept this novel concept of equity jurisdiction that would open the courts to claims for injunctions against "temptation," and would deem potential "temptation" to be a sufficient basis for the issuance of an injunction. Indeed, it would appear that jurisdiction over "temptation" has heretofore been reserved to the churches. . . .

Fifth. Finally, the challenged decree bars the Union from controlling, directly or indirectly, the fees charged by any lawyer. The complaint alleged that the Union sought to protect its members from excessive legal fees by securing an agreement from the counsel it recommends that the fee will not exceed 25% of the recovery, and that the percentage will include all expenses incidental to investigation and litigation. The Union in its answer admitted that prior to 1959 it secured such agreements for the protection of its members.

United Mine Workers upheld the right of workers to act collectively to obtain affordable and effective legal representation. One of the abuses sought to be remedied by the Mine Workers' plan was the situation pursuant to which members "were required to pay forty or fifty per cent of the amounts recovered in damage suits, for attorney fees." The Mine Workers dealt with the problem by employing an attorney on a salary basis, thereby providing free legal representation for its members in asserting their claims before the state workmen's compensation board. The Union in the instant case sought to protect its members against the same abuse by limiting the fee charged by recommended attorneys. It is hard to believe that a court of justice would deny a cooperative union of workers the right to protect its injured members, and their widows and children, from the injustice of excessive fees at the hands of inadequate counsel. Indeed, the Michigan court was foreclosed from so doing by our decision in *United Mine Workers*.

In the context of this case we deal with a cooperative union of workers seeking to assist its members in effectively asserting claims under the FELA. But the principle here involved cannot be limited to the facts of this case. At issue is the basic right to group legal action, a right first asserted in this Court by an association of Negroes seeking the protection of freedoms guaranteed by the Constitution. The common thread running through our decisions in NAACP v. Button, *Trainmen,* and *United Mine Workers* is that collective activity undertaken to obtain meaningful access to the courts is a fundamental right within the protection of the First Amendment. However, that right would be a hollow promise if courts could deny associations of workers or others the means of enabling their members to meet the costs of legal representation. That was the holding in *United Mine Workers*, *Trainmen*, and NAACP v. Button. The injunction in the present case cannot stand in the face of these prior decisions.

Reversed.

[Justice Stewart took no part in the decision. Justice Harlan concurred in part and dissented in part. Justice White, with whom Justice Blackmun joined, concurred in part and dissented in part.]

Would the Illinois motorists, whose failed effort to lower legal fees began this chapter, win today if they described their association as a "collective activity undertaken to obtain meaningful access to the courts"?

The United Freelancers Association

The gig economy has called renewed attention to the needs of men and women in the arts and journalism who have no employer, either because they don't want one or because the job market has contracted. Yet they do have legal problems. They need advice and representation on the law of privacy, defamation, contracts, tax, and copyright, among other subjects. A company's general counsel would routinely address most such needs, but these freelancers don't work at a company.

Several enterprising individuals decide to organize a non-profit entity—The United Freelancers Association (TUFA)—that will employ one or more lawyers to provide members with a defined menu of legal services. TUFA will offer other benefits as well, including group medical and dental insurance plans, financial advice, and monthly forums and workshops. The membership fee would initially be $535 yearly, a bargain considering that a lawyer would charge at least $400 or more hourly for the same work. A poll reveals that 1,855 freelancers are willing to join. The organizers identify Rafaela Begnini as the lawyer they want to hire. More lawyers may be hired as needed. Begnini asks your advice on the safest way this can be done, if at all.

B. FOR-PROFIT ENTERPRISES

"Can Viktor Be Our Partner?"

"My name is Olga Denov. I am a partner in a three-person law office whose clients are émigrés from the former Soviet Union. We help them with most every legal problem they have—immigration, landlord, credit, government benefits, bankruptcy, orders of protection, employment—except criminal, which we refer. My parents and I came from Samara when I was eight. I have two partners, Yelena, born here to émigré parents, and Andres, born in Estonia. We make a modest living. I'd be embarrassed to tell you. Sometimes we'll represent a person for free or next to free. If he prospers, he may continue to hire us. We see ourselves as public interest lawyers who happen to work in a (minimally) for-profit law firm.

"Much of what many clients need is not strictly speaking legal advice or help, or not only that. They need the help social workers give, often better than lawyers. Dealing with bureaucracies, getting them settled, kids in school, shopping advice, medical care, ESL lessons, opening a bank account. Even learning the currency. My friend Viktor Portnoi is a social worker with a non-profit humanitarian group. Sometimes he helps us, but he's got his own clients. We need to hire a social worker. It would be more efficient and better for the clients. So I asked Viktor, would he be interested. Viktor said he would be interested, yes. We're also on the lookout for a lawyer (must speak Russian).

"I do not want Viktor to be our employee. He is senior to us and at this work longer. He knows more than I do in the area of overlap between social work and law. I want him to have a stake in the firm. It won't matter to his income, but it will matter to his pride and sense of belonging. It also gives him more credibility with clients and bureaucrats. And it's important to us. It shows respect. Much of what Viktor will do resembles what we do, though of course he won't practice law. He will work on his own where a client needs only the help he is permitted to give. And he will work with one of us when a client needs legal help, too.

"Can Viktor be our partner?"

"Can We Make This Deal?"

"Even though there are 1.3 million lawyers in the United States, give or take, some counties have none or very few. People may have to drive a hundred miles to see a lawyer. I grew up in one of those counties. Most of my friends left but many stayed, mostly to manage a farm or a family business, open a shop, work in tourism, or teach school. I left too. I went to law school in Indiana and then practiced five years at a small firm.

"I'm thinking of going home and opening a law office. The Law Office of Andrea Marie Bowman. I know enough to do a competent job on most tasks people and small companies need. I'll put in nonbillable time to learn what I don't know. But I'm married, I have a son, and I'm expecting a daughter. Teddy, my husband, teaches high school math. He will have no trouble finding work, but the pay is modest. We have savings for the down payment on a house.

"A good friend, Christina Dale, never left. She now manages a store in town that sells everything. Like Walmart but not Walmart. She said she'd be willing to rent me a private space in her store for a law office for $350 monthly. She said I could get a bank loan for the rent and to equip the office. I don't think I could get a bank loan in addition to a home mortgage. And I don't want to add to my debts. I'm still paying off student loans. So Christina offered to skip the rent and equip the office. In return, I would pay her 10 percent of my gross billings each month with a cap of $500 monthly. So if I gross $2,500 in a month, I pay $250 in rent. If I gross $5,000, I pay $500, the maximum. I can change to a traditional rent any time if I reimburse her cost for equipping the office plus 3 percent interest.

"Of course, Christina will have no say in the clients I accept or know anything about them or how I represent them. Can we make this deal?"

AmazonLaw.com

Much of what lawyers do every day is apply established (legal) rules to information to achieve a client's particular goals. Much of this work is repetitive and requires little or no judgment. Rules. Information. Goals. Artificial intelligence can be easily programmed (trained?) to do much of this work, even some parts that require some judgment. And it can do it at lower cost, faster, and with a lower risk of error than when lawyers do the same work. Not all of it, of course, but a lot. How many people do their taxes on Turbo Tax rather than pay an accountant? How many accountants use Turbo Tax (or an equivalent) to do their clients' returns?

Imagine that Amazon has decided to create a virtual law firm accessible on a new website, AmazonLaw.com. (It hasn't, but once it reads this business model it might.) It plans to advertise on television, online, and in print. After two years of research, programmers identified 14 distinct legal tasks that account for 82 percent of the nonlitigation services individuals and small businesses need. Highly advanced coding, advice from lawyers in all U.S. jurisdictions, and machine learning from hundreds of thousands of transactions will enable clients to purchase jurisdiction-specific advice and completed forms without intercession from a lawyer or even a person. An electronic record of the entire exchange will be retained for ten years.

Clients who want more guidance can talk to either of two robots—Ruth or Oliver—depending on whether they prefer a female or male voice. Ruth and Oliver are programmed to recognize (so far) 91 percent of the follow-up questions clients ask, as shown through eight months of empirical testing. If Ruth or Oliver cannot resolve the problem, clients can talk to a (human) paralegal and then, if they wish, to a lawyer licensed in the relevant jurisdiction, all without extra charge. All conversations are recorded.

> Economies of scale will enable AmazonLaw to do tasks that hundreds of thousands of American lawyers routinely do as much or part of their practice, but for half the cost. Subscribers to Amazon Prime will get a 7.5 percent discount. Should this be allowed? Is it allowed today?*

We have so far discussed nonprofit organizations that are not seeking to earn a fee for the work a lawyer does for a client (other than through a fee-shifting law as in *Primus*). The constitutional protection afforded their conduct can be seen to depend on the issues they seek to raise and their nonprofit status (*Button, Primus*) or on the right of the members of an organization to pool their purchasing power to reduce the cost of legal help (the union cases) or both. If we remove these characteristics, what constitutional protection remains? May a state constitutionally forbid lay ownership of or profit participation in entities that offer legal services for a profit? May it constitutionally prohibit organizations like the Motorists' Association of Illinois, which lost the case described at the outset of this chapter?

We have a partial answer to these questions from the Second Circuit. The plaintiff challenged New York's rule forbidding nonlawyers from *passively* investing in for-profit law firms. It said that it had received "numerous offers" from "prospective non-lawyer investors . . . who are prepared to invest capital in exchange for owning an interest in the firm." It cited the First Amendment's rights to petition the government and of association, the union cases, *Button,* and *Primus*. The court rejected the challenge. Those cases recognized a First Amendment right not for lawyers but for "political advocacy groups or in individuals seeking the vindication of their own rights through not-for-profit counsel." Jacoby & Meyers, LLP v. Presiding Justices of the First, Second, Third and Fourth Depts, 852 F.3d 178 (2d Cir. 2017).

Jacoby & Meyers does not *necessarily* foreclose a constitutional argument by Olga Denov or AmazonLaw.com—the plan of neither involves a passive investor in a for-profit law firm as in *Jacoby & Meyers*. Viktor Portnoi would not be "passive" and AmazonLaw might claim that it is not a "law firm." But the decision would likely prevent Andrea Marie Bowman's arrangement with Cristina Dale.

Apart from the constitutional question, we should ask a policy one. Should we let Viktor be Olga's partner and Andrea make her deal with Christina? Should we permit the AmazonLaw business model? The reason usually given to oppose lay participation in the profits of law firms is that the laypersons, whether they are passive investors or equity partners, might cause the firm's lawyers to betray clients in order to maximize profit. This risk arises because the layperson's income depends on the profitability of the enterprise and she

---

* Of course, this is only a hypothetical—at the moment. If it can surmount the regulatory impediments, do we doubt that Amazon or someone else will do this?

may have the clout to get her way. This explanation takes a rather dim view of the integrity of nonlawyers and the ability of lawyers to resist pressure to betray clients.

There are exceptions to the prohibition of lay influence. Bank lines of credit of any amount are allowed because a loan is debt, which means that the *amount* of the bank's interest does not depend on the firm's profits. But repayment of the loan does depend on the firm's solvency, which may lead the bank to seek to influence how the firm practices law. Another exception allows a law firm to give nonlawyer "employees" an interest "in a compensation or retirement plan, even though the plan is based in whole or in part on a profit-sharing arrangement." Rule 5.4(a)(3).

Efforts to rewrite Rule 5.4 to allow Olga Denov and Andrea Marie Bowman to do what they wish to do have been vehemently opposed. The rule has been called the third rail of legal ethics. Don't touch it or confront fierce opposition! Yet, as stated, in mid-2020, the Utah Supreme Court adopted revisions to Rule 5.4 and other rules to allow fee sharing with nonlawyers and nonlawyer ownership of law firms. Arizona followed. Supreme Court Order R-20-0034 (Aug. 27, 2020). For the Utah revisions, go to https://sandbox.utcourts.gov.

Doesn't the fear that nonlawyers will be tempted to put money ahead of service to clients also apply to lawyers? Are we assuming that lawyers are more trustworthy than laypeople or less interested in money? After all, we allow nonlawyers to run large companies, major charities, and universities, and to occupy positions of power in government. True, a lawyer can be disciplined if he betrays a client, or pressures another lawyer to betray a client, or succumbs to the pressure of anyone, whereas the bar has no equivalent authority over nonlawyers. Civil claims would still be possible.

As with some other rules limiting or prohibiting conduct based on predictions of human behavior, we have no empirical evidence to support the fear that greedy nonlawyers will corrupt their lawyer colleagues in the pursuit of profits. In Washington, D.C., Gene Shipp, the longtime D.C. Bar Counsel, told the ABA 20/20 Commission that there had been no reported problems with its Rule 5.4 (in effect since 1991). That rule does allow nonlawyers to be law firm partners, although only a few firms have sought to use it.[*]

The tone of the preceding sentences is decidedly skeptical. Is it perhaps too dismissive? Not every ethical rule that excludes competition and, predictably, raises the cost of legal services is necessarily unwise or ill-motivated. Can't a state legislature or court validly apprehend excessive risk to clients of a for-profit law firm that includes nonlawyer owners? On the other hand, Walmart and other retail stores offer medical care through employed health

---

[*] Possibly this reluctance is explained by the bookkeeping nightmare. If law firms with a D.C. office have nonlawyer partners, they would need to keep two sets of books to ensure that the nonlawyers did not share in money earned by firm lawyers elsewhere. ABA Opinion 91-360. Money can flow in the other direction, however—from a nonlawyer to a lawyer.

care professionals on site. Rachel Abrams, "In Ambitious Bid, Walmart Seeks Foothold in Primary Care Services," N.Y. Times, Aug. 7, 2014. Surely, lawyers would be able to resist the bad influence of their nonlawyer partners and the lay owners of the businesses that employ them. Or maybe we should also worry about the doctors.

Nonlawyers at the Borders

Despite the effort to lock nonlawyers out of the legal industry's income stream, they are finding ways to enjoy it anyway. This is no surprise because despite the occasional financial woes of the profession, the law business remains financially attractive. Here are several ways in which nonlawyers — or lawyers working through organizations that are not law firms — are circumventing the exclusionary rules, often with the support of lawyers.

Licensed Paralegals. In 2012, the Washington Supreme Court became the first U.S. jurisdiction to recognize what we might call a licensed paralegal. Washington Practice Rule 28 created the position of Limited License Legal Technician (LLLT). An LLLT could perform limited services for clients for a fee in designated areas of practice. The court imposed educational, CLE, and testing requirements, and a character review for LLLTs. Initially, LLLT work was limited to family law matters, but expanded practice areas were contemplated. In June 2020, the court (over the dissent of Justice Barbara Madsen) ended the program because, it said, of the "costs of sustaining the program and the small number of interested individuals." In her dissent, Justice Madsen cited a study by the Public Welfare Foundation, which concluded that the program "was significant in helping create access to justice." As a "testament to this," she wrote, "Utah, California, Oregon, Colorado, New Mexico, Minnesota, Massachusetts, and Connecticut" were "considering adopting similar licenses."

In late 2019, Utah created the position of the Licensed Paralegal Practitioner, who can advise on family court matters, landlord tenant disputes, and those debt collection matters within the jurisdictional limit of the small claims court. They cannot appear in court. There are education and examination requirements, including in ethics. See Utah Supreme Court Rules 14-802 and 15-705.

The trend to adopt these limited licenses is driven by need. In recent years, there has been increased discussion of access to justice and the inability of persons of modest means to afford counsel. "According to the Legal Services Corp., 86% of low-income Americans' civil legal needs are not being met, including with health care, housing conditions, disability access, veterans' benefits and domestic violence." Aebra Coe, "Like or Not, Law May Open Its Doors to Nonlawyers," Law360, Sept. 22, 2019. In 2015, the National Center for State Courts found that in a single year, 76 percent of civil matters in ten large cities had at least one litigant with no lawyer.

Aside from the expense, a distinct problem is the absence of lawyers in rural areas, leading to the existence of "legal deserts." "Of the 3,100 counties in the United States, 1,300 have fewer than one attorney for every thousand residents, and 54 counties have no attorneys at all, according to . . . the ABA's annual 'Profile of the Legal Profession' report." Emma Cueto, "COVID-19 Threatens to Worsen US Legal Deserts," Law360, Aug. 2, 2020. This reality has led New Mexico (among other states) to study the Washington model. Twenty-one percent of New Mexico's counties "have five or fewer lawyers, and two counties have" none. RJ Vogt, "Legal Deserts Push NM to Consider Nonlawyer Services," Law360, June 2, 2019.

Under some proposals, the inquirers in "The Landlord's Lawyers Are a Mean Bunch" (chapter 12C) would be able to get a license to do what they describe and even appear in housing court.

Opposition to this trend is, however, intense and vocal and likely to get more so. Many lawyers complain that by licensing "legal technicians" (whatever we call them), the courts dilute the value of their law degrees. They also predict harm to clients because the technicians will not have had a traditional three-year legal education. One California lawyer told the state task force studying the issue, "This is going to erode the quality of legal services in the state. It's going to devalue my license and hurt the public." Of course, those are two different arguments. What do you think of them?

Online Document Production Services. As described in chapter 12C, these operations walk a customer through a series of online choices—a decision tree—at the end of which the customer can print a form: a will, a partnership agreement, corporate by-laws, a lease, and so on.

Litigation Funding Companies. Companies like Burford Capital Limited invest in lawsuits in exchange for a substantial portion of the recovery if a case is successful. Here's how it works. Say a law firm is asked to represent a plaintiff in a personal injury case for a contingent fee. But the case will require the firm to make a substantial investment of time and money for expert witnesses, investigation, and discovery. In addition, the firm will not see any fee unless and until there is a settlement or a judgment, which can take years. The firm would like to spread the risk. Maybe it can't afford the investment of money. After studying the merits of the case, a litigation funder offers to accept some of that risk in exchange for a percentage of the recovery. The funder gets nothing if there is no recovery. But it gets a lot if there is one, much more than it would get in interest for a traditional loan. The funder's profit comes out of the law firm's fee, not out of the client's recovery. The funder and lawyer stipulate that the funder cannot influence the firm's work and will have no access to privileged communications.

Now imagine that the funder doesn't want to rely on a single possible recovery for its profit. So it offers to fund a portfolio of the law firm's contingency cases, maybe most of them. It will be entitled to its full profit from the recoveries in any of them. That way it reduces its risk. As cases conclude, new ones may be added to the portfolio along with new funding and a revised return on the funder's investment. Still, the funder's profit comes out of the law firm's fees, not from the client's recovery.

There is another kind of litigation funding—consumer funding. It is less common. Remember Mary O'Meara's plight in chapter 5A3? She needed money for food, rent, and medical bills in the years her personal injury case was creeping through the courts. Her lawyer was willing to help her out, but Rule 1.8(e) would not allow him to do so. Without help, she would have to settle for less than her claim is worth. However, if Mary's case is promising enough, she might be able to make her own deal directly with a litigation funder. Her lawyer is likely to know funders and may make an introduction. In exchange for financial support while the case is pending, Mary would promise the funder a portion of her recovery. This deal is between the client and the funder. Nothing comes out of the lawyer's fee.

The champerty doctrine should have spelled doom for litigation funding in jurisdictions that recognize the doctrine, as most do to some extent. Indeed, the Chamber of Commerce has fiercely opposed litigation funding citing the champerty doctrine and other arguments. Often, Chamber members will be the ones sued by the funded plaintiffs. In court, funders have successfully resisted challenges to their business, no doubt because they fill a need. Some jurisdictions have, however, rejected funding categorically, or in the particular circumstance, often citing their rules against champerty and maintenance. Laws against gambling and usury may also apply. See generally Odell v. Legal Bucks, LLC, 665 S.E.2d 767 (N.C. Ct. App. 2008). Good introductions to the phenomenon can be found in Maya Steinitz, Follow the Money? A Proposed Approach for Disclosure of Litigation Finance Agreements, 53 U.C. Davis L. Rev. 1073 (2019) and Jean Xiao, Heuristics, Biases, and Consumer Litigation Funding at the Bargaining Table, 68 Vand. L. Rev. 261 (2015).

The South Carolina Supreme Court, which has rejected the champerty doctrine, has offered these factors for deciding whether a finance agreement will be enforced:

> The court may examine (1) whether the respective bargaining position of the parties at the time the agreement was made was relatively equal, (2) whether both parties were aware of the terms and consequences of the agreement, (3) whether the borrowing party may have been unable to pursue the lawsuit at all without the financier's help, (4) whether the financier would retain a disproportionate share of the recovery, and (5) whether the financier engaged in officious intermeddling. A financier becomes an officious intermeddler when he or she offers unwanted advice or otherwise attempts to control the litigation for the purpose of stirring up strife or continuing a frivolous lawsuit. After analyzing these factors and any others the court deems relevant, the court may enforce, modify, or set aside the financing agreement.

Osprey, Inc. v. Cabana Ltd. P'ship., 532 S.E.2d 269 (S.C. 2000).

Legal Process Outsourcing Companies (LPOs). Companies like Pangea3 and Integreon perform legal work abroad for American law firms and general counsel, using nonlawyers (or lawyers, but not U.S. lawyers) at a small fraction of traditional U.S. rates.

More about any of these companies and their competitors can be learned by Googling their names. See also John Dzienkowski, The Future of Big Law: Alternative Legal Service Providers to Corporate Clients, 82 Fordham L. Rev. 2995 (2014) and Stephen Gillers, A Profession, If You Can Keep It: How Information Technology and Fading Borders Are Reshaping the Law Marketplace and What We Should Do About It, 63 Hastings L.J. 953 (2012).

Other Nations. Changes to lawyer regulation abroad are even more dramatic and legislatively or judicially recognized:

> In England and Wales, the 2007 Legal Services Act liberalized the provision of legal services. Provisions of the Act that went into effect in late 2011 permitted "law firms [to] seek investment from third parties for the first time and companies that are not law firms [to] provide legal services." The Act was dubbed the "Tesco Law" after a large British grocery retailer: with retailers allowed to offer legal services, the law was thought to make it as easy to buy legal services as it was to buy beans. In Australia, the Legal Profession Acts permit "incorporated legal practices" and allow revenue sharing with nonlawyers. As a result of the Australian reforms, the firm of Slater & Gordon became the world's first publicly traded law firm; its IPO raised twenty-nine million dollars. After the English reforms of 2011 were implemented, Slater & Gordon then purchased the U.K. firm of Russell Jones & Walker for eighty-five million dollars.

Cassandra Robertson, Private Ordering in the Market for Professional Services, 94 B.U. L. Rev. 179 (2014).

Self-Assessment Questions

1. Rule 5.4(a) provides: "A lawyer or law firm shall not share legal fees with a nonlawyer." One exception to this rule, in paragraph (a)(3), states that "a lawyer or law firm may include nonlawyer employees in a compensation or retirement plan, even though the plan is based in whole or in part on a profit-sharing arrangement." There are other exceptions that are not relevant to this question. Your client is a personal injury and class action law firm. The firm uses paralegals for much of its work although a lawyer will review the paralegals' work. The paralegals have been trained to do many things a first- or second-year associate might do elsewhere, including drafting documents, Westlaw and Lexis research, and interviewing witnesses. All of that is permitted so long as a lawyer supervises the work. Many of your client's

cases result in substantial recoveries. The paralegals are salaried. Your client wants to recognize the paralegals' work and incentivize them by giving paralegals who work on a case a small percentage of the fees earned in that case. Advise her.

2. Benson, Edwards & Thale (BET) is a medical malpractice law firm. It represents plaintiffs on a contingent fee basis. While the lawyers at the firm are knowledgeable about medical procedures and medicine generally, they are not doctors. Over the years, they have consulted Dr. Anita Gately when deciding whether to accept a case and when medical issues arise in cases. Dr. Gately does not testify as an expert witness. Her work for BET is solely as a consultant on an as-needed basis. She has routinely charged an hourly fee for her work. BET and Dr. Gately are now exploring a different compensation scheme.

One possibility is for Dr. Gately to be on a quarterly retainer for all consultations, within certain parameters, that BET seeks during the quarter. The amount of the retainer can be renegotiated from quarter to quarter.

A second possibility is for Dr. Gately to receive a percentage of the recovery the firm receives in a matter if it consults Dr. Gately on that matter, with the percentage in any matter dependent on the amount of consultation on the particular matter.

A final possibility is for Dr. Gately to have a separate retainer agreement with any client on whose matter she is asked to work, under which she will bill the client for an agreed-upon percentage of the client's recovery, if any. The firm asks you whether each of these compensation schemes is allowed.

PART FIVE

FIRST AMENDMENT RIGHTS OF LAWYERS AND JUDICIAL CANDIDATES

XV

Free Speech Rights of Lawyers and Judicial Candidates

A. PUBLIC COMMENT ABOUT PENDING CASES

> Over the weekend, just days before jurors in the Harvey Weinstein case were set to begin deliberations, his lead defense lawyer, Donna Rotunno, wrote an opinion piece imploring them "to do what they know is right."
>
> The article in Newsweek magazine infuriated the Manhattan district attorney's office, and on Tuesday the lead prosecutor, Joan Illuzzi, called Ms. Rotunno's behavior "inappropriate," and tantamount to jury tampering.
>
> The judge ordered the defense team not to speak to the news media until after a verdict is reached.
>
> "Defense team you are ordered to refrain from communicating with the press until there is a verdict in the case," Justice James M. Burke told Mr. Weinstein's lawyers. "I would caution you about the tentacles of your public relations juggernaut."
>
> —Jan Ransom, "Weinstein's Lawyer Wrote an Article Addressing Jurors. The Judge Is Unhappy," N. Y. Times, Feb. 21, 2020

We can use the trial of Harvey Weinstein as a hypothetical to explore rules limiting trial publicity, but first some background.

Rules 3.6(a) and 3.8(f).   Rule 3.6(a) instructs lawyers to refrain from making certain public statements about their matters: "A lawyer who is participating or has participated in the investigation or litigation of a matter shall not make an extrajudicial statement that the lawyer knows or reasonably should know will be disseminated by means of public communication and will have a substantial likelihood of materially prejudicing an adjudicative proceeding in the matter." The balance of the rule identifies particular comments that are not forbidden and comment [5] identifies the kinds of comments that "are more likely" to violate paragraph (a).

Most cases in which issues of improper public comments arise are prosecutions of high-profile defendants or of notorious crimes, locally if not nationally. It's easy to see why. Routine criminal trials are not newsworthy. Nor is nearly any civil trial. So the media will ignore whatever publicity a lawyer or her client may generate. One exception is Maldonado v. Ford Motor Co., 719 N.W.2d 809 (Mich. 2006), where the Michigan Supreme Court upheld dismissal of a sexual harassment case because the plaintiff and her lawyers repeatedly publicized inadmissible information after the judge had warned them not to do so.

Rule 3.8(f) requires prosecutors to use "reasonable care" to prevent law enforcement personnel from making statements to the press that the prosecutor herself may not make and tells prosecutors that, with narrow exception, they must "refrain from making extrajudicial comments that have a substantial likelihood of heightening public condemnation of the accused." In re Brizzi, 962 N.E.2d 1240 (Ind. 2012), is a rare case publicly reprimanding a prosecutor—the elected prosecuting attorney of Marion County (Indianapolis), Indiana—for violating Rules 3.6(a) and 3.8(f) in a press release.

Gag Orders. Some trial judges seek to reduce the incidence of pretrial comment, attributed or not, by issuing "gag" orders that forbid lawyers, their clients, and persons working with either side to talk to the media, except perhaps to repeat matters of public record or to state the general nature of a charge or defense. A gag order has double value. Unlike legal ethics rules, a gag order can restrain both lawyers and nonlawyers, most notably investigative agencies. And because violation of a gag order can result in a contempt conviction, it may get more respect than underenforced ethics rules.

Gag orders have three problems: (1) Although violations are easy to detect (there's the news story, after all), the leakers can be hard to identify, especially if the source is in a government agency, where many people may have access to the information; (2) the investigation and prosecution of leaks as a contempt of court may depend on the very agencies whose personnel are among the suspected; and (3) appellate courts differ in their views of gag orders when challenged under the First Amendment as prior restraints. Compare United States v. Brown, 218 F.3d 415 (5th Cir. 2000) (in prosecution of prominent Louisiana political figure, upholding gag order forbidding public comment that "could interfere with a fair trial or prejudice any defendant, the government, or the administration of justice") and United States v. Cutler, 58 F.3d 825 (2d Cir. 1995) (holding lawyer in contempt for violating gag order in prosecution of his client John Gotti), with United States v. Salameh, 992 F.2d 445 (2d Cir. 1993) (vacating gag order as overly broad prior restraint in trial of persons accused of 1993 World Trade Center bombing).

In the trial of former Illinois Congressman Aaron Schock, which attracted much media attention, the government asked the district judge to impose a gag order. She declined. She demanded a greater threat to the fairness of a trial for a gag order than is needed to prove a violation of Rule 3.6. "In this Circuit, a court can limit defendants' and their attorneys' free speech rights where their conduct poses 'a serious and imminent threat to the administration of justice.'" That burden was not met. United States v. Schock, 2016 WL 7176578 (C.D. Ill. 2016).

The Press Has a Role. To understand this subterranean world a little better, consider, in each case and generally, the motives of each side for revealing information to the media. (What were Dominic Gentile's motives in the case following?) Also, which side is likely to have greater media contacts? Which side generally has more to gain if a case escapes public attention?

Wait a minute. How many sides are there? If you said two, count again. This play has a third character: the press and other media. If ever there was a time when courts could hope to try controversial cases out of the full glare of media attention, 24-hour cable, online publications, and social media have changed all that—putting aside, as we must, the quality of the analysis (or lack thereof). For the fact is, pre- or post-cable, some cases are big news. The press was going to cover the investigations and prosecutions of Harvey Weinstein, O.J. Simpson, Bill Cosby, Michael Avenatti, Bernard Madoff, Roger Stone, Martha Stewart, Penn State coach Jerry Sandusky, Timothy McVeigh (the Oklahoma City bomber), and the NFL's Aaron Hernandez, come what may.

We must also remember that we are talking about talking—about speech—so what are the First Amendment limits on Rule 3.6? The Supreme Court had to define those limits in the next case. The Nevada rule at issue in *Gentile* was almost identical to Model Rule 3.6 as it originally read. It was amended after *Gentile*, as discussed hereafter. There are three opinions in *Gentile*, two of them long. Four Justices, in an opinion by Justice Kennedy, wrote that Dominic Gentile's press conference did not create "a substantial likelihood of materially prejudicing an adjudicative proceeding," as the rule required (then and still). Five Justices, in an opinion by Chief Justice Rehnquist, concluded the opposite. The two opinions interpreted the words "substantial likelihood" differently. Gentile won only because Justice O'Connor, who otherwise joined the Rehnquist majority, also agreed with the vagueness analysis in the Kennedy opinion, creating a majority of five on that narrow issue.

So what did Dominic Gentile do?

CASE NOTE: GENTILE v. STATE BAR OF NEVADA

Gentile's client, Grady Sanders, was accused of stealing drugs and money from a vault located at a company called Western Vault, which he owned. The drugs and money were part of a police undercover operation. Gentile claimed that the drugs and money were stolen by a police officer and that Sanders was set up to take the fall. In Gentile v. State Bar of Nevada, 501 U.S.

1030 (1991), Justice Kennedy (for himself and Justices Marshall, Blackmun, and Stevens) wrote:

> Hours after his client was indicted on criminal charges, petitioner Gentile, who is a member of the Bar of the State of Nevada, held a press conference. He made a prepared statement . . . and then he responded to questions. . . .
>
> Some six months later, the criminal case was tried to a jury and the client was acquitted on all counts. The State Bar of Nevada then filed a complaint against petitioner, alleging a violation of Nevada Supreme Court Rule 177, [which is] almost identical to ABA Model Rule of Professional Conduct 3.6. . . .

The Southern Nevada Disciplinary Board recommended that Gentile be privately reprimanded. Gentile waived confidentiality and appealed to the Nevada Supreme Court, which affirmed. Here is some of what Gentile said at his press conference:

> When this case goes to trial, and as it develops, you're going to see that the evidence will prove not only that Grady Sanders is an innocent person and had nothing to do with any of the charges that are being leveled against him, but that the person that was in the most direct position to have stolen the drugs and money, the American Express Travelers' checks, is Detective Steve Scholl.
>
> There is far more evidence that will establish that Detective Scholl took these drugs and took these American Express Travelers' checks than any other living human being.
>
> And I have to say that I feel that Grady Sanders is being used as a scapegoat to try to cover up for what has to be obvious to people at Las Vegas Metropolitan Police Department and at the District Attorney's office.
>
> Now, with respect to these other charges that are contained in this indictment, the so-called other victims, as I sit here today I can tell you that one, two—four of them are known drug dealers and convicted money launderers and drug dealers; three of whom didn't say a word about anything until after they were approached by Metro and after they were already in trouble and are trying to work themselves out of something.

Kennedy acknowledged that Nevada's rule did not specifically say that the public statement must present a "clear and present danger" to a fair trial, only that it must create a "substantial likelihood of materially prejudicing" one, as does Rule 3.6. Kennedy read the rule to require the equivalent of a clear and present danger anyway. "The drafters of Model Rule 3.6 apparently thought the substantial likelihood of material prejudice formulation approximated the clear and present danger test." However, Kennedy spoke for a plurality of four Justices on that question. So he proceeded to decide the case under the majority's interpretation of the rule and concluded:

> The record does not support the conclusion that petitioner knew or reasonably should have known his remarks created a substantial likelihood of material prejudice, if the Rule's terms are given any meaningful content. . . .
>
> An attorney's duties do not begin inside the courtroom door. He or she cannot ignore the practical implications of a legal proceeding for the client. Just as an attorney may recommend a plea bargain or civil settlement to avoid

the adverse consequences of a possible loss after trial, so too an attorney may take reasonable steps to defend a client's reputation and reduce the adverse consequences of indictment, especially in the face of a prosecution deemed unjust or commenced with improper motives. A defense attorney may pursue lawful strategies to obtain dismissal of an indictment or reduction of charges, including an attempt to demonstrate in the court of public opinion that the client does not deserve to be tried. . . .

Rule 177 is phrased in terms of what an attorney "knows or reasonably should know." On the evening before the press conference, petitioner and two colleagues spent several hours researching the extent of an attorney's obligations under Rule 177. He decided . . . that the timing of a statement was crucial in the assessment of possible prejudice and the Rule's application. . . .

A statement which reaches the attention of the venire on the eve of *voir dire* might require a continuance or cause difficulties in securing an impartial jury, and at the very least could complicate the jury selection process. As turned out to be the case here, exposure to the same statement six months prior to trial would not result in prejudice, the content fading from memory long before the trial date. . . .

Petitioner was disciplined for statements to the effect that (1) the evidence demonstrated his client's innocence, (2) the likely thief was a police detective, Steve Scholl, and (3) the other victims were not credible, as most were drug dealers or convicted money launderers, all but one of whom had only accused Sanders in response to police pressure, in the process of "trying to work themselves out of something." He also strongly implied that Steve Scholl could be observed in a videotape suffering from symptoms of cocaine use. Of course, only a small fraction of petitioner's remarks were disseminated to the public, in two newspaper stories and two television news broadcasts. . . .

Much of the information provided by petitioner had been published in one form or another, obviating any potential for prejudice. The remainder, and details petitioner refused to provide, were available to any journalist willing to do a little bit of investigative work. . . .

Petitioner's judgment that no likelihood of material prejudice would result from his comments was vindicated by events at trial. While it is true that Rule 177's standard for controlling pretrial publicity must be judged at the time a statement is made, *ex post* evidence can have probative value in some cases. . . .

The trial took place on schedule . . . with no request by either party for a venue change or continuance. The jury was empaneled with no apparent difficulty. The trial judge questioned the jury venire about publicity. Although many had vague recollections of reports that cocaine stored at Western Vault had been stolen from a police undercover operation, and, as petitioner had feared, one remembered that the police had been cleared of suspicion, not a single juror indicated any recollection of petitioner or his press conference.

At trial, all material information disseminated during petitioner's press conference was admitted in evidence before the jury, including information questioning the motives and credibility of supposed victims who testified against Sanders. . . .

Kennedy's plurality gained a fifth vote from O'Connor (and became a majority) on an issue other than interpretation of the words "substantial likelihood." The Court held that the rule's language was too vague to support the charge against Gentile. It did not clearly tell him what was and was not allowed.

> As interpreted by the Nevada Supreme Court, the Rule is void for vagueness, in any event, for its safe harbor provision, Rule 177(3), misled petitioner into thinking that he could give his press conference without fear of discipline. Rule 177(3)(a) provides that a lawyer "may state without elaboration . . . the general nature of the . . . defense." Statements under this provision are protected "notwithstanding subsection 1 and 2(a-f)." By necessary operation of the word "notwithstanding," the Rule contemplates that a lawyer describing the "general nature of the . . . defense" "without elaboration" need fear no discipline, even if he comments on "the character, credibility, reputation or criminal record of a . . . witness [which is otherwise forbidden]," and even if he "knows or reasonably should know that [the statement] will have a substantial likelihood of materially prejudicing an adjudicative proceeding."
>
> Given this grammatical structure, and absent any clarifying interpretation by the state court, the Rule fails to provide " 'fair notice to those to whom [it] is directed.' " A lawyer seeking to avail himself of Rule 177(3)'s protection must guess at its contours. The right to explain the "general" nature of the defense without "elaboration" provides insufficient guidance because "general" and "elaboration" are both classic terms of degree. In the context before us, these terms have no settled usage or tradition of interpretation in law. The lawyer has no principle for determining when his remarks pass from the safe harbor of the general to the forbidden sea of the elaborated. . . .
>
> The prohibition against vague regulations of speech is based in part on the need to eliminate the impermissible risk of discriminatory enforcement, for history shows that speech is suppressed when either the speaker or the message is critical of those who enforce the law. The question is not whether discriminatory enforcement occurred here, and we assume it did not, but whether the Rule is so imprecise that discriminatory enforcement is a real possibility. The inquiry is of particular relevance when one of the classes most affected by the regulation is the criminal defense bar, which has the professional mission to challenge actions of the State. Petitioner, for instance, succeeded in preventing the conviction of his client, and the speech in issue involved criticism of the government.

Chief Justice Rehnquist, joined by Justices White, Scalia, and Souter, dissented. Rehnquist quoted other parts of the press conference. A few are excerpted in the footnote.[*]

---

[*] " . . . because of the stigma that attaches to merely being accused — okay — I know I represent an innocent man. . . . The last time I had a conference with you, was with a client and I let him talk to you and I told you that that case would be dismissed and it was. Okay?

"I don't take cheap shots like this. I represent an innocent guy. All right? . . .

"[The police] were playing very fast and loose. . . . We've got some video tapes that if you take a look at them, I'll tell you what, [Detective Scholl] either had a hell of a cold or he should have seen a better doctor."

Petitioner maintains . . . that the First Amendment to the United States Constitution requires a State, such as Nevada in this case, to demonstrate a "clear and present danger" of "actual prejudice or an imminent threat" before any discipline may be imposed on a lawyer who initiates a press conference such as occurred here. . . .

When a state regulation implicates First Amendment rights, the Court must balance those interests against the State's legitimate interest in regulating the activity in question. The "substantial likelihood" test embodied in Rule 177 is constitutional under this analysis, for it is designed to protect the integrity and fairness of a State's judicial system, and it imposes only narrow and necessary limitations on lawyers' speech. The limitations are aimed at two principal evils: (1) comments that are likely to influence the actual outcome of the trial, and (2) comments that are likely to prejudice the jury venire, even if an untainted panel can ultimately be found. Few, if any, interests under the Constitution are more fundamental than the right to a fair trial by "impartial" jurors, and an outcome affected by extrajudicial statements would violate that fundamental right. Even if a fair trial can ultimately be ensured through *voir dire*, change of venue, or some other device, these measures entail serious costs to the system. Extensive *voir dire* may not be able to filter out all of the effects of pretrial publicity, and with increasingly widespread media coverage of criminal trials, a change of venue may not suffice to undo the effects of statements such as those made by petitioner. The State has a substantial interest in preventing officers of the court, such as lawyers, from imposing such costs on the judicial system and on the litigants.

The restraint on speech is narrowly tailored to achieve those objectives. The regulation of attorneys' speech is limited—it applies only to speech that is substantially likely to have a materially prejudicial effect; it is neutral as to points of view, applying equally to all attorneys participating in a pending case; and it merely postpones the attorneys' comments until after the trial. While supported by the substantial state interest in preventing prejudice to an adjudicative proceeding by those who have a duty to protect its integrity, the Rule is limited on its face to preventing only speech having a substantial likelihood of materially prejudicing that proceeding.

The Rehnquist plurality, having lost its majority, rejected the conclusion that the rule was unconstitutionally vague.

Questions and Comments About *Gentile*

1. In 1994, to eliminate the vagueness problems in the rule, the ABA deleted the words that allowed a lawyer to state the "general nature of" the defense "without elaboration."

2. Also in 1994, the ABA added paragraph (c), which gives lawyers a right to reply to prejudicial publicity initiated by others. It provides:

Notwithstanding paragraph (a), a lawyer may make a statement that a reasonable lawyer would believe is required to protect a client from the substantial undue prejudicial effect of recent publicity not initiated by the lawyer or the lawyer's client. A statement made pursuant to this paragraph shall be limited to such information as is necessary to mitigate the recent adverse publicity.

3. If we assume that voir dire can discover and eliminate pretrial prejudice—an assumption that courts routinely make in denying motions to change venue—what legitimate state interest supports a curb on a lawyer's public statements? Or perhaps we should reverse the question: If in fact voir dire will remedy prejudice, why do lawyers engage in publicity in the first place?

4. In a remarkable observation, Justice Kennedy wrote:

> An attorney's duties do not begin inside the courtroom door. . . . [A]n attorney may take reasonable steps to defend a client's reputation and reduce the adverse consequences of indictment . . . including an attempt to demonstrate in the court of public opinion that the client does not deserve to be tried.

Can it be that four Supreme Court Justices (but only four) were then prepared to vest lawyers with the right, perhaps the duty, to advocate for their clients in the media? If that position is correct, why have a pretrial publicity rule at all?

5. In an omitted portion of his opinion, Justice Kennedy (again, for four Justices) wrote:

> Still less justification exists for a lower standard of scrutiny here, as this speech involved not the prosecutor or police, but a criminal defense attorney. Respondent and its *amici* present not a single example where a defense attorney has managed by public statements to prejudice the prosecution of the State's case. Even discounting the obvious reason for a lack of appellate decisions on the topic—the difficulty of appealing a verdict of acquittal—the absence of anecdotal or survey evidence in a much-studied area of the law is remarkable.

If the First Amendment gives the defense lawyer greater protection than it gives prosecutors and police (assuming it gives them any at all) haven't we created an unlevel playing field that benefits the defense?

6. Rule 3.6 prohibits certain statements that "have a substantial likelihood of materially prejudicing an adjudicative proceeding." The ABA has repeatedly rejected a "clear and present danger" test. Justice Kennedy would read the "substantial likelihood" test to refer to statements "that create[] a danger of imminent and substantial harm." The Third Circuit invoked its supervisory powers to require district courts within its jurisdiction to use the ABA standard. United States v. Wecht, 484 F.3d 194 (3d Cir. 2007). *Wecht* said that only three states—Illinois, New Mexico, and Oklahoma—had a test affording speech more protection than does Rule 3.6.

7. Whatever the test, a lawyer prepared to make a statement must try to predict the "likelihood" of the effect of that statement on any subsequent trial. How is a lawyer to know in advance? If the lawyer is disciplined, how can a disciplinary committee know in retrospect if a statement violated the test at the time it was made? *Gentile* held that the violation occurs, or not, at the moment the statement is made, regardless of what happens thereafter. That means that Gentile could have violated the rule even though no prospective juror had ever heard about his press conference. That fact, as Kennedy wrote, may be some evidence that the rule was not violated.

8. *Gentile* construed the Nevada rule to apply only to lawyers who speak about matters with which they are or were associated, not to all lawyers. This is not what it or the ABA rule then said. After *Gentile*, Rule 3.6 was narrowed to cover only a lawyer "who is participating or has participated in the investigation or litigation of a matter." Lawyers who sound off about a case with which they have no connection (which seemed to be true for about half the bar during the O.J. Simpson and Weinstein trials) enjoy as much First Amendment protection as everyone else.

People v. Harvey Weinstein

Let's return to the Weinstein prosecution and civil lawsuits against him. The national media were all over this story, with coverage comparable to that in O.J. Simpson's murder case. Nearly all news stories were specific and harmful to Weinstein. They detailed violence toward the victims named in the indictment and toward many other women whose allegations were too old to prosecute. Weinstein's lawyer and public relations people could issue denials and they did. They could claim, as they did, that the stories were all false, that all of the sex was consensual or didn't happen. They could claim, as they did, that the women who had sex with Weinstein did so to advance their careers. Assume that the government was not behind these news stories, that they were the result of press investigations and other women choosing to come forward. The press can't be stopped. The First Amendment forbids it. In this way, the United States is unlike some other common law countries, including the U.K. and Australia, which restrict reporting to public records and whatever transpires in the courtroom.

Can we be confident that Weinstein's trial was not tainted by the thousands of stories in the electronic and print media recounting accusations against him by women whose public charges of sexual assault were not the basis for the prosecution and who would not be subject to cross-examination? Can we be confident that the voir dire of potential jurors was adequate to get an impartial jury? Weinstein moved for a change of venue, which was denied. Should it have been granted?

Immunity for Allegedly Defamatory Statements During Litigation

Discipline is not the only risk lawyers face for statements in connection with pending or impending court cases. There is also the risk of defamation. Courts nationwide grant an absolute privilege (or absolute immunity) for some statements made during a pending litigation, although the privilege may depend on when and where the statement is made. In Florida, an absolute privilege is limited to statements made in court, court documents, or formal discovery. Delmonico v. Traynor, 116 So. 3d 1205 (Fla. 2013). Other statements, so long as they are "connected with or related to the subject of inquiry in the underlying lawsuit," enjoy a qualified privilege, which can be defeated with a showing of "express malice." New York recognizes an absolute privilege for statements "relevant . . . in judicial or quasi-judicial proceedings . . . irrespective of an attorney's motive for making them." If a proceeding is not yet filed, the privilege will protect the statements only if they "are pertinent to a good faith anticipated litigation." Front, Inc. v. Khalil, 28 N.E.3d 15 (N.Y. 2015).

B. PUBLIC COMMENT ABOUT JUDGES

#SourOnHoney

The State of New Grace elects its judges for six-year terms. Honey Mellenkamp has been a trial judge in New Grace for 11 years and is running for reelection. Murray Clarkson is a civil trial lawyer in New Grace. Mellenkamp and Clarkson have clashed several times. Once she nearly held him in contempt. He has twice moved to recuse her from his cases, citing her hostility to him. She refused both times. Clarkson appealed the second denial and lost.

Clarkson decided actively to oppose Mellenkamp's reelection. He started a Twitter hashtag (#SourOnHoney) and a website called "Dump-HoneyMellenkamp.com." He picketed her campaign appearances, where he handed out leaflets and carried a sign that read "SHE'S NO SWEETIE: FIRE HONEY MELLENKAMP." The leaflet had the Twitter hashtag and the website URL. The leaflet and the website say the following:

- Mellenkamp has been reversed by appellate courts more often than any other judge on her court.
- Mellenkamp consistently gives the harshest sentences and the highest bails compared to any other judge.
- Mellenkamp takes longer to issue her opinions than any other judge. Justice DELAYED is Justice DENIED.
- Mellenkamp is overbearing, emotional, confused, unprepared, and shrill on the bench.

Mellenkamp in fact has the fifth highest reversal rate among 18 judges on her court. Her sentencing and bail decisions are only moderately higher than the mean for her court. She is the sixth slowest judge to issue opinions. After Mellenkamp is defeated, she files a grievance against Clarkson citing Rule 8.2(a). You are on the court charged to determine whether Clarkson acted unethically. What else would you want to know and why? How would you rule?

Judges are public officials. In a long line of cases beginning with New York Times Co. v. Sullivan, 376 U.S. 254 (1964), the Supreme Court has held that public officials and public figures who sue for defamation must prove by clear and convincing evidence that the defendant acted with "actual malice." Actual malice, a subjective test, requires knowledge of the statement's falsity or reckless (that is, conscious) disregard of whether it is true or false. The plaintiff must also prove that the alleged defamation is false. Phila. Newspapers v. Hepps, 475 U.S. 767 (1986). *Gentile* gave less First Amendment protection to lawyers who make pre-trial statements about their own cases than the rest of the world (including other lawyers) enjoys. Does a lawyer's statement about a judge also get less First Amendment protection than the *New York Times* line of cases affords for statements about other public officials and figures? Less protection than a nonlawyer's statements about a judge? Yes.

The following case tells the story of Elizabeth Holtzman, former comptroller of New York City, former Brooklyn district attorney, former member of the House Judiciary Committee during the Watergate investigation, and twice a candidate for the U.S. Senate. She did not fare as well as Gentile. Why not?

IN RE HOLTZMAN

78 N.Y.2d 184, 577 N.E.2d 30, 573 N.Y.S.2d 39 (1991),
cert. denied, 502 U.S. 1009

PER CURIAM. . . .

The charge of misconduct that is relevant to this appeal was based on the public release by petitioner, then District Attorney of Kings County, of a letter charging Judge Irving Levine with judicial misconduct in relation to an incident that allegedly occurred in the course of a trial on criminal charges of sexual misconduct, and was reported to her some six weeks later. Specifically, petitioner's letter stated that:

> Judge Levine asked the Assistant District Attorney, defense counsel, defendant, court officer and court reporter to join him in the robing room, where the judge then asked the victim to get down on the floor and show the position she was in when she was being sexually assaulted. . . . The victim

reluctantly got down on her hands and knees as everyone stood and watched. In making the victim assume the position she was forced to take when she was sexually assaulted, Judge Levine profoundly degraded, humiliated and demeaned her.

The letter, addressed to Judge Kathryn McDonald as Chair of the Committee to Implement Recommendations of the New York State Task Force on Women in the Courts, was publicly disseminated after petitioner's office issued a "news alert" to the media. . . .

[Holtzman was found to have engaged in conduct that "adversely reflected on her fitness to practice law" in violation of DR 1-102(A)(6) of the New York Code after her allegation was determined to lack evidentiary support.]

The conduct . . . allegedly demonstrating petitioner's unfitness to practice law, included release of the letter to the media (1) prior to obtaining the minutes of the criminal trial, (2) without making any effort to speak with court officers, the court reporter, defense counsel or any other person present during the alleged misconduct, (3) without meeting with or discussing the incident with the trial assistant who reported it [in memoranda], and (4) with the knowledge that Judge Levine was being transferred out of the Criminal Court, and the matter would be investigated by the Court's Administrative Judge as well as the Commission on Judicial Conduct (to which the petitioner had complained). . . .

Petitioner relies primarily on two arguments. First, she asserts that the allegations concerning Judge Levine's conduct were true or at least not demonstrably false. Second, petitioner asserts that her conduct violates no specific disciplinary rule and further that DR 1-102(a)(6), if applicable, is unconstitutionally vague. These contentions are without merit.

[P]etitioner made false accusations against the Judge. This charge was sustained by the Committee and upheld by the Appellate Division, and the factual finding of falsity (which is supported by the record) is therefore binding on us.

As for the contention that petitioner's conduct did not violate any provision of the Code, DR 1-102(A)(6) provides that a lawyer shall not "[e]ngage in any other conduct that adversely reflects on [the lawyer's] fitness to practice law." As far back as 1856, the Supreme Court acknowledged that "it is difficult, if not impossible, to enumerate and define, with legal precision, every offense for which an attorney or counsellor ought to be removed." Broad standards governing professional conduct are permissible and indeed often necessary. . . .

Rather than an absolute prohibition on broad standards, the guiding principle must be whether a reasonable attorney, familiar with the Code and its ethical strictures, would have notice of what conduct is proscribed.

Applying this standard, petitioner was plainly on notice that her conduct in this case, involving public dissemination of a specific accusation of improper judicial conduct under the circumstances described, could be held to reflect adversely on her fitness to practice law. Indeed, her staff, including the person assigned the task of looking into the ethical implications of release to the press, counseled her to delay publication until the trial minutes were received.

Petitioner's act was not generalized criticism but rather release to the media of a false allegation of specific wrongdoing, made without any support other than the interoffice memoranda of a newly admitted trial assistant, aimed at a named Judge who had presided over a number of cases prosecuted by her office. Petitioner knew or should have known that such attacks are unwarranted and unprofessional, serve to bring the Bench and Bar into disrepute, and tend to undermine public confidence in the judicial system. . . .

Petitioner contends that her conduct would not be actionable under the "constitutional malice" standard enunciated by the Supreme Court in New York Times Co. v. Sullivan. Neither this Court nor the Supreme Court has ever extended the *Sullivan* standard to lawyer discipline and we decline to do so here.

Accepting petitioner's argument would immunize all accusations, however reckless or irresponsible, from censure as long as the attorney uttering them did not actually entertain serious doubts as to their truth. Such a standard would be wholly at odds with the policy underlying the rules governing professional responsibility, which seeks to establish a "minimum level of conduct below which no lawyer can fall without being subject to disciplinary action." [Citing the Code.]

Unlike defamation cases, "[p]rofessional misconduct, although it may directly affect an individual, is not punished for the benefit of the affected person; the wrong is against society as a whole, the preservation of a fair, impartial judicial system, and the system of justice as it has evolved for generations." It follows that the issue raised when an attorney makes public a false accusation of wrongdoing by a Judge is not whether the target of the false attack has been harmed in reputation; the issue is whether that criticism adversely affects the administration of justice and adversely reflects on the attorney's judgment and, consequentially, her ability to practice law.

In order to adequately protect the public interest and maintain the integrity of the judicial system, there must be an objective standard of what a reasonable attorney would do in similar circumstances. It is the reasonableness of the belief, not the state of mind of the attorney, that is determinative. . . .

Holtzman was disciplined under a Code provision forbidding conduct that "adversely reflects on the lawyer's fitness as a lawyer." This language remains in New York Rule 8.4(h), but it is not in the Model Rules. Holtzman's comment might also lead to discipline under Rule 8.2(a) of both the New York and Model Rules. The New York rule forbids a lawyer to "knowingly make a false statement of fact concerning the qualifications, conduct, or integrity of a judge." The Model Rule does the same and also forbids such statements made with "reckless disregard."

Questions and Comments About *Holtzman*

1. In a public statement issued after the decision, Holtzman said: "The court's decision is a blow to those who value freedom of speech and who care about the treatment of rape victims by the courts." Is she right?

2. Should Holtzman's position as D.A. give her a greater obligation to "get it right" than is imposed on others who criticize judges? Or a greater obligation to speak up? Or maybe both?

3. Does the court's standard—"whether a reasonable attorney, familiar with the Code and its ethical strictures, would have notice of what conduct is proscribed"—give adequate notice of what DR 1-102(A)(6) (now N.Y. Rule 8.4(h)) forbids? Compare *Gentile*, where the Court said Gentile did not have adequate notice of what he could not say. *Holtzman* was decided four days after *Gentile*, but the *Holtzman* court did not cite it. Should the court have applied *Gentile's* vagueness analysis? Holtzman's certiorari petition was denied.

4. In any event, why wasn't a memorandum from a lawyer on her staff—albeit a "newly admitted" one—a sufficient basis for Holtzman's response?

5. Is the court correct that if the *subjective New York Times* libel defense standard were available, a "reckless" attorney would escape responsibility for false accusations against judges? *New York Times* would not protect a statement made with "reckless disregard" for its truth or falsity, but that inquiry asks about the defendant's subjective state of mind. Like *Holtzman,* most (but not all) courts ask whether the lawyer's statement was *objectively* reckless. What would a reasonable lawyer believe based on the available information? Lawyer Disciplinary Bd. v. Hall, 765 S.E.2d 187 (W. Va. 2014) (reviewing cases and adopting an objective test under the Model Rule). So a well-meaning but mistaken lawyer can be disciplined for statements concerning a judge's qualifications or integrity. A few jurisdictions use a subjective test. See, e.g., In re Colin, 448 P.3d 556 (Nev. 2019).

6. A statement about a judge will get less First Amendment protection in discipline than it would get in a libel case. Is there any reason to coddle judges? After all, they are, like state legislators and mayors, public officials. Defenders of Rule 8.2(a) offer this answer. Does it persuade you? First, the rule is meant to protect public trust in the courts, not to compensate judges for harm to their reputations, which is what libel claims do. Second, judges are not free to respond in kind, unlike other government officials, because confidence in the courts would suffer if judges engaged in a public debate over their own integrity.

7. Holtzman was disciplined for making a false statement of fact. Can a lawyer be disciplined for an opinion about a judge's qualifications? In re Colin, supra ("No matter the offensive or unkind nature of an attorney's statement, [the rule] is limited to statements of fact as opposed to opinion because only statements of fact can be true or false."). Were any of Clarkson's comments about Mellenkamp opinion? How about "Mellenkamp is overbearing, emotional, confused, unprepared, and shrill on the bench." A few of these are adjectives men have used to describe women, less often to describe men. Are they protected as opinion nonetheless?

8. Judges sometimes use abusive language in characterizing the reasoning of other judges. Why should lawyers be held to a higher standard? Consider In re Wilkins, 777 N.E.2d 714 (Ind. 2002), modified, 782 N.E.2d 985 (Ind. 2003). In a note in a brief, Wilkins questioned the legal and factual accuracy of the lower court opinion. He wrote that "one is left to wonder whether [the court] was determined to find for [the opposing party] and then said whatever was necessary to reach that conclusion (regardless of whether the facts or the law supported its decision)." The majority said this statement violated Rule 8.2(a). The dissent, although finding Wilkins's language "tasteless," could not "see how this footnote differs from the charges occasionally leveled by judges at other judges." As have others, it cited Justice Scalia, who in one case wrote that "seldom has an opinion of this Court rested so obviously upon nothing but the personal views of its members," and in another case said that Justice O'Connor's position was "irrational" and "cannot be taken seriously." Scalia characterized Justice Sotomayor's opinion for the Court in Michigan v. Bryant, 562 U.S. 344 (2011), this way: "Today's tale . . . is so transparently false that professing to believe it demeans this institution." Yet the Code of Conduct for U.S. Judges requires judges to be "dignified, respectful, and courteous" to those "with whom the judge deals in an official capacity." A lawyer who said these things about a judge might find himself facing discipline.

C. JUDICIAL CAMPAIGN SPEECH

"I Got These Questionnaires"

"My name is Marta Rojas. I'm a lawyer in private practice. I am running for an elected spot on the state high court. I've been in practice 23 years and active in the bar association. I do a lot of pro bono work for immigrants, especially for Latinx persons because Spanish is my first language. All around, I think I'm a pretty good citizen of the profession and of my state.

"In connection with my campaign, I got these questionnaires from three different groups. One is from a right-to-life group. It lists a bunch of statements and asks me to say whether I agree, disagree, am undecided, or decline to answer. One statement is: 'I believe that the unborn child is biologically human and alive as of the moment of conception and that the right to life of human beings should be respected at every stage of their biological development.' Another is 'I believe that no provision of the state constitution protects a right to abortion.'

"A second questionnaire is from a group that works for the rights of tenants. It asks whether I agree that the state constitution should be read to guarantee tenants who satisfy certain financial criteria free counsel in eviction proceedings.

"A final questionnaire is from the state affiliate of the National Rifle Association. It asks me whether I agree with this statement: 'The state constitution guarantees residents the right to own automatic weapons, to carry loaded handguns in public and in public buildings, and to purchase any weapon lawfully on sale without a waiting period. I will so rule if elected.'

"Now, I have tentative or strongly held views on some of the statements in these and other questionnaires and no view on other statements. I'm not asking for your campaign advice. I know I don't have to reply. My question is, may I tell my views under our state Code of Judicial Conduct, which is the same as the ABA Code? And if I do respond to a question and get elected, am I thereby disqualified from any appeal raising that issue?"

———————

At least 39 states elect some or all of their trial and appellate judges. In this, they vary from the federal model. Whether election or appointment is the better policy, or whether the answer depends on the particular court, is not the question here. States can choose election. But for decades, states have also limited the campaign speech of judicial candidates in ways that the First Amendment would not tolerate for candidates for political office. The limitations, though sometimes differently worded by different states, drew on provisions of the ABA's various Codes of Judicial Conduct and appeared in state judicial conduct codes.

The following opinions address the constitutionality of one limitation, called the announce clause (which Justice Ginsburg capitalizes; Justice Scalia does not). The Republican Party of Minnesota and Gregory Wersal, a candidate for the Minnesota Supreme Court, sought a declaratory judgment that the announce clause violated the First Amendment. He lost in the Eighth Circuit and appealed to the Supreme Court. The announce clause prohibited a candidate to "announce his or her views on disputed legal or political issues." Another clause, called the pledges and promises clause, was not before the Court then and has not been since. But it figures in Justice

Ginsburg's dissent. It prohibits judicial candidates from making "pledges or promises of conduct in office other than the faithful and impartial performance of the duties of the office." The precise meaning of and relationship between the clauses is disputed, which partly explains the differences between the majority opinion and the Ginsburg dissent. Ginsburg predicts that the Court's decision on the announce clause will permit candidates to circumvent the pledges and promises clause through artful construction of campaign statements.

Minnesota's defense of its restrictions on judicial campaign speech relied on the state's legitimate interest in judges who are and appear to be impartial. But what does "impartial" mean and was the announce clause a constitutional way to ensure impartiality and its appearance?

After *White*, states undertook to rewrite their judicial conduct codes. In 2007, the ABA added language in its Code of Judicial Conduct to bring it into compliance with *White*, as discussed below.

REPUBLICAN PARTY OF MINNESOTA v. WHITE
536 U.S. 765 (2002)

JUSTICE SCALIA delivered the opinion of the Court. . . .

II

Before considering the constitutionality of the announce clause, we must be clear about its meaning. Its text says that a candidate for judicial office shall not "announce his or her views on disputed legal or political issues."

We know that "announcing . . . views" on an issue covers much more than *promising* to decide an issue a particular way. The prohibition extends to the candidate's mere statement of his current position, even if he does not bind himself to maintain that position after election. All the parties agree this is the case, because the Minnesota Code contains a so-called "pledges or promises" clause, which *separately* prohibits judicial candidates from making "pledges or promises of conduct in office other than the faithful and impartial performance of the duties of the office"—a prohibition that is not challenged here and on which we express no view. . . .

III . . .

The Court of Appeals concluded that respondents had established two interests as sufficiently compelling to justify the announce clause: preserving the impartiality of the state judiciary and preserving the appearance of the impartiality of the state judiciary. Respondents reassert these two interests before us, arguing that the first is compelling because it protects the due process rights of litigants, and that the second is compelling because it preserves public confidence in the judiciary. Respondents are rather vague, however, about what they mean by "impartiality." . . .

A

One meaning of "impartiality" in the judicial context—and of course its root meaning—is the lack of bias for or against either *party* to the proceeding. Impartiality in this sense assures equal application of the law. That is, it guarantees a party that the judge who hears his case will apply the law to him in the same way he applies it to any other party. This is the traditional sense in which the term is used. It is also the sense in which it is used in the cases cited by respondents and *amici* for the proposition that an impartial judge is essential to due process. . . .

We think it plain that the announce clause is not narrowly tailored to serve impartiality (or the appearance of impartiality) in this sense. Indeed, the clause is barely tailored to serve that interest *at all*, inasmuch as it does not restrict speech for or against particular *parties*, but rather speech for or against particular *issues*. To be sure, when a case arises that turns on a legal issue on which the judge (as a candidate) had taken a particular stand, the party taking the opposite stand is likely to lose. But not because of any bias against that party, or favoritism toward the other party. *Any* party taking that position is just as likely to lose. The judge is applying the law (as he sees it) evenhandedly.

B

It is perhaps possible to use the term "impartiality" in the judicial context (though this is certainly not a common usage) to mean lack of preconception in favor of or against a particular *legal* view. This sort of impartiality would be concerned, not with guaranteeing litigants equal application of the law, but rather with guaranteeing them an equal chance to persuade the court on the legal points in their case. Impartiality in this sense may well be an interest served by the announce clause, but it is not a *compelling* state interest, as strict scrutiny requires. A judge's lack of predisposition regarding the relevant legal issues in a case has never been thought a necessary component of equal justice, and with good reason. For one thing, it is virtually impossible to find a judge who does not have preconceptions about the law. As then-Justice Rehnquist observed of our own Court: "Since most Justices come to this bench no earlier than their middle years, it would be unusual if they had not by that time formulated at least some tentative notions that would influence them in their interpretation of the sweeping clauses of the Constitution and their interaction with one another. It would be not merely unusual, but extraordinary, if they had not at least given opinions as to constitutional issues in their previous legal careers." Laird v. Tatum, 409 U.S. 824, 835 (1972) (memorandum opinion). Indeed, even if it were possible to select judges who did not have preconceived views on legal issues, it would hardly be desirable to do so. "Proof that a Justice's mind at the time he joined the Court was a complete *tabula rasa* in the area of constitutional adjudication would be evidence of lack of qualification, not lack of bias." Ibid. The Minnesota Constitution positively forbids the selection to courts of general jurisdiction of judges who are impartial in the sense of having no views on the law. . . . And since avoiding judicial preconceptions on legal issues is neither possible nor desirable, pretending otherwise by attempting to preserve the "appearance" of that type of impartiality can hardly be a compelling state interest either.

C

A third possible meaning of "impartiality" (again not a common one) might be described as openmindedness. This quality in a judge demands, not that he have no preconceptions on legal issues, but that he be willing to consider views that oppose his preconceptions, and remain open to persuasion, when the issues arise in a pending case. This sort of impartiality seeks to guarantee each litigant, not an *equal* chance to win the legal points in the case, but at least *some* chance of doing so. It may well be that impartiality in this sense, and the appearance of it, are desirable in the judiciary, but we need not pursue that inquiry, since we do not believe the Minnesota Supreme Court adopted the announce clause for that purpose.

Respondents argue that the announce clause serves the interest in openmindedness, or at least in the appearance of openmindedness, because it relieves a judge from pressure to rule a certain way in order to maintain consistency with statements the judge has previously made. The problem is, however, that statements in election campaigns are such an infinitesimal portion of the public commitments to legal positions that judges (or judges-to-be) undertake, that this object of the prohibition is implausible. Before they arrive on the bench (whether by election or otherwise) judges have often committed themselves on legal issues that they must later rule upon. More common still is a judge's confronting a legal issue on which he has expressed an opinion while on the bench. Most frequently, of course, that prior expression will have occurred in ruling on an earlier case. But judges often state their views on disputed legal issues outside the context of adjudication—in classes that they conduct, and in books and speeches. Like the ABA Codes of Judicial Conduct, the Minnesota Code not only permits but encourages this. That is quite incompatible with the notion that the need for openmindedness (or for the appearance of openmindedness) lies behind the prohibition at issue here.

The short of the matter is this: In Minnesota, a candidate for judicial office may not say "I think it is constitutional for the legislature to prohibit same-sex marriages." He may say the very same thing, however, up until the very day before he declares himself a candidate, and may say it repeatedly (until litigation is pending) after he is elected. As a means of pursuing the objective of openmindedness that respondents now articulate, the announce clause is so woefully underinclusive as to render belief in that purpose a challenge to the credulous. . . .[11]

. . . Justice Ginsburg greatly exaggerates the difference between judicial and legislative elections. She asserts that "the rationale underlying unconstrained speech in elections for political office—that representative government depends on the public's ability to choose agents who will act at its behest—does not carry over to campaigns for the bench." This complete separation of the judiciary from the enterprise of "representative government" might have some truth in those countries where judges neither make law themselves nor set aside the laws enacted by the legislature. It is not a true picture of the American system. Not only do state-court judges possess the power to "make" common law, but they have the immense power to shape the States' constitutions as well. Which is precisely why the election of state judges became popular. . . .

[The Court held that the state's announce clause violated the First Amendment.]

JUSTICE GINSBURG, with whom JUSTICE STEVENS, JUSTICE SOUTER, and JUSTICE BREYER join, dissenting. . . .

I . . .

Legislative and executive officials serve in representative capacities. They are agents of the people; their primary function is to advance the interests of their constituencies. Candidates for political offices, in keeping with their representative role, must be left free to inform the electorate of their positions on specific issues. Armed with such information, the individual voter will be equipped to cast her ballot intelligently, to vote for the candidate committed to positions the voter approves. Campaign statements committing the candidate to take sides on contentious issues are therefore not only appropriate in political elections, they are "at the core of our electoral process," for they "enhance the accountability of government officials to the people whom they represent."

Judges, however, are not political actors. They do not sit as representatives of particular persons, communities, or parties; they serve no faction

---

11. Nor do we assert that candidates for judicial office should be *compelled* to announce their views on disputed legal issues. Thus, Justice Ginsburg's repeated invocation of instances in which nominees to this Court declined to announce such views during Senate confirmation hearings is pointless. That the practice of *voluntarily* demurring does not establish the legitimacy of *legal compulsion* to demur is amply demonstrated by the unredacted text of the sentence she quotes in part from Laird v. Tatum, 409 U.S. 824, 836, n.5 (1972): "*In terms of propriety, rather than disqualification,* I would distinguish quite sharply between a public statement made prior to nomination for the bench, on the one hand, and a public statement made by a nominee to the bench." (Emphasis added.) [This footnote was moved from a deleted portion of the opinion.]

or constituency. "It is the business of judges to be indifferent to popularity." They must strive to do what is legally right, all the more so when the result is not the one "the home crowd" wants. . . .[1]

II . . .

[T]he Court ignores a crucial limiting construction placed on the Announce Clause by the courts below. The provision does not bar a candidate from generally "stating [her] views" on legal questions; it prevents her from "publicly making known how [she] would *decide*" disputed issues. That limitation places beyond the scope of the Announce Clause a wide range of comments that may be highly informative to voters. Consistent with the Eighth Circuit's construction, such comments may include, for example, statements of historical fact ("As a prosecutor, I obtained 15 drunk driving convictions"); qualified statements ("Judges should use *sparingly* their discretion to grant lenient sentences to drunk drivers"); and statements framed at a sufficient level of generality ("Drunk drivers are a threat to the safety of every driver"). What remains within the Announce Clause is the category of statements that essentially commit the candidate to a position on a specific issue, such as "I think all drunk drivers should receive the maximum sentence permitted by law." . . .

The Announce Clause is thus more tightly bounded, and campaigns conducted under that provision more robust, than the Court acknowledges. Judicial candidates in Minnesota may not only convey general information about themselves, they may also describe their conception of the role of a judge and their views on a wide range of subjects of interest to the voters. Further, they may discuss, criticize, or defend past decisions of interest to voters. What candidates may not do—simply or with sophistication—is remove themselves from the constraints characteristic of the judicial office and declare how they would decide an issue, without regard to the particular context in which it is presented, *sans* briefs, oral argument, and, as to

---

1. In the context of the federal system, how a prospective nominee for the bench would resolve particular contentious issues would certainly be "of interest" to the President and the Senate in the exercise of their respective nomination and confirmation powers, just as information of that type would "interest" a Minnesota voter. But in accord with a longstanding norm, every Member of this Court declined to furnish such information to the Senate, and presumably to the President as well. Surely the Court perceives no tension here; the line each of us drew in response to preconfirmation questioning, the Court would no doubt agree, is crucial to the health of the Federal Judiciary. But by the Court's reasoning, the reticence of prospective and current federal judicial nominees dishonors Article II, for it deprives the President and the Senate of information that might aid or advance the decision to nominate or confirm. The point is not, of course, that this "practice of voluntarily demurring" by itself "establish[es] the legitimacy of legal compulsion to demur" (emphasis omitted). The federal norm simply illustrates that, contrary to the Court's suggestion, there is nothing inherently incongruous in depriving those charged with choosing judges of certain information they might desire during the selection process. [This footnote was moved from a deleted portion of the opinion.—ED.]

an appellate bench, the benefit of one's colleagues' analyses. Properly construed, the Announce Clause prohibits only a discrete subcategory of the statements the Court's misinterpretation encompasses. . . .

III

Even as it exaggerates the reach of the Announce Clause, the Court ignores the significance of that provision to the integrated system of judicial campaign regulation Minnesota has developed. Coupled with the Announce Clause in Minnesota's Code of Judicial Conduct is a provision that prohibits candidates from "making pledges or promises of conduct in office other than the faithful and impartial performance of the duties of the office." Although the Court is correct that this "pledges or promises" provision is not directly at issue in this case, the Court errs in overlooking the interdependence of that prohibition and the one before us. In my view, the constitutionality of the Announce Clause cannot be resolved without an examination of that interaction in light of the interests the pledges or promises provision serves. . . .[4]

B . . .

Uncoupled from the Announce Clause, the ban on pledges or promises is easily circumvented. By prefacing a campaign commitment with the caveat, "although I cannot promise anything," or by simply avoiding the language of promises or pledges altogether, a candidate could declare with impunity how she would decide specific issues. Semantic sanitizing of the candidate's commitment would not, however, diminish its pernicious effects on actual and perceived judicial impartiality. To use the Court's example, a candidate who campaigns by saying, "If elected, I will vote to uphold the legislature's power to prohibit same-sex marriages," will feel scarcely more pressure to honor that statement than the candidate who stands behind a podium and tells a throng of cheering supporters: "I think it is constitutional for the legislature to prohibit same-sex marriages." Made during a campaign, both statements contemplate a *quid pro quo* between candidate and voter. Both effectively "bind [the candidate] to maintain that position after election."

---

4. The author of the Court's opinion declined on precisely these grounds to tell the Senate whether he would overrule a particular case:

> "Let us assume that I have people arguing before me to do it or not to do it. I think it is quite a thing to be arguing to somebody who you know has made a representation in the course of his confirmation hearings, and that is, by way of condition to his being confirmed, that he will do this or do that. I think I would be in a very bad position to adjudicate the case without being accused of having a less than impartial view of the matter."

[The footnote has been moved.—ED.]

And both convey the impression of a candidate prejudging an issue to win votes. Contrary to the Court's assertion, the "nonpromissory" statement averts none of the dangers posed by the "promissory" one.

Gray Areas Post-*White*

The Supreme Court returned to these issues in 2015. In Williams-Yulee v. Florida Bar, 575 U.S. 433 (2015), the question was "[w]hether a rule of judicial conduct that prohibits candidates for judicial office from personally soliciting campaign funds violates the First Amendment." It did not, wrote Chief Justice Roberts, applying strict scrutiny:

> The Florida Supreme Court adopted Canon 7C(1) [of the state's judicial conduct code] to promote the State's interests in "protecting the integrity of the judiciary" and "maintaining the public's confidence in an impartial judiciary." The way the Canon advances those interests is intuitive: Judges, charged with exercising strict neutrality and independence, cannot supplicate campaign donors without diminishing public confidence in judicial integrity. This principle dates back at least eight centuries to Magna Carta, which proclaimed, "To no one will we sell, to no one will we refuse or delay, right or justice." The same concept underlies the common law judicial oath, which binds a judge to "do right to all manner of people . . . without fear or favour, affection or ill-will," and the oath that each of us took to "administer justice without respect to persons, and do equal right to the poor and to the rich." Simply put, Florida and most other States have concluded that the public may lack confidence in a judge's ability to administer justice without fear or favor if he comes to office by asking for favors.

Like *White*, *Williams-Yulee* divided the Court 5-4, except this time the liberal wing of the Court (Justices Ginsburg, Breyer, Sotomayor, and Kagan), joined by the Chief Justice, was on the winning side. The conservatives (Justices Scalia, Kennedy, Thomas, and Alito) dissented. Distilling the two opinions, the question they pose is stark. Its answer requires reconciling two important values: In order to protect the role and especially the reputation of the judiciary as nonpolitical (despite the fact that most state judges are elected), can a state impose restrictions on speech and campaign activities that in other circumstances would violate the First Amendment?

Lower courts both before and after *Williams-Yulee* have been grappling with this question. For example, after *Williams-Yulee,* the en banc Ninth Circuit unanimously rejected a First Amendment challenge to clauses in the Arizona judicial conduct code that taken together

> do not allow [a candidate], while running for judicial office, to personally solicit funds for his own campaign or for a campaign for another candidate or political organization, to publicly endorse another candidate for public office, to make speeches on behalf of another candidate or political organization, or to actively take part in any political campaign.

Wolfson v. Concannon, 811 F.3d 1176 (9th Cir. 2016). Six months later the Sixth Circuit addressed similar questions:

> At issue today are several clauses in Kentucky's judicial canons—from prohibitions on [1] "campaign[ing] as a member of a political organization," to [2] "endors[ing] . . . a candidate for public office," to [3] "mak[ing] a contribution to a political organization," to [4] making any "commitments" with respect to "cases, controversies, or issues" likely to come before the court, to [5] making "false" or "misleading" statements.*

The court struck the prohibition in [1], upheld the prohibitions in [2], [3], and [4], and held that the prohibition in [5] against "false" statements was facially valid but not as applied in the case before it. The ban on "misleading" statements was held invalid. Winter v. Wolnitzek, 834 F.3d 681 (6th Cir. 2016). In Platt v. Board of Commissioners on Grievances & Discipline of Ohio Supreme Court, 894 F.3d 235 (6th Cir. 2018), the same circuit upheld rules preventing judicial candidates from soliciting campaign funds and forbidding them to make speeches for or against candidates for other public office.

This summary of post-*White* circuit court opinions can only skim their reasoning. Eventually, the Supreme Court is likely to return to these issues, if only to resolve differences in how lower courts have addressed them.

What about the ABA? It was, after all, an ABA rule that *White* rejected. In 2007, the ABA changed its Code of Judicial Conduct. The new code eliminates the "announce clause" and includes an expanded pledges and promises clause with commentary. Rule 4.1(A)(13) says that a judicial candidate (whether via election or appointment) shall not,

> in connection with cases, controversies, or issues that are likely to come before the court, make pledges, promises, or commitments that are inconsistent with the impartial performance of the adjudicative duties of judicial office.

The same limitation applies to sitting judges. Rule 2.10(B). Commentary to Rule 4.1 explains:

> [13] The making of a pledge, promise, or commitment is not dependent upon, or limited to, the use of any specific words or phrases; instead, the totality of the statement must be examined to determine if a reasonable person would believe that the candidate for judicial office has specifically undertaken to reach a particular result. Pledges, promises, or commitments must be contrasted with statements or announcements of personal views on legal, political, or other issues, which are not prohibited. When making such statements, a judge should acknowledge the overarching judicial obligation to apply and uphold the law, without regard to his or her personal views.

On the meaning of "impartial," around which Justice Scalia built much of his opinion, the ABA chose the first and third definitions for the code's terminology, which now provides:

---

* The bracketed numbers have been added for ease of reference.

"Impartial," "impartiality," and "impartially" mean absence of bias or prejudice in favor of, or against, particular parties or classes of parties, as well as maintenance of an open mind in considering issues that may come before a judge.

Finally, Rule 2.11(A)(5) is a backstop. Even if the First Amendment protects particular campaign speech, that very speech may require the judge to recuse himself or herself if "[t]he judge, while a judge or a judicial candidate, has made a public statement, other than in a court proceeding, judicial decision, or opinion, that commits or appears to commit the judge to reach a particular result or rule in a particular way in the proceeding or controversy."

What advice, then, would you give Marta Rojas, the judicial candidate in "I Got These Questionnaires," set out above? Assume the ABA's post-*White* rules apply.

How About Supreme Court Nominees?

The majority opinion in *White* and Justice Ginsburg's dissent both recognize that at confirmation hearings, Supreme Court nominees routinely decline to give their views on issues likely to come before the Court. Justice Scalia says this is not because they cannot, but because they choose to demur. That in turn means that the Senate, if it wished, could insist on answers to questions about reproductive freedom, affirmative action, campaign finance laws, gun control, and other unresolved constitutional issues. The nominee might cite the risk of disqualification if she answered and decline to do so. The Senate could condition confirmation on getting the answers anyway. Why doesn't it? Maybe senators are happy not to know the answers. It makes casting a vote easier. Further, would the nominee who, for example, said she agrees or disagrees with Roe v. Wade be disqualified if the Court revisited Roe v. Wade? A judge cannot sit if her impartiality might reasonably be questioned.

Self-Assessment Questions

1. Your state high court is considering an amendment to Rule 3.6 that would narrow it in one or more of several ways.
   - Limiting its reach only to cases that will be tried to a jury.
   - Limiting its reach only to criminal cases that will be tried to a jury.
   - Limiting its reach only to public statements within 30 or 60 days of the commencement of jury selection in civil or criminal cases or only criminal cases.
   - Limiting its reach by changing the reference to statements that "will have a substantial likelihood of materially prejudicing an adjudicative proceeding" to "statements that present a clear and present danger of materially prejudicing an adjudicative proceeding."

You are on a bar committee that will issue an opinion on which if any of these proposals should or should not be adopted. What do you recommend?

2. As stated above, after *Gentile*, the ABA deleted the words that allowed a lawyer to state the "general nature of" the defense "without elaboration." Would Gentile's press conference violate the rule today?

XVI

Marketing Legal Services

Have you been seriously injured in a recent accident?
Get a FREE consultation with an injury attorney near you and find out if you have a claim.[*]

* * *

Filing For Divorce? Get Legal Help Today
Speak with a Local Divorce Attorney about Preparing for Divorce
If you're considering filing for a divorce, it's essential that you understand your legal rights.[†]

* * *

The estate of Jacqueline Fox won a $72 million dollar verdict against Johnson & Johnson based on its claim that Fox's longtime use of the defendant's talc products caused the ovarian cancer that killed her. Jim Onder, the plaintiff's lawyer, told the St. Louis Post-Dispatch, that after Fox received her diagnosis she contacted lawyers based on a TV ad about talc. "The sad part is, she had to learn about it from lawyer ads, while Johnson & Johnson tried to hide the truth from her," Onder said.
—Kim Bell, St. Louis Post-Dispatch, Feb. 23, 2016[‡]

"The Top Ten"

Donna Kennelly is a successful criminal defense lawyer. She has a good reputation with judges and in the bar. But she feels that she has not received recognition commensurate with her successes. She divides the criminal defense bar in her city into three groups. There's the top ten, the second ten, and "others." As she sees it, the bar views her as in the second ten, but she believes she belongs in the top ten. So she sets out to change that in the following ways.

---

[*] From a personal injury website.
[†] From a divorce website.
[‡] In October 2017, an intermediate appellate court overturned the verdict on jurisdictional grounds.

She writes a book about her cases but includes only those she won or where she secured a good plea deal. On the back jacket she includes laudatory references from former clients, who consented to this use. She self-publishes her book on Amazon. The title is: *Not Guilty: How I Beat the Prosecutors*. She gives copies to prospective clients.

She advertises the book on media websites along with the laudatory quotes (again with consent).

She hires a PR firm to get media interviews and television appearances where she can talk about her wins and comment on the headline trials of other lawyers.

She gives talks to lawyers about how to defend a criminal case in which she uses her wins as examples and sells her book.

She writes articles about her work for print and online media sites. Each article includes tales of her courtroom prowess. She does the same on social media.

She describes her big wins (under the title BIG WINS) on her firm website, using only publicly available information. The site also displays the title page of her book. Visitors to the site can buy it directly.

She sends a free copy of the book to anyone who she learns has been indicted, or who is on the verge of being indicted, if they appear able to pay her fees.

None of her publicity reveals confidential information. Kennelly's name begins to appear on random surveys of the top ten defense lawyers in the city.

Do any of these efforts violate ABA Rules 7.1 et seq.?

Marketing Legal Services: An Introduction

If you are the age of most readers of this book, you won't recall a time without legal advertising. Lawyers' ads might not be as common as ads for smart phones and Big Pharma, but you've probably seen or heard hundreds of them in your life—in newspapers, on radio and television, online, in glossy business magazines—and thought nothing of it. Yet for most of the last century, legal advertising was banned, with a few very narrow exceptions. A lawyer whose career straddles the watershed year 1977 may still be amazed at the change. Some may wonder whether it has been for the good.

Three distinct but interlocking trends will continue to make the rules that regulate law firm marketing (a generic term that some view as less pejorative than "legal advertising") important to lawyers. First is the growth of law firms in want of new clients in new markets. Second is the fact that the American lawyer population has for decades grown faster than the population generally, a trend that shows no sign of abating. This trend heightens competition for clients and encourages advertising (tasteful or not). Third, the internet (and perhaps technology yet unknown) can make lawyer marketing easy, cheap, and even respectable.

We are unlikely to see the level of court attention to lawyer marketing that we witnessed in the final quarter of the last century. After the Supreme Court opened the First Amendment door a few inches in 1977, it and lower courts as well as state rulemaking bodies struggled to identify boundaries for this new freedom. By century's end, that activity had subsided, perhaps because the contesting parties—on one side, lawyers who supported greater freedom to market legal services, citing its informational value for prospective clients who might be unaware of their rights or whom to call; on the other side, lawyers who found the phenomenon unprofessional or even offensive and economically threatening to their clients or themselves—had reached a standoff. In the current century, the issue has reappeared in some lower court cases, but it is largely dormant. We seem to have adopted a treaty.

Some firms like to liven up their print ads with pictures. Some want those pictures to be of an animal whose presumed qualities the firm would like the public to associate with its lawyers. So no poodles or kittens. But how about a lion? A bear? A snake? A shark? A pit bull? A panther? It fell to the Florida Supreme Court to decide whether to allow the pit bull (the other creatures have all been tolerated*). The court held that the pit bull (and an 800 number that spelled out "pit bull") violated Florida rules against characterizing the quality of the lawyer's services and permitting only information objectively relevant to hiring counsel. Florida Bar v. Pape, 918 So. 2d 240 (Fla. 2005).

A. DEFINING THE BORDERS: *BATES* AND *OHRALIK*

For many, success comes too late or not at all. For some lawyers at the New York firm of Olwine Connelly, success came too early.

In 1962, Life magazine published a gushy article about the firm with the help of some Olwine partners and associates. Maitland Edey, "Behind the Scenes Tour of Today's Legal Labyrinths: Lawyers Who Try Not to Try Cases," Life, Mar. 9, 1962.

The article, accompanied by photographs, described the firm as "blue-chip" and one that enjoyed "the cream of corporate business," a bit of an exaggeration. The participating partners were censured for fostering "self-interest publicity," but the associates were let off because the case was one of first impression. In re Connelly, 240 N.Y.S.2d 126 (1st Dept. 1963).†

---

* Earlier editions of this book have said that no firm had adopted the shark. Professor Jerome Snyder has given me three examples to the contrary.

† Olwine Connelly closed shop many years later. It fell victim to economic trends that saw the demise of many medium-sized New York law firms. Olwine was an odd choice for this story. It would not have been viewed as part of Big Law, even if that label had then existed, or as a Wall Street law firm, a description that refers to the kind of work a firm does and the identity of its clients, not geography. Maybe more prominent firms had all declined the magazine's invitation.

Partial vindication came 14 years later. Bates v. State Bar of Arizona, 433 U.S. 350 (1977), said advertising by lawyers was commercial speech entitled to First Amendment protection. *Bates* is usually credited (or blamed) for all those late-night television ads for legal services, even though it involved a stripped-down print ad. The rationale and effect of *Bates* was not limited to advertising. By freeing lawyers to talk to the media and to publish books and articles about their victories, which in a prior age might be condemned as "self-laudatory," *Bates* spurred broad efforts in public relations and self-promotion. These efforts in turn facilitated growth of the "legal press" and increased attention to lawyers by the popular press. The National Law Journal and the American Lawyer began publication after *Bates*. Today, law firms compete for media attention. Many retain costly public relations experts as consultants. Large firms hire marketing professionals. An article like the one about Olwine Connelly would today be "to die for."

But we're getting ahead of the story. Let us return to the 1970s and the anemic ad that started a revolution. It was headlined "Do You Need A Lawyer? Legal Services at Very Reasonable Fees." It had a drawing of the scales of justice and a list of services and costs (e.g., uncontested divorce $175; change of name $95; individual bankruptcy $250). That's it.

Arizona gave six reasons why it could forbid all legal advertising. Legal ads, it argued

- would have an "adverse effect on professionalism" and encourage "commercialization,"
- were inherently misleading,
- would stir up litigation,
- would increase the cost of legal services,
- would encourage shoddy work, and
- were difficult to monitor against abuse.

The Supreme Court rejected each of these reasons, examined the ad before it, and said it was protected commercial speech. But the Court also said that a state could prohibit false, deceptive, or misleading ads, might be able to require a warning or disclaimer in legal ads, and could possibly restrict quality claims because they were hard to verify.

Of Arizona's six reasons, it is the first that still resonates: the idea that professionalism (good) is at war with commercialization (bad) and that advertising encourages the latter (very bad), with the result that lawyers become consumed with making more money than the lawyer next door (even worse), leading inexorably to a change in the culture of practice, all to the detriment of clients and the justice system (absolutely awful). In response to those predictions, Justice Blackmun wrote:

> But we find the postulated connection between advertising and the erosion of true professionalism to be severely strained. At its core, the argument presumes that attorneys must conceal from themselves and from their clients the real-life fact that lawyers earn their livelihood at the bar. We suspect that few

attorneys engage in such self-deception. And rare is the client, moreover, even one of modest means, who enlists the aid of an attorney with the expectation that his services will be rendered free of charge. . . .

Moreover, the assertion that advertising will diminish the attorney's reputation in the community is open to question. Bankers and engineers advertise, and yet these professions are not regarded as undignified. In fact, it has been suggested that the failure of lawyers to advertise creates public disillusionment with the profession. The absence of advertising may be seen to reflect the profession's failure to reach out and serve the community: Studies reveal that many persons do not obtain counsel even when they perceive a need because of the feared price of services or because of an inability to locate a competent attorney. Indeed, cynicism with regard to the profession may be created by the fact that it long has publicly eschewed advertising, while condoning the actions of the attorney who structures his social or civic associations so as to provide contacts with potential clients.

It appears that the ban on advertising originated as a rule of etiquette and not as a rule of ethics. Early lawyers in Great Britain viewed the law as a form of public service, rather than as a means of earning a living, and they looked down on "trade" as unseemly. Eventually, the attitude toward advertising fostered by this view evolved into an aspect of the ethics of the profession. But habit and tradition are not in themselves an adequate answer to a constitutional challenge. In this day, we do not belittle the person who earns his living by the strength of his arm or the force of his mind. Since the belief that lawyers are somehow "above" trade has become an anachronism, the historical foundation for the advertising restraint has crumbled.

Bates did not address the "electronic broadcast media." In his conclusion, Justice Blackmun tried to limit the reach of the opinion to ads like the print ad in question, but the next decades proved it to be no limit at all. Four Justices dissented.

Today, generations later, we can ask whether Arizona's fears (and those of many states at the time) have come to pass. The practice of law may seem more commercial now, but is that because of lawyer marketing or for other reasons? And does legal practice merely *seem* more commercial (because we see the ads) or because it *is* more commercial in fact and would be so even without *Bates*? And last, and most important, has *Bates* encouraged a greater interest in the moneymaking side of practice that in turn has harmed professionalism, however defined?

Commercial speech has its limits. A year after *Bates,* the Court was highly deferential to Ohio's reasons for curtailing a different kind of speech promoting a lawyer's services. Whereas *Bates* concerned a public advertisement, Ohralik's speech targeted two potential clients in person, behavior that is commonly labeled "solicitation." How would you (how did the Court) explain the difference? It's easy to see why the Court might have chosen Ohralik's case as the vehicle to differentiate solicitation from advertising. Ohralik's conduct managed to conform to the public's very worst image of the bar.

OHRALIK v. OHIO STATE BAR ASS'N

436 U.S. 447 (1978)

JUSTICE POWELL delivered the opinion of the Court.

In Bates v. State Bar of Arizona, this Court held that truthful advertising of "routine" legal services is protected by the First and Fourteenth Amendments against blanket prohibition by a State. The Court expressly reserved the question of the permissible scope of regulation of "in-person solicitation of clients—at the hospital room or the accident site, or in any other situation that breeds undue influence—by attorneys or their agents or 'runners.'" Today we answer part of the question so reserved, and hold that the State—or the Bar acting with state authorization—constitutionally may discipline a lawyer for soliciting clients in person, for pecuniary gain, under circumstances likely to pose dangers that the State has a right to prevent.

I

Appellant, a member of the Ohio Bar, lives in Montville, Ohio. . . . On February 13, 1974, . . . appellant learned . . . about an automobile accident that had taken place on February 2 in which Carol McClintock, a young woman with whom appellant was casually acquainted, had been injured. Appellant [visited] Ms. McClintock's parents, [who] explained that their daughter had been driving the family automobile on a local road when she was hit by an uninsured motorist. Both Carol and her passenger, Wanda Lou Holbert, were injured and hospitalized. In response to the McClintocks' expression of apprehension that they might be sued by Holbert, appellant explained that Ohio's guest statute would preclude such a suit. When appellant suggested to the McClintocks that they hire a lawyer, Mrs. McClintock retorted that such a decision would be up to Carol, who was 18 years old and would be the beneficiary of a successful claim.

Appellant proceeded to the hospital, where he found Carol lying in traction in her room. After a brief conversation about her condition,[1] appellant told Carol he would represent her and asked her to sign an agreement. Carol said she would have to discuss the matter with her parents. She did not sign the agreement, but asked appellant to have her parents come to see her.[2] Appellant also attempted to see Wanda Lou Holbert, but learned that she had just been released from the hospital. He then departed for another visit with the McClintocks. . . .

1. Carol also mentioned that one of the hospital administrators was urging a lawyer upon her. According to his own testimony, appellant replied: "Yes, this certainly is a case that would entice a lawyer. That would interest him a great deal."

2. Despite the fact that appellant maintains that he did not secure an agreement to represent Carol while he was at the hospital, he waited for an opportunity when no visitors were present and then took photographs of Carol in traction.

. . . [A]ppellant [first] detoured to the scene of the accident, where he took a set of photographs. He also picked up a tape recorder, which he concealed under his raincoat before arriving at the McClintocks' residence. Once there . . . [a]ppellant discovered that the McClintocks' insurance policy would provide benefits of up to $12,500 each for Carol and Wanda Lou under an uninsured-motorist clause. . . . The McClintocks [] told appellant that Carol had phoned to say that appellant could "go ahead" with her representation. Two days later appellant returned to Carol's hospital room to have her sign a contract, which provided that he would receive one-third of her recovery. . . .

[Appellant later] visited Wanda Lou at her home, without having been invited. He again concealed his tape recorder and recorded most of the conversation with Wanda Lou. . . . [A]ppellant told Wanda Lou that he was representing Carol and that he had a "little tip" for Wanda Lou: the McClintocks' insurance policy contained an uninsured-motorist clause which might provide her with a recovery of up to $12,500. The young woman, who was 18 years of age and not a high school graduate at the time, replied to appellant's query about whether she was going to file a claim by stating that she really did not understand what was going on. Appellant offered to represent her, also, for a contingent fee of one-third of any recovery, and Wanda Lou stated "O.K."[4] . . .

[After a disciplinary hearing, the Supreme Court of Ohio affirmed the finding that appellant had violated a provision of the Code that prohibited this solicitation and suspended him indefinitely.]

II . . .

A

Appellant contends that his solicitation of the two young women as clients is indistinguishable, for purposes of constitutional analysis, from the advertisement in *Bates*. . . . But in-person solicitation of professional employment by a lawyer does not stand on a par with truthful advertising about the availability and terms of routine legal services, let alone with forms of speech more traditionally within the concern of the First Amendment. . . .

B

The state interests implicated in this case are particularly strong. In addition to its general interest in protecting consumers and regulating

---

4. Appellant told Wanda that she should indicate assent by stating "O.K." which she did. Appellant later testified: "I would say that most of my clients have essentially that much of a communication. . . . I think most of my clients, that's the way I practice law."

In explaining the contingent-fee agreement, appellant told Wanda Lou that his representation would not "cost [her] anything" because she would receive two-thirds of the recovery if appellant were successful in representing her but would not "have to pay [him] anything" otherwise.

commercial transactions, the State bears a special responsibility for maintaining standards among members of the licensed professions. "The interest of the States in regulating lawyers is especially great since lawyers are essential to the primary governmental function of administering justice, and have historically been 'officers of the courts.'" While lawyers act in part as "self-employed businessmen," they also act "as trusted agents of their clients, and as assistants to the court in search of a just solution to disputes." . . .

[A]ppellant has conceded that the State has a legitimate and indeed "compelling" interest in preventing those aspects of solicitation that involve fraud, undue influence, intimidation, overreaching, and other forms of "vexatious conduct." . . .

III

Appellant's concession that strong state interests justify regulation to prevent the evils he enumerates would end this case but for his insistence that none of those evils was found to be present in his acts of solicitation. . . .

Appellant's argument misconceives the nature of the State's interest. The Rules prohibiting solicitation are prophylactic measures whose objective is the prevention of harm before it occurs. The Rules were applied in this case to discipline a lawyer for soliciting employment for pecuniary gain under circumstances likely to result in the adverse consequences the State seeks to avert. In such a situation, which is inherently conducive to overreaching and other forms of misconduct, the State has a strong interest in adopting and enforcing rules of conduct designed to protect the public from harmful solicitation by lawyers whom it has licensed.

The State's perception of the potential for harm in circumstances such as those presented in this case is well founded. The detrimental aspects of face-to-face selling even of ordinary consumer products have been recognized and addressed by the Federal Trade Commission, and it hardly need be said that the potential for overreaching is significantly greater when a lawyer, a professional trained in the art of persuasion, personally solicits an unsophisticated, injured, or distressed lay person.[24] Such an individual may place his trust in a lawyer, regardless of the latter's qualifications or the individual's actual need for legal representation, simply in response to persuasion under circumstances conducive to uninformed acquiescence. Although it is argued that personal solicitation is valuable because it may apprise a victim of misfortune of his legal rights, the very plight of that person not only

---

24. Most lay persons are unfamiliar with the law, with how legal services normally are procured, and with typical arrangements between lawyer and client. To be sure, the same might be said about the lay person who seeks out a lawyer for the first time. But the critical distinction is that in the latter situation the prospective client has made an initial choice of a lawyer at least for purposes of a consultation; has chosen the time to seek legal advice; has had a prior opportunity to confer with family, friends, or a public or private referral agency; and has chosen whether to consult with the lawyer alone or accompanied.

makes him more vulnerable to influence but also may make advice all the more intrusive. Thus, under these adverse conditions the overtures of an uninvited lawyer may distress the solicited individual simply because of their obtrusiveness and the invasion of the individual's privacy, even when no other harm materializes. Under such circumstances, it is not unreasonable for the State to presume that in-person solicitation by lawyers more often than not will be injurious to the person solicited. . . .

Accordingly, the judgment of the Supreme Court of Ohio is affirmed.

[Justice Marshall concurred in part and in the judgment. Justice Rehnquist concurred in the judgment. Justice Brennan did not participate.]

A Prophylactic Rule

Ohralik is the only lawyer commercial speech case in the Supreme Court to uphold a permanent and categorical ban on a type of communication, but the actual holding, in light of the facts, is narrow: in-person solicitation of an accident victim by a lawyer in a for-profit law firm. You should recognize the state interest that permitted the Court to distinguish *Bates*. *Orhalik* has itself been limited in part. What if the prospective client was not a young woman injured in a car accident but a Fortune 500 CEO at the athletic club?

In Edenfield v. Fane, 507 U.S. 761 (1993), Fane, an accountant, had successfully built a practice advising small- and medium-sized businesses in New Jersey. He often obtained clients through "direct, personal, uninvited solicitation," which New Jersey allowed. Fane moved to Florida, which prohibited that conduct, and he challenged the prohibition. Eight Justices said the prohibition was unconstitutional. Only Justice O'Connor dissented. How did the Court treat *Ohralik*? Justice Kennedy's opinion said:

> While *Ohralik* discusses the generic hazards of personal solicitation, the opinion made clear that a preventative rule was justified only in situations "inherently conducive to overreaching and other forms of misconduct." . . . Unlike a lawyer, a CPA is not "a professional trained in the art of persuasion." A CPA's training emphasizes independence and objectivity, not advocacy. The typical client of a CPA is far less susceptible to manipulation than the young accident victim[s] in *Ohralik*. Fane's prospective clients are sophisticated and experienced business executives who understand well the services that a CPA offers. In general, the prospective client has an existing professional relation with an accountant and so has an independent basis for evaluating the claims of a new CPA seeking professional work.

What is left of *Ohralik* after *Edenfield*? May lawyers do what accountant Fane did? May they solicit a client in person in a commercial matter? Ohralik approached and surreptitiously recorded his own prospective clients soon after their auto accident, revealed Carol's confidences to Wanda (a "little tip"), and may have had a conflict in representing both clients. That behavior was alone enough to sink him. He was a bad candidate for defining the limits of in-person solicitation bans.

Someday the courts may tell us how broadly or narrowly to read *Ohralik.* The ABA isn't waiting. In 2018, it amended Rule 7.3 on solicitation to limit *Ohralik*'s reach. Rule 7.3(b)(3) now permits live in-person contact with a "person who routinely uses for business purposes the type of legal services offered by the lawyer." Of course, that would not have helped Ohralik himself.

Occasionally, like a volcano that erupts episodically, a state (or its bar) will decide things have gotten way out of hand and seek to impose new limits. Then former opponents will resurface for a miniature reenactment of the prior century's wars. Court challenges will follow, the issues will be (temporarily) resolved, and the volcano will subside until next time. When in response to a request from the state bar, the New York courts adopted new advertising restrictions in 2007, the opposition was quick to challenge them. Alexander v. Cahill, 598 F.3d 79 (2d Cir. 2010), struck down most of these efforts, including prohibitions against testimonials from current clients who consent, portraying a fictional judge in an ad, the use of techniques to attract attention that are irrelevant to choice of counsel, and some uses of a nickname, moniker, motto, or trade name.

B. DEFINING THE CENTER: *ZAUDERER* AND *SHAPERO*

Bates and *Ohralik* define the boundaries in the debate over legal advertising. The methodology has remained similar whatever the particular challenge. We first ask if the speech is commercial speech. If, instead, it is traditionally protected speech, the constitutional protection is greater. If it is commercial speech, we next ask if it is a type of communication so conducive to evils the state can prevent that it may be banned categorically. That's *Ohralik*. If it is not, we ask what showing the state must make to justify the challenged regulation, whether it has done so, and whether there exists a less intrusive way to achieve the goal. The next two cases address challenges to rules restricting lawyer advertising or solicitation.

1. *Targeted Advertisements*

ZAUDERER v. OFFICE OF DISCIPLINARY COUNSEL
471 U.S. 626 (1985)

JUSTICE WHITE delivered the opinion of the Court. . . .

I . . .

In the spring of 1982, appellant placed an advertisement in 36 Ohio newspapers publicizing his willingness to represent women who had suffered injuries resulting from their use of a contraceptive device known as the Dalkon Shield Intrauterine Device. The advertisement featured a line drawing of the Dalkon Shield accompanied by the question, "DID YOU USE THIS IUD?" The advertisement then related the following information:

> The Dalkon Shield Interuterine [sic] Device is alleged to have caused serious pelvic infections resulting in hospitalizations, tubal damage, infertility, and hysterectomies. It is also alleged to have caused unplanned pregnancies ending in abortions, miscarriages, septic abortions, tubal or ectopic pregnancies, and full-term deliveries. If you or a friend have had a similar experience do not assume it is too late to take legal action against the Shield's manufacturer. Our law firm is presently representing women on such cases. The cases are handled on a contingent fee basis of the amount recovered. If there is no recovery, no legal fees are owed by our clients.

The ad concluded with the name of appellant's law firm, its address, and a phone number that the reader might call for "free information."

The advertisement was successful in attracting clients. . . .

II

There is no longer any room to doubt that what has come to be known as "commercial speech" is entitled to the protection of the First Amendment, albeit to protection somewhat less extensive than that afforded "noncommercial speech." . . .

III . . .

Because appellant's statements regarding the Dalkon Shield were not false or deceptive, our decisions impose on the State the burden of establishing that prohibiting the use of such statements to solicit or obtain legal business directly advances a substantial governmental interest. The extensive citations in the opinion of the Board of Commissioners to our opinion in [*Ohralik*] suggest that the Board believed that the application of the rules to appellant's advertising served the same interests that this Court found sufficient to justify the ban on in-person solicitation at issue in *Ohralik*. We cannot agree. Our decision in *Ohralik* was largely grounded on the substantial differences between face-to-face solicitation and the advertising we had held permissible in *Bates*. In-person solicitation by a lawyer, we concluded, was a practice rife with possibilities for overreaching, invasion of privacy, the exercise of undue influence, and outright fraud. In addition, we noted that in-person solicitation presents unique regulatory difficulties because it is "not visible or otherwise open to public scrutiny." These unique features of in-person solicitation by lawyers, we held, justified a prophylactic rule prohibiting lawyers from engaging in such solicitation for pecuniary gain, but we were careful to point out that "in-person solicitation of professional employment by a lawyer does not stand on a par with truthful advertising about the availability and terms of routine legal services."

It is apparent that the concerns that moved the Court in *Ohralik* are not present here. Although some sensitive souls may have found appellant's advertisement in poor taste, it can hardly be said to have invaded the privacy of those who read it. More significantly, appellant's advertisement—and print advertising generally—poses much less risk of overreaching or undue influence. Print advertising may convey information and ideas more or less effectively, but in most cases, it will lack the coercive force of the personal presence of a trained advocate. In addition, a printed advertisement, unlike a personal encounter initiated by an attorney, is not likely to involve pressure on the potential client for an immediate yes-or-no answer to the offer of representation. Thus, a printed advertisement is a means of conveying information about legal services that is more conducive to reflection and the exercise of choice on the part of the consumer than is personal solicitation by an attorney. Accordingly, the substantial interests that justified the ban on in-person solicitation upheld in *Ohralik* cannot justify the discipline imposed on appellant for the content of his advertisement.

Nor does the traditional justification for restraints on solicitation—the fear that lawyers will "stir up litigation"—justify the restriction imposed in this case. In evaluating this proffered justification, it is important to think about what it might mean to say that the State has an interest in preventing lawyers from stirring up litigation. It is possible to describe litigation itself as an evil that the State is entitled to combat: after all, litigation consumes vast quantities of social resources to produce little of tangible value but much discord and unpleasantness. "[A]s a litigant," Judge Learned Hand once observed, "I should dread a lawsuit beyond almost anything else short of sickness and death."

But we cannot endorse the proposition that a lawsuit, as such, is an evil. Over the course of centuries, our society has settled upon civil litigation as a means for redressing grievances, resolving disputes, and vindicating rights when other means fail. There is no cause for consternation when a person who believes in good faith and on the basis of accurate information regarding his legal rights that he has suffered a legally cognizable injury turns to the courts for a remedy: "we cannot accept the notion that it is always better for a person to suffer a wrong silently than to redress it by legal action." [*Bates.*] That our citizens have access to their civil courts is not an evil to be regretted; rather, it is an attribute of our system of justice in which we ought to take pride. The State is not entitled to interfere with that access by denying its citizens accurate information about their legal rights. Accordingly, it is not sufficient justification for the discipline imposed on appellant that his truthful and nondeceptive advertising had a tendency to or did in fact encourage others to file lawsuits. . . .

The State's argument that it may apply a prophylactic rule to punish appellant notwithstanding that his particular advertisement has none of the vices that allegedly justify the rule is in tension with our insistence that restrictions involving commercial speech that is not itself deceptive be narrowly crafted to serve the State's purposes. . . . The State's argument, then, must be that . . . there are some circumstances in which a prophylactic rule is the least restrictive possible means of achieving a substantial governmental interest. . . .

The State's argument proceeds from the premise that it is intrinsically difficult to distinguish advertisements containing legal advice that is false or deceptive from those that are truthful and helpful, much more so than is the case with other goods or services. This notion is belied by the facts before us: appellant's statements regarding Dalkon Shield litigation were in fact easily verifiable and completely accurate. Nor is it true that distinguishing deceptive from nondeceptive claims in advertising involving products other than legal services is a comparatively simple and straightforward process. . . .

IV

[The Court subjected the State's restriction on illustrations in legal advertising to the same First Amendment test it used to protect the text of the ad itself. The Court rejected the argument that prohibiting the illustration of the Dalkon Shield could be justified on the ground that "some members of the population may find [it] embarrassing or offensive." It also rejected the argument that the use of illustrations in lawyer ads "creates unacceptable risks that the public will be misled, manipulated, or confused." The Court was "not persuaded that identifying deceptive or manipulative uses of visual media in advertising is so intrinsically burdensome that the State is entitled to forego that task in favor of the more convenient but far more restrictive alternative of a blanket ban on the use of illustrations."]

V

[The Court upheld Zauderer's discipline for violating Ohio's requirement that contingent fee advertisements specify that the client might in any event be liable for costs. But the Court reversed Zauderer's reprimand insofar as it was based on his use of an illustration and his offer of legal advice in the advertisement.]

. . . [T]he judgment is reversed.

[Justice Powell took no part in the consideration or decision of the case. Justices Brennan and Marshall concurred in part. They generally agreed that a state may require a lawyer to disclose that a client, regardless of the case's outcome, would ultimately be liable for costs, but dissented on procedural grounds from the Court's decision to uphold the discipline here.]

––––––––––

Justice O'Connor, joined by Chief Justice Burger and Justice Rehnquist, dissented from the Court's conclusion in Part III. "In my view," Justice O'Connor wrote, "the use of unsolicited legal advice to entice clients poses enough of a risk of overreaching and undue influence to warrant Ohio's rule." She continued, sounding a theme that would resurface in her 1988 *Shapero* dissent below:

> At least two persuasive reasons can be advanced for the restrictions. First, there is an enhanced possibility for confusion and deception in marketing professional services. Unlike standardized products, professional services are by their nature complex and diverse. Faced with this complexity, a layperson may often lack the knowledge or experience to gauge the quality of the sample before signing up for a larger purchase. Second, and more significantly, the attorney's personal interest in obtaining business may color the advice offered in soliciting a client. As a result, a potential customer's decision to employ the attorney may be based on advice that is neither complete nor disinterested.

The Court relied on *Zauderer* in Milavetz, Gallop, and Milavetz, P.A. v. United States, 559 U.S. 229 (2010). There it upheld provisions in the Bankruptcy Abuse Prevention and Consumer Protection Act (BAPCPA) that require lawyers (as well as others) who offer bankruptcy services to "clearly and conspicuously disclose in any advertisement of bankruptcy assistance services or of the benefits of bankruptcy directed to the general public . . . that the services or benefits are with respect to bankruptcy relief." BAPCPA also requires the advertiser, including lawyers, to say the following (or its equivalent): "We are a debt relief agency. We help people file for bankruptcy relief under the Bankruptcy Code."

2. Targeted Mail

The issue in the next case was whether a state could prohibit lawyers from sending solicitations by mail to persons likely to need the advertised service. These mailings are called "targeted" because they are aimed at specific persons and not prospective clients generally. The case is also instructive because of Justice O'Connor's argument for overturning *Bates*. The Kentucky rule discussed in *Shapero* was based on an earlier version of ABA Rule 7.3, since revised.

SHAPERO v. KENTUCKY BAR ASS'N
486 U.S. 466 (1988)

Justice Brennan announced the judgment of the Court and delivered the opinion of the Court as to Parts I and II and an opinion as to Part III in which Justice Marshall, Justice Blackmun, and Justice Kennedy join.

This case presents the issue whether a State may, consistent with the First and Fourteenth Amendments, categorically prohibit lawyers from soliciting legal business for pecuniary gain by sending truthful and nondeceptive letters to potential clients known to face particular legal problems.

I

In 1985, petitioner, a member of Kentucky's integrated Bar Association, applied to the Kentucky Attorneys Advertising Commission for approval of a letter that he proposed to send "to potential clients who have had a foreclosure suit filed against them." The proposed letter read as follows:

> It has come to my attention that your home is being foreclosed on. If this is true, you may be about to lose your home. Federal law may allow you to keep your home by *ORDERING* your creditor [sic] to *STOP* and give you more time to pay them.
>
> You may call my office anytime from 8:30 A.M. to 5:00 P.M. for *FREE* information on how you can keep your home.
>
> Call *NOW*, don't wait. It may surprise you what I may be able to do for you. Just call and tell me that you got this letter. Remember it is *FREE*, there is *NO* charge for calling.

[Ultimately the Kentucky Supreme Court held that the letter violated Rule 7.3 of the Model Rules, which, as it *then* read, prohibited mail solicitation that was targeted to persons known to need legal services if a "significant motive for the lawyer's doing so is the lawyer's pecuniary gain."]

II . . .

Our lawyer advertising cases have never distinguished among various modes of written advertising to the general public. Thus, Ohio could no more prevent Zauderer from mass-mailing to a general population his offer to represent women injured by the Dalkon Shield than it could prohibit his publication of the advertisement in local newspapers. Similarly, if petitioner's letter is neither false nor deceptive, Kentucky could not constitutionally prohibit him from sending at large an identical letter opening with the query, "Is your home being foreclosed on?," rather than his observation to the targeted individuals that "It has come to my attention that your home is being foreclosed on." The drafters of Rule 7.3 apparently appreciated as much, for the Rule exempts from the ban "letters addressed or advertising circulars distributed generally to persons . . . who are so situated that they might in general find such services useful." . . .

Of course, a particular potential client will feel equally "overwhelmed" by his legal troubles and will have the same "impaired capacity for good judgment" regardless of whether a lawyer mails him an untargeted letter or exposes him to a newspaper advertisement—concededly constitutionally protected activities—or instead mails a targeted letter. The relevant inquiry is not whether there exist potential clients whose "condition" makes them susceptible to undue influence, but whether the mode of communication poses a serious danger that lawyers will exploit any such susceptibility.

Thus, respondent's facile suggestion that this case is merely "*Ohralik* in writing" misses the mark. In assessing the potential for overreaching and undue influence, the mode of communication makes all the difference. Our decision in *Ohralik* that a State could categorically ban all in-person solicitation turned on two factors. First was our characterization of face-to-face solicitation as "a practice rife with possibilities for overreaching, invasion of privacy, the exercise of undue influence, and outright fraud." [Citing *Zauderer*.] Second, "unique . . . difficulties" would frustrate any attempt at state regulation of in-person solicitation short of an absolute ban because such solicitation is "not visible or otherwise open to public scrutiny." Targeted, direct-mail solicitation is distinguishable from the in-person solicitation in each respect.

Like print advertising, petitioner's letter—and targeted, direct-mail solicitation generally—"poses much less risk of overreaching or undue influence" than does in-person solicitation. [*Zauderer*.] Neither mode of written communication involves "the coercive force of the personal presence of a trained advocate" or the "pressure on the potential client for an immediate yes-or-no answer to the offer of representation." Unlike the potential client with a badgering advocate breathing down his neck, the recipient of a letter and the "reader of an advertisement . . . can 'effectively avoid further bombardment of [his] sensibilities simply by averting [his] eyes.'" A letter, like a printed advertisement (but unlike a lawyer), can readily be put in a drawer to be considered later, ignored, or discarded. In short, both types of written solicitation "conve[y] information about legal services [by means] that [are] more conducive to reflection and the exercise of choice on the part of the consumer than is personal solicitation by an attorney." Nor does a targeted letter invade the recipient's privacy any more than does a substantively identical letter mailed at large. The invasion, if any, occurs when the lawyer discovers the recipient's legal affairs, not when he confronts the recipient with the discovery.

Admittedly, a letter that is personalized (not merely targeted) to the recipient presents an increased risk of deception, intentional or inadvertent. It could, in certain circumstances, lead the recipient to overestimate the lawyer's familiarity with the case or could implicitly suggest that the recipient's legal problem is more dire than it really is. Similarly, an inaccurately targeted letter could lead the recipient to believe she has a legal problem that she does not actually have or, worse yet, could offer erroneous legal advice.

But merely because targeted, direct-mail solicitation presents lawyers with opportunities for isolated abuses or mistakes does not justify a total ban on that mode of protected commercial speech. The State can regulate such abuses and minimize mistakes through far less restrictive and more precise means, the most obvious of which is to require the lawyer to file any solicitation letter with a state agency, giving the State ample opportunity to supervise mailings and penalize actual abuses. The "regulatory difficulties" that are "unique" to in-person lawyer solicitation [*Zauderer*]—solicitation that is "not visible or otherwise open to public scrutiny" and for which it is "difficult or impossible to obtain reliable proof of what actually took place"—do not apply to written solicitations. The court below offered no basis for its "belie[f] [that] submission of a blank form letter to the Advertising Commission [does not] provid[e] a suitable protection to the public from overreaching, intimidation or misleading private targeted mail solicitation." . . .

[Parts I and II of Justice Brennan's opinion were joined by five other Justices. In Part III, not included here, a plurality of four Justices rejected the Bar Association's "contentions that [Shapero's] letter is particularly overreaching, and therefore unworthy of First Amendment protection." Justices White and Stevens, who joined in Parts I and II, were "of the view that the matters addressed in Part III should be left to the state courts in the first instance."]

JUSTICE O'CONNOR, with whom CHIEF JUSTICE REHNQUIST and JUSTICE SCALIA join, dissenting. . . .

III . . .

Bates was an early experiment with the doctrine of commercial speech, and it has proved to be problematic in its application. Rather than continuing to work out all the consequences of its approach, we should now return to the States the legislative function that has so inappropriately been taken from them in the context of attorney advertising. . . .

One distinguishing feature of any profession, unlike other occupations that may be equally respectable, is that membership entails an ethical obligation to temper one's selfish pursuit of economic success by adhering to standards of conduct that could not be enforced either by legal fiat or through the discipline of the market. There are sound reasons to continue pursuing the goal that is implicit in the traditional view of professional life. Both the special privileges incident to membership in the profession and the advantages those privileges give in the necessary task of earning a living are means to a goal that transcends the accumulation of wealth. That goal is public service, which in the legal profession can take a variety of familiar forms. This view of the legal profession need not be rooted in romanticism or self-serving sanctimony, though of course it can be. Rather, special ethical standards for lawyers are properly understood as an appropriate means of restraining lawyers in the exercise of the unique power that they inevitably wield in a political system like ours. . . .

Imbuing the legal profession with the necessary ethical standards is a task that involves a constant struggle with the relentless natural force of economic self-interest. It cannot be accomplished directly by legal rules, and it certainly will not succeed if sermonizing is the strongest tool that may be employed. Tradition and experiment have suggested a number of formal and informal mechanisms, none of which is adequate by itself and many of which may serve to reduce competition (in the narrow economic sense) among members of the profession. A few examples include the great efforts made during this century to improve the quality and breadth of the legal education that is required for admission to the bar; the concomitant attempt to cultivate a subclass of genuine scholars within the profession; the development of bar associations that aspire to be more than trade groups; strict disciplinary rules about conflicts of interest and client abandonment; and promotion of the expectation that an attorney's history of voluntary public service is a relevant factor in selecting judicial candidates.

Restrictions on advertising and solicitation by lawyers properly and significantly serve the same goal. Such restrictions act as a concrete, day-to-day reminder to the practicing attorney of why it is improper for any member of this profession to regard it as a trade or occupation like any other. . . .

Reading Justice O'Connor's views on lawyer advertising more than 30 years after *Shapero*, the word that comes to (my) mind is *quaint*. The competitive marketplace for the sale of legal services has changed so much in the intervening decades that O'Connor's wish to return to an earlier era can seem as fanciful as the desire to restore the level of civility that some lawyers believe once characterized the bar.

The Response to *Shapero* and the Response to the Response

The ABA responded to *Shapero* by rewriting Rule 7.3 to permit targeted direct mail to potential clients. However, where the communication is aimed at a person "known to be in need of legal services in a particular matter," the words "Advertising Material" must appear "on the outside envelope, if any, and at the beginning and ending of any recorded or electronic communication," unless the recipient is a lawyer, a member of the lawyer's family, or someone with whom the lawyer has a "prior professional relationship." The "Advertising Material" label made it more likely that the communication would be ignored. The 2018 amendments to Rule 7.3 deleted even this provision.

As we know from *Ohralik*, accident victims are most likely to be viewed as in special need of protection. Florida adopted a rule forbidding lawyers to solicit accident victims or their survivors by mail for 30 days after the occurrence of the accident. The rule was challenged as a violation of *Shapero* and commercial speech cases generally. The Supreme Court rejected the challenge in Florida Bar v. Went For It, Inc., 515 U.S. 618 (1995) (5-4). New York has also adopted a 30-day ban on solicitation of accident victims or their survivors. New York Rule 4.5.

What state interest justified Florida's 30-day ban? Although Florida asserted various interests in earlier stages of the litigation, in the end it relied solely on protecting the reputation of the bar. Evidence of reputational harm came from the bar itself and was statistical and anecdotal. For example, a "survey of Florida adults commissioned by the Bar indicated that Floridians 'have negative feelings about those attorneys who use direct mail advertising.'" The anecdotal evidence was drawn from newspaper articles quoting

Florida residents. One article described a resident who "was 'appalled and angered by the brazen attempt' of a law firm to solicit him by letter shortly after he was injured and his fiancée was killed in an auto accident." Is that enough evidence, or should even a temporary ban on commercial speech require more proof?

In upholding the restriction, the Court stressed that it was "limited to a brief period" and that lawyers had other ways to make their availability known to clients, including through television, radio, newspapers, and other media. The Tenth Circuit relied on the Supreme Court's emphasis on the temporary nature of the Florida ban to invalidate New Mexico's permanent ban on direct-mail contact of personal injury victims and their families. Revo v. Disciplinary Bd. of the S. Ct. for the State of N.M., 106 F.3d 929 (10th Cir. 1997).

Since *Went For It*, courts have addressed other temporary bans and found them wanting. A Maryland rule required lawyers to wait 30 days after a charging document was filed before communicating with a criminal accused or a person charged with a traffic infraction that carries a period of incarceration. Ficker v. Curran, 119 F.3d 1150 (4th Cir. 1997), invalidated the rule. Distinguishing *Went For It*, the court held that the state's poll results did not show that the reputation of the profession suffered when lawyers contacted criminal defendants. Further, unlike personal injury actions, where a person ordinarily has years to sue, a criminal accused is already in litigation and needs a lawyer quickly. "Defendants can lose rights if unrepresented for thirty days after arrest."

The United States Congress relied on *Went For It* to limit contact with victims of airline accidents or their families. In 1996, Congress passed legislation forbidding "unsolicited communication concerning a potential action for personal injury or wrongful death . . . by an attorney . . . or any potential party to the litigation to an individual injured in the accident, or to a relative of an individual involved in the accident, before the 45th day following the date of the accident." 49 U.S.C. §1136(g)(2). Notice the words "or any potential party to the litigation." This is a salutary addition, often omitted from rules forbidding lawyers to contact accident victims. It extends the temporary restriction on communication to agents of the airline and possibly its insurers.

C. DEFINING THE METHODOLOGY

The Supreme Court's methodology in legal marketing cases raises interesting questions about governance and craft. Actually, we find two competing methodologies, nicely captured in the *Shapero* plurality and dissent. Both methodologies have to identify how much weight to give the speaker's First Amendment interests. Both have to identify how much respect to give the purported dangers the state fears and wishes to prevent. And both have to identify what deference to give to the means a state has chosen to prevent those dangers. The courts then evaluate the causal relationship between the state's means and its goals. Lurking about these issues is a further riddle, eloquently addressed in Justice O'Connor's *Shapero* dissent: the relationship between legal marketing (and the pursuit of wealth it signifies) and professionalism. She thinks the former harms the latter. But she can't prove it. Maybe it does. Maybe not. But if it does, what *constitutional* difference should that make?

1. How Does the Court Know Things?

Ohralik contains many uses of "likely" and "may." How does the Court know that in-person solicitation is as dangerous as it says it is? How does the Court know that the conduct in *Shapero* is not as dangerous as Kentucky (and many other states) believed it to be? What assumptions is the Court making about motivations and especially about how money influences the behavior of lawyers? Compare Village of Schaumburg v. Citizens for a Better Environment, 444 U.S. 620 (1980), which also reviewed a state law that made certain assumptions about money and behavior. A village ordinance barred door-to-door and on-the-street solicitations of contributions to charities unless the charities used at least 75 percent of their receipts for "charitable purposes," defined to exclude the cost of solicitation. In striking the ordinance, the Court suggested that there were less intrusive methods for protecting privacy interests, such as the ordinance's provision permitting homeowners to bar solicitors from their property by posting signs reading "No Solicitors or Peddlers Invited."

Citing *Ohralik,* the village argued that the ordinance furthered the goal of preventing fraud. The Court responded: "Unlike the situation in *Ohralik* . . . charitable solicitation is not so inherently conducive to fraud and overreaching as to justify its prohibition." Is the Court really saying that lawyers are more prone to dishonesty than people who canvass for charities, justifying greater intrusion on the lawyers' First Amendment rights? Or is it saying that a state can conclude that prospective clients are more susceptible to overreaching than donors to charity? How does the Court know any of this? Justice O'Connor (appointed after *Schaumburg*) seems to believe that the Court is not equipped to evaluate the relative risks inherent in legal advertising; accordingly, she counsels deference and would give the states greater (but not unfettered) discretion to fashion rules limiting it.

Florida Bar v. Went For It, supra, purported to rely on evidence, not intuition. It cited two investigations to justify deference to the 30-day moratorium on solicitation of accident victims by mail. But the data was pretty soft. While it claimed to show public disapproval of such solicitation, the evidence amounted to little more than some newspaper quotes from individuals who were unhappily solicited and poll conclusions like these: "A random sampling of persons who received direct-mail advertising from lawyers in 1987 revealed that 45% believed that direct-mail solicitation is 'designed to take advantage of gullible or unstable people'; 34% found such tactics 'annoying or irritating'; 26% percent found it 'an invasion of your privacy'; and 24% reported that it 'made you angry.' "

Curiously, the Court seems to have been unimpressed with the fact that each of these percentages stated a minority view. In other words, between 55 percent and 76 percent of respondents *disagreed* with one of the quoted statements. Beyond that, if the public is truly hostile to lawyer direct-mail advertising, shouldn't we expect the effort to backfire, in which case lawyers would not employ it?

2. *Professionalism and Money*

Justice O'Connor made two assumptions in her *Shapero* dissent. She wrote first that membership in a profession "entails an ethical obligation to temper one's selfish pursuit of economic success." Second, she said that constraints on attorney advertising will "act as a concrete, day-to-day reminder to the practicing attorney of why it is improper for any member of this profession to regard it as a trade or occupation like any other." Accordingly, she questioned *Bates* itself.

The first assumption has broad support. At some level, pursuit of a profession and pursuit of money are at odds. Money may not be the root of *all* evil, but we know from both history and today's headlines that it can explain much of it. If the bar comes to be seen as motivated solely by money, it would risk losing any right to self-governance that it may now enjoy. The Preamble to the Model Rules, after pointing out that "[t]he legal profession is largely self-governing," stresses the profession's "responsibility to assure that its regulations are conceived in the public interest and not in furtherance of parochial or self-interested concerns of the bar." It warns that "[t]o the extent that lawyers meet the obligations of their professional calling, the occasion for government regulation is obviated." The ABA Commission on Professionalism instructed lawyers not to make "the acquisition of wealth a principal goal of law practice" and urges "good sense and high standards" in legal ads. But what follows from this instruction?

For Justice O'Connor, what follows is the conclusion that strict rules against legal advertising will serve to remind lawyers that they are professionals, not merchants, or so a state may properly conclude. She recognizes that it is not possible to *prove* that increased legal advertising comes at the expense of professionalism in fact (or leads to a heightened concern with wealth), although the relationship may have intuitive appeal. O'Connor and the *Shapero* dissenters believe the causality sufficiently probable to render it a legitimate state interest that will support "fairly severe constraints on attorney advertising" despite the First Amendment. In other words, overrule *Bates*.

Opponents of this view argue that restrictions on advertising and solicitation discriminate against consumers who are unlikely to know that they have a legal problem or to know which lawyer to see when they do. Wealthy and corporate clients do not need ads to know these things. Critics also argue that an interest in money is a good thing. It increases the chances that rights will be vindicated. Given the contingent fee, a lawyer's economic self-interest may inspire the search for clients (perhaps via the internet or social media) who may be unaware of legitimate claims — claims that, if asserted, will benefit the clients *and* enrich the lawyer. That's what happened in Jacqueline Fox's case against Johnson & Johnson cited at the top of this chapter. But critics of lawyer advertising reply that, coupled with the contingent fees, it encourages lawyers to seek out clients with weak claims who are willing, cost-free, to gamble on a lawsuit.

In one forum or another, this debate will live on.

Self-Assessment Question

1. A law firm wants to hire an actor to perform the following script for an advertisement to be shown on cable television:

> My debts were piling up after I was laid off at the construction site, and it looked certain that I was going to lose my home and car. I didn't know what to do. I called Crutch & Bly because I had seen their ads on TV. I made an appointment to see a lawyer who told me about bankruptcy. I didn't think it was for me at first, but I didn't want to lose all I had worked for. The lawyer told me I'd be able to keep my home and car and most of my savings. I decided to go ahead. I did keep my home and car and most of my savings. The construction site began rehiring and I'm back on my feet now. I owe a lot to Crutch & Bly.

Feel-good music will be on the soundtrack. Then another actor will step from behind a desk. What appear to be diplomas are visible behind her. Scales of justice are on the desk. The actor will say:

> Bankruptcy isn't for everyone, but sometimes it's the right choice. Crutch & Bly will show you how it works, answer your questions, and help you decide if it's for you. Give us a call. There's no obligation for a consultation.

Is this ad protected by the First Amendment? Is it truthful even though the actors are pretending to be what they're not: a real client and a real lawyer describing a real matter? Assume that the actor playing the lawyer is especially telegenic and looks nothing like any lawyer at Crutch & Bly. Assume that the first actor is filmed against the backdrop of a construction job site having no connection to the firm's work and that the second actor is filmed at an expensively furnished office with a gold-plated view of the city. But it was rented for the occasion and is unlike the rather plain, dark offices of the firm.

If Crutch & Bly came to you before broadcasting the ad, which lines or scenes, if any, would you advise the law firm to change or delete? What would you add? If you were writing your state's version of the marketing rules for lawyers, would you permit this ad?

Answers to Self-Assessment Questions

Chapter 2[1]

1. Lem cannot block the settlement. Settlement decisions belong to the client. Lem should explain why the offer is inadequate and give Sheelah time to think about it. But in the end, it's her choice. Nor can Lem change to an hourly rate and charge her more than the one-third contingent fee to which he agreed. First, he made a deal and he's bound by it. He knew or should have known that the decision to settle belongs to the client who can accept a settlement that is lower than her lawyer believes is fair. In fact, the client can drop the case entirely. Lem took that chance. Second, letting Lem switch to a time charge now interferes with Sheelah's right to decide to settle by making it costly for her to do so. Although Sheelah would still walk away with $200,000, accepting Lem's decision to switch to an hourly rate can in other cases lead to situations where the client walks away with little or nothing or actually owes the lawyer money, which gives the lawyer veto power over the client's freedom to decide whether to settle.

2. Yes, she does. The question here is not whether Holly's research was competent or whether her prediction of what the law would turn out to be will prove correct. The decision whether to settle the alimony case belonged to Shack. Holly was required to give her the information she would reasonably need to make this decision wisely. That includes whether, despite Holly's reasonable view of the law, there were arguments to the contrary—i.e., that the property was part of the marital estate. If there were such arguments, Shack's husband would have had to take that into account in making his settlement offers. Let's say there's a one-third chance that the law will favor Shack and make the property part of the marital estate. Let's say that the property is worth $90,000. If Holly is wrong, Shack would be entitled to $45,000 or half the amount. But there is only a one-third chance that Holly is wrong. So in negotiation, Shack can claim two-thirds of one half of the $90,000 or $30,000. That is, the uncertainty means that she has this negotiating leverage. Her husband

---

1. Answers to the self-assessment questions offer one way to address them, but not the exclusive way. Students may see angles or issues not raised here. That does not make them wrong.

has to be aware of the risk that all of the money will be included in the marital estate and Shack will get $45,000.

3. Under *Upjohn*, Caspone's interview notes with current employees are privileged if the communications were on matters within the scope of their employment. Notes of communication with former employees may or may not be privileged depending on the court's view of conflicting decisions on privilege for such communications. The company's privilege will also prevent Snoot from asking current employees about their communications with Caspone (or the company's other lawyers) at their deposition. Nor can he ask former employees about their communications with Caspone if these occurred while they were employed or, in the view of some courts, even thereafter.

Chapter 3

1. The safest course would be to get the approval of a judge ex parte. However, despite *Hammad*, the "authorized by law" exception should offer complete protection. The prosecutors are acting through third persons, not personally engaging in the subterfuge. There is no reason here to provide a fake subpoena so there's no need to worry about that sliver of *Hammad* that survives, at least in the Second Circuit. The prosecutors can rehearse the questioning with the informants but should make it clear that they are not to ask about communications with the company's lawyers to avoid learning legally protected information. In fact, all the prosecutors want to learn is what the company would tell any of its clients who asked the same questions. Although lawyers are forbidden to engage in deceit, this prohibition does not apply to law enforcement.

2. You know the state has counsel in the matter. Apart from the fact that the adverse party is a government entity, where the First Amendment may have something to say, the safest course would be not to interview anyone who is within the *Niesig* categories or comment [7] to Rule 4.2. That might include the "officials" but not the "line" lawyers. Of course, you should be careful not to seek attorney-client communications. The fact that the adversary is the government raises the question of the First Amendment right to petition the government. But the right to petititon may not be helpful because what you want to get is evidence to help you win your case, which is not within that right as ABA Opinion 97-408 views it. Also, even where there is a First Amendment right to interview persons otherwise covered by Rule 4.2, the ABA has opined that adverse counsel should be notified before you do, which you might not wish to do.

3. This question requires a straightforward application of *Niesig* and comment [7] to Rule 4.2. Snoot knows the company has counsel on the matter. Snoot can talk to former employees but he must be careful not to seek privileged information—i.e., their conversations with Morkett's lawyers about the matter. There may be none. He can talk to current employees

who are not implementing the advice of counsel, empowered to obligate Morkett, and whose conduct is not imputed to the company for liability purposes. He should describe who he is and why he wants to talk to them as *Niesig* and Rule 4.3 require.

Chapter 4

1. A first question is whether Rule 1.8(a) applies to a fee renegotiation after formation of the attorney-client relationship. It does in some jurisdictions but not others. If so, Tony had better observe its requirements, including its writing and disclosure requirements. The disclosure should include an honest assessment of the strength of Muriel's claim for the greater sum. Muriel must have an opportunity to consult independent counsel. In fact, Tony would be wise to insist on it and put that insistence in writing. Even if in the jurisdiction, Rule 1.8(a) does not apply to postretainer fee agreements or revised agreements, Tony would be advised to follow its requirements anyway because, as the next chapter tells us, Tony and Muriel have conflicting interests. Rule 1.7(a)(2). Complete disclosure of the pros and cons of making the change must be provided in writing. Muriel should be told "worst case" outcomes. This does not look like a good deal for Muriel if the likelihood of a $1.5 million verdict (or more) is strong. It means that settlement well above the $600,000 claimed in the complaint is quite possible. That could net Tony a coningent fee many times his expected hourly fee. Tony should also make it clear that his proposed contingency—25 percent—is negotiable.

2. Quarter-hour increments can be reasonable or not depending on the circumstance. A lawyer who spends six hours and 20 minutes researching a matter would bill 6.5 hours. Rounding off there does not appear abusive. But a lawyer who spends one minute reading and signing a short letter she dictated the day before (having charged for the dictation) is earning 15 times her hourly rate. That is abusive. And if she does five such tasks in a day, but not in the same quarter hour, she should not be able to bill for 15 minutes for each one (for a total of 75 minutes) when the cumulative time is actually, perhaps, 10 minutes. You can recommend that the practice be allowed subject to "billing judgment" but that gives lawyers little guidance. Requiring six-minute increments means the lawyer who worked six hours and 20 minutes must bill 6.4 rather than 6.5 hours even though 6.5 hours would not be abusive. A six-minute requirement avoids most abusive situations at little cost. It may solve problems that aren't there as well as those that are and provides a "brighter" line.

3. A question like this requires you to understand all the moving parts in Evans v. Jeff D. and then to distill all the alternatives available to your boss—their advantages and disadvantages. Your state may, but is not obligated to, follow *Jeff D*, which was a federal case. A state can have different rules. Any of the options discussed in the opinions in the case and

assessed in the note following are plausible and defensible. This question requires you to identify them and then defend the one you choose.

Chapter 5

1. In *Wheat*, Iredale, the disqualified lawyer, was *personally* conflicted. Gillen was not. Only Parker was. The court recognized that Campbell's waiver sufficed to eliminate any post-trial challenge by him. But Greene did not waive. The court held Campbell's right to counsel of choice "hostage" to Greene's wish not to be cross-examined by Gillen. It did this by "imputing" Parker's conflict to Gillen, citing Rule 1.10, but it did not explain why the imputation doctrine should defeat Campbell's right to counsel of choice. Imputation may be fine in a civil matter, but it should not outweigh a constitutional right to counsel of choice where the defendant is willing to consent to any conflict that the firm, but not Gillen, may have.

   Despite the court's statement that "the fairness of Campbell's trial . . . would have been called into account by . . . Greene," Greene had no standing to do so. Maybe the court meant that Greene, who testified, could challenge the fairness *to him* of letting the partner of his former lawyer cross-examine him, which is not the same thing. But apart from the erroneous use of the imputation doctrine, the court did not inquire whether Gillen even knew the confidential information that Parker would have learned in representing Greene. If he did not know it, there was no threat to Greene that Gillen would misuse it. Campbell lost his counsel of choice, a Sixth Amendment right, for no reason at all.

2. This question requires you to evaluate whether the firm's work for *B*, whether in court or not, is adverse to its client *A*, within the meaning of the conflict rules, because it could engender antitrust claims against *A*, which has the same policies. On one hand, the firm is not directly opposing its client. Nor will a victory for *B* necessarily establish *A*'s violation of antitrust laws because a judgment against *C*, which has "nearly" the same policies as *A*, will not be legally binding against *A*. *A* would get the chance to fully develop the facts and defend itself. It may even have defenses unavailable to *C*, especially as its policies are not identical. On the other hand, a victory for *B* against *C* (or even knowledge of the firm's advice that the policies are illegal) will surely interest *A*'s customers in bringing a similar claim against it. *A* would therefore view the firm's work as adverse to it, although its views are not controlling. *A* may even feel impelled, although not happily, to change its pricing policies to avoid trouble. Also, a court decision favoring *B* may be binding precedent on the legal theory in the matter against *A* if cases against *A* are brought in the same circuit court. If not, they may be influential.

   Solutions to this question require considerations of competing policies. On the one hand, we want to enable *B* to get the lawyers it desires and we want to recognize the lawyers' interest in developing their practice. On the other hand, we have to ask how the firm's work for *B*—especially the litigation—will affect *A*'s relationship with the firm and whether creation of legally binding precedent is so consequential that it should be considered to be adverse. A good answer will address the competing interests. I think the better answer is that the firm should be allowed to represent *B*, including in litigation. True, *A* may view the firm's work as adverse, and it can fire the firm if it chooses, but creating precedent that is harmful to a client's business interest, although not on a question on which the firm represents the client, should not be considered adverse within the meaning of the conflict rules. See pages 213–214. A contrary answer, emphasizing the immediate and foreseeable harm to *A* if the firm succeeds for *B*, is also possible.

3. This question is based on Judge Berman's opinion in United States v. Zarrab, 2017 WL 946334 (S.D.N.Y. 2017). The best argument for disqualification is that the Wishon firm is representing DeQuesto, along with Mirapoli, but there are things it cannot do because of its representation of two of the alleged victims. These are things that an unconflicted lawyer would be expected to be able to do. The firm might even have confidential information from its work for two of the victims that could be useful to DeQuesto, but cannot use or reveal that information.

On the other side of the ledger is the fact that DeQuesto is entitled to counsel of choice. Further, there is no actual threat to confidential information because the lawyers at Wishon who will assist Mirapoli have not and will not work for Credentia and Pashion. So even if the firm has relevant confidences, these lawyers do not. Also, and perhaps most important, Mirapoli will do all the work in court except possibly arguments on questions of law, not fact, that do not depend on confidential information in Wishon's possession. So DeQuesto will be fully represented. She is not asked to forego any defenses. Wishon's presence only adds to DeQuesto's defense. It subtracts nothing because whatever Wishon cannot do will be done by others. However, because there is a limit on what Wishon can do, DeQuesto's informed consent is required. Judge Berman refused to disqualify the firm in the position of Wishon & Bonderant on similar facts.

Chapter 6

1. Baker & Bly can argue that the private nuisance action is not adverse to its former client, the City of Greenwood, which is not a party. It can also argue that the second lawsuit is not substantially related to the first one because the elements of a claim of private nuisance differ from those for public nuisance. No Greenwood confidences are at risk. And because the clients in the second lawsuit are seeking money damages only, even if they win, the terms of the settlement that Baker & Bly secured for the City will not be disturbed.

The City of Greenwood can argue that the language of Rule 1.9(a) requires only that the former client's *interest* be adverse in the new matter, not that the former client be a *party* to the new matter. The City's interests are adverse because if MMM cannot use Second Avenue, the original dispute over truck traffic in the City will revive and the value the law firm created for the City through the settlement will be undone. While it is true that the private nuisance plaintiffs are seeking money only, not an injunction against the use of Second Avenue, the prospect of substantial damages, both retrospectively and prospectively, may cause MMM to avoid Second Avenue and use other city streets. That is what the City hired the law firm to prevent.

Next, the two matters are substantially related because the facts that will determine success of the second lawsuit will be largely the same as those that resolve the first lawsuit. Even though the plaintiffs differ—a public body in one lawsuit and private plaintiffs in the other—they both charge a nuisance arising out of the same conduct. Because the matters are substantially related, it is conclusively presumed that the law firm has confidences from the first matter that can be used against its former client in the second matter.

Last, Rule 1.9(a) protects more than confidential information, which is not even mentioned in the rule. Here, the law firm would be working to deprive the City of the value of the settlement. The case is Zerger & Mauer LLP v. City of Greenwood (8th Cir. 2014) (disqualification affirmed).

2. The first question is whether Kara worked on any QQQ matters while at Adams & Quincy. If she did not, there may not be a problem because on her departure, conflicts imputed to her while she was at Adams & Quincy will no longer be imputed. But even if she did not work on a QQQ matter, she may have learned confidential information about QQQ while at Adams & Quincy. For example, she may have attended an in-house CLE where QQQ work was discussed. If that is not so (and let us now assume it is not) and she did not personally work on any QQQ matter, then the inquiry ends. Moss & Michael is then not conflicted and in fact Kara herself may work on the BBB negotiations.

However, if Kara did work on a QQQ matter, the next question is whether any such matter is substantially related to the BBB work within the meaning of Rule 1.9(a). We can't say more because we do not know exactly what that work entailed, or what the new BBB work will entail. However, if Moss & Michael is unsure, it should, to be safe, screen Kara before it accepts the BBB work. The screen must be in place before the work begins. To the extent allowed by Rule 1.6(b)(7), Kara can share details of her work at Adams & Quincy with lawyers at Moss & Michael to identify whether screening is required.

3. Because Lois participated personally and substantially in the first two matters, she would have to be screened under Rule 1.11(a) and (b), unless the SEC gave "its informed consent, confirmed in writing." Also, Lois

could not share in any fees from the matters and the SEC must receive prompt written notice of the screen so it could ensure compliance with Rule 1.11. For the third matter, if Lois has *confidential government information* about JJJ (a term defined in Rule 1.11(c)) that "could be used to the material disadvantage" of JJJ, she cannot participate at all and must be screened and receive no part of the fee. In addition, the notice requirements of Rule 1.11(b) will apply if Lois participated "personally and substantially" in the third matter.

Chapter 7

1. The problem suggests that there is a gap in Rule 3.3. Selma did not lie (we assume). At least, the person putting the question to us does not know that she lied. But he does know that her testimony on fact *X* is false. A co-defendant's lawyer ("Jo") also knows this. But Selma was questioned by a different co-defendant and we are assuming that its lawyer does not know that her testimony is false. The inquirer is asking on behalf of himself and Jo whether they may say nothing and argue the false inferences that Selma's false testimony reasonably supports. Literally read, Rule 3.3 would allow this. The inquirer did not "offer" this evidence within the meaning of Rule 3.3(a)(3). So there is no remedial duty. Rule 3.3(b) is inapplicable on its face (no knowledge of "criminal or fraudulent conduct"). Lawyers (other than prosecutors) may ask the jury to draw inferences they know are false if rationally supported by admitted evidence. Should this "gap" in Rule 3.3 be corrected? I don't think we can do so. False evidence may be unwittingly introduced by an *opposing* lawyer, who has failed to see its harmful implications. Would a "corrected" Rule 3.3 require remedial measures then as well? To say yes would be inconsistent with the premises of the adversary system.

   Jo's presence introduces a second issue. By answering the question not only for the inquirer, but also for Jo, is the lawyer forming an attorney-client relationship with Jo? He is giving Jo legal advice through a colleague. Safety suggests saying, "I'm not telling Jo what to do or not do and you shouldn't either."

2. This problem is taken directly from United States v. Crawford, 533 F.3d 133 (2d Cir. 2008), which you may consider a wonderful gift from the Second Circuit for its direct bearing on the lessons here. (Much of the opinion concerns standards for reopening after summation, which are not relevant here.)

   Defense counsel's summation sought to create a reasonable doubt over whether the defendant possessed the gun (he claimed he was being framed). Counsel argued that the jury should have a doubt based on the absence of a trace report for the gun. But the defense lawyer knew there was a trace report because the prosecutor had given it to him. The government failed to introduce it, however. When the jury asked about the trace report, the trial judge let the government reopen the case to introduce it (it had very little if any probative value, which may be why the government did not offer it). The government was then also able to shoot holes in the defense counsel's credibility by revealing that *he* in fact had the report but had nonetheless stressed its absence in his summation.

The circuit's reversal of the conviction establishes that defense counsel did nothing wrong in asking the jury to draw an inference from the absence of a trace report in the record but which he knew existed. The record was the record. It lacked a trace report. Counsel could build an argument based on that absence. It didn't matter what non-record facts he knew. Judging by the jury's question, it looked like the argument had some traction, strange as it may seem. Defense counsel, contrary to what the district judge said in allowing the government to reopen its proof, did not "play games" or violate any rule by leaving "an erroneous impression with the jury." Leaving an erroneous impression is what trial lawyers sometimes do (excepting prosecutors). It's part of the job. Indeed, failing to do it not for strategic reasons, but because you find "leaving an erroneous impression" to be distasteful, could be malpractice.

3. This is an entirely realistic problem and I presume it has arisen many times. It is true that immigration status can turn on the date of entry into the country. Asking the client "When did you enter the country?" is of course unobjectionable but it may yield an answer harmful to the client. If she says "2011," can the lawyer ask "Are you sure it wasn't before 2011, because it if was then . . ."? If the client says, "Oh, right, it was 2010," isn't it pretty obvious that the lawyer knows otherwise? On the other hand, if the lawyer gives the client the cutoff date before asking when the client entered the country, is she steering the client to lie while remaining free to claim that she does not *know* the client is lying? Maybe the answer "2010" is true, not a lie. So we can say that the lawyer does not *know* it's a lie because it may be true. Yet can there be any legitimate reason for telling the client the cutoff date before asking when she arrived other than to enable the client to provide a false date in the event she arrived in 2011 or later?

A partial defense for the lawyer might be the fact that the client will then have to satisfy the immigration authorities that she arrived before 2011. So the lawyer will next say, "That's good. But we need documentary proof. Something with your name on it, a U.S. address, and dated before 2011. A phone bill. A receipt from a merchant. You need to get those."

The problem suggests that the lawyer in "The Immigrant" will have a harder time defending her conduct than will Biegler. I think so. Lt. Manion would not likely know the elements of the defenses to homicide. Biegler's education enables Manion to assist in his own defense. There is no such complexity for the purely factual question about the year a client entered the country. So Manion needs an explanation but the immigrant does not.

Chapter 8

1. Destruction of these emails would be obstruction of justice because a proceeding is foreseeable. This is true even if there would be valid evidentiary objections to their use in court, which does not seem to be so in any event. The risk to your client from destruction is, at the very least, a negative inference instruction to the jury or possibly even a refusal to allow certain proof or affirmative defenses. Also, the client should understand that the emails could likely be unearthed even if they were deleted and the hard copies are destroyed. You would tell Tony to make sure that the company's document retention and destruction policy did not destroy the emails. To protect the client, you would keep a copy of the emails in the event they are later successfully sought in discovery.

   Unlike *Ryder*, the emails are not illegal to possess. And unlike some of the criminal cases, the problem envisions only a foreseeable civil matter. So there is no turnover duty at this point assuming the jurisdiction would otherwise impose one in a criminal case. But that will change if they are sought in discovery.

2. This question requires you to apply *Brady* and also Rule 3.8(d). For *Brady* you would need to know the other evidence against Kiplinger so you could evaluate whether impeachment of the expert's testimony with proof that he had lied (was not merely sloppy) in three other cases would have changed the outcome. The burden is to show a "reasonable probability" that it would have done so. You also need to know if the prosecutor or law enforcement agencies possessed the results of the investigation in the other state because they have no obligation to disclose what they do not have. It would seem that a finding that a state expert lied under oath in three prior prosecutions on the same kind of testimony as in the current one would be devastating to his credibility and satisfy the *Brady* causation requirement.

   For the 3.8(d) analysis, you need to take and defend a position on whether the rule merely incorporates *Brady*, imposing no broader duty on prosecutors, or whether it requires more. These arguments and the division in the court decisions on this question were addressed in the chapter. Pages 389–391. The division of authority may not matter if the failure to disclose violates the more demanding *Brady* test because then it would also be a violation of the rule. But even if not, there would be a Rule 3.8(d) violation in some jurisdictions because of the failure to timely deliver the later report if the prosecutor was aware of it.

Chapter 9

1. This problem is not unlike those in chapter 2C on autonomy in the professional relationship. Can a lawyer be a nice person if it seems to work to the disadvantage of a client, at least in the immediate term? Sometimes,

the answer is yes. A factually close ABA opinion (86-1518) supports this conclusion. The opinion says the lawyer can reveal the mistake, although it takes no position on whether the lawyer has to inform the client and no position on whether the lawyer has authority to reveal the mistake even if the client instructs him not to do so. On the other hand, the opinion says the lawyer is not ethically required to point out the error. However, if the lawyer does not, there is always the possibility of an action for reformation should the other party later discover it. The client must then be told of that risk if the decision is made to remain silent. In Stare v. Tate, 98 Cal. Rptr. 264 (Ct. App. 1971), on which the problem is loosely based, the lawyer did not reveal the error and when the other side discovered it, the court did reform the settlement agreement.

A good answer here could argue that lawyers should not exploit arithmetical errors. They should exploit information imbalance, when lawful, and differences in legal skill (ditto). There are contrary arguments that would also be defensible.

Michelle wishes to formulate her response so as to accept the bottom line without accepting the formula used to arrive at it. That is a very fine distinction, though a distinction. Michelle is not actually endorsing Kate's methodology. In fact, she rejects it and just accepts the bottom line. I think a reformation action could succeed anyway, but that is a substantive law question and it may be a risk Chester is willing to take.

One other point is worth stressing: Even when a lawyer can legitimately exploit another lawyer's drafting error—or indeed any error—she should not assume that her client may wish to do so. There may be ongoing business relationships that the client does not want to jeopardize. In the problem, Chester may not want to take advantage of Kate's error even if he could. A client may find it morally objectionable to take advantage. A lawyer who plans not to reveal the error where the lawyer has discretion must tell the client, who may prefer to make the correction.

Bottom line: Michelle, with Chester's agreement, can respond: "We don't agree to your formula but are willing to compromise at $500,000." This is less than the (erroneous) demand, decouples the settlement from the formula, and may deter Kate's curiosity that discovers the error. But it is not so much less than the demand that it will impair settlement.

2. This is the sort of information you would tell your client right away. But that will mean that Chandra will know that what she represented is at least misleading. So one question is whether, under substantive law, she would then have a duty to correct what she said. If she has this duty and refuses to correct it, continuing to represent her may violate Rule 1.2(d) if her silence is considered fraudulent. Rule 1.0(d) says that to be fraudulent the conduct must have a "purpose to deceive." Even if it is not fraud, her failure to correct may under substantive law enable Planit, if it acquires Equips, to sue for damages on the ground that Chandra had a duty to disclose. Furthermore, you are Chandra's (or her company's)

agent, so your silence may, under substantive law, also support a damage claim even if you don't tell your client. And, of course, if your silence would be fraudulent should you continue to represent Equips, you will subject yourself to damages and discipline.

But maybe Chandra, who did accurately summarize the terms of the contract with Mekanics, has no duty to inform Planit after you have told her what you have learned. After all, Planit can read the contract itself and find the provision allowing Mekanics to terminate it in the event of an acquisition. It can then act to protect itself, including by asking Chandra whether she has any reason to believe this provision will be invoked. Or it can ask Mekanics. In other words, Planit's due diligence could discover the impending acquisition. Chandra's summary did not mention this provision but she did not purport to detail every part of the contract and she did not say anything that negated the existence of this provision.

Your responsibility now is to research substantive law and do what needs to be done to protect your client and yourself, which should be the identical thing. Keeping your client in ignorance of what you have learned makes no sense because you are her agent and your knowledge will be imputed to her. Furthermore, your fiduciary duty and Rule 1.4 require you to keep your client informed of important information regarding the representation.

Chapter 10

1. This question requires you to work through the tests from the ABA and the Restatement in part B3 of this chapter—they are not the same tests—to figure out if adversity to a separate second-tier subsidiary will be a conflict. Is WAII a client for conflict purposes given the firm's representation of another second-tier subsidiary? Should that more attenuated identity matter if the various tests in the ABA and Restatement positions are satisfied?

   There is a lot of information you do not have here that you need to solve the problem. The first challenge is to identify the right questions to ask and the second is to say how the answers may or will affect your analysis. The questions to ask will be identified if you look at the various tests for conflicts in corporate family representations.

2. This little question has profound consequences. The Dodd-Frank legislation, placed atop the Sarbanes-Oxley (SOX) exceptions to confidentiality, offers lawyers the possibility of a large cash reward for a client's confidential information. The SOX rules have confidentiality exceptions that may be broader than the exceptions in a lawyer's licensing jurisdiction. That's significantly so, for example, for the New York and California rules and even, somewhat, for the ABA rules. So one question is whether a lawyer may reveal information that falls only within an SEC exception

but where disclosure is forbidden by the rules of the lawyer's licensing jurisdiction. The SEC's reporting-out exceptions are permissive, so one might say that a lawyer can satisfy a jurisdiction's prohibition against revelation by not revealing without thereby violating the *permissive* SEC rules. Perhaps.

But what if the lawyer wants to reveal? Could she argue that the SEC's permissive exceptions override a licensing authority's prohibition against disclosing the same information? In other words, the state's rule may not be enforced in discipline—or even in civil litigation—against a lawyer who discloses in compliance with the federal authority. We don't know, but the answer may be that the SEC rule governs. Even if your client may disclose and hope for a reward, that action may become public and affect the client's career. "She betrayed her client for money." Of course, she may not care if the reward is big enough, but you can't be certain.

Chapter 11

1. With regard to due process, the answer is most likely that Prosser is not recused. The best argument would be that outsiders contributed 86 percent of the funds for Prosser's campaign. But that is equally so for his opponent (85 percent). This was not true in the lopsided Benjamin race in *Caperton*. The amount spent for Prosser as a percentage of all sums spent by both candidates (just over 50 percent) is far less than the equivalent number in *Caperton*. Also, unlike *Caperton*, the donors are not parties to the case. (Compare Chief Justice Roberts's Socratic questions in *Caperton*.)

   Would either candidate, if successful, be recused on the ground that his or her "impartiality might reasonably be questioned" because of the spending? We are assuming that it could be proved (improbable) that all spending for Prosser was because of a single question headed to the court. Here, you should identify how to analyze these words: "Might reasonably be questioned" by whom? (A reasonable person knowing all the facts.) Must there be a finding of partiality in fact? (No.) What's the reason for this rule? (Public confidence and litigant confidence in the outcome, although the litigant is not the imagined objective observer.) The answer would need to be the same for both candidates. If either would be disqualified because his or her impartiality might reasonably be questioned, that would largely if not entirely remove the incentive to spend in support of their election.

2. In United States v. Kaba, 480 F.3d 152 (2d Cir. 2007), citing precedent, the court vacated Kaba's sentence and remanded to a different judge. It wrote:

   > Our decision in *Leung* controls our resolution of this appeal. There, the district court had made two remarks in the course of its sentencing

proceeding that were subsequently contested. The first addressed the defendant's request for a downward departure based on her difficult childhood in China:

> Indeed frequently when I sentence folks who are not American citizens—she is a Canadian citizen who comes from mainland China—frequently when I sentence non-American citizens I make the observation which may to seem [sic] cynical but it is not intended to be cynical, it is intended to be factual: We have enough home-grown criminals in the United States without importing them. And I don't see this as a case if [sic] for downward departure in any manner, shape or form. And I decline to downwardly depart.

Second, the district court explained its reasons for imposing the sentence it chose:

> The purpose of my sentence here is to punish the defendant and to generally deter others, particularly others in the Asiatic community because this case received a certain amount of publicity in the Asiatic community, and I want the word to go out from this courtroom that we don't permit dealing in heroin and it is against president [sic] law, it is against the customs of the United States, and if people want to come to the United States they had better abide by our laws. That's the reason for the sentence, punishment and general deterrence.

The *Leung* court noted its "confiden[ce]" that the district judge whose sentence it was reviewing "in fact harbored no bias." It nonetheless vacated the sentence because "there [was] a sufficient risk that a reasonable observer, hearing or reading the quoted remarks, might infer, however incorrectly, that Leung's ethnicity and alien status played a role in determining her sentence." And the court distinguished Leung's case from others where we had held that "mere passing references to the defendant's nationality or immigrant status at sentencing" were not grounds for vacating a defendant's sentence.

The comments of the district court that led to a remand in *Leung* resemble those at issue here. In both cases, the district court referred to the publicity a sentence might receive in the defendant's ethnic community or native country and explicitly stated its intention to seek to deter others sharing that national origin from violating United States laws in the future.

The government argues that the district court's comments were a natural and logical response to arguments and submissions by both parties. This does not meaningfully distinguish this case from *Leung*. The mistake that the district court made was not its consideration of the defendant's background as an immigrant from Guinea. It was the court's apparent suggestion that the sentence was based, at least in part, on the defendant's identification with the West African community. That was no less error because the government seems to have invited it.

Chapter 12

1. Courts differ on what they will allow a claims adjuster to do without crossing over to law practice. If we are in South Carolina, *Linder* tells us that the adjuster can negotiate the value of the destroyed property. But she cannot construe the language of the insurance contract to respond to the insurer's claim that the loss is not within the policy's coverage, either because the policy does not cover the particular cause of loss or does not cover the value of certain destroyed property. The adjuster can deal with the insurer directly in negotiating value. In a different jurisdiction, one that agreed with the *Linder* dissent, the adjuster would be able to negotiate the meaning of the contract terms as well as value. In yet other jurisdictions, the adjuster can evaluate the loss and tell the client but may not negotiate that value with the insurance company.

2. The answer to this question depends on the meaning of "temporary" as used in Rule 5.5(c). If the lawyer's virtual and physical presence in the state is not deemed "temporary" because of frequent calls and emails coupled with occasional trips to Georgia, the lawyer will be engaged in unauthorized practice and cannot use any of the "safe harbors" in the rule. One fact you need to know is how long the lawyer will be in Atlanta during his trips.

   If the lawyer's presence is "temporary," then Rule 5.5(c)(1) and (4) may be available. The lawyer can work with a local lawyer on the issues. However, there may not be a local lawyer with the expertise that will allow him or her to "actively" participate in the matter, as the rule requires, which is why the client reached out to this lawyer in the first place. Rule 5.5(c)(4) will allow the temporary work if it is "reasonably related" to the lawyer's practice. To satisfy the quoted words, comment [14] requires that the work be governed by "federal, nationally-uniform, foreign, or international law." The problem assumes as much.

3. The issue in a question like this is pretty clear. Does Stern have the "requisite moral character and fitness" for bar membership? You might claim that the whole idea of character committees should be rejected because it's not really possible to predict future behavior. But that claim, although intellectually interesting, has been universally rejected. So what else can you argue? The accumulation of unpaid debt continued for years (1993-2005). Some efforts to repay the debts occurred as the bar application loomed or thereafter. That's not good because it suggests a motive other than a true sense of obligation to the creditor. The older debts permit a defense that the client has reformed, but that's not possible with newer ones or those paid in the shadow of bar admission. You would also argue that, in any event, all debts have now been paid or if any have not, their sums are small and the client has a plan to repay them. Another argument is that none of the debts were to individuals, but rather to institutions. Nor did he keep money belonging to another. This has some

(weak) value because the court might see a risk that as a lawyer he would misuse client money.

As for the relationship with the 15-year-old when he was ten years her senior, the opinion makes it clear that a sexual relationship did not begin until she had reached the age of consent. The court does not say why the relationship before that was "inappropriate." In any event, a strong argument can be made that the relationship has no bearing on character as a lawyer unless Stern was taking advantage of a girl for whom he was in effect, if not legally, a guardian.

A final goal, if the application is rejected, is to ask the court to allow Stern to return after the passage of some time, which is what the court actually did. In re Stern, 943 A.2d 1247 (Md. 2008).

Chapter 13

1. The most obvious basis for liability is negligent misrepresentation, which would require proof that McGrath should have known that what he said about the hospital's policies was wrong. Because the accurate information was in his possession, this should not be a hard fact to prove. But there's another theory of liability as well. In the actual case, the court relied on it because at the time New York law did not recognize negligent misrepresentation as a basis for lawyer liability to a third person.

   McGrath's insistence that the policy limit was $200,000 rendered him liable under the New York definition of scienter as "a reckless indifference to error," "a pretense of exact knowledge," or "(an) assertion of a false material fact 'susceptible of accurate knowledge' but stated to be true on the personal knowledge of the representer." So even if McGrath truly believed that what he thought he knew was correct, as the court assumed, the fact that it turned out to be false subjected him to personal liability under New York law.

   To avoid this risk, McGrath could have attributed what he said to his client, not himself. He could have said that his client informs him that the insurance limits are X. The adverse party is less likely to accept that statement as true than it is to accept a representation from McGrath. The question is based on Slotkin v. Citizens Casualty Co. of New York, 614 F.2d 301 (2d Cir. 1979).

2. This question looks a bit like Nichols v. Keller in chapter 2B6. That's the case in which the law firm was held liable for not telling a workers' compensation client that he might also have a tort claim arising out of the workplace accident and should see other lawyers if he wished to bring such a claim. The limitations period on a tort claim expired and the client, now aware of the tort claim, sued the law firm. The court held that the firm should have explained the tort liability because it arose out of the same accident.

DPW will have to distinguish that case. The most obvious distinction is that DPW's client was sophisticated and could itself have known the liability theory it claims the firm should have told it. The retainer agreement specified only contesting the IRS claim. Further, in *Nichols* the client had multiple claims arising out of the same incident. Here that is not so. The client has (potentially) two theories of non-liability and has asked the law firm to defend it under one theory in a particular venue against a particular opponent. The firm had no duty to review the documents the client gave it to find another theory of non-liability, one the client either did not see or did not retain it to pursue. Last, there is no proof that the client's theory that it was not primarily liable would have been upheld even if made. It's only a theory. Even if the firm failed to see it, that doesn't make it negligent and liable for malpractice. The question is very loosely based on AmBase Corp. v. Davis Polk & Wardwell, 866 N.E.2d 1033 (N.Y. 2007).

3. Even though this conduct is not related to Carl's law practice, a lawyer can be disciplined for conduct in his private life. Here are the things you want to know and which a thoughtful answer will address:

   - Does Carl have prior discipline and if so, for what?
   - Was Carl physically provoked or threatened?
   - Is there a psychological explanation Carl can offer?
   - Does he acknowledge the wrongfulness of his conduct?
   - Has he apologized and offered to compensate the victim including for medical bills?
   - Is there any history of Carl acting in a physically aggressive manner in practice?
   - Was Carl's conduct spontaneous or did he approach the victim intending violence?
   - How serious are the victim's injuries?

   If you decide that Carl should be disciplined, the next question is under what rule. Rule 8.4(b) prohibits "criminal conduct" that "reflects adversely" on a lawyer's "fitness." You also have to decide what sanction you will seek and why. If this conduct was aberrational and spontaneous and there is no prior discipline, a public censure would seem appropriate.

Chapter 14

1. A good answer to this question would first recognize that the exception in Rule 5.4(a) does not by its terms *explicitly* allow your client to do what she wishes to do. You would have to be clear about that. But that does not mean she cannot do it. The language of the exception does not *explicitly* forbid it either. It talks about a "profit-sharing arrangement" and permits employee "compensation" to be based on one. The client's goal is in fact profit-sharing, albeit profit from a single case, not firm profits.

One interpretation is that the language is not meant to refer to case-specific profits, but total profits from all cases. Supporting that interpretation is the underlying policy. If we're worried about lay influence, the incentive of a paralegal to interfere with his or her boss's decisions in a specific matter in which the paralegal has a small compensation interest, or to do improper things in that matter, is marginally greater than if the paralegal's compensation is tied to gross firm profits.

A good answer to this question would identify and discuss the policy behind fee-splitting with nonlawyers—i.e., the risk of a layperson influencing the lawyer to misbehave.

The Wisconsin Supreme Court allowed the matter-specific compensation. It saw no difference between a plan tied to profits from all work, which the rule certainly permits, and compensation based on the profitability of a specific case on which the paralegal works. In re Weigel, 817 N.W.2d 835 (Wis. 2012).

2. The first option is fine. The firm can seek help with its work on a retainer basis for all of its questions within a quarter. True, the money comes from its profits as a law firm but it is not dividing a legal fee in any particular case with a nonlawyer in violation of Rule 5.4(a). This is no different from the current arrangement except that Dr. Gately's compensation will be a fixed sum per quarter rather than on an hourly basis. Indeed, all law firm compensation, whether to employees or consultants, comes from profits.

Rule 5.4(a) would, by its terms, forbid the second option—a percentage of the firm's actual recovery on a matter-by-matter basis. Dr. Gately's compensation is tied directly to the amount of the firm's fee in each matter, which the rule forbids. The exception in Rule 5.4(a)(3) for "compensation" tied to a profit-sharing plan, even if read to allow matter-specific compensation, is aimed at compensation for "employees," not consultants. Does this distinction make sense? The defense of it would cite the greater ability of a law firm to guard against employee misbehavior.

The third option is permissible assuming that it is otherwise legal for a medical consultant to work on a contingency. Dr. Gately is contracting with the client. The firm is not in the picture. Dr. Gately's payment is not tied to the firm's fee but to the client's recovery and the client, not the firm, is paying it. It does not matter whether the fee is determined on an hourly basis or as a percentage of recovery.

Chapter 15

1. A good answer will take into account where the risks to the trial really lie. Civil cases rarely attract media attention. The very few that do are likely to get only sparse media attention. There is not much to worry about in cases tried to a judge with no jury, although there remains the concern that the public might *think* the judge's ruling was influenced by

the publicity. So the first two limitations deserve serious consideration (and in fact each *was* considered in debates about the rule but not implemented). The limitation to 30 or 60 days or less before trial is harder to defend because high-profile criminal cases can attract intense media attention for many months before a trial. Further, media attention can escalate in the 30 or 60 days before trial, which argues in favor of preserving the lawyer's ability to respond to adverse publicity he or she does not instigate.

A 30/60 cutoff seems arbitrary. The amount of time before trial the statement is made should be relevant as one factor but not a dispositive one in evaluating the risk. If there is a 30-day (or similar temporal) cutoff, it can be coupled with express authority for a judge to extend the prohibition against comment to a longer period. The greater the amount of time before trial, the less likely it is that public comments will have an effect on trial, especially given the availability of voir dire to eliminate biased jurors (*if* they can be identified).

Changing the "substantial likelihood" test to "clear and present" danger or its equivalent is probably inconsequential. More a semantic than a real difference. The result would likely be the same under either test. For one thing, as we see in *Gentile*, the term "substantial likelihood" can be interpreted differently by different judges. Also, we already have many years of experience with the current test, with precedents building on it, so we would upset that jurisprudence if we made the change.

One other thought this question should prompt: While getting an unbiased jury in fact is the main goal of this rule, public confidence that a jury was unbiased—unaffected by pretrial publicity—is another goal. The public exposed to much pretrial publicity might have diminished confidence in the accuracy of a verdict. The level of confidence may be impossible to test, but a fair argument can be made that our tolerance for any risk at all should be low.

2. It was the vagueness argument that enabled Gentile's victory and the deleted words are those that five Justices cited as creating the problem. Now the rule says only that a lawyer may state the "defense involved." "General nature" and "without elaboration" are removed. Justice Kennedy wrote that both "general" and "elaboration" are "classic terms of degree." Is the word "defense" subject to a vagueness challenge? It would be a hard argument. It seems that a lawyer can say only that the client is innocent, or misidentified, or far away at the time, or acted (for example) in self-defense. Perhaps the lawyer could say that the client is being framed, but to say more (e.g., "by the police," as Gentile did) would be "forbidden."

But not all vagueness has been or can be removed. Paragraph (c), the right of reply provision added in 1994 after *Gentile* when "general" and "elaboration" were erased, allows statements that a lawyer reasonably believes are "required" to respond to the "substantial undue prejudicial effect of recent publicity." (This was Gentile's motive and today he would cite that provision.) When indictments are announced in a high-profile case, there is a great deal of publicity, all of it prejudicial by definition because the indictment is. Indictments, unless briefly under seal, are public documents. They can be and often are quite detailed. Elaboration is what they are all about and few rules restrain a prosecutor's choice of what to include. Paragraph (c) allows comments even if they would otherwise violate paragraph (a).

So it would seem that a lawyer can often and in good faith believe that elaboration of the defense is "required" to protect a client from the publicity generated by the indictment or other documents a prosecutor files or the press publishes. Even though the right of response is limited to what "is necessary to mitigate the recent adverse publicity," that phrase is itself a bit vague. It will rarely be clear what is "necessary." Result: vagueness.

Chapter 16

1. This problem asks first whether an ad may properly use an actor to impersonate a client and a lawyer. Literally, the actor is misrepresenting himself or herself. But doesn't everyone know that? Maybe not. A viewer could easily believe that the client is in fact a firm client and that the lawyer is either Crutch or Bly (or another firm lawyer). Perhaps the ad should indicate "Actor, Not a Real Client" or "Actor, Not a Real Lawyer." A professional conduct rule could require that, consistent with the First Amendment, and some do. Your answer should address that issue.

The actor playing the client is describing a particular situation and outcome. Does the firm have any client in the same position and who was able to keep the property the actor described? If not, a viewer could walk away with a misimpression of what is possible. So if you're advising the firm, you may want it actually to have clients whose situations substantially mirror those described in the ad. You may also want to ensure that the TV client's outcome is common, not rare or unique. If you were writing the professional conduct rule you might require the same. Or you might require a disclaimer to the effect that every case is different and there is no guarantee that every client will achieve the same outcome as the client portrayed in the ad.

What about the music? If you were writing a rule, you might forbid music or other content not relevant to the decision whether to hire a lawyer or which lawyer to hire. But the ad works better with music, so that rule will hurt the marketing effort. A rule forbidding music would seem to interfere with the goal of producing an ad that gets attention. Because the music makes no deceptive or misleading statement, the ban on music or other attention-getting strategies would seem to violate the firm's commercial speech rights. That was the holding in the Second Circuit's decision in Alexander v. Cahill, cited at the end of part A.

As for the gold-plated office, it is obviously intended to telegraph that the firm is a lot more posh than it may be. Probably, using the rented space is not a good idea because clients will be startled when they visit the real law firm. But can it be done? The best argument that it can be done is that the discrepancy, and what it says about the firm's integrity, will be immediately apparent to prospective clients. No indication "Not Our Real Office" is needed.

Table of Cases

Principal cases are indicated by italics.

A. v. B., 220
Abdullah; State v., 306
Adams; People v., 204
Adkins v. Dixon, 571
Aetna Life Ins. Co. v. Lavoie, 469
"Agent Orange" Prod. Liab. Litig., In re, 252
Akzo Nobel Chems. v. Commission, 37
Alexander v. Cahill, 672, 706
Allen, In re, 40, 41
Allen v. Lefkoff, Duncan, Grimes & Dermer, 558
Allen Cnty. Bar Ass'n v. Bartels, 584
Allied-Signal, Inc., In re, 488
Ambac Assurance Corp. v. Countrywide Home
    Loans, 220
AmBase Corp. v. Davis Polk & Wardwell, 702
Amella v. United States, 359
Amendments to Rules Regulating the Fla. Bar, In
    re, 143
American Airlines, In re, 244
American Bankers Mgmt. Co. v. Heryford,
    203, 204
American Continental Corp./Lincoln Sav. &
    Loan Sec. Litig., In re, 432
American Fed. Group v. Rothenberg, 567
Americas Mining Corp. v. Theriault, 127, 137
Analytica, Inc. v. NPD Research, Inc., 21, *240,* 244,
    246, 248-250, 255-258
Anders v. California, 70, 71
Andrades; People v., 305
Andrus v. Department of Transp., 22
Anonymous, In re, 515
Antar; United States v., 463
Aponte v. Chicago, 116
Arkansas Teacher Ret. Sys. v. State St. Bank &
    Trust Co., 122
Armstrong v. McAlpin, 263, 264, 265
Aronson v. Brown, 490
Arthur Andersen LLP v. United States, 374
Asch v. State, 215
Association of Am. Railroads v. South Coast Air
    Quality Mgmt. Dist., 361
Attorney Grievance Comm'n of Md. v.
    Atkinson, 583
Attorney Grievance Comm'n of Md. v.
    Hess, 121

Attorney Grievance Comm'n of Md. v.
    Kenney, 597
Attorney Grievance Comm'n of Md. v.
    Kreamer, 21
Atwood; United States v., 465
Augustson v. Linea Aerea Nacional-Chile, 81
Ausherman v. Bank of Am. Corp., 411
Austern, In re, 574

Baker v. Wood, Ris & Hames, 556
Balla v. Gambro, Inc., 428
Balter; United States v., 99
Banco Popular N. Am. v. Gandi, 572
Bant, In re, 582
Bar v. Adorno, 22
Barker v. Capotosto, 571
Barnes v. Turner, 82
Bates v. State Bar of Ariz., 15, 666-669, 671-673,
    676, 679, 683
Belge; People v., 377, 378
Bellino, In re, 584
Bennett v. Stirling, 336
Bergantzel v. Mlynarik, 535
Berger v. United States, 201, 384, 488
Bergman, In re Matter of, 586
Bertelsen v. Harris, 562
Bevill, Bresler & Schulman Asset Mgmt. Corp., In
    re, 439
Bilzerian; United States v., 44
Binday; United States v., 103
*Birbrower, Montalbano, Condon & Frank, P.C. v.
    Superior Court,* 503, 516, *524,* 528, 529, 533
Blair v. Ing, 555
Blanchard v. Bergeron, 116
Blowers v. Lerner, 64
Bluebird Partners v. First Fidelity Bank, N.A., 614
Board of Educ. v. Nyquist, 252
Board of Prof'l Responsibility v. Casper, 124
Boatwright; State v., 50
Bobbitt v. Victorian House, Inc., 451
Boehringer Ingelheim Pharms.; FTC v., 41
Boogaerts v. Bank of Bradley, 54
Bowen; United States v., 52
Bowers v. Ophthalmology Group, 245

Boy Scouts of Am. v. Dale, 490
Bozelko v. Papastavros, 552
Bradshaw; State v., 57
Bradwell v. State, 502
Brady v. Maryland, 287, 386-391, 475, 695
Brennan's, Inc. v. Brennan's Rests., Inc., 249
Brizzi, In re, 638
Brobeck, Phleger & Harrison v. Telex Corp., 111,
     115, 117
Bronston v. United States, 319-322
Brookhart v. Janis, 55
Brown, In re, 514
Brown v. Board of Educ., 6, 287, 607, 613, 615
Brown v. County of Genesee, 423
Brown v. Legal Found. of Wash., 111
Brown; United States v., 638
Brown & Williamson Tobacco Corp., In re, 127
Bryan, In re, 43
Buck v. Davis, 601
Buckley v. Fitzsimmons, 385
Burger v. Kemp, 180, 185
Burlington, City of v. Dague, 136

Cabrera; Doe v., 489
California Retail Liquor Dealers Ass'n v. Midcal
     Aluminum, 135
Caliste v. Cantrell, 465
Campbell; United States v., 196, 234
Canton, City of v. Harris, 389
Caperton v. A.T. Massey Coal Co., 47, 463, *467,*
     473-478, 491, 698
Capoccia, In re, 577
Carey, In re, 244
Carle v. Steyh, 60
Carlton, In re, 530
Carona; United States v., 99, *100,* 102, 103
Cenco, Inc. v. Seidman & Seidman, 568
Certified Envtl. Servs.; United States v., 387
Chambers; State v., 307
Chan v. Wellington Mgmt. Co., 361
Charge of Judicial Misconduct, In re, 62 F.3d 320
     (9th Cir. 1995), 462
Charge of Judicial Misconduct, In re, 91 F.3d
     1416 (10th Cir. 1996), 462
Charge of Judicial Misconduct or Disability, In re,
     85 F.3d 701 (D.C. Cir. 1996), 462
Charges of Unprofessional Conduct, In re, 530
Chase, In re, 587
Chen v. Chen Qualified Settlement Fund,
     123, 562
Cheney v. United States Dist. Court, 541 U.S. 913
     (2004), 484
Cheney v. United States Dist. Court, 542 U.S. 367
     (2004), 484
Cherkasky, In re, 587
Chicago Bar Ass'n, People ex rel. v. Motorists'
     Ass'n, 605

Choice Hotels Int'l v. Grover, 57, 59
Chrysler Corp. v. Carey, 248
Chujoy; United States v., 323
Cinema 5, Ltd. v. Cinerama, Inc., 217
Citizens United v. Federal Election Comm'n, 476
City of. *See name of city*
Clair v. Clair, 44
Clark v. Beverly Health & Rehab. Servs., 93
Clark v. Virginia Bd. of Bar Exam'rs, 514
Clarke's Estate, In re, 562
Cleland, In re, 581
Clemens v. New York Cent. Mut. Fire Ins. Co., 123
Cline v. Reetz-Laiolo, 358
Cohn, Matter of, 464
Colin, In re, 650-651
Columbus Bar Ass'n. v. Barns, 23
Commodity Futures Trading Comm'n v.
     Weintraub, 444
Commonwealth v. *See name of opposing party*
Complaint of Judicial Misconduct, In re, 495-496
Complaint Under the Judicial Conduct &
     Disability Act, In re, 496
Connelly, In re, 665
Connick v. Thompson, 389
Continental Res. v. Schmalenberger, 252
Cook, Flanagan & Berst v. Clausing, 551
Cooperman, In re, 61
Costco Wholesale Corp. v. Superior Ct., 40
Cottle; State v., 188
Crawford; United States v., 693
Crews v. Buckman Labs. Int'l, 428
Crickett v. Admiral, 254, 262
Cromley v. Board of Educ., 255, 258, 259, 261
Cross v. United States, 55
Crossen, In re, 96
Crowe v. Tull, 8, 572
Cruz-Aponte v. Caribbean Petroleum Corp., 591
C.R.W., In re, 515
Curry, In re, 95, 96
Curtis; United States v., 295
Cutler; United States v., 638
Cuyler v. Sullivan, 179, *181,* 185-187, 218, 598

Dandamudi v. Tisch, 502
David; State v., 334-335
Decora v. DW Wallcovering, 246
Delmonico v. Traynor, 646
DeZarn; United States v., 321
Disciplinary Counsel v. Brockler, 102
Disciplinary Counsel v. Chambers, 424
Disciplinary Counsel v. Cicero, 29
Disciplinary Counsel v. Detweiler, 585
Disciplinary Counsel v. Moore, 585
Disciplinary Proceedings Against Siderits, In re,
     574, *581*
Discotrade Ltd. v. Wyeth-Ayerst Int'l, 459
Diversified Indus. v. Meredith, 45

Dr. Falk Pharma GMBH v. Generico, LLC, 450
Doe v. *See name of opposing private party*
Doe v. Doe, 577
Doe; United States v., 45
Doughty v. State, 55
Douglas v. California, 70
Duncan v. Louisiana, 522

Eastern Trading Co. v. Refco, Inc., 568
Edenfield v. Fane, 671
Eisenstein, In re, 105
Estate of. *See name of estate*
Evans v. Jeff D., 138, 142-143, 152, 689
Evanson; United States v., 231
Evitts v. Lucey, 598

Faretta v. California, 70, 72
Farinella; United States v., 336, 341
FDIC v. United States Fire Ins. Co., 159, 231
Feland, In re, 391
Fiandaca v. Cunningham, 209, 210, 213-216, 222
Ficker v. Curran, 681
Fiedler, State ex rel. v. Wisconsin Senate, 7
Finley v. Home Ins. Co., 229
Fire Ins. Exch. v. Bell, 415
Firestone Tire & Rubber Co. v. Risjord, 222
First Nat'l Bank v. Lowrey, 64
Flanagan v. United States, 197
Florida Bar v. Martocci, 591
Florida Bar v. Pape, 665
Florida Bar v. Scott, 416
Florida Bar v. Taylor, 169
Florida Bar v. Went For It, Inc., 680, 682
Florida Bd. of Bar Exam'rs, In re, 515
Foley-Ciccantelli v. Bishop's Grove Condo.
    Ass'n, 215
Fordham, In re, 119, 121, 575
Formal Advisory Opinion 10-1, In re, 215
Forrest, In re, 423
Fortune v. State, 347
Frankhauser; United States v., 375
Franzoni v. Hart Schaffner & Marx, 248
Fremont Indem. Co. v. Fremont Gen. Corp., 216
Friend, In re, 43
Front, Inc. v. Khalil, 646
FTC v. *See name of opposing party*

Gabapentin Patent Litig., In re, 221
Garcia, In re, 574 A.2d 394 (N.J. 1990), 583
Garcia, In re, 315 P.3d 117 (Cal. 2014), 502
Garcia v. Kozlov, Seaton, Romanini & Brooks,
    P.C., 567
Garner v. Wolfinbarger, 50-51
Garrett v. Bryan Cave LLP, 567
Garrett v. Derbes, 572

Garza v. Idaho, 69
Geer, In re, 587
Gellene; United States v., 157
General Motors Corp. v. City of New York,
    263-265
General Motors Corp. Pick-Up Truck Fuel Tank
    Prod. Liab. Litig., In re, 22
Gentex Corp. v. Sutter, 349
Gentile v. State Bar of Nev., 639, 645, 647, 650,
    662, 704
Giaimo & Vreeburg v. Smith, 80
Giambrone v. Meritplan Ins. Co., 248
Gibbs v. Breed, Abbott & Morgan, 567
Gibson v. Berryhill, 469
Gidatex, S.r.L. v. Campaniello Imps., 95
Gideon v. Wainwright, 68, 108, 110, 274
Giuffre v. Dershowitz, 232
Glass, In re, 508
Glasser v. United States, 183
G.L.S., In re, 515
Goldberger v. Integrated Res., 137
Goldfarb v. Supreme Court of Va., 505
Goldfarb v. Virginia State Bar, 131, *132*
Gonzalez v. State, 231
Gonzalez v. United States, 69
Gonzalez; United States v., 221
Gonzalez-Lopez; United States v., 198
Goodrich v. Goodrich, 448
Gorokhovsky, In re, 172
Gorski; United States v., 46
Gould, Inc. v. Mitsui Mining & Smelting Co., 251
Graf; United States v., 439
Grand Jury Investigation, In re, 46, 49
Grand Jury Proceedings, In re, 45
Grand Jury Subpoena, In re, 46, 441
Grand Jury Subpoena Under Seal, In re, 435
Green v. Nevers, 115, 131
Greenberg, In re, 582
Greene v. Frost Brown Todd, LLC, 226
Greycas, Inc. v. Proud, 411, 415, 572
Grievance Adm'r v. Deutch, 586
Griffin v. Illinois, 70, 109
Griffiths, In re, 502
GSI Commerce Solutions v. BabyCenter, LLC, 450
Guilden v. Bank of Israel. *See* Sussman ex rel.
    Guilden v. Bank of Israel

Hager, In re, 165, 574
Haggerty, In re, 22
Hall v. Small Bus. Admin., 488
Halverson, In re, 585
Hammad; United States v., 98-101, 103, 688
Hanover Ins. Co. v. Rapo & Jepsen Ins. Servs., 220
Hansen v. Anderson, Wilmarth & Van Der
    Maaten, 416
Harrill & Sutter, PLLC v. Kosin, 80

Hartford Accident & Indem. Co. v. Sullivan, 571

Haugabrook, In re, 583

Hausmann; United States v., 166

Hayes; People v., 306

Hays v. Ruther, 8

Hearst; United States v., 168

Hefron, In re, 125

Heintz v. Jenkins, 572

Hempstead Video, Inc. v. Village of Valley Stream, 214

Henderson v. United States, 359

Hensley v. Eckerhart, 136

Herman, In re, 583

Herr; People v., 13

Hill, In re, 596

Hill v. Shell Oil Co., 87

Hinton v. Alabama, 601

Hird; United States v., 322

Hitch v. Pima Cnty. Superior Court, 381

Holland v. Florida, 58, 59

Holloway v. Arkansas, 182-183, 186, 187

Holmes, United States ex rel. v. Northrop Grumman Corp., 458

Holtzman, In re, 647, 650

Hoover, In re, 360

Hopson v. Riverbay Corp., 341

Houston v. Cotter, 123

Hoyt Props., Inc. v. Production Res. Group, 417

Huffman v. Montana Supreme Court, 505

Hunt v. American Bank & Trust Co., 488

IBM v. Levin, 217

Imbler v. Pachtman, 385

Inorganic Coatings v. Falberg, 88

In re. *See name of party*

Iowa Supreme Court Attorney Disciplinary Bd. v. Box, 86

Iowa Supreme Court Attorney Disciplinary Bd. v. Clauss, 222

Iowa Supreme Court Attorney Disciplinary Bd. v. Gottschalk, 81

Iowa Supreme Court Attorney Disciplinary Bd. v. Kress, 583

Iowa Supreme Court Bd. of Prof'l Ethics & Conduct v. Erbes, 576

Iowa Supreme Court Bd. of Prof'l Ethics & Conduct v. Herrera, 86

Ironshore Europe DAC v. Schiff Hardin, LLP, 416

Irwin v. Surdyk's Liquor, 7

ISC Holding AG v. Nobel Biocare Fin. AG, 478

Ivory; United States v., 57

Jacoby & Meyers, LLP v. Presiding Justices of the First, Second, Third and Fourth Dep'ts, 628

Jae Lee v. United States, 64

Janik v. Rudy, Exelrod & Zeiff, 63

Jicarilla Apache Nation; United States v., 50, 441

Johnson v. Avery, 536

Johnson; People v., 303, 304, 306

Johnson v. Superior Court, 220

Jones v. Barnes, 56, *70,* 73, 75, 79

Jones v. Clinton, 36 F. Supp. 2d 1118 (E.D. Ark. 1999), 312, 314, 324

Jones v. Clinton, 57 F. Supp. 2d 719 (E.D. Ark. 1999), 324

Jones v. Rabanco, 82

Jordan, In re, 515

JP Morgan Chase Bank ex rel. Mahonia Ltd. v. Liberty Mut. Ins. Co., 449

Juniper v. Zook, 390

Kaba; United States v., 698

Kachmar v. SunGard Data Sys., 44, 81, 428

K.A.H., In re, 169

K&L Gates LLP v. Quantum Materials Corp., 60

Kansallis Fin. v. Fern, 556

Karstetter v. King Cnty. Corr. Guild, 428

Keefe v. Bernard, 40, 41

Kellington; United States v., 376

Kellogg Brown & Root, Inc., In re, 40, 41, 222

Kelly, United States ex rel. v. Boeing Co., 204

Kentucky Bar Ass'n v. Guidugli, 514

Kentucky Bar Ass'n; United States v., 14, 199

Kevlik v. Goldstein, 215, 216

Khani v. Ford Motor Co., 247

King v. NAIAD Inflatables of Newport, 81

Kirschner v. KPMG LLP, 569

Kline, In re, 390

Kloess; United States v., 376

Knight, In re, 514

Krasnoff, In re, 124

Kyles v. Whitley, 391

Labair v. Carey, 567

Lafler v. Cooper, 601

Laird v. Tatum, 654, 656

Lama Holding Co. v. Shearman & Sterling, 82

Lawrence, In re, 115

Lawyer Disciplinary Bd. v. Hall, 650

LeClerc v. Webb, 419 F.3d 405 (5th Cir. 2005), 502

LeClerc v. Webb, 444 F.3d 428 (5th Cir. 2006), 502

Lee; People v., 378

Lee; United States v., 387

Leis v. Flynt, 517, 522

Lennar Mare Island, LLC v. Steadfast Ins. Co., 228

Lerner, In re, 122

Letourneau, In re, 64

Leung; United States v., 698-699

Levine v. Kling, 570

Lewis, In re, 585

Leysock v. Forest Labs., 96

Ligon, In re, 207

Liljeberg v. Health Servs. Acquisition Corp., 478, 483, 487, 497

Lincoln Sav. & Loan Ass'n v. Wall, 431

Linder v. Insurance Claims Consultants, Inc., 533, 535, 536, 700

Lindsey, In re, 441

Linegar v. DLA Piper, LLP, 417

Link v. Wabash R.R. Co., 54

Lipin v. Bender, 105

Litchfield; United States v., 311

Liteky v. United States, 486, 488, 490

Litz, In re, 33

Lofton v. Fairmont Specialty Ins. Managers, Inc., 81

Louisiana State Bar Ass'n v. Bensabat, 586

Lowery v. Cardwell, 295

Lucas, In re, 86

Lund v. Myers, 106

Macheca Transp. Co. v. Philadelphia Indem. Ins. Co., 231

Madison Teachers, Inc. v. Walker, 497

Maldonado v. Ford Motor Co., 638

Manville, In re, 513

Maples v. Thomas, 58, 59

Marcum v. Scorsone, 252

Marentette v. City of Canandaigua, 422

Maritrans GP Inc. v. Pepper, Hamilton & Scheetz, 244

Mar Oil v. Morrissey, 125

Marshall, In re, 597

Marshall; People v., 331

Martin Marietta Corp., In re, 45

Martino; United States v., 102

Mashaney v. Board of Indigents' Def. Servs., 571

Maslowski v. Prospect Funding Partners, 614

Matter of. *See name of party*

Mayberry v. Pennsylvania, 470

McCormick, In re, 103

McCoy v. Louisiana, 73, 75, 599

McDaniel, In re, 583

McDowell; State v., 307

McKinley; State v., 215

McMann v. Richardson, 598

McMillian, In re, 513

McNulty; SEC v., 59

McRae v. United States, 187

Meredith; People v., 377, 380-382, 384

Meyerhofer v. Empire Fire & Marine Ins. Co., 43

Meyer v. Wagner, 543, 552

Michigan v. Bryant, 651

Mickens v. Taylor, 186-188

Milavetz, Gallop & Milavetz, P.A. v. United States, 8, 676

Milbank, Tweed, Hadley & McCloy v. Boon, 60

Miller; State v., 85, 103

Missouri v. Frye, 64, 601

Mitchell v. Association of the Bar of the City of N.Y., 586

Mitchell; Commonwealth v., 306

Mohawk Indus. v. Carpenter, 34, 46

Mok v. 21 Mott St. Rest. Corp., 421, 422

Monaghan, In re, 591

Montejo v. Louisiana, 86

Moores v. Greenberg, 64

Morales, In re, 536

Morrell v. State, 378, 380

Morrissey, In re, 634 N.Y.S.2d 51 (1st Dept. 1995), 125

Morrissey, In re, 898 N.Y.S.2d 1 (1st Dep't. 2010), 125

M.R., In re, 79

Mullaney v. Aude, 352, 353, 356

Murchison, In re, 470

Muriel Siebert & Co. v. Intuit, 93

Murphy; United States v., 486, 490

Murphy & Demory, Ltd. v. Admiral Daniel J. Murphy, U.S.N. (Ret.), 451, 574

Murray v. Carrier, 601

Murray v. Metro. Life Ins. Co., 231, 233

Musick; People v., 586

Mutual of Omaha Bank v. Kassebaum, 612, 613

Mutuelles Unies v. Kroll & Linstrom, 552

NAACP v. Button, 606, 607, 612, 613, 615-619, 621-625, 628

Nadler, In re, 583

Napster Copyright Litig., In re, 46

Naranjo v. Thompson, 151

Nash; People v., 381

National Inst. of Family & Life Advocates v. Becerra, 594

National Med. Enters. v. Godbey, 221

National Tank Co. v. 30th Jud. Dist. Court, 41

Neville, In re, 161, 164

Newman v. Highland Sch. Dist. No. 203, 41

Newspapers v. Hepps, 647

New York v. Hill, 69

New York ex rel. Stephen B. Diamond, P.C. v. My Pillow, 523

New York City v. McAllister Bros., Inc., 359

New York Cnty. Lawyers' Ass'n v. Dacey, 537, 538

New York State Club Ass'n v. City of New York, 494

New York Times Co. v. Sullivan, 647, 649, 650

Nichols v. Keller, 62, 63, 701-702

Nickol, In re, 587

Niesig v. Team I, 13, 89, *90,* 93-95, 688-689

Nix v. Whiteside, 294, 303-306, 310, 598

Nixon; United States v., 368

Noble v. Kelly, 57

North Carolina State Bd. of Dental Exam'rs v. Federal Trade Comm'n, 134, 539

Odell v. Legal Bucks, LLC, 632
Office of. *See name of office*
O'Hagan; United States v., 33
Ohralik v. Ohio State Bar, 619, 620, *668,* 671-674, 677-678, 680, 682
O'Keefe, United States ex rel. v. McDonnell Douglas Corp., 99
Oklahoma Bar Ass'n, State ex rel. v. Smolen, 169-171
Oklahoma Bar Ass'n, State ex rel. v. Stout, 585
Oklahoma Bar Ass'n, State ex rel. v. Ward, 390
Oklahoma Bar Ass'n, State ex rel. v. Worsham, 424
Olfe v. Gordon, 78, 557
Olsen; United States v., 388
Olwell; State v., 378, 381
Original Grand Jury Investigation, In re, 33
Osprey, Inc. v. Cabana Ltd. P'ship, 612, 613, 632

Pacific Pictures Corp., In re, 45
Padilla v. Kentucky, 64, 600
Parallel Iron, LLC v. Adobe Sys., 83
Paramount Commc'ns v. QVC Network, 352
Parents Involved in Cmty. Schs. v. Seattle Sch. Dist. No. 1, 594
Parker, In re, 514
Parker v. Brown, 133, 135, 136
Parkinson v. Bevis, 30, 61, 561
Pautler, In re, 103
Pegram, In re, 23
Pena-Rodriguez v. Colorado, 175
Pennwalt Corp. v. Plough, Inc., 251
People v. *See name of opposing party*
People ex rel. *See name of related party*
Perdue v. Kenny A., 137
Perez v. Kirk & Carrigan, 26, 29, 33
Persels & Assocs. v. Banking Comm'r, 7
Petition to Stay the Effectiveness of Ethics Opinion, In re, 390
Phansalkar v. Andersen Weinroth & Co., 562
Phillips, In re, 515
Phillips v. Washington Legal Found., 111
Picker Int'l v. Varian Assocs., 251, 258
Pinto v. Spectrum Chems. & Lab. Prods., 143
Pittsburgh History & Landmarks Found. v. Zeigler, 50
Platt v. Board of Comm'rs on Grievances & Discipline of Ohio Supreme Court, 660
Plotts v. Chester Cycles LLC, 238
Polin, In re, 513
Pony v. County of Los Angeles, 143
Post v. Bregman, 13
Potero; State v., 189
Potts, In re, 410
Powell, In re, 115
Powell, In re Estate of, 555
Prager, In re, 513

Precision Specialty Metals v. United States, 360
Preston v. Stoops, 7
Primus, In re, 606, 613, 615, *616,* 621, 628
Professional Adjusters, Inc. v. Tandon, 536
Public Defender v. State, 23
Public Serv. Mut. Ins. Co. v. Goldfarb, 230
Purcell v. District Attorney for Suffolk Dist., 49

Quattrone; United States v., 374
Quest Diagnostics; United States v., 457, 458

Radtke v. Board of Bar Exam'rs, 514
Ragin; United States v., 600
Railroad Trainmen v. Virginia ex rel. Virginia State Bar, 621-625
Randall v. Sorrell, 477
Reed v. Town of Gilbert, 595
Remodeling Dimensions, Inc. v. Integrity Mut. Ins. Co., 229
Republican Party of Minn. v. White, 653, 659-661
Revo v. Disciplinary Bd. of the Supreme Court for the State of N.M., 681
Rex v. *See name of opposing party*
Reyes; United States v., 347
Richardson-Merrell, Inc. v. Koller, 221-222
Rico v. Mitsubishi Motors Corp., 106
Riehlmann, In re, 597
Riek, In re, 390
Riel; People v., 306
Riverside, City of v. Rivera, 116
Rizzo v. Haines, 557
R.M. v. Supreme Court, 577
Robertson, In re, 576
Robeson, In re, 43
Robnett; People v., 43
Rodriguez v. Disner, 559, 562
Rodriguez v. West Publ'g Corp., 22
Roe v. Wade, 661
Rogan; State v., 334
Rojinski v. Rojinski, 544-545
Roosevelt Irrigation Dist. v. Salt River Project Agric. Improvement & Power Dist., 221
Ross; United States v., 573
Rossi v. Blue Cross & Blue Shield, 36
Rothgery v. Gillespie Cnty., 98
Ryder, In re, 381 F.2d 713 (4th Cir. 1967), 372
Ryder, In re, 263 F. Supp. 360 (E.D. Va. 1967), 369, 379-381, 384, 575, 695

Sage Realty Corp. v. Proskauer Rose Goetz & Mendelsohn, 81
Saladini v. Righellis, 612, 613
Salameh; United States v., 638
Sallee v. Tennessee Bd. of Prof'l Responsibility, 122

Sanchez; People v., 372
Sanders v. State, 198
Santa Fe Int'l Corp., In re, 220
Santa Fe Pac. Gold Corp. v. United Nuclear
  Corp., 220
Sarwari; United States v., 320, 321
Schaeffler v. United States, 220
Schaumburg, Village of v. Citizens for a Better
  Env't, 682
Schiessle v. Stephens, 256
Schiff, In re, 356, 574, *589,* 591
Schlumberger Tech., In re, 44
Schneider, Estate of v. Finmann, 555, 556
Schock; United States v., 639
Schoepfer, In re, 581
School Dist. of Abington Township v.
  Schempp, 177
Schwarz v. Kogan, 143
Schwarz; United States v., 180
Schwimmer; United States v., 219
Scott, In re, 584
Scott v. City of New York, 124
SEC v. *See name of opposing party*
Seed Co. v. Westerman, 552
Shapero v. Kentucky Bar Ass'n, 676, 680-683
Shapiro, In re, 582
Shaughnessy, In re, 64
Shaw v. Mfrs. Hanover Trust, 125
Shenwick v. Twitter, 220
Shorter, In re, 323
Shurance v. Planning Control Int'l, Inc., 222
Silver Chrysler Plymouth v. Chrysler Motors
  Corp., 260
Simpson v. James, 222, 244, 563, 567
Singleton v. Cannizzaro, 385
Skilling v. United States, 167
Skinner, In re, 33
Slotkin v. Citizens Cas. Co. of N.Y., 701
Smith v. Berg, 464
Smith v. Cain, 387, 389
*Smith v. Haynsworth, Marion, McKay & Geureard,
  557,* 558, 559
Smith; State v., 196
Snow, In re, 583
Sobol v. Perez, 521
Solow; United States v., 374
Sorrells v. United States, 102
Spanos v. Skouras, 528
Special Proceedings, In re, 385
Spectrum Sys. Int'l Corp. v. Chemical Bank, 40
Speedee Oil Change Sys.; People v., 214
Sperry v. State ex rel. Florida Bar, 536
Stanton, In re, 585
Stare v. Tate, 696
State of. *See name of state*
State v. *See name of opposing party*
State ex rel. *See name of related party*
State Farm Mut. Auto. Ins. Co. v. Hansen, 229

Stearnes v. Clinton, 95
Stender v. Blessum, 558
Stern, In re, 701
Stile v. AxiMartin, 254
Strickland v. Washington, 185, 187, 188, 198,
  296-300, 599-600
Strickler v. Greene, 386, 391
Strigler v. Board of Bar Exam'rs, 513
Stropnicky v. Nathanson, 587, 588
Sturdivant v. Sturdivant, 250
Sullivan v. Cuyler, 185
Sullivan Cnty. Reg'l Refuse Disposal Dist. v. Town
  of Acworth, 249
Supreme Court of N.H. v. Piper, 504
Supreme Court of Va. v. Friedman, 504, 505
Sussex Justices; Rex v., 461
Sussman ex rel. Guilden v. Bank of Israel, 358
Swedish Hosp. Corp. v. Shalala, 137
Swidler & Berlin v. United States, 34
Swinomish Indian Tribal Cmty. v. BNSF Ry.
  Co., 360

Taboada v. Daly Seven, Inc., 352
Talao; United States v., 100-102
Tamm, In re, 33
Tante, In re, 555
Tante v. Herring, 553, 554, 584
Taylor, In re, 323-324
Taylor v. Illinois, 54, 56, 59, 361
Taylor v. State, 188
Taylor Lohmeyer Law Firm v. United States, 31
T.C. Theatre Corp. v. Warner Bros. Pictures, 244
Tekni-Plex, Inc. v. Meyner & Landis, 441
Teleglobe Commc'ns Corp., In re, 218
Tessier v. Plastic Surgery Specialists, 251
Thiery v. Bye, 30
Thomas v. Tenneco Packaging Co., 352
Thompson, In re, 582
Thompson v. Hebdon, 477
Thompson v. Paul, 417
Thomsen, In re, 352
Thorsen v. Richmond S.P.C.A., 555
Thul v. OneWest Bank, FSB, 362, 363
Tidwell, In re, 586
Togstad v. Vesely, Otto, Miller & Keefe, 21, 244, *546,*
  551, 552, 557
Toledo Bar Ass'n v. Stahlbush, 122
Tonderum, In re, 33
Torre, In re, 164
Toste Farm Corp. v. Hadbury, Inc., 615
Transcraft, Inc. v. Galvin, Stalmack, Kirschner &
  Clark, 543
Trapnell v. United States, 599
Trepca Mines, Ltd., In re, 612
Triplett v. Colvin, 22
Trone v. Smith, 249
Tumey v. Ohio, 463, 468-470

Unauthorized Practice of Law Comm. v.
     American Home Assurance Co., 605
Unauthorized Practice of Law Comm. v. Parsons
     Tech., 537, 538
Unified Sewerage Agency v. Jelco, Inc., 250-251
United Mine Workers, Dist. 12 v. Illinois State Bar
     Ass'n, 622-625
United States v. *See name of opposing party*
United States ex rel. *See name of related party*
United Transp. Union v. State Bar of Mich., 622
Upjohn Co. v. United States, 37, 40-42, 88-91,
     434-435, 438

Van Asdale v. International Game Tech., 44, 428
Van Kirk v. Miller, 227
Vargas, In re, 502
Vega v. Jones, Day, Reavis & Pogue, 415
Village of. *See name of village*
Viner v. Sweet, 12 Cal. Rptr. 3d 533 (Ct. App.
     2004), 566
Viner v. Sweet, 30 Cal. 4th 1232, 70 P.3d 1046 (Cal.
     2003), *563*, 566
Virginia v. Hicks, 594
Vogel, In re, 584
Voss, In re, 585

Wagenmann v. Adams, 557
Wahlgren v. Bausch & Lomb Optical
     Co., 571, 572
Walker v. Pierce, 618
Wal-Mart Stores v. Independent Elec. Workers
     Pension Trust Fund IBEW, 50
Ward v. Monroeville, 469, 470
Warhaftig, In re, 575, *579*, 580
Washington State Physicians Ins. Exch. & Ass'n v.
     Fisons Corp., 314
Wasmann v. Seidenberg, 573
Watkins v. Trans Union, LLC, 246
Wecht; United States v., 644
Weigel, In re, 703
Weil, Gotshal & Manges, LLP v. Fashion Boutique
     of Short Hills, 553
Weinstein; People v., 645
Weissman; United States v., 440
Wemark v. State, 380

Westinghouse Elec. Corp. v. Kerr-McGee Corp.,
     21, 242, 250
West Virginia v. Douglass, 378
Wheat v. United States, 180, *190*, 196, 231, 234, 690
White, In re, 352
Whittenburg v. Werner Enters, 336-337
Wiesmueller v. Kosobucki, 505
Wiggins v. Smith, 601
Wigod v. Wells Fargo Bank, N.A., 362-363
Wilcox, United States ex rel. v. Johnson, 295
Wilkins, In re, 651
Williams v. BASF Catalysts LLC, 350
Williams v. Pennsylvania, 475
Williams; United States v., 361
Williamson v. Bratt, 24
Williamson v. John D. Quinn Constr. Corp.,
     527-528
Williams-Yulee v. Florida Bar, 659
Wilson, In re, 580
Wilson; United States v., 340
Winkler, In re, 105
Winkler v. Keane, 129
Winkler; People v., 129
Winter v. Wolnitzek, 660
Winterrowd v. American Gen. Annuity Ins. Co., 528
Wisehart, In re, 105
Wolfson v. Concannon, 660
Wood v. Georgia, 172, 186

Xcentric Ventures v. Stanley, 216

Yarborough v. Gentry, 544
Yarn Processing Patent Validity Litig., In re,
     215, 251
Young, In re, 62
Young v. United States ex rel. Vuitton et Fils S.A.,
     200, 203

Zapata v. Vasquez, 338
Zarrab; United States v., 691
Zauderer v. Office of Disciplinary Counsel, 170, 613,
     672, 676, 678
Zolin; United States v., 46-48
Zulandt, In re, 586

Table of Codes, Rules, and Restatement Provisions

ABA MODEL RULES OF PROFESSIONAL CONDUCT

Rule		
1.0	227	
1.0(b)	65	
1.0(c)	158, 214	
1.0(d)	696	
1.0(e)	44, 65, 159	
1.0(f)	294	
1.0(m)	293, 302, 406	
1.1	11, 22	
1.2	51, 65, 409	
1.2(a)	65, 69, 72, 79, 143, 294	
1.2(b)	286	
1.2(d)	4, 402, 407, 573, 696	
1.3	61	
1.4	64, 65, 66, 697	
1.4(a)	65	
1.4(b)	79	
1.5	115, 119, 124	
1.5(a)	117, 120	
1.5(b)	125	
1.5(c)	116, 125	
1.5(d)	129	
1.6	28, 30, 31, 33, 35, 36, 42, 48, 167, 261, 266, 406, 407, 456, 457, 458, 597	
1.6(a)	32, 34, 35, 44, 407	
1.6(b)	32, 293	
1.6(b)(1)	47, 48	
1.6(b)(2)	11, 47, 48, 407, 408, 410, 458	
1.6(b)(3)	11, 47, 48, 408, 410	
1.6(b)(5)	42, 43, 81, 566	
1.6(b)(6)	408	
1.6(b)(7)	261, 692	
1.7–1.10	232	
1.7	155, 158, 173, 209, 210, 211, 213, 215, 216, 217, 219, 220, 227, 228, 231, 440	
1.7(a)	158, 214	
1.7(a)(1)	156, 208, 209, 213, 216	
1.7(a)(2)	156, 161, 164, 165, 166, 209, 210, 211, 213, 216, 258, 559, 584	
1.7(b)	227	
1.8	158, 170, 584, 585	
1.8(a)	65, 124, 125, 161, 164, 689	
1.8(b)	31, 32, 44	
1.8(d)	167	
1.8(e)	168, 169, 170, 632	
1.8(f)	171	
1.8(h)(1)	227	
1.8(j)	43, 555, 584, 585	
1.9	215, 231, 238, 240, 246, 247, 263	
1.9(a)	158, 238, 240, 244, 248, 251, 252, 262, 267, 442, 443, 692	
1.9(b)	255, 260, 262	
1.9(c)	31, 44, 158, 262	
1.9(c)(1)	32	
1.9(c)(2)	32	
1.10	173, 238, 261, 263, 690	
1.10(a)	157, 158, 172, 180, 214, 215, 245, 254	
1.10(a)(2)	158, 255, 261	
1.10(b)	262	
1.11	158, 261, 263, 266, 693	
1.11(a)	266, 692	
1.11(a)(1)	262	
1.11(b)	266, 692, 693	
1.11(c)	266, 693	
1.13	11, 159, 408, 432, 454, 456, 457, 458	
1.13(a)	427, 451	
1.13(b)	456	
1.13(c)	32, 36, 48, 408, 457, 458	
1.13(f)	42, 440	
1.14	79	
1.15	579	
1.16	81, 273, 290	
1.16(a)(1)	407	
1.16(b)(4)	273	
1.16(c)	251	
1.16(c)(1)	251	
1.18	21, 29, 214, 250	
3.2	433	
3.3	293, 297, 302, 303, 310, 312, 316, 406, 407, 693	
3.3(a)–(c)	408	
3.3(a)	323	
3.3(a)(1)	361, 362, 421, 578	
3.3(a)(2)	363	
3.3(a)(3)	293, 693	

3.3(a)(5)	423
3.3(b)	693
3.3(c)	32, 48
3.3(e)	421
3.4	421
3.4(a)	372
3.4(a)(3)	421
3.4(e)	336
3.4(f)	93
3.5(b)	52, 464
3.6	639, 640, 644, 645, 661
3.6(a)	637, 638
3.7	158, 231, 233
3.7(a)	231, 232
3.7(b)	232, 233
3.8	384
3.8(a)	392
3.8(d)	286, 386, 389, 390, 391, 399, 695
3.8(f)	638
3.9	302, 406, 408
4.1	51, 402, 407, 409, 410, 411
4.1(a)	96, 361, 410, 417, 422
4.1(b)	406, 407, 408
4.2	85, 86, 87, 88, 89, 90, 93, 94, 98, 100, 101, 102, 103, 104, 688
4.3	29, 93, 423, 440, 689
4.4	107, 424
4.4(a)	352, 356, 358
4.4(b)	106, 107
5.1	389
5.3	389
5.4	629
5.4(a)	633, 702, 703
5.4(a)(3)	629, 703
5.4(b)	539
5.4(c)	171
5.4(d)	539
5.5	11, 523, 524, 529, 530, 533
5.5(c)	700
5.5(c)(1)	524, 700
5.5(c)(4)	700
5.5(d)	529
6.1	144, 145
6.3–6.5	145
6.3	145
6.4	145
7.1 et seq.	664
7.3	672, 676, 677, 680
7.3(b)(3)	672
8.2(a)	647, 649, 650, 651
8.3	424
8.3(a)	596
8.4	323
8.4(a)	87, 96, 102, 402
8.4(b)	97, 596, 702
8.4(c)	95, 96, 102, 103, 323, 361, 402, 410, 422, 423, 578
8.4(d)	176, 352
8.4(e)	352
8.4(g)	176, 331, 424, 588, 592, 593, 594, 595
8.4(h)	356
8.5	12, 159
8.5(b)(1)	254

ABA MODEL CODE OF JUDICIAL CONDUCT

Rule	1.2	494
	2.3	493, 494
	2.3(B)	494
	2.3(C)	331, 355, 494, 593
	2.3(D)	331, 355, 494
	2.9A	464
	2.10(B)	660
	2.11	489
	2.11(A)(5)	661
	2.15	596
	3.6	493
	3.6(A)	491, 494
	4.1	660
	4.1(A)(13)	660
	7.6	477

ABA MODEL CODE OF PROFESSIONAL RESPONSIBILITY

Canon 1

1-102(A)(6)	648, 650

Canon 5

5-104	161, 162
5-104(A)	161, 163
5-105	217

Canon 7

	358
7-13	201
7-104(A)(1)	90, 91, 92, 98, 99

Canon 9

	252

RESTATEMENT OF THE LAW
GOVERNING LAWYERS

Section

16(3)	553
37	560, 562
49	553
53	567
60	220
73	40
75	218, 221

76	221
76(1)	220
85	50
99	86
99(2)	87
101	94
102	94
121	156, 449
122	227, 228
132	221, 244
134	229

Index

ABA. *See* American Bar Association
Actors, attorneys as, 282
Admission to bar, 502-531
  admission pro hac vice, 517-522
  in Canada, 531
  character inquiries, 506-513
  Civil Rights Movement and, 520-522
  criminal conduct, effect of, 513
  dishonest journalism, effect of, 508-513
  education requirements, 505-506
  in European Union, 530-531
  examinations, 505-506, 513-514
  exclusion from, 502
  in federal system, 515
  financial probity, effect of, 515
  geographical exclusion, 504
  geographical restriction, 504-505
  immigrants, 502
  lack of candor, effect of, 513-514
  law professors, 523
  law school, dishonesty or lack of integrity
     it, 514
  mental health, effect of, 514-515
  misconduct, effect of, 513-514
  mishandling of funds, effect of, 506
  multijurisdictional firms, 516-531
  non-profit organizations and, 522-523
  outdated nature of, 503
  overview, 502-503
  racial bias, effect of, 506-507
  services other than litigation, 522-531
  states, authority of, 502-503
  transient attorneys, 516-531
  unauthorized practice of law and, 503, 515
  women, 502
Adversary system, 276-287
  actors, attorneys as, 282
  advocacy. *See* Advocacy
  attorneys, role and responsibility of, 276-278
  literature, portrayal of attorneys in, 284-285
  partisan justice and, 279-281
  popular culture, portrayal of attorneys in, 272
  popular image of attorneys, 282-284
Adverse legal authority, obligation to reveal,
     362-363
Advertising by attorneys. *See* Marketing of legal
     services

Advise, duty to. *See* Inform and advise, duty to
Advocacy
  adverse legal authority, obligation to reveal,
     362-363
  bias, appeal to by attorneys, 331-336
  boundaries of proper argument, 336-349
  contempt and, 324-326
  cross-examination and, 326-331
  ethics in, 271-276
  false statements, obligation to disclose, 291-294
  "hardball" in, 351-358
  incivility in, 351-358
  literal truth, 315-326
     Clinton and, 317-319
     contempt and, 324-326
     perjury and, 319-324
  misstatements of facts, precedent, or record,
     359-362
  perjury and. *See* Perjury
  spoliation and, 349-351
  zealous advocacy, 356, 358
Advocate-witness rule, 231-233
  public policy, 231-232
Affirmative action, 593-595
Agency relationship, 54-60
  abandonment of client, effect of, 59
  judicial admissions, 60
  vicarious admissions, 60
American Bar Association (ABA)
  Canons of Judicial Ethics, 462
  Canons of Professional Ethics, 9, 252
  Code of Judicial Conduct, 331, 462-464,
     477-478, 593, 660
  Code of Professional Responsibility, 9
  Commission on Professionalism, 683
  Criminal Justice Standards, 600
  Ethics 2000 Commission, 10-11
  Kutak Commission, 9-10
  Model Rules of Professional Conduct, 8-12
  Multijurisdictional Practice (MJP)
     Commission, 11, 529
  Standards for Imposing Lawyer Sanctions, 575
  Standing Committee on Ethics and
     Professional Responsibility, 389
  Task Force on Corporate Responsibility,
     10-11, 456
  20/20 Commission, 11

American Civil Liberties Union (ACLU), 616-621

Americans with Disabilities Act of 1990, 514

Andrews, Carol, 1-2

Announce clauses, 652-658

Antitrust law, unauthorized practice of law and, 539

Appearance of impropriety, successive conflicts of interest, 252

Arthur Andersen, 374

Assistance of counsel. *See* Effective assistance of counsel

Attorney-client privilege, 37-42
  authority of court to determine, 48
  concurrent conflicts of interest and, 218-219
  confidential information, 31-33. *See also* Confidential information
  confidentiality, duty of, 24-54
  corporations and, 41-42
  in criminal cases, 368, 376-383
  effect of exceptions, 48-50
  exceptions, 42
  public policy, 34-35

Attorney-client relationship, 19-84
  abandonment of client, effect of, 59
  agency relationship, 54-60
  autonomy in, 66-80
    civil cases, 75-80
    criminal cases, 66-75
    diminished capacity, clients with, 79-80
    scope of, 79
  competence, duty of, 22-24
  confidentiality, duty of, 24-54. *See also* Confidential information
  creation of, 20-22
  diligence, duty of, 61-62
  fiduciary relationship, 60-61
  identification of client, 20-22
  implied relationship, 20-21
  in camera review, 46-47
  judgment, duty of, 24
  loyalty, duty of, 61-62
    successive conflicts of interest, 248-249
  malpractice for incompetence, 23
  opposing parties, communication with, 85-104
    attorney as party, 86
    circle of secrecy, 93-94
    civil cases, 88-97
    class actions, 86
    client-to-client communication, 87
    competing interests, 87-88
    consent, 86
    corporate and entity parties, 88-94
    criminal cases, 97-104
    deceit, use of, 102
    government parties, 94-95
    knowledge requirement, 86
    McDade Amendment, 99-100
    overview, 85-87
    testers, 95-97
    third parties and, 87

  overview, 19-20
  termination of
    by attorney, 81
    by client, 80-81
    by drift, 82
    episodic clients, 82-83
  vicarious admissions, 60

Attorneys' fees, 109-152
  billing guidelines, 122-124
  billing judgment, 124
  conflicts of interest, forfeiture for, 222-227
  contingent fees, 126-131
    advantage of attorneys in, 127
    conflicts of interest and, 127-128
    controversies regarding, 129-131
    criminal cases, prohibition in, 129
    matrimonial cases, prohibition in, 129
  court approval, 122-124
  court-awarded fees, 136-144
    common fund, 137-138
    derivative cases, 137-138
    fee-shifting, 117, 136-137
    proper amount, 136-138
    waiver, settlement conditioned on, 138-144
  excessive fees, discipline for, 119-120
  fee agreements
    post-retainer fee agreements, 124-125
    writing requirement, 125
  inflating bills, 121-122
  IOLTA accounts and, 110-111
  lodestar, 116
  malpractice, forfeiture and disgorgement for, 559-562
  mandatory pro bono plans, 144-151
    culture of commitment and, 146-148
    as "welfare for rich," 148-151
  marketplace, role of, 111-117
  minimum fee schedules, 131-136
  overview, 109-111
  time vs. value, 115-117
  unethical fees and billing practices, 117-125
  value billing, 115-117

Australia
  Legal Profession Acts, 633
  nonlawyers in, 633

"Automatic reversal" debate, 197-198

Autonomy in attorney-client relationship, 66-80
  civil cases, 75-80
  criminal cases, 66-75
  diminished capacity, clients with, 79-80
  scope of, 79

"Bad client problem," 4, 403-410

Baldwin, Roger, 176-177

Bankruptcy Abuse Prevention and Consumer Protection Act of 2005 (BAPCPA), 676

Bar examinations, 505-506, 513-514. *See also* Admission to bar

Barratry, 612-615

Behavioral legal ethics, 14
Bennett, Robert, 311-312
Bias
    admission to bar, effect of racial bias in, 506-507
    appeal to by attorneys, 331-336
    discipline of attorneys
        discrimination in client choice, 587-588
        racist and sexist speech and conduct, 588
    judges, expressions of bias by, 490-496
        in courtroom, 494-495
        discriminatory organizations and, 494-496
        LGBT persons and, 490-492
        private clubs and, 492-494
Billing judgment, 124
Boundaries of proper argument, 336-349
Brady obligations, 386-391
Brandon, Henry, 373-374
Breach of fiduciary duty. *See* Fiduciary duty, breach of
Brougham, Lord, 19-20, 273
Browning, John, 53
Burford Capital Limited, 631
Business and financial interests, client-attorney conflicts, 160-167
Business deals, client-attorney conflicts, 164
"But for" test, malpractice and civil liability, 566-569
    entity representation and, 568-569
    fiduciary duties and, 567-568
    litigation and, 566–567
    transactional matters and, 566
Butterfield, Alex, 368

California
    Evidence Code, 220
    living expenses, providing to client, 170
    Model Rules in, 10
Campaign funds
    appearance of partiality and, 475-477
    solicitation by judges, 659-661
Canada, admission to bar in, 531
Candidates for judicial office
    campaign funds, appearance of partiality and, 475-477
    campaign speech, 651-661
    solicitation of campaign funds, 659-661
Candor, discipline of attorneys for lack of, 583-584
Canons of Professional Ethics, 9, 252
Causation, malpractice and civil liability, 562-571
    "but for" test, 566-569
    in criminal cases, 569-571
    entity representation and, 568-569
    fiduciary duties and, 567-568
    litigation and, 566-567
    transactional matters and, 566
Champerty, 612-615
Change of corporate control
    confidential information and, 442-448
    conflicts of interest, 442-448
Character inquiries, 506-513

Charging decision, 392-395
Cheney, Dick, 484-486
Christie, Chris, 435
Civil liability. *See* Malpractice and civil liability
Civil Rights Attorneys' Fees Award Act of 1976, 138-142
Civil Rights Movement, 520-522
Clark, Marcia, 383
Class actions
    concurrent conflicts of interest, 209-213
    successive conflicts of interest, 252-253
Clean Water Act of 1972, 136
Clerks, disqualification of judges for service as, 488-489
Client-lawyer relationship. *See* Attorney-client relationship
Clinton, Bill, 311-312, 317-319, 321, 324
Clinton, Hillary, 311
Closely held entities
    confidential information and, 451-454
    conflicts of interest, 451-454
Cluelessness as reason for violations of rules, 575
Cochran, Johnnie, 382-383
Code of Conduct for United States Judges, 462
Code of Judicial Conduct, 331, 462-464, 477-478, 593, 660
Code of Professional Responsibility, 9, 252
Cohen, Michael, 574
Cohn, Roy, 464
Commercial speech, 666
Commission on Evaluation of the Rules of Professional Conduct (Ethics 2000 Commission), 10-11, 125
Common fund attorneys' fees, 137-138
Common interest agreements, 219-221
Companies, representation of. *See* Entity representation
Competence, duty of, 22-24
    judgment included in, 24
    malpractice for incompetence, 23
Concurrent conflicts of interest, 155-235
    advocate-witness rule, 231-233
        public policy, 231-232
    in civil cases, 207-228
        advance consent, 227-228
        attorney-client privilege and, 218-219
        attorneys' fees, forfeiture, 222-227
        class actions, 209-213
        common interest agreements, 219-221
        confidential information and, 218-221
        consent, 227-228
        "directly adverse" conflicts of interest, 213-214
        imputed conflicts, 214-215
        malpractice, 222-227
        overview, 207-209
        standing, 215-216
        unrelated matters, 216-218
        waiver, 227

Concurrent conflicts of interest (*continued*)
    client-attorney conflicts, 160-178
        business and financial interests, 160-167
        business deals, 164
        deals with clients, 165
        fee-payer interests, 171-172
        financial assistance, 168-171
        gender, 173-178
        interests adverse to clients, 166-167
        living expenses, 168-171
        media rights, 167-168
        personal relationships, 172-173
        race, 173-178
        real estate brokers and salespersons,
            160-164
        religion, 173-178
    in criminal cases, 178-207
        "automatic reversal" debate, 197-198
        defense attorneys, 178-200
        disqualification of defense attorneys,
            188-198
        effective assistance of counsel, 181-188
        habeas corpus and, 181-185
        Holloway error, 186-187
        overview, 178-181
        prosecutors, 200-207
        shadow counsel, 197
        waiver, advising clients regarding, 198-200
    insurance and, 228-231
        identification of client, 229-231
        obligation to defend, 229-231
    overview, 157-158
Conduct unrelated to practice, discipline of
            attorneys for events in, 586-587
Confidential information
    authority of attorney to determine, 48
    concurrent conflicts of interest and, 218-221
    confidentiality, duty of
        confidential information, 31-33
        consent to disclosure of information, 44-45
        corporations, 41-42
        crime-fraud exception, 45-47
        death, effect of, 34
        effect of exceptions on privilege, 48-50
        entity representation, 434-454. *See also* Entity
            representation
        exceptions, 42-51
        fiduciary exception, 50-51
        improper acquisition of confidential
            information, 104-107
        inadvertent disclosure of confidential
            information, 106-107
        legal claim exception, 42-44
        metadata, 107
        "noisy withdrawal" and, 51
        organizational clients, 36-42
        potential clients, 29
        prevention of crime and fraud, exception
            for, 47-48
        prevention of death or bodily harm,
            exception for, 47-48
        privileged information, 31-33, 48
        public policy, 34-35
        self-defense exception, 42-44
        social media and, 51-54
        unauthorized disclosure of confidential
            information, 30, 33
        waiver, 44-45
    crime-fraud exception to confidentiality, 45-47
    entity representation and, 434-454
        change of corporate control, 442-448
        closely held entities, 451-454
        corporations, 41-42
        internal investigations, 434-441
        organizational clients, 36-42
        parent and subsidary, 448-450
    government attorneys, successive conflicts of
            interest, 266
    inform and advise, duty to, 62-66. *See also*
            Inform and advise, duty to
    public policy, 34-35
"Conflict of rules," 159
Conflicts of interest, 155-267
    competing interests, 159-160
    concurrent conflicts of interest. *See* Concurrent
            conflicts of interest
    "conflict of rules," 159
    contingent fees and, 127-128
    default rules, 159
    defined, 155-156
    "directly adverse" conflicts of interest, 213-214
    entity representation, 434-454
        change of corporate control, 442-448
        closely held entities, 451-454
        internal investigations, 434
        overview, 159
        parent and subsidiary, 448-450
    government attorneys, 158
    imputed conflicts of interest, 158, 214-215
    inform and advise, duty to, 65-66
    judges, 465-490
        campaign contributions and, 475-477
        death penalty and, 475
        Due Process Clause and, 463, 467-475
        personal relationships or interest, 484-487
        probability of bias test, 473-475
    with witnesses, 158
Congressional power over ethics rules, 8
Consent
    concurrent conflicts of interest, 227-228
    confidential information, consent to disclosure
            of, 44-45
Constitution, U.S.
    Due Process Clause, 463, 467-475
    First Amendment. *See* First Amendment
    freedom of press, 639
    freedom of speech. *See* Freedom of speech
    Free Exercise Clause, 595

Privileges and Immunities Clause, 504
prosecutors and, 203
Sixth Amendment. *See* Sixth Amendment
Supremacy Clause, 199, 537
Thirteenth Amendment, 151
Consumer protection, 572-573
Contempt, 324-326
Contingent fees, 126-131. *See also* Attorneys' fees
advantage of attorneys in, 127
conflicts of interest and, 127-128
controversies regarding, 129-131
criminal cases, prohibition in, 129
matrimonial cases, prohibition in, 129
Corporations
attorney-client privilege and, 41-42
change of corporate control
confidential information and, 442-448
conflicts of interest, 442-448
closely held entities
confidential information and, 451-454
conflicts of interest, 451-454
parent and subsidiary
confidential information and, 448-450
conflicts of interest, 448-450
representation of. *See* Entity representation
Court-awarded attorneys' fees, 136-144
common fund, 137-138
derivative cases, 137-138
fee-shifting, 117, 136-137
proper amount, 136-138
waiver, settlement conditioned
on, 138-144
COVID-19 pandemic
cross-border practice, effect on, 503
law schools, effect on, 505
"legal deserts" and, 631
Crime-fraud exception to confidentiality, 45-47
application of, 46-47
in camera review, 46-47
Criminal prosecution, 367-399
admission to bar, effect on, 513
autonomy in, 66-75
civil liability of attorneys
causation, 569-571
to third parties, 573
conflicts of interest in, 178-207. *See also*
Concurrent conflicts of interest
constitutional protections in, 597-602
contingent fees, prohibition of, 129
effective assistance of counsel in, 597-602
evidence in, 367-384
attorney-client privilege and, 368, 376-383
destruction of evidence, 369-376, 381
discipline for concealment of, 369-373
duty to turn over, 380-381
ethical duties regarding, 368-373
obstruction and, 369-376, 381
overview, 367-369, 384
source, relevance of, 381-383

spoliation, 368-369
Watergate and, 368, 373-374
negotiation, threatening prosecution in, 423-424
opioid epidemic and, 430-431
prosecutors, 384-399
Brady obligations, 386-391
charging decision, 392-395
conflicts of interest, 200-207
defendants, communication with, 98-104
disclosure obligations, 385-391
overview, 384-385
victims' interests in decisions of, 395-399
Cross-border practice, 503
Cross-examination, 326-331

Dean, John, 9-10
Defamation
judges, against, 647-651
during litigation, 646
Defense of Marriage Act of 1996 (DOMA), 289-291
Defenses
discipline of attorneys, 597
in pari delicto defense, 568
malpractice, 562-571
Demanding bosses and clients as reason for
violations of rules, 574
Depression as reason for violations of rules, 575
Derivative cases, attorneys' fees, 137-138
Dershowitz, Alan, 232-233
Destruction of evidence in criminal prosecutions,
369-376, 381
Diligence, duty of, 61-62
Diminished capacity, autonomy in attorney-client
relationship and, 79-80
"Directly adverse" conflicts of interest, 213-214
Discipline of attorneys, 574-597
defenses, 597
disciplinary systems, 577
evidence, concealment of, 369-373
grounds for, 577-597
conduct unrelated to practice, 586-587
discrimination in client choice, 587-588
dishonesty, 577-583
excessive attorneys' fees, 119-120
failure to report misconduct, 596-597
inappropriate touching, 596
judges, public comment about, 646-651
lack of candor, 583-584
LGBT policy, 595
neglect, 583-584
pending cases, public comment about,
637-646
private life, events in, 586-587
racist and sexist speech and conduct,
588-595
sexual relations with clients, 584-586
unauthorized disclosure of confidential
information, 33
inform and advise, violation of duty to, 64

Discipline of attorneys (*continued*)
   negotiation, threatening discipline in, 423-424
   purposes of, 575-576
   reasons for violations of rules, 574-575
      bad mentoring, 574
      cluelessness, 575
      demanding bosses and clients, 574
      depression, 575
      financial exigency, 575
      overwork, 575
      rationalization, 574
      substance abuse, 575
      venality, 574
   sanctions, 64-65, 576
Disclosure of information
   Brady obligations, 386-391
   confidential information
      improper acquisition of, 104-107
      inadvertent disclosure of, 106-107
   defendant committing perjury, disclosure to
      court, 303, 310-311
   false statements, obligation to disclose, 291-294
   prosecutors' obligations, 385-391
Discrimination. *See* Bias
Discriminatory organizations, judges and, 494-496
Dishonesty, discipline of attorneys, 577-583
Disqualification of attorneys
   "automatic reversal" debate, 197-198
   in civil actions, 221-222
   for conflicts of interest, 188-198
   in criminal cases, 188-198
   imputed disqualification, 253-262
      presumptions, 259-262
      removing conflicts from former firms, 262
   shadow counsel, 197
Disqualification of judges, 465-490
   duty to reveal information, 489-490
   ethical disqualification, 477-484
   extrajudicial source doctrine, 487-488
   law clerks, service as, 488-489
   personal relationships or interest, 484-487
   statutory disqualification, 477-484
District attorneys. *See* Prosecutors
District of Columbia
   contingent fees in, 125
   criminal prosecution, threatening in
      negotiation, 424
   living expenses, providing to client, 170
Dodd-Frank Act of 2010, 432, 454-459
Drinan, Robert, 13
Due Process Clause, 463, 467-475
Duty of confidentiality, 24-54. *See also* Confidential
      information
Duty of diligence, 61-62
Duty of fiduciary. *See* Fiduciary duty, breach of
Duty of loyalty, 61-62
   successive conflicts of interest, 248-249
Duty to advise. *See* Inform and advise, duty to

Education requirements for admission to bar,
      505-506
Effective assistance of counsel
   in criminal prosecutions, 597-602
   "farce and mockery" standard, 599
   habeas corpus and, 181-185
   Holloway error, 186-187
   inform and advise, duty to, 64
   procedural defaults and, 601-602
   "reasonable probability" of different result, 600
   "reasonably competent assistance" test, 599
   Sixth Amendment and, 23, 185-186, 381,
      598-599
   tests for, 187-188
Elections of judges
   campaign funds, appearance of partiality and,
      475-477
   campaign speech, 651-661
   solicitation of campaign funds, 659-661
Entity representation, 427-459
   cash for confidences, 457-459
   closely held entities
      confidential information and, 451-454
      conflicts of interest, 451-454
   confidentiality, duty of, 434-454
      change of corporate control, 442-448
      closely held entities, 451-454
      corporations, 41-42
      internal investigations, 434-441
      organizational clients, 36-42
      parent and subsidiary, 448-450
   conflicts of interest, 434-454
      change of corporate control, 442-448
      closely held entities, 451-454
      internal investigations, 434
      overview, 159
      parent and subsidiary, 448-450
   contract interpretation and, 447-448
   corporate wrongdoing and, 428-433
   Dodd-Frank Act and, 432, 454-459
   government attorneys and, 440-441
   identification of client, 427-428, 439-440
   internal investigations
      confidential information and, 434-441
      conflicts of interest, 434-441
   malpractice, causation, 568-569
   Model Rules and, 454-459
   obligations of attorneys, 431-433
   overview, 427-428
   Sarbanes-Oxley Act and, 432, 454-459
   secret settlements and, 433
   Upjohn warnings, 434-435
Episodic clients, 82-83
Epstein, Jeffrey, 232
Ervin, Sam, 368
Escrow agreements, civil liability to third parties,
      573-574
Estates, malpractice and, 555-556

Ethics
    in advocacy, 271-276
    attorneys' fees, unethical fees and billing
        practices, 117-125
    authority, ethics rules as, 12-13
    autonomy and, 4
    "bad client problem," 4
    behavioral arguments, 6
    behavioral legal ethics, 14
    borderless market for legal services and, 12
    Canons of Judicial Ethics, 462
    Canons of Professional Ethics, 9, 252
    charging decision, 392-395
    client-centered nature of bar, 4
    Code of Conduct for United States
        Judges, 462
    Code of Judicial Conduct, 331, 462-464,
        477-478, 593, 660
    Code of Professional Responsibility, 9, 252
    Congressional authority over ethics rules, 8
    criminal prosecutions
        charging decision, 392-395
        evidence in, 368-373
        prosecutors' disclosure obligations, 385-391
    Ethics 2000 Commission, 10-11
    inherent powers doctrine and, 7-8
    "in service of other theories" theory, 5
    judges, authority over ethics rules, 7-8
    judicial ethics, 462-464
    justice and fairness model, 5
    Kutak Commission, 9-10
    lawmakers, power of, 7-8
    malpractice, ethics rules and, 556-562
    Model Rules of Professional
        Conduct, 8-12
        historical background, 9-12
        overview, 8-9
    Multijurisdictional Practice (MJP)
        Commission, 11
    normative arguments, 6
    one size fits all approach, 11-12
    other sources, 13
    overview, 1-2
    politics of, 5-6
    "poor lawyer problem," 5
    "professional conspiracy theory," 5
    professionalism, 14-15
    prosecutors
        charging decision, 392-395
        disclosure obligations, 385-391
    real ethics, 14
    Rules of Professional Conduct, 331
    Task Force on Corporate Responsibility, 10-11
    "tempted lawyer problem," 4
    theory of, 2-5
    20/20 Commission, 11
    Watergate and, 9-10
Ethics 2000 Commission, 10-11, 125

European Union, admission to bar in, 530-531
Evidence
    in criminal prosecution. *See* Criminal
        prosecution
    spoliation
        advocacy, 349-351
        criminal prosecutions, 368-369
Examinations for admission to bar, 505-506,
    513-514. *See also* Admission to bar
Ex parte communications by judges, 464-465
Expert testimony, malpractice and civil liability,
    556-562
Expression. *See* Freedom of speech
Extrajudicial source doctrine, 487-488

Fair Debt Collection Practices Act of 1977, 572
False Claims Act of 1863, 457-458
False statements, obligation to disclose, 291-294.
    See also Perjury
Family, client-attorney conflicts, 172-173
"Farce and mockery" standard, 599
Federal Rules of Bankruptcy
    Procedure, 323-324
Federal Rules of Civil Procedure, 360, 422
Federal Rules of Evidence
    attorney-client privilege, 31
    confidential information in attorney-client
        relationship, 106
    confidentiality, duty of, 37
Federal Trade Commission (FTC), 135
Fee agreements
    post-retainer fee agreements, 124-125
    writing requirement, 125
Fee-payer interests, client-attorney conflicts,
    171-172
Fees. *See* Attorneys' fees
Fee-shifting, 117, 136-137
Fiduciary duty, breach of
    civil liability for, 567-568
    malpractice vs., 552-553. *See also* Malpractice
        and civil liability
Fiduciary relationship, 60-61
Financial exigency as reason for violations of
    rules, 575
Firms, nonlawyers investing in, 606, 625-630
First Amendment
    freedom of press, 639
    freedom of speech. *See* Freedom of speech
    Free Exercise Clause, 595
    governmental parties, communication
        with, 94
    political vs. commercial motives, 615
    right to petition, 94
Florida, mandatory pro bono plans in, 145
Ford, Gerald, 368, 374
Former clients, conflicts of interest. *See* Successive
    conflicts of interest
Frankel, Marvin E., 279-281

Fraud
    crime-fraud exception to confidentiality, 45-47
        application of, 46-47
        in camera review, 46-47
    malpractice for, 415-417
Fraudulent concealment
    advocacy and, 349-351
    criminal prosecutions, 368-369
Freedom of press, 639
Freedom of speech, 637-662
    announce clauses, 652-658
    defamation during litigation, 646
    gag orders, 638-639
    judges
        campaign speech, 651-661
        defamation against, 647-651
        public comment about, 646-651
        solicitation of campaign funds, 659-661
    marketing of legal services and, 665-666, 683.
        See also Marketing of legal services
    nonlawyers, solicitation of clients by, 615
    pending cases, public comment about, 637-646
    prejudicial publicity and, 643-644
    prior restraint, 638
    substantial likelihood of prejudice standard,
        640-645
    Supreme Court nominees, 661
    unauthorized practice of law and, 537-539
    unions, legal services provided by, 622
Free Exercise Clause, 595
Friends, client-attorney conflicts with, 172-173

Gag orders, 638-639
Gender issues, 173-178. *See also* Bias
Geographical exclusion on admission to
        bar, 504
Geographical restriction on admission to bar,
        504-505
Georgetown Journal of Legal Ethics, 13
Georgia, imputed conflicts of interest in, 215
Gig economy, nonlawyers and, 625
Giuffre, Virginia, 232-233
Government attorneys
    conflicts of interest, 158
    entity representation and, 440-441. *See also*
        Entity representation
    prosecutors. *See* Criminal prosecution
    successive conflicts of interest, 262-267

Habeas corpus, conflicts of interest and, 181-185
"Hardball" in advocacy, 351-358
Hernandez, Aaron, 383
Holloway error, 186-187
"Hot potato" rule, 250-251

Identification of client
    attorney-client relationship, for purposes
        of, 20-22

concurrent conflicts of interest and, 229-231
entity representation, for purposes of, 427-428,
        439-440
successive conflicts of interest and, 249-250
Ignatieff, Michael, 2-3
Illinois, mandatory pro bono plans in, 145
Immigrants
    admission to bar, 502
    threatening to report undocumented
        immigrants, 424
Impeachment of judges, 462
Imputed conflicts of interest, 158, 214-215
Imputed disqualification, 253-262
    presumptions, 259-262
    removing conflicts from former firms, 262
Incivility in advocacy, 351-358
Ineffective assistance of counsel. *See* Effective
        assistance of counsel
Inflating bills, 121-122
Inform and advise, duty to, 62-66
    civil liability, 64
    conflicts of interest and, 65-66
    discipline, 64
    effective assistance of counsel, 64
    sanctions, 64-65
Inherent powers doctrine, 7-8
In pari delicto defense, 568
"In service of other theories" theory, 5
Insurance
    client-client conflicts, 228-231
    fee-payer interests, client-attorney conflicts,
        171-172
    unauthorized practice of law and, 533-536
Integreon, 633
Interest on Lawyer Trust Accounts (IOLTA
        Accounts), 110-111
Intermediaries, 607-625
Internal investigations of entities
    confidential information and, 434-441
    conflicts of interest, 434-441
IOLTA accounts, 110-111

"Jailhouse lawyers," 536-537
Joint representation. *See* Concurrent conflicts of
        interest
Judges, 461-498
    announce clauses, 652-658
    authority over ethics rules, 7-8
    bias, expressions of, 490-496
        in courtroom, 494-495
        discriminatory organizations and, 494-496
        LGBT persons and, 490-492
        private clubs and, 492-494
    campaign funds, 475-477
    campaign speech, 651-661
    Canons of Judicial Ethics, 462
    Code of Conduct for United States
        Judges, 462

Code of Judicial Conduct, 331, 462-464, 477-478, 593, 660
conflicts of interest, 465-490
    campaign contributions and, 475-477
    death penalty and, 475
    Due Process Clause and, 463, 467-475
    personal relationships or interest, 484-487
    probability of bias test, 473-475
defamation against, 647-651
disqualification of, 465-490
    duty to reveal information, 489-490
    ethical disqualification, 477-484
    extrajudicial source doctrine, 487-488
    law clerks, service as, 488-489
    personal relationships or interest, 484-487
    statutory disqualification, 477-484
ex parte communications, 464-465
impeachment of, 462
judicial ethics, 462-464
public comment about, 646-651
recusal of
    ethical disqualification, 477-484
    extrajudicial source doctrine, 487-488
    personal relationships or interest, 484-487
    statutory disqualification, 477-484
removal of, 462
solicitation of campaign funds, 659-661
Judgment, duty of, 24
Judicial admissions, 60
Judicial Conference of the United States, 462-463
Justice and fairness model, 5

Kansas Consumer Protection Act (KCPA), 7
Keating, Charles, 432
Kitzhaber, John, 441
Kornstein, Daniel J., 327-330
Kutak Commission, 9-10

Labor unions, legal services provided by, 606, 620-625
Lack of candor, 583-584
Law clerks, disqualification of judges for service as, 488-489
Law firms
    migratory attorneys, 253-262
    nonlawyers investing in, 606, 625-630
Law schools
    COVID-19 pandemic, effect of, 505
    dishonesty or lack of integrity in, effect on admission to bar, 514
    law professors, admission to bar and, 523
Lawyers' Manual on Professional Conduct, 13
Lay persons. *See* Nonlawyers
Legal authority, obligation to reveal, 362-363
"Legal deserts," 631
Legal ethics. *See* Ethics
Legal fees. *See* Attorneys' fees
Legal opinions, reliance on by opposing attorneys, 417-419

Legal process outsourcing companies (LPOs), 633
LegalZoom, 538-539
LGBT persons. *See also* Bias
    Defense of Marriage Act of 1996 (DOMA), 289-291
    judges, expressions of bias by, 490-492
Licensed paralegal practitioners, 630
Limited license legal technicians (LLLTs), 630
Lincoln Savings and Loan, 432
Literal truth, 315-326
    Clinton and, 317-319
    contempt and, 324-326
    perjury and, 319-324
Literary rights, client-attorney conflicts, 167-168
Literature, portrayal of attorneys in, 284-285
Litigation funding companies, 606, 631-632
Living expenses, client-attorney conflicts, 168-171
Loyalty, duty of, 61-62
    successive conflicts of interest, 248-249

Macey, Jonathan R., 148-151
Mail, targeted, 676-681
Maine, Model Rules in, 10
Maintenance, 612-615
Malpractice and civil liability, 543-574
    attorneys' fees, forfeiture and disgorgement of, 559-562
    breach of fiduciary duty vs., 552-553
    causation, 562-571
        "but for" test, 566-569
        in criminal cases, 569-571
        entity representation and, 568-569
        fiduciary duties and, 567-568
        litigation and, 566-567
        transactional matters and, 566
    clients, liability to, 544-555
    conflicts of interest, 222-227
    defenses, 562-571
    estates, 555-556
    ethics rules, 556-562
    expert testimony, 556-562
    fraud, 415-417
    for incompetence, 23
    in pari delicto defense, 568
    judgmental immunity, 552
    misrepresentation, 415-417
    sexual relations with clients, 555
    standard of care, 551-552
    third parties, liability to, 571-574
        consumer protection, 572-573
        criminal law, 573
        escrow agreements, 573-574
        negligent misrepresentation, 572
        professional negligence, 555-556
    vicarious liability, 556
    wills, 555
Mandatory pro bono plans, 144-151
    culture of commitment and, 146-148
    as "welfare for rich," 148-151

Marketing of legal services, 663-685
   Bates case, 666-667
   as commercial speech, 666
   First Amendment and, 665-666, 683
   methodology in Supreme Court cases, 681-684
   overview, 664-665
   professionalism, relationship to, 666-667,
      683-684
   prophylactic rule, 671-672
   solicitation of clients, 668-672. *See also*
      Solicitation of clients
   targeted advertisements, 672-676
   targeted mail, 676-681
Marriage
   matrimonial cases, prohibition of contingent
      fees, 129
   opposition to marriage equality, 289-291
   successive conflicts of interest and, 237-238
McCarthy, Joseph, 464
McDade Amendment, 99-100
Media rights, client-attorney conflicts, 167-168
Mental health, effect on admission to bar, 514-515
Mentoring as reason for violations of rules, 574
Metadata as confidential information in attorney-
      client relationship, 107
Migratory attorneys, 253-262
Minimum fee schedules, 131-136
Misrepresentation, malpractice for, 415-417
Misstatements of facts, precedent, or record,
      359-362
Mistakes by opposing attorneys, exploiting, 403,
      419-424
Mitchell, John, 343-345
Model Rules of Professional Conduct, 8-12
   historical background, 9-12
   overview, 8-9
Moral accountability of attorneys, 287-291
Mortgage fraud, 429
Motorists' Association of Illinois, 605
Mueller, Robert, 440-441
Multijurisdictional firms, 516-531
Multijurisdictional Practice (MJP) Commission,
      11, 529
Multiple representation. *See* Concurrent conflicts
      of interest

National Association for the Advancement of
      Colored People (NAACP), 607-612,
      615-616, 621
Neglect, discipline of attorneys, 583-584
Negligence. *See* Malpractice and civil liability
Negotiation, 401-426
   "assisting" fraud or violation of duty, 406-408,
      415-417
   attorneys as negotiators, 402-403
   attorneys' own statements, liability for, 403,
      410-419
   "bad client problem," 403-410

   criminal prosecution, threatening, 423-424
   discipline, threatening, 423-424
   exploiting opponents' mistakes, 403, 419-424
   legal opinions of opposing attorneys, reliance
      on, 417-419
   lessons for attorneys, 415-417
   material statements, 410-411
   "noisy withdrawal," 408-410
   representation of facts by opposing attorneys,
      reliance on, 411-414
   undocumented immigrants, threatening to
      report, 424
   unrepresented persons, with, 423
New Jersey
   contingent fees in, 125
   Model Rules in, 10
New York
   Judiciary Law, 614
   Model Rules in, 10
Nixon, Richard, 9-10, 368, 373-374, 376
"Noisy withdrawal," 51, 408-410
Nonlawyers, 605-634
   barratry and, 612-615
   champerty and, 612-615
   gig economy and, 625
   intermediaries, 607-625
   investment in for-profit legal organizations,
      606, 625-630
   legal process outsourcing companies
      (LPOs), 633
   limited legal services provided by, 606
   limited license legal technicians (LLLTs), 630
   litigation funding companies, 606, 631-632
   maintenance and, 612-615
   nonprofit entities, 607-625
   online document production services, 631
   in other countries, 633
   overview, 605-607
   paralegals, 630-631
   public interest organizations, legal services
      provided by, 606-620
   solicitation of clients, 615-616
   unauthorized practice of law. *See* Unauthorized
      practice of law
   unions, legal services provided by, 606, 620-625
Non-profit organizations, 522-523
North Carolina, unauthorized practice of law
      in, 439

Online document production services, 631
Opinions, reliance on by opposing attorneys,
      417-419
Opioid epidemic, 430-431
Opposing parties, communication with. *See*
      Attorney-client relationship
Organizations, representation of. *See* Entity
      representation
Overwork as reason for violations of rules, 575

Pandemic. *See* COVID-19 pandemic
Pangea3, 633
Paralegals, 630-631
Parent and subsidiary
    confidential information and, 448-450
    conflicts of interest, 448-450
Partisan justice, 279-281
Pending cases, public comment about, 637-646
Pennsylvania, contingent fees in, 125
Perjury
    defendant committing, 294-301
        avoiding knowledge vs., 307
        disclosure to court, 303, 310-311
        epistemological problem, 305-307
        ethical solutions, 303-305
        full cooperation with defendant, 303
        narrative approach, 304-305
        non-verbal communication, 308-309
        overview, 312-313
        persuading defendant not to commit
            perjury, 303
        refusal to permit defendant to testify,
            303-304
        withdrawal from representation, 303
    ethical context, 323-324
    legal context, 319-323
    literal truth and, 319-324. *See also* Literal truth
    witnesses committing, 312-313
Perrin, L. Timothy, 305
Personal relationships causing client-attorney
    conflicts, 172-173
Pharmaceutical claims, 430-431
Playbook information, 246-248
"Poor lawyer problem," 5
Popular culture, portrayal of attorneys in, 272
Popular image of attorneys, 282-284
Post-retainer fee agreements, 124-125
Post, Robert C., 282-284
Prejudice. *See* Bias
Press, freedom of, 639
Prior restraint, 638
Private clubs, judges and, 492-494
Private life, discipline of attorneys for events in,
    586-587
Privileged information. *See* Attorney-client
    privilege
Privileges and Immunities Clause, 504
Pro bono plans. *See* Mandatory pro bono plans
Product liability, 429-430
"Professional conspiracy theory," 5
Professionalism
    ethics and, 14-15
    marketing of legal services, relationship to,
        666-667, 683-684
Professional negligence. *See* Malpractice and civil
    liability
Pro hac vice admission, 517-522
Prosecutors. *See* Criminal prosecution

Public image of attorneys, 274-275, 282-284
Public interest attorneys, 606
Public interest organizations, legal services
    provided by, 606-620
Public policy
    advocate-witness rule, 231-232
    attorney-client privilege, 34-35
    confidential information, 34-35
    confidentiality, duty of, 34-35

Quicken Family Lawyer (QFL), 538

Race. *See also* Bias
    admission to bar, effect of racial bias on,
        506-507
    appeal to bias by attorneys, 331-336
    client-attorney conflicts, 173-178
    discipline of attorneys
        discrimination in client choice, 587-588
        racist and sexist speech and conduct, 588
Rationalization as reason for violations of
    rules, 574
Real estate brokers and salespersons, client-
    attorney conflicts, 160-164
"Reasonably competent assistance" test, 599
Recusal of judges
    ethical disqualification, 477-484
    extrajudicial source doctrine, 487-488
    personal relationships or interest, 484-487
    statutory disqualification, 477-484
Relatives as basis for client-attorney conflicts,
    172-173
Religion
    client-attorney conflicts, 173-178
    Free Exercise Clause, 595
Religious Freedom Restoration Act of 1993
    (RFRA), 595
Removal of judges, 462
Representations of facts, reliance on by opposing
    attorneys, 411-414
Restatement (Third) of Agency, 54
Restatement of the Law Governing Lawyers
    attorney-client privilege, 40, 218
    breach of fiduciary duty, 553
    common interest agreements, 220-221
    concurrent conflicts of interest, 156, 218,
        227-229
    conflicts of interest, 156
    opposing parties, communication with,
        87, 93-94
    parent and subsidiary, entity representation
        and, 449-450
    as source of ethics rules, 13
    successive conflicts of interest and, 244, 252
Rhode, Deborah L., 146-148
Rifkind, Simon H., 276-278
Right to counsel, 98, 188, 197, 274
Right to petition, 94

Roberts, John, 473-474
Rosenberg, Ethel, 464
Rosenberg, Julius, 464
Rowling, J.K., 30
Ruben, Ann, 329
Ruben, Emily, 329
Rules of Professional Conduct, 331

Sanctions, 64-65, 576
Sarbanes-Oxley Act of 2002, 10, 368, 375, 432,
        454-459
Scalia, Antonin, 484-486
Schock, Aaron, 638-639
Screening, 266-267
Secret settlements, 433
Securities and Exchange Commission (SEC), 10,
        43, 454-458
Sexist speech and conduct, discipline of
        attorneys, 588-595. *See also* Bias
Sexual relations with clients
    discipline of attorneys, 584-586
    malpractice, 555
Shadow counsel, 197
Shakespeare, William, 282
Simpson, O.J., 167, 382-383
Sixth Amendment
    autonomy and, 79
    defendants, communication with, 98
    effective assistance of counsel, 23, 185-186,
        381, 598-599. *See also* Effective
        assistance of counsel
    right to counsel, 98, 188, 197, 274
"Slut shaming," 356-358
Social media, confidentiality and, 51-54
Solicitation of clients. *See also* Marketing of legal
        services
    accident victims, 668-671
    nonlawyers, by, 615-616
    prophylactic rule, 671-672
    public interest attorneys, by, 616-620
Solid Waste Disposal Act of 1965, 136
Speech. *See* Freedom of speech
Spoliation
    advocacy and, 349-351
    criminal prosecutions, 368-369
Sporkin, Stanley, 431-433
Standing
    concurrent conflicts of interest, 215-216
    successive conflicts of interest, 251
Starr, Kenneth, 311
Stewart, Martha, 374
Subin, Harry, 342-343, 345-346
Subsidiaries
    confidential information and, 448-450
    conflicts of interest, 448-450
Substance abuse as reason for violations of
        rules, 575
Substantial relationship test, successive conflicts
        of interest, 244-248

Successive conflicts of interest, 237-267
    appearance of impropriety, 252
    class actions, 252-253
    former vs. current clients, 250-251
    government attorneys, 262-267
        agenda setting, 266
        confidential information, 266
        screening, 266-267
    "hot potato" rule, 250-251
    identification of client, 249-250
    imputed disqualification, 253-262
        presumptions, 259-262
        removing conflicts from former firms, 262
    loyalty, duty of, 248-249
    migratory attorneys, 253-262
    overview, 158
    playbook information and, 246-248
    in private practice, 237-253
    standing, 251
    substantial relationship test, 244-248
    "thrust upon" conflicts, 251
    waiver, 251
Suits in Admiralty Act of 1920, 359
Sullivan, Ronald S., Jr., 288-289
Supremacy Clause, 199, 537
Supreme Court, U.S.
    ethics and, 462-463
    nominees, freedom of speech and, 661

Targeted advertisements, 672-676
Targeted mail, 676-681
Task Force on Corporate Responsibility, 10-11
"Tempted lawyer problem," 4
Termination of attorney-client relationship
    by attorney, 81
    by client, 80-81
    by drift, 82
    episodic clients, 82-83
    withdrawal from representation
        defendant committing perjury, 303
        ethical considerations, 273
        "noisy withdrawal," 51, 408-410
Testers, communication with, 95-97
Third parties, civil liability to, 571-574
    consumer protection, 572-573
    criminal law, 573
    escrow agreements, 573-574
    negligent misrepresentation, 572
    professional negligence, 555-556
Thirteenth Amendment, 151
"Thrust upon" conflicts, 251
Transient attorneys, 516-531
Traver, Robert, 308-309
Triangle Shirtwaist Company fire, 326-331
Tripp, Linda, 312
Trollope, Anthony, 284-285
Trump, Donald, 441, 464, 574
Truthfulness
    Clinton and, 317-319

contempt and, 324-326
false statements, obligation to
disclose, 291-294
literal truth, 315-326
perjury and, 319-324. *See also* Perjury
20/20 Commission, 11

Unauthorized practice of law, 531-539
admission to bar and, 503, 515
antitrust law and, 539
claims adjustment and, 533-536
computer programs, 538-539
exceptions, desirability of creating, 532-533
freedom of speech and, 537-539
insurance companies and, 533-536
"jailhouse lawyers," 536-537
nonlawyers. *See* Nonlawyers
overview, 532-533
Supremacy Clause and, 537
Undocumented immigrants
admission to bar and, 502
negotiation, threatening to report in, 424
Unions providing legal services, 606, 620-625
United Kingdom
Legal Services Act 2007, 633
nonlawyers in, 633
Unrepresented persons, negotiation
with, 423
Upjohn warnings in entity representation, 434-435
Utah, licensed paralegal practitioners in, 630

Venality as reason for violations of rules, 574
Vicarious admissions, 60
Vicarious liability, 556

Victims of crimes, interests in decisions of
prosecutors, 395-399

Waiver
attorneys' fees, settlement conditioned on,
138-144
concurrent conflicts of interest, 227
advising clients regarding, 198-200
confidentiality, duty of, 44-45
successive conflicts of interest, 251
Washington
limited license legal technicians (LLLTs)
in, 630
undocumented immigrants, threatening to
report in negotiation, 424
Watergate, 9-10, 368, 373-374
Weinstein, Harvey, 288-289, 637, 645
Williams, Edward Bennett, 373-374
Wills, malpractice and, 555
Withdrawal from representation
defendant committing perjury, 303
ethical considerations, 273
"noisy withdrawal," 51, 408-410
Witnesses
advocate-witness rule, 231-233
public policy, 231-232
conflicts of interest with, 158
cross-examination of, 326-331
perjury, committing, 312-313
Women, admission to bar, 502
Wyoming, imputed conflicts of interest in,
214-215

Zealous advocacy, 356, 358